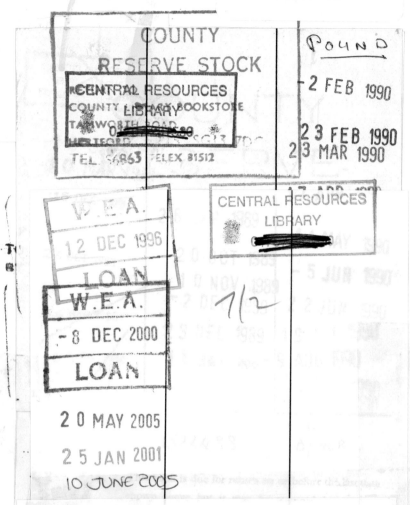

NORTHCLIFFE

ALFRED HARMSWORTH, AGED TWENTY-NINE,
AFTER THE PORTRAIT BY SEYMOUR LUCAS, R.A.
EXHIBITED AT THE ROYAL ACADEMY, 1894

NORTHCLIFFE

REGINALD POUND

AND

GEOFFREY HARMSWORTH

CASSELL · LONDON

CASSELL & COMPANY LTD

35 Red Lion Square · London WC1

and at

MELBOURNE · SYDNEY · TORONTO · CAPE TOWN

JOHANNESBURG · AUCKLAND

———

© Geoffrey Harmsworth 1959

First published 1959

Printed in Great Britain by The Shenval Press

London, Hertford and Harlow

F. 459

Introduction

A NEW book on Northcliffe may no longer be acclaimed as a literary event: two were published in his lifetime, nine in the decade following his death and three others within the last few years. Apart from these fourteen books there were at least three other biographies which were completed or in preparation but never published. In addition there have been many other books in which Northcliffe is the central or one of the central characters.

The 'debunkers', as well as the apostles of the 'Northcliffe-could-do-no-wrong' school of thought, have all had their say. It seemed that any writer who could claim acquaintance, close or casual, with the subject, felt impelled to set down his verdict for a credulous if at times a reluctant posterity. From all these accounts—including those dealing with Northcliffe's life in the hereafter—there emerges a legendary figure, dimly seen through a haze of conflicting statements and opinions, 'a man so various' that a reader may be excused for wondering whether, outside the realm of fiction, such a mixture of truth and caricature ever existed.

The present, long-awaited work, apart from its heroic size, differs in at least one important respect from its predecessors. None of the previous writers had access to the Northcliffe or the Harmsworth family papers. As far as I am aware, no approach was made in the past by or to an author with a view to compiling a full-scale, definitive life of Northcliffe. My own part in this venture stems from conversations I had with H. G. Wells far back in the 1930s. He suggested that I should write the story of the Harmsworth family—a suggestion which is recorded in his *Experiment in Autobiography*.* He himself had witnessed and shared in some part of that story himself, from the days when he taught at Henley House School, St. John's Wood, the scene of young Alfred Harmsworth's first exploits into journalism, to the First World War, when he assisted Northcliffe in the propaganda blitz on Germany.

With an insight which will become apparent in the pages of this book, Wells described the romantic rise of the Harmsworth brothers as being 'absurdly like the Bonaparte adventure'—and offered *The Harmsworth Adventure* as a suitable title. With this thesis in mind I set about my task. Much of the relevant material lay close at hand in the Harmsworth family papers. Several of Northcliffe's brothers and sisters were then alive, as well as some of his closest associates and contemporaries. All were eager to help.

* Gollancz and Cresset Press, 1934.

It was perhaps not surprising that the would-be biographer of a brotherhood composed of such diverse and powerful personalities as the Harmsworths should run into difficulties. Closely attached as they were, and bound together by an unassailable sense of family loyalty, the elder brethren were not of one mind as to how the saga should be unfolded in print. Eventually, and with keen regret, I decided to put my unfinished MS. to one side, against the day when it would no longer be necessary to consult family sensibilities in completing the work.

At the end of the Second World War, twenty-three years had elapsed since Northcliffe's death. It seemed that something more than the H. G. Wells idea of a *Harmsworth Adventure* was now needed. The full-scale definitive biography of Northcliffe still awaited an author. Those closest to Northcliffe—and their number was dwindling—were concerned that in the swiftly turning pages of history he should be accorded his rightful place. My brother Harold★ and I decided that it was our duty to ensure, as far as it lay within our power, that the often wildly inaccurate and apocryphal statements and stories of previous biographers should not pass to future generations as facts. We felt that unless this was attempted within our lifetimes, with all our personal knowledge, and the results of our years of intensive research, an authentic, fully documented portrait of Northcliffe would never be completed. Over and above that intention, there was a stronger and more impelling motive inspired by our gratitude to Northcliffe for having brought enduring fame and honour to the Harmsworth name. In short, the task which we took upon ourselves was to be our own memorial to the family, and, in particular, to the fountain-head of its manifold endeavours and achievements.

Thus from the great mass of material brought together or located for the unfinished *Harmsworth Adventure* there emerged a larger canvas which began to assume form and colour ten years ago. The first of the projected three volumes was nearing completion when, following my brother Harold's sudden and lamented death, more urgent responsibilities were thrust upon me and the whole project had once more to be laid aside.

In 1953 I decided to start afresh with a new collaborator, Reginald Pound, an old friend of mature Fleet Street experience who had recently received the W. H. Heinemann Foundation award for his biography of Arnold Bennett. The collaboration has proved to be a profitable one. Reginald Pound brought to the task a fresh and penetrating mind, an exceptionally keen eye for the significant detail and an inexhaustible capacity for research and the translation of biographical material into an orderly and coherent narrative. Inevitably, we have not always seen eye to eye about the delineation of each aspect of Northcliffe's character and personality, but Reginald Pound's objective approach to the subject has

★ Sir Harold Harmsworth (1897-1952), second son of the late Sir Leicester Harmsworth, Bt.

cancelled any tendency on my part to allow considerations of family loyalty to overshadow cold, biographical truth, and there has been no suppression by me of the other point of view. Indeed, if this book should prove to be a worthier monument to Northcliffe than its predecessors it is due to our smooth-working partnership no less than to the able planning and perseverance of Reginald Pound, whose part in our collaboration cannot be overstated.

As the first biographers to have access to the Northcliffe archives we have enjoyed a completely free hand and there has been nothing in the nature of censorship on the part of the Harmsworth family throughout the whole undertaking. Only where it has been thought that needless pain or distress might be caused to living persons have we exercised the right of restraint. Wherever possible, Northcliffe himself speaks through the pages of this book, in his letters, his messages to his staff, in his writings and speeches. It is his voice that is heard throughout.

We have followed the suggestion of our publishers by keeping the biography within the bounds of one volume, and what we feel would have been Northcliffe's own advice by reducing footnotes and references to a minimum, giving the sources and dates of correspondence and other quoted matter in the text itself. There are no elaborate appendices at the end (designed, as they often are, to give an air and pretence of scholarship) but, for the benefit of the student and the omnivorous reader of 'Northcliffiana', a comprehensive bibliography has been included. The index has been prepared with great care, industry and perception by Mr J. S. Maywood.

Apart from the Northcliffe archives, to which I have had unrestricted access since I embarked on *The Harmsworth Adventure*, we have made considerable use of the family documents and papers in my own collection. These include the diaries and letters of Alfred Harmsworth, snr., Northcliffe's father; the personal papers of Geraldine Mary Harmsworth, Northcliffe's mother; Northcliffe's own diaries for 1888 and from 1891 to 1906—a vitally important part of the story—and the large collection of books (many of them annotated by my father) and family documents which I inherited from my father and my brother, Sir Leicester and Sir Harold Harmsworth. In addition I am indebted to my cousin Esmond, the second Viscount Rothermere, for permitting us to include a number of early letters from his father to Northcliffe which, with characteristic brevity, trace the beginnings of the Harmsworth invasion of Fleet Street. My cousin Desmond, the second Lord Harmsworth, has placed the diaries and unpublished *Harmsworth Memorials* compiled by his father at our disposal and these have provided exciting glimpses of Northcliffe at every stage of his life. Among the surviving family witnesses, my aunt, Lady Hudson, Northcliffe's widow, with her long and unimpaired memory, has recalled many events of which all record has been lost. My uncle, Vyvyan Harmsworth, Northcliffe's youngest brother and the last to survive, passed from the scene before this volume went to press, but his boyhood memories and later recollections, as well as those of my aunt, Christabel Burton, have added greatly to our story.

To Sir Winston Churchill—'my affection for your uncle was deep'— I am grateful for permission to include early manuscript letters exchanged with Northcliffe.

From his unrivalled knowledge of what was happening behind the scenes in the First World War Lord Beaverbrook has given me sound advice and guidance and has allowed us to explore and quote from the Lloyd George papers in his keeping. For his warm encouragement, involving global correspondence over a long period, I express my deep appreciation.

Sir Campbell Stuart, the only surviving senior executive of Northcliffe's time, has been of great help to us in authenticating the part played by Northcliffe in the British War Mission to America in 1917 and in the direction of Propaganda against Enemy Countries in 1918.

Other sources of reference have included the Royal Archives, Windsor, the library of the Foreign Office, the library and private papers at *The Times* (by courtesy of Lord Astor of Hever and Mr John Walter), the Asquith papers at the Bodleian Library, the Evelyn Wrench diaries in the British Museum, the files at Northcliffe House, Carmelite House, Fleetway House, and those of the British Museum at Colindale.

In addition we would like to place on record our appreciation to the following for having given permission to publish correspondence, quotations from books, or for assisting us in our task in many other ways:

H.H. the Begum Aga Khan; Sir Norman Angell; the late Mr H. P. Arnholz; the Hon. David Astor; Mr R. H. Atkinson; Mrs Auchinloss.

The Earl of Balfour; Mrs G. Bambridge; Mr W. Barker; Sir William Beach Thomas; Mrs C. I. Beattie; Mr F. I. Beattie; trustees of the late Captain A. S. Beaumont; Mr Clive Bell; the Hon. Michael Berry; Mr T. G. Best; the Earl of Birkenhead; executors of the late Mr Arthur Birnage; Mr James Bone; Mr Henry Borden; Mr L. W. Bowley; Mr Percy V. Bradshaw; Mr George Brazier; Mr F. Brightling; His Grace the Archbishop of Brisbane; trustees of the late Mr Arthur Brisbane; Sir Harry Brittain; Mr R. Brook-Caws; the late Mr Collin Brooks; the late Mr Joseph Brunnbauer; Mr S. Burridge; the Right Hon. R. A. Butler.

Mr Hector Caird; Mr R. F. d'A. Carr; Lady Carson; Lady Cecil of Chelwood; trustees of the late Mr Joseph Chamberlain; Mrs Ivy Clark; Mr Adrian M. Conan-Doyle; Mr John Connell; Mr H. R. Cummings.

The Hon. Mrs Dawson; Mr W. J. Deverall; Mrs Dyke Marsh.

Viscount Elibank; Viscount Esher.

Mr Bernard Falk; Mr Leonard Farquhar; Lord Fisher of Kilverstone;

Sir Newman Flower; Mr Charles Folkard; Sir Frank Fox; Frances, Countess Lloyd George; Mr Norman Freedman; Mr A. S. Frere.

Mr R. Gadd; Mr R. Gale; trustees of the late Mr John Galsworthy; Sir Philip Gibbs; Mrs M. Gordon; Mr Philip Gosse; Mr Peter Goudie; General Sir Hubert Gough.

Earl Haig; Messrs W. and F. Haldane; Sir William Haley; trustees of the late Mr and Mrs Thomas Hardy; Mr R. G. B. Harper; Mr A. S. Harrison; Lord Henderson; Mrs V. Heddon; executors of the late Cardinal Hinsley; Mr J. B. Hobbs; Mr E. O. Hoppe; the late Lord Horder; Mr A. W. Horsman; Mrs Liv Nansen Hoyer; Mr Derek Hudson.

Lady Iddesleigh; Lord Iliffe; the Right Hon. G. H. Isaacs; Mr P. W. D. Izzard.

Mr F. Jacob; Mr W. E. Jealous; Sir Roderick Jones; Sir Vincent Jones; Miss E. Johnson; Mr Sidney Josland.

The Kedleston Trust; Mr W. Kennedy Jones.

Mr E. Laird Clowes; Mr G. Langelaan; Lady Lee; Mr A. Le Grande; Lord Lloyd.

Mr Samuel McCoy; Mr Hugh MacGregor; Dr R. McNair Wilson; the Hon. Mrs H. Macneile Dixon; Mr Anthony Marlowe, Q.C.; Mr S. Mason-Springay; Major John Maxse; Mr J. S. Maywood; executors of the late Mr Arthur Mee; Mr G. H. Messer; Lieut-General Sir E. Miller; Mrs W. H. Miller; the late Viscountess Milner; Miss E. Moberly Bell; Mr C. G. M. Morrison; Mr D. J. Mossey.

The late Sir Frank Newnes; Mr C. F. Nias.

Mr O'Connor; the Earl of Onslow.

Mr Arthur W. Page; Mr H. J. Parker; Mr John Parkhurst; Sir Neville Pearson; Mr H. Peddar; Mr Alfred Pemberton; the Hon. J. W. Pickersgill; the late Mr H. E. Pine; Mrs Harry Pirie-Gordon of Buthlaw; Mr Alan Pitt Robbins; Mr Frederick Poke; Mrs A. Powell; the late Mr H. G. Price; executors of the late Mr John Prioleau; Mr F. G. Prince White; Mr J. Privett.

Mr Peter Quennell.

Mr Leonard Raftery; Dr H. Raven; Mr J. A. Read; the Marquess of Reading; Mr Douglas Reed; Sir Bruce Richmond; Mr R. P. Riley; Sir Brian Robertson; the Earl of Rosebery; Sir William Rothenstein.

Mr C. J. Scott; Lieut-Colonel Bruce Seymour Price; the Earl of Shrewsbury and Waterford; Mr Harold Snoad; trustees of the late Mr J. A. Spender; Miss E. W. Stead; Major W. H. Stephenson; Mrs Herbert Stokes; the late Sir George Sutton; Mr Hannen Swaffer.

Mr S. Taylor-Rogers; Mr Leslie Thomas; Lady Tweedsmuir.

Mr Russell Wakefield; Edgar Wallace Ltd.; Mr John Walter; Mr G. Ward Price; A. P. Watt & Son; executors of the late Mr H. G. Wells; Mr S. V. B. Wenham; Mrs E. Wheeler; Mrs Wickham Steed; Mrs F. W. Wile and Mr Frederic W. Wile, jnr.; Sir Arthur Willert; Mr R. H. Williams; Mr J. B. Wilson; the late Mrs A. Wilson; Sir Evelyn Wrench; executors of the late Mr Orville Wright; Mrs C. Wyman-Smart.

The late Mr B. W. Young; the Earl of Ypres.

Lastly, I would like to express my warm personal appreciation to

Mr R. N. Rose, who has toiled diligently in the background to ensure the accuracy of statements made in this book, to my secretary, Mrs Ethel Howson, and to Miss I. C. Nicolson, both of whom have given invaluable aid to Reginald Pound and myself at every stage of the work.

April 1959

GEOFFREY HARMSWORTH

Contents

BOOK ONE
'Schemo Magnifico'

BOOK TWO
Napoleon of the Press

CONTENTS

BOOK THREE
War and Peace

List of Illustrations

Frontispiece: Alfred Harmsworth, aged twenty-nine,
after the portrait by Seymour Lucas, R.A.

ILLUSTRATIONS

BOOK ONE

'Schemo Magnifico'

Chapter One

The Family Face

THIRTEEN miles down the Great West Road from Hyde Park Corner and six miles north of Windsor is the once deeply rural and secluded village of Harmondsworth, a name commonly diminished to 'Harmsworth' in the bucolic local speech that prevailed before the urban invasion. Parts of the parish church of St. Mary have been there nearly eight centuries and its guardian yews appear to have gathered the dust of many of them. Close by is the great fourteenth-century tithe barn, one of the largest of its kind surviving from medieval times. Resting on foundations of the local rust-brown 'pudding' stone, the barn is 191 feet long and 38 feet wide, its interior a noble perspective of towering oak posts and arching beams and cross-ties, giving the building an air of past importance and continuing dignity. It has the majesty of a cathedral nave.

Before the coming of the internal combustion engine at the turn of the century the people of Harmondsworth cared little about what was going on in the wider world. The spongy soil was ideal for their market gardening, which supplied vegetables and soft fruit to the markets of the fast-growing metropolis to the east, with its increasing suburban pressures. Generations of villagers had come and gone untroubled by the threat of encroachment. Their inns were weatherboarded, their cottage thatch mossy with age, their streams too lazy to move; a countryside of eccentric charm appealing only to the connoisseurs of landscape.

The new arterial road which slashed through that peaceful scene gave the village its last remaining years of rusticity. The old wooden fingerpost pointed 1¼ miles to Harmondsworth and its Gothic barn. But the final breathing space was brief. The flat broad acres which for centuries had supplied the simple living of the people were pegged out for bounding stretches of concrete and tarmac, runways of the airliners which now

3

operate there through all the hours of day and night. London Airport, sprawling offspring of the Second World War, routed the last vestiges of peace and quiet from Harmondsworth. The spectacular rise in the world of two sons of the long line of generations which has borne the contracted version of the Harmondsworth name had helped to decide the fate of the village.

The first appearance of the name of Harmsworth in one of its earlier varied spellings is in a Middlesex fine, or land sale, dated 1316. More than one expert investigation of the Harmsworth family line has been made. The most complete and exhaustive of these researches, recently carried out and accepted by the Royal College of Arms, establishes the direct descent of Alfred Harmsworth, Viscount Northcliffe, from Robert Harmsworth (1500–1557), archer, of Southampton.

The pull of the land was strong in the Harmsworth blood. Some of the men were market gardeners, others farmers. John Harmsworth, directly descended from Robert, the archer (who may have been a farmer also), moved from Tadley to Basingstoke, six miles away, to become overseer of the poor in that town. Through several generations the Harmsworth men's names alternated between Richard and Thomas. The farmhouse of the third Richard (baptised 1672) is still there in a part of Odiham locally known as Poland, a corruption of Poleing Lane End. The fifth Richard (born 1759) was Northcliffe's great-grandfather.

That Richard Harmsworth and his wife, Mary Martin, had four sons and four daughters. The seventh child and third son, Charles, was Northcliffe's grandfather. Born June 17, 1805, Charles Harmsworth was baptised in Odiham Chapel and went to Odiham Grammar School, a foundation of the seventeenth century for boys who would later serve their time as apprentices to a trade. It continued as a school until 1950, when in pursuance of the 1944 Education Act it was closed, the event being marked by a valedictory speech from a member of the county education committee who said: 'We want more schools like Odiham School. They turn out individuals who become capable citizens.' In the eighteenth and nineteenth centuries a number of the boys of the Harmsworth line attended the school.

When Charles Harmsworth left Odiham School he went to work as a carrier. His journeys sometimes took him to London and it was during one of them that he met the young woman who became his wife. She was Hannah Wickens, née Carter, a childless widow. Her birthplace was Swallowfield, near Reading, in Berkshire. A romantic rumour clung to her name. Her father, it was said, was of the royal blood. The name of George IV's brother, the Duke of York, was hinted at. Some small credence was given to the story by the complete absence of documentary evidence of Hannah Wickens's birth and by a message sent to North-

4

cliffe's father, Alfred Harmsworth, by an old nurse who on her death-bed was said to have had a secret to impart about his mother's origins. While Alfred Harmsworth, senior, may not have had Mr Yellowplush's bland self-assurance about his quality, temperamentally he was not impervious to the glamour of such a possibility, though there is no record of his having responded to the summons. Friends of his who were fellow members of the Sylvan Debating Club, of London, remembered his habit of announcing, with pontifical upraised hand, when he was elated by wine: 'I am descended from kings!'

Sir Leicester Harmsworth, one of Northcliffe's brothers, made notes of a discussion between himself and another brother, Cecil (Lord Harmsworth), in 1932. Each knew that their father had the habit, in the circumstances mentioned, of claiming illustrious forebears. They believed that he 'probably knew more than he told'. They agreed that certain facial resemblances in the family were remarkable in that connection, though wholly presumptive, 'but, even so, not entirely unconvincing'. There was the extraordinary likeness of Aunt Sarah Miller, their father's sister, to George III, 'especially as she grew older'. Another of the Harmsworth women 'had much the same look', and a Harmsworth grandson 'in laughing profile is exactly like the Prince of Wales'. Sir Leicester Harmsworth added to his note of the discussion:

Cecil hazarded a suggestion which, in the philosophic way, I regard as very strong. He said: How could one expect people like our father and Aunt Miller, of great distinction of manner and appearance, to come merely from a very humble Hampshire peasant circle? He remarked that it was unthinkable to him that they could have originated in that way. My own opinion is that the story is unprovable by evidence, at least so far as is at present known, but that it is undoubtedly based on sound surmise.

Hannah Carter had become Hannah Wickens by marrying, in 1822, a soldier of that name who had served in the Peninsular wars. She was sixteen and she signed the marriage register by 'making her mark'. He was thirty-seven and ended his days, in early middle age, as a Chelsea pensioner. He left his estate of £200 to a ward sergeant of the Royal Hospital; nothing to Hannah. They had no children and Hannah went back to her Berkshire hamlet, a few miles north of Odiham, to keep a grocer's shop.

Hannah has come down in the family records as a woman whose bearing and mental distinction were memorable in the sense of suggesting that an aristocratic principle was at work in her. Although she had a local accent, her contemporaries had no difficulty in recognizing that she was of superior fibre. She married Charles Harmsworth about 1833; no record of the place and actual date has been found. They went to live at 27 High Street, Portland Town, London, where they opened a greengrocer's business. Later they had a tobacconist's shop and also dealt in coal.

Portland Town as a name, and largely as a place, vanished from the London scene under the advancing tides of building which followed the industrial revolution. It was a district of cream stucco villas spaced over wide open ground. The unmade roads were soon to be improved into the naphtha-lamp lighted avenues and terraces of the polite new suburb of St. John's Wood. Its few shops and offices were concentrated in its short High Street, which was the Harmworths' address for a number of years: it is now St. John's Wood High Street. Bounded on the south side by Lord's cricket ground and The Regent's Park—its formal name, long abandoned—the chief amenity of Portland Town was its sylvan northern fringe. Right up to Hampstead on the heights there were fields. Kate Greenaway, who lived in Church Row, Hampstead, found daisies to paint in them and straying town children were startled by the sudden wonder of nightingale song from copse and hedgerow. Jerome K. Jerome, author of *Three Men in a Boat* and *The Passing of the Third Floor Back*, remembered Hampstead when it was 'a pleasant country town, connected with London by a three-horse bus. A footpath ascended from Swiss Cottage, through cornfields, to Church Row; and a pleasant country road, following a winding stream, led to the little town of Hendon.' Those northern suburbs-to-be remained aloof from the life of the metropolis which lay far down in the valley under its own smoky sky.

As a business man, Charles Harmsworth branched out from shopkeeping into building and small property ownership. He had a cousin, George Harmsworth, who was a bricklayer. Together they put up a number of small houses in Victoria Terrace, Portland Town Road and Barrow Hill Road, St. John's Wood. Charles drank too much. He died of alcoholism in his early fifties, after a long illness. Hannah was a widow again, now with two children to support. They had been married some twenty-four years. Their eldest child, Alfred, was born in the year that Victoria came to the throne, 1837. Alfred grew up with his mother's looks and more than a little of her personal style, the suggestion of impregnable inner dignity which had made her stand out among her class and kind. Between him and his sister Sarah Anne there was a wide gap in years caused by the death of several who died in infancy. The result for Alfred was a certain isolation and because of it his parents tended to make too much of him. With the idea of correcting that bias, they at first sent him to a small school for boarders at Kensal Green, and here he is, aged nine, writing to them with the lisping deference evoked by the unchallenged parental authority of those times:

Kensal Green,
December 10th, 1846

My Dear Parents,—It gives me much pleasure to announce to you that our vacation will commence on the 17th inst.

My endeavours have been exerted to progress in the branches of education assigned as most likely to benefit me in my future pursuits.

I beg most thankfully to acknowledge your constant kindness and care of me, and I trust that all my acts will be obedient, and evince my gratitude and respect for you.

Mr and Mrs Bilney desire me to present my very best respects to you. Give my love to Sister and all friends.

I am,
My dear parents,
Your affectionate son,
A. HARMSWORTH

Authority in another guise may have been at the boy's elbow as he wrote. The juveniles of the period were taught what was known as the epistolary art and were expected to show particular care in practising it in their letters home. There was a manual of instruction: '. . . to your superiors write with a becoming confidence, neither assuming nor servile; to your equals with an engaging freedom; to your inferiors with an affability that may prevent their feeling their inferiority; to all with respect'.

Stirrings and prompting among the keepers of the national conscience had led to the setting up in 1839 of a committee of the Privy Council to deal with funds voted by Parliament for education needs. By the time that Alfred Harmsworth was ready to go out into the world education was on the march and his mother had decided that there was a career for him as a teacher. The same decision was made by many mothers of 'bright' boys of the lower middle order of society. It reflected the Victorian emphasis on self-improvement and carried with it the respectable white-collar implications of a profession rather than a trade. At fourteen Alfred Harmsworth was entered as a student at St. Mark's College, Chelsea (now known as the College of St. Mark and St. John), established in the 1840s as one of the first teachers' training centres. Housed in a building linked romantically with an heiress of the Bowes-Lyon family and with Nelson's Emma, the college undertook the training of young teachers for the Church schools, receiving them at the age of thirteen or fourteen and sending them forth again at seventeen or eighteen into whatever teaching posts they might secure. Although the syllabus was thought advanced, few of the students reached matriculation standard and for several years they passed out from the college without examination. When, in Alfred Harmsworth's time, an examination system was instituted, there appeared

7

simultaneously in the college account books the note: '£2 10s. for wines and brandy given to students who were low and nervous.' The National Union of Teachers is commonly thought to have been conceived if not born under a tree in the college garden. The idea of forming it was discussed by some leaving students who had foregathered there for celebrations.

Alfred Harmsworth was at the college three years. He left at seventeen to go to his first teaching post, a junior mastership at the grammar school of Truro in Cornwall. The school had lately been moved, at the headmaster's own expense, from its original dilapidated building in St. Mary Street to Ryderville House, Fairmantle Street. There Alfred Harmsworth lived and worked for the next two years. One of his letters at the time, to a schoolfriend in London, was signed 'Army', a nickname which became 'Harmie' when in later years he was a familiar of the Middle Temple, London.

Of his two years at Truro there is almost no record, but life there may well have had its attractions for his highly sociable nature. The railway had not yet come from Plymouth and the last stage of the journey was still being done by coach. Not easy of access, Truro developed a self-sufficiency that made it commercially prosperous and socially busy. Tin from the ancient Cornish mines was brought in for stamping at the Coinage Hall, where the Duchy dues were fixed. The vice-warden of the Stannaries presided over the court which dealt with legal matters to do with the mining, and lawyers' offices were said to be as numerous in the city as shops. For a short spectacular period Truro was the Cornish metropolis, its winters gay with soirees and concerts and balls patronized by the county families, who did not care to make the long and occasionally hazardous journey to London for the season. Alfred Harmsworth had arrived in Truro by coach. He left it by coach, in 1857, two years before the railway joined the city to Plymouth. His father's life was ending and he returned to London to find his mother battling with her husband's affairs as a builder and petty landlord, presenting the then rare spectacle of a woman in business.

Science has not proved an hereditary factor in alcoholism, but it soon became obvious to those around him that Alfred Harmsworth, the schoolmaster, had a liking for drink. Partly, no doubt, it was due to his easy popularity. He had more than one man's share of charm. He had his mother's presence. He carried himself with the casual air of one whose instinct tells him that he was born to better things. A few glasses of wine and he behaved as if he had been raised to the peerage. The mother of his closest friend, Frederick Wood, who became a Civil Servant, wrote to her son stating her wish that he should not go into lodgings with Harmsworth, whom she thought too extravagant in tastes and 'too grand' in style. He had a romantic imagination. His sister Sarah, in his eyes, was the most beautiful of women. There was not a man in the world, he later used to say, who was good enough to be the husband of his eldest daughter, Geraldine. In his friendships he was warmly staunch. He attracted men's regard; from some the limits of devotion. It was one of the notable things about him that his friends were mostly men of distinction. Running through his life was a religious faith which survived many falterings, deepening his remorse for follies from which it was never strong enough to save him. His positive social gifts were offset by his manifest lack of will and purpose as a professional man. He preferred good company, the pleasures of conversation, the easy way; one of those men who are never fired by ambition to exert their best powers or to prove their true quality.

★   ★   ★

Back in London, he entered on a phase of his schoolmastering life that has always been a blank in the family records. Nothing is known of how he supported himself for the next three or four years. It is thought that he filled temporary teaching posts. As to means, his mother had a small income from rents in St. John's Wood that were not always regularly paid. Then, in 1861, he was chosen from thirteen applicants for the place of fourth master at the Royal Hibernian Military School, Dublin, a civilian appointment in a predominantly military establishment. The school had been founded in 1764 as a 'Hospital for Maintaining, Educating and Apprenticing the Orphans and Children of Soldiers in Ireland'. George III gave the project his formal blessing in 1768 with a charter authorizing the erection of a handsome range of buildings in Phoenix Park. The school was one of three to have the privilege of colours granted and presented by the Sovereign, the others being the Royal Military College at Sandhurst, and the Duke of York's School at Dover, with which last the Royal Hibernian School has since been amalgamated. At that time religious instruction headed the curriculum, though the masters were all Army trained. Alfred Harmsworth's arrival on the staff was one of the results of a scheme of reorganization designed to bring in teachers from a purely academic background.

Dublin's social and cultural allurements could hardly have failed to attract a young man of Alfred's easy habits and small resources. The move was doubtless congenial to his temperament, which was capable of being oppressed by his mother's insistence on the virtue of 'getting on', the over-riding passion of the Victorian middle class mind. Values were different in Dublin, with its Georgian door knockers echoing through drawing-rooms in which the songs of Tom Moore were sung at untuned pianos and where the conversation was apt to be at its wittiest on the subject of funerals. The city had lost some of its political importance since the Act of Union of 1800 but none of its eighteenth-century resistance to provincialism. It was recovering a consciousness of its old standing as a capital not only of Ireland but of Europe. Plans were in being for the opening of its National Gallery on the site of the Great Industrial Exhibition of eleven years before. It had been a matter of civic pride that a large part of the exhibition had been 'reserved for the fine arts'. Another exhibition was being organized, 'to display the existing state of manufactures in Ireland, to note the progress they have made, and to discern what capabilities the country and the people possess for the development of new departments of industry'. Although at any moment tensions might flash forth like black lightning from brooding Irish hearts, a new optimism was in the Dublin air. To view the city from the platform of Nelson's Pillar in what was to become O'Connell Street was a memorable local experience. You looked down on the stir and colour of Dublin life and on tangy autumn mornings it was said that you could smell, up there, the good coffee they made at Jude's Hotel and catch the drifting strains of the music played at Fortune's Refreshment Saloon.

It was in the Dublin of the 1860s that Alfred Harmsworth met the girl who was to become his wife and the mother of one of the most remarkable families of modern times.

*   *   *

Geraldine Mary Maffett was a comely and pleasing young woman. Photographs and the testimony of her contemporaries have left no doubt of it. Her auburn hair, worn in a roll on the nape of her neck, and fine fresh complexion were to be a striking feature of her appearance all her days. She was to retain as long, too, her sweet singing voice. She was born in 1838, the daughter of William Maffett, land agent, of Dublin, who was then aged fifty-seven. He was twice married. Geraldine was the fifth of his eight children by his second wife, Margaret Finlayson.

William Maffett, who had started out in the world as a grocer's errand boy, had a harsh reputation as a business man and that he was domestically tyrannical is suggested by his custom of 'seeing' each of his children for a quarter of an hour each day, an interview which Geraldine said she always dreaded. His office was at 24 South Frederick Street, Dublin; his home at 27 Pembroke Place. Born in County Down in 1781, he could remember duels in Dublin, and sedan chairs. He was of wholly Scottish descent rooted in the small town of Moffat, in Dumfriesshire. Margaret Finlayson was also of Lowland Scottish stock, with a single deviation into the French on her mother's side. Both families were staunch in their attachment to the Protestant faith.

William Maffett's people had long lived in County Down. They were yeoman farmers and ministers of the Presbyterian Church. Their connections ran distantly through a number of those leading Ulster-Scottish families which contributed much to the public life of the northern province and still more to the greatness of the British name overseas. While the ancestral background on both sides was exclusively Lowland Scottish, the environmental influences were Irish, and of some of the Maffetts, and particularly of Geraldine's eldest brother Willie, it was said that they were as Irish as the O'Connells of Kerry or the Joyces of Galway. In that sense, Geraldine herself stood apart. Her temperament remained true to her Scottish heredity. She seemed to be resistant to local influences and, for example, never had a marked Irish accent. She had not been to school; she was educated, with her sisters, by French and German governesses. She had precisely the qualities of mind that Alfred Harmsworth did not have; theirs was a meeting, and in due course a union, of sympathetic opposites, a subject which inspired Alfred to not wholly coherent philosophic reflections in a letter of many pages written to her during their engagement:

. . . As love is not within my control, I ask myself in whose hands is it? The question requires no answering here. He who can penetrate the hidden subtleties and dissect at a glance the complete mechanism of human character, who comprehends from the first to the last step the consequences, who has appointed each one to his task in the great Laboratory of life. He has appointed also the help-mate, and has wisely and beautifully pointed out who is fit for whom not by presenting an estimate of character, but by the subtle, thrilling and uncontrollable impulse bringing two from opposite ends of the globe, maybe, and of exactly opposite temperaments, it most often is, and draws them into the Union, so mysterious, if I might dare, but the Proprieties say no, I could show you how mysterious is this Union of being . . .

Soulful verbosity was characteristic of Alfred Harmsworth's style of thought and expression. 'I want your love,' he went on to inform Geraldine, 'and if you can give me that with no reserve, trusting happily to that love, then is my life complete', adding with quivering pen the peroration: 'If distrust or worldly teaching blight your budding affection, I am indeed alone and my life has no flowers.' The courtship lasted two years. Geraldine said that it was Alfred's laugh which had first attracted her to him. To her he was a knightly figure, capable of releasing her from the abiding dullness of the Maffett family life. She was ambitious. She had the Scottish urge to go forth into the world. She had been to London, an unsettling experience. She had seen the grey-haired Duke of Wellington outside Apsley House and Madame Tussaud taking the money at her waxworks show. Provoked by her family's opposition to the match, she spurred Alfred along the path of self-advancement. She appreciated his intellectual resource. Too often she saw it wasted in talking. Dublin was full of failures who could talk. For her the teaching profession gave neither social status nor security. She insisted that it held no future for him and that he would be wise to read law. Constantly she goaded him by a will which was stronger than his own. She often said, then and later, that he needed 'stirring up'.

That in due course Alfred became a barrister was a triumph of her faith in him and possibly also of her determination to prove that her instinct in marrying him had been sound. The choice of the Middle Temple was made because members of the Irish bar gained in prestige by being 'called' in England. Alfred never practised in Ireland. He went to London to be formally admitted as a student early in 1864. While he was there, Geraldine's favourite sister Sidney died. In his letter of sympathy to Geraldine, Alfred was moved to quote lines 'from one of my own poems' and subjoined the hopeful thought that 'your Papa will be softened by his loss'. There was that little house at Chapelizod, just outside Dublin, he reminded her, which they had been to see together and in which he felt that they could be completely happy as man and wife. 'I am afraid of its being let if I do not stir myself. We should save something by vegetables. There is a nice greenhouse. Think of it, darling, and speak to your Mama. Ever your true Alfred.'

They were married 'according to the rites and ceremonies of the United Church of England and Ireland', at St. Stephen's Church, Dublin, on September 22, 1864. The marriage certificate gave Alfred's occupation as 'Gentleman', not 'Schoolmaster'. It described his father as 'Gentleman', not 'House Owner'. He was twenty-seven, she a year younger. 'Geraldine looked exceedingly pretty', Alfred's sister Sarah wrote in her diary. 'The chariot for the happy pair had a postilion.' Some of the Maffetts had said that they would not go to the wedding, persisting in the view that a poor schoolmaster was not the right suitor for their attractive sister and conveniently forgetting that their father had himself begun life in a lowly way. Old William Maffett retorted to this show of snobbishness with peremptory vigour. Those of the family who were not at the wedding would be cut out of his will. All the Maffetts were at the church. But it was not until the fame and power of Geraldine's eldest son had spread across the continents that the marriage became at last acceptable to them.

After a £10 honeymoon in County Wicklow, at the beauty spot of Glendalough, about which Thackeray said a tune should be written, Alfred and Geraldine Harmsworth settled down to the married state in the small house of their dreams at Chapelizod, called Sunnybank. It stood behind a wall screening it from the main road running westward out of Dublin and had a garden sloping down to the Liffey, with a small orchard at the side. Time's mark was on Sunnybank, as on the rest of Chapelizod, a decaying Georgian charm. It was to take the fancy, in due course, of a new residential class who would turn the village into a favourite Dublin suburb without finally destroying the reputation given to it by poets as eminent as Tennyson and Swinburne, who regarded it as the source of the Isolde legend. Also surviving are the ivy-hung remains of an old house which figures in one of the weird tales of Sheridan le Fanu. The change had scarcely begun when the Harmsworths went to live at Chapelizod. They paid £20 a year, conforming with some nicety to the imperative of Victorian domestic economy that rent should represent one-tenth of income. Between them at that time Alfred and Geraldine Harmsworth had £220 a year. Seven months after the marriage William Maffett died, aged eighty-four, leaving an estate of about £30,000. His death was a cause of dismay to Alfred Harmsworth. Both he and Geraldine now felt themselves exposed to the unhindered ill-will of those Maffetts who had been against the marriage. Alfred wrote home to his mother:

Sunnybank,
Tuesday

. . . I have never seen so large a private funeral. Every one testified their respect for Mr M. His bankers sent a note of condolence directly they heard of his death. . . . I was present at the reading of the will. His estate is estimated at £33,000. The two younger sons seemed much surprised that it was not larger. Charlie was to have had, but refused, the office, although the work is of the lightest and easiest, being something like that of a private banker's to sit and receive money which you can dispose of again to best advantage—being exactly like that of an Army agent's. I wish I had the chance.

. . . It will probably add £100 to our income but it puts an end to hopes I had begun to entertain of getting into the office some day and, anyway, Mr M. is a powerful friend gone. Mr M.'s decease was always the period I fixed for our stay in Ireland, that is to say, I determined, unless anything very much better presented, to stay here till then. But he being gone, I shall now look to London and strive to bring G. there to supply in you and my friends a warmer home than that she has lost here.

Everard Hamilton is staying here; his poor father, when in the will Mr M. alluded to his dear deceased daughter Adelaide, the wife of John Hamilton, Esq., went into such paroxysms of grief as I think I never saw. He has never mentioned her since her death and the least allusion to former times makes him shake all over and his face twitch with pain. He is the kindest friend we have and I shall never forget it, I hope.

Ever yr. fond
ALFRED

Alfred's desire to find a more congenial home for Geraldine was to remain unfulfilled for two more years. He was not sufficiently well advanced in his law studies to risk a gamble with his future, more especially as a first child was expected and new charges on his income had to be faced. Preparing for that event, he undertook spare-time tutoring with a family named Ferrier of Glenmaroon Lodge, Chapelizod, and sought also to earn something extra by writing for *The Dublin Saturday Review*, a journal with a brief, ineffectual history. He wrote two stories for it, but received no payment for the work.

Harsh as old William Maffett may have been as a man of business, a touch of whimsical gallantry appeared in his will, in giving tokens of remembrance to 'my good friend Eliza Finlayson . . ., my sincere friend Ellen Finlayson . . ., my fair friend Catherine Bayly . . ., my sweet friend Mary Denauvineux . . ., my kind friend Hannah Carey . . . .'. His business instinct complicated the will to so great an extent that expectations from it were frustrated by long drawn-out legal proceedings, a result of family disputes. The Maffett children were to receive £3,000 each. Alfred Harmsworth's diary suggests that hopes of that amount for his wife were never realized. A final settlement was not forthcoming until well on into the present century, by which time the value of the estate had fallen heavily. The diary refers to small payments coming to Geraldine from Ireland from time to time, usually when Alfred and his family were in serious need and ascribed by him then to the intervention of 'a higher power'.

*　　　*　　　*

Late in the afternoon of Saturday, July 15, 1865, Alfred Harmsworth was in the garden of Sunnybank when the family doctor, James Maguire, who lived at Belgrove, just across the river, came downstairs to announce that Geraldine had given birth to a boy. The father's response to the news was to pull off his tasselled smoking-cap and throw it joyfully into the air. His excitement marked an event of greater consequence to the Harmsworth name and fortunes than he would ever know, a fact that was to become a source of infinite regret to the son born that day. Having been allowed by the doctor to see mother and child for a few happy minutes, Alfred Harmsworth sat down at his bureau to fill in the letters which he had drafted in skeleton form in advance, leaving a space for the child's sex to be written in, with the precise time of the birth. The first of the letters was sent off at once to his mother-in-law:

> Sunnybank,
> July 15th, 1865

Dear Mrs Maffett,—Mrs Harmsworth was safely delivered of a son this evening at 6.50 o'clock. In haste. Yrs. very sincerely Alf: Harmsworth, Sunnybank, Chapelizod.

In the birth certificate, the father's occupation was given as 'School-master at the Royal Hibernian Military Academy'. The child was taken to the parish church of Chapelizod—where his parents were members of the choir—to be christened on October 12, 1865. He was named Alfred Charles William: Alfred after his father, Charles after his paternal grand-father, the Hampshire carrier turned London greengrocer and builder, and William, after his maternal grandfather, the Dublin land agent. He was spoken of at the time as 'a strangely quiet child', and as having 'solemn blue eyes'. He had an unusually large head. His head seemed to grow faster than his body.

During the next few months the situation in Ireland became menacing. The Fenians represented a revolutionary movement which, in those middle 'sixties, created fears and tensions as far afield as Australia and North America, where in 1866 some of its more fanatical adherents began an invasion of Canada over the Niagara river, one of history's forgotten episodes. Others shocked English public opinion, and shook English nerves, by dynamiting a hole in the wall of Clerkenwell Prison, killing and injuring a number of innocent people. That year, 1867, the Harms-worths left Ireland, their going hastened by a rumour that Alfred Harms-worth, as an Englishman living in Ireland, had been 'spotted as fair game' by the Dublin Fenians. When Geraldine Harmsworth hurried in from the village, to tell her husband what she had heard of the threat, he noted it in his diary and added: 'Reading law with my sword on my knee. *Dieu nous garde.*' By then a second child had arrived, a girl. The father's occupa-tion was given as 'Barrister', though he had not yet been called to the Bar. She received the names of Geraldine Adelaide Hamilton.

On March 12, 1867, the two babies were wrapped in blankets and carried to a waiting cab. It took them and their parents into Dublin: 'Sunnybank abandoned for ever', is noted in Alfred's diary. The family stayed a short time with Geraldine's brother-in-law, John Hamilton, another Ulster-Scot living in Dublin, and then went on to one of her sisters in Armagh and from there to Belfast and London. A few evenings before leaving Dublin, Alfred had gone to a Dickens reading. 'One of the greatest treats I ever had,' he wrote in his diary. 'I cannot attempt to describe my sensations on first beholding this wonderful man.' Geraldine Harmsworth left her native land with anything but a heavy heart. Loyal in sentiment to her Ulster connections, she had no great love for Ireland, holding the over-simplified view that the North was constructive and the South destructive. Patriotism is not a feminine virtue; besides, her home life had been dull and unadventurous until the arrival of Alfred Harms-worth from England. Her greatest personal devotion throughout his life was to him, the Englishman by whom she had fourteen children in a succession of pregnancies continuing to her forty-seventh year. Her

15

attitude to her children was matriarchal rather than maternal. She could write to one of her boys on Christmas Eve and forget the season's greetings, scribbled afterwards on the back of the envelope. What she had to give was not deep feeling but moral strength. Hers was the nature of the Roman matron in whom a sense of justice is stronger than the affections. To the last, though never in a forbidding, imperious spirit, she dominated her family. An exceptional truthfulness was one of the outstanding qualities that bound them to her. Cecil (afterwards Lord Harmsworth), her third son, said: 'She was the most entirely truthful human being I ever knew.'

They stayed for a few weeks with Alfred's mother, at 6 Eaton Terrace, St. John's Wood, until they found a house of their own. Hannah was wiser in years and experience. Geraldine had the advantage of a better start in life: she impressed her mother-in-law by singing in Italian and by her piano playing. That she had a true idea of her husband's family background and circumstances until she arrived in London is a matter of some doubt. Her upbringing, by governesses, had been directed to social ends and the subsequent drudgery of her married life must have been hard to bear. Possibly by way of contrast and relief, she took part in public readings from Shakespeare and Dickens at the schoolroom in Victoria Mews, Belsize Road.

Their first London home was at 6 Alexandra Terrace, St. John's Wood, later 30 Alexandra Road (since demolished), ten minutes' walk from the Eaton Terrace house. Instead of the Liffey making music at the bottom of the garden, there was the Great Northern Railway and sulphurous smoke. At first, Alfred Harmsworth did not take kindly to the new surroundings; 'misgivings that we may not be so happy as at pretty little Sunnybank with its sunny memories', and it is possibly significant that soon he was writing in the same place, in his scrappily kept diary: 'Made a fool of myself last evening. No more drink', and that increasingly he sought his pleasures farther afield, usually at public-houses grandiloquently named.

His income was coming from the small emoluments of an assistant secretaryship in the London Office of the Commission inquiring into the revenues of the Established Church in Ireland. The appointment lasted only nine months, at the end of which time he received a written testimonial to the value of his services. He was continuing his legal studies in what appears to have been a somewhat desultory way and at the same time battling unsuccessfully with his weakness for drink. 'Took too much wine.' 'Very seedy, my own fault, too much drink again.' The confessional note recurs in pathetic successive phases of self-reproach and heaven-sped promises of reform. Readily given to morbid thoughts, he was much cast down in spirit by an ice-skating calamity in Regent's Park, when forty lives were lost: 'Thousands gazing at the mournful search for bodies.' A regular churchgoer at St. Augustine's, Kilburn, after the ice accident he discovered in himself a growing tendency to religious doubt and the torment of it drove him to The King of Prussia and next-morning remorse. 'Very seedy, owing to my own folly.' Left briefly to himself on the evening of his thirtieth birthday in 1867: 'I muse on my fleeting years and purposeless life. *Cui bono.*'

The baby Alfred, who was to cut such a tremendous figure in the world, was often sickly: 'Poor little Alfred', 'little Alfred poorly again', 'Baby Alf very unwell with his head', 'little Alf very unwell—Dr. says congestion of the brain'. These attacks were spoken of in the family as 'little Alfred's fits'. Entries about the child's health occur frequently in the diary during what seem to have been two critical years. The last, in June 1868, reads: 'Sunny a little ailing in his head—God preserve him.' The child was remarkably silent; he rarely uttered a cry. His mother thought his silences 'were almost alarming'. The Dublin relatives said among themselves, when she left for London, that they did not believe she would rear him. She was not the kind of mother to have dreams and visions for her first-born, to imagine him as a young eagle who would one day raise them all aloft on the pinions of incredible good fortune.

'Little Alfred' became thereafter 'Sunny' in his father's diary. Nicknames were common currency in the family of Alfred and Geraldine Harmsworth. 'Dot' and 'Bunny' and 'Buffles' and 'Puggy' and 'Bonchie' and 'Pop' and 'Boo' survived among them long after their romping days were done.

The arrival of 'Bunny' was another family event of great consequence: Harold, born at 6 Alexandra Terrace on April 26, 1868, and destined to become the first Lord Rothermere and a principal architect of the family fortunes. In his birth certificate, contrasting with the previous entries for Alfred and Geraldine, his father's occupation was given as 'Student at Law'. His nickname stressed the timid side of his nature. In the following year a third son was born, Cecil Bisshopp. The family name for him was 'Buffles', for buffalo, because of his shaggy head of hair.

Chapter Two

A Toy Printing Set

ALFRED HARMSWORTH, senior, was called to the bar in 1869, having regularly 'eaten his dinners' in term time at the Middle Temple. He had sat for the Trinity term examination, in which there were written and oral tests in constitutional law and legal history, equity, common law, real property, jurisprudence and civil and international law. He was placed in a middle position with somewhat uneven markings: good in equity, not so good in common law. Still, an achievement for one with his by no means propitious start in life and excuse enough for his admiring wife's assertion at a later time that her sons owed their success to his intellectual brilliance.

His family was increasing, his income falling. At the outset of his career as a barrister he had to support a wife and four children. He had several of the qualities which would have enabled him to make progress in his profession; a quick mind, genuine eloquence, a good presence. There was something indefinably memorable about Alfred Harmsworth as there had been about his mother, a quality which apparently impressed itself everywhere but in the courts. The horse bus drivers on the 'Atlas' route from the City to St. John's Wood were attentive in saluting him and his tall hat was always solemnly raised in response. Sir Max Pemberton, the novelist, said that it was impossible when talking to him to believe with Carlyle that the grand manner had perished with the French Revolution. And no one was to know that, frequently, he had to borrow the bus fare from one of his sons.

His manner with the barmaids of the sumptuously named public-houses was not less agreeably formal; a polite bow from the waist, the flourished hat, a greeting in a voice that was like no other man's, firm but caressing and conveying a sense of hidden excellence which was never finally eclipsed, though as likely as not before the evening was out he would feel sufficiently exalted to proclaim himself 'a descendant of kings'. And, indeed, the portrait of him exhibited by his friend, Seymour Lucas, R.A., at the Royal Academy in 1874 and now hung in the Treasurer's Room at Middle Temple, shows him to have had the Brunswick look, an ancestral face with the bloom of gentility on it. While the physical suggestion of high breeding was strong enough, the verbal allusion may have been nothing more than a jesting echo of his sojourn among the Irish.

Lord Lytton had referred in print to St. John's Wood as 'the Grove of the Evangelist', and in doing so had embellished the conversation of Alfred Harmsworth, the barrister. He delighted in the poetry of it and often wrote it at the top of his letters. In that suburban square mile or so he found many congenial associates, by no means all of them fellow patrons of the public-houses. Many celebrated persons lived in what a local historian said was not so much a parish as 'a metropolitan oasis'. Illustrious names adorned the directory: artists, writers, politicians, people of the theatre. In the houses of some of the older families the tapping of crinoline hoops was still to be heard as the last of their wearers, usually servants, descended the stairs.

Ruefully surveying his career, as he often did in his diary, Alfred Harmsworth could console himself with having originated at that period an institution which has made its mark on more than the social and in-tellectual amenities of St. John's Wood. A direction to his most prominent talent, that of being able to speak well, had proposed itself to him when one evening, journeying homeward by bus, he had the notion of starting a debating society. Most of his friends were drawn from the circles of literature and art. 'Harmie', as some of them called him, had no difficulty in securing their help in forming, in 1868, what became the Sylvan Debating Club, a name which, in its suggestion of a classical rural context, was extravagant even then.

Four of his sons became members and the club's minute book has a note of an evening during one of its less prosperous periods when the Harmsworths made up half the total attendance. The club's president, Judge Sir Sherston Baker, said that the future Lord Northcliffe was at one time regular in his attendance and spoke frequently. Northcliffe gave the club a loving-cup, which it still cherishes. As a founder-member, Alfred Harmsworth, senior, was for twenty-one years the club's vice-president; curiously, never its president. He mentions in his diary, as if it had been a personal reflection on him, that having at the start been made secretary he was outvoted from that post immediately afterwards. There it is recorded that he took part in debating a variety of controversial topics: 'Horseflesh as Food', 'The Morality of Music Halls', 'Government Super-vision of the Social Evil', 'Abolition of Capital Punishment', and 'Marriage with Deceased Wife's Sister', which latter, he noted, 'fell flat'. At one of the meetings he was 'dreadfully alarmed' by the prospect of losing the toss-up for a round of drinks, 'I have no money. Very low spirited indeed. Never worse.' He wrote his advice on public speaking to his son Cecil:

I am glad you are going in for oratory. You ought to have picked up hints at the Sylvan. You should write out first the principal parts of your intended speech, and this until you acquire such practical skill as to be able to dispense with such aids. Read the best speeches, but above all read the best poets. Study the management of the voice—in this every Irish speaker I have heard failed altogether.

The Sylvan Debating Club survives as London's second oldest society of its kind. Through the changes of the greater part of a century it has provided a platform and often a distinguished hearing for speakers who subsequently became prominent at the bar and in politics and other spheres. It remembers Harmsworth, senior, as a loyal supporter and an outstanding exponent of the art of public debate. His son Cecil left notes of his visits to the Sylvan, whose meetings were first held at the Princess of Wales tavern and afterwards at the Eyre Arms Hotel, a name commemorating a well-known St. John's Wood property-owning family. From the grounds of the hotel some of the early aeronauts made balloon ascents and much later in the century it developed an important boxing connection which led to the formation of the National Sporting Club. Cecil Harmsworth wrote:

As a boy I often attended Sylvan meetings . . . and it was a pleasure to me to observe that my father was almost always the orator of the evening. 'How wonderfully this Irishman speaks!' said a visitor to the club who sat next to me on one of these occasions. But the orator was an Englishman of pure Hampshire stock.

Most of Alfred Harmsworth's work as a barrister consisted of 'devilling' for busier men of the profession, in which it was generally agreed that he himself might have been a success but for the reputation, justified or not, gained for him by his drinking habits. Whether drink was an indispensable ingredient of his existence cannot now be judged. The evidence of his diary suggests that he was most given to drinking because other men were thirsty, that he enjoyed above all the social side of drinking, that he had not the power of will to detach himself from convivial company.

What may be an imperfectly understood fact of social history was the extent of the contemporary belief in drink as a medical prophylactic. The Victorians lived in dread of consumption, as tuberculosis was commonly called, diphtheria, smallpox, typhoid, scarlet fever, scourges capable of wiping out families and a source of far-spread anxieties. Many drinkers doubtless rationalized a bad habit on account of its alleged preventive or remedial value. Others genuinely resorted to it as a guard against infections which the doctors seemed powerless to ward off or cure. These fears were real. There may have been a deeper relevance than was seen in the popular songs which glorified drink. While Alfred Harmsworth may not have been a fastidious drinker, he could appreciate the pleasures of good wine. A solicitor friend of his, a connoisseur who was in the habit of sending his best sherry for a voyage to China and back, one evening at dinner brought out some specially prized port. 'What do you think of it?' he asked his guest, whose glass was empty. 'I will give you the answer,' Harmsworth replied, 'when we've finished the bottle.'

In the courts Alfred, senior, attracted notice by his use of language as well as by forensic skill. Appearing once for the London and North Western Railway Company, he spoke for nearly four hours and, on sitting down, received 'much praise' from the judge and his fellow members of the bar. He had a gift for repartee. Cross-examining a man said to have stolen a leg of mutton, he asked: 'What did you do with it?' 'I threw it into the doctor's garden,' was the reply. 'No doubt to be cured,' said Harmsworth with the effortlessness that was one of his chief characteristics as a speaker. There was a time when he aspired to the higher reaches of the law and fancied his chances of gaining a county court judgeship. His hardly characteristic enterprise, on that occasion, in gaining the support of a number of influential colleagues was not rewarded by fortune. He had no better luck when he sought preferential consideration for employment in the humbler role of legal adviser to the governors of a lock hospital. He practised on the south-eastern circuit, at the Middlesex, Essex, Hertford, St. Albans and Colchester sessions. His chambers were at 4 Garden Court, Temple, where Oliver Goldsmith had lived in another building on the same site; at 6 Pump Court, where Fielding lodged; and in his last year at 3 Essex Court, where John Evelyn had lived. He appeared from time to time for the Great Northern Railway Company, without securing the permanent retainer he had hoped for from that connection. Twice he lost his voice as a result of throat weakness, compelling him to give up practice. He appeared in court several times with a deputy to speak for him. The second visitation of what has always been regarded in the Harmsworth family as a congenital ailment deprived him of a livelihood for many months. His second son, the late Lord Rothermere, remembered that during that time there was often only bread for breakfast and more than once no Sunday lunch. A point of extremity was reached at which the youngest children were wrapped in newspapers at night, for want of blankets. Freemasonry may have helped him to survive the worst crises. He was for five years a member of the Honor and Generosity Lodge of that order in St. John's Wood.

Geraldine Harmsworth's staunch character did not unfailingly rise above these vicissitudes. She had many despondent hours. The comforts of being a Maffett daughter were in sharp contrast to the woes of being a Harmsworth wife. There had been a time when, for instance, she could gaily follow the fashions of the day. Now her clothes often came from the wardrobes of relatives and friends. From her own resources she had to make do with the homely cape and bonnet, while her better-off St. John's Wood neighbours were draped in gowns with skirts built up in successive flouncy layers and displaying the 'polonaise' open effect in front with more bows, more flounces, more tucks. They wore little ruffles at the neck and had their hair done up in a 'chignon' at the back. The colours of their gowns were chemically bright.

Behind Geraldine Harmsworth's domestic inexperience there was a certain ineptitude; she could not sew or knit, a handicap in that sometimes impoverished household. Beef was fivepence a pound, coal seventeen shillings a ton, but the shadow of penury hovered constantly near. 'Harmie' had his moments of good fortune. He returned early one day from chambers to fling three sovereigns and three shillings on the kitchen table, an event for celebration, his usual fee being half a guinea or less. He ordered Geraldine to go forth and buy salmon for supper; they would have a treat. Like Dora Copperfield, she came back with a whole salmon flapping from her basket. She had not known that it could be bought by the pound.

There was a short period of comparative affluence in which Alfred Harmsworth felt justified in taking into his service a black boy with the name of Jack Wasp, to wait on him in the Temple or at home, as required. The boy was put into the clothes of a *valet de chambre*, which suited his name as well as his person. That in a few weeks he had disappeared with his master's watch may have had more than moral implications.

*   *   *

Geraldine's stand-by in every domestic crisis, of finance or of temperament, was Alfred's sister Sarah, who had gone over to Dublin for the wedding, receiving much esteem from Geraldine for doing so, and, incidentally, hearty approval of her good looks in that city of good-looking women. Married to Thomas Hendry, a Writer to the Signet, and after his death to Francis Miller, a London solicitor—'Mr Miller', always, in her references to him—Sarah had the good looks that were exaggerated into sensational beauty by her brother's lively imagination, a sympathetic nature, and the mysterious aristocratic core. She was known in her early twenties as 'the belle of St. John's Wood'. One of her accomplishments was beautiful handwriting. She was a good talker, fastidious about not using the same word twice in a sentence, and remembered also for her clear, sweet, sympathetic voice, heard with great effect in her readings from Dickens. She lived at 16 Cavendish Road, St. John's Wood. In 1886, she launched a weekly paper of her own, the *Kensington Advertiser* (later *Kensington Society*), a daring project for a woman in those days. The paper had a life of three years, long enough to bring about a cure of the depression into which she had fallen after the death of her young son. Pertaining to that sorrow, it was a satisfaction of hers to say that she had erected over his grave a cross 'which can be seen a long way off'.

Another relative who proved to be also a friend was one of the Irish cousins, Florence Hamilton, daughter of Geraldine's sister Adelaide. 'Flo' was admiringly recalled by Cecil Harmsworth as 'a dashing brunette with the raven hair and brilliant complexion of an Irish colleen. We Harmsworths', he wrote, 'have always regarded the Hamiltons with particular affection. Not because of their double relationship with us, but because of their loyal friendship in bad times and good.' The Hamilton and Maffett lines had been joined by marriage in 1754. The Hamiltons sprang from the stock of the dukes of that name and of the earls of Haddington. Receiving that information, Alfred Harmsworth communicated his satisfaction in it to his diary. A close examination of the Hamilton and Maffett connection was made in 1891 in *The Hamilton Memoirs* by Everard Hamilton, B.A., of Dundrum, Co. Dublin, reprinted in 1920. Later investigation has produced new proofs that Northcliffe's mother came from an ancestry that was wholly Scottish until, in the seventeenth century, it took fresh root in Ireland. An earlier William Maffett had married into the famous Dublin silversmiths' family of Walker, whose works have long been collectors' pieces.

The Maffett side of the family was the more positive and robust. Yet it did not impose itself in obvious physical terms on the Harmsworths. The second Harmsworth son, Harold, had the slightly pendulous lower lip of his Maffett grandfather. With that small exception, the Harmsworth sons and daughters showed a remarkable degree of genetic unanimity in resisting the Maffett impact. They all took after their father. His facial imprint is not less strong in the second generation of Harmsworths.

★   ★   ★

Soon it was clear that Alfred Harmsworth's meagre earning power could not support the expenses of 6 Alexandra Terrace, and a move was made to a small wooden box of a house in the Vale of Health at Hampstead. It is a part of Hampstead Heath that had gained notoriety in earlier times from the laundresses who obtained a concession from the lord of the manor to use it as a drying ground. They made it their exclusive territory and were belligerently jealous in protecting their rights. There were people still living who could remember the last clothes-line posts held by licence under that ancient grant. 'Vale of Health' was a picturesque invention of a man named Woods who had later bought the low-lying, swampy part of the original Heath for development purposes. He drained it off and built a row of little weather-boarded houses which became known as Woods' Cottages. It was the era of a popular song acclaiming the charms of life at Hampstead on its hill: '*Hampstead is the place to ruralize-ri-ti-larooralize. . . .*' The little house the Harmsworths moved to was one of Woods' Cottages. It was known as 'Rose Cottage', until Ernest Rhys, editor of 'Everyman's Library', went to live there. Satisfied that it had been occupied in former times by Leigh Hunt, the poet and essayist and allegedly the original of Harold Skimpole in Dickens's *Bleak House*, Rhys re-named it 'Hunt Cottage', as it continues to be called. An old iron pump at the back had its place in literary history. Leigh Hunt, heard pumping furiously at it, was said to be working off his bad tempers. At any rate, in April 1870 Alfred Harmsworth moved his fast-growing family to a scene that had been familiar to Byron, Keats and Shelley.

Older residents had heard their grandfathers speak of a time when highwaymen lay in wait along the track leading from Jack Straw's Castle to the Spaniard's Inn. The dome of St. Paul's Cathedral, looking like a floating silver bubble in the haze of a summer's day, was visible across miles of fields where the urban future did not begin to declare itself until the eye reached Primrose Hill. Beyond, Islington and Marylebone were beginning to lose their identity in the spreading roof huddle of the capital. 'A courteous old farmer invited us into one of his fields with a good view of Harrow', whose God-pointing spire stood solitary in the rural north-west. Alfred Harmsworth was writing in his diary at the end of a day's outing with his two eldest boys, Alfred and Harold. They had been blackberrying at Hendon.

Signing the tenancy agreement for 'Rose Cottage', Alfred, senior, was much vexed by his personal circumstances. Lincoln Bennett, the hat people, had called again: 'Wrote them a sharp note.' Lodge, the butcher, was inquiring about his bill: 'Wrote to him, excusing payment.' *Chambers' Journal* had declined the articles he had been submitting: 'My usual luck.' There was 'a black Thursday' when he had been obliged to part with a Dutch still life which he had long treasured. It came up at Christie's: '£9 15s.' His midday meal, in Hall at the Middle Temple or at one of the Fleet Street eating-houses, was often no more than a plate of soup with a roll. He complained of feeling weak and tired from too little food. An ironical fate delivered at the door of his chambers a glass case of stuffed tropical birds, sent by a client in lieu of fees. Lodge, the butcher, served him with a writ: 'Monstrous piece of pettifogging.' His mind, he wrote in the diary, was 'fearfully disturbed at our state'. He had repetitious dreams of fat cattle, naked boys, open Bibles, of catching a swallow in flight. 'Geraldine and I do not bear our troubles well', he wrote in the same place. There were quarrels. Geraldine would wait for him to come home and, hearing his stumbling footsteps, would go to the door and meet him with anger in her voice.

He had a rueful humour. After listening to one of his recitals of financial distress, a friend of his remarked: 'You don't appear to be worrying much.' Harmsworth answered: 'I imagine my creditors are doing all the worrying that is necessary.' Unlike Oliver Goldsmith, he had no genius for poverty. The mood of elegy is rarely absent from his diary pages. They are those of a low blood pressure temperament which finds life not so much a burden as a mystery which exhausts the spirit. The death of Dickens in that year of the family's removal to the Vale of Health was an occasion for noting, with peculiar satisfaction, that only the previous day a manuscript of his had been rejected by Dickens for *Household Words*. 'All the world shocked. Universal gloom', and he wrote the great name in large capital letters as if he found the news unbelievable, omitting to surround it with the heavily inked black border with which he often solemnized such entries. He had been in the audience at the St. James' Hall for Dickens's last reading, when the novelist had shut the volume of *Pickwick* before him and spoke his moving goodbye: '. . . from these garish lights I vanish now for evermore.' On the day of the funeral he and Geraldine rose early to join the mourning throng at Westminster Abbey. 'The coffin in open ground strewn with flowers. His head at Handel's feet and Sheridan lies at his.' These and other details are noted with the almost epicurean relish that marked Victorian morbid sentiment. Great new hopes of more abundant living were paralleled by a more intense preoccupation with dying.

*   *   *

The Harmsworths lived in the Vale of Health for three years. Three more children were born to them there: Robert Leicester, on November 1, 1870, Hildebrand Aubrey, March 15, 1872, and Violet Grace, on April 11, 1873. Alfred and Harold were the inspiration of a *Punch* drawing. They had been to tea at a neighbour's. Harold became silent at table. 'I know what *he's* thinking about,' said Alfred blithely. 'He's thinking about cake—he's *always* thinking about cake.' The remark reached the ears of George du Maurier, who lived nearby. He took it for his purposes as a *Punch* contributor and, with a change of sex, it appeared as a caption for a drawing on April 27, 1872.

Imposing events figure in the *memorabilia* of the period: the outbreak of the Franco-Prussian war, the declaration of the Third Republic of France, England's Elementary Education Act; the proclamation of the German Empire by Bismarck. At the outbreak of war, Alfred Harmsworth noted a story told in the City about the French being in wild flight from the enemy, 'throwing away their arms and accoutrements as they ran'. His feelings, like those prevailing in the English middle classes, were anti-French, not only because the ideas of the Revolution had continued to be intellectually current and active in England but because the French had given support to the Fenians. Also, two of Geraldine's sisters were married to Germans, the memory of the Prince Consort had gained lustre in the nine years since his death, and Queen Victoria's eldest daughter was the wife of the future Kaiser Wilhelm II.

The Elementary Education Bill had been introduced in the House of Commons by the Right Honourable W. E. Forster, vice-president of Committees of Council on Education in the Gladstone Government. He commended the bill in a peroration which stressed the urgency of creating more mental skills to counteract 'the smallness of our numbers'. The voting had sent the traditional deep-throated murmurs of parliamentary approbation reverberating through the country. It was the first step in a social advance which transformed the nation, for up till then only one person in seven in England could read and write. Religious objections remained in the arena of controversy for some time after the passing of the Act. Other voices were raised in fear that national education would expose the people to the contagion of revolutionary ideas from the Continent.

A small occurrence in the summer of 1873 may have been not less consequential in its effects than some of the resounding events of the time. Among the neighbours of the Harmsworths at Hampstead was a family named Jealous. George Samuel Jealous was a Lincolnshire man who had graduated into journalism, like George Augustus Sala, and other Fleet Street personalities of the day, from the mechanical side of publishing. In 1860 he had founded his own paper, the *Hampstead & Highgate Express*, which still serves its neighbourhood. He was a Liberal idealist who was active in philanthropic causes, working for popular education and world peace. As a writer, he had qualified for membership of the Savage Club, which gave him access to a wide circle of distinguished literary and artistic acquaintances. Harmsworth, senior, was often his guest there. As 'Sunny' Harmsworth obviously relished being allowed into the *Hampstead & Highgate Express* composing room on press days, George Jealous gave him a toy printing set for his birthday. 'That was how I came to know printers and their ways', Alfred, junior, told a printing trade unionist nearly fifty years after.

Among the family memories of those Vale of Health days were the visits of their German relatives. Grace Maffett's husband was Albert Maximilian Selss, of Coefeld, Westphalia, professor of German in Dublin University, a massively handsome man of great learning. Caroline Maffett married Carl Borntraeger, of Wiesbaden, remembered as a man of good presence and, for a German, of uncommonly easy manner. Caroline went to live in Germany. The Selsses, going there from Dublin during university vacations, always called on the Harmsworths on their way through London. They travelled as if equipped for an expedition. Their luggage, their umbrellas, their hats, were protected by neat linen covers. Cabmen they regarded as enemies and the Harmsworths dreaded the altercations with hansom drivers on the doorstep. To the Harmsworth children their uncle Selss was anything but formidable and they long remembered the treats he gave them at the confectioners' and especially following him and their father up to the Bull & Bush to drink all the ginger-beer they wanted. Later, by the misfortune of war, those German connections were to become embarrassing to the Harmsworth family.

$$\star \qquad \star \qquad \star$$

'Sunny' Harmsworth was not sent to school until he was eight years old. His father, the ex-schoolmaster, now maintained that formal education should not begin too soon. Early childhood, he said, must be 'natural and free'. Circumstances as much as sense may have helped to form that judgment. School fees were to be a source of new worries in a household in which the breadwinner's gross income for 1872, for example, was not more than £140. Not long afterwards he was writing: 'Acct. overdrawn, and without a shilling. We in great distress, at last ebb and almost in despair. . . . Nevertheless, full of trust in God, tho' not as full as I could wish.' The cloud lifted: a nought had somehow gone astray in the reckoning. 'Harmie' set out with a thankful heart to the Bull & Bush and from there into town for the rejuvenation of a Turkish bath. Three days afterwards there appeared on his breakfast plate 'a disagreeable letter from W. H. Maffett saying that whole share of residue coming in must be devoted to paying off my debt to the estate'. In the following week his mother died at 6 Eaton Terrace. Time had given to the strange exceptional quality in Hannah Harmsworth a sanction which history withholds. Her peasant context seemed to diminish with her advancing years. Her facial outlines and expression had acquired a dignity of more than age. She died in 1894 and her son's anguish at their parting appears in his diary entries of her calling for him with her last gasps of breath: 'Alfred!' 'Alf!' 'Alf!'

The eldest of the family, passing through the plastic boyhood years, received a deep abiding imprint of the frustrations besetting his father. Looking back he would speak of them as a reminder to others that he had been at close quarters with misfortune. He would say: 'As long ago as I can remember, I was determined to be rid of the perpetual and annoying question of money.' What no one ever discovered was the extent to which he had felt the humiliations of middle-class poverty, those incitements to psychological protest which have had a far-reaching effect on the affairs of men. Proud-lipped and determined, if the young Alfred Harmsworth had been hurt by the ignominies of the family situation he never showed it. Possibly that was because he realized his destiny at an age when most young men are still dreaming.

By now the family had moved again, back to St. John's Wood, to 13 Grove End Road, a small Georgian house formerly occupied by the Misses Knight who had been kind to Alfred Harmsworth, senior, in his young days. He wrote in his diary his satisfaction at being able to take his family to live in that house of heart-warming associations. The new house had a garden with trees and the sturdier Harmsworths spent most of the first days there watching the passing traffic from the tree tops. The third boy, Cecil, the Lord Harmsworth of the future, cherished his memories of the garden. 'To this day', writing in his closing years, 'the peculiar scent of pear blossom brings instantly to mind the delights of that earthly paradise.' One of the trees enclosed within the walls was a horse chestnut. Its spring brilliance was another of his fixed recollections. By Cecil's special pleading with the local authorities the tree was spared when 13 Grove End Road, with other properties close by, was demolished to make way for a large block of flats known as South Lodge, and it is still there, growing out of the pavement.

The young Alfred had been taught nothing but behaviour. All that he knew up to that time he had learnt from looking and listening. What seems to have been his natural instinct as an observer was sharpened during those early years. It was in itself invaluable education. Had he gone to school earlier his course in life might have been different. His power of observation was exceptional and no doubt it supplied directional bias to his career. He learnt the alphabet almost entirely with the help of the printing set which George Jealous had given him. After one or two experimental terms at small local establishments of the 'dame school' sort, he was put in the care of Miss Berry, who kept school at Wykeham House in the nearby Boundary Road. Soon afterwards, Miss Berry retired and the school was taken over by Miss Alice Budd, one of her teachers, who was then joined by her sister Florence. The elder Miss Budd was impressed from the first by young Harmsworth's cleverness at composition. She used to take his essays round to the mothers of her other pupils as an example of the progress to be made under her tuition.

A later pupil recalled the elder Miss Budd as resembling the Duchess in *Alice in Wonderland*. The school was dignified by the socially approved name of 'Academy' and it was for boys only. Latin and French were among the subjects. The school day always began with a hymn and young Alfred Harmsworth's voice, upraised in *All Things Bright and Beautiful*, often rang out on the morning air of St. John's Wood. The music teacher, Thomas Rich, a brother-in-law of the Misses Budd, was impressed, at that early time, by the Harmsworth boy's quiet firmness of manner. 'We all foretold a future for him.' One of Alfred's first acts of self-assertion as a new boy was to fight off an older boy who was attacking another newcomer, a small Jewish lad named Henry Arnholz. 'You fought my battles for me,' Arnholz wrote to him in a subsequent letter of recollection. 'He was extraordinarily attractive', that old schoolfellow recalled later. 'He had golden hair and blue eyes and carried himself in a commanding way. People often turned to look at him in the street.'

★　　　★　　　★

Two more children came, the sixth and seventh sons, Charles Harmondsworth and William Albert St. John. The family moved again, to Burghfield House, 94 Boundary Road, St. John's Wood, a larger house than any they had lived in before, and next door to the Misses Budds' school. Five more children were born, three of whom died as infants. The survivors were Christabel Rose and Vyvyan George. Not long before her fourteenth and last child arrived, a boy named Harry Stanley Giffard who died at eighteen months, Geraldine Harmsworth was seen running upstairs, at the age of forty-seven, with the energy of a young unburdened woman. The eleven living children grew up at 94 Boundary Road. It was the last house in which the Harmsworths lived together as a family.

As in many and perhaps most large families, where the mother is preoccupied with the latest arrival, the eldest Harmsworth children helped to bring up the younger ones. At Boundary Road the young Alfred Harmsworth assumed a prefect's role. He exercised it by a condescending exemplariness, leaving the more practical forms of discipline to his eldest sister, Geraldine, who, when driven to it, would knock her brothers down. Himself unnaturally silent as a child, young Alfred had an acute dislike of noise even as a boy. He had larger ear orifices than most young people. Miss Budd said that she had known him to be 'thoroughly upset' by noise as he worked in school. It may have been the reason why at home there was a 'down' on crying. Crying was not allowed. Geraldine, junior, smacked and clouted unsparingly in her efforts to suppress it. When she failed, Alfred would seek sanctuary upstairs, away from the hullabaloo.

A cousin remembered:

My brother and I, with considerable care and some expense, made a doll's house as a birthday present for Geraldine. It did not last more than an hour or so after its arrival at Boundary Road. No toy lasted more than an hour or so at Boundary Road; it was smashed irretrievably in the Harmsworth *mêlée* that filled the house with noise and explains why the schoolroom, as it was called, on the ground floor at the back, was so sparsely furnished and why the garden was a wilderness of scooped-out earth and ill-treated shrubs.

If the din became too great, their mother bribed the elder children to vanish for the day with pennies for buns and lemonade. The nearness of Hampstead Heath and Ken Wood was for them the call of the wild. They roamed tirelessly over the Heath's eight hundred acres of woodland, scrub and rough common ground, pockets bulging with 'conkers', stones, birds' eggs in season, returning home with stockings down, dusty knees, holes to be mended. More than once, through a long summer's day, they wandered as far as Totteridge, four or five miles, passing a fine Queen Anne mansion, Poynters Hall, which, unbelievably then, would become their mother's home for many years. 'Almost all the way from West Hampstead to Barnet, a mile or two farther on, was then a country road with hawthorn hedges on both sides,' was Cecil Harmsworth's recollection, 'and cow parsley shoulder-high on the banks where we often played hide-and-seek.' Dwelling more lovingly and perhaps more often on those old familiar scenes of childhood than his brothers and sisters, Cecil wrote that he could scarcely believe the urban developments which changed them almost beyond recognition in the years that followed. Old Totteridge, at least, has not yet been engulfed by the northward spread of London.

When he was in the mood to join in the games of the younger ones Alfred brought romance into their play. He was the Arthurian king dubbing his knights on the eve of battle. Hoops, hopscotch and the other commonplace games of the period did not interest him. The youngest Harmsworth son, Vyvyan, recalled the Boundary Road years, chiefly because of the oppressive weight of seniority which he could not escape. To him the future Northcliffe seemed remote but entirely heroic—'and extraordinarily good-looking, the handsomest chap of his age I ever saw. I was awfully proud to think he was my brother'. Of the rough-and-tumble life in the family he remembered in particular the ruthless raiding of an adjoining garden when the apples were ready. 'It must have been terrible to have had us for neighbours.' He remembered the occupant of the house next door, 'a little bearded man named Bedford', flinging open his window one morning and calling out to the older Harmsworth children: 'Why don't you come right in and take what you want? I know you'll have it, anyhow—you might as well have it honestly!' The neighbour on the other side was a City man named Turner who suffered reverses and committed suicide. His wife and children received the news with shrieks of anguish that haunted the Harmsworths for days after.

★   ★   ★

At the age of eleven, Alfred left the Misses Budd and was sent on the advice of a solicitor friend of his father to Stamford Grammar School in Lincolnshire. The school stands on the site on which it was originally built in 1548. One of its first pupils was that William Cecil who became the Lord Treasurer Burghley. St. John's, Cambridge, has always had a close connection with it and is represented on the governing body by a Fellow. In 1822 the number of pupils was only sixteen. A few years before Alfred Harmsworth went there the school's fortunes were revived and ensured by a grant of money from a local hospital charity. Called Browne's School in his day, it is now known as Stamford School (Radcliffe & Browne's Foundation). Benevolence was apparently not the emotion with which the school chiefly impressed Alfred Harmsworth. He was consistently 'picked on' by the headmaster, a fork-bearded clergyman named Edward Coulson Musson, formerly vice-principal of Queen Elizabeth's College, Guernsey, who caned him three times a week for two years, according to the victim.

In after-years a school contemporary named Nottingham recalled Harmsworth getting 'four on each hand and as many strokes from the nape of the neck to the calf of the leg as could be given without overlapping'. Stripping for a bathe in Freeman's Hole, Uffington Meadow, the boys saw 'the blue-black marks of the strokes' as Harmsworth undressed with the rest. He had been caught escaping from confinement by a knotted sheet let down from a window. 'Musson was certainly a man to inspire fear', it is stated in the *History of Stamford School*, published for the school in 1954, 'and instilled Latin by frequent applications of the cane.' His violence resulted in Harmsworth's removal. A caning had split the boy's thumb. It kept him out of class for a term, after which Harmsworth, senior, declined to send him back. Alfred, junior, showed more intelligence out of school than in it. He never took the lessons seriously enough for his Stamford headmaster, whose reiterated 'Go to my room!' can hardly have been undeserved all the time.

Various old boys of Stamford School recalled the Harmsworth of their day in anecdotal reminiscence, all citing the rare good looks. He was remembered for his temperamental liveliness and unpredictability, his practical joking, his fast running. His school nickname was 'Dodger', one of a group of boys to whom Dickensian nicknames were attached. Reminded of it later by an old Stamford schoolfellow, met in Chicago, he showed some displeasure: 'His mobile face was clouded with a frown.' He left the school in the summer of 1878, taking with him the memory of what he afterwards spoke of as the two unhappiest years of his life. Perhaps giving rein to a sense of triumph, he later allowed himself to be elected a 'co-optative Governor' of the school, founded a number of 'Harmsworth prizes', and accepted the presidency of the Old Boys' Club. A time came when the Rev. Mr Musson applied to him for help in securing another kind of appointment. His old pupil had not forgotten and, unhappily, could not forgive.

Mrs Charles Harmsworth, née Hannah Carter, Northcliffe's
grandmother. A photograph taken in 1863

Alfred Harmsworth, senior, Northcliffe's father. A photograph taken about the time of his engagement to Geraldine Maffett

Chapter Three

The Young Freelance

BECOMING a day boy at a typical small struggling private school of the period, Henley House, St. John's Wood, Alfred Harmsworth entered on what may have been a first vital identifying phase in his life, though again it showed his intelligence working more effectively outside the classroom than in it. He was thirteen, and to the point almost of mental distress he could not then, or after, give his mind to matters which did not interest him in a primary sense, taking his attention at once. Arithmetic, for example, bored him exceedingly and he would allow himself to be defeated by its simplest exercises and problems, cheerfully risking consequences which, it is true, were less dire at Henley House than they would have been at Stamford School. 'All mathematics were a sore trial to him', one of his masters wrote in after years. His best subjects were spelling and composition.

He had not needed formal schooling to develop the penetrating power of observation which was one of his more remarkable characteristics. Cecil Harmsworth believed that his brother's exceptional alertness of eye and ear was in some degree trained by the 'memory game' which they often played at home. Each member of the family was required to go out of the room, while the others rearranged the furniture and other objects in it. 'Alfred had an uncanny perception. The booby traps we set for him always failed ridiculously.' Cecil said that Alfred's power of perception sometimes astonished them by enabling him to detect symptoms of illness in advance of the patient's knowledge of it.

Henley House School was in Mortimer Road, Kilburn, an address exalted by new boundary arrangements into Mortimer Crescent, St. John's Wood. The proprietor and headmaster was a shy and lisping Aberdeen man, John Vine Milne. With his brother Alexander, he had taken over the decrepit goodwill, valued at £100, of a school previously conducted there and, without much improving its financial status, made it a better school both academically and socially. It was the local senior school for many of the boys who had been at the Misses Budds'. J. V. Milne was a type of schoolmaster new to Harmsworth, patient, tolerant, gently humorous, encouraging his pupils to live up to the best that was in them, a master for whom teaching was above all a vocation. H. G. Wells, who, after Harmsworth's time, joined the Henley House School staff, said that 'within the limits of his means and opportunity, Mr Milne was a very successful teacher indeed'. Wells describes the school in his *Experiment in Autobiography*, where he says that it was housed 'in two rather battered villas'.

It drew its boys from the region of Maida Vale and St. John's Wood; the parents were theatrical, artistic, professional and business people who from motives of economy or affection preferred to have their sons living at home. . . . The playground was a walled gravelly enclosure that had once been two back gardens. It was too small for anything but the most scuffling of games.

Although Alfred Harmsworth showed no promise in the schoolroom, Milne thought him one of the brightest of his boys and the handsomest. The good looks were a recurring theme in all the recollections of his early years. 'Extraordinary beauty'; 'fine eye and brow'; 'the face of a young Apollo'; 'a splendid-looking chap': masters and schoolfellows at Stamford and Henley House joined in agreement on that subject. If he was not precisely their Steerforth, most of the other boys were David Copperfields in their admiration for Harmsworth, A. C. W., known at Henley House as 'Billy', the fair-haired day boy with the forelock which he often had to shake away from his left eye and whose air of effortless superiority was intimidating enough to gain him the captaincy of the school cricket and football teams, though he was not first among them as a player of either game. The testimony of one of the hero-worshippers, a boy named Sheldrake, was that although Harmsworth was no match winner they all enthusiastically voted him into top place, which he filled as a natural leader rather than by prowess. An onlooker, seeing him play in a cricket match on the old Eton and Harrow ground now obliterated by Ellsworthy Road, London, N.W., made the remark that 'young Harmsworth looked as if he was not interested'.

His fag at Henley House, a boy named Goodrich, wrote reminiscently: 'He was a pillar of the school, one of the giants among us. Timid and obedient then, I recall with what mingled pride and fear I obeyed his commands—carrying his books, minding his bicycle.' The bicycle was a source of wider veneration; he had a half share in a 48-in. Coventry 'ordinary' with a high front wheel and a smaller one behind. The cycling revolution was just over the rim of time. Alfred Harmsworth sensed its excitements and was winning new esteem by his uphill riding in and around St. John's Wood; he and his bicycle, with its shining steel spokes and hub caps, became a legendary partnership in the school's history. To his hard riding of the cumbersome 'Coventry' he owed the strong wrists of his manhood. It also brought him the admiration of a Merchant Taylor's schoolboy, Max Pemberton, son of a Mincing Lane rice broker. The Pemberton family lived at 34 Clifton Hill, St. John's Wood. Young Pemberton and Alfred formed a lasting friendship. They first met when Pemberton had a bicycle fall in Hamilton Terrace, near by. Alfred helped him to his feet and saw him home after the accident.

The cycling boom which came with the invention of the 'safety' frame and pneumatic tyres was still a few years away, but already cycling clubs were raising clouds of dust along the highways and rivalling one another in smartness of turn-out and whatever was *le dernier cri* in fashions awheel. The club of which Alfred Harmsworth became the leader sported a uniform and one of the members carried a bugle for rallying purposes. Among his fellow riders were the sons of W. P. Frith, R.A., painter of 'Derby Day', A. E. Stoddart, who became a famous athlete, and a son of John O'Connor, a Lyceum scene-painter. Theirs was the first generation to take to wheels in the popular sense. While the excitements of cycling seem tepid in the light of later experiments with speed, the bicycle then was a fascinating means of escape from the routine of travel as well as from work. At last the individual was free of the bondage of the railways and the annual swarming of the industrial masses to the sea.

Soon after that first meeting, Max Pemberton and Alfred went on a club ride to St. Albans. They returned to St. John's Wood at midnight. As they were dismounting, someone called out of the darkness: 'Who'll ride with me to Eastbourne?' There were cries of remonstrance and jeering. Two figures rode into the night for the journey of over fifty miles. One of them was Harmsworth. He and the challenger set off for the Sussex coast. At 4 a.m. they ran into thick fog and had to lie under a hedge near Uckfield. When daylight came they pressed on, reaching Eastbourne at ten o'clock. After a short rest, they rode back to London. Another of his journeys was to Bournemouth and back. On some of these longer rides it was his satisfaction to boast that he had not dismounted *en route*, rides often entailing uphill tests which may have been physically harmful.

*　　　*　　　*

Milne, the headmaster, recorded later that young Harmsworth was 'something of a puzzle' to him. He had come to the conclusion that, for

35

all the boy's intelligence, he would never pass any examination containing arithmetic, which ruled him out as a candidate for the professions. Milne had noticed how well Harmsworth expressed himself in written composition, that he was better in that respect than the average schoolboy. He was better read too. He knew his Dickens and was well acquainted with the works of Defoe, Smollett, and Oliver Goldsmith. He was now reading Thackeray. For those reasons, Milne gave his consent when Harmsworth came to him with a scheme for starting a school magazine. 'He begged me to start it. When I told him I was too busy, he said: "Let me do it, sir. It shall give you no trouble." '

The first number of *The Henley House School Magazine* was published in March 1881. Under the title was printed the line: 'Edited by Alfred C. Harmsworth', who was not quite sixteen. It can be seen now as part of the emulating processes which drove the boy on to achievements that were to give him a place in history. Editors were men of importance, 'Mr Editor' the presiding deity of Victorian journalism. The family friend, George Jealous of Hampstead, was editor of a paper which people took into their homes. His talk about local affairs, about council meetings and votes of confidence, was sometimes lifted to a level of higher interest for Alfred Harmsworth by his familiar references to Sala of the *Daily Telegraph*, and others well known in the world of writing and print and publication. Mr Jealous was a great man to the young Harmsworths. He was impressive apart from his public status, with his local-preacher style of garb and his staunch and purposeful idealism. Going about his little journalistic affairs in North London, George Jealous was the pattern for a career far more notable than his own.

The school magazine gave young Alfred his first smell of a printer's shop, the hot occupational attar of ink and oil and metal which perfumes a long tradition. The early issues were printed by a Kilburn printer named Ford who, with his two compositor sons, produced a small and unsuccessful local paper, *The Kilburn Post*, at 5 High Road, Kilburn. Like Jealous, Ford was an archetypal figure in young Harmsworth's life, the craftsman who could compose one's thoughts and ideas into ordered reality, the exciting permanence of the printed page. The printed pages of *The Henley House School Magazine* have a surprising freshness of appearance, a professional bloom which was doubtless supplied by Ford, the printer, but which reflects also the eager assent of the very young editor. Milne, remembering, said that Harmsworth was in his element in the printer's shop. 'He used to hurry off to Ford's with his "copy" to superintend operations there. Ford was profuse in promises but Harmsworth haunted the place until the printer, in desperation, got on with the task. This boy of fifteen had found his life's work', and, incidentally, provided the model for the schoolboy editor named Cossington in H. G. Wells's

THE HENLEY HOUSE
SCHOOL MAGAZINE.

EDITED BY ALFRED C. HARMSWORTH.

No. 1. Vol. I.] MARCH, 1881. [Price THREEPENCE.

CONTENTS.

THE SCHOOL MAGAZINE.

IT is hoped that the opportunity now afforded of
appearing in all the dignity of print will be an
inducement to many Henley House Boys, to cultivate early in life the power of giving expression to
their thoughts. "Writing maketh an exact Man,"
and boys who will take the trouble to form the habit
early in life of clothing their thoughts with appropiate
language, will find that they gain clearer ideas. They
will know what they know ; that is, the mist of their
minds will clear away and there will be definite forms.

Our knowledge has been compared to a circle of
light surrounded by darkness. The larger we make
our circle of light, the greater is the circumf
of darkness, It is a quantity   ringing home
to us the truth that the more we know, the more do
we become conscious of our ignorance. But besides
the light and the necessary darkness, there is in our
minds too often a great deal of mist—that is inexact,
confused, half-knowledge. The practice of writing
down our thoughts tends to resolve this mist, and we
perceive what part is knowledge, and what part is ignorance. We often hear the excuse; " I know, but I
can't express myself." There is good reason for doubting such knowledge.

Now the ability to *think consecutively,* and to *write
clearly and to the point* is only attained by study and
practice. Some act on the principle enunciated by
one of Shakspeare's characters. Dogberry said " To
write and read comes by nature;" but then he is
hardly an authority. I can hear some saying "Oh, it's
such a fag." Well, things worth having generally are
obtained by labour. Many of us would like to be
Musicians, but shrink from those wearisome Scales
and necessary but uninteresting exercises.

In former days, every gentleman was required to
be skilful with the Sword ; unfamiliarity betrayed the
want of breeding. In the present day he must wield
the Pen ; and, even if he does not enter public life, he
must at least be able to write a letter. The conflict
was formerly in the field: it is now in the political journal, the scientific magazine, or the ponderous review.

As there would be no writers if there were no
readers, a word will be said about reading. Some
read too little ; but there are also those, and their representatives are in this School, who read too much.
The former starve their minds ; the latter suffer from
mental indigestion. A great writer once said, if he
had read as much as most people, he would have been
as foolish. What a comforting reflection, some of
you say. But the philosopher's meaning was that he
had thought deeply on what he had read, and not filled
his mind with a mass of loose, half-worked-out
thoughts. To sum up in Bacon's words, "Read not
to contradict and confute ; nor to believe and take for
granted ; but to weigh and consider."

J. V. M.

HIBERNIA'S LAMENT
ON THE MODERN HOME RULER

Hibernia weeping cries, " My poor degen'rate Son,
  " No wit, no learning hath, no genius and no fun,
" Mere *dull* obstruction is with him the vogue ;
  " He's nothing left that's Irish but the brogue."

C. N. Warton.

"ENTRE NOUS."

I have it on the best authority that the *H.H.S.
Magazine* is to be a marked success.

* * *

The weather has not permitted much Football
lately, but the last few days have been brightened by
occasional glimpses of the Sun.

* * *

We have, as our readers are doubtless aware, a new
Captain and Secretary, I am sure both these gentlemen will find us some matches and that in them, we
shall deserve success, if we cannot command it.

Editor at Fifteen

novel, *The New Machiavelli*. 'I have it on the best authority that this paper is to be a marked success', he had written in the first issue. And in the second issue, as if he felt free to confess his private belief that he had the touchstone, he announced: 'I am glad to say that my prediction as to the success of this magazine proved correct.'

There can be no doubt that the boy who got out the little four-page paper was able if imitative. He saw the point of establishing in readers the habit of looking for the same feature in the same place in each issue, grasping an editorial principle that was to serve him well in his later career. His self-expression took a more direct form in the column of gossip headed 'Entre Nous'. In it he ranged over a variety of school topics and in doing so gathered experience of a branch of journalism that would contribute greatly to the extraordinary success which lay ahead of him. *The Henley House School Magazine* was the forcing ground of a talent which was to become the most formidable personal power of its kind in modern times.

The journalistic gift, for his age, was obvious if not remarkable. It is now clearly seen that the root of the matter was in him. Once Milne kept him in for some slackness in class when the other boys were given time off for play. Harmsworth settled down to produce some verse to suit the occasion:

KEPT IN

Here I am, myself bemoaning, under impositions groaning.
The still schoolroom all alone in on this pleasant afternoon;
Oh! how wearing 'tis here sitting, with no prospect of soon quitting,
And the moments slowly flitting by this sunny day in June.

Listening to the clock's slow ticking, at this sickening Virgil sticking,
Horrid Latin words out-picking, feeling overcast with gloom;
Tantalising sunbeams eyeing, watching happy birds by flying,
For the flower-decked meadows sighing, pent within this wretched room.

Now no more my task I'm shirking. Will is aiding me in working,
Hope upon my breast is lurking, soon no fetters more shall hold me;
Soon shall I have finished writing, soon have ceased this stuff inditing—
All my wrongs are quickly righting—now I draw my breath—I'm free!

A. C. HARMSWORTH

A. C. Harmsworth, at sixteen imitating rather than experimenting with contemporary poetic forms, had also learnt to play the piano without bothering to read music. No one remembered his having had a lesson, but he played with sufficient assurance to perform at school concerts. He also figured prominently in school theatricals. 'Harmsworth made a most imposing Dr Whackem in "Birchington Academy",' said the *Boys' Own Paper*. The role was not an uncongenial one, judging by an editorial note on school discipline in the magazine: 'We regret that Harmsworth's plan, committing the discipline of the school to a Committee of boys, is not yet elaborated on paper. He throws out the idea, and leaves the very trifling details to be worked out by inferior minds.' The mind of the editor of *The Henley House School Magazine* was stimulated to its best flights by extra-mural activities, as Milne had discovered. The school holidays, for instance, were a more formative influence in Alfred Harmsworth's life than the hours in class. Aware of his absorbed interest in producing the magazine, George Jealous gave him small holiday reporting jobs to do on his *Hampstead & Highgate Express*. It was an act of kindly encouragement that may have been decisive in helping him to identify his future with the profession which ultimately he would dominate. A minor effect of those brief exciting professional forays was that for him Hampstead and its history became a subject of abiding interest. '*Hampstead—the spot which most of all I love. The place of which I never yet have tired.*' If it hardly inspired his best lyrical expression in the school magazine, his feelings about it remained sufficiently strong to draw him back there many times in the years of success and fame to visit scenes familiar to him as the schoolboy reporter.

Mrs Jealous said that a chief attraction of their home for 'Sunny' Harmsworth, as she always called him, was the variety of books, newspapers and periodicals that arrived at her husband's office. He used to bring them home and 'Sunny', visiting the house to get away from 'the others', would draw his legs under him in an armchair and settle down to read them by the hour. She remembered him from those days as 'silent and thoughtful', and marvelled at 'what was in him, all mysterious, all silent'. No other person had appealed to her as he had, she wrote. 'I never saw any child, man or woman in the same clear light. I could know nothing of the worldly success that awaited him, but there was a spirit there and I knew it.' In summer time, she said, 'Sunny' would come quietly to the open window, gently push back the curtains, and ask, always most politely: 'May I come in, please?' The preternaturally quiet boy was none the less capable of the mischief of his years. Under cover of darkness someone moved the 'To Let' and 'For Sale' boards from houses in Boundary Road to other properties not in the market. The discovery was followed by excited conjecture and summary threats. It had been young Alfred's practical joke, in idea and in execution.

There were now eleven Harmsworth children, the oldest sixteen and a half, the youngest a few months. The family was constantly oppressed by want of money. At times there was not enough bread. The deep hurt of that time showed itself sixty years after to a visitor to Dornoch, one of the several homes of the second Harmsworth son, Harold, Lord Rothermere. At dinner the second course was one of the lowlier kinds of fish, made into a tasty dish by his Italian chef. On being told what it was, Rothermere, ordinarily unemotional, burst into tears and left the room. He returned in five minutes, apologizing. He had been reminded, he said, of his childhood. 'We lived on that fish for days at a time. My mother couldn't afford to get us anything else.'

In the evenings, home from school, Alfred would brood over get-rich-quick ideas. He experimented with photographic reproduction and, in doing so, spoilt some prized family photographs which might otherwise have survived to illustrate the present work. In the course of the same endeavours he ruined a bedroom carpet. His father's hair pomade suggested the idea of a 'silk hat reviver'. He made up a viscous mixture, put it in bottles, and advertised it, without result. He then developed an adolescent frenzy for making a fortune out of pills. Pill-making had brought fabulous wealth to some men—to 'Professor' Holloway, for example, £5,000,000. Morison, Parr, Holloway, Cockle, were household names. They had made fortunes out of the real and imagined infirmities of the people. Their hideous black-letter advertising was in all the papers. Though the number of those who could read even the boldest print was still relatively small, it was by advertising that the golden harvest had been reaped. A newcomer to the trade, Joseph Beecham, was beginning to catch up his rivals with the slogan: Worth A Guinea A Box. And it may not have escaped Alfred Harmsworth's notice that there was a proprietorial connection between Parr's Life Pills and *The Illustrated London News*. Stimulated by a Christmas present of £5 from one of his father's rich friends, his acquisitive imagination busied itself with the making and marketing of 'Tonks's Pills' and that on no skittish impulse. 'Tonks's Pills' were made to a formula in which kitchen soap was a main ingredient (as at that time it was commonly said to be of some brands of pill) and a credulous public was given a chance of judging their merits. The brothers and sisters at 94 Boundary Road were enrolled as packers and dispatchers. Ford, the printer, received an order for handbills. Small shops in St. John's Wood and Hampstead were canvassed by a good-looking young traveller who shook his hair out of his left eye as he showed his samples. 'Tonks's Pills—Cure All Ills' was actually displayed in shop windows. On New Year's Eve 1881 the elder Harmsworth children stayed up into the early hours packing pills, an episode described by one of the girls as 'Tonking the New Year in'. Calling at the shops for cash results, Alfred was depressed at finding that there were no repeat orders. 'Tonks's Pills' rapidly declined into a Harmsworth joke. Destiny had reserved the family name for more imposing enterprises.

★   ★   ★

Alfred left Henley House at the end of the Christmas term, 1881, when he was sixteen and a half. Keeping up his contribution to the school magazine, though having ceased to edit it, he appears to have offered articles there which had failed to find acceptance elsewhere. A marked competence of expression is noticeable in 'The Glorious Fifth', sketching contemporary Guy Fawkes Day celebrations. 'Newspapers', describing the latest developments in Fleet Street, was signed by him, his article concluding with the peroration:

The net income of *The Times* is actually £1,003,600 a year, its daily sale 80,000 copies, and the cost of a column for advertisement from £40 to £100 a day. It has immense influence in politics, home and foreign, and is generally conceded to be the premier journal of the world.

Alfred Charles Harmsworth
(Ex-Ed. H.H.S.M.)

Later, watching with astonishment the Harmsworth rise, the brothers Milne were as pleased to claim the Old Boy association as Alfred was to acknowledge it. 'Though I was not much of a student . . . the generous and thoughtful way in which I was educated at Henley House must have had a great influence on my career.' Alexander Milne, the younger brother, kept in touch with him, from time to time asking him to guarantee his account at the bank, which Alfred did for many years. According to the autobiography of A. A. Milne, playwright and *Punch* contributor, Alfred ignored a request from his father, J. V. Milne, to help him in the purchase of a large school property, 'price £7,000', on the Kent coast. Writing to Alexander Milne, on January 9, 1915, Alfred (then Northcliffe) said: 'I am very glad to renew your guarantee, which I enclose, although I really think that your nephew, who is making a fortune out of *Punch* by attacking me, might do something for his uncle.'

Alfred Harmsworth, senior, had no encouragement to give to his son's journalistic hopes. 'None of my friends will have anything to do with you', he told young Alfred. For the father there was only one calling, though it had failed to bring him more than passing satisfactions. Barristers and journalists were neighbours in Alsatia, but the bar had won from society a recognition withheld from the journalists, with their lack of a unifying code and their confusion of standards. The elder Harmsworth's opposition to his son's journalistic ambitions was not entirely unreasonable. Much of the journalism of that time was a degradation of civilized values.

A barrister of the Middle Temple, Edward Abinger, wrote of seeing the Harmsworths, father and son, dining together in Hall there. He recalled Harmsworth, senior, as 'a dear old Bohemian gentleman'. The young Alfred he described as 'having the face and figure of a Greek god'. Abinger remembered that one of the elder Harmsworth's dining companions in Hall was Cosmo Gordon Lang, afterwards Archbishop of Canterbury, and that young Alfred sometimes joined them in an after-dinner game of whist. No doubt Alfred Harmsworth, senior, cherished the hope that his eldest son might succeed where he had failed. He had influential friends who could be of help. There was Edward Clarke, a future leading advocate and Attorney-General, whose dapper, bewhiskered figure was to make him popular with the cartoonists. Young Alfred had been taken to the St. Stephen's Club to meet him. There was Charles Greville Prideaux, Q.C., the authority on Church law. There was Augustine Birrell, who made a greater reputation as an essayist and after-dinner speaker than he did at the bar or in politics. In him Alfred Harmsworth, senior, had an admirer as well as a friend. Meeting 'Harmie' on the Embankment one morning, Birrell commented on his not looking well. Alfred Harmsworth remarked that it was not a matter of health so much as the cares of a large family. The encounter was recalled long afterwards by Winston Churchill at a banquet. 'Ten years passed', he told the company. 'By that time it was a case not of protecting Mr Harmsworth's children from the world, but rather—er—' and the ensuing Churchillian grin was taken up in prolonged laughter.

Brief consideration of the possibility of being coached for Cambridge renewed Alfred Harmsworth's hopes for his son's future. But the young Alfred knew what his father refused to believe, that he had no gift for sustained study. He gave out the opinion, later on in life, that a year at a university may be a very good thing but that three years 'is often a waste of time'. When, presently, he was receiving a constant flow of applications from university men for posts on his staffs, he had a stereotyped answer for them: 'University and public school education are often of benefit but in the practical affairs of life they as often require living down.' Yet his first thought, when fortune came, was to arrange for his three youngest brothers to go to universities. On the subject of education, the founder of the popular and useful *Harmsworth's Self-Educator* was perhaps never fully at his ease. He was coached for a brief period by a tutor named Jocelyn, whose fees, it is believed, were paid by one of the elder Harmsworth's friends.

The friends of 'Harmie' were unusually sympathetic to him in his struggles. One of them, George Robinson, of Stonegate, Leicester, engineer to the local gas company, which his family owned, supplied funds enabling the third Harmsworth boy, Cecil, to go to Trinity College, Dublin. Alfred Harmsworth had acknowledged Robinson's earlier generosity by naming his next son Robert Leicester. There were other benefactors, the Yeos, for instance, the well-to-do St. John's Wood builders. All this practical warmheartedness was a tribute to the likeable qualities of Alfred Harmsworth, whose misfortunes did not embitter him, so that an intimate friend could say: 'It is always a pleasure to help "Harmie".'

★   ★   ★

The problem of young Alfred's future went into abeyance when, not long after leaving Henley House School, he had pneumonia, a result of one of the long-distance cycle rides, which were the hobby of his youth. His convalescence was passed in reading, mostly of the periodical kind. A personal column advertisement in *The Times* caught his eye. The advertiser wished to hear of a secretary-companion for a Continental tour, all expenses paid, 'musical tastes preferred'. Alfred answered the advertisement. He had to wait some time for a reply, which then requested fuller particulars about himself. He gave them, withholding his age. Asked to call at 33 Great Cumberland Place, Marble Arch, London, he was interviewed by the advertiser, the Reverend and Honourable E. V. R. Powys, third son of the third Lord Lilford. Powys was an amiable and cultivated young man of twenty-seven. Alfred Harmsworth was seventeen, amiable and, if not cultivated in the finer sense, at least personally presentable and with his own youthful charm. Powys said afterwards that, young as he was, Harmsworth impressed him at their interview, and subsequently, with his general knowledge, his mental quickness, his flow of conversation. He engaged him as his companion for the holiday, not knowing that for Harmsworth the decision meant anxiety as well as satisfaction: there was the awkward question of clothes. His parents had some difficulty in fitting him out for the journey. He and Powys went off together in the summer of 1882. As his brothers and sisters followed him out on to the pavement at 94 Boundary Road, where a hansom cab was waiting, Alfred turned and said sternly: 'Please don't crowd round. You know I hate fuss.' The jingle of hansom cab harness could make romantic music and it can be imagined as an exhilarating accompaniment of his thoughts as they reached out towards the novel experiences ahead of him.

The Continental tour took him through France and Germany, though details of the itinerary are lacking now. Powys found in him the right travelling companion. 'He showed such keen intelligence and pleasure in all he saw and heard. He proved to be delightful company. We never had a dull moment together.' At the hotel at Aix-le-Bains they met a French admiral who became their acquaintance for a few days. As they prepared to move on, the admiral addressed Powys: 'Si votre jeune ami est un modele de la jeunesse Anglais, je vous felicite de tout mon coeur, c'est un charmante garcon, d'une intelligence suprenante.' Reporting the compliment, Powys said that Harmsworth 'attracted all sorts and conditions of people wherever we went'. They drove out together for a picnic in the Val de Suzon, near Dijon. Their *cocher* disappeared. He returned, after being away some time, with a large bunch of wild flowers picked expressly, he said, 'pour le jeune Monsieur'. Powys said that the man must have gone far afield for such a varied collection of flowers. 'Harmsworth was delighted. He said to me: "It's awfully jolly of him! Just fancy an English cabby bothering to do such a thing!" ' What impressed Powys particularly was 'his kindly thoughtfulness for others and his devotion to his mother, of whom he always spoke with affectionate gratitude. It was charming'. Powys liked to think that the tour encouraged Alfred's regard for France and the French which coloured many of his later activities as a journalist and maker of public opinion. There is no doubt that he returned to London decidedly better in health, mentally invigorated and fortified in his resolve to be a professional journalist. Like many first-time travellers, he had the feeling of unique and privileged experience and an urge to communicate it.

*　　*　　*

Unwillingly, his father gave him a letter of introduction to Samuel Carter Hall, founder and editor for forty years of *The Art Journal*, author of a variety of books and composer of hymns, an old man who could look back on a life of endeavour in the cause of temperance, early closing, hospitals and better conditions for nurses and governesses. He was prominently concerned in founding the Brompton Hospital. He and Charles Dickens had been friends, and it was believed in literary circles that Hall was, in part at least, the original Pecksniff. That, in itself, made the interview memorable for Alfred Harmsworth. The old man wore the knee breeches, the velvet jackets and the frilled shirts of a vanished age and his reputation was eminent enough to cause Alfred to tremble as he rang the bell at the Kensington flat in which Hall lived out his last days. Their meeting was cordial and frank. Recalling it a few years after, Alfred said: 'My ideas of fame and fortune were considerably knocked on the head by what he told me of the trials of authorship.' The old man wrote out a letter of introduction to the editor of *The Queen* and handed it to him with a pinch of snuff. He stressed the importance of never wasting an editor's time: 'the contributor who is perpetually calling or writing soon gets into disfavour'. Alfred said it was the most valuable advice he had received as a freelance writer. 'I took it to heart and any success I had I largely attributed to the fact that I never troubled any editor with correspondence.' The letter of introduction brought him no good. His articles at that time were rejected by *The Queen*. He also had to swallow a dose of discouragement from George Augustus Sala, whom he met through one of his father's friends. Sala, an authoritative if not entirely reliable personality of the Fleet Street scene, advised young Harmsworth to avoid it. A few years later it was Sala who was gratified to be able to call on Harmsworth.

Studying the literary markets with renewed determination. Alfred turned his eye on the stream of publications for the young coming from Red Lion Square over the imprint of James Henderson. *Young Folks' Tales, Weekly Budget, Scraps, Lots o' Fun, Comic Life,* all appeared to thrive, and all were written in a simple straightforward style that young Harmsworth could easily make his own. Henderson was a genial bearded Scot who had moved south, *via* Leeds and Manchester, in a series of professional steps giving him the experience he needed to justify his ambition to meet the challenge of London. Calling on him as a would-be contributor, Alfred Harmsworth quickly decided that Henderson had 'a keener instinct for business than for the literary side of things'. He was unlikely to have known then that Henderson had rendered a considerable service to the cause of press freedom. As the publisher of the first halfpenny evening newspaper, *The Glasgow Evening Mercury,* and of the first penny daily newspaper, *The Glasgow Daily News,* he had wilfully ignored the disabling advertisement and stamp duties of the time. This led to his being summoned to appear at the bar of the House of Commons. Questions put to the Government before the appointed day elicited the announcement that it was not intended to proceed. Henderson had gained one of the victories which helped to abolish the taxes on knowledge.

Established in London, with his *Weekly Budget* selling 200,000 copies and his income reckoned at £15,000 a year, Henderson made it his custom to invite writers for his papers to foregather for lunch in his office at one o'clock on Thursdays so that they could meet members of his staff and exchange ideas. Sometimes the gatherings assumed the form of debates on current affairs. James Henderson took a liking to young Harmsworth and occasionally put him up for the night at his house at Herne Hill. 'Your father was so kind to me as an aspirant,' Northcliffe wrote to Henderson's son Nelson nearly forty years after, 'that I would be delighted to see anyone you ask me to see.' One of the contributors who at intervals joined those gatherings was invariably referred to as 'the man from Bournemouth'. Alfred remembered his dark, unkempt appearance and his 'shining gaiters', his Western backwoodsman air. This contributor wrote a serial story for *Young Folks* (at 12s. 6d. a column), giving it the title of *The Sea Cook.* Henderson's editor changed it to *Treasure Island.* 'The man from Bournemouth' was R. L. Stevenson. Later contributors included Max Pemberton and C. Arthur Pearson.

His acquisitive instincts sharpened by the worries about money at home, Alfred Harmsworth was delighted to be earning half-guineas by his own wits, a first taste of success which was presently communicated to Milne at Henley House School. In the June 1881 issue of the school magazine the 'Entre Nous' column started by Harmsworth was headed by a paragraph which read:

It will interest all readers of the School Magazine to hear that a Henley House boy—and one who is still a boy, too—whose contributions to our paper are always so welcome, has developed into a journalist. He is now on the staff of several papers, daily and otherwise.

Harmsworth's desire to shine in the journalistic firmament was eager enough but it was an exaggeration to claim for him that he was a Fleet Street pluralist as early as that. What the writer of the paragraph, Alexander Milne, who had taken the magazine over after Harmsworth, meant to convey was that the former editor was now a freelance writer who contributed to various papers. Alfred was eighteen and making £3 a week by his pen. 'He was so set and so serious, so precocious and ambitious,' wrote a Hampstead contemporary of his who became well known in the printing trade, Frank Colebrook, 'that one might say he had no youth save in the sense that he was always boyish.' He freelanced for four years, with the exception of a period of staff work on a paper called *Youth*, published from *The Illustrated London News* office in a top room at 198 Strand. The paper was edited by Edward Morton, some time dramatic critic of *The Referee*. He wrote the musical comedy *San Toy* which had a long run at Daly's Theatre. A contributor to *The Times* in 1931 recalled a visit to the office of *Youth* during Morton's editorship. 'I found a boy with bright eyes and fair hair correcting proofs. Morton said: "This is my young friend Harmsworth. He's going to be editor of *The Times* some day."' According to Alfred Harmsworth's testimony, as editor of *Youth* Edward Morton 'neglected his duties' for his more remunerative labours outside the office.

Youth belonged to the Ingram family who owned *The Illustrated London News*. It was the new name given to a combination of two older publications, *The Boys' Newspaper*, founded in 1880 by Cassell, Petter & Galpin, of La Belle Sauvage Yard, E.C., and *Boys' Illustrated News*, already owned by the Ingrams. Neither paper had been a success and *Youth* was an attempt to appeal to a generation more willing than any that had gone before to be instructed as well as amused by reading. For its illustrations it relied too freely on wood engravings used in *The Illustrated London News*, and its literary quality, too, was often above the heads of the readers whom it was hoped to reach. Stories for *Youth*, as for a good many other papers, were usually written round ready-made illustrations, a saving in costs. 'Writing to cuts', as the practice was called, was a literary commission well known in periodical publishing up to the 1890s and the coming of the half-tone block. Alfred Harmsworth wrote one of its

46

serials, *Fame and Fortune*, describing the progress of a young man named Reginald Oliver from provincial poverty to editorial success in the metropolis. He afterwards said that it was 'largely autobiographical'. Its tone was highly moral. Reginald said his prayers and believed that they were answered. Somewhere at the back of *Youth* was an unformulated policy of opposing the shoddy types of publication which supplied much of the reading of the young at that time. They catered for the lowest tastes at a level of sensationalism rarely equalled by the worst excesses of twentieth-century journalism. Crime, sex, violence, were exploited with a thoroughness which some critics saw as an open conspiracy against society. Others regarded it as part of the French infection.

Morton left the editorial chair of *Youth* to write for the theatre rather than about it, and Alfred Harmsworth took it over as editor at the weekly salary of £2. A veteran newspaper man, Aaron Watson, who met him at that time, said that he had the air of 'a careless onlooker at life. Nothing appeared to concern or ruffle him or greatly to interest him. His general good looks were much out of the common.' If that was fairly observed, there was also the fact that his onlooking mind missed precious little. *Youth* gave him the chance to show it not only by the quickness with which he acquired technical competence but by giving him, also, the freedom of *The Illustrated London News* organization, of which his paper was an insignificant part. It was his first opportunity to mix with editors, artists, writers, wood engravers, electrotypers, distributors and advertising men. He made the most of it.

Soon after he had become editor of *Youth* he was the victim of a practical joke at Eton. Eric Parker, some time editor of *The Field* and an old Etonian, told how his fagmaster, Hatchard, who was captain of the school, had the idea of sending invented items of Eton news to *Youth*. Among them were descriptions of non-existent school customs:

Another curious custom at Eton is 'Slunching the Paddocks'. On a certain day all the Collegians and Oppidans are provided with a coarse sort of pudding, which is put to the following use: After dinner is over they all go to Weston's and School Paddocks and throw this pudding all over them. This is called 'Slunching the Paddocks', the pudding being called 'Slunch'. It is supposed to be derived from the fact that when Queen Elizabeth visited Eton College 'she lunched' (s'lunched) in College Hall, and the students sprinkled the paddocks with dry rice in her honour.

Apparently flattered by attention from that quarter, the editor of *Youth* made it known that he would like to be asked down 'to see things for himself'. A visit was arranged and Hatchard was struck by his 'charm of youth and guilelessness' and appears to have been self-reproachful for having 'so easily taken him in'. The visit, which included lunch in college, went off pleasantly, and an account of it appeared in the paper. A privately printed booklet, *Eton As She Is Not*, gave permanency to the hoax and that formal version of it has become a collectors' rare item.

Alfred Harmsworth's energy and ideas could not offset the effects of the inadequate budget on which he was obliged to produce *Youth*. He said afterwards that its title was a handicap, because young men of seventeen and eighteen did not like asking for it under that name. Advertisers were not attracted into a paper selling to readers with no spending power to speak of and the end was almost certainly in sight from the beginning. The Ingrams were glad to get rid of the paper to John Baxter Boyle and his printer partner, D. G. Macrae, for £100. They in turn sold it for £300 to Horatio Bottomley, who likewise had no success with it, though it may have served a purpose as part of his complicated business activities. Publication of *Youth* was suspended in 1888. In later years Bottomley wrote that Alfred Harmsworth had been a sub-editor on his staff. It was a claim that had to be refuted. He never worked for Bottomley.

Running *Youth* gave Alfred Harmsworth more than technical experience. It showed him that in the publishing world ideals are apt to be tumbled down by economics, that success was more likely to come from following the public taste than from trying to lead it.

★   ★   ★

Precisely when Alfred Harmsworth left home to live his own life is not known. There are grounds for thinking that he left in 1882 after a quarrel with his father and that relations between them were strained for some time. There are no references to his father in the scrappy diary he was keeping though it records his often calling at his father's chambers at 6 Pump Court, Temple.

He went to live at first with a friend of his earliest years, Herbert Ward, at Duncan Cottage, South Side, Hampstead Heath (now 99 South End Road). Apparently to relieve the family pressure, he sometimes had one of his younger brothers to stay there with him. St. John remembered sharing his bed at Duncan Cottage. 'I suppose Herbert was home from one of his voyages,' he wrote to Alfred many years afterwards, 'because I well remember your telling him to moderate his language. I suppose you thought it too robust and seafaring for my hearing.' Ward was the elder by three years. 'I can remember when you wore sailor suits', Alfred said to him a long time after. 'Yes,' said Ward, 'and I can remember when *I* had to blow your nose for you.' Spoken of as 'a pocket Hercules', Ward, who was a nephew of Roland Ward, the Piccadilly taxidermist, had already had a remarkably full and adventurous life, though he was still only twenty or so. He had left Mill Hill School at fifteen and had sailed to New Zealand in an emigrant ship. For a year he lived with the Maoris. He had been round the world before the mast. He was exceptionally strong for his size; 'a bull', it was said of him, 'with an artistic temperament'. For Alfred Harmsworth he was an entirely congenial companion whose unusual self-reliance, the result of paternal neglect in his formative years, was to find fuller scope in journeys and adventures which provided material for books, lecture tours and a series of sculptural studies of the Central African savage that have for many years been part of the permanent collection of the Smithsonian Institute at Washington. Ward's travel experiences probably influenced Harmsworth's imagination when, later, his support was sought for more than one expedition of scientific interest and importance.

They had not long been housekeeping at Duncan Cottage when word came that the Ingrams had sold *Youth*. 'The news was a blow of the moment,' Alfred Harmsworth said. 'With all the confidence of eighteen, I decided to write all sorts of wonderful things which would replace the salary I had lost.' Meanwhile, though he had a cheque book, he had no money except the payments coming in from the serial story, *Fame and Fortune*, for which the rate was very low. 'I had practically nothing to live on, unless I chose to return to my parents', which meant confessing to the failure predicted for him when he left home. Ward's situation was not much better, his father having suddenly gone off to California to seek his fortune in the land boom there. Ward, junior, had been trying his hand at art and his father, like Harmsworth's, had objected. But Ward's father, unlike Harmsworth's, was able to make his son a small allowance. 'With this and what I earned from the serial story we lived together in one room in a very small house in Lavender Sweep, Clapham,' Alfred Harmsworth told an interviewer for the weekly paper *M.A.P.* (*Mainly About People*) in 1898. 'We were very hard up indeed.' They shared everything, including a suit of evening clothes. Harmsworth was inclined to worry about his appearance, thinking of its effect on the editors of Fleet Street. He was always pleased, he said, when cabmen hailed them as likely fares. 'It shows we look all right,' he would say. Every Sunday Alfred went home to his parents for the midday meal. There were some Sundays when he went on foot from Clapham to St. John's Wood, six or seven miles. He could not afford the bus fare. To save postage, he often delivered his contributions by hand to the offices of the papers for which he was writing.

Ward was driven by need as well as by his love of adventure to offer his services to Stanley, the explorer, then preparing his expedition to the Congo. He was accepted and underwent great privations. His great feat of courage and endurance was to paddle alone by canoe for fifteen hundred miles through cannibal country to get help for the sick men of

Stanley's party. Max Pemberton took his place as Alfred Harmsworth's companion. Pemberton was just down from Cambridge and thinking of a career at the bar. He was beset by the same urgent need of money. Aspiring to meet his needs by casual journalism, he went to the British Museum reading room to look up facts about Robert Burns. Coming out, he met Alfred Harmsworth, whom he had not seen for some time. 'Nobody wants to read your opinion of Burns,' Alfred told Pemberton. 'Give editors the kind of thing they want—less British Museum and more life.' Following that meeting the two went into lodgings together at 11 Boscable Gardens, Regent's Park, near Lord's Cricket Ground. There they shared a silk hat. Pemberton's mother supplied them with stiff white paper bands to hide their soiled shirt cuffs.

Pemberton said that although Harmsworth was mentally energetic beyond the average of his age, he often surrendered to moods of lethargy and disinclination to work, periods of indulgence which he probably looked back on longingly when time had laid on him its immense burden of responsibility and power. There were moments, for instance, in which he fancied himself as a composer of light music. He composed 'The Ellen Terry Waltz', a topical title which may have done as much as the music to secure its publication by the firm of Klein & Co., of 3 Holborn Viaduct. The tune had come to him as he was strumming on the piano at the Anchor Inn, Ripley, Surrey, a noted place of call for the early cycling clubs. 'Contains the ingredients of a good waltz. Though written in the style of Johann Strauss, it has many individual characteristics', is the comment on the tune by Messrs Chappell & Co. to whom it was recently submitted for a professional opinion. Family recollection has it that Alfred's father was displeased by the idea of his son 'writing a tune about an actress'. There is little doubt that young Alfred dreamed of fame as a composer of popular songs. At that time he was calling on Henry Klein every day to talk over ideas and to submit lyrics.

His freelance journalism was interrupted by an illness that brought him near to pneumonia again, this time after a bicycle ride from Bristol to London in pouring rain. He was now lodging with Pemberton at 37 Sheriff Road, West Hampstead, but spent that Christmas in bed at 94 Boundary Road, in his mother's care. The effects of the illness were to remain with him in the form of a liability to throat trouble. They made a lasting mark on his constitution.

Alfred Harmsworth to Henry Klein:

> 94, Boundary Road,
> St. John's Wood.
> December 28th, 1885

My dear Klein,—Thank you for your cheering letter. It has done me more good than all the medicine I have taken since I saw you. You see that I am under my mother's wing—not a bad place, I can assure you, only I am anxious to be out into the world again.

If you care for the verses on the other side keep 'em for a New Year's gift— if you don't like them tell me and I will do you another set.

I have not forgotten my debt to you.

Yours ever,

ALFRED C. HARMSWORTH

The verses, over which he had written the three possible titles of 'Sleeping and Waking', 'Asleep' and 'The Sleepers', opened with the sonorous lines:

> *O'er Palace gates and Prison bars, o'er sorrow and o'er woe*
> *The Midnight Chimes are floating with measure soft and slow,*
> *Hushed are the weary voices, the laughter and the strife*
> *The Morrow's tide comes creeping across the sands of life. . . .*

He had begun keeping a diary in which the name 'St. Vincent' was frequently written. 'St. Vincent', West End Lane, West Hampstead, was the home of a family named Milner. Robert Milner had begun his business life as a clerk in the West Indies sugar trade. He was now a partner in the importing firm of Shaw & Milner, later Shaw, Butt & Company, of Wood Street, London, E.C. The introduction of sugar beet from Germany adversely affected the West Indies trade and Robert Milner's business suffered. In the middle 1880s, he had been fairly prosperous, able to keep servants and to provide French and German governesses for his children. At that time, the Milners were better off than the Harmsworths. Like the Harmsworths, like many families in their social layer, they had their dreams of vanished grandeur. Mrs Milner's family name was Wilmot and Wilmot was the family name of the Rochester earls. There had been not wholly disheartening genealogical forays in that direction.

Mary, more often called Molly, was the eldest of the three Milner girls; there was also a son, Harry, who as a boy was a 'chum' of Alfred Harmsworth's. Mary was *petite*, graceful and vivacious, a legatee in those respects, it was thought, of a French great-grandmother. She had exceptionally fine brown eyes, also a 'wonderful head of hair'. She and Alfred Harmsworth had met first of all at a children's party long before and she continues to remember, these eighty years after, her mother's admonition on that occasion: 'Now, Molly, don't dance *all* the time with the best-looking boy in the room.' For several years Molly Milner and Alfred Harmsworth were no more than casual friends, not often meeting except in each other's homes. Now, affectionate references to her were appearing in Alfred's diary. Other entries tell of 'quarrels at St. Vincent', referring to tensions between Robert Milner and his son Harry, who was later sent out to Australia on an emigrant ship with £5 in his pocket to start a new life.

Alfred Harmsworth, resuming the life of the unattached writer, with its smattering opportunities for self-education, dealt with a number of different papers and a profusion of topics. The articles he was writing showed that at twenty he was an efficient compiler and purveyor of factual material for the more popular types of journal. They showed him to have been the born journalist, a professional who reached competence without serving a formal apprenticeship to letters. His lack of specialized training seems to have caused him some later misgivings, which had to be covered up by romantic versions of his experiences as an amateur reporter on the *Hampstead & Highgate Express*. He often claimed to have worked and mixed with the *élite* of that branch of news gathering. He knew the pangs of editorial rejection, commending them afterwards to others as a necessary and valuable part of experience. One of the editors was the influential Frederick Greenwood, of the *Pall Mall Gazette*. 'Mr Greenwood did me a great deal of good. He rejected most of the articles I wrote for him. I had some fifteen or sixteen MSS. returned, but there was always a kindly little note which did much to take the bitterness out of the disappointment.' Looking back to those freelancing days, he was able to say with an inflexion of pride that 'though I was hampered by continual ill-health, I kept the wolf from the door'.

Temperamentally, perhaps constitutionally, he was not drawn even to the milder excesses of the Bohemian life. He set foot in the taverns of Fleet Street only for the midday meal. If his father's example was not finally discouraging, he saw other men staggering to professional disaster. One whose fate stamped itself on his memory was Leopold Lewis, who wrote *The Bells*, in which Henry Irving had made history at the Lyceum Theatre. 'I often saw him, up and down the Street, a poor old wreck.' His freelancing experiences gave him a lasting insight into the realities of a branch of journalism mostly ignored by proprietors and disdained by editors. He knew perfectly well that while there were many hacks among the Fleet Street freelances, in their ranks, too, were men and women whose gifts had enlarged the reputations of editors sitting at their desks. He demonstrated his sympathetic attitude generously in his later years as editor and newspaper owner. He remembered the meagre cheques he had received for his articles in *Cassell's Saturday Journal*: on one occasion '14/– for a column of facts'. He always recalled those old freelancing transactions with pleasure. It seemed to be important to him to identify himself with the common struggle for existence when he had risen far superior to it. Other experiences were less congenially remembered. One year he joined a goose club. He drew the winning ticket and took home the goose for the family Christmas at Boundary Road. Reminded of it long after by an old Savage Club friend of his father, he a little too obviously changed the subject.

There was a day when he and Pemberton had no luck in placing their ideas for articles. Alfred was depressed because the editor of *Society*, who had previously taken some of his work, said that he had no room for more. Alfred rejoined Pemberton, who had waited for him on the Fleet Street pavement, and together they turned into Farringdon Street and walked towards Holborn, to take a bus home to St. John's Wood. Pemberton noticed a *Tit-Bits* poster outside a tall neglected-looking building on the opposite side of Farringdon Street. They crossed over to look at it. George Newnes, a Congregational minister's son and former traveller in the fancy goods trade, had lately brought his paper to London from Manchester. 'This chap pays a guinea a column,' Pemberton said. 'Let's go up and see him.' Mounting to the first floor, they found themselves in a large untidy room in which a man, with a beard the colour of badger's hair, sat eating his lunch off a proof-littered trestle-table. He was George Newnes, the founder and proprietor of *Tit-Bits*, who, without realizing it, had become a force in the modern world by setting in motion the greatest publishing development of the age. His *Tit-Bits* had been conceived in the spirit of a hobby, a scrapbook of 'interesting bits' clipped from newspapers and periodicals. He could have told his two young visitors precisely how it had come about. He had gone home one evening in Manchester and, with his feet up, had read a local paper to his wife. One of the items told of an engine driver's little daughter who was left briefly alone on the footplate of her father's engine. The engine started to move, gathered speed, and was soon rushing along the line. The engine driver jumped on another engine, set off in pursuit and, climbing from one engine to the other, stopped the runaway. Newnes's wife had said: 'There ought to be a paper full of tit-bits like that. A lot of people would read it.' The steam from James Watt's kettle was not more momentous in its consequences than this later domestic incident.

The success of *Tit-Bits* was largely the result of lucky timing. It became a symbol of the mental emancipation of the generation most immediately affected by the 1870 Education Act, the source and fount of the successive waves of publishing enterprise which have expressed as well as ministered to a longing not only for more reading but for more life. Long before 1870, John Cassell, the psalm-singing founder of *Cassell's Saturday Journal* and other 'improving' papers, had found a steadily growing public for his *Working Man's Friend* (1850), which reached a sale of 100,000 copies in a few months. He anticipated and in some measure prepared the advent of the *Tit-Bits* type of publication. Cassell's journalism was earnest and crusading, he having been a fearless preacher in the courts and alleys of Clare Market, where Aldwych now is, then one of London's disreputable quarters. His name is perpetuated in the imprint of the well-known book publishing House. Newnes was content to imbue his *Tit-Bits* with general moral ideas, leaving piety out of it.

Looking up from his lunch, Newnes asked the two young callers their business, and on being told that they wanted to become *Tit-Bits* contributors, he asked bluntly: 'What subjects?' Neither had thought as far as that. Pemberton, neatly improvising, said: 'Jerry-builders.' He said afterwards that the idea had come to him from 'the crazy nature' of the Newnes building. The article was written and sent in and paid for in cash by registered post, all within a few days. Harmsworth followed it with 'Some Curious Butterflies', written by hand on ruled copybook paper. Other subjects confirmed the bias of his professional inclinations: 'A Visit to W. H. Smith & Son', 'Newspaper Special Editions: How They Are Made' and 'How Some Fortunes Are Made', describing the effect of copper-plate engraving methods on the popular taste. 'Q.C.s And How They Are Made' no doubt owed something to his sojourns in the Middle Temple with his father. 'Organ Grinders And Their Earnings' set him wandering in the alleys of Clerkenwell in search of material. Writing in the 1,000th issue of *Tit-Bits*, Newnes recalled that Harmsworth was 'almost daily in the building for a time, bringing in most interesting copy'.

Alfred Harmsworth's imagination had been lit up by meeting Newnes, not because Newnes was an inspirational figure but because he had a success on his hands. If Newnes, why not Harmsworth? The implied question was one of opportunity rather than of talents. George Newnes, thirty-five to Alfred Harmsworth's twenty, seemed to the younger man to be middle-aged, heavily painstaking and unprofessional. That Newnes would develop a masterful personality was clearly not foreshadowed in his first encounter with Harmsworth in Farringdon Street, any more than it was vouchsafed that the same street would presently become the headquarters address of the world's greatest periodical publishing organization, the Harmsworth brothers' Amalgamated Press.

Pemberton believed that this meeting with Newnes was decisive in the career of Alfred Harmsworth. He remembered Alfred coming into his bedroom one morning soon afterwards to talk about the phenomenon of Newnes's success. 'The Board schools are turning out hundreds of thousands of boys and girls who don't care for the ordinary newspaper. They'll read anything that is simple and sufficiently interesting. The man who has produced this *Tit-Bits* has got hold of something bigger than he imagines. I shall try to get in with him.' Discussing the future with his eldest sister, Alfred told her: 'There'll be a huge demand for good, wholesome stories.' She never forgot his saying it. 'He was still only a boy. It showed how his mind was working.'

From there he went on to consider the chances of finding capital to start a paper like Newnes's. Pemberton's father, in the City, was approached; he was not interested. Pemberton then secured an introduction to a wealthy Park Lane hostess, Lady Meux, and laid the scheme before her. 'She agreed to the venture and would have gone on with it but for the intervention of the family solicitor.' Mary Milner's father showed interest and then regretted, in a letter, that he did not see his way 'quite clear about capital'. He afterwards put his few hundreds into an umbrella business, with results which, according to Alfred, were awkward enough to require an urgent family conference at seven o'clock one morning.

George Newnes had experienced the same sort of frustration. His most promising hope of capital had been from a Manchester business man whose interest evaporated unexpectedly in the course of the crucial interview, leaving Newnes disappointed to the point of nervous collapse. Lost in gloomy thoughts on his way home, he tripped over a kerb and lay half-conscious on the pavement. A policeman, flashing his bull's-eye lamp, accused him of being drunk and Newnes was hard put to convince him otherwise. The capital on which *Tit-Bits* was founded came from 'The Vegetarian Company's Saloon', started by Newnes with no capital at all. When he had made £400 he gave up catering for the hypochondriacs of Manchester and went into publishing. As a vegetarian restaurant proprietor, he was more than once seen in another part of the city eagerly disposing of a midday steak.

Alfred Harmsworth's emulating energy was given a new direction when the publishing firm of Iliffe of Coventry offered him the editorship of *Bicycling News*. He had been writing articles for other cycling papers, among them *The Cyclist*, owned by the Iliffes, and *Wheeling*, a rival paper edited by one of the cycling personalities of the time named McCandlish. Alfred wrote to him on March 7, 1886: 'As you were good enough to introduce me to Iliffe, I shall be glad in return to make you known either to Cassell's or the *Morning Post*.' Iliffe negotiated in the first place through his London manager, Septimus Smith, known as 'The Colonel' for his sartorial elegance. Smith offered Harmsworth a salary of £2 10s. and arranged for him to travel to Coventry to sign an agreement with William Iliffe personally. Harmsworth had recently been turned down as an applicant for the sub-editorship of *Society* and it seems to have been with some relief that he wrote in his diary for January 7, 1886: 'Heard of certainty of getting work on *Bicycling News*. Thanks to Smith', and to the cycling misadventure which had befallen him shortly before. He had been away on one of his self-imposed endurance rides and, after a severe drenching, had been ill with congestion of the lungs. The doctor urged him to find work away from London. The agreement with Iliffe was signed on March 27, 1886. Later that day, Alfred returned to London to spend the weekend at 'St. Vincent'. His diary entry for that Sunday reads: 'Awfully happy with my darling.'

        ★   ★   ★

The momentum of the industrial revolution was mounting fast. Steel manipulation—the word survives as 'manip' in the important steel tube trade of today—was accelerating the social revolution. The bicycle, until then a ridiculous-looking machine which none could ride with grace and few with ease, was evolving into its finally popular form. *The Times* had published a leading article: 'The bicycle has . . . now surmounted the difficulties of construction and adapted itself to human capabilities—it augments at least threefold the locomotive power of an ordinary man. Society used to be divided into the equestrian and pedestrian orders: these people have found a third rank.'

Coventry's metropolitan place in the bicycle industry was the result of the disturbing effects of the new pace of invention and exploitation. The city had previously known the shocks of unregulated enterprise. Its fairly extensive worsted, woollen and silk frilling trades had been hit by foreign competition, which later depressed other local industries, the making of watches and sewing-machines among them. The city of Tennyson's 'three tall spires', with its coal and steel resources, turned to bicycle manufacturing as to a sheet anchor in a stormy sea. The skill of the watchmakers and sewing-machine mechanics was invaluable to the cycle trade. A population of 40,000 was expanded to 70,000 by the cycling boom, which received its most decisive impetus when a Sussex farmer's son, J. K. Starley, introduced the 'diamond' frame, and J. B. Dunlop, a Belfast veterinary surgeon, patented the pneumatic tyre. In 1889, not more than three or four bicycles had air-filled tyres. Two years later, cycle manufacturers began sending their wheels to the Dunlop firm to be fitted with the new tyre. Cycling was becoming safe and enjoyable and soon 'the wheels of chance' of a topical Wells novel were spinning to the farthermost parts of the land.

The coming of the bicycle brought new business to the Coventry printing houses and the demand for catalogues and technical literature increased the turnover of the Iliffe firm, which did jobbing work, with wallpaper dealing as a sideline. Iliffe's compositors were setting new bicycle trade names almost every week, some to become household words, some not: 'Premier', 'Spinaway', 'Rover', 'Humber', 'Invincible', 'Rudge', 'King of the Road', 'Raleigh'. There were others less solid-sounding and some as fanciful as the orders in the books of their opportunist promoters. William Iliffe's shop was at the corner of Vicar Lane and Smithford Street. In time he was joined there by his son, William Isaac Iliffe, whose soundness of judgment was mainly responsible for the rise of the firm in the realm of trade journal publishing. He it was who took the decision to publish the paper on which the family's prosperity was founded, *The Cyclist*.

It is difficult to understand now that the advent of so simple a method of getting about was met by begrudging and sometimes bitter resentment from other users of the road and from the press. In spite of the sympathetic prescience of *The Times*, the bicycle as a means of personal locomotion was actively despised by many people of the class from which that newspaper's readers came and the superior social attitude has persisted down to our own time. As late as 1939, when a writer proposed to a leading London publishing firm a book based on a bicycle tour of England, he was told that 'the best booksellers would not be interested'. In the 1880s there were still a few remaining coaches on the English roads and, like the watermen of the Thames of an earlier time, when the hackney coach first appeared in the London streets, the coach drivers and guards saw a threat to their livelihood. A guard of the London–St. Albans coach was fined £5 for endangering a cyclist's life by throwing an iron ball and chain into his front wheel as they passed on the road. Another angry man was given six weeks' hard labour at the Thames Police Court for a similar kind of assault. Encouraged by the harsh denunciations of the new pastime in a racing journal, *The Sporting Times*, a party of horse-lovers attacked a number of cyclists with some violence on the Ripley Road in 1887. It was a common thing for cyclists to be lashed by the whips of passing coach and wagon drivers.

Cycling journalism in England started in the 1870s. One of the first publications of the kind was *Ixion*, a shilling monthly published at 125 Fleet Street. It lasted three months, just long enough for it to forecast the coming of heavier-than-air flying machines. *The Bicyclist*, a penny monthly, was published in 1875 from Herne Hill, a centre of the early cycle racing meetings. Next came *Bicycling News*, in 1876, published by Benjamin Clegg, a Covent Garden printer who was also an Essex publican. The paper was bought by William Iliffe for £50 in 1885. Iliffe already owned two or three other cycling papers and in 1879 he added *The Cyclist* as the first fruits of his partnership with a Weymouth schoolmaster named Henry Sturmey, who originated the Sturmey-Archer gear and who later printed on his business notepaper the doubtless fully-justified opinions of a dozen newspapers that he was, also, a pioneer of British motoring. He was the first editor of *The Autocar*. *The Cyclist* at first declined advertisements, but in three years its circulation of 6,000 was supported by twenty pages of advertising and the paper could be considered a commercial success. Though its sales were not large, its tone and integrity gave it the highest standing among papers of its kind.

Other cycling papers sprang into being, some of them overnight and doomed as quickly to disappear. The rivalries were fierce. Most of the papers were given several subsidiary titles, invented to monopolize the field and to keep out intruders. For that reason the Iliffes were denounced as 'the Coventry ring' and their success with *The Cyclist* in particular brought them abuse of a sort that could not flourish in print under our later laws of libel. When they launched a new paper called *Wheel Life*, it was hailed by a contemporary as 'another broken-kneed horse from the Coventry stable'. The editor of *Wheel Life*, stung into disregarding the Iliffes' policy of ignoring attacks, retorted in kind: 'Garbage and inanity have spread their foul wings over each issue, while vulgarity jostles with mendacity for the first opening left by the other two.' There was in those papers resentment of new ideas as well as of new rivals. The Dunlop innovation was derided as 'the exploding tyre'.

* * *

Alfred Harmsworth, aged twenty-one, unpacked his bag in the Coventry of those absurd journalistic antagonisms early in April 1886. William Iliffe had found accommodation for him at 5 The Crescent, Holyhead Road, a small terrace house occupied by Miss Louise Mercer, who had been governess to the Iliffe children and now let rooms. He paid £1 a week for his bed and board and had a courtesy share in the sitting-room with another lodger, the Rev. H. H. Devenish, curate of St. John's Church, Coventry. Alfred attended services there. He also went with the Iliffes to Queen's Road Chapel. He soon hit on a nickname for the curate—'Devilfish'. They became good companions, so that nearly twenty years after Devenish was able to write to him that 'the old friendship is as true as ever', by which time the curate had become rector of Kinwarten, Warwickshire, and Alfred Harmsworth famous in the land. Alfred charmed Miss Mercer in particular by his piano playing, his ability to rattle off the latest tunes. It was the only luxury he could afford, the few shillings a week for piano hire. He had only to hear any piece once and he could play it immediately, an odd little gift with which he impressed many people.

Henry Sturmey said that when Harmsworth first went to Coventry, 'his entire belongings were contained in a small handbag'. He described Harmsworth as being 'a somewhat loosely built figure with a very earnest manner', and said that his jaw was 'strong and determined'. As co-proprietor of cycling papers with Iliffe, Sturmey was impressed by 'the superabundant energy which he put into his work'. According to a member of the staff of *The Coventry Standard*, Alfred was 'poorly off for clothes'. Iliffe's personal assistant, named Woodward, said that he had to mend Harmsworth's jacket before he could attend a cyclists' rally. The *Bicycling News* cartoonist, George Moore, told how he had 'more than once lent Harmsworth a shirt'. It was always understood that Iliffe's London representative, Septimus Smith, lent Alfred a morning suit for the interview with William Iliffe. It is hard to accept such reports, for all this unanimity of reminiscence. Alfred Harmsworth had taken pride in his appearance as a vendor of editorial ideas and he had been seen in Fleet Street wearing the Inverness cape and glossy silk hat which were the period's hallmark of the well-dressed man. Shabbiness for him had a Bohemian context for which he had no taste.

There was no questioning the impression which his good looks made on his Coventry colleagues. One of them wrote: 'He was distinguished-looking, loose-limbed, carrying himself with an air of freedom which you seldom see in a man. I often walked with him in the streets and could not help noticing the number of people who turned back to take a second glance at him. Some would ask me afterwards: "Who was that fine-looking chap you were with?"' This same colleague, named Carson, remembered how profuse Alfred Harmsworth was in his thanks for the smallest service rendered. 'He was always very grateful. He had a way with him which quickly made friends and inclined people to do things for him.' There was another contemporary with whom he left the recollection of 'exceptional and even arrogant self-confidence'. A writer in *The Coventry Standard* later recalled him as having 'a good deal of vanity; imperious in a way, but an excellent friend and companion'. The admiring note was echoed by his fellow lodger, Devenish. 'I was captivated by this handsome young stranger. Most young men are apt to be awkward at a first meeting. Harmsworth walked into my dingy little sitting-room with the aplomb of a diplomat entering a salon.'

*   *   *

The sales of *Bicycling News* had fallen to 300 copies a week, and the Iliffe's first move was to improve its circulation, and its dormant advertising appeal, by combining it with two of their other journals, *Wheel Life* (started as *Hum of the Wheel*) and *Wheel World*. Alfred Harmsworth had contributed to *Wheel Life* while he was still in London. He wrote a series of articles, 'Chats with Celebrities', the 'stars' of the cycling world. He had written articles and sketches for *Bicycling News* before going to Coventry, signing them with his Henley House School name of 'Billy'. They showed, clearly, that he had a flair for writing. He was then seventeen.

Shortly before his arrival in Coventry, there appeared in *Wheel Life* a fairly flattering outline of his so far sketchy career. It gave a list of the papers to which he had contributed and ended on the bold assertive note that 'his success is generally considered quite out of proportion to his years and a brilliant career is very generally expected of him'. If in those days of his youth tongue-in-the-cheek egotism came naturally, it might be fair to doubt whether he himself had prompted that crude manifestation of it. He had been seconded for the Coventry post by 'The Colonel', Septimus Smith, and Alfred's diary shows that Smith had been 'touching' him for small cash sums. He was earning no more than he had made as a freelance. But money was coming in regularly. Besides, he was enjoying again the peculiar pleasures of being an editor, of having one's favours sought instead of having to seek them from others.

Bicycling News soon responded to the Harmsworth editorial touch Its circulation rose. Inside a fortnight he had given the paper a fresh complexion. He adapted a well-known advertising slogan to read: *It Comes As A Boon And A Blessing To Men, The Popular Penn'orth, The Racy B.N.* His ideas were good for circulation, bad for office morale, it seemed. The nominal editor was Lacey Hillier, a noted cycle racing pioneer and amateur champion, oracular on bicycle history, and obstinately resistant to the technical improvements which were to make cycling a popular pastime. He was by profession a stockbroker and worked in London. Iliffe had decided that the time had come for the editor to work in Coventry; hence the new arrangement. It left Hillier with the job of writing leaders while Alfred did the office work in Coventry. Hillier would not admit that he had been superseded by the younger man who, he insisted, was manager of the paper, not its editor. He led a revolt against Harmsworth. Angry because his technical successor had broken up his articles into briskly readable paragraphs, Hillier, who could be crushing when roused, wrote to William Iliffe complaining that 'this yellow-headed worm has cut my copy to rags'. Iliffe, a man of good sense, took no notice. But the uncomplimentary epithet of 'yellow-headed worm', shortened to Y.H.W., took the place of 'The Kid', as he was known at first to the printers at Vicar Lane. Years later, when Harmsworth answered a letter from Hillier, he signed himself 'Y.H.W.' instead of 'Northcliffe'.

Another aggrieved writer for the paper said, apropos of Hillier's outburst, that Alfred Harmsworth's blue-pencilling was often so drastic that 'I could hardly recognize my mutilated offspring'. Particularly irritating, said this contributor, was the fact that Harmsworth knew so little of the subject on which they were experts. 'I did know everything at that period about practical cycling. A. C. Harmsworth certainly did not.' Aware of the deficiency and not being particularly bothered by it, Harmsworth was able to call on the services of a number of well-informed men who were specializing in cycling subjects. One of them was Arthur Morrison, writing as 'Nym' in the Iliffe papers, and later well known as the author of *Tales of Mean Streets* and other stories of East End of London life which are beginning to be accepted as minor Victorian classics. Alfred Harmsworth's lack of specialized knowledge was offset, for his proprietors, by his instinctive understanding of what bicycle enthusiasts would read. His keen contemporary sense saw, for instance, that photography might become part of the pleasure of riding about the countryside and the space which he regularly gave to it helped to popularize the camera.

For him, the bicycle was not simply a new form of movement. It was a social portent. Most significant was his insight into its effects on the future of women. The woman cyclist, then, was a derided figure, her appearance a signal for abuse from passers-by; there were instances of cycling women being stoned by outraged anti-feminists. *Bicycling News*, under Harmsworth, broke new ground by acquiring a woman correspondent, Lilias Campbell Davidson, sometime president of the Women Cyclists' Association, whose role it was to write articles creating a more favourable public opinion. It may be an insufficiently acknowledged fact that the Coventry cycling journalists were an important influence in the freeing of women from domestic bondage. Before long, women were joining the men in their club rides and dispelling for themselves the prejudice that met them in the streets. No one would have forecast that change even two or three years before it came about. Some of the impetus behind it can be traced to the enfranchising journalism of the young editor of *Bicycling News*.

His enterprise went beyond the editorial sphere. He organized the paper's advertising and added usefully to the revenues. His facility as a provider of ideas was drawn on for other Iliffe papers. For *The Cyclist* he invented a mysterious Chinese character whom he called *Ah Fong*. This personage, according to various printed reports, all of which flowed from young Alfred Harmsworth's pen, was due to arrive in Coventry by bicycle a few days before Christmas and, it was hinted, a public reception was being arranged. His mission was understood to be one of trade and goodwill, and manufacturers, it was urged, would do well to advertise their products to time with his coming. Local interest rose to a high pitch of expectation. *The Cyclist* advertisement columns were filled. Many applications were received from persons wishing to attend the reception. Ah Fong arrived in the form of the paper's Christmas Number. It was a Harmsworth hoax and so successful that everybody laughed and regarded it as one of the funniest episodes in cycling journalism. Another of his editorial inventions was a column of scraps from books and periodicals to which readers were invited to contribute. The common thread was cycling and the open road, but the idea cast a longer shadow. It was the sort of journalism which was to be the foundation of his success. Within a year the circulation of *Bicycling News* had moved rapidly upwards, and the curious position had to be faced of a paper selling more than it could afford to print because the advertisement revenue had not kept up with the sales. The Iliffes had never wanted *Bicycling News* to succeed to the point at which it might eclipse *The Cyclist*, which came first in their sentiments as in their balance-sheet.

Harmsworth soon became the target for abuse from the rival factions. They referred to his paper as 'The Hotch-Potchery'. He wrote some of the articles under a pen-name, calling himself Arthur Pendennis, taken from Thackeray's hero, whose personal style he had always admired. 'That little tradesman', was one of the sneers thrown at him. It was considered to be specially offensive, and it evoked the printed retort that 'Mr Arthur Pendennis, by the by, has been a student for the Bar', the writer of the paragraph being Harmsworth himself. 'Arthur Pendennis's charming prose is only marred by the writer's want of practical knowledge of his subject', was a more bearable comment. Stung by a scurrilous article, 'in what we regret to be obliged to term our contemporary', he carried the attack for once deep into the enemy lines, heading it 'Pro Bono Pimlico'. His Arthur Pendennis articles were well done, considering his years.

Recoiling possibly from the crude polemics and the social harshness of the Coventry scene, he apparently asserted the Pendennis affinity with unaccommodating disdain. He was heard to say that he would 'eventually get a peerage'. When he was stopped by a policeman for riding a bicycle on the towpath, he at first gave the name of 'Lord Pendennis'. Sturmey remembered one occasion when Harmsworth was hauled off his bicycle by a policeman who caught him riding without a light after dark. He gave the policeman his father's London address in the Temple. Nothing more was heard of the incident. There were Coventry characters of that period whose mentality he can hardly have respected, for all that they were acquiring the financial solidity which he conspicuously lacked. One of them was having a new house built. The architect asked: 'Which aspect do you prefer?' 'What aspect is ——'s house going to have?' the client asked, naming a rival in the bicycle industry. 'South', he was told. 'Then give me two south aspects', was the order.

Like his father, Alfred was capable of impressing others with his instinctive civility. There was in Coventry a well-known cycling man, A. J. Wilson, who was deaf, and who, for that reason, used the pen-name of 'Faed'. Alfred had lessons in the deaf alphabet from George Moore, the cycling cartoonist, taking the trouble to do so to make conversation easier for Wilson. Referring to it in a letter written in 1933, Wilson, who became an intrepid motor-cycling pioneer, said: 'Many years afterwards, when Harmsworth had become Northcliffe and the owner of Sutton

Place, in Surrey, I went to lunch with him there. After our meal, at which various other people were present, he took me up to his sanctum and sat beside me on a sofa and talked on his fingers to me for over an hour.'

Writing to an acquaintance in 1939, Mrs Walter Welford, whose husband was editor of one of the Coventry cycling papers and who herself practised professional photography in Hagley Road, Edgbaston, recalled Alfred Harmsworth as one of her first sitters. He was in Birmingham with members of Iliffe's staff for a cycling event. They all had their photographs taken. Harmsworth was 'not an easy subject. His polished manners undid my posing. He *would* keep springing up to move this and lift that for me. I could not keep him still.' In a group photograph, taken at that time, he looks half-crushed in the throng of cycling nabobs, squeezed between Lacey Hillier and H. H. Griffin. He is seen wearing a bowler hat, too old for his years, and in his gloved hand he holds a cigar, confirming that impression. In a few years several of his seniors in the group would be asking favours of him.

The petty professional strife of Coventry often annoyed him, sending his thoughts back to London, the city of his future. He was heard to say to the 'Cyclist Poet', Fred Smith, whose verse was popular with *Bicycling News* readers: 'One of these days, I'm going up to London to start a penny weekly like Newnes's *Tit-Bits*. Only I shall let the great British public ask the questions.' Smith, who was also Iliffe's head reader, used to say in his turn: 'I knew Alfred Harmsworth when all he had to jingle was a few coppers and a bunch of keys.' His other colleague, Carson, walked back with him to Miss Mercer's one day when they talked about the future. 'This Coventry life,' Harmsworth remarked, 'is too middling—you are not quite down, but you are by no means up.' Carson recalled his 'brilliantly shining eyes' as he declared: 'I must be up!' Carson said that he was 'a strange mixture of optimism and pessimism, somewhat flighty in his work, but full of ambition'. Carson said that Harmsworth was often to be found at the local reference library, which he spoke of as being 'full of quaint and curious literature, enough for a lifetime of writing for *Tit-Bits*'. He was still sending articles to that paper and could not understand why Carson did not exploit the same opportunity. Carson was knowledgeable about the Coventry past and Harmsworth was always willing to explore the older parts of the city. 'Let us walk in the footsteps of kings', he would say, as Carson and he set out on a Saturday ramble.

He wrote to his brother in Dublin for Christmas, 1886:

8, The Crescent,
Coventry

My dear Cecil,—. . . I expect you have to scrape pretty hard. It won't do you any harm. Lots of fellows have to live close at college.

I am going to town on Thursday till Tuesday and shall be at 94 on M's birthday. Send her a card and a letter. I shall try to give her a substantial present. I expect you are rather pushed for Xmas presents and card money, so I send you all I can spare. Mind not to run into debt. I can always send something at a pinch.

I have got a rise to £190 from Iliffe. I expected £220 but shall not get that till I am married. However, I have a series running through Henderson's *Young Folks* that will run for 2 years and that brings me in £70 or £75 a year in fact, besides occasional articles there and about £1 a week from *Tit-Bits*.

Your affectionate brother,
ALFRED

Writing to the same brother a week or two later: 'I send you ten bob, as Ma tells me that it will come in handy. I hope you are working hard and are paving the way to getting into a good set.' Cecil had gone to Trinity College, Dublin, from the Philological School in Marylebone Road, London (now Marylebone Grammar School), where Harold had been educated. Leicester was also a pupil there; his education was interrupted by rheumatic fever, which permanently injured his health. Hildebrand was at Dublin High School as part of an arrangement by which, to relieve the pressure at home, he was being looked after by Maffett relatives. The Marylebone school reports showed that Harold was 'particularly good at arithmetic'. At other subjects he gained poor places. Even so, he had a liking for school and almost resented the holidays. Cecil did better than Harold and went on to win prizes at Trinity College, Dublin, where he was Senior Moderator in Modern Literature and Stewart Scholar in Literature. Of the three, it was Leicester who made the best showing at the Marylebone School. Cecil carried a painful memory of the school down to his last days. 'It was the odious practice to summon from class, in the loud voice of the school porter, embarrassed urchins (myself sometimes among them) whose fees were in arrears and whose attendance was required by the school collector. After sixty years I recall with indignation the humiliations imposed on a shy and sensitive boy by the callous stupidity of the school authorities.'

Geraldine Maffett, Northcliffe's mother. A photograph taken in Dublin
shortly before her marriage to Alfred Harmsworth, senior, in 1864

Sunnybank, Chapelizod, near Dublin, where Northcliffe was born on July 15, 1865

Chapter Four

'Answers to Correspondents'

ONE of the most far-reaching inventions of an inventive age was the paragraph. Skilfully exploited by the new impresarios of the printed word, it was a portent of greater moment than many of the more spectacular developments which heralded the twentieth century. Alfred Harmsworth considered that its true begetter was Edmund Yates, of *The World*, a proprietor-journalist whom he as a younger man had much admired. Newnes in *Tit-Bits* was exploiting the brevity which was the secret of catching the attention of the new literate public. A page in his paper, headed 'Answers to Correspondents', contained many paragraphs of two or three lines only. Although 'Answers to Correspondents' was a convention of periodical journalism before Newnes appeared on the scene, he grasped the value of it as a 'feature' more firmly than any editor had previously done and continued to give readers' letters his personal attention long after he could afford to pay others to do it for him. His biographer, Hulda Friederichs, said: 'For years he took these letters in bundles twelve inches high, and higher, went carefully through them, and answered them so wisely, so fully, and so well, that in course of time people belonging to every social class sought help and advice from that source. Nor was there any part of his work which he found more interesting or more stimulating.'

As a schoolboy, Alfred Harmsworth had used the idea of 'Answers to Correspondents' in *The Henley House School Magazine*. When he left the school, the heading for that column in the magazine was reduced to 'Answers'. Newnes's realization of the value of 'snappiness' had set him on the road to riches. Harmsworth's more ruthless energy took up the running and soon enabled him to overtake and pass the older man in achievement and rewards. Newnes had hit on a profitable formula for meeting the mental needs of the superficially educated new generations. It was:

D

Information as entertainment. It made a strong appeal to the mind of Alfred Harmsworth. Ruminating in bed one morning during his last weeks at Coventry, he resolved to put up to the Iliffes the notion of a popular weekly, on *Tit-Bits* lines, to be called *Answers to Correspondents*. He had given readers' letters prominence in his cycling paper. He knew that they were an editorial asset. William Iliffe listened to his scheme, for young Harmsworth had proved that he could secure circulation; also, he was attractively eager in his enthusiasm. Iliffe's verdict was against the idea. It meant a digression from the trade paper publishing in which the firm was most experienced and into which they had put much of their capital. Harmsworth's new paper would have to stand alone. It could not be fitted into their existing arrangements for advertisement canvassing, and so on; in short, it was a gamble. As a parting friendly gesture, Iliffe offered to print such a paper for him on credit for a few weeks if he decided to launch it. Alfred left William Iliffe's office with that generous promise in his pocket. He was twenty-one and as aggressively sure as any young man of that age can be that there was no time to lose.

A newcomer to the Iliffe staff at that time, a cycling champion of the early 1880s named George Gatehouse (later advertisement manager of *The Autocar*), was asked by William Iliffe shortly after Harmsworth had left: 'What are they saying about it in the town?' The reply was given: 'They're wondering why you let him go.' Iliffe pondered the point before making any comment. Then he said: 'He was too hot for me.' Harmsworth had saved the fortunes of *Bicycling News*. They declined again after he had left Coventry. The paper was later sold and incorporated in a Birmingham sporting publication. It was natural that Coventry should not detain him longer than he needed to learn the lesson that, as he afterwards said, 'not all the wisdom of the British Isles resides in London'. Although Coventry had put valuable technical skill into his hands and added solidly to his experience of printing and publishing, it was inevitable that he should return to London to make the more consequential discoveries awaiting him there. Love, money, ambition, frustration, may have combined to give force to his decision to leave Iliffe. Mary Milner was in London; and we can see from his diary how often she was in his thoughts. All the best writing markets were in London; the highest rates of literary payment were made there. In London he could find the most stimulating and productive opportunities for self-expression, especially as he knew by instinct what he wanted to do. Or, he may have been attracted back more positively by hearing that a friend of the Maffetts in Ireland was in a position to provide finance for the paper he was eager to start.

* * *

William Fry Carr, from Dublin, was one of the thirteen children of Canon Carr, of Christ Church Cathedral, Dublin, rector of Whitechurch, Rathfarnham, Co. Dublin, and editor of *The Church of Ireland Gazette*. A brother of William's who died in infancy had been named D'Argaville, after his maternal grandmother. When William Fry Carr's *fiancée* heard it, she exclaimed: 'Oh, what a lovely name!' and insisted on calling him by it, William being too prosaic for her liking. Assenting to the change and amending the spelling to Dargaville, Carr crossed the Irish Sea to seek a career in London. He brought with him £1,500 for investment in any reasonable undertaking on behalf of his wife-to-be, Geraldine Maffett's closest girlhood friend, the daughter of Dr Gordon, of Hume Street, Dublin. It was her dowry. Carr also brought a Maffett introduction to Alfred Harmsworth. He had what is sometimes called 'a fine eye' and his brogue was music in the ear. He was a good athlete who excelled as a cross-country runner.

Carr had travelled to Coventry for his first meeting with Alfred. Devenish, the curate, said that Alfred asked for the private use of the front parlour for the duration of the interview, saying that he could not hope to impress his visitor in his bed-sitting-room. The interview was successful, resulting in what seems to have been an impulsive fusion of interests. Carr agreed to go in with Alfred on a business footing. Within a few days, Alfred left Coventry and went into lodgings with Carr at 77 Iverson Road, Kilburn, one of the many local streets of an aspidistra-cherishing community which asserted its character in strictly whitened front door-steps and close-drawn curtains of Nottingham lace. It was from there that Carr and Harmsworth embarked on a business relationship based on the capital which the former had brought with him from Ireland. They took a room in a first-floor office belonging to the publishers of *Horner's Penny Stories* at 26 Paternoster Square, just off Ludgate Hill; rent 15s. a week. For privacy's sake, the room was divided by a matchboard partition which gave them an office eight feet by ten feet. The other part, twelve feet square, became the publishing office. It was too small to admit more than two or three newsagents' men at a time; others had to wait their turn in a passage outside. Carr, the sentimental Irishman, was touched to learn that the carpenter who put up the partition had sixteen children, several of them ailing. An office whip-round for him produced four shillings. The partnership agreement between Alfred Harmsworth and Dargaville Carr provided for two others to join them, Edward Markwick, of 3 Elm Court, Temple, a barrister friend of Harmsworth, senior, and Markwick's half-sister, Annie Rose Rowley, of 159 High Street, West Norwood. In the deed of partnership she is described as 'Typewriter', Markwick as 'Sub-Editor'. Markwick had dropped his original surname of Johnson in favour of his middle name. He was born in Limehouse in 1850, the son of a mariner, and was called to the Middle Temple in 1883. He wrote leading articles for the *Daily Telegraph* and was legal adviser to the *Encyclopædia Britannica* publishers. He and young Alfred Harmsworth were often seen together in the Temple and Fleet Street. Carr was named in the deed as 'Business Manager', Harmsworth as 'Editor'.

Otherwise, the staff in the beginning consisted of a youth named Tom McNaughton, who looked after the 'trade counter'. He was joined shortly afterwards by an office-boy, B. W. Young, son of the landlady at Iverson Road. At home Young had to call the two lodgers every morning, and Alfred Harmsworth, he remembered, 'never liked getting up'. He recalled the Harmsworth of that time as being 'decidedly handsome' and having 'a feminine pallor'. The Young boy was given his job in the office by Carr and Harmsworth was annoyed about it. Young overheard him say to Carr: 'You might have consulted me. I have several brothers whose future I am responsible for.'

At Carr & Co. money was frequently short. Young was more than once sent round to the City Bank, Ludgate Hill branch, to ask if there was a balance to cover 'a very small cheque'. Possibly the capital provided through Carr was forthcoming only in instalments. There appears to be no warranty for the statement made in *The History of The Times*, volume 3, page 102, that Alfred 'risked £1,000 of his own savings from journalism upon a journal of his own'. There had been no chance for him to save so much money. It is doubtful if he saved any.

A visiting American expressed surprise at finding a mimeograph duplicator in that small and cluttered office. 'If we were as go-ahead as your people,' Alfred Harmsworth told him, 'we might have the telephone, too.' The telephone was beginning to be used in London business houses but official fears that the revenue from telegrams would be prejudiced hindered the development of a public telephone service. Although less than two decades remained of the nineteenth century, its shadow still lay heavily on that London in which Alfred Harmsworth was trying to establish himself. That he was looking ahead was shown by a long article headed 'Typewriters' which he contributed to *The Queen* of April 10, 1886. It reviewed the possibilities of a development soon to be socially significant as well as technically unique.

The activities of Carr & Co. ranged from the publication of a treatise on biliousness, price a shilling, to *A Thousand Ways to Earn a Living*, by A. C. Harmsworth, which was published by them in collaboration with George Newnes. It began with accountancy and ended with yacht building and had a good sale, helped by publicity in *Tit-Bits*. Dealing with newspaper work as a calling, the author told his readers: 'It gives no scope for genius.' Carr's also published *All About Our Railways*, by A. C. Harmsworth, the first in a proposed *All About —— * series which went no farther. He wrote the railway book as a result of a talk with a signalman during a long wait at a small station outside Coventry. Among the firm's failures were *Famous Breach of Promise Cases*, *The Way to the Winning Post*, and a 'potted' biography of W. G. Grace. The company held the agency for *Recreation*, subtitled 'The Gymnasium News', a penny monthly sponsored by the National Physical Recreation Society which had for its object the 'promotion of physical recreation among the working classes', a possibly redundant ideal which, as Carr & Co. found, offered no scope for journalistic success. *The Volapuk Journal*, 3*d.* monthly, was dedicated to 'the spread of a universal language'. But the subjects of Queen Victoria remained firm in their belief that the creator had already decreed the official language of the universe and Carr & Co. could make no progress with the Volapuk heresy. Their hopes for a time were centred in *The Private Schoolmaster*, official journal of the Association of Principals of Private Schools, of which J. V. Milne, of Henley House School, had been secretary. The paper was edited for Carr & Co. by Markwick, the barrister member of the firm. Its sales were never more than 300 copies a month and advertisers were not interested in it for the further reason that as a class schoolmasters represented no worthwhile purchasing power. Harmsworth thought that the paper had a certain prestige value and kept it going for some time at a loss. Lasting four years, it has a pioneering place in the history of educational journalism.

Carrying himself as if confident that his destiny had been arranged as he would wish, Alfred did not allow the firm's poor prospects to cloud his days or even disturb his temper, though he had a fight in the office with a cousin, Arthur Hendry, whom he had temporarily employed. Young remembered that there were days when Harmsworth and Carr did nothing whatever but talk. 'When he was not talking to Carr, he was talking to the newsagents' "reps", asking them every sort of question about their jobs and picking up a lot of information that was useful to him later.' Max Pemberton, calling one afternoon, observed that his friend was wearing a morning coat in a shade of fawn, with a rosebud in the buttonhole. 'He seemed very happy, though he did not disguise from me that business was not flourishing.' His careful dressing, which Pemberton was equally careful to note in detail, was possibly influenced by the research he had been doing for an article called 'Purple and Fine Linen', contributed to *Pictorial Society*. In it he held up Brummell and Pendennis as exemplars which the men of 1886 sadly needed.

The business was not producing a living for the partners. Dargaville Carr had no liking for office life. Alfred was still dependent on his freelance work. As for the young man at the trade counter, Tom McNaughton, he had so little work to do that he went off to become one of the McNaughton Brothers, a famous music-hall double act, and later to marry a sister of Marie Lloyd. Alfred was angry because he left without giving notice. His place was taken by another young man named J. M. Blanch, well known in Fleet Street, later, as one of the managers of the *Observer*.

★   ★   ★

'Times have never been so bad,' Alfred Harmsworth, the barrister, wrote to his son Cecil at Trinity College, Dublin, adding with amusing disdain of the logic of their situation: 'Do not demean yourself to the vulgarity of a tramcar unless absolutely necessary.' There were times when Cecil could not afford to ride even by tram. Harmsworth, senior, was sensitive also to the social unworthiness of football as a pastime for would-be gentlemen. 'Cricket is the first of all games and calls out the best faculties of mind and body.' Cecil's mother wrote to him in a more severely practical tone. 'You had better make your underclothes last two weeks, not wearing the vest at night.' White marble oilcloth on his dressing-table, she suggested, would be an economy, and in reply to a complaint from him about college laundry charges she wrote: 'Your neckties should be wide enough to cover all', a hint of makeshift hardly conforming to the personal dignity insisted on by the head of the family. 'You do not say if you have heard of anywhere where they have early Communion. See to it', and in her next letter: 'We shall of course be delighted to have you back for the vac. if the money can be found, but it has been fearfully scarce.'

Alfred Harmsworth, senior, to Frederick Wood:

> 6, Pump Court,
> Temple.
> 24th March, 1886

My dear Fred,—I wish I had been a little more pressing in asking you to speak to Heneage on my wish for a judicial appointment of the nature of a County Court judgeship. Yesterday I saw in the papers an announcement that the County Court Judgeship of Preston was vacant. I wrote at once to the Lord Chancellor for it, and he replied saying that the post was in the gift of the Chancellor of the Duchy and that he had reason to know that he had filled it up.

There are other County Courts in his jurisdiction and other legal posts of like character, and if you are on sufficient terms I would ask you to mention the fact that I am an aspirant for such an office with such terms of commendation as you think proper, and if you can go so far bespeak beforehand a nomination when a vacancy occurs.

Write to me as to your views.

> Ever sincerely,
> ALFRED H.

A hope, later that year, that he would receive a post as Official Referee soon faded. 'There are political rivals in the field', he wrote and his Johnsonian Toryism no longer carried the old respect. His disappointment was shrugged off with the Micawberish comment: 'It is something to have made them hesitate.' He had colleagues at the bar who did not doubt that his abilities entitled him to consideration for professional advancement. They spoke of him as a sound lawyer and an excellent advocate whose gifts of speech compelled attention from every side.

Meanwhile, he watched the rise of contemporaries and friends. 'There are 14 new Q.C.s,' he wrote in a letter to Cecil. 'Mr Harris and Mr Nasmith have both got silk gowns. I have been retained by a City Guild, the Carpenter's Company. I am looking forward to much venison and turtle.' There being few briefs, he had sublet his Temple chambers at what may have been a small profit to himself. He was now spending much of his time at home, shut in the room he called his 'den'. Increasingly he withdrew from the society of his children, retaining his closest intimacy with the eldest girl, Geraldine, whom he called 'Lady Dot'. Resigned apparently to the prospect that life had nothing more to offer him, he would sit blinking through the haze of endless pipes of tobacco, reaching forward now and again to jot down lines of uninspired verse on devotional or patriotic themes. He lapsed into a world of reverie. When the hall ceiling crashed down outside his room door, followed by cries of alarm and running feet, he did not stir from his chair.

A few days after the great national spree of June 20, 1887, when Victoria, fifty years enthroned, had gone in state to St. Paul's Cathedral and her people had lit the bonfires of rejoicing on every beacon height and drank and feasted and sung and laughed a long day through, ten of the eleven Harmsworth children assembled at 94 Boundary Road for a private celebration, their father's fiftieth birthday. The family seemed to have outgrown the twenty-three years' span of their parents' married life. Alfred was just on twenty-two, Geraldine twenty, Harold nineteen, Cecil seventeen, Leicester sixteen, Hildebrand fifteen, Violet fourteen, Charles thirteen, St. John eleven, Christabel seven and Vyvyan six.

It was July 3, just before the law term ended for the long vacation, when for the successful barristers there was a lessening in the flow of briefs. Harmsworth, senior, was denied that contrast in his affairs. He had not had a brief for three months. His last £1 had been retained by the bank in respect of back dues. The discovery, made the day before, was particularly upsetting because Geraldine Harmsworth had counted on the money for domestic needs. In the fullness of time, and crowned by its irony, her husband's amiable character and feckless career would be commemorated in the Middle Temple by an Alfred Harmsworth Memorial Fund of over £60,000. He would have been hardly less astonished to hear that his portrait has a permanent place in the Benchers' Room. Cecil Harmsworth's recollections confirmed the seriousness of the family's situation. They were 'struck all of a heap', he said, when it was realized that there was 'absolutely no money in the bank'. Alfred was apparently absent from the party. It may have been the period of his estrangement. They were resigning themselves to the likelihood of having to forgo the meal of celebration when it was remembered that the fourth boy, Leicester, had not yet come in with his Civil Service salary of 14s. When he arrived, the sum of 10s. was 'borrowed' by their mother, who bustled off to the shops, returning with 'a cushion of bacon and a large quantity of green peas'. Meanwhile, the youngest of the children had laid hands on two duck eggs, which they gravely presented to their father.

Harmsworth, senior, pronounced his birthday lunch the most delicious he had ever had: 'Never in my life have I enjoyed anything more', and he went on to ask what food could a man desire *better* than bacon and green peas? Come to think of it, he had a rich friend who actually preferred bacon and green peas to all or any of the more expensive dishes he could so easily afford. . . . Grace then being said, he retired to his room to read Shakespeare, fortified by the contents of a jug which stood on the table at his elbow.

★ ★ ★

Alfred, junior, was preoccupied by his plan for bringing out a paper of his own. There is no doubt that it was based on Newnes's idea. Both of them were likely to have known of an earlier paper called *Replies* which had the secondary title of 'A Journal of Question and Answer'. It had appeared two years before Newnes started *Tit-Bits*. Having been conducted with no success by the Co-operative Publishing Company, of Catherine Street, Strand, London, it was taken over by a firm of moneylenders in Mark Lane, E.C. They changed its name to *Oracle* and made it a medium, no more fortunate, of advice to investors. An American paper, *Queries*, had been put on sale in London a few months before Carr & Co. started in business. It failed to tap a market which Alfred Harmsworth was firmly determined to exploit. Both Newnes and Harmsworth, too, would have known that the supply of good reading matter in periodical form was restricted to about half a dozen periodicals of which the most widely circulated were *The Family Herald*, *Household Words*, *The Penny Magazine* and *The London Journal*. *The Family Herald* had made its readers' letters a source of attractive 'copy'.

Alfred Harmsworth was not content to emulate. He was out to excel. *Tit-Bits* had made readers' letters one of its chief attractions. In Harmsworth's paper they were to be *the* feature; hence its original title, *Answers* to Correspondents, a kind of Notes & Queries for the unscholarly average man thirsting for information rather than for knowledge. Notes & Queries may be entitled to fuller acknowledgment as an incentive to the new journalism. It had been appearing for nearly half a century as a fount of information supplied by its specialist and erudite readers for their mutual interest and help. Alfred Harmsworth drew attention to its existence later in announcing one of his new editorial developments, expressing the opinion that the circulation of Notes & Queries would benefit if the paper were published 'at a more popular price'. In considering his Answers to Correspondents idea, his imagination had been projected beyond the printed word. 'If the paper pays,' he said to a friend, 'I propose to have experts in to answer questions personally. For a shilling, anyone will be entitled to call at the office to ask a question and get an answer on the spot. I believe the place would be packed all day with people in need of information.'

Newnes was not a journalist by instinct or training. Someone said of his Tit-Bits that it was 'the greatest literary fluke of the century'. Harmsworth was a born journalist. 'Somehow I knew from the first just what people wanted to read—at least, that is a fair assumption, I think', he told an English Illustrated Magazine interviewer in 1896. He could write, he could originate ideas, he could handle type. He had studied Newnes's paper with a keen professional eye and had no difficulty in convincing himself that he could improve on it.

Neither among his family nor his friends did he find encouragement for what to them seemed a grandiose conceit. Shown the Answers 'dummy', the manager of a large wholesale newsagents' business, named Williams, saw nothing in it of interest to the trade. Without challenging that negative verdict, Alfred Harmsworth quietly stated his sale-or-return terms for the paper when it appeared. Another visitor, N. C. Davidson, whose business was with Outing, was astonished when, after showing him the 'dummy', Alfred said: 'We're not going to have any advertising. We don't believe in it.'

He talked about the paper with a number of other people without impressing them. His was the sort of temperament which prompts shrewd judges of men to say: He will either make a fortune or go bankrupt. The judges in this instance might have been confirmed in their doubts if they had seen the brown-paper covered folder containing young Harmsworth's ideas for the future. It showed that he was dreaming, fantastically, of starting not one paper but a number of papers. Pasted across the front of the folder was a label with the doggerel inscription in large drawn capitals: SCHEMO MAGNIFICO.

As he had earlier found, the first of all problems was money: where and how to procure the necessary capital. Carr & Co. were in no position to finance a paper. Urgent discussions took place in the back half of the shabby little office in Paternoster Square. At one of them, Markwick, the barrister partner, suggested that he might take financial soundings of a man he knew who had 'married money'. The possible speculator to whom Markwick proceeded to write a letter was Alexander Spink Beaumont, formerly of the Royal Welch Fusiliers. Markwick threw in the hint that 'it might not be unprofitable' to invest 'a small sum' in Carr & Co.

How and when the paths of Beaumont and Markwick had first crossed is not known. Beaumont was the son of a major-general who had dropped the surname of McCumming for Beaumont, one of his other names. Why his son took the name of Spink has remained an unanswered question to subsequent generations of the family; it was the married name of one of his aunts. Having seen service in India, Alexander Spink Beaumont retired with the rank of captain to marry, in 1872, the widow of William Savage, of Midsomer Norton, Somerset. She was the daughter of the Rev. Sir Erasmus Griffies-Williams, Bart., of Llwyny Wormwood Park, Carmarthenshire, and a woman of wealth. By the time that Alfred Harmsworth came to know him, Beaumont had grown a beard which made him look more sailor than soldier, so much so that Alfred referred to him in letters as 'the Admiral'. He had no means of his own. Presumably because she controlled the cash, Mrs Beaumont became known in the office of Carr & Co. as 'the C.-in-C.' She was fourteen years older than her husband. A friend of Harmsworth's referred to her in a letter to him as 'charmingly uncommon'. Very soon after they became his backers, Alfred Harmsworth was signing his letters to the Beaumonts in terms of affection: 'With love and kisses from us all', 'Our love to you both', and so on.

Beaumont was a chess player of considerable attainments whose name is remembered by the *cognoscenti*. From his London home, 1 Crescent Road, South Norwood Park, S.E., he organized important tournaments and exerted himself tirelessly to promote the growth of the game. A trophy given by him in 1904 continues to be competed for by leading women chess players. Music was another of the passions of his life. His compositions were heard at the Crystal Palace concerts. Sims Reeves, the celebrated Victorian tenor, chose one of Beaumont's songs, 'The Garden of Roses', for his 'grand final farewell concert' at the Albert Hall in 1891. The amount of his original investment in Carr & Co. was £1,000. It was primarily devoted to pushing the English sales of *Outing*, an American journal of amateur sport for which the Iliffes had held the London agency until Carr & Co. took it over. *Outing* was edited and printed in New York and its chances of success in this country can never have been bright, its articles being almost wholly American in appeal. Its circulation in England was about 1,000 copies a month. Its owner was Poulteney Bigelow, son of Lincoln's ambassador to France, a traveller in strange regions and correspondent for *The Times* of London during the Spanish-American War.

Not long after Carr & Co. had taken over the agency for *Outing*, advertising the magazine in *The Private Schoolmaster* as a journal 'eminently suited to the requirements of a school reading room', Bigelow sent his right-hand man of affairs, Colonel Warman, to look into the prospects for *Outing* in London. The visitor overawed the office staff at Paternoster Square with his splendid fur coat and his large embossed card bearing the address: 239 Fifth Avenue, New York City. Unable to conceal his surprise at the humble office of Carr & Co., he found it possible, none the less, to apply the very latest American colloquialism to young Harmsworth— 'a live wire'. Possibly he had seen the letter which Alfred had written to Beaumont about *Outing*:

. . .We are to hire six superior sandwichmen, dress one as a shooting man with a gun, game-bag, etc., a second as a hunting man, a third as a football player, a fourth as a fisherman, a fifth as a cricketer, and a sixth as a yachting man. They will all have good clothes and first-class guns, cricket bats, etc. Each, that is to say, will represent some popular sport. Each will carry an advertisement of *Outing* and all day long will parade the West End.

The appearance of this queer cavalcade in 'the best' streets of the metropolis had no advantageous effect on the sales of *Outing*. The magazine failed but it may be entitled to more than passing notice in the history of periodical publishing. The size and make-up of its pages were followed closely by Newnes in *The Strand Magazine* when in 1891 he launched that subsequently celebrated publication. A contemporary critical comment on the first issue of *The Strand* was that 'it looks too much like an inadequate copy of a good American magazine to be altogether satisfying'.

For Alfred Harmsworth there were other preoccupying matters at that time. He wrote to Mary Milner:

Midnight, Monday-Tuesday,

30-12-87

My very dear darling,—I have just got the enclosed from Grimwood. It came by the last post, but I did not see it in the letter-box till I was departing for bed. I really could not call you 'dear Mary', so you must excuse the 'very dear darling'.

I will come, then, at 6.30 Wednesday.

Your loving devoted,

A.

*　　　*　　　*

Alfred Harmsworth was drawing no more than £60 a year from Carr & Co., a fact which he took care to bring to the notice, in writing, of Captain Beaumont. His income at that time, 1888, was not likely to have been more than £200 a year. Money, the ever-present problem, did not deter him from contemplating a step which would complicate his finances. His mother had written to Cecil: 'I hear Alfred really talks of getting married in April. I have written to him remonstrating but do not hope that it will avail. They are both *quite too young*.' According to a member of the Markwick family, it was Markwick who lent Alfred the cash to buy an engagement ring for Mary Milner. Alfred wrote to his Aunt Sarah's second husband, Francis Miller, the solicitor:

CARR & CO.,
Publishers.
Telegraphic Address 'Outing, London'.
Cheques should be crossed 'City Bank'.

26, Paternoster Square,
London, E.C.
15th March, 1888

Dear Uncle,—I enclose, with many a bitter tear, the first payment of my debt. Please lay in a dozen smart clerks to collect the rest. Also kindly arrange to keep the 11th of next month clear. You have an important engagement at 2 o'clock at Hampstead Parish Church on that date and there will be wedding cake for sampling later on.

Yours with wailing & gnashing of teeth,
ALFRED C. HARMSWORTH

Signor Francisco Millero.

On that same day, 'Dot', the eldest Harmsworth girl, who was learning to typewrite in the office at Paternoster Square, when free of home duties, wrote to Cecil at Trinity College, Dublin:

Your appeal for clothes has not been in vain. Harold has handed over his short black coat, which I have mended and sent on its way to Perth, as we have agreed that it is worth dyeing. As to 'bags', I am sorely afraid that I can do nothing for you.

THE WEDDING is to be on April 11th. I understand from Alfred that the presents are pouring in, in fine style. They already have three cruets. I am vacillating between a screen and a little table, the sum in hand being 12s. 6d. . . . The bridesmaids' dresses are already chosen, they are all white and I am sure such a bevy of beauty will never be equalled—at least in 'our' day.

Tell me what you think of this performance. I see a good many faults but this time I am able with truth to say it is the fault of the type-writer.

With much love,
Your affectionate sister,
DOT.

The officiating clergyman at the wedding was Alfred's companion of the Continental tour of six years before, the Rev. and Hon. E. V. R. Powys, who held a living not far from Coventry. Alfred had kept in touch with him and had cycled out to consult him just before leaving Coventry to ask his advice about the Church as a vocation for his brother Cecil, who was thinking of taking Holy Orders. At the same time, he mentioned his approaching marriage and Powys had offered to perform the ceremony. Recalling it, Powys wrote: 'It was one of the prettiest weddings imaginable, the extreme youth and good looks of the bride and bridegroom being most attractive.' Alfred was above middle height, though not tall, and the good looks of his school days had become those of the handsome young man. Mary's prettiness was set off by a milk-and-roses complexion which was the envy of her sex. Their happiness glowed about them. It was much remarked on by those present. Alfred had sent his mother a little note by hand from his lodgings the first thing that morning:

In Bed,
My Wedding Day.

My darling Mother,—Give the bearer my brown portmanteau. I hope the weather will clear up. Am feeling very, very happy.

Your very loving son,
ALFRED

The wedding was reported in George Jealous's *Hampstead & Highgate Express* of April 14, 1888, in the resounding *clichés* of local journalism: '. . . bride charmingly attired . . . long tulle veil . . . bouquet of liles-of-the-valley . . . six bridesmaids in costumes of white china silk with hats *en suite*. . . .' Lilies-of-the-valley were thereafter the bridegroom's favourite flower. The presents were 'unusually numerous and costly', and the paper printed a list of ninety-five of them, including a variety of framed engravings, tea and coffee services and sets of apostle spoons. Mr and Mrs Arthur Pearson gave asparagus tongs. (Pearson was managing *Tit-Bits*.) The list was rounded off with 'a pair of milking stools (Mr Jack Hughes)'. The report concluded: 'In the evening a dance, confined in the new fashion exclusively to young unmarried friends of the bride and bridegroom, was given.' The reporter of the wedding overlooked an interesting point for comment. Both the bridegroom and his best man, Markwick, had sticking out of their jacket pockets a folded 'dummy' copy of *Answers to Correspondents*. It had been Alfred's idea that the unpublished new paper should receive some of the blessings of the day. He wrote to his mother on the first day of the honeymoon:

18, Alexandra Gardens,
Folkestone.

My darling Mother,—Just a line to tell you how happy we are, and how com-

77

fortable. What will please you, I know, is that we are having a very, very economical honeymoon.

What a happy day yesterday was. The happiest in all my life. Good-night, my dearest Mother.

Your loving Boy,
ALFRED

I cannot tell you how it pleased me to see you kiss my darling so affectionately. It is what I have wished for for years.

During the honeymoon, Markwick arrived from London for a further talk about the production of the paper destined to become known as *Answers*. Alfred had worked out the costs and had resolved that £1,000 would be needed to launch it with safety. That took into account the promised printing credit from the Iliffe firm. The only chance of getting the money seemed to be in Markwick's power to persuade the Beaumonts to put more capital into Carr & Co. Markwick had undertaken to try. He had already made an unsuccessful approach for £500 to a *Daily Telegraph* colleague, Hall Richardson.

His call on the Harmsworths at Folkestone was a break in his journey to Viarreggio, where the Beaumonts had a villa. Alfred and Mary saw him off by steamer to Boulogne. As they walked together to the pier, Alfred's attention was caught by a piece of orange-coloured paper floating down to the pavement from an upper window. He went forward and picked it up, liking the colour. When the steamer left harbour, he wrapped the bit of coloured paper round the 'dummy' copy of *Answers* which he was carrying and waved goodbye with it. Markwick had promised to telegraph if his journey succeeded. The telegram consisted of one word: 'Joy.' It meant that Beaumont was willing to put up another thousand pounds.

Alfred Harmsworth, senior, to Cecil Harmsworth:

3, Essex Court,
Temple.
30th April, 1888

My dear Bouffles,—The wedding as you hear was very splendid. My only disappointment in the ceremony was the absence of yourself and Hildebrand. Boo [Vyvyan aged 7] wouldn't go—said he 'wasn't going to fag up to Hampstead'.

Money is very scarce and demands very plentiful but you are not forgotten.

I have an offer of a stool in a stockbroker's office for one of the boys. I wanted rather for Bunny [Harold] to go in for it, but as there would be no salary for the first year, he hesitates. The offer of course is a very valuable one and opens up a fair prospect not only of a competence but of a fortune in the future . . . .

Your loving father,
ALFRED H.

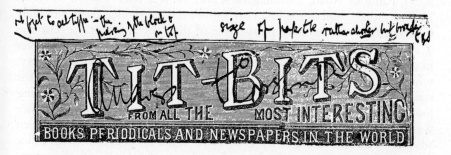

Alfred Harmsworth's 'Dummy' headline for his new paper, roughed out on a copy of *Tit-Bits*

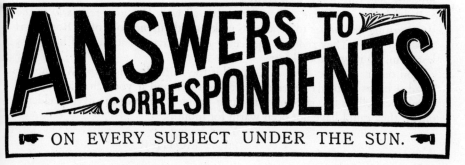

Title block for the paper which later had a world-wide circulation as *Answers*

Alfred and Molly returned from the honeymoon to begin married life at 31 Pandora Road, Dennington Park, N.W., later known as West Hampstead, a small house in a newly-built terrace, which figures bravely if forlornly in the dazzling perspective of their social ascent. Its rent was £26 a year. Though the name had its suggestion of luck, Alfred never liked Pandora Road. A trade journal proprietor, Greville Montgomery, who later founded the Building Exhibition, remembered going down the stairs of his office in Adelphi in that year, 1888, and meeting 'a striking looking young fellow with shining eyes' who asked where a certain office was. A publication on the top floor had failed and the furniture had been advertised for sale in the *Daily Telegraph*. 'What do you want with office furniture?' Montgomery asked, struck by his youthfulness. 'Oh, I'm starting a new paper,' was the reply. 'I see,' said Montgomery, privately amused by the young man's assurance. 'And what are you going to call it?' 'Answers to Correspondents,' the young man said and went bounding on up the stairs towards his remarkable future.

Geraldine Mary Harmsworth to Cecil Harmsworth in Dublin:

> 94, Boundary Road,
> 4th May, 1888
>
> My dear Cecil,—I enclose a small cheque which will meet the present emergency and hope to be able to send you a little more shortly. As we gave a picture for you, Alfred ought to send you the money you told him to keep for the present. The happy pair have returned. I have not seen them yet. I hear there is an account of the wedding in the 'Ladies' Pictorial' of last week giving all the presents, etc. I have not seen it myself.
>
> Papa's voice is still bad, otherwise we are all well. Dot goes regularly to the type-writing and hopes to be able to make a little money out of it. Bonchie is at school again. They reduced the fee to £2 this term on account of his illness last term. So it was not all lost.
>
> You ought to look Aunt E.F. up, also the Miss Flemings, 17, Wellington Road. I believe Tuesday evenings suit them best and if you can spare time it would be well, as it is the duty of young people to enliven the lives of elderly ones if they can. I have not been warm for months.
>
> Your loving
> MOTHER

Molly Harmsworth had been receiving an allowance from her father, Robert Milner. Now, Alfred insisted on providing it, apparently not liking the implication that he was in no position to do so.

While the future beckoned him with brilliant hopes, the late 1880s saw the fortunes of his family decline to their lowest point. It was reached in social as well as economic terms when arrears of rent forced them to give up the house in Boundary Road. It had been their home for eleven years.

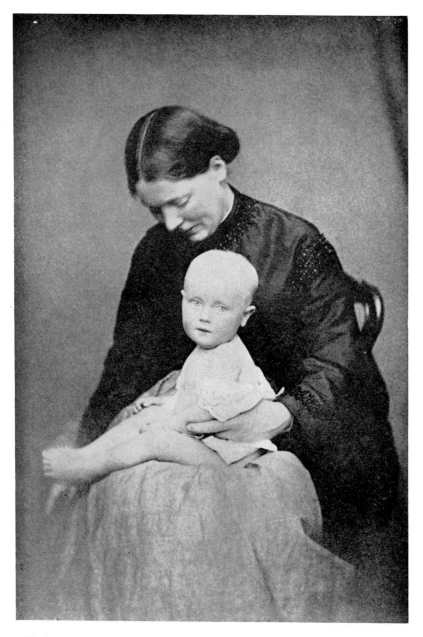

Alfred, aged two, with his mother. As Northcliffe, he wrote on a copy of
this photograph: 'Note early development of swollen head'

Rose Cottage, Vale of Health, Hampstead, with (*left to right*) Harold, Alfred, and their eldest sister Geraldine

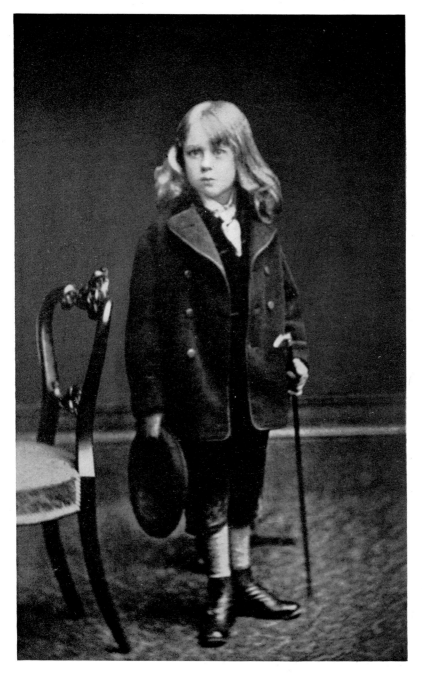

Alfred, aged seven-and-a-half, shortly before he went to his first school in
St John's Wood

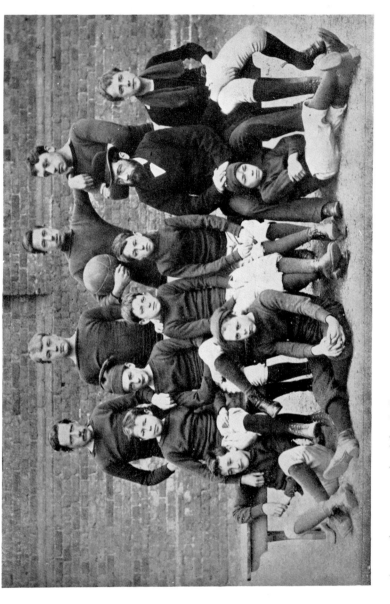

The Henley House School football team, 1881. Alfred Harmsworth is second from the left in the back row

It had seen the high spirits of childhood pass into the grave purposefulness of youth. The house had contained them all in roomy if sparse comfort and it had afforded privacy if not peace for Alfred Harmsworth, the father. Taking with them what remained of their furniture, they moved into a small lately-built terrace house in the neighbouring suburb of Brondesbury. Its front windows overlooked a cemetery. Soon after they had arrived there, Harmsworth, senior, happened to lean on the mantelpiece in the front parlour. It broke away from the wall under his weight and fell in pieces about the fireplace. Unlike fallen pictures, collapsed mantelpieces do not customarily evoke superstitious fears. The debris swept up that day at Fairlight, 2 Hulse Terrace, Salusbury Road, Brondesbury, can be seen now as a symbol of the imminent dissolution of the family as a domestic entity. The 'high cabal of time and the ocean' was about to work a momentous change in the Harmsworth circumstances.

The Salusbury Road house was always an uncomfortable memory for the older children. The fourth boy, Leicester, wrote of their time there as 'those terrible days'. Their father wrote to Cecil: 'No money is stirring. I feel I am thrashing the wind.' He was served with another writ. A bailiff followed it. The man sat in the small front hall, where the younger children took turns in keeping him company. Occasionally there were scenes between Geraldine and her husband. The children dreaded them.

★   ★   ★

Having roughed out a final 'dummy' of his proposed new paper on a copy of *Tit-Bits* (dated April 14, 1888), Alfred Harmsworth scribbled instructions to the printer in the margins giving it the serial number 3 in place of the number 1 normally denoting a first issue. The meaning of the figure 3 was that the title of the paper implied the existence of readers whose queries were being answered. Numbers 1 and 2 were not produced until the volume for the year had been completed, when a limited supply of copies bearing those numbers was specially printed for readers wishing to have the full set for binding.

According to the evidence of the bound volumes, the first issue of *Answers to Correspondents*—'ridiculously named', said a trade paper—was dated June 2, 1888. It had twelve pages. Number 3, with sixteen pages, is dated June 16, and is believed by some members of the Harmsworth family to have been the first issue seen by the public. But the problem is boldly faced in the editorial introduction to the June 2 issue: '. . . this number is a necessary makeshift (how could we answer questions before we had any?). . . .' Doubt remains about which in fact was the first published issue of this historically interesting periodical. One of Iliffe's compositors, George Shuttleworth, said that Number 2 was the first issue:

'just a few No. 1s were printed, that was all.' (Neither was the final issue of *Answers*, dated February 18, 1956, seen by the public. A printers' strike prevented it from being put on sale.)

The first copy to be sold over the counter at 26 Paternoster Square, on what Alfred later recalled as 'a sweet June morning', was bought by Max Pemberton. 'Mr Carr had the honour of selling it to him', Alfred told a shareholders' meeting in 1896. Of that issue, 12,000 copies were sold, nearly all by street vendors operating within a narrow radius of Fleet Street. They were particularly active at horse-bus stops, leaping aboard and bullying passengers to buy the new paper. It is probable that a much larger number of copies was printed: 60,000, according to a trade paper report. In *Answers* for May 28, 1892, Alfred Harmsworth disclosed that he had 'hit upon the plan—since imitated until the public are thoroughly weary of it—of giving away an immense number of copies of the earlier issues in order to familiarize the multitude with the journal and create a demand'.

A journalist, Frank Boyd, who later became editor of *The Pelican*, bought a copy of the first issue of *Answers* on Ludgate Hill and was amused because the newsvendor offering it to him said: 'Fust number of *Hawnswers to Correspondinx*.' Boyd recalled it as 'a mean, wretched-looking little production with "amateur" written all over it'. He said that 'it looked as if it had not a million to one chance of succeeding'. The paper did not begin to sell until the following Saturday. Price one penny, and printed on cream-coloured paper, it had no cover and no advertisements. 'What the Queen Eats' ('game she cannot bear'); 'Strange Things Found in Tunnels', 'Narrow Escapes from Burial Alive', 'Do Women Live Longer Than Men?', 'How to Cure Freckles', 'What has become of Tichborne?' (echo of the century's *cause célèbre*), 'Why Jews Don't Ride Bicycles', 'Remarkable Arrests'—this was the formula for flattering the self-esteem of the beneficiaries of the new elementary education system and the stuff of the Philistinism which Matthew Arnold feared was about to take charge of the world. 'We are a sort of Universal Information provider. Anybody who reads our paper for a year will be able to converse on many subjects on which he was entirely ignorant. He will have a good stock of anecdotes and jokes and will indeed be a pleasant companion.'*

Alfred Harmsworth addressed wrappers, folded circulars and wrote all the articles, paragraphs and jokes for the early issues. The guinea for a short story was for some time his only outside payment. He and his wife cut articles from American newspapers and magazines and rewrote them for English readers. The jokes which were used as 'fill-ups' all through the paper were lifted freely from sources nearer home, not excluding *Tit-Bits*, and they are of biographical significance in that they reflect a sense of

---

* *Answers*, February 16, 1889.

humour that never developed much above the *Answers* level. His brother Cecil, reading at the British Museum during a vacation, made some notes about the origins of the Bank of England. Alfred insisted that they were to be written out in the form of a reply to a reader: *Can you give me any facts about the history of the Bank of England?* asks 'Joint Stock'. In that form Cecil's contribution appeared in *Answers* for August 25, 1888. After a few months outside contributors were encouraged. One of them, in that first year, was H. G. Wells, who said that it provided him with 'a few useful shillings a week'. Another was Lovat Fraser, who became one of the leading newspaper controversialists of the First World War and after.

Informing the journalism of George Newnes, and in a less earnest if not necessarily less sympathetic sense that of Alfred Harmsworth, was an awareness of the urge towards self-improvement which pervaded mid-Victorian morality and hallowed contemporary business instincts. In that respect, George Newnes had the advantage of more than age; his experience in the Manchester fancy goods trade can hardly have been useless to him in his career of popular publishing. Neither was well-educated, though Newnes had been for a few terms at the City of London School, where a future Prime Minister, H. H. Asquith, was a pupil at the same time. Both were susceptible by upbringing and temperament to the self-help gospel proclaimed by Samuel Smiles in a book, first published in 1859, which has gone on selling ever since. His *Self-Help* supplied the moral justification of their activities, which encouraged knowingness rather than the pursuit of knowledge.

For eight months the future of *Answers to Correspondents* and of Alfred Harmsworth's grand imaginings in 'Schemo Magnifico' were in jeopardy. The paper might easily have failed, like other imitators of Newnes's idea. Alfred himself made no secret of that possibility. He was heard to say at the Priory Lawn Tennis Club at West Hampstead that he had had no luck so far as a publisher and that if *Answers to Correspondents* failed he would be 'in a bad way'. Reviewing those early struggles at a meeting of shareholders some years after, he said: 'This business went through a period of great adversity.' The circulation of 12,000 had not been maintained after the first week; it had dropped to 8,000. In the following three months it did not rise above 20,000. 'I can't make it pay!' he said repeatedly to Harold one evening, seeming desperately worried as he paced the attic room at Pandora Road which was his office four days a week.

The paper was still being printed in Coventry on credit allowed by the Iliffe firm. It was an awkward arrangement, requiring weekly journeys to the Midlands, involving time and money. Often Alfred found it necessary to telegraph late material to Coventry or to notify changes in the make-up. It could only be done by permission of the Iliffes' London manager, Dawbarn, and was a further source of difficulty. Near press time at Coventry with one week's issue, he found a third of a column not filled. There was no overmatter to fit the space. He immediately wrote a 'filler' for the waiting machines, heading it: 'Can Monkeys Smoke?' It produced a correspondence which went on for months. Shuttleworth, the compositor, remembered the future Northcliffe moving restlessly about the printing shop 'when the scissors and paste were at work'. Writing twenty-five years later, Shuttleworth recalled 'a scene' about overtime work. 'You were so anxious to get the paper out to the trade. You and Mr Iliffe were often at loggerheads.' A member of the *Coventry Standard* staff remembered William Iliffe following Alfred along Smithford Street, Coventry, calling after him in a tone of extreme annoyance, and Alfred shouting back at him over his shoulder: 'You lack the manners of a gentleman!'

The Iliffes' printing bill ran up to £750, according to the recollection of William Iliffe's younger son Edward, now Lord Iliffe. William Iliffe decided that the time had come to tell Harmsworth that he could have no further accommodation. Holding him off with reassurances, Harmsworth gave him bills for three, six and nine months and had the printing contract transferred to Allen & Scott, at 30 Bouverie Street, London, the printers of *Tit-Bits*. This was an economy of both space and time. It reduced the distance between the editorial offices and the printers from a hundred miles to half a mile.

*   *   *

George Newnes had made a great thing of competitions as a means of advancing the circulation of his paper. He was not being original in doing so. A competition prize of £1,000 had been offered by a journal of the 1860s. But competitions had as much to do with the growth of *Tit-Bits* as its reading matter. In 1883, 'Tit-Bits Villa', Dulwich, London, S.E., a seven-room freehold house awarded as first prize in one of his competitions, had become a place of pilgrimage for Sunday trippers. Buried gold was another of his circulation schemes. Clues scattered through the instalments of a serial story written for the purpose enticed readers into taking part in what became a great public treasure hunt, with five tubes each containing a hundred gold sovereigns as the prize. They had been buried in the verge by the roadside near St. Albans. Within a few hours of the appearance of the last instalment of the serial a cyclist rode out from Hatfield and dug up the 'treasure'. The widespread publicity which *Tit-Bits* received marked a new chapter in periodical publishing. Newnes had applied his experience of business life to journalism. As well as his early training in the Manchester warehouses, he had an arithmetical mind; he happened also to be a good chess player. Realizing that he sold space to advertisers who were concerned with its circulation rather than with its contents, he set about exploiting the something-for-nothing instinct in human nature, creating a kind of community preoccupation which we have since seen reproduced to its limit of intensity by the football pools. Over many years the competitions in the weekly papers, ranging from picture puzzles to 'missing words' and many variations of the anagram form, were an indirect educational influence. They helped to make a literate nation.

As the founder of *Answers to Correspondents*, Alfred Harmsworth had seen the point of competitions and had given them prominence from his first issue. He made it a condition that entries should be by postcard only and that each entry must be accompanied by the names and addresses of five persons as witnesses. It was a way of forcing the name of *Answers* upon the public. But Harmsworth had less money to play with than Newnes, who was by now making good profits. In the issue of October 6, 1888, it was jauntily announced that since *Answers to Correspondents* was started, £106 had been paid out in prize money. George Newnes may have smiled. He had given away a great deal more than that.

An unexpected general fall in circulations that autumn was ascribed to widespread and lasting fog. It lay over London and several other cities for some weeks. Alfred Harmsworth believed that another factor that was depressing the public was 'the Jack the Ripper scare'. The Harmsworths at Salusbury Road were as jumpy as everyone else. One night a noise was heard in the coal cellar. They sat rigid with fear, afraid to speak.

From the beginning, the office staff had abbreviated the name of the paper to *Answers* and Alfred now decided to make that the formal title. Later, in 1893, he wrote that the public found the old name too long, 'and they themselves dropped the concluding words and called it *Answers*', which was what old James Henderson, of Red Lion Square, had predicted to him they would do. At the same time, Alfred made some modifications of his original plan for the paper. He printed an adventure story and invited readers to send in others. He introduced interviews with well-known persons. He also devised a cover. Its colour was the vivid orange which had caught his eye that day in Folkestone when he and his bride were seeing Markwick off to Italy. He equated orange with gold and after that *Answers* was referred to editorially as 'The Golden One', while readers became 'Answerites', and 'Mr Answers' was the style given to the paper's roving reporter, Max Pemberton. The fashion of the coloured cover had been started by Newnes, who had decked out his *Tit-Bits* in green. *Answers'* orange cover first appeared in the autumn of 1888.

Mail order methods had much to do with the early growth of *Answers*. An Easter offer of 'Beautifully coloured reproductions of famous art works' was an inducement of 1889. The paper arranged readers' trips to the Paris Exhibition of that year, charging £2 12s. 6d. for return fare and a week at an hotel and budgeting, even so, for 'a profit of from 5s. to 10s. on every ticket sold'. 'Prize packets' of books, boxes of 'chemical tricks', pens and other articles were offered to readers at temptingly low prices, always with the idea of bringing in a direct profit as well as of making the paper better known. The offer of a junior clerkship in the office of *Answers* as the prize in a competition blandly disregarded Newnes's first use of the same idea some years before, when the successful entrant had been a young man named Cyril Arthur Pearson, soon to become a competitor of both Newnes and Harmsworth in the business of publishing periodicals. The *Answers* offer was glossed with the novelty of making women eligible, an intuitive touch of Alfred Harmsworth's which brought in over 10,000 entries.

The telephone and the typewriter were to effect a remarkable change of emphasis between the sexes, a process begun by the women factory workers for whom the revolution in industry provided a way of escape to economic freedom. The growing pace of invention and production was bringing into existence new kinds of business concerned with financing, distributing and marketing, and these in their turn generated the many forms of administrative activity which have evolved into modern office life. The telephone and the typewriter did much to release women from their classic servitude. Though not among the list of accomplishments expected of entrants in its 'Prize Situation' competition, typewriting was a new development justifying a long article in *Answers*, which boasted editorially of employing 'four lady typewriters' to help deal with the 2,000 letters received each week. Alfred Harmsworth wrote in his 'Editorial Chat': 'The type-written letters we send out from the office attract a good deal of curiosity, and many are the applications we receive for information as to the method in which our correspondence is conducted. . . . There is no doubt that within a very short time the vast majority of banks, insurance companies and commercial houses will use a typewriter almost to the exclusion of the pen.' The confident editorial forecast was accompanied by the reminder that the originating impulse to produce a typewriter had been English and that the Americans had been 'very smart' in perfecting it. Meanwhile, Queen Victoria declined absolutely to look at any document which was not written by hand and a Q.C. publicly refused a typewritten brief.

Classes for instruction in typewriting were being formed in London, and the go-ahead young editor of *Answers* was commending them to his 'lady readers' as a sign of the coming new times. 'We are strongly of the opinion that, in many departments of commercial and literary life, ladies are superior to their admirers.' Instead of the subsequently familiar exercise line, 'Now is the time for all good men to come to the aid of the party', the apprentice typists of the period were taught to tap out texts and moral maxims like 'The wages of sin is death' and 'Clean hands and a sound conscience'.

Iliffe's compositors at Coventry had often complained about Alfred Harmsworth's 'shockingly bad' handwriting, from which they had to set their 'copy'. He became a willing apprentice to the typewriter and had evidently made some kind of bargain with the London agents for the Remington machine. An advertisement for it appears as a printed footnote on the sheet of office paper which he used one evening for typing a letter to his mother, who had just left on a rare visit to her relatives in Ireland. The ribbon was Cambridge-blue and his use of the touch-bar far from assured.

26, Paternoster Square, E.C.
9th October, 1888

My darling Mother,—By this time you are having the worst of it and I am sitting here in Paternoster Square (5 o'clock) trusting there is not much of a sea on.

I do hope that you are going to make up your mind for real enjoyment of your holiday. There is no cause for worry, & even if there were it would not do you or anyone else any good. Make up your mind for a complete rest. I will ask Dotty to keep at home as much as possible. You ought to look sometimes on the cheerful side of life. You have a fine and fond crop of sons going out into the world and all doing well. Do, my darling Mother, make up your mind for a cheerful holiday; enjoy yourself, go about as much as possible and stay in bed as late as you can so that the stay may do you good. Give my love to my aunt & remember me to my uncle and cousins.

Your fond boy.

Geraldine Harmsworth was fifty. The lowness of spirit may have been associated with her time of life. Despondency was not a characteristic of her nature. But with the moral strength which distinguished it there went a diffidence rarely perceived by those who met her casually. Contrary to the legend which has grown up about her, she was a woman of strong presence rather than of strong mind.

In eight months *Answers'* circulation had risen to 30,000 copies a week. It was fair progress, but the paper was not yet a money-maker and it was still unknown to a host of potential new readers in the north of England particularly. There Newnes's *Tit-Bits* held undisputed sway. No chance to add to the circulation figure was neglected. When Carr announced that his two sisters were coming to England from Dublin, Harmsworth urged him to arrange that they should get out of the train at every stop and ask for *Answers* at the bookstall. Obligingly they did so.

New competition ideas were tried with varying effects on the paper's fortunes. A serial, 'The Confessions of a Ticket-of-Leave Man', the outcome of a chance meeting between Alfred Harmsworth and an ex-convict, proved a decided success. A surviving member of the staff of Carr & Co. remembered the ex-convict as being 'somewhat refined'. He called regularly at the office where Alfred asked him questions and out of his answers composed each instalment as it was required. Prison life was unfailing in its interest for Alfred Harmsworth. He visited Wormwood Scrubs prison and the Black Museum at Scotland Yard on the same day. Soon afterwards he was shown over Pentonville Prison. Next on his list of similar experiences was Borstal: 'Spent a most interesting day there.'

Alfred wrote to the Beaumonts:

> 26, Paternoster Square,
> London, E.C.
> 1st March, 1889
>
> My dear Captain and Mrs Beaumont,—You will be glad to hear that the present week has been quite our best so far. In fact, with the exception of Iliffes' acccount, we feel that almost for the first time since we started we can breathe. I hope you have noticed the improvement in the quality of the paper.
>
> It is really wonderful that the circulation has increased at all, for we have been having diabolical weather, snow, hail and rain, without half a day's sunshine. I trust that it is not so with you. We have received about 30,000 postcards in the Great Advertisers' competition, and may look for some increase in circulation when we publish the result the week after next.
>
> This week's *Tit-Bits* is very bad. The Wine Merchant has been away for two months straight off. Perhaps it is the effect of that stuff he has drunk for the past eight years.
>
> With love from all of us,
> Yours very sincerely,
> A. C. HARMSWORTH

'Wine Merchant' was a reference to George Newnes's partnership or investment in a business of that kind. It may also have been a gibe at his drinking habits, which later became a problem for others as well as for himself. He was a diabetic whose personal history suggested that he drove his powers well past their limit. His energies in the first years of his career as a publisher were severely taxed by the need for keeping ahead of imitators of *Tit-Bits*. Within six months of its appearance on the bookstalls, twelve similar papers were brought out by would-be rivals and by the end of a year the number was twenty-two. 'It has always been the unhappy lot of *Tit-Bits* to be imitated by persons with no ideas of their own', he complained in his editorial columns. Now he was faced with the challenge from young Harmsworth: 'the first real opposition I have had', he said. While his sense of grievance may have been tempered by his earlier necessary dependence on literary material in other periodicals for the success of his own, George Newnes not only had to endure, in isolation, the satire of *Punch* but the provocation of seeing the younger man plagiarizing, also, his methods of reaching the public. Harmsworth's venture had to survive in a period of exceptional publishing enterprise. In the year which saw the birth of *Answers*, 1888, just on two hundred new periodicals were launched, a considerably higher figure than that for the first year of *Tit-Bits*.

A friend of Alfred Harmsworth's, calling at the Paternoster Square office on a dark November day, tripped over a pile of *Answers* on the floor, 'I know it's not much of a paper,' Alfred said in his quietest, almost whispering tone, 'but you needn't be so rough with your criticism.'

Chapter Five

'A Pound a Week for Life'

'CIRCULATION still going up,' Alfred wrote to the Beaumonts at the end of March 1889, 'but the financial position still causes anxiety. We do not think the paper has increased so rapidly before at any time and we shall print for next week, 33,000. We are striving might and main to meet Allen & Scott's account for next month. We have three weeks to get the money in and we have £70 towards it at the bank.'

With the appearance of *Answers* in its bright orange cover, an advertising agent, T. B. Browne, of Queen Victoria Street, on the look-out for new business, undertook to try to sell its advertising space on commission, at the rate of £30 per page. When he booked a first order for a quarter page series, Alfred Harmsworth and Dargaville Carr waltzed round the little office.

The weekly printing bill of £60 was a continuing worry, increased when Newnes announced that *Tit-Bits* would pay £100 to the next-of-kin of any reader killed in a railway accident with a copy of the paper in his pocket. The offer startled the public. It exploited a familiar sentiment, the gloomy Victorian view of human life as a funeral procession from the cradle to the grave. But it did not at first produce the circulation tonic which presumably Newnes had hoped for. A woman whose husband had been killed in a railway smash in the West of England had written to him asking for monetary help and Newnes's biographer stated that the idea of 'free insurance' arose from that incident. Three years later, Alfred Harmsworth insisted in his editorial notes in *Answers* that free railway insurance had originated in France. 'It is not an English invention. It was used in France, and also in America, long before it was adopted here.'

Having announced his offer, Newnes found himself in conflict with the Inland Revenue authorities. Every insurance policy was liable to stamp duty; penalty for infringement, £20. 'If this view be correct,' he wrote editorially, 'we have laid ourselves open to fines of several hundred millions sterling . . . sufficient to pay off the National Debt.' He received a writ, later withdrawn: the law, in its own measured time, allowed free insurance to go forward. Adapting it to suit his circulation-raising purposes, Newnes initiated rivalries that long outlasted his day. The intense and sometimes unseemly 'free insurance' battles between the popular daily newspapers of the 1930s, in which the benefit offered to the individual reader rose as high as £10,000, were in direct line from the *Tit-Bits* £100 scheme of the late 1880s.

Young Alfred Harmsworth was having a disagreeable foretaste of the competitive violence to come. He wrote to the Beaumonts in a tone of alarm: 'We cannot cope with the enemy if they are to have such a material advantage.' He was in negotiation, he added, for a £200 free insurance scheme in *Answers*: it was a matter of getting the best quotation from one of several insurance companies. The printing bill of £300 was five weeks in arrears. 'We have every reason to hope that we shall be able to meet it. 'He suggested that there was consolation in the news that the Commander-in-Chief of the British Army, the Duke of Cambridge, had bought a copy of the paper. 'Let us hope that His Royal Fatness enjoys it.' A week after announcing the *Answers'* free insurance offer, he was able to send Beaumont the welcome words: 'Our best week.' The public had responded. There was a marked improvement in the paper's sales. He reported at the same time that *Tit-Bits* was 'becoming rather wild' and that Newnes had had a row with his printers and was imitating *Answers* 'very closely'. The *Answers'* free insurance offer contained a curious proviso: 'Suicides will not under any circumstances share in the benefits of the above insurance.' No one in the office had noticed the absurdity until readers drew attention to it. Meanwhile, a new publicity tag was beginning to repeat itself with threnodic persistence in the minds of railway users: WHEN YOU TRAVEL BY THE TRAIN, STICK TO ANSWERS MIGHT AND MAIN.

Markwick, the barrister, had been concerning himself with editorial matters which Alfred considered outside his province. Markwick took his stand on the fact that he had introduced the Beaumonts and their money and that he was their spokesman in the office. Dargaville Carr, happy-go-lucky Irishman, not interested in bookkeeping, was proving unequal to the responsibilities of his job. A rearrangement of the affairs of Carr & Co. was clearly necessary. The company's most valuable asset was still the mental inventiveness and optimism of Alfred Harmsworth. *Answers* was taken over from Carr & Co. by a new company known as Answers Company Limited. The capital of £3,000 was divided into 600 shares of £5 each. Beaumont and his wife held 150, Markwick 140, his half-sister, Miss Rowley, 10, Carr and his wife 100, and Alfred Harmsworth and his wife 200. Against his signature on one of the Board of Trade documents, Alfred wrote 'Gentleman', whereas he was officially described as 'Journalist'. The original partners, with the exception of Miss Rowley, became directors of the new company, which required a company secretary. The position was offered to Alfred's brother Harold, aged twenty-one. He was in the Civil Service, working at the Mercantile Marine Office, a branch of the Board of Trade, on Tower Hill, London. He had started there as a boy clerk at 12s. a week after leaving Marylebone Grammar School. He worked in the Engagement Room where ships' crews were formally signed on. His duties consisted of copying the agreements and keeping records of the crews. At the time of his being offered the *Answers* post, he was earning 25s. a week and, as he was twenty-one, he acted on occasions as deputy superintendent of his department, where the most he could hope ultimately to earn was £600 a year.

It had been at Harold's suggestion that *Answers* should be detached from Carr & Co. and become a company in its own right. He had been doing evening work at 26 Paternoster Square, helping to count the swelling stream of competition postcards and also trying to unravel the tangles of Dargaville Carr's bookkeeping. The story has descended in the Harmsworth family that Harold was so dismayed by what he found, and did not find, in the books that he wept at his desk. He had no need to tell his brother Alfred what he thought, that if matters were not at once righted the whole structure of the company might come tumbling down. Alfred had his own misgivings.

Alfred Harmsworth to Captain and Mrs Beaumont:

26, Paternoster Square,
E.C.
11th April, 1889
Thursday

My dear Captain and Mrs Beaumont,—As I am staying in town late tonight on account of the Easter Number, I take this opportunity of writing in case I have to be at the printers all day tomorrow. Black fog and gas burning all day, with rain here, yet paper has increased. We hope to say good-bye to the figure 3 now and I hope that after the Easter Number we shall commence at 40,000.

Allen & Scott's account was a great worry and kept me awake a good deal, but it is all right. Money sailing in. We have to pay them £311 odd, including five weeks' *Answers*, 1 *Recreation* and 1 *Private Schoolmaster*. If things go on like this, our bill will be £500 or £600 within three months. A few weeks ago we thought 40,000 was our limit this summer. Now 50,000 is our goal.

Probably Carr or the old man [Markwick] will have written to tell you about the proposal to take my brother Harold in as financial manager. He has asked for a week to decide as he will give up a good berth in the Civil Service (Board of Trade Department). Now we are a Company, we must be very careful to obey the stringent rules of the Companies' Act or we shall get into a hole and the returns and turnover have got quite out of Carr's hold. It takes him all his time to collect accounts. Harold is 21, very cautious and used to managing a large department. We should have liked to consult you, but knew you would approve the choice. Bookkeeping is as much his hobby as trying to lick *Tit-Bits* is mine.

I have been a bit sleepless and headachy the last two weeks and shall spend Easter at the seaside. Mary was in here today and joins me in love to both and 'Answers Limited' sends its embraces to the C.-in-C. and Chairman.

Excuse damnable handwriting, it is freezing.

Yours very sincerely,

A. C. HARMSWORTH

Harold Harmsworth had not decided to give up a Civil Service career without much worrying thought. Cecil Harmsworth said that it was a subject of 'anxious debates in the family' His cast of mind was more sober than Alfred's. He tended to be suspicious of his fellow men and there was a strong strain of pessimism in his nature. His humour was sardonic. Physically, he was the taller. In appearance and stamp of personality he was rigid and somewhat unbending in his earlier years.

Unlike each other in outlook, those two Harmsworth brothers were in effective antithesis: in kinds of ability and in temperament each complemented the other, some would say perfectly. Alfred's instinct for journalism and the public taste amounted to genius but he had no mind for figures or arithmetical propositions, as his school record showed. Harold's competence in that line of thought and practice could fairly be called masterly. He could reduce the most intricate financial problem to the terms of a simple mental calculation.

Alfred's charm and good looks, the fine lines of his nose and mouth, his poise, came from his father. Harold had the more stolid characteristics of his mother, inheriting through her some of the brusqueness of William Maffett, the Ulster-Scots grandfather from Dublin. Alfred carried himself as if he were invisibly plumed and spurred; he had a natural panache. Harold's personal style was the reverse of romantic. If people ever turned to look at him in the street, as they did at Alfred, it was only towards the end of his days when he could be pointed out as the nation's third richest man.

Nothing had exercised Harold's mind more up to the time of joining his brother in the business of *Answers* than the good sense, or otherwise, of taking that step. For him it was probably an intensely worrying time. He had always been a victim of nervous indecision. He was known to walk up and down outside a house at which he had been invited to call before he could bring himself to ring the door bell. Cecil Harmsworth said that Harold's shyness came from their mother, 'in an exaggerated form'.

Harold Harmsworth to the Secretary of the Local Marine Board:

Mercantile Marine Office,
St. Katherine Dock House,
Tower Hill, London.
10th May, 1889

Sir,—Having accepted an appointment in a publisher's office, I beg most respectfully to place in your hands my resignation of the post I now hold in this office. With your kind permission, I will leave on the 1st prox.

I would take advantage of this opportunity to ask you to convey to the Local Marine Board my thanks for the great kindness which has been shown me during my period of service here. With your self, Captain Watson, and the other gentlemen with whom I have served, my relations have been equally happy, and if for this reason alone, it is with great reluctance that I sever my connection with an office where I have spent so many pleasant days.

I am, Sir,
Your most obedient servant,
HAROLD HARMSWORTH

Writing at the same time to his father's friend, Fred Wood, the Board of Trade official whose influence had helped him into the Mercantile Marine Office, Harold expressed his sensibility of kindnesses received and mentioned that his salary in the new post would be higher than that of his rank in the Civil Service. He added, deferentially: 'I hope that my action in this matter will escape your censure.'

'Be wise, Harold, be wise,' Wood wrote in a reply of many pages rich in Biblical allusion. 'Hearken unto the voice of wisdom and the lips of experience. Strive to advance, certainly, but hold fast until the next step is secure. *The hours are so short.* You will go farther and fare worse. Be not weary of well-doing. Never resign except with a pension.' Cecil Harmsworth regarded Harold's letter of resignation from the Mercantile Marine Office as 'the most important single document in the history of the family'. Harold left the Civil Service on June 1, 1889, a few weeks after his twenty-first birthday. The following Monday morning he walked into 26 Paternoster Square to begin work as secretary and business manager of Answers Co. Ltd. at £4 a week. He found the office in a state of subsiding turmoil. *Answers* had been having a great success with the latest of its novelties, a puzzle called 'Pigs in Clover', consisting of a glass-topped box containing seven coloured balls, which had to be enticed into position over corresponding coloured and lettered squares, spelling out ANSWERS. The idea had been brought into the office by a visiting American, identified in a trade journal as 'Mr Sam Loyd, the famous chess problemist and puzzlist'. Alfred took the original specimen to his friend Klein, the music publisher, and they tested it together in Spiers & Pond's restaurant in High Holborn.

It was nearly rejected because the box weighed too much for the penny post. Then Alfred chanced to see a jar of coloured sweets in a confectioner's window. He bought a sample supply and solved the problem of weight. Soon he was writing to the Beaumonts:

26, Paternoster Square, E.C.
20th May, 1889.

My dear Captain and Mrs Beaumont,—We are so hard pressed with work that we have scarcely time to eat. The 'Puzzle', which we send, is by far the greatest success we have ever had.

Three factories are at work but we cannot get them fast enough. It is a small oblong box in fancy colours and contains seven balls. The object it to get these balls in a row. People seem quite mad about it and although we charge threepence for it, it is occasionally sold for a shilling.

The profits are large, but it is the advertisement for which we are looking. Being called the 'Answers' puzzle and having a lot of puffs of 'Answers' upon it will stamp the name of the paper upon everyone's mind. . . .

Newnes was blackballed at the Savage Club the other day. I will tell you of this in person.

This typewriter is a bit out of order, so kindly excuse horrible writing. Excuse more just now. With love and kisses.

Yours very sincerely,
A. C. HARMSWORTH.

The effect of the puzzle's success on the fortunes of *Answers* was important in point of time as well as accountancy. The circulation had more than once been pushed up to beyond 30,000 by special offers and competitions, but it had not gained stability at higher than that figure, which meant that it was still not doing more than pay its way. Now, thanks to the puzzle, sales had shown a sharp upward movement, soaring to 45,000 and staying there. This result was attained not only by the appeal of the puzzle as a new toy, but by astute promotion schemes in provincial districts where *Answers* was still little known. Travellers were sent out to organize *Answers* puzzle clubs in Glasgow, Birmingham, Leeds, Manchester, Edinburgh, Liverpool and Belfast. Prizes were offered through the paper to those readers 'who can achieve the feat of spelling out the name of *Answers* in the shortest time'. Two hundred competitors from all parts of the kingdom, including Scotland and Ireland, met in eager rivalry at *Answers* office. A boy of fourteen broke all the records and won £50.

'Wherever the puzzle goes it is acting as an ambassador,' was the grandiloquent editorial claim. 'It is being done in trains, at the seaside, and everywhere,' Alfred told the Beaumonts. A City of London bank manager wrote in protest to the editor of *Answers*: 'Whenever my back is turned, my clerks neglect their work to try shaking the little balls into the right order.' Soon the warning was unctuously sounded in the paper: 'We inform those journals which are so fond of appropriating our ideas that the *Answers* puzzle is fully protected and any infringement will be severely dealt with by the proprietor', who may or may not have seen himself as an authority on the difference between legal infringement and bold buccaneering imitation. It was stated in *Answers* that there were over a hundred imitations of the puzzle. 'We had nine factories making it. Including the American, Australian, French, German and Russian sale, two and a half million puzzles were issued.'

Newnes had published two of Alfred Harmsworth's shilling books in conjunction with Carr & Co. Now that *Answers* was becoming a serious rival to *Tit-Bits*, he petulantly dropped them from his list, earning more scorn from Alfred. 'The opposition is taking practical shape. The great Judge of Wine has removed the advertisements of "1000 Ways" and "All About Our Railways" from his paper and is advertising wretched books published long ago, which he told me only sold poorly. This is cutting off his nose to spite his face with a vengeance, for he draws quite as much profit as we do from the works in question. It shows what *Answers* is doing.' Alfred was pleased to report, a little later on, that Newnes, too, was in arrears of payment to his printers; also that he had been disappointed by the *Tit-Bits* publicity at the Paris Exhibition. 'What we are going to do in the future we shall reveal in good time,' it was stated in the heavy-father tone of Victorian editorial omniscience. 'We have many plans and projects, and the large section of the public which is interested in watching the developments of journalistic enterprise will derive amusement in watching the contest of popularity now being waged between this and a very well-known contemporary whose strenuous struggles to maintain its place against the new-comer are only equalled by our determination to get to the very top of the tree.'

The ominous word 'boycott' was heard coming out of Manchester. A local reading-room announced its committee's decision to stop *Answers*, 'because it is likely to interfere with a rival which has been established as many years as we have months', was an *Answers* comment. The 'rival' could only be *Tit-Bits*, with its Manchester origin. Another *Answers* paragraph implied that Newnes was the author of the *canard* that the articles by the ticket-of-leave man were a fraud. Harmsworth gave notice, in print, that £500 had been deposited at the bank for payment to any person providing proof of the statement. The bickering between him and Newnes went on for some years. When Harmsworth drew attention to the novelty of printing an *Answers* article heading in shorthand, Newnes retorted that he would issue a complete shorthand edition of *Tit-Bits*. The younger man's attitude to Newnes was that of a borrower who dislikes to admit that he is one. His resentment took the familiar form of

Alfred Harmsworth, senior, barrister-at-law; a photograph taken shortly
before his death in 1889

The Harmsworth brothers. (*Left to right*) Alfred, St John, Cecil, Hildebrand, Leicester, Harold, Vyvyan in front

patronage. An *Answers* article, entitled 'Popular Editors', combined pseudo-magnanimity with editorial flair.

Mr Newnes resides at a handsome establishment known as 'Wildcroft,' Putney Heath, but he is frequently abroad. *Tit-Bits* is not the only venture in which Mr Newnes has been interested. Some years ago he started the *People's Lawyer*, and this year he made another journalistic endeavour with a weekly called *Play*. These journals, however, are now defunct.

In addition to his paper, Mr Newnes is a shareholder in The Scientific Dress-Cutting Association; he has just finished a sort of railway between Lynton and Lynmouth; he has an interest in a wine merchant's establishment, and has several other smaller concerns in hand. The profits of *Tit-Bits* fluctuate between £22,000 and £28,000 a year.

An echo of the old Coventry malice was heard. *Answers* had published an article on cycling. Complaining of its treatment of the subject, *Wheeling* pointed out to its readers that '*Answers* is managed by the youth whose assumption of the *nom-de-plume* of "Arthur Pendennis" was an index to his character'. Alfred's father walked one morning that year along the Strand with another barrister, Louis Distin Powles, of the probate registry at Norwich. As they passed St. Mary's Church, Harmsworth, senior, stopped and put his hand on his friend's shoulders. 'Powles, old man,' he said with deep feeling, 'I have a marvellously clever boy. We shall see him come up right to the top of the tree!'

*   *   *

Bores, calling at the office and wasting his time, obliged Alfred to work at home several days a week. 'Why should a man who has invented a pocket fire-escape bring it to me? The bore I loathe most violently is the perpetual caller, the individual who has learnt my name, and who calls early and late "on a matter of great importance, which can only be divulged to the editor in secret".' He published an article on 'Champion Barbers'. Shortly afterwards 'a short, dapper gentleman' called at the office, asking to see him. 'He was at first taken to be the head of a deputation of the unemployed, for behind him was a small crowd of a dozen others of generally out-of-work appearance. Upon inquiring, it was discovered that the dapper gentleman had read the article . . . and had come to give us ocular proof of his supremacy with the razor over all the lightning shavers described in it. He proposed to shave the "deputation" before my eyes and forfeit a sovereign if he "left a hair on their faces at the end of five minutes".'

Importunity increasing with the circulation, a few months later he felt it necessary to write an editorial note: 'My undertaking with the public is to supply them with the best paper I can produce every week. I do not guarantee to tell them how they should curl their moustaches or cure their stammering. . . .' When an article writer doubted whether grass could grow within five miles of the highly urbanized district of Widnes in Lancashire, evidence to the contrary made life at *Answers* office difficult for several days after. 'For the last four weeks envelopes and packets crammed with grass have been pouring in. . . . There is enough grass now in the editorial department to build a good-sized hayrick. One blade of grass would have satisfied us but the men of Widnes did not think so. One packet weighed 48 lb., and we paid ninepence extra postage, under the impression that it was a present from a friend in the country.'

At Pandora Road he had a typewriter, 'a very fair little library', a supply of periodicals from which he would cut or compile paragraphs for *Answers*, and the active help of his wife. There he wrote columns of replies to readers' real or invented inquiries and many of the miscellaneous articles which added variety to the paper. There were weeks when he made up future issues in the little front room, with proofs draping the backs of chairs and scissors and paste in constant use at his elbow. Many years after, looking back to those days, he said with quiet regret that he had never been so happy. He thought nothing of walking the four miles or so to Paternoster Square and walking back to West Hampstead at the end of the day. Sometimes on the return journey he would knock at doors and hand in a copy of *Answers* as an introduction to possible new readers. 'Oh, I remember the Edgware Road,' he remarked years later to a member of his staff who mentioned having seen a Chaplin film in that part of the town. 'I often walked down it to Fleet Street when I hadn't the price of a bus fare from Hampstead. The Edgware Road has changed since those days,' he reflected, adding: 'I suppose I helped to change it.' He made frequent tours of the bookstalls and newsagents' shops, inquiring about the paper's sales and trying to discover which part of its contents 'pulled' best. It gave him a knowledge of circulation which few editors had the opportunity to acquire.

His rapidly-expanding ego imprinted itself on the paper in terms of his youthful enthusiasms: success, money-making, journalism and authorship, Dickens, and an exuberant curiosity about life in general. In all the early issues there is an article on Dickens, in some more than one article, though the novelist had died nearly twenty years before. Dickens was for some years the chief object of Alfred Harmsworth's never obsessive capacity for hero-worship. Of anecdotal reminiscence about the novelist the founder of *Answers* could not have enough and he was probably correct in supposing that his readers could not either. It was an enthusiasm which led him to make a fine collection of Dickensiana. Part of it consisted of not less than three hundred photographs of Dickens and it might be a misjudgment to think that the intensity of his admiration was centred in the flamboyantly successful man of the world rather than in the reforming writer.

While social conscience in a doctrinaire sense had no place in Alfred Harmsworth's life, he was far from insensitive to the disparities of human fortune. Referring to the discontents of General Post Office workers in 1891, he wrote: 'The present profits of the Post Office are about three millions a year, and in the opinion of many people, at least two-thirds of this should be handed over to those who earn it.'

*   *   *

A symbolic reader-figure only vaguely emerges from the early *Answers* volumes. It is a predominantly male figure. The era of the conquering 'woman's angle' has not yet arrived. This typical reader appears to be given to wearing the white collar of the clerk with the rolled-up sleeves of the artisan, a class composite reflecting social change and a cautious adjustment to circulation possibilities. He has an appetite for processed mental meals in the form of one-sentence paragraphs of information 'about everything under the sun'. To his arbitrary fear of sudden death is joined a recurring dream of sudden wealth or of meeting royalty on equal terms. With a relish for details of the hangman's private life there goes an aspiration to the higher knowledge, hinted at in articles on the careers of artists and scientists and the successes of self-educated persons in realms other than commerce.

His gambling instincts are provided for by competitions ranging from those involving spectacular guesses to others requiring him to count accurately the total of words or the number of times the letter 'b' occurs in a given issue. The fair comment to be made on those often puerile preoccupations is that before the new literacy the only 'flutter' open to the ordinary man was by means of street-corner betting. As a sharer in the infinite dullness of life in lower middle class England, the typical *Answers* reader found that while the paper satisfied some of his longings it generated others still more alluring. That Alfred Harmsworth would have stated it as a formula is unlikely, but with his precise intuition he later exploited it in other publications and added considerably to his wealth and prestige in doing so. The secret has since been rediscovered with highly profitable results by the editors of the mass-circulation women's papers which dominate the latter-day periodical publishing scene.

In the early *Answers* issues the ingenuous enthusiasm of the former schoolboy editor shows itself in numerous articles on journalism and authorship. Unimpressed by the older race of editors, he did not pose as an Olympian. He took his readers into his confidence from the beginning, gave them frequent glimpses behind the editorial scenes, made them feel that he too was involved in the struggle for existence. He appealed to them for patience and understanding as well as, frankly, for pennies. A subtler insight is shown in articles which stressed the gamble of starting a new paper and warning would-be speculators of the risks. Two columns are given to one such article, which purports to tell the experiences of an unfortunate journalist who launched his own paper and lost everything. Professionally, the competent touch is demonstrated when the editor reprints criticism of his paper's contents and policy:

'Answers To Correspondents' is but one more rod for our backs. All such papers are useful only to the lazy ignorant. They encourage educational sloth and impart a patchwork quality to a man's mental training. So many men's writing plagiarised, so much ruthlessly cut from context, so much scissor work! Who is the editor of this excerpt publication and where will he and his brother conspirators ultimately go? The intellect of the few, their wit and humour, joys and sorrows, all are shot into the machine, the handle turned, everything is bruised, crushed, and pulverised; then comes the mixing powder of adulteration, and this dreadful weekly 'Answers To Correspondents' is ready for issue. May we have the strength to bear with it!

The total impression received from an examination of the early issues of *Answers* is of an ingenious exploitation of the popular mind, which had been taught to read but not to think. The periodicals which owed their prosperity to that fact were a powerful and constant force in the growth of modern democracy. Not that any of them could boldly proclaim a political faith, even those which mirrored the hopes of the widest class of reader. 'We do not care to express an opinion on Socialism', it was stated in *Answers* for June 29, 1889, a year in which the streets of London were thronged with processions of dockers on the march to better times. A reader 'of Radical sympathies' who wrote deploring the many references in *Answers* to 'the Conservative gang' received the reply that 'politics play no part whatever in the management of this paper'.

*   *   *

Popular education after 1870 created demands that had existed only in a limited form before. One of them was cheap paper. Low-priced books and magazines, penny weekly papers, leading on to penny and halfpenny newspapers, became an incalculable community influence as a result of technical development perhaps more profound in its effects than any other produced by the industrial revolution. The paradox remained that paper making was never of the first importance among the manufactures of the nation. Up to within about twenty years of the emergence of the *Tit-Bits* kind of journalism, paper making had relied almost entirely on rags as its material of origin. Much of the supply came from the Continent. The Crimean War, with its need of bandages, diminished it. A little later on foreign countries put a duty on rags for export and began making their own paper and sending it to England. For three or four years the English manufacturers were in difficulties. A letter was circulated to parochial clergy all over the country asking their help in organizing rag supplies. 'A little industry, a little intelligence and an established system would perfectly secure us from failure in an important branch of art and trade.'

The troubles of the paper makers were brought before the nation in a more spectacular way by Gladstone's insistence on abolishing the paper duties, regarding them as part of the 'taxes on knowledge' which it was his Government's policy to remove. Opposition from within the trade, as well as from fiscal experts, led to delay and, at one point, to Gladstone's threatened resignation. Repeal came, by a narrow margin, in 1861. Gladstone was reported to have said, with dramatic emphasis: 'The paper duty has gone. For the full results of its removal, man must wait until we of the nineteenth century are gone.' In seven years the paper output of the country had considerably increased. Largely, the crisis was overcome by the introduction of esparto grass from North Africa. By 1880, the year before *Tit-Bits* appeared, the esparto import had reached 200,000 tons. Because England had the chemical means of treating it, esparto grass became the chief material in paper making and a factor of far-reaching social change. Greater demand set in motion the search for other new sources of supply. The uses of wood in paper making had been investigated as far back as 1800. They did not become important until late in the century, when mechanical production of wood pulp was superseded by chemical methods. 'Wood pulp,' wrote Alfred Harmsworth (by then Northcliffe) in the eleventh edition of *Encyclopædia Britannica*, 'is at the roots of the expansion of the modern newspaper.' One of the many company prospectuses of 1889, when *Answers* was one year old, sought capital for wood-pulp mills in Norway. Repeal of the paper duty had come just before the education advances of 1870 and they were largely implemented by it.

★   ★   ★

'If we can manage to keep from quarrelling, we may touch 100,000 with the Christmas number and exceed that quantity next summer regularly. We are absolutely unknown in the greater portion of the country.' Alfred Harmsworth was writing to Alexander Beaumont, addressing him 'My Dear Captain', a style condemned as 'bad form' in *Answers*' etiquette column only a short time before. The reference to quarrelling is not clear.

There appear to have been office tensions. 'Harold has gone off to the Ardennes for ten days. He was breaking down, as you know.' Harold had been working twelve hours a day. His own notes concerning that period state that he was 'getting tired of the unpleasant state of affairs at the office'. His services were retained only when he was given shares in the company by the insistence of Alfred. For that purpose, Carr surrendered 100 shares, Beaumont 30. The transaction was left to Markwick, as the legal expert, and according to Harold's notes it was followed by 'a row' between Markwick and Beaumont, as a result of which Markwick was 'ousted from Beaumont's house'.

Writing at a later date about that stage of the paper's development, Alfred said that there were 'the usual breakers to get through before we reached the smooth sea of success. Our troubles were not diminished by dissensions among the crew.' Because he had founded the paper and believed he knew exactly what its readers wanted, he was aggrieved at not being its chief proprietor. 'I resolved that unless I obtained the absolute editorship I would start another publication and prepared one accordingly.' Of this alternative enterprise there is no record in document or memory. He added to the disclosure: 'Circumstances, however, favoured me, as I must say they usually do. In 1889 I received not only a much larger share in the proprietorship but the absolute control of the concern, whereupon I resolved to go ahead.' Another of the brothers, Hildebrand, called 'Brandy' in Alfred's letters to Beaumont though never in the family, had joined the circulation staff. He was seventeen and had been educated at Dublin High School by the Maffett relatives. His brother said that already he was bringing results by his energetic canvassing of newsagents' shops and whole streets of houses, door to door.

Harold's rigid watch on expenditure soon had an effect on the Answers Company affairs. He had begun to prove what he was abundantly to confirm in the future, that there are phases of publishing experience in which managerial judgment is more important than the editorial function. It was a concession of opinion which Alfred was never able to make un-grudgingly. At the board meeting held on the first anniversary of the founding of the paper, Harold announced a steady sale of 48,000 copies a week and a gross profit for the twelve months of £1,097 3s. 1d. The board meeting was held in a newly-rented upstairs boxroom used for storing *Answers* back numbers. The piles of copies served as seats. At this meeting, conducted by the secretary sitting at a small deal table, it was decided that new offices must be found, for preference in Fleet Street. Someone mentioned vacant accommodation at 108 Fleet Street, down at the Ludgate Circus end, 'over Spence's men's outfitting shop'. Not long afterwards Alfred wrote to Beaumont: 'I saw the new office thoroughly for the first time yesterday. It could be made really charming. I think there is no doubt that we shall get it.' Youthful exuberance was shading into sober confidence, though there were worries. Iliffe's bill was still unpaid and *The Private Schoolmaster* was running at a loss. But for Answers Company Limited the future looked bright enough and it was with a hopeful heart that Alfred went off with his wife for their summer holiday on the Kent coast.

*   *   *

On Saturday afternoon, July 12, 1889, Alfred Harmsworth, senior, and Geraldine, his wife, were at Hendon for a garden party given by the widow of an old friend of his named Day. The weather was overcast and there was a lowering temperature. Alfred, the elder, who liked to cut a figure on those occasions, wore his lightest clothes with thin-soled shoes, 'nicely-dressed and jolly and genial', young Alfred said in a letter written nine days later from 4 Flint Cottages, Broadstairs, to his brother Cecil in Dublin. 'He made the mother so proud to be with him. He had not been so genial for years.' Returning from that happy outing, Harmsworth, senior, did not feel well. At seven o'clock, he said: 'Now I'll toddle', and went up to bed. In a few minutes he was calling out for his wife. She hurried up to his room. He was vomiting blood. Leicester was sent by Underground Railway to fetch the family doctor, Allen, from Fairfax Road, St. John's Wood. Told of the symptoms, the doctor took a serious view of the case. As soon as he saw the patient he said there was no hope. 'Our concern was that he should survive until Tuesday,' Leicester afterwards wrote. 'Monday was Alfred's birthday and we all felt that it would be specially poignant for him if we lost our Father on that day.'

Young Alfred wrote to Cecil in Dublin:

He lingered on peacefully and painlessly till 4.15 a.m. Tuesday, when he died, looking, as Leicester told me, perfectly happy. On Sunday he said, 'I think I am dying,' but mother, who was much shattered by the shock, did not think he really knew his danger. He was quite insensible for hours before he passed away. Auntie, Uncle, and our people were all by his bedside in the little room at the top of the stairs.

I knew nothing till all was over and the shock was terrible. I am getting over it now, for the dear soul is away from all the petty worries of this world. We buried him yesterday in the family grave and should have liked you to have been with us.

It will be a bit of a struggle to keep the family in its place. *But we will do it,* and we must make our folk powerful and prosperous, where the father would have loved to have seen us. Our business grows apace. 'Answers' did 57,000 last week.

. . . Do not grow depressed at the terrible occurrence. There are many things about it that should make the father's death less of a trial than it should otherwise have been. We must all set to work to make the mother's life the happiest possible. Harold will be the father of the house and we must improve it and make it more habitable. The turn of our financial tide has come.

Your loving brother,
ALFRED.

The cause of Alfred Harmsworth's death was medically given as cirrhosis of the liver. It was virtually a repetition of the death certificate of his father, who had died at fifty-three. Alfred was fifty-two. The telegram to Alfred, junior, at Broadstairs, announcing his father's death, had been followed by a letter from Geraldine Harmsworth saying that there was 'no money to bury him with'. He wrote to Henry Arnholz, who had been at Henley House with him:

Your little card of condolence, coming from so old a friend, gratified me much. . . .

I gather from your envelope that you are already entered upon your professional career, of the success of which there can be no doubt. I hope that I may at some time or other be able to influence your work.

My own concerns have prospered beyond my expectations. If you ever have an idle moment to waste look at a copy of 'Answers,' a weekly paper I edit and partly own. Will you please convey all my best remembrances to Mr & Mrs Arnholz and your sister?

Yours sincerely,
ALFRED HARMSWORTH.

Henry Arnholz was the small and nervous Jewish newcomer to the school whom Alfred had championed against the bullying of older boys. From Broadstairs at the same time Alfred wrote to his father's old friend Wood of the Mercantile Marine Office:

My dear Fred,—I address you thus to keep up my dear Father's custom. My little wife and I shall expect you between now and September 21st and remember you come in and go out when you please, and NO questions asked.

Now we expect you and there will always be a vacant room at 31 Pandora Road, West Hampstead, near unto the Grove of the Evangelist, for you.

Come.

Yours, hoping to be as his father was to you, and for as many years,

ALFRED.

Geraldine Harmsworth, senior, to Cecil Harmsworth:

4, Flint Cottages,
Broadstairs, Kent.
12th August, 1889

My dear Cecil,—. . . I came down here last Thursday to stay with Alfred and Mary for a little time. They have a nice little cottage and are making me as happy as it is possible for me to be at present.

I am glad to tell you that Bonchie [St. John] is going to Mr Milne's school and Boo [Vyvyan] to Miss Budd's.

The Church here is just across the road, very high. I don't like it as well as St. Augustine's [Kilburn] but the service is so spirited and earnest I much prefer it to the dead and alive services to be found in some places. The clergy wear birettas, they have more candles than at St. Augustine's and ring a bell sometimes during the high celebration. The music is very good and they have musical instruments as well as the organ. It is just four weeks today since dear Papa was dying and it seems to me like half a life-time. Everyone says it is all for the best, but I find it hard to agree.

Your very loving
MOTHER.

The Sylvan Debating Club formally recorded its members' regret. 'In a few well-chosen words, the president of the club, Sir Sherston Baker, Bart., Recorder of Barnstaple, paid a tribute to the late founder. Mr Robert Mansel, the new vice-president, referred to his late predecessor's abilities which, he said, had always charmed them and whose eloquence and courtesy had commanded their respect. Mr Frederick Wood, of the Board of Trade, spoke most feelingly. . . .' There were affectionate remembrances of him in courts and chambers. He had been more popular than the family realized.

Later that year Cecil, at Trinity College, Dublin, gained the first of his university prizes. His mother sent him family congratulations. 'We are all quite overcome by the joyful news. How delighted your dear father would have been.' She took the opportunity to add: 'I hope his children will ever remember how clever he was and that to him they will owe any intellectual success they may attain to.' He remained evergreen in her memory. One of the Maffett nieces heard her say: 'I have a fine large family, but I would rather have my husband back.' In her next letter to Cecil, who had been over to stay with her at Broadstairs, she counselled him to be 'all that is discreet' and to keep a watchful eye on Hildebrand. 'You must admonish him, as I am rather anxious about him, so much left to his own resources at his age, and I trust that he will be preserved from all evil.' She went on to tell Cecil:

I hear 'Answers' is doing great things, but I have not seen it lately. I am reading Sydney Smith's life and letters, edited by his daughter, Lady Holland.

I was very sorry not to have been able to go to Finchley with you and I hope the next time you see the grave it will be what it should be.

I am sorry you did not see our old landlady. She seems to think you ought to have paid her a visit. She was telling me this evening that she quite remembers the rejoicing at the Battle of Waterloo—and asked me what it was all about.

I have walked the young people nearly off their feet. To Margate and back before dinner on Saturday and no refreshment on the way—not even a glass of beer. I took them to see ANSWERS [a large-scale poster of the paper].
Your loving
MOTHER.

*　　　*　　　*

Answers for October 12, 1889, contained the following announcement, under the head, *An Important Move*:

The proof of the pudding is in the eating, and of a journal the circulation. We have altogether outgrown 26 and 27 Paternoster Square, and three weeks hence take possession of handsome offices at
108 FLEET STREET
lately occupied by a well-known evening paper. We were fond of the quaint old premises where our journal was started, and we endeavoured by taking up extra rooms next door, to remain; but 'Answers' went up, up, up in the world until we have been obliged to make a departure. The change to the commodious first-floor overlooking Ludgate Circus is now positively necessary.

We hope to make the new premises a model of what the home of a journal should be; the Editorial Department promises to be a decided novelty in journalistic offices.

For the present our friends will kindly address us at our old quarters.

We feel sure that all will join in wishing the paper the same good luck in its new premises that it has hitherto experienced.

A week later the oncoming gloom of the London winter was relieved by the sight of strings of sandwichmen ambling along the kerbsides with orange-coloured boards bearing the slogan: A POUND A WEEK FOR LIFE! The pavement throngs were urged to buy the current issue of *Answers* in which were to be found particulars of 'The Most Gigantic Competition The World Has Ever Seen'. A note of highly topical novelty was struck when a week or so later *Answers* repeated its announcement of the competition in huge shorthand characters, 'kindly written for us by Mr Pitman himself'.

A paragraph in the financial page of *The Times* had given young Alfred Harmsworth the idea of the competition. It stated the value of the gold and silver lying at the Bank of England on the previous day. *Answers'* £1-a-week-for-life prize was offered to the reader who most nearly guessed the exact amount of gold coinage in the banking department of the Bank of England at the close of business on Wednesday, December 4, 1889. Readers' guesses were to be sent in on postcards only. Each postcard was to bear the names and addresses of five witnesses, who must not be members of the entrant's family or live in the same house. Readers were free to send as many guesses as they wished, subject to that rule. There is reason to believe that the origin of the prize, as distinct from the competition, had been in an encounter by Alfred and Harold Harmsworth with a tramp. They were walking on the Thames Embankment one evening when a destitute man asked them for money. They talked to him. He wanted to know what they did for a living. Prize competitions were mentioned. 'There's only one prize I want,' the man said—'a pound a week for life.' It was a poor man's dream of wealth. Alfred saw at once its universal appeal.

The offer took the public fancy as no previous competition had. It was an astonishing success. As a subject of current comment in innumerable lower middle class and working class homes, *Answers* rivalled the prevailing strikes and labour demonstrations, in the leadership of which the names of John Burns and Cunningham Graham were just then prominent. A Fleet Street trade paper of the time said that the competition had inaugurated 'a period of popular excitement unquestionably without precedent in journalistic history. Never before had the newspaper reports of the Bank's balances excited such profound interest.' The task of sorting the entries was formidable. Two temporary clerks were overwhelmed; they had to be reinforced by eighteen more. Dot, the eldest of the Harmsworth girls, who had been earning pocket money by giving music lessons, hurried off down to Fleet Street to lend a helping hand. Leicester, nicknamed Puggy, likewise gave part-time assistance: he was paid 10s. a week. He was nineteen and in the Claims Department of the Inland Revenue; soon afterwards he joined the Answers Company at 25s. a week. Cecil, having taken his degree at Dublin, now also joined the firm. Hildebrand was still working, like Leicester, on the outside staff of the Answers Company, pushing up circulation in the provinces. Hearing of Cecil's examination result he wrote:

> 90, Coburg Street,
> Plymouth.
> [Postmarked September 29, 1889]

Dearest Cecil,—Bravo!!! My heart throbbed with delight and I scarcely slept a wink last night. Bravo! Bravo!! Bravo!!!

I can see that we shall be if not the first in the realm, certainly among the foremost families of the day. I, as you know, am going (no boasting, really) in for M.P.s and politics whenever my screw gets large enough and I propose that you and Leicester should rule the clergy and you be the Archbishop of Canterbury and Leicester Bishop of London, Alf at the top of the literary world, I to hold the reins of politics in the Conservative Government, Harold to be Chief Sec. of Ireland and the rest to hold minor posts.

I can't keep from chorusing Bravo! to you, my much-loved brother, and you can know my feelings when I get up at 7.30 to write this and am waiting to post it. It is indeed marvellous in our eyes and since you put the announcement of your success in such an unpretentious manner you are doubly loved by me.

The family is in splendid condition and how darling father would have rejoiced to see the leap we have made. We shall be the biggest firm in London yet. I work like a nigger, hard at work which you know I am not accustomed to, but work I will and shall like anything till the toppermost rung of the ladder of success is at my and my brothers' feet.

My dear Cecil, your kind advice is and has been followed to a T. I spend my evenings writing, drawing and 3 a week replenishing my mind at the Public Library with the sayings and doings of our British Statesmen from immortal Chatham's time, a glorious star of our nation, to Lord John Russell, Canning and his rival, Robert Peel, Palmerston, John Bright and Beaconsfield and Gladstone . . . they occupy my mind all day long. *Non sibi, sed patriae* will be my motto when I rise Hildebrand Harmsworth, Esq., M.P.★ . . . I hope you don't think I'm too self-laudatory, but you know my spirit is so keen on bettering itself that I can't help it. It's better to be ambitious than to be a sluggard. The early bird catches the worm, but the slug is left to the sluggard, an impromptu joke, that. 'Answers' is booming here and it will be a wonder if in eighteen months we don't outdo 'Tit-Bits'.

I am quite a toff now, no seedy bags or small 6¾-ish caps and dark brown— supposed to be white—collars. I save about 15/- a week. 'Answers' is 80,000 this week, marvellous. I leave for Cornwall on Saturday, Bodmin, then Truro, Penzance, Falmouth, and finish up my tour with Exeter and Salisbury. I don't smoke and am teetotal to a T. There are heaps of temptations but I hold myself aloof with a lofty contempt.

This is long enough and with bravos my dearest bro,

Yours,

H.

Answers office bustled with undisciplined energy, fervent inexperience. The editor sat in a large room described in an article as 'an extremely luxurious chamber'. From his window, leaning out, he could look up Ludgate Hill. Opposite, over the roof tops, soared the spire of St. Bride's. Below it was St. Bride's Avenue (demolished 1900) gracefully rounded at its Fleet Street corners by early Victorian shop windows. There, for forty years, *Punch* had its office. 'The view from our office is intensely kaleidoscopic,' *Answers*' editor told his readers. Twice a day, the pavements were shimmering streams of silk hats. This was the Street of Adventure which young Alfred Harmsworth would make still more adventurous. We see it through the contemporary eye of the young and tragic author of *Mightier than the Sword*, Alphonse Courlander:

Heavens! What a world of paper and ink this was, to be sure. The doors,

★ He was an unsuccessful candidate for Parliament in 1900 and again in 1906. He was made a baronet in 1922.

the windows and the letter-boxes bore the titles of newspapers—all the news-papers that were. Every room on every floor was inhabited by the representa-tives of some paper or other: on the musty top windows the titles of journals in Canada and Australia; great golden letters bulged across the buildings telling of familiar newspapers . . . and over and above the irregular roofs the wires spread thin threads against the sky, wires that gave and received news from the uttermost ends of the earth. Every branch of human activity, all the intricate complexities of modern life seemed to be represented either by a room or the fifth part of a room in Fleet Street.

Max Pemberton, twenty-seven, was 'contributing bright replies to our pages', at a guinea a column, chiefly on theatrical subjects. Harold did not share Alfred's faith in Pemberton's journalistic abilities: 'He is a silly fellow and always seems to miss opportunities.' A young Lord Mountmorres was constantly in and out of the office. Having succeeded the Irish peer of that name who was mistakenly assassinated by gunmen at Clonbur in 1881, he was in need of income when he came down from Oxford and gained 'Mr Alfred's' approval by going out into the streets disguised as one of *Answers'* vendors and getting himself arrested on suspicion of having burgled his own chambers. Later, he contributed many articles to the paper and succeeded Max Pemberton in the role of 'Mr Answers'. A young member of the circulation staff, Willie Scott, who had been at night classes with Leicester Harmsworth and who later was linked by marriage with the Harmsworth family, arranged with a theatrical designer, Fox, of Covent Garden, to design a dress coat of orange satin with broad black lapels and cuffs, and a vest and breeches of orange silk. In this eccentric attire he went to fancy dress carnivals, receiving 'a perfect ovation' (*vide Answers*) at a great ball held at Olympia in 1891. He gained new publicity for the paper when he rode along the Strand at night with the first electric lamp ever fitted to a bicycle.

Harold Harmsworth leapt up the office stairs two at a time. He was much given to pacing his room, hands deep in his trousers pockets, as if pondering great matters. If he sat down it was only for a brief moment. Then he would leap to his feet and begin pacing again. Even 'The Admiral' felt rejuvenated and, when at home at South Norwood, often travelled up to the office to experience at first-hand the excitements of being the backer of an enterprise on the brink of success. The office visits of Mrs Beaumont were remembered for another reason. She made a habit of buying meat pies from Lockhart's eating house two doors up the street and distributing them regally to the staff. No one in the office fancied food from that lowly establishment. The 'C.-in-C.'s' bounty was invariably tipped into the waste-paper basket.

A total of 718,218 postcards had been received in the 'greatest ever' prize competition, which was won by a member of the staff of the

Ordnance Survey at Southampton, Sapper C. D. Austin. The purchasing power of the pound at that time was such as to enable him to marry at once. His guess of the amount of gold coin at the Bank of England on the appointed day had been within £2 of the correct figure. No one else came within £100 of it. One of the last incoming posts brought 295,000 postcards, a phenomenon which the Postmaster-General mentioned in his official report for the year. Queer detracting rumours were put about: the winner would, of course, be someone very old; he was bound to be the editor masquerading under another name; and so on. On the morning when the figure was posted up outside the Bank, according to custom, a large crowd gathered in Threadneedle Street. The police were called to control it. The London evening papers had 'special runners' to carry the result to Fleet Street. *The Naval and Military Argus* reported that 'the excitement in Southampton was tremendous'. Sapper Austin was invited to visit London at the expense of *Answers*. 'After he had been interviewed at our office,' it was editorially announced, 'he was invited by Captain Alexander S. Beaumont (late of the Royal Welch Fusiliers), Chairman of the Answers Company, to visit him at South Norwood, where the young soldier stayed the night'. When he died eight years later of tuberculosis, Alfred Harmsworth had a final cheque of £50 sent to his widow, who was left in poor circumstances.

The result was given in the 28-page Christmas Number of *Answers*, 1889. Of that issue 205,000 copies were sold. Only eighteen months old, *Answers* was amply justifying its title of 'The Golden One'. 'Capitalized, £1 a week for life represents about £1,100,' Harmsworth wrote later in *Answers*. 'For £1,100 I managed to excite the interest of nearly five millions of people in this journal, for it should be remembered that every person who entered that competition had not only to sign his own name on a postcard, but to get five other people to add theirs also.' Fleet Street prophets of doom sat back and waited, telling each other that the true test of the Harmsworth finances and ability would come when bigger and better prize competitions were needed to maintain the paper's progress. The public appetite had been stimulated. Now it would never be satisfied. Newnes, of *Tit-Bits*, took another line. He gave it as his opinion that guessing competitions were demoralizing, 'a hit at us, obviously', Beaumont wrote to Alfred. Alfred's confidence was unshaken. His policy was to consolidate the future of *Answers* by a firmer editorial touch, by making the paper acceptable on its merits as reading matter, by a stronger assertion of his journalistic gifts.

An editorial paragraph in the issue dated January 4, 1890, reaffirmed the constitution of the Answers Company in response to a letter 'from one of our readers who resides at 40 Norfolk Street, Glossop', a town whose 'good people', the editor surmised, were 'particularly suspicious'.

The Editor of this paper is not at all afraid to publish his name, but he certainly would object to thrust his personality before the public week after week.

But if it interests anyone to know it, the Editor begs to state that his name is Alfred C. Harmsworth. *Answers* is the property of a limited company, of which Mr Harmsworth holds one-half the shares. The other principal shareholders are Mr Edward Markwick, Barrister-at-Law and a well-known literary man, who is also Vice-Chairman, Captain A. Beaumont, late of the Royal Welch Fusiliers, who is Chairman of the Company, and Mr Harold Harmsworth, who is its Secretary.

Mr W. D. Carr, who has been connected with the head office since the start, now goes to Dublin, to open up an Irish office for the journal, further particulars of which will shortly be published.

As a holder of a sixth share, Dargaville Carr was perfectly content to leave the running of the company to the brothers. Harold wrote in a memorandum to Alfred that as an office worker 'Carr is no good'. Cecil Harmsworth said of him that 'he was entirely innocent of the practical affairs of life'. His pay in London had been £5 a week. Now he was given the sole agency for *Answers* in Ireland at the same rate of remuneration, plus commission. Later, as the representative in Ireland for all the Harmsworth publications, he received a good income, with offices and staff at James's Street, Dublin. 'My brother was jolly glad to get back to the social life of Dublin,' Canon F. R. Carr, of Penzance, told the late Sir Harold Harmsworth in 1950. 'He had no gift for business life at all. He was the nicest fellow you ever met. All of us were devoted to him.' Complications in Dargaville Carr's personal affairs were the subject of a number of austere memoranda from Harold Harmsworth to his brother Alfred after the new arrangement had been made. 'I will truly do my very best, I can assure you I am sick of debts,' Carr wrote to Alfred, 'and I realize perfectly what a fearful thing it would be for me and for my poor little wife if I lost the agency.' Writing to Alfred about Carr at a later stage, Harold said: 'His misfortunes are all of his own making. He has had so many opportunities that I do not feel inclined to pity him. We shall have to do something. He owes us more than £300.'

Carr's departure from the office in Fleet Street coincided with the arrival there of another young man destined to figure more conspicuously in the Harmsworth adventure. Alfred now felt himself entitled to the services of a full-time secretary. Harold had written to him: 'In regard to a correspondence clerk, you should certainly do something to relieve yourself of the mass of purposeless communications.' In reply to an advertisement which had offered 'a splendid opening for ambitious young man', a clerk from the counting house of *The Star* newspaper presented himself at 108 Fleet Street. Shown into 'Mr Alfred's' room, the applicant, who was tall and spare in build and troubled by a slight stammer, took down a letter in shorthand at the editor's rapid staccato dictation. The young man passed the test and was engaged at 35s. a week. His name was George Augustus Sutton, the son of a coachman. He was born at 1a Devonshire Mews East, Marylebone, on September 21, 1869, and he may have been named after George Augustus Sala, then one of the foremost Londoners. His manner was discreet, deferential, quiet, and reliable. He might have been designed by nature to be 'Mr Alfred's' confidential clerk. A nervous habit of fingering his necktie, pulling it leftward and then straightening it again, reflected the indecision of which he was a lifelong victim. Socially, he did not qualify as a 'good mixer'. The set of his eyebrows was deemed by his colleagues at 108 Fleet Street to be Mephistophelian. Soon 'Sutton' was corrupted into the office nickname of 'Satan'.

★   ★   ★

'Mr Alfred' had been working early and late. He wrote in *Answers* that editing a weekly paper meant a sixteen-hour day. Those around him could not say that he was exaggerating. An attack of influenza, in what is recorded as London's first epidemic of that infection, brought him a warmly-worded invitation from the Beaumonts to stay with them at Viareggio. It was his first Continental holiday since the tour with Powys, the clergyman, eight years before. He benefited from the change of scene and routine but was quite unable to rest. Every post had to be caught with editorial instructions and suggestions and manuscripts of articles written by himself. He wrote some lines which were posted up in the office for all to read:

> Clear the sun, and bright the skies,
> Say, oh newsboy, what's the rise?
> Sweet the scent of bud and flower,
> Are we piling every hour?
> Green the grass, and blue the sea,
> How's the circ. and L.S.D.?
> Rare the palms, the chamber's gay,
> What's the boom? Now, varlet, say!

The circulation was going up but not at a rate to satisfy his ambition, which had fixed on a quarter of a million as the summit of its immediate satisfaction. In his 'Editorial Chat' for the issue of May 3, 1890, he wrote:

I don't like betting, and I don't and won't bet, but there is a genuine British fashion of backing one's opinion, and if the circulation of *Answers* has not touched 250,000 copies by or before August 13th next, I will send a £50 note to the sender of the first telegram I receive after eight o'clock in the morning reminding me of this offer. I do not mind saying candidly that unless something unforeseen happens I shall not be obliged to relinquish my hold of that £50.

Eager to reach the quarter of a million for *Answers*, and no doubt still more keen to announce it to the public and his rivals, he experimented with a variety of novel ideas. The *Answers* pipe, made by Messrs Frankau, a City tobacco firm whose business later supplied some of the background scenes for a best-selling novel of the First World War, *Peter Jackson, Cigar Merchant*, by Gilbert Frankau, brought publicity for the paper. Alexander Beaumont composed 'The *Answers* Waltz'. It was published for the paper by Klein, who had brought out 'The Ellen Terry Waltz', Alfred Harmsworth's own composition. There were *Answers* cigarettes, an *Answers* prize dog, an *Answers* fountain-pen, an *Answers* toothache cure, *Answers* coffee, *Answers* silver medals for heroes of the year. 'The toothache cure is efficacious,' Harold wrote to Alfred. 'Several of our clerks have taken it with good results.' The paper's free insurance offer was raised to £500, then to £1,000. 'Mr Answers', the paper's special correspondent, was sent out on a series of 'extraordinary adventures'. He was put to sleep by a stage mesmerist. He spent a night in a haunted house. He was 'shadowed' in the streets by detectives from Scotland Yard. He learnt to ride one of the new 'safety' bicycles.

The circulation responded to those different incentives but with no spectacular rise and Alfred Harmsworth peremptorily announced a greater-than-ever prize offer: £2 a week for life in another Bank of England guessing competition, on the same lines as before. At once the Treasury Solicitor stepped in, threatening proceedings under the Lotteries Act. Counsel's opinion confirmed the official view that money prizes for guesswork were illegal. The competition was withdrawn. In Fleet Street it was thought and said and no doubt hoped that young Harmsworth with his 'penny phenomenon' had overreached himself. The general manager of the House of Cassell, Mr (later Sir) Wemyss Reid, predicted in Max Pemberton's hearing that 'Messrs Harmsworth will be in the bankruptcy court before another year has passed'. Recalling the Treasury action two years later, Alfred Harmsworth wrote: 'Among many of the public, and especially those jealous of my success, the universal opinion was expressed that *Answers* was done for.' In fact, the circulation mounted to a figure which it had not reached before, 230,000 copies, though it fell shortly afterwards. Alfred Harmsworth sent a cheque for two hundred and fifty guineas to the Balaclava Heroes' Fund as a sign of his financial integrity. It rounded off an episode which had gained *Answers* considerable advertisement and some public sympathy: why had the previous guessing competition been permitted if it was not legal?

In the editorial notes for August 23, 1890, an amusingly cryptic paragraph informed readers that 'an offer of £50', made in the issue of May 3, had produced 'a large number of telegrams'. New readers might, not quite foolishly, have inferred from it that *Answers* was engaged in a philanthropic enterprise about which it was becomingly modest. It was a confession of disappointed hopes. Reading it, George Newnes may have smiled behind his beard. His *Tit-Bits* was selling over half a million copies a week. The average weekly circulation of *Answers* was 180,000. Its net profits were rising. They were now nearly £150 a week. 'We have some startling schemes in view', Alfred announced in print when the fuss about the banned competition had died down. This was the point at which one of the partners, Edward Markwick, the barrister, took what proved for him and his family a ruinous decision. His sober legal outlook on affairs had never finally adjusted itself to the Harmsworth pace, that of men much younger than he. His measured thought made little impression on Alfred's headlong faith in the future of the business. The talk of 'startling schemes' apparently frightened 'the Old Man', the name by which Markwick was often referred to in Alfred's letters to Beaumont. To his later and sadly reaffirmed regret, he parted with his 140 shares in Answers Company Limited. Few signatures on a share transfer document have been personally more fateful than that of Edward Markwick when in 1892 he made over his shares in the Answers Company to the Harmsworths and Beaumont.

It was in that year that the second part of 'Schemo Magnifico' became a practical possibility. The Pandora Publishing Company, named after the road in West Hampstead where Alfred and Mary Harmsworth had begun their housekeeping together, was founded with a capital of £500. Alfred and Harold were the shareholders. The brothers believed that there was a chance for a new type of humorous paper to be sold at a halfpenny, then an untried price in the periodical market. They saw it mainly as a publicity medium for *Answers*, though they had hopes of invading the realm of publishing too long dominated by the 'penny dreadful'. With their recent memories of the sort of trash put on sale to young readers, those two in their early twenties had a large contempt for the sordid stuff which degraded the 'juvenile' journalism of the period. Alfred particularly deplored the fact that some 'penny dreadfuls' gave away toy pistols and daggers as an enticement to new readers. 'To any such publisher wanting to "lift" his circulation,' he wrote in *Answers*, 'I recommend a barrel of dynamite.' *Comic Cuts*—'100 Laughs for a ½d.'—would be derided in tone and price as appealing to the tastes of errand-boys, as contributing nothing to the moral elevation of its readers. Made up in the style of the early issues of *Tit-Bits*, and owing even more to the successful existence of a crudely humorous weekly called *Ally Sloper*, it consisted of eight pages of snippets arranged in columns that ran down the length of the page under headings like 'Smiles' and 'Jokes' and 'Tiny Chips'. 'Smiles' announced that a boy had swallowed a revolver cartridge. 'His mother doesn't dare to wallop him in case he goes off.' 'Jokes' had this as a sample: Artist's Friend: 'I like your picture of your uncle. But is his face quite so red?' Artist: 'My uncle? That's a sunset!' 'Tiny Chips' stated as one-line facts that 'salmon can jump ten feet' and 'England has engaged in 127 naval battles'. There was a ruthless pillaging of American papers for jokes and drawings.

For *Comic Cuts*—'Edited by A. C. Harmsworth'—the slogan, 'Amusing Without Being Vulgar', was chosen. As soon as the decision to bring it out had been made, Alfred developed a fanatical eagerness to see it on sale. He took a man named Houghton Townley from *Answers* staff and ordered him to have the new paper ready in four days. The effect on Townley was curious. He was so unnerved by the sudden responsibility that he was kept up all one night vomiting with anxiety. Number 1, out May 17, 1890, sold 118,864 copies, largely as a result of the advance 'booming' given to it in *Answers*. It was a basic concept of 'Schemo Magnifico' that there was to be a constant interplay of publicity for the various publications comprising it. This was to lead to difficulties: meantime, it had handsomely proved itself in the fine circulation secured for *Comic Cuts* from the first issue. In a few weeks a steady sale of 300,000 copies was reached; later it was to go much higher. Newspaper readers were amused to learn that on the previous afternoon a member of the House of Commons, none other than the former Deputy Speaker, Sir Lyon Playfair, had been seen lolling in his accustomed place, furtively reading a copy of *Comic Cuts* concealed in 'Orders of the Day'. The paper had nothing to recommend it as a literary production, even in the Pickwickian sense. But it helped to kill the 'penny dreadful'. In two years it was making more money than *Answers*, the parent paper. '*Comic Cuts* is now the milch cow of the business, and not *Answers*', Harold wrote, February 3, 1892. *Comic Cuts* was to hold its place for sixty years, a far longer life than its founders presumed for it. It became part of English folklore.

Ten weeks later, the Harmsworths announced a second paper, a 16-page production, price a halfpenny, which they claimed to be 'the only paper of its kind in the world'—*Illustrated Chips*, quickly shortened to *Chips*. The formula was the same as for *Comic Cuts* with the addition of line drawings, most of them crudely drawn, all crudely reproduced. *Chips* had a central character, 'Mr Chips', invented by an artist named Dodds. The first issue appeared on July 26, 1890, and much publicity use was made of the fact that two papers could be had for a penny a week. As with *Comic Cuts*, the best that could be said for the newcomer was that it helped to restrict the scope for the still less desirable types of publication. These

Harmsworth papers were published for immature minds, but in those early days, as always afterwards, Alfred and Harold Harmsworth were unyielding in their policy of not pandering to the lowest tastes of all. Alfred wrote in *Answers*: 'It is always a gratifying thought to us that it is universally admitted that no harm can come from the reading of any of our publications, and that by encouraging the taste for pure literature we are rendering a service to the times in which we live.' The humorous writer, A. A. Milne, wrote that 'Harmsworth killed the penny dreadful by the simple process of producing a ha'penny dreadfuller'. The gibe was barbed by what seems to have been its writer's long cherished animosity towards his schoolmaster father's old pupil.

If there was little in the Harmsworth 'juveniles' that was positively high-minded, there was nothing that was obscene. Alfred particularly scorned the productions of a Fleet Lane firm which published *Smiles* and *The World's Comic*: 'disgusting drivel' was his term for them. There were those who considered his boys' papers silly to the point of idiocy, that *Chips*' 'Weary Willie and Tired Tim' tramp characters made fatuous reading for young minds. Writing about the growth of the business in *Answers* Christmas Number for 1891, Alfred said: 'The firm has never published a solitary line of reading matter unsuitable to the most refined home circle.' That statement expressed his personal preferences. What the critics did not grasp was that then, as now, there were immature minds for which the printed word had no charm. They were the original 'comic strip' audience, now world-wide. The 'comic strip' idea was first developed in those Harmsworth papers and it was a famous black-and-white artist, Tom Browne, who drew some of the most popular at that time. He claimed that his inspiration for them came from 'Don Quixote'.

Chips took the public fancy, as *Comic Cuts* did, and the sceptical minds which had thought it unrealistic publishing economics to bring out a new paper that was virtually a copy of the one immediately preceding it from the same source, had to admit the soundness of the Harmsworth strategy. By producing two papers more or less alike, the brothers successfully anticipated and warded off the competition of rivals from outside. Alfred afterwards put it on record: 'I foresaw that our policy was to rain paper after paper upon the public and thus raise our prestige and block competition.'

In a private report on juvenile papers in general, the result of a study commissioned by the Congregationalist theologian, Dr J. B. Paton, founder of more than one moral crusade for the young, it was stated: 'The "dreadfuls" have been hit very hard by such papers as the Harmsworths' and are not read to such an extent as they were. Not that the Harmsworth and similar papers are much better, but they look respectable. Scarcely anyone objects to them and even the best newsagents stock them. Thus they have supplanted the old "dreadfuls" and secured a circulation never dreamed of. Although they are less crude and horrible, they are if anything more vulgar.' That opinion was evidently shared by the proprietors of *Punch*, who reacted with all too little humour when *Comic Cuts* was spoken of by Alfred Harmsworth as 'the poor man's *Punch*'. They sent him a solicitor's letter.

A Harmsworth innovation which brought the newsagents many complaints over their counters was the practice of starting a serial story in one paper and continuing it in another. 'A very aggravating habit', and they begged the Harmsworths to stop it. A number of newsagents, foreseeing damage to the penny periodical trade, refused to deal in the two new halfpenny papers. Readers of both, as also of *Answers*, were kept informed about the boycott and were asked to help in its defeat. Soon the Harmsworths were able to announce a combined circulation of just on 500,000 copies a week. The newsagents had to bow to the popular demand.

Now, Alfred Harmsworth was going down to Fleet Street only on *Answers* press day or for other special occasions. Sutton, his secretary, joined him at Pandora Road immediately after breakfast most mornings. In the afternoon, they would walk on Hampstead Heath. Sometimes, on those walks Alfred would talk to his fox terrier, Bob, but would say no word to Sutton. They would be back for tea and then resume work, often till midnight.

Alfred Harmsworth to Leicester Harmsworth:

ANSWERS

FREE £1,000 INSURANCE

Editorial Department,
108, Fleet Street, E.C.
6th August, 1890.

My dear Leicester,—I am glad to hear you enjoyed the Bank Holiday. We have Dot's future husband staying with us and we all like him immensely.

You must not be disheartened because Derby is a small town compared with Nottingham. The population of Derby is 80,000. . . . Once you get a good circulation in these small towns, it sticks much more firmly than in the large ones, because there is not as much competition. We sold 605,000 papers last week altogether. Not so bad is it?

Harold and I have agreed to let Hildebrand have a 10th share in both 'C. Cuts' and 'Chips', provided he agrees that you will have £300 per annum out of the shares, if, that is to say, they produce sufficient. This ought to make you work extra hard so as to keep the sale up. . . .

ALFRED

Leicester Harmsworth, Esq.,
69 Nottingham Road.
Derby.

117

During that late summer of 1890, Alfred Harmsworth received the first unmistakable assurances of coming prosperity. At twenty-five, he was hardly intent on acquiring power and influence. His ambition was not formulated in the arbitrary Victorian terms of personal progress. To an undoubted single-minded passion for journalism, there was joined a no less positive identification of himself with professional exemplars, successful journalists, successful editors, successful publishers. 'I thought of nothing else,' he told his friend Pemberton. The identifying processes of youth are more usually activated by a wish to emulate than by the will to excel and the Harmsworth dream of success was no exception. For example, realizing that success was near, Alfred's first thought was to escape from the routine of existence in the small house in Pandora Road, West Hampstead. He reacted violently against the possibility of becoming absorbed into the endlessly repeated pattern of suburban life. He had cherished the idea of living at Broadstairs ever since he had been taken there to recover from one of his infant illnesses. Dickens's associations strengthened his attachment to the place. Betsy Trotwood's cottage was said to be one of the little houses clustered above the small enclosed harbour. Nearby is the Royal Albion Hotel where part of *Nicholas Nickleby* was written. Dickens had been lyrical about Broadstairs in a letter to Forster, his future biographer: 'It is more delightful here than I can express. . . . O, it is wonderful!' And to a friend at Cambridge, Massachusetts, he had written in 1843: 'This is a little fishing place; intensely quiet; built on a cliff whereon—in the centre of a tiny semi-circular bay—our house stands: the sea rolling and dashing under our windows. Seven miles out are the Goodwin Sands . . . whence floating lights perpetually wink after dark, as if they were carrying on intrigues with the servants.'

The Harmsworths spent a succession of summer holidays at Broadstairs. During the earliest visits, they stayed in rooms at a villa called Oakleigh. For later holidays they took 4 Flint Cottages furnished. Max Pemberton was sometimes their weekend guest, and he has told how they found the property which became Alfred's favourite place of residence during the rest of his life. They had a dogcart in which they were often seen jogging through the dusty Thanet lanes. 'Returning from an expedition to Sandwich one day, we drove through the village of St. Peters, and beyond it the ancient village of Reading Street, which was then but a small collection of cottages. . . . At a turning, our horse decided upon a little reflection and, pausing to admire the view, he allowed us to see over a high wall, beyond which lay as beautiful a garden as Thanet could show.' Further along the wall was a 'for sale' board. Alfred asking about it the next morning, was told the price, and inspected the property, which was known as Elmwood. Almost from the first glance he had decided that it must be his.

Harold Harmsworth to Alfred Harmsworth:

> Wiesbaden.
> [Undated].

My dear Alfred,—We are having a very jolly time here. The Mater is in fine form.

I hope you have arrived at a decision about 'Elmwood'. I should think you could pay £500 down and if you have to raise the remainder of the purchase money by a mortgage you could discharge the mortgage by quarterly payments of £500 each. I should advise you not to undertake definitely to do this as in the event of any unforeseen contingency it might cause you great anxiety to fulfil the terms of the mortgage.

In any case, I should not be led by the auctioners to bid against unseen would-be purchasers. You have made another offer, I presume, and I should not under any circumstances advance the offer by so much as a £5 note. It is the only way to deal with these people.

Any mortgage you may enter into should have plenty of alternative conditions securing you from its being foreclosed.

In any case, if you do not secure 'Elmwood', I, from my point of view, think it will be to your advantage. At the end of 5 years' time an estate of 1,000 acres or so will be more in your form. It will obtain for you a county standing which will, of course, be very nice. Can you not again approach them as to renting 'Elmwood'?

I should like to be able to tell you how much money you may reckon to receive during the next 12 months. I do not, however, like to make any definite statement. Exercising every economy, I should think it would not be less than £10,000. If you in buying 'Elmwood' make your arrangements on the basis of receiving £5,000, you cannot very well go wrong. If anything then happens you can satisfy yourself by the knowledge that you adopted every precaution. I, as well as every other member of the family, will, I know, think that your happiness is the first consideration.

> Yours,
> HAROLD.

Alexander Beaumont to Alfred Harmsworth:

> The Normandy Hotel,
> Rue de l'Echelle,
> Paris.
> 21st September, 1890.

Dear Alfred,—I have only to interview my bankers and you to have the mortgage drawn up and the money will be yours.

We are so very pleased to think that 'Elmwood' is now yours—you might have searched the world over and not found a place to suit you so well. I should like 'Grannie' [Mrs. Beaumont] to see the place and you two in it—you will have to call it 'Arcadia'.

> Yours, as ever,
> ALEX. S. BEAUMONT.

Elmwood, St. Peters, Kent, about a mile inland from the North Foreland shore between Broadstairs and Margate, was a Tudor farmhouse come to manorial status by various inharmonious additions of rooms and quarters over the years. Much re-facing of its brick and flint had already obliterated its origins. Standing in about nine acres of wood, garden and pasture, behind flint walls guarded by red pillared gateways, with splendid views of the sea, it no doubt seemed to Alfred Harmsworth the 'eminently desirable property' of the house agents' advertisements, capable of providing the social requisite of 'background'. A rambling house, it had uneven staircases and low large rooms, full of comfortable corners. The windows overlooked meadows to which the iodine coming off the sea gave a rich perpetual greenness. Tall, thin elms and fir trees screened the house. Southward, there was a fine sloping view down to the edge of the chalk cliffs of Joss Bay. The property cost him £4,000, his first purchase out of the profits of *Answers* as distinct from earnings. He was able to commit himself to a short-term mortage, paid off in twelve months. A diary note states that, in addition, it cost him £1,600 'to get into the house', meaning, no doubt, repairs, decorations and furnishing. Thus at twenty-five he was master of a small estate and one to which he remained sentimentally attached for the rest of his life. He always preferred Elmwood to any other house he owned or lived in. It was his nearest realization of home, though for him home in its most compelling sense was always where his mother lived.

For her, at the same time, he bought a London house, 112 MaidaVale, to the gift of which he added furniture and a carriage and pair. A little later on she became the owner of their old home, 94 Boundary Road, St. John's Wood. Harold wrote to Alfred, in March 1892, to say that he had cleared off the last small mortgage instalment on her behalf; it was bought as an investment. After twenty-five years of marriage, in the course of which she had known as much hardship as happiness, she could enjoy again the comforts of her former state and no one was more gratified than her eldest son who made it possible. Her first thought, when security came, was to present a stained glass window to St. Augustine's Church, Kilburn, in memory of her husband.

Alfred was promptly generous, too, in providing for his brothers and sisters. Leicester, who, like Cecil, had thought of going into the Church, was sent to study at Oxford, without entering the university. Hildebrand was put with a tutor at Windsor, the Rev. Gilbert Edwardes, before going up to Merton College, Oxford. 'I've told him on no account to play baccarat with the Prince,' Alfred wrote to his mother, 'as he comes of a respectable family.' St. John, who had been at Henley House, where H. G. Wells was teaching science and writing for the school magazine which Alfred had founded, was sent to Fauconberg Grammar School, at Beccles, in Suffolk, an early eighteenth-century foundation with a good record of preparation for the university. He went up to Christ Church, Oxford. Vyvyan was sent to Charterhouse and Cambridge. 'I'd like my brothers to be better equipped than I am', Alfred told Comyns Carr, the barrister-playwright, on one of their fishing trips. Geraldine, or 'Dot', who had recently gone out to India to marry Lucas White King, of the Indian Civil Service, was given a belated trousseau and a money allowance. Likewise, he made arrangements for the education and future security of his younger sisters, Violet and Christabel. 'Remote Irish cousins', as Cecil Harmsworth called them, received less sympathetic consideration. To their requests for loans and bank guarantees Alfred was curiously unresponsive.

Cecil Harmsworth to his sister, Geraldine:

112, Maida Vale,
N.W.
Dec. 29th, 1890.

My dearest Dotleins,—You can imagine that we felt rather doleful for some time after your departure, but we are really such a busy family now that we haven't much time for grief. What with settling down in the new house, and bringing out the three rags every week we have always enough to do without indulging in unnecessary sentiment. Besides, it would be rather too comical for us to be shedding buckets of tears over here when you are looking forward with joy to the happy meeting with your own.

Methinks I see you seated at the entrance to a rather shabby-looking tent (like a wigwam) watching a large pot merrily simmering over a fire. The thermometer registers some 250 in the shade, and you are airily attired in one of your numerous cotton gowns. A hat, four feet in circumference, adorns your rippling, sunshine hair. Tropical large-leaved trees shut out the surrounding scenery and birds of gay plumage flit from bough to bough.

Don't be astonished at all this nonsense. The stories I read in manuscript for 'Answers' are vitiating my mind and I find myself unconsciously adopting their style and manner.

Alfred and Mary are getting on with the arrangements at 'Elmwood,' and it won't be long before they are away too and then we shall be left alone together. Mother is reasonably cheerful and on the whole as comfortable as the heart could wish. The kids are as boisterous as ever. . . . In fact, all goes well and as cheerily in the House of Harmsworth as is possible without dear Dotkins. I find that I have only room to enclose boundless love and affection and to remain,

Your loving bro,
CECIL.

Geraldine's departure for India may have prompted a paragraph in an *Answers* article on story writing, which Alfred almost certainly wrote: 'Most plots, we believe, are derived not from real facts, but from facts which suggest themselves to us as possible in connection with people we know. What if Miss Smith, who is going out to India to marry her *fiancé* there, should fall in love with somebody else during the voyage. . . .' All was grist to that mill. His editorial enterprise was at the same time reaching out for the coming new writers:

> Masongill House,
> Kirkby Lonsdale.
> 24th December, 1890.

Dear Sir,—I shall be happy to do a story at the rate of £5 per 1,000 words, which is my present scale. Let me know at once if that suits you.

> Yours faithfully,
> A. CONAN DOYLE.

Never forgetting his experiences as a freelance in Fleet Street, Alfred now made a strong editorial point of paying his contributors 'on acceptance', writing in his 'Editorial Chat': 'I can state, without boasting, that the system of immediate payments is entirely due to *Answers*. At one time authors were obliged to wait often for weeks, sometimes for months, and occasionally years, for payment for pigeon-holed contributions.' He returned to the subject in later issues. 'The modern tendency to increase the payment of authors cannot be too widely commended', he wrote as part of a special announcement to contributors. Until the arrival of Newnes and Harmsworth, rates of literary payment were humiliatingly low, often half-a-crown for a paragraph or a set of verses and ten shillings for a column. 'Our usual rate of remuneration is £2 per column—about 1,200 words', Sidney (afterwards Sir Sidney) Low, of *The St. James' Gazette*, wrote to Lord Mountmorres, of *Answers* staff. For the professional writer, Alfred Harmsworth maintained the considerate attitude throughout his life, although in his early publishing years he was satisfied to commission a serial story of 52,000 words for £75. No other proprietor or editor, before or since, has shown a more practical understanding of the writer's economic position.

While he was making his plans for raising the family's standing in the world, he imposed on himself a course of reading for the preliminary Bar examination. Possibly because he had no chance of going to a university, as he was enabling his younger brothers to do, he felt a need to improve his personal qualifications to match theirs. 'I can't read without emotion of Alfred's lessons in Latin and history amidst all his intense preoccupations with the business', Cecil Harmsworth wrote on seeing, years afterwards, his brother's diary notes about that aspiration of his. Alfred had written for January 18, 1891: 'Wrote to Mr Giffard, asking him to use his influence to excuse me from the Bar prelim. examination.' Mr Giffard, a relative of the then Lord Chancellor, replied that he would do his best.

Ten days later, Alfred noted that a barrister friend of the family named Seddon had 'promised to do what he could in the way of seeing the Benchers of Lincoln's Inn about getting me in'. Then came word that Seddon's friend, an examiner, had resigned: 'so I shall not be able to get through the Bar prelim. examination that way'. In those first months of 1891 he was studying regularly, paying Seddon three guineas a week as his coach. 'Worked at my papers in the evening', he wrote on March 16, after a busy day at Elmwood, and again, on March 22: 'Did Latin in the afternoon', it being Sunday. Harold, too, was seeing Seddon at that same time and, as far as can be gathered, for similar reasons. He had gone straight into the Civil Service after leaving Marylebone School. 'Do not expect me Saturday,' he wrote to Alfred in May 1891. 'I must do work for Seddon.'

As has been suggested, Alfred probably thought it unsatisfactory that as the eldest of the family he should have to acknowledge an inferior position scholastically. Of the legal life, to which it seems unlikely that he was aspiring at any time, he wrote much later: 'Legal training, and the law's delays, never seemed to me to be concomitants of initiative, energy, action and decision.' On June 3 he wrote: 'My exam, I think, is a success', leaving the nature of the 'exam' to be guessed and also its result; there is no further mention of it in the diary. It does not appear that he went on with his extra-mural studies beyond May 1891. The profession of the law probably did not lose a great advocate. On the other hand, legal training might have been of considerable value to Alfred Harmsworth, whose mental processes lacked *esprit de suite*. The motive for his studies remains in doubt, the more so as the demands on his editorial and publishing qualifications were becoming heavier. For instance, Newnes was making much of the fact that his *Tit-Bits* was now selling more than 500,000 copies a week. Celebrating the 500th number, he proudly announced that the orders for the special issue had reached 620,000 copies. 'There is a half-penny daily paper in France which claims to sell a million copies per issue and we see no reason why there should not be a penny weekly in England to do the same.' Meanwhile, pursuing the obsessional policy of the paper, he wrote that if all the copies of *Tit-Bits* sold since its start could be piled one on top of another, 'we could positively build a monument 3,993 times as high as the Monument of London'.

Dargaville Carr to Alfred Harmsworth:

> 14, Lower Sackville Street,
> Dublin.
> March 11th, 1891.

My dear Alfred,—What a vile temper you must think I have.

Did I display my bad qualities in that line so forcibly in London that you think every letter you write must 'annoy and enrage' me? My Father knew all about my money difficulties, so your letter was no surprise to him. My Father is very anxious for my success in life, he and I never fall out. I never had a single quarrel with him, and I hope I never shall.

You are quite mistaken if you think he looks upon me as a Rothschild, he knows my income, thinks I have done well, and he blames nobody but myself for leaving the firm. Can you expect a Father to feel quite satisfied that his son is making about £600 a year and his son's late partner £10,000 a year? He does not quite realise your brains and my want of them. But I assure you he never says anything of you and Harold except in praise.

Now, Alfred, you have given me many a good jaw, let me give you one.

Every letter you write me is full of guesses. In one you guess I am extravagant, in another that I am going about cursing you and that my Father is doing the same. There are lots of other things you surmise without any right. I ought not to mind them because I know they all emanate from some recess of your own brain. Don't guess any more, like a good man.

Very kind regards to your wife, hoping that the air of Elmwood, St. Peter's, Kent, will suit her.

Yours affectly., and not in a rage,
CARR.

Carr wrote again a few weeks later to assure Alfred that he was doing his best 'to try and get square', and that he was spending nothing that he could possibly avoid. He added as postscript: 'You never tell me what you are doing now. Is your income very large?' If Alfred answered that inquiry he was likely to have done so with an optimism not shared by his brother. Harold was watching the firm's fortunes with a particularly gloomy eye just then. '20th April, 1891—I find that *Answers* literary account is still increasing at a tremendous rate. Up to this date we have paid for April £180 or, if nothing more is paid this month, £45 a week. Unless something is done, *Answers* finances will be approaching a chaotic condition.' He wrote a reminder a few weeks later: 'Literary account still terrific.' Alfred, meanwhile, had the satisfaction of noting in his diary: 'Paid off nearly all debts', presumably including Iliffe's printing bill, which had been outstanding an embarrassingly long while. He was able to indulge the luxury of having his shirts specially made for him and took care to note that, too. A social occasion, recorded at the same time, gave him a chance to enjoy an experience which had been well known to his father, as a friend of George Jealous: 'Saturday Night Dinner at the Savage Club with Harold and Max Pemberton. A very amusing evening. I enjoyed Mr Odell's recitations particularly', a reference to a celebrated personality of the Bohemian world.

Alfred and Mary Harmsworth moved into Elmwood on April 15, 1891, a day on which Alfred noted: 'This is one of the latest springs on record. The trees are only just beginning to shoot.' They had been lodging at 36 Albion Street, Broadstairs, 'Miss Gillman's, over Parsons Library', while Liberty's of London were carrying out interior decorations and furnishing at Elmwood. The telephone was installed. It was still so much of a new thing that Mudford, editor of the *Evening Standard*, declined to have it in the office or at his home. Mr Gladstone remained obstinately confused about the difference between the telephone and the phonograph.

Cecil Harmsworth wrote to their cousin Everard Hamilton in Dublin: 'Alfred and Mary look quite different when they are down there and always seem to be in the best of spirits.' He added: 'Alfred is the life and soul of the business. He is brimful of ideas.' Cecil himself was the subject of a memorandum to Alfred from Harold: 'June 4—He might as well have that editor's column in *Comic Cuts* again. He has not so much to do now and it would mean an extra half-guinea a week in his pocket. His stuff is quite good. . . .'

Alfred Harmsworth to Everard Hamilton:

> Elmwood,
> St. Peter's,
> Kent.
> IV. VII. 1891.

My dear Everard,—My wife and I are exceedingly desirous that you should visit us this summer. If you would name any time between August and December we should be much rejoiced. We are dull folk and beyond an occasional country dinner party I can offer no more amusement than tennis and driving. Nevertheless, you must come.

In writing to you I am reminded of a passage in a letter written by my dear father at the time of the death of Grandfather Maffett. My father was writing from Chapelizod and he says (to his mother): 'Everard Hamilton is staying here. His father is the kindest friend we have and I shall never forget it, I hope.'

With many good wishes for you and yours.

> Yours most sincerely,
> ALFRED HARMSWORTH.

Beaumont had been seriously ill: 'We have been very anxious about our Chairman', Alfred wrote to Mrs Beaumont. He went on to tell her:

I prophesy that in December of this year, health being good, *each of our three papers* will be ahead of the biggest circulation in the world. Our organisation is getting complete and we have £21,000 a year to play with.

Yesterday I was at 'Elmwood' for 2 hours, or rather 1¾ hours, getting there at 2.15 and leaving at 4. It looked charming in the snow and I never felt so pleased with the bargain.

> Your thoroughly respectable and affectionate
> ALFRED.

When Mrs Beaumont replied that her husband's convalescence was accompanied by much depression of spirits, Alfred wrote to him in a tone of cheeky disregard for the wide difference in their years, heading his letter, 'from the garden at Elmwood':

My dear Cap,—We all have our troubles, you know, some time or other, and you have escaped many that make the lives of other men a burden. You have no pecuniary cares, no worrying family, no enemies, no regulation round of humdrum toil, while you have *friends*, at least average health, success and prosperity, and many interesting pursuits and hobbies. Cheer up, my dear Cap., life is all right. You look at it through those blue specs of yours and they give you the 'blues'. Probably you are both still tired from your journey. We don't like to think of any of *us* being in low spirits.

'Answers' is exceeding expectations and I'm fairly sure of 250,000 this year. This week we did 200,500.

There are many things waiting completion for your advice and approval. This place is a dream and I can work here admirably. My ambition is to free 'Elmwood' by Xmas and so get rid of your clutches, you grasping, greedy, Jewish sixty per cent.-loving miser. If all goes well, I can nearly do it.

There is a nice fat sum waiting for you at the office.

Yours always,
ALFRED.

In another letter to Captain Beaumont, Alfred referred to his intention of placing 'those near to me beyond the fear of financial ups and downs'. He was anxious, he wrote, 'to secure for me and mine a large amount of solid capital', which he proposed to put only 'into two things, Consols and Railway Debentures'. After that, he planned to 'do what you do, speculate with the interest, the capital being safely locked up'. The letter ended with the appeal: 'I wish you would get a photograph of yourself and Gran. I haven't a decent one of you. Yours always, Alfred.' While it seems that, with the expansion of the Answers Company's business, Harold Harmsworth tended to become intolerant of Beaumont's part in it, the correspondence shows that Alfred's footing with their backer was friendly, often cordially so, up to the summer of 1891, nearly five years after their original transaction together. He had written in his diary for February 17, 1891: 'Capt. Beaumont came to lunch and agreed to advance £500 out of his profits for each new paper we started, and also agreed to add a codicil to his will to the effect that our family should have the first opportunity of buying his "Answers" and "Comic Cuts" shares in the event of his death at a 3 years and 18 months valuation respectively.' The swift development of the business brought to its young founder and his still younger brother new complexities of work and responsibility and these in turn produced temperamental situations which had not been foreseen in 'Schemo Magnifico'.

Alfred Harmsworth to Leicester Harmsworth:

ANSWERS,
Editorial Department,
108, Fleet Street, E.C.
25th July, 1891.

My dear Leicester,—I am very glad to find there is plenty of room for our work in the town.

This was our best week, 760,000 papers. Next week the first orders for *Answers* are 232,000. That is the holiday number, of course; perhaps we may do 240,000. If we do, it will be very satisfactory progress. *Comic* keeps up well and *Chips* doesn't go down.

I have not heard from Hildebrand for a long time. What is his address?

I suppose you know you are coming to London for the boys' paper and going to blossom out into a full-blown sub-editor.

ALFRED.

Leicester Harmsworth, Esq.,
15, Frederick Street,
Accrington.

Soon their sales touched 800,000 copies weekly. The million mark was now well in sight. For them it was in itself a goal of attainment, a summit to conquer before they climbed still higher. Despite the accountants' testimony, there were sceptics who believed that the Harmsworths were bluffing.

An older resident of St. Peters was watching their progress with an increasingly nervous eye. He was Edwin J. Brett, who lived at Oaklands, nor far from Elmwood. He had surrounded himself there with a collection of armour about which visiting neighbours were apt to be sarcastic among themselves. He had made money out of a series of lurid 'dreadfuls', which he published from 173 Fleet Street. A contemporary of his remembered 'the Fleet Street newsagents' boys fighting in Brett's offices for supplies of his papers'. Apparently as a gesture of social worthiness, he launched a weekly called *The Boys of England*, for which he secured royal patronage, and a prosperous circulation. The weekly continued through to the end of the century, absorbing several others and immortalizing Jack Harkaway as a boys' fiction hero. At one time Brett's publishing list consisted of a dozen titles, papers of varying fortunes. *Boys' Comic Journal* was one of his money-makers, founded in 1883. The Harmsworths may have owed him some acknowledgment for inspiration in the same line. He died a man of wealth. The business was then moved to 'Harkaway House', West Harding Street, Fetter Lane. There it failed. Pitiful requests for help were afterwards written to Alfred Harmsworth by members of the Brett family: 'As you know, he was first in the field.' The early appeals were generously answered. They were followed by awkward personal calls at his London house which seem to have finally disengaged his sympathy.

Chapter Six

History of a Quarrel

'IF we stick to our work, we shall soon pass £40,000 a year, which Newnes points to with so much pride.' Harold Harmsworth was writing to Alfred, for once a long letter instead of his usual terse weekly progress report, e.g.: *My dear Alfred,—Answers* 207,000, *Comic Cuts* 338,000, *Chips* 197,000. *Yours, Harold.* The letter showed the alternating current of that subsequently eminent business brain, caution amounting to pessimism contrasting with exhilarating hope. Gloomy about the rise in *Answers* 'literary expenses', about advertisers' suspicions 'that there is still a great deal of shoddy about *Answers*', and the increasing risk of 'one or two insurance claims' damaging the paper's finances, Harold was at the same time capable of visualizing the company owning its premises and moving on from that stage to a public issue of shares. 'I may be sanguine, but if we had six or seven flourishing publications we should make £70,000 or £80,000 a year.'

A third Harmsworth company was formed in November 1891, 'The Periodical Publishing Corporation Limited', with a capital of £500. Alfred held 300 shares, Harold 150, Cecil 10, Leicester 10, the Harmsworth Trust 30. The Trust had been founded to provide for the education of members of the family who were as yet too young to take part in the business. The immediate purpose of the new company was to launch a penny weekly paper, *Forget-Me-Not*, aimed at the potentially immense new reading public of women. Few papers were dealing exclusively with women's particular interests. Those which did were mostly printed on poor quality paper and trafficked in sentimental articles and stories and insipid poetry and gave away cheaply reproduced fashion plates. In a higher and more expensive class were journals like *The Queen*, the *Ladies' Field* and the *Lady's Pictorial*, with small, exclusive circulations. For the advanced members of the sex, who smoked cigarettes in public, read *The*

Alfred Harmsworth in his late twenties

Mary Elizabeth Milner; a photograph taken a few years after her marriage to Alfred Harmsworth

Alfred Harmsworth, aged thirty

26 Paternoster Square, the first office of *Answers*

Yellow Book, and talked of the vote, there was *Woman*, edited by Arnold Bennett. *Forget-Me-Not* was planned to give better value for a penny than the few existing women's papers did at a higher price.

'In its wrapper of delicate forget-me-not blue, *Forget-Me-Not* will be as bright and pure as the flower from which it gets its name.' The touch was fairly certainly Alfred's. Its sub-title was: *A Pictorial Journal for Ladies*. Among its first advertised attractions were the 'Diary of a Professional Beauty' and 'Confessions of a Wallflower'. Etiquette was an indispensable topic: 'Trains should be held with the right hand', and the paper stuck rigidly to the niceties of social intercourse by referring always to 'ladies' and 'gentlemen' in dealing with the sexes. Women in durance vile were 'lady convicts'. Its illustrations were light and graceful, filigree drawings showing 'ladies' in the semi-devotional postures required by decency as well as by fashion. The tone was excessively proper in the governess sense approved by the dominant social influence, the court of the ageing Queen.

Forget-Me-Not started uncertainly along the path to its ultimate success. There was a difficult period in which Harold wrote: 'The circulation is still as limp as ever. *F-M-N* is undoubtedly in a very critical condition.' There were rumours of its being a failure and the Harmsworths decided not to discourage them, so that their triumph was the more complete when *Forget-Me-Not* was seen to dominate the market for women's papers—'in point of time, absolutely the most successful publication ever issued', was Alfred's claim in writing. 'It has a circulation larger than all the ladies' journals that have been established for 20 years.'

Harold Harmsworth to Alfred Harmsworth:

108, Fleet Street,
E.C.
30th September, 1891.

My dear Alfred,—Re 'Forget-Me-Not' and Captain Beaumont's tenth share. I duly wrote to Captain Beaumont asking for £1,000 and pointing out the conditions under which he was to participate. I said that the £1,000 was to be paid in any case, whether the journal paid or not. To this he takes exception.

Under these circumstances, I am of opinion that the offer should be withdrawn and that he should not participate in any way whatever. We should be prepared to risk £1,000 and if we keep our heads cool there is absolutely no reason why any money should be wanted at all. I will engage that if the journal begins to pay within three months you will not be asked for any money whatever.

I can run the thing on credit and pay off when it shows a profit but, of course, if the liabilities reach £1,000 I will let you know immediately.

My argument, briefly, is that if the journal pays, the £1,000 will not be wanted, but if the journal does not pay the £1,000 will not go very far.

Captain B's tenth share I consider to belong to the boys. They can do a great deal more for our business than Captain Beaumont's odd thousand pounds.

You have now been relieved of the liability of 'Elmwood' (£1,000 going to you today) and are quite in a position to risk £500 during the next three months. If it pays, then one-tenth share, instead of being worth £1,000, will be worth £10,000.

I am quite willing to go to the extent of £500, if necessary.

We are not bound by any honourable engagements to continue the offer to Captain B. He has objected to the terms, which is tantamount to a refusal. Wire me on receipt and I will write him saying the matter is off.

Yours,
HAROLD.

Harold Harmsworth to Alfred Harmsworth:

108, Fleet Street,
E.C.
1st October, 1891.

My dear Alfred,—Answers 221,000, Comic Cuts 345,000, Chips 199,000. In reference to Beaumont and his first letter to me, I should say that he did not refuse to pay £1,000 for a tenth share, but that from his letter he appeared discontented with the provision that the £1,000 would be divisable by all the proprietors in proportion to the shares owned by them. He described it as 'news to him' and said the £1,000 or balance might be divided 'provided the money was not required for pushing the paper'.

These remarks appear to me to be reflections on ourselves, and after the manner in which we both, and particularly yourself, have treated him, I consider they are most unmerited. I have, however, written to him in the terms of your letter and told him that the tenth share can be obtained for £2,500.

Beaumont has apparently an idea that he is the central pivot on which this business turns. For my part, I am quite willing to contribute my share of the necessary capital, as well as give something very handsome towards obtaining the other tenth for the boys.

I have no particular faith in Beaumont. He would have invested in 'Pearson's Weekly' unless we had put our feet down.

Yours,
HAROLD.

Harold Harmsworth to Alexander S. Beaumont:

108, Fleet Street,
E.C.
1st October, 1891.

Dear Captain,—I have again heard from Alfred in reference to the tenth share in *Forget-Me-Not*. He now thinks a tenth share in the publication is worth £2,500 (two thousand five hundred pounds) and in this I fully agree with him. Would you therefore let me know whether you are prepared to go in at this price? My letter of the 28th ulto. should read with the alteration of £2,500, instead of £1,000.

As you know, the plan of publication has entirely changed and instead of bringing out a cheap novelette, we are now producing a high-class penny journal for ladies.

Candidly speaking, we do not require the venture to be financed, as both Alfred and myself are quite willing to do this. In this kind of business skill and ability account for everything and capital for nothing.

Yours sincerely,

HAROLD HARMSWORTH.

Alexander S. Beaumont to Harold Harmsworth:

South Norwood Park,
S.E.
2nd October, 1891.

Dear Harold,—As I accepted the offer made in your letter of the 28th ulto., in my reply to you dated 29th September, you cannot alter the sum agreed upon for my one-tenth share in *Forget-Me-Not*, which amount had been settled verbally many weeks previously.

Had you told me that Alfred wished to run the journal by yourselves (the straightforward course) I should not have objected, but, as you did not, I hold you to the offer, which I accepted.

Yours as always,

ALEX. S. BEAUMONT.

Harold Harmsworth to Alfred Harmsworth:

108, Fleet Street,
E.C.
6th October, 1891.

My dear Alfred,—Re Beaumont, we shall have some difficulty in this matter, but I think I see the way clear ahead. In regard to Beaumont's financing the undertaking, I have always desired to forget the fact so long as matters went smoothly that much more of the financing was done by you and, in a much less degree by myself, than by Beaumont. All the advertising, prizes, and insurance money have been really capital outlays.

You and I have had to contribute our quota, as well as put in all the necessary work required to conduct the paper. As you know, after I came to the business, no money was put in, but notwithstanding this, something like £7,000 has been spent which otherwise might have been paid in dividends. Of this sum, according to the present holding of shares, you have contributed £3,850 while I myself have put in about £1,300. Beaumont on this basis has contributed the first £1,750, total £3,500. You have therefore paid for about 30% of your shares and received only 25% for editing.

This, to my mind, is a preposterous position and your interests should be supplemented if there is unpleasantness by a salary of at least £3,000 a year. My salary should bear a proportion to yours, so that you should not have to pay anything. Cecil, too, should have a good salary.

Bennett [chartered accountant] has often put this matter before me in the proper light, but, as you know, I am very conservative in my habit of mind, and much averse to a change unless need arises.

I shall send you tomorrow a copy of my correspondence with Beaumont. If he will not accept a straightforward offer for his shares we ought to know what to do.

Yours,
HAROLD.

Writing in his diary for the next day, October 7, Alfred noted: 'Received a rather stirring letter from Beaumont. Went up [from Broadstairs] to see Harold, who made some startling statements to me about the matter.' The diary note continues discursively: 'Came back by the Granville Express. Parnell died today and W. H. Smith yesterday. In the evening I gave an entertainment consisting of magic lantern and tea to the village school here. Received the result of my first roll of Kodak pictures, with which, on the whole, I am pleased.'

Alexander S. Beaumont to Harold Harmsworth:

South Norwood Park,
S.E.
7th October, 1891.

Dear Harold,—Of course, I plainly see that you do not want me in the new venture, but, I must remind you, that when I handed over to you and Alfred the greater number of the Shares I had purchased from Markwick at the same price I had given for them I did so because it was an understanding between Alfred, you and I that I should do so.

I could have put an extra price on them, or could have demanded instant payment for them, but I carried out my part of the arrangement loyally. In the same way, it was arranged and agreed between Alfred, you and I that I should have the one-tenth share in the new penny journal for £1,000, and the one-tenth in the new halfpenny journals for £500 each—and I expect you both to be as loyal to me as I have invariably been to you, not only in the case of the Markwick shares, but from the very beginning.

Yours as always,
ALEX. S. BEAUMONT.

On October 9 Alfred made a diary note: 'Paid Capt. Beaumont £450, which cleared me of all debts to him for Elmwood and Markwick's shares. He promised to invest £1,500 extra in *Forget-Me-Not*, if necessary, making £2,500 in all.' On October 12 he recorded that 'Capt. Beaumont forwarded me the receipt for my last payment on Elmwood and £1,000 for *Forget-Me-Not*, together with a letter, which I filed. I wrote to him

132

that I did not think he ought to bargain about *Forget-Me-Not* considering the handsome treatment he had received at our hands'.

In the history of the estrangement of the Harmsworths and Beaumont, finance was the factor assisting the breakdown of a relationship already jeopardized by differences of another kind. Harold, in particular, had strong personal reservations about Beaumont, whose part in the business he clearly begrudged. Unlike his brother, who was not invariably realistic in money matters, he refused to regard it as indispensable. He had not been early enough on the scene to share Alfred's gratification at having capital made available to him for the furtherance of his ambition. The story has persisted in the family that, outraged by Beaumont's conduct in the office, Harold once pushed him out of a room. A long surviving member of *Answers* staff remembered hearing Mrs Beaumont say with haughty emphasis as she left 108 Fleet Street with her husband after one more stormy scene: 'We will go now where we can find some *gentlemen*! . . .' There were grievances on both sides. Beaumont was much upset by Alfred Harmsworth calling on him for money to pay a printer's bill at a time when he was ill in bed and unfit to talk business.

Harold Harmsworth to Alfred:

> 108, Fleet Street,
> E.C.
> 1st December, 1891.

My dear Alfred,—Beaumont has nobbled the shares of Miss Rowley, who has resigned. As a counter move, I have on Graham's approval [William Graham, solicitor] got sworn statements re Beaumont from Scott, Skinner, and Ebden. I shall get two more tomorrow. Graham says the case is strong enough to hang a cat.

When you come up on Monday you can read the statements. Graham says that if there is the least nonsense, we must at once tell Beaumont about the evidence.

I am on the alert and ready for any move.

> Yours,
> HAROLD.

Although Harold had given him the good news that there was a chance of the business making £50,000 the next year, the crisis brought nervous tensions for Alfred, who wrote in his diary that he was 'quite prostrated' and had to stay in bed all day as a result of the news about Miss Rowley, to whom he wrote expressing surprise and regret. 'When you are rested, don't let any false pride forbid you returning. Let me say that after four years of happy work it is distressing that your peace of mind should suffer because of other people's differences.' His favourite Aunt Miller had cause to write to him.

Warrior House Hotel,
St. Leonards-on-Sea.
4th December, 1891.

My dear Alfred,—I did not answer your letter before as it caused me a good deal of pain.

I cannot resist saying that had the positions been reversed I should not have written to you as you did to me, and also that had I had a little of your wordly wisdom when I came into my poor little income of £200 a year about seventeen years ago, I should not have required to ask a loan from my rich nephew.

No one but Mr Miller knows of my having written to you, and that was when it was *un fait accompli* and the only favour you can do me now is to keep the matter to yourself.

Your ever affectionate
AUNT.

His aunt had lost money by the failure of her journalistic enterprise, *Kensington Society*, which had made its *début* in the same year and month as *Answers*. Like her, Alfred was feeling the strain of proprietorship. His family sentiment, normally strong, reasserted itself more characteristically when he received the news that his eldest sister, in India, had become a mother.

Alfred Harmsworth to Geraldine White King:

Editorial Department,
'ANSWERS.'
108, Fleet Street,
London.
15th January, 1892.

My dearest sister,—When I got home to Maida Vale last night I found the joyful news of the safe arrival of a little niece. Terrific excitement among the tribe immediately ensued and everyone is in the full dignity of Aunt and Uncle, not to forget Grandmama.

Boo's [Vyvyan's] remark was: 'If I am uncle, what's Leicester and Hilder?' He is sorely puzzled over the problem. Aunt Pop in very fine form. I am seeing my solicitor just now with a view to settling £50 on my niece and godchild, who will not be forgotten in my will, also being made today.

The babe arrived on the very best financial day in the history of the family. *All* our four papers increased by £1,000 a year yesterday, besides a niece.

Mary's full of excitement. Dear little soul, she has not been blessed and perhaps will not be, but some nice little nephews and nieces will please us quite as well.

Kiss the little one for me dear,.

With lots of love to all three, my dearest sister,
Yours devotedly,
ALFRED.

He had been staying at the Hotel Metropole, London, where on the back of a bill he scribbled evidence of his mental agitation: '. . . *being egged on by some cheap hungry solicitor.* . . . *Why choose this particular time when I am hampered by lack of assistants, illness and Xmas numbers?* . . . *Rude tone of letters not like you.* . . . *Why have you suddenly decided to throw over your own good luck and take someone else's advice?* . . .'

The old cordiality had evaporated. Alfred wrote now, 'Dear Beaumont', and signed himself 'Yours truly', recording in his diary that the worry was giving him sleepless nights. There are references to Beaumont's 'utter recklessness', to his 'remarkable conduct in ignoring the shareholders' interests', to his 'spreading lying rumours about us', to the fact that there was no means of getting rid of him 'without a public scandal'. A closing entry for 1891 is: 'Found that Beaumont has been up to his tricks again. I cannot sit on the same board with him.' From that time forward, with clinching finality, Alfred Harmsworth proclaimed himself as 'Founder and Editor' on *Answers* page one. In 1892 he was named as founder and editor at the top of each page in several successive issues. Up to then, he had been content with being publicly known as its editor.

The Harmsworth-Beaumont quarrel is by no means completely documented. A few letters, Alfred Harmsworth's staccato diary notes, a dictated memorandum by Alexander Beaumont stating his dissatisfaction at the use of *Answers* for advertising other Harmsworth publications, some notes made by Harold (as Lord Rothermere) years after, and the distant inconclusive recollections of no more than two or three survivors of the period, comprise the evidence for the opposing points of view. The story follows a familiar pattern where mental services are equated with financial backing. 'For all your sakes, I shall be thankful when the severance is complete and you may be congratulated,' an old friend wrote to Alfred Harmsworth. 'I hope you haven't paid too much. If so, I shall be vexed at those lawyers.' Legal intervention amplified and then pacified the grievances. Beaumont had resigned his directorship of the Answers Company, and the chairmanship of the Pandora Company, in December 1891, according to Alfred Harmsworth's diary 'on the score of ill-health'. On August 8, 1892, Beaumont and his solicitor, Hargraves, called on Alfred 'to try to arrange a settlement'. The diary note continues:

After 3 hours' discussion we adjourned till 6 o'clock when the discussion again commenced, and after between two and three hours more, it was settled and agreed that we sign an agreement whereby Capt. Beaumont is to have a bond for £8,000 on the joint and sole security of our three companies with interest at 30%.

On August 24 he wrote that Beaumont and his solicitor had called again. 'In an hour we settled the matter satisfactorily to all concerned.' There is no documentary evidence of the transaction in the Harmsworth files. It is believed that there was a variation of the original settlement, as a result of which Beaumont received an annuity of £2,400 a year, a not unfavourable return for his investment of £2,000. Difficulties concerning Markwick's half-sister's shares flared up again the following year. There was a threat of legal proceedings, 'a great nuisance', Alfred Harmsworth wrote in his diary, 'when I thought all the trouble was over'. On July 21, 1893, he was relieved to write: 'We settled our quarrels with Miss Rowley today.' He dined that evening with Markwick at the National Liberal Club. There he was seized with 'a very bad fainting fit'.

The luxury of a month's holiday abroad was crowned by the news, on Alfred Harmsworth's return to Fleet Street, that the circulation of *Answers* had reached 300,000 a week. He had been pleased to see, when ashore at Gibraltar, that 'the soldier who had charge of the Visitors' Book in the Galleries was reading *Answers*, which, by the way, I had seen in Sicily and at Port Said and other places'. Sales of the paper had been helped by a Conan Doyle serial story, *The Doings of Raffles Haw*; price £150. During the negotiations for the serial, that rapidly rising newcomer to authorship had written from 12 Tennison Road, South Norwood: 'Forget whether I told you that I live now as above, having given up my professional work in Wimpole Street.' Doyle says in his autobiography that it was from that address that he set out to live entirely by his pen. Raffles Haw was a prodigiously wealthy man who tried to do good with his money and who, when he saw the effects of his benefactions on weaker characters, committed suicide 'from a broken heart'. A cautionary tale which the more calculating philanthropists of the era probably found much to their taste. It was followed by *Convict 99, or Penal Servitude for Life*, by Marie Connor Leighton. Her gifts as a story-teller had been commended to Alfred Harmsworth by Hall Caine, the novelist, two or three years previously. *Convict 99* was the true prototype of the serial story which had the loyalty of a vast reading public until the paper shortages of the First World War compelled its abandonment by newspapers and periodicals in general. It was so great a success that after its original publication in *Answers* in 1892 it was several times reprinted in other papers.

The serial story vogue was created by Alfred Harmsworth. Three years previously he had tested, in *Answers*, the public interest in prison life with his ticket-of-leave-man series of articles. *Convict 99* took the miscarriage of justice theme and introduced into it new elements of drama. It was announced as being more than 'just a piece of enthralling fiction'. It was a social document which raised the question: 'Can prison sufferings be mitigated? The walls of our convict prisons', wrote the editor of *Answers*, 'hide lives as terribly tried as those of the prisoners of Siberia. Charity beginneth at home. Let us first inquire into the sufferings of the British criminal before we try to reform the Czar.' The public response showed that the formula was as sound as the instinct which had impelled him to secure all the rights in the story for *Answers*. He supervised each chapter and was several times obliged to jump into a hansom cab and drive off to 29 Grove End Road, N.W., to induce its amusingly temperamental author to change an episode or devise a more striking 'curtain'. He was ruthless in his demand that every instalment should have what he called 'a news finish'. He may himself have suggested names for some of the characters. The heroine was called Geraldine. Her surname was Lucas, the first name of the man whom Geraldine Harmsworth had gone out to India to marry.

Marie Connor Leighton's daughter Clare, an artist of the woodcut, has recalled how in later years she more than once saw Alfred Harmsworth at the house lying on a sheepskin rug in the drawing-room, 'flat on his stomach, his head buried in his hands'. Her mother, explaining this odd behaviour, told her that 'he can think best when he is flat on his stomach. The blood doesn't have to make the effort of running uphill to the brain'. He rewrote parts of another Leighton serial, *An Amazing Verdict*, in the course of several visits to Grove End Road. It gave him, he noted, 'a lot of bother'. One night he worked so late that they had to give him a bed. He was delighted when the Leightons' small son, aged three, offered him a cigarette, 'on his own account'. Marie Leighton, writing to him in her florid Italianate hand, with letters two inches high, sought to touch him sentimentally by recalling the incident when in 1913 her long series of writing contracts with the Harmsworths came peremptorily to an end.

Launching *Convict 99* gave him a fine opportunity to proclaim his faith, as an editor, in the appeal of a better sort of fiction than was being supplied by some publications. Reading the first part of the story, he wrote that he was reminded of something that Charles Dickens had said about the immense power for good or evil wielded by the writer of stories. 'The Editor . . . has long wished that *Answers* might not only be a journal of instruction and amusement . . . but that the minds of its mighty army of followers might be influenced for the alleviation of the sorrows and sufferings of their fellow-men.'

The Harmsworth brothers were now in a position to claim that the combined sales of their publications was a million copies a week. 'The trade' was sceptical. It might mean copies printed: what about copies sold? An answer was forthcoming with the effect of a sledge-hammer. Dated June 4, 1892, a certificate, signed by E. Layton Bennett, chartered accountant, of Cornhill, London, E.C., confirmed that the *net* sales of the Harmsworth publications exceeded a million copies a week. The exact figure was 1,009,067 copies weekly. For some time past the circulation figure for

Answers had been regularly given in that paper. The net sales certificate for all the company's papers led into a campaign with far-reaching effects on the newspaper and periodical publishing trade of the country. 'Net sales' was to become a generally adopted, but also fiercely disputed, practice of the new century. Aware that the scope for misrepresentation was being widely exploited, Alfred Harmsworth warned advertisers against 'sham circulations' and urged them to probe 'the *real* sale of many journals claiming immense circulations'. When they discovered the truth, he wrote, their eyes would be opened 'very wide indeed'. In later times the 'net sales' question was to loom up still more powerfully in the intensely competitive atmosphere of Fleet Street, where today it is considered by competent judges to have been a destructive campaign in its emphasis on quantity as against quality in periodical circulation especially. Alfred Harmsworth's idea of issuing a net sales certificate was a bold stroke of publishing policy which echoed down the years.

Favourable comment on *Answers*, earlier that year, by Lord Randolph Churchill, had been followed by a friendly message from Mr Gladstone. A general election had taken him on a speaking tour in the north of England and in Scotland. At Dalmeny Park, where he was the guest of Lord Rosebery, he was approached by 'Mr Answers' for an interview. 'Mr Answers' on that occasion was the young Lord Mountmorres, a fact which may have accounted for Mr Gladstone's amiable co-operation. He said: 'I consider the gigantic circulation of *Answers* an undeniable proof of the growth of sound public taste for healthy and instructive reading. The journal must have vast influence.' Privately, Mountmorres reported that the movement of Mr Gladstone's eyebrows had held the audience spellbound. Lord Randolph Churchill had said: 'Your new literature is simple, but is none the less instructive and valuable for that.' He went on: 'Let us take the case of one fresh from school, who reads in your pages not only interesting things about every department of life but gathers also interesting facts about literature itself. What is he likely to do? Certainly not to relinquish the reading habits he has acquired. There is no reason at all why he should not go on from your pages to the pages of the monthly magazines, from those to the quarterlies, and again from those through all the English classics.' He gave it as his opinion that the Harmsworth sort of journalism would be far from evanescent, that it would become a permanent feature of our time.

Inspired by the Gladstonian blessing, Alfred reviewed his editorial responsibilities anew in *Answers* for July 23, 1892:

Great care is taken in our office that every line of information should be weighed and balanced by all sorts and conditions of men before it makes its way throughout the world. . . . The spoken word vanishes, the printed word

the man into
protestations.
keen," said
accepting the
thinking it a

- discovered
top-coat was

often wears
tobacco.

was one- of
if he took

father, who is
do you part

very ill with
cce of will."

was only fatal

re frequently
insanity and
you suppose
?"
yı: "I expects
n."

ous! Have
Caneby and

en them face
were dwawn,
a turn-down

ce the other
n.
," insinuated
the desk.

ou," he said
reller.
repeated the
across the
knob, and it

Sir Charles Russell, a not easily fatigued speaker, on the occasion of his two days' speech before the Parnell Commission, drank nothing but hot coffee, which he declared was not only good for the voice, but an excellent stimulant.

THE sculptor is the most likely of all men to cut a figure in the world.

GILES: "I suppose that literary man you introduced me to reads a great deal?"
Merritt (a novelist): "Not at all.

many times?
part their h.
man's life is
stamps are p
London omr
cock crows i
in a London
would grow

No, it is n
you think of
body else,
instances.

A LITTLI
After a whi
thought. L
" Mamma,
" Because
" Oh, yes.'

CHARLIE S
you have sa
hair?"
Alice: "(
haven't got.'
Charlie: "
Alice: " A

NEIGHBOUI
fence): "I an
garden so ea
reward."
Tommy (t
be, but I've
and haven't

FLOSSIE w
brother a fig
right hand ai.
Handing t
she said, " M
" Yes," was
" Thank yc
with me," wa

" I'VE got
inventor.
The capit:
calculating n
answered, " V
use it."
That night
another appli

remains. Every word of the 100,000 we print every week is carefully considered before it appears. For this purpose there are retained on my reading staff a clergyman, and an honours man of Trinity College, Dublin [his brother Cecil]. The gentleman who interviewed Mr Gladstone this week is an Oxford man and promises to be of distinction in the literary world. These are in addition to a number of well-informed journalists who are instructed to be most careful in their revision of what we print.

Harold Harmsworth to Alfred Harmsworth:

'ANSWERS.'
108, Fleet Street,
London, E.C.
15th July, 1892.

My dear Alfred,—Answers 375,000, Comic 420,000, Chips 212,000, *Forget-Me-Not* 83,000. Total, 1,090,000.

Hildebrand is the essential cause of my not running down today. In my absence he has been wearing my tennis clothes and the laundress will not have them ready for me until late tonight.

Yours,
HAROLD.

Alfred Harmsworth to Frederick Wood:

Elmwood,
St. Peter's, Kent.
13.8.1892.

My dear Fred Wood,—. . . Things move apace with us. Harold is engaged to a charming girl, Leicester is married, my sister has a baby, Hildebrand is just going up to Oxford, St. John is preparing for the Army, and Vyvyan for Charterhouse. The Mother thrives and looks much younger than ever.

Many thanks, my dear Fred Wood, for your congratulations on our worldly prosperity. Fortune is a fickle creature and hath strange whims. We are making just on £50,000 a year and don't want half of it. Ten years ago we should have thought a fiftieth part of it affluence. People call us miserly because we save all we make, but as I said, Fortune is a coquettish lady and may turn her back on us one of these days, so we are preparing against her. These figures are private, of course, and are known only to some half-dozen persons, though 'Harmsworth, Limited' may next year be floated and we shall have then to reveal.

Would that the dear old Governor could have seen his son's luck. He was quite a believer in the family.

Yours always affectionately,
ALFRED C. H.

In the issue of *Answers* dated September 17, 1892, there was a conspicuously 'boxed' announcement headed 'ANSWERS INCOME'. It told readers that the pence and halfpence paid by them to the newsagents for *Answers* and the other Harmsworth papers 'amount, when added up, to £3,800 every week or within three thousand pounds of £200,000 a year'. The announcement also supplied the information that, in addition to that sum, there was an average weekly revenue of £500 from advertisements. That flourish in print was excused by the conjunction of youth with extreme good fortune. The results it flaunted before the public had been the accomplishment of only four years. It encouraged Alfred Harmsworth to extravagant flights of optimism. Discussing the outlook for *Answers* at the end of that year, he wrote: '1900 is a long way off but, given good health and strength, I would not be at all surprised if our weekly sale reaches from ten to fifteen million copies a week.' Meanwhile, the *Manchester Guardian* was pointing out that while 'America is supposed to be monopolizing the publication of English literature, yet the attainment of the largest circulation of periodical journalism in the world can be ascribed to a British editor, Mr Alfred C. Harmsworth.' Already, it appeared, Alfred Harmsworth was seeing himself the master of a wider domain. A note in his diary for September 7, 1892, records: 'Lunched with Iliffe at Anderton's Hotel, Fleet Street, to discuss whether I should purchase his Coventry paper.'

To spur a flagging circulation, Alfred had been greatly daring with his £1-a-week-for-life competition in *Answers*. It had been remarkably successful in its publicity effects. When the legal attitude to 'guessing' competitions had been formally defined, he proceeded to reinforce his gains in circulation by editorial improvements rather than by new methods of advertising. His journalistic gifts found more satisfaction in devising plots for serial stories and in suggesting interviews and articles. He knew by then that mysterious forces affected competitions, that the entries would come flooding in, while for the next competition the response would be small. This unpredictable flux was a subject of editorial comment: 'It is curious to watch the rise and fall of crazes.' In February 1891 he had written concerning an abortive *Answers* prize offer: 'We don't know what competitions are coming to. There were only three competitors. Times have indeed changed.' The year before that a picture puzzle competition in *Answers* had brought in more than 40,000 entries. A few months later, in a similar form of competition, the entries numbered fewer than 1,400.

Near the end of 1891, the dormant public interest had broken out afresh in the craze for 'Missing Words', a competition organized by *Pearson's Weekly*. The founder of that publication, Cyril Arthur Pearson, was the son of a Church of England clergyman and a great-grandson of the author of *Abide With Me*. His father, the rector of Drayton Parslow, Buckinghamshire, had made a hobby of inventing the more erudite kinds of mental puzzle and spent much of his time in his study thus occupied. Young Pearson's upbringing and education had included two years at his father's old school, Winchester. He had not gained much from his schooling. Concerning it, he was in the habit of saying that he had 'preferred tennis to Tennyson and cricket to Carlyle'. Shortsighted, with a jerky manner which had earned him the school name of 'Pigeon', he became a journalist because the profession appealed to him more than the job in a City bank which his father had in view for him. He had countered the parental plan by winning the *Tit-Bits* competition in which the prize was a job in George Newnes's office, at £100 a year. The competition, called 'Inquiry Column', comprised a general knowledge test extending over many weeks; and Pearson, who was eighteen, had shown spirit and resource by making weekly journeys totalling 180 miles on an old-fashioned high bicycle to look up reference books in the Free Library at Bedford. There were 3,000 entrants in the competition and the scrutineers in London had to check 39,000 examination papers before declaring Pearson the winner. Having acquired the publishing rudiments in Newnes's office, he asked for a rise in salary. At the end of six years he was getting six pounds a week. When Newnes retorted that he would never be worth more than £500 a year, Pearson, with the help of another Newnes man, Peter Keary, drew up his own version of *Tit-Bits* and *Answers*, put it in a pink cover, and called it *Pearson's Weekly*, with the front-page motto, 'To Interest, To Elevate and To Amuse'. It was financed to the extent of £3,000, advanced by a friend of the Pearson family. The first issue carried a free railway insurance policy of £1,000 and there was a competition for clergymen only, with annuities as prizes. It sold a quarter of a million copies. One of the articles in that first issue was headed 'Curiosities of Blindness'. It had been written by Pearson himself. For him eyesight was a fateful topic. He published his paper from Temple Chambers, E.C., where he started in four rooms with a staff of four persons. Keary said that unsold copies of the first issue filled the office, seriously hampering work there. Then W. T. Stead gave the paper an approving mention in the *Pall Mall Gazette*, with helpful effects on its circulation. As the sales rose it was realized that more capital would be needed, at which awkward moment the investor of the original £3,000 lost his remaining capital in an Argentine speculation and wanted his money back from Pearson. Sir William Ingram's interest was sought because he was an old Wykehamist as well as a successful publisher. He provided new money and afterwards said that he had not been attracted by the paper but by the possibility of having young Pearson at hand to succeed John Latey as editor of *The Illustrated London News*.

Like Alfred Harmsworth, Pearson wrote nearly all that appeared in the first issues of his paper. As a worker, he drove himself excessively hard.

He called on every leading newsagent and most of the lesser ones, travelling England, Scotland and Wales by train, sleeping in third-class compartments, living almost exclusively on sandwiches, and writing articles between stations. He had always worn glasses and believed that he damaged his eyesight by his constant reading and writing in trains. The turning point in his fortunes has been attributed to 'Missing Words'. He himself said that the tide changed in his favour when he announced a house-to-house distribution scheme as 'A Helping Hand to those Out of Work'. It brought him the services of a large number of willing canvassers and the good will of new readers who thought they were supporting a philanthropic enterprise. According to Pearson, 'Missing Words' extended the circulation gained by the earlier scheme. He had been correcting the proofs of a Christmas number of his paper and had struck out the last word on one of the pages, 'as I did not think it quite properly conveyed the author's meaning'. In the act of searching for a better word, 'it occurred to me that a good form of competition would result from leaving the space blank and asking readers of the number in question to fill in the gap'.

Launching the competition in his paper, Pearson made it a condition that each entry should be accompanied by a postal order for a shilling. The response was only moderately encouraging. It took six months to reach a total of 20,000 entries a week. Inexplicably, from then on the competition became a people's mania. The 20,000 entries rose to a total in one week of 473,574, representing nearly £24,000 in shilling postal orders. 'The entries came in so thick and fast,' said R. D. Blumenfeld, who shortly afterwards joined Pearson's staff, 'that it was impossible to keep control. Office boys were found with their pockets stuffed with postal orders. Those that were crossed they shoved down the drains and choked them up.' Relays of members of the Young Women's Christian Association were engaged as temporary clerks, presumably as an insurance against further dishonesty as well as to cope with the rush. Eager to exploit the public mood, other papers started the competition. More than once the overworked General Post Office mixed the entries for one paper's 'Missing Words' with those of another.

There was surprise in the publishing trade that *Answers* was a slow starter in the 'Missing Words' race for circulation. *Pearson's Weekly* touched the million mark, to settle down at half a million. The Harmsworths' caution was probably due to their earlier encounter with the law. Not even 'Missing Words' had eclipsed their £1-a-week-for-life offer in intensity of public interest. They used 'Missing Words' in the first place as a way of drawing attention to their new paper, *Forget-Me-Not*, without giving it special prominence as a competition. Not until Pearson had been running 'Missing Words' for nearly a year did they seriously accept the challenge. Then they undercut him by inviting readers of *Answers* to send in two entries, in place of one, for a shilling. To their offer they attached the announcement that a halfpenny in every shilling would be deducted for the 'Free Breakfasts Fund' for children which *Answers* had been sponsoring. That good-natured enterprise had not met with much success. Now it was given a considerable 'lift', and nearly a million hungry mouths were fed as a result. It had been Alfred Harmsworth's inspiration to link the Fund with *Answers*. He was more sensitive to its appeal than perhaps its founders knew. As a mark of good faith, he engaged a clergyman, the Rev. C. W. Sparkes, to supervise the opening of the competition entries, the value of which rose to £3,000 a week. Before long, Harold was sending Alfred a memorandum: 'The mixture of parson and business man is not a success.'

The Harmsworths' reluctance to exploit 'Missing Words' was not unwise. As the interest grew to be nation-wide, the moral issue was raised in ever louder tones. Churches and other bodies and groups declaimed their views. Bigoted persons were noisy with prophecies of national degeneration. Would-be public informers rose up to do their dubious duty. The *Daily News* attacked *Answers* in a leading article, to which the *Financial News* replied with a charge of hypocrisy: 'It is pleasant to know that, although every encouragement which "latest intelligence" can possibly give to gambling in cotton futures, or time bargains on the Stock Exchange, or betting on the Turf will still be forthcoming, the abandoned people who get up "missing word" competitions will be hounded to their just doom . . . put in the pillory, to be pelted with pious platitudes of pharisaical censure.' The editor of *Answers* rejoined in lighter vein. He considered the *Daily News* article to be an example of 'brilliant journalism', and hoped that the anonymous writer of it would communicate with him. 'We should like to call his attention to the fact that we pay one guinea a column (700 words). We should be glad to have something from his pen.' Argument on the legal side was mainly pedantic and involved much paring away of shades of meaning. Little was said about the likely if imperceptible advantages of seducing the attention of younger readers in particular from the betting sheets and such 'penny dreadfuls' as remained. On that score 'missing words' may have had a credit side.

Proceedings were taken against *Pick-Me-Up*, one of the smaller weeklies which had been running 'Missing Words'. It was as if the entry of *Answers* into the general scramble for prestige and profit to be gained from the competition had once again stirred the official conscience. With other papers, *Answers* was served with a summons. At Bow Street magistrate's court, Sir John Bridge ruled that 'Missing Words' constituted a lottery and was therefore illegal. His decision was followed by the Treasury demand that all those papers concerned in the competition should return the money sent in by competitors during the previous week. Pearson's £24,000 was impounded, pending a ruling in the Chancery Court. The ruling was given in February 1893. It upheld the decision in the other court. The social impact of the verdict is stated in emotional terms in Arnold Bennett's well-known novel, *These Twain*. There a character maintains 'that it is inconceivable that any English court of justice should ever interfere with a pastime so innocent and so tonic for the tired brain. Now the fearful blow had fallen . . . to bring indignation and affliction into tens of thousands of respectable homes'. An *Answers* editorial comment mentioned that at the height of the boom copies of the paper were in demand at 2s. 6d. each. That climax of the 'Missing Words' craze gave Alfred Harmsworth the cue for his first after-dinner speech. He was the guest of Herbert Ward at 'Ye Sette of Odde Volumes', a literary dining club. Unexpectedly called to his feet, he said: 'While I am always ready with my "Answers" every Tuesday, I regret that I am unable to produce them tonight. I have never made a speech in my life before and most of my words are missing.'

'Saw Pearson,' Alfred wrote in his diary for January 4, 1893. 'He seemed very anxious for some sort of co-operation between the two firms.' On January 13 Harold wrote to Alfred: 'Pearson called today. No hint of pecuniary embarrassment.' While Alfred Harmsworth did not believe that 'Missing Words' had been specially profitable to any publisher—advertisers had not responded to the temporarily increased circulations—the competition had ensured Pearson's future. His pink-covered weekly now held its place alongside the green-covered *Tit-Bits* and the orange-covered *Answers* in the important front-of-the-counter position on the bookstalls, a familiar trio of the lower middle-class scene, and of railway travel, through thirty years.

*   *   *

'The father's vision of the Bench and the Woolsack may not be fulfilled. There is, perhaps, a grain of comfort in the fact that his son's venture earns enough money not only to pay the Lord Chancellor's salary but that of ten judges into the bargain.' The quotation is from a trade journal which in 1893 surveyed with boasted exactitude the Harmsworth achievements up to that time. It was responsible for the statement that *Answers* had shown no sign of becoming a success until Harold Harmsworth was brought in to take charge of the business side. 'He then found the firm in a semi-bankrupt condition . . . but soon put it on a sound and paying basis.' Writing to Alfred, Harold spurned the comment as 'very silly and one which I can understand caused you to anathematize. There are many obvious mistakes but this one is nonsense—very.' The implication of 'semi-bankrupt' was hardly justified, since the possibility existed of Beaumont being prepared to come to the rescue; moreover, there were signs of improvement at the time of Harold's arrival on the staff. Loyal and modest though it was of Harold to disclaim the credit, his part in the business at that stage was probably decisive and indispensable. He had his brother's full confidence. In the later years Sutton would stand in that relationship. For the present, it was undeniably Harold's restraining hand that was steering the company firmly on its course. His outstanding service consisted of eliminating waste and getting things done more cheaply than before. No detail was too trivial for his scrutiny. The price paid for paper, the costliest item in their outgoings, was thought to be less than that paid by any comparable concern. George Newnes Limited, a business of similar character and size, did not show nearly the same rate of profit to turnover.

Harold Harmsworth's realism balanced Alfred's buoyancy. Harold was a human gyroscope, steadying the momentum of the business. He saw that the clue to their success was in buying raw material at the lowest possible price and selling it at a profit in processed form. His financial keenness was capable of exasperating Alfred. The profits for 1893 were over £30,000. Studying one week's accounts for *Answers*, then approaching the 400,000 circulation level, Harold complained that the cost of over-set matter was thirty shillings: 'Will you caution the Literary Department?' Alfred had arranged that members of the staff should be paid the paper's ordinary rate for any articles or stories contributed by them in their spare time. Harold demanded that they should work at half-rates. 'I think that by revision of these payments a sum of £20 a week might be saved.'

It was by such sharp-eyed economies, such unremitting concern for the safety of the business, that Harold was able to write to Alfred on September 1, 1893: 'I have banked for you today £10,466 13s. 4d. There will be a little more to bank in a day or two.' Alfred had never had so much money. Summing up in 1892 the results of their four years in business together, Alfred had written in a prominently displayed article in *Answers*: 'During 1889 my brother, Mr Harold Sidney Harmsworth, left the Civil Service to join *Answers*, of which he has since become business manager. Though his work is not of the showy nature which meets the public eye, his financial abilities and sound business judgment have helped *Answers* to obtain much greater financial prosperity than it would otherwise have reached.'

Alfred, then, was the journalistic genius, Harold the man of business; in their circumstances, an unassailable combination. On the surface they fitted neatly together in a partnership of intuitiveness with practical common sense. Alfred was a creator, Harold an organizer. Their temperaments were displayed in their conspicuously different handwriting, Alfred's oblique, restless and imperative. Harold's clear, neat and clerk-like.

Below, there were materials of conflict in the unconscious gambling instincts of the one and the nervous fears of the other. Alfred was aflame with ideas that were to emblazon the Harmsworth name across the sky. Harold was incapable of any such excitements. He did not share Alfred's view of the importance and permanency of the kind of publishing they were engaged in. He considered it essentially an ephemeral form of trading and believed that they were wise to grab—his favourite word in that context—as much money as possible as quickly as possible. As an expert of the balance sheet, he thought well of cash in hand. In his brother's uncomfortably frank attitude Alfred saw criticism of the quality of the publications which he alone had evolved. Harold's usual designation of them as 'rags' quite likely irritated him; at any rate, soon there were differences of opinion and policy between them. Their brother, Sir Leicester Harmsworth, wrote later that 'the great divergence, not to say cleavage', between the two elder brothers had begun to reveal itself as far back as 1892 to 1893. In 1892, for example, Harold stood out against Alfred in the matter of purchasing *Black & White*, an illustrated weekly with an unsatisfactory balance sheet which subsequently led to its being merged in *The Sphere*. He intervened successfully in more than one other proposal to acquire papers with a doubtful future.

The future Rothermere's part in the Harmsworth rise has not been disputed. That of the younger brothers who worked to consolidate the early achievements of Alfred and Harold has received less than fair notice. Surveying the growth of *Answers*, Alfred himself wrote in May 1892: 'In 1888 I stood alone with a little band of loyal adherents. In 1892 I have the assistance of my brothers, Harold Sidney Harmsworth, Cecil Bisshopp Harmsworth and Robert Leicester Harmsworth.' Not long afterwards, he told an interviewer: 'My progress, or whatever you like to call it, is to be attributed to good fortune, hard work, the help of most able brothers and a loyal and enthusiastic band of workers.' They in their turn accepted their eldest brother as the dominating force at all times, then and later. He it was whose ideas meant most to the business, whose editorial flair was its greatest asset, whose leadership frequently seemed inspired. In the Fleet Street precincts, the younger brothers came under the rule of Harold as manager of the firm. He required them to conform as strictly to office regulations as other members of the staff. He wrote a note to Alfred: '18th January, 1892.—Will you send that letter to Cecil and Leicester that I suggested? The points are: 1. Time of arriving at the office. 2. Half an hour for lunch. 3. Must not leave the office before 6 p.m., unless on business.'

★   ★   ★

Quickening their pace, the Harmsworths experimented with an all-fiction

Answers Supplement, sold separately from the parent paper, and when it failed after a few months' run they called it *Home Sweet Home*, sought by means of it to popularize Bible reading, and showed that in publishing nerve is as vital as capital and ideas. The paper provided the early editorial training of a man who was to become influential as a pioneer of the half-tone block printing which brought in the era of the picture paper. His name was Arkas Sapt, an unpredictable Fleet Street personality who left his mark on newspaper history without gaining for himself the security or the recognition his talents deserved. Harold Harmsworth complained about Sapt: 'His notions are eccentric.' Alfred, whose nominee Sapt was, declined to be moved by the criticism. He kept Sapt on the staff, with consequences that were important in later and more spectacular developments of the business.

The combined sales of the firm's publications had increased by forty per cent in a year, standing at the total of 1,473,000 in June 1893. It was a circulation Niagara, with a swelling flood of receipts. Exactly twelve months earlier an announcement on page one of *Answers* had denied rumours that the proprietors were planning a public flotation. 'The statements have no foundation whatever.' In fact, Harold had several times urged his brother to assent to a public flotation. He raised the matter again in a letter written during his honeymoon in Scotland, he having married Lilian Share, the eighteen-year-old daughter of George Wade Share, a City hardware merchant, of Forest Holme, Queen's Road, Forest Hill. Romance had to make way for the reflection that 'there is an almost unlimited supply of money waiting for suitable investment. There are several reasons why we should not hesitate.' One of them, perhaps, was the successful flotation of George Newnes Limited. Concerning that event, Harold had written to Alfred: 'The actual price he [Newnes] will receive for his business I figure out at between £600,000 and £700,000.'

There were several reasons, too, for caution. The Liberator frauds of that year, bringing into prominence the name of Jabez Balfour, had caused investors to be shy even of Government securities. Industry, especially in the North, was disturbed by strikes and there were hungry mouths in Lancashire. London business houses were involved in a series of Australian bank crashes. The general mood of uncertainty dipped into depression at the news of the ramming of the Mediterranean flagship *Victoria*, with a calamitous loss of life. The Harmsworths were advised to postpone their flotation. For once, Harold was impervious to pessimism. Alfred wrote in his diary for May 2, 1893: 'Harold and I discussed whether or not we should form a limited company of our business, with a view to paying off the mortgage and paying for our new printing machinery.'

In June 1893, Answers Limited (changed two years later to Answers Publications Limited) was formed. In a passing reference to the paper's brief successful history and glowing future, its founder drew attention to the fact that 'of all the hundreds of papers that have appeared since we issued *Answers* in 1888, only one of a similar kind remains. A few linger on in a bankrupt or semi-bankrupt condition, but the majority have disappeared long ago.' The capital required to take over the copyright and goodwill of *Answers* was put at £275,000, of which 125,000 7 per cent preference shares of £1 each and 50,000 ordinary £1 shares were offered to the public. The first directors were Alfred and Harold Harmsworth, who undertook to receive no salaries or commissions until earnings of £40,000 had been reached in a year, Dargaville Carr, and Robert Leighton, husband and writing partner of Marie Connor Leighton. Carr telegraphed jubilantly to his Dublin relatives: *Answers shares real jam*. The prospectus was cast in the tone of patronizing idealism characteristic of its time. 'From this day forth *Answers* will be known as a Co-operative Company.' The shares were offered in particular to wholesale and retail newsagents, stationers, booksellers, 'and their families and assistants': all were invited to invest in a business which could boast 'a rate of progress probably unexampled in the history of the periodical Press'. It was not less sound business strategy because it induced cynical comment about the expectation that newsagents who bought the shares would give a preferential display to the Harmsworth publications.

New offices were opened at 24 Tudor Street. 'I am rather sorry that we have been obliged to leave historic Fleet Street,' Alfred told his readers. 'Fleet Street has for centuries been regarded as "the highway of letters" in London, but at present it is rather more than full up . . . the newspaper world has overflowed into other streets in the immediate neighbourhood.' He added: 'The present habitation of *Answers* presents a very cheerful appearance and those who have heard terrible tales of the dens in which London editors perform their work would be not a little astonished at the brightness and comfort of the interior of *Answers* offices, Tudor Street.' The editor's room was described in *The World* as being 'prettily decorated and hung with Hollyer's reproductions of Rossetti and Burne Jones'. It was reached by an exceptionally deep staircase, with the door of the editor's room opening directly on to it. 'Makes it easier for me to kick people down,' Alfred said. A caller, Henry Leach, the golf writer, thought the editor's room sombre. At one end of it, curtained off, Sutton had his desk. Leach said that Sutton 'seemed all pins and needles, instant in the service of the restless and enormously energetic young head of the concern'. Sutton had just married. Sending him congratulations, a friend named Manning, who became a doctor, wrote: 'I was talking of you to my wife. I said that if I had a room full of sovereigns and had to go on a long journey, I would not hesitate to entrust you with the key. What is more, I would not count the sovereigns.' Sutton valued the tribute. He kept the letter all his days. His loyalty matched his honesty. He spent his summer holidays of those years near Broadstairs, so that he might be at hand if 'Mr Alfred' needed him.

The moustache crop at 24 Tudor Street was lush: the young men of the period chose to look older and, as they thought, wiser than their years. 'Mr Harold' and 'Mr Cecil' led the movement. 'Mr Alfred' remained outside it, his classical features requiring no embellishment. They were remarked on in *The World* at that time: 'A firm, powerful face, despite its youthful character, abundant masses of light brown hair shading a broad brow, with a strong, square lower jaw.' Leach said that he 'spoke rapidly, in short and somewhat jerky sentences, with a manner of decision', and his wide-set eyes had 'a peculiar attraction'. He was surrounded by men of his generation; the emphasis was decidedly on youth. Young, Small, Sutton, Sumpter, Linforth, Haydon, Garrish, Whitefoord, Birnage, Anderson, were all in their twenties and all grew up with the business to become its managers, editors and directors. The women were young and zestful too; for them it was an adventure to be out in the world, apart from the excitements of working with the all-conquering Harmsworths. Jean Skinner, Maud Bown, Ethel Maycock, Rose Logan, Lily Dibben, look out of the pages of an early pamphlet about the business with eyes that appear to be fixed on a resplendent star. Habitually, proudly, they spoke and wrote not simply of *Answers* but of 'Mr Alfred Harmsworth's *Answers*'. To them he was 'Alfred the Great'.

Women office workers then were a London novelty and social convention did not allow them to lunch out at restaurants patronized mainly by men. The *Answers* young ladies had their lunch in the office, behind a screen. One of them, the former Miss Ethel Maycock (Mrs Sumpter), remembered that during an *Answers* competition 'a Harmsworth younger brother' picked up a sack full of competition entries from readers and emptied it over the head of Whitefoord, Harold Harmsworth's secretary. The elder Harmsworths were angry because it was press day and office routine was upset. They made their younger brother go down on hands and knees and sort out several thousand scattered letters because some editorial correspondence had been lost among them. As a result, the staff was kept behind until ten o'clock that night. All the competition correspondence was thereafter dealt with at another address.

A subsidiary company was formed in 1893 primarily to take over the firm's printing work. Alfred and Harold were in instant accord about naming it The Geraldine Press, after their mother. It enabled them to expand their already huge weekly periodical circulations. New boys' papers had been launched: *The Wonder* (1892), *The Marvel* (1893). They were quickly followed by *Union Jack*, reviving a title with which G. A. Henty had unsuccessfully tried his luck some time before, and *Boys' Friend*.

In the pages of *The Marvel* 'Sexton Blake, Detective', began a career of fifty years as the office-boys' Sherlock Holmes. *Union Jack* undertook to publish 'only pure, healthy stories'. Both papers were advertised as 'one more nail in the coffin of the penny dreadful'. Crusading with its stable companions against 'unhealthy literature', *The Marvel* hit hard at the sensationalism of the more scurrilous 'juveniles', but the main weight of the Harmsworths' attack was delivered in the *Boys' Friend*, which called the writers who contributed to the baser sorts of paper 'beer-swilling wretches' and condemned them not only for the kind of work they did but for the surroundings in which they did it, allegedly public-houses and the kitchens of common lodging-houses. There was equally harsh criticism of a practice which Alfred Harmsworth had himself been a party to as editor of *Youth*, under William Ingram of *The Illustrated London News*, that of buying up old blocks of illustrations and having articles and stories written round them. The *Boys' Friend* professed, also, a strong distaste for the short paragraphs, 'of at most five lines', which were a feature of the 'penny dreadful' writing technique. Yet the short paragraph had been an important and perhaps vital fact of the Harmsworth publishing success.

Answers broke new fiction ground by publishing the first of its serials to have war as a theme, a reflection of the rising tide of twentieth-century nationalism and of the armament rivalries that would presently divide the world. The paper disavowed any political line but the story, called *The Poisoned Bullet*, had been planned by Alfred Harmsworth and William le Queux, its author, to 'promote public interest in the idea of a larger Navy'. A treaty had been negotiated between France and Russia and the visit of the Russian Fleet to Toulon in 1894 gave new force to speculations about when, rather than where, a world war would break out. *The Poisoned Bullet* assumed that it would be in 1897, the belligerents those two countries against Great Britain. When the serial had been running three weeks, Harold Harmsworth complained to his brother: 'The instalments do not contain enough war scenes. I should cut down to a minimum the hero and heroine's part and give plenty of battles, naval and land. So far, three long instalments have appeared and the only execution done is the bombardment of Newhaven and Brighton.' Very soon there came instalments headed 'The Battle of Beachy Head', and 'The Massacre of Eastbourne'. Later, it was the turn of Birmingham and Manchester to face the foe. 'The provinces were awe-stricken.' Everywhere, 'the carnage was terrific'.

Announcing the serial, Alfred had quoted from a leading article in *The Times* of November 16, 1893: 'The question of Naval Defence and its unquestionable sufficiency is a question which vitally affects every citizen of this country, and most of all its poorest citizens. There would be no question of "a living wage" if we once lost command of the sea.' In the issues of *Answers* containing the early instalments of the serial, he 'boxed in' quotations from speeches or statements made by leading naval authorities, among them several retired admirals. They stressed the dangers which *The Poisoned Bullet* was dramatizing with such lurid success.

The propaganda reflected the earlier symptoms of a more potent general fear and no doubt helped to exacerbate it, a circumstance which incurred the censure of later historians who saw in it the makings of an enmity which was to erupt in the great wars to come. The Pan-German League had been founded four years before, in 1890, the year of Bismarck's dismissal. There were leading Germans who made no secret of desiring an end to the political appeasement of Great Britain. Long before that, in 1870, the Positivist philosopher, Frederick Harrison, had asked: 'Why are we to take the future freedom and peacefulness of Germany on trust? Prussian rule has always been defiant of public opinion.' Earlier still, in the 1830s, Bulwer Lytton wrote in his *Pilgrims of the Rhine*: 'The ideal is passing slowly away from the German mind. The memories that led their grandsires to contemplate, will urge the youth of the next generation to dare and to act.' In making his paper one of the mouthpieces of a growing sense of uneasiness, young Alfred Harmsworth was again following a trend rather than initiating it, and it would have been unrealistic to expect to find him, at his age, demonstrating the wisdom and restraint of older men. He showed at least common sense in taking the opportunity to rebuke, in print, those who 'possess a ridiculous arrogance by which we are led to underrate our opponents'.

Lord Roberts to Alfred Harmsworth:

> Grove Park,
> Kingsbury,
> Middlesex.
> March 26, 1894.

Dear Sir,—I entirely concur with you in thinking it most desirable to bring home to the British public in every possible way the dangers to which the nation is exposed unless it maintains a Navy and Army sufficiently strong and well organised to meet the defensive requirements of the Empire.

> Believe me,
> Yours faithfully,
> ROBERTS.

★   ★   ★

For Alfred Harmsworth this was a period of fluctuating health. There was much resorting to bed, 'feeling not at all well', 'suffering from overwork', *vide* the diary. There were many attacks of faintness, unaccounted for.

There were recurring headaches, frequently noted. Harold was concerned about him. He wrote to Alfred: 'I hope you are taking care of yourself. I should lay by for a few days, if I were you, and let the business go hang.' He was medically advised to take a course of treatment 'lasting six or eight weeks and to go abroad for at least three months'. Taking a precaution uncongenial to most men of his years, he made his will. Before doing so, he consulted a solicitor about what might happen if he did not make a will. From his youth up it was observed that he often looked tired, while showing no physical awareness of it. A hidden factor of *malaise* seemed to be a constant of his life. The family assumption was that his health had been undermined by the strenuous cycling feats. Later medical consideration of one of his health crises of those years has suggested that the diagnosis should have been rheumatic fever, with its sometimes baleful after-effects. A more than ordinary severe attack of influenza had laid him low not long after he had started *Answers*. It left him with a deep-seated nervous concern not to risk that form of infection again. 'It is nothing to laugh about', he said severely to a member of the staff who suggested a prize for the best influenza joke.

He was now much at Elmwood, going to bed early, rising late. 'No sense in getting up until the day has been well aired', he would say. Daytime callers would find him lying on a sofa, his head resting amid heaped pillows, the floor around strewn with newspapers and magazines and proofs and sheets of his scribbled notes. The implication that he was resting was solemnly respected by those closest to him. Visitors were not always so ready to understand. Some saw in it a gesture of self-importance in a young man. But the reclining habit, to which he became more addicted as time went by, appears to have expressed his sense of a need to guard his strength. His accountant, Layton Bennett, whom he had first met at the Priory Lawn Tennis Club at West Hampstead, remembered that at the Pandora Road house, when they had been dining, Alfred rose from the table and flung himself at full length on a sofa. 'Excuse this,' he said. 'I always have to rest after my evening meal.' Later, he said that his after-meal rests were made necessary by 'flushings of blood to the head'. He sometimes gave the same excuse for his irritable outbursts. From the sofas of villadom, he graduated to luxuriously deep armchairs, which were as familiar a part of the furnishing of his offices as of his homes. 'The Harmsworths are squatters', their mother used to say. Alfred's reserves of good health were never brimming over, and often he appeared to mistrust them. He had hypochondriacal moods, possibly associated with the low blood pressure which was part of his medical history. He experimented with various self-treatments involving fasting, dieting and similar disciplines. When he had been in occupation of Elmwood for some months, a friend commended to him the virtues of sea water for the morning bath.

Orders were given to the gardeners to fetch, every day, a supply of fresh sea water from the North Foreland shore, five hundred yards across the fields. The bracing effect had been less than was forecast. It was found that the gardeners had become tired of sea-water hauling. They substituted well water and soaked seaweed in it.

Alfred's spells of semi-invalidism sent him in search of the restorative pleasures of fishing in lake and stream, a hobby of his boyhood. His diary of the early years at Elmwood mentions many fishing excursions, always in fresh water, always with zest, except for an inhibition about eating what he had caught. In *Answers* he printed a letter, suspiciously provocative, condemning fishing as a cruel sport. He had a share, with Comyns Carr, the barrister and dramatic critic, and Haddon Chambers, the playwright, in 'an ugly little pillbox of a cottage' by the railway line alongside Piscator's river Lea, which was in fact hardly more than a stream. Mrs Comyns Carr thought him 'quiet and extraordinarily modest', though success was already well within his grasp. She heard him say to her husband about the growth of *Answers*: 'Yes, I seem to have a nose for the thing. I don't know where it comes from.' He had a schoolboy relish for a bobbing float and liked to show by apt quotation that he was well acquainted with *The Compleat Angler*, which appears in the design for his bookplate. Landing his first salmon, a twenty-pounder from the Tay at Cargill, Perthshire, in 1896, he was moved by excitement to fall on his knees and kiss it. Tender-minded as he was about eating the fish he caught, there was in his nature a contradictory vein of juvenile cruelty. It was said that in his bathroom at Elmwood he had for a brief period an aquarium with two compartments, in one side of which were goldfish, in the other a young pike, and that when the mood was on him he would raise the glass partition and watch the ensuing panic.

When work became more pressing and he had less time for travelling to distant waters, he caused a pool to be made in the garden at Elmwood and stocked with fish. Its sporting scope was extremely limited and a visitor was amused to see on the adjoining grass an apparatus of rods, lines, reels, landing nets, folding chairs and sandwich tins, as if for an elaborate expedition. Every time Alfred took a fish from the pool he threw it back. The same visitor wrote: 'Fish hooks haunt this house. You are afraid of finding them in your bed.' What was not realized even by some of those nearest him was that the fish pool was also an insurance against fire, of which he had an abnormal dread. His interest in fishing gave him a liking for anglers whose prowess was greater than his own, subject to their being congenial in less specialized ways. He valued the company of men like R. B. Marston, editor of the *Fishing Gazette*, G. A. B. Dewar, author of various books on outdoor pursuits and an accomplished dry-fly fisherman, and C. H. Cook, who wrote as 'John Bickerdyke', an authority on both deep sea and fresh water fishing. Another of his more constant companions of the rod in later years was a compositor friend, G. H. Messer, who helped him to improve his private fishing stream in Hampshire.

Among the visitors to Elmwood at that time was Markwick, the barrister, who had so unluckily for himself and his family severed his business connection with the Harmsworths. Alfred wrote in the diary, July 12, 1893: 'Had interview with Markwick at which we made up our differences.' A few days after that he went to Markwick's house at Norwood; and they also dined together at the Savoy Hotel in London. On September 22 both Alfred and Mary Harmsworth were Markwick's guests at Norwood and a little later in the year Markwick was one of the guests at a dinner party given at the Savoy by the Harmsworths. There is no reason to doubt this evidence of harmony restored, while there is reason to print it because of a belief in the Markwick family circle that Markwick had been wrongfully deprived of his interest in the Harmsworth business. Subsequent correspondence between Alfred Harmsworth and Markwick, when they renewed their old friendship after a long later lapse, provides no support for any such conclusion. Hoping no doubt to resume touch with journalistic fortune, Edward Markwick later started one or two journals of his own. One of his ventures was *The Newspaper Review*, which had a short life. Alfred invited him to write for *Answers* and he was its regular contributor on legal matters for nearly twenty years.

At the end of that year, 1893, Alfred wrote in the diary: 'This has been a good year for us in many ways. The circulation of our papers has not increased much, though we established a new one which promises to be a success, making seven in all, and we have practically completed our printing works. My investments have also considerably increased. I have settled Elmwood and £21,000 on my wife, £51,000 on my mother and have, in addition to the settlement, invested in the printing works and other securities something like £18,000.' He omitted to note that earlier in the year he had been attracted to cycling journalism again. He had put money into a new paper in which R. J. McCredy, well known as an Irish racing cyclist, and Charles Sisley, former editor of *Cycling* and of *The Rambler*, were associated editorially. Sisley had started a paper, *Up-To-Date*, which has a place in journalistic history as the first halfpenny illustrated paper. Doomed to fail, it may not have been without its significance for Alfred Harmsworth, with his keenly acquisitive instinct for new publishing possibilities.

A contributor who was much at Elmwood that year noted in him the symptoms of an occupational disability of periodical publishers and editors. 'He was usually ignorant of the day of the week and often, it seemed, quite uncertain which week of the month it was.' As editor of *Answers*, 'which appears on Tuesday with the following Saturday's date on it', the paper having gone to press three weeks in advance, he himself complained of the muddling effect of that publishing necessity. Probably it accounted for his habit of writing undated letters.

One of his later associates, H. W. Wilson, who was often at Elmwood, had no doubt that those early years there were the happiest of Alfred's life. 'He had not overworked himself, as he did later. He had the resilience of triumphant youth. He did not torment himself with care. It really seemed as if he had a magical power to command success. Everything about him prospered and he was touchingly eager to make others successful with him.' He cherished Elmwood for more than pride of possession, as the first visible mark of his great good fortune. It gave him a restorative peace which he would never find anywhere else. His diary references to it show an attachment that grew with the years, though the house was incurably damp in winter—the piano needed tuning every spring. Late in his life, his thoughts went constantly back to the garden in which he spent so many happy days. He liked to recall breakfast in summer under the copper beech on the lawn, the table heaped with peaches from the green-houses and the fine fresh air coming off the sea.

He was taking fencing lessons and learning to play the mandolin, a romantic period craze. He was going again to Sylvan Club meetings. He was giving sittings to Seymour Lucas, R.A., who had painted his father. 'My portrait much criticized', he wrote on private view day at the Royal Academy of 1894. The artist had perhaps made him look too proudly sure of his destiny.

Chapter Seven

The Siege of Portsmouth

'IT is not a venture we should tackle yet. If the magazine fell flat the loss would be very great.' Harold Harmsworth was being pressed by Alfred for co-operation in starting opposition to *The Strand Magazine* (1891–1950), from which Newnes was gaining personal prestige as well as professional success. Alfred's enthusiasm for his latest idea, to be called *The Harmsworth Magazine*, was temporarily diverted by another venture which had suggested itself to him during a wet day's fishing at Bricket Wood, near Watford. A title flashed into his mind—*The Sunday Companion*. He saw instantly what it might be, a new kind of journal for Sunday reading, a paper which would not attach itself to any of the denominations, but which would promote the Christian faith in general and, with that proviso, be all things to all men. 'A task for the angel Gabriel himself,' said its first editor. Alfred Harmsworth's religious sincerity was as casual and as conventional as that of most young men. He had retained a genuine if undefined respect for religious principles as the imprint of his upbringing. His brother Leicester said that he 'could safely be described perhaps not as devout or devoted, but certainly a member of the Church of England'. He often went to the village church at St. Peters. For many years he attended the Easter morning service there with his mother. In 1931 Wickham Steed mentioned in a *Week-End Review* article that Alfred Harmsworth, as a youth, had enlisted in the Salvation Army. Commissioner T. H. Kitching, of the Salvation Army, is quoted in St. John Ervine's biography of General Booth, as having heard him say to Booth: 'You know, I was once one of you.' The story was not known to any member of the Harmsworth family. Inquiries at Salvation Army headquarters in London have produced no confirmation of what may have been the result of a passing adolescent mood. Alfred admired the work of the Salvation

Army. He was for many years a subscriber to its funds. When casual labour was wanted for his businesses his standing order was that the Salvation Army should always be given the first chance of supplying it.

While he was unlikely to have shown much intellectual curiosity in the currently spreading waves of agnostic doubt, or to have been specially sensitive to the distresses which they caused in many hearts, he may have seen in *The Sunday Companion* an insurance policy against the daring combativeness of the new scientific spirit. Such a paper would gloss his enterprises generally with a moral respectability which might be a business asset, an endorsement of his 'clean journalism' policy. It would impart the touch of popular appeal to a branch of publishing which, with but one or two exceptions, had long been wanting in editorial novelty and freshness. The first issue of *The Sunday Companion* was dated July 1894. On its front page it bore a message: 'I wish your new unsectarian paper every success.— Samuel Smiles.' That celebrated professional moralist was interviewed inside the paper, which chiefly reported his interest in mechanics' institutes. There was the inevitable article headed 'At Church with the Queen'. It was decorated by skimpy little line drawings showing Her Majesty seated in lonely eminence in front of a congregation. Much of the material might have come from *Answers*; some of the paragraphs, under 'Wise & Witty', from *Comic Cuts*. Turning to the last page, readers were confronted by a full-page black-letter advertisement for Beecham's Pills—'Worth A Guinea A Box'.

By the Harmsworth standards, *The Sunday Companion* was not an immediate success. For some time it showed no sign of making a profit. Harold Harmsworth urged his brother to stop publication—'knife it', was his advice. From the beginning there was sectarian criticism. The Rev. Michael Baxter, more usually known as 'Prophet Baxter', who had gained a large circulation with his *Christian Herald* by periodically predicting the end of the world, foretold impending doom for *The Sunday Companion*: 'It won't last six months.' When that forecast was falsified, there were imitators to be fought off. Arthur Pearson, of *Pearson's Weekly*, came out with the *Sunday Reader*. Roberston Nicoll, whose *British Weekly* dealt with world politics as well as religion, started *The Christian Budget*. A firm which published a comic paper called *Sketchy Bits* launched *Illustrated Christian News*.

Before long, Harmsworth's paper remained alone in the arena with Baxter's *Christian Herald* and *Horner's Penny Stories*, a fortnightly publication with a religious tone. For *The Sunday Companion* he engaged as editor, Hartley Aspden, a Newnes man who had been a *Manchester Guardian* reporter. Aspden's early journalism had taken him to denominational gatherings, the congresses of the Established Church, the meetings of the Baptist and Congregational Unions, the synods of the Presbyterians. 'I knew what divided as well as united them.' He kept a particularly watchful eye on the Salvation Army's *War Cry*, which had been running several years and used lurid headlines and an American-style make-up. *Sunday Companion* posters were often startling. One of the earliest showed St. Paul's Cathedral attacked by aircraft dropping bombs into fire and devastation below. It bore the inscription: 'In that Great and Terrible Day.' Novel circulation schemes were tried. Jordan water, imported from Palestine 'by Turkish permission', was distributed with a certificate of authenticity for the christening of readers' babies. American organs were offered to missionaries. A musical instrument called the 'Harp of David' was another of the prizes. Medals were struck for Sunday School teachers' long service. Nearly one hundred thousand children were enrolled in a 'Bible Band' and given a *Sunday Companion* badge to wear. Out of this impetus to good works there came a charitable undertaking called 'The Barefoot Mission', which supplied boots and clothing to the children of London's neediest poor. 'There are no salaried officers and no expensive establishment,' announced the Harmsworth papers in unison. 'Everything is done out of love for the poor, suffering little ones.' Soon the results of this concerted publicity overtaxed *The Sunday Companion* organization and 'The Barefoot Mission' was taken over by the Ragged School Union, whose leader, John Kirk, had the startling experience of being knighted on the spot by King Edward VII in the course of a conversation about his self-sacrificing labours.

In two years *The Sunday Companion* justified its founder's inspiration and its editor's keen sense of salesmanship by showing a profit of £2,000. In ten years it was making £20,000 a year. Later, it touched £30,000 a year, with its circulation standing at 500,000 a week, equalling that of all the leading denominational papers combined. Apart from the need for holding off new competitors, which it had been successful in doing, *The Sunday Companion* was followed up from inside the office in accordance with the Harmsworth master plan. A batch of similar papers was invented: *Sunday Stories*, instantly popular; *Sunday Circle; Home Companion; Golden Stories*, the last-named using the early work of a writer who became a figure of the world fiction market, Ethel M. Dell. It was as part of this scheme of protective expansion that *Horner's Penny Stories* took Alfred Harmsworth's attention. Once a four-page Gospel tract, it was by now a thriving paper of twenty-four pages, published every other week. Thanks to the extraordinary magnetism of a writer using the pen-name of 'Fannie Eden', some of its issues reached a sale of 400,000 copies. Hartley Aspden was commissioned to negotiate a purchase for which the Harmsworth shareholders were asked to find £50,000. He turned the paper into a weekly, exploited the infallible pen-name, and doubled the revenue. Another money-making property had been found by the Harmsworths.

English readers do not make a show of their religious loyalties and these papers were never a conspicuous part of the ubiquitous bookstall trade. Their sales were largely conducted on the basis of direct delivery by the newsagents to the homes of the people. Alfred Harmsworth and the men and women around him both discovered and created a great new public and it could hardly be otherwise than that the influence of their ideas and energies was a contribution to morals rather than to faith. It was with more than merely acquisitive satisfaction that presently they were able to flaunt across the front cover of *The Sunday Companion*: 'Largest Circulation of any Religious Paper in the World.' Of an ambitious and unpopular editor of one of the Harmsworth 'religious' journals it was long remembered that his layout for the cover of a Christmas issue included two lozenge-shaped illustrations, one captioned 'Our Saviour' and the other, alongside it, 'Our Editor'. A rival editor of the group ensured that a 'pull' of the cover appeared on Alfred Harmsworth's desk. 'Splendid!' Alfred exclaimed on seeing it, bringing his fist down with a bang. 'Now I can get rid of him,' and did.

The Harmsworth publishing domain was being consolidated at other points, particularly among the 'juveniles'. *Pluck Library* and the *Boys' Home Journal* had been added to the list, with results that by no means alleviated Harold Harmsworth's worries. Despite sometimes alarmingly fluctuating circulations, the papers in this class sold in their hundreds of thousands and yielded their quota of profits. The editorial policy was the same in each instance: the cultivation of physical fitness in the young, the encouragement of adventure abroad and enterprise at home. In all of them the bugle-call of patriotism was loudly sounded, pride in Great Britain and the Empire. 'No more penny dreadfuls!' was long the ruling theme and in at least one of the new Harmsworth boys' journals it was stated in those words. Students might find the period more faithfully reflected in these papers than in many adult publications, in that they expressed the moral ideas and social interests that were thought to be best suited to the juvenile tastes of the time. The quite extraordinary success which attended most of those new ventures enabled Alfred Harmsworth to detach himself more completely from the detailed editorial supervision which he had been giving to his publications. They now numbered thirteen. In Harold he had an extremely able deputy who could be depended on to keep an unrelenting watch on costs and circulations. In Cecil, Leicester and Hildebrand, he had no less eager partners, who were supported in their turn by a keen staff consisting entirely of members of the same youthful generation. All were given a share in the profits as well as salaries; generally, sixpence for every thousand of circulation up to 100,000 copies and a shilling per thousand

Harold Harmsworth (later the first Viscount Rothermere), aged about thirty

Elmwood, St Peters, Thanet

after. The basic salary averaged £5 a week for each paper. Between them they devised and produced a stream of publications which, by intellectual standards, fell far short of their opportunity to shape the future while having an undoubted influence upon it. Alfred Harmsworth was not an architect of the new democracy. He was one of its master-builders. Projecting and editing his series of periodicals over seven or eight years gave him an intimate and perceptive knowledge of the public taste and of what, especially, the average man expected and was not getting from his newspapers. The experience and insight which he gained from his proprietorship of domestic, juvenile, religious and, particularly, women's papers, were to be imprinted deeply and lastingly on a more influential part of the Fourth Estate.

★   ★   ★

A visit, his first, to the United States of America combined a search for journalistic inspiration in New York with tarpon fishing in Florida, which latter experience he drew on for the chapter he afterwards wrote for *The Badminton Library*, and for articles in the *Fishing Gazette*. He owed much to American journalism. The first issues of *Answers* had drawn freely on American newspapers and magazines for articles and paragraphs. They continued to be a fertile source of editorial ideas. He paid his respects to several publishers, walked through their offices and printing plant, looked with a particularly keen eye into their distribution methods. He studied the New York newspapers with close comparative interest. Lunching with representatives of the International News Company, he was handed a telegram: *Answers* 350,000. It was a figure with which to make an impression in that *milieu* of mainly local circulations. He was not over-impressed by this first sight of New York. He was surprised to see 'mud in the streets'. His visit was not reported. Hardened to spectacular personal success, the New York interviewers ignored him.

Returning to London, he was met at Euston by his mother, waiting in her smart new carriage-and-pair. His talk was of the addition which he was going to make to the house at St. Peters, a building in the style of the American wooden-frame houses he had seen from the train during the journey from New York to Florida. It was to be a retreat in which he saw himself working in isolation from the domestic and social routine of Elmwood. He gave the order for its construction within the next three months. Known thereafter as 'the bungalow', it finally consisted of a large central room with two box-like rooms adjoining, the whole fronted by a veranda. The bungalow became the setting for activities of sometimes far-reaching consequence, the nerve centre of Alfred Harmsworth's world for years to come. In it he put the desk which had been almost the only piece of furniture in the Paternoster Square office where he had started *Answers*.

An American polar expedition was in preparation. Alfred knew about it before he left for New York and he had evidently given some thought to its being countered by a British effort along the same lines. A week or so before sailing, he had telegraphed to Archangel for news of a young traveller of his acquaintance, Frederick George Jackson, whom he knew to be keen to win the laurels of a successful explorer. Jackson had made adventurous journeys into the Australian outback and had crossed the frozen tundra of Siberia. Alfred Harmsworth returned from the United States apparently strengthened in his view that a British attempt to reach the North Pole should be made.

Not yet a proprietor of newspapers, he could hardly be charged with sponsoring a North Pole expedition as a 'stunt' in the interests of *Comic Cuts* or his women's papers, while *Answers* was an established success, needing for the present no new stimulus of publicity. 'The expedition is in no way connected with *Answers*,' he told that paper's readers. 'So far as I am concerned, it is a personal hobby', the possible cost of which had been the subject of an apprehensive note from Harold. Expedition headquarters had been opened at 119 Pall Mall. Its sponsor's interest in the undertaking was strong enough to draw him frequently away from his work in Fleet Street to help in the arrangements at what he called his 'Polar office'.

Jackson sailed in the *Windward* on July 12, 1894, taking with him as far as Archangel, Alfred Harmsworth's old friend, Herbert Ward, and Cutcliffe Hyne, who had been commissioned to write travel articles for the new Harmsworth magazine. Alfred was twenty-nine on July 15. For his birthday he went down to Cowes and was there 'sent for by Prince Henry of Battenberg and congratulated on the organization of the Polar expedition'. During their three years away, the party encountered 'two wild men in dirty rags, black with oil and soot, with long uncombed hair and shaggy beards'. One of them was Fridtjof Nansen. He and his companions had been wandering for nearly twelve months, trying to find a way out to Spitzbergen and home. In his book, *Farthest North*, Nansen made it clear that the Jackson-Harmsworth expedition had brought them aid only just in time. Describing the meeting in the solitudes, he recalled the 'exquisite pleasure' of a moment in which he smelt soap after being so long deprived of it.

Jackson's journeys were extensive and his long explorations important. They covered nearly 15 degrees of longitude and over eighty miles of latitude. In 1895, during a boat journey of great danger, he reached a bold ice-capped promontory of 2,000 feet which he named Cape Mary Harmsworth, after Alfred's wife. The expedition did not reach the Pole. It named its chief base Elmwood, and also added to the map the name of Alfred Harmsworth Island in the north of the Franz Josef group, the scene of its principal labours. Jackson was able to prove that the Franz Josef territory was not a land mass, as had been thought, but an archipelago of numerous small islands. Ice had deceived the earlier explorers. His geographical work was accompanied by valuable scientific observations and collections.

George Newnes was animated by a similar wish to see his country's prestige extended to the snowy wastes. His expedition to Antarctica in 1898 cost him £38,000. He remarked, with a shrug of resignation, that all he got out of it was 'one stuffed penguin'. His name, too, found a place on the Arctic charts. Alfred Harmsworth's trophies were a *Windward* lifeboat, which was put on show in the garden at Elmwood, St. Peters, and a stuffed Polar bear. 'That cost me thirty thousand pounds,' he used to tell visitors to Elmwood, where it stood in the hall. He presented *Windward* to Lieutenant (later Admiral) Robert Peary, of the United States Navy, for use in the preliminary surveys which led to his reaching the North Pole. By way of acknowledgment, he was made a member of the American Geographical Society.

Fridtjof Nansen to Alfred Harmsworth:

Godthaab,
Lysaker.
1st October, 1896.

Dear Mr Harmsworth,—Hearty thanks for your very kind letter. Certainly it is quite unnecessary to assure me that neither you nor any member of your expedition has used the word 'rescue' with reference to myself or my pleasant meeting with Mr Jackson. And, after all, if the word had been used what would it matter? I hope you do not think me so frivolous as to mind it.

I would have written to you long ago, as I feel I have so much to thank you for, having been your guest nearly two months, and having been treated with such a genuine English hospitality in the inhospitable North.

Yours sincerely,
FRIDTJOF NANSEN.

★   ★   ★

Alfred was beginning to establish a system of personal habits designed to increase efficiency: to see as few people as possible, to write as few letters as possible, to do no work after 9 p.m., and to start the day at 6.30 a.m. That was his expressed formula. 'The bungalow' supplied the conditions for carrying it out. Callers at the house, in person or by telephone, would be told unflinchingly that he was not in when he was only a couple of hundred yards away, in favouring temperatures bent over his desk in white silk pyjamas. Alfred Harmsworth, thus attired, trailing newspaper galley proofs, was a memory of many Elmwood visitors. Older acquaintances had recollections of seeing him make use of one of the first portable telephones, recalled as 'a massive piece of equipment about the size of a sewing-machine', which he lugged with Sisyphus labour from room to room as a demonstration of his primacy in the art of keeping in touch. He was continuing to experiment with the phonograph (not yet known as the gramophone) as an instrument of professional efficiency. Edmund Yates, founder of *The World*, went to Elmwood to hear Harmsworth using it for dictation purposes. He spoke into the long tubular horn of an Edison machine and his words were played back out of a comical confusion of overtones. Rapidly developing as a means of communicating more than talk, the talking machine became for him a perennial pleasure. His interest in it as a source of entertainment led him to publish the first regular reviews of new gramophone records. 'For this one act alone,' wrote Alfred Clarke, head of the H.M.V. company, 'the trade in general owes him a lasting debt of gratitude.'

Already the glow of the rising new century was becoming brighter over the horizon. Having helped to popularize the bicycle, with its incalculable social effects, Alfred Harmsworth told the readers of his papers that electricity was about to be a means of propulsion as well as of a more general system of lighting, that man's ancient dream of conquering the air would be realized sooner than they imagined, and quoted with approval, in an article on the new development of photography, Emerson's poetic second-sight: 'We make the sun paint our portraits now; bye-and-bye we shall organize the echoes as we now organize the shadows.' Neither did he fail to observe that the twentieth-century promise was threatened by forces more menacing than any the passing century had known. An *Answers* article, 'Why the Germans come to England', condensed in popular terms, in 1891, fears which would change the history of the world. Others of his contemporaries were not less eager to speed the march of time. None had more spectacular opportunities than young Alfred Harmsworth of expressing their impatience. Editorial prescience was varied by the valedictory mood. 'Ruskin Growing Old' an *Answers* heading announced. It epitomized the new generation's intolerance not of a lawgiver but of an age.

'Schemo Magnifico' had been accomplished in firm outline; the filling-in process could go on indefinitely, following the requirements of the market place. The situation of the firm was still being reported to Alfred Harmsworth almost daily by his brother Harold.

ANSWERS
Tudor Street, E.C.
20.7.94.

My dear Alfred,

Answers	335,000
Comic Cuts	425,000
Chips	282,000
Forget-Me-Not	141,000
Wonder	184,000
Home-Sweet-Home	66,500
Marvel	144,000
Union Jack	132,000
Sunday Companion	45,000

1,754,500

I hope that we shall be able to pay the same dividend next year and put £5,000 to reserve fund. To do this *Answers* circulation will have to keep up, and this is what I fear it may not do. A serious fall in *Answers* circulation would, from a dividend-paying point of view, place the Company in great difficulty. I have been looking at *Answers* last six numbers and it is certainly very bad.

'Mr Answers on a Tread Mill' and articles like it have been done time out of mind. There is not a corner in a prison with which readers are not now thoroughly acquainted. I think agitations like 'Britain for the Britons' are a mistake as they give the paper a quasi-political status which is not desirable.

Altogether I think *Answers* will need the most careful nursing during the next few months. It is in a perilous position.

Yours,
HAROLD.

Harold, the multi-millionaire in the making, was passing through one of his timid phases. He repeated to Alfred his opinion that *Answers*, the cornerstone of their undertakings, was 'in a distinctly parlous condition'. His fears were communicated in a number of letters to Alfred in 1894, a year which saw the family's fortunes spread out in a way that not even Alfred's buoyant imagination had foreseen.

There is no sign in Alfred's diary or letters that he shared his brother's pessimism at that time or let it influence his attitude to their fast-growing business. Soon, indeed, he would assert himself vigorously against it. Harold's impulse to 'knife' any paper of theirs which did not show a profit in sometimes a most unreasonably brief trial period was a matter for earnest discussion among the younger brothers of the firm. In later years Leicester Harmsworth wrote a memorandum on the subject.

It was one of the chief concerns of the younger members of the family (myself, Cecil, and Hildebrand) to dissuade Harold from these courses. If our arguments and appeals to him did not seem likely of success, we resorted to Alfred to exercise his final authority. Alfred was always with us in these matters. In this way the *Sunday Companion* was saved: a journal which produced great profits and which was the parent of other journals which produced good profits, but which would not have seen the light if the *Sunday Companion* had been 'knifed'. The same story has to be told about the *Boys' Friend* and the publications of which it was the parent. The *Boys' Friend* did not pay for some time. Harold insisted that it should be stopped and the editor discharged. However, his views were not allowed to prevail, fortunately for him and the rest of the business. *The World and His Wife* was killed, in my absence, as a result of this policy. *Forget-Me-Not*, one of the most promising and profitable of our journals, was set upon the path of extinction largely by Harold exercising his authority to have it printed on paper of almost indescribable poorness. If one wished to describe in a sentence the opposing tendencies in this matter, one would say that Alfred was a creator and Harold a cutting-downer. Harold's financial value to the business—very, very great value—was almost entirely due to his gift of cutting down, and getting things done cheaper than they had hitherto been done. No item in the business was too small for his eye in these matters.

Clashes of business judgment did not follow the brothers into the family circle, where they came under the authoritarian rule of their mother and were united in their devotion to her. B. W. Young remembered the 'minor squabbles' of those days in Tudor Street, and that Harold once refused to get out a balance sheet 'while Alfred behaves so rudely to me'. Such incidents were in the normal flux of temperament. Irreconcilable differences never arose, though the distance between some members of the family was greater than between others, as, for instance, between Alfred and Hildebrand in their later years. Cecil Harmsworth left this testimony: 'Alfred's attachment to his family clan was second only to his devotion to our mother. What concerned them, concerned him. Throughout his life he maintained an affectionate interest in all matters affecting their well-being and their advancement.'

For most of that summer of 1894 Alfred was at Elmwood, working, fishing, cycling, watching cricket, playing tennis, receiving visits from members of his editorial staffs, relishing the satisfaction of owning a kennel of pedigree Irish terriers and of being able to stroll through his own peach and orchid houses, and having recourse to what an enthusiastic neighbour described as 'the finest billiard-room in Thanet'. He did not care for billiards or any other game. He preferred strumming on his little yacht piano. It was a pleasant mode of life for a young man whose career had hardly begun. Molly Harmsworth had made an exceptionally comfortable home of Elmwood, though there were visitors who went away thinking that the attempt to reproduce, in the dining-room, the black-oak antiquity of Holyrood Palace was perhaps over-ambitious. Spreading palms graced the drawing-room. All round it were long, low bookshelves. The furniture was covered with scarlet flowered chintzes. Pink-shaded lamps stood on every bedside table.

Cecil and Leicester went off on a world tour in July, as part of their general education and to make business arrangements in Australia. They left on July 26 and the next morning Alfred worked for the first time in his newly-built bungalow in the garden. He had recently shown much pleasure, on a bird's-nesting ramble round his grounds, at finding a crumbling bit of flint wall in which time and ivy growth had made a recess giving a fine southward view across the meadows to the Channel. He had it shaped by a mason into what became known as his 'pulpit'. In the years that followed he was often seen standing there gazing out to sea.

As chairman of Answers Limited, presiding at the ordinary general meeting of the company in the Memorial Hall, Farringdon Street, London, on July 20, he had drawn attention to the success attending the publication of their two new papers for boys, *Union Jack* and *Marvel*.

It can safely be said for them that, in addition to being money-earners for the shareholders, they are doing excellent work in killing what was at one time a widespread cause of mischief, and even of crime. I refer, of course, to the 'penny dreadfuls', which, to my certain knowledge, have been steadily dying for the last few years. The unexpected appearance of the *Marvel* and *Union Jack* has given them a blow from which they will not, in the opinion of those competent to speak, recover.

To those shareholders for whom the moral aspects of publishing for the juvenile population were secondary to dividends, this class of paper was an attractive investment because the circulations were sustained by successive waves of new readers. The profits for 1894 were £30,059. The chairman announced a dividend of fifteen per cent.

Enjoying the pleasures of wealth, Alfred was already experiencing some of its embarrassments. Klein, the High Holborn music publisher who had brought out 'The Ellen Terry Waltz', was in financial difficulties: 'lent him £200'. An American named Christie called to discuss a gold-mining venture: 'he bored me with his endeavours to get finance'. His friend Mountmorres, now editing *The Artist*, 'came to ask me to help him in a difficulty, but I declined to give him any money'. W. E. Henley, the poet who edited the *National Observer* (originally the *Scots Observer*), wanted him to buy or finance that far from flourishing but virile weekly paper. An offer was made but nothing came of it. Of greater moment was the diary entry for August 15: 'Boyle, publisher of the "Westminster

Gazette", proposed to us that we should purchase "The Evening News & Post". Messrs. Tracy and Kennedy Jones came to see us on the subject and promised to inquire into the matter.'

'Schemo Magnifico' had not included developments outside the market for periodicals. Alfred Harmsworth may or may not have had his visions of wider domain. His brother Leicester believed that he had, that he was 'dreaming and planning to base his fame as a journalist, mainly, upon newspapers'. Earlier that year, using an intermediary, he had made inquiries about the chances of acquiring the *Islington Daily Gazette*, a London suburban paper; nothing had come of them. When the prospect unexpectedly opened before him of becoming the owner of a London evening newspaper, he did not leap to seize it. 'Was going up to town on the "Evening News & Post" matter,' he wrote on August 18, 'but didn't feel well enough and didn't go.' Instead, he sauntered about the streets of Ramsgate.

★   ★   ★

Opposite the Harmsworths' office in Tudor Street, E.C., was the office of the evening newspaper called *The Sun*, founded in the Liberal interest by T. P. O'Connor, M.P. Workers on *The Sun* often saw young Alfred Harmsworth going in and leaving his office, success evident in his proudly held chin and energetic walk and in the smartness of his office building. A new weekly paper, *The Sketch*, had sent an interviewer down to Tudor Street to see him. 'There were flowers on his desk and flowers in boxes on all the window sills, all through the summer red geraniums and yellow calceolarias, while his room was as full of flowers as a leading lady's dressing-room. The dinginess of Tudor Street was redeemed by the floral display of the three-story building which bore a large gilt sign, "Answers", across its white-painted front.' By comparison with every other building in its locality, 24 Tudor Street looked so cheerfully inviting that it was occasionally invaded by revellers mistaking it for a public-house. Today it is overshadowed by the lordly propinquity of Northcliffe House.

To the older generation of staff men the young Harmsworth was still a fly-by-night figure who was making the most of his luck while it lasted and stood for none of the solid virtues, editorial or financial, which counted for success in Fleet Street. One man on *The Sun*, Louis Tracy, frankly admired Harmsworth, without having met him. Tracy was a Liverpool man who had worked on *The Northern Echo* at Darlington. After further experience at Cardiff and in India, he arrived in London to join T. P. O'Connor on *The Sun*. It was he who had suggested to Boyle, of the *Westminster Gazette*, that it might be worth while tipping off Harmsworth about the sale of the *Evening News & Post*. In doing so, he advanced the Harmsworths' fortunes without notably improving his own.

In 1894 London had five penny evening newspapers, the *Pall Mall Gazette* (1865–1923), *The Globe* (1807–1921), the *Evening Standard* (1827), the *St. James's Gazette* (1880–1905) and the *Westminster Gazette* (1893–1921), and four halfpenny evening papers, *The Echo* (1868–1905), *The Star* (1889), *The Sun* (1893–1906) and the *Evening News & Post*. Their combined circulations totalled less than any one of the three evening newspapers which hold the field today. In policy they were as varied as the tints of the paper on which they were printed (tinted paper being cheaper than white). Few were making money. Unlike the morning papers of the day, the London evening papers, some of them, at least, were preparing to meet the needs and tastes of the new reading public which was put off by weighty opinions and long unbroken columns of news dispatches containing more descriptive stuff than news. Editing the *Pall Mall Gazette* in the 1880s and risking its reputation as 'a gentleman's paper', W. T. Stead had brilliantly imagined a kind of journalism which was to prevail later. His energy of mind was given to expressing itself in sensational articles and in a keener response generally to events previously thought beyond the scope of London evening journalism. His flamboyant policy was ahead of its time, but as an inspirer of the livelier trend in newspaper editing he could claim some of the credit later given to Alfred Harmsworth. *The Star*, under T. P. O'Connor, had also set the pace with its bold American-style headings and the virile writing of its contributors, some of whom were later to make great names in the world of letters. Claiming to crusade for two lumps of sugar, instead of one, in the charwoman's tea, *The Star* made Radicalism almost gay.

O'Connor was one of the first newspaper editors to grasp the trend towards a more concise journalism. 'We shall have but one daily article of any length and it will be usually confined within half a column.' He had heeded the implications of *Tit-Bits* and *Answers* and, later, he was to follow them in a weekly paper of his own. He had written a masterly article, headed 'The New Journalism', for *The New Review*, October 1889. There he referred to the parting of the ways between 'the long, lifeless columns' of the older newspapers and 'the more personal tone' of their later rivals. He made much of the discrepancy between the fastidiousness which decried 'any allusion to the personal appearance, the habits, the clothes, and the home and social life of any person' and the respect which was generally accorded to history as written by Macaulay, Carlyle and Green, 'who scorned no detail, however trifling, which threw a light on the habits and character of historical personages'. Nearer at hand, there was the dictum of Disraeli that 'it is the personal that interests mankind'. Forced after three years to resign from *The Star*, which he had made a literary but not a financial success, O'Connor started *The Sun*, capitalizing there the considerable personal reputation he had made as a political writer and commentator on the current scene. While he wrote his articles straight on the typewriter at what for those days was thought to be an incredible speed—'the bell of his machine never stops *pinging*', according to a colleague of his—the brunt of getting out *The Sun* every afternoon was being borne by Louis Tracy as assistant editor, and William Kennedy Jones as chief sub-editor. Uncertain of their future under 'T.P.'s' editorial reign, both had their eyes open for better jobs.

Looking down into Tudor Street one morning from *The Sun* office, Jones saw a smart carriage and pair draw up at *Answers* building opposite. Out of it there sprang a young man in morning coat and top hat who helped out after him an attractive and particularly well-dressed young woman. 'Alfred Harmsworth and his wife', Jones was told when he asked who the couple were. He was impressed.

By the end of the summer of 1894 *The Sun* was in trouble. The flat-racing season was ending and not all the paper's readers were to be wooed into continuing allegiance by 'T.P.' writing on politics 'at the top of his voice', as a critic remarked. The paper was making a loss of £30,000 a year. O'Connor wrote to Harmsworth suggesting 'a combination of interests'. The plan was frustrated by political differences. A committee appointed to study the position took the opportunity of considering the outlook for other London evening papers, as a result of which it was learned that the *Evening News & Post* was for sale. It had been financially supported by Coleridge Kennard, partner in a London banking house and for several years Conservative member of Parliament for Salisbury. He supplied more than £100,000 to keep it alive, bringing the total loss on the paper to a quarter of a million pounds. In 1894, he notified his solicitor, Bernard Parker: 'I'm going to stop the *Evening News*. I can't keep it going any longer.' Listening to a plea for time, he gave Parker six weeks in which to make arrangements for the paper's future. His sudden death threw the responsibility for the sale on to his executors. They were left with a debt of £15,000 on the *Evening News*. It was only as the last week was expiring that a way out of the *impasse* was found. Parker managed to interest Harry Marks, Conservative M.P. for Thanet and chief proprietor of the *Financial News*. Marks, who was a pioneer of City journalism, undertook to keep the paper going. But the process of resuscitation seemed likely to be prolonged and after a few months he gave notice of withdrawal. Then a paper maker issued a writ which would have stopped publication. Another paper maker was persuaded to take up debentures, extending the time margin for further negotiation. In July 1894, both Conservative and Liberal money was offered and a final Conservative bid of £17,000 was being considered by Parker on behalf of the Kennard family and Marks.

At this point the impending sale was mentioned to Alfred Harmsworth by Boyle. Tracy and Kennedy Jones of *The Sun* had seen the books of the *Evening News & Post* under the pretext of procuring information on which their editor, T. P. O'Connor, might make an offer, although a condition of sale was that the paper should be continued in the Conservative interest. Both were surprised to find that the paper had a useful circulation, touching 100,000 copies. They resolved to try for an option, with the idea of selling it on terms which would include contracts for each of them and, if possible, a cash consideration. They had no capital and had no luck in finding any until, within a day or two of the close of their option, a *Sun* colleague, Harry Jones, mentioned Alfred Harmsworth's name. When they doubted his ability to purchase the paper, Jones said that Harmsworth had told him that the profits of Answers Limited exceeded £40,000 a year.
Harold Harmsworth to Alfred Harmsworth:

> Wedderburn Cottage,
> Wedderburn Road,
> Hampstead, N.
> [Undated]

My dear Alfred,—Kay Robinson has not a very high opinion of Tracy and Jones. He says they have not got that reputation as journalists which they would like us to believe. He, however, fully believes that the E. News might be made to pay.

I have written to Tracy that under no circumstances would we consent to either he or Jones holding more than 10% of the shares. This will make him cool off, I think, and in that case it will be as well to let the matter slide.

If we could pick the paper up for a song it would be worth our while to have it, but not otherwise.

> Yours,
> HAROLD.

Harold wrote to Alfred on August 16: 'I must say I am not keen on the venture. I have no wish to identify myself with the Conservative Party and it would certainly not suit your purpose to do so either.' The following day Harold wrote to say that he had made an offer for the *Evening News*. 'It is that we pay £5,000 down and take over debts amounting to £15,000. Tracy says it will be accepted.' Harold added: 'I think there is money to be made out of it.' He foresaw that 'the sporting element' would have to be encouraged. 'The paper will not sell a copy without it.' He appended to his letter, as was his habit, the latest sales figures of their existing publications: '*Answers* 356,000, *Comic Cuts* 438,000, *Chips* 283,000, *Forget-Me-Not* 145,000, *Marvel* 153,000, *Sunday Companion* 38,000, *Union Jack* 140,000, *Home-Sweet-Home* 73,000.'
Tracy said that delays during the negotiations gave him and Kennedy

Jones sleepless nights. That experience was apparently not shared by the brothers Harmsworth. Their correspondence gives no sign of elation at the prospect of newspaper ownership. Alfred noted on August 27: 'In great doubt all day whether we should get the *Evening News* or not, there being other competitors and matters difficult to arrange.' One of the competitors was the Wolverhampton newspaper proprietor, Thomas Graham, who believed that the paper's heavy losses would dispel any stipulation about its future policy. He planned to secure it for the Liberals, but failed because his partner-to-be insisted that there should be no racing news. The sale agreement with the Harmsworths was signed on August 28 at the price of £25,000 including plant, machinery and fittings. As a preliminary to completing it, Alfred Harmsworth went to Coutts' Bank to arrange for the disposal of some of his securities. The manager deemed it prudent to say that in his banking experience there were several ways by which a man might be certain of losing his money and none of them more certain than running a newspaper. Undeterred, Alfred put his signature to the documents. He then went back to Tudor Street to dictate a note to Tracy and Jones confirming that they were to receive between them fifteen per cent of the profits of a company formed to acquire the *Evening News & Post*.

On August 31, 1894, the leading article in the *Evening News & Post* had for its heading: 'The Evening News'. It announced that at four o'clock the previous afternoon the proprietorship of the paper had passed into new hands. An unctuous preamble about the future moral and social policy of the paper conformed to long-established editorial custom. Rarely has any new periodical or newspaper been started, or a change of ownership publicly notified, without it. *Free from fad or prejudice, it will preach the gospel of loyalty to the Empire and faith in the peoples united under the British flag. . . . Strongly and unfalteringly Conservative in Imperial politics . . . will occupy an advanced democratic platform on all social matters. . . . Progressive in municipal reform . . . non-sectarian in all questions affecting the religious beliefs of the community . . . sympathetic towards Labour . . . friendly to every phase of communal advancement. . . .*

Night after night Alfred and Harold, with Kennedy Jones, met in the ramshackle building at 12 Whitefriars Street, trying to find out why, as Alfred wrote later, 'the *Evening News* was such a failure that the wags of the Radical Press used to amuse themselves by having its shares put up for sale in bushel baskets and informing the world that such shares realized a few pence each'. A Fleet Street acquaintance met them one night going into the *Evening News* office. Returning his greeting, Harold said moodily: 'We're going to take another look at our gold brick. This', he said, indicating Jones, 'is the man who sold it to us.' Their room in the office building was an attic. It had only a small roof light with broken panes.

For the week before the transfer to the Harmsworths the loss on the paper was £100, the average for many previous weeks. In the first week of their ownership a net profit of £7 was shown. In the third week it was £50. The paper struck a lucky vein in its racing tips, although, against Jones's advice, Alfred had cut down the racing news from fourteen columns to nine. It earned its purchase price in three years. Harold had already made his presence felt. Under the old management, everything had to be paid for at high rates because the continuance of the paper depended on long credits. Now all that was changed. Tracy said that it became a joke in the office to say that when Harold had a couple of minutes to spare he would send for the paper agent and knock off another two and a half per cent discount. The four new stockholders dined in celebration at Kettners. Harold refused to see any reason for high spirits. 'It will take us years to wipe off those debentures', he glumly reminded Alfred in his next week's report.

By the end of two months Tracy's thrustful partner, Kennedy Jones, had succeeded him as editor. Tracy was given the post of manager. Not proving successful, he sold his seven-and-a-half per cent interest in the paper to Harold Harmsworth and took over the management of a racing sheet called *Paddock Life* in which Harmsworths had a small financial interest. Finding that unprofitable, he went to the *Allahabad Pioneer* and afterwards settled down to the life for which his talents best fitted him, that of a novelist. One of his novels, *The Final War*, was widely read. 'Tracy, who is a great friend of mine, did not hold on to his shares,' Alfred Harmsworth wrote in 1921. 'Had he done so, he would have made a fortune, but he is happy without it.'

Kennedy Jones, known and remembered in Fleet Street as 'K.J.', liked to boast that he had been born in the same Glasgow street as Sir Thomas Lipton, 'only at the better end'. He was the same age as Alfred Harmsworth and his Welsh name capped a mixed ancestry of Scots and Irish. He had raven black hair, scars on his forehead, and an untamed look in his eye. As a boy, he sold newspapers in the streets. He learned his journalism in Glasgow and had worked on newspapers in Leicester and Birmingham before coming to London to make what he could of qualities which were mainly mediocre but which he did not hide under a bushel. 'I'll be a rich man in five years', he had bragged on leaving Birmingham. Before finding his feet in London, he knew hard times. Keighley Snowden, a respected Yorkshire journalist, met him walking Fleet Street in the search for work. Jones was even then invincibly sure of himself. 'I'm getting to know this bloody town like my shirt. Inside twelve months, laddie, I'll be making a thousand a year.' He himself wrote that he had been forced at that time to go into an eating-house in Poppins Court, Fleet Street, and order a meal for which he could not pay. 'I was hungry. I had had nothing to eat since breakfast. I was twenty-seven and of robust build. My luck was out.' It may have been in recoil from that shabby Bohemianism that later, at a picnic, he bawled loudly that the cold chicken had not been boned, threw the bird over a hedge, and drove ten miles to a seaside grand hotel for lunch.

A man of sardonic moods, flaring tempers and no-quarter aggressiveness when it came to beating down rivals, 'K.J.' had almost none of the elements of personal popularity. He had many enemies whose existence seemed to give him pleasure. 'They say I'm brutal and autocratic!' he would repeat with a grin of self-approval. When he had a major surgical operation, an old colleague of his said to him: 'Directly I saw you were going to be cut open I knew it would be all right. There couldn't be any complications in your case—you never had any bowels.' His sense of humour was ruthless, despite his engaging smile. 'They say a sub-editor I sacked jumped into the Thames. They're wrong—it was two sub-editors.' The Irish in him softened his harsh Glasgow accent. Possibly the same strain showed itself in his facts of unproclaimed generosity. Having once dismissed an editorial man, he continued to pay the victim's salary out of his own pocket until a new job was found. A colleague of his of many years insists: 'Under the roughness there was a heart of gold.' 'He was a just master,' wrote the Fleet Street essayist, E. T. Raymond, who edited the *Evening Standard*.

In Fleet Street the part played by Kennedy Jones in the Harmsworths' affairs has probably not been fairly estimated. Harold Harmsworth, who championed Jones as an office colleague, said that if Jones's contribution could be stated in figures he would put it at ten per cent. Leicester Harmsworth contended to the last that 'the part played by Kennedy Jones in the success of the *Daily Mail* was very small indeed'. In encouraging the view that he was one of the founders of the Harmsworth fortunes, 'K.J.' was conforming to his instincts but hardly to the facts. He was also overlooking the inconvenient truth that he had gained his original footing with the Harmsworths as part of the purchase terms for the *Evening News* rather than for his journalistic prowess. His newspaper training, and his experience of the mechanical side in particular, was probably invaluable at that time and it cannot be doubted that he more than anyone else helped to transform Alfred Harmsworth from a weekly paper journalist into a newspaperman.

★   ★   ★

As a comment on Alfred's intuitive processes, a picturesque remark was made about him soon after he had acquired control of the *Evening News*: 'He has a mental searchlight which reveals to him glimpses of the future.' He had almost no experience of news handling but from the first he fashioned the *Evening News* as a prototype of his more daring newspaper venture to come. He changed the character of the paper almost overnight. New type was used. A break was made with solid make-up methods. Leaders were cut down. Instead of one topic, three or four might be discussed in the leader column. The old diffuse political reporting was banished. A daily short story was made a feature of the paper (as it still is). A women's column was an innovation. 'God, man, you're not going to turn the paper into an evening *Answers*, are you?' Kennedy Jones asked him. Some of the articles were actually 'lifted' from back numbers of that weekly: for example, a full account of the recovery of the body of the Prince Imperial from the Zulu battlefield. Other articles in the *Answers* vein were 'Evils of Baby Farming', 'Burials Alive', 'Secrets of the Dissecting Room'. A series headed simply 'Anarchy' in the boldest of black type made an impression on London readers who earlier in the year had been startled and made angry by the news that a Frenchman had been blown to pieces in Greenwich Park by the explosion of a home-made bomb he was carrying. There was vague public consternation over a club of foreign anarchists in London. Desperate characters were popularly believed to be plotting in back rooms off the Tottenham Court Road.

The women's column was soon expanded into a 'Women's World' page. What was daily journalism coming to? Remotely anticipating the greatest gambling urge of our time, the football pools, the *Evening News* in 1894 invited readers to send forecasts of winning teams, enclosing a penny stamp with each forecast. In the best weeks the revenue in penny stamps reached £200 and as the weekly prize outlay was a £5 note, the difference justified Harold Harmsworth's grudging assent to the expense. He never finally believed in 'literary' ideas, while admitting that Alfred's magazine touch was of great value to the *Evening News* at that time of transition. He could not deny the merit of Alfred's innovations. Alfred's insistence on having the news simplified and explained and his constant call for maps, more maps—those were new touches that had a great deal to do with the paper's widened appeal.

A sign of success for the Harmsworths' newspaper venture was that the advertising position soon improved. 'Lipton, Tea Planter, Ceylon', in bold black type, heralded the coming of the chain grocery store and an outstanding career of swaggering individualism. 'Epps' Cocoa', 'Kops' Ale', 'Holloways' Pills and Ointment' and 'Hudson's Soap', manifested in a similarly crude fashion the incunabula stage of advertising. It was still largely an affair of ill-arranged display type. Illustration was not yet an indispensable visual aid to selling goods. Impatient for profits, Harold raised the *Evening News* advertising rate to £40 a half-page. It was thought absurd by some of the older advertising men. Those young Harmsworths, they said, were out of their depth in the newspaper shoals and reaches. The journalistic revolution, in which they were taking the lead, was gaining in force every day. The revolution in advertising, which was to pile up wealth for them, had hardly begun.

*   *   *

In town, Alfred and Mary Harmsworth rented a house, 9 Charles Street, Mayfair, but Alfred travelled constantly to Broadstairs, working at Elmwood as often as possible. His wife did not share so fully his regard for the place. In London, if she was away, he preferred to stay at the Constitutional Club or at an hotel. He had a bachelor's inclinations but no instinct whatever for looking after himself. His brief daily diary notes were now kept for him by Sutton, whom he was more usually addressing as 'Sutkin'. From the biographical standpoint, the servant was even less communicative than the master. 'Worked in the morning. Went to town by the Granville. Attended "Evening News" meeting. Best week so far—profit £168. Slept Metropole, Room 173.' 'Granville' recurs constantly, the 'Granville Special Private Express', a train running between Cannon Street, London, and Ramsgate in an hour and forty-five minutes. Over the years Alfred Harmsworth became one of its most conspicuous and no doubt best-attended passengers. In it he did a great deal of office work, reading articles, correcting proofs, writing his 'Editorial Chat' for *Answers*. Hearing that Pearson, travelling to his Surrey home by train each night, worked with the aid of a 'portable electric lamp', he had the fact noted in the *Evening News*, as if it was a wonder of the age. A result of Sutton's loyalty as an amanuensis is that we are told much less than before about 'Mr Alfred's' health, to which he himself had previously made many diary allusions. 'Stayed in bed working until lunch', is one of the few hints now given to show that he was still having to take care of himself. Harold wrote him a warning note from 10 Lansdowne Place, Eastbourne: 'I hear you are going to Paris on Thursday. I think you want a change. You should drop as much work as possible. At the present pace we shall be nervous tired-out men by the time we reach forty.'

Before leaving for Paris, Alfred had agreed with Kennedy Jones, as the *Evening News* editor, that the paper must be the first in the field with its reports of the trial of James Canham Read for the murder of a young woman at Prittlewell, near Southend. The arrest of Read, at Mitcham, Surrey, after a hunt lasting several days, had kept newspaper readers on tiptoe with excitement. On September 29, Alfred had visited Chelmsford Prison in the company of an *Answers* contributor, Major Arthur Griffiths, sometime governor of Millbank Prison, London, acting editor of *The Fortnightly Review*, and author of books on crime and criminals. They had talked with Read for an hour in his cell. Coming away, Harmsworth had no doubt that the trial would create the highest pitch of public interest. Informing Kennedy Jones of his belief, he left for Paris.

Working each morning in his room at the Hotel Chatham, sightseeing every afternoon, theatre-going every evening, enjoying, in particular, being escorted 'round the thieves' quarter' with a detective, he fitted in several talks with the proprietor of *Le Petit Journal*, M. Marinoni, whose four-page paper with its trenchant front-page leading articles sold 650,000 copies daily, exceeding the total for all the London morning and evening newspapers together. *Le Petit Journal* was said to be making £150,000 a year. The importance of the meetings may or may not have been obvious to Sutton, as he took down the dictated diary entry on 'Mr Alfred's' return to London: 'Drafted plan for our new daily.' If the plan had been forming in Alfred Harmsworth's mind during the Paris visit, it probably received an invigorating new impulse from a telegram sent by Kennedy Jones on the last day of the Read trial, November 15, 1894: *Evening News sold 390,000.*

Only a few months previously, Alfred had spoken out strongly in *Answers* against newspaper exploitation of crime; 'not a fact of which we as a nation should be proud'. He may not have known, then, that Delane, as editor of *The Times*, had been an enthusiast for 'a good murder'. Whatever his private feelings were about the *Evening News* treatment of the Read murder case, Alfred Harmsworth would have had to admit that it gave him a valuable first lesson in the methods of news-getting and particularly in the expert use of the telegraph and telephone. For that he owed more than he may have acknowledged to 'K.J.'

Alfred Harmsworth to brothers Cecil and Leicester:

> Elmwood,
> St. Peter's,
> Kent.
> October 22, 1894.

My dear Boys,—This will arrive at Vancouver a long time before you get there, but I write it because the wife and I are off to live in Paris for the month of November. Either from Mother or the newspapers you will have learnt that we have bought the 'Evening News'. It was a big venture for us. We had to pay £25,000, but we have so far made about an average of £150 a week out of it. On the whole we think it a bargain inasmuch as we got all the machinery thrown in. Its circulation is 40,000 a day more than that of 'The Star' and 60,000 a day more than that of 'The Sun'.

All the papers are doing well: 'Forget-Me-Not' has been fluctuating between 145,000 and 148,000 for a long time. The autumn double number, price 2d., went well, doing 148,000. 'Home-Sweet-Home' is 75,000. 'Answers' is as high as it was this time last year. We are giving away for a Christmas prize a flourishing shop in any kind of business the winner chooses. The halfpenny books, the 'Marvel' and the 'Union Jack', are rising splendidly. We are just about to start another which will appear November 26th called 'The Pluck Library'. The 'Wonder' is doing more than it ever did before. 'Chips' went down but is now rising. 'Comic Cuts' is steady, 425 [425,000].

Our next scheme is a daily paper which we talk of starting in February.

We are all looking forward to seeing you again. I expect by the time you get to Vancouver you will be tiring of your travels and anxious to come home to work. . . .

ALFRED.

P.S. 'Sunday Companion' rising steadily.

In its first year under the Harmsworths the *Evening News* made £14,000. The second year's profit was £25,000: 'Since we purchased the *Evening News* last September,' Alfred wrote in *Answers*, May 25, 1895, 'we have added nearly 400,000 copies a week to its circulation. We paid £25,000 for the paper, lock, stock and barrel, and we would not sell it for £100,000, or, indeed, for any figure.' He recalled, pleasurably, that when he and his brother had taken over the paper only a few months before, it had been confidently stated 'that there is no money in halfpenny evening papers'. He had noted 'a sincere disposition to shake hands and wish us joy of the *Evening News*'. Now joy had come of it. 'We are more than satisfied with our new venture. It has answered well.' There followed an accountants' certificate of 160,000 copies a day sold.

For the first time he knew the exclusive satisfaction of being near the centre of events, of having direct contact with the makers of history. From Paris he had written to Lord Salisbury to inform him what had been accomplished with a newspaper on which the Conservative Party had lost a great sum of money. Lord Salisbury, who in a few months was to take Lord Rosebery's place at 10 Downing Street, expressed pleasure at hearing about 'the good prospects which have opened before the *Evening News*'. He remembered 'how gloomy they were in the days of my poor friend Coleridge Kennard'. Two days after his return from Paris, at the end of November, Alfred Harmsworth breakfasted with Cecil Rhodes and Starr Jameson. 'Afterwards walked with Cecil Rhodes from the Burlington Hotel to Ebury Street', a perambulation which he would not have been likely to share as the proprietor of *Answers* or *Comic Cuts*.

'*December* 18, 1894.—Slept to half-past 10. Worked at office. Decided on issuing another weekly paper for women. Home to Elmwood by the Granville.' The previous evening Alfred had been at the Sylvan Debating Club's meeting: 'Made a speech on Mr Rhodes's policy.' For the moment, Mr Rhodes's policy was engaging his attention more closely than his editorial responsibilities. He had come under the spell of one of the few men to whom he could accord heroic stature. 'Cecil Rhodes was the only statesman for whom I ever heard Alfred express unqualified admiration,'

Cecil Harmsworth wrote in later years. Alfred was seeing the British world through Rhodes's eyes and the vision was stirring him in a way that no party political creed or issue had before.

The new weekly for women was to be his reply to Pearson's *Home Notes*, which Harold estimated was making a profit of £12,000 a year. Harold was still much bothered about the future of the *Answers* company. 'The more I looked into it, the more I see it wants support. To be in a thoroughly good position, it should have further sources of profit to the extent of not less than £100 weekly.' Thus incited, Alfred had asked Clement K. Shorter, who had founded *The Sketch* for the Ingrams, to visit him at Elmwood. Shorter was having a personal success with *The Sketch* by using the new metal process blocks for printing pictures instead of engravers' wood blocks. It meant speedier reproduction, an important development in printing and journalistic history. Shorter was making use of the new method to fill *The Sketch* with pictures of beautiful actresses. Those who knew him only in his later years, the shambling book pundit whose hair bobbed on his shoulders as he walked, could not easily believe that he had been an enterprising, sought-after editor. Alfred Harmsworth had hoped to persuade him into a change of allegiance. Harold stepped in with the reminder that they were not yet in a position to pay the salary which Shorter would ask.

The new Harmsworth paper for women was called *Home Chat*. Apart from being a counter-move against Pearson's *Home Notes*, it came into existence on the assumption that the Harmsworths, better than anyone else, could produce for a penny what had before been sold at sixpence. The result was a feather in the cap of young Leicester Harmsworth, aged twenty-five, flaunting his first moustache and impressing his women callers with his earnest appreciation of their work for the paper. Young as he was, he had grasped the fact that the 'new' women, who smoked cigarettes and were becoming aggressive about the vote, had identical interests with all other women, whatever their age and class, and that while a change of status was decidedly in the air women themselves did not essentially change. He was ably helped by two sisters on the staff, Maud and Flora Bown. A little later, Maud Bown was made editor and she faithfully and successfully reflected the proprietors' policy for many years. *Home Chat*'s line was cosy domesticity, tinged with the gentle snobbery which professed intimate knowledge of persons in high places: 'The Queen's daughters invariably address her as "Mama".' Making those concessions to established prejudices, it discouraged the submissiveness of women by publishing articles on careers and new outlets for women's creativeness. Its 'signed' society gossip page was a journalistic innovation: its free paper patterns another. It published, also, one of the first 'comic strips', a feature called 'Jungle Jinks' which gave enduring pleasure to the young of succeeding generations and gained for the paper a sound and solid part of its circulation. 'Give them plenty of animals', Alfred Harmsworth had said in the tone of inspiration as Leicester showed him 'dummy' pages of the children's part of the paper.

The rush for *Home Chat*, when its first issue was put on sale in March 1895, was exceptionally heavy, outrivalling that for any of the group's publications up to that time. It was a sign of the confidence of 'the trade' in the judgment of Alfred Harmsworth and those around him. That promising start was like a morning on which the sun shines too soon. It was followed by anxious times, due in part to printing troubles, to keen competition from Pearson and, in Harold Harmsworth's opinion, to faulty advertising arrangements. The number of returns from the news-agents caused him to write despondently: 'I do not at all like the outlook.'

Harold Harmsworth to Alfred Harmsworth:

12th June, 1895.

My dear Alfred,—Answers 442,400, Comic Cuts 391,000, Home Chat 185,800, Marvel 164,000, Boys' Friend 145,750, Chips 265,000, Forget-Me-Not 145,000.

Decline in the sale of *Home Chat* is getting very serious. There is no sign of it abating. Leicester is going carefully through all the ladies' papers and is drawing up a list of the additional features that might be dealt with. It seems to me that we must make up our minds not to see any profit out of this paper until next year. If the fall is not arrested, we shall have to make good a very heavy loss this year. The paper is not nearly so good as it might be.

Yours,
HAROLD.

Before long the prospect brightened again and in a year or two the latest Harmsworth paper for women was gaining an increasingly pro-minent place in the company's balance sheet. It continued publication until its demise in 1959. An 'Aunt Molly', impersonated in the early days by young Leicester Harmsworth himself, was still in charge of the junior pages, where a shadowy Jumbo recalled the once overwhelmingly popu-lar hilarities of 'Jungle Jinks'.

*   *   *

For May 4, 1892, Alfred had written in his diary: 'Dined with Graham [presumably William Graham, solicitor] and his partner, to discuss my going in for politics.' The general election of that year appears to have given a new direction to his thinking about the future. He had not shown more than a casual interest in politics. Now he was seeing himself as a Member of Parliament, an inspiration likely to have had social as well as political implications. Politically, he was given to expressing sentiments rather than to holding opinions. That he was sympathetic to the arbitrary views of his favourite author, Dickens, can only be suggested; but Dickens's belief in a benevolent autocracy was the sort of notion, sustained by a flexible logic, that would have appealed to the young Alfred Harmsworth, intolerant with the conceit of his years of the authority of professional politicians. This over-simplified attitude expanded and contracted, but never deepened, in his later career. Politics involved argument and for that he had no liking. Cecil Harmsworth wrote in his private memoranda: 'I have often wondered what Alfred's politics really were.' This brother thought that they were chiefly inspired by 'a firm faith in the Anglo-Saxon future'. There was a latent Radical in Alfred, but he was strongly susceptible to Disraelian imperialism. He was endorsing Joseph Chamberlain's 'bigger and better Britain' policy in the *Evening News*, giving Chamberlain, his eyeglass, his orchid and everything that was his, generous notice. Chamberlain's passion for reform, shown with forceful sincerity in local government, his combination of adventurous radicalism with imperialistic fervour, his view that 'the great problem of the future was how to promote the happiness of the people', his concern for pensioning the aged, were so much admired in the Harmsworth family circle that a newly-arrived boy of its next generation was given the first name of 'Chamberlain'.

Having declined nomination for Folkestone in 1894, Alfred accepted an invitation to stand as Unionist candidate for Portsmouth in the General Election of 1895. He was unanimously adopted on March 29. In a fortnight he had descended on that town with what the editor of the local Liberal *Evening News* said was 'a shattering impact'. Taking up residence at 51 Clarence Parade, Southsea, he opened negotiations by which a local paper, the Conservative *Evening Mail*, owned by the well-known Portsmouth family of Holbrook, was purchased in the names of his brother Harold and Kennedy Jones. 'I do not doubt that something could be done with it,' Harold had written to his brother on April 20. 'Of course, to be a success it would have to be run on broad general lines with your candidature as a side issue. If we could get a special wire laid on from the "Evening News" office [in London] we could play havoc with the opposition rag.'

Receiving the Harmsworth imprint, and later, some months after the election, given the new title of *Southern Daily Mail*, the paper was transformed from a staid local journal into a go-ahead newspaper with all that the Fleet Street hallmark could mean in technical and financial resources. 'We come to do our utmost; regardless of effort, careless of cost, and heedless of fatigue', it announced editorially. A bright particular idea of Alfred's was to run a serial story portraying the destruction of Portsmouth as a naval base in the great war which, according to Old Moore, was imminent. The story was designed to play on local fears and local patriotism, no part of the kingdom being more sensitive to the recurring war scares that flashed the growing might and defiance of Germany across the European scene. William Le Queux was invited to go down to Southsea to discuss the idea. In reply, he wrote to Sutton: 'The doctor says I have overworked myself and has ordered me a rest. I regret this exceedingly, for to Mr Harmsworth I owe whatever success I have obtained as a writer of serial fiction.' *The Siege of Portsmouth* was written to Alfred's order and under his close supervision by Beckles Willson, a young and dandyish Canadian freelance journalist, in collaboration with William Laird Clowes, a leading naval historian who was eloquent if not fanatical about Britain's unpreparedness at sea. He supplied the technical information, while Willson was responsible for the civilian side of the story. Alfred left no doubt in the mind of either that plot mattered less than authenticity of atmosphere. Readers were to be impressed above all by its scientific authority, important in view of local expert knowledge. Willson was told to identify by name certain Portsmouth personalities who might be relied on in a war emergency to live up to the highest patriotic principles, while the dockyard workers, whose support was vital to the election, were to be shown valiantly contending with war conditions. For that purpose, he studied the Portsmouth directory, ticking off names from the lists of members of local political parties. 'Put in old Jack Palin,' he was commanded by Admiral Lord Charles Beresford. 'He was a boatswain under me and he taught Prince George to swim!'

The serial was advertised to the public on hoardings everywhere in the town and along the roads leading to it. Large posters showed a bayonet charge by waves of foreign soldiers, identifiable according to readers' prejudices as German, Russian or French. The Town Hall was seen crumbling to dust under shell fire, while townsfolk reeled to their deaths in front of the stricken citadel. History itself postponed the destruction of Portsmouth Town Hall, from enemy action, for fifty years. According to a note of Harold Harmsworth's, the story was not a marked success as a circulation raiser. Perhaps the hot summer made it uncongenial reading. Besides, the town was *en fête*. An Italian naval squadron had arrived on an official visit and the streets were bright with decorations and busy with civic formalities. It was difficult to induce a war mood. Beckles Willson was impatiently taking time off at Portsmouth from his London job of helping to prepare the monthly magazine which was to be the Harmsworths' reply to Newnes's highly successful *Strand*. Willson had written in his diary after a first discussion with Alfred about the serial: 'What a strikingly handsome fellow he is—a most engaging figure!' Appointed editor-to-be of the new magazine at £500 a year, Willson visited Elmwood, which he found 'all very luxurious and very ravishing and very stimulating'.

He was not to know that already Harold Harmsworth was worrying about the preliminary expenses of the proposed magazine. 'It is costing £40 a week in overheads and, so far as I can see, there is not the least chance of its coming out for another twelve months.' He added to his note to Alfred: 'We have a very heavy financial struggle with *Home Chat*, and we could not stand another.' Characteristically, Alfred had gone ahead with the magazine plan, not deterred by questions of cost, until politics took his attention from it. Meanwhile, Beckles Willson, whose devotion to the Mother Country later found passionate expression in a book, *England: By an Overseas Englishman*, had begun work on the Portsmouth serial. When it was finished, Alfred ordered him to write a patriotic song to arouse audiences at the Empire music hall, Portsmouth. Thereafter, while the election lasted, an attractive young woman enrobed in the Union Jack walked on to the stage there twice-nightly to sing the doggerel refrain:

> The soldier brave fights for his flag,
> His martial valour shields it.
> The sailor staunchly mans our Fleet
> But here's to the lad who *builds* it!

To make sure that the song would be heard, and heard again, by the dock-yard workers and their sweethearts and wives, Kennedy Jones hired twenty loud-voiced young men at sixpence apiece and free gallery tickets to demand repeated encores. Beckles Willson reported that the arrangement 'gave much offence' to the professional performers in the wings. While there were moments in which he had to pretend not to have heard catcalls from roughs in the streets, the candidate with 'the pleasing smile and unusual lock of golden hair flowing over his forehead' (from a contemporary Portsmouth account) was an unqualified social success during the campaign. He and his wife, whose appearance unfailingly evoked the epithet of 'charming' in the locally printed accounts of their activities, were strict in their observance of all that was expected of them. Alfred's punctilio was flawless. He never kept a meeting waiting. He was at every sort of function. He gave money to forty-seven different local charities, institutions and causes, as various as children's outings and old people's treats, a Church of England roof repair fund, Roman Catholic schools, the Church Lads' Brigade, the Christian Brothers, several cycling clubs, educational classes in Hebrew, the P.S.A. Brotherhood movement, the Royal Navy Pensioners' Protection Association, with the most substantial donation of all going to the local Conservative Association. His domestic life was complicated by the need to take care in patronizing the local tradesmen. The names of several grocers, fishmongers, dairymen, green-grocers and bakers, among others, appear in his account books for the period, indicating that he was aware of the risks of discrimination.

He cheerfully let himself in for dances at memorial halls, for receiving deputations of chief petty officers, naval writers, naval coopers, navvies and stokers, for trips in destroyers, for taking the first and second degrees of Freemasonry, and submitting to the rites and ceremonies of Druids, Buffaloes, Foresters and Oddfellows. The Harmsworth carriage-and-pair was the smartest of its kind; the horses, high-stepping it through the streets of Portsmouth and the avenues of Southsea, made passers-by turn and stare in admiration. An artist member of the Harmsworth staff, Roland Hill, who had been sent down from London, wrote privately to a friend: 'A.H. has played the game for all it is worth, never missing a chance for *effect*—standing up in an open carriage, illuminated by torches, with one arm lovingly twined round the slender form of his young wife—tableau— cheers.' More perhaps to his taste was the sitting requested by *Vanity Fair* on behalf of 'Spy' (Sir Leslie Ward), though the result was one of the feeblest likenesses ever achieved by that celebrated cartoonist. There were visits to Dickens's birthplace at Portsea; house-party compensations, too, at Broadlands, home of the Ashleys, where he mingled with society per-sonages whose names Sutton dutifully recorded in the diary. Alfred Harmsworth's patrician fellow Conservative candidate in the election, the Hon. Evelyn Ashley, was puzzled by the gauche manner of Kennedy Jones, who closely attended his chief during the campaign. Ashley had been Lord Palmerston's private secretary. He knew personally half the aristocracy of England and appeared to find much entertainment in his association with 'those pushful young men' from London.

As a speaker, Alfred soon realized that his voice was too narrow in compass to command a large audience. It was a gentle voice to come from a personality so manifestly charged with vital force. Its undertones were pleasing and gave it a rare quality of memorableness. It suggested con-versational *finesse*, not oratorical power. Those who knew him intimately remember that in relaxed moments it was his whim to speak barely above a whisper and that at times of decision he would use a tone of intimidating quietness. 'Because I say so', confirming a challenged private verdict, was likely to be said in the mincing way of a self-righteous maiden aunt. Colonel (later Sir) Arthur Holbrook, of Portsmouth, coached him in style and in topics, but before long, in place of speech making, he was finding it more satisfactory to both sides for him to invite questions from the audience and to give individual and informal replies. He faced his in-terrogators about lower deck conditions, dockyard discharges, Indian troopship deficiencies, local voices uttering local grievances, with an assurance which owed more to nerve than to knowledge. At one of the meetings his instinct for gauging the public mind failed him. He gave it out that he was strongly in favour of men being commissioned from the lower ranks. 'If we don't do it now, a time will come when we shall be glad to do it.' Agitation from the chairman drew him aside for a platform consultation. 'For God's sake, don't say that,' Holbrook whispered. 'These chaps hate the idea of not being officered by gentlemen!' Primed by Holbrook, he spoke out strongly against the restrictions of the drink trade and demanded that the brewers should be relieved of some of their tax burdens. This involved him in an unexpected back-of-the-hall altercation. A heckler rose up with the question: 'Don't you publish a lot of papers?' Alfred Harmsworth answered: 'I do—and I'm proud of them.' The voice continued: 'Is one of them called *The Sunday Companion?*' 'That is so,' was the reply. 'It's one of the best.' The voice was immediately heard again. 'Didn't you say in that paper last week that the drink trade is the curse of the country and that no publican can be a Christian?' Pausing and then speaking quickly as if to cover his hesitation, Alfred answered: 'I don't know. I'm not the editor. I've not seen the issue you refer to.' Thereafter, the editor's name was printed on the front cover of the journal, causing jealousy among the firm's other editors who were obliged to toil on in the traditional anonymity of their kind.

On the eve of the poll, a prominent Portsmouth figure made an unexpected platform appearance on behalf of the Liberal opposition. Father Dolling was an Anglican priest whose devoted labours as head of the Winchester School Mission at St. Agatha's, Landport, had won him a large and loyal following in the dockyards. A broad-shouldered, thick-set County Down man, whose father was of Huguenot descent and whose mother had Scots and North of England ancestors, Robert Radclyffe Dolling had worked as a land agent in Ireland after leaving Harrow and Cambridge. From boyhood he had been intent on entering the Church of England and before being ordained, at the age of thirty-four, he gave himself unstintingly to the service of London's poor.

From Alfred Harmsworth's diary we learn that he had made a point of calling on Dolling early in the Portsmouth campaign and that he attended services at St. Agatha's. He noted Dolling's unusual gift for organization, displayed in all that he undertook. 'He not only knew how things ought to be done. He was able to make the most unlikely people do them.' Dolling's last-minute intervention made him the central figure of a great open-air meeting. He appealed to the men of the Royal Dockyard not to split their votes. 'If you cut yourselves in two, you never deserve to have a vote again.' They respected his forthrightness as they respected his self-sacrificing work for them and their people. Their spokesman promised that they would vote 'straight and solid' and the meeting broke up with volleying cheers for the speaker of the evening. He had been particularly concerned to secure support for the party favouring licensing restrictions. Amid the election excitement, the appearance of a priest espousing the Liberal Party, for one of whose candidates he had signed the nomination form, passed without the wider notice it might otherwise have received. Following Dolling's appeal, Alfred Harmsworth made what Lord Edmund Talbot, one of his official supporters, afterwards described as 'a last forlorn effort' to speak to the dockyard men. He had little success.

Polling was on July 16, the day after Alfred's thirtieth birthday. The four candidates, Sir John Baker, clothier, and Walter Owen Clough, cloth manufacturer, for the Liberals, and the Hon. Evelyn Ashley, son of the Earl of Shaftesbury, and Alfred Harmsworth, for the Conservatives, were driven around the town in open carriages. Bands paraded the streets, followed by throngs of children released from school for the day. 'Went to the Town Hall in the evening' is written in Alfred's diary, 'when the result was declared against Ashley and I [sic], the figures being: Baker 10,451, Clough 10,255, Harmsworth 9,717, Ashley 9,567.' Quoting the figures for the previous election, he added as a gesture to his self-esteem: 'So I polled more than the winning man in 1892.' Ashley had been 'hopeless' as a candidate, it was said by his supporters. They agreed it was he who lost the election for the Party. The speeches of the successful Gladstonian candidates after the declaration of the poll at the Town Hall were bitter against the opposition. Their animosity was clearly directed at the youngest and least experienced candidate and his methods. 'I don't wish to have your congratulations,' snapped one of them, Clough, when Alfred Harmsworth, in his speech, made courteous remarks about him. 'That may be your way of accepting victory,' Alfred retorted. 'It would not be mine.' For the Liberals, Portsmouth was a rock in a tempestuous sea. In the rest of the country they suffered heavily and the new Parliament assembled with a Conservative and Liberal Unionist majority of 152. Alfred Harmsworth had no place in it but Portsmouth had compensated for his disappointment by giving him the friendship of Robert Dolling. Together during the next few years they were to bring hope and happiness into many drab young lives.

'At my age a defeat does one good. Too much success in life is bad for one,' Alfred remarked when the Portsmouth result had been given out. 'Besides,' he added, half seriously, 'my place is in the House of Lords where they don't fight elections.' Summing up the campaign, one of the Portsmouth journalists wrote: 'Harmsworth nearly wore us out.' He returned at once to London, where in the rush to overtake arrears of work and decision he had no great difficulty in forgetting his defeat. The experience had made it clear to him, and to those around him, that he had none of the parts that go to the making of a success in politics. His dislike of public speaking was joined to a preference for action which could hardly have tolerated long debates and committee work. Nor would it easily have accommodated itself to the discipline of the Party whip. His was the cross-bench temperament. He shared Cecil Rhodes's aversion from 'the purely parliamentary type of man', though both he and Rhodes may have resented the fact that, in a democracy, it is the parliamentary man who has the ultimate power. Thereafter, his attitude to political life appears to have been that of John Morley, who, as editor of *The Fortnightly Review*, considered himself to be the equal of twenty-five members of Parliament.

Why, then, did he divert time and energy to a course for which he had so little aptitude? The question mark looms larger when we realize that he had already committed himself to a decision which would make him a more formidable national figure than he might expect to be as a Member of Parliament. 'Our next scheme is a daily paper which we talk of starting in February', quoting from the letter which he had written to Cecil and Leicester on their world tour in October 1894. In November, Harold had written to him: 'The new rag must be out before the next County Council elections, which are due about 15th March. There is going to be a big fight.' In his diary for December 6 Alfred wrote: 'Harold and Lilian dined with us and we drafted the plan of our new daily.' Meanwhile, the *Southern Daily Mail* was giving the brothers a small insight into provincial newspaper publishing which may not have been without its effect on their later activities. The paper remained in Alfred's possession until 1907, when it was voluntarily liquidated. At the final casting of accounts, he received £8 10s.

Alfred had fought the Portsmouth election against a background of wavering health states which brought him, at the end of the campaign, close to a breakdown. That was no doubt the reason for the diary note, a few days before the election: 'Murrell [his doctor from London] came to see me.' 'Dr Raven said I must knock off all work of any kind altogether', the diary recorded on July 26. Thereafter, 'Elmwood' and 'pottering about the garden' recur in the diary as an indication that he had taken the doctor's advice.

* * *

'K.J.', visualizing his future in the light of the Harmsworths' lucky star, urged on Alfred the idea of producing a chain of halfpenny morning papers in the main provincial centres. It was 'Schemo Magnifico' again, transferred to the newspaper realm, and for Alfred there was still a residue of inspiration in that sweeping original publishing concept of his. Jones's keenness had a more immediately practical source. The General Post Office was granting 'private wire' facilities to newspapers between 6 p.m. and

6 a.m. daily. For £500 a year, which included the services of a trained operator at either end, news could be fed direct from London to all the chief cities and towns of Britain. Jones saw the 'private wire' as the instrument of a development which would greatly enlarge the Harmsworths' newspaper power and, in doing so, handsomely improve his own prospects. Where existing newspapers could not be acquired, new ones would be started. A beginning was made with that grandiose plan, largely, it appears, under the pressure of Jones's enthusiasm. The brothers bought the *Glasgow Mail & Record*, a title merging two older papers, one of them the *Glasgow Daily Mail*. They bought at the same time the antiquated gas-powered plant of the *Glasgow Echo*, founded as a result of a lock-out of the staff of the *Glasgow Citizen*. The paper had trade union support, but lacked capital. It had shut down in May 1895. A total outlay of not more than £7,000, most of which came from Harold's pocket, gave the Harmsworths useful new experience. Their Glasgow paper, published at a halfpenny, was the proving-ground of the London *Daily Mail*.

'K.J.' later explained that because the Glasgow paper did not succeed in the first year they were driven back to consider 'the converse idea, namely, to produce a daily paper in London which should be on sale in every city of the United Kingdom at an early hour of the day'. The implication appears to be that had the Glasgow venture more quickly justified itself, they would have gone ahead with the scheme for a provincial chain. Well before 1895 had passed, Alfred was fully preoccupied by his important new project in London. There is the annotation to be made here that there are interesting likenesses between the typography and make-up of the Glasgow *Daily Record* of 1895 and the London *Daily Mail* of 1896. The fortunes of the Glasgow *Daily Record* took a turn for the better when one night a selection of racing tips was put over the wire from London. Later, the paper passed into Harold Harmsworth's personal ownership and, helped by the well organized news service of the London *Daily Mail*, it became Scotland's most widely circulated daily. In 1924, Harold Harmsworth, by then Viscount Rothermere, sold it for over £1,000,000. It has its place in the history of journalism as a stepping-stone towards one of the most influential newspaper developments of the age.

★　　　★　　　★

Perceptibly, now, the era was moving towards its close. The perspectives, constants, values, of a seemingly immutable order were subject to revision in the light of a dawning new century. The old seemed older, and the young younger, than their years. Alfred Harmsworth had arrived at the age of thirty with the adolescent shyness which softened his personality. He could subdue it to the demands of his calling, but he preferred anonymity to publicity. When *Who's Who* requested an entry from him, he restricted it to thirteen lines. Shyness was a dominant characteristic of the Harmsworth boys, in Harold awkwardly so. A contemporary who often saw Alfred at the Temple Restaurant in Tudor Street said that he always showed a marked diffidence in making his way to his regular place there, yet as soon as he entered everyone was psychically aware of his presence. 'Quiet, acute and self-contained,' Arnold Bennett wrote in his diary after seeing him at the theatre one evening at that time. 'He might be a young *Saturday Review-er* or a *Yellow Book* editor. Never did a man's appearance so belie his character.' If it was somewhat ungraciously presumed, the anomaly undoubtedly existed. The novelist-to-be was accurately reporting an inconsistency between Alfred's achievements and appearance. He still had his freelance air. It seemed at odds with success and influence and suggested that an occult favouritism was at work on his behalf. He had reached, in those middle 1890s, the full extent of his physical height, 5 feet 8 inches, without showing any sign of the weight which would mock the classical compliments bestowed on him in youth and become a dangerous obsession of his middle age. To some observers at the time he seemed to have a feminine softness of contour, as if he needed rough exercise. His looks and bearing were those of a young man of quality as well as of substance. That bright new illustrated weekly, *The Sketch*, had recently referred to his 'clear-cut, senatorial face'. The physical refinement was offset by an unmistakable air of authority, of governance, which is the most distinctly masculine attribute. To some he seemed imperious, but that was an older, superficial trait, a chin-up defiance belonging to the years of economic and social insecurity and always subservient to his natural charm, which was formidable in its power to make amends. He had not outgrown, either, the boyishness of heart which was for long a memorable thing about him. An interviewer for the *English Illustrated Magazine* went down to see him at Elmwood in the spring of 1896. 'I seemed to be in the company of a boy concerned with boyish pleasures and boyish hobbies, of one to whom the busy world outside is unknown.' Like Plato's wondering child-man, he seemed to see all life with the vivid intensity of a first vision.

On R. D. Blumenfeld, then of the *New York Herald* and for forty years afterwards editor of the *Daily Express*, he made the impression of 'a forceful youth whose whole outlook was cast in the direction of youth'. H. W. Wilson, who became one of his editorial associates, saw him 'playing trains' at Elmwood. The diary has a note in 1895: 'Bought a new model engine with carriages.' He still gave careful attention to the contents of the boys' papers. Their editors, writers and artists were frequently called down to Broadstairs. He liked commissioning stories about wild animals. One of his editors said that he always showed 'a strange excitement when wolves were discussed'. This persisting boyishness was attractive and enviable. The sense of fun that went with it made a good impression but it was not easily turned inward. He laughed at himself only at the prompting of others, usually women, when it was a matter of *amour-propre*. He had a preference for the immature sort of joke known as the leg-pull but did not like having his own leg pulled. Two Edison Bell gramophone records, one of sneezing, the other of snoring, were capable of reducing him to helpless laughter long after they had ceased to amuse anyone else.

As editor of *Answers*, he had absorbed a bewildering miscellany of factual information and, like the average of his readers, he had little sense of the relation of things. He was almost entirely without the power of sustained thought or of abstraction. In Hazlitt's words, he saw his objects always near, never on the horizon. Caught by an idea, he was capable of the mental leaps of genius. In circumstances requiring reasoned discussion he was given to lapsing into silence, often construed as the brooding of an intellect which he did not possess. He was acutely responsive to the living minute. For him it was a new world every day. By now he was confirmed in his habit of walking quickly, eating quickly, talking quickly. His metabolism, it seemed, was geared to a fundamental anxiety. Speculatively, one recalls here the abrupt displacement from the attention of his mother by her rapid childbearing. Only a catastrophic sense of dismay, it seems, could have fashioned the psychic bond that made him her adoring slave. 'This is our day', he would write, cable or telephone on his birthday. His deference to her was as complete in opinion as in sentiment. So profound an attachment meant that he could never give himself fully to any other person and those who were enticed into intimacy with him were apt to suffer from his mercurial interpretation of that state. That, increasingly, he seemed to be a lonely figure was not wholly due to his public eminence.

BOOK TWO

Napoleon of the Press

Chapter Eight

May 4, 1896

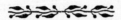

AT 1 a.m. on Monday, May 4, 1896, there was mounting tension at 2 Carmelite Street, London, E.C., premises which had been taken over from Sir George Newnes, who had used them for the business department of his *Westminster Gazette*. They were about to be the scene of a more dynamic enterprise, young Alfred Harmsworth's spectacular leap into the twentieth century. Lord Nelson, challenging fate before the battle of Cape St. Vincent, had cried: 'Westminster Abbey or glorious victory!' Less flamboyantly, Alfred Harmsworth said to Kennedy Jones as together they waited while the machine men made ready: 'Bankruptcy or Berkeley Square!' Editorial workers, some of them in frock coats, trooped down the stone stairs to the basement. Other members of the staff whose duties were done for the day stayed on to witness the climax of weeks of anonymous effort. Many of them had been present at an inaugural party given by Alfred and Molly Harmsworth two nights before at their temporary London home in Charles Street, Mayfair. 'There was a bucket of champagne at every man's feet', according to one of the guests, who also reported that 'A.H.'s drink was ginger-beer'. It was noted with still less approval that the company was not invited to share his taste in cigarettes, large, long 'Khedivials', supplied to him from Cairo. They were the first personal luxury that he had allowed himself when he began to make money.

At 1.20 a.m. the three new fast rotary presses throbbed into life. Out of the subterranean roar and clatter the first copies of the *Daily Mail* were flung into the world, telling of war in Bulawayo, assassination in Persia, atrocities in Cuba, murder at Reading. An editorial scorned 'the exquisite nonsense' of the three-miles-an-hour limit for the newest form of road vehicle, the motor-car. There was the first instalment of a serial, *Beauregard's Shadow*, by an unnamed author. A page headed 'The Daily Magazine' was described as 'a practical attempt to provide something more than the mere news of the day'. Another section was 'Women's Realm', a still greater novelty. The paper's front page was filled with small advertisements. Its back page proclaimed in ugly black-letter type the merits of Bovril, Dr Tibbles' Vi-Cocoa, Erard Pianos and Krog's Patent Malted Food for Horses, the latter looking like a joke drawing from *Comic Cuts*.

Alfred Harmsworth's diary reported that the moment of the birth of the *Daily Mail* had been reached only 'after a severe struggle and with many misgivings'. Up till then, newspapers had been folded by hand, usually by the newsagents' womenfolk. In many middle-class households it was the maid's first morning duty to take in the paper with the milk and iron the fold in readiness for the master's descent to breakfast. The new *Daily Mail* printing presses had a mechanical folding device, concerning which the two suppliers of the presses, Foster of Preston and Hoe of London, came into legal conflict about patent rights. According to a printing trade paper, the threat of an injunction hung over the *Daily Mail* that first night. There were other difficulties. The London wholesale newsagents were not satisfied with the Harmsworths' terms. A deputation was sent to the office. Tempers ran high, with the distributors on one side and Alfred Harmsworth and Kennedy Jones on the other, before a settlement was reached.

The first copy of the *Daily Mail* to come off the machines was formally handed by the head printer to Alfred Harmsworth, who autographed it and had it sent at once by messenger to his mother at 112 Maida Vale. He signed about a hundred other copies for members of the staff. 'Slept at the Salisbury', in Salisbury Square, Fleet Street, his diary tells us. A different account appeared in *The Rise of the Daily Mail* (1916). 'I did not leave the office for the first two days and nights, and then went home and slept for twenty-four hours.' Yet another version was given by Sir Winston Churchill: 'I remember lunching at Londonderry House on the day the *Daily Mail* first came out, and Alfred Harmsworth sat as the guest of honour at a very small party.' That occasion is not entered in the diary, where we read: 'A big success, I think, bigger than was anticipated. Sold 390,000 copies. Letters and telegrams of congratulation pouring in on the *début* of the *Daily Mail*.' He had anticipated a sale of 100,000, while hoping for 150,000.

Number 1 of the *Daily Mail* was not the first issue of that newspaper to be produced, though it was the first to be published. There is at the British Museum a token issue dated February 15, 1896, a slip bearing the name of the paper, for copyright, and some Stock Exchange prices. Between that date and May 4, sixty-five experimental four-page issues were printed, unknown to the public and, for that matter, to most people

One of the 'trial-run' editions of the *Daily Mail*

in and around Fleet Street, where there were recurring waves of speculation about what was going on at 2 Carmelite Street, down by the river. When navvies were seen at work there digging out the foundations, someone remarked: 'That'll be the grave of the Harmsworths' new paper.' It proved to be a pit for the old journalism.

No newspaper was more carefully planned. During eleven weeks a staff went through the motions of getting out a succession of 'dummy' editions. The nucleus of a news and cable service had already been established. Offices were opened in Paris and New York. Reporters went out on 'stories' which none but themselves and their colleagues would read. There was special training for the subs—vernacular for sub-editors—in the art of cutting down verbosity, the curse of the older newspapers. They were the forerunners of a new race of Fleet Street craftsmen. Before 1896, news was commonly printed as it came in, its importance judged by its length. At *The Times* the make-up of the news pages was left to the discretion of the head printer. Harmsworth would have none of that. Also, as an essential part of his trial-runs, 'copy' was set up by the new linotype machines. The rehearsals had required the paper to go to press with the same efficiency as if it were being put on sale next morning. To shield its character from too inquisitive eyes, misleading features were included in the make-up. The paper's title was set in Roman capitals instead of the intended Old English. As publication day drew nearer, a touch of impishness appeared. 'A £1,000 note would not purchase this copy of the *Daily Mail*.' Alfred Harmsworth later explained: 'We were all somewhat overwrought by a fortnight's final work.' Copies of the rehearsal issues were sneaked into rival newspaper offices. The strategy was apparently effective: 'The Harmsworths' new rag hasn't a chance.' There were less impetuous opinions. To some it seemed that young Harmsworth had the Midas touch, that he could not go wrong, that he had but to say which course he would follow and the way was made mysteriously clear for him. His income for 1896 was £42,255. At Coutts' Bank, in the Strand, where he had opened his main personal account in 1891, he was now received by one of the partners, instead of a manager, as before.

Daily Mail was not the first choice of name. 'Arrow', 'Express', 'Herald', had been chalked on the blackboard in the bungalow at Elmwood. 'Arrow' was Alfred's first preference. He believed in one-word titles, his faith in them confirmed by his experience with *Answers*. Kennedy Jones claimed to have converted him to *Daily Mail*, which had long been in use in the provinces. Leicester Harmsworth told Alfred how, as an *Answers* representative in Birmingham, he had heard the newsboys there shouting 'Mail!' as they sped through the streets with their supplies of the *Birmingham Daily Mail* and how he thought then that it was 'a good penetrating cry for Smiths' boys'. Finally, Alfred wrote his verdict on the blackboard:

Daily Mail. It was seen there for some years after. The word 'Mail' by itself, he told Leicester, 'gave no clue to the periodic character of the paper'. Soon, hoardings in London and the Home Counties flared DAILY MAIL in bold yellow letters on a blue ground. According to Kennedy Jones, experiment had shown that those two colours were the least susceptible to the changing light of day. For that reason, he said, he chose them as his racing colours when the *Daily Mail* made him rich enough to own a stable. He claimed also to have suggested the date of the paper's first appearance. 'I was born on May 4. It was an early ambition of mine that if ever I helped to found a newspaper it should be born on my birthday. Fortune favoured.' Leicester Harmsworth said that in choosing the first week of May, his brother had been influenced by a less sentimental consideration. 'News was always more prolific at the opening of the London season.'

Before any new Harmsworth publication came out, it was Alfred's custom to hold a round-table talk about it with Harold, Cecil, Leicester and Hildebrand. A message from him: 'Be at Sweetings' at one-thirty for a chat', meant that there was something more important than the menu to discuss. The 'chats' were rarely held at the office. Sometimes the younger brothers were summoned to Broadstairs. When the *Daily Mail* moved to the top of the agenda, Harold was less often present. The other brothers were aware that, as between the two eldest, business discussions had become a contest in which Alfred's ideas about journalism were joined with Harold's about economy. Engrossed in his newest venture, Alfred had let Harold work his will on the periodicals, not always with happy results. In their early talks about the *Daily Mail*, Harold had urged the use of tinted paper because it was cheaper than white. Alfred summarily banished the idea: 'They'll think we're another sporting sheet.' He and Harold had already been in disagreement over the same matter in regard to the *Evening News*, which printed its later editions on pink paper. His attitude now stiffened. From the first he had planned to print the *Daily Mail* on good white paper. It would flatter the halfpenny newspaper reading public. He may also have had in view the growing use of illustrations in newspapers. For that, white paper was a practical necessity.

In consequence, Harold's part in starting the *Daily Mail* was little more than that of a newsprint buyer, though he had supervisory powers over the business management. A state of dissent had developed in which Alfred not only asserted freedom of action but became secretive about it. Leicester Harmsworth said: 'The chief reason for Alfred's monopoly of decision regarding the new paper was his fear of Harold's ideas of economy. Alfred planned great expenditure on foreign telegrams and the getting of news in general. Harold, he had no doubt, would work against such a policy', and, using an intermediary, Harold did so.

Alfred, then, was the sole founder of the *Daily Mail*. 'My Coming Daily Paper' headed a display announcement signed 'A. C. Harmsworth' in *Answers* early that year. He wrote in the diary for May 18, two weeks after the paper had started publication: 'Harold came to the office, first time for weeks.' In later years, Harold was in the habit of speaking of the *Daily Mail* as 'really an afterthought', the result of the morning paper experience which Alfred and he had gained in Glasgow. He ignored the long gestating period disclosed in Alfred's diary and in the letter written to Cecil and Leicester during their world tour of 1894. He forgot that Alfred had told *Evening News* shareholders in November 1898 that the *Evening News* had been bought 'with a view to the eventual establishment of the *Daily Mail*'.

Twelve days before the advertised publication date, another new morning paper appeared, the penny *Daily Courier*. The paths of Newnes and Harmsworth had crossed again. In the field of daily journalism, Newnes had been well ahead of Harmsworth, as he had been with his *Tit-Bits*. His evening *Westminster Gazette*, printed in good clear type on green paper to temper the eyestrain of readers using the poorly lit suburban trains, had come out on January 31, 1893, a thoughtful, well-written newspaper published in the Liberal interest. His *Daily Courier*, likewise, made no submission to popular taste and rumours that it was to forestall the *Daily Mail* were soon discounted. Seeing the first issue, Alfred Harmsworth was not much impressed. He thought it 'rather a muddle'. Its sixteen pages were of the size and make-up of a weekly review. It bore the marks of amateur inspiration. Its editor, W. Earl Hodgson, was a magazine journalist who had worked on *Blackwood's*. He was said to have required his sub-editors to transform every paragraph into a gem of literature. An advertisement for the *Daily Courier* appeared in the second issue of the *Daily Mail*: 'An Important New Departure in Daily Journalism.' Soon, departure was seen to be the operative word. The *Daily Courier* stopped in August, a praiseworthy, impracticable essay in newspaper production. Only its size endured, perpetuated in the 'tabloid'* papers to come. As a newspaper experiment it confirmed a difference of character between Newnes and Harmsworth. Both made daring mistakes. Newnes's were touched with idealism. His *Daily Courier* had little chance of success. His *Westminster Gazette* was read by an intelligent public which did not know that he was losing between £5,000 and £10,000 a year to keep it going, his total loss being £100,000. Harmsworth had his quixotic moods, too, but he was scared of bad luck.

There was nothing to startle the attention in his new daily, designed though it was to be of 'the greatest interest to the greatest number'. Yet its crisply edited news pages seemed to reflect a sense of the adventure of

* See reference to the word 'tabloid' on page 266.

living at the dawn of a new century. To a printer's eye it had more 'white' in it than was usual among newspapers then. To a visitor from New York, it might have been more than a casual reminder of Charles A. Dana's *Sun*, which had been far ahead in the art of news condensation. 'Anything more depressing to contemplate than a page of any of the penny papers ... it would be difficult to imagine. No one with a zest for news or views could face those rows of solid columns of the smallest print. It would be true on the whole to say that Alfred Harmsworth changed all that.' The passage is quoted from the autobiography of Wilson Harris, for twenty years editor of *The Spectator*, sometime Independent Member of Parliament for Cambridge University. Concerning the 'solid columns of uninteresting matter', the Fleet Street trade journal, *Newspaper Owner and Manager*, stated that 'even the correctors of the press have yawned as they have dealt with it'. Sir John Robinson, for many years editor of the *Daily News* (now *News Chronicle*), wrote: 'As regards opinions, the cheap press does not differ greatly from the dear press that preceded it. In every other respect it is immeasurably superior.'

On May 4, 1896, leading articles in *The Times* filled 81 inches of space, in the *Daily Telegraph* 32 inches, in the *Morning Post* 53 inches, in the *Daily Chronicle* 55 inches and in the *Daily News* 41½ inches. The *Daily Mail* leading articles for the same day filled 17 inches, divided into four short topics. It was a radical change of practice, involving office arguments which nearly ended in leading articles being dropped altogether. The matter was in doubt until Friday of that first week, when it was decided that the paper needed a platform from which, as Kennedy Jones said, 'to explain the drift of events'. A few months later an article in the *Westminster Review*, headed 'The Decline of the Leader', mentioned that 'even *The Times* has recently come out on occasion with one leader only', an example soon widely copied. 'That vulgar little halfpenny paper', despised particularly by the *Yorkshire Post*, had successfully defied an august tradition, principally sustained thereafter by the long and often admirable front-page leaders of J. A. Spender in the *Westminster Gazette*.

Contemporary critics of the new cult of brevity missed the obvious objection, its tendency to confuse incidents with events. Instead, they dwelt on its bad effect on parliamentary reporting. Up to the coming of the *Daily Mail*, leading politicians could count on their speeches being printed *in extenso*. Spender remembered newspapers which gave 'solid pages of Parliament to which were added solid pages of platform oratory' (*The Public Life*, 1925). For that practice it could be claimed that it helped to steady such public opinion as existed. But the new classes of reader, who had been enfranchised by the Third Reform Bill of twelve years before, had no use for the long speeches which filled the newspaper columns. 'To report parliament at length, or even to report it fairly at all, was to bore and estrange them.'* Thereafter, who said it and how it was said were to be matters of more public curiosity than what was said, in and out of parliament. Harmsworth journalism changed the relationship of press and public. It destroyed the old enlightened view that reason would prevail. The argument of the leading article gave way to the comment of the paragraph.

Rather less vulnerable to the hostility of the older grandiose school was Alfred Harmsworth's insistence on simplification, on first paragraphs which at least gave a clue to what followed, on illustrating foreign news by maps, always for the readers' convenience. His order was 'Explain, simplify, clarify!' Foreign currency figures must be made clear in English money terms. Foreign language quotations were discouraged. A staff writer who used the phrase *fait accompli* in an article found it asterisked next morning in the paper, with a footnote supplied by the proprietor: 'Mr Hands means "accomplished fact".' He objected to slang. 'Omnibus' was not allowed to appear as 'bus'.

The new types of sub-editor whom Alfred Harmsworth had caused to be specially trained in his paper's 'style' were held ruthlessly to their task of making many paragraphs where few were used before. He had seen what other editors had not, that for the jostled travelling reader paragraphs were necessary signposts. He also insisted that the paper's regular features should appear in the same place day after day. 'Readers must know where to find what they want.' For the first time, large numbers of City-bound readers could be sure of having a good grasp of the day's news by the time their morning journey was done. There were no long columns of matter to be got through in a hurry or to be taken home for perusal at night. It was a refreshing change in the routine of newspaper reading.

Still more important for the Harmsworth future was Alfred's belief that women could be induced to become newspaper readers. The penny papers had mostly ignored their special interests. It followed from his personal psychology, as well as from his previous publishing experience, that women would figure with great prominence in the immense new circulation vistas that were unfolding before him.

Movements in women's world—that is to say, changes in dress, toilet matters, cookery, and home matters generally—are as much entitled to receive attention as nine out of ten of the matters which are treated of in the ordinary daily paper. Therefore two columns are set aside exclusively for ladies.

That mildly expressed declaration of *Daily Mail* policy might have been lifted from *Home Chat*. Behind it there was a clash of views between Alfred and 'K.J.'. Jones was at first against what he called the unnecessary

* R. C. K. Ensor, *England: 1870-1914* (Clarendon Press).

PENNY NEWSPAPER
FOR
ONE HALFPENNY.

Daily Mail.

THE BUSY MAN'S
DAILY JOURNAL

NO. I.   (REGISTERED AS A NEWSPAPER)   LONDON, MONDAY, MAY 4, 1896.   ONE HALFPENNY.

BUSINESS NOTICES.

PERSONAL.

BIRTHS.

MARRIAGES.

DEATHS.

HOTEL CECIL.

THE ILLUSTRATED CARPENTER AND BUILDER.

THE WEEKLY PAPER
1d. ALL THE BUILDING INDUSTRIES.

REYNOLDS NEWSPAPER
LARGEST, CHEAPEST, AND BEST.

THE BEST WEEKLY NEWS.
PAPER FOR SUNDAY READING.

'We've struck a gold mine!'—Alfred Harmsworth in 1896

sacrifice of space to domestic matters, though he recanted later. For the moment, he wanted more space to be given to racing, his favourite sport; there were few days on which he did not have a bet. Alfred had no interest in racing then or after. He retorted by ordering an improvement in the tone of the racing news and notes already appearing in the paper. At that time, the quality of racing journalism in general was poor. Alfred's intervention resulted in considerable changes for the better. He invented the pseudonym of 'Robin Goodfellow' in the *Daily Mail*, a racing name still respected in the sporting world. He reformed the City page, ordering a newly appointed City editor, Charles Duguid, to 'make a page that is independent and interesting'. Till then, City journalism had been neither: it had consisted of the publication of prospectuses and company reports without comment or criticism, except for the 'puffs' of promoters' agents. The investing public had been given almost no guidance or protection. The *Daily Mail* revealed the news in company prospectuses and share dealings. It changed the character and improved the quality of financial journalism.

Alfred Harmsworth had announced the *Daily Mail* as 'the busy man's paper', a slogan which he printed day by day in the little spaces called 'ears' on either side of the title at the top of the front page. He was opposed to newspapers published in the clubman tradition. They affronted sympathies crystallized in his relationship with his mother. Installed by that time as the chatelaine of a fine town mansion, 2 Great Cumberland Place, Marble Arch, she was an arbiter whose judgments touched the lives of far more people than had ever heard of her. The critics of the Harmsworth revolution all overlooked the truth that 'woman appeal' was the heart and soul of it.

*   *   *

Among the messages which Alfred Harmsworth received on 'that glorious May morning'—description 'K.J's'—was one from Mr Gladstone. He had assisted the fame of Mrs Humphrey Ward's novel, *Robert Elsmere*, by writing an article on it in *The Contemporary Review*. His commendation of the *Diary of Marie Bashkirtseff* had also gone forth to the world. His telegram to Alfred Harmsworth: *The Daily Mail appears to be a most interesting experiment to which I give my heartiest good wishes*, may not have been meant to be taken in the same testimonial sense, though *Answers* had always been immensely respectful to him. His message was conspicuously 'played up' in the paper. A. J. Balfour, who professed not to read newspapers, wrote privately of his 'high appreciation'. Knowing the skill, energy and resources available to the *Daily Mail*, he said, he could not doubt its success. 'You have taken the lead in newspaper enterprise and

Monday 4 (125-241)

A by Lucas, I think, bigger than we anticipated.

Sold 397,000 Letters & telegrams of congratulation pouring in on the debut of "The Daily Mail".

Kept at the Salisbury

Diary entry for May 4, 1896, dictated by Alfred Harmsworth to Sutton

both you and the Party are to be heartily congratulated', though the Conservative Party would not invariably find aid and comfort in the *Daily Mail* of the years to come. There was also a telegram praising 'a wonderful halfpennyworth'. It was signed 'Newnes'. Alfred Harmsworth would have been not less gratified to know that 'Labby' (Henry Labouchere) of *Truth* had studied his copy of the *Daily Mail* that morning in his rooms at 5 Old Palace Yard and that he had put it down with the prophecy: 'This paper will go.'

Returning to the office on the afternoon of that first publishing day, 'K.J.' noted with satisfaction that the white-coated newsvendors in the streets were selling their copies fast. Many people paid a penny for the new paper, not realizing that the price was a halfpenny. At Carmelite Street he had to push his way through a crowd of men waiting for further supplies. The printing machines of the *Daily Mail* could not meet the demand, which totalled 397,215 copies and was not far short of the combined sales of the London penny papers. The *Evening News* printing, publishing and circulation staff had gone into action on behalf of the new paper. The presses of three other newspapers were standing by. We have Kennedy Jones's word for it that Alfred Harmsworth returned to the office that day to savour the beginnings of a success which in part he attributed to the weather. It had been a day of brilliant sunshine, flooding London with the zest of spring. 'It is a singular fact,' Alfred wrote not long after, 'that every one of the Harmsworth journals has been blessed by a fine opening day.' Without venturing to regard it as a dispensation of providence, he avowed that it counted for a good deal. 'Well, how goes it?' he was asked by Kennedy Jones, who had been given a seven and a half per cent interest in the new paper. 'Orders still pouring in,' Alfred told him. 'We've struck a gold mine.'

Alfred Harmsworth's instinctive judgment had flared up in a masterstroke of divination. Mentally, he was allied to the mass of his readers, but he was enormously more active within that range. He knew what the people wanted because their prejudices were his own. Backing his certainty that a newspaper is the creation of its time and environment was a realistic acknowledgment of the fact that the costs of production had been brought down by the new wood pulp making processes and the arrival of mechanical typesetting. Newsprint had only once been cheaper in the previous ten years. It was now £11 a ton. He summarized the position as he saw it in 1896: 'On going thoroughly into the £. s. d. question it became clear that most of the existing dailies were really halfpennyworths sold at a penny. The proprietors had simply pocketed the difference instead of sharing the advantage with the public.'

There was no novelty in publishing the *Daily Mail* at a halfpenny. A number of provincial dailies had been published at a halfpenny and for a short time there had been a halfpenny morning version of *The Echo*, one of London's evening papers. In the 1880s, *The Times* had published *The Summary* at a halfpenny, withdrawing it after twelve months. *The Morning* had been published at a halfpenny in May 1892, beating the new halfpenny *Morning Leader* by two days in a race to reach the news-stands first. Partly because their news services were not so well organized as Harmsworth's, they did not succeed with the public and the identity of *The Morning* was absorbed by the *Daily Express*, while the *Morning Leader*, which was ahead of its rivals in the use of illustrations, is embalmed with the *Daily News* in the vaults of the *News Chronicle*. There were those who believed that just as Alfred Harmsworth had taken his idea for *Answers* from *Tit-Bits*, the *Daily Mail* owed its inspiration to those two defunct halfpenny papers. The originality of the *Daily Mail* was in its enterprise, in its policy of giving a pennyworth for a halfpenny. Better value—that was the secret of Harmsworth's success. He could not see why the news agencies should be looked on as the main fount of news supply, why so many of the world's cities and towns were never 'date-lined' in the news columns, why the only news to come out of America was about cyclones.

In his resolve to make a better newspaper he was drawing on his experience with the *Evening News*. Taking over that paper, he made the discovery that newspaper sales were subject to extraordinary ups and downs. Some days, sales would rise for no obvious reason. On other days, there would be an equally unaccountable fall. The news of the smashing of the Spanish fleet off Santiago during the Spanish-American war of 1898 did not sell a single extra copy of the *Evening News*, which had gone to considerable expense in making special cable arrangements *via* New York. The battle of Omdurman, which made Kitchener a popular idol, was not a selling cry for the *Daily Mail* newsboys and neither was the great Dreyfus trial. Public feeling responded more reliably to the news of the death of Gladstone, which sold many extra editions. Alfred also recorded that sports news, for which readers had shown an insatiable appetite over two or three years, suffered a slump in 1899. Those often mysterious fluctuations brought their own problems. The answer, as he saw it, was to provide a consistently interesting newspaper which would steady the public demand. Hence the growth of the 'feature' journalism of the modern newspaper. He wrote that it was his 'good luck' that the older newspapers gave no sign of occupying the position which he had staked out for his paper. 'Their lack of initiative and their subservience to Party was a direct invitation to the assault administered by the *Daily Mail* on Monday, May 4, 1896.' It was part of his good luck that the opposition of the distributing trade to halfpenny newspapers was by then losing its force.

Reviewing his paper's early progress, he implied that the strategy of deception employed during the rehearsal period was carried over into the first months of the paper's existence. London Letters, appearing in the provincial press, suggested that 'because of heavy losses the price of the *Daily Mail* will be raised to a penny'. The rumours were not denied. They may have been inspired. Alfred Harmsworth commented: 'People will usually believe what they want to believe. That kind of talk kept competitors away and helped to make our foundations secure.'

The first *Daily Mail* leading article mentioned a development which was more significant than the tactics of the trial-run period or the evasions that came after. 'It is no secret that remarkable new inventions have just come to the help of the Press. . . . It is the use of these inventions on a scale unprecedented in any English newspaper office that enables the *Daily Mail* to effect a saving of from 30 to 50 per cent and to be sold for half the price of its contemporaries. That is the whole explanation of what would otherwise be a mystery.'

The chief of these new developments was linotype setting, which quickened the pace of newspaper production by applying the principle of the typewriter to the automatic casting of type, hitherto an operation of skilled hands. 'So mechanical an art as the setting and spacing of a line of uniform type was bound to be accomplished by machinery, sooner or later, and the revolution is now being quietly effected in thousands of printing offices in all parts of the world.' Such was the text of an advertisement issued by the Linotype Company, of 188 Fleet Street, in 1899. There was a consoling paragraph for printers who might be stirred by Luddite impulses. 'Does this mechanical line-setting imply that the hand compositor's occupation is gone? By no means. It indicates that his higher and truer avocation is that of an artist in type. As a line-setter, he cannot hope to compete with the machine operator. But as a display hand he has as fine a field open to him as any handicraftman can command.'

Prejudice, ignorance, custom, trades union bigotry: the new device was met by strong resistant forces. Machines were wilfully mishandled. Some were sent back to the makers because the men refused to work them. One-pound shares of the company fell to half-a-crown with no takers. A prominent journal described the linotype as 'a hopeless invention'. Alfred Harmsworth showed no interest until 1893: 'Went to see the Linotype and was much struck by it.' The prototype machine had been brought from America in 1889. The *Railway Herald*, in Chancery Lane, installed three machines that year. Provincial newspapers, the *Leeds Mercury* first, were ahead of the London newspaper press in taking up the new development. The first London newspaper to do so was *The Globe* in 1892. In that year, the Linotype Company profits were £2,100. In the following three years they rose to £59,000; in three years more to £180,000. It was a rate of progress akin to that of the Harmsworth businesses, to which it was probably as indispensable as cheap paper and the 1870 Education Act. Newspaper progress was indebted also to the General Post Office, which had made remarkable strides in the telegraphic transmission of news and other 'copy'. From a pedestrian eighty words a minute, it had worked up to six hundred words a minute. 'I really believe we have made the Press', claimed the engineer-in-chief of the General Post Office, Sir William Preece, and there were Fleet Street realists who said 'Hear, hear'.

*　　　*　　　*

How much did it cost to start the *Daily Mail*? The original financing was apparently not a subject of documentary record. A preliminary announcement in *Answers* told readers of that weekly: '£100,000 is at stake. It is quite possible that the undertaking may not be a success. So far we have met with no failure.' In *The Romance of the Daily Mail*, published in 1903, Alfred Harmsworth named half a million pounds as 'the initial cost of machinery, buildings, ink factories and the like, and this was altogether apart from the capital required for daily working expenses'. He was writing seven years after the event and appears to have been reckoning the cost of establishing the paper as a property around which there was about to be grouped, in 1905, a new company formation, the Associated Newspapers Ltd. of our day. In *The Mystery of the Daily Mail*, published in 1921, it was stated: 'The total initial capital was less than £15,000.' The reliably compiled history of modern newspapers, *The Street of Ink*, by H. Simonis,* also names £15,000 as the sum, 'and the whole of it was never required'. John Baxter Boyle, manager of the *Westminster Gazette*, who had kept in touch with the Harmsworths from the time of their purchase of the *Evening News*, left a record of lunching with Alfred at Schuler's Restaurant, Ludgate Circus, 'when he told me that the *Daily Mail* had taken only £12,500 of the £25,000 which he had provided. He showed me a list of the securities in which he proposed investing the surplus £12,500 of the fund which he had set aside to establish the paper.' *The History of The Times* states that 'the paper had been started with a mere £15,000 got together by the two Harmsworths and Kennedy Jones', but there is no warranty for supposing that either Harold Harmsworth or Jones had any part in the financing. There was a tenacious rumour that Cecil Rhodes had provided some of the money. It was alleged that 'the wicked South African policy' of the *Daily Mail* was due to the flow of Rand gold into the Harmsworths' pockets. Alfred wrote in *Journalism as a Profession*†:

Many years ago I was unwise enough to purchase a number of shares in the Chartered Company, and, as Mr Labouchere remarked, 'a certain number of fools were let in at £8. 10s. each'. I was one of the fools, and still hold the shares, but, in addition to the depreciation in their value, I have never received a dividend, and have been overwhelmed with abuse in Parliament and elsewhere, and quite rightly, I think. It never occurred to me when I purchased these shares that there would be a South African war, and, had it occured to me, I should never have considered it possible that one's critics would suppose that such a property would bias one's judgement of national affairs. But I resolved then and there that under no circumstances would I ever again lay myself open to very just suspicion.

The disclaimer was not everywhere accepted. Down to the present day the belief has persisted in some quarters that Rhodes's money was behind the *Daily Mail* in 1896. What is not in doubt was Harmsworth's ample capacity to finance his *Daily Mail* venture himself. In May 1896 he had £80,000 worth of securities, apart from his large holdings in his companies. Helping to keep production costs down was the availability of the *Evening News* machinery and business organization. There was also the advantage of substantial and continuous publicity in the Harmsworth periodical press, with its millions of copies going out each week to all parts of the country. Each succeeding issue of the paper clearly

---

* Cassell, 1917.
† Hodder & Stoughton, 1903.

indicated that exceptional resources of finance, energy and enterprise were behind it.

In his diary for May 7, 1896, Alfred noted: 'Went to dinner of the Anglo-Saxon Club, where I was the guest of the evening.' Among those present was Sir Charles Dilke, M.P., sometime candidate for the highest political office, an enigmatic figure in public life. The day after the dinner he wrote to a young journalist named George Warrington Steevens, who was beginning to make a reputation for himself on the *Pall Mall Gazette* when he was impelled to resign in sympathy with its editor, Harry Cokayne Cust, M.P. Cust had left after a disagreement about policy with the proprietor, William Waldorf Astor. The resignation of Cust and some of the principal members of the staff was of itself a considerable news 'story'. Steevens was of the company which had gathered in the editor's room and solemnly sung the *Nunc Dimittis* before their final departure.

Charles Dilke to Steevens:

> House of Commons
> 8th May, 1896.

My dear Sir,—I met last night perhaps the most remarkable man I have ever seen—though I know Bismarck and knew Gambetta well. It is Harmsworth. The similarity of ideas between those of this Bonaparte First Consul and yourself suggests to me that it is possible that he might like to catch for some of his journalistic undertakings so cultivated, so intelligent, and so modern a journalist.

He is very young and his speech showed that he rates Rhodes too high. Rhodes is as strong as Bismarck, and youth rates strength too high, but Rhodes was never sharp and has become stupid. Harmsworth himself is superior, in that he is (probably) both strong and sharp.

> Very truly yours,
> CHARLES DILKE.

Steevens, a slight dark man of twenty-seven who wore *pince-nez* and looked at the world with shy observant eyes, was known as one of the most distinguished young scholars of the day. He may not have been a pre-destined journalist because his two first names were those of the character in *Pendennis* who wrote for a *Pall Mall Gazette* of Thackeray's imagination, but on the real paper of that name he had shown high promise. He had gone up to Oxford from the City of London School. A Balliol senior scholar, he gained a first in 'Mods' and 'Greats' and a fellowship to Pembroke College. Whether or not as a result of Dilke's intervention, he was soon in Harmsworth employment. 'Tell me what you can do', Alfred had said to him at their first interview. 'I think I can do anything from tying parcels downward', Steevens had replied 'in his queer shy cynical way'. He was given leaders to do but failed in that line of work. He was put on to reporting the Richmond Horse Show. Alfred Harmsworth said: 'He showed genius in his extraordinary power of observation and his entirely new way of recording what he had seen.' His prose was vigorous and memorable, like Kipling's. Describing a Lord Mayor's Show, he wrote: 'There were the usual number of unborn babies in the crowd.'

Chiefly, the *Daily Mail* staff had been recruited from the *Evening News*. John Hood Lingard, known as 'Daddy', who had worked in a theatre box-office, and John Cowley, thought by some to look like Sherlock Holmes, were brought in as stalwarts of the counting-house. Safe men, not 'big' men, were wanted there. Leicester Harmsworth said that Alfred made Lingard manager of the *Daily Mail* in order to keep Harold at a distance. Consequently, Harold 'took up' Cowley, using him to influence Lingard. The situation created mistrust of Cowley in Alfred's mind. It persisted for many years. Cowley profited greatly by his later association with Harold. Thomas Marlowe and Walter Evans supplied editorial experience. Another of the key men was George White, also from the evening paper, a pale thin man of guaranteed calm in a crisis. It was he who succeeded in getting the *Daily Mail* on to more breakfast tables outside London than any other metropolitan newspaper. Marlowe was Irish-born of English stock, educated at Queen's College, Galway. He said that he was first attracted to Fleet Street by reading the essay on Richard Savage in Johnson's *Lives of the Poets*. After serving under T. P. O'Connor on *The Star*, he joined the *Evening News* and made his mark by interviewing E. T. Hooley, the notorious financier of the cycling boom. It brought him to the notice of Alfred Harmsworth, who made him the *Daily Mail* news editor for the trial run period. Evans, a Birmingham man, had been assistant to Kennedy Jones on the *Evening News* and had also worked on the *Southern Daily Mail* at Portsmouth. He was small and scholarly-looking, with a prominent Adam's-apple and a cavalry officer's moustache. He did his work amid clouds of strong-smelling shag tobacco smoke and was said to subsist for long periods on an egg a day.

Alfred Harmsworth himself retained the title of editor. A tireless organizer of the paper's affairs, 'K.J.' was given editorial authority without the rank in Alfred's absence. The man in charge from day to day, responsibe for 'getting out' the paper, was J. E. McManus, a solicitor who had never practised and who had been editorially trained on *The Freeman's Journal*. He served some time as a leader writer on the *Leeds Daily News*. Then he came to the *Evening News* in London and outlasted several of its editors. Bohemian in his habits, he survived Alfred Harmsworth's distaste for them long enough to be the first recipient of a form of communication that was to become celebrated in newspaper annals, the personal comments on the *Daily Mail* by the chief proprietor which were posted up in the office every morning through the later years.

McManus stayed in the delicately balanced chair of an acting editor for two and a half years, the occupant of a curtained-off corner of the untidy gas-lit newsroom at 2 Carmelite Street. The main part of the room was used by six sub-editors and a varying number of reporters whose instant source of contact with the world outside was a single wall telephone. The days of Harmsworth office affluence were not yet. After McManus, who left to edit *The Morning*, there came Arthur Hungerford Pollen, son of a former professor in the old Catholic University of Dublin who was secretary to the Marquess of Ripon. Like McManus, he gave up the law for journalism. His *Daily Mail* time was short, not necessarily because he had been likened in appearance to Napoleon by T. P. O'Connor, writing in his new weekly, *M.A.P.* [Mainly About People]. Pollen had little news sense. He was more successful when he became a writer on naval topics.

Next on the scene was S. J. Pryor, a Liverpool telegraph operator who had worked in the New York office of an international news agency, and had then come back to England as assistant to the London representative of the *New York Journal*, Julian Ralph, afterwards well known as a war correspondent. Apt to be over-impressed by New York experience and given to raising expectations unencumbered by promises, Alfred invited Pryor to join the *Daily Mail*. He did so in the belief that he would become its editor. His new proprietor consulted him too often for the peace of mind of others in the office. The growing sense of crisis in South Africa made it desirable to open a *Daily Mail* news centre in Cape Town. Kennedy Jones was perhaps unduly enthusiastic about Pryor's qualifications for the job, with the result that Pryor reluctantly went. Returning after a few months with a bayonet as a souvenir, thereafter seen on every desk he used, he found that he had been superseded by Marlowe. He had received no intimation of the change and there ensued an office comedy, a daily race by Pryor to be ahead of Marlowe in reaching the editor's chair. It was said that because of his foresight in the matter of lunchtime sandwiches Marlowe finally won the contest. The situation caused much private amusement, tinged with the suggestion that no one was enjoying the joke more than the chief proprietor. His attitude was criticized when Marlowe was confirmed in authority over Pryor. Pryor was thought to have been badly treated. Taking his bayonet with him, he went to the *Daily Express* and then became editor of the ill-fated *Tribune*, one of Fleet Street's most spectacular failures. A capable and responsible journalist, he figures as the editor in Sir Philip Gibbs's novel of newspaper life, *The Street of Adventure*. Later, he worked on *The Times*. In 1918, he was given the newly-created post of press secretary at Buckingham Palace.

Pryor carried himself like a briskly preoccupied clerk. Marlowe walked with a commodore air. It seemed not merely expedient that he should eventually be made editor of the *Daily Mail*. He was designed by nature to adorn that position. As a figure-head, he was superb. He was also a first-class news man. He was three years younger than the chief proprietor but his greying hair gave him a look of seniority. Gruff and deep-voiced, with a glint of secret humour in his grey eyes, he had a quiet masterfulness that commanded respect. He had a reputation for standing up to his chief. Their relationship was governed on his side by prudence. If he never let himself be browbeaten, there were situations in which his silence was undignified. After his term as news editor, he was made acting editor, like those others before him. When Alfred Harmsworth was forced by sheer weight of work and responsibility to delegate some of his authority, Marlowe was given full status. He held it for twenty-seven years, a great servant of the paper.

Reversing a dictum of the character in *Pendennis* who dreamed of a newspaper 'written by gentlemen for gentlemen', Lord Salisbury is supposed to have said that the *Daily Mail* was 'run by office-boys for office-boys', a sneer that had as much truth as Bismarck's gibe at Salisbury, that he was 'a lath painted to look like iron'. The *Daily Mail* was being written and edited by men whose intellectual attainments were hardly inferior to Salisbury's: G. W. Steevens, H. W. Wilson, King's Scholar of Durham School and a scholar of Trinity College, Oxford, where he took honours, Arthur Hungerford Pollen, M.A. (Cantab.), Mayson Beeton, of Marlborough and Oxford, Ignatius Rubie, of the Sorbonne, Arthur Lynch, with several university degrees, G. A. B. Dewar, another Oxford man, who wrote the parliamentary sketches, and Max Beerbohm, one of the paper's regular writers on literary matters. For the first time, a staff of men with good minds was engaged in the production of a popular newspaper.

The man who took Marlowe's place as news editor was Lincoln Springfield, in later years part-proprietor and editor of a well-known weekly, *London Opinion*. Before taking over from Marlowe, he was asked down to Elmwood. At tennis and billiards he beat his host with easy superiority. 'Look here, Springfield,' Alfred Harmsworth said, 'do you think you're being quite tactful?' Springfield remembered 'the boyish laugh'. As news editor, Springfield was paid ten guineas a week, rated then as 'good money'. Harmsworth had made as complete a break with custom in wages and salaries as with other traditional practices in journalism. He sent them soaring at a time when £6 a week was reckoned a worthwhile salary and a thousand-a-year-man was the object of respectful salutations in 'the Street'.

There was the potent attraction of more money. There was the glamour of working for a wonderfully successful newspaper. There was Alfred Harmsworth's personal magnetism. 'We were all inspired by him. He would come into your room and leave behind him a trail of eagerness to do well.' Such was the testimony of one who joined the business department before the paper came out. 'It is difficult to convey the almost adoring respect in which Alfred Harmsworth was held by some of the younger members of the staff,' wrote another staff man who was then a junior reporter. 'There was a little chap named Mildred who said to me in an awe-stricken tone: "Do you know, I think Mr Alfred is such a great man that when I hear him coming up the stairs, I tremble all over!"' George Mildred, long regarded as an ideal Carmelite House employee, became one of Alfred Harmsworth's secretaries and it was put about that he always instinctively bowed on hearing his master's voice on the telephone. On being told of it, Alfred ordered another member of the staff to ring up Mildred and say that 'the Chief' wanted to speak to him. Then, slipping into the little room where Mildred sat at the telephone, waiting, Alfred called out: 'You needn't bow this time!'

It was the job of a young reporter named Vaughan Dryden to collect paragraphs for the column of book notes. In one of them he referred to books being preferable 'to papers which live on useless information'. He was summoned to 'Mr Alfred's' room. 'Let me tell you, young Dryden,' Alfred said with a meaning glance at a bookcase filled with *Answers* bound volumes, 'that this newspaper is founded on useless information.' Dryden remembered seeing him walk through the newsroom on specially busy nights with a large box of cigarettes which he took by the handful and scattered in front of the toiling 'subs'. McManus's son Clive, later of the *Daily Mail* staff, was startled, he said, by Alfred Harmsworth's looks on being introduced to him in the newsroom at that time. 'His hair was golden. He wore a light-grey frock coat. He was the handsomest person I had ever seen.' Copying their hero, several of the younger *Daily Mail* men wore their hair as he did, well smoothed down, with the bold parting and the pendant forelock. Imitation of Alfred Harmsworth was as keen if not as immolating a cult as that of Napoleon's young officers.

The frock coat was a symbol of professional worth which Alfred easily discarded when his abounding success had put him beyond the need to impress others. No one responded more readily than he to the new monarch's preference for informality in dress. From about 1901, he more usually wore a blue serge suit with the white-spotted red silk tie which became his hallmark. He bought the silk by the roll from Beale & Inman, of Bond Street, who kept the pattern exclusively for him. His *Daily Mail* men were expected to uphold the paper's prestige by dressing well. When Lord Salisbury's secretary complained of the 'unseemly attire' of a *Daily Mail* reporter who called at Hatfield House, Alfred put up a notice in the news-room calling attention to the importance of a good appearance. It was taken down when one of the older men arrived at the office in a morning suit which all too obviously had been made for an ampler figure. 'X— is the best reporter we have,' Alfred said, 'but in a frock coat he's a disaster.' He told his reporters: 'When you go to Belgrave Square you must be dressed for the front door. I won't have my people looking as if they ought to be sent down the basement steps.'

An old newsvendor whose pitch was outside King's Cross railway station told the *Newspaper Owner & Manager* (later the *Newspaper World*) that the *Daily Mail* was being bought by 'thousands of working men who never bought a morning paper before'. The same trade journal stated the opinion: 'There is no doubt that the *Daily Mail* has discovered a new reading public.' The old journalism was too cumbersome for the heirs of national education, advancing trade unionism and the extension of the franchise. Multiplying appetites rather than forming tastes, the wider development of education was dissolving 'the mysterious majesty of print', shifting the source of its power from the educated few to the mass. It was hardly the fault of the popular press if its readers were ill-equipped to digest what they read and had a poor sense of values. Alfred Harmsworth's thinking on the subject may not have been as lofty as that of the ancient administrator who said: 'These are not the best laws that I can make. They are the best that my Athenians can bear.' His new paper suited their preferences by giving them information in an easily assimilated form and it was for the schools, from which they were coming in increasing numbers, to train their inclinations. The pugnaciously opinionated 'K.J.' had his own view of the origin of the prevailing low levels of taste. The new types of newspaper reader, he said, were 'the children, the grandchildren and the great-grandchildren of a people accustomed to public hangings, public whippings, pillories, ducking stools and stocks. Was the taste engendered by such sights during the centuries to be outbred by the cheap schooling of a single generation?'

Meanwhile, Harmsworth journalism supplied many of the ingredients of self-education. 'Newspapers do some of the best work that used to be done by books,' John Morley told the citizens of Arbroath when opening their new public library in 1898. 'Intellectual curiosity has been stimulated enormously by this popularization of knowledge on subjects once regarded as the exclusive province of the specialist,' wrote A. J. Cummings, the political and social critic of the Liberal *News Chronicle*, in his book, *The Press* (Twentieth Century Library, 1936). 'If the *Daily Mail* had not been produced by the Harmsworths, something very similar must have taken its place. A literate nation sooner or later will demand a vital and popular press.' This is how Alfred Harmsworth himself saw the change which he had wrought:

Before the *Daily Mail* was published, journalism dealt with only a few aspects of life. What we did was to extend its view of life as a whole. This was difficult. It involved the training of a new type of journalist. The old type was convinced that anything which would be a subject of conversation ought to be kept out of the papers—the only thing that will sell a newspaper in large numbers is news and news is anything out of the ordinary.

The *Manchester Guardian* put it in another way. Harmsworth's *Daily Mail* 'made life more pleasant, more exciting, for the average man'. The same newspaper recorded also that 'even those journals which decided not to try to compete with the *Daily Mail* by imitating it had to improve their news services, their make-up, their typography, their commercial arrangements; those that would not or could not improve usually perished'. Echoing a famous voice in history, Alfred Harmsworth could say: 'I am the revolution.' The days of the old newspaper aristocracy were numbered. Soon, *The Saturday Review* was deriding the 'snippet' journalism of the new daily, while a trade journal surmised that 'some day there will be a daily paper consisting entirely of paragraphs'. The demand from the newspaper reading public inevitably fixed the character of the supply, which in itself was governed by the curiosity stimulated by the new literacy. Considering the breadth of its appeal the *Daily Mail* was a better newspaper than it need have been.

★   ★   ★

From the beginning the paper sacrificed advertisement space to news. The penny papers had been in the habit of publishing advertisement supplements of sometimes as many as five pages in an eight-page issue, adding to their income, subtracting from their convenience to the reader. 'The note of the *Daily Mail* is not so much economy of price as conciseness and compactness', the older newspapers being awkward to handle in train and bus. Advertising had to be kept in its place. 'The advertisements in the *Daily Mail* will never be allowed to encroach upon the literary matter.' They produced revenue but in Harmsworth's sight they 'spoilt the paper'. First and always a journalist, he was professionally resentful of the advertisers' growing power, reinforced though it was by his own inventiveness and success. The *History of the Times* fails to take note of a deep-rooted prejudice in stating that the prosperity of the *Daily Mail* was based on the lesson which '*Answers* had taught them'—the Harmsworth brothers—'that money was made out of selling space to advertisers and, moreover, to the same advertisers time after time'. It had been Alfred's unrealistic hope to do without advertising in *Answers* because so much of it was of the disfiguring patent medicine kind. Yet no one was more pleased than he when Beecham's Pills took a trial series of quarter pages, just as later, while objecting to the unsightliness of advertisements in the *Daily Mail*, he never thought of reproving his outdoor publicity staff for plastering the hoardings of the London, Brighton & South Coast Railway with *Daily Mail* posters that were an eyesore to many travellers through a pleasant southern landscape.

Leicester Harmsworth said that Alfred's attitude to the advertisement side of the paper might have brought serious difficulties. 'He was rigid in excluding more than a certain number of advertisements. On one occasion, further capital had to be raised as a result of that policy.' There is possible confirmation of that statement in Alfred's bank account with Coutts's, which shows that he drew cheques in favour of the *Daily Mail* to a total of £19,000 a few months after launching the paper.

Although advertising orders had been turned away for the first issue, there was no great pressure of demand by advertisers during the paper's first weeks. With an angler's cunning, Harmsworth inserted free advertisements of Newnes's publication on the front page. He said that when it was seen that his chief rival thought the space worth having, confidence would grow. The declaration on June 1 of a daily average sale of 171,121 copies had not impressed the better class of advertiser, who continued to equate halfpenny papers with low purchasing power and lower tastes. There were many newspaper readers, also, who regarded the halfpenny coin as a social blemish, like Cockney speech and a taste for margarine.

Classified or 'small' advertisements were a mainstay of the *Daily Mail* income in the beginning. Alfred Harmsworth introduced a novel way of attracting them. He printed in the paper a replica of a post office telegraph form. Readers wanting jobs or having something to offer were invited to fill in the form at the G.P.O. inland telegraph rate of a halfpenny a word. The response was overwhelming. The advertisement manager worked the clock round, snatching sleep in his office chair. Later it was claimed that 'the telegraph form idea has been copied all over the world'. In fact, it appears to have been copied in the first place from a Croydon paper, which used the idea years before.

A number of London business houses, led by Thomas Wallis & Company, the Holborn drapers, tried to buy 'display' space on the front page but were refused. Later, they were allowed to advertise 'below the fold' only. A change came when an advertiser applied for a 'below the fold' position on the magazine page, which had a direct appeal to women readers. It soon proved to be the paper's best-selling space and enabled Harold Harmsworth to raise the advertising rates. Seizing the inference, Alfred set about creating the Women's Page, an inspiration which developed the force of a second wave in the journalistic revolution begun on May 4, 1896.

Chapter Nine

'A Factory in Bohemia'

ALFRED HARMSWORTH announced 'the greatest progress in the tide of the company's prosperity, a profit of £53,000: dividend, 22 per cent for the year', at an Answers Publications Ltd. ordinary general meeting in July 1896. In less than eight years the company had earned the equivalent of nearly half its capital. His brothers' world tour of the previous year was beginning to show results in increased overseas circulations. 'I can remember when a publisher who thought to circulate his publications in, let us say, New Zealand or British Columbia would have been considered a visionary.' He did not conceal his personal satisfaction in announcing that the company had 'handed to its authors and writers more than ten thousand pounds' during the twelve months. Congratulating the shareholders, Layton Bennett, the accountant, reminded them that they had so far received £113,000 in dividends. 'I think that is something to be proud of. There are very few companies at the present day which can point to a balance-sheet like this.' He felt sure that he 'had the sense of the meeting', he said in the platitudes of his calling, 'in proposing a vote of thanks to the chairman and directors', and there was still more admiring applause when the chairman rose to announce: 'We are making today considerably over sixty thousand pounds a year. I hope to maintain, and even increase, that figure for the whole of this year.'

Before the year had ended, an extraordinary general meeting was called. As Leicester Harmsworth took his place with his brothers in the Memorial Hall, Farringdon Street, he heard a shareholder say: 'Why, they're just a lot of boys!' The purpose this time was to sanction the conversion of Answers Publications Ltd. into Harmsworth Brothers Ltd., to take over all the existing Harmsworth businesses, except the newspapers. Between them, Answers Publications, Pandora Publishing Company, Periodical Publishing Corporation and the Geraldine Press, were earning

216

profits at the rate of £126,000 a year. The chairman was careful to tell the shareholders: 'With the newspaper part of our business the new company will have nothing to do.' He referred to a point of criticism. 'It is in the minds of some people that this is a one-man show. That is not so. Necessarily, there must be someone at the head of it. But it is evident that one man cannot run fourteen papers and my brothers and I are connected with eighteen in all. I make no secret of that.' He went on to suggest that the figures given to the shareholders showed that there was no neglect of their interests. Deploring the need to equip the new company's printing works with French and American machines because of their superiority to the British, he told the shareholders that tickets would be issued to any of them and their friends who cared to see the companies' papers being printed. Not everyone present may have recognized in the invitation one more move in the rivalry with Newnes, who had built a visitors' gallery in the big basement machine-room of his new building in Southampton Street, Strand, and was encouraging the public to go in and watch his *Tit-Bits* being printed.

The directors of the new million-pound Harmsworth company were Alfred, Harold, Cecil, Leicester and Hildebrand. Their respective ages were 31, 28, 27, 26 and 24. They could say that the average age of their staffs, 'not including the office boys', was 24 and that in no more than eight years they had built up the largest periodical publishing business in the world. Speaking as a retiring director, Robert Leighton said at the extraordinary general meeting that 'in his shrewdness at judging the necessities of the public, Mr Alfred Harmsworth is really a genius' (Applause). The new company prospectus named Alfred as the founder of the business, Harold as conducting it with him. On October 21 the *Daily Mail* reported that the issue of Harmsworth Brothers' shares had been heavily over-subscribed. 'By an oversight', the announcement of the new company, with its fourteen papers, did not appear in *Answers*, the parent of them all. Cecil was the editor. His sense of Fleet Street inadequacy may have been still further sharpened by the laughter which he had to face soon afterwards when, in his editorial column, he referred to the firm's newest publication, *The Girls' Friend*, as 'a huge woman's journal'.

★ ★ ★

Alfred had been warned again by his doctors, Murrell in London and Raven at Broadstairs. Murrell had been emphatic about the need for him to rearrange his work and hours. 'He gave me some serious advice.' Both doctors ordered more relaxation. He sought it in more theatre-going and from the diary it seems that he had a preference for bad farce. But he was at the first night of Irving's production of *Cymbeline* at the Lyceum. 'Afterwards to supper behind the scenes. Met Henry Irving and Ellen Terry. Liked both.' He saw *The Geisha* twice, *The Importance of Being Earnest* three times. 'Been reading novels a good deal.' With difficulty, he kept away from the office for a fortnight. Instead, he was visited at Charles Street by a stream of callers. Among them were Herbert Ward, Grant Richards, who had been working with Stead on *The Review of Reviews*, and who had dreams of going into business as a book publisher with Harmsworth's help, G. W. Steevens, Max Beerbohm, and William Graham, the solicitor, who was constantly summoned to his side. Directors' meetings were held at the house. Too much business, private and professional, was being done there. 'A Mr Beauclerk came to borrow money. Not so well tonight in consequence.' A few days later: 'I am thoroughly run down', a state which a fishing trip to the Norfolk Broads failed to relieve. He bought a new 'Premier' bicycle and rode the 120 miles from Norwich to London in two days. A day or two's rest and he pedalled off down the Portsmouth Road, with enervating results. 'Stayed the night at The Anchor, Ripley. Found several of the old people dead since I was there eleven years ago.'

On November 14, 'to see the motor-cars start on their trip to Brighton. Little better.' Thirty-five cars made history that day, setting forth from Northumberland Avenue, London. About half that number reached Brighton. The event marked the freeing of motorists from the three-miles-an-hour regulation, originally framed to restrict the speed of traction-engines. The 'Emancipation Run' of 1896, commemoratively repeated each year since, inaugurated the motoring age. A leader note in the first issue of the *Daily Mail* had called attention to the anomaly of Britain concentrating on sea power while neglecting the coming revolution on the roads. Alfred Harmsworth's newspaper influence, campaigning against the law's absurdity, gave inventors and manufacturers the incentive to overtake French and German internal combustion developments, which had not been hampered by legal limits. In those countries the number of motor-car manufacturers was already numbered by the score. In England there were six.

His health did not sufficiently improve. A complete severance from work was ordered by the doctors. On November 30, a cousin of the Ravens at Broadstairs, Reginald Nicholson, spoke of India as a change of scene. The following day he was asked to book passages for Alfred and Molly Harmsworth, with himself as their guide. Ten days later the three left for Brindisi, there embarking for Bombay. On December 25, Alfred wrote in his diary: 'Don't like my first Christmas away from home.'

Refreshed by the voyage out, his first impulse on landing at Bombay was to call on the editor of *The Times of India* and to seek out the local representative of the *Daily Mail*. The diary is exclamatory throughout the tour and tells little of his impressions. 'Saw Taj Mahal by moonlight.' An elephant ride and a visit to the Holy Man of Benares are as casually noted. A tiger beat produced 'a most enjoyable day, full of novel experience', of which we hear no more. Between excursions, he was occupied by 'letters from the office', writing articles for the *Daily Mail* on plague and famine in India—subsequently published as a pamphlet, *Hard Facts from India*—and contemplating the steady progress of his newspaper towards a commanding position in the world's press. Its circulation had passed the 250,000 mark and was still rising.

* * *

George Bernard Shaw hailed the *Daily Mail* as 'the most important recent development in London journalism'. He wrote to Alfred Harmsworth on the first anniversary of the paper, May 4, 1897: 'Why don't you place your political criticism on the same footing as your dramatic and literary criticism? Then it would be influential and interesting. Party politics are the last and most obstinate of the follies you have inherited from the Old Journalism.' In fact, the paper had no strong political affiliation for the good reason that commitments of that kind were already a drag on the fortunes of the newspapers it was designed to supplant. From the beginning, the editorial viewpoint was flexibly independent of the parties. It was not in the nature of Alfred Harmsworth to be tied to a faction. He required to be free to support any person, cause or institution that might serve his genuine if not always coherent wish to further the national interest. His aim was to produce a newspaper for the people.

For anniversary purposes, the paper prominently repeated its policy of 'all the news in the smallest space', and proclaimed that 'it owed nothing to sensationalism, tittle-tattle or indecency'. Most of its success, it declared, 'is due to the inspiring thought and labour of a very devoted band of young workers'. Credit was given to 'the unstinted efforts' of Kennedy Jones. Looking back from a later time, Alfred Harmsworth could say: 'They were joyous days.' Men spoke of them with the fervour of Napoleon's old soldiers who could proudly claim: 'We were with the Army in Italy!' H. W. Wilson, who had become chief leader writer, recalled them as 'days of youth, full of romance, which will live in the memory of all who shared those early triumphs'.

In the second week of May that year, 1897, the Harmsworths went to live in Berkeley Square, indulging the spectacular alternative to bankruptcy which Alfred had visualized on the night of 'putting the paper to bed' for the first time, a year before. The house was number 36. In one of its sitting-rooms Gladstone had proposed to the lady who became his wife.

Its small white-painted front gave it a *bijou* modesty next to number 38, the stately town mansion of Archibald Philip Primrose, 5th Earl of Rosebery, who, having become Prime Minister in March 1894 at the age of forty-seven, had resigned after sixteen uncomfortable months in office. He and Harmsworth were already known to each other.

October 8, 1896.—To Dalmeny to endeavour to interview Lord Rosebery for the *Daily Mail*. Succeeded in doing so. Lunched and spent a most pleasant time there. Met Mr Asquith.

It was not so much a formal interview as a meeting at which Rosebery had declined to discuss the topic of the hour, his departure from Downing Street. 'I thought the *Daily Mail* came from the other camp,' he observed, to which Harmsworth promptly replied: 'The *Daily Mail* is independent and Imperial.' In the printed account of what passed between them were the 'personal touches' of the new journalism. 'The man who had this morning startled the world appeared as merry and sunburned as though he had just returned from the moors or the links. Dressed in a comfortable suit. . . .' When the sacred name of Gladstone was mentioned, 'there was, I thought, a tone of sadness in the cheery voice'. Passing from room to room, the would-be interviewer noted that 'there were pictures of Mr Gladstone's most famous gatherings, a portrait of Mr Gladstone and, over the indicator of a bell, the words, "Mr Gladstone's bedroom".' That same day, Rosebery noted: 'Mr Harmsworth came to interview me. I lunched him instead. An interesting young man.' There was no further communication between them until a year later, when Roseberry sent in a note to 36 Berkeley Square:

My dear Mr Harmsworth,—I hope you like our excellent and respectable neighbourhood. I tried to find you one day to give you the accolade of a freeholder but you were in all the agonies of a concert. Sincerely, ROSEBERY.

It was the first of a long series of usually brief communications written to Harmsworth by Rosebery. More often than not, they were addressed 'Dear Neighbour'. Some were signed 'Neighbour'. The relationship between the two is easier to understand from Harmsworth's side. For him, Rosebery was not only an admired political and social figure, a Whig among the Radicals, heroic, still, in the sight of those Liberals who remained unprejudiced by his having won the Derby. He was Arthur Pendennis in exalted degree, gifts and charm. What power of attraction Harmsworth had for Rosebery, an aristocrat of the intellect as of birth, is less readily suggested; perhaps his tenacity, which the older man decidedly lacked, perhaps what may have seemed to him to be, even so, the lightly won success, which Rosebery, to the detriment of his reputation, always coveted—'the palm without the dust'—perhaps simply the unconcealed admiration which Harmsworth had for him at that time. There were passing political sympathies of no significance to either or to history. Cecil Harmsworth wrote that 'undoubtedly Alfred had some thought of supporting Rosebery's Liberal League both in the press and financially', but that Rosebery's indecision was 'out of tune with Alfred's eager spirit'.

When, as I recollect Alfred telling me, the old Duchess of Devonshire assured him that in supporting Lord Rosebery he was backing the wrong horse, he had probably begun to entertain doubts of a leader who had all the talents but that of leadership.

The two men had embarked on a closeness of personal acquaintance which never became friendship. They walked together two or three times a week when in town, their goal a tree on the west side of Hyde Park. Reaching the tree, they would gravely touch it with their sticks and turn and walk back to Berkeley Square. Those ritualistic perambulations may not have been inspired by the fact that Rosebery's father had written a pamphlet on physical exercise. If anyone, seeing them striding by, assumed consanguinity between them, he might have been excused. They had a similar facial stamp of 'fine carelessness'. Rosebery is remembered by Lady Hudson, then Molly Harmsworth, waiting patiently in the hall at 36 Berkeley Square for Alfred to come down from his room. Cecil Harmsworth thought Rosebery 'a solitary man', and said that his house, number 38, 'had some beautiful things in it but was untidy'.

Socially, Alfred Harmsworth's rise kept pace with his extraordinary success as a publisher, the latest evidence of which was that Harmsworth Brothers Ltd.—'the company which bears the name of my family', to quote the proud boast of the chairman at the annual general meeting of 1897—had declared a net profit of no less than £178,000 and that the rapid growth of the *Evening News* called for a quarter of a million pounds of new capital. His bankers' orders for West End club subscriptions now amounted to £300 a year. Within a week or two of his launching the *Daily Mail*, he was notified of his election to the Carlton Club, rendezvous of the Conservative hierarchy. He had been presented to the Prince of Wales at a St. James's Palace levee. Glitter was added to his widening range of acquaintance by the Dukes of Edinburgh and Abercorn, Sir Arthur Sullivan, of the famous Savoy partnership, and Sarah Bernhardt. He had a lease of box 53 at the Royal Opera House which cost him £402. He and his wife stayed again at Broadlands with the Ashleys and were on the weekend guest list of the Onslows at Clandon Park. He lunched with W. G. Grace at Lord's on June 3, 1897, and, returning to the office, found the following letter awaiting his pleasure:

Dear Mr. Harmsworth,—Why should you not run down to The Priory, Reigate (1 hour from London), and spend Monday night next with us? You will find a very beautiful place, a few agreeable people, and a warm welcome from

Yours truly,

GEORGE N. CURZON.*

The diary tells us that the visit took place later that year, when the Asquiths, the Alfred Lytteltons and Austen Chamberlain were of the party. 'I heard a great many interesting things about the inner life of politics and much about Gladstone and Rosebery.' Walking the Surrey lanes on that occasion with Margot Asquith, 'she told me a great many political matters, especially a good deal relating to the quarrel between Rosebery and Harcourt', spoken of as 'that clash of flint with steel'.

The Saturday Review sneered that he had 'grown rich and got into smart society' from a kind of journalism which it could not sufficiently deplore. Enjoying, naturally, the pleasures of being admired for his success as well as for his personal attributes, he was not then or at any time socially active in the crude and thrusting sense. For him the attractions of social advancement were not in knowing 'the right people' but in having access to those of exceptional achievement. His professional instinct was always sharper than his social bias. 'What are we dining *about*?' he would ask his wife on occasions for which an array of distinguished persons had been asked. He was earning the reputation of a self-effacing host. He would preside silently at table, often taking the smallest part in the conversation while being wholly attentive to it. Only rarely did he seem to be insensitive to the social nuances. Shortly after he had moved to Berkeley Square, he invited some of his old angling acquaintances to dinner. When the party broke up, he was so prompt in helping one of the more garrulous guests into his overcoat that the man turned on him with the angry demand: 'I say, what's the 'urry, 'Armsworth?'

In his private circle, which had its most constant centre at Elmwood, there were always one or two men who could claim friendship with him without necessarily being encouraged to assume permanence in that standing. Herbert Ward remained his closest friend, though his journeys severed communication for long periods. 'I suppose I know Herbert better than anyone in the world', Alfred would say. After Ward, it was Max Pemberton who had known him longer than anyone outside the family. Pemberton had become a Harmsworth employee and the process of making a friend into a colleague had not been altogether successful. 'Why do you have Max down to stay?' Harold asked Alfred. The answer came promptly: 'I don't have to think when I'm with him.'

The names of a number of close acquaintances recur in the diary of the

* Later, Marquess Curzon of Kedleston.

222

middle 1890s, mostly of tennis and fishing enthusiasts who could be relied on to fill in the Elmwood weekends. There was Neville Jackson, a neighbour of the Harmsworths in the Pandora Road days. He had Stock Exchange connections, and his wife wrote a standard work on the art and history of the silhouette and edited *Home Chat*. Much later, she was commissioned to telephone Alfred Harmsworth every morning, to give him a 'woman's angle' on the day's news. There was 'Tuppy' Hayter, a young man about town who was given a post on *The Rambler*, a short-lived Harmsworth weekly which, ignoring the Johnsonian derivation of its title, catered for the fresh-air seekers left over from the cycling boom of 1895. Hayter had been secretary-companion to Harmsworth on the fishing trip to Florida. There was Gilbert Burgess, freelance art critic, the son of a Royal Academician. There was Lord Mountmorres. All were in some degree dependent on him, an important if not a prime qualification for admission to his circle. Max Beerbohm was not an intimate friend, nor was he a dependent, although a letter shows that he cherished the hope that Harmsworth would buy a collection of his cartoons on view at the Carfax Gallery. He was seeing much of the Harmsworths. 'They are very charming people', he wrote to William Rothenstein; he thought Alfred 'quite amazing and interesting'.

Standing apart in years and experience, but within the same personal radius, were the naval historian William (later Sir William) Laird Clowes, Sir Douglas Straight, the Old Harrovian editor of the *Pall Mall Gazette*, William Graham, the solicitor, of the firm of Nicholson, Graham & Jones, 24 Coleman Street, London, E.C., Edwin Ward, the portrait painter, a prominent member of the Savage Club, and Robert Radclyffe Dolling, the Anglican priest of Portsea, who had reached a depth of understanding with Alfred attained by few others in his circle, then or after. But for Dolling's death, that might have been the friendship of Alfred's life. A little later there came Charles Whibley, the scholarly, opinionated critic and essayist who wrote 'Musings Without Method' in *Blackwood's Magazine*.

From 1896, it is Reginald Nicholson's name that occurs most often in the diary. He was four years younger than Harmsworth, the son of a Master in Lunacy at the Royal Courts of Justice. After Charterhouse, he had gone to India as assistant traffic manager of the Bengal-Nagpur Railway Company. He and Alfred Harmsworth had first met at Broadstairs. Of easy manners, naturally companionable, 'Reggie' Nicholson soon made himself useful to his new friend, at first, and for several years, keeping his personal accounts. His spinsterish handwriting fills the pages of a series of ledgers recording tradesmen's bills, investments, annuities, gifts and loans, and crediting himself with £62 5s. a month for his services. It is clear that Alfred counted on him for help of a kind that Sutton was less well qualified to give, particularly in a social way. Nicholson could grace a lunch or dinner table with his tactful charm. He was constantly in attendance on the Harmsworths and became virtually comptroller of their households. Later, he was to fill important newspaper posts. Like the others, he found it difficult to maintain the friendly status on any but Alfred Harmsworth's terms. As the eldest of a large family, Harmsworth may not have needed friendships. He had arrived at a summary judgment on that matter. 'After thirty we make many acquaintances, but few friends', he told Max Pemberton. Some who had known the pleasures of being in his intimate circle and the pain of banishment from it may have agreed that, like David Garrick, according to Oliver Goldsmith, he 'cast off his friends as a huntsman his pack, for he knew when he pleased he could whistle them back'.

Alfred and Mary Harmsworth were becoming resigned to their fate of childlessness. As time passed, it had been thought desirable to seek medical advice. The best consultants in England and on the Continent were invited to give an opinion. All agreed that there was no discoverable reason why the Harmsworths should not be parents. That consummation continued to be denied them. Alfred had a poetic way of disposing of sympathetic allusions to the subject. He would say: 'There is always a crumpled rose leaf.' It cannot be doubted that it was a lasting disappointment to him not to have a son whom he could bring before the world as heir to his name and place. When a boy was born to Cecil, Alfred wrote: 'Despite our lack of fortune in these matters, the news will, I know, give my dear wife very great pleasure. I am glad', he added, 'that it's another little son to head yet another branch of a family for which I am so ambitious.' Receiving word of the child's death at the age of only a few months, he broke his holiday in France to go over for the funeral at the Marylebone Cemetery, London. Among the three or four notes at the back of his diary for 1899, one refers to the death of 'my dear little godson', ten months before. As for his more intimate frustration, no doubt too much might be read into his use of gynaecological language when speaking of his new papers as they appeared. 'Pain and anguish', 'lusty child', 'birth pangs severe', 'promising child', are phrases taken from his diary notes and letters concerning those events.

He gave to children the spontaneous affection which few of their elders drew from him. 'The Nicholson children are a great joy to us', occurs in the 1899 diary. He recorded there his fondness for Edwin Ward's 'dear little Bluecoat son, Frank'. He had a triumphant instinct in his dealings with the very young: he always sat with them on the floor. Almost it seemed that he wilfully regressed in imagination to his earliest years as a member of a large family. Many of his letters to his mother were signed 'Your first-born'. He inscribed books and photographs to her in that same way. His personal attitude to her was always that of a child seeking guidance. A friend who was often at Elmwood remembered watching him playing in the garden with some local children whom he had invited in to pick flowers. 'It was as if he had renounced the world. He seemed completely happy.' There was no truer testimony to his generous good nature; all children felt at home with him.

Meanwhile, he and his wife were happy in their married companionship. 'We wire to each other twice a day', he noted in the diary in 1897, when he was fishing in Scotland. She is usually referred to in the diary as 'the wife', sometimes as 'the little wife', as 'wifie', and as 'wifelet'. Their early years together had been marred by her ill-health; the double pneumonia at Broadstairs had left a legacy of heart trouble. Embellishing her husband's success as well as keeping pace with it, she assumed her share of its duties with remarkable assurance, as if some patrician strain had leapt the generations to flower once more. Charming his enemies and friends alike, her performance of the role of hostess was deeply admired, not least by her husband, who through the changing years was unchanging in his respect for her. Often severely tested, her sagacity was never found wanting. He was always impressed by her physical fearlessness and no doubt envied her for it. 'My little lion-heart', he called her. 'I have no fear', she would say, mounting the worst-tempered horse in the stable. She was one of the first women to ride in a motor-car and the early models could not go fast enough for her. She was one of the first women to go up in an aeroplane. She descended the world's deepest mine without a claustrophobic qualm. Nerve of that sort could put Alfred at a disadvantage. Climbing a scaffolding thirty feet high, he had to turn back 'white with fear and wet with perspiration', according to one who was with him.

Good taste came as naturally to his wife as the poise. It was reflected in her personality rather than in her domestic surroundings, which she tempered to her husband's more limited and conventional preferences. Sir William Rothenstein, the artist, who knew Alfred from those years, said that he had 'a quite sincere bad taste'. In furnishing, for example, comfort came first. When, after being abroad, he found that his wife had changed some of the rooms at Elmwood, he had everything put back as before, including the wallpaper. He ordered the decorators to lay in a large stock of the same wallpaper for future use. Discovering that a cheap china ornament, a fairground souvenir of his Hampstead boyhood, had been thrown out during the renovations, he wandered round the junk shops of Ramsgate looking for another like it. His professional life had opened too early, and had been too absorbing, for him to have a chance of forming sound tastes. He lacked the higher cultural refinements, but he could not be charged with blindness to that truth, nor was he a Philistine

I

despiser of the arts. He had never read systematically. His quick brain harvested information which was not ripened into knowledge. His hurrying spirit left him no time for reflection. His library, formed at Elmwood round his prized Dickens's first editions, was by no means an impersonal part of his existence. Volumes from it went on his travels— Oliver Goldsmith, Izaak Walton, Dr Johnson and the modern novelists, Hardy first among them. When he said that he could not afford to buy art masterpieces, he was probably thinking of his brother Harold, whose art education enriched dealers and their go-betweens. In the early 1900s, Alfred commissioned his friend, Charles W. Furse, an A.R.A. who had more respect for the New English Art Club than for the Royal Academy, to buy pictures by modern artists with the idea of forming what Furse told him would be 'a collection which would challenge the Chantrey Bequest'. A start was made with works by Steer, Sargent and Whistler. The untimely death of Furse apparently put an end to the project. Alfred took more obvious pleasure in showing off 'my Canaletto', one of his few old-master purchases. In music he remained the strumming amateur for whom Chaminade's 'Automne' was a master work. More adult was his appreciation of the natural scene. If it no longer stirred him to lyrical expression as in the Hampstead days, he was often moved to write about it with genuine feeling in his letters.

★　　　★　　　★

Eight years before he had been glad to receive a guinea for an article, even half-a-crown for a paragraph. Now, he was making £80,000 a year, an income that was only at the beginning of its astounding momentum. The beginnings, too, of physical change were to be seen in him. Without losing the crucial boyishness, the engaging charm, the good looks, he was acquiring an air of substance beyond his years. His face lines were hardening in the mould of success. His nose, someone noticed, was like Napoleon's. Ecstatically, his serial writing contributor, Marie Connor Leighton, decided that his mouth also was 'just like Napoleon's'.

She was not the only visitor to Elmwood who read significance into the cipher 'N' on the Sèvres sauceboats. There were others who wondered whether their host cherished the notion of affinity. Like his friend Cecil Rhodes, he was a collector of books on Napoleon. Engravings of Napoleon helped to furnish the bungalow in the garden. A bust of Napoleon stood on its mahogany *torchere* in the drawing-room. There were physical resemblances for all to see. They were evident not only in the drooping forelock, Napoleon's made familiar to the world by Delaroche's celebrated 'snuffbox' portrait. Alfred Harmsworth was like the Napoleon of the early Consulate period. Each had the bone structure that made him look physically more substantial than he was. Both walked as if on springs, head tilted acquisitively forward from the shoulder. Their pallor of complexion, their eye colour, was the same. Those who were astrologically interested noted the fact that each had the same zodiac sign. R. D. Blumenfeld said that from the first he was struck by Alfred's 'Napoleonic gestures and peculiarities', including the habit of 'lolling luxuriously in an armchair'. It would be possible to find more support for the fancy that the imperious spirit which descended on a cradle in Ajaccio in August 1769 also visited Chapelizod in July 1865. The Bonaparte father, failing at the law, was attached to the legend of past family grandeurs. The Bonaparte mother, burdened by an immense destiny, ran over the mountains of Corsica; the Harmsworth mother, heavy with child at forty-seven, bounded up the stairs of St. John's Wood. Both dominated large families. Both knew the sensations of extraordinary fortune. Like Napoleon Bonaparte, Alfred Harmsworth's personality was of the kind which disturbed the emotions of other people, abasing them with fear, uplifting them with admiration. He had his Corsican moods. Those around him had to be prepared to meet devastating rancours and heart-stirring kindnesses. The equating procedure might lead us to the conclusion that the journalist's revolution was mightier than the general's.

Whether or not Alfred Harmsworth, at thirty-one, was identifying himself with Napoleon Bonaparte as a force of history, at his age he could hardly fail to be impressed by the flowing tide of his own success. It was bearing him on and up to a professional and public eminence which made his seniors review their careers with a rueful awareness of lost opportunities, if not of failure. The poet, W. E. Henley, wrote to him from Stanley Lodge, Muswell Hill, on June 1, 1897: 'How I wish you'd been on the old *National Observer*! We had a run for our money, as it was, but with you! . . .' T. P. O'Connor wrote to him from Oakley Lodge, Upper Cheyne Row, Chelsea, on May 6, 1898: 'I only wish it had been my good fortune to have been associated with you.' The same note was echoed in a letter written to Max Pemberton in July 1897 by Sir Wemyss Reid, general manager of the Cassell publishing firm, who had predicted bankruptcy for the Harmsworths and had now met Alfred for the first time. 'The impression he made on me was far beyond my expectations. I thought him a most strikingly interesting person.' Power was coming to him as to no other man of his generation. It ranged over a rapidly widening domain of print and publication and gave new impetus to the operations of paper mills, ink factories, type foundries and other kindred industries. 'Napoleon of the Press' was perhaps not so extravagantly effusive as was thought by those who were amused by his Napoleon cult at Elmwood or heard later of his exclamatory pleasure after trying on Napoleon's hat at Fontainebleau: 'It fits!' In fact, the Napoleon legend was largely fastened on him by the cartoonists and professional humorists, among them E. V. Lucas, in his *Change for a Halfpenny* lampoon on the popular press. No doubt Alfred was pleased when the Marchioness of Granby, later the Duchess of Rutland, did a pencil portrait of him. Asked why she had written 'Napoleon' against his name, she replied: 'Because he seemed to me to be very like Napoleon—shape of head—lock of hair on forehead —earnest look under his brows—and eyelashes like a child!'

Like Bonaparte, but without the elements of farcical comedy, Alfred Harmsworth founded a dynasty. If he did not exalt his mother and the rest of his family to heights of splendour, he brought them wealth and position and made them immensely proud of the Harmsworth name. Only the older ones remembered the bad times. 'Dot', the eldest daughter, repressed her memories of them perhaps more wilfully than the others. She never mentioned the Salusbury Road address to her children, who grew up unaware of the family's early circumstances. Harold, who had laid the foundations of what would be the greatest Harmsworth fortune, had three sons and was living at North End House, Hampstead, once the home of the elder Pitt. Leicester, handicapped by ill-health but sustained by good humour and a firm religious faith, had married the sister of a Somerset House colleague of his named Scott and he and his wife were established at Reveley Lodge, Bushey Heath. Cecil married a Maffett cousin, Emilie; they were living at Hadleigh Wood. Hildebrand was still unmarried. He had an apartment in Curzon Street, Mayfair. The younger brothers and sisters were living with their mother in Maida Vale.

Cecil Harmsworth's private memoranda are entirely modest about his part in the family success and warmly generous in attributing the larger share to his elder brothers. 'Without Alfred, I would never have gained any sort of foothold in Fleet Street, never having credited myself with the quickness of mind and the intuitive sense for news or the sleepless interest in the passing events of the day that are essential to the make-up of the true journalist.' The editorship of *Answers* was an avuncular role well suited to his personality. He was kind and gentle and he had the right tone of voice, richly benevolent. His bias is seen in his frequent use of the word 'gentleman' in his editorial musings. A small tradesman wishes to trace his lost soldier son, a private of the 4th Hussars. 'The missing gentleman's name', Cecil tells his readers, whom he invites to take part in the search, 'is John Wilson.' A chimney sweep has a debt of £13 and is bowed down by it. 'I advise this gentleman', writes Cecil, 'at all costs to keep away from moneylenders.' Alfred often spoke of Cecil as 'the gentleman of our family', and it was true that while Cecil was a Harmsworth in physical appearance, he had little of the mental force and drive of his elder brothers and no taste whatever for the competitive life. It was often said of him that he would have made an ideal bishop or ambassador. His *Little Fishing*

Book was written with the engaging charm of a gentle essayist and his unpublished diary often delightfully expresses his pleasure in the pastoral scene.

The sixth son, Charles, had been delicate from birth and took no part in the business or in the affairs of the family. He was medically advised to live out of London and spent most of his sixty-eight years in Sussex, well provided for by Alfred and Harold and leading the life of a country gentleman with his own servants and carriage-and-pair. Alfred often visited him in the early years of his illness and later took him on travels abroad. His rare appearances at family gatherings delighted the younger nephews and nieces; to them, he was always 'a pleasant surprise'.

The two remaining brothers were St. John and Vyvyan, the latter named after a Disraeli hero. St. John—'Bonchie' at home—had no fancy for journalism though his temperament was closer to Alfred's than that of any of the other brothers. He had a flair for games that came near to genius. He rode, ran, played cricket, football, tennis and billiards—at the last-named he was reckoned unbeatable—with a perfection of grace and accuracy that was spoiled only by his refusal to take himself seriously. In consequence, he did not gain prizes. At Oxford, he played in the first international Rugby football match against France. He came down with his degree but not with the blue that he had seemed certain to win. Neither did Vyvyan, the youngest brother, have the journalistic temper. Cecil wrote of him: 'He had the outdoor spirit and London was death to it.' His only venture in Fleet Street, after Charterhouse and Cambridge, was a period of informal apprenticeship in the machine-room of the *Evening News*. He soon surrendered to the pull of the countryside exerted through his Hampshire forebears. His brothers said that when he was called to London on family or business affairs he was always in a hurry to catch the next train back to the Weald of Sussex, where he long made his home. In physical appearance he was considered to be most like the father of them all. 'Such devoted companions as he,' Cecil wrote in his private notes, 'are beyond rubies in such a brotherhood as ours.'

Cecil challenged the assumption that Alfred's intense family loyalty prejudiced the careers of other men in his employment. 'There was, I say, nothing of nepotism in Alfred's business relations. By his munificence, and that of Harold, we younger brothers enjoyed, very early, financial independence, but not so as to be free of service to the business. We were *hors concours* in respect of promotion in the several editorial departments and that fact redounded often to the advantage of aspirants to advancement working under us. We were not in the running against them and could encourage talent without fear or jealousy of perhaps brighter spirits who might in time come to supersede us.' Cecil added here: 'I remember Sir Arthur Pearson deploring the weakness of his position in

Fleet Street compared with Alfred's. *He* had no band of brothers to help him at every turn.'

The Harmsworth editors had orders not to mention the chief proprietor's name in their columns except by his consent. He had no taste for self-advertisement. He was still more reticent about seeming to take advantage of his position as head of a powerful publicity machine. He wrote many articles for his papers but only in special circumstances, such as the trip to India, was his name put over them. He may have had his dreams of power, but there was no overt sign that he saw himself as a leading performer on the stage of history. Even so, from 1897 onward the anonymity which he preferred could no longer contain his growing prominence as a director in the wings. It was as if the *zeitgeist* was drawing him up out of his generation to be moulded into a dynamic twentieth-century figure.

*   *   *

On the evening of June 21, 1897, the Harmsworths gave a party at Berkeley Square. The invitations were inscribed: *To Meet The Colonial Premiers*, who were in London for the Diamond Jubilee. Leaders of London society, ambassadors, members of both Houses of Parliament, famous actors, professional beauties, thronged the house. A foreign princess said that nowhere had she seen more splendid floral decorations—'not even in royal and imperial palaces'. A Parisian restaurateur, with his staff, had been brought over to provide a banquet. Paderewski played the piano. Melba sang. The next day Alfred wrote in his diary that he had seen 'the most magnificent spectacle I ever beheld or ever can behold', the Diamond Jubilee Procession. 'We had a room at 66 St. James's Street, which I took chiefly for Mother.' He had to rush away through the crowds as soon as the procession had gone by, to resume work at the office where, *vide* the diary, he was 'worrying them about the *Daily Mail* Golden Extra', an eight-page souvenir printed in gold and sold at sixpence. In printing history it was not an exceptional novelty. *The Sun*, in 1838, had printed its coronation number in gold. There was a great demand for the 'Golden Daily Mail' and years later specimen copies became collectors' items. In contrast, the *Evening News* circulation fell heavily on Jubilee Day, for the unexpected reason that the newsboys found more profit in selling programmes and paper handkerchiefs. As their contribution to a notable event, Harmsworth Brothers Ltd. had already published *Sixty Years a Queen*, an illustrated popular history issued in ten sixpenny parts. It was hailed as 'the publishing triumph of the Jubilee', and its sale of nearly 300,000 copies led to far-reaching developments in the Harmsworth business.

The note of the Diamond Jubilee was benevolent imperialism and its fervour vibrated far and wide, though the old Queen was by then failing in her responses to all but the more domestic sentiments. To some on-lookers that day she seemed a scarcely animate figure being dragged through the streets as a symbol rather than as the sentient ruler of great realms. The crowds were smaller than they had been for the Jubilee of ten years before, but the emotional density was not less great. It was given perfect expression in Rudyard Kipling's *Recessional*, published in *The Times* on July 17 and acclaimed even by the unofficial laureate's Liberal-Pacifist friends.

Looking down on the resplendent procession as it passed St. James's Palace, Alfred had been caught in the waves of feeling which his *Daily Mail* had helped to generate. This was the new imperialism. It was exhibited with a swagger implying that (in the vernacular of a later time) it could not care less about the resounding consequences of the defeat of the old imperialism in 1776, but also with a humility posing the imperial idea as sentiment rather than as policy. That concept exactly suited Alfred Harmsworth's temper. It called for no precise thinking and only the vaguest convictions, for a generous patriotism but no political profundity. The marvellous procession was the vanguard of a movement which would expel disorder from the British cosmos. For him, the imperial idea meant an extension of the efficiency for which his soul had always craved, perhaps in recoil from the chaos of his early circumstances. His reverence for order had in it a visionary element that went well beyond mere competence. It had made him the admiring disciple of Cecil Rhodes, who had added an immense territory to the Empire and who dominated any assembly, however distinguished, proving to Harmsworth's satisfaction that men mattered more than their politics. Broadly, that remained the measure of his political thinking. It was the more congenial to him because it provided a formula by which he could justify his independence as a newspaper controller.

Announcing with more confidence than insight that he was personally responsible for 'the political aspect of our papers', Alfred told a share-holders' meeting that he had no use for old-fashioned Conservatism, which was as dead as old-fashioned Radicalism. 'We are Unionist and Imperialist. We have no sympathy whatever with the politicians of the 'sixties, the 'seventies or the 'eighties.' Declaring that he and his papers stood for 'the unwritten alliance of the English-speaking peoples', and that their advocacy of a big navy, among other causes, had evoked charges of Jingoism, he added: 'It is possible that we suffer from the arrogance of youth', a point which a critical posterity has largely ignored in assessing his influence—'that of the strongest combination of newspapers in the United Kingdom, if not in the world'—on popular feeling about South Africa or the rise of German power.

An incident during the Jubilee march reflected something other than the good humour of the London crowds. In January 1896 the German emperor had telegraphed to Paul Kruger, president of the Transvaal, congratulating him and his people on repelling the Jameson raid. In the Diamond Jubilee procession, the German representatives, headed by the Kaiser, were booed at some points of the route and at one place, where there was a brief unexpected halt, a cockney voice called out to the Kaiser's brother: 'There's a post office round the corner, if you want to send any more telegrams!' Behind the caustic London wit was a growing national mistrust of German ambitions. It was shown on a larger scale that day in the full-throated cheers which greeted the strong processional contingents from the Empire and colonies. Many readers of the *Daily Mail* had been disturbed by the reiteration in its pages of warnings about Germany. In its first year they were told that 'the keynote of modern Germany is militarism' and that there was world danger in 'the inherent brutality of the German character, which the saving grace of the art of music has never destroyed'. The writer was Alfred Harmsworth's friend Burgess, the R.A.'s son. He had been sent to Germany to write about what he saw there.

On September 24, 1897, the paper published the first of sixteen eye-witness articles, headed 'Under the Iron Heel', by George Warrington Steevens, commissioned to follow up Burgess's tour of investigation. Steevens came back convinced 'that Germany will keep her hands free to deal with us. Let us make no mistake about it. For the next ten years fix your eyes very hard upon Germany.' It transpired that the German emperor had been keeping his eye on the *Daily Mail*. In his personally compiled chronology of world history from 1878, he named the founding of that newspaper as one of the principal events in Great Britain in 1896. For many observers, Germany was the ultimate menace but in the foreground of world affairs there was a rapidly deteriorating position in South Africa, where the Jameson Raid of 1895 had stirred up passions that had not been subdued by Dr Jameson's imprisonment. The rally of Imperial strength for the Diamond Jubilee was a comforting reminder of likely help in time of trouble and a consolation in particular to those who were unable to make up their minds whether the decline of the British Empire had begun with the surrender of Majuba Hill nearly twenty years before or with the opening of the Kiel Canal in 1895. Alfred Harmsworth was having both possibilities of history pointed out to him in 1897 in letters from Admiral Lord Charles Beresford and the Hon. James Lowther, a future Speaker of the House of Commons.

According to the diary, it had been 'a very tiring season', and as soon as the official festivities were over, rounded off by the great naval review at Spithead, Alfred went down to Elmwood to enjoy 'a completely idle holiday in beautiful weather'. One of his weekend visitors was Max Beerbohm, not yet the mocking bird of English letters. Another visitor was Charles Dickens's youngest son, Henry, who had gone down to Broadstairs to give readings from his father's works at a Dickens fete, which Molly Harmsworth helped to organize. Henry Dickens afterwards wrote to Alfred: 'It is true that my father wrote a Life of Our Saviour. He wrote this for his children and the original ms. is now in the hands of my aunt, Miss Hogarth. With the fullest sanction of the family, she would adopt every feasible means in her power to prevent publication.' The interdict was broken thirty-five years later, when the *Daily Mail* paid £40,000 for the serial rights.

On July 21, Alfred had been called to London by an office complication: 'Narrowly escaped being sent to Holloway [prison] for contempt of court by the *Daily Mail*.' A week later, he drew £20 petty cash from Reggie Nicholson and went to Stamford, Lincolnshire, to present prizes at his old school. On his way south again, he visited his mother at her holiday house, Wentworth Lodge, Aldeburgh. He passed his few days there riding a bicycle through the quiet Suffolk lanes: 'delightful'. Before August was out, he travelled to Scotland for a fishing holiday with his American friend, Carson, who had worked on some of the early issues of *Answers*. There were compensations for the poor fishing. 'Morning at Dunvegan Castle, home of the McLeods, where Johnson and Boswell went; a delightful experience.' On the homeward train, 'G. R. Sims joined us', a first encounter with the popular playwright and contributor of 'Mustard and Cress' to *The Referee*. 'He amused us much.' Back in London, he was met by his wife: 'We were delighted to be together again.' Next day, 'left 2.30 to stay with Mother at Aldeburgh', once more. 'In evening to church with Mother.' 'I had a walk with Mother', always with the capital M. 'At Cromer played golf for the first time and liked it.' That second stay at Aldeburgh enabled him to meet Mayson Beeton again. Beeton had been a *Daily Mail* staff correspondent. He lived at Horsey, on the Norfolk coast, and he was to be much concerned in the years to come with developing the raw materials supply for the Harmsworth publishing empire.

The tremendous expansion of his undertakings was causing Alfred Harmsworth, in 1897, to review his personal status in relation to that of his nearest rival. He unburdened himself in a letter to the Earl of Onslow, Under-Secretary of State for India, dated October 18:

Dear Lord Onslow,—My opponent and friend Sir George Newnes started the *Westminster Gazette* and Lord Rosebery promptly recognised his journal by a reward that in the formation of his company this year proved of enormous commercial advantage to him.

On our side, owners of newspapers of comparatively slight influence are rewarded and my predecessor in the *Evening News* received recognition, though the journal was a failure.

However, I would rather say nothing more on the subject: the Party leaders are no doubt quite ignorant of the revolution which the *Daily Mail*, in its infancy at present, is making in London journalism. They have never even enquired as to the new provincial offshoots I am preparing. The Government has an enormous majority and can dispense with young men and, moreover, such of the leaders as know me are aware that I would never sacrifice my belief in the need for a strong Imperial and Foreign policy to any personal disappointments and annoyance at the favouring of opponents.

Pardon that worst of bores, the man with a grievance, and again allow me to thank you most sincerely for your disinterested thought.

Faithfully yours,
ALFRED C. HARMSWORTH.

Alfred was giving his mother £4,000 a year. She had the Victorian reverence for property. 'Some more freeholds', she would say when her sons asked what she wanted for a birthday present. That Christmas, all the family except 'Dot', who was in India, gathered at the fine old house which the elder Harmsworth boys had bought for their mother, a Queen Anne mansion with thirty-five acres laid out by 'Capability' Brown in the rural fringe six miles north-west of Hampstead. They paid £9,000 for it. She wrote to Cecil shortly after taking possession in the late autumn of 1897:

Poynters Hall,
Totteridge,
Herts.

My dearest Cecil,—The letter signed by you all which Hildebrand handed to me came as a great surprise. I had no idea that my dear boys meditated an improvement in my income, already a very handsome one—and I can only say that I am deeply touched by it and very grateful.

Your very loving
MOTHER.

*　　*　　*

What the new psychologists were diagnosing as 'the strain of modern life', sent Alfred to Egypt in search of rest early in 1898. There was a letter from the poet Henley, just before he left: 'Would that I, like you, were for Egypt! I am much worried and bedevilled by things in general and health in particular.'

Alfred Harmsworth to Frederick Wood:

Dahabieh 'Horus,' Assouan.
9.2.98.

My dear Fred,—One of the many crimes of middle age is that I am so absorbed in business that I neither see nor write to old or, indeed, any friends. Indeed I am become a sort of hermit.

They, and you as my dear father's oldest and warmest of friends, are often in my mind and it was most annoying to me to miss you at Totteridge the other day.

This is the existence you would enjoy. We are living in the classics. You must let me pack you off here one day. To be able to survey thirty civilizations in three or four weeks, to look upon works and records of folks who had put in four thousand years of culture B.C., makes one regard the Greeks and Romans, whose work is as plentiful here as anywhere, as people who lived the day before yesterday.

We live in a kind of glorified houseboat and sail thirty or forty miles a day, shooting, exploring, photographing, as we choose. That piece of brown stuff I enclose I took from a tomb 4,000 years old. It is a piece of mummy cloth. As my dear father would have said, from journalism to robbing the dead is but a natural and brief step.

I have been reading here of all things a 'History of Mary-le-Bone.' Lord, how it takes me back to the time when you and I—or was it the Gov'nor and you?—fought the neighbourhood boys as we made our way along the Finchley Road.

You *must* come and see us on our return.

Affectionately yours always,
ALFRED C. H.

The reference to middle age, at thirty-three, had actuarial warranty then which a later generation finds it hard to accept. The thought of middle age had been with Alfred Harmsworth on his thirtieth birthday, though it was perhaps also part of his uncertain health context, the measure of which could be judged by the exceptional buoyancy of the diary note: 'The Nile trip is a boon and a blessing. Never felt so fit in my life', on February 17. On February 5 he had written: 'I do not remember being so well for years.' His self-satisfaction received a rebuff on February 18: 'Gloomy because of the death of two English lady visitors.' A sudden swelling of the lip sent him uneasily to the doctor, who relieved his fears with the information that it 'results from cold'.

Alfred Harmsworth to Cecil Harmsworth:

S.S. 'Clyde.'
6th March, 1898.

My dear Cecil,—In nine or ten days from this writing I shall, I hope, be at work again and in better trim than I have been for years.

From Max [Pemberton] I hear that the preparations for the magazine go on apace. Its production should greatly increase the prestige of our business, for pre-eminent as that is at home, it is depressingly unknown among the class who go to the parts of the world we have just left. *The Strand*, *Pearson's*, and the others are everywhere. I have been studying all the magazines, English and American, closely. Except in printing matters, I shall be amazed if we cannot get the first place. A more interesting field of operations I cannot conceive.

You must take Emilie, to whom my fond love and Mary's, to Egypt one of these days. It was the most surprisingly delightful trip of our lives. As for dahabieh life, with companions one loves and a goodly store of books, I know nothing like it.

Newnes has ordered a huge steel dahabieh. Mug! One can hire them in plenty in Cairo. He takes a noisy crew about with him, they tell me, and by no means adds to the reputation of our trade.

Your affectionate brother,
ALFRED.

The magazine idea had come up for consideration a number of times in the previous three years, to be pushed away by more pressing concerns. 'Our old project' was Harmsworth's diary reference when Louis Wain, an artist who made his name and wrecked his mental health by drawing nothing but cats, discussed it with him early in 1893. Cutcliffe Hyne, inventor of one of the period's celebrated fiction characters, Captain Kettle, had been commissioned to write articles as part of the preparations. Later, in 1895, Beckles Willson had produced several 'dummies', only to be told that publication was being deferred for twelve months. Willson wrote in his exercise-book diary: 'What *will* people say? My reputation will be ruined. I shall not be able to face my friends. Harmsworth has put me in a false position.' The postponement had not been wholly due to Alfred's concentrated labours on the newspapers. His brother Harold was going through one of his panicky phases. He was despondent about the future. War clouds were gathering over South Africa. So overwrought was he that he begged Alfred to agree to their selling out altogether, lest ruin should come. Harold was persuaded to take a rest at Seaford, Sussex, followed by a voyage to Egypt. Alfred, meanwhile, went calmly ahead with the magazine plan, intending to give as good value for threepence as Newnes was giving in *The Strand* for sixpence.

The first issue of *The Harmsworth Magazine* came out in July 1898, ten years after the first issue of *Answers*. W. H. Smith & Son declined to deal with it on the terms offered by the Harmsworths. To that elephantine resistance there was added the mosquito sting of *The Saturday Review*, edited by Frank Harris, who attacked Alfred's writing in the new magazine as 'brainless, formless, familiar and impudent'. What is referred to in his diary as 'our war with Smith's' was momentarily offset by a national advertising campaign which sold 780,000 copies of the magazine's first issue, a considerable number of them in drapers' and chemists' shops. Lipton, the provision merchant, conferred with his managers about distributing copies through his chain of shops. The *Daily Mail* and the *Evening News* reported the clash with Smith's as if a battle raged: 'Magazine War: News from the Front.' 'What America Thinks of Our Fight.' 'The Bookstall War.' For some readers the war of 1898 had nothing to do with the conflict between Spain and the United States. When, in addition to the trade aspects of the dispute, Smith's were accused of censoring the contents of the publications they distributed, Alfred Harmsworth received letters of support from other publishers and editors and from literary figures of the day, Conan Doyle and Kipling among them.

Having produced a penny newspaper for a halfpenny, he had expected to repeat the formula of success by publishing a sixpenny magazine for threepence. For once, the Harmsworth touch failed. The price of *The Harmsworth Magazine* was raised to 3½d., then 4d., with no very remarkable results. The magazine began to succeed only when it moved into the sixpenny class, along with *The Strand*, *The Windsor*, *The Royal* and *Pearson's Magazine*, and used the 'names' it had affected to despise. Meanwhile, Alfred Harmsworth had renewed his self-confidence by bringing out a threepenny magazine for a penny. Under the title of the *Penny Pictorial*, it was a bookstall favourite over many years.

*   *   *

Before the old century had ended, Alfred was governing his swiftly growing publishing realm from a sumptuously appointed room on the first floor of the big new five-storey building of red brick with stone mullioned windows that was changing the face of Carmelite Street and Tallis Street, round the corner. He had moved in before the builders had moved out. First called Harmsworth Building, it was renamed Carmelite House, commemorating the monastic order on whose sanctuary lands the votaries of the young new century were trespassing with indecent haste. Because its foundations were sunk in soil reclaimed from the Thames, the building was for a long period exempt from rates, a saving of £1,000 a year. It had cost nearly half a million pounds and it brought the Harmsworth periodicals and newspapers under one roof. An art gallery had been one of Alfred's ideas when the plans for the building were being drafted. It was not found possible because the Harmsworth papers soon overflowed every floor. A wit referred to the building as 'a factory in Bohemia'.

The new printing establishment across the river, in Lavington Street, Southwark, costing £40,000, had been completed too. From it would flow a continuous stream of Harmsworth weekly papers. Many of them were devised in response to mechanical imperatives rather than to meet a public demand, though the keenest judgment was often shown in deciding what type of publication stood the best chance of finding a market. Mostly, they were printed in six-point or even smaller type on grey paper and the combination may have been harmful to eyes not so good as Alfred Harmsworth's. Other works at Gravesend and Northfleet were designed to print *The Harmsworth Magazine* and the more substantial publications of the group. Alfred was now able to tell his shareholders that they owned and operated more rotary presses than any other company. He also told them that they were spending £100 every working day on 'literary contributions', an item of the balance sheet which he rarely failed to stress. St. John, not long down from Oxford, had been brought on to the board. Sutton was similarly promoted. *Answers* had beaten *Tit-Bits* in circulation by several hundred thousand copies a week, a fact announced to the shareholders in 1899.

At one of the company meetings of that year a tall slim young reporter on the staff of the Commercial Press Association rose from his place in the Memorial Hall, Farringdon Street, to make a suggestion about procedure which was favourably received by the chairman. After the meeting Alfred Harmsworth had a brief talk with the young man, who, he suggested, might apply for a post with Harmsworth Brothers Ltd. Nothing came of it and yet for the young man, William Berry, of Merthyr Tydfil, perhaps everything did. He was twenty and probably not impervious to the glamour of the young head of the Harmsworth enterprises. Strong identifying urges may have been set in motion, for Berry had come to London two years before with barely defined ambitions. Finding direction, they bore him on to his own outstanding success in Fleet Street, crowned by his proprietorship of the *Daily Telegraph* and, later still, after Northcliffe's death, by his acquisition of the Harmsworth periodicals group. As Lord Camrose, he died in 1954.

'Big rooms, big ideas', and Alfred Harmsworth's Room One at Carmelite House had the effect of amplifying his psychic presence so that men knew when he was in the building though they had not seen him. Room One was boldly spacious and ornate. Its walls were panelled in mahogany. Rows of expensively bound volumes of the Harmsworth publications gleamed in mahogany bookcases. Each mahogany overmantel, above its fireplace at either end of the room, was as solidly assertive as the pediment in classical architecture. Above one of them was a copy of Poussin's 'Arcadian Shepherds'. The imposingly virtuous business impression was tempered by an assortment of Empire furniture which made the room look half-boudoir, an effect embellished by the thick pile carpet which cost a thousand pounds and a crayon portrait of Molly Harmsworth resting on an easel amid masses of embowering flowers from the garden and conservatories at Elmwood. A bust of Napoleon stood in a window recess. There were silver-framed photographs of his mother, and of his father in wig and gown, on the broad leather-topped desk. At night the room was radiant with the glow of hidden lights. Sutton was always at hand next door. An office-boy in an Eton suit and collar sat sedately in a corner of the secretary's ante-room. Seeming to enlarge, also, Alfred Harmsworth's personal authority, his occupancy of Room One was followed by a new note of respect in addressing him. He was less often 'Mr Alfred', more often 'Chief'. A printing trade paper commented in the year 1900: 'The American custom of calling a chief editor "the Chief" seems to be spreading in British journalism. We rather like it.' It did not spread far in British journalism. There was no one else then, or after, to give it the same compelling sanction as Alfred Harmsworth.

His *Daily Mail* was already established as one of the few London newspapers that were making money. Pearson was losing £1,750 a week on his *Daily Express*. A sign of the ascending popularity of the *Daily Mail* was the frequency with which it was mentioned on the music-hall stage. Under an agreement of April 28, 1898, it had been taken over by a private company with a capital of £200,000. Alfred had been appointed chairman and given 'literary and political control of any papers issued by the company during his life'. Harold was made 'manager and deputy chairman during his life'. Alfred took 95,000 shares, Harold 48,000. As in the case of Harmsworth Brothers Ltd., Alfred saw to it that his younger brothers were well looked after. Cecil got 16,000 shares, Leicester 15,000 and Hildebrand 10,000. Kennedy Jones's allotment was 15,000. The *Evening News* was now making £50,000 a year at a time when evening newspapers were not highly regarded as an investment, four of them having changed hands in recent years. Its circulation had reached 800,000 copies a day and was still rising. Its shares, valued at 3d. when the Harmsworths took it over, now stood at £3. The paper gained greatly from the news resources of the *Daily Mail* and had secured what was then the record price for a single advertisement, £400. The Harmsworth periodical house was paying dividends of thirty per cent. Newnes was paying ten per cent, Pearson fifteen per cent. With its nineteen publications, it was reaping further profits in a branch of publishing first explored by Cassell of London and Chambers of Edinburgh, the issuing of works of literary and educational value in fortnightly parts. Cassell had made £50,000 out of a *Life of Christ* by Dean Farrar, who sold it outright for a comparatively small sum and never got over it. The Harmsworths' *Sixty Years a Queen* was written for them by Sir Herbert Maxwell, Bart., who received £250 for all rights in the work which showed a final profit of £15,000. This was followed by *Nelson and His Times* and Sir John Lubbock's *Hundred Best Books*—'an entire library of one hundred volumes, containing 48,235 pages, 310 illustrations and 20 coloured maps'—and the sale of those works led to the production of others which easily eclipsed anything of the kind that had gone before. They were more rewarding in personal prestige than *Comic Cuts* journalism, though Alfred had never had any false modesty about that and, indeed, occasionally flourished its success as one of the exploits of his youth.

For June 22, 1898, he wrote in the diary that he had 'spent two hours at *The Times* office discussing with Mr Walter negotiations in regard to that paper'. The diary for July 27 notes that Moberly Bell, manager of *The Times*, dined with him. The *History of The Times* states that 'in March 1898 Harmsworth came for the first time to Printing House Square and there learnt from Walter's lips that the sale to him of any share or portion would not be admitted'. The diary has no note of the meeting. Arthur Walter, the scholarly Old Etonian head of his family, would have been likely to resist any attempt by a young man of thirty-three to influence the affairs of *The Times*, that preserve of venerable experience and practice.

It was known in Fleet Street that *The Times* was in difficulties. Apart from the very considerable loss of prestige and money incurred through the Parnell-Pigott case, the controlling owners, the Walter family, were enmeshed in the clauses of a will that was likely to become more onerous with the passing of time. The shares in *The Times* were divided and sub-divided to a point of absurdity. Moreover, its organization and methods were out of date. Whether, thus early, Harmsworth was concerned to acquire *The Times* we do not know, though the *History of The Times* states that it was for him 'a glittering prize'. For the moment, his interest had been provoked by a letter from a Walter granddaughter, Mrs Sibley, owner of a fortieth share. Dissatisfied with the management and its possible effect on her beneficial interest, she had resolved to take action which would force an inspection of the books. Thinking that Harmsworth might be a valuable ally, she wrote to him. Hence, no doubt, the meeting with Arthur Walter. He also went to see the eminent solicitor, Sir George Lewis, who told him: 'If you purchased the Sibley share, you would be purchasing a lawsuit which would be remunerative to the lawyers, but not to you.' The 1898 talks being abortive, he was content to play the waiting game. It seems that he also had acquisitive ideas about the *Daily Telegraph*, a newspaper which it pleased him to call the 'Daily Bellow-graph' when its policy was out of tune with his own. Hall Richardson, manager of the *Daily Telegraph* for many years, wrote in his volume of Fleet Street recollections: 'To me, he never disguised his ambition that he might one day own the paper.' The *Daily Telegraph* was an important competitor of the *Daily Mail* and their rivalry had reached a point at which the *Daily Mail* was challenging the claim of the older newspaper that it had the world's largest circulation, asserted daily on the front page.

Early in 1899, the *Daily Telegraph* announced that it was going to publish seven days a week. The *Daily Mail* reacted at once, as if its future was at stake. It, too, would publish a Sunday edition. Both papers began Sunday publishing on April 9, 1899. The *Daily Mail* published six Sunday issues, the *Daily Telegraph* seven. Both had to bow before the storm of public resentment worked up by religious leaders who fought stoutly for the puritan legacy of the English Sabbath, with its millions lounging about in consecrated idleness. That institution of ancient decree was thought to be threatened by the indifference to it of an equally ancient people, represented by the proprietors of the *Daily Telegraph*, the Lawsons. The President of the Newspaper Society reminded readers of the London evening newspaper, *The Echo*, that the initiative in seven-day newspaper publishing had been taken by 'one who belonged to a race that does not recognize our Sunday'. Powerful articles in *The British Weekly* and *The Methodist Times* led the attack. There were votes of censure from the Presbyterian, Congregationalist and Baptist boards of ministers in London. Secular resistance, inflamed by the possibility of 13,000 workers being deprived of their day of rest, was organized by the Retail Newsagents & Booksellers Union. The *Daily Mail* scored tactically by printing opposition views in its columns.

> 29, Delamere Terrace,
> Westbourne Square, W.
> 24th March, 1889.

Dear Sir,—Since you are good enough to urge me to express my views about Sunday newspapers, I must honestly tell you that—although I have no conscientious scruple about encouraging their circulation—I think them exhausting and unnecessary. I have never taken in a Sunday newspaper and I am glad to have one day a week unlike the rest. The whole conception of a Sunday newspaper appears to me to accentuate the hurrying, wearying and trivial monotony of experience which is the curse of life nowadays.

> I am,
> Your obedient servant,
> EDMUND GOSSE.

There was a remarkable concentration of American attention on the Sunday newspaper question in England. In the previous year, American churchmen had spoken out strongly against the generally lowered tone of the nation's Sunday journalism. *Sell's Dictionary of the World Press* (1900) states that 'no event in English life since the introduction of the first Home Rule Bill in 1886 attracted more attention in the United States than the attempt made in the spring of 1899 to issue seven-day journals in London. Each stage of the experiment was recorded by cable in the American press and commented on in the editorial columns and when the attempt failed, various explanations were put forward in the American newspapers and magazines'. The real explanation was that the three main wholesale newspaper distributing companies, and particularly W. H. Smith & Son with their railway bookstall monopoly, were solidly against Sunday work for their staffs. Smiths' had declined to supply *The Observer* to the Duke of Connaught in camp at Aldershot because it meant a Sunday delivery. There was no explanation of the obstinacy of the Lawsons and the Harmsworths in persisting in a venture which could hardly succeed without that co-operation. Why, then, the venture at all? *The Newspaper Owner & Manager* suggested that the *Daily Telegraph* proprietors had 'expensive machinery and facilities which they do not care to see idle on one day in seven'. *The Financial News* believed that the decision on seven-day publication had been taken because, by long custom, company prospectuses were issued on Saturday and supplied a substantial part of Sunday paper revenue from the rates paid for printing them.

On a morning in the second week of May 1899, two men were talking on the kerb outside Carmelite House. One was George White, the *Daily Mail* publisher, the other James Read, a young *Sunday Daily Mail* 'rep' working the provinces. 'You see those three men going into the lift?' White said. 'That's Alfred Harmsworth, his brother Harold, and Kennedy Jones. They're going in to kill the *Sunday Daily Mail*.' Yet both White and Read had no doubt that the paper would have survived the agitation: they had their fingers on the public pulse. The *Sunday Daily Mail* stopped on May 17, 1899, the *Sunday Daily Telegraph* a week later, the end of an inglorious Fleet Street chapter. Within thirty-six hours over twenty thousand approving letters were delivered at Carmelite House. The *Sunday Daily Mail* announced that it would be transformed into 'a complete, artistic, illustrated weekly newspaper, fully recording all the week's news and presenting it in a handy and attractive form', for sale on Saturday morning. The new name for the paper was *Illustrated Mail*. It was not a success, though the Boer War gave it impetus as an experiment leading on to the new daily picture journalism. It had an art staff of talented young enthusiasts: St. Mar Fitzgerald, whose line drawings gave new distinction to newspaper illustration, Oliver Onions, who became a writer of distinguished fiction, Percy V. Bradshaw, founder of the Press Art School, David Whitelaw, later editor of *The London Magazine* and a popular novelist, Barnard Lintott, and Penrhyn Stanlaws, the American magazine illustrator, who brought some of the Dana Gibson charm to his work for the paper. The *Illustrated Mail* paved the way for the *Overseas Daily Mail*, which supplanted it in 1904. The *Sunday Daily Telegraph* retired from the fray with the announcement that its 'Page for Women', its serial story by Miss Braddon, its special articles by Sir Edwin Arnold, and its chess and acrostics columns, would in future appear in the Saturday issue of the *Daily Telegraph*.

* * *

Thackeray had complained about 'the thorns in the cushion' of the editorial chair, the heedless unending calls on an editor's energy and time. The assault on Alfred Harmsworth's attention was more intense than anything of the kind known to Thackeray as editor of *The Cornhill Magazine*. A long admired tenor of the Victorian age, Sims Reeves, begged out of the bitterness of bankruptcy at seventy-five for support for a self-proposed national testimonial. 'I thought my birthday, October 21st, would be suitable, as it is also the anniversary of Trafalgar. How often have I sung "The Death of Nelson" and, I add, with very great success. I can sing it now, not perhaps with the same stentorian power, but with the same expression of feeling. I must go on working to live.' Herbert Beerbohm Tree was worried because the *Daily Mail* no longer mentioned his theatre, Her Majesty's, in its 'Green Room Gossip'. The Countess of Warwick, at her castle, pleaded for 'a page or two a month in your magazine' in which to put forward her ideas of social reform. Lord William Nevill, writing from 72 Eaton Place, S.W., was 'much distressed' because the *Daily Mail* had recalled his conviction and imprisonment of two years before. 'You are a wealthy man of great influence. I am now down at the bottom of the ladder. Don't let your paper prevent me from trying to get up, if it is only a few, a very few, steps', and Alfred Harmsworth pencilled a note on the letter: 'I have replied personally, as I thought we were rather unkind to him.' W. H. Mallock, known for his *Critical Examination of Socialism* and other works, was anxious to be rid of the incubus of *The British Review*: 'Would you consider purchasing the shares?' Ellen Terry implored his help for her charity matinee at the Lyceum Theatre: 'Won't you appear as Napoleon crossing the Alps on a little gee-gee? That would be most splendid!! Please, do help me all you know. I don't think you dislike me—much!!' Conan Doyle had a sister who wanted to write for publication and 'would there be a chance for her work to find a place provided that it in every way came up to your standard?' Hall Caine requested an appointment to discuss the action of the National Club in asking him to resign, 'a sequel to *The Eternal City*. My offence is sympathy with the Catholic Church. I should like to see you.' Lady Randolph Churchill's son Winston had written a short story entitled *Man Overboard*, which she sent to the *Daily Mail*: 'Will you please let me know its fate?' Sir Douglas Straight, editor of the *Pall Mall Gazette*, was upset 'because having nodded to you the other night at Drury Lane, you met my recognition with a stony stare. I am sore and hurt.' The Marquess of

Granby drew 'Mr Harmsworth's attention to the regrettable account in the *Daily Mail* of the sad circumstances of the death of his sister, Lady Katherine Manners'. Lord Kelvin, writing from Aix-les-Bains, desired to reply to *Daily Mail* criticisms of that resort. Madame Melba had been annoyed by 'several people saying that they taught me to sing. Will you print a letter, if I write a nice one?' Clement Scott wished to be allowed 'to introduce a very clever girl who has a great gift for writing'. H.R.H. Princess Christian, at Cumberland Lodge, Windsor, wrote on behalf of Surgeon-Major-General Taylor, 'a man of *great* culture and having *talent* with his *pen*'. Lord Curzon requested that 'your writer about my poor wife's illness be a little more circumspect'. Clara Butt, asking 'forgiveness for troubling you, would like to introduce a friend, Mr Branscombe Wood, who has done a great deal of literary work in Australia . . .'. Mrs Beerbohm Tree, at 77 Sloane Street, sent a reminder 'not to forget to put Herbert up for the Automobile Club'. The artist, G. F. Watts, 'wants to know if you will take up the case of education and hammer away at the futility of stuffing children's brains with the dry details of our present system'. Lady Dorothy Nevill, hostess of an age that was passing, wrote in her large hand on diminutive notepaper enclosed in a stamp-size envelope, asking for attention to be given to a new book by her son, Ralph Nevill. Hall Caine urged that it 'would be God's work to expose those nasty rats of music-hall agents', because of their behaviour to women. His heart 'had been made to bleed the other day by hearing what happened to a pretty young thing of 17'. The editor of *The Quarterly Review*, G. W. Prothero, sought advice on conducting that eminent periodical: 'I should be really grateful if you would jot down any ideas on the subject.' Max Pemberton wished 'you would put the wife nominally on your staff', so that she might qualify for a free voyage to Madeira. Cecil Rhodes desired the publication of a speech by him on the tariff question. 'You can add an extra sheet to your paper. It is a good speech and should be published.' Lillie Langtry asked permission for a member of the *Daily Mail* staff, Sidney Dark [later editor of *The Church Times*], to write 'advance paragraphs' for her. Madge Kendal appealed 'to Mr Harmsworth's kindness and generosity' for publicity for one of her charity shows. W. T. Stead sent a man 'who is walking round the world, earning his living as he goes'. Sir Arthur Sullivan enclosed a letter from H.R.H. Princess Louise, who was 'handicapped by the want of means and overshadowed by others who know how to put themselves more prominently forward. I am so fond of her. I should very much like to bring you together.' Lady Charles Beresford 'wants to bring to your favourable notice a friend of mine, Mr Arthur Symons, distinguished poet and critic: he begs me to introduce him to you'. H. W. Massingham, editor of the *Daily Chronicle*, would like 'to enlist your sympathies on behalf of a young lady who used to work for

The Star when I was on it'. H. H. Asquith, of 1 Paper Buildings, Temple, complains that the *Daily Mail* has 'given currency to a report that I am about to retire from the bar. Kindly have it contradicted.' The Poet Laureate, Alfred Austin, begs acceptance of some lines—'such as I have had printed for the Queen'—for publication: 'I cannot help thinking that a large sale would result.'

* * *

Father R. R. Dolling to Mrs Alfred Harmsworth:

> Elmwood,
> St. Peters.
> [Undated]

My dear Mrs Harmsworth,—We said the General Thanksgiving in the tent —for four perfect weeks without one single hindrance. It is wonderful. I half think you and Harmsworth guessed what you have accomplished for us, but you can only guess it. I know it and am, therefore,
> Yours gratefully and appreciatively,
> R. R. DOLLING

Alfred's admiration for Dolling had grown steadily since their first meeting at Portsmouth, during the election campaign of 1895. Having fallen out with his bishop on ritual matters, Dolling had left Portsea to work in the East End parish of St. Saviour's, Poplar, with its attached Church of England school. Alfred was attracted by the Franciscan spirit which Dolling showed in his life and work, his concept of religion as joyous experience. Dolling's biographer, the Rev. C. E. Osborne, wrote that Alfred was 'the most intimate friend of Dolling's last years'. He was Dolling's financial mainstay at St. Saviour's. Catechizing the pupils of the school, Dolling asked: 'Now, boys, who is the patron saint of this parish?' A shout came from several parts of the classroom at once: 'Please, sir, Mr Harmsworth!'

In 1898, Alfred had bought Joss Farm, adjoining Elmwood. It added a farmhouse, land and cottages to the property. Joss Farm fields ran down to the North Foreland cliffs. There, at Dolling's suggestion, Alfred started a boys' summer camp. It provided a month's holiday to hundreds of boys of St. Saviour's school and parish. Many had not seen the sea before. 'The outdoor life to most of them', Cecil Harmsworth wrote, 'was pathetically unfamiliar.' Grateful memories survive. One of the 'old boys' of the camp recalls Alfred's visits, 'in a dazzling white summer suit', his fox terrier, Bob, at his heels. He always tried to be present at the weighing of the boys at the end of their holiday. 'To the boy who had put on most weight, he gave a sovereign.' The present Archbishop of Brisbane,

Australia, was a young curate at St. Saviour's, the Rev. Reginald Halsey. He remembers speaking to Alfred about the future of St. Saviour's boys after leaving school. 'I will always give a promising boy a chance in my businesses', Alfred told him; and the Archbishop recalls that more than one boy did well as a result. Alfred told the camp commandant, the devoted headmaster of St. Saviour's Boys' School, Frank Matley, to let him know of suitable St. Saviour's boys when school-leaving time came. 'What would my poor East End boys do without Harmsworth?' Dolling wrote. 'No one can tell what he has done for my dear lads.'

Maintaining the camp wholly at his own expense for sixteen years, contributing to the funds of a similar camp for St. Saviour's girls, run by Dolling's sister, and later to the home of rest at Worthing which commemorated Dolling's life and work, as well as making a regular annual allowance to Dolling for his church school, cost Alfred Harmsworth large sums. He had his reward in the gratitude of Dolling and his boys and in the opportunity to live up to his most generous impulses.

Chapter Ten

Dawn of a New Age

ALFRED could afford now to leave the management of the periodicals, which were still multiplying almost with parthenogenetic ease, to his brothers. Harold was in control of the finances. Cecil was looking after *Answers* and *The Harmsworth Magazine*. The younger brothers each had a department with a group of editors under him. *Answers* page proofs were still being sent to Alfred, and the editor of any of the publications who fancied himself beyond the reach of proprietorial observation was likely to get shocks when he least expected them. 'Why do you allow your artist to draw thin policemen? Surely you are aware that the public prefers its police to be fat and kindly?' Sometimes the tone was arbitrary: 'I don't care for ——'s serial story. Wind it up in your next issue. Get a better writer.' Omniscience could be harsh if the editor was about to depart on his annual holiday or the serial writer was in arrears with his rent.

Primarily, Alfred was concentrating on the realities of newspaper power. Up to that time, he had been content with the routine life, the daily round of complicated high-speed decision and action which is for ever a mystery to the public whose interest it serves. He had written about it with a novice's enthusiasm in the first number of *The Harmsworth Magazine*:

When you casually and carelessly open your newspaper of a morning, how often do you realize, even if you are aware, that it is the product of a score of busy organizations, with tentacles spread over the whole world, the operation of which involves the best brains and machinery of the age; that unlimited capital and thought are devoted to its daily production; that its continual appearance has created a new class of men who work at night and sleep by day; that its distribution requires the use of special trains, and the gathering of its news the opening at night of telegraph, cable and telephone offices; that the public appetite for reading is sweeping away vast Scandinavian and American forests for the manufacture of the wood pulp of which the paper itself is made; and that the very journal you are reading may have formed part of a growing tree a month ago!

There was in daily journalism a dynamic drive not to be found in periodical editing and publishing. His determination that the *Daily Mail* should have an unrivalled news service secured a considerable part of the million circulation which it had attained by the end of 1899. His resolution in that matter had been reinforced by a news story which had stirred the nation in 1897. The *Daily Mail* had beaten its rivals with its account of the grounding of the P. & O. liner *Aden* off Socotra, in which many lives were lost. Forty-five persons had spent seventeen days on the wave-swept ship, hourly expecting death. At the height of the storm, on June 20, they had sung the national anthem as a Diamond Jubilee salute to Queen Victoria. The night editor struck out that part of the story, thinking it an inventive touch by the Aden postmaster, from whom the news had been procured. It was afterwards confirmed by the survivors. Commending the night editor's desire to avoid sensationalism, Alfred Harmsworth resolved to create a world-wide network of accredited *Daily Mail* representatives. He wrote: 'This meant nothing less than the appointment of special correspondents in every important centre throughout the world; the whole face of the earth being so mapped out that nothing could happen anywhere without coming under the immediate cognizance of a paid representative having facilities for transmitting the news direct to the London office.' He lost no time in setting up his hemispheric news corps with the help of the able men around him and Kennedy Jones in particular. There was to be no counting the cost. Soon the paper had a news service unequalled in scope by any other newspaper and eclipsed only in authority by that of *The Times*. The success of the *Daily Mail* was largely built on that reputation.

At this point it is appropriate to bring forward for examination the statement which has appeared in the several reprintings of the historical survey, *England: 1870–1914*, by R. C. K. Ensor, that a *Daily Mail* news story of the Boxer Rising in 1900 was 'evidence of the length to which it would go for sensationalism'. The paper had received a cable from its Shanghai correspondent (appointed on the recommendation of a well-known British firm of China merchants and, according to H. W. Wilson, chief leader writer of the *Daily Mail*, 'highly paid and peculiarly well qualified to sift news from Chinese sources') reporting the murder of the German minister in Peking, Baron von Ketteler, and the burning of foreign legations. The message was referred at once to the Foreign Office, which replied that no word had come from Peking for three weeks and that there were grounds for believing that a massacre had occurred. The Shanghai man was asked for confirmation. He replied emphasizing the importance of the news. Meanwhile, in London, every source of likely information was consulted, while the foreign editor of the *Daily Mail* cabled Shanghai again, urging 'extreme caution'. The correspondent re-affirmed the reliability of his information and another Shanghai newspaper representative endorsed it. In the House of Commons, the Under-Secretary for Foreign Affairs said: 'We can hardly dare to hope that in substance the reports of the massacre are inaccurate.' Kennedy Jones recorded: 'There was no confirmation of the news but all admitted its extreme possibility. Finally, we decided to publish the cablegram.' It had been held back three days while the inquiries were made. At the same time, the message was communicated to other London newspapers, with a statement of its origin. They printed it, *The Times* among them. There-after, there was a silence of several weeks: no further reports came out of North China. *The Times* published obituary notices of presumed victims. A memorial service was arranged at St. Paul's Cathedral. On August 15, an international force reached Peking. It found all safe except the German minister, who had been murdered, as the original cable had stated.

Alfred Harmsworth ordered an immediate on-the-spot investigation. W. J. Evans, who had become editor of the *Evening News*, was chosen to conduct it. He left for China by the first available passage. The Shanghai correspondent, he found, had too literally accepted rumours put about by the Chinese Government for inscrutable reasons which, it was believed, counted on a favourable reaction of public opinion when it was seen that the rebellion had been magnified by the foreign press. As recently as 1955, *The Times* printed a letter from a reader quoting the book mentioned above as authority for denouncing that old *Daily Mail* news story as 'pure invention'. *The Times* could have looked back to its file for 1900 to find that it made the following comment in publishing a letter from Charles Watney, the foreign editor of the *Daily Mail*: 'The documents which have been sent to us with this letter from the *Daily Mail* office correspond in all respects with the description of them given in the letter, and are con-clusive as to the good faith of the *Daily Mail* in publishing the story of the massacres in Peking transmitted by its correspondent in Shanghai.' Moberly Bell, the assistant manager of *The Times*, wrote later that the *Daily Mail* 'quite innocently misled us, owing to the over-zeal of a corre-spondent in Shanghai'.

There were readers who, while not questioning the paper's good faith, were upset by the lurid headings used in presenting the story. One of them was the rector of Hamworthy, Dorset. His letter of protest dis-turbed Alfred Harmsworth, who since his *Answers* days had been parti-cularly sensitive to criticism from clergy of the established Church. R. D. Blumenfeld, doyen of Fleet Street editors between the two world wars, recalled that the publication of the Peking atrocity story caused

Harmsworth 'intense anxiety'. Blumenfeld asserted: 'He was innocent, completely innocent.' The chief sub-editor of the *Evening News*, William Colley, through whose hands the Peking story also passed, said that there was never any doubt about the good faith in which it was published. 'I verily believe that Alfred Harmsworth would readily have sacrificed every sou he had to repair the shock to the public conscience. His honour never shone brighter than on that occasion.' Later investigations showed that the correspondent in Shanghai was not as well qualified for that position as had been supposed. The *Daily Mail* foreign editor was insufficiently informed of his credentials, a procedure made difficult in a sudden news crisis such as that of the Boxer Rebellion.

Although 'yellow press', the opprobrious American epithet, had often been flung at Harmsworth's newspapers by those to whom a halfpenny paper was necessarily the invention of cheap minds, his personal attitude to irresponsible journalism was never tolerant. Sensationalism is not necessarily exaggeration or untruth. In the Harmsworth press it was the violent energy of a new generation challenging the smug assumptions and methods of the old. Those who charged Alfred Harmsworth with its worst excesses might have been more accurate in citing his tendency to confuse news with views. In that matter he was very much the victim of his temperament. World events had enlarged his perspective of personal power. They made it impressively clear that life had more in it for him than the writ of the blue pencil, the green eyeshade and the rotary press. Journalism, he saw, could be more than the making of a newspaper. It could be leadership. He had brashly tested that implication in the winter of 1898 by offering a prize for the best suggestion for a new Liberal Party programme. Thousands of postcard entries were received from members of Liberal and Radical associations and clubs urging a revision of Liberal policy and the selection of a more actively alert leader than Sir William Harcourt, the Whiggish aristocrat with the ship's prow jaw. The official Liberal press treated Harmsworth's audacity with scorn. It became consternation when Harcourt resigned. Harmsworth had shaken if not convulsed a great English political party.

His voice echoes from the close of a famous decade: 'The great world is becoming very interesting. Parish pump politics are giving way to world affairs.' The stormy international atmosphere of 1897–1900, with its war between Turkey and Greece, between the United States and Spain, the clash with France over Fashoda (in the course of which the *Daily Mail* assailed the French Government with lashing scorn), the 'scramble for China', the German Emperor's 'mailed fist' proclamation, the fighting in the Sudan and South Africa, had shown that he was now in a position to propagate information and opinion about global happenings. He had made preparations for reporting the war in South Africa on a scale never before attempted by a newspaper. He engaged special trains, called them the 'Daily Mail war express', and by reaching out to the Midlands and the North of England pushed the paper's sale up to a million copies, the world's largest daily circulation. While his special writers, G. W. Steevens, Charles Hands, Julian Ralph and Edgar Wallace, were keeping a mass of readers better informed about far-off events than any newspaper public had been before, he was meeting the policy-makers at the centre and finding himself elevated to the rank of formidable opponent, important ally. He could meet Salisbury, Cecil Rhodes, Rosebery and Balfour as one of the men of his time. He could invite his oldest rival to dine with him in Berkeley Square. Sir George Newnes was still living in Putney.

Historians of the period have taken up a sternly critical stance in reviewing his attitude to the Boer War, as reflected in his newspapers. Few have been fairly disposed towards him as a young man commanding larger resources of publicity than anyone else and using it as an instrument of the popular mind. There is a lack of realism in requiring early fortune to be matched by magisterial responsibility; and if the reputation of the young Alfred Harmsworth was vulnerable, it was also exposed to indictments that were a condemnation of a general sentiment rather than of individual wickedness. He acted in the light of his day, which blazed with patriotic excitement. He divined the public mood. He did not initiate it. That was both a reaction from Benthamite Liberalism and a response to the reviving warrior spirit in Europe. The South African war was the latest stage in a long ferment of history which had still not reached its climax. By stirring the brew with his imperialistic fervour, his reiterated scorn of Little Englanders, his whipping up of popular feeling when it seemed to be drooping from war weariness, his 'Absent-Minded Beggar Fund', based on Kipling's unheroic jingle by which the Daily Mail raised £107,000 for soldiers' families, Alfred Harmsworth incurred the displeasure of posterity without compromising his integrity as a journalist. He had decided, after earnest consultations, not to attack the appointment of Sir Redvers Buller to the war command, thinking it against the national interest to do so, though he had no faith in Buller. He had publicly approved Marlowe's judgment in suppressing a war message that was found to be false, though it was printed by other newspapers whose editors had the same choice. The consequent destruction of thousands of copies of the Daily Mail that had already gone to press was a direct loss and caused much ill-feeling among the newsagents. 'But public confidence was intensified and letters of appreciation poured in from all parts of the country.' At an Evening News company meeting in 1899, he had congratulated Kennedy Jones 'particularly on the way he has kept your paper free of war sensationalism'. As editor of Pearson's Daily Express, R. D. Blumenfeld was a diligent watcher of the Daily Mail. He could write also as a former news editor of the *Daily Mail*: 'Alfred Harmsworth was a careful and conscientious purveyor of news. I never knew him unwittingly to disseminate inaccurate information.'

Encouraging the nation's aggressive instinct, he was a no less thoroughgoing critic of Government half-measures and muddling in the prosecution of what was to be known as 'the unnecessary war'. When his special correspondents disclosed British artillery weakness at the front, he raised the call for more and better guns. Remembering the Sudan, he wrote a leading article calling for an investigation of the medical services in South Africa, declaring them inadequate. His independent attitude led to a serious clash with Whitehall, which retaliated by cutting off the supply of official information to the *Daily Mail*. When the paper published the information, made available to it by other London papers, its editor was accused of bribing War Office clerks, a charge which the proprietor announced would be followed by a writ for libel if the Secretary of State for War, St. John Brodrick (later Lord Midleton), repeated it out of Parliament. An attempt made to have Harmsworth summoned to the bar of the House of Commons was defeated by 222 votes against 128. Those crises between the Harmsworth press and Parliament raised constitutional issues of importance to the later relations of Fleet Street with Downing Street. The pattern of protest was to be repeated on a dramatically intensified scale in the greater war that was to come.

Throughout the Boer War, Alfred Harmsworth was closely in touch with Government circles. He was friendly with Balfour. He was in frequent and intimate correspondence with George Wyndham, Under-Secretary of State for War. Lord Selborne, Under-Secretary for the Colonies, wrote privately and persuasively to him when his *Daily Mail* policy appeared to hinder that of the Government. Salisbury's private secretary, Schomberg Macdonnell, was constantly in his company. Harmsworth had access to Salisbury personally, although the Prime Minister was defiant of newspaper power. They discussed Germany. Harmsworth asked the Prime Minister whether it was not possible to come to a final understanding with the Germans. Salisbury, after one of his alarmingly long silences, had replied: 'We find Germany a very expensive friend', and from then on Harmsworth deemed it his duty to keep his readers informed about the trends of German policy, first sketched in the reports of his special writers visiting Germany in 1896-7. Of what those trends might lead to, he seems to have had no doubt. Before the Boer War had ended, he was foreseeing war with Germany. 'Tomorrow may be the day of world-wide conflict', his paper proclaimed in 1900 and he urged his fellow-countrymen to be ready. He told R. D. Blumenfeld: 'My own view is that the Germans are being led definitely and irrevocably to make war on the rest of Europe and that we will have to take part in it.' He opened his columns to an argument by Winston Churchill for more naval expenditure and refuted it in a leader: 'England must remember a fact with which Mr Churchill does not deal—that the Navy is a purely defensive force. We must be able to strike as well as to ward off blows, unless in the contests which the future may force upon us we are content to see hostilities languish on for an indefinite period.' The voice may have been the voice of needless doom; its undertones were undeniably sincere.

In June 1900 news came from South Africa that G. W. Steevens, the *Daily Mail* war correspondent, had died of enteric fever, drinking a last glass of champagne and sighing: 'This is a sideways ending to it all.' On receiving the news, Alfred Harmsworth called for his fastest car and, with Richard Harding Davis, the American newspaper correspondent, went to see Steevens's widow, at Merton, near Wimbledon. The art critic and sometime editor of *The Academy*, C. Lewis Hind, was with Mrs Steevens when they arrived in 'a very emotional condition'. Hind said that 'A.H. was sobbing and saying that he could never forgive himself for sending George to Ladysmith and that the blow had destroyed his power to think and work'. There were poignant recollections of the dead young scholar having told a friend that he had often recited to himself during night sojourns in the desert Stevenson's lines: '*Under the wide and starry sky*. . . .' Retreating from 'a painful scene', Hind went into the garden, where Davis, 'an interesting and rather fierce-looking man in khaki', told him that Harmsworth wanted him to take Steevens's place in South Africa. 'He asked me to drive down here with him so that he could give me final instructions. Will he be long?'

Recriminations were mingled with regrets. When Steevens had been in the Sudan for the *Daily Mail*, where he had done much to create Kitchener's reputation of invincibility, Alfred Harmsworth had undertaken to form and equip, 'regardless of expense', an ambulance unit which would take modern nursing methods to a battlefield in which there were more deaths from sickness than from wounds in action. The War Office declined the offer. It might have led to Army nursing reforms and a consequent saving of life in the Boer War that followed.

W. E. Henley to Alfred Harmsworth:

St. George's Lodge,
Chesswood Road,
Worthing.
20th January, 1900

My dear Harmsworth,—I have done all I could. I am too sick about the dear boy to do more. Here is the stuff.

The *In Memoriam* will, I think, be liked by his wife.

This death has shocked us terribly. It is so wanton, so miserable, so unnecessary. I remember but one in my life that can begin to vie with it for utter sadness.

Oddly enough, I dreamed of him this morning. His voice is in my ears as I write.

Yours most sincerely,
W. E. HENLEY.

The poet was further moved to write that 'there was lost in George Steevens as fine a spirit, as rare and as completely trained a brain, and as brave a heart as we have to show', and Rudyard Kipling, also, was inspired to pen valedictory lines. Steevens's death was one of Alfred's lasting sorrows. He was obsessed to the point of horror by the notion that he was responsible for it. He had a portrait of Steevens posthumously painted by the Hon. John Collier. The death in action of another member of the staff, Sergeant Gilham, a young assistant in the *Daily Mail* library, touched him hardly less deeply. 'The tears would fill his eyes when he spoke of Gilham years after', said H. W. Wilson, the leader writer. He gave a rifle shooting trophy bearing Gilham's name. Two years after Steevens's death, the special scholarships committee of the City of London School accepted an anonymous offer of £3,000 for founding G. W. Steevens's scholarships in journalism. In the official history, *City of London School* (Blackwell, 1937), Alfred Harmsworth is named as the donor of 'a munificent anonymous present', and confirmation of it is to be found in Coutts Bank ledgers. Several prominent Fleet Street careers had Steevens's scholarships as their springboard.

Henry W. Lucy ('Toby, M.P.', of *Punch*) to Alfred Harmsworth:

42, Ashley Gardens,
Victoria Street, SW
March 6, 1900

Dear Mr Harmsworth,—As an old journalist I cannot refrain from telling you with what pleasure I hear of your munificent provision for Mrs Steevens. The action is worthy of him and of you.

Yours faithfully,
HENRY W. LUCY.

*   *   *

The coming of the motor-car had enabled Alfred Harmsworth to widen the circumference of his domestic life. Mainly, it had been centred in 36 Berkeley Square and Elmwood. But Elmwood was not the kind of country house in which Molly Harmsworth could take much pride. It was too much of a business conference centre, affording little scope for her social gifts. In August 1899 he had taken a furnished tenancy of a large Georgian country house, Calcot Park, near Reading: according to the diary, 'for a year's trial'. In September of the same year he took Thorrington Hall, Darsham, Suffolk, for the pleasure of his friends who liked shooting, a sport which he avoided. It gave him no satisfaction whatever to kill birds. Also, he was always preoccupied by thoughts of work and feared the risks of absent-mindedness when carrying a gun. Thorrington did not suit him; he suffered from 'intense and infernal' chills there, 'painful and exasperating', he told Sutton. 'I would rather be ill in London.'

His expanding prominence was accompanied by a contracting relish for the more extravagant amenities of wealth. For him, one of the chief pleasures of being the tenant of Calcot Park was its nearness to Hurley, on the Thames, where Reginald Nicholson rented a cottage. Alfred spent almost as many of his weekends there as at his country mansion. A time would come when he would abandon the ornate splendours of Room One at Carmelite House and be often found at work in its small annexe and when he would indulge the eccentricity of exchanging his own bedroom for his valet's in large hotels.

He had bought his first motor-car, a 6 h.p. Panhard-Levassor, price £800, in the spring of 1899, though he had motored in France before then. His mother was one of his first passengers, W. E. Henley another. The poet celebrated the experience by writing what proved to be his last poem, a set of uninspired verses entitled *Song of Speed*, dedicated to Alfred Harmsworth. The motor-car was still sufficiently novel to rank as an excuse for absences from the office, and Alfred's motoring, from 1899 onward, gave a decisive impetus to the revolution on the roads. His little yellow high-seated 6 h.p. Panhard was the first motor-car seen in many of the towns and villages of south-east England and a ride in it was an exclusive treat for the crippled boys who could not join in the games at Elmwood camp.

In July 1899 he had started off, 'at a moment's notice', to drive to Oldham to help Winston Churchill in an election campaign there. On the way north, he stayed a night with the Iliffes, 'whose children I had not seen since I left Coventry in 1887'. Five punctures, one after the other, frustrated the attempt to reach Oldham: 'very disappointing, though pleasant trip'.

Winston Churchill to Alfred Harmsworth:

35a, Great Cumberland Place,
W.

July 7th, 1899

My dear Harmsworth,—I write you only a very brief letter—just to thank you for your kindness in supporting me during the Election in the *D.M.*: and for your adventurous expedition in the motor-car.

I am sorry that neither of our enterprises were successful in connection with Oldham. But I don't expect my career or your car will be seriously damaged. Once more thanking you.

Yours sincerely,
WINSTON S. CHURCHILL.

On August 8 he had set out to visit Rudyard Kipling at Rottingdean, but got no further than Wimbledon because of breakdowns. Driving over to Broadstairs, his French chauffeur panicked at the sight of a horse crossing the road and steered the car so sharply to the side that it ran up a bank and overturned, pinning its owner underneath. He was pulled out, badly shaken, his arms temporarily paralysed. It was one of the first recorded motor-car accidents. The occasion is remembered by Max Pemberton's son Alfred (after his father's great friend). Alfred Harmsworth had been taken to The Gore, an Elizabethan farmhouse near Minster, where the Pembertons were then living, not far from the scene of the accident. Alfred Pemberton writes: 'I was five years old. It was my first meeting with Alfred Harmsworth. I recall him then as a fair, handsome man who greeted me with a smile that would have melted a glacier, and the words: "Hullo, cocky!" '

Soon England was as full of strange noises as Caliban's isle and not a few of them issued from the varied assortment of cars that filled the coach houses of Calcot Park that summer: several Gardner-Serpollet steam-cars, a Locomobile, a 6 h.p. Daimler, a single cylinder Renault, a 12 h.p. Panhard, a 20 h.p. Panhard and a 40 h.p. Mercédès. Calcot Park was the first stop (for a champagne breakfast) in the 1,000 Miles Trial of the early spring of 1900, when sixty-five out of eighty-three entered cars toured the country on a run which had its base line between London and Bristol and its apex at Edinburgh. Describing the event as 'a really great and picturesque idea', *The Autocar* stated that 'no better plan for familiarizing the public with cars and their capabilities could possibly have been devised'. In June, a motor show at Richmond had been a considerable attraction, but 'the British public was not to be inveigled from its love of and belief in the horse merely because the cars disported themselves in the grounds of the horse show. Something more practical was wanted'. At that point, Claude Johnson, first secretary of the Automobile Club of Great Britain and Ireland ('With which is Incorporated the Self-Propelled Traffic Association'), afterwards The Royal Automobile Club, went to Harmsworth with the plan for the 1,000 miles trial run. Johnson wrote: 'He at once put his purse at the club's disposal and he gave the scheme the utmost possible support in his papers at a time when other journals were scoffing at the automobile as being a disagreeable and unnecessary plaything of a few cranks.'

Alfred Harmsworth took part in the run as far as Manchester, driving his 12 h.p. Panhard, with Kennedy Jones as passenger. The car was considered 'the last word', admired as much by the experts as by the gaping sightseers along the route. 'Everything about it was wonderful,' according to *The Autocar*, 'and the man who was lucky enough to get a lift on it over any section of the tour was cross-examined by all so that they too might realize the bliss he had experienced. There was a great deal of harmless idolatry and quite as much harmless covetousness over that Panhard.' In it, Alfred covered distances which were regarded as exceeding the mileage of the small engine power then available. He thought nothing of driving to Scotland, with an overnight stop at York. In 1900, he motored hundreds of miles in France. Those pioneering ardours were afterwards considered to have been as detrimental to his health as the extravagant cycling feats of his early youth. He was enchanted by the new sensation of speed. He found a poetic phrase for it. 'It is like being massaged in a high wind.'

His sensitiveness to coming change was shown in his perception of the successive stages by which the motor-car would be established as a social force. Claude Johnson, writing later as managing director of Rolls-Royce, could testify:

It will be impossible for me ever to forget an occasion on which, in 1899, he saw in front of him and explained to me a vision of the future of the motor-car movement. He saw coming the increasing hatred of the motor-car by all classes, except a few enthusiasts, then the recognition of the facilities of transport which the motor-car could afford, and, consequently, the inevitable purchase of motor-cars by the rich. Then a consequential increase in the dislike of the motor-car by the poor, until the opposition of all classes would be swept away by the institution of the poor man's motor-car—the motor-bus.

When, early in the century, John Scott-Montagu, M.P., the future Lord Montagu of Beaulieu, started his sixpenny weekly, *The Car Illustrated*, Alfred Harmsworth stated in its first issue his belief that the motor-car 'will revolutionize the life of England to a degree not yet properly foreseen by any leader of thought, with the exception of Mr Balfour'. *The Car Illustrated* had for its secondary title: *A Journal of Travel by Land, Sea and Air*. The air qualification was a visionary one, although in no more than six years it would be justified in practical terms. Meanwhile, motoring was still so much of an adventure that Montagu and his editorial staff would rush to the office windows, overlooking Piccadilly, at the sound of a motor-car engine in the traffic below.

Alfred Harmsworth's contributions to the journalism of the motor-car were embodied in more permanent form in *Motors and Motoring*, being volume 29 in *The Badminton Library*, a book publishing enterprise begun by Longman's in the 1880s under the patronage of the Duke of Beaufort. More immediately effective was the letter he wrote to the Automobile Club on July 7, 1900, urging the club to start a campaign against the county councils of England and Wales, which were resisting the coming of the motor-car. As a direct result of the letter, the Local Government Board was persuaded not to take action on the recommendation of the councils, 'until the members knew a little more of their subject'. Deputations from the councils were invited to meet members of the club and to 'gain knowledge concerning motor-cars by taking drives in them'. Two years later he was predicting that by 1920 'traffic will be regulated by policemen on motor bicycles', and that 'fruit, flowers and vegetables will be arriving in cities from the country by means of swift motor delivery vans'.

Demands for Harmsworth's advice as a motorist were adding new burdens to his correspondence.

> 12a, George Street,
> Hanover Square.
>
> Dear Mr Harmsworth,—I hear you have a Frenchman with your cars who understands those built by Panhard. There is something wrong with mine but neither my engineer nor myself can make out what. It would be awfully kind if you cd. let your man just see mine—any morning about nine o'clock.
>
> Yours truly,
> SHREWSBURY & TALBOT.

Another motoring peer, Lord Onslow, asks for figures of car maintenance. 'I wonder if you keep any accounts which would enable me to estimate the cost. Of course, I could not afford the infinite variety of cars that you possess; but I am seriously considering whether it would not be worth while to put down all horses except hacks.' There were now fewer references in Alfred's diary to 'The Granville', the Pullman train which for so many years had carried him to Broadstairs. Soon there would be no more.

*　　*　　*

While he was enjoying all over again, with fresh excitements, the pleasures of the open road, the rapid expansion of his publishing activities was already taxing the resources of Carmelite House and an overflow building was acquired in Bouverie Street. Carmelite House vibrated with professional enthusiasm and 'Mr Alfred'-worship. 'It was like being behind the scenes at a theatre,' was the reminiscent comment of one who worked in the art department. 'Always there was the feeling of the unseen presence of Alfred Harmsworth. You felt compelled to give of your best, even though, night after night, you missed your last train home.' Members of the mechanical staffs stepped out to a near-by public-house for a break at 11 a.m. On their return, they made a habit of bowing in mock gravity towards Room One.

In a five-minute interview with a slightly built, lively minded Cockney clerk named Wareham Smith, Alfred created the advertising department. Until then, advertising had functioned automatically as part of the business side, under Lingard. 'Don't go out after your advertisers,' Alfred commanded Smith. 'Wait for them to come to you', and soon they were lining up to buy the paper's increasingly expensive space. A 'white sale' display advertisement by the London drapery house of D. H. Evans Ltd. had a convulsive effect on the growth of the new advertising science. When rival drapery houses illustrated their *Daily Mail* advertisements with line drawings of women in underwear, Wareham Smith's desk was heaped with letters of moral protest.

Advertising not only enabled Alfred Harmsworth to pay the highest wages and salaries and rates to contributors but to boast about it. Yet his underlying resistance to the advertising necessity was never finally quelled. He would comment in writing that 'Wareham Smith is a damned nuisance. He has ruined today's paper.' He would tell his editors to throw out too-obtrusive advertisements. He himself often cast them aside within minutes of an edition going to press. Opening the *Daily Mail* one morning soon after Wareham Smith had been appointed, he wrote on seeing a certain advertisement that he had 'felt like a bird wounded with an arrow'. Yet he would hardly have been amenable to the argument that the press is a parasitic part of the national economy, producing no wealth of itself and using great quantities of imported raw material, whereas advertising directly stimulates the processes of production and distribution.

Patronizing his advertisers, reacting violently from their wrong stresses and false claims, educating them in the more intelligent uses of type and display, Alfred Harmsworth's *Daily Mail* assisted the integration of advertising into a far wider framework than that of Fleet Street. More than any other newspaper, it shaped the advertising future by encouraging the art of salesmanship through print. So, too, *Daily Mail* advertising policy established a new status for advertising agents. Up to 1900 or so, they were mainly space brokers. Responding to the pressures of Harmsworth censorship, they enlisted the talents of artists and typographers to make advertisements more attractive and therefore more efficient. Advertising acquired a professional code embodying principles which had been formulated in the first instance for the *Daily Mail*. Once again puritanism and opportunism had been joined with eventful results.

Another department was developing the arts of publicity in new and original forms. The America's Cup race between Sir Thomas Lipton's *Shamrock* and the American defender *Columbia* was an affair of the greatest curiosity in two continents and for the 1899 race the *Evening News* devised the 'cineyachtograph', a pictorial screen which enabled large numbers of people gathered on the Thames Embankment to follow the yachts' course as news of them was flashed from a chartered steamer off Sandy Hook to Carmelite House. It was the forerunner of a long series of enterprises serving the national interest as well as the good will of the Harmsworth newspapers.

At night, the windows of Carmelite House bloomed with the weird dawn light of the new age of picture journalism. It was a flaring pale luminosity with a ghoulish smell. The Boer War had stimulated the demand for topical pictures. Newspaper offices in Fleet Street had shown war maps in their windows. Only one or two displayed photographs. They caused crowds to block the pavement. Line drawings were still the chief source of newspaper illustration.

Speed was the bedevilling urge, the need to save what the aggressively edition-conscious Kennedy Jones chose to call 'golden minutes'. Down in the big bays on the ground floor, where the delivery vans picked up their supplies of *Daily Mail* and *Evening News*, the noises of internal combustion engines now mingled with the clatter of horses' hoofs. The *Daily Mail* war trains, taking the paper to Midland and Northern breakfast tables, had been an innovation that was quickly copied by rival London newspapers. To keep its circulation supremacy, the *Daily Mail* had established an office and printing plant in Manchester, taking over a derelict school at Gorton for that purpose. The claim that the paper was read simultaneously in Brighton and Newcastle-on-Tyne was soon extended to include the farthest points in Scotland and Ireland, alarming the proprietors of old-established local journals by its ruthless trespass. Permanent Manchester headquarters were acquired in Deansgate in 1902. The *Daily Mail* was in the true sense Britain's first national newspaper.

In 1898, a newspaper trade journal had reported a persisting antipathy to women as newspaper workers. In 1901, the same journal recorded the opinion that women were not suited to the newspaper life, though by then there were several well-known newspaperwomen, among them Miss M. F. Billington, of the *Daily Telegraph*, Miss Flora Shaw, of *The Times*, and Mrs Crawford, of the *Daily News*. One of them recalled, as an early experience, being asked to leave a committee meeting at which there was to be a discussion of soldiers' underwear.

The *Daily Mail* did much to dispel a powerful prejudice. In the beginning, the paper had only one woman on the staff, Mrs Mary Howarth, who had been on *Answers*. She was in charge of the 'Women's Realm' feature in the *Daily Mail*. The 'Absent-Minded Beggar Fund' brought more women workers into Carmelite House, where the sex revolution had not been foreseen by the architect, with resulting embarrassments. Those women were the harbingers of change. Soon doors were opened to women editors, women specialist writers and women reporters, then one of the rarer novelties of women's changing status. From Room 50 at Carmelite House there presently came the prototype twentieth-century woman journalist, who owes more than she realizes to Alfred Harmsworth's instinctive appreciation of her possibilities.

*   *   *

One of his larger personal commitments in 1900 was Sutton Place, near Guildford, Surrey, the splendid Tudor mansion built between 1520 and 1530 by Robert Weston, faithful servant of Henry VIII, who executed his son, Francis Weston, without apparently incurring the father's enmity. 'To Sutton thronged the great nobles of England', writes Charles Whibley in *The Pageantry of Life* and to Sutton came the twentieth-century newspaper proprietor, enticed not less strongly by the green immemorial blandness of its setting than by its historical magnificence. He took a lease of it for twenty-one years, paying £1,700 a year rent, to include the home farm and shooting. He signed the five-figure premium cheque in a flurry of relief. Up to the last moment of the negotiations uncertainty hung in the air. Another would-be tenant held fast to a prior claim. 'Very much distressed', he had written in the diary for June 22 on hearing that his offer might not go through. Before long, he was experiencing if not recording kindred emotions as the responsible occupier of one of England's show places. Neighbouring property rights had to be newly defined at considerable legal expense. Unsuspected defects were found in the house, entailing costly renovations that took a year to complete. There were difficulties about rights of way, overhanging trees, drainage. The presence of magnesium sulphate (Epsom salts) in the water suppply was not without its inconvenience. Getting the house ready was a business of several months. While the work was being done, the Harmsworths used Sutton Park Cottage for their weekends on the estate.

Announcing that Alfred Harmsworth had declined a knighthood, *The Newspaper Owner & Manager* followed it with a paragraph surmising that he would be offered a baronetcy. His income was capable of supporting a dukedom. It was close on £150,000 a year, his net capital worth in 1901–2 being estimated at £900,000, a figure which included a valuation at cost of his shareholdings in his own companies. He had increased his mother's allowance to £6,000 a year and had arranged handsome annuities for his sisters, with one of £500 a year for his aunt, Sarah Miller. To his wife he was aboundingly generous: 'he gave me *everything*'. He was also giving annuities to members of his wife's family.

Beyond those family benefactions, he was supplying the needs and assuring the future of a number of people who had no direct claim on him; for example, more than one indigent member of his father's generation at the bar and of the Sylvan Debating Club. He continued to pay his father's old friend, Frederick Wood, £300 a year and made an allowance to his daughter, Eleanor Wood, who wrote: 'Your generosity is overwhelming.' He was paying the school fees for several of his friends' children at Eton and elsewhere. He was helping Henry Klein, the Holborn music publisher, who had encouraged his earliest aspirations and whose fortunes were in decline. Loans to him of more than £2,000 eventually became a gift. When Klein died, his widow received £200 a year from Alfred Harmsworth for the rest of her life. Grant Richards, the book publisher, was lent £2,500 'as a personal favour', none of it repaid. Old Mrs Jealous of Hampstead was helped, on one occasion with £500. A Thanet barber's assistant, Frederick William Smith, who attended Alfred at Elmwood, was lent £800 to start his own business in Harbour Street, Ramsgate. The money was paid back and the barber was always held in esteem by his benefactor. He advanced large sums from his personal accounts to enable members of his staffs to buy shares in his companies and to others to qualify for their directorships. He seldom failed to show sympathy with those beset by private money problems. One of them was Edgar Wallace, risen from Ludgate Circus newsboy to war correspondent who had 'scooped' the Boer War peace terms for the *Daily Mail*. 'He saved me from ruin', and the bank guarantee for £1,000 which had ensured that result had finally to be cleared by Alfred Harmsworth himself. Other writing men of the time had cause for gratitude: Henley, William Le Queux the serial writer, Laird Clowes the naval historian, Pollen, sometime acting editor of the *Daily Mail*, Edwin Pugh, remembrancer of London life, Harold Begbie, were among them. Lord Mountmorres's place as a supplicant had been taken by another journalistic peer, Lord Rosslyn, who had started *Scottish Life* with Harmsworth help and had no success with it. Max Pemberton, Dargaville Carr, Gilbert Burgess, Nevill Jackson, Reginald Nicholson, John Baxter Boyle, Beckles Willson, Alfred E. T. Watson, editor of *The Badminton Library*, Claude Johnson, did not ask in vain. He had provided Steevens's widow with an annuity of £500 a year. At Henley's death he undertook to pay his widow's rent at Park Mansions, Battersea, and continued to do so for nineteen years after. 'For all you have done,' she wrote in 1916, 'the deepest gratitude of my heart for *ever*.' He saved careers, reputations, homes. A mortgage foreclosure on Broome Park, Kent, later the home of Lord Kitchener, is believed to have been averted by his timely aid. A distracted Thanet postmaster, in debt to a moneylender, was rescued from his plight. J. W. Robertson Scott, founder of *The Countryman*, looking far back to the days when he first knew Alfred Harmsworth, wrote: 'All the time, there is remembrance of his kindness', and the full tale of it will never be told.

It was not the facile kindness of a man with money to spare. Often it expressed a warmth of consideration that is the essence of generosity. Wives of harassed editorial men would receive hampers from Harrods or Fortnum & Mason, although they had never met 'the Chief' whose compliments were inscribed on the accompanying card. Baskets of fruit and flowers would arrive at hospitals and nursing homes for invalids who had no reason to suppose that he knew of their illnesses. The peace and comforts of Elmwood were made as freely available to those who could not afford a holiday as to the directorial class of guest.

The 'princely beggar' of the London Hospital, the Hon. Sydney Holland, later Lord Knutsford, often turned to him for help in promoting his meritorious if sometimes too pushful fund-raising enterprises. But Alfred Harmsworth preferred to spread his donations to charity in smaller amounts over a wide range of institutions: the Newsvendors' Provident Fund, the Baptist Children's Fund, the Actors' Orphanage, the Soldiers & Sailors Association, the Royal Earlswood Institution for Mental Defectives, the Gardeners' Orphan Fund, the National Council for Combating Venereal Disease, the South Western Orphanage, the Newspaper Press Fund, St. John's Hospital for Diseases of the Skin, Little Sisters of the Poor, the Royal Literary Fund, the Sandwichmen's Christmas Dinner Fund, the Royal General Theatrical Fund, the Artists' Benevolent Fund, are picked out at random from the record of his donations for 1902–3. Always at the top of the list, from the days of his *Answers* success, were the Salvation Army and the Society for the Protection of Women & Children. He subscribed to both for most of his life.

He showed no pride in his wealth. For him, it was one of the conveniences. Acquiring money in great amounts, he was often without any in his pocket. Borrowed half-crowns appeared on the debit side of his chauffeurs' accounts. If he was not utterly incapable of ostentation, it was never shown in money terms. Apart from the honesty of his pleasure in being able to help others (and there was no doubting it), his personal attitude to money can be stated simply. He liked having it in plenty because it enabled him to buy the best: the best suits and shirts, the best motor-cars, the best cigars, and, above all, the best medical advice. Presumably, it was with the same indulgent satisfaction that, in 1900, he had subscribed £5,000 as a third-share of the capital on which *The Connoisseur*, the sumptuous monthly magazine for collectors of the best in art and antique furniture, was founded. He put money into less glamorous enterprises: for example, £500 in George R. Sims's much-advertised hair restorer called 'Tatcho' (in

which Cecil and Leicester invested £1,000 each), and an unrecorded sum
into the 'Normyl' cure for inebriacy.

Rudyard Kipling to Alfred Harmsworth:

> The Elms,
> Rottingdean, Sussex.
> 15th December, 1899

Private

Dear Mr Harmsworth,—. . . Now I want money. It's the old, old tale.
Eminently respectable female servant seduced by eminently respectable Tommy.
Tommy ordered to S. Africa. Kid to be born in a few months. Virtuous female
employer proposes calmly to turn her out into the street but (thank God!)
has a fleeting notion that perhaps I might help ere she sacks her. There are some
few calls on my purse just now. Please send what you can and I'll account. I'd
like £20 for sudden calls.

> Ever yours sincerely,
> RUDYARD KIPLING.

*   *   *

Cecil, Leicester and Hildebrand had been Liberal candidates for Parliament
in the autumn of 1900. Cecil was defeated at Droitwich by 268 votes.
Leicester had been returned for Caithness in a four-cornered contest by
28 votes. At Gravesend, Hildebrand had been beaten by his Conservative
opponent, Gilbert Parker, a novelist, by 738 votes: 'I knew he would get a
licking', Alfred wrote in the diary. Leicester had lately bought a paper of
his own, *Golf*, paying £1,350 for it. Cecil and Hildebrand had established
a magazine property, the *New Liberal Review*, which chiefly demonstrated, not journalistic or business *flair*, but esteem for Joseph Chamberlain and political independence within the inner Harmsworth circle. Those
diversionary enterprises did not mean discord, although feelings between
Alfred and Hildebrand had hardened since Alfred had discovered that
brother's addiction to playing billiards in Fleet Street saloons during office
hours. A member of the *Daily Mail* staff was dismissed for keeping him
company. Both Leicester and Hildebrand had sold some of their family
shareholdings to Alfred, and Leicester, it seemed, had already decided on a
change of direction in his career. Meanwhile, Alfred had commissioned
Edwin Ward, of the Savage Club, to paint a portrait of each of his
brothers.

There was a Golden *Daily Mail* to mark the last day of the century,
which the cartoonist, Max Beerbohm, depicted as a leather-clad, heavily
goggled entity, rushing with headlong speed into the future. A leading

article, which flouted the standing order for brevity by filling nearly a column and a half, sounded a recessional note. 'We are entering stormy seas and the time may be near when we shall have to fight in very truth for our life. Athens fell, who was the civilizer of the world, because her parties quarrelled among themselves and because she failed to realize the all-importance of armed strength. But if we are true to ourselves', etc. In Westminster Abbey, Canon Gore, later Bishop of Oxford, leaned over the pulpit and flung his words down the aisles. 'The spread of education has given a vast impulse to journalism and popular literature, and has produced an enormous number of persons wishing to be clerks, but it is doubtful whether these things are promoting character.' In St. Paul's, Canon Mason, of Canterbury, reviewed the advances of science and invention in relation to the moral progress of mankind. Outside the cathedral, a vast crowd was assembling. The *Daily Mail* recorded the scene:

The hand of the clock has reached the quarter, and is pressing on imperceptibly to midnight, the hour that marks the doom of the nineteenth age of the Christian era. The crowd has grown strangely quiet. The triangular space that separates the minute-hand from the hour of twelve diminishes slowly. The angle becomes acute, the hand steals on, is blended with its fellow. The nineteenth century is gasping out its breath—Boom!

The first stroke of midnight crashes through the frosty air, and is hailed by an annihilating roar of jubilation. The succeeding strokes are almost unheard; they are all but lost and drowned in the tumult of cheering. Hurrah! The twentieth century has dawned.

*　　*　　*

In New York, *The World* reported that the new century was hailed in City Hall Square and Lower Broadway by a crowd of 100,000 cheering people. The New Year's Day issue of that paper bore across the top of its front page a 'banner' with the strange device of a message in reproduced handwriting: *I ask America for an impartial verdict on this 20th century Newspaper.—Alfred Harmsworth.* The paper was changed in size and appearance. There were readers who thought they had been hoaxed.

Alfred Harmsworth had arrived in New York the previous day. With him were his wife and 'Reggie' Nicholson, who was acting as Alfred's secretary. Alfred had written to his mother during the voyage:

R.M.S. 'TEUTONIC'

Darling Mother,—We had it rough from Liverpool to Queenstown . . . and I have been anxious about the dear wife, but her wonderful pluck and the digitalis have kept her going, though she looks pinched and ill.

I am all but bored to death, tired of reading, of rolling, of wondering how far we have gone and when we shall arrive, and, oh, so regretful that we did not go to delightful Cannes. Never again do we venture on the wild Atlantic at Christmas time. Your lilies of the valley bloom still and I shall walk ashore at New York wearing some. Fond greetings for the day have gone from our hearts to you across the sea.

Wife says you did not understand that you were to keep £500 as a present. I thought you did, dear.

ALFRED.

Leaving the ship, he had been handed a message from the owner of *The World*, Joseph Pulitzer, the most powerful of the New York newspaper proprietors. It invited him to take charge of *The World* for one day, remodelling it in the light of his ideas of newspaper development in the twentieth century. Pulitzer promised 'no interference'. He would give Harmsworth complete editorial powers. Pulitzer had read an article which Alfred had written for *The North American Review*, forecasting 'the simultaneous newspaper', an earth-girdling production which was to be backed by an organization of Standard Oil vastness. To some readers it may have sounded like an echo of the Napoleonic world throne dream translated into the newspaper realm.

Alfred accepted the invitation, which was also a challenge. That night the front of *The World* building dazzled the crowds with a pyrotechnical display of coloured electric lights, saluting the New Year. As a compliment to the visiting editor, Pulitzer ordered his staff to work in evening dress. One man, Pomeroy Burton, the news editor, refused, considering it 'an affectation'. His terse independence did not escape Alfred Harmsworth's notice. Neither did his quick thinking when mechanical adjustments were urgently called for by Alfred's change in the size of the paper.

All through the hours of going to press that night, the Harmsworth watchword was: 'Keep it down, gentlemen!' He moved constantly through the newsroom repeating his injunction to be brief: 'No story of more than two hundred and fifty words!' He was imposing 'tabloid' journalism on a public which had rejected it some years before, when Munsey, another of the New York newspaper owners, had tried it in his *Daily Continent*. Much of the comment on Alfred Harmsworth's version of *The World* was that the real novelty was in his term, 'tabloid', which was claimed to be the copyright of a British firm of manufacturing chemists. Later, they issued warnings against infringement. The Harmsworth edition of *The World* was for some time one of the permanent exhibits at the New York Public Library.

The World for January 1, 1901, made Alfred a transcontinental celebrity

The World, New York, January 1, 1901

for nearly twenty-four hours. The newspaper clippings harvest was immense. There seems to have been no American newspaper that did not pass judgment on 'the Harmsworth experiment', thereby justifying what was thought to be his conceit in presuming to address the American nation through a metropolitan newspaper. He had abolished 'screaming' headlines. He had cut down the use of illustrations. He had subordinated advertising to news. A printing trade journal wrote:

His tremendous energy made itself felt in every department. The entire staff carried out his suggestions to the letter, although some of these were revolutionary in character. The keynote was: all the news in sixty seconds. At midnight editors and reporters joined Mr Harmsworth in drinking a toast in champagne to the dawn of a new century.

His thoughts may have gone back to that midnight in May, not quite five years before, when he and his *Daily Mail* staff had raised their glasses to the future of that newspaper. Now he was bracketed in bold type with the tyrants of American newspaper proprietorship, Joseph Pulitzer, James Gordon Bennett, Frank Munsey, William Randolph Hearst. Compared with 'those volcanically forceful personages, who are more intent on telling you how great they are than on letting you find it out for yourself', wrote Julian Ralph, the American war correspondent, 'Harmsworth stands out, easy, well-controlled and polished in manner, the most prepossessing and picturesque figure in journalism on either side of the Atlantic'. William Randolph Hearst wrote editorially in his newspapers: 'Would you like to look at Mr Harmsworth? Imagine a face that presents a mixture of Napoleon, Edison and the left-hand cherub leaning over the frame of Raphael's "Sistine Madonna".' Hearst went on to tell his readers: 'He is trying to buy the London *Times*. He wants to own "a great paper, the greatest paper". Therefore he knows that he owns no such paper now. May he get *The Times*; and when he gets it, may he show us the real Harmsworth editing a real newspaper', a jibe not so much at the visitor as at Pulitzer. In New York, Alfred made no secret of his desire to own *The Times*. Catching the local atmosphere, he seems to have bragged about it; for instance, to the publicist Nathan Straus, who was more passionately interested in his propaganda for pasteurized milk for babies.

The World, on that first twentieth-century morning, was sold out by nine o'clock. Extra editions, totalling 100,000 copies, were called for. Later in the day, copies were selling at a premium. It was a subject of considerable criticism and the balance of professional opinion went against it. Seen in relation to the imminent half-tone block revolution in the newspapers, its temporary editor's drastic attitude to illustration was like an aberration of judgment, perhaps because he was a conspicuous victim of the crude line drawing then prevalent in American journalism. To millions of readers he was made to look like one of the patent medicine addicts whose testimony to tonics, ointments and pills filled the advertising columns. Comment was sometimes amusingly personal, as for example: 'He knows more about journalism than he does about hair-dressing.' The *Minneapolis Times* suggested that the name of Harmsworth might be better remembered for its association with a class of periodicals that had killed 'sordid literature for the young'. The tribute was a balm for the irritation which he felt on reading in an Atlanta newspaper that he was American-born and had gone to London in his youth to rejuvenate the British press. But it may not have excused the reference to him in the *Minneapolis Tribune* as 'Al' Harmsworth. The broad general verdict on his *World* venture appeared to be that, after all, he was not the Christopher Columbus of twentieth-century journalism.

Alfred Harmsworth to Geraldine Mary Harmsworth:

> Holland House,
> New York.
> January 12, 1901

My darling Mother,—We have had a most extraordinary visit here. People say that no young man's coming has ever stirred up the United States so much before. The articles and pictures that have appeared about the name of Harmsworth number many thousands. But I shall be glad to escape from the turmoil.

It might please you to know that distinguished people from all parts of the United States have come here to meet me. I am to have a private audience with the President and have been treated, generally, in a way that quite amazed me. What is more satisfactory is that I think it will be profitable to the business.

Nearly all the articles which are appearing about me are invented and they, nearly all, make me praise the paper in which they appear. They all invariably state that the editor of the *Daily Mail* receives a salary of £15,000 a year and are particularly anxious to inform their readers that I was born in Ireland, in order to please the Irish here.

This is the most progressive and growing of countries. The wealth and energy appal one.

Should any articles about us appear in any English papers, reprinted from here, don't believe one word. *All are invented.*

Your devoted adoring,

FIRST BORN.

'Mark Twain in great form,' he wrote in the diary. Also: 'Went to see Edison. Spent the day with him.' There is no mention of meeting the President. But the crux of the 'turmoil', undoubtedly, was the splendid Whitney ball at 871 Fifth Avenue, where the Harmsworths were announced with the Vanderbilts, the Astors, the Jays, the Harrimans and the Reids, 'the finest private social function ever held in New York', *The World* told its readers. Molly Harmsworth, who had triumphantly defied the indifferent talents of the newspaper artists, was at her best, evoking a frankness of admiration that was less rare in New York than in London. On the day of his arrival, the hotel reception clerk had said, glancing up as Alfred gave his name: 'When is your father checking in?' The Harmsworths' good fortune was not in wealth alone.

During that first week of 1901, an influenza wave struck New York. Alfred was named in the newspaper lists of 'distinguished victims'. The attack was sharp and he left for Florida with its fever still upon him. A gossip writer hoped that he would have better luck than to catch 'a tabloid tarpon'. In fact, the sport yielded a brave array of fish but none of the big game variety that he was after. He noted in the diary that the singing of the mocking-bird reminded him of Elmwood. Within a few days virulent malaria was superimposed on the influenza.

His diary tells of 'very bad pain', of his wife's alarm at his state and of her 'splendid nursing', of his 'enjoying a course of Hardy's novels while still feeling very ill', and of his being peremptorily ordered back to New York. There was one bad day when he feared the worst, that he might not see England again. During the voyage home in the *Oceanic*, he endured the classic *sequelae* of malarial depression. 'Cannot bear to be alone. Cannot read or keep my attention on anything.' The tale of woe recurs in the diary, from January to May, with its grimmer visitations underlined: *'Extremely depressed'*, and *'Very depressed indeed'*. Five exclamation marks are set against the entry for April 16: 'Lunched Automobile Club and to office.' The next day he was at work again but 'left tired and in pain'. Thanet irresistibly called him. '18*th April, Thursday.*—Went to Elmwood, to which I have been looking forward so much for weeks. Found it looking lovely, the daffodils more numerous than ever. Good deal of pain.' The next day: 'Felt better.' Doctors came down from London, one ordering complete rest, another a holiday in Paris. Ten days later he was forced to admit: *'Very depressed again today.* Prostate pain', and the theme of depression, sometimes acute, runs through the diary of the weeks which saw spring pass into summer. The Paris prescription worked its miracle. '20*th May, Monday.*—A lovely day and felt so well. Drove in Bois. Life worth living. Sent £10,000 to London Hospital on my recovery.' It provided modern equipment for the hospital. His later medical history suggested that the malarial illness had produced side effects which reverberated in his constitution through the rest of his life.

A casual diary note for June 19 illustrates the changing personal fortunes to which he was always nervously susceptible. 'Went to see Mother and Dot off to Switzerland. Office all day. Sir George Newnes to see me in the evening about the sale of his business.' Newnes's position was deteriorating. He was a diabetic and the progressive course of his illness endangered his judgment. He invested too heavily in early colour printing processes. He gave disastrously excessive print orders. Surrendering to the drink habit, he went into hiding for long periods, leaving his associates without power to act. The effect on the highly esteemed firm of George Newnes Ltd. was chaotic. In 1901, he started a new illustrated paper called *The King*, presumably hoping to supersede *The Queen*. The venture lost money from the beginning. Meeting a tea broker friend named Wade in Regent Street at that time, Newnes sounded him about a personal loan of £200. Of the tone of the discussions with the Harmsworths there is no record. On June 29 Alfred noted: 'To the Savoy to meet Sir George Newnes in regard to the purchase of his business. He would not accept our terms.'

'Spent the day at Sutton Place,' he wrote on July 23. 'House nearly ready. Drove up to the Stracheys [St. Loe Strachey, editor of *The Spectator*, was then living at Newlands Corner] in the evening. Wife had three fainting fits.' On July 30, he took Pearson, the publisher, 'for a midnight ride', and another of his passengers was Lord Rosebery, who hoped that it might cure his insomnia. The Harmsworths went into residence at Sutton Place on August 24. 'Thoroughly enjoyed my new home,' Alfred wrote. 'Slept fairly well.'

Alfred Harmsworth to his mother:

Sutton Place
by Guildford
Surrey.
Sunday, 29th August, 1901.

My darling Mother,—The first letter I write in our new home is to the dear one I love so much.

ALFRED

What he had noted in his diary as the 'sad news of Cecil Rhodes's death', in March 1902, did not affect him so deeply as did the death of his friend Robert Dolling, the Anglican clergyman, in May, at the age of fifty-one. 'Whitsuntide party at Sutton Place, but we are gloomy by reason of Father Dolling's death.' Alfred had been called to the bedside in Dolling's last hours, 'to say goodbye'. He was a central figure in the mourning throng that had overflowed St. Saviour's Church, Poplar, for the funeral service. He was active in ensuring that a worthy successor was found to carry on Dolling's labours in London's East End. The Bishop of Stepney wrote to say that his wishes would be respected. 'I am doing all I can . . . to get the right sort of man for St. Saviour's . . . a man of whom you would approve. It would be an enormous *lift* to him if he felt that some, at least, of the generous support which you gave to Dolling might be renewed to him.'

'*25th May.*—Busy about negotiations re *The Times*.' The hint of higher-altitude activity is not followed up; there is no further reference to it in the diary of the period. R. D. Blumenfeld said that early in October 1900 Harmsworth had empowered him to go to the Walters with an offer for *The Times*, remarking: 'I do not think they are getting on too well over there. If I went to them, they would at once refuse me. I've got a million pounds in Consols and I authorize you to pay up to that sum.' According to his accountants' statement for the year, his capital worth was £886,000. In the months that followed, his name was more than once linked with rumours of change at Printing House Square. When they appeared in print in America, Arthur Walter, head of the owning family, issued a strong and final denial.

To the Edwardian courtier, Lord Esher, who lunched with him on October 29, 1901, Alfred was the young *arriviste*—'clever, vain, not very intelligent about anything except organization and money-making, but full of aspirations for power. The man interests me, as all self-made men do.'

*　　*　　*

For Alfred, 1902 was mainly a holiday year. In February he left for

France, driving down to Monte Carlo in 'my steam travelling carriage', a term which does not seem to have belonged to its early twentieth-century context. But his Serpollet steam car was one of the wonders of the world to many people in the parts of France through which he drove it that year. During a mechanical crisis on the road at Ancy-le-France, a cloud of steam and flame went up from the engine. A passing peasant woman fell to her knees, in terror of the devil's work. Reaching Monte Carlo, he noted: 'Saw Santos Dumont fly over the sea.' That early adventure in a dirigible balloon by the young Brazilian inventor might have been thought to merit a less prosaic comment but Alfred Harmsworth's epoch-making response to the challenge of aviation was not yet kindled. He had been content, thus far, to publish an occasional article in *Answers* about men's dreams of aerial navigation and to report the early experiments in his newspapers. 'Went about a good deal with Santos Dumont', he wrote. Their talk was chiefly of airships.

There was a car excursion to Strasbourg, extended by train to Stuttgart. 'It was my first sight of Germany', and the effect of it seems to have stirred a deeper level of feeling than that of romantic sentiment. A dæmonic force was rising in Europe. He gazed long and earnestly eastward from the Vosges, and was impelled to write again in his diary: 'I shall never forget my first sight of Germany.'

As one of the first owner-drivers, his motoring that year confirmed his view that the new development in transport would quickly expand beyond the pleasures of the few. In the *Daily Mail* he had a powerful accelerator of public sentiment but, being a journalist rather than a propagandist, he allowed public sentiment to be fairly reflected in that newspaper; and public sentiment was hostile to the coming of the motor-car. He published letters from those who detested the internal combustion engine as well as from those who saw in it an instrument of that progress which, through science, was to set men free and therefore make them happy. His impartiality worried some of the pioneers. One of them, the Hon. C. S. Rolls, begged Claude Johnson, secretary of the Automobile Club, to intervene. Johnson's subsequent letter to Harmsworth, dated September 15, 1902, is a social document.

I enclose a letter from Charlie Rolls. The points seem to me to be as follows: (1). Cars have come to stay. (2). They will very shortly to a very large extent replace the horse. (3). Road travel must be considerably accelerated and can be accelerated without danger. Loss of time on the road means loss of money, just as much as loss of time elsewhere. (4). Our hereditary instincts are shocked on seeing anything on the road faster than the horse, but as our senses become educated we shall recognise the fact that speed of itself is not dangerous but the inability to stop is dangerous. (5). It is therefore no good for people to get hysterical because motor cars are driven fast, as it is certain that they will be

'A Reader from No. 1', September 1897: Alfred Harmsworth, taken shortly
after the founding of the *Daily Mail*

Leicester Harmsworth (*left*) and Cecil Harmsworth (later the first Lord Harmsworth), in their twenties

Hildebrand Harmsworth (*left*) and St John Harmsworth (*right*), in their twenties

Sutton Place, Guildford

driven fast. (6). We want to encourage the legitimate use of automobiles and to discourage (and, if practicable, render impossible) the illegitimate use of automobiles. (7). Cars must be numbered.

'I don't bow to the belief that time is money', Alfred wrote, testifying that, on the contrary, he was in search of the rest and recuperation which the motor-car enabled him to find in places hitherto inaccessible to mechanical transport. Johnson's letter was none the less important as a directive. It gave point and force to what had largely been an opportunist attitude to the new era on the roads. It encouraged the proprietor of the *Daily Mail* to adopt a more coherent and constructive policy, with incalculable effects on society.

In the summer he had been with his mother on a pilgrimage to Truro to see the old grammar school where his father was once a junior master. Together, they spent 'a very delightful week, which we both enjoyed very much'. In the early autumn there came 'a most enjoyable trip, full of variety', to Scotland. It was followed in November by a visit to Dalmeny, where Lord Rosebery was entertaining the German emperor. The diary has nothing to say of Harmsworth's encounter with a monarch whose power he would help to bring to dust. Through that year, his offices, staffs, periodicals, newspapers and professional responsibilities generally, were hardly mentioned in the diary. For him, 1902 seems to have been *annus mirabilis*, in which he was more free of care than he ever would be again. 'Diary not kept,' he wrote in France for the week of February 13 to 20, 'but our daily life consists of motoring, lunching, walking, dining, plenty of sleep, sun and fresh air, a good time altogether.' His playgoing in London was given more emphasis than his work, though his taste for such pieces as *The French Milliner*, *Three Little Maids* and *Frocks and Frills* was at odds with Arnold Bennett's impression of him at a Haymarket Theatre first night as having 'the head of a poet, a thinker'.

More than usually congenial, too, was the social activity in which he was involved. There was 'a day with Rudyard Kipling'. At Mentmore, Lord Rosebery's place in Hertfordshire, he had 'a long talk with Winston Churchill'. That thrustful young politician had for some time been in the habit of writing to him in advance of his public appearances in the hope that the *Daily Mail* would give heed to them. Nine years younger than Harmsworth, Churchill was admiringly aware of his influence and attracted to his personality. They were to get to know each other well through the next quarter of a century, their friendship intermittently slackening and tightening in response to the play of events and recalled in the warmest terms by the Sir Winston Churchill of a later time. Another of Alfred's ripening social relationships was with John Scott-Montagu, of Beaulieu, a man of much private and public virtue. Montagu had been with him on the French holiday earlier in the year. Not a club-man by nature, Alfred was going fairly often to The Beefsteak Club to which he had been elected two years before. There, Bohemianism was sanctified by Debrett.

At Sutton Place, the pages of the vellum-bound visitors' book were rapidly being filled with distinguished signatures, representing literature and journalism, politics, the stage and fashionable society. Many Americans went there, receiving a welcome which was stirred to vivid recollection and important consequences in the years to come. Not that old friends were forgotten. Fred Wood and Max Pemberton were often summoned to be of the company. Wood had dress scruples. For one of the Sutton Place garden parties he arrived in an ancient uniform, with gold lace and cutlass, which had formerly graced his post in the Mercantile Marine Department of the Board of Trade. Pemberton treasured his memories of 'summer afternoons in the gracious old-world garden', and he wrote of 'the Chief standing in the doorway, beaming like a schoolboy'. Yet Alfred was not completely happy at Sutton Place and there may have been more than physical significance in his inability to sleep there. His pride in the beautiful old house was largely a reflection of his admiration for his wife's social graces, for which it was the perfect setting.

Lord Curzon of Kedleston to Alfred Harmsworth:

> Viceroy's Camp,
> India.
> October 30, 1902.

Dear Harmsworth,—. . . You would have laughed had you seen me two days ago, in a State carriage and 4, making a triumphal entry into a native city. It ran away with me in the main street, turned clean over, and I landed heavily on the head of the Maharajah in a ditch. Are tours worth the making? Who can doubt it after such an experience?

> Yours sincerely,
> CURZON

Again there had been warnings from the doctors: 'Go slow.' As before, he went to Paris for rest and remedy, taking as his guests Max Pemberton, Claude Johnson, Lord Rosslyn and a young Scotsman, Campbell Muir, whose name recurs in the diary for a year or two but who remains a shadowy figure in the *entourage*. Within a week, Alfred was writing: 'I do not ever remember picking up strength quicker', indicating a recuperative facility that may have been medically suspect. Crossing to England a few days later to be with his mother for Christmas, his *malaise* returned. For him it was Christmas Day in bed. A more thorough change of scene was recommended. He decided to go to St. Petersburg.

The visit was recorded in his customary staccato way, e.g. 'Went to the ballet. Czar was present but did not appear.' The diary has nothing to say of an Austrian floor waiter, Joseph Brunnbauer, at the new Hotel National, who was to become his confidential valet through the next decade, and who was lighting candles to his memory fifty years after. The homeward journey from Russia took him through Berlin. 'Didn't think much of it', was his first comment on that city, modified by the spectacle of the Unter den Linden 'in the evening glow, very fine'.

He was ill again and at Elmwood in the first weeks of the spring, 1903, but enjoyed the rest it imposed on him. 'Frankly, I like it,' he wrote to his friend Laird Clowes. 'Here I am at home with my books, my bottles of good Burgundy and my nux vomica. I am not hurrying to get well' (April 28). He was more concerned about his mother's health and well-being. That summer he wrote in the diary: 'She is evidently ageing fast', but she was to live another twenty-two years. He insisted that they take holidays together more often. 'We were very sad at parting', he wrote after travelling with her to the Black Forest that year. He bought the freehold of Sunnybank, Chapelizod, where he first saw the light. It was a link with her past, rather than with his, that could not be broken.

In October 1903 he suffered a return of the liver trouble which was thought to be part of the malarial aftermath. 'Feeling wretchedly weak and in a good deal of pain.' There was protracted neuralgia. 'Having electricity, massage and medicine, the result of too much work', he told Sutton. A new medical name comes into the records, Dr Vernon Jones. 'He ordered me to the seaside', and as always Elmwood supplied the balm of sleep and good air. Vernon Jones urged him to cut down his working day to one of five hours, not more. 'It is most difficult to carry out', his patient complained in the diary. There was also a new entry in his 'Private Loans' ledger: 'Vernon Jones, £900.'

A young ex-Etonian, Evelyn Wrench, who had become a business prodigy by exploiting the picture-postcard vogue, met Alfred Harmsworth for the first time in the autumn of 1903, describing him as 'a man obviously of Nordic stock, with steely blue eyes, clear-cut features and a Napoleonic lock of hair hanging over his broad forehead'. As they walked to their table for lunch in the Savoy Hotel restaurant, 'I noticed people nudging their neighbours to point him out'. Wrench was struck by 'his extraordinary power of absorption in whatever he was discussing'.

★   ★   ★

At some earlier point in his life, Alfred had read that in the French Revolution only one Paris newspaper had continued publication. It was able to do so because its proprietor owned a paper mill. In March 1903 *The Halifax Morning Chronicle*, of Nova Scotia, forecast great industrial developments in that territory and linked the name of Harmsworth with them. Concessions, it was stated, were being sought from the Government of New Brunswick. Subject to water supply tests, the project would go forward.

Last fall, Mr Harold Harmsworth and one or two other Londoners visited New Brunswick and inspected several possible sites for pulp and paper making. The Grand Falls location in Gloucester county was among the number. If all is satisfactory, Messrs Harmsworth will, it is announced, launch some 2,500,000 dollars in the enterprise and build at Grand Falls on the Nepisiquit River.

The Boer War had given the Harmsworths their first experience of rising paper prices, from £11 13s. 4d. a ton in 1900 to £16 6s. 8d. in 1901. As consumers of huge quantities of paper, they were much concerned. There were grave risks in their dependence on the open market. Vast acreages of forest in Canada and Scandinavia were being heedlessly torn down to meet American demands. The New York *World* was consuming the timber of seven acres of forest every day. Already it was clear that those were not inexhaustible sources. A precarious situation might be made the more so by forest fires, not less devastating than the axe. Rushing torrents could sweep away a year's cutting of logs overnight. In summer, there was the chance of a drought which could stop the water flow, indispensable to pulp making. In winter, ice could jam the turbine wheels as well as interrupt navigation. All those were largely uninsurable hazards. Harold was responsible for maintaining the enormous Harmsworth momentum. It was an increasingly worrying task. The prosperity of their undertakings was at stake; no less.

The splendours of Sutton Place had not dimmed Alfred's feelings for Elmwood and may have heightened them. He continued to invite old friends and members of his various staffs to join him there for weekends and sometimes longer periods. In the autumn of 1902 he had spent a week there with Harold, Sutton, Mayson Beeton, Max Pemberton, Fred Wood and an American-born circulation man named Dubbs, who had the unusual first name of Marine, which not even his closest friends could be induced to use. Over dinner one evening, Alfred said to Harold: 'What would happen to our publications if war broke out in Europe?' Harold answered perfunctorily: 'No doubt it would be very serious.' Falling silent for a while, Alfred then spoke his mind. 'We must not continue this risk. Harold, you and Beeton must go to Newfoundland, get timber concessions and build mills.' Recording the occasion in a letter to Frederick R. Poke, then proprietor of *Everybody's Weekly*, Dubbs wrote: 'That is how it happened. I heard it. Harold and Beeton sailed that week.' Beeton had already shown a firm grasp of economic geography in articles which he had written for the *Daily Mail* after investigation of the West Indies sugar industry. Although the Harmsworths were getting a large part of their paper supplies from Scandinavia, Alfred in particular had no faith in long-term investment in that region. He believed that Germany would seek to dominate Europe and its raw materials within the next decade. Their raw material, wood pulp, must be procurable within the British realm. It was vital to their future that they should have complete control of the source of supply.

While that fragment of historical information from the French Revolution had been fermenting in Alfred's mind, he expanded the range of Harold's anxieties by buying an ailing Sunday newspaper, the *Weekly Dispatch*, making an offer for the *Birmingham Gazette*, sending his personal representative to scout the prospects for a new morning paper in Newcastle, and inventing the *Daily Mirror*. The *Weekly Dispatch*, which was a hundred years old, had passed after many vicissitudes into the hands of Sir George Newnes. His Congregational affinities prevented him from developing the paper along the sensational lines of its chief competitors, *Lloyd's Sunday News* and the *News of the World*, which had practically driven the *Weekly Dispatch* out of the market. With its circulation down to 5,000 copies, Newnes was glad to get rid of the paper to the Harmsworths for £25,000. It flourishes in this modern age as the *Sunday Dispatch* with a readership of millions. Nothing came of the proposed Birmingham and Newcastle ventures.

As for the *Daily Mirror*, it appeared with the force of an impulse rather than with the assurance of a need. The make-up was finally settled on October 25, 1903. Ten days later the paper was in the hands of the public. Either ignoring the trend towards sex equality or interpreting it much too freely, Alfred Harmsworth was caught up by the idea that women should have their own daily paper. What is more, they should write and edit it. He may have been spurred on by a rumour that a group calling itself the Women's International Progressive Union had been meeting at the offices of W. T. Stead to discuss a woman's paper run exclusively in the interests of that body.

He wrote in his diary for November 1, 1903: 'Came down to the "Mirror" office, found Kennedy Jones in full swing, and after the usual pangs of childbirth produced the first copy at 9.50 p.m. It looks a promising child but time will show whether we are on a winner or not.' The birthplace was 2 Carmelite Street, where the *Daily Mail* had first seen the light. As a birthday gift, readers in many parts of the country received a gilt-and-enamel Pompadour-style hand mirror. The next day Alfred wrote: 'Numerous letters and telegrams of congratulation on the appearance of the new child. Great demand—machines going until the afternoon; total 276,000.' The elaborate rehearsal lessons of the *Daily Mail* had been swept aside. The first issue of the *Daily Mirror* looked like an illustrated daily edition of *Tit-Bits*.

The editor was Mary Howarth, who had been in charge of the *Daily Mail* women's features. She was supported by 'a large staff of cultivated, able and experienced women', to quote from a preliminary announcement. Half a dozen trained editorial men had been brought in, perhaps to reassure the proprietor rather than the ladies. When someone remarked that the office was like a setting for a French farce, 'with women rushing in and out', a colleague ungallantly retorted: 'In a French farce they would be beautiful.' The strain of getting out the first few issues was intense. There were several fainting cases among the women. Alfred had champagne sent in to revive them. Over the office hung the menace of the *double-entendre*. Proof-readers were seen hurrying like fugitives into corners where they could bring the latest horrifying example to the attention of editorial men. The *Daily Mirror* ladies upset even their ardent champion, the proprietor, by using words like 'soupçon' and 'yclept' in their copy. Soon the men were moved up into command. The change was made abruptly during a weekend. On Friday night, the woman editor's room was like a boudoir. By Monday morning the scene was transformed. Gone were the dainty wall mirrors, the chintz curtains and the Queen Anne chairs. Masculinity had taken over, surrounded itself with varnished deal office equipment and filled the room with pipe smoke and cynical laughter. The new editor was Hamilton Fyfe, brought over from the *Morning Advertiser*, organ of the licensed victualling trade. Fyfe, who had been secretary to G. E. Buckle, editor of *The Times*, was a good-looking Scot in his early thirties. He had an actor's face and voice but was a little too plodding to be the romantic figure that he undoubtedly supposed himself to be. To him fell the ungracious task of dismissing the *Daily Mirror* women with three months' salary in lieu of notice. 'They begged to be allowed to stay. They left little presents on my desk. They waylaid me tearfully in corridors. It was a horrid experience—like drowning kittens.' Prefacing his letters of dismissal Fyfe wrote: '. . . in view of impending changes that are to be made in the paper.'

Changes were not merely impending. They were a matter of desperation. Nothing, it seemed, could stop the downward plunge. Three presses had been needed to produce the first day's issue. Soon, one of them was idle, then two. The *Daily Mirror* ran headlong into a loss of £3,000 a week. By the time the lowest sale of 24,801 copies was reached, Harold Harmsworth was going about like a stricken man. 'There was consternation at Carmelite House.' The words are Cecil Harmsworth's. 'Alfred had for once completely misinterpreted the popular mind.' It was the worst setback that his reputation had suffered. Nothing like it had befallen any previous Harmsworth venture.

Because his innovation of the *Daily Mail* women's page was a success, he had seen in it the inspiration of a larger aim. He believed that women could be seduced for a penny from their allegiance to the sixpenny *Queen* and *Ladies' Field*. The class note had been sounded in the preliminary publicity: it was to be 'a daily newspaper for gentlewomen'. Apparently his highly charged emotional respect for women had coloured his vision to a point of absurdity. It is hard to counter the opinion that in its original form the *Daily Mirror* was a ridiculous production. The spectacle of the austerely dressed, would-be efficient women in the *Daily Mirror* office who, as Alfred Harmsworth told a friend, 'wore the most manly collars and cuffs', should have convinced him that women aspired to a greater identity of interests with men, that his notion of separateness was a clumsy if not a profound misreading of their instincts. It cost the Harmsworths £100,000. A large part of that sum came out of Alfred's pocket. When Harold suggested cutting the loss and stopping the paper, Alfred shook his head like a punished prize-fighter and vowed to go on until the problem was solved.

The means of salvation was the half-tone block, adapted to the speed of newspaper printing. Arkas Sapt, on the staff of the *Illustrated Mail* (formerly *Sunday Daily Mail*) had begun experiments several years before as editor of another Harmsworth periodical, *Home Sweet Home*. In certain of his moods Sapt was mistaken for a genius, an impression deepened by his casual attitude to time and money. Alfred Harmsworth's belief in him was a tribute to Sapt's abilities, his style of life being Bohemian, in Alfred's vocabulary a term of contempt. By the perversity of existence, Sapt's personal tastes saved the Harmsworths' money; his improvidence forced him to commute his commission on *Daily Mirror* sales for a few hundred pounds. He might have been an extremely well-off man.

Supporting Sapt morally and financially, in particular against Harold's pessimism, Alfred prevented a Fleet Street fiasco. Hamilton Fyfe wrote that 'he dramatically disappointed all who believed that his career was broken. He had snatched victory from the jaws of defeat'. It was too generous a testimony. It overlooked the threat to Alfred's self-esteem. He had not shown the divination, the sure touch, of his earlier ventures. Apparently the single-mindedness which had been one of his most distinctive and, for that matter, most profitable characteristics, was blurred by his multiplying preoccupations. In New York, three years before, he had objected to newspaper illustration, declaring it 'unnecessary, a mere matter of habit'. In London, his *Illustrated Mail* (superseding the *Sunday Daily Mail*) was a lavish user of line drawings, some of them the work of accomplished artists. On January 28, 1904, the *Daily Mirror* was renamed the *Daily Illustrated Mirror*: 'A Paper for Men and Women.' Its price was lowered to a halfpenny. Three months later, on April 28, it became the

Daily Mirror again: 'An Illustrated Paper for Men and Women.' Its page size was reduced and its make-up was based on the principles which Alfred had established for his twentieth-century version of the New York *World*. The wedding of an American heiress was given six inches of space; the death of a famous historian two inches. Readers learned that Mrs Cornwallis-West 'has a piquant cheekiness', and that 'several women are making handsome dress allowances out of their victims at bridge'. Here was London's first 'tabloid' newspaper.

He had published a personal statement: 'How I Dropped £100,000 on the Mirror', admitting 'flat, rank and unmitigated failure'. With equal candour, he forecast success. 'If the *Daily Mirror* had not failed, I should not have found out so promptly that the public wanted a daily picture paper.' The statement may have been thought arrogant by the proprietors of the *Daily Graphic*, who had been publishing that penny illustrated paper with moderately good results through the last fifteen years. But they had no Sapt in their office. They still relied chiefly on woodcuts and line drawings for their illustrations, only tentatively using half-tone. Also, their printing speed was slow, 11,000 copies an hour. Sapt was certain that he could do better and Alfred Harmsworth gave him a Hoe rotary press to play with. No one had yet managed to print half-tone on a fast machine. Taking his 'pulls' every morning to Harmsworth, Sapt did it. The first results looked like child's play. 'What a ghastly mess!' Alfred exclaimed on seeing one of the first page proofs of Sapt's handiwork. It drew a letter from a member of the staff of Raphael Tuck & Sons, the fine art printers: 'I know you will not mind my poking fun at the *Daily Mirror*, but the illustrations have been so killingly funny that they are really puzzle pictures. In the *Daily Mirror* you have an excellent publication, but the illustrations are so very, very wanting—*and it is all due to the photographs requiring special treatment before being reproduced*.' It was a valuable hint, presumably acknowledged. Retouching enabled the *Daily Mirror* to print better pictures. Better quality ink made its impression in more than the mechanical sense, while a young and exuberant circulation staff, led by the aggressive, fierce-eyed Dubbs, clinched those necessary improvements by reporting increased sales everywhere.

Ludicrous emergencies arose before the tide turned. There was only one dark room, nearly always in use. Late night crises were caused by over-eager news photographers dashing into the room while plates were being developed, spoiling results. Acids from the engraving room, flushed into drainpipes and sewers, led to difficulties with the sanitary department of the Corporation of London. One night the office electricity fuses blew out with a cataclysmic flash. The editorial staff worked on in flickering candlelight and got the first edition on to the machines only a few minutes late. Blocks went astray between the office and the art department, which was in another building, and in some editions the pages had blanks in them. Someone on the art staff suggested that the spreading interest in amateur photography should be encouraged by an invitation to readers to send in pictures. The result was a deluge. Mailbags emptied thousands of useless 'snaps' into the office. Not all of them bore the senders' names and addresses. Confusion reigned for weeks.

With the recovery of circulation and the vindication of his judgment, Alfred Harmsworth detached himself from his close preoccupation with the *Daily Mirror*. It was said of him in the office, disparagingly, that he did not understand picture journalism. He appeared to make no effort to do so, conceivably because it meant laying hold of a new set of techniques and values at a time when, uncertain health apart, he was beginning to be aware of his years. He may have learned the lesson of his overwhelming success, that it was all too likely to involve him in still more effort, still greater struggle. He was thirty-seven and, by the life-span arithmetic of his generation, 'getting on'. Moreover, his journalistic experience (which had never been, strictly, training) was based on the literary tradition of Fleet Street. He tended to regard the *Daily Mirror* as a by-product of his publishing inventiveness, though the begrudging spirit could have been in part due to the embarrassments caused him by the paper's near failure.

At a meeting of the Illustrated London News and Sketch Ltd., on February 26, 1904, Sir William Ingram, Alfred Harmsworth's old employer, was asked by a nervous shareholder what might be the effect of the new daily illustrated journalism on the future of their company. Replying that 'the question is difficult to answer', Ingram added: 'The proprietors of the *Daily Mirror* are very clever and wonderful people.' Referring next day to the meeting, the *Daily Mirror* told its readers that the proprietors of the sixpenny illustrated weeklies were 'feeling the strain', and suggested that no one would want to wait a week for pictures that he could now see within a few hours of the events being illustrated. 'A new element has entered into the world of newspapers', and for the Harmsworths it was a new source of wealth. The paper was owned by the Pictorial Newspaper Company Ltd., registered on February 29, 1904. The Daily Mail Publishing Co. Ltd. held 27,393 shares, Alfred Harmsworth 10,000, Kennedy Jones 2,500, Harold Harmsworth 1,000, Leicester Harmsworth 750.

Alfred was content to leave the general financial and business control of the *Daily Mirror* to his brother Harold and the editorial direction to Alexander Kenealy, with final authority on that side given to Kennedy Jones. Kenealy came from the *Daily Express*. He had also worked on the *New York Herald*. Alfred brought him in to assist Fyfe in the day to day running of the paper. Kenealy soon showed that he had a more realistic view of the public taste than Fyfe, who wanted to infuse the paper with his cultural preciosity. Soon Kenealy superseded him. The son of the eccentric barrister who defended the Tichborne claimant, Kenealy was short and rotund and afflicted with a nervous cough and a mild compulsion mania, a habit of tearing up pieces of paper as he talked at his desk, scattering them over his blotter and then carefully scooping them up and dropping them into the wastepaper basket. It was a neurotic routine that had to be gone through many times a day.

Kenealy was and is still credited with being 'the man who saved the *Mirror*', and his touch was at times brilliant. He was served by a group of ardent young enthusiasts for the new-style daily journalism who gave the paper the effervescence which it has retained through more than fifty years. Before long, the daily sale was 400,000 copies. Later, a change of editorial tone would send it soaring into the millions. Writing privately of the lowered standards which led to that spectacular climax of the paper's fortunes, Cecil Harmsworth said with emphasis that 'if they had been promoted under the proprietorship of Alfred, there would have been short shrift indeed for those responsible'. In that event, the *Daily Mirror* would have been unlikely to justify its technically impressive mid-century claim to 'the largest daily sale on earth'.

*   *   *

Mary Harmsworth to Alfred Harmsworth:

Sutton Place,
by Guildford,
Surrey.
[Undated]

My darling 'Sir Alfred,'—I must be the first to tell you how glad and happy I am to know that you have gained recognition for the hard work of years. No one, dear, deserves it more than you—but the happiest thought of all to me is that *we began* life together and have been together through all the years of work which have earned you distinction and fortune so young. My fond love and every congratulation from

Your loving
Wife

A laconic diary note for February 26, 1904: 'Conversation with the King', may have had no bearing on the fact that his name appeared among the baronets in the Birthday Honours List issued on the evening of June 23, 1904. The growth of the popular press had already received acknowledgment in the form of official honours. Two London newspaper proprietors had been made peers during the past few years. Newnes had long been a baronet. Several journalists had been knighted. Acquainting

Newnes with the Sovereign's wish, the Prime Minister had referred to his 'services to popular literature'. There was no similar Harmsworth citation. The diary tells us: 'Over 200 telegrams received at Berkeley Square before midnight', and, the next day: 'Such a day of congratulations as amazed me.' The day after that, at Sutton: 'Wife and I dealing with avalanche of letters and telegrams.'

Among the letters that he preserved was one from Henry Arnholz, the solicitor: '17 *Great Winchester Street, London, E.C.* Little did I think in the far-off days when you fought my battles for me at school, and when you gave me birthday presents (one of which—a box of chemicals—I still possess), that I should have the privilege of congratulating you on receiving a Birthday Honour.' The letter touched a sympathetic chord. Arnholz had been given occasional opportunities of acting legally for his old school champion. Now he was able to add to the japanned deed-boxes a brand-new one inscribed: *Sir Alfred Harmsworth, Bart.* For Arnholz, Alfred remained the hero of his boyhood years, an admiration that he never lost. Fearing perhaps to risk it by familiarity, he maintained a strict punctilio in his dealings with his old friend. Often Alfred wrote to him as 'My dear Henry'. Arnholz always responded formally, a habit that he never relaxed, though their association became more intimate as time went by.

The Times and the *Morning Post*, pillars of the Party which had honoured him, gave only a few lines to the news of his baronetcy. The *Daily Telegraph* said that 'to few men has it been given to win so much success in so limited a time'. The *Daily Chronicle* said that 'Mr Harmsworth's is the name of the most general interest in a list that is more remarkable for quantity than quality'. Touching on the importance of opportunity in relation to personal fortune, the newspaper stated that 'he has done as much as any man living to revolutionize British journalism'. *The Bystander* quipped that he controlled thirty periodicals, 'and an indeterminate number of brothers'. Only a little while before the chief proprietor of the *Daily News*, George Cadbury, had written to thank him for 'a kindly notice' of his connection with that newspaper and had said that it was his policy 'to urge that personalities be avoided as far as possible'. His writ did not run on this occasion. The paper hinted at a disparity of public service between Harmsworth and Edward Elgar, 'the composer of *The Apostles*', one of the new knights.

Any hurt feelings that Alfred may have had were solaced by the ovation he received at a dinner given in his honour ten days later by two hundred senior members of his newspaper and publishing staffs. 'Surprised to find that I thoroughly enjoyed it. Much touched by the kind feeling shown to me.' He concocted a small joke which went the office rounds: 'I was tired of hearing so-and-so call me "Mr 'Armsworth". It'll be a change to hear him say "Sir *Halfred*".' In the office, his elevation in the social hierarchy set the seal on the practice of calling him 'Chief'. Now he more often used that term in signing his written communications to the staff.

It seemed to those around him that his naturally dominating personal style had gathered new force. It had become more commanding, intimidating his fellow men with the notion that while he did not scorn their compliments, he preferred the approval of the gods. His capacity to impose himself on others, to charm but also to repel, had increased. He alternated ominously between the much adulated boyishness of heart and gloomy preoccupation in which he seemed remote even from his friends. His movements had become more jerky, as if reflecting inner restlessness. 'Ferrier, the great nerve specialist, examined me', he wrote in the diary for March 22, 1904. Like his rotary presses, his brain was working twenty-four hours a day.

He was putting on weight and worrying about it to the extent of repeatedly checking it on the scales. He made notes showing constant fluctuations between eleven and twelve stones, his marginal comments reading: 'Not so rosy', 'Down again, thank goodness', 'Triumph of self-denial', 'Good boy'. His chest measurement, recorded by Poole of Savile Row, was $41\frac{1}{2}$ inches, waist 41 inches. But his figure was still that of a young man, he still had the sinewy grace, his shoulders were still firm and broad, maintaining the look of deceptive physical strength. The forward thrust of the head could be more aggressive now, and the face was set in his father's distinctive mould, tempered by a pink and white delicacy of feature which was Byronically combined with muscular vigour. T. P. O'Connor had lately written of him with a characteristic flourish: 'The extraordinary thing is the almost girlish transparency of the complexion. The whole face suggests the almost ethereal beauty of the cameo.'

His way of opening a conversation had become needlessly abrupt, his silences more forbidding. Himself quick-witted, he had never found it easy to be patient with those who were laborious in explanation. Now, he was often brutal about it. He would thrust out a hand, say 'Good day', and turn aside, leaving the other person floundering in mid-speech. When, as often happened, the dismissal was accompanied by his best smile, the victim would be made still more unhappy. He had no talent for dissembling his feelings. When he was bored he could not help showing it.

Some of those closest to him surrendered the rare privilege of calling him 'Alf'. Pemberton wavered between 'Alfred' and 'Chief'. Kennedy Jones who had pronounced it 'Allf' and never called him 'Chief', compromised with 'Allfred'. His fishing companion, Nevill Jackson, persisted with 'Harmy'. Louise Owen, Alfred's personal secretary for a number of years, recalled that a new member of the *Daily Mail* staff whom Alfred addressed by his Christian name for the reason that he had known the young man's father, vanished from the Harmsworth scene after a fatal day on which he had presumed to respond on the same familiar basis.

The autocratic attitude may have expressed something quite other than self-importance. He had enough of the family diffidence to be uneasy about the exceptional good fortune that had singled him out from his fellows. He would speak of it as 'my luck' and his tone could have been thought apologetic. He had been borne up so rapidly on the pinions of success that, like Polycrates, he dreaded bad luck. 'Anything but failure'— it was Cecil Rhodes's motto and Alfred Harmsworth's too. He sought to rationalize his situation by taking the fatalistic view. He would invoke Kismet. He would say: '*Che sara sara*', what will be, will be. Apparently he required to placate a feeling of being mysteriously as well as marvellously fortunate. The arbitrariness which he tended more often to show in his behaviour, the less stable moods and the petulance which could bring dismay to those who thought they knew him well enough to be immune from it, all this argued some psychic discomfort, almost as if he resented his relative immunity from the blows of fate.

Chapter Eleven

No Longer an Island

READING the *Daily Mail* one day towards the end of October 1904, Alfred Harmsworth sent a memorandum to the editor:

Exactly what's wrong with the modern washing machine is that we put all the clothes in the boil at once and the colours run, then you wring 'em and fold 'em and iron them into neat squares and out they come all of a pattern. For the sake of variety and individuality, don't, I beg.

The machine analogy was apt enough. He conducted his newspapers by a series of explosions, suggesting imperfect internal combustion. Even so, what he had set in motion eight years before had become the best equipped and most efficient organization of the kind anywhere. Recently, the *Daily Mail* had conquered its last territory in the circulation battle of the time by appearing on breakfast tables in the West of England, where formerly it had been arriving two hours later. No commendation of that feat of production and distribution gratified Alfred Harmsworth more than a letter sent to him by three members of the Herefordshire county council education committee, who wrote: 'You are conferring a great boon on us.' Pleased by that testimony to his emancipating power, he told his secretary: 'Send them a nice reply.' The record-breaking Great Western Railway locomotive, *City of Bath*, racing through the night, helped to make more than newspaper history in 1904. If it also lent force to Lord Melbourne's fear of general education 'filling the people's heads with nonsense which it would be impossible ever to get out of them again', it was enabling many more people to make exciting discoveries about the world they lived in. Every day, the *Daily Mail* brought the breath of adventure into hundreds of thousands of homes. No newspaper before had done as much. There was dithyrambic gush about the birth of princes and the death of kings, but there was also a great deal of information, social, political and economic, that had not previously been within the reach of the multitude. Alfred Harmsworth's *Daily Mail* was a powerful instrument of change in the lives of the people. It linked them, however tenuously, with the intellectual resources of the nation, broadening and deepening their interests and giving them vicarious access to new kinds of experience. His own general curiosity was a magnification of theirs. The *Daily Mail* had no more eager reader than he. 'In a sense, he was the only completely convinced democrat that I ever knew,' was said of him by a critical commentator. 'He did really believe that things ought to be decided by the mass-opinion about them. To find out what that was, or what it was going to be, and to express it powerfully, seemed to him not only profitable but right and wise.'*

That conviction of Alfred Harmsworth's made the *Daily Mail* the medium of a public spirit which was exceptional among wielders of newspaper power not in kind but in breadth of social impact. The scornful might say that this or that campaign—better motoring, standard bread, intensive gardening, ideal homes, young farmers' clubs, smallholdings, sweet pea growing, aviation, daylight saving, prize roses—was invented and conducted primarily as a circulation stimulant. Branded as 'stunts', such activities expressed not only Harmsworth's instinct for leadership but often drew inspiration from a source unsuspected by readers of his paper, namely, the approval of his mother. She was strongly susceptible to the notion that a newspaper should have a moral justification as well as a material purpose, that it must acknowledge the overriding proprietorship of humanity. Alfred rarely failed to consult her before committing himself to those extra-mural enterprises.

The *Daily Mail* battled for the installation of the telephone in every London police station, one of its longer struggles in the name of common sense. It seconded the adoption of the clanging bell for fire engines. Oppressed by the fate of eight fire office workers who died in a fire in Queen Victoria Street, Alfred Harmsworth initiated other fire brigade reforms. His *Daily Mail* prevented a proposed vast extension of the London tramways system, which would have further complicated one of the greatest traffic problems of modern times. 'The motor-bus is coming', was his reiterated warning to the London Traffic Commission, which had begun gathering evidence for a report to be published in 1906. Capital had already been sought for the London General Omnibus Company.

Starting the *Overseas Daily Mail* in November 1904, he was less interested in its then slender commercial prospects than in establishing it as a 'bond of Empire', a newspaper connection between the mother country 'and the scattered hundreds of thousands of Britons in the far corners of

* I. A. Spender.

287

the world'. Evelyn Wrench, aged twenty-one, was given the editorship. He remained in active association with the paper for fourteen years. To him, Alfred Harmsworth was 'just like a light-hearted young uncle or elder brother', who told him: 'Businesses grow old rapidly. I make a rule never to bring in anyone from outside over the age of twenty-five.' Wrench subsequently wrote:

He sometimes advanced young men too rapidly and in the first flush of enthusiasm made promises which were not carried out. The cynics in the office, when some recently discovered youthful genius was introduced to the Chief, used to smile knowingly and wonder how long the newcomer would survive the trials which awaited him later on, when the sun was no longer shining, and when he had to make his way painfully through the valley of discouragement and disapproval.

Men already established in his offices were encouraged to expect promotion that never came. There was an angry letter from one of his earliest employees, Houghton Townley, who felt himself disparagingly overlooked if not forgotten; 'though I do not come and throw bricks at your window'. Undoubtedly there was harshness, not all of it derived from Alfred Harmsworth personally. He was blamed for the behaviour of his departmental heads. Kennedy Jones's methods brought him undeserved epithets. It was 'K.J.' who originated the system of engaging almost any likely applicant for an editorial job on a three-months' trial basis, usually at a rate of pay well beyond what he had earned before. When, for lack of competence or some defect of personality, the arrangement was not renewed, the disappointed young journalist would enlarge the legend of a ruthlessness which generally recoiled on Alfred Harmsworth personally. He was himself capable of indifference to the fate of those who did not conform to his standards of proficiency, for him an indispensable aspect of character. He liked men to be quick in thought and action. He preferred that they should have what he called a good-shaped head. A man with a large head was likely to make a stronger impression on him than a man with a small head. He was not always so discriminating in his approval of services rendered and men who thought that his smile or an appreciative memorandum meant security of favour were sometimes cruelly disillusioned. There were rumours of the suicide of victims of his capriciousness, the tragic element in the lives of weak men being exaggerated into an indictment of a personal power which, considering its scope and duration, was not often abused. Documents of the period show his impulses being most generously touched by personal crises and Sir Evelyn Wrench has told in his autobiography how at the age of twenty-one he was saved from financial disaster by Alfred Harmsworth's ready help. To set against

Sir Alfred and Lady Harmsworth, at Sutton Place

Northcliffe (*centre*) at Pau in 1909, with (*left to right*) Kennedy Jones, A. J. Balfour, Wilbur Wright and Arthur M...

the generosity, there was the experience in 1905 of the subsequently
eminent King's Counsel, Sir Edward Marshall Hall, who in a libel action
had made a tasteless reference to Harmsworth's wife. Thereafter, by Alfred
Harmsworth's strict command, he was referred to in all *Daily Mail* law
and social reports as 'Mr M. Hall'. That petty revenge was made the
ground for scornful comment on Harmsworth by critics who did not
know that he had refrained from retaliating on an earlier occasion when
Marshall Hall had attacked the Harmsworth press in highly intemperate
language.

Yet, at the same time, Alfred was showing the greatest solicitude for
the young editor of *Answers*, S. J. Summers, who was over-exerting himself to the detriment of his health in making a success of his job. Summers,
Alfred insisted, was to move into a room next his own, 'so that I can keep
an eye on him'. The young editor's death was an emotional shock which
Alfred could not conceal. 'I was amazed', he scribbled in his diary; and for
some time after he could not bring himself to go into Summers's room.

*　　*　　*

Fiscal controversy was the dominant political theme, with Joseph Chamberlain planning to sweep the country with Tariff Reform and H. H.
Asquith in charge of the Free Trade demolition squads following his
every move. For the moment Alfred Harmsworth's mercurial politics
were steadied. He was a Chamberlain man. In the beginning he was inclined to oppose Chamberlain and the 'stomach taxes', as he called them
in the *Daily Mail*. He had proposed that Rosebery should put himself at
the head of the Free Trade movement and make speeches in conformity
with a whirlwind campaign to be worked out between them. Rosebery
did not care for the idea. From that time the two 'neighbours' of Berkeley
Square parted company. In J. A. Spender's hearing, he described Rosebery
as 'hopeless'. He had evidently been prepared to risk the displeasure of a
considerable part of his *Daily Mail* public, for that newspaper was not a
Liberal organ. Cecil Harmsworth believed that the effect of so violent a
policy change 'might have been disastrous'. He also wrote: 'Alfred was
never a supporter of the whole programme of any political party.' When,
some years after, Spender was challenged by Leicester Harmsworth for
having named Alfred as a Tariff Reformer, Spender replied: 'I am my own
witness in this matter, for I knew your brother intimately in those years.
In his talks with me he was always a Protectionist and we had many arguments on the subject. He always, in those days, attributed what he called
the "colossal" success of the U.S.A. to protection.'

In an undated letter to Lord Robert Cecil, Alfred wrote: 'You know
that I am a very keen Tariff Reformer, but that is not the discussion at the

moment. The brutal fact is, of course, that we are all under the influence of the invalid at Highbury [Chamberlain], who is never allowed to hear the truth. I do not, however, take so pessimistic a view as to the result of the Election as you do.'

April 1, 1905, was another of the Harmsworth red-letter days. The *Daily Mail*, the *Evening News*, the *Weekly Dispatch*, and their subsidiary publications, were incorporated in a company to be known as Associated Newspapers Ltd., with a capital of £1,600,000. It was an edifice crowning Alfred's years of inspiration, hard work and good luck. Bank staffs worked through the night, coping with the rush of applications for shares.

Visiting Paris, he often complained that no London morning paper was to be had there until much later in the day. The only available newspapers printed in English were the *Daily Messenger*, formerly *Galagnani's Messenger* of ancient lineage, and the Paris edition of the *New York Herald*, both poor productions by his standards. The Entente Cordiale having created a better atmosphere, he resolved to print and publish in Paris an edition of the *Daily Mail* which would circulate in many parts of the continent, reaching readers several hours earlier than any of the London papers.

The technical challenge was in itself an incitement. It was a daring idea, transmitting the contents of a London newspaper by telephone and reproducing it in print in the French capital each morning. There were more compulsive considerations. He disliked the idea of an American newspaper gaining a monopoly of English-speaking readers in Europe. There were those around him who doubted whether enough circulation could be secured to justify the additional heavy expense of transmitting news and other matter by private wire from London every day. It had always pleased him to defy the doubts of business men. If he presumed that such a newspaper would still further extend his sphere of influence, he also believed that it would have a missionary purpose, that the *Continental Daily Mail* would serve the interests of England abroad.

The *Daily Messenger*, nearing its last gasp, had been offered to him by its manager, Ralph Lane. He would not buy it, but intimated that he would employ Lane, who had the qualifications to help him start the Paris *Daily Mail*. 'Will fifty thousand pounds be enough, with a further fifty thousand in reserve? You can make three major mistakes and I shall not hold it against you. After that, we'll see.' Organizing the telephone and telegraph arrangements from the London end was Andrew Caird, who had to deal with Governments as well as with individuals. The French authorities made it a condition that there should be no French domestic politics in the paper. Northcliffe reminded the staff: 'We are guests of the French people. It is not polite to discuss our hosts' internal affairs.' Prominent on the editorial side was W. M. McAlpin, Paris correspondent of the London *Daily Mail*. The first issue of the *Continental Daily Mail* appeared from 3 Place de la Madeleine on May 22, 1905. Lane, who under his middle names, Norman Angell, wrote *The Great Illusion* and became a Nobel Prize winner, was a Socialist and a frank critic of the Harmsworth kind of power, while remaining an admirer and friend of Alfred Harmsworth, with whom he worked in harmony for ten years. In his autobiography, *After All* (1951), he considered 'the Chief's' reputation for ruthlessness. He said that it was exaggerated. 'If he felt that a sacking was called for, he generally made an attempt to find another place for the victim.' After an angry outburst, Alfred remarked to Angell: 'A man as powerful as I am ought not to let his temper get away with him.'

That same month he bought *The Observer*. Apart from its long history and tradition of independence, which quite naturally appealed to him, the paper provided him with an opportunity to show his capability of winging to the higher flights of journalism. He paid about £5,000 for a circulation which swung curiously between 2,000 in winter and 4,000 in summer, knowing that he could expect no prosperity from it until the sales had somehow been pushed up to at least 40,000. It involved him in heavy expense and a variety of mechanical and editorial problems. By then he was thoroughly assured of his resources. His net income for the year ending March 31, 1905, was £115,000. Apart from his heavy shareholdings in the family businesses, he had stock worth £300,000. He at once offered the editorship of *The Observer* to J. L. Garvin, then editing *The Outlook*, a sixpenny review, and writing for the *Daily Telegraph*. Garvin was not yet ready to make a change which was eventually to provide scope in plenty for his splendid journalistic gifts.

Harmsworth put money into the *Manchester Courier* in an attempt to make it 'the leading Conservative organ of the North', a venture which became an expensive nuisance to him over several years. He acquired an interest in the bright social weekly *Vanity Fair*. He paid £14,000 for the controlling shares in *The World*, Edmund Yates's old paper, persuading himself that 'it might be converted into a "town and country" journal, making a strong bid for business monopolized by *Country Life*'. He put £10,000 into the East of England Newspaper Company, of Norwich. None of those enterprises responded satisfactorily to his practised touch. Examining the position of the East of England Newspaper Company, his solicitors, Lewis & Lewis, found that he had shown small concern for the safety of his money. It transpired that he had invested his £10,000 in the character of a friend rather than in the prospects of a business, which had in fact lost £36,000. The friend was Edward E. Peacock, sometime manager of the *Morning Post* and honorary secretary of the Savage Club. Yet when another and closer friend, Hugh Spottiswoode, of His Majesty's Printing Office, wrote in considerable stress of mind asking for a loan on ample security, he answered (October 25, 1905): 'I am not a moneylender and have usually found that loans are an effective means of parting private and business friendships.'

Reaching his fortieth birthday that year, he was a brisk-moving man with the appearance of excellent health and retaining the distinctive good looks of his youth. 'Merely to know him, to have the privilege of his companionship, was to be exhilarated': such was the testimony of one of his better known editors, J. A. (later Sir John) Hammerton. 'He exhaled a certain tonic quality which, by some—and assuredly by myself—was definitely experienced in his presence.' Hammerton wrote that 'in every Harmsworth publication, no matter how slight his personal part in its production may have seemed, some measure of his own vitality, his own enthusiasm, his own optimism, had been communicated to its editor. He was thus the coadjutor of all his numerous editors.'

He chose on occasions to speaks of his staffs as 'one big happy family', a simile which may have gratified him personally but which may have seemed dubious to those who knew of the jealousies and feuds under the surface loyalties. Moreover, there were changes in the Harmsworth inner circle. St. John, who had no flair for the journalistic life, had recently decided that his future lay elsewhere. Alfred had hoped that St. John would fill a directorial post on the *Continental Daily Mail* and had sent him to France to improve his French, saying: 'At least one of us ought to be able to speak that language well.' On holiday with his tutor, St. John was shown a spring of bubbling water in the orchard of a doctor named Perrier at Vergeze, near Nimes. The spring had been known to the Romans. Its reputation was still only local. The elder Harmsworths were astonished to learn that St. John was planning to sell his family shares in order to buy the Perrier spring. Encouraged by Molly Harmsworth, but with a good deal of opposition from other members of the family, he took the first steps towards establishing the internationally known Perrier water business. 'The thought of it, the management and control of it, and its advertising, were all his,' Cecil Harmsworth wrote. 'The shape of the familiar bottle was his idea, taken from Indian clubs lying in a corner of his room. The labels on the bottle were of his design.' St. John was not yet thirty.

In 1905, Hildebrand left the Amalgamated Press Ltd., after having given some of his best years to that extremely successful concern; while Leicester, who had been even more successful as a departmental head and who shared with Hildebrand one-sixth of the profits over £150,000, was preparing his exit too. Alfred asked Sutton to try to persuade Hildebrand to take over *Vanity Fair*: 'I am quite sure that if he puts in £10,000 or £15,000 and *works*, he will make money. Not much, but enough, and the social position is good. He *ought* to have more work to do and Mother is most anxious that he should.' Differences between the two brothers widened when Hildebrand's chauffeur came before the courts on a serious motoring charge. Alfred was extremely angry because the case brought the family name into the police reports. Hildebrand undoubtedly tended to take life too easily, but behind his light and chaffing manner was an astute business brain. Though he lost £80,000 as the proprietor of a London evening newspaper, *The Globe*, from 1908 to 1911, he held on doggedly to his family shares and by judicious management built up a fortune of £1,600,000, part of the residue of which he left to Merton College, Oxford.

Leicester Harmsworth's departure from the boardroom of the Harmsworth periodicals business in 1906 severed its most valuable family connection, excepting that of the two oldest brothers. Partly because of enduring ill-health, partly because a publication which he had sponsored two or three years previously had been 'knifed' in his absence by Harold in one of his pessimistic drives for economy, Leicester had decided to follow his own star. He bought shares in the company making the Darracq motor-car and within a year was richer by £100,000. He then joined Sir George Newnes and others in oil company flotations, in which he lost a small fortune and made a large one. As a preliminary to those ventures he needed ready money and to get it put his Harmsworth shares on the market. Alfred objected, more particularly as Leicester was proposing to sell them to Sir John Ellerman, the shipping magnate. Leicester was stiffened in his resolve to put himself beyond Alfred's summary jurisdiction. 'It is not easy to find people you would care to be associated with', he wrote to Alfred. There was never a quarrel. The two brothers were on amicable terms through the years that remained.

In 1905, Alfred and Harold were expanding their power and opportunities into new realms. Ever since the South African war they had been concerned to have behind them a full year's supply of paper to meet emergencies. The emergency they most feared was war in Europe. Mayson Beeton, camped in a tent on the banks of the Grand Falls of the River of Exploits in Newfoundland, recommended them to buy timber limits in that region, where there were abundant spruce and lakes and rivers to supply the huge quantities of water required for high-capacity paper mills. The Harmsworth's foresight, plus Beeton's judgment, was creating an enterprise which would enrich Newfoundland and ensure the continuance of a popular press at home. Out of their imagination and resolution came the Anglo-Newfoundland Development Company, with its 3,100 square miles of territory, its townships, railways, mines, harbours, line of steamships and massive output of wood pulp, raw stuff of papermaking for the vast newspaper and periodical circulations of congested, industrialized England. Harold Harmsworth was the principal organizer of the project and its resources. It is his monument.

There was an afternoon in 1905 when B. W. Young, the former *Answers* office boy who had risen to be secretary of the Harmsworths' periodical group, heard angry voices in 'the Chief's' room. Immediately afterwards he was sent for by Sir Alfred. 'He looked white-faced and upset.' Beaumont, the original backer of *Answers*, had just left. Alfred Harmsworth told Young that Beaumont was suing him for fraud. 'That was the word he used', Alfred said to Young. The *Standard*, owned by C. Arthur Pearson, announced that 'Sir Alfred Harmsworth is the principal defendant in a gigantic case of newspaper litigation', stating that Captain A. S. Beaumont was alleging that he had been induced to part with 'extremely valuable shares' under false pretences. Other newspapers gave similar reports, as a result of which a consolidated action for libel was brought by Alfred Harmsworth. He obtained a full apology from the offending newspapers. A writ had been issued against him by Beaumont but the action never went for trial. It was an eruption of the quarrel of nearly twenty years before. As part-author of the Harmsworth success, Beaumont no doubt coveted a larger share of the royalties. In 1905 the Amalgamated Press, which Beaumont's money had helped to found, paid a dividend of forty per cent, against Newnes's ten per cent and Pearson's fifteen. He may have been spurred to legal action by that opulent declaration. In the light of the known facts it was unlikely that his case could have succeeded.

Substantially contributing to the extraordinary Amalgamated Press profits, which in 1905 were £255,000, was the 'part works' publishing department which Alfred had inaugurated in 1897 with *Sixty Years a Queen*. It had been followed by similar works covering the life of Lord Nelson, the South African war, another and more intimate biography of Queen Victoria immediately after her death, the war between Japan and Russia, and the *Harmsworth Encyclopædia*. The *Harmsworth Self-Educator*, which followed, an even more abounding success, was a source of keen personal satisfaction to Alfred, who had 'the heart that seeks the public weal', and who could claim that if such publications were animating rather than educative they kindled a wish for knowledge in innumerable minds. The *Harmsworth Self-Educator* was so popular that copies were snatched from the bookstalls as soon as a new issue appeared.

Dating from that time, an office association of Arthur Mee, an earnestly sincere Nonconformist from Nottingham, with Hammerton, the lithe Anglo-Scot, soon made the Amalgamated Press imprint respected by the book trade, bringing out a succession of best-selling instalment works and the well-found volumes which gave them permanence. Mee's greatest personal triumph was the *Children's Encyclopædia*, which he called 'the book of my heart', a work of irreproachable character, its pages radiant with his naïve idealism, a golden treasury for children of all ages and many lands. 'It will give delight to hundreds of thousands, probably millions, of little people,' Alfred Harmsworth wrote to him. 'And that fact ought to be a great joy to you, as it is to me.' In 1946, Hammerton estimated that fifty-two million volumes of the *Children's Encyclopædia* had been sold. It is still selling all over the world.

A telegram was handed to Alfred Harmsworth at Hurley, where he was staying with Reginald Nicholson, on the morning of December 9, 1905. It read: '*I am feeling very proud today fond love.—Mother.*' Her eldest son, the morning papers announced, had been raised to the ranks of newspaper peers. Once again, telegrams and letters of congratulation flowed into Carmelite House. Once again, there were murmurings of disapproval. What had Sir Alfred Harmsworth done to justify his elevation to the same lofty sphere as Sir Algernon Borthwick (Lord Glenesk) of the *Morning Post*, or Sir Edward Lawson (Lord Burnham) of the *Daily Telegraph*? He himself was more immediately concerned with the title which should appear in his letters patent: Lord Broadstairs or Lord Kingsgate? Young Evelyn Wrench, who had all the qualities of the perfect aide-de-camp, was kept running on armigerous errands between 'the Chief' and the College of Arms.

Lord Avebury, who, as Sir John Lubbock, had invented Bank Holidays and in doing so jeopardized the quieter amenities of more than the shores of Kent, wrote to him from 6 St. James's Square, London, S.W.: 'I hope you will not take the name of Kingsgate. Why not St. Peter's—a very pretty name, if you do not like the perhaps more imposing one of Broadstairs.' When someone else thought of Elmwood for his title, he pretended to shudder and said 'Goodness, no—it's the wood they use for coffins'. The name of 'Sir Alfred Harmsworth' was on the point of being displaced by 'Lord Broadstairs' when he was seized by the more euphonic inspiration of Northcliffe, taken from a neighbouring part of the coast. Evelyn Wrench was sent back to the College of Arms to register it on December 15. The right to flourish the Napoleonic cipher 'N' may have appealed to him more light-heartedly than some people were disposed to think because bees were incorporated in his coat-of-arms, like Napoleon's. The motto chosen for the barony was *Beni qui sedulo*, which a scholarly leader writer of Fleet Street rendered into 'Blessed is the busybody'.

'You are the youngest peer who has been created,' Balfour said to him, putting his arm round his shoulders and adding with an unexpected show of feeling: 'I am very proud of you!' Quoting an earlier remark of Alfred Harmsworth's that 'when I want a peerage I will pay for it like an honest man', the *History of The Times* states categorically: 'In fact he did pay for his peerage.' Aware of the source of the statement, Northcliffe's biographers are surprised that credence should have been given to it in that authoritative work. The most searching inquiry has disclosed no final reason for believing that he was party to such a transaction. Harold, who joined him in the House of Lords some years later, said: 'One of the advantages of being a newspaper proprietor is that you do not have to pay for a title if you want one.' It is more than likely that Alfred's provincial newspaper activities in 1905 were considered sufficient to justify an honour for which Balfour, as Prime Minister, presumably thought him already well qualified. He had been in close touch with Balfour and other leaders of the administration about the future of the *Manchester Courier*, and his investment in the newspaper group at Norwich represented a similar readiness of co-operation. His *Southern Daily Mail* venture may also have come into the reckoning. The *Manchester Courier*, published in the Conservative interest, involved him in a total cash outlay of nearly £50,000, which alone might have been counted the price of a barony. No profit came to him, either, from East Anglia.

A. J. Balfour to Lord Northcliffe:

Whittinghame,
Prestonkirk, N.B.
January 17, 1906.

My dear Lord Northcliffe,—The present situation profoundly interests me. In part the movement in the constituencies is no doubt due to the old familiar causes—the swing of the pendulum, and so forth, and, in so far as this is the case, there is nothing about it worthy of much more. But I am quite confident that there are much deeper causes at work than those with which, for the last 20 years, we have been familiar.

I regard the enormous increase in the Labour vote (an increase which cannot be measured merely by the number returned of Labour members strictly so-called) as a reflection in this country—faint I hope—of what is going on on the Continent; and, if so, 1906 will be remarkable for something much more important than the fall of a Government which has been 10 years in office!

Yours sincerely,

ARTHUR JAMES BALFOUR.

Northcliffe had come back from Monte Carlo for the general election, which swept the Liberals into power. He lunched with Joseph Chamberlain, had talks with Balfour, and supervised the public screening of the election results by *Daily Mail* magic lanterns operating on the Embankment and in Trafalgar Square. Coloured signal rockets fired from the highest roofs, to tell more distant watchers how the election was going, gave a carnival touch to a night which a visitor from abroad might have thought was dedicated to a great sporting event rather than a serious democratic process.

36, BERKELEY SQUARE.
W.

Your son's a peer. Just
had King's letter
AC

Will call one o'clock

Alfred's note to his mother, the day before the announcement of his elevation
to the peerage

Joseph Chamberlain to Northcliffe:

> Imperial Hotel,
> Torquay.
> February 3, 1906.

Private

My dear Northcliffe,—Balfour showed himself so determined against any advance in my direction last night, and was also cold to my suggestion of joint organisation, that I was forced to the conclusion that he has finally decided to stand with the Free Traders rather than with the Tariff Reformers. In any case, he will for the present continue the policy of the last two years which, in my judgment, has been injurious to the Party, the Cause and to himself.

I can't follow him on this path, but if he was to offer the leadership to Long [Walter Long, later Viscount Long of Wraxhall, Secretary of State for the Colonies] I see no reason why I should in that case hold aloof.

I doubt if this solution would commend itself to A.J.B., but I wanted you to know that, as far as I can command, I should see in it an acceptable arrangement.

> Yours very truly,
> J. CHAMBERLAIN.

*   *   *

'To Totteridge with Mother', Northcliffe noted in his diary on March 17, 1906. 'Mother's display of wild crocuses wonderful and she in great form.' He added: 'This is the first time I have touched my diary this year.' For months its entries had consisted merely of engagement notes kept by his worshipping personal secretary, George Mildred. After ten days the pages were blank again, except for monosyllabic entries such as 'Office', 'Sutton' and 'Elmwood'. Much of his time and attention was absorbed by the business of consolidating Associated Newspapers Ltd.

Late in June he sailed for New York, Boston, Montreal, Quebec and Newfoundland, a major trip of convalescence after a minor operation on his knee, performed by the eminent Sir Victor Horsley. It was to give him his first sight of Newfoundland, where Mayson Beeton and his pioneers of the Anglo-Newfoundland Development Company were laying out the site of a new town on the edge of the wilderness and harnessing a giant waterfall to the gargantuan Harmsworth appetite for paper. Northcliffe wrote to his mother, addressing her as 'Mummy dear', about the 'vast prosperity of Canada; no poor, homes for millions unborn'.

He had given power of attorney during his absence to Reginald Nicholson, whom he told to sell the Berkeley Square house as he was 'getting tired' of it. He complained that his sleep was disturbed in the early hours by a motor van grinding its way up the Square past the house. Nicholson was ordered to write to the police about it. They found that the van carried copies of the *Daily Mail* from Whitefriars Street to Paddington. Nicholson said that Northcliffe took the joke against himself 'very well—in fact he was delighted'. Nicholson was also instructed to pay £12,000 for a nine years' lease of 22 St. James's Place, once the home of Samuel Rogers, the banker-poet, whose 'breakfasts' became part of literary history. A charming small house overlooking the Green Park, sandwiched among the great town residences of the older nobility, its threshold had been crossed by Sir Walter Scott, Wordsworth, Coleridge, Sydney Smith, Byron, Turner and Dickens, some of the names on Rogers's lush visiting list. His friends called the house 'Memory Hall'. He lived there fifty years, surrounded by art and book treasures so numerous that when he died in 1855 Christie's took eighteen days to sell them. Northcliffe to Edmund Gosse, librarian of the House of Lords: '22 St. James's Place, S.W.—Leo Maxse told me that Austin Dobson is writing an article about our little place here. I wonder if you and he would do us the honour of lunching one day in the room where Byron met Lady Caroline Lamb.'

*   *   *

On the night of July 18, 1906, St. John Harmsworth was motoring back to his mother's house at Totteridge from Horsey Hall, Norfolk, where he had been staying with Harold. That day he had played several sets of tennis, one of the games at which he excelled. Tired, he gave over the wheel to his chauffeur. Near Hatfield, on the Great North Road, the chauffeur misjudged a corner and drove on to the verge. The car overturned, throwing St. John against a telegraph post. Recovering from the shock, he found that he was almost completely paralysed. He could not move a muscle or even close his eyes. A passing motor-cyclist undertook to ride into Hatfield for medical help. Dr Charles Hall, a local general practitioner, arriving on the scene, saw that nothing could be done. St. John's spine was fractured. He was taken with infinite care to a cottage across the road, where he was made comfortable on the parlour floor. He was forced to remain there several weeks, too dangerously hurt to be moved. The tenants were persuaded (and compensated) to leave. The cottage was taken over by doctors, with frequent visits from Harley Street specialists. When finally it was thought safe to take him to a London nursing home, he was packed in sand to protect him from being jolted. He never walked again. His life from then on was one of successive operations, frustrated hopes and splendid courage. He was an exemplary sufferer, facing the problems of his new existence with undaunted spirit. His expanding 'Perrier' business was controlled from a wheeled chair. The motor-cyclist who had brought aid to him as he lay on the roadside was an advertisement clerk, F. A. Procter, on the staff of Lever Brothers at Port Sunlight. For twenty-seven years thereafter he received an annuity of £52 from St. John Harmsworth, whom he never saw after the accident.

Receiving the news, Northcliffe had at once cut short his business trip in North America and returned to be with his crippled young brother. His care was as tender as a woman's. It was an affecting sight to see him cutting up St. John's food in hotel dining-rooms on their travels together. Writing to him, Northcliffe had usually addressed him as 'Dear Boy'. Now it was 'My dearest Boy'. There was a reference to his feelings in a letter from his aunt, Sarah Miller: 'I am so frightened you will forget me, you always have so much to think of, and now added to your cares is your terrible anxiety and loving care for dear Bonchie.'

★   ★   ★

Whether it was the spirit of Samuel Rogers still pervading 22 St. James's Place that inspired Northcliffe that autumn to start a regular *Daily Mail* supplement to be called 'Books' is a matter of conjecture. He had always insisted that books should be given what he called 'a good show' in the paper, which picked out new works of literature for review by distinguished critics of the day. His literary supplement was applauded by authors and publishers but it did not succeed, probably because he had put Edmund Gosse in charge of it. Gosse wrote to him after six months: 'In a less depressed time of the publishing trade, and when there are fewer distracting and depressing influences abroad, I am sure that our experiment would have had a commercial success. In younger hands than mine, it may yet have.' Gosse was followed by Archibald Marshall, newspaper correspondent turned novelist, whose personal problems created office difficulties, and Ford Madox Hueffer, another staff man, added to Northcliffe's increasing boredom with the supplement. For him there were always distractions at hand and he was giving attention just then to procuring the release of Colonel Arthur Lynch, who raised an Irish battalion to fight with the Boers and who was the last British subject up to that time to be condemned for high treason. Lynch, a man of good intellect, had worked on the *Evening News*. While not condoning his military activities, Northcliffe continued to be a friend to him. He provided for Lynch's wife and children throughout his imprisonment.

That autumn of 1906 Santos Dumont, whom Northcliffe had seen flying a dirigible at Monte Carlo, made the first recorded European flight in a heavier-than-air machine, covering twelve yards, following it with another flight of two hundred and fifty yards. Northcliffe was angry because his newspapers neglected what to him was an epoch-making occurrence. A Scots sub-editor, on late night duty, 'afflicted', Northcliffe said, 'with the caution of his race', had condensed the report of the second flight into a four-line paragraph for the 'News in Brief' column. Telephoning from Elmwood to the news editor at his home early next morning, Northcliffe demanded: 'Don't you realize, man, that England is no longer an island?' He challenged public interest everywhere by offering a prize of £10,000 for a flight from London to Manchester. *The Star* derisively offered £10,000,000 to any airman who flew five miles. *Punch* joined the gleeful chorus, offering large rewards for a flight to the moon. A *Daily Mail* leading article which suggested that 'some considerable time' would pass before England's insularity was finally threatened brought a telegram of rebuke from Northcliffe to its writer, H. W. Wilson. In another eleven years German aircraft were crossing the shores of England to drop bombs on London. It was Northcliffe who suggested a *Daily Mail* model aeroplane competition that year. The flights were made at the Alexandra Palace, North London, with twisted elastic supplying the motive power. In default of a first prize winner, a special award of £75 was made for the best performance to a young engineer named A. V. Roe. His 'Avro' company was to become one of the great names in the British aircraft industry.

On December 1, 1906, the *Daily Mail* announced an edition for the country's 40,000 blind persons. It was Northcliffe's own idea, carried out by Evelyn Wrench. An edition in Braille was set up by blind compositors and the proof readers were also blind men. The business experts at Carmelite House pointed out that the edition could never be run at a profit, but Northcliffe insisted on its publication. It was continued at a loss for eight years, until the outbreak of the 1914 war. He was proud of being its originator and referred to it with manifest satisfaction in more than one of his office bulletins.

F. W. Wile, *Daily Mail* correspondent in Berlin, to Northcliffe (April 29, 1907):

It was intimated to me today, indirectly, that the British ambassador in Berlin is not pleased with the 'zeal' with which the *Daily Mail* has followed the inception and course of the reigning spell of Anglophobia in Germany. I have borne vividly in mind an injunction of yours, given in the midst of our walk through the grounds of Sutton Place last September, that the *Daily Mail* representative in Berlin is not expected to get his political inspiration from His Majesty's Embassy. I can readily understand why diplomats would prefer that we pay no attention to the press campaign against England that has been so incessantly in progress here, but I have never been able to reconcile their desires with my obligation to report glaringly obvious facts.

Northcliffe complained of 'burning' eyes and went to see a specialist, Anderson Crichett, who upset him by suggesting that he might have to have an operation and in the meanwhile prescribed glasses. Another medical consultant, James Goodhart, talked to him about sleep. 'Take what sleep comes to you. You can do on four and a half hours', and there was doubtless no logical consequence in the letter he received the next day from Mrs Alice Stuart Wortley, a diligent political hostess, addressing him as 'Poor dear Napoleon'. She complained that he did so little to encourage her desire 'to bring sympathetic people together'. His social elusiveness troubled other ardent hostesses. He disliked dinner parties and the affectations of formality. Also, he was not a gifted conversationalist but an interesting talker who was apt to fall into long silences after pronouncing upon whatever topic was in the air. The author of *The Green Carnation* and *The Garden of Allah*, Robert Hichens, who was almost a professional diner-out, said that he only once met Northcliffe at dinner outside his own home. Then, 'everybody was amazed'. Northcliffe also had a habit of excusing himself at the last minute from his wife's evening arrangements with the increasingly unconvincing explanation: 'I must go and put the paper to bed.'

Through Pomeroy Burton, the former New York *World* news editor who had recently joined the *Daily Mail* as an executive with unspecified powers, another newcomer from America arrived that year on Northcliffe's personal staff, Alfred Butes, an Englishman who for some years had been confidential secretary to Joseph Pulitzer, the New York newspaper proprietor, who had made him one of his trustees. Butes knew all Pulitzer's private business and was practically irreplaceable in that role. Pulitzer never forgave Northcliffe for a defection which had in fact been originated by Butes himself. He had begun life as a young reporter on the *Salisbury & Winchester Journal* and wanted to work in England again. A persistent frock-coat wearer with the solemn air of a Sunday School superintendent, he moved about his business with silent efficiency, taking care to contract no awkward alliances and consequently being regarded with distrust by those around him. 'The best secretary God ever made', was Northcliffe's ultimate verdict.

Northcliffe was away from England for much of 1907. It was understood in his offices that his eyes were in need of rest from the clamant demands of the printed word; also, that the doctors had urged him to go slower for his general health's sake. There was a still more pressing reason for his absence from London that summer. The *Daily Mail* and its associated papers were being sued for libel by Lever Brothers, the soap makers, and by a number of smaller firms in the industry. Northcliffe's solicitor advised that he had better remain beyond the reach of the process servers. He wrote a hurried undated note to Sutton from Paris:

I urged K. J. to stop soap on score that I cannot carry increasing burden of work, unless free from all complications. Told him none of us can be cross-examined on motives of soap cases and that if I am examined should be obliged to tell truth and that therefore Sir G. L. [Sir George Lewis, solicitor] had from outset decided that I could not be put into box. Nor could, in my view, he [K. J.].

The *Daily Mail* and its associated newspapers had been attacking Levers' proposed soap trust. Northcliffe's knowledge of America, and perhaps even more his friendship with Theodore Roosevelt, the 'trust buster', had made him suspicious of trusts, in spite of his own rationalizing attitude to newspaper publishing. He did not believe that such concentrations of industrial and economic power were necessarily in the public interest and might be against it. A subjoined prejudice was his resentment of the increasing use of American capital in English undertakings, such as underground railways, shipping lines and tobacco companies. A bank failure in New York, followed by a Wall Street panic, had adversely affected the London markets. The bank rate rose to seven per cent. There was a slump in trade. Northcliffe was unfavourably disposed towards American financial and business methods. 'We already have the tobacco trust operating here,' he said, 'Where is it going to end?' There was another reason for objecting to the Lever amalgamations. They would reduce overheads and, inevitably, advertising expenditure.

If Levers were justified in improving their trading position, he was equally entitled to defend his interests. He launched the campaign with 'muck-raking' enthusiasm. Levers were cheating the poor. They were using unsavoury substances in soap making. Their schemes would throw large numbers of people out of employment. They were cornering raw materials. The attacks, carried on day after day in the *Daily Mail*, the *Evening News* and the *Daily Mirror*, were conducted 'in the public interest' under headlines which punched home the Lever menace: 'Squeezing the Public', 'Cruel Blow to the Poor', 'How Fifteen Ounces make a Pound', 'Trust Soap Already Dearer'. The *Daily Mirror* cartoonist, W. K. Haselden, had fun with 'Port Moonshine' and readers were urged not to buy 'Sunlight' soap. Levers' sales fell sixty per cent. Their two million preference shares dropped heavily. A *Daily Mail* front page heading told the nation: 'Public Opinion Smashed the Soap Trust.'

Lever (later Lord Leverhulme) went to his lawyers, who consulted F. E. Smith (later Lord Birkenhead). They asked for an immediate opinion. After a day's hunting in Leicestershire, Smith sat up all night with a mass of documents, a bottle of champagne and two dozen oysters, producing the result of his cogitations by breakfast time. 'There is no answer to this action for libel and the damages must be enormous.' They proved to be the largest ever awarded by a British jury up to that time. The litigation dragged on through many months, with Carson appearing for Lever (not for Northcliffe, as *The Times* official history states) and Rufus Isaacs (later the first Marquess of Reading) for the *Daily Mail*. The reading public found it almost as enthralling as the celebrated Druce case which came later in the year. At the opening trial, held at Liverpool Assizes in July 1907, the jury awarded Lever Brothers Ltd. damages of £50,000. Gloom settled like a pall over Carmelite House when the news came through. Reporting the verdict, the *Daily Mail* said that 'a somewhat embittered controversy' had been entered on in 'a no doubt mistaken sense of public duty'. *Truth* got a laugh at Northcliffe's expense by parodying a famous cartoon in which a tramp was seen writing a testimonial to the makers of Pears' Soap: 'Six weeks ago I *abused* your soap, since when I have *abused* no other.'

By an extraordinary mischance, the *Daily Mail* solicitors and counsel did not ensure that the settlement terms marked on the brief were final. It left the Lever people free to issue a series of minor writs. As a friend of both parties, Sir Thomas Lipton, the tea merchant, went to Lever with the suggestion: 'Aren't you pressing the Harmsworths a bit hard?' Lever demanded £30,000 to dispose of the last of his actions. Lipton said that the Harmsworths might be willing to pay £20,000: 'What do you say to that?' Lever went to his desk and scribbled a note: '£40,000 and costs.' Handing it to Lipton, he said 'My last word'. 'But you have already suggested thirty thousand,' Lipton said, surprised. 'You didn't agree, so it's gone up', said Lever laconically. Lipton went back to Northcliffe, whose answer was: 'Very well. We'll fight.' Lever did not get his £40,000. The jury awarded him £500. 'Frankly, the result was a great triumph for you. This is very private,' Lever's counsel, F. E. Smith, wrote to Northcliffe. 'None was more disgusted than I at another *rechauffé*, especially after the extraordinarily liberal offer your people made.' Smith, familiarly known as 'F.E.', and Northcliffe were secretly meeting through the later proceedings, which 'F.E.' had hoped to round off, he said, by 'a final and friendly dinner' with Northcliffe and Lever at the table. He wrote to Northcliffe: 'If you feel that you have placed yourself at any disadvantage by discussing the case intimately with me, I am quite willing to withdraw from it—if you don't, I hope you will let us meet anyhow, for, God knows, there are many subjects of interest to discuss besides soap.' He also asked Northcliffe to realize 'that we lawyers are made for man and not man for us lawyers' (April 19, 1909). Notes made by Northcliffe's confidential secretary suggest that Smith was particularly anxious not to forfeit Northcliffe's good will and support in politics. 'He can help me greatly', presumably meaning Northcliffe. 'L.', presumably Lever, 'of no use to me. I don't want his money. Would much rather never have seen him.'

Certain smaller firms had been encouraged by Lever's example to follow suit, piling up damages and costs to a total of £151,000. Discussing the cases with Carson some time afterwards, Northcliffe remarked: 'You're the biggest enemy I ever had.' Carson retorted: 'Why didn't you employ me, then? I daresay you'd have won.'

While the ultimate responsibility was his own, Northcliffe appears to have pondered the position of his chief editor, Marlowe. A letter from H. W. Wilson, the *Daily Mail* chief leader writer, had a cause to plead: 'I do hope that you will do all you can for so faithful and devoted a servant as Marlowe. As I have known you so well, I feel sure you will be magnanimous, the more so as I have received so many kindnesses from you, and know what you really are. I quite agree with what you said, that the libels must be stopped.' For Marlowe it was a possibly anxious time. His political decisions had not pleased Northcliffe, who was particularly critical of a *Daily Mail* attack on Winston Churchill. Marlowe felt obliged to reply: 'I have carried on your paper, sometimes under circumstances of great difficulty, for eight years and I have always endeavoured to carry out your wishes when I have been informed of them. When I have not been so informed I have acted according to the best of my judgment and ability and I must have failed lamentably if there is any justice in the criticisms you now make.' Marlowe suggested that Northcliffe's own judgment had been prejudiced 'by recent events', presumably a reference to the soap case. 'I think you have been a little depressed and this probably makes you feel things more than you otherwise would.'

It seems that Marlowe's tact hid grave doubts about Northcliffe's judgment. According to a letter written by Marlowe to a friend nearly twenty-five years after, his faith in Northcliffe had been severely shaken. He claimed from that distant standpoint: 'Northcliffe conducted that affair personally', meaning the campaign against Lever, 'and everybody concerned in it who published the things he told them, taking their truth for granted, was badly let down'. 'Afterwards', Marlowe wrote, 'it was the rule among my staff that anything coming from him must be verified with extra care.'

Harold Harmsworth, more depressed than his brother and anxious about the balance sheet, urged that there must be economies: 'Every expense of the company should be cut down to the bone.' He ran into trouble when he also urged that the cost of the law suits should come out of profits. There was a protest in the name of members of the staff at Carmelite House. John Cowley, one of the directors, wrote to Northcliffe: 'The deduction of Soap expenses from the profits would mean, approximately, cutting in half the year's income of nearly all the recipients under the profit-sharing arrangement.' Northcliffe came to the rescue by paying a considerable part of the damages out of his own pocket. At Carmelite House, the shadow of the soap litigation lay heavily across the year.

Chapter Twelve

Printing House Square

THE Henley House pupil who had written in the school magazine about the majesty of *The Times* had transmuted his patriotic glow into a recurring dream of ownership. In the year of his starting the *Daily Mail*, 1896, he had spoken to H. W. Wilson of his resolve to become the arbiter of the paper's power and fortunes. 'He made no secret of it,' Wilson wrote, 'and often referred to it after 1900.'

In those first years of the new century there were many rumours that *The Times* was changing hands. Andrew Carnegie was named as one of the possible proprietors, so was Alfred Harmsworth. As has been recorded, he made direct approaches to the Walter family who owned the paper. In 1906 the rumours so strongly connected him with the paper's future that a new Liberal newspaper, *The Tribune*, was started with a view to rivalling *The Times* in quality and importance, it being confidently expected that *The Times* would deteriorate under his hand. That dangerous fancy cost its backers more than £350,000 in two years, by which time *The Tribune* declined into being merely a background for a popular novel of newspaper life, *The Street of Adventure*, by Philip Gibbs.

The rumours were based on the known fact that *The Times* was in low water as a business concern, though its reputation was still high in the world. The story of its rise from modest beginnings as *The Daily Universal Register* of 1785 is traced in great detail and with complete authority in the *History of The Times*, written, printed and published at Printing House Square (1935–1952). Its founder was John Walter, a prosperous coal merchant who had failed as an underwriter at Lloyd's. It was called *The Times* from 1788. The second John Walter, who took the paper over in 1803, was a man of exceptional force of character, courageous and independent, contending against Pitt and his Government and standing out as an exemplary figure in an age of servility. By introducing steam printing he initiated revolutionary changes in newspaper production. He brought in two great editors, Thomas Barnes, 1817 to 1841, and John Thadeus Delane, 1841 to 1877. Both were exceptional journalists. Walter and they were powerfully united in a policy governed by one thought and rule, the national interest. Those three men made the world's greatest newspaper.

The pre-eminence they created had lasted until the early 1880s. By then, other newspapers were challenging *The Times*. *The Standard* and the *Daily Telegraph* became serious competitors, while the *Morning Post*, nearest rival of *The Times*, dealt it a blow by dropping in price from threepence to a penny. Bad advice let the paper in for the long and extremely expensive Parnell Commission of 1888 and after, with resulting ill effects on its reputation. Gravely weakened, the paper did not respond to the introduction of new machinery or to the enterprise which exploited the then despised telephone as a means of quicker communication. The till at Printing House Square was often short of cash. In 1898, two American business men, Horace Hooper and W. M. Jackson, arranged that *The Times* should sponsor the ninth edition of the *Encyclopædia Britannica* at a reduced price. It had been completed in 1889, and brought up to date by supplementary volumes. Pushed by *The Times*, what was known as the tenth edition sold well and, as the outcome of a sort of partnership with the two promoters, the paper received enough money to pay its bills through a critical period. Many old readers were embarrassed by the transaction. One of them was Max Pemberton, who wrote:

Well do I recollect being startled at eleven o'clock at night by a telegram which met me in a lonely part of Suffolk. The reply to it was paid, and the messenger despatched by the local post office believed that it was mightily urgent. I found in it an intimation that my last chance of obtaining the *Encyclopædia Britannica* expired at noon the following day. It was signed 'Manager of *The Times*, Printing House Square, London.' Many thousands of these telegrams had gone over the wires that night, scaring invalids in their beds, and the source of alarm to many innocent people. Not only this, but those who lived in remote districts often had to pay a heavy surcharge for the delivery of the far from exciting tidings.

A more ambitious book-selling experiment embarked on in the paper's name in 1905 was a further shock to the sensibilities of those to whom *The Times* was a sacred institution. Hooper and Jackson organized *The Times* Book Club, which offered its subscribers at £3 18s. a year a daily copy of the paper and access to all the new books, with the right of purchase of any new book after a certain period. Soon what was known as 'the book war' raged in London, with the Publishers' Association, the

Booksellers' Association and several authors formed up in battle array against Printing House Square. The publishers stopped supplies of books to the Club and took their advertising away from *The Times*. While the Book Club did not succeed as a method of bringing in many new readers of *The Times*, it rendered some service to the publishing trade and so to authorship. The press of 'carriage folk' outside its premises at 93 New Bond Street is still remembered by old subscribers.

Those extraneous activities were intended to restore the financial standing of *The Times*. To some of the paper's numerous proprietors they seemed not only infelicitous but positively injurious aids to recovery. As a property, *The Times* had been divided by the first John Walter into two clear-cut parts, the newspaper and the printing works. The first part had been divided into sixteen shares, subdivided over the years into numerous smaller parts, each with unlimited liability. The printing business, with its machinery and the freehold premises at Printing House Square, remained the property of the Walter family. In 1885, there were a hundred owners of shares or parts of shares in the newspaper, with Arthur Walter, appointed by deed sole manager of *The Times*, receiving on behalf of his family £32,000 a year, in good years and bad. In earlier times, the amount had been as high as £80,000 a year, halved between the Walters, as printers and publishers, and the owners of *The Times* shares. In the 1880s and 1890s, while the Walters continued to draw their considerable annual income from printing and publishing the paper, the shareholders received less and less for their interest in it, in some instances nothing.

In 1906, Dr Knowsley Sibley, whose mother, Mrs Clara Sibley, had been in touch with Alfred Harmsworth in 1898, issued a writ against the reigning Walter, asking leave to procure a full statement of affairs, 'and a declaration that the property be transferred to a limited liability company' (*History of The Times*). Sibley was staunchly backed by Miss Brodie-Hall, another of the shareholders and a relative of the Walters. It was the beginning of a series of protests which the dissidents succeeded in working up into what was virtually an anti-Walter crusade. On July 31, 1907, the Chancery court ordered the dissolution of *The Times* partnerships and the disposal of the assets, property and effects of the newspaper through a judge in chambers.

*　　　*　　　*

One night in the latter part of 1907, the Northcliffes dined at the house of Sir Alexander Henderson, a City financial expert who became Lord Faringdon. He was an adviser of Pearson and a backer of his newspaper enterprises. There was fog, and Northcliffe, always the unwilling diner-out, asked his wife to make their excuses. When it was mentioned that

Paderewski had promised to play the piano after dinner, Northcliffe changed his mind. There was talk during the evening about the impending amalgamation of two leading railway companies. 'And', it was remarked casually, '*The Times* with *The Standard*.' *The Standard* was one of Pearson's papers and the remark was not lost on Northcliffe, who telephoned his solicitor, Lewis, the first thing next morning. 'Find out what you can,' he said. Lewis went to Moberly Bell, the manager of *The Times*, who replied that he had heard nothing of the proposed amalgamation. Northcliffe would not let the matter rest there. Twelve years later, writing to a member of *The Times* staff, G. Murray Brumwell, Northcliffe recalled: 'Lord Faringdon nearly became the Proprietor of *The Times*, and but for a chaffing remark made to me by Lord Stuart of Wortley, he *would* have been the Proprietor.'

Leaving for France, he charged Sutton to keep in close touch with Lewis. Sutton pursued his own line of inquiry and soon discovered that plans were well advanced for Pearson to take over *The Times* as part of a newspaper group which he was to control. *The Times* chief proprietor, Arthur Walter, had been secretly negotiating with Pearson. Neither Moberly Bell, the manager, nor G. E. Buckle, the editor, had been taken into his confidence. Buckle to Arthur Walter (January 6, 1908): 'It has been a shock to me, as the principal servant of the Paper, and your friend of nearly thirty years' standing, that you should arrange to bring an outsider into the heart of the office . . . without consulting me.'

A paragraph in *The Observer* on January 5, 1908, had told the world that 'important negotiations' affecting the future of *The Times* might 'place the direction in the hands of a very capable proprietor of several popular magazines and newspapers'. It was the first intimation that workers on *The Times* had of coming change. Those who did not think that Northcliffe was the proprietor referred to were prepared to believe, none the less, that his was the hand that wrote the paragraph for tactical if not mischievous purposes. They were right. He admitted it in a message to *The Times* office exactly a year later.* It was largely with an intention of depriving him of any possible advantage, as well as of disposing of rumours, that on January 7 an announcement about the negotiations was given in *The Times*. 'The business management will be reorganized by Mr C. Arthur Pearson, the proposed managing director.' The announcement was qualified by the proviso that court sanction might be required.

Pearson at least was confident. Messages of congratulation confirmed him in that state, none more so than one from Northcliffe, who suggested that he be interviewed for the *Daily Mail*. C. Arthur Pearson to Northcliffe:

---

* 'I put that paragraph in *The Observer* which exploded the Pearson *conspiracy*.' (The italics were Northcliffe's.) January 4, 1909.

The Standard, London, E.C.
January 7th, 1908.

My dear Northcliffe,

I am very sorry to have refused, but I believe you will realise the position I am placed in. All this publicity for me is rubbing things in very much so far as the Walters are concerned, and from the point of their feelings I do not want to be seeming to push myself at all. Believe me, I very much appreciate all that you have done, and I will be very glad, if you still think it worth while, to have a talk with the *Daily Mail* after I have been in *The Times* office a few days. . . .

Northcliffe's response took the form of an article about Pearson the following day. It quoted Chamberlain's eulogy of Pearson as 'a hustler', a commendation unlikely to win the hearts of the *Times* proprietors, its staff or its readers.

It was on that same day, January 8, that Sutton wrote to Northcliffe outlining the terms of the reorganization. Sutton's letter did not suggest that Northcliffe was urgently concerned at that stage. 'If you thought anything of it, I could run over and tell you the whole business', which does not support the *Times* historian's implication of subtle manipulations by Northcliffe from the beginning. Sutton had heard that some of the *Times* shareholders would resist the proposed arrangements. It was on that basis that he thought 'the Chief' might be interested.

An article inspired by Northcliffe in *The Observer* on January 12 was likewise construed as an attempt to undermine confidence in Pearson. 'Mr Pearson is still young; he is a little over forty. . . . He has done strong as well as sensational things.' He was congratulated on his business acumen. 'Mr Pearson has the opportunity of his life and it is evidently quite baseless to imagine he will set himself to fail in the most obvious of all ways by playing it too low.' Kennedy Jones put it on record that the article sincerely represented Northcliffe's views. 'It was not a blind to enable him to get behind a rival, as it has been often and most unfairly asserted' (*Fleet Street and Downing Street*, 1920). Alfred Butes, the confidential secretary, was with Northcliffe at the Pavilion Hotel, Folkestone, staying overnight on their way to France. Butes said that they spent the evening 'writing out a long and amusing article' about the competition for *The Times*. 'It was a piece of camouflage, a smoke-screen for Northcliffe himself.' The article was sent by train to Sutton in London early the next morning, with instructions that he should deliver it personally to Garvin, for the following Sunday's *Observer*. 'Where did this come from?' Garvin asked Sutton. Sutton answered: 'It blew in the window.'

Kennedy Jones wrote that he had considered ways and means of gaining control of *The Times* for his own purposes. He discussed them (according to his account) with Lord Curzon, to whom he proposed the editorship. Curzon declined, whereupon Jones telegraphed to Northcliffe in France:

Are you prepared to come into a deal which will upset negotiations eventually acquiring business ourselves? Profits on paper have for eight years never been below thirty thousand scheme would require three fifty thousand ... would have to be carried through by some big man or syndicate who would save organization for Empire Sutton can start tonight.

Pearson was busily making his dispositions. He had ordered his head printer to 'take over' at Printing House Square by a given date and was forming a general staff to assist him in his task of rejuvenating the greatest of all newspapers by incorporating it with *The Standard*. There is a surviving memory of a dinner to mark his impending arrival in Printing House Square. The Savoy Hotel chef reproduced the *Times* clock in ice as a table centrepiece. It was a singularly ironic symbol of Pearson's hopes, for the manager of *The Times*, C. F. Moberly Bell, was secretly engaged in a transaction which would bring them to nothing.

Moberly Bell's loyalty to *The Times* was as fiercely exacting of himself as of those around him. In his devotion to the paper he was wholehearted and selfless. He was never in favour of Pearson as controller and energetically applied himself to obstructing that possibility when it was made obvious that there would be no place for him in the Pearson hierarchy. He had good cause for resentment at the governing proprietor's action in publishing the notice of January 7. It virtually deprived him of his public standing as the *Times* manager. When Harcourt Kitchin, of the city office, asked him: 'What are you going to do about this Pearson business?' Bell replied: 'Smash it.'

Bell's personality dominated the transformation scene in negotiations which now seem to have contained a number of pantomime effects. Limping slightly from an old accident, he looked like a professional conspirator who had no need to wear a cloak. The illusion owed something to his powerfully curved nose and piercing eyes set in a sallow complexion which some people wrongly ascribed to eastern origins. He was born in Egypt of English parentage and environment had counterfeited heredity. He was a man of energy and gusto who contrived to make his most trivial acts seem significant. Roused to indignation, especially over a moral issue, he could be formidable. He worked long hours, never took a holiday, and never seemed tired. Like others on the *Times* staff, he retained a touch of the amateur and it did not endear him to men like Northcliffe and Kennedy Jones that he hated the telephone, despised secretarial help and wrote his letters by hand.

In 1908 he conceived it to be his supreme duty to save *The Times* and not from Pearson alone. There were reasons for believing that alien interests were lurking in the wings. An American syndicate was supposed to be putting on pressure. The shadow of cosmopolitan finance fell across the stage. Bell let Wickham Steed, *The Times* correspondent in Vienna, know that a group, 'supported by Britons of the name of Koch and Speyer', were seeking to gain control. Steed's reply was a footnote to later European history:

I fear Speyer and Koch. Even if they have no direct commission from the German Government, they are German Jews, and five years' experience here has taught me one thing: for some unexplained reason, interest, clannishness, unconscious linguistic or racial fanaticism, every Jew in this part of the world is a strong pro-German who looks towards Berlin as the Musselman towards Mecca. I have studied them, high and low, rich and poor, learned and ignorant —in their heart of hearts they are pro-German to a man.

Steed felt so strongly that he proposed, 'as an extreme resource', that the staff should revolt or strike 'in case of purchase by the Speyer's or by the Sibley-Pearson gang'. Northcliffe told Ellis Powell, a financial journalist: 'Emil Koch was not the only foreigner who made us fearful', and twelve months afterwards he let it be known in a message to the *Times* office that Koch was 'one of those who negotiated for *The Times* on behalf of the Japanese Government'. Meanwhile, Bell came to the conclusion that the great thing was to save *The Times* from the Walters.

He had not been immediately ready and willing to work with Northcliffe. He tried to find more congenial backing, but he had no gift for high finance and little understanding of the subtler ramifications of business thought. In his dilemma, he 'hit upon one expedient to help him to a decision', his daughter wrote (*The Life and Letters of Moberly Bell*, 1927):

He made a list in alphabetical order of all the prominent people known to possess sufficient wealth to be possible purchasers of *The Times*, and submitted it to Lord Cromer, to some of the Rothschilds, and to various other of his acquaintances whose judgement he trusted, asking them to cross off the names of any to whose connexion with *The Times* they would take serious exception. No one crossed off Northcliffe's name.

He had met Northcliffe two or three times, 'on pleasant terms', he recalled in a letter to Northcliffe. Now they were in touch again, brought together by Horace Hooper. Their opening interview in the negotiations took place at 38 Sackville Street, Piccadilly, where Northcliffe had taken offices for his private accountant, T. E. Mackenzie. Butes was there to receive Bell, who, he said, greeted Northcliffe bluntly. Butes then left them together. 'Mr Bell,' Northcliffe said, with equal bluntness, 'I am going to buy *The Times*. With your help, if you will give it to me. In spite of you, if you don't.' Moberly Bell answered: 'I will help you.' The interview was brief. Thereafter, the matter was carried along by Kennedy Jones, Sutton, Bell and by Northcliffe's solicitor, William Graham. A secret code of communication was agreed on. Northcliffe was 'Atlantic', Bell 'Canton', Kennedy Jones became 'Alberta' and Sutton 'Buffalo'. The name of Pearson was changed to Dawson in letters and telegrams.

Northcliffe conducted his side of the preliminary negotiations from the Hotel Crystal-Bristol, Boulogne, where he stayed under another name. Butes said that much of his time, over several weeks, was passed in coding and decoding telegrams. Northcliffe put it about that he was in the South of France, taking a rest cure. There was no sign of his adopting the Napoleonic stance, gazing with brooding eyes across the Channel and planning the invasion of Printing House Square. Bell, too, enjoyed using the apparatus of mystification. Later, he was delighted to tell others that vital messages at that time were passed to him by his wife in Arabic. In his years at *The Times*, he had always worked in his office with the door open. Now, for the first time, it was closed.

Fortified by Northcliffe's power, he had gone to the governing Walter with the information that he had succeeded in finding a more suitable backer than Pearson but could not for the time being disclose his name. Arthur Walter, harassed beyond his powers of resistance, accepted a situation which a stronger man would not have tolerated. He agreed to wait on Bell's deliberations, content with Bell's assurance: 'I am acting solely in what I believe to be the best interests of *The Times*.' Buckle, the editor, was still guessing. He believed that Hooper and Jackson, the Americans, were behind Bell, and he told Bell that it was a combination which he did not like. In fact, it was Hooper who in an introductory sense was behind Northcliffe. He had been in private talks with Kennedy Jones and had urged on Bell the advisability of working with Northcliffe.

New names gave life to the rumours—Lord Strathcona, Lord Brassey, Sir Hugh Bell, the Rothschilds, Lord Swaythling, Lord Iveagh and also Sir George Newnes, who promptly dispelled any idea that he was interested. Northcliffe himself had considered a scheme which would give Pearson the managing directorship 'under our guidance', telling Sutton: 'The *Mail* is in my judgment a very much greater power than *The Times* will ever be and we can make it an infinitely greater thing than it is.' Concluding his survey of the position as he saw it in the first days of the new year, he advised Jones and Sutton (January 9, 1908): 'Do not allow yourselves, either of you, to be carried away by zeal. Personally, as I told you here when you spoke to me two months ago, I am content with what we have. You have also to remember that anything either of you does will be ascribed to me. Walk warily.' Lord Esher, at 2 Tilney Street, Park Lane, made a diary note that week, after dining one night with John Morley at the Ritz: 'He told me a good thing of Lord Northcliffe. Someone, Donald, of the *Daily Chronicle*, I think, was saying how he proposed to run his paper on *sound* lines, no modern journalism, but good solid stuff, etc. "Yes," said N., "and, my dear fellow, why not print it in Gothic type?"'

Moberly Bell, writing to Northcliffe on January 29, recorded 'a singular change' in Walter's attitude to him, showing anxiety to get out of the Pearson agreement, and saying to Bell: 'Directly it is upset I shall come to you. Of course, I guess who it is, but I'm not going to say anything.' Bell asked Northcliffe where he could see him for a talk. 'Couldn't I go to some suburb and you pick me up in a motor—or will I come to you like Nicodemus by night!' He was able to report: 'I see no signs of being shadowed yet.' Harcourt Kitchin, who saw Bell frequently at that time, wrote that 'he entered so thoroughly into the spirit of the game and enjoyed every minute of it so wholeheartedly'.

Northcliffe himself entered so far into the spirit of it that he was prepared to mystify Bell. He came over to London on a secret flying visit without telling Bell. Having an easy adaptability to domestic circumstances, he stayed the night with the Suttons at their Belsize Park villa and, on a second trip, at Butes's flat. Bell wrote to him on January 30, stressing the 'secrecy' and 'mystery', and asking for more names to be added to their private code: 'Caesar'—General Sterling, a belligerent *Times* shareholder, and 'Naples'—William Sharp, solicitor, acting for Miss Brodie Hall. Bell wrote a letter to Sharp which had an important bearing on the paramount issue of who would finally direct the destiny of the newspaper. It was dated January 30, 1908.

Dear Mr Sharp,—Except that this letter, though written on official paper, is only the expression of my personal views and not as Manager of *The Times*, there is nothing in it which is private—to any one of the Proprietors.

The position is briefly this. *The Times* is a great national institution, first and foremost. I have given the last 18 years of my life wholly to its interests and if at any time during that period I could have furthered those interests by my retirement, I should have made the sacrifice without hesitation though not without regret. Compared to that big national interest, the claims of the Walters the Brodie Halls, the Sibleys or the Bells are not worth consideration.

I find those interests endangered by a deplorable Agreement with a Mr Pearson. If that agreement, or any other agreement, had been beneficial to *The Times*, I should have welcomed it, though it meant loss to all those other interests I have mentioned, including my own.

Because I know it spells disaster to the interests of *The Times*, I oppose it openly and avowedly. The fact that it is not beneficial even to the Walters, the Brodie Halls, the Sibleys and the Bells is a coincidence not affecting my attitude.

The extent of the disaster caused by that Agreement no one can judge but myself. I put it very moderately when I say that if on the 1st of January of this year *The Times* was worth £300,000, today it is not worth £200,000.

The great immediate question, Bell went on to assert, was how disaster could be avoided. 'If the only remedy possible involved the ruin of all the other interests I have mentioned, I would cheerfully support it.' He informed Sharp that he had 'been able to formulate' a scheme that would benefit all the proprietors in a way that none of the other schemes put forward could do. 'My scheme gives the present proprietors the first charge on all the assets, so that in the event of failure they remain the proprietors.' The earlier schemes gave first charge to those who found the cash. Still more important, Bell's plan stipulated that the whole political direction of the paper should remain in the hands of the existing staff and that the editorial side should be conducted on the same lines as before. Bell put it to Sharp:

If you and your clients have really at heart the continued existence of *The Times*, let me beg you to use your influence to put an end to these undignified squabbles between one section and another of the proprietors. If their object is simply and purely nothing but £. s. d., I cannot do more than tell them that every week that their quarrel is prolonged is costing them more than the most efficient management could replace in 3 months. It is no exaggeration to say that it will take 3 years to recover the damage done in the last 9 months.

Let them sink their personal grievances—which I admit exist—and unite for the *big interest*, which happens to be their own.

The solicitor replied on January 31, acknowledging Bell's 'admirable letter', and undertaking to try to 'bring about an early end of all the litigation', subject to Bell's readiness to supply proofs of his statements. Bell retorted that there was no statement that he could not prove, 'except of course those that refer to the future. Time will prove those.' To attain a final solution, he declared, 'I would sacrifice everything that I have.' His sincerity helped to bring about the unanimity indispensable to the negotiations at that point. It had been hardly less efficacious in his dealings with 'X', Bell's private pseudonym for Northcliffe, who already knew him for a man of principle. On February 9, Bell secured a written understanding to act as managing director of *The Times* for five years in the event of Northcliffe becoming the new governing proprietor. In the letter covering the arrangement Bell undertook to carry out Northcliffe's 'absolute instructions', on the assumption 'that the present policy of the paper in Home & Foreign affairs should be continued under the editorship of Mr Buckle and Mr Valentine Chirol', head of the foreign department. Bell had not lightly signed away authority to Northcliffe. But Northcliffe, through Sutton, made it clear that he would withdraw from the negotiations unless such an undertaking was given. Bell was faced with the danger that Pearson might come forward again and so he signed.

On February 20, solicitors issued a letter on behalf of Dr Sibley and his fellow dissenters. 'If anyone desired to make a proposal for the purchase of *The Times* and will send the proposal to us, it will duly be brought before the judge.' The *Daily Chronicle* referred to the announcement as being 'like a passage from a Gilbertian opera'. Sutton, hearing North-cliffe's name more often in talk about *The Times*, deliberately injected the name of Rothschild into the gossip. His daily reports to Northcliffe read like extracts from the minutes of meetings of a cabal. 'Alberta ['K.J.'] and I had a long interview this morning.' 'Adriatic [Sir George Lewis] arrives in London today.' 'Demerara [Jackson] has now 82 per cent of the proprietors in his favour.' 'There are many rumours that Atlantic [Northcliffe] is negotiating.' 'Calgary [Hooper] is in Paris to go to Fontainebleau. Please don't go there.'

On February 28, Sutton wrote that 'we have had some shocks'. Counsel had warned him that a shareholding minority might carry proceedings beyond chambers to the court of appeal. It was feared that Sir Alexander Henderson was preparing to submit a formidable offer. Miss Brodie-Hall had a scheme, drafted in association with Panmure, Gordon & Co., the City financing house. Sunday, March 1, according to Sutton, was 'such a day of excitement' that it was 'unsettling'. There had been telephoning all day, 'and hasty consultations in out of the way streets'. Henderson had been in personal touch with Walter (Manitoba), who now said that he wanted no scheme which included Dawson (Pearson), whereupon Hender-son had said: 'Very well, let us eliminate Dawson.' On that, Walter con-sulted his solicitor, Soames (Navarino), who advised him to be 'very careful lest there was a trick'. So the game was played, with Northcliffe far from poker-faced but giving few signs of overwhelming desire to lay his hand on the prize. He was still keeping in the background, his identity as a bidder still kept secret by Bell. On March 8 he wrote to Bell that he had returned from the Continent because he had heard that Walter had given assurances that he was not the person concerned in the offer which was to go before the court. 'As you know, I am that person', and he told Bell that if the court approved the offer he would not wish Walter to be in ignorance of his identity. 'I beg that you will at once therefore inform him. In the interests of the anonymity of the paper, I think that the in-formation should be confined for some years to Mr Walter only.' Bell gave the information to Walter under a pledge of secrecy, which Walter immediately broke by telling Godfrey and John Walter and, after them, Buckle.

Writing to Butes, Northcliffe's 'cover' man, Bell said that Walter's indiscretion had made him 'mad', and that he was 'sick of the whole d——d thing'. Mrs Walter had been to London specially to see him, bringing her husband's apologies and promising that he would 'never do it again, that he would stay at his house until I told him that he might come in to town. He would see no one and write to no one.' Mrs Walter told Bell that her husband 'was crushed and unaccountable'. He was un-doubtedly a sick man. But Bell thought fit to close his letter to Butes with he comment: 'What can one do with such idiots!' The next day, March 13, he telegraphed to Northcliffe through Butes: *Have effectually prevented further leakage have got him safely away.* For Bell, it had been a bad time. He was disinterested in motive but his career was in the balance. He had been deeply disturbed. He continued to put the paper first. He asked Butes to tell Northcliffe on March 13: 'I want you in no way to consider me. Whatever the result, you have treated me generously and as squarely as I have treated you. I only regret that I had to deal with such a hopeless fool on the other side.'

The devious course of the bargaining for *The Times* is followed with exactitude in the official history, which with curious obtuseness refers to Northcliffe throughout the negotiations as Harmsworth. Sutton reported to Northcliffe on March 15 that the previous day Pearson had told Hooper at lunch that he had 'found out in time to get out', the crucial discovery being that 'the finance of *The Times* was too unsatisfactory'. Sutton added: 'There have been many suggestions as to the ownership, but Alberta ['K.J.'] and I have been busy spreading the Rothschild version.' At Sutton's club, the Devonshire, it was confidently being said that the new owner was Northcliffe, and Sutton affirmed: 'I think I have been useful there.' Garvin had told him: 'There is a strong impression at Printing House Square that it is Northcliffe.'

★   ★   ★

The small green japanned deed-box which went everywhere with him was full of letters to be answered. Henry Klein, retired music publisher, wrote:

The Bays,
Burwood Park Road,
Walton-on-Thames.
8th March, 1908.

My dear Lord Alfred,—Some time ago you asked me if I had any early writings of yours. Looking through old letters, it seems to me like yesterday, so vividly are those scenes before my mind—what happy times they were on the Holborn Viaduct when you came to see me every day. I remember when you brought me the first proof of 'Answers To Correspondents' to read, and the first 'Puzzle,' which we tried while at lunch next door (Spiers & Pond's).

What a good friend you have been to me! What and where would I be without you!

If you have a late likeness of yours to spare, I should so much like to have one. I have only the one with the terrier.

God bless you, dearest friend, with the best of health and contentment.

Your affectionately grateful
HENRY KLEIN

317

Rufus Isaacs was importuning him again on behalf of his sister: 'She is very anxious to do some editorial work for you.' The vicar of St Saviour's Poplar, to whose yearly stipend Northcliffe contributed £50, inquired when he might expect the next instalment. Robert Donald, editor of the *Daily Chronicle*, apologized for publishing comments on the peerage, about which Northcliffe had complained. There was correspondence to be dealt with regarding the possibilities of the sands at Skegness as a scene of aeroplane trials. Gaston Mayer, director of the Theatre Française at the New Royalty Theatre, London, regretted that his experiment there had failed, in spite of 'your lordship's personal and generous support', which cost Northcliffe several hundred pounds. Frank Millar, Glendower, Chiswick Lane, London, W., alleged anti-Catholic bias in the *Children's Encyclopædia*. Ford, the Kilburn printer of the Henley House School Magazine, was in dire distress and begging for help. L. J. Maxse, editor of the *National Review*, deplored Northcliffe's absence from the country 'as a real national calamity', at a time when the First Lord of the Admiralty, Tweedmouth, was obsequiously corresponding with the Kaiser about the Royal Navy. 'It is the greatest outrage that has happened in our time. I did not know where to communicate with you and felt quite helpless.'

Northcliffe to his mother:

Versailles.
14th March, 1908.

Darling Mumlo,—We are still continuing our vagabondage and at present are at the Hotel des Reservoirs, where you and I lunched and where I should very much like to stay with you some time this year. I can imagine nothing more happy than that we two should be wandering about the Park and Palace.

Exactly when we shall return depends upon events with which I shall acquaint you and of which you know the purport. So far those affairs go well, though there have been, already, rumours of indiscreet talk on the part of the members of our family—who certainly *know* nothing. The very appearance of your firstborn on the scene in a struggle of this kind brings in others. 'What is good enough for Lord N.,' they say, 'is good enough for us.'

We may move away from here on Tuesday. All depends on events as I have said. We are most anxious that if the thing is accomplished it shall not be known for several years, until we have had time to demonstrate that we are not so erratic as our enemies suppose.

I hope all is well at Poynters. I shall be very glad when I am able to relinquish the life of an exile.

Your devoted
FIRSTBORN

Bell had himself taken the draft sale contract to Versailles for Northcliffe's signature. Northcliffe peeped through the keyhole of Bell's bedroom at the hotel. 'He was lying fast asleep, worn out with his journey and industry.' He had left London at 9 p.m., crossed to Paris, arriving at 5 a.m. He had slept till 10 a.m. and had then worked with Northcliffe until night, leaving for London at 9 p.m. Reaching Victoria station at 5 o'clock the next morning, he went straight to the *Times* office and worked until 7 p.m. He was sixty-two. He telegraphed from London to Northcliffe at Versailles late in the afternoon of March 16, 1908: *Gone through as we wanted*. It was the end of the struggle for *The Times*. Northcliffe had won. It would prove to be a Pyrrhic victory.

The purchase price for the copyright of the newspaper and its allied publications was sanctioned by the judge at £320,000. To enable Bell to pay the full amount into court if required, Northcliffe placed cash to that value at the Bank of England in Bell's name. It was a superb gesture of confidence in Bell. 'I could go down with a sack, draw all that money out, and bolt with it,' he told Kitchin. His face glowing, he paid his tribute to Northcliffe: 'A splendid fellow! He insisted on depositing the money in my sole name.' Northcliffe afterwards explained that action. 'I wanted to show old Bell that I, at any rate, believed in him. He had made all sorts of conditions for *The Times* and for the staff, yet made no condition for himself. So I decided to hand the purchase money over to him. It was the least that I could do.' He told his solicitor, William Graham: 'Moberly Bell could easily have got the capital elsewhere.' When the deed was signed, Bell remarked to Northcliffe: 'I don't know *how* you will make it succeed, but I am sure you will.'

Northcliffe told his mother: '16th March, 1908.—I could not wire you that I have been successful in the matter that has engaged me so long and kept me abroad so much, as the Post Office is the sure way of revealing secrets; but I have just received a telegram saying so. I shall try to make my work worthy of you, my dear, but *it is a secret*.' Adelaide of Demerara (Hooper and Jackson) to Atlantic (Northcliffe): 'Monday evening, March 16, 1908.—Not only the British public, but all friends of Great Britain will some day know what a great good you have done for the nation.' Arthur Walter wrote to Bell that same day: 'Your telegram caused me great relief. I trust we shall have peace now.' Lady Northcliffe to Sutton: 'Tuesday [undated].—Hooray! I am glad—and I know you are too—glad that the strain is over. The Chief has been a perfect brick and borne the suspense wonderfully. It has been dreadfully trying for him being exiled while the fight was going on. It is so right that he should have this thing—he is the only person in the world who could run it!'

Bell's desk was piled with telegrams and letters of appreciation and congratulations from *The Times* well-wishers at home and abroad. To some of them he was the St. George of Fleet Street and Pearson the vanquished dragon. The messages gave no hint that any of them realized that Northcliffe was the new force behind the paper. Soon after the completion of the purchase, Bell wrote to Lady Northcliffe asking her acceptance of a souvenir, 'as a token of gratitude I shall always feel to your husband for his whole action towards an institution with which I have been so long associated that I regard it as a part of myself!' There were others in the office who were grateful to Northcliffe, Bell testified, 'even without knowing his name, for the consideration he has shown throughout this period of transition'. The secret was so well kept that Admiral Sir John Fisher wrote to him from the Admiralty on July 23, in the course of a letter referring to 'this entrancing new vista of wireless in sea war', making the suggestion: 'Why don't you buy *The Times* and make Garvin editor? That would be Napoleonic in conception and Cromwellian in thoroughness! Pearson came to see me when he thought he had it, but he was neither Napoleon nor Cromwell, but only a babbler!'

During one of their many talks about the paper, Bell had shown Northcliffe the small notebook in which for years he had kept a record of the daily circulation. He told the new chief proprietor: 'We are suffering from lack of abuse. Other papers used to attack us with every sort of accusation —financial trickery, of being in the pockets of the politicians, of sending coach-loads of unsold copies of *The Times* to Brighton and dumping them in the sea, so that we could say that we sold more papers than any other London paper. There were personal reflections on the character of John Walter. One rival actually referred to us as "the bloody old *Times*".' Northcliffe said: 'Don't worry about a lack of abuse, Mr Bell. When I reveal my identity as controller of *The Times* you will get all the abuse you want.'

Early one morning, shortly after the signing of the contract, the head printer at Carmelite House, Tom George, was shaken out of his sleep at his Dulwich villa by his wife with the news that a cab was at the door. 'They want you at the office.' He arrived there at nine o'clock. Northcliffe, his brothers Harold and Cecil, with Kennedy Jones and Sutton, were standing together at one end of Room One. 'K.J.' was the spokesman. 'You know Parbury,' he said, referring to Pearson's mechanical expert who had been installed at Printing House Square. 'Go across and tell him to put his jacket on.' George went to the *Times* office and was refused admittance on saying that he had come from Lord Northcliffe. 'Don't know anything about Lord Northcliffe,' the hall porter said. George asked for Parbury's room. 'What are *you* doing here, Tom?' Parbury asked him when he was shown in. 'We've bought *The Times*,' George told him. 'I've been sent to tell you to put on your jacket.' Parbury refused to believe him. 'Don't be silly—*our* guv'nor's bought it!' Pearson's man had to make way for John Bland, an old Stamford School

Lady Northcliffe, after the portrait by Philip de Laszlo, 1911

(*Left*) Northcliffe in Scotland with George Sutton and (*right*) with Kennedy Jones and Graeme Sutton in Nancy of a Hall of

boy who had become an expert printing engineer. Before long he was ordered to throw out much of the antiquated machinery at Printing House Square and authorized to spend £60,000 on giant new Goss presses and the latest Monotype composing machines.

Moberly Bell received a letter from an old colleague who had gone over to Pearson's *Standard*. Congratulating Bell on the success of the negotiations, his correspondent told him (March 19, 1908): 'Though it would undoubtedly have been to my benefit had the Pearson arrangement come off, I heartily rejoice that it fell through. I feel confident that neither you nor Messrs. Walter have any conception of what *The Times* has escaped. I have, for all the chickens had already been carefully counted and their various roles in life—with the accompanying emolument—duly apportioned. A reign of splendid incompetence and nepotism, parsimony and prodigality, would have been inaugurated in Printing House Square. There would have been a little colony of poor relations absorbing fat salaries and doing God knows what in return.' The writer begged to be acquitted of malice or ulterior motice. 'A few years spent in the *Times* office has a peculiar effect—it engenders a spirit of *je ne sais quoi* which cannot be shaken off. I left my heart in Printing House Square—not with persons, but with the undying institution.'

The Times had informed the world on March 17: 'There will be no change whatever in the political or editorial direction of the paper, which will be conducted by the same staff on the independent lines pursued uninterruptedly for so many years.' Valentine Chirol, head of the *Times* foreign department, to Moberly Bell: 'Many thanks for your very interesting and reassuring letter of March 23. What you tell me about X [Northcliffe] reminds me of what St. Loe Strachey said of him to me: "I hate his methods but there is something very big about him. He seems to me to be cast in much the same metal as Cecil Rhodes, whose methods were often equally repugnant, but whom everyone admits to have been a big man." ' Northcliffe to G. E. Buckle, editor of *The Times* (undated): 'You have gone through a very nerve-racking time and if you and Mr Bell did not possess the constitution of giants, you would have both broken down.' If his weight statistics were an index, Northcliffe himself had thrived on the tensions and excitement of buying *The Times*. That year he reached his highest recorded maximum, fourteen stones. 'Exact', he wrote in his weight book. 'Horrible.'

Northcliffe to Coutts' Bank, April 7, 1908: 'My brother Harold tells me that it will be necessary to charge my securities for the purpose of the purchase of *The Times*. I hereby authorize you to charge *part* of my stocks and shares as your security for the loan. I would point out that these stocks and shares are worth at least £3,000,000.' A message from General Sterling, who had been the largest single holder of shares in *The*

Times after the Walter brothers, congratulated Northcliffe on the 'straight-forward and generous manner' in which he had carried out the transaction (April 13). Northcliffe to General Sterling: 'Paris, Easter Sunday.—It is pleasing to me to think that I was able to assist Mr Bell in keeping *The Times* in the hands of the English people.' Arthur Walter, writing on April 14 after 'a long spell of trouble and anxiety', wished Northcliffe to know that he had been throughout 'very sensible of the generous manner in which you have acted both towards the Proprietors and myself'.

Insisting that he must have a holiday from the affairs of Fleet Street and the world, after the recent weeks of suspense, Lady Northcliffe persuaded Northcliffe to go with her to Seville. J. L. Garvin and his wife, Charles Whibley, and Owen Seaman, editor of *Punch*, went with them, with Evelyn Wrench acting as Northcliffe's secretary and Lady Northcliffe's chamberlain of the household. Northcliffe enjoyed the colourful Spanish scene, especially after the monotony of his days at Boulogne, but his mind constantly ran on *The Times* affairs. Wrench walked with him for two hours near the Moorish ruins of Alcala, ten miles from Seville. 'He opened his heart and discussed his problems and the difficulty of finding his "generals" for various undertakings, among them *The Times*.' More consequential for Wrench was their exchange of views, during the same walk, about his plan for starting the Overseas League, 'a great non-party society to promote the unity of the British Commonwealth'. Northcliffe was 'much interested'. He promised Wrench the free and full use of the *Overseas Daily Mail* for promoting the idea.

He returned to London in May to study developments in Printing House Square and, where possible, to initiate them. Brumwell, one of Buckle's best sub-editors, was told to 'stand over the printer' every night and supervise the make-up of the paper. It was the end of the long dominance of the printer over that function. Northcliffe's personal policy was one of watchful discretion. He had deputed Kennedy Jones to organize the practical side of the changeover and 'K.J.' had dropped his I'm-telling-you mode of approach, and, surprisingly, was winning friends and influencing people at *The Times* by his tact, while impressing them no less by his efficiency in dealing with make-up congestion and case-room delays. At Carmelite House, 'K.J.' usually wore the short black jacket and striped trousers of a City man. Visiting Printing House Square, he thought it more seemly to put on a heavily braided tail-coat. He gained the confidence of Arthur Walter, who told him with tears in his eyes that he had never expected to inherit the family responsibility of controlling *The Times*. It had come to him by the accident of his elder brother's drowning on the family estate in Berkshire. Dramatically, he had found himself called to a position for which he had neither training nor taste. His heart was in the life of the countryside, in 'the Volunteers', and in cricket.

He and his brother Godfrey were changed men away from Printing House Square. They would ask members of the staff to join them in weekend cricket games at their country homes, where they were kindly and companionable hosts. Meeting the same staff people the following Monday in the *Times* corridors, they would pass by with chin-high aloofness.

Northcliffe did not go down to Printing House Square in the first months of his authority there. He gave a dinner, instead, for the purpose of meeting senior members of the various departments. Until then, Moberly Bell was the only one of their number who had seen him. What conquests his personality made on that occasion were not a subject of record. Not all the officers of the sinking ship persisted in deploring Northcliffe as coxswain of the lifeboat because he had not been to Oxford. The official history tells us that 'he looked as if his thoughts were far away'. After his victory over Pearson, he had shown few signs of elation at having secured control of the paper. Reclaiming its circulation from the 38,000 mark to which it had fallen meant new burdens of work and worry, the latter increased by weakening eyesight. His oculist prescribed dark glasses. Northcliffe wore them indoors and out, fearing the fate of total blindness that had befallen Pulitzer of New York. He had always read himself to sleep. Now, to spare his eyes, he had someone to read to him in bed, a practice continued to the end of his days. It might not be unfair to say that, on the whole, his pleasure in that proceeding was greater than that of those deputed to read to him. By no means all his bedside servitors were enthralled by Dickens.

There were weekends of lively social occasion at Sutton Place that spring. John O'Connor, Nationalist M.P., Lady Betty Balfour, Austen Chamberlain, Reginald McKenna, M. Delcassé, ex-Foreign Minister of France, Alfred Lyttelton and Jan Paderewski are named in the diary, while Cecil Harmsworth was noting: 'Sutton Place, Sunday, May 10, 1908.— Alfred and I birds'-nesting in the morning. Sheets of lovely narcissi out on the terrace lawn.' Up in Manchester, Northcliffe's local partner in the *Courier*, A. F. Stephenson, the Southport newspaper proprietor, wrote in a letter (May 11): 'How Churchill does hate the Chief!'

Northcliffe to Winston Churchill:

22, St. James's Place,
S.W.

11th May, 1908.

My dear Churchill,—I was amazed to hear from Mrs Garvin that she had heard from her husband that you considered our criticisms a personal matter.

There was a well understood agreement between us that we should use our stage thunder in the furtherance of our mutual interests.

As we have got to live together more or less in public life in more ways than you know, for, I hope, a great many years, I propose that we take a walk in St. James's Park some morning this week and thrash the matter out.

You have criticised me very hotly in and out of Parliament and I have never felt the least put out about it, as you must have seen by our recent meeting at Lord Lansdowne's.

Yours sincerely,
NORTHCLIFFE.

A writ for libel against the *Manchester Courier* had been issued on Churchill's behalf. Northcliffe wrote to him again on May 13, disclaiming any knowledge of the circumstances. 'I am advised, and indeed consider, that any endeavour to connect me with something over which I have no control, which took place when I was absent from England, and in a matter in which I am only one and not by any means the largest share-holder, would be an act of grave injustice, and I shall personally consider it an act of hostility.' He had heard it hinted, he went on to say, that 'some mutual friend has suggested I have at some time experienced some doubts of you', and he asked Churchill 'to bring that friend forward, as I should like to confront him'. There was no warranty for such a belief. 'I do trust that in future you will neither deduce from nor attach im-portance to rumour or listen to the words of busybodies.' Churchill answered the next day with the hope 'that our personal relations will be all the better for the misunderstanding which you have so completely re-moved from my mind'.

Northcliffe's annoyance at the *Daily Mail* criticism of Churchill was shared by Lady Northcliffe, whose social circle included many friends of the Churchill family. Marlowe, as the responsible editor, wrote on May 15: 'My dear Chief,—I am extremely sorry that you should have had so much trouble—and especially grieved that Lady Northcliffe should have suffered annoyance on my account.' Shortly afterwards, Northcliffe to Churchill: 'I am delighted to think that the only cause of friction between us has been cleared away. My feelings towards you have always been of admiration and esteem, and I shall look forward to a long if somewhat critical friendship.'

He was intensely interested in the news coming from Kill Devil Hills, North Carolina, where the Wright brothers, the cycle-repair mechanics, on December 17, 1903, had flown their heavier-than-air machine a dis-tance of eighty hundred and fifty-two feet against a twenty-miles-an-hour wind. That accomplishment had been followed in 1904 by a circular flight, an event in itself, and then by a straight-line flight of three miles. In May 1908 Northcliffe asked for private reports to be sent to him by the *Daily Mail* New York man, W. F. Bullock, who was ordered to watch developments. His reports kept Northcliffe closely informed and North-cliffe in turn passed on much of the information to the *Daily Mail*, whose readers were left in no doubt about its founder's conviction that the conquest of the air would soon be front-page news. Bullock cabled him on May 10: *Have paid several visits to camp and two Wrights past week stop found them eminently agreeable stop scene of their experiments is weirdly desolate stop some six coastguardsmen myself and one or two other spectators only witnesses of their marvellously intricate flights conducted amid roar of far-sounding Atlantic breakers over endless waste of sand dunes stop.*

Bullock further reported that the Wrights were going to France in June to negotiate a sale of their patents to the French Government, while hoping that the United States Government would intervene to their advantage. *Aeroplane primarily intended war machine stop* Bullock cabled, *travelling speed forty miles an hour stop able if all goes well overtake any modern warship and as it can be manoeuvred utmost ease any direction navigators have claimed should have no difficulty dropping bomb greatest nicety on any object attack stop.* Soon, Northcliffe was talking of the pioneering brothers as if he knew them personally. 'They never go up together', he was heard saying, 'in case both get killed. They toss a coin to decide which should make a flight. Before an ascent, they embrace each other.' They appreciated his personal interest, while not invariably being as communicative on technical matters as he wished. A little later that year he was approached on their behalf with the suggestion that he should form an English company holding their British and Colonial patents, 'and thus become the moving spirit of flying in England'.

The spirit that moved Northcliffe as a promoter of aviation was not commercial and not exclusively journalistic. Neither was it scientific, with the result that his money prizes tended to encourage those preferring the easy triumph rather than the ardours of research. It drew its impelling force from the growing general fear of war with Germany, which cast shadows over the last years of the brief and gay Edwardian interlude. In 1906, Haldane, the Secretary of State for War, had gone to Germany to study the organization of the War Office there. At a parade on the Tempelhofer Field, Haldane watched from a carriage the Kaiser reviewing his troops.

He galloped up to me and held a conversation, I standing in the carriage. 'A splendid machine I have in this Army, Mr Haldane, now isn't it so? And what should I do without it, situated as I am between the Russians and the French?'*

While the historians have not agreed whether iniquity or folly was the greater sin to be charged against the Governments and leaders of the day, some writers on (not necessarily of) history arraigned Northcliffe as an

---

* Richard Burdon Haldane: *An Autobiography*, 1929.

arch-conspirator against the peace. One of them, the American Professor S. B. Fay, in *The Origins of the World War*, a frequently reissued book from 1928 onward, blamed him for anti-German reporting in *The Times* eleven years before he acquired control at Printing House Square. Even his old Paris colleague, Sir Norman Angell, could believe that as a newspaper proprietor Northcliffe had a vested interest in war. In *The Press and the Organization of Society* (1933), Angell wrote: 'Are we to assume that the Harmsworths rampaged for the Transvaal because they owned South African mines? There is a much simpler explanation. The gold mine of Lord Northcliffe was nearer home. It was in the expanded circulation of the *Daily Mail* and the *Evening News*.' But Northcliffe insisted that wars are not favourable to newspapers. Circulations fluctuated, advertising was uncertain, staffs were overworked, paper supplies jeopardized. Increasing costs and currency problems added to the difficulties. No newspaper proprietor in his senses had reason to suppose that he, above all others, would emerge unscathed from what then threatened to be the greatest human struggle ever known. Certainly Northcliffe did not believe that when the final clash came it would be anything but a most destructive business, rending the civilized world apart. More than most of his fellow countrymen, he had reason to dread the imponderable power of the warrior state that was rising up in Europe. His special sources of information all too clearly confirmed the reality of the German preparations, whatever the logical force behind them, that an energy was being generated in Germany which she could not contain. She aimed at transcending the historic balance in Europe by a reorganization which would give her the hegemony of more than a continent. By 1908 the German lust for power and place was becoming a world danger. For drawing attention to that fact Northcliffe was condemned from the Liberal side of the House of Commons as 'a footpad of politics and an enemy of the human race'. When, four years earlier, he had committed his *Daily Mail* to the principle of compulsory service—'defence, not deference' was his slogan—threatening and abusive letters poured into the office, most of them addressed to him personally. The paper continued to point out that the rise of great armies on the Continent brought urgent new problems into British life and politics.

War is a horrible and dreadful thing for everybody, and the only way for England not to have war with Germany is for England to get ready. Never mind the English people who say there is no danger of Prussia precipitating Germany upon us. There is danger. And every Englishman who lives in Germany knows that there is danger. (*Daily Mail*, July 13, 1906.)

All the fine words in the world cannot disguise the fact that the naval competition between England and Germany is intense, and that Germany is now building a great fleet with the express object of meeting the British Navy at sea. (*Daily Mail*, April 24, 1907.)

Northcliffe's appointment of Frederick William Wile as Berlin correspondent of the *Daily Mail* was a prescient act, for Wile was an American newspaperman (*Chicago Daily News*) of experience and resource whose nationality would be an asset when war came and whose reporting in what remained of the peace was marked by vigilance and accuracy. The British Embassy, yearning for a quiet life, hinted that it would welcome his transfer to some other capital. The German authorities pressed for his removal. Northcliffe paid no heed. He had no doubt of the sureness of his judgment in choosing Wile for the Berlin listening-post and stoutly maintained him in it.

His private information service from Central Europe was valuably augmented by *The Times*, with its uniquely authoritative sources of news and opinion. *The Times* had been condemned by the Kaiser in 1905, a year in which the British Fleet had appeared in the Baltic, as the great mischief-maker between the two countries and he had spoken of its Berlin correspondent, George Saunders, as 'a first-class swine'. Winston Churchill, in May 1906, addressing a gathering of German editors at the offices of the Liberal *Daily News*, warned them against 'the patriotic Press on both sides of the North Sea'. Haldane had personally met members of the *Times* editorial staff that same month with a view to persuading them to modify their anti-German sentiments. According to high German report, he had found them incorrigible. 'The attitude of *The Times*,' states the official history, 'as perhaps that of the Germans, was hardening under the pressure of developments which were rendered all the more menacing by the increasing weight of the armaments which backed the respective policies of the Great Powers.' The paper's attitude was not likely to be re-cast under Northcliffe. Harcourt Kitchin, the new assistant manager, recorded that Northcliffe said: 'I shall leave the editor unrestricted control unless he should fail to warn the British people of the coming German peril. I insist on that duty being discharged.' Haldane to Northcliffe on July 17, 1908: 'I have not the least doubt that an enormous amount of information is collected by foreign officers here, especially Germans, but they do it when they are on leave and not under any commission. I am going not so much on an affirmative proof but rather by the knowledge of what our own officers do when they are abroad. Like yourself, I have not any notion of how to stop it.'

Paderewski, the Polish musician-statesman, told of an evening in 1908 when he was dining in London with Lord Charles Beresford, Northcliffe and one or two others. Paderewski said: 'A war, I think, is in store for you in a few years.' He was asked: 'What war?' 'With the Germans', he answered. Northcliffe commented: 'You are undoubtedly right. They are already preparing for it, though no one believes it.'

Admiral Sir John Fisher to Northcliffe from Tarasp, Switzerland:

Private & Confidential.   29.8.08.

Dear Lord Northcliffe,—You can rely on enclosed, but please don't make it public. We spend a lot on Secret Service and I am sure of my information. Nevertheless, it would be simply madness of the Germans to make war on England. However, Lord Salisbury once said to me when Prime Minister: 'One never can tell what some great gust of popular passion may not sweep a nation into doing in the shape of some act of madness.'

I am 36 miles from the nearest railway and 1,000 miles [*sic.*] from the Admiralty and no motors allowed by the Government and only cart horses, so it took me 7 hours on a level road to get here from the station, but I am 4,000 feet above the sea, the thermometer 70 in the shade, the air delicious, a rushing snow river under my window and everlasting sun and blue sky since I arrived a week ago—so I am in paradise!

Yours very truly,
J. A. FISHER

Northcliffe complained of overwork that summer to his brother Harold. 'There have been only three days in the last 365 when I have not worked and mostly all day long, from 7.30 in the morning.' He wrote to Lord Selby: 'On Friday, Lady Northcliffe and I went to a little house we have by the sea to get away from worries. On Saturday, there began a shower of telegrams and telephone messages.' They came from Imre Kiralfy, organizer of the Franco-British Exhibition which was being held at the White City, London. 'The whole of my weekend was devoted to trying to understand the general muddle at the Exhibition.' It seemed to him, he wrote to Harold, that 'the business is getting out of hand', and was it a fact that new papers were being started at the Amalgamated Press without his knowledge? 'After all, I am the chairman.' Leicester wrote to him: 'I am glad to learn that you are at last realizing that you cannot do everything. Your latest responsibility is alone sufficient for any man.'

His latest responsibility was answering well to his hand at the wheel. Buckle, the *Times* editor, who had mistrusted him, had written an amicable letter on June 23:

Thank you very sincerely for your kind appreciation. . . . In the last few years circumstances have naturally weighed our spirits down; but the new arrangements and your vigorous personality have infused hopefulness and buoyancy into us all. It has been, if I may say so, a matter of very special satisfaction to me to find that the things which I care most about in the Paper are highly valued by you; and I fully realize the great advantage of most of the suggestions you have made for alterations in our system of management. We must not, however, go too fast. There must be no doubt that the Paper is still *The Times* in essentials, but improved in every respect, brought thoroughly up to date, and made as nearly the ideal newspaper as possible. It is because I know that these are your views that I now look forward without misgiving to the future.

On July 11, Lord Esher, the courtier and public servant, wrote in his journal that he had seen Northcliffe, 'who lives in Sam Rogers' house in St. James's Place. He lives simply, his house is furnished with taste, without display, or ostentation of his enormous wealth.' They had talked chiefly about *The Times*, 'and the method, half skill and half luck', Esher wrote, 'of its purchase'. Northcliffe had written him 'a curious letter, a confession of his idea in buying the control of the paper, and his intentions in regard to it, should he die. Both are creditable to him.' Northcliffe had explained the origin of the letter to Buckle, editor of *The Times*, two days previously. 'Lord Esher came to me this morning with a very direct statement about *The Times* that I could not deny, emanating, as it obviously did, from a very high quarter. I told him the facts but so that there should be no possible misunderstanding in that quarter, I reiterated the gist of my conversation in a letter, a copy of which I enclose.' Esher considered that Northcliffe's mind was that of 'an organizer and speculator, not of a politician. He evidently loves power, but his education is defective, and he has no idea to what uses power can be put, except by deputy.' The confidant of kings then went fatuously astray in his judgment as he wrote: 'He enjoys the sensation of appointing or dismissing an editor. But he could never inspire an article and still less could he edit a paper.' He did not doubt that Northcliffe would convert *The Times* from a bankrupt concern 'into a fine property'. Dated July 9, Northcliffe's letter to Esher confirmed a statement in the *Westminster Gazette* of the previous evening that the policy of the paper would not be affected by the new arrangements.

My position is merely that of one who wishes to see this country represented to the world by an absolutely independent newspaper, always, I trust, in my lifetime, worthy of its high tradition; the organ of neither parties, sects nor financiers; its columns open to every shade of politics; a newspaper run not as a profit-making machine at all.

The Times is, in fact, in my life what a yacht or a racing stable is to others—it is merely my hobby.

I propose, if I am spared, to leave in my Will an endowment and a suggestion for its direction by such a committee as that of the British Museum to preserve it, perhaps, for some generations.

Yours sincerely,
NORTHCLIFFE

When Buckle read the letter, he wrote to Northcliffe: 'As a considered statement of your views with regard to *The Times* it is, of course, an historical document of permanent importance. I hope', he added, 'that Esher understands how desirable it is for the present that he and his illustrious friend should not spread their knowledge abroad', a reference to the King's interest in the change of ownership and what it might portend. The *Times* history implies that the monarch's interest inspired Northcliffe's declaration to Esher. In fact, the tone of his dealings with Bell, from the beginning, was that of a sensitive regard for the paper's traditions and standing, if hardly for its management. Bell had been gratified when, early in the negotiations, Northcliffe had let him know that he wished to see the paper conducted in the future as it had been in its best years. It was more than a move in the game. It was a genuine sentiment. That he should give it testamentary significance meant no startling change of mind on his part.

The accountant, E. Layton Bennett, whom he had employed from the *Answers* days, reported to him after an inspection of the books at Printing House Square: 'Our friends' ideas of bookkeeping are of an exceedingly vague character.' Northcliffe to Layton Bennett: 'I hope you have been tactful in your inquiries, as no one likes the intrusion of newcomers. You would not yourself if you had been established in business for 120 years. We want the Printing House Square people to get to like us.' He was exerting his social and personal charm to that end, while remaining the unobtrusive new controller. He proposed longer holidays to Bell and Buckle—'two months, at least'—and other senior members of the staff. He asked them to lunch with him privately at St. James's Place. There were weekends at Sutton Place. Their wives received courtesies never shown them by the old proprietors. Mrs Moberly Bell to Northcliffe (September 29, 1908): 'We enjoyed our weekend immensely and I can never explain to you what a different complexion our life and work have now.'

G. E. Buckle, editor of *The Times*, to Northcliffe:

> The Rectory,
> Crickhowell,
> Breconshire.
> 11th August, 1908.

Dear Lord Northcliffe,—. . . Will you forgive me if I refer to a somewhat delicate matter? You have treated me so courteously and straightforwardly, and in all your dealings with *The Times*, so far as I know them, have been so considerate and high-minded, that I venture to tell you how grieved I am, and how bad I think it to be for the Paper, that you and Walter should be on such unfortunate terms. He is a very old friend of mine, and, until last winter, had in all essentials—barring his unhappy manner—behaved to me in a most generous way, giving me throughout steady support. I cannot understand his action, either in regard to the Pearson arrangement, or his negotiations with you, without attributing much to the bad state of his health since the autumn. But it must be plain to him and to you that the Paper cannot satisfactorily go on if the Principal Proprietor and the Chairman of the Board are at logger-heads. . . .

While Walter is very sore, and, as is usual with him, thinks he has been in the right throughout, I can see that he would welcome better relations if his pride were salved. . . .

Believe me,

Yours sincerely,

G. E. BUCKLE

Northcliffe reprimanded the *Times* advertising manager, James Murray Allison, for making possibly doubtful claims regarding the paper's circulation and warned him in stronger terms about the 'bad taste' of some of the advertisements. 'I would rather see no advertisements at all in the paper and pay the dividends out of my own pocket, than have the whole of the good work of the Editorial staff marred in this way.' It was a subject that exercised him constantly in the early weeks of his co-proprietorship. He made his intention clear to Allison: 'I am determined to get this matter put right.'

The paper's distinguished foreign editor, Valentine Chirol, wrote to Northcliffe on August 17: 'Do you know Ibsen's "Master Builder" with its eternal refrain: "Youth is knocking at the door"? I wish there were a little more of it knocking at our door.'

The official historian of *The Times* presumes to state (Volume 3, page 639) that in his first year of control Northcliffe was 'so fascinated by *The Times* that, at that time, he could think and plan and read and talk of nothing else'. History has sometimes corrected biography; here the process may justly be reversed. Northcliffe was not so obsessed by *The Times* as to be unable to divert his attention at will to a subject of rather larger consequence, the rising tensions in Europe which almost daily were becoming a greater threat to peace. He was so anxious that he directed H. W. Wilson, of the *Daily Mail*, to prepare a long and reflective memorandum on the subject to be laid before Balfour under the heading, 'Why England believes that Germany is making War Preparations'. Northcliffe himself supplied some of the factual material for the document. L. J. Maxse, *National Review*, to Northcliffe (August 20, 1908): 'A friend of mine was taken in to dinner a few days ago by a Cabinet Minister, who said to her: "If the public knew what we know as to Germany's war preparations there would be a tremendous panic." An interesting comment on Churchill and other types. I am very anxious to have a talk with you.' F. W. Wile, *Daily Mail* office, Berlin, to Northcliffe: 'I had a chance to meet Admiral von Tirpitz, First Lord of the German Admiralty. We were cornered off by ourselves for nearly half-an-hour. He was unmistakably interested in the *Daily Mail* attitude towards German naval development and let me know that he didn't like it! The interview was, to my mind, mainly significant in its proof of the value the highest quarters in Germany put upon the power and influence of the *Daily Mail*.' Northcliffe to Arthur Mee (August 22, 1908): 'Some weeks ago you wrote urging me to print an article asking the Germans to destroy their airships. When the Zeppelin airship was burnt the other day, Germans at once subscribed over £100,000 in sums varying from a penny upward. I wish you would spend one of your holidays in Germany and try to realize the situation. Every nation has its characteristics. Our people have sang froid, the French jealousy, the Spaniards pride, the Americans boastfulness, the Germans envy and suspicion. The present state of affairs is a very unhappy one, produced, however, almost entirely by well-meaning preachers and politicians unacquainted with the German character.' Northcliffe to the same (August 28): 'I agree with you that nearly all wars begin by suspicions, and suspicions can be best allayed, in my judgment, by saying nothing.' He wrote again to Mee: 'Germany is new, masteful, alive, brutal, and horribly *nouveau riche*.' He was at the same time in touch with Balfour about another matter, the failure of the local Tories to support the *Manchester Courier*, 'which has arrived at one of its quinquennial crises'. He was studying and taking action on Mayson Beeton's long reports from Grand Falls. He was worrying the head printer of his periodicals group, J. H. Newton, about the quality of ink being made at the company's ink factory. When Harold wrote to him in July that he was proposing to take up coal land options in Newfoundland on behalf of the Grand Falls company, Northcliffe reverted to the topic of overwork. 'Apart from the burden of finance there is the burden of management to be considered, and personally I can do no more than I am doing—in fact, I must do less.' He was corresponding with the Hon. Sydney Holland (later Lord Knutsford) of The London Hospital about the new pathological department to which he was giving £500 a year. Holland to Northcliffe: 'Its splendid work has been made possible by your help.' Northcliffe to Holland: 'It is a pity that we have not a national institution like the Pasteur Institute in Paris. Sir Victor Horsley is writing an article for the *Daily Mail* showing exactly what vivisection has done. I propose leaving the country and then publishing it!' Northcliffe to Percy T. Martin, 'a considerable shareholder' in Associated Newspapers Ltd.: 'I do not know why, without any knowledge, you should say that I am not taking any interest in the *Daily Mail*. As a matter of fact, I have not yet taken any holiday and have been working consecutively at the paper—with only three days' intermission—since August, 1907.' The Rev. R. J. Campbell, of the City Temple, to Northcliffe: 'To speak frankly, I do not like your newspapers, but they are not in my judgment as dangerous to the moral well-being of the community as the religious hypocrites who profess the loftiest motives while in reality doing what I suppose the press in general does—championing the cause that pays.' W. T. Stead, *Review of Reviews* office, to Northcliffe: 'It is a constant marvel to me how you ever keep in touch with one-tenth of the business you have in hand. Nevertheless, I want to solicit your interest for a really practical scheme for founding a National Theatre in London.' Arthur Brisbane, *New York Journal*, to Northcliffe: 'Your letter of invitation to stay with you is most kind and thoughtful. How in the world do you manage to remember so many people and so many different things? But I cannot think of getting away. I am rented out to Hearst for nine more years. My job is writing something—however trashy—*every* day in the year and fussing more or less around this office. So I must stay, and write, and fuss. Come over here and get naturalized and go into politics. That isn't an insult, it's a compliment.' A. G. Hales, the novelist and war correspondent, to Northcliffe, after appealing for monetary help: 'I wrote to you in a moment of utter weakness. I was a cur to give way and I deserved the lash that came by post. I am not done yet, as England will learn some day.' Northcliffe to Ray & Flowers-Ellis, solicitors (August 26, 1908): 'My friend, Mr S —— [of Carmelite House] seems, through no fault of his own, to have got into financial difficulties that are rather serious. I shall be glad to help extricate him.' He was not so obsessionally beset by *The Times*, either, to spare time for the consideration of local and parochial matters. The vicar of Woking, the Rev. F. J. Oliphant, was disturbed by a rumour that a day school near Sutton Place was to be staffed by nuns. Northcliffe wrote to him, August 28:

Sutton Place has been the property of a distinguished Roman Catholic family for three hundred and eighty years and prior to that date there existed here a chapel of St. Edward, dating back to the time of Edward the Confessor. The only church on the estate is a Roman Catholic one. The nearest County Council school is far too distant for children, some of whom are under-fed, to walk there and then begin study.

The teacher's distressing illness has been brought under the notice of Lady Northcliffe and myself. We very gladly agreed to assist in her retirement and in providing the school with a teacher whose religious views we have not asked. In this we have had the assistance of the Rev. Mr Hinsley, a Roman Catholic clergyman who is the chaplain to the owner of this estate. We have also undertaken to provide a vehicle to bring the little ones from a distance and to take them home.

We shall be glad to assist the church to which we belong. But we would naturally not interfere with the traditions of the local family—a tradition preserved by them for so many hundreds of years.

Yours sincerely,

NORTHCLIFFE

Hinsley had thanked Northcliffe for his 'kind, strong words' about the school, and for all 'your goodness in this as in so many other matters', and begged to remain his 'devotedly in C.J.' The future Cardinal Archbishop of Westminster wrote again: 'I never forget to pray for you daily. Believe me, my Lord, whatever I can do at any time to repay all your goodness to these children and all the kindness you have shown, will be to me a welcome and eager privilege.'

However oppressive the claims of *The Times*, they did not preclude him from going off lightheartedly at the end of August for a holiday on the Continent. 'We leave tomorrow (thank goodness) and I am going to ponder your *Times* scheme,' he told St. Loe Strachey, of *The Spectator*. 'I think I can see a way out of all the difficulties.' Strachey's *Times* scheme, worked out at Northcliffe's suggestion, set forth his ideas 'regarding the best way of establishing *The Times* by your will as a national institution'. He proposed that the paper should be placed in the hands of trustees, men of national eminence such as the Archbishop of Canterbury, the Speaker of the House of Commons, and the Lord Chancellor. Before leaving London, Northcliffe sent a gift to Winston Churchill, who was shortly being married. 'I have now been twenty years wedded and find the experiment quite a success. We both hope that you and Mrs Churchill may have every possible sort of happiness.' Churchill sent his thanks by return with the hint (August 30, 1908): 'Tell your "old paper" [*The Times*] to report me *verbatim* at Dundee, at Manchester, and at Newcastle, and I will see that they get good copy.'

*   *   *

Northcliffe had put young Evelyn Wrench in charge of the export side of The Amalgamated Press and Wrench had gone to Canada on the business of his department. In Toronto he went down with typhoid. Northcliffe sent him a cable of good cheer every day, also a daily picture-postcard, and sent two long letters to him every week. 'No parent could have done more for his son than he did for me,' Wrench said. One of the letters, written in pencil, covered twelve sheets of notepaper; 'the longest letter I ever wrote', Northcliffe said in a postscript; 'begun 15th, ended 18th September'. Lady Northcliffe also 'wrote long, kind letters', telling him: 'Your Chief has been very anxious about you', and 'the Chief' paid the expenses of a convalescence in Jamaica for both Wrench and his sister, who was looking after him.

Picture-postcards, Northcliffe's favourite form of communication on holiday, told where he was on his Continental holiday, but not what he was doing, not, for instance, that he was consulting a leading German oculist, Dr Solm, at Frankfort, who advised him to read *The Times* only with a magnifying glass, 'and not at all by artificial light'. He sent picture-postcards to his mother, brothers and sisters, to Sutton, to his editors and to his secretaries. Sutton was frequently addressed as 'The Sutton, The Amalgamated Press, London'. Sutton's wife, at 14 Belsize Square, N.W., had a card with the message: 'He *must* have a holiday.' Sutton took the holiday and before the end of it received a picture-postcard of Bremgarten, inscribed: 'No more slacking—get to work.—Chief.' Kennedy Jones to Northcliffe (September 30, 1908): 'An interview I had today with a big physician made it obvious that I have got to walk warily and take exceeding care. I am going to take it easier, difficult though that will be, knowing that *The Times* wants reorganizing in every department, save, perhaps, the editorial.'

Before leaving with his wife and his mother for New York in the *Lusitania* on October 3, Northcliffe had talks with Arnholz, who was to present a scheme for incorporating in his will his wishes regarding the future of *The Times*. Chiefly, he wanted to make certain that the paper should never fall into alien hands. The main point to be decided was whether *The Times* could be made the subject of a charitable trust which would conduct the paper on a non-profit basis, while giving full effect to the policies of its editor and a body of trustees in disseminating 'reliable news and the expression of views and opinions upon all questions of public interest as free as possible from all party or other bias or prejudice and the promotion and upholding of the national honour and welfare at home and abroad and the good government, prosperity and wellbeing of the British Empire generally'.* The sentiment was presumably Northcliffe's, the drafting undoubtedly Arnholz's. An incidental proviso was the 'fostering and encouragement of a high standard of honour and patriotism amongst journalists generally'. A tabulated list of suitable candidates for the trusteeship included most of those suggested by Strachey, with the addition of 'a distinguished Nonconformist divine, a distinguished member of each of the two Services, and a person distinguished in Art or Letters'. Counsel, on being consulted, had 'no doubt that a scheme which is designed to provide for at least one leading newspaper of the country to be published purely in the interests of truth and for the promotion of the benefit of the Empire, free from party rancour and unbiased by party prejudice, would be regarded by the court as a public object of the highest utility and accordingly "charitable".'

* *The Times* trust, formed in 1924, was largely based on Northcliffe's plans for the future of the paper.

Counsel's opinion was sent to Northcliffe in New York, where he seems to have had no difficulty in detaching himself from *Times* affairs. 'We are going to have a complete holiday this time.' In New York, he and Marconi were given a dinner by the editors of the *New York Times*. Northcliffe was to have sent a wireless message to London, but word was received from R. A. Fessendon in charge of the equipment: *Nova Scotia and Irish stations not working tonight*. He made a point of calling on Professor Hornaday, of the New York Zoological Society, to discuss acclimatizing the American robin (*Planesticus migratorius*) and the grey squirrel in England, an experiment he had long wished to make. Hopefully, he bought several pairs of both species and had them sent to him at Sutton Place.

In Toronto, he was entertained at the Canadian Club. In Ottawa, he stayed with the Governor-General, Earl Grey. They talked about the formation of the Canadian Army cadet corps, which Grey thought 'the most important thing' that had happened in Canada during his term. 'Canada has no officer class. The corps will help to save the British Empire.' It was urged on him, 'by everybody from the Governor downwards', that Canada had a great need of the best type of British emigrant to counteract the flow of people of alien blood from over the border. 'The Chief Justice, Sir Charles Fitzpatrick, made two long journeys in Canada to impress this upon me.' Northcliffe took serious note of the fact 'that, with the exception of Lord Milner, Canadians have hardly seen an English public man of any position. There is not one English financial house of any importance with a branch in Canada.' He drew the attention of a number of prominent persons at home to the matter, among them Churchill, whom he urged to pay his first visit to Canada as soon as he could do so. Churchill replied (November 24, 1908): 'I am quite alive to what you say; and I shall watch for an opportunity to bring it about. I ripen and mellow as the years pass, and almost any autumn might see me in the land of the maple leaf. The moment must, however, be well chosen.'

A letter that followed Northcliffe back to New York *via* Toronto took his memory back to the days when even *Answers* was only a dream. It was from Mrs Leader Williams, of The English Tea-Rooms, Palermo, daughter of Dr Gordon, of Dublin, the father-in-law of Dargaville Carr. 'I feel that even as my father gave you your first lift, so you—who like to help success—might give *me* a shove! He gave £1,500 and never asked interest or security, or repayment, only gave it for your business to do what you would with. I only ask £500, repayable in five years.' Northcliffe replied: 'The circumstances of advancing the capital are not as you state. The capital was advanced to your brother-in-law, Mr Carr, who, as a result, has always received a very large income from the business [as the sole representative in Ireland of the publications of The Amalgamated Press]. It has been one of the most profitable investments ever made. Now, if he will help you, I will help you in like proportion. That, I think, is a fair offer.'

Harold had written to warn him that the 'soap actions' were still not finished; he thought that there was no chance of an agreement with Lever. 'As far as we can learn, he has still at the back of his head an idea that he can get anything up to £250,000. Even the flabby Rufus Isaacs does not think he can get more than £10,000, *in toto*, for the remaining actions.' Harold was able to give the more encouraging news that 'every part of the business is doing well'. Sutton, writing nine days later, informed him that Associated Newspapers' profits were £3,500 down on the previous year and that the 100,000 copies that had been put on to the sale of *Answers* by Marie Connor Leighton's 'powerful new serial story', entitled *Greed*, 'were not being held'. A number of old *Times* employees had been dismissed, having outlived their usefulness to the paper. Some of them were writing Northcliffe bitter protests. He talked with Moberly Bell about individual cases and, where there was injustice or hardship, saw that it was relieved.

Towards the end of December, *The Times* correspondent in Berlin, George Saunders, telegraphed the substance of a statement made by Professor Hans Delbruck, one of the Kaiser's advisers, on the political situation in Europe. 'England regards the German Empire today as its real opponent and rival and there is a party in the Island which considers it necessary to provoke a passage of arms with Germany.' H. W. Wilson, who had reliable Admiralty channels of information, wrote confidentially to Northcliffe: 'The range tables of the new Krupp guns that have been secured by the Intelligence Department staggered the Admiralty.'

The year closed with a great snowstorm. Northcliffe telephoned to Moberly Bell 'a little suggestion' that *The Times* should have an article on birds in the snow. He also annotated 1908 with the observation: 'This is the first time since motoring became general that we have had heavy snow.'

Chapter Thirteen

A Climacteric Year

NORTHCLIFFE was forty-three. He had wealth, place and power. Few men's dreams were more extravagantly realized in the terms of conventional ambition. His income by that time averaged £200,000 a year. His place was indisputably that of one whose advent was a particular incident in the history of civilization. His power was, on the whole, politically nebulous if not impotent, but it was socially massive; an energy of mind that animated the lives of innumerable people who never read his newspapers. And it was unique in that, unlike the power of the politicians, it was subject to no sanctions but his own.

He had not sought those satisfactions at the bidding of a voracious appetite. They were the 'great expectations' of the moralizing society into which he was born, rather than the consummations of an aggressive individual urge. By a calculated act of emulation he had come to know early in life the heightened sense of existence called success, Stevenson's 'topmost point of being'. Its intoxication drove him on to more exacting demonstrations of his talents and in doing so imposed on him strains and fatigues which were about to culminate in the unpleasant climacteric afflicting many larger-than-life men in middle age.

He had come back from America, as he invariably did, with a renewed zest for work. Over there they unreservedly admired his brand of success. They also had a keener appreciation of the place of the publisher and journalist in society and accepted him as paramount chief of the tribe, the more readily because it was discreetly understood that he could now claim the last word in the affairs of *The Times*. There was private recognition of him in that role in New York if, as yet, little of it in London. Once again he had sipped the heady wine, and its consequence was to generate more energy than his already impaired organism could safely contain. 'Your activities in America were so great,' Buckle of *The Times* wrote to him, 'that they produce for us more American matter than we are able to digest', a rejoinder intended also to offset Northcliffe's proposal that the paper should give more space to Canadian affairs. An encyclopædia publishing contract which he made in New York for his Amalgamated Press showed a marked lack of judgment. Averting its worst effects, and finally scrapping the project, cost the company several thousand pounds.

To some, at that time, he seemed to be unnaturally excited, like a man in a fever. Hammerton, of the Amalgamated Press book department, wrote that 'the Chief talked to me for hours on end, until he had exhausted himself so that he was on the verge of collapse' (*With Northcliffe in Fleet Street*, 1932). Evelyn Wrench thought that the years 1909–10 were crucial in Northcliffe's health history. Max Pemberton said that there was a lessening of his 'amazing vitality' and that 'many of his intimate friends perceived this about the year 1909'. Lady Northcliffe wrote to Sutton, at The Amalgamated Press, in the first weeks of that year: 'This is in confidence—will you help me to urge the Chief to take as long a holiday as possible? I see every sign of coming fatigue—and dread a breakdown. He is working at very high pressure and the strain seems to tell on him more than it used to. You are the only person he will listen to.' His mother remarked to another member of the family: 'I know Alfred is unwell. For the first time in his life he has contradicted me.' When, early in January, one of the best-known of The Amalgamated Press editors, Hamilton Edwards, stung by 'the Chief's' criticisms of his department, wrote out his resignation, Northcliffe retorted in a pencilled scrawl, 'Don't be ridiculous. If I am unusually irritable, just try a dose of ptomaine poisoning and you will understand.' He believed that he had 'picked it up' in the *Lusitania*, homeward bound.

Whatever its real nature, the illness of 1909 was enlarged into a legend of crisis when it was reported one evening that he had been seen climbing up beside the driver of an *Evening News* horse van as it was about to leave Carmelite House. His brother Harold was alarmed. Alfred had never behaved like *that* before. A search party of clerks was sent out. The van was traced to Waterloo. The driver, Jim Berry, explained that 'the Chief' had ordered him to drive to the station, where he was catching a train to Guildford, for Sutton Place. The episode was talked about as if it was necessarily a mental aberration. Presumably, no one remembered the Austrian Archduke John who vanished from the court for ever, disguised as a seaman. Perhaps Northcliffe, too, was tired of the tyranny of established ways. His absence from his offices that year totalled seven months.

H. G. Price, who became a member of his personal staff in the spring of 1909, saw in 'the Chief' no marked sign of deteriorating health. Neither did Pine, the chauffeur, nor Joseph, the valet, and all three were constantly at his side. Equally positive is the evidence of his correspondence. It was as

lively and wide-ranging and prolific as before and it preserved no record
of introspective dealings with the doctors. He was sending pertinent
comments, criticisms and suggestions to *The Times* office in the form of
communiques and in letters to Moberly Bell. They were not a sign of
'infatuation with his new connexion' (*vide* the *History*), for he was sending
similar communications to the *Daily Mail*, and less regularly but not less
effectually to the *Evening News*, *Weekly Dispatch* and *Continental Daily
Mail*. Parenthetically, he was corresponding with Professor W. T.
Hornaday, of the New Zoological Park, about the American robin and
the grey squirrel.

He told Sutton that his symptoms were those of the neurasthenia he
had 'after the malaria', and that he had 'gone through a terrible time. I
have been feeble, slow, cross and lacking interest in the sex, always a bad
sign with your devoted Chief' (February 1909). Sir Victor Horsley examined him and diagnosed 'pancreatic trouble'. Lady Northcliffe was successful in persuading him, no doubt with Sutton's help, to let her take him off
to Pau, where within a few days she was able to write to Sutton: 'He is
really *much* better. All the tiresome symptoms are disappearing, but it
seems that he has been quite ill.' The brothers Wright were carrying out
trial flights at Pau and Lady Northcliffe told Sutton: 'The Chief likes the
Wrights immensely and it has been an excellent thing for him to have the
interest of them here. I keep the work down with a firm hand.'

The high summer of his life and career had been a blaze of prestige. His
psychic protest against the coming of autumn was all the more exhausting.
Arriving at the point of ordained change with depleted nervous reserves,
he never fully recovered the buoyant spirit that had been part of his
magnetic charm. Nonetheless, the charm was still potent enough and
his voice, for instance, was specially attractive to those who ears were
attuned to its soft cadences. For women it could have enchantment. It
was not only the seductive tone. Meeting him was always an event, as
Hugo had said of Gautier. His blue-grey eyes had the compulsion of a
handshake; they gripped with a firm focus of attention. No photograph
ever caught their arresting luminosity.

He stooped a little more than before and he was putting on weight.
Yet the aura of the boy still clung to him, made visible by the forelock
ingenuously brushed over his left brow. Remarkably enough, the intensity of his years had left no lines on his face, though there was a slight
sagging of the cheeks and mouth and often a severity of expression that
was made to seem uncharacteristic when he smiled. His smile had always
been a means of conquest which both men and women found it hard to
resist.

Yet, for all the goodness to him of the gods who contrived his birth,
he had never stuck the feathers of personal vanity in his cap. No one ever

saw him glancing at himself in a mirror. Such vanity as he had was shown in harmless if sometimes foolish boasting about the power of his papers or in showing off on the telephone as he demonstrated his summary authority over some hapless individual or proved his ease of access to those in high places. 'Get Lloyd George,' he ordered Price, the secretary, during an Elmwood weekend. When Lloyd George answered, Northcliffe asked him brusquely: 'Do you want the freedom of the City of London?' and, receiving the affirmative, slammed down the telephone; his way of showing others present, among them the Surgeon-General of the British army, that Cabinet Ministers were his to command. His imperious dominion was exhibited to equally startled witnesses on another occasion when a new young Canadian secretary named McGillivray joined him in Paris for a spell of duty. Cursorily acknowledging the young man's salute, Northcliffe asked him: 'Have you brought your typewriter?' The answer was no. 'Then go back to London and get it', was Northcliffe's command and it was obeyed.

His vitality diminishing, he became more readily irritated and, to the greater dismay of those who knew his better side, vindictive. The current of his warm and friendly nature, which friends and colleagues found so constantly pleasing, even enchanting, would suddenly fuse in a violent flash, destroying the good will of years. Angry because a news story in which he was personally interested was not printed in his *Weekly Dispatch*, he telephoned to the office of that Sunday newspaper, demanding to speak to the editor. When the editor came on the line, Northcliffe snapped: 'Who is that?' 'Editor, *Weekly Dispatch*, Chief,' came the answer. 'You *were* the editor,' Northcliffe retorted and banged down the receiver. The editor was replaced within a week. There were men close to him, J. L. Garvin, for instance, and Norman Angell, who never saw that side of his temper, perhaps because they could answer back. To Evelyn Wrench 'the Chief' was a splendid Olympian figure until Northcliffe one day turned on him with a vehemence which, at the time, shocked him deeply.

The chief proprietor of the *New York Times*, Adolph Ochs, wrote to his London manager in 1911: 'Your report of your interview with Northcliffe shocks me. I can only believe that he was unnerved and harassed and lost control of himself.' Northcliffe's so-called brainstorms were dreaded by those who had been within their penumbra. They saw a changed man whose readiness to wound made the timid shrink from his presence. The tenebrous moods passed as quickly as they came and he was known often to seek to rectify immediately the harm that had been done—as, for example, summarily dismissing the doorkeeper at Carmelite House and within ten minutes reinstating him at a higher wage. Seeing a messenger boy named Fairbrass go into Marlowe's room with his cap on, Northcliffe angrily snatched it off the boy's head, which was bald from a skin infection. Later in the day the boy received an envelope containing two half-crowns and a note of apology: 'I am sorry I insulted you.' 'I never knew him *not* to make amends when he had behaved badly', wrote John Prioleau, the motoring correspondent, who went with Northcliffe round the world.

What some of his staff did not know was that he was capable of simulating the frenzies which they found so alarming. The managing director of the Imperial Paper Mills at Gravesend, Stanley Cousins, was called to Printing House Square to explain a series of paper 'breaks' which had delayed *The Times* printing. In the room with Northcliffe when Cousins was announced was the head printer at Carmelite House, Tom George. 'Now', said Northcliffe to George, who had been told to stay in the room, 'you're going to see how I treat a man when I'm angry.' He met Cousins with threatening fists and rough words. George saw with amusement that he 'puffed out his face to make it look red and indignant'. He was impressed because Northcliffe's furious tirade included not a hint of bad language—'quite a feat, I thought'. Cousins had put his bowler hat on a chair. Northcliffe made a dive for it, opened the door, and gave the hat a straight kick off the toe which sent it bounding along the landing. Cousins went after it and, shutting the door on him, Northcliffe resumed his talk with George as if nothing had happened to interrupt it.

Dealing with statements that Northcliffe ruled by fear, one of his secretaries has written: 'I am of a timid disposition. Had I ever felt such fear I should not have been able to hold a pencil in my fingers to take his dictation, nor would Price and others whom I could name.' To one of the Paris editorial men he remarked: 'I'm called "The Old Man" behind my back, I believe', and added: 'You all regard me with little affection but much fear.' If he never knew the extent of the affection which many men felt for him, he exercised a paternalism which was an immensely potent force in holding his staffs together. Men and women who rarely met him were delighted to receive letters signed 'Your attached Chief'. Some would undergo miseries of self-examination if he signed himself simply as 'Chief', while a stark 'N' at the foot of a letter could cloud the day. A manager of *The Times* attempted to describe the feelings of those who worked at all closely with Northcliffe. He defined them, 'chiefly as alarm and adoration'.

*   *   *

Like all men of peremptory will, he hated the inexorable. A fear of death constantly agitated him. 'Think how many readers of Part One will have died before you reach Part Fifty', he said in a tone of awe to Arthur Mee, who was planning another encyclopædia in fortnightly issues. Passing a churchyard or meeting a funeral, he always looked the other way. Given an account of the illness which had caused the untimely death of an Amalgamated Press man, 'he squirmed and shivered', wrote Sir John Hammerton, 'as though he himself were already suffering from the same disease'.

An empty chair at table would cause him unrest. 'He had a peculiar horror of it', according to Hammerton, who said that he knew Northcliffe to be upset to the point of being 'unable to enjoy his food'. Thirteen at table was another of his anxieties (his mother's too). He was seen to wait until a long line of traffic had passed before stepping off a narrow pavement to avoid walking under a ladder. He observed the ritual of turning the silver coins in his pocket when he saw a new moon through a window. During his absence in America the Amalgamated Press board chose the 13th of the month as the publication date for a new magazine. He cancelled it by cable. Wednesday, he believed, was his lucky day.

Concern about his health became as obsessive as his fear of death. He sought to justify it by inventing an aphorism. 'One often looks at one's bank balance, so why not at one's health balance?' The American newspaperman from Chicago, Edward Price Bell, who knew him for twenty years, said that 'his non-robustness of constitution was evident'. There were the persisting low blood pressure symptoms. When a doctor referred to them in the course of an overhaul, Northcliffe said: 'My circulation is in my newspapers.' Throughout his life he had been subject to sudden unpredictable losses of energy. In a phase of impatience with Harley Street professionalism, he turned to 'nature cure' under the direction of one of his former magazine editors, Leslie Willson, who had set up as a health specialist in London. Reading an obscure vegetarian journal, the *Herald of Health*, some time in 1909, Northcliffe saw a reference to a 'new health' society calling itself 'The Wallaceites'. He suggested it as a good subject for a *Daily Mail* article, and asked that a reporter should 'get the facts'. Before the article was written, he had sent for the reporter and questioned him eagerly about the new movement and the theories behind it.

His colleagues often found him lunching in the office on a raw apple, dry biscuits and a bottle of Perrier. He had never been self-indulgent at table. He was rather less than a moderate user of alcohol. No one saw him the worse, or the better, for drink. He developed a neurotic dislike of eating in public and in later years if he agreed to go to a restaurant it was on condition that a place was reserved in 'a quiet corner'. At public banquets he would decline all but the simplest dishes. Frequently he took a meal at home before those occasions and then refused the menu with the excuse that he was dieting. It suited him to quote a remark which he attributed to King George V: 'Food tastes better in small houses.' His preferences were expressed in what he called his ideal meal, 'a picnic consisting of a dozen

343

plovers' eggs and half a pint of champagne'. A director of Selfridge's, the London department store, saw him in Oxford Street 'eating plums out of a paper bag'. As for so-called business lunches, he held those in some scorn. Invited to lunch by Sir Harry Brittain, of the Empire Press Union, he replied: 'I do not like luncheon engagements. I do not find that anything happens as a result of them. I believe that half an hour's solid talk in a room will do more good than any amount of lunching.'

*   *   *

His brain force was far in excess of that of most men, endowing him with a masterful grasp of his environment. His ideas flowed incontinently and were subject not to the disciplines of the syllogism but to a power of concentration which, while it often quickly exhausted itself, could be ruthlessly applied. For sustained reasoning, as for abstractions, he had a womanish disregard. Yet he respected few human attributes more than efficiency, while not disdaining to change his convictions with what to some was bewildering adroitness. Charged with opportunism he answered: 'Of course! A man should learn more as his years pass. Only fossils stay put.' When a friend told him that he had been seeing Conan Doyle, Northcliffe said positively: 'There's nothing in spiritualism. I've looked into it. I've tried to believe in it, but I can't.' Less than a year afterwards, he told the same friend: 'There is a great deal in it—there must be when men like Doyle and Lodge make it their life work and stand by it.' The difficulty for his admirers was that the inconsistencies were too often the stirrings of expediency on the surface of a mind that had breadth but not depth. It was suffused with a sense of moral responsibility but there was insufficient anchorage for philosophy or firm principle, though his hatred of falsehood, for example, was sincere and unremitting. He had scruples rather than standards and it meant that he was apt to do the right things in the wrong way.

Serving him in place of the settled view was a super-acute sense of seeing and hearing, which made the living minute intensely and perenially interesting. The well-known chronicler of the countryside, Sir William Beach Thomas, said that he 'excelled in perfection of sight', and Garvin said that 'he carried microscopes in his eyes and microphones in his ears, so that it was not safe for anyone within reasonable range of him to assume that the least sign went unnoticed or the lightest sound unheard'. His solicitor, Henry Arnholz, spoke with astonishment of Northcliffe's 'X-ray eye', which enabled him instantly 'to pick out a single line in a complicated legal document engrossed in handwriting on brief paper, and say: "I want that altered", though he had not seen the document before.'

His powers of observation were often striking. At office functions, among hundreds of faces, he would instantly spot newcomers to his staffs. Arriving at a dinner of circulation representatives, a gathering of two hundred and fifty persons, he at once went up to two men talking together and said: 'You are not my people, I believe.' They had been 'smuggled in' as guests of one of the managers. Walking the seashore, he would flick lost coins out of the sand with his walking-stick. He would read out small-type notices in shop windows as his car flashed past. He skimmed all experience with the glancing swiftness that he brought to bear on the printed word.

The resultant superficiality would occasionally lead him to strange assumptions—about ducks, for example: that they cannot live without water. No one ever succeeded in convincing him otherwise. Seeing ducks by the wayside, he would stop the car and go in search of the nearest pond in the hope of guiding them to it. If there was no pond he would come back shaking his head, as if quite unable to comprehend their situation. An agricultural show secretary was threatened with unpleasant publicity in the *Daily Mail* when Northcliffe saw some penned ducks which in his opinion were suffering from a lack of water.

One could not be much in his company without realizing that he had a great amount of information without profound knowledge of any particular subject. He never saw a subject whole or entire. He had exploited the paragraph because he thought in paragraphs. It was the explanation of his exceptional facility in dictating letters. All his secretaries were impressed by it. He never faltered and never went back to change a word.

Good talkers he tended to bracket with glib talkers and to mistrust them. Like his gestures, his own talk was quick and darting and showed little respect for the better usages of conversation. 'I am putting this into a letter because your mind works so much more quickly than mine that conversationally I can never manage to state more than about half a case to you,' Norman Angell wrote to him. At the same time, he could be an admirable listener, particularly to his intellectual superiors. To them he would speak deferentially. 'But, of course, *you* know that,' he would say, or: 'I do not have to tell *you* that.' He preferred the company of men of simple humour. There was a Hampshire publican who had a rich resource of dialect and local lore. Northcliffe would make long detours by car to call on him. Crossing Salisbury Plain, it pleased him to stop the car and go in search of an old shepherd with whom he liked to talk. In the naïve and unapologetic prejudices of the tenth Earl of Wemyss (1818–1914), he found unfailing delight.

*   *   *

In some ways his was the temperament of the artist, though, unlike the true artist, he was rarely doubtful about the results of his endeavours. He was an artist at guessing, sometimes an inspired one, reaching conclusions not by reflection or deduction but by recondite cerebration. His mother would say that 'he could see what was on the other side of a brick wall without looking over it'. Claude Johnson, managing director of the Rolls-Royce company, passed on to him in conversation the news that leading medical specialists had pronounced the doom of a friend of them both. 'They say he has cancer and will probably die in a few months.' Northcliffe listened with sombre attention. He struck the palm of one hand with the fist of the other. 'It is not cancer', he said. He repeated it four times. The doctors were wrong. The assumed victim lived on in good health for many years.

E. T. Raymond, who had worked for him and was later editor of the London *Evening Standard*, referred to his 'uncanny way of arriving at the results of thought without thought itself'. Against that pronouncement Leicester Harmsworth wrote marginally in the volume in which it appeared: 'How very true.' Northcliffe's 'sixth sense', as he liked to call it, his remarkable faculty for divining the course of things, had served him well in his pristine years, but something of the old magic seemed to have gone, and there is no substitute for the occult in the lives of men. The world was too much with him. The latent poet had long since been suffocated by the thick undergrowth of topical journalism. The self-taught pianist was excited by the new syncopated rhythms of the seaside concert parties. He went more than once to hear Elgar's *Dream of Gerontius*, but he had no time in which to cultivate musical sympathies or to seek more than casually what was excellent in any of the arts. It was possibly from a sense of deficiency that he felt constrained to refer frequently in his communiques to *The Times* to the need for more effective criticism of books and music. '*I think music is a matter that requires very serious attention*' (underlined), he wrote on December 28, 1908. In his communique for the following day he mentioned a new Elgar symphony and thought himself competent to pronounce it 'the most important piece of English composition for many years'. Nor had he any compunction about proposing that *The Times* drama critic, A. B. Walkley, should moderate his taste for French quotation. Moberly Bell to Northcliffe (September 22, 1908): 'Your paragraph shall be sent to him in the hope that he will confine himself, in the future, to one language.' It had no effect.

At all times, books supplied his most satisfying mental recreation. There were always books at his bedside, wherever he happened to be, and often they were read to him as he lay receptively ready for sleep after the labours of his day. One of his secretaries wrote: 'In dictating to me, he made many apt quotations from the poets and authors. I did not doubt that he had read widely and retentively. I often "read him to sleep". I was never asked to read trash. I remember his interest in Pierre Loti and Flaubert as well as in Dickens and Kipling.' His friend Charles Whibley, he bookman and critic, wrote of him in *The Times* that 'he took pleasure in so severe a work as Elton's *Origins of English History*, and turned with equal interest to the volumes of the *Annual Register*, upon which Burke has set his mark'. Whibley also wrote that 'Hobbe's *Thucydides* entranced him', and that while he was entirely sympathetic to the 'ancient fashion of speech', the long s's irritated him: 'an old book was well enough; an old printing press was an outrage'. One of his favourite biographical subjects was the life of Cardinal Wolsey. He had a particular preference, also, for county histories and parish records. 'Snappiness' was the note of his journalism, but he wholeheartedly commended the prose splendours of the Book of Common Prayer, which had been part of his literary nourishment as a boy. From it, no doubt, he derived his preference for pure English, 'in which', as *The Times* history states, 'he never allowed his taste, or his judgment, to be deflected by his love of novelty and change'. He told Moberly Bell in March 1909: 'One thing that does not seem to have gone to seed is the style of the writing in *The Times*. For that I am humbly grateful.' He heartily disliked slang in his newspapers. To *The Times* (January 27, 1909): 'Is "shut down" good English?' He asked the editorial staff to discard the use of 'chauffeur' and 'garage', substituting 'motor driver' and 'motor house', a ruling which failed in its purpose of purifying the language. He objected to slovenly usage in private correspondence as in his papers. He criticized Pryor, of *The Times*, for writing 'par' for paragraph and 'sub' for sub-editor, in a letter. 'Above all, do not use any Americanisms.' He, who admired the Americans, resisted their influence on the English tongue. 'Somebody should stand by with a coke-hammer and smash every American and other foreign word that tries to get into the building. Our own language is quite good enough. American is very amusing to talk, but it should not be allowed to be printed in *The Times*.' On his instructions words like boom and slump were printed between inverted commas.

While in such matters he had an aspiring mind, his imagination was not capable of soaring far above the mundane clamour. But if he was a stranger to ecstasy, he had an eye for a fine sunset and could be as delighted as a child in the more readily accessible pleasures of field and wood and stream. At Elmwood, he would often step into the garden at night to look at the stars, which was not to say that he was contemplating them. He was not oppressed by the universal mysteries. In religion he remained an Anglican who conformed mainly at his mother's bidding. He gave £2,000 to rebuild the spire of the Victorian Gothic Church of St. Augustine's at Kilburn, which his parents had attended; he paid or contributed to the stipends of a number of Church of England incumbents; he rendered great and lasting service to Westminster Abbey. Aspects of Roman Catholicism attracted him; but his religious sense was chiefly contained in a generalizing acceptance of the realities of the unseen. For him it was more convenient to believe in fate than to exercise faith.

In matters of conduct he was content to abide by the Confucian maxim that 'he who follows the way of a gentleman is a gentleman'. He had an unrelenting objection to *risqué* stories and was always censorious of coarse language. He banned advertisements containing the words 'constipation' and 'rupture', and an example of his less predictable fastidiousness was his last-minute refusal to sanction the publication of photographs of the degrading Jeffries–Johnson fight in 1910. 'Don't argue,' he told the picture editor of the *Daily Mail*, who pointed out the considerable cost of getting the photographs. 'I won't have them.'

*   *   *

It was believed outside his circle that he demanded a handsome fee of flattery in return for even the semblance of his friendship. He liked his praises to be sung, but it mattered who sang them. The sycophants of his domestic and professional circles amused rather than repelled him. They encouraged his Napoleonic posturing, to him a source of schoolboy pleasure, self-conscious play acting. One of the *Daily Mail* staff correspondents, J. M. N. Jeffries, wrote that 'he accepted their adulation as the badge of his rank and accomplishment', and that he was capable of divesting himself of it at any challenge from the world outside, 'where he was always ready to give as good as he got'. He discountenanced more flatterers than he endured. Given that he liked, and was liked, one had the passport to dissent from his views and actions without forfeiting his good will. Yet so mercurial was his vitality, so iridescent his temperament, that his inconsistencies continued to disturb those who had been longest exposed to them. His faults were in proportion to his best qualities; in combination, they proclaimed the magnitude of his personality. The voice of J. L. Garvin is heard testifying (*The Observer*, August 20, 1922): 'If you once had felt affection for him and had known the kind fascination of his best moments, you could never escape wholly from the spell. Nothing could extinguish it even when public or journalistic difference involved direct or deadly antagonisms, and you stood at sword's point and in diameter of combat. Often he had to be resisted, but in intercourse few men were harder to resist.' There was a day at Elmwood when he harshly criticized Price, the senior secretary. Price said that he would resign. Northcliffe left with no further word. Just before lunch, bent over his typewriter, Price felt a touch on his shoulder. 'I am sorry, Price,' Northcliffe said in his gentlest tone. 'I was unjust. If it is any consolation to you, it spoilt my morning.' His capricious displeasure could retard the healing processes. 'I spoke severely to you on the telephone,' he wrote in memorandum to S. J. Pryor, 'and I hope you will understand that, fond as I am of you, I meant every word of it.' Charles Duguid, the City editor of the *Daily Mail*, was 'filled with reassurance and delight' at receiving a New Year message from him (December 28, 1913): 'I am glad you still like me, as the impression you have sometimes conveyed is that you think me a silly fool. Thus in my liking and admiration for you I pocket the unintended insult and try not to be disheartened.' His dæmon could reduce men to tears. 'I have been perfectly miscrable since receiving your letter', one of his oldest Fleet Street friends, Alfred E. T. Watson, editor of *The Badminton Magazine* and racing correspondent of *The Times*, wrote to him. 'A word of encouragement from you is priceless.' His gifts of intimacy could make the heart dance. 'After all, my life has not been quite such a failure and muddle as I often regard it,' his fishing companion G. A. B. Dewar, whose Fleet Street experience included the editorship of the *Saturday Review*, wrote (July 15, 1913): 'It cannot be, or I should not have got such a letter as you have written to me. It has stirred me all through.'

His kindliest impulses remained always strong and active and compassion if not magnanimity was rarely missing from the scale of his feelings. The *Times* official history, with its undertones of antipathy, placed it on record that 'he could inspire devotion and hold it through endless trials. In Printing House Square all those who worked with him remember him with pride and affection', a tribute chorused by his old Carmelite House colleagues who had known him through so many more of the trials.

Through his newspapers he helped innumerable charitable causes. Personally, he seemed to have no promptings to take his place among the spectacular philanthropists. His gifts of £10,000 to the London Hospital, £5,000 to the Prince of Wales's Fund and £5,000 to the Westminster Abbey restoration fund, were examples of his largest gestures of public munificence, in modest contrast with the princely benefactions of his brother Harold (Rothermere). Instances of the readiness of Northcliffe's response to private misfortune have been given: it came from the heart and went to the heart. There is a letter written to him in 1913 by Marlowe, who had lost a son in a motoring accident: 'One of your most wonderful qualities is that sympathetic imagination by which you realize the feelings and sufferings of others even more keenly and "practically" than they do themselves.'

His thoughtfulness often surpassed that of ordinary courtesy, making his friendship the more grievous to lose. A friend or employee may not have told him his birthday. He would find it out for himself and mark it by a letter or telegram or an equally unexpected gift. He may not have been told that a wife or child was ill, but there would be messages of comfort for the patient and most likely flowers and fruit and books.

Garvin said that 'in the small offices of friendship he was incomparable for happy thought and invention'. In the midst of his heaviest labours and gravest responsibilities he would turn aside to do things that were a constant source of wonderment to his friends.

His forethought travelled in many directions, expressing itself in a rare excellence of tact. Taking Max Pemberton with him on holiday, he wrote beforehand: 'People like me are much too apt to imagine that all the world moves on gilded wheels. I have no right to take you away from your work, work that you may be relying on, without seeing that you do not suffer thereby. We will talk of that when we meet.' He saw a red-eyed young messenger girl on the stairs at Carmelite House. 'My dear,' he asked her in his tenderest tone, 'what is the matter?' She had raging toothache. He went back to his room, spoke on the telephone to his dentist in Wimpole Street, and arranged for the girl to be seen at once. An Amalgamated Press editor, proud of being able to send his young sons to a good preparatory school in Surrey, was taking a day off to play in the fathers' match. Northcliffe asked him: 'What car are you going in?' When he was told, he said: 'That won't do. You must go in my Rolls-Royce. It'll give your boys a thrill.' At Hook, in Hampshire, where he had fishing water, he admired the clean and tidy interior of a labourer's cottage. He told Pine, the chauffeur: 'Find out what they have to live on.' Pine reported that the family's income was 19s. a week. 'They must have a hard time of it,' Northcliffe said. 'Do you think they would be offended if I gave them something?' Pine made more inquiries, following which the family received a regular allowance from Northcliffe's private purse.

A member of the Carmelite House staff, J. E. Privett, was sent as a boy to the bungalow at West Clandon with letters for Northcliffe, whom he had never seen. When Northcliffe heard that the boy had started at 7 a.m., he asked sternly: 'Who sent you? I wonder how *he* would like to go all that time without food.' A table was spread with good things to eat and the boy was sent back to the office with the injunction: 'If you ever see anything in the paper which you think ought not to be there, find out where I am and tell me about it.' Privett never forgot 'the Chief's' consideration for him. 'He made me feel that I was not, after all, just a messenger boy.' Hearing that his old school teacher of St. John's Wood, Miss Florence Budd, had become a poorly-off invalid he made her a weekly allowance of money until she died. It was typical of him that he arranged for her sickroom to be redecorated and newly furnished; 'so that she may have the benefit', he wrote, 'of more cheerful surroundings'.

Looking for the springs of human action is rarely satisfying. Northcliffe's impulses to be kind may have been indicators of a diminished apacity to enjoy life by direct participation, sometimes the fate of men of wealth and power. But he could impart a moving quality of tenderness to his kindnesses, perhaps because of the maternal influence which suffused his being. Garvin said that Northcliffe's devotion to his mother 'was exquisite; to me, the most beautiful thing. . . . A better son never lived.' It was not in Geraldine Harmsworth's nature to make that claim; besides, she had other sons. Those who saw her and Northcliffe intimately together were not reticent about making the claim for her. She remained the one fixed point in the turmoil of his existence. He depended on her as on no other woman, not even on her who graced their married years, embellishing his career as well as sharing his life.

Against his mother, in every kind of situation requiring sagacity of judgment, no other woman could hope to prevail with him, though there were women who deluded themselves that they did, and all profited without knowing it by her matriarchal sense of justice. No one could say of Northcliffe what was said of Napoleon, that he was 'not a gentleman' in his relations with women. His personal charm, a certain magnetism and the glamour of his situation in the world, made him formidably attractive to the sex. Inevitably, there was gossip about that side of his life. When it came to his ears it was apt to be a subject of joking remarks to his nearest secretary. He referred in a letter to H. G. Price to 'a certain talkative lady' and the 'inference that those infants are mine, which is always thrown out everywhere, is passing off my back like water. I am certainly one of the most numerous parents in England. As a matter of fact, the little girl is a bright pet. I wish she *were* my daughter.'

*   *   *

He told his brother Harold that the best medical opinion was that he 'would not be much good' for some weeks. The doctors advised him to spend all the time he could in the open air, which hardly fitted in with his own diagnosis of ptomaine poisoning. That was in January 1909. He was writing from Pau in the Basses-Pyrenees. 'I do not see why I should not transact a little business and so, inasmuch as at the end of the year we shall be thinking of nothing but Newfoundland, I really think we ought to have a good talk over the whole of our affairs.' After suggesting dates, he announced that he was 'tremendously annoyed by the flagrant puffs of a medicine in which I hear Percy Burton is interested'. Percy Collingwood Burton had married their youngest sister Christabel in 1905. He was a handsome athletic Irishman who had a partnership in the St. James's Advertising Agency, Norfolk Street, Strand. 'I have been fighting puffs in the *Daily Mail* for years' (Northcliffe to Harold) 'and I thought I

351

had killed them. It is an outrageous abuse of our family influence', an·
was the beginning of a quarrel which led to Northcliffe ordering hi
newspaper managers to accept no advertising placed by Burton's agency
to its intended victim a disabling blow.

Northcliffe to Arthur Mee (January 26, 1909): 'I am always sorry t·
scold you or anyone, but really, after eighteen months' hard work, an·
but one holiday, it is hard that you should involve me with the Jews. *I*
little time ago it was the Roman Catholics, and I know from Roma·
Catholic friends that they felt very seriously about it. For the last twelv·
months I have been assailed by the Nonconformists, Roman Catholic
and Jews too. I suppose your next onslaught will be against the Churcl
of England. Now, do please be more careful in future.' Northcliffe to th·
editor of the *Jewish Chronicle* (January 29, 1909):

You have known me for nearly twenty years as a very keen friend an·
student of Israel. At the moment your letter reached me I was reading D·
Adler's most interesting book on the Jews in Spain and Portugal. My newspapers are so judaphil that a great number of people are under the impressior
that my family are Israelites. Sometimes I have criticised Jewish action; especiall·
did I do so in regard to the Alien Immigration Act, the wholesale oppositior
to which by Jews placed upon them the odium of the admission of anarchists,
and the hordes of thieves and other undesirables in Soho. For that action I wa·
very strongly attacked by the Jewish and especially some Yiddish journals. I
hope that the Jewish Board of Deputies, in justice to my businesses, in whicl
many Jews are engaged, will make some expression of regret for their attack
upon me.

*   *   *

At Pau, on a cold February day of 1909, the doors of a big wooden shed,
standing at the edge of a wide grassy plain with a wonderful view, were
opened to reveal a mysterious-looking apparatus of wire, wood and
canvas which was hauled into the light by an equally nondescript array
of helpers. One of them was A. J. Balfour, in a long box overcoat and a
deerstalker cap, who was making little more than a token show of
physical exertion. Another, more obviously energetic but less readily
recognized, was Northcliffe, wearing a huge fur motoring coat that hung
shapelessly to his feet. Balfour had come over from Biarritz as his guest.
A small eager-looking man with eyeglasses clipped on his nose was
Arthur Mee, editor of the *Children's Encyclopædia*. They were assisted by
several men of the chauffeur type and watched by a small crowd of
sceptical local residents who stood with their hands deep in their pockets
and stamped their feet for warmth. A little man in a leather jacket was
in charge. His name was Wilbur Wright.

When he clambered up into the fragile machine, the crowd was in a barracking mood. Mee said that as Wright called out to the party pulling on the rope 'One!' the crowd jeered back 'Un!' 'Two!' Wright shouted. 'Deux!' jeered the crowd. 'Three!' Wright shouted again and there was no jeering. He had cast off the rope and was rising in the air. Soon he had flown off into the middle distance and seemed to be bouncing along the lower slopes of the Pyrenees. Then he turned and came straight back over the heads of the crowd. Jeers turned to cheers.

Northcliffe had written to Moberly Bell (February 4, 1909): 'If you want a little holiday, do not forget that Pau is an excellent place. I can provide you with very nice accommodation here, and show you a man flying in the air, which would wake you up a bit.' And to Mrs (later Dame) Ethel Locke King, Brooklands, Weybridge, Surrey (February 5, 1909): 'I had a talk with Wright about Brooklands. Apparently, aeroplanists do not like trees. Would you let me know if there are any trees at Brooklands? An expert here estimates that there will be five thousand people flying at the end of the present year. Farman is teaching people at Châlons and two other people are also giving lessons. I see there is a Captain Moore Brabazon [later Lord Brabazon of Tara] flying at Châlons. Could you not get hold of him for Brooklands?' Soon, he was communicating his newest enthusiasm to more highly placed persons. He wrote to the Secretary of State for War, Haldane, on February 19:

I wonder if I may bore you on the subject of aeroplanes? I notice that the Germans and French have military representatives here watching the Wrights' machine, which Mr Balfour came to see. As I am constantly being chaffed by these foreign gentlemen with regard to the British army aeroplane, which they have nicknamed 'the steamroller', it occurs to me that, if it is worth the while of Germany and France to be on the spot, one of your young men might be sent down here to find out why it is that this aeroplane gets off the ground, and can fly for ten minutes or ten hours, if it chooses, and your Aldershot aeroplane, which is a very bad copy of the bad French aeroplanes, is unable to leave the ground. . . . Pray pardon this effusion.

He wrote more strongly to Esher (February 26):

Our national muddle-headedness has rarely been seen to worse disadvantage than in this particular matter, aviation. Here, some seven hundred and fifty miles from London, is a machine which can fly perfectly at forty miles an hour, at any height up to about a mile. It is stated by the German and French officers here to be practically 'unhitable'; provided with wireless telegraphy, the operator can scout an enemy's positions in a way possible by no other means. Despite the fact that this machine is only twenty-two hours' distant, nobody has been here from the War Office.

He had already told *The Times* office: 'Our national position in aviation is truly pathetic.' He told Strachey, of *The Spectator*: 'Flying must revolutionize scouting in war', and reiterated that no British officer had been sent to Pau. 'Germans, French, Italians, Spanish and Japanese were all there.'

Every new mechanical device, from aeroplanes to pencil sharpeners, was capable of exciting his interest. One day Marlowe found him winding up a clockwork toy clown which he set tumbling across the floor of Room One. 'Send me, very kindly, some of these new "safety razors" and ten dozen blades', he wrote to W. F. Bullock, the *Daily Mail* correspondent in New York. He took the opportunity of chiding Bullock for criticizing the New York *World* in one of his cabled reports. 'Those who live in glass houses should not throw stones', and he touched on the problem of a newspaper proprietor's responsibility when it is diffused through a myriad human channels. 'Personally, I am always at the mercy of the thousands of journalists in my employment, and many of them do quite as foolish things as the Americans.'

* * *

Kennedy Jones wrote from his sickbed to complain about affairs at *The Times* with particular reference to Moberly Bell, for whom he still used the code name 'Canton' in correspondence; just as he used 'Atlantic' for Northcliffe long after the need for secrecy had passed. 'Here are the main facts which will enable you to judge his uselessness as a manager.' Having set them out, Jones added: 'In all the twelve months Canton has never attempted to, nor, indeed, is he capable of grappling with these vital yet primary questions of managing.' Northcliffe had already let Bell know that 'K.J. is a good deal disturbed about the expenses of *The Times* and its financial outlook' (February 13, 1909). Two days later he wrote more explicitly to Bell:

The new proprietors have not, I think, borne their burden badly. They have paid an exorbitant price, have exorbitant fixed charges to meet, and have left the whole business absolutely in the hands of the staff of the paper, and they have no chance of getting any interest on their investment for a long time, and under the present system not at all. My own feeling is that *The Times* is heading on to another financial crisis.

He did not wish to hurry Bell, he said, 'in the disentanglement of the great Printing House Square muddle'. He acknowledged his own responsibility in adding 'considerably to the expenses by several suggestions

I have made', including opening an American office on Fifth Avenue, New York. Kennedy Jones's investigations had roused him to what he clearly considered to be necessary action. His letters to Bell were longer and more frequent and often they were full of pungent comment and occasionally forthright criticism, as when Jones reported that much of the 'copy' sent to the printer was still being written by hand. 'I hate carping criticism, and you know that I do not indulge in it, but I make these complaints to show that I have always found that muddle in a newspaper office always shows in the newspaper itself' (February 18).

The editorial staff was embarrassed and puzzled by his acute comparisons of the contents of the paper with those of its rivals. '*The Times* is behind other papers today in news of Sport and of the Theatres. There is no report of the Amateur Billiard Championship, London Section Final. No report of Caius College (Cambridge) sports, and Oriel College (Oxford) *v*. Clare (Cambridge), nor of Eton Senior and Junior Steeplechases. All these events are reported in other papers.' Such pedantry in referring to the colleges of the two universities may have been thought needlessly gratuitous by the men of *The Times*, but Northcliffe declined to be overawed by their scholastic exclusiveness. He had been bold enough to write in a communique a few days before: 'I hope the Greek is all right in the report of the Assistant Masters' meeting. Some of these gentlemen might inquire why it is that one can go through British colonies and find hundreds of their pupils occupying menial positions, and why men with businesses such as I have, while straining every nerve to use public school boys, rarely find more than ten per cent of them any good.'

Nothing appeared to miss his eagle eye, which was known to be alert at any early hour every day, but which, in the case of *The Times*, pounced on infinitesimal errors of punctuation or small technical flaws such as a slipped rule or a battered letter. 'My copy this morning was from No. 4 machine. Page 8 is spoilt through not taking the ink properly.' 'The Weather Chart on Page 14: Some of the arrows are very indistinct today.' 'There was a stupid mistake yesterday where *The Times* spoke of "trooping the colours". This is a well-known trap for every junior sub-editor. It should be "trooping the colour".' Frequently there would be appended a list of news items 'NOT in *The Times*', a comparison which usually told heavily in favour of the *Morning Post* and the *Daily Telegraph*. Even the most hardened *Times* staff men had to respect Northcliffe's extreme diligence. His determination that they should do so was reinforced by the well-kept secret of 38 Sackville Street, Piccadilly. A room had been set apart for S. J. Pryor, the former *Daily Mail* man who had rejoined Northcliffe's staff after several years with other newspapers. Pryor was acting as his *Times* watchdog. It was he who was supplying the information on which Northcliffe's omniscient observations rested. Pryor's

work there started at 6 a.m. Sending a long and full report on the issue o
The Times for February 20, 1909, Northcliffe did not scruple to tel
Moberly Bell that 'such an analysis, even trained as I am, occupies at leas
two hours'.

Hardly less provocative was his firm grasp of the history of the paper
He surprised members of the staff with whom he talked by his intimate
awareness of the paper's past, his instinct for protecting its traditions, hi
knowledge of its best and worst periods, and of matters which wen
beyond the editorial competence. He knew more than most of them
about the standing of Delane with the Walters and about the family and
professional pre-eminence of John Walter the second. It was not merely
the random information of a naturally acquisitive mind. '*The Times* was
made not by the lax habits of the last twenty years, but by its vigilance
in news gathering between 1820 and 1870.'

His sensibility was offset by the oppressiveness of various *Times* practices and methods which had not been revised since the great days.
Asking what had been done about a scheme which he had proposed as an
aid to circulation on the Continent, he wrote to Bell (February 22, 1909):

What has happened? What nearly always happens in attempting to improve
The Times. One is always, to use *The Times* expression, 'up against' some vested
interest, some unreasonable prejudice, or some meaningless habit.

I am so accustomed to be able to reorganise without vested interests and
muddle that I wonder whether I shall live long enough to see this old institution
free from mistakes, old news and late news, and seen as of yore in the hands of
every Englishman abroad, as well as made lucid and clear and ceasing to be the
labyrinth of which Lord Rosebery complained.

He wrote to Bell two days later: 'I do wish you would take my letters
in a more reasonable frame of mind.' Bell had told him that he wanted
'no persistent urging that we devote more space to this and to that', and
Northcliffe rounded off his appeal by saying: 'When you know me better
you will understand my method of criticizing and co-operating.' The
same day, February 24, he telegraphed to Bell's wife at 22 Park Crescent,
Portland Place, London: *If I am worrying Mr Bell please let me know stop
I fear he does not understand my rough ways*. The following day, he wrote
again to Bell: 'I am sorry you take my criticisms so much to heart.' And
on February 26: 'I hope the staff do not think I am ungrateful or interfering. I certainly am not ungrateful, and have no wish to interfere. I have
no other ambition in life than that it shall be said in England when my
obituary appears on the personal page that I assisted in maintaining the
only national newspaper in the world. I have no goldmine idea of *The
Times*.' He wrote in a different vein on March 7:

Hotel Ritz,
Paris.

My dear Mr. Bell,—I was sorry to hear that Layton Bennett and K. J. had succumbed in the matter of accounts to the mephitic atmosphere of Printing House Square. 'Abandon scope all ye who enter here' should be written over the portals of that mid-Victorian barrack.

I see before me now a vision of the choicest spirits that I have gathered around me bedrowsed into a state of torpor and love for the obsolete. If it only ended there it would not be so bad, but this particular brand of Upas tree not only carries its victims back almost into the depths of ancestor worship, but inculcates in them a love of the inaccurate and a perverted appetite for printers' errors. Your Roman seems to have enjoyed his oyster after its fourteen days cross-country journey from Colchester or Burnham-on-Crouch. Your *Times* sub-editor has an equally morbid taste for ancient news.

But it is a fine day and I will not be kept indoors even for *The Times*.

It will not be unreasonable to reassert that the official historian of *The Times* erred in assuming that Northcliffe was so bemused (not to say bewildered) by his association with the paper in 1908 and thereafter that he could give his mind to little else. The historian was writing without access to a large amount of documentary evidence to the contrary. Northcliffe to Strachey, editor of *The Spectator* (March 10, 1909): 'I have read with much interest your article on newspaper gambling. I have been trying to stop it for some years, but the matter is more complicated than you think. No newspaper, from *The Times* downwards, can afford to dispense with betting, because its readers are immediately diverted to another paper. For the moment I should be satisfied with the stopping of prize competitions, and I have urged two successive Solicitor-Generals to take the matter up.' Northcliffe to Winston Churchill (March 17, 1909): 'Will you and Mrs Churchill come and lunch here next week, whichever day suits you? I do not think you have seen our little house, which was for fifty-five years the home of Samuel Rogers, the banker. On entering our dining-room a little time ago old Lord Wemyss said, "I have not been in this room since 1855".' He was personally conducting an inquiry into the 'pulling power' of serial stories in *Answers*. It meant reading reports from circulation representatives in many parts of the country, seeing editorial men and women, calling in writers to discuss plots. He found time to remember old family friends. Frederick Wood to Northcliffe: 'Another present—your generosity is overwhelming! I am ever poor in thanks. Wrist shaky. The Sylvans had a good debate on the eternal Irish problem.' Katharine Wright to Northcliffe (March 28, 1909): 'If the flying did something for your vacation at Pau, will you not believe that you and Lady Northcliffe did much to make our stay very pleasant and interesting to us? With kindest remembrances to you both, in which

Wilbur and Orville join me.' Sutton to Northcliffe: 'Thank you ever so much for your kindness. I am very grateful to you. I am sure you know that if there is anything I can do to show my appreciation of your goodness, I shall be glad to do it. I can at any rate try and show it by my work. That is the best way to thank you.—Sutkin.' Northcliffe to his mother (April 11, 1909, by telegram): *Our twenty-first very happy wedding day dear Mother and we send you Easter greetings.—Alfred.* J. L. Garvin to Northcliffe (April 13): 'There was a superstitious sort of feeling about spending my 41st birthday with you. I feel twenty years younger than when we started together and hope to be a real help to you yet.' Alfred Butes to John Cowley, a director of Associated Newspapers Ltd. (April 16): 'The Chief is distressed to hear that two men, Slater and Ruinets, have been dismissed with the very short notice of one month, after five or six years' service. The men should have received at least two or three months' notice. The Chief wishes in future to receive the name of every person dismissed, with the reason and length of service in each case.' Northcliffe to R. D. Blumenfeld, editor of the *Daily Express* (April 17): 'I particularly dislike taking anyone from Mr Pearson during his illness. [Pearson was having the first of the eye operations which did not save him from eventual blindness.] We are thinking of starting an out-door paper under Mr Beach Thomas, and he wanted the assistance of Mr Izzard. If this will in any way inconvenience Mr Pearson, I would postpone the publication of the paper. Everyone admires the courage with which he is facing his ordeal, one that I am well able to appreciate.'

Northcliffe told Beach Thomas, who was long in his service as a special correspondent, that in his view 'the countryside had never been properly treated as a source of news'. He cited on that occasion his favourite example of the 'howlers' made by urban writers on country topics: 'The crack of the rifle on the moors', on August 12. Beach Thomas wrote: 'Lord Northcliffe's idea was that natural history of all sorts, the farm and the garden, were proper sources of news which people would be glad to read about and ought to read about. The idea was novel, in regard to daily newspapers, at any rate on the scale which he envisaged.' The new paper of the countryside was indefinitely postponed. Beach Thomas was engaged to write for *The Observer* and the *Daily Mail*, while P. W. D. Izzard was encouraged by Northcliffe to contribute 'A Countryman's Diary' to the *Daily Mail*, where it appeared every day for twenty-seven years. The little feature had no more devoted reader than 'the Chief' himself. Travelling abroad and receiving bundles of recent copies of the *Daily Mail* from London, his first thought was to turn to the little daily article over the initials 'P.W.D.I.'

Beach Thomas's articles on French intensive gardening brought such a heavy extra delivery of letters to Carmelite House that Northcliffe considered starting a paper to be called *Golden Soil*. Instead, he set up an experimental vegetable growing research station of his own at Sutton Place, at an estimated cost of £2,290 in the first year. The work done there, under scientific direction, made 'copy' for *The Times* as well as for the *Daily Mail*. The 'Daily Mail Farm' on the Great North Road, near Grantham, was so overrun by weekend sightseers that its operations were seriously impeded. That was Beach Thomas's doing. Izzard wrote for the flower and vegetable gardeners of England with the authentic note of amateur passion.

★   ★   ★

At *The Times* Moberly Bell had stubbornly continued to fight the battle of the accounts. Northcliffe complained again: 'What I personally want, with all my numerous responsibilities, are accounts that I can look at as at a barometer. What I have never been able to obtain from *The Times* yet is, how much money we have made this week, how much money we made this week last year and the year before, and what *The Times* has made since the beginning of the financial year.' He wrote again: 'It is because I believe that the directors of a newspaper should be able to see each week exactly what they have made that I plead for a system which will ensure this result. I see this. Layton Bennett sees this. Kennedy Jones is beginning to see this. Why should you be the one old Tory who won't admit it?' Against a mention of Bell in a letter from a member of the Walter family, Northcliffe wrote: 'He only understands the coke-hammer.' Again, as to editorial matters (March 10, 1909): 'During the past year I have been shutting my eyes to mistakes, because I know that I am dealing with a number of people who have been associated with a proprietary which deliberately allowed *The Times* to be deprived of its advertisement and other revenues year after year without any effort, and, in addition, did not trouble to make a daily comparison with the rival newspapers that were injuring it, or even to read *The Times* itself.' And the next day: 'I often wish my suggestions were followed without so wry a face. I never make them without careful consideration, though I am sometimes wrong and I am sometimes right.' To which Bell replied: 'You say yourself you are "sometimes right and sometimes wrong". Personally, I think you are generally right in everything connected with the editing and production of the paper, but I am very much mistaken in you if you are not the last man to wish a servile acquiescence in every idea that you propound without we, on our part, giving to it such consideration as our poor intelligences may suggest. In fact, you yourself have repeatedly said: "My notes are hurried and are to be taken as suggestions only." '

Being asked to swallow his words was not pleasant medicine for Northcliffe. Not many men among those on his staffs had cared to risk the prescription. Moberly Bell was a rock-like character with no crystal gleam of imagination. He did not easily perceive himself to be at fault. Northcliffe's patience was becoming strained but he managed it with exemplary firmness for the time being and could show good feeling, as in writing to Bell on March 13, 1909, about the young John Walter. 'I like him extremely. He does not seem to have had a chance, and seemed quite pleased to get an appointment on *The Times* [as correspondent in Madrid]. I believe that if he had two years' education in the mechanical and editorial part of the business he would be able, with good advisers, to take charge of *The Times*. If he shows any capacity in Madrid, and any desire to regain *The Times* for his family, I should certainly feel disposed to leave my interest to him on very easy terms, and would indeed prefer that to my present scheme of forming the control into a national trust. I am impulsive and sometimes too quick in my judgments, but I do not think I have made a mistake in John Walter.'

The Governor-General of Canada, Earl Grey, had told Northcliffe that there would be value in a visit to Canada by the editor of *The Times*. Northcliffe had been urging Buckle to go. 'The Canadians see nothing but the riff-raff of our cities and the worst products of our public schools. I know that the too numerous Battle of Quebec and Canada Club dinners, during the customary loyal toasts, always show that "Canada is loyal to the backbone". The great mass of the people by reason of its ignorance is indifferent or contemptuous, and in the West openly pro-American. But one cannot say so, and I can only do my best by guiding opinion in England carefully and judiciously where one is acquainted with facts.'

Intending to be helpful, he proposed, if Buckle decided to make the trip, to ask the Canadian Pacific Railway to provide special facilities. Buckle replied at once: 'I have never accepted any favour of any sort from any corporation or individual; and am much too personally and editorially proud to place myself and *The Times* under the obligation that such acceptance would involve. To show you my feeling, I may say that I have never been to a theatre since I was editor without paying for my seat.' Northcliffe was equally quick in rejoinder. 'I abominate such things as free passes, because they are in the nature of bribes. None of the newspapers I am connected with accepts free tickets or passes, with the exception of tickets for dramatic critics, which we accept on legal advice that comments of an uninvited critic might be considered libellous. My idea of a newspaper, and especially of *The Times*, is that of an entirely independent and impersonal organ. It is for that reason that I do not allow my name to appear in my newspapers if I can help it.'

Northcliffe to John Galsworthy:

> 22, St. James's Place,
> S.W.
> 22nd April, 1909.

Dear Mr Galsworthy,—. . . As to the war question, it is one of the most difficult in the world at the moment. Nobody in this country wants war.

If you care to study the question as my guest in Berlin for a few days, I shall be very glad to invite you. I shall be there about the 13th May. If you can write anything calculated to stop war between England and Germany, I shall be very glad to print it. But I think it best that you should ascertain the German view first.

> Yours sincerely,
> NORTHCLIFFE.

Moberly Bell announced his wish to put *The Times* porters and messengers into uniform and suggested dark green with gold braid: 'Is this too flamboyant for your taste?' Replying on April 23, 1909, Northcliffe admonished Bell for a letter 'written in your own hand at the expense of the shareholders of The Times Publishing Company Limited', and gave it as his opinion that 'a tail-coat and grey trousers—something like the uniform worn in institutions like the Bank of England and Coutts & Co.—would be best for *The Times*. To put your messengers into a costume of the Lyons' Popular Restaurant type would be to alter the tone of Printing House Square.' 'Forgive me for writing "with my own hand",' Bell wrote by return. 'It is 11 p.m. and all my type writers have left. Added to which it is ten times as pleasant to write to you as to dictate to you!'

John Galsworthy to Northcliffe:

> Wingstone,
> Manaton,
> Devon.
> 25th April, 1909.

Dear Lord Northcliffe,—Many thanks for your kind letter. . . . I know well enough that war is not desired by this country, but there has grown up a vicious habit amongst responsible men of saying that it is inevitable. From that to a general belief that it is so is but a short step, and from such general belief to a war is shorter. . . .

> With kind regards from
> Yours sincerely,
> JOHN GALSWORTHY.

Receiving word that a 'bucket shop' advertisement had been accepted for the *Family Journal*, Northcliffe wrote peremptorily to the advertising director of The Amalgamated Press (April 27): 'I have ordered the cheque to be returned. The explanation given me is that such advertising is being taken by *John Bull*. The Amalgamated Press is not *John Bull* and has, I hope, higher ideals than that publication. Quite apart from the moral aspect, it is foolish to take such matter because it keeps good advertising out of the paper.' A popular ventriloquist, Arthur Prince, was making friendly references to the Harmsworth Press in his patter. Northcliffe went to see his performance. Next day (April 28) the performer received a message from Carmelite House: 'Lord Northcliffe desires me to say that he notices that you are continually improving.'

His crisis of the nerves had left him less springy of step. His movements now seemed more deliberate. His brain was still alert to every tangential flick of circumstance. The novelty of telegraphing pictures was one of his interests just then. A *Daily Mail* art department man, Thorne Baker, who had obtained remarkable results in colour photography, was experimenting in long-distance transmission. 'I have got over the difficulties,' he wrote to tell Northcliffe, 'and I hope that very shortly now we shall be getting half-tone pictures regularly and with certainty from Manchester.'

Northcliffe to John Galsworthy:

> 22, St. James's Place,
> S.W.
> 28th April, 1909.
>
> Dear Mr Galsworthy.—I expect to be in Berlin about the 20th May. I hope we shall be able to meet. I feel my own personal responsibility in this matter very greatly, and having German relations, and knowing intimately the feeling in both countries, I wish to make readers of my newspapers as well acquainted as it is possible to be with the exact state of affairs. Two of my greatest difficulties are, firstly, English ignorance of Germany, and, secondly, the Germans' somewhat natural indignation at our suggestion that they should alter their navy to please us.
>
> Yours sincerely,
> NORTHCLIFFE.

Two London dramatists characterized him recognizably in stage plays, J. B. Fagan, in *The Earth*, produced at the Kingsway Theatre, London, on April 14, and Arnold Bennett, in *What the Public Wants*, at the Aldwych Theatre, London, on May 4. Bennett disclosed that in his play, 'Harmsworth is the hero, and the press and the theatre the subjects. What *my* Harmsworth wants is not to be continually slighted by intellectual people. This play is the story of his disappointment in this desire.' (Letter to Mr and Mrs W. W. Kennerley, October 7, 1908.) Bennett considered his Harmsworth to be sufficiently close to life to warrant his doubting whether the Stage Society would risk producing the play. The *Daily Mail* drama critic in a discreet notice said that it was 'very amusing and well written'. After its presentation by the Stage Society, it was put on at the New Royalty Theatre, London, with Charles Hawtrey as the newspaper proprietor. It was again well received, but its run was short. The earlier play, *The Earth*, had little to commend it, despite the distinguished efforts of Norman McKinnell at portraying the millionaire proprietor of the newspaper which gave the play its title. Garvin wrote to Lady Northcliffe, after seeing it: 'I was furious to think that we had all been so preposterously indulgent to so crude a piece of puzzle-headed claptrap. These futile attacks only mean that the Chief is a great man and when they pass they will leave him a still greater man.'

*   *   *

Preparing to leave for Germany, he had the little green deed-box sent up to his room at 22 St. James's Place, and spent a morning answering the 'pending' letters from his bed. 'I cannot be keener than I am about the removal of our national art treasures to the United States', he wrote to Charles E. C. Jerningham, of *Truth*, who wanted him to campaign for 'a Commission to investigate the country's treasures'. Northcliffe further informed him: 'I am all the keener since I have seen some of them in the houses of their new owners on the other side of the Atlantic, in the houses of people who in no way appreciate them at all, and where many of them are being destroyed owing to the terrible heat of the rooms there.'

Haldane, the War Minister, had written to tell him that 'we have at last elaborated our plans for the foundation of a system of Aerial Navigation for the Army and Navy and constructed a real scientific Department of the State for the study of aerial navigation' (May 4, 1909). Having studied the composition of the committee charged with carrying out the plans, Northcliffe replied to the War Minister: 'I hope you will not mind my saying that it is one of the most lamentable things I have read in connection with our national organization. There is no practical aviator on the committee and the list of subjects is such as would have been discussed fifteen years ago.' He wished, he wrote, to turn to 'a more pleasant topic', and proposed a military rehearsal of the press censorship as it would operate in a European war. 'The training of Press censors might be commenced this year [1909]. One knows how Moltke and Bismarck watched the Press and in those days it was in its infancy.' Haldane replied: 'I think there is a great deal in your suggestion. We will talk about it.' He assured Northcliffe: 'The Naval and Military experts have demonstrated to the Defence Committee that dirigibles and still more aeroplanes are a very long way off being the slightest practical use in war.' Visiting his old university of Gottingen, he had found, he said, that the Prussian

Government had set up a chair of aviation. It was the purpose of the British Government, he told Northcliffe, to encourage the inventor in every way. 'Rightly or wrongly, our principle is that without science progress in this difficult matter will be very slow.' Northcliffe had urged the appointment to the War Office committee of men like Royce and Napier, the motor-car pioneers. 'They are very able constructors and men of business,' Haldane agreed, 'but in this big affair much more than that is needed.'

Garvin had written again: 'Fond as I am of *The Observer*, never think for a moment that I want to keep it for my own purposes like a log tied to your leg. Give me your confidence fully, always, and you will never repent, for I never cause friction when trusted.' Replying to 'My dear Garvino', Northcliffe told him that he was wrong in fearing that *The Times* necessarily diverted proprietorial attention from *The Observer*. 'Personally, I never proposed to manage *The Observer* and, as you know, I was always endeavouring to buy *The Times*, since I approached Mr Walter ten years ago.' He interpolated his regret that too much prominence had been given to a Perrier Water advertisement, 'which should not have been there because the Water belongs to a brother of mine, and it looks as though we were favouring him'. Memo from Northcliffe to Kennedy Jones: 'I have been gradually finding out that *The Times* is not a good "puller" ', referring to advertising results.

Hilaire Belloc, M.P., denounced the 'war scare' journalism of the *Daily Mail* in a speech to Liberals at Salford, Manchester. One of the Associated Newspaper directors, Andrew Caird, reminded Northcliffe in a note: 'You were rather kind to Mr Belloc when he got into Parliament and since, and this is the reward.' Ostensibly he was going to Germany for another consultation with the Frankfort oculist, Solm. The news of Pearson's failing sight had increased his concern about his own.

The visit was to have an important secondary purpose. He was determined to find out what he could about the internal German situation, with its ominously growing potential for disturbing the peace. His *Daily Mail* staff had been called 'the footpads of politics' by the Liberals, angered by the paper's 'scaremongerings'. Northcliffe was 'an enemy of the human race'. Reluctantly, Asquith and Grey informed the House of Commons that the Germans were building Dreadnoughts with priority speed, imperilling the whole position of the British Navy. That was in March 1909. Northcliffe had given the facts to the public six months previously. He now told his newspaper readers that the humble submission of Serbia to Austria, backed by Germany, marked the triumph of might over right and was a menace to the future of England.

Examined by the German oculist during the second week of May 1909, he wrote to Butes: 'Solm says there is no disease, but he is worried that

I am constantly requiring stronger spectacles. I expect his report to be sent on to me in Berlin.' Awaiting it, he dictated a long letter to his friend Sir Douglas Straight.

I am rather like a spider enmeshed in a web of its own making. One thing has led to another in my career, and lately there has come *The Times*, which I did not want but which I did not wish to see ruined. I trust and hope that in future it will conduct itself with the minimum amount of interference from me. It has been a back-breaking task these last fifteen or sixteen months, involving very early rising on my part and the neglect of exercise, but the results are very satisfactory in every department.

He proceeded to say something about other sides of his life as a newspaper owner. There was the *Daily Mail*, involving 'an immense amount of work', and requiring a great deal of editorial caution. 'The slightest error in a paper with such a circulation is seen and magnified by the public. Quite lately, the same little mistake in a Reuter telegram occurred in *The Times* and in the *Daily Mail*. *The Times* did not receive one correction. The *Daily Mail* received hundreds.' Very few people, he continued, realized what the management of a paper read by several million a day means. The periodical side of his business, he told Straight, did not worry him at all, though it was much bigger than all the other parts of the business combined.

I have, therefore, to think what I can relinquish. Something I must relinquish because of the report of the oculist, which I understand I am to receive this afternoon, is not favourable unless I take things much easier. The unfortunate part of our business is that it brings forward everyone, from Royalty downwards, asking for support for this, that, or the other thing. The latest request is that the *Daily Mail* should raise a Dreadnought. My reply was that our business was to publish news. My correspondence alone requires four people to attend to it now.

He was asked, he said: Why are you embarking on your Newfoundland enterprise? His answer was that he had to consider the situation of his newspapers in the light of the possible activities of a paper-making trust, which might 'squeeze the life out of English newspapers'. As regards the weight and pace of his work in general, it was easier to *say* stop than *to* stop it; italics his.

No one is more anxious for more domestic life than I. No one has a more charming chatelaine and more charming chateaux than I. But until I can organise some reduction of business, the only time the chatelaine and I get together is when we are abroad [May 15].

The oculist's report was a serious warning. 'Unless you exercise the greatest care and restraint, it will be necessary for you to retire altogether from active participation of [*sic*] business in three or four years if you wish to retain a proper use of your eyes.' Northcliffe wrote to Butes: 'Unless I am to go about with a dog and tin cup in the next few years there has got to be some alteration in my career.' Receiving, as every senior member of his staffs did, a copy of the report, Garvin wrote at once: 'For God's sake, take what care is now possible and let everything else go to the devil. Of course, I have been long enough with you and near enough to you to know that you are caught in the colossal machine you have created; and it is hard to get out; but don't let it destroy you. If you took even for a year the real irresponsible life-giving rest you have never taken, free from any thought of shop, your papers would rub along somehow and you would come back like Titan refreshed.'

Moberly Bell saw in the prognosis an opportunity to impress Northcliffe with some hopefully sage advice. 'You must really content yourself with idleness. You can do much more in the way of general inspiration if you will avoid that minute inspection which must be trying. Seriously, your eyesight is too precious to be wasted in the detection of blemishes which while evident to you are not recognized by the casual reader.' Northcliffe to Bell: 'It was most kind of you to write. I am of course somewhat disturbed', in which state of mind he telegraphed to *The Times* advertising manager (May 15): *Fridays Odol advertisement horrid.*

To Kennedy Jones, he wrote: 'I must try to organize my life and business accordingly. I have no desire to become a second Pulitzer.' Concerned above all to avoid that catastrophe, he told Pine, the head chauffeur, to see that extra blinds and shutters were fitted to the Rolls-Royce, so that he could ride, if need be, in shaded light. To F. E. Smith: 'I have been finding out a good deal about Germany. What a great pity more of our people do not spend their holidays here.' He gave an interview to a German news agency representative. 'An admirable way of helping to avoid a struggle between the two nations would be by the exchange of visits; not merely by Burgomasters and Members of Parliament, but by a great extension of travel between the peoples as a whole. If only I could send here the readers of the *Daily Mail*!'

He affirmed: 'The present state of mutual suspicion is particularly unfortunate, because there is no antipathy towards Germans in England or towards Englishmen in Germany, and because the two countries have so much to learn from one another.' Much of the misunderstanding, he suggested, 'arises from the fact that your governing people do not understand that secrecy begets suspicion and that suspicion is the feeder of agitation'. Representing 'The Peace Society of the City of New York', Andrew Carnegie sent him a message of warm approval; the interview, he said, was 'a fine thing'. But Northcliffe warned Garvin: 'I do not believe that any visits or writings will affect the inevitable purpose of these people', and he wrote to H. W. Wilson: 'Every one of the new factory chimneys here is a gun pointed at England.'

Reports of alarming rumours at home about Zeppelin airships carrying out secret night trials over East Anglia, prompted him to telegraph to Kennedy Jones (May 20): *Do you want me to cable anything about this ridiculous airship rubbish in England stop amused and contemptuous.* It was made-in-Germany scorn, parts of the German press having wilfully amplified the rumours and used them as an excuse for satirical writing about the English character. 'No one over here takes the rumours very seriously', he was told by Wilson, the *Daily Mail* leader writer. Northcliffe passed back word to his editors that the real danger-signals were not in the sky but at sea, though he had told the German public in his interview that their dirigibles were not such 'a dangerous bird as the Wright aeroplane'. His messages to the *Daily Mail* put an end to the airship scare of 1909.

He visited the great German engineering and chemical plants; looking into the German labour exchange system, 'which seems to me admirable', as did German efficiency in town planning; thought the Rudolf Virchow Hospital 'most magnificent', and went over it a second time, saying: 'We have nothing like it'—with the reservation that English nurses were superior. He let the Berliners know through their newspapers that he was 'not an out-and-out admirer' of their city, 'despite its delightful open spaces and its handsome ladies'. To him, a travelled man, it was 'not much more than a huge provincial town'. He deplored the Berliners' habit of staring, 'the infallible hall-mark of the provincial'.

Of exceptional interest to him was the visit with John Galsworthy to the Moabit Prison, an eagerly seized chance of indulging an old and still vigorous curiosity. He concerned himself with the fate of a murderer, Heinrich Gabel, who had been in solitary confinement for thirty-three years. 'I shall see if the Kaiser will pardon him', he announced to Galsworthy, and a plea was sent in their joint names for presentation to the emperor. Months afterwards the man was released and Wile, the *Daily Mail* man in Berlin, wrote to Northcliffe: 'I think you are partly responsible', a tribute which the ex-convict might not have endorsed because on going out into streets now clamorous with the sounds and sights of internal combustion engines he was so bewildered that he begged the warders at the gate to let him in again.

'There is no fear of my journals going back as to the German danger,' he wrote to Hall Caine on May 26. 'They never have misunderstood the German situation. I began to understand it some eight years ago, when I first made a regular practice of visiting Germany, that wonderful unknown country. Foolish airship panic mongers merely cause us to be despised in Germany. As to the Navy, the quicker we get to work and prepare the better.' And to Garvin the same day: 'I have learned a great deal in Germany, but nothing that does not increase my belief in the need for preparation by land and sea and in education.' He deemed it equally politic to arrange for the publication that year in the *Daily Mail* of a series of articles by 'A German in England', introducing them in a leader with the sentiment: 'Nothing is more likely to produce a happy effect on the future relations of the two great Empires than a better knowledge of each other.'

His stay in Berlin was abruptly concluded when he woke one morning to the embarrassing discovery that a chambermaid at the Hotel Adlon had thrown away his denture. He left for Paris at once to get it replaced.

Chapter Fourteen

Front Page Story

THE first Imperial Press Conference, held in London in June 1909, was more than a pleasant outing for newspaper proprietors, editors and journalists from many parts of the British Empire. It brought about reductions in cable charges and abolished obstacles in the channels of news distribution. Those were among the chief results of its formal deliberations, to which Northcliffe contributed as one who had given encouragement and practical help to its originator, Harry (later Sir Harry) Brittain, formerly secretary to Sir William Ingram of the *Illustrated London News* and founder of the British section of the Pilgrims' Society. More effective still were the informal conversations, including those of a memorable day when the delegates wandered in the grounds of Sutton Place. They helped to solidify sympathies which stood firm in the years of peril ahead. The delegates had come to London with no clear realization of the mounting European tensions. A speech of welcome from Rosebery, who, Wilson of the *Daily Mail* wrote privately, tried at the last moment to get out of his promise to be present and 'had almost to be brought up to London by force', sounded a note of warning that rang out uncongenially on the summer air. He told his audience that 'there never was in history so threatening and overpowering preparation for war'. The visitors were startled. At Sutton Place, a few days later, they crowded round Northcliffe to hear his first-hand impressions of Germany. Garvin said that they were noticeably impressed—'and some depressed', although it was a purely social occasion. Northcliffe had once again remembered old friends: the names of Pemberton, Markwick and Fred Wood were in his list of 160 guests. When Admiral Sir John Fisher wrote from the Admiralty to congratulate him on the success of the Conference, he disclaimed all credit for it—'one of the most important gatherings that has ever taken place in England'.

His hospitality at Sutton Place was sometimes a valuable unofficial adjunct of the diplomacy of the period. There was a letter from a new Canadian cabinet minister, Mackenzie King★. 'June 18, 1909.—I have thought of Lady Northcliffe and yourself so often, and of the happy hours at Sutton Place. It is a source of gratification to have a seat in the cabinet and to be able to share in a larger way in the affairs of government and to co-operate with those who are working for the upbuilding of the Empire.' He had read the reports of Northcliffe's German interview. 'While there may be cause for concern, England does herself an injustice in either provoking bitterness or belittling her strength and position.'

Northcliffe was still corresponding with Professor Hornaday in New York about the American robins: 'I have released seven of the birds and they have taken to English life quite as readily as some of your millionaires do.' The grey squirrels were 'a little unsettled', and a subsequent generation of agriculturists in England had cause to regret that they were ever introduced, though Northcliffe was not wholly responsible.† A young Australian journalist, Frank Fox, was walking with him at Sutton Place when a gardener came forward with a net full of sparrows caught eating food put down for the robins. Obviously hoping to impress with his zeal, the gardener proceeded to wring the sparrows' necks. It was too much for Northcliffe. He turned hurriedly aside. Fox wrote: 'I thought he was going to faint.'

His heads of departments, he complained, were 'being worked to a standstill'. 'Everyone', he told his brother Harold, 'is working up to the last ounce of capacity.' Kennedy Jones, to whom he had written from Germany expressing 'relief at having someone so reliable as you at the other end of the wire', had gone away, 'completely knocked up'. Sutton, another victim of overwork, was being given treatment which put him to the peculiar necessity of taking a cold bath at night and getting into bed without drying. Pomeroy Burton's position as general business executive was to be reviewed. 'He has many faults', wrote Northcliffe in a summarizing note to Harold. There was also Andrew Caird, equally prominent among the senior men at Carmelite House. 'I am well aware of his great merits, but he is not doing himself or the business any good by his vulgarity and *brusquerie*', and Northcliffe considered whether to 'force his resignation', on the ground that 'the rising up of a bully is a menace to the organization'. Marlowe's deafness was increasingly a handicap. Northcliffe said that 'it is such a struggle telephoning to him'. Cowley, the manager of the *Daily Mail*, was leaving to start a new newspaper, the *Evening Times*, taking with him Charles Watney, the news editor, Edgar

★ Prime Minister of Canada from 1921-30 and 1935-48.
† The grey species had originally been acclimatized at Woburn, about 1890.

Wallace and Bernard Falk. When Harold wrote deploring Cowley's departure, Northcliffe countered with the objection that 'his cutting down and sudden dismissals have caused us much trouble'. Harold was urging 'a thorough overhaul of the *Daily Mirror* finances', the highly satisfactory revenue of £5,267 in one week showing an actual loss of £51. He also indicated the need for a considerable amount of new money for the Anglo-Newfoundland business. The Punch-like circulation manager of *The Observer*, Valentine Smith, had pushed its sales up to 39,000, at which they obstinately remained, to Garvin's dismay. 'We cannot put up our advertising rates, and so make a profit, until we pass the 40,000 mark.' His editorial exertions caused Northcliffe to write to him: 'I am anxious about your health.' At the same time, he wrote to Buckle: 'Dr Shadwell told me that your sleep is not as it should be. I trust you will not think this merely impertinence or an intrusion', and to Monypenny, who had been Buckle's assistant: 'Room and quiet here [at Sutton Place] are ready for you at any minute. This is a very fine place for recuperation.'

At The Amalgamated Press, Hartley Aspden, who had made a success of the company's religious publications, beginning with the *Sunday Companion*, was being forced by bad health to give up his post. Hearing 'the very sad news', Northcliffe wrote to him (June 11, 1909): 'I shall feel your going as the personal loss of a dear friend and associate. Harold and I have this morning discussed terms by which you will have ample provision for many years.' Hamilton Edwards, who had conducted several of the company's papers, was again threatening to resign. The manager of the *Continental Daily Mail*, Ralph Lane (Norman Angell), was suffering from pernicious anaemia. 'I am not buying any more papers', Northcliffe replied impatiently on June 26 to an old Fleet Street acquaintance, Lucien Wolf, who wrote to tip him off about a weekly journal that was for sale. 'I have several that I would like to sell. Kind regards.'

Sutton was the one predictable being on whom Northcliffe could count in all circumstances. He was Northcliffe's watchdog at The Amalgamated Press, whose flood of publications, from encyclopædias to 'comics', was swelling everyone's income but his own. So devoted was he to 'the Chief' that for many years he tolerated a situation in which he drew a smaller salary than some of the editors and advertising men who worked under him. In 1910, his salary was increased to £1,000 a year and he was given a very small percentage of the profits above £200,000. He might have been dismayed to know that 'the Chief' was still referring to him as 'my secretary', as, for example, in a letter to Lord Rothschild in January 1909.

'It is easy to *say* stop, not so easy *to* stop.' There was no reason why he should put himself to the trouble of writing a homily to the Carmelite House clerk who, having been dismissed for petty embezzlement, begged to be taken back.

It is quite impossible to employ people who have been guilty of theft. You should consider yourself very lucky that you are not in prison, where you would be but for your wife's health. If you were allowed to return, it would be most unfair to those other clerks who are worthy. I have given instructions that the expenses of your wife's forthcoming confinement are to be paid and some small allowance made to her while she is recovering. I hope you will realise that you are very fortunate. Your thefts were continuous.

It was exasperating, no doubt, to have to write memoranda on matters which others were well paid to attend to. 'Yesterday I went down to Carmelite House at twelve o'clock. The visitors' room was in a neglected condition. The paper bag from which the head porter eats his cherries or winkles was lying on the floor and there was general untidiness.' Marlowe was not bestirring himself sufficiently in the *Daily Mail* campaign against the cruelty to old horses being shipped to the Continent. 'You do not quite realize', Marlowe replied, 'that it is impossible for us to go any further without libelling the shipping companies.' There was more satisfaction in being able to tell the ornithological professor in New York on July 13: 'I have now thirty-six young robins hopping about my park. Some are beginning to scatter; they have been seen as far away as two miles.' The owner of Sutton Place had intimated a change of mind about selling it and had given Northcliffe the first offer. Northcliffe answered: 'The fact is I want no further possessions of any kind. I have too many already. At one time I had an idea that if Sutton Place was ever for sale I would buy it for the nation. Since then, I have seen a number of things that have been given to the nation and have seen how they are neglected or otherwise misused.'

On July 17, 1909, he entertained the editorial staff of the *Daily Mail* at Sutton Place. It was an opportunity for him to throw off some discursive remarks to the company about newspaper responsibility.

One runs a newspaper, as one must do, with a number of men who have very strong feelings. I think that we are rather more inclined to favour in reporting the party whose views we editorially support and that, I think, to be wrong and unwise, a relic of the days when Dr Johnson said that in reporting the House of Commons he made the Whig dogs suffer. We had a case the other day. It was the great annual meeting of the National Liberal Club, at which all the distinguished Liberal leaders were present. I saw that we dismissed it in two lines, a great pity. There were present all the important men in and out of the House of Commons on that side of politics, men whom we think to be misguided, but who, at any rate, represent the opinion of perhaps half the people in England. We practically ignored that gathering. I do ask our staff to try to make the paper as absolutely impartial as possible. It is very important that so gigantic a power as ours should be used fairly.

Moderation in headlines, he told his hearers, was likewise important. He deplored the constant use of words like 'disaster' and 'tragedy', while recognizing that, 'owing to the narrowness of our columns', headline writing was a difficult art. He would not care to see the *Daily Mail* reverting to the alleged practice at Printing House Square in headlining the assassination of a Head of State simply: 'Foreign News', a story which although symptomatic was untrue, but caused laughter to echo back from the mellowed brick walls of Sutton Place.

We have got to be moderate. The way some of the morning newspapers use those two words must greatly impair their influence with the public, who know that the running over a child by a motor-car, though it is a very sad thing, is not a 'disaster'. We should not call one sailor drowned at sea a 'naval disaster'. It is what Jones and I have often called the 'the danger of the mega-phone'. I remember that there were headings which used to worry the life out of me when we first took over the *Evening News*. 'Baby in a Barrel' was one of them. That was my first acquaintance with bad newspaper habits.

He had noticed at the lunch, he said, what a young and alert-looking body of men they were who brought out the *Daily Mail* each day. 'We have our faults, our blemishes', but they were maintaining the paper's huge circulation against great competition, in the course of which they could claim to have taught others how to run a modern newspaper.

When I look back to the newspapers that were in existence before we started the *Daily Mail*, when I glance back, as I have done lately, at some of them, I feel that even those of us who are concerned in our work do not fully realize what we have done—the enormous variety of new topics that we have introduced into a newspaper. We have increased the size of newspapers, which may or may not be a blessing; at any rate, it has led to the doubling or trebling of employment for British journalists. In particular, we have enormously increased in newspapers the amount of news from the far distant parts of the world. Even the greatest of the penny papers in 1896—the year in which Harold and Mr Jones and I started the *Daily Mail*—dismissed the United States in short Reuter telegrams. Since then, every one of them has been obliged also to follow us into the realms of specialized news, of a kind which the older newspapers did not think worthy of printing—such things as those about which Mr Beach Thomas, for example, and his colleague, Mr Izzard, now collect for us. Agriculture was dismissed in a thing called a 'Crop Report'. At present, as you know, our agricultural imports cost us something like £150,000,000 a year. I hope we can succeed, through our agricultural journalism in the *Daily Mail*, in reducing that amount.

There were other achievements, he said, which he would like to see to the paper's credit. 'I think we might do something to help English music.'

He thought the paper might also do more, much more, to 'encourage the people' generally. He deplored the pessimism of the leading articles written by H. W. Wilson.

I never liked it. I have tried to stop it, but it is so hard to stop that kind of thing, and those things kept appearing. You may express your regret that such and such a view was expressed in yesterday's paper; it does not alter the fact that it appeared. This country has just snatched a £7,000,000 contract for rebuilding the Spanish navy. If the contract had gone to Germany, I am quite sure that Mr Wilson would have made it a national disaster. [Laughter.] I was talking the other day to a very distinguished gentleman at Cambridge. It was in the afternoon and he raised his teacup and said—'Here's to England—the coming country.' We can do a great deal to encourage our people.

He had spoken longer, he told them, than he had intended. 'I shall not be seeing you again for some time', and announced his forthcoming departure 'to inaugurate our vast enterprise in Newfoundland—perhaps the vastest of its kind in the world'. Some of those who had been with him from his eager-youth days saw in him a new stature, a potential realizable perhaps in some wider field of action. Neither he nor those around him showed any profound insight into the forces of suggestion and persuasion at their command. They appeared to be unaware of the warnings which Tocqueville, for example, had bequeathed to the moulders of modern democracy. None of them, it seemed, thought to examine the risks for society inherent in their policy of 'giving the public what it wants'.

*   *   *

'Should not something be done about the aeroplanists who are now assembling at Calais to fly the Channel?' Northcliffe had asked in his *Times* communique of July 1. It was a prod for those men of *The Times* who were unwilling to pay attention to any *Daily Mail* activity, whatever its significance. 'I think it is most likely that they will succeed', the more especially as the two most promising contenders for his prize of £1,000 were Frenchmen. His contacts and talks with French inventors and engineers at Pau and elsewhere had given him the belief that they would carry the great flying adventure beyond the stage reached by the Wright brothers, whom he admired and had encouraged but whose self-satisfaction convinced him that others would soon move on ahead of them. They refused to believe that soon, very soon, their clumsy launching method of weight, chain and pulley would be superseded.

The first Channel attempt had been made on July 19 by a young

French sportsman with an English name, Hubert Latham. He and his machine had been picked up seven miles out by a French destroyer. From then on, the two neighbouring nations awaited events with almost breathless unanimity. The *Daily Mail* had set up wireless stations on both sides of the Channel, imparting an added note of twentieth-century novelty to the days of waiting. From dawn to sunset, crowds gathered at Dover and Sangatte to scan the sky between. It was known that Latham intended to fly again. There was a general hope that he would succeed. He went to bed on Saturday night, July 24, trusting his mechanic to call him if the weather promised well. At dawn, the mechanic decided otherwise and went to sleep again. Half an hour or so later a limping man was seen wheeling a small monoplane from a shed farther along the sands. 'Ou est Dovre?' he asked one of the watchers. Someone pointed northward. At 4.41 a.m. his frail dragonfly of a machine sputtered forward and took the air. Twenty-seven minutes later its pilot, Louis Blériot, inventor of a motor-lamp, put it down in a sloping grass field under the walls of Dover Castle.

The most controversial Budget in English history was pushed off the front page. The call for more Dreadnoughts was drowned by the applause for Blériot. The suffragettes screeched their slogans in vain. What Northcliffe had imagined he had also helped to accomplish, giving the world one of the greatest news stories in the history of journalism and animating the public scene with classical excitement. He at once resolved that his prize should be handed to the victor in the most impressive circumstances possible at twenty-four hours' notice. Wareham Smith, his advertising director, week-ending on the Sussex coast, was called out of bed after midnight and commanded to drive immediately to London to arrange a banquet for two hundred guests at the Savoy Hotel. Northcliffe's only comment as he entered the room was: 'Not enough French flags.' It amused him to tell afterwards that when he presented the gold trophy and the cheque for £1,000 to Blériot, Madame Blériot reached forward and took the cheque.

He rejoiced in the French success and not only as an admirer of France. It was a salutary rejoinder to Germany's pride in her Zeppelin performances. His offer of £10,000 for a flight from London to Manchester was still open and was no longer scoffed at. (It was to be won by Louis Paulhan, a French aviator, in 1910.) Northcliffe supplemented it by another offer, £1,000 for a circular mile flight by a British pilot in an all-British machine. It was won that same year by Moore-Brabazon, who, as Minister of Aircraft Production in a British Government of thirty-five years later, put his name to orders for machines capable of flying ten times as fast as his mile-a-minute flight of 1909. On the day of that flight Louis Paulhan went up in an aeroplane from Brooklands to reach a

record height of 720 feet, 'twice the height of St. Paul's Cathedral!' wrote
Hamilton Fyfe, sharing his astonishment with readers of the *Daily Mail*

*   *   *

In a message to the *Times* office on January 11, 1909, Northcliffe had
written of the Chancellor of the Exchequer: 'The emptiness of Lloyd
George's head is becoming painfully apparent to the country.' As Chancellor, and more specifically as a Radical, Lloyd George was in opposition
to the bigger navy campaign having for its slogan, *We Want Eight and
We Won't Wait*, a popular parrot call for two additional Dreadnoughts
in answer to the expansionist keel-laying in German navy yards. With
an eye to the social legislation nearest his heart, he had pronounced himself in favour of smaller ships, capable of harrying enemy trade routes in
time of war. Northcliffe's uncomplimentary remark may also have derived from a prevailing fear that the Budget of 1909 would show class
feeling being used as an instrument of policy.

On the afternoon of August 3, 1909, Cecil Harmsworth, then Member
of Parliament for Droitwich, espied his brother, Northcliffe, in the peers'
gallery of the House of Commons. It was so unusual to see him there
that Cecil went up to talk to him. Northcliffe asked if as a peer he could
take tea in the members' tea-room of the House of Commons. His
arrival caused many heads to turn inquisitively in his direction. He was
greeted by Henry Dalziel, one of Lloyd George's newspaper-owning
friends, who discovered that Northcliffe and Lloyd George had not met.
Dalziel immediately excused himself, returning in a few minutes to say
that the Chancellor would be glad to see Northcliffe in his private room
behind the Speaker's Chair. 'He is very keen to meet you', Dalziel said.

So off we went [wrote Cecil Harmsworth]. There were cordial greetings.
N. and I stayed with Ll. G. for upwards of an hour. The whole of this time
Ll. G. devoted all his powers to capturing N. It was a dazzling performance.
Private secretaries and Ministers looked in at the door, to be wafted away by a
wave of Ll. G's hand. The spell was not to be broken by anybody or for any
purpose.

On the main provisions of the Budget, amendments to which were
being laboriously worked through the House of Commons that summer
and autumn, Northcliffe was impervious to Welsh eloquence. Perceiving
it, Lloyd George changed his emphasis from the general to the particular,
commending the Development of Roads Bill to Northcliffe's support.
Cecil Harmsworth wrote in his diary:

Then Ll. G. did a very bold thing. Would Lord Northcliffe like to see the draft proposals which he was to submit to the House the next day? N. replied that he supposed it to be quite out of order, as it most certainly was. But Ll. G. was after big game. He produced the draft from a drawer of his table, handed it to N., and told him to make any use of it he pleased in the *Daily Mail*. N. was taken aback as they say, and so was I. 'What, in tomorrow's *Daily Mail?*' he asked incredulously. 'Before the House itself has heard it?' There was no trace of faltering in Ll. G's manner. He waved objections aside. To him, N's support was worth all risks. N. put the precious draft in his inner pocket and we left.

Northcliffe, his brother said, 'delighted in Ll. G's splendid imprudence'. It was the beginning of friendliness but not of friendship. Lloyd George's action on that occasion brought him much abuse from his fellow-Liberals. Cecil Harmsworth afterwards wondered 'whether it was worth it. There was the gain of a support that was always uncomfortably independent. Against that there was to be set the implication that the most influential Ministers were not independent of the Press.' While Lloyd George went boldly forth to face the consequences of his audacity, a *Daily News* commentator was making mischief out of Northcliffe's visit to the House, suggesting that he had moderated his opinion of the Budget and that, as a result, 'the political situation has undergone a change'. The writer of the paragraphs quoted *The Times* as foreshadowing 'a collapse of the obstruction which exhausted the house', during the passage of the Budget through the Commons. Enclosing the *Daily News* cutting, Garvin wrote to Northcliffe on August 5:

You know my affection for you. You know I am not one of your sycophants. You know I want nothing from you at all; and that you can get from me the opinion of an honest and fearless man with a touch of prophecy in him. Opinion of that kind, better than flattery 'priceless to Kings,' as some one said, ought not to be useless to you! I have a conviction that you don't really believe in my insight, but if you could only see it, I am *right, right, right* in entreating you not to encourage by indirect means in your papers thoughts of a surrender on the Budget which would ruin the Empire. In my admiration for your genius, and seeing you growing as I thought every day, I boasted that you were 'a Napoleon who would never come to his Moscow.' But now I am not so sure; and I am more alarmed for *you* than for the Empire and the party.

Oh, believe me, half England will not sit down to be despoiled without fighting; and if your papers won't fight their battle they will turn to the papers that will.

Yours ever,
J. L. GARVIN.

'The *Daily News* statement is an entire concoction', Northcliffe told the *Times* staff. To Garvin he was content to reply, on August 11: 'For the last six months you have been in an extremely nervous condition HEALTH comes first. It is very necessary that you should preserve your health not only for the public interest, but for the sake of your family I have placed this view on record, and I hope you will preserve this letter.' Garvin's answer was that his appearance of nervous tension was merely physical. 'I am equally full of nerves and nerve and, strange as it may seem, times of crises are my times of mental rest.' He promised to be sensible and 'not overstrain this curious new vitality'. Northcliffe had asked him to go with him to Newfoundland, where there was to be a ceremonial opening of the new paper mills. Garvin accepted with delight, then abruptly withdrew. 'I must stay at my post to fight the Budget,' as if he feared that Northcliffe was under a Celtic spell. 'Whether it is killed by direct rejection or amended to death, it must go. The alternative of submission is unthinkable. We must get ready to fight for our lives.' In his loin-girding pose, Garvin's protuberant eyes looked like twin moons reflecting an inner prophetic light. With his impassioned politics Northcliffe had little patience. He regretfully acknowledged Garvin's decision and left it at that, turning his attention to a plan for encouraging public school boys and university men to emigrate to Commonwealth countries. 'I am tremendously keen on your scheme,' he wrote to Philip Kerr (later Lord Lothian), 'and will do all I can for it.'

★   ★   ★

At Printing House Square, Moberly Bell was stoutly maintaining his defences against threatened proprietorial encroachments. Northcliffe had said that he would not interfere, while Bell had made formal submission to his overlordship. Each was finding it hard to stick to his bargain. The official history states (vol. 3, p. 642) that 'the economic side of it', namely, of The Times newspaper, 'was for the first moment for twenty years requiring no attention', and it was true that the new money which Northcliffe brought in averted the day-to-day crises which Bell had faced over a long time. Nonetheless, Northcliffe continued to be worried by the financial outlook for the paper. He was kept informed of it by Kennedy Jones.

G. E. Buckle, editor of The Times, to Northcliffe:

Printing House Square,
E.C.
9th August, 1909.

My dear Northcliffe,—I do not know whether you were speaking seriously when you told Bell and me at St. James's Place on Thursday that you contemplated transferring at Christmas your interest in The Times to some one who would run it from the purely commercial point of view, if the financial situation of the Paper had not by then been settled to your satisfaction.

My reasons for doubting whether you were speaking seriously are that less than a year ago you told me that you had made a will providing that, in case of your death, your interest in the Paper should pass to a set of trustees who would conduct it in accordance with its traditions; and that, at about the same time, you also told me that you recognized that the re-establishment of *The Times* must be an affair of time, and that you were content to wait five years for any pecuniary return. It is now less than a year and a half since the Court sanctioned the agreement under which we are working.

But, assuming that your statement was serious, there are one or two considerations which I think I ought to lay before you. You suggested that the worries connected with *The Times* had affected your health; and, of course, if that is your sole or principal reason, I can have nothing to say. If, however, as I trust, your health will permit you to continue, it certainly appears to me that you will seriously damage, not only *The Times*, but your own journalistic reputation, by abandoning us in this premature fashion. That *The Times* would be heavily damaged by a second change of Proprietors within two years of the first, is too obvious to need any argument. But you would suffer with it. The man who puts his hand to the plough and looks back has never any honour from either Christian or pagan. It is certain that, after associating yourself with the first Paper in the world and then giving it up in less than two years, you would occupy a very different position in public estimation to that which you hold now. I may perhaps also remind you that any such action on your part would be completely at variance, not only with the language which you have held in the past year and a half to Bell and me, but also with the speech you made, a little more than two months ago, to the staff of *The Times* at Bell's dinner. . . .

Are we to blame if we hesitate to follow implicitly precedents which, though they may well have answered well elsewhere, do not seem entirely applicable to a unique journal like *The Times*? I admit that we are conservative in journalistic matters, but a great part of our reputation is bound up with this conservatism. If you hustle *The Times* too much, you will change its character and destroy its influence. Hitherto you have always seemed to recognize this. I ask you to return again to that sound opinion.

Meanwhile, pray believe that I am ready to co-operate in reducing expenditure as far as may be without injuring the reputation of the Paper; but I cannot think the time you suggest—a little over four months—is at all sufficient.

You will, I am sure, forgive the frankness of this letter. You are a frank man yourself.

Yours very truly,
G. E. BUCKLE.

That shrewd and judicious communication was answered by its recipient the following day. Writing from Elmwood, Northcliffe said that he had assumed that Buckle would have realized that he was 'trying to get Bell to move'.

We have done our best by persuasion, but without effect. I am sure you realise as well as I do that the old man is one of the most difficult characters with which to deal. He is perfectly straight, and yet most elusive; most amiable and gentle, and yet, on the other hand, inordinately vain and obstinate; most industrious, yet doing little real work; and, above all things, tactless. He has the faculty of placing others in most difficult positions.

As a step towards tightening his personal control, a week later he appointed Reginald Nicholson as assistant to Bell in place of Kitchin. Nicholson, who had first joined Northcliffe's circle in 1895, had for some time been helping with the management of the *Daily Mirror*. He was one of the few men on the staff of any of the Harmsworth papers who could claim to be a close friend of 'the Chief'. He told Buckle some time later: 'Northcliffe asked me to go and work at *The Times*, not entirely because of my business capacity, but because he knew his own impulsive character so well.' He soon made himself popular at Printing House Square, as he was wherever he worked. He was not the kind of man to make hurried decisions and he established himself in such a good relationship with Bell that the latter wrote to Northcliffe about 'the debt of gratitude I owe you for giving me the help of Nicholson, who has won golden opinions from all and is invaluable to me'. Nicholson cited himself as a restraining influence on Northcliffe. 'If I may humbly say so, it was in this way all through my connection with him that I was of the greatest use to him in his career.' (Letter to G. E. Buckle, *circa* January 1935.)

Not only the money side of *The Times* bothered Northcliffe. The chief advertising canvasser, James Murray Allison, a romantically-minded Australian who had been press agent to Sandow, the physical culture man, and who wrote not-bad verse and painted in watercolours, had reported that 'much of the circulation was dead—a circulation that went into Government offices and dentists' waiting-rooms and places where the paper was not opened'. Northcliffe also pointed out that to find the news of the day, 'readers were obliged to wander all over the paper'. Sometimes news items were printed twice in the same issue. 'An important statement' on military aviation was made by Haldane in the House of Commons, 'but you had no reference to it'. He thought it desirable to remind the news department that 'Halley's comet is now approaching us', and there was outside criticism to support him.

Came to me in the House of Commons, one Gosse, a librarian, gravely concerned about *The Times* news. 'I have always thought,' said he, 'that *The Times* was a complete newspaper, and have not taken any other; but now, my own family circle is in grave anxiety in regard to the missing steamship "Waratah," and I find no word in *The Times*.' He looked at me cloudily and suspiciously, as who should say: 'What are you doing with *The Times*? In the old days, etc., etc.' I did my best to mumble something but he went away looking very doubtful. . . . [August 4, 1909].

In his dealings with *The Times*, Northcliffe was bothered by a social consciousness which led him into amusing differentiations. 'One Gosse, a librarian', was needlessly offhand seeing that he had himself engaged Gosse to edit the *Daily Mail* book section, In a communique to the *Daily Mail* he named Sir Thomas Lipton as 'the well-known sporting personality'. In a message to the *Times* office a few days after he referred to him as 'the food man'.

He showed appreciation in his messages: the staff could not hold it against him that he was unmindful of good work. He may in his turn have appreciated the justice of Buckle's comment to him in writing: 'It is a wonder to me how generally correct and well-merited your observations are. When the criticism is of individuals, please bear in mind how keenly they feel any blame from you.' Buckle had insisted on having his salary of £3,000 cut to £2,500. 'This is a matter which touches my personal honour. I find that there is a deficit on the working of the Paper. In my view, it would be clearly wrong for me, as a Director, to vote myself my full salary while the Paper cannot pay its way.' He had assumed that an importunate would-be contributor had been sent to him on Northcliffe's recommendation. Northcliffe wrote to him: 'You may be sure that I do not do that kind of thing. I have a horror of it, because I so often suffer from it personally.' Sending a statement on Newfoundland, 'and your great enterprise there', by Sir Edward Morris, Prime Minister of the Colony, Buckle inquired whether Northcliffe had any objection to its publication in *The Times*. He replied: 'I have a horror of seeing my name in papers with which I am connected. I have taken the liberty of slightly altering the article by eliminating my name.' For Buckle, this was unimpeachable behaviour which had the awkward effect of making Northcliffe seem still more enigmatic in his dealing with 'the Paper'. Probably Buckle was both relieved and puzzled when Northcliffe went off to Canada, taking Bell with him. 'For once in your life,' Northcliffe had told Bell, 'you must take a holiday.' The *Times* historian interpreted it as a move to get Bell out of the office, leaving Nicholson free to make what changes he deemed necessary. 'Nicholson was a man of sympathy and understanding', in which judgment of the historian Northcliffe himself would have concurred.

Valentine Chirol, head of *The Times* foreign department, had a letter from Northcliffe at that time, giving the opinion that the 'troubles at P.H.S. are due to that infernal Book Club', and that they were faced with bankruptcy. 'As an organization, *The Times* is heartbreaking. I can assure you that were it not from a sense that this thing is a national duty I would have gone off six weeks ago with my rod to my pleasant streams and forests across the Atlantic.' Chirol did not hesitate to suggest that difficulties had been caused by 'the lavish expenditure' which Northcliffe had encouraged. Northcliffe's reply admitted responsibility 'for much of the extra cost', and was content to claim that 'it had created a good impression', a justification which might have embarrassed his investigating accountant, Layton Bennett. 'Please do occasionally accept some suggestions,' he begged the advertising manager. 'I know it is a hard job to teach old dogs to do new tricks, but the *Times* dog is the most difficult animal I have tackled yet.'

With his wife, their friend Katharine Furse, widow of Charles Furse, A.R.A., Moberly Bell and Evelyn Wrench, Northcliffe arrived in Canada in the first days of September 1909. They entrained at Quebec for Vancouver, went from there to San Francisco and thence across Arizona to Chicago, Montreal and Newfoundland. It was a journey of five weeks which left Bell with a feeling that he needed more rest than when he started, and fortified young Wrench's ardour for the future of the English-speaking peoples, while considerably diminishing his sense of mission as sales manager of the Harmsworth periodicals. 'Thank heaven', he wrote, 'there were no thought readers about!'

Mrs Furse could find but one adjective for the trip, 'amazing'. She wrote home to her mother: 'Northcliffe is an extraordinarily good companion on a journey like this, his unfailing interest and immense knowledge of odd facts keeping everyone's wits alert.' She thought it surprising that he could correctly name, 'straight off', every one of the States in the Union. She assumed, because he spent much time in his private compartment on the Canadian Pacific Railway, that he was 'resting'. In fact, he was reading the local newspapers, bought at every stop. Sometimes Wrench would return to the Pullman staggering under a load of twenty or thirty papers. 'He would spend hours poring over these papers, looking for ideas for his own publications', and ignoring the warnings of the German oculist.

Wrench was troubled by 'the Chief's' treatment of 'old Bell'. Twenty years younger, Northcliffe often showed scant consideration for Bell's seniority. Wrench said that there were 'unpleasant scenes'. Bell wrote that Northcliffe had every day some new project to be written or telegraphed about. 'An hour ago he said to me: "Now I am going to have three days of absolute peace, nothing to read, no one to abuse." Ten minutes ago he hammered at my door. "Just look at this," showing me a local paper with some figures about immigration. "We're not taking it seriously enough. Wire to Cook, write to Buckle, leave letters for Grigg. Try to get hold of Amery." ' Bell was disposed to think: 'I have no doubt that I shall be all the better for it in the end.' Other men had found ways of

working satisfactorily with Northcliffe through the stresses of daily newspaper life. It was Moberly Bell's misfortune that he never did so.
Northcliffe to Kennedy Jones:

Private Car 'Independence,'
Kansas City.
September 27th, 1909.

My dear K.J.—Shortly after this reaches you, old Bell will arrive home. He is under the impression that we are trying to deprive him of his rights and privileges at Printing House Square. He has been on the whole not a more difficult travelling companion than I expected, but quite difficult enough, and I hope that you will instruct Reggie [Nicholson] and Pryor [S. J. Pryor, to whom Northcliffe had given 'a watching brief' at *The Times*] to report to you immediately any interference. I am convinced that the only way to deal with him is to jump on him at once. When he sees you are in earnest, he becomes duly obedient. The truth of the matter is that the old man is older than his years.

Like all old people, I suppose, he is a mass of prejudice and sees just what he wants to see. I think also he is inclined to be an intriguer. He is elated at the least sign of prosperity of *The Times* and doesn't believe there is any need for watchfulness. What he really thinks is, if we leave *The Times* alone, all will be well and 'Belled'.

While it gratified Northcliffe to go about the world as chief proprietor of its 'greatest newspaper' and the *Times* historian, writing forty years after, felt entitled to say that he was 'inevitably fascinated by the opportunity, the right, and the power to mould it', Moberly Bell saw for himself that 'the Paper' was only a part of Northcliffe's complicated existence. Travelling across the North American continent, Northcliffe's mind turned constantly to happenings in Europe and what they might portend for England and the empire. Wearing a battered soft felt hat and, surprisingly, a high wing collar that looked as if it had been borrowed from Bell, with the unvarying red-and-white spotted tie, a fat cigar pendant from the side of his mouth, he had been interviewed for the *San Franciso Chronicle* on the likelihood of 'an early war between England and Germany'. Bell was present at the interview and the newspaper reported: 'That this war is as inevitable as was the clash between Germany and France in 1870 and the struggle between Japan and Russia in 1904 was declared unequivocally by each.' Bell was quoted as saying that 'the situation was like that of two trains rushing towards each other on a single track'. The *Chicago Tribune* invited Northcliffe to state his views in an article which was widely quoted in the United States and Canada. 'I see it suggested in the American papers that there is some kind of a scare in England. I wish there were', and he said that the nation's leaders, both politicians and laymen, had sounded warnings, 'but without avail'.

The official figures of German naval development were disturbing enough, 'but we know that these figures are just as inaccurate as were the figures made public by Germany prior to the Franco-Prussian war in 1870. We know that the German Press is prohibited from telling the truth.'

The pro-German Press in the United States and Canada had begun to attack him before his arrival. They now denounced him as 'a leader of the growing war party in Great Britain'. He retorted that the fact that Germany refused to discuss her armaments was 'more than significant—it is threatening', and he reminded the American public of Germany's record 'in making unprovoked attacks on other nations'. He was asking for readiness, 'not for war'. It was thought that his views helped to weaken German propaganda in the United States, while Canadian sentiment was stirred by his picture of the Mother Country being deprived of vital food supplies as one of Germany's first measures against her if war came. Medill McCormick, of the Chicago newspaper-owning family, who had been educated in England, wrote for Northcliffe's attention a warning letter about the growth of German influence in America. 'We not only exchange professors with the German universities; we import historians, psychologists and chemists for our best chairs. A generation ago we looked to Oxford and Cambridge for inspiration. Now we turn to Heidelburg and Leipzig.' Northcliffe commissioned Robert Blatchford, editor of the Socialist weekly, *The Clarion*, to go to Germany and write about what he saw there, as Steevens had done before him.

*   *   *

At Grand Falls, Newfoundland, a wide triumphal arch spanned the night with electric lights spelling out WELCOME TO THE CHIEF. Two days of festivity had come to an end. The Governor-General of Canada and his retinue, and the Premier of Newfoundland and his Cabinet, had departed. Thanks largely to Lady Northcliffe, 'everything was splendid'. Nothing had been left out of the arrangements, except perhaps a culminating firework display, considered too great a risk in that wilderness of standing timber. Northcliffe stepped out into the garden of the extremely comfortable house which he had built for himself and his wife—'a little bit of England', was his order to the architect. He stood gazing alone into the darkness that was falling on the township and the vast silent forests beyond. For him it was a moment of the deepest feeling. 'I felt humbled by that great responsibility.' Financial writers had warned investors against the project, some calling it 'a wild-cat proposition'. Hydraulic engineers had said that the Exploits River could not be harnessed for

>ower because of winter ice. Labour authorities had predicted that the Newfoundlanders would never submit to industrial conditions. Wood pulp experts had argued that the perpetual fogs made the climate too moist for paper-making. Hearing all sides and then forming their own judgments, Harold Harmsworth and Mayson Beeton had confidently leased the timber lands and put up the pulp and paper mills.

The two days of festival crowned their three years' work, setting the mills in motion. Caird, the level-headed executive from Carmelite House who preceded Northcliffe as a visitor to Grand Falls, had been 'astonished by the magnitude of the concern'. What moved the largest shareholder, Northcliffe himself, still more, was the faith in him and the Harmsworth name of hundreds of small investors at home. He told those who had assembled for the inauguration:

There was, you may remember, a distinguished Canadian statesman who gave it as his opinion that the Canadian Pacific Railway would never earn its axle-grease. That did not deter the British investor. He trusted his leaders and today he is the largest financial factor in the whole of the vast railway system of Canada. I pay my tribute to my shareholders at home because I am grateful to them, because they poured millions of dollars into this superb creation at Grand Falls.

Standing there, he could see gleams of silver where the fading light touched the broad westward winding river. He recalled, 'with a touch of sadness', that on that beautiful river the last canoes of a dying race had been seen less than a hundred years before. He had told 'Muzzy' Beeton in two letters written before he left England: 'I want this to be *the* great event in the modern history of Newfoundland.' His wish had been granted. 'Unique and unparalleled', was the verdict of the *Royal Gazette and Newfoundlander Advertiser* ('Printed and Published by John W. Withers, Printer to the King's Most Excellent Majesty, at his Office, Gazette Building, Water Street, St. John's.') Northcliffe to Kennedy Jones (October 20, 1909): 'The opening ceremonies were a magnificent success and did us a world of good in this very suspicious island.' Northcliffe to his brother Harold on the same day: 'These ceremonies have done us a great deal of good and we are now in a position to get any concessions out of this country that we wish. The more I investigate the property, the more convinced I am that we have a magnificent investment.' Hearing that Harold had appointed an assistant to Beeton, he wrote to his brother: 'Vincent Jones is the most likely Englishman I have ever seen for sending to the Colonies. I much prefer an Englishman to any other nationality. I notice, by the way, that many leading Americans have an entourage almost entirely English. Pierpont Morgan, for instance, is entirely surrounded by Englishmen', and he might have mentioned Pulitzer's similar preference.

He proposed an immediate reconstruction of the Grand Falls company involving new capital of £3,000,000. 'Everything here most satisfactory Wish you were here.' Harold's reply was a cold draught of common sense 'Are you prepared to take the Chairmanship of such a company, with all its responsibility, and with the knowledge that you would be tied to the enterprise for practically the rest of your life? Once the huge company is launched, with its tens of thousands of shareholders you would, so far as I can see, never be able to recover your personal freedom. I abhor the issue of vast amounts of capital. That way disaster lies', and the subject was closed.

Northcliffe to J. L. Garvin (October 21): 'When the Budget and the Germans have captured England, we must all come and live here. We will give you a nice free homestead, and you can turn your pen into a plough-share. I only hope your furrows will be more distinct than your writing.' Northcliffe to Kennedy Jones (November 1): 'It is rather hard to drag ourselves away from this monster enterprise to the smoky squalor of Printing House Square. Grand Falls is equal to all we have done put together.' From Carmelite House, his brother Harold, in charge during Alfred's absence, was instructing Sutton (November 4): 'It is a first-class opportunity of overhauling the entire expenditure side of Mee's depart-ment', the book publishing branch of The Amalgamated Press. 'Will you get in, and cut everything down?'

* * *

Showing signs of fatigue, Northcliffe returned to London at the beginning of December. He had been writing to Leslie Willson, his 'nature cure' man, from Newfoundland, taking what amounted to a 'keep fit' corre-spondence course. On December 6 he wrote to his physician, Vernon Jones, of Arlington Street, St. James's: 'I wonder if you think I ought to see you with some other consultant in regard to these attacks. I can now trace them for ten years. Last year was certainly the worst.' Jones replied: 'I advise you to let me call in Dr Bertrand Dawson. He has given very special attention to your particular form of trouble', recurring phases of nervous exhaustion. 'Alfred is not taking proper care of himself', St. John had written to Cecil. Northcliffe self-prescribed an old remedy, Paris. His wife wrote to Sutton within a few days of their arrival: 'The Chief is *much* better—I cannot tell you how relieved I am. He delights in the crowds here', but too many people were trying to see him, 'from Pierpont Morgan down', he himself told Sutton.

G. E. Buckle, editor of *The Times*, to Northcliffe:

Braddon Hall,
Braddon Hill Road East,
Torquay.

15 Dec. 1909.

My dear Northcliffe,—No doubt, I am by temperament an optimist; otherwise I should hardly preserve, as I hope I do, some trace of youthfulness after 26 years' editorship of *The Times*. But, in what I wrote to you about the improvement in the advertisements, circulation, and expenses compared with last year, I based myself solely on facts, presented to the Board weekly by your Nicholson, and admitted in conversation with me the other night by Kennedy Jones. I know we have still an uphill fight before us—in part owing to the extra expenditure incurred on your representations last year. But it does not seem to me to be common sense to ignore the actual improvement, because there is still a long way to go.

I do not know to whom you refer as nullifying the efforts of Jones, Nicholson and Pryor; *I* am endeavouring to help them. Nor do I understand what you mean by saying that it is lamentable that every communication you send has to be put into the hands of those who ungratefully resent your efforts to save the Paper. . . . Probably you are referring to Bell; if you mean more, please tell me.

For your kind references to me I thank you, and I am quite sure that you are sincere in what you say. But what is the present position, in relation to you and Jones, of the three directors who actually carry on the work of the Paper? You have absolutely lost confidence and for half a year have never hesitated to say so in decided language, in the Managing Director, the pivot on whom turned the whole negotiation by which you acquired your commanding interest in *The Times*. In these circumstances, nothing but duty to the Paper, to which he is wholly devoted, can keep him at his post. Your entire disbelief in him is in itself a serious matter for the Board, and especially for Chirol and me, his friends, who realize all that he has done for the Paper. . . .

I have delayed answering your letter, partly owing to holiday laziness, and partly in order that I might carefully consider the terms in which I should place before you the views which I (and, I believe, my fellow directors) hold. I will, according to your wish, preserve your letter, along with others couched in very different terms; perhaps it would be well if you were to keep this letter of mine.

Believe me,
Yours very truly,
G. E. BUCKLE

The same:

64, Warwick Square,
S.W.

24 Dec. 1909

My dear Northcliffe,—This is to wish you and Lady Northcliffe a very happy Christmas, and to trust it may find you recovered from your indisposition.

I am very sorry that there has been any misunderstanding between us, and apologise to you for anything I may have done to cause it. After my talk with Nicholson I have no doubt that your feelings towards me at any rate, and I hope to the Directors of *The Times* generally, have undergone no change; and I will not allow my confidence in you to be shaken.

With Nicholson's very efficient aid, I hope that next Christmas may see *The Times* in a position to meet its obligations. At any rate we will work hard to that end.

Believe me,
Yours very truly,
G. E. BUCKLE

Northcliffe to G. E. Buckle:

Hotel Majestic,
Paris.
December 28th, 1909

My dear Buckle,—I was very glad to get your letter, because your previous one greatly upset me and those who work with me.

We have only one desire and that is the rehabilitation of *The Times*. That can only be effected by the diminution of waste, and the consequent provision of funds for the development of *The Times*.

It should not be forgotten that so long as we squabble and misunderstand each other, the exercise of initiative is impossible. I have given you the best man I have, Kennedy Jones, easily the ablest newspaper manager in England; Nicholson, who was at my right-hand for fifteen years; Allison, incomparably the best Advertising Manager; Digby, who will, I believe, restore the absolutely essential lost small advertisements of *The Times*; Pryor, who knows the technique of newspaper expense and administration perfectly, and his man Hardman, who, he believes, is a first-rate newspaper carpenter for night work. I have deprived my other businesses of these men at a considerable loss to those businesses.

What are wanted now, allow me to say with great respect, are, (1) Editorial initiative, (2) Publishing initiative: *The Times* is holding its own and that is all.

It would be well, I think, if more of your Staff knew the real financial facts of *The Times*, and also that we have to combat daily the mal-administration of Hooper-Jackson regime, and that the task of rehabilitation is a stupendous one.

Yours sincerely,
NORTHCLIFFE

★   ★   ★

Blatchford's articles on Germany had been published in the *Daily Mail* in the middle of December, a harsh-sounding note in the grand Christmas concord. His explanation, as a Socialist editor, had been forthright. 'I write hese articles because I believe that Germany is deliberately preparing to destroy the British Empire, and because I know that we are not able or ready to defend ourselves against a sudden and formidable attack.' It was more than the Liberals could bear. 'Ravings', was the *Daily News* word for it. *The Nation* ridiculed the fancy that 'Germany contemplates a wanton attack on a good neighbour'. When the *Manchester Guardian* dismissed the articles as a Tory trick to turn the impending general election away from the Liberals, 'deliberately raking the fires of hell for votes', Blatchford was quoted in retort: 'Votes? What has the danger to the Empire to do with votes? I wrote these articles for men and women, not for votes.' Congratulating Northcliffe on publishing the articles, L. J. Maxse, of the *National Review*, took the opportunity of saying (January 1, 1910): 'At all the election meetings I go to the only name that draws on the other side is Lloyd George. The mention of Winston Churchill used to be faintly cheered, but there has evidently been a great slump in that quarter. It must indeed be a bitter pill for him. Men who are too obviously playing for their own hand don't permanently impose on the English people, thank God!'

On January 4, the King's friend, Esher, wrote: 'We have never been nearer a revolution since 1688 and probably *never* nearer to a big and sudden European conflict. The tension between Germany and England is a newspaper tension, but it is severe for all that.' Shortly afterwards he reported in another letter written from Windsor Castle to the same correspondent: 'The King began about Germany and lamented Blatchford's violence. He is writing the Emperor a letter of congratulation on his birthday, and proposes to say that the two countries have no cause for quarrel or jealousy, and that the Press should not be allowed to stir up ill-feeling.'

Northcliffe, meanwhile, had inquired into charges of 'Kaiser-baiting' by the Berlin office of the *Daily Mail*. The resident correspondent, F. W. Wile, replied with a list of news stories about the Kaiser which had been sent from his office. They supported his claim that 'none ever sent by me is deliberately unfriendly. All are scrupulously accurate' (January 6). The *Times* correspondent in Berlin was Hubert Walter, son of John Walter III, who had been given the post by Northcliffe twelve months earlier. He wrote to Northcliffe on January 8, 1910: 'I agree with you that Germany has no intention of invading us, and that her victories, if any, will be diplomatic. The longer I remain here the more impressed I am by the fact that Germany's policy consists mainly of absolutely unscrupulous bluff, in the presence of which it behoves us to remain so strong that we can afford to value it at its proper worth.'

Northcliffe commissioned Wile in Berlin to write a book which would explain Germany to the English people. 'We tend to think of Germany as a land of stuffy professors,' he told Wile. 'I am asking you to give a fair picture of Germany as she is today. Write in a way that all can understand.' The *Daily Mail* was to sponsor the book as a contribution to better general feeling. Ineptly titled *Our German Cousins*, it did not attract much attention. Failure did for Northcliffe what prayer did for others; it gave him strength. 'The Book That Will Not Sell!' he proclaimed in large type in the *Daily Mail* and offered a prize to the reader who sent in the most convincing explanation. In a fortnight two hundred thousand copies were sold.

On a Sunday afternoon of that year, 1910, the Polar explorer, Captain Scott, called to see Marlowe, at Carmelite House. Northcliffe had sent him a cheque for £50 to buy wine for the wardroom of his ship, *Endeavour*, soon to leave for the Far South. Having asked Marlowe to convey the thanks of himself and his officers to Northcliffe, Scott said, 'I want to ask you a question which you may be able to answer. When will the war with Germany start?' The editor of the *Daily Mail* was not given to prophecy. 'I can only tell you,' he said, 'that there is a well-informed belief that Germany will be ready to strike in the summer of 1914 and it is thought that she may do so.' Scott looked reflective. 'By that time I shall be entitled to command a battle cruiser of the *Invincible* class,' he said. 'The summer of 1914 will suit me very well.'

*　　*　　*

At last, Sutton summoned the nerve to bring to 'the Chief's' notice his situation as the underpaid managing director of an enormous and still expanding publishing house—the world's largest. 'I think I ought to have another thousand a year salary. The Amalgamated Press should pay me more. I am not asking for it on account of length of service, that I know is not everything, but because many of the more recent newcomers to the A.P., who have never had anything like the responsibilities and worries I have had, are better paid. I know you will realize that I dislike worrying you' (January 14). There was no reference to the matter in the letter which Northcliffe wrote to him on January 22. It showed that he had taken some recent financial advice of Harold's seriously to heart:

The most important business thing that might arise in my absence is the *Mirror* flotation. On no account is it to be over-capitalised. The burden of disgrace, in case anything should happen, would fall upon me; the burden of effort to maintain profit always falls upon me. Our greedy grabs in the past have been very serious sources of anxiety and but for great good luck, we should have had trouble. £475,000 is the maximum I will allow it to be capitalised at.

The *Daily Mirror* was fast overtaking the *Daily Mail* in number of copies sold, a fact in which Northcliffe did not specially rejoice. He looked on the *Mirror* as the bastard of his journalistic family. No one ever heard him speak of it in the warmly possessive way that he spoke of '*my Daily Mail*'. He would say: 'People are always telling me that it is not a newspaper.' It was showing a *gamin* liveliness which often caused him to avert his eyes from its activities, which included 'buried treasure' hunts, fashion parades and beauty shows. The arrival of a newcomer to picture journalism, Hulton's *Daily Sketch*, had put the *Mirror* staff on their mettle and their exuberance often jarred Northcliffe's sensibilities, as when they offered prizes to the holders of tram and bus tickets with certain numbers and sent readers chasing across London after City bees powdered with flour as part of an experiment to discover how far bees travel in search of nectar. He had to acknowledge, as often, the nerve of the *Daily Mirror* photographers who got pictures from Zeppelins in flight, secretly 'snapped' criminals in the dock, and risked their lives in a succession of Balkan wars, all for £3 10s. a week. 'The Chief', making one of his rare appearances in the *Daily Mirror* office, noted with dissatisfaction that the reporters were 'untidily dressed'. He gave an instruction that any man applying for a salary increase should receive it only on condition that he undertook to buy a new suit.

The *Daily Mirror* staff of that time, outside the office and in it, was the most resourceful of any in the Harmsworth groups. In charge of what was called the art department was a born journalist named Hannen Swaffer, who for all that he was constantly employed looked like an out-of-work actor of the Irving school. Northcliffe called him 'Poet', and in 1913 wrote of him to Kenealy, the editor: 'I have only just realized what an important part Swaffer played in the building up of the *Daily Mirror*.' Swaffer's assistant, a youngster named Bartholomew, likewise made his mark as one of the first experimenters in a kind of journalism which has proved to be the most typical of our age.

*　　　*　　　*

'I am not very well', Northcliffe wrote to Sutton on February 5, 1910, putting at the top of his letter 'The Asylum, Manchester Street, W.' It was his name for the nursing home to which he had been sent by his latest medical consultant, Bertrand Dawson, for 'complete rest'. He complained of the nursing home being 'like a prison'. He hoped to leave in a month, but there was no chance of his getting back to work before June. Meanwhile, he was pleased to hear that a first small consignment of Grand Falls paper had reached Carmelite House and was being used for the 6.30 edition of the *Evening News* of January 27. He hoped 'to be allowed to see the *Mirror* prospectus', but his newspaper reading was cut down to the *Daily Mail* and *The Observer*. 'Dawson is very strict.' Vernon Jones told Butes that there was 'inflammation of the pancreas'. Northcliffe dictated a message to Sutton: 'This slow illness is a great nuisance. I feel tied hand and foot. Dawson, who is the Prince of Wales's doctor, is *insistent* on no business until June. This is evidently the same illness that I have had again and again.' Evelyn Wrench said that it was spoken of as 'neurasthenia' in Northcliffe's private circle. There was a letter from Rufus Isaacs, K.C.: 'If only you would be content to be less active! That you cannot is doubtless one of the secrets of your gigantic success.'

Arthur Walter's death on February 22 made way for the accession of John Walter, the fifth in his line to step up into the chairman's place at Printing House Square. He was thirty-seven and had been working at *The Times* for twelve years, first as an assistant to Moberly Bell, afterwards as the paper's correspondent in Spain and Portugal.

Northcliffe wrote to him on February 24:

Will you kindly convey to Mrs Walter and accept yourself my expression of sympathy in this great loss?

I would have been present at the last ceremony had I not been for some weeks in medical hands in this place [the nursing home].

As we may possibly not meet for many months you will not, I ask, regard it as an intrusion if I say now that you will always have my earnest support in your endeavour to maintain the Paper in the high station your greatly respected father desired it to hold in the worlds of Government and of Letters.

I do firmly believe that when we are rid of some of our inevitable initial troubles a bright era will dawn at Printing House Square, and I know that the Directors, and my personal colleagues, will cordially assist and make your life there happy and prosperous.

Yours sincerely,
NORTHCLIFFE.

In April, he went with his wife, Garvin and Whibley to Paris, *en route* for Valescure, St. Raphael. Sutton wrote to Lady Northcliffe in Paris about 'certain rumours' in London concerning 'the Chief's' health. Lady Northcliffe replied from the Hotel Ritz: 'The rumours are very bad here too. This running away from London will not help to allay rumours there! What do you think of his condition?' From St. Raphael, a week or two later (April 3, 1910), she was able to tell Sutton that 'he makes a little progress every day, but is still very easily fatigued—nervous—and a long way off work yet'. The doctor, she said, had insisted on absolute rest and no mental effort. 'I am, as you may imagine, very happy to be with him and am able to keep even the tiny daily cares away from him. Charles [Whibley] and Garvin are very loving, delightful friends but they are so full of vigour that I only let him see them for a quarter of an hour each day.' A scribbled note reached Sutton a few days later, requiring him to send Northcliffe copies of all the London papers. 'I think very much of you, my dear Sutkin', was scrawled down the margin. To Hamilton Fyfe: I am weary of the roses and the nightingales of Valescure and long for Fleet Street.' To his mother: 'Darling Mums,—I am sticking to my cure closely. It is a very slow business. I am so weak.' The sudden illness and death of King Edward VII was an excuse for mentioning to her that his new medical adviser, Dawson, 'was the youngest and ablest by our dear king's bedside'. He wrote to John Walter (May 7):

So far as you and your little son are interested, I want *The Times* to be once more *The Times* and John Walter to be John Walter, not as you amusingly say, a phantom chairman. Your letter shows me that, unlike the attitude of narrow suspicion I have faced these two years, your sole desire is the good of the paper. I rejoice to hear from Nicholson that you are rapidly mastering the details of the business. A good deal of my long illness has been due to the perpetual combat with men who did not know, and who loftily jettisoned upon the willing mules of Carmelite House the Book Club, the printing, and other nuisances that savoured of what it is easy to call 'commercialism.'

He had the idea that some of the Fleet Street rumours which were current about his health came from his brother-in-law, the advertising agent. He asked his mother: 'Do keep P. Burton from gossiping about me. When well I shall deal with him.' His mother had been disturbed by the talk and went to meet him in Paris, on his way back from St. Raphael. 'I thought I was getting on a bit better,' he wrote to tell Harold on May 19, 'but yesterday I went to Versailles with Mother and had a very bad day. She was alarmed at it and so was I.' It was being put about that he was in a state of complete nervous collapse, which Lady Northcliffe firmly denied. There is the supporting evidence of Garvin's correspondence. He had been staying with Northcliffe and had no compunction about writing him very long letters about *The Observer* and topical affairs, beginning one of them: 'Your jolly letter came this morning so vigorous and sound that nothing could be less like a man in need of a rest.' Even so, Garvin suggested that 'such mental energy' required relaxing and wished it were possible 'to keep you chloroformed for six weeks'. Another of his staff men, Hammerton of The Amalgamated Press, again noted a tendency in 'the Chief' to talk 'for hours on end', bouts of verbosity which he invariably concluded with some such remark as 'Now, get on with your work—you do nothing but talk, talk, talk. I am quite tired out'. In May, Dawson wrote out his conclusions for Northcliffe's guidance. 'You are really gathering up strength all the time, and ultimately you will be quite well and able to fill your place in the world—and that is saying a good deal when one considers what a place you have filled. You will not be able to do quite the same kind of work as before, but then that will no be necessary.' Cecil Harmsworth met his brother at Boulogne on May 2c and wrote in his diary: 'Alfred apparently a good deal better after his res at St. Raphael.' Evelyn Wrench also made a diary note (June 10, 1910) 'The Chief looked bronzed and not so fat, but restless, and his health i unquestionably getting on his nerves.' Sir George Newnes had just died a spent and broken man. Northcliffe himself dictated the obituary notice for the *Daily Mail* and *The Observer*.

J. L. Garvin to Northcliffe:

> 9, Greville Place,
> N.W.
> July 28th, 1910.

My dear Chief,—I must write you like a human man. Why don't I get a word I hear that you are really better and it rejoices me. I also hear that you are making things hum in various directions and see by various unmistakable signs that it is so. In the meantime, the cessation of all business communication between us for months is making the situation difficult as well as absurd.

I went to Valescure simply because you were not well and to do you what good I could. I went not only as a friend genuinely concerned but broke in a moment for your sake certain engagements, and did this in a way that caused me great difficulty. . . . Nobody could have come nearer to a sentimental idiot, so it has seemed since; but then and always I had been as slow to worry you on my own account as quick to answer your call. . . .

If we have ceased to understand each other it is sad and bad. If not, let us talk as we used. That won't make you less happy and will make me more so.

> Yours ever,
> J. L. GARVIN.

Garvin was concerned about his future and that of *The Observer*, which was showing a small uncertain profit. He was summoned to Elmwood. The reassurance he was given was not enough. He felt obliged to write on August 10: 'As there is no reply to my suggestion about security, I take it that it is useless to proceed', namely, with the drafting of a new contract. 'Remember always that before we came together I warned you of a conviction that I was not really "your sort".' Northcliffe telegraphed his readiness to 'make any arrangement that pleases you', adding in a second telegram, the warning that he could not continue as a director of *The Observer* 'if it is to be a perpetual source of worry'. He affirmed that he was not interested in the financial success of the paper. 'I only care that it affords the Empire a peep at your great vision.' He urged Garvin to keep his readers informed about Germany, 'that great unknown quantity', and stressed in particular: 'As to grievances, let them wait until I get back. I have mine too. At present I am beset from seven a.m. till bedtime.' Working for *The Times* he described as 'the damnable grind of a semi-bankrupt business'. He called attention to the neglected appearance of the boardroom at Printing House Square. 'It should be swept and garnished. At present it seems to be a repository of oleographs and disused silk hats.'

Harold Harmsworth to Northcliffe:

> Carmelite House,
> Carmelite Street, E.C.
> 2nd November, 1910.

My dear Alfred,—I do wish you would do as little work as possible. All your strength should be reserved for the purposes of recuperation. Business does not matter a rap when your own health is concerned. Even if anything did go wrong, what does it matter if the dividends of The Amalgamated Press are 25% instead of 40%, when the dividends are 25% you are in good health, and when they are 40% you are in bad health?

I hear you are coming back next week, and I should like to spend a day or two with you, but I do hope you will not exert yourself, or exhaust yourself.

> Always yours,
> HAROLD.

Northcliffe was in Paris, on his way home from a second visit to Newfoundland, in the course of which he found less to be enthusiastic about than on the trip of exactly a year before. He saw signs of coming labour troubles at Grand Falls and had sketched out for his fellow directors a report which pointed to other problems that might have to be faced.

The trip was to be part of his convalescence, supplying the fresh air and rest considered essential to his full recovery. He was glad of the proximity of a young medical man, Philip Seymour Price, who was going out to report on health conditions at Grand Falls. Northcliffe had asked Guy's Hospital to recommend a suitable doctor and Price was the candidate. Influenced perhaps by the example of Pulitzer, the American newspaper magnate, who had just appointed an English doctor, a brother of Eden Phillpotts, the West Country novelist, to be his personal medical adviser, choosing him from 730 applicants, Northcliffe attached Seymour Price to his staff, on a retainer basis. Thereafter Price took charge of the medical side of Northcliffe's life. They had known each other only a few weeks when Price had to submit to the criticism of being 'slow in the uptake', a defect which he promised to remedy. 'I am watching my faults of character,' he let Northcliffe know from Grand Falls. 'Procrastination is being fiercely attacked.' From a letter that the Hearst newspaper writer, Arthur Brisbane, wrote to Northcliffe after seeing him in New York, it appeared that he was flouting the expensive medical advice that he had been receiving. 'It isn't rest for you to be three thousand miles from your office but next door to a cable, sitting neck deep in newspapers, with one eye bunged up and the other glued to the editorial page of *The Times*— that is not rest.' Soon Price won back the esteem he had lost by discovering signs of valvular damage to Northcliffe's heart.

Preparing to cross to London, Northcliffe developed an agitated interest in the numerous papers published for the young by his Amalgamated Press, copies of which he had ordered to be sent to him at the Hotel Ritz. He accused his editors of depraving juvenile tastes and threatened sharp action if improvements were not made at once. 'I will not have such vulgarities. I shall send a man to the printers to take them out. If I don't like a serial story, I shall stop it without warning. Because Mr and Mrs Robert Leighton once wrote us a very good convict story, *Convict 99*, is no excuse for filling our papers with bad convict stories.' Using the word 'loathsome' to express his feelings, he took the matter up with Sutton, declaring that the publications 'have got out of hand during my absence. There are now hundreds of vulgarities and indecencies in the papers. Either they improve or I leave the business. One or the other' (November 7, 1910). To Evelyn Wrench, sales manager of The Amalgamated Press, on the same day: '*Merry and Bright*, No. 3. The front page is occupied by a fat man and an over-developed young woman. Page 2 is "The Girl Without a Home". Page 3 is not quite so bad but vulgar. On Page 6 there is a man holding a revolver. I never allowed revolvers in the papers at all.' To A. H. Mann, an Amalgamated Press editor (November 7): 'It is incumbent on every responsible person to watch our papers closely. They constitute an immense power for good. At the outset of the business, the papers were such as one could be proud of. Please refer to the early files, when they were morally healthy publications in every way. The number of prison stories, detective stories, bad girl stories, sensational and always very badly drawn pictures is deplorable and will be vigorously dealt with. I should like to see our business what it was, a great educational and moral "uplift", to use a slang word.' Again on November 7, Northcliffe to Sutton, by telegram: *Stop today all headings in papers such as Behind Prison Walls etc. Go over all page proofs yourself and remove vulgarities.*

The sudden censorious onslaught could not have been more violent if his mother had inspired him to act; and she never hesitated to express her views on any of his papers. It may have been the delayed action of a fuse lit by an Old Bailey judge who, four months before, trying a case in which it was held that frauds had been committed through advertisements, said that if he could have his way the costs of the prosecution would be paid by those owners of publications in which the advertisements had appeared. The list before him included a number of Amalgamated Press publications. Northcliffe would have resented at any time n his career papers of his being named in those circumstances. As conroller of *The Times*, he was now much more sensitive. The explosive point seems to have been reached when Harold Harmsworth lauded in a letter the merits of a young editor, whom he claimed to have 'discovered' and who was sending the circulations of two or three papers soaring to heights not reached since the days of *Comic Cuts* and *Chips*. When Sutton pleaded that the newcomer be 'given a chance', Northcliffe replied: 'I have no desire to be over-severe on any young man in the office. Of course, he might, by going on in this way, get a circulation of 600,000 a week or a million a week. Anybody could do it', and he concluded that young man, 'whom I have never seen', must be 'a bounder'. Northcliffe then repeated his ultimatum. 'Either I have no responsibility for The Amalgamated Press or I must be able to control the publications.'

Harold, who had been made a baronet 'for public services', had sold his *Daily Mail* shares and severed his connection with the paper in order to develop other financial interests, while still giving time and attention to The Amalgamated Press. He was announced as the founder of a King Edward VII professorship of English Literature at Cambridge University, with the provision that 'citizens of the great English-speaking American Republic may be eligible for appointment to the chair'. Its first occupant was Sir Arthur Quiller-Couch, 'Q' of the Cornish novels. Cecil Harmsworth had bought Dr Johnson's house in Gough Square, Fleet Street, and was restoring it from a ruined state as a gift to the nation.

From Berlin, the *Daily Mail* correspondent, Wile, wrote to tell Northcliffe that the proprietor of the *Lokal-Anzeiger*, *Die Woche*, 'and their various affiliated properties', had asked him to 'sound you as to your inclination to consider purchasing his entire establishment'. From 17 Church Row, Hampstead, H. G. Wells wrote a letter marked 'Very Private' suggesting that Northcliffe might 'help to save India for the Empire' by creating 'a new vernacular Press' in India. 'Jails and suchlike antiquated methods will never suppress sedition. A series of vividly intelligent, copiously illustrated vernacular newspapers could transform it into helpful energy.' Wells believed 'it could be done if you sailed in there with the right men', in reply to which Northcliffe wrote: 'I realize my tremendous responsibility', and proposed that they meet for a talk. Wells to Northcliffe: 'I would break almost any engagement for a talk with you.'

He was annoyed because Evelyn Wrench was caught up in his vision of Empire and no longer happy in his job of pushing the sales of the Amalgamated Press publications. 'Don't chase butterflies', was his offhand advice when Wrench tentatively referred to the subject. The Overseas League, which had been Wrench's own idea and creation—'Headquarters: Carmelite House, London, E.C., England'—already had 267 branches and Wrench was conceiving it as the British Empire's answer to the German Navy League with its 1,100,000 members. Arthur Mee had to be reminded of the importance of concentrating on his job when Northcliffe heard that he too was 'going in for sideshows', in his case local government in his part of Kent. 'I have merely tried to be a good citizen,' Mee explained. 'But I will give it all up. I will do nothing that you consider distracting or jeopardizing in any way.' He had lately started the *Little Paper*, which was to become better known as the *Children's Newspaper*.

Northcliffe to Arthur Mee:

> Hotel Ritz,
> Place Vendôme,
> Paris.
> November 1st, 1910.

My dear Arthur,—When I was your age, in 1894 or '95, I felt impelled as a duty to go into politics, and I became candidate for Portsmouth. That took up a year of my life. I found that my duty lay elsewhere. I found that my business left my control, and that people were leaving me. I found that politics—and this applies to local as well as national politics—consume a vast amount of time, more time than an onlooker would imagine. I realized then that I could do more good with my Press than with my person. I found that the pressure of modern life requires all one's energy in one concentrated task. I found that if my hand was taken from the tiller the ship went wrong.

Because of illness over the last two or three years, he wrote, many things had displeased him in the business. Now that he was getting well, slowly, he had no doubt that those things would 'get right again'. The journey to Newfoundland had been 'very fatiguing'. But for it he would have been back at Carmelite House, 'among you all, where I love to be'.

You hold in your hands the nucleus of a magnificent opportunity. Very slowly, we are awakening to the duties of the individual and the State towards the child. We are beginning to realize that the child is father to the man, and that the collective strength of the individual is the strength of the nation. Few men in England have such power in their hands for good as you, if your *Children's Encyclopædia* and the *Little Paper* were absorbed by even a small proportion of the children of the Empire. Your work is in itself most delightful work. You are free and untrammelled. And the fact that you are part of a vast machine hardly ever affects your surroundings. Yet you must remember that, for good or ill, you are part of that machine. You have the opportunity of using your influence to make that machine a better machine.

Meanwhile, remember that concentration is one of the great secrets of effective progress.

> With much affection,
> Your devoted
> CHIEF.

He had seen Vernon Jones again, to be told (November 14, 1910): 'A little work will now do you good rather than harm, but it must be only a little. I advise you to limit it to two days a week. I am sorry, after all these months of enforced rest, but I am absolutely certain that it is *for the present* a necessity.' Seymour Price, who had stayed on at Grand Falls to deal with a typhoid outbreak, wrote to him on November 16:

I shall not rest content until I know that you are *quite* fit. I do not, however, expect you to be able to work as hard as you have done in the past, or anything approaching it, because it seems to me that you have done the work of about ten men of normal ability for eighteen years and brain effort is, of course, the greatest strain possible on the whole organism.

Northcliffe told Sutton that he intended to abide by the doctor's advice and did not propose 'to resume really active work for a long time'. He feared that he had been 'worrying everybody. Forgive me, my dear Sutkin, if I have been cross. I was not cross with you, but with the various people who needed hauling over the coals.' Writing to Chirol of *The Times*, who was critically ill, he concluded:

Of more importance is the question of health. It might amuse a cynic to find one invalid writing strenuously to another about mere temporal affairs, but this particular invalid who is writing has something in hand in regard to Anno Domini. Like another invalid, he is nervous and if not Latin at any rate Celtic, by temperament. This invalid, however, is guarding himself by escaping such pinpricks in the daily round as he may.

Disturbed by 'persistent rumours' about her husband's health—'everyone in London says that Lord Northcliffe has an incurable disease'—Lady Northcliffe wrote to Sutton on November 16: 'The Chief looks to me better than he has done for ten years—younger, firmer—better altogether. He eats well and sleeps perfectly. *But* he is rather nervous about himself and more inclined to run away from London.'

Northcliffe to the Rt. Hon. A. J. Balfour:

The Times
Printing House Square, E.C.
December 14, 1910.

My dear Mr Balfour,—I hope you will not think it an impertinent intrusion if I suggest that you now go away for a good rest.

You have given the Party a magnificent lead, but they are selfish folk and will work you unstintingly. Not before in my life has our country been so greatly in need of leadership, for I notice, from a careful scrutiny of the German Press—of what it is printing and also what it is not printing—that our friends across the North Sea are in no wise slackening their preparations, while we are amusing ourselves with an unnecessary General Election.

Yours sincerely,

NORTHCLIFFE

When he sent Balfour some 'Notes on the Navy' made by H. W. Wilson, for private perusal, Balfour replied in acknowledgment: 'The difficulty I feel in dealing with the Navy on platforms is that it is so hard to make the public understand the danger of the position without saying things about Germany which hardly seem discreet in the mouth of an ex-Prime Minister!' Through his secretary, J. S. Sandars, Balfour complained to Northcliffe about statements in Harold Harmsworth's Glasgow newspaper. Northcliffe replied: 'My brother and I are great personal friends, but I have nothing to do with his political career and I never see his beastly paper. He and my brothers Leicester and Cecil have Radical bees in their bonnets. Harold is a particularly obstinate and determined man.'

The 'unnecessary general election', as he called it, had brought him a long letter from Lord Robert Cecil at 4 Paper Buildings, Temple, E.C. (November 18, 1910). 'The Unionist Party appear to me to be rushing on to their destruction. There is only one power than can save us, and that is the Press. If you should wish to see me, I am entirely at your service.' Bonar Law, pessimistically contesting the North-West Manchester division, had written to Northcliffe on November 22 intimating the likelihood of his defeat, while hoping that *The Times* would not print anything to that effect. 'If you could prevent it I should be much obliged.' L. S. Amery, formerly of the *Times* staff and a future Cabinet Minister, was also electioneering and had sought Northcliffe's help. 'My Press is at your disposal', Northcliffe told him (November 29). 'I hope Mrs Amery does not mind photographers, who are absolutely essential. To be unknown by the democracy is to be damned by them.'

★   ★   ★

His younger brothers begged him to take up golf. St. John had been a player of the first rank before his car accident. Vyvyan, who was working on Leicester's paper, *Golf Illustrated*, was winning laurels of his own at the game. Leicester himself was one of the best players in the House of Commons. Northcliffe was persuaded, with results that went far beyond those of medical significance. He called in James Braid, a reigning champion, to advise on the making of a nine-hole course at Sutton Place. Braid found him a coach, 'Sandy' Thomson, the professional of the Hampstead Golf Club, a genially sardonic gnome whose skill as player and instructor was impervious to his liking for whisky. He taught North-cliffe all that he knew about golf and in doing so helped to accelerate its popularity everywhere. Between them, they ruined its sanctuary value for the few and opened the fairways to what became a multitude.

Northcliffe rarely approached the eighteenth hole with his chin held high. But he was the best of good losers, taking defeat as if he knew it to be a tonic for the soul. He could feel sorry for himself, but his temper was rarely if ever influenced by golf. He was never known to use bad language (on or off the golf course) or to break his clubs. His salmon fisher's wrists gave him a force and directness of drive from the tee that others envied. Early in his learning period, he stood on the sixth tee at Sutton Place, made 284 consecutive drives of good length and, collapsing from exhaustion, had to be helped back to the house. Within two years he was playing down to a handicap of twelve. Incidentally, he was finding his business vocabulary usefully varied by golf terms. 'I have had to smite Roome [a *Daily Mirror* director] with my niblick over and over again to get him to pay attention to improved printing methods. Even now I do not think that I have got him out of his bunker.'

Golf became part of his journalism as of his life. He joined golf clubs at home and abroad and was a subscribing member of more than twenty. He was amused and flattered when, on one of his American trips, the *Chicago Tribune* printed a headline in its Sunday edition—'Northcliffe's Golf Not as Bad as Expected'. He hired the best players to write for the *Daily Mail* and the *Evening News*. One of them was Henry Leach, who wrote golf books and for many years contributed the gentle essay called 'The Heart of Things' to *Chambers' Journal*. Leach had no doubt that it was Northcliffe more than anyone else who made golf popular, though Northcliffe himself gave some of the credit to a fellow newspaper pro-prietor, Riddell, of the *News of the World*. Leach wrote: 'Before Northcliffe started to play golf the newspapers under his control had devoted little attention to the game. Everybody knows what happened afterwards, and what the result has been.' At *The Times* there was Bernard Darwin, writing for the connoisseurs who disliked the popularizing process and winning many non-golfing readers by the urbanity of his style. He showed Northcliffe that golf could be a help to circulation. Northcliffe thereupon gave golf reporters equal status with special correspondents. The great players of the game were made a subject of interview and gossip para-graphs. They were entertained at Sutton Place, where American cham-pions were made a fuss of for more than golf's sake. The publicity of the Northcliffe newspapers created the 'gallery' at golf tournaments. They broadened the appeal of the game into a pastime for the middle classes.

Northcliffe did not sleep well at Sutton Place and in 1910 he was of the opinion that he never would sleep well there; it was 'too low-lying'. A neighbour, Lord Onslow, of Clandon Park, offered him the use of a bungalow, built as a play house for the Onslow children on a secluded slope called Merrow Down at West Clandon, a few miles from Sutton Place. For rest and quiet, it was ideally situated and Northcliffe took it on a long-term lease, furnishing it with plain comfort. On Merrow Down he found a peace which not even Elmwood could offer; at the bungalow his wants were ministered to by no more than a housekeeper and a secretary. And he slept there so well that he got into the way of spending his day at Sutton and retiring to rest for the night at the bungalow: 'It is a famous sleeping place,' he told an American friend. 'It is between five and six hundred feet above sea level, on dry chalk soil on those great Surrey Downs about which Kipling has written so charmingly.' He wrote to Lord Onslow:

The bungalow is a success, but I am sorry to say has given rise to a considerable local scandal, the suggestion being that my habits are not as moral as I tell people they are. Aye, and worse than that, that his Lordship, the Lord of the Manor, doth resort there in my absence. However, it is well to be able to face the world with a clear conscience, as you and I can.

Chapter Fifteen

What the Public Wants

A YEAR of coronation, 1911, was itself crowned by a splendid summer. There were weeks of shimmering heat in which all England seemed to be at the seaside. For the survivors of a generation then emerging from adolescence to experience far sterner than that which they had been prepared for in the schools, it was a halcyon period which remained in the memory as of a rare and blessed dispensation. 'Before the war', to those who reached their twenties between 1914 and 1918, was a phrase for a most poignant nostalgia, for paradise lost, for a wonderful succession of blue days, each seeming to outbid the calendar's longest, and nights that glittered fantastically with all the jewellery of heaven. There was tension, there was fear, there was unrest. In London, Balfour had told Northcliffe that 'even Lloyd George and company are really anxious about the growth of German power'. In Berlin the Kaiser had lectured the British military attaché on the folly of England's alignment with the decadent French. 'All my life I have worked for a good understanding with England' (March 3, 1911). He had come to London in May for the unveiling of the Queen Victoria memorial in the Mall. He wore the full-dress uniform of a British Admiral of the Fleet and the crowds received him well, fortified by the knowledge that Great Britain would soon possess 'the greatest battleship in the world', H.M.S. *Neptune*, and two new Dreadnoughts.

There were deepening apprehensions in the inner circles of diplomacy. They did not reach down to the crowds watching the scarlet and gold State procession moving against the background of fresh green St. James's foliage that spring, or to those sprawling in the sun that summer. Lord Roberts could ruffle the surface of their indifference. He could not bestir them to ponder seriously the trend of events. 'We are no better prepared for war than we were in 1899', he wrote to tell Northcliffe on February 26, and again on March 19: 'No one in the House of Commons seems to care about our military position.' In the first days of July the public felt the peripheral waves of tension set up by the intimidating behaviour of a German gunboat in the port of Agadir in French-controlled Morocco. The isle became suddenly full of rumour, centred in the supposed mobilization of the Royal Navy. Soon, all was as before. Agadir had gone from the headlines. The pierrots sang and joked about 'paper-bag cookery'. People bathing, listening to Blue Hungarian bands, dozing in their deckchairs, would look up to seek the source of a popping mechanical noise coming from the sky. 'There it is! There it is!' the keenest observers would cry out as if stationed on a peak of history, and a moving speck in the blue distance would come into focus as a monoplane from which the heavily goggled pilot leaned out to wave in greeting as he soared and banked over the beaches. He was a French aviator named Salmet who had been engaged by the *Daily Mail* to give exhibition flights at holiday resorts. A vast majority of holidaymakers had not until then seen a flying machine. Their excited cheers followed Salmet all through that summer round the coasts of England.

A constitutional crisis threatened the future of the House of Lords but there was little popular interest. 'We have had very few letters about it', Northcliffe mentioned in a memorandum about the competing themes of sweet peas and 'standard bread'. His mother, back from a motor drive, had told him of her pleasure in seeing cottage gardens in Hertfordshire full of flowers. An idea took root in his mind as she spoke: Why not give a prize for the best bunch of sweet peas? 'It'll be an excellent hobby for people shut up all day in offices and shops.' His mother nodding her approval, he impulsively fixed the prize at £1,000. It would help to popularize the gardening articles in the *Daily Mail*. It would also divert readers' attention from the critical politics and the succession of strikes which made today's paper look too much like yesterday's. 'We have got into a groove,' he objected to Marlowe. 'Our leading articles are like gramophone records.' He still had no serious interest in, and certainly no insight into, politics; and he was at one with the people in their preference for simpler enthusiasms. He telephoned the sweet pea competition idea to Carmelite House with orders that it was to be announced in the paper at once. It brought in 38,000 bunches, which were put on show at the Crystal Palace, where the judges gave the £1,000 prize to a Scottish grower.

Northcliffe's 'standard bread' campaign was potentially more constructive and actually less successful. He had hoped 'to restore the delicious old farmhouse and cottage bread which made the bone and sinew of Englishmen and the beauty of Englishwomen famous before the craze for white starch began'. The rhetoric was backed by a first prize of £100 and a sixty-guinea cup, with £500 in other prizes, for the best 'standard loaf, containing at least eighty per cent of the whole wheat'. Northcliffe put the *Daily Mail* medical correspondent, Dr Hugh Riddle (brother of the Baroness van Hutten, the novelist), in charge of the drive for better bread. Loaves poured in on Carmelite House from all directions. More than 3,000 of them were exhibited at the Agricultural Hall, Islington. Much interest was roused but few appetites. Hardly anyone wanted to eat 'standard bread'. His editors begged to be allowed to drop the subject. Piqued, maybe, but more decisively influenced by his oldest journalistic maxim, that reiteration was the secret of 'getting at' the public, he ordered an article on 'standard bread' to be printed every day for a year, giving ill-natured minds an excuse for suggesting that he was financially interested in the flour milling industry. The 'standard bread' campaign was commonly spoken of as another of his 'stunts', but there was a sincere public purpose behind it, and behind Northcliffe was his mother, urging him to persevere. Preaching the merits of 'standard bread', it appeared, was part of his credo as a food reformer. He chose to reveal himself as 'what is called a crank' in a letter to a correspondent (February 28, 1911): 'I believe that much of our national trouble is due to our bad food.' He also believed that tea-drinking 'enervated the nation'.

He had evidently made a good recovery from the profound *malaise* of previous months, disconcerting in particular those who, as Lady Northcliffe herself heard, had spoken in whispers of his being in the grip of 'an incurable disease', and demonstrating the therapeutic value of the game that he had none too eagerly started to play. He was showing himself on several golf courses. 'Steal one working day a week for this game,' he counselled Garvin. 'Nothing ever did me so much good.'

Northcliffe to Charles Whibley:

The Times
Printing House Square, E.C.
March 20th, 1911.

My dear Charles,—Why am I silent?

1. Because my leisure is eaten up by the learning of golf.

2. Because I have determined to make 1911 see *The Times* in its old position, and am reorganizing it from cavern to cupola; so that when I am not swearing in the country I am swearing at what cynical Rosebery calls the 'city branch of your Oxford Street business' [The Times Book Club].

So that I am lost for the time being to my friends. The quacks insist on the golf, and after three long years of *Times* muddlers, it is essential that I smite them as vigorously as I try to the golf balls.

As soon as may be, I shall escape my bondage and fly with you somewhere as you will. If you would learn the game, we could make many excursions. It makes one walk and does good therefore.

Your very affectionate
N.

In May, A. J. Balfour went down to Sutton Place to open Northcliffe's new nine-hole course, at that time the finest private golf course in England and possibly in the world. Its three thousand one hundred yards undulated enticingly over the slope between house and river. It was beautifully secluded and its best holes, three good short ones and two long, were a delight to play. Gathered to watch Balfour's raking inaugural drive was a house party that would have set Henry James reaching for his pen. Four of the guests had flown over from Brooklands and Hendon. Northcliffe walked forward to greet them with the air of a proud godfather. 'I suppose', Cecil Harmsworth wrote in his diary, 'a more original or interesting afternoon party has rarely been given.' Behind the first tee was the splendid hundred-yards-long wild rose hedge, just coming into scented bud, a minor gardening wonder of the world and a subject of some of the early colour-photography experiments which Northcliffe had been sponsoring. The Sutton Place lawns were another sort of masterpiece, the setting that day of one of those animated social occasions of the period which viewed through time's ever-extending telescope look like charades without a meaning. The ladies at Sutton Place followed the peculiar usage of the 'high' handshake to which they, or their social exemplars, had been habituated at the crowded soirées of Stafford House and the other great mansions of Mayfair. It was not so much Northcliffe's day as his wife's. Once again she had triumphed as the chatelaine of Sutton Place. There was no one who did not bow the head to her in that role. She made the Sunday luncheon parties memorable events for many distinguished persons in those pre-war summers. The new young secretary, Russell Wakefield, wrote of them as 'exquisitely favoured days', on which the Northcliffes' hospitality drew around such varied personalities as Bonar Law and Selous, the big-game hunter; H. B. Irving—'always talking of crime'— and Lady Betty Balfour, the ardent feminist; Gervase Elwes, the singer, and Alfred Lyttelton, county cricketer and sometime Colonial Secretary; Grahame-White, the pioneering airman, and Lady Dorothy Nevill, custodian of Victorian memories. Wakefield heard Austen Chamberlain, another guest, drawling suavely to the host who was going out to golf: 'I cannot conceive how you can have fallen prey to that lamentable pastime. Its nomenclature alone revolts me—those "bunkers", "bogeys" and "slymies".' ' "Slymies?" ' echoed Northcliffe. 'You're thinking of the popular name for politicians.'

Interviewing Wakefield at Printing House Square before taking him on to his staff, Northcliffe had said: 'So you're just down from Oxford. Did you read for Honours?' Wakefield replied that he did; 'but I only got a second, I'm afraid. I played too many games.' Northcliffe's comment was a rebuke. 'Never make excuses. No one believes them; not even yourself, if you're sensible.' He went on: 'Do you know what I'd have done if you'd told me you'd got a first? Reluctantly shown you the door. I should have known you had a tired brain. This country is ruled by tired brains, and they all took firsts at the university. I will not have them in my businesses. A second is an excellent degree. It reveals intelligence but also a refusal to be prematurely worked out.' He changed the subject by asking: 'Do you play golf?' Wakefield told him that he got a blue for it. 'You did?' Northcliffe exclaimed. 'When can you start?' Wakefield noted his 'formidable eye'. He did not grasp that he was engaged. 'You mean, sir—?' 'I mean that you're my personal private secretary, if you want the job. Did you win your match against Cambridge?' Wakefield replied that he had won it, 'by a fluke, really'. Northcliffe commended his modesty. 'Always take credit for your good luck and blame yourself for your bad.' He concluded the interview with the instruction: 'Report to Mr Price at Carmelite House on Monday morning at nine o'clock. If we don't suit each other, there will be little harm done. If we do, your fortune is made. Good day, my boy.'

*   *   *

He had been 'tightening things up' (his phrase) at Carmelite House. As a result, Marlowe was able to report increased efficiency in several departments. 'Mr Pomeroy Burton's systematic activity' was producing 'stimulating and beneficial results'. 'Mr Caird is now one of the strongest members of the staff.' 'Mr Wilson [the leader writer] is still the mental backbone of the paper.' Marlowe deprecated any suggestion of lowering the tone of the paper to secure a still wider readership. 'The middle-class reader, to whom we have always appealed, is very sensitive to any change of this kind. I am sure that by aiming high we can always command the attention of the lowest. By aiming low we should lose everything.' He wrote as a peroration: 'I should like to see the *Daily Mail* enjoying the literary reputation of *Figaro*, the commercial prosperity of the *Daily Telegraph* and the prestige of *The Times*. Here is work to keep us all busy for years to come.' From his pinnacle, Northcliffe declaimed the proprietorial sense of duty in a letter to Sir Joseph Compton-Rickett, P.C., M.P.:

I regard my position as that of a public trustee, with immense responsibilities. I do not feel that I have any right to send my undiluted opinions into one out of every six houses in this country every day. I enclose, for example, an article by Philip Snowden [the Labour leader] which appeared in the *Daily Mail* a few days ago.

Over at Printing House Square the outlook discouraged firm assurance.

There were complexities still to be resolved. 'I know now that I ought not to have undertaken the task', Northcliffe had written on January 4, 1911, to George Saunders, the *Times* correspondent in Paris, appointed there after a long and influential term at Berlin. He was relieving his feelings yet again about the work and worry of his connection with the paper. 'The thing is so eaten up with old personal antagonisms and jealousies with which I have no concern, mismanagement has gone so deep, that had I not been restored to health I should be obliged to pass my burden on to another.' He seemed to be baffled by his impotence as one who had fertilized so much fruitfulness in the vineyards of Fleet Street. And 1911 he considered to be a year 'of greatest crisis for the Paper', which, he told Nicholson, had been 'little more to me than an annoyance the whole way through'.

Northcliffe to John Walter:

The Times
January 23, 1911.

Dear John Walter,—The very first things I had to greet me this morning on returning from a brief semi-holiday were a number of messages from my little nieces and nephews and the sweet picture of your dear little son.

If I mistake not, that face has in it firmness, wisdom and kindliness. I think the top part of the face is very 'Walterish'. I have such an entire belief in heredity that I cannot say anything better than that.

I have often thought of the well-filled nursery at Bear Wood [country home of the Walter family], not necessarily in envy, because I always think that these things are best arranged for us.

Lately reading Jesse's *Life of George III*, I was struck by the prominence *The Times* had already attained very early in the nineteenth century. I had not realized that so well as I should.

Yours sincerely,
NORTHCLIFFE

He had put in his private observer, Pryor, to report on the progress of the departmental changes on which he had insisted some time before. Pryor told him: 'Some of it has been done, but much of it has not', and Northcliffe, writing to 'K.J.', referred wearisomely to 'the abominable amount of drive' required to achieve the improvements he desired. When Bell said that something could not be done, Northcliffe snapped at him: 'There you go again, Bell, saying can't, can't, can't. It runs through the office, a steady, deadly opposition to every new idea. It won't do, it really won't do. You must break yourself of the habit or we shall quarrel.' He complimented Richmond, the editor of *The Times Literary Supplement*, on an article about the Post-Impressionists, and observed: '*The Times* seems to regard pictures as furniture or decorations or, even worse, as the means of making money by sale to the Americans. In music, we seem to have got as far as Strauss and Debussy.' He hoped to see 'men like John, Steer, Tonks, Orpen and Nicholson getting a little recognition' in the paper. To Clive Bell, who wrote sardonically from Bloomsbury about the inadequacy of the *Times* art criticism, he replied: 'If you watch *The Times*, you will begin to see some signs of grace. You must be patient—some three years' ownership of *The Times* has taught me that, among other things.' Soon Bell was writing to him again: 'It must be true what they say—you are omnipotent. You have reformed *The Times* in a week.' He asked to be allowed to thank Northcliffe, 'for myself, for a group of friends and', he added, 'for all genuine artists and all who care about the significant things of life'.

'They are not encouraging,' was the comment of W. F. Monypenny, long Buckle's assistant and now one of the directors, on the business figures which Northcliffe had sent him concerning *The Times*. 'My mind has long been prepared for more heroic measures.' Doubtless Monypenny, like others among his colleagues, feared that such measures would involve an open breach of Northcliffe's undertaking not to interfere. Northcliffe was visiting Printing House Square more often. One day he found Buckle opening the editorial mail with his thumb, which may not have been his excuse for a subsequent angry outburst in the editor's room. There was an intimidating suggestion that he might shortly occupy that part of the establishment known as the Private House. There was the further anxiety that Moberly Bell's strength as a bulwark was being undermined. Bell's wife had told Northcliffe (January 24, 1911): 'I had that overhauling done —not very satisfactory. Heart the trouble—it is too feeble for the size of the body. The doctor advises slowing down. I write this as you asked me to have him overhauled.' Northcliffe wrote to her in reply:

I only wish that he could be induced to do what I did—cut himself off from work and worry until the doctor approves. . . . If the present *Times* experiment is not a success, further great steps must be taken, which will impose more work upon Bell and everybody else, and I do beg that every effort be made to rest him as speedily as possible.

Sir Victor Horsley once said that I had a keen eye for diagnosis. I diagnosed a case a fortnight ago, and held my opinion against two doctors, as to one of our people, with, I regret to say, most unfortunate accuracy; and I am bound to say that I was disturbed when Bell came into my room a few days ago.

Bell's life for many years has been a most anxious and harassed one. You know that, contrary to many opinions expressed at headquarters, I believe that *The Times* might not have been in existence but for his efforts in the early 'nineties. What those efforts must have cost him no one can tell.

I need not tell you, my dear Mrs Bell, that, despite all our fallings in and out, these three years have greatly endeared Bell to us. We may not see him as you do, but we do see a most courageous, indefatigable, devoted servant of *The Times*. His cheery optimism often carries one merrily through dark places.

The *Times* history does not sufficiently credit Northcliffe with the good feeling which he showed in his transactions with the Nestors of Printing House Square. The tone of the correspondence between him and Bell was frequently genial. He was amused, for example, when Bell suggested as New Year resolutions: 'For Lord N. To think twice before he telephones. For M.B. To think thrice before he writes letters.' He could write to Buckle in 1911: 'Please don't think that I am at all ungrateful for what is being done. I do thoroughly realize the tremendous task before all of us and hope that if I am granted good health I may be able to help.' Replying to good wishes from Buckle: 'Your kindly letter has just reached me. I hope that everything good will come to you and yours in 1911.' It was the postscript to a letter in which he had written: 'The situation is difficult and delicate. A number of men of very different origins, training and experience, all of them with the defects of their qualities, have been brought together to repair the errors of past Squires of Bearwood [the Walters]. The process is one demanding great mutual forebearance, which has, I think, been shown on all sides, and will, I trust, result in the ultimate success of this most difficult enterprise.'

The mutual forebearance was severely strained in the spring of 1911, when the *Daily Mail*, the *Evening News* and the *Weekly Dispatch* took a strong line against the ratification of the Declaration of London, which in wartime would deprive the Royal Navy of the right to intercept materials of use to an enemy. *The Times* advocated ratification. Buckle wrote on March 1 his 'great regret' at hearing from Bell and Nicholson of Northcliffe's 'strong disapproval' of the policy of assent. 'I was unaware that this was a matter on which you had a decided opinion. You had never mentioned it to me', and the policy had been formulated and maintained in the paper since the change of proprietorship. Buckle's letter was a carefully balanced exposition of the policy and of reasons for persisting in it. 'Deeply as I regret that the opinion held in the office should differ on this important question from yours, I feel no doubt that it is impossible for *The Times*, if it wishes to maintain its reputation, to go back on the line it has taken up.' Northcliffe to Buckle, in reply (March 3, 1911): 'I thought Nicholson had made it plain that I will not devote one farthing of my fortune to supporting that which I know would be an injury to this country, and this, therefore, is to acknowledge, with much regret, the receipt of your letter and is my final communication on this subject.' He intimated to Nicholson: 'If resignations are offered, accept them.' There is no reason to doubt what he wrote to Buckle or that he considered the Declaration of London to be inimical to the national interest. The *Times* historian suggests that Northcliffe was mainly actuated by a fear that the 'superior political influence' of the paper might 'render vain the efforts of his other newspapers', exposing him 'to the taunt that their campaign was ill-judged or badly led'. He had stated his position again to Bell also on March 3: 'I have made up my mind what I am going to do about it and I shall act very definitely.'

Refusing to accept 'sea law made in Germany', the *Daily Mail* organized a protest meeting in the City. Balfour, who had been invited to speak, answered that he 'knew nothing of the subject'. Northcliffe wrote to him: 'I hope you will not think it presumptuous, or lacking in a sense of proportion, when I say that I believe this matter to be much more vital than any of the measures now being discussed.' Balfour replied: 'I mean to do my best—if I am alive after the Coronation ceremonies!' He was persuaded to give up a Saturday to reading what had been written in favour of the Declaration of London and a Sunday to hearing arguments against it. The following Tuesday, he attended the meeting and declared himself against ratification. Two days later, he spoke to the same effect in the Commons and helped to secure the rejection of the Naval Prize Bill, embodying the Declaration, before the House. What seems scarcely believable at this distance was the obtuseness of the supporters of the Declaration in not acknowledging that in a war it would greatly prejudice the country's food supplies, always at the mercy of extraneous circumstance.

Northcliffe to Reginald Nicholson:

Carmelite House,

March 6th, 1911.

My dear Reg,—Buckle wrote to me about the 'independence' of *The Times*. I have learned a good deal of the 'independence' of *The Times* during the last three years, and I know something of its 'independence' since the Jameson raid, and am ready for that sort of nonsense if required.

Would indeed that *The Times* were independent. It has about as much independence on certain matters as the hall porter at the Foreign Office or a Bond Street picture dealer's assistant.

I am just off to Sutton Place to look after my golf links. I played at Ranelagh yesterday and did not like it. Stoke Poges spoils one for other places.

CHIEF.

From that time, the worthies of Printing House Square believed that it was Northcliffe's intention not only to break his implied bond of non-interference with the editorial policy, but, still more offensive to them, to align 'the Paper' with his papers. In huddled debate, they considered a united act of resignation, but, largely at the spirited call of Moberly Bell, decided to face what storms were coming. Their heroics were as nearly disinterested as it is possible for the human heart to be. For them only 'the Paper' mattered. They girded their loins anew to the task of preventing *The Times* from becoming 'an *edition-de-luxe* of the *Daily Mail*'.

Their situation can at this distance be simplified into a clash between age and youth or dramatized as the agony of an older generation watching the rise of a younger, represented by a master in the middle forties as against their average of sixty. Standing apart, while stoutly defending his office fellows, Moberly Bell was splendidly tolerant of Northcliffe's wilful temperament and worst moments, arguing that Northcliffe himself was as much a victim of them as those around him. 'His remarks hurt me,' Bell said, 'only because I really like him. He is a good fellow.' Bell's self-command, admired by those who also deplored it, was sustained at greater cost to himself than was realized. His daughter wrote of him coming home in those latter years 'night after night, tired out'.

On April 2, 1911, Bell reached his sixty-fourth birthday. His family agreed that his health and spirits had 'markedly improved; he was looking, and said he was feeling, better than he had done for many years'. On April 5 he sat at his desk writing one of his firm-handed, clear-headed letters, the subject being the Copyright Bill before Parliament. His secretary, at her desk, heard his pen clatter to the floor. There was no movement from Moberly Bell. His secretary thought that he had fainted. He was dead.

Northcliffe to Mrs Moberly Bell:

> Hotel Ritz,
> Paris.
> 7th April, 1911.

My dear Mrs Bell,—They wrote me from Printing House Square, and I read in the paper, about the passing of your dear man. Everyone I have met who knew him has the same thought: the end he would have chosen.

No consolation to you, dear Madame Wise, who know that he was a victim of that vast greedy machine at Blackfriars. I was at Versailles yesterday, where three years and three months ago he and I bridged the crevasse of 1908, the second or third time he had saved the situation, and I came away sorry and melancholy at the conviction that had I done my duty and *insisted* on an Egyptian trip for him, we might have had him with us still.

When the times comes, dear Madame Wise, I hope that you will often be in our homes. My wife is very fond of you.

> Yours very sincerely,
> NORTHCLIFFE.

He wrote to Sutton: 'Old Bell's death, an unexpected trouble, makes life burdensome and my golf today was a hopeless failure. How I shall manage to stick it at Biarritz I don't know, as I always carry great business burdens. I often wish I had been born a peasant. I have been urged to go over for the funeral but have unhappiness enough.' Mrs Moberly Bell replied to his letter: 'You must not even dream that a holiday or absence from the office would have made any difference, and, as you know, he always made holiday grudgingly and hurried back to his desk.' She wrote again on April 21: 'I wanted to thank you the very first moment for your generous goodness. I did not know of your extraordinary forethought in sending me that £300 to go on with—that touched me very much.' In another letter to Northcliffe, after hearing the directors' decision to provide for her future, she wrote: 'I cannot say how deeply grateful I am—it puts me out of anxiety about my children's careers—and it is such a loving tribute to my dear "Man" who would love most of all that you should be so good to me. I just take your kind hand in mine and thank you.' Northcliffe wrote to Monypenny: 'If you could take the opportunity of telling Mrs Bell anything that would interest her about The Times, I would be greatly obliged. It has been part of her life for so many years that I can well understand that this sudden break in the continuity of interest, in these early days of her grief, may add considerably to her burden. I have always found Mrs Bell not only interested in The Times but an extremely good critic of it.'

Bereft of Bell, the 'Black Friars'—a Northcliffe nickname for the men of Printing House Square—had to accept the likelihood of unimpeded pressures from him. He had put Nicholson on the board in Bell's place. Through 1911, Buckle was uneasy about his future and still more uneasy, it will be just to assume, about the future of 'the Paper'. Northcliffe was going over his head to consult individual members of the staff—Chirol, head of the foreign department, Wickham Steed, the Vienna correspondent, and Dr G. E. Morrison, known as 'Chinese' Morrison, a notable figure in the annals of Far East news gathering. Morrison had gone to see Northcliffe and wrote to him on February 16, 1911:

I cannot thank you too warmly for all the kindness you and Lady Northcliffe have shown me since I came to England. I count it among the greatest privileges I have enjoyed in England, the opportunity you have given me of meeting and talking over with you our hopes and aspirations for the future of The Times. I will keep in touch with you and let you know from time to time how things are going. There will, I believe, in the future be no further suppression of facts that conflict with the prejudices of our foreign editor.

Thanks to you I go back to China more contented than I have been for a long time past, for I know that I can always communicate with you should need arise.

A young All Souls graduate named Geoffrey Robinson, recommended by L. S. Amery, had come into the office from the foreign staff; he had been serving as the *Times* correspondent in his capacity as editor of the Johannesburg *Star*. A protegé of Milner in South Africa, his knowledge of Empire problems and his sympathy with the Imperialist idea commended him to Northcliffe, who spoke of him thus early to Evelyn Wrench as 'a future editor of *The Times*'. Buckle had already notified Nicholson: 'I told Northcliffe that I felt doubtful whether, in the new conditions, it would not be better that I should make way for a younger man of his own choice. He was good enough to protest against the suggestion. But it has never been long out of my mind. . . .' Soon he would have cause to feel still more isolated in his post. Valentine Chirol, head of the foreign side and one of his oldest colleagues, was preparing to retire.

*   *   *

In 1911, too, Northcliffe and Garvin parted political and journalistic company, Garvin exclaiming in a letter: 'God help the Empire!' and subscribing himself with the assurance: 'I love you all the same.' In one of his recent articles Garvin had referred to Northcliffe as a 'weathercock' in politics. Far from being affronted, Northcliffe was amused to address Garvin as 'My dear Wetterhahn' when in Germany, and as 'My dear Girouette' when in France. He sold *The Observer* in April 1911 to Waldorf Astor for £40,000. 'Garvin and I do not see eye to eye,' he told Charles Russell, the solicitor in the transaction, 'though our relations are otherwise more than kindly.' They had disagreed over Tariff Reform. He wrote to a newcomer to politics and journalism in England: 'My dear Aitken [Max Aitken, M.P., later Lord Beaverbrook],—So far as I am concerned, *The Observer* is nothing. It is everything to Garvin. . . . Under no circumstances will I continue in *The Observer* with him. I am extremely fond of him, but I think he acted with great unwisdom. . . .' The break had come over Imperial Preference. It was not unwelcome to Northcliffe. *The Observer* had been improved as a vehicle of opinion rather than of news. Its circulation had been increased eightfold in three years, but Garvin was writing outside the paper and Northcliffe liked his editors to be single-minded. Because he himself had too little time to give to *The Observer* his interest waned. Garvin to Northcliffe: 'It has been a horrible upset but the best solution as things are. Nothing will ever alter our affectionate friendship for you both.' Northcliffe to Garvin: 'I know that the association of these several years between ourselves and our sweet ladies has made us like and understand each other and I hope that both of you will adorn our future years.' The letter stirred Garvin to write with yet deeper feeling:

414

The whole thing has been a bit desolating, but it would have been an utterly miserable business had it meant a severance of our friendship. That must never be. Yet how sorry I was and am to part with the old situation. I feel like an orphan. Enough that we may have had many a good hour together. You will always find me the same obstinate but staunch and fundamentally affectionate man.

I am tired to death and rather feeling that no salt has any savour. Well, life is a queer business. It makes me laugh and it makes me sigh. Who will I talk shop with now? Let us try to be closer friends than ever; there's nothing now to interfere; but it may be long indeed before I have three more such vital years as those we have spent together.

Ever and always,

Your affectionate

GARVE

Northcliffe had taken Lord Onslow's bungalow 'for peace and quiet', and had attained neither. 'My day is marked out in minutes,' he told Max Pemberton, 'and I have to see my friends when I can. It has practically come to this, those who have no telephone I never see.' He answered a fishing invitation from Lord Orford with the confession: 'I have become a slave to the machine.' Letters followed him to the bungalow, as everywhere. He told Marlowe: 'I have two men here opening them from morning till night.'

There was Sir Sidney Lee, the historian, thinking it desirable to remind him: 'You have never done anything yet to help in stemming the exodus of masterpieces across the Atlantic.' Northcliffe wrote in reply: 'I do not like the way these picture sales are worked, and, as late proprietor of *The Connoisseur*, I have some knowledge of it. There is a very unpleasant background to the situation. That is why I do not interfere.' When a Fleet Street acquaintance, Arthur Lawrence, asked permission to write a biography of him, he answered curtly: 'I think such publications are indecent.' To the editor of the *Newspaper World* who asked for a photograph of him for use with some articles on newspaper proprietors, he wrote: 'I hope you will not insert a picture of me in the series to which you refer. If I wanted publicity for myself I could get it in many millions of copies each day. I thoroughly hold with Dana and Delane that a newspaper owner should be "read" and not seen.' And to *The Times* news staff: 'Would you kindly see that neither my name nor that of Lady Northcliffe appears in *The Times* except in official announcements of attendance at public functions? I should not trouble you had it not been that my name has appeared so repeatedly in *The Times* of late, despite the wish I expressed when I became principal Proprietor.' Objecting to certain aspects

415

of *Daily Mirror* journalism, he drew the following reply from the editor Alexander Kenealy:

I quite agree with your letter about the bad taste and ignorance of some of the things that appear in the *Daily Mirror*. I have been trying to stop them.

Highly-educated men, I find, as a rule have no sense of news. They always want to write about ancient Rome or what happened to Jupiter. They regard the death of King Edward as unimportant because it is recent. We have Oxford men here and Eton men. None of them can write gramatically or spell, and they are woefully ignorant of anything that has happened since 42 B.C.

I heard one of our Eton young men asking a Board School office boy, who hadn't an 'H' to his name, who 'this man Chamberlain' was. The office boy told him. The Eton man has not been with us for some time.

Seymour Price, the physician, was getting married at Holy Trinity, Sloane Square, and going to live and practise in Sloane Gardens, S.W. 'I hope you won't think me extravagant in having the ceremony at so fashionable a church. My idea was solely that it might be a judicious advertisement in the area. . . . I owe so much to you for advice, philosophy and finance.' Northcliffe, in reply: 'I know I can look forward with confidence to see you gain great eminence in your profession. Your patient thinks a great deal of his quack.' Memo to the editor of the *London Magazine* [formerly *The Harmsworth Magazine*]: 'Alter the title of the article on the Kaiser to "The Kaiser—A Friendly View".' Horace Hooper, of The Encyclopædia Britannica Co. Ltd., wrote from 125 High Holborn, giving his side of a dispute between him and his partner Jackson. Northcliffe to Hooper: 'It is a great pity that two such straight and able men, who produce great results, should not be working together.'

John Galsworthy to Northcliffe:

> 14, Addison Road,
> London, W.
> 7th April, 1911.

Dear Lord Northcliffe,—I do beg of you to use your great influence to try and bring about an understanding between nations that the air is to be left alone —free from the machines of organized murder. It seems to me that there is a fearful responsibility on the leaders of nations now to check at its birth this horror hanging over the heads of the unborn generations.

If it is not stopped now, it will gather too much momentum. I can imagine them saying in A.D 2000. 'May God curse those who lived in 1911 . . .!'

> Believe me, dear Lord Northcliffe,
> Yours very truly,
> JOHN GALSWORTHY

Northcliffe to John Galsworthy:

The Times
Printing House Square, E.C.
May 4, 1911.

My dear Galsworthy,—Will you kindly tell me how you are to approach
foreign nations? If you approach Germany, they at once think that you are
interfering with them. I have very little doubt that you are right about the
views of posterity.

Yours very truly,
NORTHCLIFFE

Strachey, of *The Spectator*, was writing to him, often at inordinate length,
in his large, scrawling hand, on national affairs. Another of his more per-
tinacious correspondents was Maxse, of the *National Review*. Both men
in some degree aspired to be saviours of the nation. Markwick, his old
partner, sent a photograph of his son and Northcliffe answered: 'The older
I get the more interest I take in young people.' As proof of it, he had sent
young Alfred Pemberton, his godson, to Canada for education and experience, keeping him supplied with cash and writing to Max Pemberton, the
boy's father: 'I hear from Alfred continually. At this very impressionable
time of his life he will learn what you and I had to learn—independence.
I have had pathetic experience of the lack of independence of gently-born
and gently-bred English boys.' He was paying the Cambridge fees of
several young men of promise, telling one of them: 'I spent a couple of
days at Cambridge the week before last and delighted in it. How much I
regretted that my own circumstances had not enabled me to go there years
ago.' He was supporting a young Furse at Eton and arranging to send one
of Marlowe's sons to Marlborough. A reader of *The Times* sent him a copy
of a school magazine brought out by two young girls named Brisley, aged
thirteen and fourteen, of Bexhill-on-Sea. Complimenting them, he invited
them to visit him if they came to London. They had tea with him in the
boardroom at *The Times*. Northcliffe to Marlowe of the *Daily Mail*: 'Will
you get an appreciation (Page Four) of Noyes, the young poet? His work
is greatly improving.'

Lord Haldane, at the War Office, hoped that *The Times* would print
his inaugural address to the Educational Congress at Oxford. 'Its purpose
will be to show that the misinterpretation of each other's ideas by Germans
and Englishmen arises out of differences of tradition and education: the
two races have in fact different standpoints.' A personal appeal from Aaron
Watson, historian of the Savage Club, on behalf of Byron Webber, an old
Fleet Street man, 'something of a poet, frail, stricken, and 74', brought a
cheque for £10 and an allowance of £1 a week. Lord Curzon, asking for

417   P

money in support of a £100,000 appeal for the Royal Geographic
Society, had little success in flattering him as 'a great and conspicuo
friend of exploration who has given nobly to geographical enterprise
Acknowledging Northcliffe's £250, he wrote: 'It absolutely kills all hop
if the friends of the society, and you are one, will do no more for us tha
this.' Ellen Terry implored him to 'be a friend to my very extraordinar
and most talented son', Gordon Craig, 'who has a great scheme of stag
decoration and scenery. I wish you would see this young fellow (my ver
dear son) and *more than once. I beg you* to take an interest in his affairs
More to his fancy was an intimation from Brenton Macnab, of *Th
Montreal Star*, that a new street in the western part of Montreal was to b
named Northcliffe Avenue; and another from Beach Thomas that th
bird boxes at Elmwood were being occupied by approved tenants. H
brother, Sir Harold, wrote discouragingly about the prospects for a nev
publication which Northcliffe had proposed. 'The sooner we get back t
the "fried fish and stewed eels" of The Amalgamated Press the better
Practically all the publications above the 1d price, at the present time, ar
failures and are absorbing quite a lot of money.' Northcliffe to Sutton
'Harold probably does not know the nature of the paper I am starting
To compare it with Hammerton's [*Everybody's*] paper is foolish. Hammer
ton is not capable of organizing or running a paper. He is a most in
dustrious, unoriginal man. Many thanks, my dear Sutkin, for your kind
ness and for all the trouble you take about my affairs. If I seem irritable, i
is only my shorthand manner. It means nothing but that I am extremely
fond of you.'

There was also a letter from his youngest brother, St. John:

I was amused, dearest Alfred, to be told at Totteridge that I was mysteriously
silent with you about my business affairs. Why should I worry you? Surely
you have enough of your own. As it is, you carry most of your relatives on
your shoulders. The Perrier business is really in a very flourishing condition and
is a valuable property. Naturally, my long illness has deprived it of its force,
but I hope to be devoting more attention to it in the future. It is true that my
private finances are troublesome. I am returning to Paris next week to continue
my treatment. The fifth year of my struggle finds me full of hope and faith
that I shall be ultimately freed. Continue, dearest brother, to render me that
valuable moral support which has been such a help to me during these long
years.

The correspondence burden was the heavier because he could not
restrain his own constantly stimulated impulses to add to it. There was no
pressing need for him to send guidance to Curzon and Haldane as public
speechmakers: it reflected the impact on a democratic society of the
accelerated pace of newspaper production. He urged them to 'decline to

peak at any place where there are not good telegraph facilities and to peak not later than half-past seven in the evening', saying that 'public men o not seem to realize that the whole newspaper situation has changed in he last ten years'. He pointed out that 'Churchill is very well aware of hese arrangements and while much of the reporting of his speeches is due o merit, a good deal is also due to his practical common sense in seeing he situation as it is'. Concerning that future statesman, he had written to Marlowe after the 'battle' of Sidney Street of January 1911 which Churchill, then Home Secretary, had supervised: 'Now that you have had our usual outburst against Churchill, I trust you will leave him alone for time. As I have to bear the whole responsibility for this sort of thing, wish you would not do it unless I suggest it.' Also to Marlowe: 'The *Daily Mail* was not made by licking Ministers' boots. I have a natural horror of that sort of journalism, and suffer a great deal from it at Printing House Square, where I am trying to break it down.' To the manager of he Manchester office of the *Daily Mail*: 'I have been much distressed to ind that there is unhappiness in the Manchester office. I am going away or a little holiday and hope by the time I come back everything will be ll right, otherwise I shall make severe trouble for the heads of the business. They have no right to ignore their humbler brethren.' He wrote to ask about Maxse's health. 'Do let me beg you to take things more easily.' He had invited a former Elmwood housekeeper, Mrs Jackson, to give him her opinion of the serial stories in The Amalgamated Press girls' papers, and, as a result, was able to startle the editor of the group with the comment: 'I am not at all satisfied with the two serials in the *Girls' Reader*—"Apron Strings" and "No Reference". They are exaggerated and improbable.' Northcliffe to Wareham Smith, advertising director of Associated Newspapers (June 5, 1911): 'My heart sank when I read the other day that you were about to start another Ideal Home Exhibition. The *Daily Mail* does not need these artificial supports. The exhibition did some good but at the present time, when business is menaced by severe competition on all sides, I think it would be better for the cobbler to stick to his last.'* There was doubtless equally good reason for drawing the attention of Monypenny, the *Times* director, to the 'very serious condition of the paper's finances' and for criticizing James Murray Allison, its advertising manager, for 'his outspoken optimism which has the effect of rendering the staff perfectly callous in regard to expenses'. A correspondent who sent in a list of 'suggestions for popularizing *The Times*', received the reply: '. . . In other words, you want to put a Punch and Judy show in Westminster Abbey.' He confided to the new editor of *Forget-Me-Not*: 'It was a little creation of my own many years ago, a delicate blossom which unfortunately has had too much varied gardening. It is a little paper for

* The *Daily Mail* Ideal Home Exhibition has been successfully continued for more than fifty years.

which I had great ambitions.' A woman applicant for a post was nc altogether relevantly informed: 'One of the reasons why I am not ii favour of the suffrage of women is the impossibility of getting them t work together properly. The friction they created among themselves a the *Daily Mirror* in the old days when that paper was conducted by ladie exceeded anything I had ever known.' To the Master of Elibank, M.P. 'If my newspapers can be of any service to whatever government may b in power, I am only too pleased.'

*　　*　　*

'I am rather under the impression that those dark, sunless rooms a Carmelite House have an effect upon one's spirits,' he wrote to Suttoi from Versailles in the early summer of 1911. 'The Italians have a saying where the sun does not enter the doctor does.' Hearing that he had madc a short flight with Paulhan in a Farman military aeroplane, his mothei wrote out on a half sheet of notepaper the following pledge, which hc signed: 'I hereby promise not to go in any aeroplane or flying machinc whatever without the written consent of my Mother.—Alfred. May 31st, 1911.' It did nothing to lessen the intensity of his interest in the development of aviation. A great new wave of popular acclaim followed the competitors for his £10,000 prize in a round-Britain air race in July 1911. At Hendon, the starting point, crowds camped out all night to see the seventeen flyers take off for the circuit of 1,010 miles in machines that looked like box-kites with engines. The race was won by a French officer flying under the name of André Beaumont. Breathlessly, the *Daily Mail* leader writer commented next day: 'A fresh revolution—the greatest conceivable—in human transit, is upon the world—is, indeed, fast being accomplished.' Northcliffe returned to London to greet the victor and to hand him the £10,000. General Seely (later Lord Mottistone) wrote to him from the War Office his 'personal thanks' for the 'great stimulus' of his money prizes 'to the science and industry of heavier-than-air machines. They will make my task much easier in building up the Royal Flying Corps.'

Apropos his short holiday, he told his mother: 'I greatly needed the change, for I had immense difficulty in getting our business into order again. It had grown rebellious. Heads swelled all round and needed heaps of reducing. They are now reduced.' He was talking more freely of his 'spies', who, he let it be known, were keeping him informed 'of many things'. The immature side of him still delighted in that sort of fiction. He used the word 'spy' in his messages to the office as a crack of the whip, meant to keep the staff on their toes. It amused im to pose as all-knowing; at the same time, it was astonishing how much he did know. Private telephone calls over office lines were supposedly reported to him. In fact, he had instructed the switchboard operators in various buildings to overhear and make notes of his own conversations with certain callers, so that corroborative evidence might be available if needed. From that precautionary tactic grew a legend which has often been used to belittle his character.

★   ★   ★

By the end of that wonderful summer he was feeling 'completely run down', and claiming that he had never been so busy as in the previous six months. He proposed motoring by easy stages to Edinburgh and, after some golf, crossing to Dublin. 'It will be rather nice to pop into the old bookshops of Edinburgh', he told Max Pemberton, whom he had chosen to be his holiday companion again. Arriving there, he expressed to Pemberton a preference for reading 'sensational novels'. Pemberton let Sutton know that 'the Chief was tired for the first few days and I thought him in very poor condition indeed. He was so tired he could hardly do anything at all.'

From the Braid Hills Hotel, Edinburgh, he wrote to his mother that 'a bad financial year' obliged him to curtail his allowance to her, 'at any rate, for 1912'. He had been giving her £6,000 a year, now cut to £4,625. He explained that the Labour troubles of the previous year—strikes at the docks, on the railways, in the mines and the shipyards—had deprived him of his *Daily Mail* profits 'for the whole of the twelve months'. His income in 1911 was £118,000. In 1912 it was £125,000. His wife had been in the doctors' hands. 'We speak together often on the telephone,' he told his mother, 'and I am looking forward to being with her again.' On October 3 he wrote to his mother from his birthplace at Chapelizod, Dublin:

Sunnybank.
In bed, 8 a.m.

Dearest Mother,—We got here in the dusk last night, but light enough to see that the garden looks very gay with geraniums. There is a considerable stir in the place at my return after 44 years' absence and there were signs of movement about and, I fear, unsupported claims to old acquaintance. 'Sure, I knew you and your dear mother when you were a little baby.' 'Did you?' I asked. 'Yes, me lard.' 'And how old may you be?' I inquired. 'Forty—or forty-five.' A vague age, truly, but it gave away the show.

Both Max and I, and Joseph too [his valet] agree that 'Sunnybank' is a model of a small house. It is well planned. Last night, all lit up, it looked quite imposing from the garden.

Max and I sat in the drawing-room and smoked, and went to bed at 10.

I read a chapter or two of *Vanity Fair* and was asleep by half-past ten. Woke up at 2.20 and listened to the river and a great rain storm, was asleep again a 3.45, woke at 7 to a bright and sunny but changeable Irish day, had my *Daily Mail* and *Mirror* at 7.15. I wonder what you would have thought of a London paper here at 7.15 on the same day in 1865. Then I wired to you, walked in the garden, examined my dear birthplace, picked this apple leaf and rose leaf, came in and am writing this in the great family bed.

I feel particularly well here this morning and am going off to church.

I cannot help thinking how wisely you chose your home, darling. As I write with the window right open, there is the steady rush of the river and much cawing of rooks. I think of you every second, darling, and thank God I have had so good and brave a Mother.

Your Firstborn

Pulitzer, of the New York *World*, died suddenly in November and Northcliffe was moved to write a column and a quarter about him in the *Daily Mail*. He dictated it with hardly a pause, producing a readable and informative valedictory which brought him professional compliments from both sides of the Atlantic. There were even echoes of appreciation from Printing House Square. Buckle wrote regretting thas 'so vigorous and picturesque a piece of portrait-painting' was not available to *The Times*. Northcliffe wrote of Pulitzer: 'Many of his critics, being unable to find a flaw in his public acts, were driven to attack minor blemishes that naturally occur in an organization carried on by one whose health necessitates continued absence from his affairs.' He may have hoped that the point would be taken by his own critics, who refrained from making play with his curious disclosure that 'it was while studying British rule in India that Pulitzer's failing eyesight received its final shock'.

There was disquieting private information from Germany, transmitted to Northcliffe by Wile, the Berlin correspondent, who had been given 'a frank and confidential interview' by the German Ambassador at Washington, Count Bernstorff. The Ambassador had been on his annual leave in Germany. 'He says that there is no exaggerating the enmity against England which now prevails in Germany. He described this enmity as "universal and widespread, from the Kaiser down to the humblest street sweeper".' Declaring himself a man of peace and a friend of England, 'he admitted that the atmosphere, the like of which he has not known since the Boer War, is deplorable and unfortunate to the highest degree. Germans of all classes are convinced that England's hostility to Germany is deep-seated and irremovable.' The temperature had been sent up by Lloyd George's speech at the Mansion House in July, when he had uttered what was taken as an official warning to Germany about the Agadir incident. Winston Churchill wrote in *The World Crisis**

* Thornton Butterworth, 1923–31.

hat the speech, which was meant to avert war, 'brought us to the very verge of it'. Pertaining to that dangerous possibility, Northcliffe had written to Churchill a few weeks earlier (September 18, 1911): 'My newspapers have never been provocative about Germany. Germany resents my printing the facts about her forces and intentions.' Wile's report to Northcliffe continued:

As an indication of the state of feeling in the highest German circles, Bernstorff told me that when he was dining with the Kaiser the other night, the speech of Lloyd George was the topic of conversation, and the consensus of opinion was that the speech was as provocative an affront to German honour as was the telegram of Napoleon III, which precipitated the Franco-German war. One of the personages at the table expressed the view that Germany ought to have gone to war with England to avenge Lloyd George's insult. Not having done so, the consequent humiliation would leave its sting for many a year.

Wile had called the Ambassador's attention to Churchill's speech at the Guildhall, London, on November 8, a few days before, in which he said that British naval expenditure would continue to rise in ratio to German expenditure. Bernstorff answered that England could not have naval peace on those terms because 'Germany will not consent to permanent acknowledgment of British naval supremacy'. He concluded the interview by likening Anglo-German relations to those of 'two bulldogs which were perpetually barking at each other and would continue to bark until one of them flew at the other's throat'. H. W. Wilson, the *Daily Mail* leader writer, said that 'the situation was far more dangerous than was generally known. For weeks we on the Northcliffe newspapers lived in apprehension.' There were ominous German troop movements. The commander-in-chief of the German navy took what were considered to be 'necessary precautions' by cruising off Scapa Flow. Wilson recorded that he had to wake 'one of the very kind and courteous attachés at the French Embassy, in the small hours of the morning, to ascertain whether war had begun'. Concerning 'necessary precautions' on the British side, Northcliff declared an unofficial censorship, ordering his editors to 'print nothing to fan the war spirit'. Few members of the public knew that the railways to the southern parts of England were being patrolled. When the Balkan War broke out in 1912, his *Daily Mail* stated that a European conflict over the question of Serbia securing an outlet to the Adriatic 'would be a blunder and a crime'.

Northcliffe wrote to Winston Churchill again that autumn. 'I think I told you one of my German relations said: "We are a nation of land crabs. If you advance, we retreat; if you retreat, we advance." ' To Churchill's acknowledgment of attentions received from the Northcliffe newspapers, which printed many of his speeches, he replied (November 11, 1911) 'I have not been in the least kind to you. I judge public men on their public form, and I believe that your inquiring, industrious mind is alive to our national danger.'

From Vienna, Wickham Steed, representing *The Times* in that capital, sent a message to Northcliffe informing him that 'the Countess de Castellane says that the French General Staff expects war next spring. The French Ambassador here has been repeating for the last three months, *Nous allons à la guerre!*' Steed doubted whether war would come within six months, 'but I should not care to predict the maintenance of peace for much more than a year'. He referred in his message to 'the precarious position of German industry and the determination of the Prussian Junker class to force on, if possible, some foreign complication in order to prevent the destruction of Junker privileges by internal reform'. Those, he considered, were the elements in the situation which made for war. He pressed on Northcliffe the need 'to get our army into order and to see that our reserves of weapons and ammunition are sufficient for all possible emergencies' (November 11, 1911).

Frank Matley, headmaster, St. Saviour's School, Poplar, to Northcliffe:

November 29, 1911.

Dear Lord Northcliffe,—On behalf of the boys and myself let me thank you with all my heart for your splendid generosity.

When I told the boys at the morning assembly that you have assured them a camp at 'Elmwood' for next year, their delight was unbounded. A holiday of this kind does mean so very, very much to them. It not only makes their sum of happiness so much greater, but it enlarges their whole outlook upon life generally.

The last thirteen camps have done incalculable good in building up the poor physique of the boys in this part of the East End, and I can assure you we all keenly appreciate your great kindness in continuing your benefactions to a neighbourhood which needs them so badly.

I remain,

Yours very faithfully,

FRANK MATLEY

★   ★   ★

Lord Roberts, campaigning for national service and sometimes speaking in half-filled halls, believed that he was working to stop war, as did Northcliffe who supported him, and who subscribed himself when writing to the field-marshal as 'Yours affectionately and with esteem'. Calling on his fellow-countrymen to be prepared, Roberts had but one aim, the safety of England and the Empire. Northcliffe, the journalist, deemed it wise as well as expedient to give British newspaper readers the German view by printing an interview with Hans Delbruck, Treitschke's successor in the chair of history at Berlin University, and a personal consultant to the Kaiser. A restrained and measured presentation of the German case, it reads now like pathetic evidence of the *impasse* to which the nations had come. Northcliffe ordered H. W. Wilson to reply, point by point, in a *Daily Mail* leading article which suggested that the Germans were living 'in an atmosphere of artificial suspicion, deliberately created for political reasons', namely, support for the naval expansion plans of Admiral von Tirpitz. 'We have said before and we now say again that the British people have every desire to live in peace with their neighbours.'

In after years, Tirpitz agreed that Great Britain had not attacked Germany at a time when there had been a good chance of success. No one, it seemed, gave her credit for keeping the peace. A document among the Northcliffe papers supplies a period footnote. A correspondent recorded that 'Lord Cawdor [First Lord of the Admiralty, 1905] told me himself, first hand, that six months before he left the Admiralty, Sir John Fisher came to his office one day and said, "Sir, if you want to smash up the German fleet, I am ready to do so now. If you wait five or six years, it will be a much more difficult job." Cawdor said: "I will tell Mr Balfour", and went along to his room and repeated what Fisher had said. Mr Balfour's reply was: "Tell Fisher we don't want to smash up the German navy—but to keep in readiness." Cawdor returned to his room and told Fisher, who said: "Very well, remember I have warned you." '

Northcliffe knew that there was a peace party in Germany but he did not believe that it would or could prevail. He chided Marlowe on January 13, 1912, for allowing the *Daily Mail* to give 'the impression that Socialist victories are of importance in international affairs. If you travel in Germany, you realize that nobody cares how many victories they win. It is misleading, because the English peace party have some foolish theory that if Socialists are returned there will be less likelihood of war.' He may or may not have been borrowing the opinion of Wickham Steed, of the *Times* foreign department, who had written two days before that armaments were the governing factor in German politics of that time. The Socialists of Germany, who were to gain one-third of the Reichstag seats at the general election, had given 'no sign of unconditional hostility to armaments. The old Socialist cry: "Not a man! Not a penny!" for the army, no longer resounds.'

In England, the Liberal writers of the *Daily News* protested that 'the leading articles of the yellow journals would be couched in a very different strain if their titled proprietors were at any personal risk of smelling powder'. *The Nation*, edited by H. W. Massingham, hugged to itself the illusion that 'on the German side, Social Democracy, with its 20 per cent of soldiers in the German Army, will stop war and the growth of German armaments'. When a special writer of the Liberal *Daily Chronicle* staff, Philip Gibbs (afterwards knighted for his services as a war correspondent), went to Germany and reported back his fear of German intentions, his editor, Robert Donald, dismissed them with the comment: 'Utter rubbish!'

With their similar characteristics, sentiments and aptitudes, England and Germany were fated to be rivals whose intrinsic parallelism would have disruptive effects on the whole human comity. Far beyond their own national bounds, they were seeking to outpace each other in manufactures, science, trade, diplomacy and prestige. Everywhere, they were jostling each other for place and power in a great secular struggle of history. 'I think Germany is in a very tight corner', Northcliffe wrote to his young nephew Vyvyan, Harold's eldest son, who was travelling in Germany: 'and I do not wonder at its anxieties—the Russian colossus in the East, a much weakened Austria, Italy a very doubtful ally, France like a hungry tiger with its claws very much sharpened of late, and one or two small English vessels in the North Sea . . .'

The efforts of posterity to discover less impersonal causes of the climax of 1914, ignoring the armaments race which began with the German annexation of Alsace-Lorraine and the intensive propaganda which glorified war in the German popular mind, seem futile and unreal. Some of the blame was fastened on Northcliffe, who was regarded by the Massinghams and Gardiners and Bellocs as a pyromaniac bent on seeing the world go up in flames. Spengler, the German philosopher-historian, was about to indict him in *The Decline of the West* as a 'master-nature' who made the people 'clamour for weapons' and forced their leaders 'into a conflict'. With what expectation of profit to himself he courted chaos those critics did not say. He had long ago learnt that while newspaper circulations multiply in war, so do production costs and working difficulties. But the success or failure of a newspaper was as nothing in Northcliffe's reckoning when balanced against the fate of the nation. His love of country was as deep and strong as the other transcendent devotion of his life, which is sufficient tribute to the intensity of his patriotic feeling. The methods of its expression might be deplored—serial stories by William Le Queux about invasion, and so on—but its sincerity could not be impugned. For Northcliffe it was a case of England, right or wrong, and particularly when the world thought England was wrong. As for the warmongering charges, those who made them would have been discountenanced to know that he was secretly planning to publish the *Daily Mail* in the capital of the expected enemy, in Berlin itself.

* * *

Kennedy Jones had a serious intestinal operation in 1912. It closed his Fleet Street career without dimming his desire to shine elsewhere, in business and politics. The *Times* history states that he was 'dropped' by Northcliffe in furtherance of the latter's ambition to gain full control of all departments of the paper, an assumption hardly complimentary to the character of the new editor whose appointment was about to be announced. Things had not been going so well as of old between Northcliffe and Jones, who had objected to Northcliffe giving what he thought to be too much time and energy to Printing House Square matters, to the disadvantage of his other interests and in particular the Newfoundland enterprise in which 'K. J.' was financially involved. There was also the fact that although 'K. J.' had been prominent in the original *Times* negotiations, and was still on good terms with the Walters, he had not been elected to the board. It appears that his deteriorated health, which impaired his usefulness as a director of Associated Newspapers Limited (Carmelite House), had some effect on his prospects in Northcliffe's dispositions. The *Times* historian suggested that Northcliffe did not think him socially fitted to be a director. Touching on his retirement, and the consequent sale of his shares to Northcliffe, the same authority thought it relevant to quote 'K. J.' as being on 'Alf' terms with Northcliffe, a statement as inaccurate as another in the same context in naming Pomeroy Burton as Northcliffe's brother-in-law; they were not related. According also to the historian, Northcliffe's motive in selling parcels of the shares that he had bought from Kennedy Jones to certain members of the *Times* staff was to 'buttress his power'. A statement from a letter written by him to John Walter should be put in (January 18, 1913): 'You will notice in the transfers of Jones's shares that I have sold them to people who I think will strengthen the active business department of the paper. It is more, very much more, than Nicholson can bear. They should form acute critics and suggesters.' 'K. J.' had made a fortune from his Harmsworth association and he did not discourage extravagant estimates of its size. Seeking an easier life, he bought a share in the furniture business of Waring & Gillow Ltd. He gave a business luncheon to a large gathering of old colleagues and friends, in the course of which he rose up to offer £5 for an advertising slogan. The prize was not won by the wittiest, scribbled on a menu card and sent up to him by E. V. Lucas, the essayist and bookman: 'See Maples and Die.'

There were important editorial changes at Printing House Square. Valentine Chirol, newly knighted, resigned as head of the foreign department and left the paper: 'one of the most able and industrious of the servants of *The Times* and one of the most familiar in international circles', to quote the History. Wickham Steed took his place, though doubting colleagues believed that he would find difficulty in settling down to head office requirements after his roving years. Buckle made way for Geoffrey Robinson, aged thirty-seven (he changed his surname to Dawson in 1917, for family reasons). Buckle's editorship had lasted twenty-eight years, exceeded only by Delane, who had broken down and retired at sixty after thirty-six years in 'the chair'. Barnes had died in harness at fifty-six. Buckle was 'feeling the strain' at fifty-eight. He had been hurt by hearing from John Walter, and not directly from Northcliffe, that the latter wished him to retire. Buckle to Northcliffe (July 11, 1912): 'I was certainly very much upset when I wrote to you, but I had no desire to use an offensive tone and I apologise for anything that was wrong in the letter.' Robinson, already known to Northcliffe as 'Robin', had been a director of The Times Publishing Company since the beginning of the year. The news of his appointment was well received, and Buckle, who was 'sore about his own treatment' (*vide* Robinson's diary) wrote him a generous, firm-phrased letter which ended with the advice: 'Try your best to keep *The Times* clear of special *Daily Mail* hobbies and policies. I feel you will not be able to do so wholly. I know you agree with me on the extreme importance of giving the lie to the taunt about "a twopenny halfpenny *Daily Mail*".' Northcliffe had told Buckle's assistant, J. B. Capper, in writing: 'The Paper is in *extremis*, and its continuance depends absolutely and entirely on the prosperity of the *Daily Mail*.' With a thought for *Times* sensibilities, he added: 'The latter part is perhaps not important for the staff to know, but they should at least understand that the most drastic economies are necessary in every quarter and that any pensions that are given by the new Proprietors are gifts from the Proprietors' pockets.' It was an opportunity for him to point out, too, that 'the new Proprietors have no responsibility whatever for the several incompetent persons who are retained as acts of kindness' (February 24, 1912). For Northcliffe's liking, too many of the *Times* men conducted themselves as if high-ranking members of the Civil Service, traditional in thought and habit, unchallengeable in tenure.

Worry was coming to him from The Amalgamated Press. A near-crisis was brought about by the action of one of its principal editors, Hamilton Edwards, who was again threatening to resign, with a demand for heavy compensation. Northcliffe's patience was unequal to this new strain. He wrote to Sutton: 'If any concession is made, I resign on the spot. I am very weary of The Amalgamated Press.' His brother Harold, with whom he was staying at Cap Martin, was embroiled in the arguments and he, too, wrote to Sutton (March 11, 1912): 'I want to get out of the whole thing. I am sick to death.' Even the uncomplaining Sutton was sorely tried. He wrote to Northcliffe (March 11, 1912):

You said the other day on the 'phone: 'You work in the trenches—I walk on the top.' Do you think this is the kind of thanks I should receive for the very serious and anxious work I have done for several years on your personal account? You have been saved much anxiety and worry, how much you really don't know, and it is not finished yet. Yet, in spite of this, plus my 23 years' association with the firm, my treatment in regard to position and finance compares most unfavourably with that of some other people in the office, who have not done a tithe of the work that I have done for the business and for you. I am sorry to write in this strain, but your remarks and the tone of your letter threatening to resign, makes it highly necessary for me to do so.

Northcliffe to Sutton:

[Postmarked Nice]
March 15, 1912.

Your letter grieved me, dearest Sut, more than you can fathom. It showed such an entire misconception of my feelings and wishes towards you, such a misconception, too, of my own life, as to make a person placed as I am despair of being understood by anyone. If you, who know me better than any, do not understand, how on earth can Buckle, for example? Why Buckle, you ask. Well, my last attempt at a holiday was spoiled by *Times* friction (of which you did not hear), just as by Amalgamated Press friction. Before that, it was Beeton and Newfoundland, and so on *indefinitely*. The business is a Frankenstein. *It gives me no peace whatever.*

As to Edwards, I regard him as a preposterous person who will bring upon himself a severe legal drubbing and be eventually bought out at a high price— and more work will fall on me, who already begins at 6–7 every morning. As to your profits, dearest Sut, I offered you shares and you would not take them. If you want any, say how many and have them. You know that I mean what I say and would rejoice in your having any you choose.

CHIEF

The next day Sutton received a telegram. *Harold told me this afternoon you would like vice-chairmanship and much increased pay rather than shares why did you not tell me yourself dear Sut you know that you can always have anything I can give and have it with much affection so take it with my best wish.—Chief.* Sutton was exhorted in a following letter: 'I wish that instead of telling others your ambitions and grievances you would speak straightly to me. You have had scores of opportunities and have not done so. Letters, you know well, do not appeal to me. I get so many. My views on letters are Napoleon's. You know well that there are in the world not more than six people to whom I am greatly attached, and that for many years you have been one of them, and will be till I pass. I had no idea that you sought further responsibility. I don't, and perhaps one judges others by one's own feelings' (March 18). Sutton thought it necessary to reply: 'I am not in the habit of asking you for things. I never have done. All the same, I felt very much that others, whom I did not think deserved as much, should be getting so much more. You apparently did not realize that I was dissatisfied. For your offer of the Vice-Chairmanship and increased pay, accompanied as it was by your expressions of goodwill and affection, I am thankful.' And Northcliffe: 'We have been together nearly a quarter of a century, dearest Sut, without friction: if ever you feel aggrieved in future *do* come and speak out. My position in my 47th year, having worked at the same trade since I was 15, is that the pressure on me *must* be reduced.' He had some advice to offer. 'Have no private friends in the business. See and be seen. Get a *very capable* gentleman secretary of tact, what I call a tall hat man. *Don't try to do it all yourself.*' He had no doubt that Sutton would in due time qualify to be chairman, and he went on to say:

The present troubles are incidental to any gigantically profitable concern and will occur sporadically. We may have to introduce profit-sharing, as Levers have done. Read Masterman's *Modern England*. Much truth therein. The old Capitalist regime has gone. We are doing it quietly in England, as usual. America will follow with dynamite and blood.

In that same year, The Amalgamated Press moved to its new headquarters at The Fleetway House, Farringdon Street, E.C. The Harmsworth periodicals had not been centrally accommodated since they had expanded beyond the confines of Carmelite House. Latterly, many of them had been published from Bouverie Street, but there were overflow buildings in several other streets, making administration costly and hampering efficiency. The Fleetway House, built on a site close to that of the old Fleet Prison, adjoined the Memorial Hall, where the success of Harmsworth Brothers Limited had been reported to the shareholders with comforting regularity over many years. It contained three acres of floor space and one hundred and ninety rooms. Considered then the last-word in publishing offices, someone remarked that it looked like the Savoy Hotel in front and Wormwood Scrubs behind. Jaded as he was, Northcliffe must have had some inner satisfaction as he sat for the first time at his desk in his fine big room overlooking Farringdon Street. On the opposite side of the street was the old building in which he and Pemberton, as young freelances, had called on George Newnes to discuss their first contributions to *Tit-Bits*.

Chapter Sixteen

The Long Impending Clash

On an impulse, Northcliffe decided to 'clear off correspondence' in Paris, taking Whibley as his companion. 'Charles and I are to report on the Paris restaurants,' he told Garvin, 'a task of much self-sacrifice and labour.' The green deed-box contained mainly letters awaiting answer but also numerous notes for memoranda of his own. To Marlowe (April 23, 1912): 'Many years ago I went carefully into the question of the remuneration and status of the captains of Atlantic liners. The poor payment of these men is a world scandal. I wired you this morning to take it up.' His thoughts, like those of most people, were centred in the disaster to the American-owned *Titanic* with its loss of over 1,500 lives. Northcliffe had known Thomas Henry Ismay, who had built up the White Star line. He had admired him for his deep interest in all that concerned the safety of his ships, 'his personal examination of every ship before it sailed from Liverpool every Wednesday, his wisdom in foreseeing that his ships might fall into the hands of a Yankee Trust, and, if they did so, his children were to be paid in gold, as they were'. He could not view dispassionately the loss of the *Titanic*, a supposedly unsinkable liner, when warnings had been given of icebergs in her vicinity, and he knew that the main function of wireless, properly used, would bring instant assistance to a ship in distress.

His feelings were deeply stirred, as he showed in a letter to Garvin, to whom he wrote on April 26, 1912, 'I am having a long bout of revision of departments, seeing to it that there are enough boats for the passengers, adding fresh officers to my ships, sometimes even a little glad that I have no second generation coming.' There was a letter from his brother St. John. Its final paragraph read: 'Good night, dearest Alfred. My heart is brimming over with emotion for your loving care for me during these six terrible years.' Pomeroy Burton had written: 'Pearson is practically

431

blind. He is to undergo a very serious operation, an operation that is regarded as largely experimental because it is quite new. I thought you would like to know exactly what his terrible plight is.' Northcliffe to Pomeroy Burton: 'For goodness sake, don't write me so often.' His impatience may not have been entirely dissociated from the fact that he was himself seeing the oculists again. They found 'three little growths, which caused my vision to be all wrong'. Wareham Smith, the advertising director, was scolded for 'the disgraceful puffing of Selfridge. No reference to Selfridge's, direct or indirect is to appear in the *Daily Mail* unless it comes under general news—a fire or some similar event.' Concerning *Times* affairs, Northcliffe told Reginald Nicholson: 'A little more liveliness, a little less divinity and education, with a steady circulation campaign, might keep the horrid wolf from the door.' He hated, he said, 'the ungrateful task of grumbling', but as his was the chief responsibility he would be lacking in his duty to the paper if he did not 'continue to urge the facts of a dark-looking situation'. Evelyn Wrench, travelling in Canada, received a cablegram: *Am surprised at lack of recognition of myself as inventor and founder of Overseas Club.—Chief.*

Evelyn Wrench to Northcliffe:

> The Over-Seas Club,
> Lethbridge, Alberta.
> 25th June, 1912.

My dear Chief,—Frankly, I do not understand your cable. At every public meeting, I have given all the credit for the success of the movement to three individuals, (1) to Cecil Rhodes, to whom we directly owe the inception of the Overseas Club idea, (2) to you for placing the *Overseas Daily Mail* at the disposal of the movement, (3) to Lord Grey, who did a great deal to interest Canadians. . . .

The chief difficulty we have had to face has been the prevalent idea that the Overseas Club was just a money-making scheme, run with a view to bringing kudos and increased circulation to the *Daily Mail*. I found on many sides a tendency to forget that it was through the *Overseas Daily Mail* that we came into being. If you still feel dissatisfied with my explanation, I would much rather that you would accept my resignation as editor of the *Overseas Daily Mail*. For some time I have felt that I must devote myself to the Empire.

Please do not think that I am ungrateful to you for all you have done for me during the past 8 years and I shall always hope that you will let me sign myself

> Your affectionate
> EVELYN

A young reporter on *Sporting Life*, named Trevor Wignall, was astounded (his word) to receive a message one morning that summer saying that Lord Northcliffe would like to see him. The message was conveyed by William Blackwood, editor of *Answers*, who explained that Northcliffe had read a short story by Wignall in *The Story-Teller*, one of Cassell's magazines edited by Newman Flower. Northcliffe fancied that Wignall could write a serial for *Answers*, in those days a handsome commission for any young writer. Blackwood asked him to draft a synopsis and a first chapter which they took along to Northcliffe at Carmelite House. The Rolls-Royce was at the door. They were ordered rather than invited to travel with Northcliffe to Broadstairs. A small, sickly-looking boy, wrapped in rugs, was on the front seat. Wignall learnt from Pine, the chauffeur, that the boy was a printer's son who was being taken down to Elmwood by Northcliffe to recuperate after an illness. Though it was a fine bright morning they rode in semi-darkness all the way, Northcliffe continually manipulating the specially fitted shutters to keep the sun from his eyes. He asked about Wignall's accent. 'Welsh', he was told. 'That's good,' he said. 'You're a change from the Scots who are always around me.' As they drew out of London, he commanded Blackwood, a Scot with a marked Dundee accent, to read the first instalment of the serial which Wignall had sat up all night to write. When the reading was over, there was a long silence in which Wignall mournfully contemplated returning to the dreary round of a *Sporting Life* reporter. It was not until they were near Broadstairs that Northcliffe spoke. He made two comments on the chapter that he had heard. 'There are no song birds in Australia. And your returning hero would not be permitted to take a railway porter at Victoria into the buffet for a drink.' At Elmwood he showed Wignall the bungalow with its bound copies of the first issue of all the Harmsworth publications, and then abruptly said: 'Now I will drive you to Margate, where you can get a fast train back to town.' On the way to Margate, he talked about young writers who did not read enough, stressing their ignorance of Dickens. At the railway bookstall he bought a paper-covered volume and thrust it into Wignall's hand. 'Read it, study it, digest it,' he said. 'Emulate its myriad human touches and you will be fit for *Answers*', and waved him to the platform. In the train Wignall proceeded to study the book. It was a sixpenny copy of *East Lynne*.

To Seymour Price, who, announcing the birth of his first child, had written: 'I am anxious that he should grow up with a full knowledge of how and whence his father's great chance in life came', Northcliffe replied: 'I do not want any more Godchildren, because the number must be approaching a hundred, I am afraid. You are aware that I have an army of relations. However, I would be delighted to stand sponsor', and at Christmas there was '£5 for my dear little Godson'. To Mrs Eva Barnes, widow of a *Daily Mirror* editorial man: 'Mr Kenealy will have expressed to you my most sincere sympathy and regret for the loss of your dear husband.

I hear that you have a little boy of six. I should like to give him a presentation to Christ's Hospital (Bluecoat School), and to look after him financially while he is there, so that he may get a good start.' To Frank Dilnot, editor of the newly-founded *Daily Herald*: 'I think it very essential to the welfare of this Empire that Labour should have a proper newspaper. We have the only representative Parliament in the world. I should like a really representative Press.' Lord Haldane to Northcliffe: 'The Kaiser has said in private quite recently things just as bad as what he said to Dr Hale [an American publicist friend of Woodrow Wilson, to whom the Kaiser had given an interview]. I am well-informed as to various conversations. On the other hand, he has, equally unpremeditatedly, said quite good things. I do not attach much importance to either the one or the other. He is an impulsive and rather excitable man—and, as is the way with Sovereigns, does not restrain himself. If all that Edward VII said in private were published there would have been rows galore. The great thing is polite manners in public. You rendered a real service to the nation when you succeeded in suppressing the American interview', in the course of which the German Emperor admitted that Germany was secretly fomenting sedition in India, and bitterly denounced England for 'betraying the white race' by the Japanese alliance. A report of the interview, secretly transmitted to Northcliffe, contained the following statements: 'Dr Hale said that he gathered from the German Emperor that his ambition was to take Egypt from the British and later the Holy Land from Turkey, thereby emulating the deeds of the Crusaders. He appeared to be very bitter against his uncle, King Edward, and accused him of trying to set the other Powers against Germany. He was very friendly towards the United States because the march of progress and the degeneration of Great Britain showed that the two dominant world forces of the future would be Germany and the United States.' Northcliffe's medium of communication was a senior member of the *New York Times* staff. Hale, an American clergyman in Anglican orders who had turned journalist, was also on that newspaper. Northcliffe's correspondent reported: 'Dr Hale told his editorial colleagues that his interview with the Emperor was so serious and direct that it was dangerous to repeat it. During the interview, the Emperor walked the floor and spoke forcefully and earnestly, delivering each word so that Dr Hale could understand him thoroughly. He seemed to be full of electricity and his eyes snapped when he spoke of England, his bitterness was so intense. I have not said a word about writing you this, because I should have been forbidden to do it. Not a line will be printed in the *Times* [*New York Times*], but you can safely rely that every word I have written to you was actually spoken by Wilhelm.'

Concerning William Bayard Hale (1869–1924), the *American Dictionary of Biography* recorded that his interview with the Kaiser was printed in the

Century magazine, but suppressed. 'The whole edition was bought up, taken on a warship into the mid-Atlantic, and burned by German naval officers. During the war, a proof of this "highly indiscreet" statement, said to have been confided to the Harvard University Library, disappeared.' Hale afterwards became President Wilson's biographer and his confidential agent in Mexico. During the First World War he was retained as German propaganda adviser in Washington in the belief that 'he held the key to the back door to the White House'. He was subsequently 'pilloried by pitiless publicity' and retired from public life.

Haldane wrote to tell Northcliffe that 'in consultation with Grey and Harcourt', he was preparing a proposal for 'a new development in international relations through—partly—the influence of the lawyer-statesmen of the U.S. and Canada'. Haldane had reported to the Cabinet that Germany was preparing for war. Northcliffe told Pomeroy Burton: 'Any person who follows current politics closely must be a plus six fool among fools if he does not realize every day that we are moving to and fro round the crater of a volcano.'

Northcliffe to his brother Hildebrand:

The Times,
Printing House Square, E.C.4.
16th July, 1912.

My dear Hildebrand,—When I came back last night, I found your sweet birthday present, with which I am decorating my room at *The Times* today.

I never see you, and am told that you live in bed. It must be trying, this hot weather!

You ought to come and see something of our business now and again. It is becoming a very wonderful thing. I could give you a very interesting day. The growth of the *Daily Mail* has been amazing. I am told that £5 each is now being refused for the shares. The circulation at the present time—the dull season—is over nine hundred thousand a day, and the advertisement revenue has been as much as £3,000 in one day.

The Gravesend paper mills are very interesting.

With much love to all of you,
Your affectionate
ALFRED

Leaving for a golfing holiday with Max Pemberton, he gave Marlowe the instruction: 'Keep Lloyd George off the contents bill during my absence.' He disliked the implication of a mention of him in *The Spectator* that he was becoming portly in appearance. Strachey, the editor, answered his objection: 'It was perhaps a little unfortunate. The suggestion of rotundity or avoirdupois merely meant the substantial power and personality of yourself as newspaper proprietor.' Holding its first banquet, the newly-founded National Union of Journalists received from him a letter which was greeted with recurring applause when it was read out to the members by Horace Sanders, the Central London branch secretary.

In the last twenty years our craft has risen from a humble, haphazard, and badly paid occupation to a regular profession, which must, in the future, offer increasing opportunities to men and women of ability. It has therefore become all the more necessary that newspaper workers should adopt the methods of other professions, and form a society for mutual protection and encouragement.

The introduction of all manner of time saving machinery within the last few years has made the work less arduous, but more nerve exhausting, and it is incumbent that journalists should unite for the obtaining of longer annual holidays and better pay.

It is my proudest boast that the changes and competition which I have introduced into English journalism have had the effect of increasing the remuneration of almost every class of newspaper writer, as well as greatly adding to the number of those engaged in journalism.

It is not, in my opinion, wise or politic for newspaper proprietors and journalists to belong to the same institution, and I have been much pleased to notice that there is nothing of the cap-in-hand and beanfeast business about your society.

There are times, of course, when newspaper proprietors and those who work with them should co-operate to uphold the dignity of the Fourth Estate, as in the recent occasion when the staff of the *Sydney Daily Telegraph* were expelled from the New South Wales Legislative Assembly. It seems to me that a self-respecting Society like yours has the opportunity of doing much for its members. Will you permit me to add that I am the more gratified at receiving your invitation because I know your properly independent attitude towards those who own newspapers?

Acknowledged as 'a tribute to the Union from the most famous living personality in British journalism', Northcliffe's letter acquired almost the status of a charter in the history of what has become familiarly known as the N.U.J. 'It holds a permanent place in our annals.' He also gave the Union the use of a column on the leader page of the *Daily Mail* for a statement of its constitution, policy and prospects. 'It's truly splendid,' wrote the secretary of the London branch. 'Fleet Street rings with it, and all the world can see that the veil of the Union's future has been moved and the glimpse given is of a shining star! It makes the heart glad, for until this year the way has been a grey one.' Approached by the president of the Institute of Journalists, James Sykes, who invited him to address the annual conference, he answered: 'I am not of a particularly resentful nature, but I really owe nothing to the Institute of Journalists, except a great deal of abuse. If you care to refer to the early records of the Institute, you will find that the proprietors of the penny newspapers used the

Institute as a means of attacking my colleagues and me. For that reason, I have never had anything to do with the Institute and do not propose to have, other than to contribute to the Orphan Fund. Sometimes plain speaking does no harm.'

He disclaimed interest also in the Olympic Games. 'I never thought it possible to revive the Greek ideal.' He demanded an explanation from Roger Casement, who, having undertaken to write an article for the *Daily Mail*, sent it elsewhere. He reminded Marlowe: 'I am not fond of employing friends or their children. Harold Pemberton, however, is an exceptional boy and is bound to our family by two generations of loyalty. I think he might be a welcome addition to our staff.' He asked Pomeroy Burton to investigate the *Daily Mail* advertising position. 'Our advertisement men are not of the social calibre to understand the situation. They forget that a lot of cheap vulgar advertisements all over the paper can just as effectively lower tone as cheap vulgar articles. I might have an article by George V, but it could be quite ruined by an advertisement, put more prominently, of two-and-elevenpenny hats.'

He inquired of Marlowe: 'Are we getting middle-aged, or what has happened, that we cannot make changes as we used? If I had been afraid of thrusting responsibility on young people, where would you and Caird have been? Please give my own methods a trial; after all, they have made these various businesses.' Edward Grigg,* of the *Times* staff, was told: 'I have had more litigation in connexion with *The Times* during my few years of proprietorship than I have had for the same period with all my other business affairs put together.' A Printing Supplement, celebrating what was then thought to be the 40,000th issue of *The Times*,† had been published on September 10, 1912. It was a success. John Walter wrote to Northcliffe that 'the Publishing Office had never known such a demand', and congratulated him on 'a great idea'. Walter was particularly gratified by the favourable comments of other newspapers. 'Their whole tone affords conclusive proof of the success which has attended your labours of the last 4 years to save this great institution from death and to endow it with new life' (September 12). Looking over his broad acres of the Fourth Estate, Northcliffe cracked his whip at Kenealy, editor of the *Daily Mirror*, warning him: 'It has been a hard year. I am going to make 1913 worse.'

On November 26, 1912, the *Times* leading article raised the paramount question: Is there no means of evading war? Northcliffe caused the substance of the article to be reprinted in his other newspapers:

The question is being asked with some bewilderment by millions of men in

---

* Later Lord Altrincham.

† Later, it was found that the serial numbering of *The Times* had been twenty-three in advance of the true number.

this country, who want to know what difficulties there are in the present situation which should threaten Europe with a general war. . . .

There are no irresistible waves of popular feeling, no gusts of angry passion such as sweep whole peoples into war before they are well aware of what they are doing.

There is no great nation in Europe which today has the least desire that millions of men should be torn from their homes and flung headlong to destruction at the bidding of vain ambitions.

In England men will learn with amazement and incredulity that war is possible over the question of a Serbian port, or even over the larger issues which are said to lie behind it.

Yet that is whither the nations are blindly drifting. Who, then, makes war?

The answer is to be found in the Chancelleries of Europe, among the men who too long played with human lives as pawns in a game of chess, who have become so enmeshed in formulas and the jargon of diplomacy that they have ceased to be conscious of the poignant realities with which they trifle.

Sir Arthur Conan Doyle, who wrote to say that he had sent 'a memorandum to the Imperial Defence Committee, which may prove another name for the waste paper basket', and that he 'could run down the Strand like old Solomon Eagle before the plague, crying out "Another hour has passed, yet another, and nothing has been done",' received with Northcliffe's appreciation of *The Lost World* the benign assurance: 'I have asked my Berlin correspondent to watch matters continually' (December 18, 1912). The apocalyptic voice would have had little chance of being heard above the nation's hilarious reiteration of the newest song-hit, *Yip-i-addy-i-ay*!

*   *   *

'I am anxious to see whether the Pathescope can be used for the education of children', Northcliffe wrote early in 1913 to the manager of the company making the film projector of that name. He ordered one to be sent to the Town Clerk of Pwllheli, Caernarvonshire, for experiment in a school there, subject to the supply 'of suitable educational films', a prescient glimpse of the visual-aids future in the schools. In the more imposing context of luxury motoring, he was watching the progress of Rolls-Royce almost with a proprietary air, though he had no financial interest in it. 'Is it not time you fitted a self-starter?' he wrote to ask his friend, Claude Johnson, the manging director. Johnson replied: 'We dare not fit anything which will ever go wrong, and we have not yet come across a self-starter which is good enough for Rolls-Royce. Royce is devoting himself entirely to the question of self-starters, but this is one surrounded with difficulty.' Northcliffe also sent Johnson a 'memo for R.R. 1913. Give electric light. Insist on safety doors. Have some new talking points.' He further suggested an advertising slogan which is still in use by the company: 'The Best Car In The World.' For Claude Johnson the 'talking point' of the moment was the Rolls-Royce share buying of Max Aitken (later Beaverbrook). Northcliffe to Claude Johnson (January 16, 1913): 'In view of what you tell me, you must not mind me saying that you have been lacking in foresight and forethought in not obtaining control of the Company, a perfectly easy thing to do. Control is essential to the peace of mind not only of the head of a business but of the humblest employee.' When doubts were expressed about the effect of Aitken's association with Rolls-Royce, Northcliffe wrote to the solicitor, William Graham: 'He is one of the straightest men in the country.' Having acquired, with Lord Selborne, the controlling shares, Aitken tried to persuade the directors to adopt mass production methods. Northcliffe intervened with a letter to Aitken dated January 15, 1913:

The day before yesterday, Claude Johnson, of the Rolls-Royce Company, told me that you and Selborne had bought many shares in the Company and seemed anxious to convert it into a larger enterprise. My interest in the automobile is that of a pioneer, and in Rolls-Royce a platonic admiration for somebody else's beautiful garden. The Rolls-Royce business is a delicate orchid which owes its success entirely to Johnson, who previously, as you know, organized the Royal Automobile Club, bringing it from bankruptcy to, I think I am right in saying, seven or eight thousand members. My head chauffeur, who is an engineer with English, French and American experience, tells me that at Derby they have assembled the finest mechanics in the world.

Johnson asked me to write to you on the matter, but I told him that I did not interfere in other people's business or disputes. Having said this I have done with it.

Aitken soon afterwards disposed of his interest in Rolls-Royce, leaving the company free to pursue its own highly individual policies, with far-reaching consequences for the reputation of British automobile and aircraft engineering. But Northcliffe was not less concerned for the health of the genius of the firm than he was for its future. He greatly admired Royce and had promoted his interests from the beginning. 'I am very glad indeed to hear that he is so much better,' he wrote to Johnson. 'Keep him away from the doctors, and expecially the surgeons, at all hazards.' Health was the perennial topic. Northcliffe had just undertaken to give Walter Heape, F.R.S., £250 a year for five years in aid of his cancer research.

A private message from New York reminded him that it was he who had proposed Walter Hines Page as the new United States ambassador in London. The appointment was made that spring. It had considerable effect on the future of Anglo-American retlaions. From his brother

Harold's beautiful villa, La Dragonnière at Cap Martin, he was sending forth a stream of letters about bad paper from Newfoundland; humane slaughtering—he wanted John Galsworthy to lead a crusade; the salary and future of the *Daily Mirror* cartoonist, W. K. Haselden—'I own to an affectionate regard for you, dear Chief'—the reduction in the price of *The Times* to 2*d*.; the disloyalty of Manchester Conservatives to the *Manchester Courier* for which he gave his guarantee of £52,500; ordering the *Daily Mirror* news staff to 'forget cricket and suffragettes: we have had enough of both'; arranging to send the British golf champions, Ray and Vardon, to play in the American Gold Cup Championship at his own expense and telling his editors that he wanted no personal publicity from it: 'persons with ample means have a duty to do such things'; offering £10,000 for the first transatlantic aeroplane flight; making life temporarily easier for Max Pemberton, who felt 'quite at a loss in the face of your magnificent kindness'; and asking Sutton to ensure 'a great quarter-of-a-century number of *Answers*, with 25 years' reminiscence articles by big people'. His brother Cecil, meanwhile, was taking a more restful view of life. He wrote from La Dragonnière:

The villa stands high among woods of pine and olive and looks out across a lovely blue bay to Monte Carlo. The lawns are emerald green and the borders gay with flowers. There are narcissi and jonquils in the new grass in the grey shade of the olive trees and the standard orange trees are carrying large golden fruits. The sweet peas are four or five feet high and in full bloom. Stocks, pansies, nemesias, wallflowers, geraniums, tall double nasturtiums and primulas of many shades make a lovely show. The air is full of the hum of bees and the sweet chatter of birds. Alfred remarkably well and gay.

From the *Times* office, Geoffrey Robinson wrote to him on March 2: 'I quite agree that the new arming of Europe is definitely serious and very difficult to handle without inflaming popular excitement and passion.' Robinson wished Northcliffe to be assured that he 'would not let the subject go', adding the opinion: 'It seems to me that the supreme danger of the moment is that the revival in France, which everyone admires, may degenerate into an aggressive jingoism which will alienate this country.' Robinson saw it as 'an obstacle to Lord Roberts' campaign, which is otherwise going admirably'.

Returning to London, Northcliffe found himself playing a walking on part in a drama of not very high finance, low politics, commercial jealousies, anti-Semitism and Roman Catholicism, which has come down in history under the title of 'The Marconi Case'. The British Government had awarded a contract to the Marconi Company for the erection of a chain of radio stations as a development in Empire communications. Rumours were put about that members of the Government had speculated in Marconi shares. A French newspaper gave names: Sir Rufus Isaacs, Attorney-General, Mr Herbert Samuel, Postmaster-General. A libel action resulted in an apology to both. It disclosed that Isaacs had bought four thousand shares in the American Marconi Company, which did not stand to benefit from the contract. He had sold the shares at a loss to himself of £1,300, while continuing to fear that an ignorant public might misconstrue his action. At that point, Harold Harmsworth wrote to his brother Northcliffe from the villa (March 10, 1913):

I know that you have always thought it judicious and prudent to help Rufus Isaacs, if the occasion arose. The occasion is now here. Isaacs has never asked us to do anything for him. *In your interests* I consider you should help him now. *The Times* and the *Daily Mail* can kill at its birth any effort that may be made by misrepresentation and calumny to raise an agitation which may compel him to resign office. I know the thing will seem ridiculously trumpery to you, and it is, except for the fact that Isaacs is destined for high judicial office. All that is wanted is a soft pedal in *The Times* and *Daily Mail*.

General interest jumped several points higher when it was known that Lloyd George, Chancellor of the Exchequer, had also bought some of the American Marconi shares. A libel suit against Cecil Chesterton, brother of 'G. K.', with Hilaire Belloc and other contributors to Chesterton's paper, the *New Witness*, in the public seats, stirred the flames of feeling. Corruption was looked for; only indiscretion was found. A select committee produced a divided result, its minority report finding 'grave impropriety', leaving the situation of the implicated officers and ministers of the Crown to be saved by a debate in the House of Commons. In an undated letter to Winston Churchill, Northcliffe wrote:

Your Marconi friends stage manage their affairs most damnably. The system of making mysteries of pieces of evidence in the inquiry, and doling them out like a serial story, has a bad effect on the public, though, as a matter of fact, the whole Marconi business looms much larger in Downing Street than among the mass of the people. The total number of letters received by my newspapers has been exactly three. The method of dragging the thing out really does make some people think that there is something behind it all, though I personally, as I had your word for it that there is not, know there is not.

Rufus Isaacs to Northcliffe (March 21, 1913):

Believe me, I am very grateful to you for your generous treatment of the American Marconi incident. I know how such a matter might be used if there was a desire and intention to injure me and that although the transaction is as innocent as any that has ever been effected, it might be twisted into an appearance to those who had not mastered the facts of something very unpleasant.

441

No one who is aware of the part you have played can ever fail to remember the kindness of your heart and the great generosity of your disposition, and in the truest and deepest sense of the words I thank you.

Lloyd George to Northcliffe (March 21):

I feel I must write to thank you for the chivalrous manner in which you have treated the Attorney-General and myself over the Marconi case. Had we done anything of which men of honour ought to feel ashamed we could not have approached you on the subject. But although the transaction was in itself a straightforward one, we were only too conscious that it was capable of exciting unpleasant comment. I therefore appreciate deeply the generosity and largeness of view which have distinguished your treatment of the matter.

Northcliffe to Isaacs (March 24):

Letters of thanks to newspapers are very rare and it was pleasant to get yours. No one who knows your record in the City or at the Bar and your care of your innumerable kinsmen could feel that you had shown anything more than a lack of foresight in this business.

Northcliffe to Lloyd George (March 24):

I adopted my line about this Marconi business because five minutes' lucid explanation showed me that it was the fairest one. Moreover, I am neither a rabid party man nor an anti-Semite. I was particularly glad to do so, inasmuch as I feel that you will now know that I am not personally hostile to you, as was twice suggested last year, by mutual friends. You gave me some shrewd blows, and I replied to them. So far as I was concerned, that was the end of it. A week-end glance at the French and German newspapers convinces me that this country has before it more urgent business than personal or party issues.

The *Daily Mirror* circulation director was with Northcliffe at St. James's Place one afternoon that summer when Lord Roberts's card was sent in. As the circulation director left to make way for the distinguished visitor, Northcliffe said: 'He's called to talk about the coming war.' Winston Churchill had been warned by General Botha, the South African statesman, who had just returned from Germany: 'Mind you are ready. Do not trust those people. They mean you mischief.'

One of Northcliffe's objectives in 1913 was to 'make definite connections with leading papers in all the great foreign centres, with German war possibilities especially in view'. A 'German War Emergency Fund' of £20,000 was to be 'placed in charge of one of the leading banks, subject to seven days' call', for special news gathering purposes. His chief executives were ordered to train understudies. The writing staff of the *Daily Mail* was to be reinforced. 'There must be more explanatory articles on world events by experts.' Northcliffe was trying to find a way of making the world believe that the pen was mightier than the sword. He was personally in touch with the new *Times* man in Berlin, J. E. Mackenzie, who had succeeded Saunders. He was constantly receiving information from Wile, the *Daily Mail* man there; for example, on July 5, 1913, in an envelope marked 'For Lord Northcliffe only', word that 'the German naval authorities have been warned to keep an eye on Mr Erskine Childers, the English writer, whose book, *The Riddle of the Sands*, came into such prominence a few years ago'. Wile wrote in *The Saturday Evening Post* (October 7, 1922):

. . . in 1913 I was summoned to London for conference with the Chief. During the preceding seven years of my service as Berlin correspondent of the *Daily Mail* and its associated newspapers, they had specialized in reporting Germany's conspicuous preparedness afield, afloat and aloft. Such developments, indeed, were the most important news Berlin produced from day to day, along with Germany's vast strides as a competitor of Great Britain in the markets of the world. I knew Northcliffe would be deeply interested in the newest manifestations of Germany's purpose to overawe or overpower Europe, but the real object of my summons was far different.

'Wile,' said Northcliffe soon after my arrival in London, 'I am going to start a Berlin edition of the *Daily Mail*.' If he had tendered me the editorship of *The Times* I could hardly have been more stunned.

Wile wrote that Northcliffe 'went on, in his impetuous way, to say how he now saw the long impending Anglo-German clash, with its incalculable world ramifications, hastening on. He was persuaded that it could be avoided and purposed using printer's ink to that end.' He believed that 'straight English talk' to the German people, day after day, might alter the distorted conception of Britain and British policy which they were getting from a Wilhelmstrasse-controlled press. 'A Berlin *Daily Mail*', argued Northcliffe, 'will open German eyes, show them the madness of their theory that John Bull is trying to encircle them, teach them that there is room enough in the world for both the Hamburg-American Line and the Cunard . . .'

Northcliffe proposed to make Wile editor and general manager of the venture. 'It may cost us a couple of hundred thousand pounds to get it established. It will be worth many times that much if we can knock the war mania out of German heads.' Wile also stated that, on his return to Berlin, 'confidential soundings' indicated that the idea would not be unwelcome there. He prepared a 'dummy' copy of what in his judgment a Berlin edition of the *Daily Mail* should be like. It tallied with Northcliffe's own ideas and was circulated to the directors in London. North-cliffe called a special meeting for its discussion. No decision was taken. Much of the argument centred in the *Continental Daily Mail*, which had cost a lot of money to establish and had only lately begun to show a profit. 'Never mind,' Northcliffe said to Wile. 'These fellows haven't any imagination. They are thinking of dividends. I'm thinking about a war. We'll have our Berlin *Daily Mail* one of these days.' Seven months later the Prussian police raided and sacked the *Daily Mail* office in Berlin. Wile presumed: 'They must have run across half a dozen copies of the original dummy edition which hitherto had never been disclosed to any German eyes except those of the printers.'

*   *   *

Answers jubilee year was duly celebrated by a Special Double Number. Letters of congratulation and appreciation flowed into The Fleetway House from readers in all parts of the world. Many of them were addressed to the founder.

Leicester Harmsworth to Northcliffe:

> Thornwood Lodge,
> Campden Hill, W.
> Tuesday.

My dear Alfred,—As a little souvenir of *Answers*' jubilee I am sending you the accompanying goblet. It is Charles the First silver dated 1637.

The last 25 years have been an extraordinary record of success for you; and I am more than glad that things at the present time are more successful than ever. I hope it will continue so.

In any case, I should not like this occasion to pass without expressing to you my appreciation of all that I and my little lot owe to you. It is not absent from my thoughts at any time.

My hope is that you may for many years continue to enjoy the success and prestige you have earned and so entirely deserved.

> Your affectionate
> LEICESTER

In that year of jubilee, Klein, his old music publisher friend, died, and so did his *Answers* backer, Alexander Beaumont, who had written what was in effect a letter of farewell. 'You are not likely to hear from me again, for I have become an old man and very infirm.' Klein's son wrote to Northcliffe: 'I should appreciate it if you would allow me to come and see you, to tell you myself to what extent your unbounded generosity softened the latter years of my father's life.' Northcliffe arranged that the payments he had been making regularly to Klein should be continued

Daily Mail

BERLIN EDITION

Giving all the News Many Hours in Advance of any 5 **other English Journal Circulating in Central Europe.**

LONDON. MANCHESTER. PARIS. NICE. BERLIN.

FIRST YEAR. THURSDAY MORNING, NOVEMBER 20, 1913. No. 1.

Daily Mail
TO-DAY'S WEATHER.

'oggy at first, then fair to dull with rain afternoon or evening; temperature rising, h freshening south-easterly winds.

CHANNEL PASSAGES.

Inglish Channel and North Sea, smooth and ty to moderate; Irish Channel, moderate or her rough.

SPECIAL FORECAST.

'or the twenty-four hours ending midnight, day, November 21.

'OR ENGLAND AND WALES.—Light variable h winds from between the south-east and south; gy to fair temporarily; rainy and mild afternoon evening.

'OR IRELAND.—Fresh or strong from between east and south; dull, rain at times; milder.

M. 5000

To popularize the Berlin Edition of the **Daily Mail** among the thousands of German and English travellers journeying between the two Countries, the proprietors, hereby agree to pay an insurance of **FIVE THOUSAND MARKS** to the legal heir or heirs of any person whose life is lost during such a trip, provided the person is proved to have carried at the time of death a late copy of this journal.

AMUSEMENT GUIDE.

THEATRES.

önigl. Schauspielhaus. Die Jungfrau von Orleans. 7½.
eutsches Theater. Emilia Galotti. 7½.
essing-Theater. Pygmalion. 8.
ammerspiele. Der verlorene Sohn. 8.
eutsches Künstlertheater. Hanneles Himmelfahrt. — Zerbr. Krug. 8.
erliner Theater. Wie einst im Mai. 8.
heater i. d. Königgrätzer Straße. Die Kronbraut. 8.
leines Theater. Gesinnung. 8.
omödienhaus. Hinter Mauern. 8.
rianon-Theater. Seine Geliebte. 8.
chiller-Theater O. Zwei Wappen. 8.
chiller-Theater Charlottenburg. Die Jungfrau von Orleans. 8.
ustspielhaus. Im grünen Rock. 8.
Deutsches Schauspielhaus. Die heitere Residenz. 8.
letropol-Theater. Die Reise um die Erde in 40 Tagen. 7.55.
'halia-Theater. Die Tangoprinzessin. 8.
Casino-Theater. Ferdinand der Tugendhafte. 8.
Rose-Theater. Im weißen Rößl. 8¼.
Gebr. Herrnfeld-Theater. Was sagen Sie zu Leibusch? 8.

OPERA, OPERETTA AND CONCERTS.

Königl. Opernhaus. Mignon. 7½.
Deutsches Opernhaus. Der Troubadour. 8.
Theater des Westens. Polenblut. 8.
Montis Operetten-Theater. Die ideale Gattin. 8.
Theater am Nollendorfplatz. Der lachende Dreibund. 8.
Residenz-Theater. Hoheit — der Franz. 8.
Philharmonie. 3. Philharmonisches Konzert. 7½.
Singakademie. Georg von Lalewicz, Klavierabend. 8.
Bechsteinsaal. A. Wagner-P. Woiku, Mod. Sonatenabend. 8.
Klindworth-Scharwenka-Saal. Liederabend Helene Glinz. 8.

MISCELLANEOUS.

Vaudeville: Wintergarten 8. Die 4 Cines-Variété-Lichtspiele. Zirkus Busch, Galavorstellung. 7½. Zirkus Schumann, Tango vor Gericht. 7½. Passage-Theater (Kino-Variété). 5.
Cabarets: Chat noir. 11. Metropol-Palast-Bier-Cab. 8. Linden-Cab. 11. Passage-Bier-Cab. 8½. à la Brady. 8. Bunte Bühne. 8¼.
Urania (Theatersaal). 15 Jahre bei den Schwarzfußindianern. 8.
Beethovensaal. Wilh. Ostwald: Monismus als Religion. 8.
Lichtspiele Mozartsaal. Der neue Spielplan. 6.
Die 7 Union-Theater (U. T.). Lichtkunstspiele. 5.
Admiralspalast. Die lustige Puppe. 8½.
Eispalast. Kunstlaufprogramm. Geöffnet von 10 Uhr vorm. ab.

MESSAGE FROM PRESIDENT WILSON

FRIENDSHIP FOR GREAT BRITAIN.

Mr. James Bryce, the former British Ambassador in Washington, was the guest of "The Pilgrims" at a dinner at the Savoy Hotel, London, last night, when Dr.

Page, the United States Ambassador in London, read the following message from President Wilson: —

Few men have done more than Mr. Bryce in strengthening the ties of friendship and of brotherhood which unite England and the United States and which have been the cause of a common inspiration and a high example to the whole world.

General Huerta to-night, it is stated from New York, decided to defy President Wilson, who has demanded his immediate resignation of the Provisional Presidency of Mexico.

President Wilson has sent a private emissary, Dr. Hale, to General Carranza, the Mexican rebel leader and General Huerta's rival.

General Huerta has decreed that all Mexican banks are entitled to make payments to any amount in notes instead of coin.

GENERAL HUERTA'S DECREE.

NO REDEMPTION OF BANK-NOTES IN SPECIE.

From Our Own Correspondent.

Mexico City, Wednesday Night.

General Huerta to-night isued a decree practically suspending specie payments.

The decree declares the half-peso (a silver coin worth about a shilling) and bank-notes to be legal tender for unlimited amounts, and the banks are authorised to refuse to redeem their notes in specie. The decree remains in force for one year.

General Huerta's decree has caused the gravest uneasiness. The half-peso, op fifty-cent piece, is purely a token coin, the alloy used in making it being far inferior to that of the peso. In releasing the banks from the obligation of redeeming their notes in cash on demand, the measure partakes of a retroactive character forbidden by the Mexican Constitution. It is feared that the prices of the necessaries of life will rise rapidly, provoking popular discontent.

The two issue banks in this city are the National Bank of Mexico and the London and Mexico Bank. Both are now controlled by French capital. The latter bank was formerly London Bank of Mexico and South America, which still retains a minority interest. In addition, there is an issue bank in nearly all the States of the Mexican Federation.

According to the decree the notes of the National and London and Mexico Banks will be legal tender all over the Republic and the notes of the State banks in each respective State. Some of the State banks are not so prosperous as formerly owing to the prolonged revolutionary disturbances.

The Prefect has two waiting-rooms for visitors. One is for men. It is dark and rather dingy. The bareness of the walls is relieved by a railway map of France and on the table is a directory.

KING FERDINAND'S FEARS.

"TO LET" PLACARDS ON HIS PALACE.

FROM OUR OWN CORRESPONDENT.

Sofia (Bulgaria), Wednesday.

In the conversations he has had at Vienna with the Emperor Francis Joseph and Count Berchtold, the Austro-Hungarian Foreign Minister, King Ferdinand of Bulgaria is reported to have again raised the question of the revision of the peace of Bucharest, urging that otherwise his position in Bulgaria is in danger.

It is impossible to verify these reports, but in responsible political circles it is not admitted that the fears, which the King is said to have expressed are based on any solid foundation.

"To Let"

placards are, however, reported to have been pasted up at the doors of the Royal Palace in Sofia, and this may be regarded as a fresh sign of resentment felt by the people.

GERMAN WAR CHEST.

JULIUS TOWER STORE OF GOLD AND SILVER.

Details are published of the prompt measures taken by the Imperial Bank to carry out the provisions of the new Defence Law in respect of the "strengthening of the Empire's financial preparedness for war."

The main feature of the scheme, as will be recalled, is the increase of the existing German war chest from Lst. 6,000,000 in gold to Lst. 12,000,000 in gold and Lst. 6,000,000 in silver. The additional gold will be stored in the vaults of the Imperial Bank, but the silver will be added to the war chest at the Julius Tower at Spandau, the "German Woolwich." Although the taxation provisions of the Defence Law do not come into effect until January 1, the Imperial Bank has already accumulated Lst. 2,500,000 of the additional gold required and placed an equivalent amount of paper currency in circulation.

The German exports for the last nine months increased by Lst. 50,000,000, while the imports increased by only Lst. 750,000. The gold reserve of the Imperial Bank, which in May 1912 was only Lst. 45,000,000, amounted to Lst. 60,000,000 last May. The Government aims at building up a reserve of Lstrl. 75,000,000.

MARRIED BY THE BRIDE'S MOTHER.

"THE NEWEST STYLE."

FROM OUR OWN CORRESPONDENT.

NEW YORK, Wednesday.

The newest style in "ethical weddings" was witnessed at Chicago to-day when Miss Gertrude Wakefield Hassler and Mr. Frederick A. Carpenter, a rich manufacturer, instead of exchanging religious vows at the altar signed and exchanged contracts.

The bride first signed and handed to the bridegroom the following:

I, Gertrude Wakefield Hassler, do by the signing of this contract give myself to Frederick A. Carpenter, to be his lawful wife, to have, to hold, and to love. I promise to be faithful so long as he proves true, and I will strive to fill with a vast measure of contentment each day our lives are thus joined.

In exchange for this the bride received the following:—

I, Frederick A. Carpenter, by this contract take as lawful wife Gertrude W. Hassler, and solemnly promise to agree to be faithful in words, thoughts, and deeds. to protect, love, and devote my life to her, to bring her the happiness and contentment she so well deserves.

After the contracts had been read, Miss Hassler's mother placed her daughter's hands in Mr. Carpenter's and said, "May all the good and truth in the universe combine to keep your hearts bright."

THE QUEEN AND MINERS.

The Queen during her visit to Lambton Castle Durham, at the and of this month, will visit the homes for aged miners in the county.

Lord Durham, the host of their Majesties, has made arrangements for the visit, and Mr. John Wilson, the Labour M.P. for Mid-Durham, will meet the Queen at the homes at Ushaw Moor, near Durham.

M. Hennion, the new Prefect of Police in Paris, has introduced reforms at the Prefecture which foreshadow those that would certainly be extended to every Government office should the Suffragettes ever acquire the political influence they seek.

KRUPP TRIAL.

BRANDT AND ECCIUS FOUND GUILTY.

LENIENT SENTENCES.

The Krupp trial was concluded yesterday afternoon.

Herr Brandt has been sentenced to Four months' imprisonment, the sentence being regarded as having been served by the accused through his detention in custody during the judicial examination. Herr Eccius has been fined 1,200 marks (Lst. 60).

Herr Brandt and Herr Eccius, the two accused, were allowed to address to the Court the last words in their defence.

Herr Eccius said that when he went to Essen he read on the Krupp monument, "Let your aim be the common weal." His work was inspired to this end.

He begged the judges to set as an argument against his complicity the fact that this had been the guiding motive of his action.

In delivering the sentence the Court declared that the Krupp firm had formerly won a special position in the matter of artillery armaments, which it had, however, lost later on account of its high prices. A search had consequently been made for a suitable person to acquire requisite information through intercourse with army men. Such a person had been found in Brandt, to whom the possibility was suggested of obtaining information from former comrades. Brandt had obtained such communications and had used them for his "Kornwalzer" (confidential reports). He had even gone so far as not only to stand drinks, but also to make

little loans or presents of money in return for these favours. An indication of Brandt's consciousness of guilt was his statement that he no longer felt a decent fellow. The acts of bribery were to be regarded as a continuous action.

BAVARIA'S NEW KING.

TAKES OATH TO OBSERVE THE CONSTITUTION.

MUNICH, Wednesday.

At ten o'clock this morning King Ludwig III. took the Oath to observe the Constitution in the throne-room of the palace. The ceremony, which was of a very impressive character, was attended by the princes of the Royal house, all the Ministers of State and the members of the Council of State and a deputation from the two Houses of the Diet.

After a speech by His Majesty the Minister of Justice proceeded to read the formula of the oath by which the King swears to rule in conformity with the Constitution and the laws of the Empire. His Majesty, with his right hand uplifted, spoke the words, "I swear."

Baron von Hertling, the Premier, thereupon addressed the King and begged him to receive the most respectful homage of the whole Ministry of State and of the Councillors of State and their vow of inviolable loyalty.—Reuter.

Northcliffe's plan in 1913: a Berlin *Daily Mail*

during his widow's lifetime. About Beaumont's death he wrote to Sutton: 'I am glad that I was kind to him some months back.' His Coutts' account showed that as from March 1913 he had been paying £150 a quarter to Beaumont. No other reference to the transaction has been found. Beaumont left £57,606 12s. 8d.

Offered a weekly paper which was for sale, he replied (April 29, 1913): 'I do not want any daily, weekly, tri-weekly, fortnightly, monthly, morning, noon or evening papers. People say that I have already more than is good for the national welfare.' In fact, he was making arrangements to sell the *Daily Mirror* to his brother Rothermere: the change-over was completed towards the end of the year. He was reading and disapproving *Daily Mail* serial stories, telling Heath Hosken, who edited them: 'You really must enlarge your circle of authors.' Sutton woefully reported to him that the *Daily Mail* medical correspondent had prescribed a hair curling lotion 'to be taken after meals three times a day in water'. The editor-proprietor of the *Manchester Guardian*, C. P. Scott, called on him to discuss the stopping of newspaper prize competitions. Northcliffe wrote to Sir George Riddell, of the *News of the World*: 'I am quite willing to consider the question. Long experience has taught me that these competitions are really more nuisance than they are worth; but if we stopped them we might find ourselves in the position of Mr Scott and the *Manchester Courier* proprietors, who years ago met and agreed not to print racing returns, with the result that a man employed in the *Manchester Guardian* printing department, Mr Hulton, saw his opportunity and founded a great business which has worried them ever since.'

He went to Grand Falls again that autumn, taking with him his wife, Mrs Algernon Douglas-Pennant, Harold Child of the *Times* editorial department, Andrew Caird, and H. Russell Wakefield as travelling private secretary. The position of Mayson Beeton, who had done as much as anyone in bringing the great enterprise to fruition, required consideration on the spot. Harold Harmsworth spoke of his 'immense services'. Northcliffe seemed less worried than his brother by Beeton's threatened retirement. Northcliffe to his mother (September 5, 1913): 'Very busy investigating, inspecting, handshaking, speechmaking, travelling. Your little sachet is under my pillow and you, darling Mum, are always in my heart. The town is electrically decorated for us. There is a huge letter N with coronet, 35 feet high on top of a tower. It looks brilliant and can be seen twenty miles away in the forest.' The same (September 19): 'Just a tiny little love letter, my dearest Mother, to tell you that we are well despite immense hard work in Newfoundland. It is 2,480 miles Grand Falls and Chicago; 1,250 miles Chicago, Washington and New York; 3,250 miles New York to London: total, 6,980 miles till I kiss my darling Mum. I have your lavender pillow under my head.'

Inspecting the sheds where the bark was stripped from the logs, he made a remark which is remembered at Grand Falls. Proud of the efficiency of the department, the manager told him: 'This place runs itself.' 'What did you say?' Northcliffe flashed back. 'Don't you know that anything that goes of itself must be going downhill? I never allow that to happen in any part of my businesses.' He wrote to Sutton (September 21): 'We had a very strenuous time at Grand Falls, but I *know* we did good and I *know* that the A.N.D.C. [Anglo-Newfoundland Development Co.] is a good thing. I was delighted with V. Jones's [later Sir Vincent Jones] work, but Muzzy [Beeton] spoils everything. He is the Old Man of the Sea, much as I like him as a friend.' After calling on Robert McCormick, of the *Chicago Tribune*, Northcliffe, in thanking him for hospitality, wrote (November 26): 'I had been to Chicago before and hated it. Now I like it. Which shows that, after all, it is people in places, not the places themselves, which really affect one.'

As always when he was in England, he spent Christmas with his mother at Poynters Hall. He arrived after a game of golf in which he got wet through. While his clothes were being dried he appeared in a morning coat lent him by his mother's butler, Mansell. Seeing him, a young Burton nephew was heard whispering to his father: 'Dad, has Uncle Alfred got Mansell's job?' On December 27 he drove over to Beaconsfield to present an illuminated address to Lord Burnham, proprietor of the *Daily Telegraph*, who was eighty the next day. It had been Northcliffe's idea, first put in a letter to Robert Donald, editor of the *Daily Chronicle* (November 7, 1913): 'If two or three of us could come together and get an Address signed by all the newspapers in England, congratulating him, it would please a very delightful old man who is always kind to his workers, and is, even today, one of the ablest of our craft.'

Yet not long after expressing the felicitations of the profession to that well-liked Jewish doyen of London newspaper proprietors, Northcliffe was involved in an ugly clash with the Jewish acting-editor of his *Weekly Dispatch*, who resigned because 'you insulted me on account of my origins'. For an Anglo-Irishman with Scots blood, one of whose oldest personal alliances outside the family was with a Jew, Henry Arnholz, the solicitor, Northcliffe was perversely given to goading the susceptibilities of both Jews and Scotsmen. Hamilton Fyfe said that 'it was more than half due to his mischievous schoolboy humour', expressed in remarks like 'I'm sure you must be a Jew—you've got such a Scotch name'. He was susceptible, like many Englishmen, to the ancient fear of Jewish will-power with its enormous unconcern for other people's ideals. It did nothing to minimize his personal feelings for Arnholz, to whom he gave tokens of his regard in the form of jewelled tiepins which have acquired heirloom value in the solicitor's family. One of them represented a snipe, with which Northcliffe sent the scribbled message: 'Note the long bill!'

Northcliffe to Stephen Paget, F.R.C.S., Secretary of the Research Defence Society:

> The Times,
> Printing House Square,
> E.C.
> December 16th, 1913.

Dear Mr Stephen Paget,—I have been assured by very distinguished foreign authorities that experiments on dogs and cats are not necessary, except as regards diseases peculiar to themselves.

I enclose a cheque for £100, but I do hope your Society will leave the dogs and cats alone.

> Yours very truly,
> NORTHCLIFFE

*   *   *

'Six years' experience of Printing House Square has taught me that "nothing happens" there. All sorts of things are *discussed*, but "nothing happens".' Northcliffe was writing in January 1914 to Howard Corbett, the new assistant manager of *The Times*. 'The Paper' was becoming again an inflammatory focal point of his attention. It had given a paragraph about the weather at Norwegian resorts. 'I do not believe that anyone wants to know what the weather is at Norwegian winter resorts. It was a waste of space, ink and composition' (January 20). 'At one time, the first indication of a great jewel robbery used to appear in *The Times* in the form of a notice offering a reward, the paper itself containing no mention of the matter', another of the 'pinpricks' which John Walter had asked him to spare 'the office' if harmony and efficiency were to be attained. Robinson, the new editor, was noting in his diary (January 19, 1914): 'Fearful worry and chaos in the office. N. raging about and giving contradictory orders.' 'Lunatic raging and nagging' (January 21). 'Another diabolical day' (January 22). Northcliffe to Robinson (January 24): 'Yesterday's inquiry into the finance of *The Times* was a revelation and does not reflect credit on the establishment. The salaries paid are eighty-four thousand pounds per annum, not including the mechanical department, and the mouse that issues is, this morning, certainly a ridiculous one.'

Not all was imperious discord. *Humbly beg for light leading article daily until I return*, he telegraphed to the editor on January 25, 1914. It was the inspiration of the *Times* 'fourth leaders', as they have long been universally known, one of his lasting legacies to the paper. The idea had sprouted from the subsoil of his experience in the Coventry days, when e had been attracted by the light leading articles in the *Daily Telegraph* id had noted his appreciation of them in *Bicycling News.*

G. Murray Brumwell, to Northcliffe (February 24, 1914): 'My dear hief,—The first letter which I have received from you in your own and overwhelms me with its all too generous expressions of praise. nd your princely gift takes my breath away and leaves me quite icapable of finding adequate words of thanks. Your kindness is upendous.' Ernest Brain, special correspondent of *The Times*, to North-iffe (February 26): 'I am always glad to do anything in my power for *he Times*, with which my life has been bound up, but the fact that one's rork is appreciated and recognized is most cheering, and for this and for our kind words of encouragement I thank you very warmly.'

Most of the office staff had a different view of 'the Chief'—a Carmelite louse genuflection not popular at Printing House Square, though Robinson, Brumwell, Wickham Steed and others used it in corre-ponding with him—from that of the travelling correspondents. Robinson vas impelled to write a long and closely argued appeal for deliverance rom the frictions which, he showed, were affecting the spirits of the taff and consequently the quality of 'the Paper'. Sardonically, Northcliffe ad remarked in a letter addressed to 'my dear Robin' on January 22: Apparently, the more friction at Printing House Square the better. This morning's paper is admirable.' Robinson had little reason to feel ppeased. *The Times* history states that Northcliffe had gone 'over his iead' in a number of matters in his province, among them editorial ppointments and dismissals. 'The staff were so upset that the Editor mburdened himself to the Chairman of the Company', John Walter, who agreed to take Robinson's memorandum to Northcliffe in Paris. Northcliffe had gone there hurriedly to see a specialist; his eyes were worrying him again. His brother Harold wrote: 'I had Pearson here the other day. He is as blind as a bat, although quite cheerful. He is a standing warning against optical overstrain. He thinks his blindness is largely due to want of care.'

Robinson's memorandum, addressed to the proprietors but meant for Northcliffe, was fair and constructive. Recognizing the need for econo-mies, it offered a fifty per cent personal salary cut, and besought the proprietors' comradeship as well as confidence. 'We are a perfectly sensible lot of people.' He pointed out that in the office there was a general feeling that certain dismissals had been a result of personal dislike, which had not taken into account the individual's value to the paper. 'The essence of the whole thing is that they should be a willing and cheerful body of workers, and under present conditions I am afraid this is too much to expect.' Northcliffe appears to have taken the point. He wrote to his *Times* henchman, Pryor, who had been consulted by him about the staff changes:

'May I hope you are going about with a more cheerful expression, ar not grumbling? I want the whole office to get into the best of spirits fc the immense task that they have before them. Everybody should be jolly as possible', an exhortation with a poignant sequel for its recipier who shortly afterwards had a cerebral hæmorrhage.

To the vexations of *The Times* and the worry about his eyesight wa added the passing annoyance of a novel, *Lord London*, by Keble Howard recognizably based on his character and career. Intended to provide ligl entertainment, it incurred Northcliffe's extreme displeasure by what l took to be its portrayal of his father as an enfeebled dotard who sper his days playing the violin in an attic. In the words of their chairman, th publishers, Chapman & Hall, found themselves 'up against a mysteriou obstacle'. Their advertising was rejected. William Heinemann, an ol friend of Northcliffe, intervened. Northcliffe told him: 'As a public mar I have to put up with publicity. But I will not have my father insulted Northcliffe's sense of humour was ever subordinate to family pride.

Northcliffe to John Walter:

> Grosvenor Hotel,
> Rue Pierre Charron,
> Paris.
> February 21, 1914.

My dear John Walter,—You do not mind me writing frankly to you. In th endeavour to save *The Times*, your family property, inefficient people hav been removed. The promotion of Steed, in place of one of the arch-muddler [a reference to Chirol] at Printing House Square, who, I believe, cost the pape some scores of thousands of pounds, is typical of some changes I have made in your interest quite as much as mine, but chiefly in the interest of the paper Yet, one of those people is going about assuring others that you disagree witl my policy, which is the only possible policy that can save the paper fron extinction.

Up to now, we have worked together extremely well in a very difficult bur human relationship—difficult for both, but, I am sure, more difficult for you than for me. Unless you join me in this struggle for efficiency and economy, the result will be failure.

> Yours sincerely
> NORTHCLIFFE

John Walter replied on February 23: 'Nothing would be more likely to do harm to the Paper both in this office and outside than the spreading of a report that you and I are in disagreement with regard to the policy being pursued at P.H.S.' Even if it were true, he wrote, he would not advertise the fact. 'Fortunately, it is not. In the main lines of our policy I agree with you entirely, as you know.' But the recent staff changes had

een made without reference to him. 'I had actually been congratulating
member of the staff on his work and discussing possible developments
f it, and then a few days later heard that he had received notice to leave.'
And on February 24: 'I am glad to hear you are not contemplating any
more reductions in the staff at present. I know that some members of the
Editorial side were very much upset by the suddenness with which the
recent changes were made. They are all working at pretty high pressure
nd we must be careful at the present moment not to increase the strain.'
Northcliffe to John Walter: 'In reply to your first letter, I have always
ndeavoured to see that you are informed of everything that goes on. It
was no lack of desire for unity or lack of courtesy or regard on Nicholson's
part. It was simply that the man was overloaded with work, which
eventually broke him down.' Replying to John Walter's second letter:
I do not see why any members of the staff should complain of haste on
my part. If they do, they remind me of the young lady who, after ten
years' courtship, affected the "this is so sudden" demeanour when the
man sought to bring her up to scratch by asking for the date' (February 25,
1914).

Northcliffe's knowledge of the economic and political history of 'the
Paper' was exceptional. He could have passed a fairly stiff examination in
the subject where some of the elder brethren of Printing House Square
certainly would have failed. For many months he had made it a practice
to read three back issues every day, in addition to his study of the current
editions. He wrote to Perry Robinson, one of the special correspondents:

The Times was created, as you know, practically by John Walter the Second,
who chose Delane, then less than half the age of the majority of the people at
present at Printing House Square, and a third of the age of a good many of
them, to carry out his projects.

The administration of *The Times* was divided between the Editor and the
Manager—a system of joint government which existed till Delane's death,
when, unfortunately, the Editor was replaced by Professor Chenery, whose
Sanskrit was stronger than his administrative capacity, and who very often did
not appear at the office at all, or communicate with it. The paper then fell into
the hands of the Manager only, and became completely centralized. This
particular Manager landed *The Times* into the Parnell trouble. He was eventually succeeded by Mr Moberly Bell, who was called Assistant-Manager, but
who, in fact, really conducted the whole establishment—engaged the staff, sent
out the foreign correspondents, altered leading articles, and who was indeed
in command, as I found in 1908, when, by the way, the paper was bankrupt.

He telegraphed from Paris to Sutton: *Could you send me little report of
the business dear Sut feel lonely without it Answers serial story very excellent.*
There was a telegram 'at urgent rate' for the advertisement manager of the

Daily Mail: Most strongly protest against your injuring my newspaper by use of such type as in Oxo advertisement please send me written explanation why you disobey my orders.—Chief. A telegram for Pomeroy Burton was pointedly addressed to his golf club at Walton-on-the-Hill, Surrey *Please attend to your business many things need attention.* W. A. Ackland whom Northcliffe had sent to Manchester to 'pull the *Courier* round' wrote to let him know that he had 'averaged two hours' sleep a night for six months', and begged: 'Give me till the end of this week to rest. Ackland was offered 'the full use' of Elmwood for 'as long as it takes to get you right again'. The same restorative facilities had been put at the disposal of Pryor and his family. A letter from an old Fleet Street acquaintance, Lucien Wolf, told of the plight of Edward Morton, the one-time editor of *Youth*, on which the young Alfred Harmsworth had secured his first editorial post. 'He has collapsed under a stroke of paralysis and I am afraid that his professional career is at an end. He has done well as a playwright, chiefly as the author of *San Toy* and the *Merry Widow*. We have been very astonished to find that out of all the money he made practically nothing remains.' Wolf added: 'I know that you and Morton had differences and if your recollection indisposes you to take any part in this business, I will not question your decision.' Northcliffe to Lucien Wolf: 'I do not remember very much about Morton, and I certainly do not remember any differences with him. I did his work and he took the money, but, on the other hand, I did learn a very great deal of the technique of journalism, which was of great use to me in my career. I will co-operate in anything that his old friends suggest.' On March 18, he was present in the House of Lords as one of the sponsors of his brother Harold, whose peerage had been announced in the New Year honours list and who was being introduced as the first Baron Rothermere of Hemsted, in Kent. Their mother witnessed the formal presentation, with its oath-taking and solemn pacing of the floor and gangways of the Chamber, the only woman, it was believed, to see two of her sons take their places in the House of Lords as first peers of their line. A third son, Cecil, became a peer after her death.

On March 10, 1914, Northcliffe dictated the news contents bill for the following morning's *Daily Mail*. It was to be: 'THE TIMES at 1*d*.' The change of price from 2*d*. was announced in *The Times* itself as taking effect on and from Monday, March 16. After months of private discussion, doubt and prevarication, and deliberately intended deception of its penny rivals, the *Morning Post* and the *Daily Telegraph*, he made a decision which increased the paper's competitive momentum sufficiently to carry it through many years to come. The big Hoe presses ran through the night to print (according to the editor's diary) 281,000 copies of a 24-page paper. 166,136 copies of the first penny issue were sold to the

ublic, settling down to an average of 145,000, with 'firm promise of
ncrease'. It was a novel and rejuvenating experience for those who had
een catering for a circulation of 46,000, though there were beards at
rinting House Square and in the clubs of St. James's which wagged
ignals of distress at the 'popular' price.

The operation had succeeded beyond his hopes against great odds and the
ntire credit was his, for he made an act of faith in the contemporary value, as
n object of trade, of the historic quality of *The Times*, and in the existence of
sufficient percentage of the penny public capable of appreciating it. And he had
een fully justified. The conviction that had prevailed in the office since 1855
ad been reversed. Every change he had made had obviously conformed with
he nature of the paper. He had reduced its price but not one of the 'old con-
titutionalists' in Printing House Square said, or could say, that he had reduced
ts essential quality. In fact, March 16, 1914, secured the future and the standards
of *The Times*. (*History of The Times*, vol. 4, part 1, p. 155.)

A letter from Moberly Bell's widow showed again his sympathetic tact.
I think it was the kindest thought that made you spare that moment to
send a note to me and I love to think that you link my husband's memory
with your new *Times* scheme. For years he longed that this moment
should be possible. I congratulate you from my heart on your success and
feel that I am sharing it' (April 16, 1914).

A third secretary was added to Northcliffe's personal staff that year, a
stammering London University graduate named Francis Herbert Mountjoy Nelson Humphrey-Davy, son of a Bournemouth doctor. Before working in the *Times* news department he had been secretary to two Members
of Parliament. He was a near passionate student of heraldry. For his first
interview with Northcliffe he attired himself in full morning dress. 'I shall
be honoured to serve your lordship', he said with his usual difficulty in
addressing a social superior, 'as I have an unbounded admiration for the
peerage.' Northcliffe looked at him curiously. 'Oh, you have, have you?'
he said. 'I'll damned soon cure you of that!'

Lloyd George, interviewed at Criccieth, had given it out as his opinion
that Anglo-German relations were on a firmer footing than they had been
for years. He saw it as a better sign that the Continental countries appeared
to be turning their energies to the strengthening of their land forces. For
some Liberals the implication was that there was no justification for naval
expansion at home. Their cry became 'Peace, Retrenchment and Reform!'
It could not dispel the nervousness which continued to underlie every kind
of European transaction, from diplomacy to street corner trading. It
needed no acute sensitivity to realize the imminence of a convulsion in
human affairs. War in Tripoli and the Balkans were the preliminary
tremors. Northcliffe could not accept the view that the time was ripe for

a great scheme of disarmament, such as the Liberal pacifists were urging
He insisted that his leader writers should defend the navy estimates against
their propaganda and make one more effort to ensure the reorganization
of the British army and the adoption of national service, which he had
made a *Daily Mail* political theme over many years. Concerning th
'scaremongering' with which he was charged by the *Daily News* and othe
organs of antipathetic opinion, a letter written to him by Wile, from
Berlin, on March 14, showed that if he was in favour of bellicose journalism
at that time his preference was being ignored by his editors.

I am very much mistaken if you have not been wondering at the milk-and
water treatment accorded the German war-scare campaign against Russia in
the Berlin dispatches of the *Daily Mail*. The 'scare' started on the night o
March 2nd. On that very day, the President of the German Navy League
launched a new campaign for more Dreadnoughts. Also, the Kruppized press
renewed the familiar crusade against English guns, with a view to encouraging
Germans to believe in the invincibility of their own 'on the day'. I told all
about these things, succinctly and briefly, and then brought in the anti-Russian
campaign—its very inauguration. What happened in Carmelite House? With
that unfailing lack of appreciation of the value of a German political event the
Russian war scare—since grown to the most important Continental political
incident of recent times—was dismissed with a four-line paragraph.

On the night of March 9, the most remarkable revelation of the whole war
scare took place—an article in the pacifist *Tageblatt* advocating a 'preventive'
war on Russia without further ado. I summarized the salient points in a dispatch. Not a syllable of it was printed. Yet *The Times* published a special summary of the dispatch and, in addition, a $1\frac{1}{2}$-column leader. It was not very
pleasant for me to have Mackenzie [Berlin correspondent of *The Times*]
remark to me at lunch: 'Wile, you seem to be missing this Russian war scare
business.'

On March 25, Cecil Harmsworth, Liberal M.P. for Luton, noted in his
diary: 'Greater excitement in the House this week than I have ever
known.' General Gough and other officers of the cavalry brigade at the
Curragh, in Ireland, had sent what was 'a virtual ultimatum' to the
Government, which appeared to be preparing measures of coercion
against Ulster. 'Liberal members all over the House gathered in gloomy
knots and anxiously canvassing the situation. I find Winston Churchill
singing blithely to himself in the lavatory behind the Speaker's Chair.
I thank him for his reassuring cheerfulness and he tells me that it is
his habit to confront difficult situations with an outward serenity of
aspect.'

Secret German influences were supposedly at work on the Irish situation. The German press attack on Russia was bold and defiant. So the
pitiful nationalistic drama was played out to its last act. When one of

Northcliffe's young nephews, Rothermere's eldest boy Vyvyan*, wrote to solicit his interest in an Anglo-German friendship club at Oxford, he replied (May 12, 1914): 'You know that I am not one of those who believe in the likelihood of friendship between the English and the Germans, but will do anything you wish. I am always glad to hear from you, my dear nephew.'

Christ Church,
Oxford.
May 13th.

Dear Uncle Alfred,—I didn't realize before that you weren't a believer in the possibility of friendship with Germany. As far as I'm concerned, I think it is a good thing to encourage good relations between the two countries, and to try to get Englishmen to understand Germans better than they do and not to despise them and misunderstand them, for they must be a wonderful race to be achieving what they are. It is gratifying too to find that such eminent men as Fürst Bülow are lending their support to the club, and showing that they are not really antagonistic to England.

Ever your loving Godson,
VYVYAN

To one of his paper experts, Vincent Jones, of the Anglo-Newfoundland Development Company, he confided his belief in the possibility of 'trouble with Germany at any minute'. It was essential, he urged, that paper and pulp supplies should be built up in England. He thought it likely that the boiling point in Europe might be reached 'between now and 1915', and said that he looked forward 'with much apprehension'. Writing in the last week of June 1914 to Stanley Cousins, head of the Imperial Paper Mills at Gravesend, about the poor quality of the paper supplied to *The Times*, he begged for a speedy increase in both supply and quality. 'I have reason to believe that there may be a great and, to most people, unexpected demand within the next two months.' Hardly less significantly he mentioned: 'At any moment it may be necessary to print photographs in *The Times*. Will you consult with Mr Bland [printer of *The Times*] as to the best kind of paper for that purpose?' An innovation of Northcliffe's, *The Times* art department in due course introduced the highest quality photographic reproduction into daily journalism and brought new prestige to the paper and new revenues to the counting-house.

*　　*　　*

* The Hon. Harold Alfred Vyvyan St. George Harmsworth was born in 1894, and was educated at Eton and Christ Church, Oxford. At Eton he took prizes in science, history and divinity including the Rosebery history prize. He was a promising young boxer and won the school welter-weight. Later, when he was at Christ Church, he gained his Blue for boxing and represented the university against Cambridge in 1914.

455

Northcliffe to his mother:

Imperial Hotel,
Enniskillen.
3rd July, 1914.

Sweet Mum,—It is difficult to write when one is up early and off for th
day, with local deputations to receive at night.

I have seen enough of the drilling of these auspicious and determined Scotc
and English Irish to know that they *cannot be put down*.

I wish my darling mother were with me. We have had excellent roads, ver
lovely country, and hotels not so bad. We passed through Armagh yesterday
Red flags on all the churches everywhere and 'We want no popery here' on a
the walls. The girls wearing marigolds and any other orange-coloured flowers

I think every hour of my darling mother and shall be with her again soon

The party in Northern Ireland which was against severance fron
England had organized a defence force. Northcliffe thought it necessary
to go over and see the state of affairs for himself. He found men everywhere parading and drilling; what Dickens had called, he remembered
with a laugh, 'allong-ing and march-onging'. He had long before decided
that the only war that would settle problems in Ireland was a war against
poverty. He had his own remedy for that and often mentioned it during
the visit. 'Let them harness their rivers, create white coal, do what we are
doing in Newfoundland. Build up industries. The political independence
of Ireland will come, but the only people to gain by it will be a few
politicians.' He thought that the Government should have 'nipped it in
the bud', the prospect of civil war, which, with the raucous activities of the
suffragettes, was helping to confirm the German belief that there was a
weakening of the English spirit. He did not take sides himself and was
irritated and bored by the spate of contrary opinion. He was often reminded in conversations of his local affinities, but, as his brother Cecil
wrote, he had never considered himself an Irishman. He had no strong
religious feelings, no large intolerances, few sentimental prejudices. He
played golf on some of the greenest courses in the world with eyes and
ears open, while trying to appear both incurious and impartial. He understood the Ulster temper in the way that he understood the impulse of any
individual or group to resist imposed authority, but he would not commit
himself or his newspapers to it. He made plans on the spot for reporting,
not supporting, what seemed to be impending calamity in Ireland. S. S.
McClure, an American magazine proprietor who accompanied him
through seven of the nine Ulster counties, was much struck by the attention he gave to the smallest details of news organization.

Arriving back in London, Northcliffe saw Asquith, the Prime Minister,
who, after hearing his impressions of Ulster, took the chance of trying
to impress on him in turn 'the importance of making *The Times* a respon-

ible newspaper'. Readers of the *Daily Mail* and probably not a few of those of *The Times* were more immediately interested in the trial of Mme Caillaux for shooting M. Calmette, the editor of *Figaro*. As for Northcliffe, a communication that had reached him privately from a source close to M. Poincaré, the French President, may have reduced the Irish imbroglio to a minor place in his thoughts. It indicated that the German war potential had reached so great an impetus in every department that it was beyond control and that there would be an attack on Belgium.

On August 2, Northcliffe played golf at Totteridge with his young secretary, Russell Wakefield, who said that 'N. was seized with mounting anxiety. Returning to town in the Rolls he would urge Pine on and then stop him to buy an evening paper, biting deeply into his cigar as he waited. We stopped four times on the drive back to town. He would scan the paper in his infinitely practised way, and then throw it on the floor of the car.' Wakefield recalled Northcliffe that afternoon as being 'very kind but distrait', and wrote: 'I can still see him crouching formidably forward in the Rolls, and Pine's imperturbable back!' Perhaps thus soon he saw the parting of the ways between the generation of the young man sitting beside him and his own.

BOOK THREE

War and Peace

Chapter Seventeen

An Army Without Shells

LIKE a general, Northcliffe deployed his men in readiness for a world conflict. Correspondents of the *Daily Mail* were under orders to leave London at a few hours' notice for their war stations; some had already gone. One was on his way to Vienna; a second had left to observe Austrian operations against Serbia; a third was posted to the Franco-German frontier, another to Switzerland, another to Holland; the last-named went off in the morning coat and silk hat in which he had been attending a London social function. Each carried two hundred pounds in gold. The youngest, newly promoted from the ranks of junior reporters, was J. M. N. Jeffries. Marlowe said to him gruffly: 'Remember a deceased correspondent is of no use to his newspaper.' The paper's local correspondents had been alerted, understudies for the travelling correspondents appointed. Similar arrangements had been made at *The Times*. Its corps of experienced men, whose names in some instances were household words in the territories of their assignment, was supplemented by a body of young correspondents sent out from Paris, some in cars, some on bicycles, to keep in touch with the French army.

In Northcliffe's papers there is a note on the activities at that time of the Kaiser's brother, Prince Henry of Prussia, who, after returning from South America, had arrived in England and been taken to see the Royal Flying Corps base at Netheravon, Wiltshire. That was in May. At the end of July, he was in London again and seeing King George V. 'This visit', according to the report, 'was to nose about on the Irish question', and it was disclosed that he returned to Potsdam for a Council Meeting at which he presented a confidential report. 'It was an important factor in determining Germany to go ahead. In his report Prince Henry expressed the view that we would not intervene.'

What none could say, right up to the last moment, was that England would fight with France and Russia. The Foreign Secretary, Sir Edward Grey, could only speak in a temporizing tone on behalf of a democracy with many voices. At Carmelite House, Northcliffe and Marlowe received a succession of French newspaper men in London. 'I was a witness of their agony,' wrote H. W. Wilson. 'I can use no other word. Night after night they came to the office. They had no doubt now that war was in sight and that, if it came and Great Britain stood aside, France faced disaster.' Wilson wrote also that 'Northcliffe had not a minute to call his own'. He was as grimly preoccupied as a minister of state and when he was not at his offices he was telephoning to them at all hours of the day and night. Wilson said that at Carmelite House it was no uncommon thing for Northcliffe in those first days of war to have calls waiting on eight or ten of its thirty telephone lines at the same time. He was regarded as a fount of information. Many of the callers were themselves men of affairs who, like him, were groping blindly through the maelstrom of events. Questions of newspaper policy which he alone could settle vexed him through anxious hours. He feared that the Germans would launch an attack by sea and air on England, and believed that they would count on the newest arm to produce the first great shock of the war. He did not believe that the British army could safely spare divisions to cross the sea; moreover, he had information which made him doubt whether an expeditionary force would be sufficiently well equipped for its offensive purposes, despite the admirable organizing efforts of Haldane and his advisers.

While these matters were agitating his judgment new situations demanding his attention were springing up hourly. There was violent selling of securities by German interests and a great rush of bills and drafts had been organized with the object of draining London of gold. Soon the machinery of credit had come to a halt. Lord Rothschild, the City banker, sent for the *Times* financial editor, Hugh Chisholm, and requested an instant change in the tone of the paper's leading articles, which, he asserted, were driving the country into war. The City, Rothschild said, stood at the brink of disaster and only a policy of neutrality would avert it. Wickham Steed recorded in *Through Thirty Years**:

Returning to *The Times* office, Mr Chisholm informed Lord Northcliffe and the Editor, and afterwards attended the daily editorial conference. Lord Northcliffe, who presided, said: 'I think Mr Chisholm has something to say.' Chisholm then repeated his interview with the financial magnate. He was still white with rage. When he had finished, Lord Northcliffe asked my opinion.

'It is a dirty German-Jewish international financial attempt to bully us into

* Heinemann, 1924.

dvocating neutrality,' I said, 'and the proper answer would be a still stiffer eading article tomorrow.'

'I agree with you,' said Lord Northcliffe. 'Let us go ahead.'

Rothschild and his brother Leopold then went to Printing House Square. Northcliffe saw them at once. It was believed that the meeting had been arranged by the Chancellor of the Exchequer, Lloyd George. They told Northcliffe that they had received news of such gravity for the future of England that her only hope was to remain neutral. German naval and military might was overwhelming. It was capable of crushing the British Empire 'in a few weeks'. They begged Northcliffe to support the neutral course.

On Saturday, August 1, he called a conference in his room at *The Times*. With him were Robinson, the editor, Marlowe of the *Daily Mail*, and Steed. He announced: 'I have trustworthy information that the Government are going to "rat". We have taken a strong line in favour of intervention on behalf of France and Russia. What do we do if the Government give way?' He turned to Steed, who had undoubtedly reported to him the information brought to *The Times* office twenty-four hours previously by George Lloyd, one of the younger Conservatives, that the Government, who, by Winston Churchill's later definition, were 'overwhelmingly pacific', were preparing 'to back down'. Steed answered Northcliffe by saying that if the Government stood aside from the conflict the paper would have to 'go bald-headed against it'. Northcliffe then asked him: 'Would you attack the Government at a moment of national crisis?' Steed replied, 'Certainly', and gave his reasons, one of them being that *The Times* would thus preserve its dignity. Marlowe 'spoke against attacking the Government. The country would never forgive us.' Geoffrey Robinson, the *Times* editor, counselled caution, pointing out that they had a weekend in which to ponder the problem. The paper was being assailed from the Liberal side for its 'fervid declarations' in support of the Entente. The editor of the *Daily News*, A. G. Gardiner, had denounced *The Times* in an article headed 'Why We Must Not Fight', declaring that the *Times* policy had 'paved the way to this stupendous catastrophe'. In the *Manchester Guardian*, H. W. Nevinson spoke of 'the abominations into which *The Times* and its attendant satellites are attempting to drag us'. A Quaker, Arthur Rowntree, was apparently hopeful of confining the conflict to a narrower sphere: 'We ought to proclaim to the world that the *Manchester Guardian* and not *The Times* represents the industrialism of the north and the wisdom of the north.' C. Roden Buxton, M.P., asked: 'What right have *The Times* and its satellites to speak for the people of England?'

On the afternoon of August 4, a young assistant in the *Times* library was told to take a reference book to Steed's room. Northcliffe entered after him. 'Well, it's come', Northcliffe said to Steed, who replied in the tones of one expressing relief from the tensions not of a week but of years: 'Yes, thank God!' They had some talk about an article for the next day's paper. Northcliffe seized the book, glanced through it with professional intensity, and ripping out one of its pages strode from the room.

In greater matters of the moment he was not necessarily so decisive. There was the overriding question of the British expeditionary force. He surprised the group of anxious men assembled for the 5 p.m. news conference in the *Daily Mail* office on Wednesday, August 5, by the vehemence of his declaration that 'not a soldier of ours shall leave these shores!' The news editor, Tom Clarke, said that he 'made quite a scene'. In the talk that followed he explained that England would be 'doing enough' with the Royal Navy, and that it would be foolish to leave the country unprotected by troops in case of invasion attempts, which he believed would be made. He was unlikely to have known that the War Council summoned that day by Haldane, the acting War Minister, was not willing, because of the invasion risk, to sanction the sending of more than four divisions of the expeditionary force to France; and among those present were Roberts, Kitchener and French. 'In any event,' Northcliffe argued, 'the French have their own Grand Army for the job of holding the Germans'. He wrote a leading article opposing the expeditionary force plan. Handing it to the head printer, at Carmelite House, Tom George, he said: 'This is for your eyes, and the eyes of your most trusted comp alone.' Marlowe had written his own leader, supporting the plan. 'I am the editor of this newspaper,' he said, striding into George's room. 'I want to see what the Chief has written.' Sharp discussion followed. Then Northcliffe capitulated. The head printer said later that Kitchener's personal secretary, Sir George Arthur, had been at Carmelite House during the evening. 'I had the job of smuggling him out by a back way.' The first edition of the *Daily Mail* that night was two hours late. Within two days *The Times* was stating that 'the time is at hand when the British Army, as well as the Navy, will have been thrown into the scale', and soon the *Daily Mail* was expressing admiration for the 'thrilling feat' of landing in France 'the largest army that ever left British shores'.

Kitchener's appointment as Secretary of State for War was held to be a triumph of Northcliffe publicity, though there was discomfort in Printing House Square about the way that Haldane had been displaced. The change had been urged on the country in a series of attacks which practically drove Haldane out of public life. But for his organizing abilities there might have been no Territorial Army and no British expeditionary force which, judging from the meagre reports, was acquitting itself with glory on the Flanders plain. Paying tribute to his services in *The World Crisis, 1911–15*, Winston Churchill referred to the 'very manly and loyal part' which Haldane took 'at all times and on every question connected with the preparedness of this country'. A great tidal war was beginning to roll across the Western world and for those of philosophic cast who left them naked to the foe the legions of lesser minds had no respect. The hour belonged to the men who made them feel safe behind ramparts of steel and clouds of battle smoke. Haldane was regarded by the army, by the public, and by the allies of Great Britain, as the friend of Germany and the leader of a pro-German section of the Cabinet. He was, moreover, a lawyer and a scholar-politician, and, as such, like Asquith, he did not make men feel safe. So, within a few days Kitchener came before Parliament as effective head of the nation's land forces and Churchill spoke for the country when he expressed his own feelings: 'I was glad that he had been appointed.' In his *Memories and Reflections** Asquith stated that he took the decision to appoint Kitchener, as 'an emergency man', on August 5. Lord Milner disclosed privately that Asquith had already appointed Haldane. After talking with Leo Amery, M.P., and others, Milner 'prevailed upon Kitchener to go straight to Asquith' (Milner's diary). Kitchener's official biographer, Sir George Arthur, wrote that 'the Prime Minister's mind was largely made up for him by the persistence of Lord Northcliffe and the insistence of the public'. There was no doubt that the Northcliffe-inspired leading articles correctly interpreted the popular mood. No other military personality of the day commanded the same esteem or could have secured so many willing volunteers for the slaughter. The tall unsmiling soldier, whose formidable moustache made a limp inverted V-sign on hoardings all over the land, was the challenging figure of the times.

✱   ✱   ✱

'What are my outgoings?' Northcliffe asked Mackenzie, his private accountant, two weeks after war had been declared. Mackenzie produced figures. Sutton Place was costing more than £15,000 a year, 22 St. James' Place nearly £6,000, Elmwood £1,700, car running and maintenance just over £3,500, annuities to relatives and friends, £16,000. 'Presents to friends' amounted to £15,771 in the previous twelve months. Sutton reported to Mackenzie that 'the rate we are getting on Lord Northcliffe's money is under 2 per cent' and he proposed a change of securities to yield 3⅝ per cent. Few men with such large liquid resources paid less heed to improving their situation. Mackenzie further showed that his regular charity subscription list totalled £8,547 for the year, that his fishing cost

* Cassell, 1928.

£218, his club subscriptions £206, his doctors £284, the boys' camp at Elmwood £350. Now the camp lay within the sound of the guns, and with particular regret he decided that it must be discontinued as from the summer of 1915. The good that it had done in its sixteen years was beyond accounting. It had given him a happiness which had its own obverse shadow, reminding him of the life with children which he had always dreamed of and never had. The camp commandant, Frank Matley, the Poplar schoolmaster, wrote to Northcliffe: 'We all feel that a great influence for good has gone, but we also feel how very generous you have been in giving us the camp for so many years and we wish to thank you over and over again for all your past kindness. We shall ever think of you with affection and gratitude.'

Northcliffe's wife and mother were asked to accept substantial cuts in his allowances to them. His sisters were faced with reductions of £100 a year each. His Aunt Sarah Miller's £500 a year was continued as before. He found that, after all, he could not bring himself to make more than token economies in those directions.

As for charities, they began to multiply under the stresses of war, and his list, still headed by the Salvation Army, the Society for the Protection of Women and Children and the Dolling Home of Rest at Worthing, grew larger. His first war charity contribution was to the Belgian Journalists' Emergency Fund. It was followed by £5,000 to the National Relief Fund (the 'Prince of Wales's Fund'). Soon his help was being sought in more personal matters. 'I have made enquiries on every possible occasion about George Cecil', the Guardsman nephew of his friend L. J. Maxse. 'Sometimes I begin to be hopeful, and then, again, I am not so hopeful. I met the American Ambassador, and, at first, he was a little hopeful, but, afterwards, he was not so hopeful.' Among the first British officers to fall in action was one of the Harmsworths' Irish cousins, Henry Telford Maffett: 'an Orangeman in politics, a good Churchman of the Evangelical Irish school, a hard rider to hounds', Cecil wrote of him. 'I cannot hope to know a more punctiliously honest man. He was indeed one of the best.'

'You know that we are in the midst of a struggle for our lives here. It is difficult to deal with one tithe of all the correspondence I receive from all parts of the world.' The gentle reminder was contained in Northcliffe's reply to Katharine Wright, sister of the Wright brothers. She had written to him about a new attempt in an American magazine to wrest from them the credit of being the inventors of the aeroplane.

I am sorry to say that Orville is far from well. In fact, I am convinced that he will go like Wilbur unless we find some relief for him. That is why I am writing to you without consulting him. He would not wish me to trouble you.

But I realize that you are, in this matter, the most powerful friend that we have in the world and I have confidence that both you and Lady Northcliffe will understand my great concern for the reputation of both of my brothers and for the health and life of the one who is still with us.

'I do not suppose that Wilbur and Orville realized the part their work would play in modern warfare,' Northcliffe told her in reply. 'You have probably read of the harrowing experiences of flying men. A great many have been killed. Please give my warm regards to Orville and tell him it is his duty to see that he is not robbed of his fame by these rogues', the promoters of a claim that the Wrights had usurped the place in history of Samuel Langley, the secretary of the Smithsonian Institute.

A message to 'the Lord Northcliffe' from the Queen intimated the royal pleasure in an article written for the *Daily Mail* by Robert Blatchford and imparted the information that 'Her Majesty has learned that there is a great feeling of ignorance, more particularly among the lower-middle class, regarding the cause of the present war'. Northcliffe was now less interested in causes than effects. 'We may not be preparing sufficiently for invasion,' he told Arthur Brisbane, the American journalist. 'I am inclined myself to think that we are not—perhaps because I should be one of the first people to be hanged if the Germans got here.'

He wrote an article for the *Daily Mail* (September 26, 1914) urging certain precautions against air attack, advice which was not taken until after the attacks had begun. Before the war, he had called for a strength ratio of four to one in the air against Germany, 'and you were ridiculed for doing it', H. W. Wilson reminded him. He had repeatedly urged, also, the development of the air arm against the submarine attacks which later brought the British cause very close to ruin. 'The next war will be the war against disease', he remarked to Dr McNair Wilson in that same month of September 1914, and his prediction echoes far and wide in the work of the United Nations Organization in these later times. He was farther-seeing than most people, too, about the duration of the war. He scorned the popular notion of its being 'all over by Christmas'. He believed that it would last at least three years, in holding which opinion, as the *Times* history states, he was practically alone among laymen. Kitchener thought that it would be 'a very long war'. General Joffre, the French commander-in-chief, forecast its duration as 'about eight months'. Wickham Steed, 'in all modesty', concurred in that estimate. Robinson, the editor of *The Times*, reckoned that it would be 'about eighteen months', and was heartened by friends who told him that it could not possibly last so long. Northcliffe held firmly to his forecast of three years. 'You are talking nonsense,' he said to a *Daily Mail* editorial man who believed that the army would be home by Christmas. 'Our men will have to face two or three Christmases out there, perhaps more.' He told the Government Chief Whip, Percy Illingworth, M.P., that the conquest of Prussia 'will be a much severer task than our military authorities realize'.

Asked for his views by the *New York Sun*, he stated: 'It is no doubt disappointing to English and American business men to learn that there are people like myself who regard this gigantic struggle as a matter of years rather than months.' He did not believe that the necessary army could be raised by voluntary service. 'You'll remember that you could not do so in 1861,' he told the Americans. 'My personal belief is that we shall be obliged to adopt conscription as you eventually did.' He concluded his statement to the American newspaper on a note which was to be amplified resoundingly by a British statesman at the outset of the greater war still to come. 'We shall fight with all the resources of our manhood, our shipyards, our wealth, our British tenacity.'

In September 1914 he wrote to Sir John French at British general headquarters in France, suggesting a campaign of propaganda designed to weaken the German spirit. His proposal was that facsimile letters and leaflets, describing the 'extremely good treatment' of prisoners in British hands, should be dropped by aeroplane over the German homeland; an acute long-term forecast of future strategy. 'As in advertising, the results will take a long time,' he said, 'but I will stake any reputation I may possess that you will get immense results eventually.' French did not take up the idea, which Northcliffe passed on to General Henry Wilson. 'He told me that, after all, it was a minor matter—the thing was to kill Germans' (Northcliffe to General Charteris, August 6, 1916).

To the *New York American*, in answer to a cabled request for a statement, he replied: 'The process of defeating Germany will be one of years rather than months.' For him that was not speculation. It was inescapable fact. Those around him noticed that as the war advanced he became more impatient of theory, waving it aside as if it were a waste of time and mental energy. 'What are the facts?' he would demand in a voice which they also noted was less often the instrument of inconsistency. The war strengthened his sense of responsibility and gave more depth to his personality. At last he could lose himself in a cause incomparably greater than newspaper success. One of the effects was that references to his health were conspicuously absent from his correspondence over long periods. 'We are fighting for our existence,' he wrote in a letter to the Prime Minister, urging him not to deny the nation information which would bring that truth home to it. 'Our people have nothing but the casualty lists and the mutilated scraps with which it is quite impossible to arouse interest or follow the war intelligently.' Asquith cited Northcliffe's letter in his *Memories and Reflections* as 'a real service to the national cause', which Northcliffe clearly hoped that it would be. Nothing troubled him more in those months than the enfeebled presentation of the truth about the war to the people whose sacrifices were essential to winning it. He had long ago advocated censorship in the event of war—censorship but not suppression. Lord Kitchener had an elephantine memory which could not forget that in the Boer War young Churchill had been a troublesome war correspondent, and that Edgar Wallace, of the *Daily Mail*, had 'scooped' the peace terms arranged at Vereeniging in 1902. Set against those activities of the press, the fact that his public reputation had largely been made for him by a war correspondent, G. W. Steevens, of the *Daily Mail*, was of small account. Now, well over a decade later, he resolved that the press should be kept in its place. Northcliffe was angry because the war correspondents were being treated like camp followers. He fought strenuously to get them accredited and blamed Kitchener for the indignities to which they were subjected by the army authorities. Discovering that Kitchener habitually smoked black cigars, he emphasized the 'black' as if it were a flaw in Kitchener's character, disparaging him also as 'a tall man with a narrow forehead'.

Fleet Street was not alone in its astonishment when a dispatch from a *Times* man at the front, Arthur Moore, was released with interpolations as well as excisions made personally by the chief censor, F. E. Smith, who apologized to the editor for his 'clumsy journalistic suggestions' and at the same time begged that 'parts of the article' be used 'to enforce the lesson—reinforcements and reinforcements at once'. The dispatch was so frank in its revelation of the 'bitter truths' of the Mons retreat that no one at *The Times* had expected it to be passed. The effect of Smith's handiwork had been to make the dispatch more disturbing, so much so that Asquith in the House of Commons denounced its publication as likely to spread alarm and confusion. He made no reference to the censor's part in it and the censor himself made a statement to the House which the *Times* history refers to as 'regrettably ambiguous'.

One of the younger *Daily Mail* men attached to the forces in France, Ferdinand Tuohy, was sent for by Northcliffe at 22 St. James's Place. Northcliffe spoke to him about Kitchener's obtuseness in regard to war news. 'What's wrong with the man? What does he think I want to do— wreck the country? This war can't be run in the dark. They can shoot me if I put anything in my newspapers that I shouldn't.' Lord Roberts, who, a little while before had told Coulson Kernahan, an Irish novelist who had helped him in his national service campaign, that Northcliffe had done more than any other individual to bring the army to its state of comparative readiness for war, called on Northcliffe before leaving on a visit to the British Expeditionary Force. He asked Northcliffe to give him a letter to Sir John French, the commander-in-chief, setting out the need for war correspondents. Saying goodbye to Northcliffe at Printing House

Square, he had remarked: 'We shall lose this war by secrecy.' Northcliffe had left him in no doubt that 'the extreme reticence practised by the Government was a danger to the nation'. He told General Wilson: 'If this war is a "walk over", then all my knowledge of Germany is wrong. The "walk over" impression is entirely due to the authorities, who suppress everything except optimistic twaddle.'

He was the leader of a powerful body of Fleet Street opinion, but for months the British censorship, under Kitchener's hand, operated on the assumption that British nerves could not stand bad news. Northcliffe wrote to Lord Murray of Elibank, P.C., the former Liberal chief whip:

What the newspapers feel very strongly is that, against their will, they are made to be part and parcel of a foolish conspiracy to hide bad news. English people do not mind bad news.

Every newspaper man that I know regards Churchill as responsible for many of the initial evils of the Press Bureau, and he himself is aware of his own letter to me about *The Times* dispatch from Amiens, which was inserted in *The Times* by the special request in writing of Mr F. E. Smith, who not only made the request but personally embellished and altered the article. My newspapers were held up in the House of Commons by Mr Asquith and others as having acted disloyally, and, in the House of Lords, by Lord Haldane, although they were well aware of the fact that Mr F. E. Smith asked *The Times* and my other newspapers to publish the article.

Some things are more than flesh and blood can stand. So far as I am concerned, I propose to keep aloof from members of this government until the war is over. I have always liked Winston personally, and he knows that.

Northcliffe was impatient of what he regarded as Churchill's obstructive attitude to Admiralty news. He was preparing to take steps to counter it when Murray of Elibank, writing another letter to Northcliffe in which he asked consideration for 'the great strain' under which Churchill was labouring as First Lord of the Admiralty, helped to restore the old friendly footing between the two men.

* * *

Near the end of 1914 Northcliffe was violently assailed in an open letter published in the *Daily News* by its editor, A. G. Gardiner, who had been stung into blasting retort by the *Daily Mail* pamphlet called *Scaremongerings*, the purpose of which—according to Gardiner—was to cover Northcliffe and the *Daily Mail* 'with honour as the true prophets of the war and the *Daily News* and other representatives of Liberalism with odium as the false prophets of peace'. The 'open letter' was a scathing polemical exercise which produced back-patting approval at the Reform Club and provoked some of Northcliffe's colleagues, led by Lovat Fraser of *The Times*, to prepare a dossier on Cadbury activities. According to the information thus collected, as the beneficiaries of a protected industry the Cadbury family preached Free Trade for others through their *Daily News*, while as supporters of the Anti-Gambling League they owned *The Star*, 'the chief organ for promoting gambling among the poor'. It was maintained that there was 'atrocious slavery' in certain primary producing areas on which Cadbury's cocoa and chocolate trade depended, while their newspapers 'had the effrontery to spread the Chinese slavery lie and to attack Belgian conduct in the Congo'. Tea was heavily taxed and could not be exported to neutral countries. 'Yet cocoa and chocolate (certainly a luxury) are not taxed and may be exported to Holland and Switzerland. This preferential treatment of cocoa reminds one of the worst scandals in the United States of America.' When Fraser wrote to Northcliffe suggesting that 'these *personal* attacks on you must not go for ever unanswered', and that 'some of us who know what you have really stood for, both in journalism and in politics, must take this matter in hand', Northcliffe replied (December 15, 1914): 'My object in showing up the *Daily News* is to spike their guns when the settlement comes, and I think I have done that. I do not in the least mind personal attacks, nor do I care what the public think about me.' Northcliffe to W. F. Bullock, *Daily Mail* correspondent in New York (December 20): 'I am sure you have had your difficulties as well as we on this side. What with the censorship, the absence of advertisements and the gradual fading away of the staff, the life of the newspaper owner has been almost intolerable. Still, the glorious work of our men in the North Sea and in Flanders makes one's trials bearable.' He expressed his pride in a fund-raising achievement of *The Times* to his friend Brisbane, of the Hearst organization in New York: 'Three million pounds for the sick and wounded soldiers breaks the record so far.' The Hon. Sir Arthur Stanley, chairman of the joint committee of the British Red Cross and the Order of St. John of Jerusalem in England, to Northcliffe (December 21): 'I must write you one line to congratulate you on the three millions and to thank you most gratefully in the name of our joint committee. You are indeed a splendid friend', a sentiment echoed in a cordial letter from Lord Rothschild on the same subject. A New Year message from Northcliffe to Norman Angell, author of *The Great Illusion*, brought in response 'the sincere hope that the next year will, to the confusion of your critics, see your career crowned by achievements that will give it a very unique place in our history' (January 4, 1915).

*　　　*　　　*

Gallipoli in February 1915, Neuve Chapelle in March—the first a splendid failure of history, the second an ignominious demonstration of political and military ineptitude disguised by the greatest man-made noise that had ever assaulted the human ear. In both instances, but above all in the second, the lack of high explosive pointed to a weakness in the central direction of the war which was already causing trepidation in the field and was beginning to be anxiously apprehended at home. For those who went into battle on the British side in 1915 no recollection had a firmer lodgment than that of 'the scandal of the shells'.

At first conceived as a naval operation, the assault on the Dardanelles was amply supported by the kinds of ammunition suited to its purpose. When the purpose failed and the operation became an amphibious one, the firing of shrapnel against the Turkish redoubts proved to be as ineffectual as against the more elaborate entrenchments of the Germans in Flanders. The British artillery at Gallipoli was known to the French as 'the one-round-per-gun force', according to Sir Ian Hamilton, the commander-in-chief, who wrote that if he had more high explosive he could advance with half the loss in lives. The thunderous din which had shattered the dawn of March 10 at Neuve Chapelle with awe-inspiring precision died away two hours later in a series of desultory fusillades suggesting no longer co-ordinated action. The lack was not disciplinary or moral. It was material. The shell supply had run out before the job had been done. Supporting divisions, lying in the fields and orchards of the Pas de Calais, were never called forward. Relying on shrapnel to force a breach which only high explosive could accomplish, the great bombardment failed. For weeks, months, afterwards the artillery which was to give aid and comfort to the men in the line from Poperinghe to Cambrai and beyond was rationed to four rounds a day. The Asquith administration was seemingly satisfied with the knowledge that the necessary high explosive shells 'had been ordered', an assertion of virtue which brought little consolation to the men who had to face, meantime, the superior firepower of the enemy.

Charges of Government neglect were vehement and not wholly fair. The problem had been authoritatively considered much earlier and a number of steps, inadequate though they proved to be, had been taken to deal with it before it became a great public issue. Some account of them is given, for example, in *Politicians and the War*: 1914–16* by Lord Beaverbrook, where it is set in a context of party and personal machinations which failed to recognize that for the soldiers in the line at that time it was the paramount problem of the day.

In his *War Memoirs*† Lloyd George wrote that 'Lord Northcliffe had for some time been receiving an unending stream of letters and statements

* Butterworth, 1928.
† Nicholson & Watson, 1933–6.

472

from men at the front about the shell shortage, but all efforts to give publicity to these complaints had been diligently blacked out of his proofs by the Censor'. The censorship prevented them from airing their greatest grievance in letters written from the trenches. It had no power over them when they went home wounded or on leave. As patients in the war hospital which Lady Northcliffe was conducting at Sutton Place, young officers had an opportunity of describing their experiences to Northcliffe in person. Some wrote to their Members of Parliament. Men of all ranks wrote to the newspapers and particularly to the *Daily Mail*, which claimed to be the 'soldiers' friend'. Many of their letters were addressed to 'Lord Northcliffe, Daily Mail, London'. Holding up a batch of the letters at an editorial conference, he remarked: 'This hospital reading public is a very interesting one—we should pay particular attention to it.' One of the letters, delivered at Carmelite House by a soldier on leave, was signed by twenty-three members of the composing-room staff who were serving in France with the second London Division. In thanking 'the Chief' for the provision made by the *Daily Mail* and its associated newspapers for their wives and families, they welcomed what he was doing to improve their situation in the front line. On two of his three visits to France he had heard Sir John French's views. He was aware that Lloyd George had threatened resignation unless action was taken. But the impatience of Lloyd George seemed for the moment to be appeased by declarations that drink among trade unionists was the devil behind the shell shortage. The King was persuaded to endorse that view in a public statement.

Disapproving the leading article in *The Times* of April 12, 1915, Northcliffe dictated some comments to Lovat Fraser, who had written it. The leading article, he said, confused the readers, lulling them into a false sense of security. 'The whole war is being unduly prolonged', and Sir John French, as Northcliffe had reason to know, was on his way over to make 'the most urgent representations' to the Cabinet. 'It must be obvious to everybody that something is wrong.' He particularly objected to the statement in the leading article that there was a lull at the Dardanelles which it was inadvisable to examine too closely. 'Why should we not peer closely into the scandal of the Dardanelles? The result of that expedition, according to General Joffre [the French generalissimo], who told me personally, is to take away available troops from the French and British armies; to bring about the fall of Venezelos, our friend in Greece; to disturb the whole of the Balkan States; and greatly hearten the Germans. It was heralded by a blare of trumpets that made a ridiculous fanfaronade around the world.'

He insisted to Fraser that 'the whole question of the supply of munitions of war is one on which the Cabinet cannot be arraigned too sharply'. He objected to *The Times* whitewashing the Government and misleading the public. 'When, recently, I saw those splendid boys of ours toiling along the roads to the front, weary but keen and bright-eyed (many of whom have given up rosy prospects and happy homes), I could not help feeling very, very bitter at the thought that many of them were on the way to certain mutilation and death by reason of the abominable neglect of the people here.'

Asserting that he rarely interfered 'with the editorial writing in *The Times*', he pointed out to the leader writer that '*The Times* has a tremendous duty and responsibility'. He felt it the more, he wrote, having made three visits to the front, during which he had spoken to many directly involved in the fighting. 'I know that, while we are talking about the alleged drunken habits of the working man (in which I do not believe), the guns at the front are starved for want of the only means of putting an end to this frightful slaughter of the best which any nation has to give.'

That was Northcliffe's temper then and throughout the war. With it there went an unremitting faith in the power of England to survive her ordeal and to emerge from it victoriously. That conviction was a burning inner light which glowed through the darkest times. The Celt in him was subdued by a Roman *gravitas* which prompted one of his younger contemporaries to write: 'He was absolutely dauntless in his belief in victory, and it was really inspiring to talk to him in bad hours' (Lord Beaverbrook, *Politicians and the War*). Wilson, of the *Daily Mail*, wrote: 'I find in my diary that I never talked with him in those dark and critical months without hearing from him words of confidence and hope.' He knew moments of the deepest gloom, but none of doubt, and he was unsparing of his contempt for those who trembled when the enemy's hammer blows were at their worst. He spoke of the German onslaught as 'this massive attempt by the second-rate to dominate the world'.

The failure at Neuve Chapelle provoked Sir John French into making public the chief cause, the shortage of high explosive shells. On March 15, Lord Kitchener told the House of Lords that he was seriously worried on that account. Five weeks afterwards, when no more than eight per cent of the shells supplied consisted of the much-needed high explosive kind, Asquith, the Prime Minister, speaking at Newcastle (April 20, 1915), denied the shortage. He said: 'I saw a statement the other day that the operations, not only of our army but of our Allies, were being crippled, or, at any rate, hampered, by our failure to provide the necessary ammunition. There is not a word of truth in that statement, which is the more mischievous, because, if it were believed, it is calculated to dishearten our troops, to discourage our Allies, and to stimulate the hopes and activities of our enemies.' The quotation was part of a balanced speech which he vigorously and convincingly defended at a later time. The fact remained that he was not regarded by many of his colleagues or by the public as an inspiring war leader. Milner wrote privately that autumn of 'the hopeless wobbling and irresolution of our rulers'. Major-General Henry Wilson, the field-marshal to be who had access to the politicians, was writing only a little later: 'Asquith has never gone to war, he is not at war now, and he never intends to go to war. He has been worth unnumbered corps to the Boche.' That extravagant opinion of a fighting Irishman corresponded to a general feeling.

Northcliffe to General Sir John French, Commander-in-Chief, British Expeditionary Force:

The Times,
Printing House Square,
E.C.4.
May 1, 1915.

My dear Sir John,

I very much regret intruding upon you at a moment of such tremendous strain as this, and I would not do so if I did not think it within your power greatly to add to the strength of the army and to make our chances of victory more certain.

The evil effects of the secrecy with regard to your army are assuming new form. On April 21st, Mr Lloyd George, in the House of Commons, said that there were thirty-six divisions at the front. That statement has been interpreted by the British and French publics as meaning that you are in command of 750,000 men. People are asking and writing to our newspapers to this effect: 'If Sir John French has three-quarters of a million men, why is he only occupying thirty miles of line? Why are we not able to give more substantial assistance to the French?' Early this week Lord Kitchener expressly forbade the newspapers to analyse Mr Lloyd George's statement, and you are therefore believed to have this vast army at your disposal.

A further phase is the palpable endeavour of the Government to silence the army. In the absence of some strong statement from you the Government have your friends at their mercy, because they are able to get their newspapers to say that any agitation for less secrecy is unpatriotic and playing the enemy's game.

As a further result of secrecy, Mr Asquith is able to assure the nation that your operations have never been hampered for want of ammunition.

A short and very vigorous statement from you to a private correspondent (the usual way of making things public in England) would, I believe, render the Government's position impossible, and enable you to secure the publication of that which would tell the people here the truth and thus bring public pressure upon the Government to stop men and munitions pouring away to the Dardanelles as they are at present.

Yours sincerely,
NORTHCLIFFE.

From May 1915 the searchlight of Northcliffe's press comment, dimmed though it was by Defence of the Realm regulations, began to concentrate on Kitchener. His years among the desert sands had given him some of the characteristics of the Sphinx. They had not fitted him to grapple with the intricacies of twentieth-century warfare. His extraordinary personal magnetism had attracted men from office, mine and factory, from farm, field and fireside, millions of them. 'Kitchener's chaps' crowded the kingdom's drill halls and barrack squares, while he, the mightest chap of them all, sat brooding in Whitehall on problems that eluded his solving, and on criticism from within the establishment by some who thought that his famous recruiting poster savoured undesirably of self-advertising in an army leader. It was even suggested that he had abrogated the place of the monarch in thus appealing to the nation. He distrusted the politicians and avoided dealings with them when he could. He gave orders over the head of the commander-in-chief in the field. He flinched from the gaze of the crowd. 'The people here do not understand me and I do not understand them!' he said, thumping the table, to Sir George (later Lord) Riddell, the newspaper proprietor. He ignored the reverent salutes of the police on duty outside the War Office. Within, he was known as 'K. of Chaos'. His weaknesses as War Secretary were becoming intolerably obvious to those who worked at the higher levels of responsibility. They were given wider publicity by a heavily censored message sent to *The Times* on May 15 by its military correspondent, Lieutenant-Colonel Repington, who wrote: 'The attacks (on Sunday last in the districts of Fromelles and Richebourg) were well planned and valiantly conducted. The infantry did splendidly, but the conditions were too hard. The want of an un-limited supply of high explosive was a fatal bar to our success.' That same day Northcliffe heard that one of his nephews, Lucas King, the son of his eldest sister Geraldine, had been killed in action, aged twenty. When Cecil Harmsworth, then Under Secretary at the Home Office, called on North-cliffe later that day at St. James's Place he found him 'full of the delin-quencies of the Government—the lax authority of the Prime Minister, the "muddling" of Kitchener, and the general ineptitude of the whole body' (Cecil Harmsworth's diary). 'He tells me that one of the most important of our Ministers (Winston, as I guess, but he does not say so) has been at him, trying to get him to attack McKenna [Home Secretary, 1911–15] and Runciman [President of the Board of Trade, 1914–16]. I reason with him on the folly of undermining one individual minister after another, there being no other Ministry, Coalition or otherwise, in sight.' The observations of another Harmsworth brother may be inserted here. Concerning Repington's dispatch to *The Times* and its reverberating effects, Leicester Harmsworth wrote a memorandum which recorded that Repington was uneasy because the purport of his message had been taken up as the theme of increasingly critical leading articles in the *Daily Mail*. 'Repington was strongly opposed to any public reference to this matter. He was timorous of criticism and exaggerated the disadvantages of exposure. Northcliffe and I had an interview with him at his house at Frognal on this and other subjects. He was desirous of currying favour at all times with the heads of the Army, with whom, privately, he stood in very bad personal odour. He resented being overborne by Northcliffe in this and in other matters. He was a spiteful and vindictive man. Afraid to hit out straight, but not above petty scandal, innuendo, and, indeed, misstatement. But undoubtedly a clever man.'

Disdaining Repington's prejudices, Northcliffe ordered the *Daily Mail* leader writers to keep up the pressure. They proclaimed the folly of using shrapnel against the elaborate German earthworks and wire entanglements. 'It is like using a pea-shooter.' On May 19 the leading article insisted that 'a great blunder' had been made in failing to order large quantities of high-explosive shell and in putting too much responsibility on Lord Kitchener. 'In his 65th year, and pretending to no experience of European warfare, he has had to carry on at the War Office during the greatest period of strain it has ever borne. We supported very strongly the appointment of Lord Kitchener, but, frankly, we confess that we should have done so with considerable hesitation if we could have foreseen the extravagant uses to which the Government have put him.' On May 20 the *Manchester Guardian* informed its readers that 'the present position of the country in the matter of the supply of arms, and above all of explosives, is not merely unsatisfactory: it is deplorable', and the paper denounced 'the sacrifice of thousands of precious lives as a discredit and a scandal'.

At Elmwood on those spring evenings, Northcliffe heard the thud of the guns at Ypres. The sound came over the water like an appeal from men beleaguered by hateful circumstance. 'You say you have not seen a green leaf,' he wrote to Hamilton Fyfe, the *Daily Mail* war correspondent with the Russian armies (May 11, 1915). 'I do not want to harrow your feelings by telling you how very lovely England is just now.' Two days earlier, the British commander-in-chief in France, Sir John French, had noted: 'I never remember a more bankrupt condition as regards the supply of ammunition.'

Late in the afternoon of May 20, Northcliffe arrived at Carmelite House and, giving orders that he was not to be disturbed, himself wrote the leader for the next morning's *Daily Mail*. His secretary said that when he had finished writing it in his own hand 'his face was white and set'. He went over the article with Wilson, who warned him that it might bring upon his head the utmost wrath of the authorities. Wilson mentioned prison. 'I don't care what they do to me,' Northcliffe said. 'The circulation of the

Daily Mail may go down to two and the circulation of *The Times* to one—I don't care. The thing has to be done! Better to lose circulation than to lose the war.' The leading article was sent to the printer. While he waited for proofs, Northcliffe called for the sub-editor who wrote the contents bills. For the next day, May 21, he ordered one bill for all editions: KITCHENER'S TRAGIC BLUNDER. In a few minutes a proof of the leading article was in his hands. He took it into Marlowe's room. Having read it Marlowe said to him: 'You realize, I suppose, that you are smashing the people's idol?' Northcliffe's reply was: 'I don't care. Isn't it all true?' 'Quite true,' Marlowe said, 'but it will make the public very angry. Are you prepared for the consequences?' To which Northcliffe retorted: 'I don't care twopence for the consequences. That man is losing the war!' Marlowe had lunched with a member of Sir John French's staff, home from the front. What he had to tell amply confirmed Northcliffe's views about Kitchener.

After seeing Marlowe, Northcliffe drove out to Totteridge, taking the leading article with him to read it over to his mother. She suggested certain changes of emphasis. He made them and then telephoned instructions to Carmelite House that the article was to 'go in' that night. Wickham Steed, who was with him in the evening, recorded that he looked 'more grim' than he had ever seen him. When Northcliffe proposed that *The Times* should join in the attack, Robinson, the editor, replied that he was not in full accord with Northcliffe's attitude. It was left to the *Daily Mail* to carry the day. The attack on Kitchener shocked the public, shook Whitehall, and threw Northcliffe's critics into new paroxysms of rage. At 11 a.m. that morning he telephoned to the *Daily Mail* circulation manager, Valentine Smith: 'What do you think of the contents bill this morning?' Smith answered: 'It will cause us a lot of trouble. We're bombarded with orders reducing supplies.' Northcliffe asked him how many readers the paper might lose. 'A hundred thousand at least,' was the reply. 'I don't care,' Northcliffe said in his quietest tone. 'What I wrote was true. Our men out there are being killed because there are no shells to smash down the German defences. I'm determined that they shall have them.' To Pine, his chauffeur, he remarked on his way to the office that morning: 'I wonder what Kitchener thinks of the *Daily Mail* today—I'll bet it made him jump!' He said also to Pine: 'I mean to tell the people the truth and I don't care what it costs.'

The Service Clubs of Pall Mall banished *The Times* and the *Daily Mail* from their midst. Individual readers cancelled their subscriptions. Fifteen hundred members of the London Stock Exchange burnt copies of both papers to a chorus of cheers for Kitchener and jeers for Northcliffe. The Liberal *Westminster Gazette* praised 'the manly and honourable impulse' of the stockbrokers, who, it was surmised at Carmelite House, were also working off an old score against the *Daily Mail* for having established the 'Daily Mail Exchange' to assist readers in their share transactions. The paper was denounced and burnt by members of the Liverpool Provision Exchange. Envelopes containing bits of charred *Daily Mail* were sent to Northcliffe. Similar demonstrations were staged at the Baltic Exchange in London and at the Cardiff Coal and Shipping Exchange. Northcliffe still did not abate his campaign. There was a moment when he stood on the brink of defying the censorship which refused publication of soldiers' letters supporting the 'shell shortage' allegations. He was dissuaded by colleagues who feared that he might imperil the future of the paper. He then gave orders that the letters should be sent to Lloyd George and Curzon. 'These letters will show them how the Press Bureau is keeping the truth from the people.' Untroubled by advertisers who cancelled their contracts, he never forgot the staunchness of Sir Woodman Burbidge, of Harrods, who declined to follow their example. Neither was he prejudiced by the resignation of his brother Cecil from a Government post which in the circumstances was embarrassing to him and his colleagues.

One of his many godsons, Alfred Pemberton, motored out to Totteridge with him on the day of the Stock Exchange demonstration. He afterwards wrote in a letter: 'I shall never forget his intense patriotism and his unaffected calm on that occasion.' Firm-lipped and resolved, he faced the worst that whipped-up resentment could do. 'As regards abuse, I am a pachyderm', he told St. John Hornby, of W. H. Smith's. The *Daily Mail* sale on the day of the Kitchener attack was 1,386,000 copies. By the end of the campaign the circulation had fallen by 238,000 copies. Northcliffe was visibly cast down by the public's attitude to him at that time; for him no Napoleonic declamation, as at the beginning of the Hundred Days: 'If there is one among you who wishes to kill his emperor, here I am!' He told an American journalist friend, Curtin: 'I've had a hard time of it these last few weeks. They would take away my property, if they could, and put me in the Tower.'

Nor did it matter to him that he was accused of worse than inconsistency in his efforts to displace a minister whose original appointment he had done much to procure. He was influenced not by antipathy but by events. The reports from his private intelligence corps helped to determine his actions. He had been disturbed by what he had learned about the armament makers and their 'ring'. It did not heighten his respect for the contracting departments of the State. In those months, he developed so great a force of criticism that Churchill wanted to shut down *The Times*, or, rather, transform it into an organ of official opinion, a harshly undemocratic proposition which Asquith declined to accept. Lovat Fraser, the *Times* leader writer, protested to Northcliffe about 'Churchill's absolutely impudent' desire to 'muzzle the press', and also suggested that his 'monstrous Dardanelles proposals to send *all* our battleships charging through the Narrows should debar him from any responsible office in the future'. Northcliffe had his own resources of vehemence. He was rarely impressed by other people's, and especially not by the *Punch* cartoon which showed John Bull trampling the *Daily Mail* underfoot as he patted Kitchener's shoulder, saying: 'If you need assurance, Sir, you may like to know that you have the loyal support of all decent people.'

The fall of the Liberal Government at the end of May 1915 was popularly ascribed to Northcliffe's influence, and some historians have assumed that he credited himself with being the sole instrument of change. They overlooked a leading article in the *Daily Mail* of May 26: 'The collapse of the late Government was due to the failure of Sir John French's appeals to the War Office for a larger proportion of high-explosive shells and to the resignation of Lord Fisher on account of disagreements with Mr Churchill.' Garvin of *The Observer* was sure that 'the explosion at the Admiralty would not have occurred when it did but for the general feeling about "shells"'.

Northcliffe had little cause to plume himself with satisfaction at the result. The new Coalition Government was headed by Asquith, and Kitchener likewise remained at his post. 'But he has, added to him, a Minister of Munitions in the powerful and energetic person of Mr Lloyd George', said the *Daily Mail*. Clearing the way for that new ministry was Northcliffe's most effective contribution to the politics of May 1915. When it was done, his brother Harold nursed a disappointment. Bonar Law had told him that but for Northcliffe's attitude to Kitchener, he, Rothermere, would have been the first Minister of Munitions. Writing in his diary for May 31, 1916, the British Ambassador at Paris, Lord Bertie, recorded that, seeing Lord Robert Cecil, he took the opportunity of saying that 'had it not been for Northcliffe we might still be blind to the shortage of shells'.

At Printing House Square, office disapproval of the Kitchener attacks—considered 'mischievous and unnecessary' by Robinson, the editor—was accompanied by annoyance that the campaign linked *The Times* in the public mind with the *Daily Mail*. Robinson complained: 'We are credited indiscriminately with anything the *Daily Mail* may have said.' The editor claimed that *The Times* had played a part in securing the new ministry, while doubting whether Lloyd George was the ideal head of it. As for Kitchener, when Carson protested in a speech at the Guildhall that he did not know of 'a poorer service that any man could do to this country than to attempt, even in the very smallest degree, to shake the confidence of the nation in Lord Kitchener', Northcliffe wrote to tell him: 'Your speech suggests that my newspapers have some motive in criticizing him. I do not know Kitchener personally, but for ten months he had the power of

Northcliffe, 1916

Northcliffe at Sutton Place with (*left*) Geoffrey Robinson (later Dawson), editor of *The Times*, and (*right*) John Walter.

Oliver Cromwell as to shells. Today he has the same power as to compulsion. Yet within the last few weeks he sends a circular to the newspapers suggesting I am wrong to urge this vital necessity. I do not trust Lord Kitchener, nor do the Scotch, and the North of England folk. The London mob know nothing of war and will cheer the Tichborne claimant or Jack Johnson.' In his letter he asked Carson whether anything could be done to minimize the 'impending catastrophe' at Gallipoli. A letter from Sir William Robertson Nicoll, editor of *The British Weekly*, suggesting that personal attacks on war leaders were apt to produce sympathy for those attacked, drew from Northcliffe the reply that 'in view of all the murdering that is going on, it is no time for niceties'. He told Nicoll that he was personally responsible for the attack on Kitchener, 'knowing that I should incur great unpopularity and be placing myself in a most difficult position'. He agreed that Lloyd George 'had taken his courage in both hands and shown himself to be a real man' (June 3). On June 7, Nicoll wrote again: 'I have had much conversation with Mr Lloyd George. He said that every word you wrote was absolutely correct. Also that you had performed and are performing an eminent service to the country. He told me a number of stories of the War Office which made my blood run cold.' Northcliffe wrote to Nicoll on June 16: 'I made my personal attack on Kitchener after very great consideration. The Reform Bill of 1832 was not passed until Hyde Park Railings had been broken down.' He also reiterated his admiration for Lloyd George. 'He has risked everything, including health, in an endeavour to save the armies of Flanders and the Dardanelles. The Dardanelles situation is, in my opinion, worse than that of Flanders, for the men in Gallipoli are without high explosives.' Suggestions that the shells outcry in 1915 was another 'stunt' of Northcliffe's, designed to cover the errors of the soldiers, were at variance with the truth. Northcliffe was not bothering about reputations. He was concerned with matters of life and death.

*　　*　　*

'My dear Chief,' Marlowe wrote to Northcliffe on July 12, 1915, 'the directors and chiefs of staffs of your various enterprises desire the honour of your company at luncheon on Thursday next at the Ritz Hotel at one o'clock to celebrate your birthday'—his fiftieth. Accepting, he wrote that he was much touched that his friends had thought of him 'at this very busy time in our history'. In the course of a necessarily brief celebration he was handed a beautifully illuminated 'address of felicitation' signed by the heads of departments representing 8,000 workers of every rank. The souvenir menu was graced with verses written by Claude Edward Cole-Hamilton Burton, who, under the pseudonym of 'Touchstone', contributed to the *Evening News* and the *Daily Mail* an average of three hundred sets of topical verse a year for forty years. He had sold his first verses to the newspapers as a boy at St. Paul's School.

MANY HAPPY RETURNS!

Chief, though your fiftieth summer now is reckoned,
　The oldest workers in your busy hive
Find you in energy not even second
　To that bright youth, yourself at twenty-five.
So much achieved, so much still worth achieving:
　That is a thought to give us hope and heart
Who in each new success of your conceiving
　Feel we must bear our part.

Ours be no empty wishes that are tendered
　For all your future—and may that be long!
No mere lip-service here today is rendered:
　The unseen bonds that bind us all are strong.
Therefore we pray all good may still befall you,
　Her kindliest blessings may Dame Fortune send,
And through long years to come may each still call you
　Not only Chief, but friend!

'The Chief' was pleased to be assured by several of his colleagues that he did not look his half century. He appeared to be fit and supple and eager. The familiar forelock might have been specially barbered for the occasion. His informal speech of thanks to his hosts delighted them with its happy reminiscent touches and impressed them with its 'inside information' about the war. Rarely had he been in better form, his good spirits possibly owing something to the news that the *Daily Mail* had more than regained the circulation lost by the campaign against Kitchener. Yet Geoffrey Robinson, of *The Times*, was writing in his diary of that time about 'N's lunatic rages' and 'brain-storms' and noting that Lady Northcliffe had been to see him 'about N's condition'. John Walter had written to him on July 11, regretting that a visit to the Red Cross organization in France would preclude him from joining the birthday party:

It is just five years since you and I became associated in the conduct of *The Times*. We began our association as you have recalled more than once, in circumstances of peculiar difficulty for ourselves and danger for the Paper; but the difficulties and dangers were overcome, and today we see *The Times* in a sounder position than it has enjoyed for a generation. For that we have others to thank besides ourselves, and I know you are as grateful to them as I am; but on this 50th anniversary of your birthday one feeling overlays all others in me— a feeling of gratitude to you personally for the strenuous work you have given to the service of our common property in spite of your many other pre-occupations, and of admiration for the skill with which you have brought the Paper through so many vicissitudes to its present state of excellence and prosperity. I wish my forefathers could visit Earth again to see how well their life's task has been continued.

Northcliffe acknowledged Walter's tribute with 'a thousand thanks'. Two days after the birthday lunch he wrote to his mother from the Hotel Folkestone at Boulogne-sur-Mer:

I jumped out of bed yesterday morning at 7.15 and at 8.30 a.m. was in the train at Victoria, having breakfasted, bathed, dressed, been to St. James's Place and done my office telephoning. Just the kind of tonic I like.

Got to Boulogne 12.30. Excellent lunch and sleep. At 4.30 had two hours of Red Cross investigation and excellent dinner with my correspondent, Beach Thomas. 8 p.m. bed.

That is how I spent the first day of my fifty-first year, my darling mother.

It was his fourth visit to the front. He had talked with many officers at British and French headquarters, among them Pétain, whom he described as 'one of the discoveries of the war'. He made numerous notes which were expanded into articles for his newspapers and later used in book form (*At the War*, 1916). He cracked the icy official attitude towards publicity for the war in a letter which his fellow newspaper proprietor, Riddell, held to be a document of 'historic importance' because it had been shown to Kitchener who, after reading it, agreed to the admission of war correspondents to the British sector in France. Northcliffe saw that the new war correspondents would need qualities entirely different from those of Russell, Forbes, Steevens and others who had made their journalistic reputation on earlier fields of battle. To the pen of the ready writer there would have to be joined the eye of the historian, able to piece together a coherent and accurate picture out of a vast jigsaw of confusing details.

By his personal influence with Delcassé, sometime French Foreign Minister, and with Tardieu, the editor of *Le Temps*, Northcliffe also helped to improve the British press liaison with the French forces. He recommended Hilaire Belloc to Tardieu as 'the best man' to write about the French army for British readers. Repington, Lovat Fraser and G. A. B. Dewar wrote to him pointing out that Belloc had launched 'a terrific attack' on him in his little paper, *New Witness*. Northcliffe replied: 'That sort of thing does not trouble me in the least.' To the Hon. and Rev. Edward Lyttelton, D.D., of Eton College, who complained about the *Daily Mail* in a long letter, he gave the short answer: 'I hold your attack upon editors and reporters in general to be as thoroughly unjust and ill-founded as your opinion of the proper function of the public press.' He appealed to John Walter to join in reducing the expenses of *The Times*, for which he had provided a bank guarantee of £50,000. 'There seems to be extravagance in all departments.' To A. D. Maitland, a member of the composing room staff of *The Times*, he wrote (July 4, 1915): 'I particularly loathe changes among my colleagues in the editorial, composing and machine-room departments. This war is breaking up every association of mine. Two of my secretaries, Mr Russell Wakefield and Mr Snoad, are in the army and I have had to call in the aid of a machine called the Dictaphone. We have got to realize that we are face to face to with changes the extent of which no man can foresee.' The *Daily Mirror* editor, Alex Kenealy, was ill. Northcliffe wrote to his sister, Dr Arabella Kenealy: 'If you thought I could do any good by cheering him up I would come at a few hours' notice. I will say anything that will save the dear fellow anguish', and he gave the greater part of a day to driving to Haslemere in Surrey, where Kenealy died. After the funeral at Hangleton, Sussex, he wrote to Kenealy's mother (July 8): 'I do not remember a more beautiful ceremony than that of that lovely afternoon. I felt that he could not lie in a sweeter part of England.' There was the contrast of his behaviour at that time to Wile, the former Berlin correspondent, who wrote to him: 'I am humiliated and hurt by your cruel personal allusions', and declined to renew his *Daily Mail* contract. Soon, Wile was addressing him in letters again as 'My dear Chief. . . .' Afterwards, Wile wrote about Northcliffe's 'brain-storms', saying that 'five minutes later he was invariably as gentle as a woman, forgiving as a lover, as generous as a doting parent'. Northcliffe to Balfour (July 11): 'The perpetual washing of dirty linen in public is not a grateful task, and I have carefully refrained from even hinting at what I know in any of my papers, hoping against hope that improvements would be made.' Northcliffe to Thomas Marlowe (July 27): 'Just a word of thanks, my dear Marlowe, for your wisdom at the conference yesterday in checking the foolishness of several, including me, in regard to reviving controversies with the *Daily News* at this time.'

From Dunglass, Cockburnspath, Scotland, where he had gone for a rest, he wrote to Sutton on August 4, 1915:

On the occasion of the first anniversary of the war, I write to thank you, my dear Sut, for a thousand hours of extra work and worry on your part that have enabled me to concentrate on my great effort to get the war fought efficiently. You relieve me each day of a great number of A.P. [Amalgamated Press] problems that would otherwise distract me and prevent that intense absorption by means of which I do believe I am helping to shorten the great struggle. Believe, dearest Sut, that although silent and distracted by my knowledge of the sickening blundering, I am not unmindful of the fact that had I upon my shoulders your daily and most unselfish burdens at The Fleetway

House, I could not, if the day were forty-eight hours long, attend to my national duties as efficiently as I trust I am.

A less personal but equally spontaneous acknowledgment was sent to Robinson of *The Times*, who was thanked for 'guidance and tolerance in the most terrific of years'. Northcliffe wished him to know that there was 'behind the irritability much warm gratitude for all you have done for the Cause and the Paper, for the thousand hours you have stolen from sleep and your friends, the affectionate care you have given to your devoted staff. Life is difficult for all of us just now, but especially for those within reach of the Ogre of Printing House Square.' The assistant manager, Howard Corbett, was asked to convey Northcliffe's thanks 'to all the business and mechanical men who have exhibited so much self-sacrifice this tremendous twelvemonth'. There was a separate letter for H. G. Price, Northcliffe's personal secretary. 'Some illegible words to give you a few thanks for hundreds of extra hours of drudgery since the war began. The mixture of hurry, worry, crankdom, responsibility and—yes, verily, profanity from the *Chief* telephonist—will mark this year as one of the most damnable in the annals of the Wembley branch of the family of Ap Rhys. I thank you, dear Price, for a thousand kindnesses to me since August 4th, and for your tolerance of my frequent use of high explosive.—N.'

An appeal for help had reached him that morning from the daughter of his father's friend, Seymour Lucas, R.A. He at once posted the money she needed. Josiah C. Wedgwood, M.P., wrote to tell him that he was discussing with F. E. Guest, M.P. (Treasurer of His Majesty's Household), 'the formation of a party to act as an Army party, in opposition to War Office and governmental incompetence' (August 20). A letter from Professor Hornaday, of the New York Zoo, drew on August 23 the admission: 'I have given up my "robin" experiment. I tried year after year, but did not succeed.' The grey squirrels (so called) were unfortunately flourishing. Wareham Smith, the Carmelite House advertising director, was warned (September 9): 'Your long holiday will soon be over, for I may return earlier than is expected.' To Vincent Jones, of the Anglo-Newfoundland Development Corporation, who was on war service in India (September 14): 'We think and talk a great deal of all those who have gone from our undertakings to this tremendous adventure, and, frankly, some of us who are left behind by reason of age wish we were with you.' 'We have had a hard fight,' he told Arthur Willert, the *Times* correspondent in Washington, 'but amid all the abuse the staff has been splendidly loyal. Hard words break no bones, and we are beginning to get the shells' (September 14). To a young former member of the *Times* clerical staff, who had emigrated to Australia, he wrote in reply to a request for advice about enlisting: 'Your place is by your mother's side and not at the war. Under our ridiculous voluntary system, all sorts of people go to the war who should not. In Germany and France, the son who looks after his mother does not go to the war' (September 14). To Northcliffe, who had supported Lord Roberts in his call for national service (which might have prevented the war), the voluntary system was more than ridiculous, it was tragic, an act of community foolishness which would cost the race of Englishmen dear in the years to come. He had sent his mother to stay in the West Country. 'Not that she is afraid of Zeppelins,' Cecil wrote. 'Alfred is afraid for her.'

'With gratitude for opportunities given over 20 years', Reginald Nicholson resigned his managerial post on *The Times* that September, severing a close personal connection with Northcliffe. Nicholson had taken an appointment in the Ministry of Munitions; later he became Coalition Member of Parliament for Doncaster. His successor, Howard Corbett, was ordered by Northcliffe to make rigid economies. Newsprint, which in 1915 had cost £9 6s. 8d. a ton, had jumped to £25 13s. 4d. a ton. When Pomeroy Burton, at Carmelite House, suggested wage cuts to meet the rising costs of newspaper production, Northcliffe replied: 'The first thing is for the directors to reduce their own income'—he was himself preparing to resign his directorship of the Amalgamated Press. 'I desire to be relieved of some of my burden.' Elinor Glyn, the novelist, declared her admiration for his 'courage in promoting England's interests above party politics', even though the *Daily Mail* had 'always been unkind and belittling' to her work. Northcliffe to Frederick Bowater (September 28): 'When a man is on affectionate terms with his paper agent after five-and-twenty-years' association, it says a very great deal for the paper agent. You know how warmly our family regard yours.'

★ ★ ★

'Thank God, there are some men of decision left in this country still,' the Quartermaster-General of the British Army, Sir John Cowans, wrote under seal to Northcliffe after seeing him for the first time in October 1915. 'Sir C. Monro has your letter re the Dardanelles. It is a truly amazing document!' General Monro was about to leave for Gallipoli to take over from the deposed commander-in-chief, General Sir Ian Hamilton. He was also to make an independent inspection and report, his first task. That step had been urged 'with great respect' on Lloyd George by Northcliffe in a letter in which he said that he had heard 'with the greatest distress' that the Cabinet had decided to increase the Dardanelles force.

Northcliffe had been worrying about the Dardanelles affair since August. He was apprehensive about the situation there being complicated by the failure of the Russians, who, he presciently believed, would be out of the war within a year. He and Wilson of the *Daily Mail* went several times to London railway termini to see reinforcements leaving for Gallipoli. 'A very touching sight,' Wilson had written on September 1. 'Large body of men drawn up on the platform. An immense crowd of women, many weeping. Atmosphere of awed silence, as of people present at a grandiose funeral ceremony. Few who leave for the Dardanelles have much hope of returning. The men were fine. They went off singing and cheering.' Northcliffe was greatly moved by those scenes. Wilson said that he took the fate of the men at Gallipoli 'very much to heart'. When an Australian journalist, Keith Murdoch, arrived in London after looking into postal conditions among the troops there, Northcliffe at once got in touch with him. Murdoch's report on what he had seen and his poor opinion of the generalship of the Dardanelles campaign was the document which Cowans had described as 'truly amazing'. As an eye-witness account, it was not accurate in all its observations and it was possibly unfair to individuals. 'This unfortunate expedition has never been given a chance. It required a great leader. It required self-sacrifice on the part of the staff as well as that sacrifice so wonderfully and liberally made on the part of the soldiers. It has had none of these things.' Allowing for its defects, the report showed that the worst features of the Crimean War of fifty years before were being repeated on a larger scale at Gallipoli. With the help of Northcliffe and Lloyd George, Murdoch was able to place his report before the Cabinet. Northcliffe wrote to him (September 30): 'If I were in possession of the information you have, involving as it does the lives of thousands of your compatriots and mine, I should not be able to rest until the true story of this lamentable adventure was so well known as to force immediate steps to be taken to remedy the state of affairs. The matter has haunted me ever since I learned about it.'

Northcliffe was more intolerant of what he called the 'cable-butchering' censorship at that period than at any other during the war. Unable to publish news of the operations, except such as was officially issued, he took the risk of denying deceptively optimistic news which created the illusion of success where none was or, as he believed, could be. There was talk of prosecuting him. Wilson, as the *Daily Mail* leader writer, noted in his diary: 'Our arrest was being considered.' The Cabinet's position was weakened by the threatened resignation of Carson, who was dissatisfied with the conduct of the war. He had gone to Kitchener for vital information. 'Only on the 9th October, 1915, did he get to the dreadful truth about the Dardanelles. On that day—it was a Sunday—Kitchener took him into his room at the War Office and pointed to a box in the corner. "There," he said, "you will find Hamilton's dispatches, which you so much want to see. You can spend the week-end over them, and damned unpleasant reading you will find them",' and Carson's biographer added: 'It was thus that Carson made his acquaintance with that terrible story which later he was to pass on to the Dardanelles Commission.'* Two days earlier, Northcliffe had sent an equally revealing American report on Gallipoli to Murray of Elibank, to whom he wrote: 'Long experience has taught me that it is useless offering my costly and very accurate service of private news to the Government. They will apparently take anything optimistic from anybody, but will not listen to anything regarding the Gallipoli catastrophe. In the hope that you may be able to make some impression on any one of them, I send the enclosed. I do not suppose the information will have the least effect, but if you happen to be talking to any member of the Cabinet you might mention it.' Lord Murray of Elibank replied to Northcliffe on October 12: 'Your offer to allow the Government to see your secret information will, I feel sure, be of immense assistance, and I am very happy to be the medium in transmitting it to them. I think you have already rendered incalculable service to them and the country in bringing Mr Murdoch in touch with them, and the statement of the American military attaché has really stirred them up. I gave Grey and Ll. G. copies.' Northcliffe told Philip Witham, from whom he leased Sutton Place (October 7): 'I am concentrating every moment of my time trying to get our poor men out of the Gallipoli trap. If they are not removed in a few weeks they will be destroyed. They are entirely dominated by the Turkish guns. Their losses have been appalling.' His brother Cecil went to see him at St. James's Place on October 12 and wrote in his diary: 'I find him in bed flanked by a telephone on either side and partially submerged under piles of newspapers. He was to have told me of fresh Cabinet disruptions but a War Correspondent from the Western front and another visitor occupy his attention and I hear nothing. N. is more dreary than ever about the war. There is nothing for it but a brand new government! What government and where from?'

Northcliffe to Sir Edward Carson:

Printing House Square, E.C.
16th October, 1915.

Dear Sir Edward,—At the risk of incurring your perpetual displeasure, I cannot refrain from again writing to you about the Dardanelles.

Since, many months ago, I communicated with you (and long before with some of your colleagues), the appalling waste of splendid life to no purpose has continued. Ever since I saw you a few days ago I have had further news of fresh horrors.

The Indian Mutiny made a mark on public memory for fifty years. It requires

* Ian Colvin, *Life of Lord Carson*, Gollancz, 1936.

no imagination to realize that the Dardanelles tragedy, which the Australians and New Zealanders are determined to reveal to the world, will be for all time a theme of universal discussion.

Yours sincerely,
NORTHCLIFFE

A correspondent of the Sydney *Sun* wrote in 1921 that he had been in Northcliffe's room at *The Times* during the Dardanelles campaign, when Northcliffe, 'having paced up and down the floor like a caged lion, threw himself into a big chair and asked in a tense tone: "How are those brave Australians to be got away from Gallipoli?" He repeated: "We must get these Aussies away. We must!" ' His constant concern about what was going on at Gallipoli, the correspondent wrote, was 'a splendid service to Australia'.

Carson carried out his threat to resign. His departure from the Government loosened an already unwieldy Cabinet structure. Northcliffe spoke of him at that time as 'a stout-hearted fellow'. Robert Donald, editor of the *Daily Chronicle*, quoted Asquith as having said that Carson had 'shown no initiative and made no helpful suggestions' during his six months as a member of the administration. Nonetheless, his going had a sequel of change which, while imperfectly illustrating the processes of cause and effect, was important alike for Government and country.

Wilson of the *Daily Mail* recorded that one of Carson's last contributions to Cabinet discussion at that time was an argument which defeated a proposal of Sir John Simon, the Home Secretary, to suppress the *Daily Mail* for printing a map headed 'The Road to India' as a reminder to readers of the 'issues at stake in that distant theatre of hostilities'. The Liberal press sought to make a crime out of its publication. 'If the Kaiser had paid £100,000 for that pro-German map it would have been worth it' (*The Star*, October 12, 1915). Northcliffe 'was accused by members of the Government of bringing Bulgaria into the war by the act of printing this map' (Wilson). The House of Commons gave up a seven hours' sitting to the matter, Simon pressing home the charge that the map 'put into the hands of the enemy material by which they might influence the East against us'. What Simon and his supporters had overlooked was that the map had been printed in the *Continental Daily Mail* with the approval of the French authorities whose censorship was not less strict than the British. Northcliffe's real offence was that, without any beating about the bush, he publicized ministerial blunderings, revealing to the nation facts which were known to all and sundry in the fighting zones but which were studiously withheld from the people at home.

Writing to his editor about Northcliffe's 'tearing, raging anti-government agitation' at the end of 1915, an American newspaper man in

London, Edward Price Bell of the Chicago *Daily News*, made the comment: 'He does not exact as the price of his friendship the servility of his friends.' Bell had been a friend of Northcliffe's for many years. The 'stories' that he had sent to his newspaper about Northcliffe were sometimes critical of him, 'yet he is perfectly friendly to me'. Bell now wished to know why a 'story' that he had sent about Northcliffe's attitude to conscription had not been printed. 'He is a great disturbing force here.' Bell's editor had given it as his opinion that if the United States had been facing 'the serious outlook which faces the British Empire we should resort to conscription if necessary to win our fight'. In reply, Bell summarized the British political attitude to the question. 'The Unionists, generally, think that conscription eventually will be necessary. The Liberals think that conscription will never be necessary.' Meanwhile, the British press generally, including Northcliffe's part of it, was 'heartily supporting Lord Derby's scheme to bring Britain through the crisis without resort to conscription'.

As an advocate, long before the war, of national service, Northcliffe regarded the appeals for volunteers with deep concern for the future. Wilson said that he remarked many times: 'They are taking the cream of our youth', and referred in that context to mistakes made during the American Civil War when volunteering 'ground up the choicest seed-corn of the nation'. Wilson said that the reference was taken from a passage in a book about the Civil War called *The Soldier in Battle*, wherein it was recorded that the voluntary method of recruiting consumed 'the young, the patriotic, the intelligent, the generous, the brave, wasting the best moral, social and political elements of the republic, and leaving the cowards, shirkers, egotists and money-makers to stay at home and procreate their kind'. Northcliffe concurred in that estimate of a system which he had family reasons for resenting, if no other.

He was altogether sardonic about the official advertising campaigns which came into play as the volunteer waves diminished. He thought that the freakish posters with their exclamatory inscriptions, 'Does the Cap Fit? If So, Wear It', and so on, were vulgar and ineffectual and, what he particularly objected to, possibly injurious to allied and neutral goodwill. In any case, the results were unsatisfactory in that such appeals called out some of the best types of men in industry, leaving behind them 'slackers' and 'firebrands' whose sense of responsibility to the future was as nebulous as their sense of duty to the country. Northcliffe now blamed Kitchener for taking the 'wrong' men as well as for not supplying the 'right' shells. Even so, Lord Derby, who was in charge of the national recruiting scheme, wrote his personal appreciation of services rendered: 'I am really grateful for all your help' (October 25) and again: 'I am indeed most deeply grateful' (December 12).

'I hate being unjust, I really did think Mr Masterman [Chancellor of the Duchy of Lancaster] was pro-German,' Northcliffe wrote to Hedley Le Bas, joint secretary of the National Relief Fund, on December 6. 'I shall take care that my staff are informed of what you say.' His impatience with the politicians of the period was given rein in a memorandum to Marlowe the next day: 'I wish you would not start "booming" Churchill again. Why do you do it? We got rid of the man with difficulty and he is trying to come back. "Puffing" will bring him back.' Winston Churchill had been dropped from the Government in the May reshuffle. 'I am finished!' he had said to Riddell, the *News of the World* proprietor, on May 20. Northcliffe, and many others, held Churchill responsible for the Dardanelles débâcle, which might have been one of the brilliant strokes of the war.

In the last months of the year Northcliffe became still more fiercely critical of the official handling of affairs. He knew Asquith's weaknesses and despised them, while respecting his finest qualities. But the area of his discontent had been deepened by information privately supplied to him in December about 'a ministerial intrigue of a most mischievous character', involving Lord Haldane; Lord Crewe, the Lord Privy Seal; Sir John Simon, the Home Secretary; Walter Runciman, President of the Board of Trade; Sir Eyre Crowe, the Permanent Under Secretary for Foreign Affairs; and in some degree Sir Edward Grey, the Foreign Secretary. Those persons were alleged to be conspiring to nullify the blockade of Germany. 'The arch-conspirator is Lord Haldane, whose influence at the Foreign Office is now paramount. Sir Edward Grey appears to have come under it absolutely. The Foreign Secretary has been spending most, if not all, of his time during the past week at Lord Haldane's office, or house, or both' (December 13). Geoffrey Robinson of *The Times* had 'got wind of' the facts and they were receiving the 'vigilant attention' of *The Times*. Sir Edward Carson was also watching the situation.

Northcliffe's private informant told him that 'Grey was particularly lachrymose on the subject of the starving German women and children'. Even more privately, Northcliffe himself was showing similar humanitarian sympathies, though his newspapers denounced them in other people. He was sending money into Germany by an American journalist for the benefit of his widowed Irish aunts who had been married to Germans. It was a serious risk, containing the possibilities of disaster to his public reputation. He took it for the sake of his mother, anxious about the fate of her sisters. To the American journalist he wrote: 'Frau Borntraeger and Frau Selss are two of my mother's sisters, widows, who were married to Germans. Ask them how they are. They will be a little cautious in speaking at first, until you tell them that you come from their nephew Alfred. Give them £125.' The money was to be handed to Frau

Selss, whose husband, Professor Selss, had been a naturalized Englishman. 'That is why I send the money to her. It is illegal to send money to Germans, therefore I cannot send anything to Frau Borntraeger. I am taking a little risk, but I do not think the Government would mind. Tell them that we are afraid the war will last for many years, as the English are determined to stop this sort of thing once and for all.'

Occasionally, the *Daily Mail* received letters from readers who suspected his German connections. Similar letters reached *John Bull*. The editor of that lively if sometimes scurrilous publication, Horatio Bottomley, prepared a stock answer to such correspondents: 'I had the privilege of knowing Lord Northcliffe's father—a finer English gentleman I never knew.' When he sent a copy to Northcliffe, he received in reply the exhortation: 'I wish you would not be such a fatuous optimist about the war.' Several citizens of Doncaster who were in the habit of meeting in a small wine merchant's for a drink and talk were surprised at being asked by a representative of the eminent London legal firm of Lewis & Lewis whether one among them had stated that Lord Northcliffe was a German. 'You will not hear any more of the matter', Reginald Ward Poole, Sir George Lewis's partner, wrote to Northcliffe (January 20, 1916). 'S—— is thoroughly frightened, and so is C——, who signed the statement, copy of which I enclose.' Towards the end of that year, Princess Blücher was dining with the German Foreign Minister, Baron von Jagow, in Berlin, when he remarked, 'suddenly in the middle of the dinner: "Is there nobody who will shoot Lord Northcliffe? He is his own country's worst enemy, as well as ours. He is more answerable for all this bloodshed and carnage than any other single individual throughout the world".'*

Northcliffe to Lord Knutsford:

The Times,

Printing House Square, E.C.

December 23, 1915.

Dear Knutsford,—I had intended to go to the House on Monday. Had I done so I should have wasted some three hours. Those three hours I devoted to a conversation with one of my spies from Germany.

If the time comes when I feel that I can do any good by going to the House of Lords, I will go there, but I hope I am not immodest in suggesting that, at the present time, my printing presses (which demand all my attention) are doing more good than could any vocal effort on my part.

Yours ever,

NORTHCLIFFE

* *An English Wife in Berlin.* Dutton, New York, 1920.

Preparing to leave the *Times* office early on Christmas Eve, he dictated a brief note to Massingham, editor of *The Nation*. 'I am not anxious about the ultimate end of the war. What does trouble me is the holocaust of those splendid men.' After talking to Northcliffe at *The Times* two days previously Massingham had written: 'I should like to say that I think you have not had justice done you in respect of your general motives, considering all the facts you have known. . . . I hope you won't think this insincere or intrusive. I only say what I feel.' With which compliment from an old adversary of the pen, Northcliffe went off to spend Christmas with his mother at Totteridge.

Northcliffe to Geoffrey Robinson:

22, St James's Place.
S.W.
December 30th, 1915.

My dear Robin,—Nearly every day in some part or other of *The Times* appears a puff of Kitchener. Twice this week he has been quite unnecessarily referred to in a leading article, and there is nearly always something about him somewhere in the rest of the paper. Lloyd George assures me that this man is the curse of the country. He gave me example after example on Sunday night of the loss of life due to this man's ineptitude. Is it not possible to keep his name out of the paper?

Yours sincerely,
N.

Chapter Eighteen

Fleet Street and Downing Street

HISTORY has not yet balanced England's account for the year 1916. That it was a year of fate for the English people has never been in dispute. What has not been finally determined is whether the sacrificial English blood flow in its great summer battles was genetically calamitous or whether racial repair has been effected by the pre-natal clinics and the bulk-purchased orange juice of the Welfare State. The Somme offensives, which began with an earth-shaking roar on July 1, 1916, were the last demonstration of what many people then and since have thought to be the follies of the voluntary system of recruitment. They completed the despoliation which had already deprived the future of much of the nation's best manhood. Indiscriminate enlistments were followed by indiscriminate slaughter.

Like everyone else who was in touch with the larger affairs of the world, Northcliffe was stretching mind and nerves in a constant wearing effort to comprehend that which was of a magnitude to defy comprehension. Moreover, he often had to appear to be 'in the know' when he was not and the fact that he did not have constant access to the inner councils that were trying to impose a pattern on the grand flux of events was as great a strain as having to keep to himself some of the disturbing news that came his way. 'There is no Prime Minister,' he told Massingham (January 17, 1916). 'The views of people with such responsibilities as you and I are necessarily crippled by lack of information. The Prime Minister gives us no lead.'

An anonymous letter, postmarked Hackney, threatened him with death by shooting 'if the Compulsion Bill is passed'. Concerning that burning topic he told the *Daily Mail* staff that there were too many 'puffs' of Lord Derby, who was head of the recruiting campaigns. 'I have done my share in creating national idols who have turned out to be no good and we ought to learn wisdom' (January 21, 1916). He complained in another communique to the office that the word 'scandal' was being used too often. 'There is nothing scandalous in what we call "The Taxicab Scandal". "Difficulty" or "Shortage" would be more to the point. "Scandal" is a very serious word, and should rarely be used.' Severe newsprint rationing meant that newspapers were about to be drastically reduced in size. 'It will mean going back to the cult of brevity which we started twenty years ago.' In his message to the *Daily Mail* of February 24, he wrote: 'What with the price of paper and the calling up of the married men, it looks as if we shall soon have nothing to print, and no one to print it.'

Strenuously determined to acquaint himself with all aspects of the great struggle, Northcliffe went off with Wickham Steed at the end of February to see the fighting at Verdun, against which focal point of the French front the Germans had opened one of the most terrible assaults in the annals of war. Getting there proved to be an adventurous business. U-boats in the Channel compelled a last-minute change to a small ship. Steed wrote in his *Through Thirty Years*: 'I had never travelled with Northcliffe before, and his cheerfulness and patience under discomfort won my admiration and that of our companions. There were but three berths left. He insisted on tossing for them, and, having lost the toss, curled himself up in a mackintosh on a seat.' The party's way through to Verdun from Le Havre was obstructed by the French military authorities, until an appeal was made by telegraph in Northcliffe's name to the Prime Minister, Briand. They drove on in a car with an engine that had constantly to be cooled by snow dug from ditches. At Bar-le-Duc, where refugees from Verdun had overrun accommodation and food supplies, Northcliffe and Steed settled down for a night in the dining-room of the Hotel du Commerce. 'On the floor in a corner I discovered a quarter of a loaf of stale bread,' Steed wrote. 'Cleaning it with our pocket knives, we hacked it into small pieces. Northcliffe excited the wonder of a heavy-eyed and slatternly maid by anointing his crust with some Worcester sauce which he detected in the recesses of an otherwise empty cupboard. And so to bed at 3 a.m.' They finished their journey by 'thumbing' a lift to General Pétain's headquarters in a French military lorry. Northcliffe climbed up beside the driver, whom he recognized as a garage proprietor from Biarritz.

Steed wrote in his account of their experiences that nothing surprised him more than Northcliffe's physical stamina. 'Though not an exceptionally strong man, he had borne exceptional strain and fatigue, with little sleep and less food, from the Thursday afternoon until 2.30 a.m. on Sunday, his mind being constantly on the alert and his pencil continually jotting down impressions in his notebook', and Steed said that no better companion in an adventure could be desired. He noticed, at the same time, that Northcliffe's mind 'worked curiously', that they both saw the same things, but while Steed saw them in a matter-of-fact way, Northcliffe saw and recorded them, unconsciously, Steed believed, 'in a form which the public would understand'. Steed decided that Northcliffe received impressions through a medium 'which might be called the public eye in miniature'. He said that Northcliffe's mind was wholly governed by an intense determination to help in winning the war.

All his observations were, in a sense, automatically censored by that resolve. He was remarkably, sometimes uncannily, intuitive, and very sensitive to atmosphere. He caught, as I caught in a minor degree, the exhilaration of the defenders of Verdun. The whole region seemed to vibrate with magnetism. The effect upon me did not wear off for weeks.

With Steed's help, Northcliffe produced a dispatch of six thousand words on the defence of Verdun. He had himself dictated much of it, supplying the background for Steed's military information. At the end of one of their relays of dictation, Northcliffe collapsed, unable to speak. Completing the dispatch by himself, Steed wrote as its conclusion: 'Verdun is unlikely to be taken.' It appeared in the London newspapers on March 6 and was reproduced in three thousand British, French, American, Italian and neutral journals. Men had come to believe that Verdun must fall. Northcliffe's dispatch heartened the Allies and, in the end, proved to be a correct forecast.

Not only the sudden sharp illness but what he saw in and around Verdun left its mark on Northcliffe. He had seen the horror of war in the eyes of men who had suffered in ways that were new in human experience. He returned to London in what some of those closest to him thought to be an overwrought state. He was so easily exasperated that his family and friends began to worry about him again. A scene at a Carmelite House news conference when he turned savagely on Marlowe for his deafness sent editorial men back to their rooms feeling that 'something is wrong with the Chief'. Sitting in his car outside the Hotel Metropole in Northumberland Avenue, where Lloyd George had just installed his new Ministry of Munitions, Northcliffe called out to Winston Churchill, who was entering the building: 'Hullo, Winston! Are you after Ll. G.'s job?' Pine, the chauffeur, said that 'Mr Churchill looked annoyed'. A day or so later Northcliffe received a small package from Churchill. It contained the ivory statuette of Napoleon which Northcliffe had given him not long before. With it was a letter of rebuke intimating that Churchill could 'no longer keep it as the gift of a courteous gentleman'. Northcliffe wrote to apologize. 'Had I thought that the remark would have wounded you, I would not for a moment have made it; and I ask you to accept an expression of my regret for having said it.'

He had been worrying about the air defences of London, which he believed would shortly be tested by daylight raids. He thought it necessary to inform the Colonial Secretary, Bonar Law (January 30): 'You may or may not know that I was the person who introduced the aeroplane to the War Office—with no result. The prizes we offered years ago for short and long flights caused me to be regarded as a lunatic by many people. If I thought it wise to express in *The Times* my views on the air defence of London, I should be thought as mad as I was considered to be ten years ago.' He wrote again to Law (February 16) in the hope of stimulating official interest in 'the best aero engine in the world', the Rolls-Royce, taking care to disclaim any financial connection with the company. 'We are not getting a full output. I am deeply concerned.' In that frame of mind he wrote also to Georges Clemenceau, of France, warning him that a British parliamentary committee, about to visit Paris, included a number of members 'who do not like the vigorous prosecution of the war' (February 19).

Lady Northcliffe wrote to Sutton (April 1):

The Chief strikes *me* as being far from what he should be—*much* too excitable and beginning his old habit of abusing his friends at his own table if they venture to disagree with him. It is most painful—and he looks puffy and generally wrong and is not very wise about his diet. I wish we could persuade him to see a doctor or in any case to take a *real* holiday where he could be quiet and regain his balance! It worries me a great deal.

Yet he showed no untoward symptom when he addressed the Sylvan Debating Club at the Tavistock Hotel, Covent Garden, on the evening of April 10. 'A larger attendance than I have ever seen at the Club,' Cecil wrote in his diary. 'Alfred speaking on his experiences during 6 visits to the Front and on the shortcomings of the two successive War Governments.' A few days later Cecil reported to Alfred that 'sitting next Carson on the Front Opposition Bench, he told me of the P.M.'s fine courtesy and great patience in the Cabinet but also of his utter lack of initiative' (April 19). Cecil had talked with Margot Asquith, who 'discussed excitedly Northcliffe's attacks on the P.M. She thinks that N. has some personal grudge—a mistaken impression I did my best to dispel.' Northcliffe to H. W. Massingham (April 26): 'You did me an injustice in last Friday's *Nation* in suggesting that I have some personal vendetta with Mr Asquith. The statement that I have some personal quarrel with him was invented by the oriental Donald of the *Daily Chronicle*. I distrust Mr Asquith because he obviously distrusts himself.'

His correspondence, heavier in 1916 than in the previous year, amply confirmed his impatience with the management of the war, but disclosed no exceptional nervous tensions. He found time to urge privately the claim to official recognition of his old rival Arthur Pearson, whose efforts for the war blinded were to bring him so much respect. Coupled with his recommendation of Pearson, he put forward the name of A. J. Wilson, his cycling colleague of the Coventry days, a champion of the deaf. 'Both are really remarkable men', he told Lloyd George. When Katharine Wright appealed to him again to support her brothers' reputation against their detractors, he replied (April 30): 'Your sweet letter touched my wife and me greatly. . . . The fact is beyond question that your brother made the first aeroplane that flew, and flew it. No specious arguments can get away from that truth.'

To friends and colleagues who thought that he should or would take a more direct part in the conduct of national affairs he gave an appreciative ear while disavowing all ambition to shine in the political sphere. Like Macbeth, he was apparently content to wait for chance to crown him. To Sir John Willison, the *Times* correspondent in Canada (April 22):

I have no anxiety to enter the Government. I believe that the rotary press is more powerful than the portfolio. If I can be of any service at any time and am invited I will enter the Cabinet, but not such a Cabinet as the existing one, which is composed of a number of faint hearts and one or two active pro-Germans. I hate the thought of the wastage of the splendid British, Canadian and Australian lives that has been involved by these people's compromise. Unless we can get rid of Asquith, Kitchener, Balfour and Bonar Law, we shall lose the war.

Hooper, of *The Encyclopædia Britannica*, had written from New York on April 18, urging him to 'deliver five or six lectures' in America, assuring him: 'There is no man in Great Britain who would get as good an audience and respect paid to his opinions as yourself. Every newspaper would give you an amount of space they would give no other living man, with the exception of the King', and Hooper hoped that it would be understood that he was 'not writing in any spirit of flattery'. A threat of resignation by Lloyd George had produced another crisis in Whitehall. Austin Harrison, editor of the *English Review*, asked Northcliffe to believe that Asquith and his friends kept the Coalition together 'in fear of you—jealousy. They fear that if the Coalition falls you may be asked to form or join a Government and they would rather lose the war than see you in office' (April 20). Northcliffe to Austin Harrison: 'I think that you over-estimate the Government's fear of the influence of my newspapers.' The Bishop of Birmingham (Dr Russell Wakefield) hoped that 'before long we may see you *directly* responsible for the policy of this country'. Northcliffe to the Bishop of Birmingham (April 21): 'When I am really wanted and asked for I will come forward. The time is not yet. We have much tribulation before us.' H. G. Wells, from Easton Glebe, Dunmow: 'I think you are playing a supremely useful part in goading on our remarkable government, but I do not see any alternative to it. I've some faith in Lloyd George, but the utmost contempt for Carson.' Wells proceeded to the proposition that 'the ultimate strength and resources of a nation lie in the sanity, energy and abundance of means of education, discussion, research and training (which a certain unheeded minority has been dinning into the English mind for forty years, from Matthew Arnold to me)'. He predicted that 1930–40 would see the downfall of the British system. It would not be averted by 'a new Air Ministry or anything of that sort'. Salvation would only come through 'a *revolution*. . . . And there is nobody in the country with the imagination, the instruments, and the prestige for revolution except yourself. The war has brought you into open and active conflict with the system as it is.' He suggested that Northcliffe had 'drifted into this position through the logic of events', rather than having deliberately taken it up. 'What you don't seem yet to publicly admit is that to quarrel with one system is to incur the obligation of starting another. You could make that formulation possible.'

Replying on April 22 to Wells's undated letter, Northcliffe considered that Wells did Carson an injustice. 'Here is a man without any personal ambition who is willing to devote the scant remains of his energy and health, not to any personal ambitions, but to the incessant need for *quickness*.' For himself, Northcliffe said that he had found that 'the only way to get anything done is to attack the Coalition incident by incident, muddle by muddle'. He assured Wells: 'I am very much with you as to the future, though I see it probably not as clearly as you do. Your thoughts help tremendously', and he brought in that expediently useful phrase which contrasted the printing press with the political portfolio. Wells then took up the subject of an alternative Government. 'The trouble is that there are no sufficiently big *reputations*. There are plenty of men who could make a ten times better government, but because they are not party politicians the press has not *built up their reputations* in the public mind. Take such men as Lord Montagu, Sir Mark Sykes, Sir Harry Johnston, for example. If any considerable section of the press decided to make a list of a score or so of *men of tomorrow* and noticed them unostentatiously, steadily and fully, an alternative government *would* follow quite naturally.' Northcliffe's comment on May 8 was: 'It is only when one looks through the world with the microscope of a newspaper that one sees how reputations are made. Unfortunately, owing to the manipulation of the press by self-advertising quacks the wrong men often rise to the surface. You must have noticed that in the scientific world as well as in politics.'

Self-advertising was one of the topics on which the editor of *The Times* had strong views and, according to a memorandum of his, he stated them unequivocally to Northcliffe on May 14 of that year. Northcliffe had given instructions that any public reference to his newspapers should be reported in them. 'The whole of the Northcliffe Press is climbing at a pace which proves that the public are realizing that we are right' (message to the *Daily Mail* staff, April 22, 1916). Night editors interpreted Northcliffe's instruction on that subject too personally, putting his name up in bold type over his dispatches from the Front. The editor of *The Times* reproached his assistants for using 'sycophantic headlines' about Northcliffe during his absence. He preferred to believe that Northcliffe was suffering from 'a bad bout of megalomania'. His comments to Northcliffe had evidently been frank and Northcliffe, he acknowledged, 'took it all very well'. Northcliffe to the *Daily Mail* office (May 19): 'I was vexed this morning to find an astounding puff of myself on the Home Page. I do not know how these things get into the paper and I shall be glad if the rule I laid down long ago is followed, namely, that nothing is to appear in which my name or the name of my family occurs without its having been submitted to me, unless, of course, it be merely a reference to an attendance at some public meeting or a speech referring in any way to myself when it would be too late at night for me to be consulted. This particular puff is an outrageous and dishonest thing because the article I wrote has very little reference to the Battle of Verdun. The paragraph is headed offensively "Lord Northcliffe at Verdun".' Robinson, the editor, said that he had told Northcliffe that the attacks on individual public men in conjunction with personal advertisement suggested that he, Northcliffe, 'wanted a job'. According to Robinson, Northcliffe answered that he 'wanted no job except to take part in the final Peace Conference'.

Lloyd George's confidant, Riddell, wrote at the end of May: 'L.G. never tells me about his meetings with Northcliffe, but I am sure they are in daily contact.' Cecil Harmsworth recalled it as 'a period of something like real friendship between them—they were collaborating for a settlement of the Irish problem'. Cecil had gone to Dublin on family business. A telegram from Northcliffe asked him to 'track down William M. Murphy, owner of the *Daily Independent*', whom Alfred and Ll. G. regarded as an essential element 'in the negotiations now going on for a settlement of the Irish question'. Cecil did not record that Northcliffe had initiated the collaboration with Lloyd George, who had been charged by the Cabinet to 'take over' the Irish problem on the suggestion of Joseph Devlin, the Nationalist Member of Parliament for West Belfast. It was Northcliffe who advised Devlin to propose Lloyd George as the negotiator.

With its circulation of 120,000 a day, William Murphy's newspaper was an important possible ally. It severely criticized the Home Rule Bill and maintained an attitude of aloofness from the Nationalist Party.

'Clearly,' Cecil wrote, 'Murphy and the *Independent* cannot be left out of any proposals for "settling" Ireland.'

Northcliffe to Cecil Harmsworth:

> 22, St. James's Place,
> S.W.
> May 24, 1916.

My dear Cecil,—Ll.G. asked me to ask you to remain in Ireland for three or four days, and he has been asked by the Government to try and effect a settlement of Irish affairs; and the Irish leaders have all been at him and seem willing to accept his ruling. One of the keys of the situation is Mr Murphy of the *Irish Independent*—a man for whom I have a profound admiration. I have telegraphed asking him to come to London, and I believe if he and I got together we could settle this damnable business; but it needs to be settled *now*, otherwise the hot-heads will get to work, both in Ulster and elsewhere. You may go and see him and tell him this, if you like and think well of my plan, *but what I want to do is to get him* to London.

> ALFRED

Reputed to be 'the ablest business man south of the Boyne', Murphy was an outstanding personality who reciprocated Northcliffe's admiration. Many years before, Northcliffe had supported him in an enterprise to which he owed his subsequent business fortune and political influence. Northcliffe now looked for his aid in the pacification of Ireland. But Murphy's will was as inflexible as his manners were polished. He made it clear to Cecil that he had 'no intention of putting his great business interests at the mercy of a peasant parliament representing only the south of Ireland'. He went to London only because Northcliffe wished to see him, he told Cecil. But he remained firm against the sorceries of Lloyd George and Northcliffe's friendly pressures. The negotiations came to nothing and no one was more disappointed than Northcliffe. He had hoped, if not believed, that destiny had reserved for him a leading part in the last act of a drama of internecine history.

'After walking in the rose garden with Mum,' he wrote on July 19, 1916, 'left overburdened with luggage for Charing Cross', *en route* for the battle fronts of France and Italy and to the neutral regions of Spain and Switzerland. His official purpose was to report on the administration of *The Times* Red Cross Fund. But he took far more notes than that task required and out of them came a flow of messages for *The Times* and the *Daily Mail* touching on various sides of the war and the personalities of some of the leaders.

Northcliffe to his mother:

> 20th July, 1916.

Sweet Mother,—I was wafted from your rose garden to the delightful chateau some thirty miles from Boulogne of General Sir Arthur Sloggett,

Chief of the medical arrangements of the whole Army, with 95,000 beds under him.

I can't write often, my darling, but you know I think of you many times each day.

Going on to British general headquarters, his first concern was to ask for facilities for sending 'a direct and immediate' telegram to London. Assuming it to be a message of business importance, Brigadier-General Charteris, of the headquarters staff, agreed to send it over a special line. Northcliffe wrote out in large capital letters a message of love to his mother. Recording the incident, Charteris noted that 'Northcliffe was amazingly outspoken in his comments on people at home; he regards Asquith as quite played out, Lloyd George as only out for his own career, but says that the latter has more vim than all the rest put together'.★ Meeting the new commander-in-chief, Sir Douglas Haig, for the first time, Northcliffe himself noted: 'I felt happier than when I saw General French at St. Omer.' Charteris wrote: 'A great deal depends on how Northcliffe and D.H. get on together: they have very little in common.' Northcliffe talked with Rawlinson of the 4th Army; Trenchard of the Royal Flying Corps, 'earnest, intelligent, anxious'; Sir Julian Byng, commanding the Canadian Corps; and Birdwood, commander of the Australian and New Zealand forces: 'deepset eyes, close cropped head, a fire eater'. It was Haig who most impressed him: 'Unusual facial angle, delicate features, strong chin, strong hands, no mysteries, no military swank, always at his maps and calculations.' Headquarters was in a house still partly occupied by a French family. He was touched to see Haig in his room one evening, 'bending over his maps', while from upstairs came the voices of children going to bed. He put into his rough notes some of the deeper feelings stirred in him during his war sightseeing.

Saturday, July 29.—A splendid day, a delightful garden, green and with a little winding pond; the roses and the sunshine are such a contrast to the bloody battle of the Somme so near this little chateau at Hesdin that I have been more melancholy and war-stricken than for many days past. The countless wounded of yesterday . . . this bloody and damnable war is a black pall on everything. The garden and foliage are almost as in England, but not quite. I ought to be happy, but I'm not. The war kills everything. *Sunday, July 30.*—Lovely morning, but roses, sunshine, church bells and guns don't mix.

At a casualty clearing station he watched 'a difficult and dangerous abdominal operation', noted 'unconscious men, some sinking'. At another, 'a pathetic and heartrending outpost', he saw 'a vitally urgent tracheotomy'. He sees 'a massing of Coldstreams and Grenadiers and Scots

★ *At G.H.Q.*, Cassell, 1931.

Guards. Our best. Will they be wasted?' Walking in the garden of the chateau before breakfast, he experiences 'a delicious moment—roses with the dew on them'. He had a final talk with Haig. 'He showed me his plans. Each time I see him I am convinced of his qualities. We talked of the wobble of the politicians.' He sent a message to Lloyd George on August 1: 'Any wavering now will cost us eventual losses beyond calculation, alarm France, and hearten a depressed Germany.' Writing to Sir Robert Hudson about Red Cross matters, he said (August 5): 'Sir Douglas Haig is the first British general in whom I have ever had any confidence.' He wrote to Lloyd George that he had found nothing 'but satisfaction at the change that has come over the Army since Sir Douglas Haig took command', and asked him to give thought to paying a visit to France to see for himself the splendid British organization that was being built up. He followed his letter with a telegram asking that copies of his letter should be sent to Carson, General Sir William Robertson, and Robinson of *The Times* (August 6). He wrote to Sutton from Le Havre: 'The confidence of the new armies of ours, the belief in the new C. in C. and the tremendous organization from this great sea port right up to the front, will *one day* seal Germany's doom.' Hearing from home of 'the intriguing against the Army command in political circles', he wrote to Sir Arthur Sloggett: 'It is a damnable thing', while to Geoffrey Robinson he confided (August 6): 'I go off to Italy with a heavy heart in this matter and half wish I were not going at all.' When Robinson doubted 'if there is much in the rumour as to inter-ference', Northcliffe discussed it with Haig and wrote afterwards to Robinson (August 8): 'There is a great deal in it.' In the same letter, Northcliffe referred to a propaganda plan which he had devised for breaking German army *morale*. Haig, he wrote, had 'instantly approved it'. Northcliffe wanted to have letters from German prisoners who wrote home about their good treatment in English hands 'photographed by the thousand dropped over the German lines'. Several months previously, he had asked to see Balfour 'in regard to the necessity of counteracting German intrigues in France, Russia, Sweden, Norway, Spain, the United States, South America, China and elsewhere. If it is a matter for Sir Edward Grey, I will most gladly call upon him.' British propaganda was still largely under unimaginative military control. It was to be nearly two years before Northcliffe was allowed to intervene forcefully in that branch of the war effort.

*   *   *

'Most darling Mother,—Hot, hot, hot—but all most interesting', North-cliffe wrote from Italy on August 13, and 'hot, hot, hot as I write in bed to my most darling and sweet mother', from the Grand Hotel, Rome, on

'Friday or Saturday, 18th or 19th. Don't know which.' He had talked for an hour with the King of Italy, who was 'aged 46, short, very intelligent and amusing, especially about the Kaiser', and had interviewed General Cadorna, the Italian commander, 'a short, lithe, quick-moving man of sixty-six, broad head, aquiline nose, merry eyes'. He visited the Italian front lines overlooking Gorizia, but 'could not face the extreme heights' of some of the Italian positions and, being driven by an Italian military chauffeur, 'I had to shut my eyes rounding curves.' He was happier in Venice, 'my first visit and on a perfect day. Infinitely more beautiful, and grander, than I had expected. I had to fill up a form giving *your* names, birthplace, and age, as well as my own. "Geraldine" was a terrible puzzler for them!' His companion, Wickham Steed, said that Northcliffe was 'left dumb with amazement' after a leisurely tour of the Venetian streets, ending in moonlight. 'He vowed that, after the war, he would live there for some months each year.' He rarely failed to mention in his letters to his mother that he was sleeping well again and evidently he had renewed his supply of nerve force, for he told Howard Corbett, of *The Times*, in a letter of August 27: 'I propose making things hum between now and Christmas', throwing in the bland comment: 'I am entirely satisfied with the progress of the war', reaffirmed in a letter to his mother of August 29: 'All goes extremely well in the war. You know how careful I have always been in my estimates of the progress. My love to all the family, especially the tiny ones', his youngest nephews and nieces.

He had told Geoffrey Robinson that 'people in high position think I ought not to go to Switzerland, which is over-run by German agents who may nab me. However, we shall see what we shall see', and he took train for Berne. Arriving there, he wrote to tell Joseph Conrad of his pleasure in reading *The Nigger of the Narcissus* and of seeing other Conrad works in Continental bookshops. Steed, who had gone off to meet the General of the Jesuits in the hope of getting his support for a plan of persuasion to be brought to bear on the Vatican which to some people appeared to be championing Catholic dynasties rather than the Christian cause, noted an instance of Northcliffe's faculty for 'reading the minds of others'. When he rejoined Northcliffe at Berne, Northcliffe remarked at once: 'You have disappointment written all over your body.' Steed's mission to the 'Black Pope' had failed.

From Geneva they returned to Paris and then went to Spain, 'to see something of German propaganda', which they had been studying with profit in Switzerland too. They found that it had a strong grip on the Spaniards and Northcliffe's staccato notes provided the material for reports as well as for newspaper articles. Some of his scribbled remarks etched a more lasting impression; for example, that every small town had 'an excellent band whose only fault is the monotony of its mournful, modern

;panish music'. Reflecting on its minor key characteristic, 'it is the music)f a people resigned to their lost position as *conquistadors*'.

Returning, by Haig's invitation, to stay again at British general head-juarters, Northcliffe was taken to see 'the newest form of arm, not to be lescribed for many days yet', namely, the tank. Steed wrote that 'North-:liffe tried to enter one of them by the manhole on the top; but as his girth was some inches larger than the hole, he stuck midway and had to be lauled down to the inside by the feet while I sat on his shoulders above. Jetting him out again was an even harder matter.' Northcliffe went to the little wooden Presbyterian church' with Haig for Sunday morning service. The padre gave out a hymn which was sung so half-heartedly that he raised his hand after the second verse, saying: ' "We will try another", and gave the number of "Rock of Ages", sung with intense devotion.' All day the guns were 'throating and sobbing', Northcliffe's phrase for the in-termittent cannonades of the Somme battles. 'Monday, 11th September.— Lying in bed here in small room with both windows wide open, cooing of wood pigeons, chattering of small birds and cawing of rooks, bright September sun shining in, reminding me of September in Norfolk. The shuddering and uneasy thudding of the guns, twelve miles off.' On the way homeward *via* Boulogne, 'called on my nephew, Alfred Harmsworth in hospital', Leicester's eldest son, seriously wounded. 'On the whole, feel well after my experiences', he wrote on September 13, 'and delighted to get to my peaceful Elmwood', where his return was saddened by news of the death of 'Freddie' Wood, 'our oldest family friend', and of Vernon Jones, the physician who had helped him through his health crisis of two years before. 'I think of you all very often and of everybody at the front at this very moving time. Yesterday at this house on the North Foreland the windows shook all day long with the bombardments on the Somme', he told Sloggett, the Surgeon-General, in a letter of September 26.

He was using Elmwood that autumn as a place of secret rendezvous with his 'spies' from Germany, mainly American and Dutch newspapermen. In London he saw them at Printing House Square, after dark, using what was known as the Private House for that purpose. They brought him much useful and some valuable information that he passed on to Downing Street. Another visitor to Elmwood then was Cecil Harmsworth's eldest son, Desmond, a preparatory schoolboy convalescing from an appendicitis operation. He hardly knew his uncle Alfred except by name and fame. He has recalled that 'there was not in Northcliffe's behaviour the slightest trace of the effort a very busy man might feel obliged to make in order to be nice to a boy guest of 12 or 13—a particularly uninteresting age'. The boy was paralysed by shyness. 'He might have been intimidating and I an embarrassment yet he talked easily and informatively about everything, and especially the war, with obvious pleasure, and I listened with complete fascination as if to someone I had always known.' Desmond Harmsworth remembers clearly the first day at Elmwood:

After dinner he took me upstairs to the library and talked on; how concerned he was for the wellbeing of St. John [Northcliffe's crippled brother], for whom he expressed great affection; how the *Daily Mail* had caught Crippen, the murderer; how a monstrous and revolutionary machine like a ship on land spouting bullets, still a virtual secret, called a tank, was going to change the course of the war. We sat on the floor while he played the gramophone, skimming the played records across the thick carpet. It was the only time I knew him. Making allowance for the magnified impressions of childhood, it seems to me that he had more outgoing force, more of the sheer genius of personality, than anyone else I have known.

In his letter to Lloyd George of August 6, Northcliffe had urged him to visit the British armies in France and see for himself the immensely efficient organization that was being built up there. Lloyd George went in the late autumn. From British general headquarters Philip Sassoon privately reported to Northcliffe that the visitor did not make a favourable impression: he kept Foch waiting an hour and a half, did not apologize, 'and sat with his arms on the table'. According to Sassoon, Foch was 'absolutely scandalized', while Sir Douglas Haig was 'terribly disappointed with him'. Sassoon gave it as his 'private opinion' that Lloyd George had no liking for Haig and concluded that 'Churchill's subtle poison' was responsible.

Northcliffe's popularity at British general headquarters just then stood high. He was the champion of the soldiers against the politicians. Haig was amused to note in his diary (September 11, 1916) that Northcliffe called Lloyd George 'a shirt-sleeve politician' and that Northcliffe told him Lloyd George 'does whatever he, N., advises!'

Northcliffe to Sir Philip Sassoon:

The Times,
Printing House Square,
E.C.
2nd October, 1916.

Dear Sir Philip,—You are dealing with people, some of whom are very thick-skinned, others very unscrupulous, but all afraid of newspapers. It is urgently necessary that they should be told, and more than once: 'Hands off the Army.' They are now definitely aware that any interference will lead to exposure. Probably Sir Douglas thinks 'Save me from my friends'. If he looks back over the incidents of the visit he will realize that it is well to nip this thing in the bud at the outset.

You may have noticed that directly the tanks were successful, Lloyd George ssued a notice through the Press Bureau that they were due to Churchill. You will find that unless we watch these people they will claim that the great Battle of the Somme is due to the politicians. That would not matter if it were not for the fact that it is the politicians who will make peace. Personally, I dread a peace made by these tricky people.

Yours very sincerely,
NORTHCLIFFE

Northcliffe was sending Haig, through Sassoon, occasional memoranda which he headed 'Jottings from the Home Front'. His subject was usually the Cabinet, whose members he described as 'a pack of gullible optimists—"detached cynics", Leo Maxse calls them—who swallow any foolish tales'. He agreed that there were 'exceptions among them, and splendid ones, but the generality of them have the slipperiness of eels, combined with the vanity of a professional beauty'.

On October 6 Northcliffe had a secret meeting with Lloyd George at Lord Milner's little house in Great College Street, Westminster, a venue chosen because it was secluded and approached from three sides, conducive to furtive entry and exit. They lunched with an unnamed third person in Milner's absence at Sidmouth, where he was nursing a cold. Returning to the *Times* office, Northcliffe wrote to Milner: 'Your charming hospitality today gave great pleasure to your three guests. The little luncheon was admirably done, and your house is perfection. We regretted much that you were not there. A great deal of important information was elicited which you ought to know', but no record remains of the purpose of the meeting.

Three days later Northcliffe gave an 'uncensored address' to members of the Aldwych Club (of advertising men), concerning which Cecil Harmsworth made the note: 'About 500 lunchers, some 1500 more having failed to obtain tickets. Alfred had a reception that would not be accorded, I think, to any one of our statesmen with the possible exception of Ll.G.' Taking the members of the club into his confidence in a way that obviously warmed their hearts, Northcliffe spoke freely about war matters, including political meddling with the army, and still more freely about certain personalities, notably Haldane, whom he charged with lending a too ready ear to peace overtures from the enemy. He was given an ovation when he sat down. At Ramsgate, on October 14, Cecil wrote in his diary:

Alfred in a most amiable mood. He tells us that he has given Lloyd George warning not to interfere with strategic affairs. Ll.G. is said to be worrying Sir William Robertson and even to have another little military expedition of his own in view.

Field-Marshal Sir William Robertson, Chief of the Imperial General Staff, to Northcliffe:

> War Office,
> 11.10.16.
>
> Dear Lord Northcliffe,—I am much touched by your letter. It *is* very hard work trying to win this war. The Boche gives me no trouble compared with what I meet in London. So any help you can give me will be of Imperial value.
> With grateful thanks,
> Yours sincerely,
> W. ROBERTSON

'The man on the spot knows best', was an article of Northcliffe's professional creed that had long been confirmed by his dealings with the *Times* foreign correspondents. He even more ardently avowed it as an observer of military events. Lloyd George believed that the army's policy of attrition was needlessly wasting lives on the Western Front, where the generals had built up a magnificent war machine which they were so preoccupied in admiring and administering that they had no time to think of the future. He favoured a strong Franco-British diversion at Salonika in support of the army of the Serbs. Northcliffe sent a message to the *Daily Mail* on October 13 in which he referred scornfully to 'mad, wild expeditions in distant places', and protested against the weakening of the army in France. 'If we continue to grind into the public mind the terrible fact that political interference means an increase of the death roll of our army, Sir Douglas Haig and Sir William Robertson will not be worried as they are at present.' He may have recalled the experience of Lord Roberts in the Boer War, which some observers believed had been needlessly prolonged by the politicians at home. According to a story allegedly told by Lloyd George's personal secretary, J. T. Davies, Northcliffe burst into Davies's room at the War Office and, when Davies made a move towards an inner door leading to Lloyd George's room, motioned him to stay where he was, saying: 'I don't want to see him—you can tell him for me that I hear he has been interfering with strategy and that if it goes on I will break him.' Lord Esher recorded the story in that form in his diary; Lord Beaverbrook repeated it in his book on war politics. The history of *The Times* gives it. Northcliffe's own version of a possibly misrepresented incident was contained in a letter which he wrote to Sir Philip Sassoon on October 18, 1916:

The news from my sector of the Home Front is that on Tuesday the 10th, hearing from a mutual friend that General Robertson was not sleeping owing to the interference, I telephoned to our Welsh friend [Lloyd George] saying that wanted to see him urgently about interference with the army. Either he was afraid to see me, or he was really away, and as I had to leave town that afternoon, I replied that I would come and express my views to Mr J. T. Davies, his personal secretary, to whom I said plainly that I shared the national gratitude for Mr Lloyd George's energy in shell matters and his attempts to settle Home Rule; that I had given him a personal hint in conversation and several hints in my newspapers that I could no longer support him and if further interference took place with Sir William Robertson I was going to the House of Lords to lay matters before the world, and hammer them daily in my newspapers. This may seem a brusque and drastic thing to do, but I think I know the combination I am dealing with better than you folks who are so engrossed in your splendid and absorbing task.

He told Sassoon that he had stopped the visits of his parliamentary correspondents 'to the ante-rooms of these great people every afternoon', at the same time assuring Balfour that they were abstaining 'out of no lack of respect for you'. He wished to make it clear that 'the help of my newspapers, or of my voice in the Lords, where I have consistently refrained from using my uncensored position, is always at the Government's disposal in the *active* conduct of the war against the enemy abroad and at home'. Since he had adopted that course, he had been informed by General Robertson that 'things are better', and Northcliffe also took it as a good sign 'that Winston has been going about libelling me in extra vigorous style'. He wished it to be understood, he said, that he 'realized to the full the necessity of smooth relations between the Secretary of State for War and the Chief of the Imperial General Staff', and pronounced himself 'a believer in the Secretary of State to a very great extent'. To Repington he wrote (October 18): 'I think if I were to join the Government I should lose what little influence I have. The people would never tolerate a newspaper owner being a member of the Government.' He was pleased to hear from the New York correspondent of the *Daily Mail*, W. F. Bullock, that 'phenomenal publicity' had been given to his war dispatches in the American press. 'Everyone agrees that they have done incalculable good in deepening American sympathies with the Allies' (October 20). A former Member of Parliament, Henry Allhusen, brother-in-law of Lord Midleton, expressed a wish to erect at his own expense a monument to Northcliffe, 'during your lifetime, as you have done more to win the war than any other man' (October 14). Northcliffe's response to a somewhat premature compliment is not preserved in the family files. He was at Elmwood passing page proofs for *At the War*, which he had compiled for Hodder & Stoughton from his war dispatches. Cecil wrote in his diary for October 16: 'Glorious autumn day. Alfred comes early for me and takes me off to Princes Golf Links at Sandwich, a splendid natural course of great difficulty. Quick and splenetic as he is ordinarily, he is one of the most placid golfers I have seen. Today he did describe one lie as "damnable", but he eschews bad language. Getting into the rough, his only comment was: "There's no fool like a fat fool." '

It was known, and noted in writing in the *Daily Mail* office earlier in the year, that 'the Chief' had been upset by the death in action of young Lucas King, the second member of the family to give his life in the war thus far. On October 24, 1916, another of his nephews, Vere Harmsworth second son of Harold (Rothermere), wrote a letter to St. John Harmsworth from 'a dugout, by candlelight', in France, which moved all who read it and not least Northcliffe, whose personal attachment to the younger Harmsworth generation was suffused with the affection of a frustrated parent. Vere Harmsworth, who had been at Osborne and Dartmouth, served in the Hawke Battalion of the Royal Naval Division at Gallipoli, and also in France, where he had not missed a day in the trenches for seven months.

We go over the top the morning after tomorrow. It will be about dawn. It is to be a terrifically big show. Our battalion goes over the 1st of our Division and we are to take about the 1st three lines of enemy trenches. If it goes all right and the artillery does not fail us, it will be an A1 show, but otherwise absolutely bloody.

We shall be very cramped and uncomfortable until it starts. Who knows what it will be like? It will be like living in a new world, far removed from this. If one comes through, one will emerge out of the new world rather dazed, and it will take some time to settle down. The awful nightmare of seeing one's own men—that one has been with so long—being struck down all round one, will never move from one's mind. One gets attached to one's own men and their loss hits one as hard as dear friends.

He wrote that they were leaving certain non-commissioned officers behind, 'in case we are all wiped out'. Speculating on that possibility: 'Somehow I have never imagined myself as an old man with the infirmities and limitations of old age. At school and in the later years I have tried to imagine myself at 50 or so. I do not seem to fit in. At business in the years to come I shall never be any good.' To him, he said, the future had 'always been rather vague, far away and unreal. I may have been born just to live my 21 years and then fade away'. He thought of his father:

He has been so good to me, and he has built up such a position for his three sons that it will be heartrending for him to have part of his life's work wasted. After all, if he has only to give up one of us three, he will be paying quite a small share compared with other families. It is the price that has to be paid for the freedom of the world.

It is curious how reserved he is with me and I with him. The feeling—

wfully strong—is there on both sides, but what is bred in the bone of every Englishman stops it coming out.

If I fall, do not mourn, but be glad and proud. It is not a life wasted but gloriously fulfilled.

VERE

P.S. I am leaving all I have for the betterment of those who have suffered through the war. Most of it for the men of my Battalion. My whole being is bound up in my men, heart, body and soul. Nothing else seems to matter.

Northcliffe described to Sassoon (October 25) a meeting with the French Minister of Munitions, Albert Thomas, 'a keen little man', whom Lloyd George, according to Northcliffe, had wished him to meet. 'The object was to convince me that military direction of the war is not always for the best, and that had the soldiers been obeyed, Paris and Verdun would have been lost; that soldiers always say a thing is impossible.' Northcliffe continued: 'I told him that so far as the Battle of the Somme is concerned—which to me is the crux of the war—I could not support any interference with the soldiers, and I gave him a good deal of information about our political geniuses and their various well-meant but ignorant schemes of strategy.'

M. Thomas, whose cousin was Lloyd George's French interpreter, was the leader of a French delegation which was returning to Paris after talks in London. Northcliffe met the delegates at Folkestone in his capacity of a newspaper proprietor who had made it clear to the Government in London that he was opposed to political interference with the army in the field. With him went Thomas Curtin, the American newspaperman who had been staying at Elmwood after the latest of his several trips into Germany. Curtin described the Folkestone proceedings in the *National Review* (February 1923). An unnamed army officer, who had also been a guest at Elmwood, travelled with them to Folkestone 'for the ride'. Curtin said that the officer's talk irritated Northcliffe. 'He wanted to *think*.' The officer could not hold his tongue. He spoke about the strategy of Napoleon in relation to the war. 'The Chief turned sharply upon him, and in a manner which might have surprised those who said that Northcliffe was a slavish imitator of the Corsican, exploded: "Napoleon doesn't count in this war, not a bit. It is a different war, fought with different weapons. We are going to discuss the facts of today at Folkestone, and I want to hear not another word about Napoleon." ' Curtin said that Northcliffe ordered his chauffeur to stop, 'following which he left us and sat on the front seat the rest of the way'.

Arrived in the council room at the Folkestone hotel, Northcliffe faced a formidable delegation. He was impatient of irrelevancies. 'We are wasting time, wasting precious minutes in side discussions', he said, and laid his watch on the table. Curtin wrote: 'I can still see M. Thomas, with large brown eyes and heavy beard, with a group of his countrymen on one side of the table, and Northcliffe, his personality filling the room making them agree with him that weakening the line in France might mean the loss of the war. In twenty minutes he had won his point and before the half hour was up he was speeding back to more work at St. Peter's.'

Sassoon wrote to him that there was no doubt that Ll. G. was much in the pockets of the French, and assuring Northcliffe that his frequent letters were appreciated. 'It is wonderful your finding time amidst all your work to write—you cannot write often enough.' A letter from the Surgeon-General, Sloggett, on October 30, informed Northcliffe: 'I have had the Duke of Connaught staying with me. He is a staunch admirer of *your* and quite realizes what you have done for the country. I was out at Fricourt three days ago and I have *never* since the war commenced seen such mud—it is positively feet deep and horses and mules have been so bogged down that they have positively had to be shot.' The flooding rains were not alone to blame. The exceptional quantities of shells which had come to the army as a result of the previous year's agitations by North-cliffe and others had destroyed the drainage network of the Flanders plain. Consequently, progress was impeded rather than accelerated.

On November 18, Haig wrote to his wife in London: 'When I come over I'll try to get Lord Northcliffe to come and lunch with us one day, as he has been such a help latterly to the Army and myself.' That same week, General Wilson called on Northcliffe at the *Times* office and 'could not get him to talk sense'.* By Wilson's volatile testimony, Northcliffe was self-contradictory and disposed to deduce impending collapse in Germany from an unprecedented rise in the price of eels. No doubt like everyone else he was distracted by the chilling autumn knowledge of the cost of summer successes. 'This is one of the gloomiest periods of the war,' Cecil Harmsworth noted. 'I have never seen so many people shaking their heads over our chances of winning.' Lloyd George himself recalled it as a nightmare time, brought about by 'the ineffectiveness and irresolution of our leadership'.† The blinds were down in innumerable English homes. They were drawn once again in the Harmsworth family. Vere had been killed, leading his men in the fighting of November 13.‡ Robinson, of *The Times*, saw Northcliffe a few days later. 'He was much cut up at his nephew's death.' It revived the old intensity of feeling that had overcome him in the South African War when he was

---

* Major-General Sir C. E. Callwell, *Life and Diaries of Field-Marshal Sir Henry Wilson*, Cassell, 1927.

† *War Memoirs.*

‡ See page 510.

Northcliffe with Henry Ford at Detroit, 1917

(*Left*) Thomas Marlowe, editor of the *Daily Mail*, 1899–1926. (*Right*) Lieut-Colonel Campbell Stuart in 1917 when

brought word of the death of George Steevens and of the young *Daily Mail* library worker, Gilham, whom he had mourned as if for a son. In the greater war his attitudes to its direction received emotional reinforcement from more intimate griefs. Imposed on the sorrows of the time were the lesser but insistent cares of reduced food supplies, increasing dissension within the governing circle, the defection of allies, and fears of worse enemy visitations to come, especially at sea; a general state of enervation which Northcliffe was unlikely to escape, though his young Australian journalist friend, Frank Fox, home from France on leave, saw 'no sign of failing' in him. 'He was full of concern for what he spoke of as "the awful muddle" .' He telephoned points for a *Daily Mail* leading article. 'Greatest characteristic of this government is indecision. More than 100 committees making up its mind for it. Idle septuagenarians like Mr Balfour and Lord Lansdowne and semi-invalids, such as Lord Grey of Falloden. Government by 23 men who can never make up their minds a danger to the Empire.' It was a time for plain speaking. When other newspapers described the comments on Balfour, Lansdowne and Grey as ill-mannered, Northcliffe ordered the *Daily Mail* leader writer to retort: 'Rude work will be required to pull the country out of danger.'

On December 3, 1916, Cecil Harmsworth noted in his diary: 'Alfred has been actively at work with Ll.G. with a view to bringing about a change.' Geoffrey Robinson, who afterwards wrote mistakenly that Northcliffe and Lloyd George 'had not been on speaking terms for several months', also noted that 'a reconciliation meeting' between Northcliffe and Lloyd George took place on December 1. Sir Max Aitken (Beaverbrook) had tried, and failed, to bring them together: 'I was very anxious that Lloyd George should make it up with Northcliffe. I had a strong belief both in Northcliffe's power and in his rigid patriotism. I did not share the dislike and disparagement of Northcliffe then rife in Governmental and political circles.'* Lloyd George remarked to his friend Riddell at that time: 'An alliance with Northcliffe is something like going for a walk with a grasshopper.' But now Sir Arthur Lee intervened to effect the meeting which occurred on December 1. The two men were together again on December 3. That night, at a quarter to twelve, a statement was issued from 10 Downing Street, announcing the reconstruction of the Asquith Government. Early the next morning, Northcliffe telephoned to his brother Cecil. 'Who killed cock robin?' he asked. 'You did,' Cecil replied. Later in the day Cecil went to see Northcliffe at St. James's Place. 'He tells me he was with Lloyd George yesterday', and Cecil noted: 'In the House of Commons, confusion and bewilderment. Most people have been growing uneasy under the nerveless direction of the P.M., but most people also regard the possible partnership of Ll.G. with dismay.' Cecil

* *Politicians and the War.*

went on to the Ritz Hotel to see Harold. 'I find him with Winston who walks rapidly up and down the room talking at the top of his voice. Home to dinner, leaving Winston declaiming.' There was a letter for Northcliffe from Lord Derby: 'The present system is not one that can possibly give us success.' Derby believed that the people were 'perfectly determined that there shall be a firmer grip taken on the management of the country' (December 5). The following day the King called a Cabinet conference at Buckingham Palace in the hope of securing agreement between the contending parties, those in favour of Asquith's continuance as Prime Minister and those who wanted a change in the leadership. When Bonar Law, representing the Tory side, declined the opportunity to form a Government, Lloyd George was invited to try and his efforts succeeded. Cecil Harmsworth, the Liberal Member of Parliament for the Luton division of Bedfordshire, noted on December 6: 'The London Liberal daily papers are full of denunciations of Northcliffe, whom they regard as the arch-wrecker of the Asquith Govt. There is truth in this, of course, but not all the truth. Grave dissatisfaction with the P.M's leadership has been growing apace among Liberals in the House and has found expression in such staunchly Liberal papers as the *Manchester Guardian* and *The Nation*.' Invited to a Liberal party meeting under Mr Asquith's chairmanship at the Reform Club two days later, Cecil and Leicester Harmsworth decided not to attend, 'having no wish to hear what may be said of Northcliffe, who has had so large a share in the present upheaval' (Cecil's diary, December 8). Seeing from a window of 10 Downing Street, Lloyd George and Northcliffe walking in earnest collusion in the garden of No. 11, Margot Asquith wrote in her diary: 'We are out!' Lloyd George was careful to say in his memoirs that Northcliffe was not brought into the consultations leading to the change of Government. Lord Beaverbrook, recording his go-between role in *Politicians and the War*, the most explicit contemporary account of those events, said so too. Perhaps the back-bencher Harmsworths were wrong, or, at least, not quite right, in assuming their eldest brother to have had a front-bencher's influence on inner Cabinet happenings at that time.

Why, then, was Northcliffe meeting Lloyd George in those crucial hours? A part explanation was supplied by a well-known Anglo-American literary agent, Curtis Brown. Shortly before the fall of Asquith, Brown received a telephone call from Northcliffe's secretary asking him to go to 22 St. James's Place. Arriving there, he was shown into Northcliffe's study. Northcliffe told him: 'Lloyd George is likely to leave the Government. This you will please regard as confidential for the present. He is a poor man, with nothing to live on except writing. I want you to let me know in the next few days what you can get for a series of newspaper articles from him on political affairs of the day.' Brown negotiated an offer, in the circumstances a matter of some discretion. It was for the inclusive English and American rights. Northcliffe sent him a curt note 'to keep off those English rights'. Apparently he had reserved them for the *Daily Mail*. But Lloyd George did not require to go into the literary market-place until a good many years had passed. On December 6, he was engrossed in the task of forming a new Government with himself as its head.

He had, in fact, discussed more than literary matters with Northcliffe: for example, the presidency of the Board of Trade, of which office Max Aitken, on the word of Lloyd George, believed that he had the reversion. He was 'so sure of the Board of Trade' that he warned his constituency to be ready for a by-election. The post was given to Sir Albert Stanley (later Lord Ashfield). If Northcliffe did not propose the appointment, on Stanley's own testimony he influenced it. Sir Albert Stanley to Northcliffe (May 9, 1919): 'It was largely through your good offices that the Board of Trade came into my hands.' Writing of his own situation in December 1916, Aitken referred to his 'extreme embarrassment'. When Lloyd George suggested a peerage, he at first declined but afterwards accepted it—'a very foolish way of escape', he wrote, from his dilemma. It would seem that Northcliffe supplied some of the propulsion by which 'the little Canadian adventurer' was launched into the rarefied upper atmosphere of the British political system.

On December 7, Lloyd George received a deputation of Conservative ex-ministers and after discussing the allocation of various offices, he announced, according to a memorandum made at the time, that he had 'no intention of asking Mr W. Churchill or Lord Northcliffe to join the Administration'. On December 8 he moved into 10 Downing Street. Before the day was out he made a personal bid for Northcliffe's good will. Max Aitken was with him. He asked Aitken to telephone a message to Northcliffe: 'The Prime Minister would like to see Lord Northcliffe at No. 10 Downing Street.' Aitken waited on the line. Northcliffe's answer was a declaration of independence: 'Lord Northcliffe sees no advantage in any interview between him and the Prime Minister at this juncture.'*

Northcliffe enjoyed his reputation as the scourge of Governments, but he never claimed that it was he who brought Asquith down. He made it known to those around him that there was much in Asquith's character that he admired and he was moved by the news of the death in action of Asquith's son Raymond, whom he had known and liked. He believed that Asquith had no firm grip on the realities of the war and that, confronted by some of its larger problems, he was incapable of acting masterfully. Asquith's biographers, J. A. Spender and Cyril Asquith, supposed that Asquith's aloofness towards journalists generally was a source of

---

* *Politicians and the War.*

Northcliffe's antagonism. They conceded that Asquith's failing was 'a certain arrogance which blinded him to the powers and qualities of men who were not of his school and tradition'. Neither a *Times* leading article written by the editor (December 4, 1916), into which Asquith read wilful mischief against himself, nor the 'hurricane campaign' of the *Daily Mail* and its associated newspapers, was alone responsible for Asquith's departure from office. Asquith failed because, as a war leader, he was a failure. That is not his epitaph in history. He was a lawyer and the lawyer element was predominant in his unwieldy Cabinet. 'But we are not at law with Germany—we are at war with her', Northcliffe insisted.

To the politicians Northcliffe was 'a swaying force, uncertain, capricious, essentially personal, potent alike for good and evil'—Winston Churchill's verdict, taken from *The World Crisis*. That intermittent friend of Northcliffe presented him to posterity as 'at all times animated by an ardent patriotism and an intense desire to win the war. But', Churchill wrote, 'he wielded power without official responsibility, enjoyed secret knowledge without the general view, and disturbed the fortunes of national leaders without being willing to bear their burdens.' Personal power is always 'potent for good and evil'. If Northcliffe 'disturbed the fortunes' of some of the leaders, he believed it to be in the national interest. Hearing that Carson had gone to the Admiralty as First Lord, he wrote to him on December 10: 'I have been a little overworked lately, but the news has come as a tonic. I feel ten years younger since I heard it.' As for his sense of responsibility, he wrote to Printing House Square on December 12: 'We should now give all the publicity we can to the new men in the Government. We must do our best to get the new ministers known, and thus strengthen their position in the country', though he doubted the war-winning capabilities of Balfour and Robert Cecil in particular. He had become a non-official statesman who was influencing events at many more points than was realized. He had helped to improve the munitions supply and also the supply of men for the forces. Without him, national service, which he deemed to be fair as well as necessary, might have been delayed even longer, although he had urged it from the beginning and, in fact, before the war began. He succeeded in stiffening the blockade of Germany in the belief that half measures were of too little avail. He criticized the unwieldy Cabinet of twenty-three, as a result of which a small inner Cabinet was created for the better conduct of the war.

Apart from what he did through his newspapers, he rendered a great amount of public service in private, communicating his ideas and suggestions to persons in authority: informing the First Lord of the Admiralty of weaknesses in coast defences; urging the Quartermaster-General to improve the fighting men's rations; conducting his own propaganda service while waiting for the nation to wake up to the supreme need for establishing one; persuading the managers of leading London hotels to fly the American flag ('it may bring us a bit of good will from American visitors'); and seeing to it that Heads of State regularly received copies of *The Times*.

He sends to the Prime Minister evidence of 'the muddling' of Neville Chamberlain, the director of national service. He impresses the Chief of the Imperial General Staff and the army commanders with the need for making better use of 'the superior civilian brains' to be found in the ranks of the new armies; and there is some reason to suppose that his representations in that matter had a direct if distant sequel in the compilation of the register of special talents which was of value at the outbreak of the Second World War. He writes to the Food Controller about public waste in hotels and restaurants, noted by himself. He passes useful information to the president of the Board of Trade. Visiting the great war stores port of Richborough in Kent, he is impressed by the efficient personality of the officer in charge, General Collard, and remarks with a half smile: 'I could not help thinking that he reminded me a little of myself in the way he goes about questioning everybody and getting matters settled.'

*　　*　　*

Railway company will not guarantee delivery of Christmas tree, he telegraphed on December 20 to the mother of one of his many godchildren. *Please buy Irene tricycle stop am sending ten pounds*. He was signing documents that gave him the sole ownership once again of Elmwood, which he had made over to his wife. In place of it, he bought her a charming little property called Buckthorn Hill at Crowborough in Sussex, 'which she much prefers'.

That day he found the time, also, to begin a brief, decisive correspondence with the women's suffrage leaders, Lady Betty Balfour and Mrs Fawcett. 'There is absolutely no movement for women's suffrage anywhere,' he wrote. 'I have made inquiries of a great many women on the subject, but they do not take any interest in it. I cannot explain the psychology, but it is the fact. Try to get up a public meeting on the subject, and I will support it.' Lady Betty wrote across the foot of the letter: 'What says our leader to this?' and sent it to Mrs Fawcett. The leader was extremely angry. 'I wrote in a white heat to Lady Betty', according to her memoirs, published in 1924. The women's movement was in suspense, she pointed out, only because the women were engaged in patriotic duties, helping to win the war. 'Because we break no windows, Lord Northcliffe thinks there is "no movement for women's suffrage anywhere".' Lady Betty sent Mrs Fawcett's tirade to Northcliffe, who, dictating letters at Totteridge on Christmas Day, wrote to Mrs Fawcett: 'I do not suggest window-breaking. I do think that some great meeting or united deputation is necessary.' He promised 'to speak to the Prime Minister tomorrow'. Receiving a copy of the letter, Lady Betty Balfour wrote to Mrs Fawcett: 'I was asked in Woking yesterday if I had heard of the latest political crisis: "Northcliffe has sent for the King." '

The joke was echoed in Cecil Harmsworth's diary for Boxing Day: 'With the two boys to see their Uncle Northcliffe at the *Times* office. We find the king-maker in the handsome Georgian parlour of the oldest-fashioned house in London. N. presents each of the boys with a one-pound note and promises them copies of his book, *At the War*. He takes us into the great machine-room where everything is ready for printing tonight's *Times*. N. is to spend two hours this evening with the Prime Minister. He is full of confidence in the result of the war.' 'I rather like the idea of a united deputation,' Mrs Fawcett wrote to one of her assistants that same day. 'I think we should consider it very carefully', and asked for the attendance, 'without fail', of other prominent figures of the National Union of Women's Suffrage Societies at a meeting which was to act on the suggestion.

Northcliffe wrote again to Millicent Fawcett on December 27: 'I talked for some time with the Prime Minister last night who is very keen on the subject, and practical too. I make the suggestion to you and Lady Betty Balfour that you get up a large and representative deputation. That will give the newspapers the opportunity of dealing with the matter. I shall speak to the editor of *The Times* on the question today. I believe he is entirely favourable.*' The asterisk indicated a footnote: '* Have done so. He is.' It marked a complete reversal of the *Times* policy. For almost half a century the paper had opposed the women's cause and missed few opportunities of damaging it. Millicent Fawcett wrote that Northcliffe's support 'was of great value', and that he was 'constantly talking to his friends on our subject'. He had earlier resisted the notion of women's suffrage. Now he pronounced an encomium on their demand for suffrage. 'The women are wonderful. Their freshness of mind, their organizing skill, have been magnificent. Men are making too great a mess of the world and need helpers without their own prejudices, idleness and self-indulgence.' In January 1917 the logic of their case was recognized in the report of the Speaker's Conference on Electoral Reform. Proudly wearing the uniforms of their war service, the women's deputation which Northcliffe had proposed waited on the Prime Minister at 10 Downing Street. Towards the end of the month the House of Commons passed, by a seven-to-one majority, a clause in a new reform bill giving women the vote.

At the War, dedicated 'To My Mother', had sold well as a Christmas gift book and an American edition was being prepared. The author had made it a condition of the contract that his royalties should go to a joint fund of the Red Cross and the Order of St. John of Jerusalem, which received over £5,000 from that source during the ensuing half year. Fifty-six thousand copies of the book were sold in the English edition. Readers of the Christmas Number of *Answers* can hardly have been enheartened by the statement, under the heading, 'When Our Boys Come Home: by Viscount Northcliffe', that 'this is not one war but many wars, and there are yet further wars to come'. He saw it, he said, as 'the mere prelude to an upheaval of the world'.

A prominent publicist connected with war charity appeals, Sir Hedley Le Bas, having given it as his opinion that Northcliffe would be in Downing Street before many months had passed, Northcliffe wrote to him (January 7, 1917): 'Heaven forbid that I should ever be in Downing Street. I believe the independent newspaper to be one of the future forms of government. Some of my friends say it is not a responsible method of helping to rule. Let them try newspaper ownership and find out.' Garvin, master of rhetoric, publicly denounced it as 'irresponsible despotism', while privately reaffirming his regard for Northcliffe as a friend. Northcliffe's attitude to others with power was riven by the same duality. Thus, admiring Balfour, he wrote: 'If I speak to him on the subject [of the blockade] he will very delightfully waste three quarters of an hour of my time and nothing will happen.' To him it was ludicrous that the velvet-gloved Balfour, as Foreign Secretary, and Lord Robert Cecil, as Under Secretary of State, should be responsible for the blockade of Germany.* He had just paid his ninth visit to the battle front in France and was in no mood to tolerate weak men or weak measures. 'Jacky' Fisher, late First Sea Lord, was sending him private information about the submarine menace, telling him (January 16, 1917): 'What you told me long since as to the production of German submarines being prodigious turns out to be Gospel truth.' Fisher suggested that they should keep in touch by telephone. '*The post is not safe.*' When, the following day, Fisher sent him a long document of enlightenment about naval strategic misjudgments, Northcliffe replied: 'All very interesting, but it is your fault that the blunderers remain in office', presumably a reference to Fisher's impulsive resignation from the Admiralty after differences with Churchill, the First Lord. 'The broadside you fired into me requires one in return,' Fisher replied on January 24 in a letter which belongs to the files of history.

You have to remember that had not McKenna [First Lord of the Admiralty, 1908–11] stood by me up to the point that twice he walked out of the Cabinet, our Fleet would not have been what it was when the war broke out, for there

---

* 'A.J.B. tells me he doesn't know and never did know anything about the Blockade.'—Cecil Harmsworth's diary, February 2, 1919.

was not one Churchillian vessel marshalled under Jellicoe. It was McKenna's administration that the world gazed on at Scapa Flow. . . . Jellicoe's appointment as admiralissimo was planned under McKenna and adopted by Churchill and fixed by me in 1905. His recent removal from the command of the Grand Fleet was the biggest naval crime ever perpetrated and on a par with the subtle trick that forced Campbell-Bannerman (who I knew very intimately) to form his government before the general election and so compelled him to include Asquith, Grey and Haldane in his government—*all of whom he hated!*

Northcliffe to his brother Hildebrand, then living at Freshwater Grove, Coolham, Sussex (January 25): 'What a chilly address!' Northcliffe to Sir Philip Sassoon (February 1): 'I saw Lloyd George the night before last about various things—chiefly in regard to propaganda in the United States, more and more essential in view of the fact that the war is now really starting.' Sir Philip Sassoon wrote to tell Northcliffe that Haig had said to him while out walking: 'How is Northcliffe—*do* write and ask him how he is and tell him how much I hope he is all right again.' Sir Hedley Le Bas to Northcliffe (February 7): 'Bonar Law is the weakest man occupying a high position that I have ever met.' Northcliffe to Lady Byng, wife of the commander-in-chief of the Canadian armies in France (February 11): 'This democracy is beginning to understand something about the war and the reckless slaughter is producing bad effects and much criticism, as I am writing to Sir Douglas Haig today.'

Northcliffe to Sir Douglas Haig:

The Times,
Printing House Square, E.C.
21st February, 1917.

Private.

Dear Sir Douglas,—I wrote a little time ago to Sir Philip Sassoon, telling him of the state of public opinion and of the views expressed in a hundred quarters—views that are obviously influencing the War Cabinet which, as you know, is, with the exception of Lord Milner, who is away, and Mr Balfour, who is occupied at the Foreign Office, hostile to you. Until yesterday I was unaware how hostile Lord Curzon is. His attitude came as a great surprise to me. . . .

So long as criticism is unjustifiable, I know that I am strong enough to defend you, but with every household in the country represented in your Army, often criticizing, and with a hostile War Cabinet, supported by a growing section in both Houses of Parliament, it would be impossible to stem the tide of clamour for drastic changes in your Army.

I would ask you to give this letter your most earnest consideration and to do everything in your power to rob these critics of their weapons.

Last August the movement against you was confined to a small circle in Society agitated by Churchill & Co. Today the movement is spreading greatly and has many representatives in both Houses of Parliament.

I very much dislike worrying one with such a tremendous responsibility, but I should not be a friend to you and your Armies if I did not tell you what is going on.

Yours sincerely,
NORTHCLIFFE

He wrote to Maxse that 'the anti-Haig movement is unjust and it is wrong. Haig is paying for the blunders of his predecessors' (February 20). Haig replied to him in a long handwritten letter of February 23. 'Very many thanks for so kindly writing and I also must tell you how thoroughly grateful I am for the very generous way you have supported me and championed the cause of the Armies in France. I feel sure that you know what my feelings are in this matter, so I will say no more now.' He was 'much surprised' to hear of Curzon's hostility. 'I think that this must be because I am of the genus "soldier" and not that he finds me personally obnoxious!' The commander-in-chief proposed to give war correspondents all the facilities required for establishing the facts about casualties, criticisms of which were 'based on ignorance'. He dealt in some detail with criticism of the generals.

All our Army commanders have been selected because of having shown ability as commanders in the face of the enemy.

1st Army.—Horne has had as meteoric a career as Nivelle!

2nd Army.—Plumer owes his selection to having done well at a critical time when Smith Dorrien (the then A. Commr.) failed. This was in F.M. French's time. I have carefully watched Plumer's methods and am satisfied that he is a good asset!

3rd Army.—Allenby has gone from G.O.C. Cav. Div. to Infty. Div., Corps and lastly Army. All in F.M. French's time and has justified his selection.

4th Army.—Rawlinson started at Zeebrugge with the 7th Divn.

5th Army.—Gough started as a Brigadier of Cavalry and has gone all through the steps of commanding Cav. Divn., Infty. Divn., Corps and Cavalry Corps and now Army.

A similar analysis of Corps and Divl. Commanders wd. demonstrate the same fact. Only those who have shown capacity for command in the field have been chosen for advancement. And if for any reason, any commander (no matter of what rank or standing) shows sign of falling below the requirements of his position, I have no hesitation in removing him. Much of the criticism now heard in London is probably due to this circumstance!

Concerning Northcliffe's complaint of the 'neglect of civilian brains', Haig agreed that 'the War Office might have done much (earlier in the war) by making out a "register of qualifications" based on the civil life of those who joined the Army. This is only another of the penalties we have to pay through not having had an organized nation before the calamity of war fell upon us!' He concluded his long letter by assuring Northcliffe that if criticism enabled him to improve his arrangements, he welcomed it.

On the other hand, if there is a great leader under me, or elsewhere, who can carry on this great army better than I am doing, I shall at once step down and try my best to help in some other capacity. As I have told you, I want nothing out of the war and only hope that I may be left alone after I have ceased to be of service to my country. Meantime, I do my best and have a clear conscience. I also believe that any man of merit will be able to rise to any height in this Army, but he must have *merit* first.

Again, ever so many thanks for your most friendly letter and with all good wishes.

Believe me,
Yours most truly,
D. HAIG

★ ★ ★

Northcliffe had made a point of going down to Thanet more often than was his habit in winter time because he thought 'it would give confidence to local people', many of whom were leaving in fear of raids. Hearing of hardship among the villagers of Reading Street, a neighbouring parish, he sent for a local resident. 'I will see the village through its trials,' he promised, and for two years he paid the food and clothing bills of the poorest families, giving the instruction: 'My name is not to be mentioned.' He was at Elmwood on the night of February 26 when a German destroyer fired a number of shells which exploded close to the house. Humphrey-Davy, a descendant of Nelson, went fearfully into his master's bedroom, suggesting a retreat to the cellars. Northcliffe refused to get up. 'If we are to die, we will die in our beds.' He referred to the raid in his communique to *The Times* on February 27:

Incidentally, the paper was nearly deprived of its chief proprietor last night— a source of mingled feelings among the staff. At 11.30 my house was lit up by some twenty star shells from the sea, so that the place was illuminated as if by lightning. For six minutes shrapnel burst all over the place, some of it hitting the library in which these notes are prepared every day, killing a poor woman and baby within 50 yards of my house and wounding two others. According to various estimates, it was the result of a destroyer raid. The authorities have no doubt that my house was aimed at, and the shooting was by no means bad.

Wilson, the leader writer, was 'horrified to learn what I have always dreaded', and begged him not to risk his life by going to Elmwood again while the war was on. 'The Germans know perfectly well that you are the

522

soul and heart of this war, and that if you were out of the way the various puppets now in office would probably run and make peace.' He had no doubt 'that you are now carrying on your back not merely the fate of Carmelite House, but something very much graver, the very honour and existence of our country'. Whether or not Northcliffe believed it, Wilson meant it, every word. The veteran reporter, Charles Hands, already a legendary figure to the younger newsroom men at Carmelite House, thought it 'a beautiful letter, which says perfectly what all of us are thinking about you. It will be a great grief to you to keep away from Elmwood, but, dear old Chief, I really and honestly think that you ought to do so, if you will forgive my saying so.' Hearing from his Broadstairs doctor, Moon, that 'more and more people are leaving', he went there again in March, 'to reassure people at a time when I much prefer the warmth of my garden in Surrey'.

In London, he had left St. James's Place and taken a furnished house, 8 Buckingham Street, S.W. It was so small that Lady Northcliffe often returned to find a visitor waiting to see him in every room. A few days before the move, there was an air raid warning and some of the domestic staff showed signs of nervousness. Northcliffe took an umbrella out into the Park, opened it, and walked up and down with it over his head until the maroons sounded the all-clear.

He had accepted at the invitation of Lord Cowdray the post of chairman of the Civil Aerial Transport Committee which was to consider the future of civil aviation in Great Britain. The announcement drew a letter of congratulation from his old rival, C. Arthur Pearson: 'The man who has done more than anyone to encourage and develop aviation is very surely the right man in the right place', and expressed the hope that 'the first official position which you have accepted will be a prelude to others of even greater importance. I am sure millions of others hope as I do.' In March, Northcliffe had talks 'with a great many Irish people', and told Geoffrey Robinson: 'This is the golden moment for a settlement.' He was the principal guest at a dinner at the Irish Club in London on March 17. 'I had rather a job to get them to drink the King's health, but, with a few exceptions, the whole room rose.' He had made it clear to the members that unless they honoured the toast he would leave the club. Writing to his mother from Bournemouth, where he went for sea air and rest in April, he described his experience as a train traveller (April 5): 'We were six a side, I having *part* of a corner seat, the prize of prizes. After my long and sleek years of snug Rolls-Roycing, it is strange to be reverting to the method of movement of my grandfathers. May the war end soon, *I* say, so that I can move about in comfort. Till Tuesday, my sweet,—Your adoring Firstborn'. He was overhauled by a Bournemouth doctor, A. E. Blackburn, who advised him to consult Sir James Mackenzie at 133 Harley Street. Mackenzie wrote later that month to tell Blackburn: 'I saw Lord Northcliffe and found the condition you describe. The systolic bruit [heart murmur] is one of those which I find occurring not infrequently in men who are over 45 years of age.' The patient was physically 'out of tone', Sir James confirmed, and advised 'a more hygienic life'; sensible suggestion, unrealistic expectation: there was no escape for Northcliffe from the entanglements which he had spun for himself.

He had lately mentioned in a memorandum to *The Times* that in the course of a long talk at 10 Downing Street, the Prime Minister 'had listened intently, but was probably thinking of something else all the time. His life is so much occupied with committees that he is unable to think out any subject in detail', a criticism of Northcliffe's own method of existence, though he was too fitfully preoccupied to realize it. Northcliffe to the *Times* office (April 18): 'In regard to the German Corpse Conversion Company, it is necessary that we reprint the evidence in facsimile from the German papers. *The Times* circulates largely in neutral countries in official circles, and I have little doubt that the Germans will attempt to deny their HORROR.' They had paid him the compliment of issuing *via* Zurich *The Great Anti-Northcliffe Mail*, a propaganda newspaper intended 'to eliminate the Northcliffe Press from the part it is playing in the war'. In size and format it was a replica of his *Daily Mail*, with twice as many pages. To Northcliffe it was interesting only as proof that there was as yet no serious paper shortage in Germany. He wrote to the *Times* office (April 24): 'The historian of the future will find a mine of wealth in *The Times* as to the gradual growth of the increasingly effective German blockade of England.' He pointed out to the *Daily Mail* staff the same day: 'Surely the question of the education of the future generation is of some importance. The school teachers are badly paid.' To the same (April 26): 'Much to my disappointment, I could find nothing in the paper to criticize this morning. I have done my best.' To the *Weekly Dispatch* editor (April 28): 'If you and your friends cannot get out a good paper with the immense abundance of varied news we have today I suggest that you take to some such occupation as agriculture.'

In his daily communications to his newspaper staffs there was a rising note of urgency on the subject of paper supplies. 'The crisis has come,' he warned *The Times* on May 3. 'We must have greater brevity in the subediting. We shall have to revert to smaller type.' Readers were to be told that all contributions and letters must be short. 'Pulp and paper ships are being sunk continuously and nothing is coming from Newfoundland. Continuing at this rate the paper will cease to exist in a few months' (May 4). 'The most important matter in all newspaper offices today is the saving of space' (May 5). The submarine attack was mounting dangerously. Fisher was provoked to send him the question, underlined heavily in red ink: 'Can the Army win the war before the Navy loses it?' While Northcliffe was exhorting his newspaper managers to drastic economy, he felt no spur to modify the outflow of his correspondence. Northcliffe to the *Daily Mail* office (May 7): 'I notice a letter about rhubarb leaves as spinach. They are well known to be poisonous. No such letter should have been inserted without consulting the authorities.' He returned to the subject the following day: 'It is a dangerous vegetable.' The esteemed poet, Sir William Watson, a candidate for the laureate-ship, composed a set of verses in which Northcliffe's service to his country was commemorated with that of Alfred the Great, 'the most graceful testimony I have received', he wrote in acknowledgment, adding: 'I have no doubt that those who, at the time I was carrying on the demand for shells, were stating that there was no lacks of shells, including the late Prime Minister in his famous Newcastle speech, are not anxious to be reminded of their crimes' (May 8). Northcliffe to H. G. Wells (May 14): 'Your articles in the *Weekly Dispatch* have removed my last faint hopes of that dukedom towards which I have been panting so long.' He was annoyed because his brother Rothermere's name had been omitted from the *Daily Mail* report of a speech made by Bonar Law, who had mentioned it in a recital of business men's services to the war effort. Rothermere had taken charge of the army clothing establishments. 'He has saved the coun-try millions, in addition to eradicating a vast amount of corruption. It was very wrong to remove his name. I should like to know who did it' (May 15).

Chapter Nineteen

The British War Mission

Two events that tower above the undulating plains of history occurred in the year 1917. One of them was the entry of the United States of America into the European war, on April 6. Three months before, President Wilson, who held office at the head of a Radical administration by a tenuous majority, had proclaimed the American wish for 'Peace Without Victory' and had told his intimate adviser, Colonel Edward M. House, that the country would stay out of the war. The Germans withdrew to a shortened line on the Western Front and, fortified also by the resources of corn and oil made available to them by the collapse of Rumania, as well as by the deteriorating Russian effort, embarked on indiscriminate submarine warfare. In that campaign the American leaders saw a declaration of 'war against mankind'. The grandiloquent peace concept, the pious hope, the 'woolly idealism' for which the editor of *The Times*, writing to his Washington correspondent, said the Americans showed no sign of being prepared to suffer, was abandoned. From then on, President Wilson considered the German Government to be 'morally condemned'. The words were those of the German Ambassador at Washington, Count Bernstorff.

Grave material shortages were hampering the war efforts of both Great Britain and France. There were also symptoms of moral exhaustion. The French spring offensive, under Nivelle, had broken down. British losses in the mud of Flanders were a matter of more than grave military concern. For Great Britain and her allies in Europe this was touch and go year. Uplifted as they were by the American decision, they could not hope for immediate support along the battle fronts. The Americans were far from ready to throw their weight into the conflict. They had no experience of organizing for war. For that reason, the President had agreed to receive at once a British mission which would consist of men competent to discuss the best means of co-operation between the two countries.

The British Mission of April 1917 was led by A. J. Balfour, the Foreign Secretary. His first task was to impress the Americans, and, above all, their President, with the seriousness of the war position. England was now the only firm bastion of the West. France was bleeding to death. Italy had little fight left in her. Russian power was crumbling away. The pendulum of time and fate was swinging in favour of Germany. Balfour was as clearly briefed on American attitudes to the war and to the prime belligerents as he was on British requirements in goods and cash. He arrived in Washington knowing that a majority of the American people did not regard themselves or their future as being menaced by the Central Powers, that they felt themselves 'to be arbitrators rather than allies', that they were committed to the battle not for glory or profit but for the triumph of democracy. He was left in no doubt of a persisting distrust of Great Britain, 'kept alive by the ridiculous history books still used in the national schools'. The line of guidance, and the quotations, are taken from 'Memorandum on American Co-operation', drafted by the head of the British Intelligence Service in the United States, Sir William Wiseman, who had the complete confidence of the President's adviser, Colonel House. The President himself had read the memorandum and had approved it as 'an accurate summary'. It was gratuitously reinforced by a letter from Northcliffe, written to Balfour on April 11. 'America is a land of pitfalls for English people. Twenty-one visits have convinced me that it needs a great deal of knowing.' He expressed the hope that Balfour would avail himself of the services of the *Times* man in Washington, Arthur Willert, and the *Daily Mail* man in New York, W. F. Bullock. 'Both have been with me many years and are not of the American-English type, as I bring them to England every year to keep their accent and viewpoints right.' Northcliffe was at the same time instructing Geoffrey Dawson (formerly Robinson) to give 'more prominence to Willert's dispatches on the American situation', in *The Times*.

Balfour found President Wilson more thoroughly committed in thought to the future of the world than to its current agonies. The President respected Balfour's experience of affairs and his high standing and he was further attracted by the likelihood of Balfour being an important figure at the peace conference. Despite the somewhat unrealistic atmosphere at Washington, and a temperament too apt to be taken for that of a cynic, Balfour achieved a notable political success during his brief American sojourn, though that was not its most obvious purpose. He helped to inaugurate a new era in Anglo-American relations, diminishing if not sweeping away the animosities remaining over from the eighteenth century.

At other levels, the Balfour mission's effective results fell short of expectations, particularly as regards finance. Northcliffe wrote to the Prime Minister on May 18: 'I have received the following private cable from the *Times* correspondent in Washington: *Congress procrastinating stop executive not yet organized stop country not given necessary leadership stop Balfour has been in broad sense conspicuously successful though his subordinates handicapped in concrete work.* The Mission had attained its chief object of communicating vital information to the President and the men around him and of making finally clear to them the need for a closely concerted effort against the common enemy. That some of the most essential information was not communicated in writing was unfortunate in view of later events. The Balfour Mission lacked the fullness of organization which would have made all its purposes effective. On the credit side, it laid a firm foundation for the publicity services by which Great Britain was subsequently drawn into a more intimate and beneficial relationship with the American people. Agreeing with House that the war was 'the biggest event' in history, Balfour said that 'beyond that he could not think; he could not grasp the details and probably would never be able to do so'.

Before returning from the United States in May, Balfour had recommended the setting up of what Lloyd George speaks of in his *War Memoirs* as 'a permanent British Mission there, to maintain liaison with the American Government and co-ordinate the activities of the various British agencies at work in the United States'. The British Government had been making extensive purchases through the export department of J. P. Morgan & Company, of New York, of which department E. R. Stettinius was in charge. As the demand for American materials grew, various officials had been sent from England as controllers of the different buying agencies, each of which became a mission in itself. Each had freedom of action. There was no central control, and a great deal of rivalry, and muddle, as a result. Lloyd George recorded that the post of head of the British War Mission was offered, first, to Sir Edward Grey, whose failing eyesight precluded his acceptance of it. At a War Cabinet meeting on May 25, Northcliffe's name was put forward as that of 'an experienced business man'. To quote Lloyd George again, there was approval of the suggestion that he might be 'a very suitable person for this appointment'.

Some weeks earlier Northcliffe had been in touch with Lloyd George about the importance of telling the Americans more about Britain's war efforts and needs. The Prime Minister had written to him, in an acknowledging letter of April 4, agreeing that 'there is no time to lose'. Shortly afterwards, Lloyd George asked Northcliffe to go to the U.S. as Ambassador and Minister Plenipotentiary. The offer of the appointment was made in the Cabinet room at 10 Downing Street, in the presence of

Edward Keen, European General Manager of the United Press Association of America. A record of it occurs in a letter written by Northcliffe to Lady Northcliffe, dated June 9, 1917: 'He pressed me to go . . . and I refused.' On June 11, Lord Bertie, the British Ambassador at Paris, noted in his diary: 'Lloyd George wanted to substitute Lord Northcliffe for Spring Rice [British Ambassador at Washington] but that was stopped.' On May 30 Northcliffe received a message from 10 Downing Street saying that the Prime Minister wished to see him on urgent business that evening, though they already had an appointment for the following day. 'I went to Downing Street', Northcliffe wrote to Lady Northcliffe, 'and he asked me again to go to the United States. On this second occasion he was very emphatic. Would I go for some months as head of the British War Mission? It was *vital*, he said, that someone known in, and who knew well, the United States, should go: it was vital to our national fortunes.' The letter to Lady Northcliffe continued:

I agreed to accept the post with more regret and reluctance than I can express. I told him that on public grounds I do not believe I am the man. Enemies at home, journalistic and political, will make my task difficult. I am so hated by the Germans in the United States that my career is likely to be cut short. I believe that my work at home has helped towards efficiency, however unpopular it has made me with Asquith & Co. I am too old to adapt myself to this new work. I urged that Churchill should go, young, half American and a picturesque figure, or Harold [Rothermere] was a real man of business for the work.

Lloyd George's clumsy insistence on Northcliffe's business qualifications was unlikely to have been accepted as a compliment by his nominee who had no title to them or pretence that he had. He was before all things the journalist who may have been offended by the ascription. 'In regard to the suggestion which you made to me last night,' he wrote to the Prime Minister, 'I should be greatly obliged if you would first offer it to my brother Rothermere. He has got the clothing business "fixed"—as they say in America—and is capable of a much bigger job.'

Northcliffe wrote to his wife:

It was decided by the War Cabinet, after consultation with Americans in London, that I was to be marked down for the difficult and delicate task, from which, in my judgment, it is impossible for anyone to emerge with credit; that does not matter. Anything I have achieved at home has been won by my press. In the U.S. I am to be without my source of influence. My coming will be resented by the Embassy, by the Missions, by the Consulate, and eventually by the Americans themselves.

Foremost among the Americans consulted in London was Northcliffe's friend, Walter Hines Page, the U.S. Ambassador at the Court of St. James. When, in 1914, Page had been made Ambassador, Northcliffe 'had taken the liberty' (his own words) of writing to the President, Theodore Roosevelt, informing him that he considered 'the appointment ideal'. On Page's side, the cordiality of feeling was such that it became a liability to Northcliffe when Page wrote about him to President Wilson in terms of scarcely restrained enthusiasm: 'an uncommonly brilliant fellow', 'a business man of extraordinary ability and energy', and so on. Wilson's attitude to Northcliffe had been influenced by Balfour and also by A. G. Gardiner, editor of the London *Daily News*, who was in close touch with House. House himself had met Northcliffe in London and had been entertained by him and Lady Northcliffe at Sutton Place. His prejudice was not so strong as that of Wilson, who was said to have regarded Northcliffe as the British equivalent of Hearst, an agent of unrest. 'I don't believe in Northcliffe', Wilson told Josephus Daniels, Secretary of the Navy, and he had telegraphed to House, on hearing of the British intention to send out someone to supervise Government war spending, giving the opinion that such action was 'most unwise and still more unwise the choice of person named', i.e. Northcliffe. The President may have remembered that *The Times* had been patronizingly critical of his call for a clearer definition of war aims, rating it as an interference by a well-meaning outsider, while Northcliffe himself had told the *New York Times* that 'the suggestion that Great Britain should consider peace can only be regarded as hostile'. Wilson had shown so little sympathy with the proposal to send Northcliffe that eyebrows were raised in Washington when it became known that, despite the President's opinion, the appointment was confirmed in London. In fact, it had been left to the State Department in Washington to review the position in the light of that opinion, a step which, by some tardiness of understanding, was not taken until it was too late. Northcliffe had sailed. On June 7, the New York newspapers announced his acceptance of the post, 'in succession to Mr Balfour'. There was no mystery about the origin of the announcement. The Prime Minister himself had passed it for publication on June 6. Lord Beaverbrook has put on record that there was opposition to the Northcliffe appointment by Balfour. Sir Maurice (later Lord) Hankey, Secretary to the War Cabinet at the time, has stated that Balfour supported the appointment.

The disparity of views between Washington and London produced a crop of speculative comments, the sum of which was that Lloyd Goerge had successfully manipulated the opportunity of putting three thousand miles of ocean between himself and a man who wielded so great a power of public criticism. Colonel House noted in his diary, later in 1917, that he had met a journalist who had been present when Lloyd George was asked why Northcliffe had been sent to the United States: was it because he was getting troublesome? 'George admitted that was the reason.' Lloyd George was an opportunist in conversation as in other matters. It may have been almost as congenial to him to pretend that he had dispatched Northcliffe from the governing centre and to entangle him in difficulties with an unsympathetic ambassador, as actually to have done it. Certainly the decision could not have been taken without Northcliffe's awareness of the personal strategy involved. Both men were capable of vengeful things. Both also could rise to the heights of great purpose. 'It is the wisdom of successful government,' Lloyd George remarks in his *War Memoirs* concerning the choice of Northcliffe for the British War Mission, 'that it should harness the powerful but unruly natural elements to some beneficent task', thus raising his appointment above the gossip of the chancelleries. What the Lloyd George memoirs, like every other record of those events, fails to state is that the beneficent task on that occasion found its assignee more ardently alert to its importance than most people, not excluding the Prime Minister himself. Northcliffe's knowledge of the Americans, gained from many visits, had given him an ample appreciation of their power and possibilities.

On the morning of June 7, men and women of the editorial staff of the *Daily Mail* departments gathered round the notice boards to read the day's message from 'the Chief'. It read as follows:

I am leaving to take over Mr Balfour's American Mission and it is essential that not one line of criticism of the United States, men, books, or anything else, should appear in the *Daily Mail*, the *Continental Daily Mail*, the *Overseas Mail* or any other publication associated with the *Daily Mail*.

There was a sneering reference to American journalism the other day in one paper, not, I am glad to say, any of those here mentioned, which, if it were cabled to the pro-German newspapers in America, would have helped the enemy propaganda.

Only those who know the attitude of Fenian, pro-German, and anti-English pressmen in America can realize the minute efforts they make to discover material for anti-British attack.

$\star$ $\qquad$ $\star$ $\qquad$ $\star$

In Washington the most vigorous opposition came from the British Ambassador, Sir Cecil Spring Rice, who lost no time in communicating his distress of mind to the President. Parenthetically, Spring Rice's qualifications as a wartime ambassador had been challenged in a letter to Northcliffe from H. G. Wells. 'He is just a miscellaneous diplomatist—Tokyo, Cairo, Petrograd, an all-covered-with orders kind of person. We might as well have a messenger boy there.' Wells 'had a brain-wave to communicate' on the subject. 'The one man to get hold of Wilson as British Ambassador is Gilbert Murray. He could talk to Wilson like a brother.'

In the light of the President's attitude to Northcliffe, House had at first hoped that Northcliffe might be 'headed off', as he put it. There was a discussion about how it might be done. When it was learned that Northcliffe was coming, House went into conference with Sir William Wiseman, who was constantly in touch with the presidential inner circle. They discussed whether to help Northcliffe or hinder him. 'It was our intention to let him run amok.' In other words, give him a chance to prove himself *persona non grata*. 'After enjoying the thought of this, Wiseman and I decided the matter was too serious. . . .' The quotation is from House's diary for June 9, 1917.

The *Times* correspondent in Washington, Arthur Willert, had been summoned to witness the perturbation of the British Ambassador. Spring Rice was greatly upset. Willert described the scene in his book, *The Road to Safety**:

The picture of the ambassador still comes to me as he looked up from his desk. A small grey figure, neat grizzled beard, metal-rimmed spectacles, delicate sensitive face, at that moment pale and drawn with angry agitation.

To Spring Rice, Northcliffe was the incarnation of all that he disliked in the twentieth century.

Lloyd George referred in his memoirs to 'one of our representatives in the States' as having written to Balfour: 'Whatever induced the Government to send Northcliffe here? May I explain, hastily, that this is not a question to which I expect an answer. It is merely a horrified note of exclamation. . . .' The effect on those nervous patriots was as if one more cyclone was about to hit America. Lloyd George referred to 'a storm of criticism'.

On May 31, Northcliffe had lunched at Downing Street with the Prime Minister. There was one other guest, the Secretary of the War Cabinet, Sir Maurice Hankey, who noted in his private diary that Northcliffe was 'very quiet and restrained'. That same day, Northcliffe presided at the first meeting of the Civil Aerial Transport Committee. Opening the meeting, he gave notice of his new appointment and moved that his place on the committee be taken by the deputy chairman, Major Baird, M.P. Thereafter, as before, Northcliffe's services to aviation were rendered outside the official sphere. A last memorandum on that crowded day instructed Marlowe to print a letter in the *Daily Mail* urging the reform of school hours for younger children.

Northcliffe spent the evening at 13 Dean's Yard, Westminster, with Sir Robert Hudson, the Red Cross administrator. He confided to Hudson

* Verschoyle, 1952.

that he had 'a strong premonition that he would not see England again'. He asked Hudson to promise to befriend Lady Northcliffe while he was away and to 'take special care of her' if he did not return. Having arranged for Arnholz to draw up a document giving Sutton control of his personal and business affairs for the next twelve months, and to draft a new will to be sent to him in America, he and his French-Swiss valet, Paul Madeux, left for Liverpool and the hazards of the Atlantic within thirty-six hours of receiving the Prime Minister's final instructions. They were seen off from Liverpool by Sutton and Price, who handed over the little green deed-box. There was a message from Lord Derby, Secretary of State for War: 'Goodbye and good luck to you. Nobody realizes more than I do the difficulties and dangers of such a task.'

In a last note to Sutton, Northcliffe had written: 'If anything happens to me, my dear Sut, I want you to have Elmwood. It is the nicest house I know and I love every inch of it, just as much as I shall hate every hour I am away from all my friends and haunts. But it must be done and I shall do it to the best of anything that may be in me', and, on the back of the envelope: 'If anything happens to me, T. E. Mackenzie [his private accountant] is to be *well* provided for.' Pine, the chauffeur, followed with the Rolls-Royce, a showpiece of British motor engineering. H. G. Price, his senior secretary, was also in the vanguard, and was recalled from active service to serve under him in the War Mission.

He thought it necessary to inform the Prime Minister, on June 2, that it was possible for him to leave the country only if Sutton, Dawson (Robinson) and Marlowe were retained in their respective positions as chairman of the Amalgamated Press, editor of *The Times*, and editor of the *Daily Mail*. 'All three desire to participate in military service but that does not assist *me*.' In other words, if they were called up he would be obliged to return, 'as I am responsible to the proprietors of the Amalgamated Press with a capital of £1,300,000, the Anglo-Newfoundland Development Company with a capital of £1,600,000, *The Times* with a capital of £850,000 and Associated Newspapers with a capital of £1,600,000'. Presumptuous though the expectation may have been that a Prime Minister should give his mind to such details in the hardest year of a great war, Northcliffe's letter affirmed:

You know that I will do my very best to help finish the war. I am a little disturbed on leaving England by facts which have reached me as to the interference of the British Ambassador at Washington with members of the Mission. I shall go to him frankly, telling him that I desire to work in every way in accord with him and wish in no way to intrude upon his province, but if, as I am told and reluctantly believe, he is a man of small parts, inclined to make mischief, I shall come back after duly acquainting the War Cabinet and the Foreign Office with the circumstances.

Northcliffe, by telegram, to his mother: Crewe, rail; 2 June, 1917.—
Au revoir my dearest.—Alfred.

★   ★   ★

On board the small U.S.M.S. *St. Paul*, Northcliffe found Isaac Marcosson, an enterprising and widely travelled American interviewer already
well known to him, Arthur Hungerford Pollen, formerly of the *Daily
Mail*, who was going out to lecture in the United States, and R. G.
Knowles, an American comedian popular with British music-hall
audiences. Northcliffe, deck-walking with Marcosson, reminded him that
their fellow passengers were different from the ocean tourists of the peace
years. 'By the time we reached Sandy Hook', Marcosson wrote, 'he knew
the story of their lives—diplomats, soldiers, aviators, historians, natural-
ists, authors, plain business men. More than one of them remarked to me:
"I had no idea that Lord Northcliffe was so simple and so accessible." '
L. J. Maxse's *National Review* later recorded an incident of the voyage.
'Never is the father of a year-old baby on the steamer likely to forget
what he proudly narrated on landing: that Lord Northcliffe had insisted
on giving him his life-saving suit as soon as he heard that the baby had no
mother.' When it was put to him that he ought not to take such a risk
in view of the task ahead, he answered: 'Kismet is my motto. What will
be, will be. See that he gets it, please.'

The submarine campaign was at its height. British shipping losses were
nearing catastrophe point. National disaster had never come so close. For
the Germans, Northcliffe was a major individual target of the war. He
behaved as if his personal jeopardy had no place in his thoughts. He was
not only crossing a perilous ocean. On landing in America he would be
exposed to other risks. He wrote to his wife:

... We went round the *north* of Ireland with a foolish procession of some ten
ships. When I awoke, it was a perfect summer morning. An American ship
following was torpedoed. We got her messages for help (S.O.S.). Then her
name and longitude and latitude. Then 'we are sinking'. Then 'all in boats'.

Daylight is at 3 a.m. and I start going through a mass of official papers soon
after. Such as are not very secret Pollen reads to me from 9 till 1. He is a beautiful reader—and flabbergasted by the figures. Incidentally, I have an army of
people, thousands all over the U.S., Canada and South America, buyers, in-
spectors, all, I hope, honest. They will naturally resent my coming, as will the
Embassy and the N.Y. Consulate, but I shall work hard for harmony.

I enclose the passenger list. It is typical of the population of the U.S. You
might post it to the P.M., telling him that these are the people I am expected
to enthuse for England.

534

Yesterday we saw a magnificent English sailing ship, all her canvas set, the first I have ever seen at sea, on her way towards England and, the American naval officers think, certain doom.

When he was not studying the documents of officialdom, he wrote long reflective letters to his family and old colleagues. Referring to his unwillingness to leave England at such a time in her history he fell into a mood of valedictory reminiscence, almost of foreboding.

My private objects are selfish. My sweet mother is nearing her 80th year and she and I have always delighted in each other's companionship. For the last few years I have lived much with her, slept in the room next to her. Her happiness and my happiness and health have benefited by my sleeping at Totteridge, for in London I sleep ill and my health goes downhill.

My domestic life, despite the children that never came, is smooth and happy. We lately moved from our delightful 22, St James's Place to a small but exquisite house at 8, Buckingham Street, Buckingham Gate. Lady Northcliffe has been a pattern to other rich women in this war time. She at once turned our beautiful Sutton Place into a hospital and *worked* in her hospital continuously. I lately gave her a home of her own at Crowborough, as dainty as her dainty self. I retained my beloved Elmwood, bought with my first *profits* (as apart from journalistic earnings). We have been married 27 years, not many childless couples so happily.

My work has been absorbing, always. My 'Times' and 'Daily Mail' and other newspapers, my periodicals, the Newfoundland adventure (for which, together with the business side of the Amalgamated Press, the business foundation and success of the 'Evening News' and 'Daily Mail', Harold is mainly responsible), all these have been my children. My journals have been burned and banned at times for doing what they believed to be their duty, but they have huge followings. These undertakings are filled with those who have proved to be my friends. I have other friendships of value. Our family is an united one, with the Mother as the centre.

My last hours in England, never so lovely as in the unique hawthorn, chestnut and lilac time of the lovely year, were a rush to settle my affairs and see heads of Government departments with whom I shall have to deal, and the farewells.

Mother and I clung together for a few moments on that Saturday morning. I saw her at her porch and then off in her car with Harold and St. John. We picked up Leicester at Golders Green and then on to Euston, where the wife and some of my staff were come to say goodbye. Those last two days in England went as in a flash.

On the Friday I had an audience at Buckingham Palace. George V. is quite unlike the popular notion of him. Animated, vivacious, and packed with facts, with a microscopic memory of his travels, he surprised me not a little.

I cannot say that I am enjoying the journey towards my great task. I slept

well at first but the heat is great and the weight of coming events is upon me.
I feel as I felt on the night of the opening of the Grand Falls mammoth, when
I walked out alone and gazed upon that vast responsibility.

I have had hours of acute regret on the voyage. *Let the cobbler stick to his last.*
I loathe leaving my home and work. But I am ordered to go and if I fail
absolutely it will be because I am not the man for the task.

He begged his wife to send photographs and 'other souvenirs of home
for my abodes' in America. The Government, he told her, would provide
him with a house in Washington, if he wanted it, and suitable accommodation in New York. 'But I must have a little country place, near
golf.' He went on to describe the task before him:

Nothing but my intimate knowledge and instinct of the grave national
danger would have led me on this lonely and dangerous venture. Even *I* had
not a full understanding till I read the gloomy documents dumped on me for
the voyage. My task is a terrific one and most delicate. I am sent forth literally
to *beg* for assistance of all kinds and in colossal quantities and from a people
whom certain of our public men and journals have attacked up till the last few
weeks. Most fortunately, I have never allowed any criticism to appear in my
Press. The Americans on this ship know it. I have always felt, as you know,
that when this war *did* come we should eventually have to ask for their assistance. On the scale on which I am being sent forth to plead, it looks as though
the British nation will be in pawn to the United States, and, though I do not
fear for the future, it is obvious that people don't realize the coming linking up
of nations. . . .

The brazen impudence of some of these Government begging suggestions
fairly staggers me. They are written by people who obviously have never been
in America and who seem to think that we are conferring a favour in allowing
the Americans to join the alliance. I shall do my utmost. I will slave 18 hours a
day. But I should like a whirlwind visit of the Prime Minister, not merely to
the East but to the money and munitions centres of the great West. We are
begging from a people who want munitions for their own army, who have
been humbugged by the censorship, so that their notion of the war is quite
different from ours, their sympathies pro-French and in many states vigorously
anti-English, with German propagandists working against my Mission night
and day.

England, 'green cloudy England', never looked fairer than when I said farewell to Mother at Totteridge. We don't realize how lovely a thing has been
this spring. The Americans on board cannot cease talking of the hawthorn and
lilac, especially the hawthorn. I am fond of the United States, entirely at home
there, and admire many fine traits in their people. But I regret my beautiful
homes and working places, my happy circle, perhaps more than I ought. . . .

On this ship alone are three people we entertained at Sutton Place; those
lovely days, and the roses, help me. In America there are more than two
thousand influential folk whom we have entertained somewhere.

Ask my friends to write to me. I shall be a very isolated person, guarded night and day and *pestered always* and always with strangers.

'This is a very slow ship,' he wrote to his mother, warning her that she would not hear from him for nearly a fortnight. 'I think of you at least once in every hour.' The day before he reached New York, he wrote to her more fully:

Sweet Mother,—Though I have not been able to send wireless messages, which are forbidden, I have been with you all across this wide sea. I keep my watch to Totteridge time and as I know your movements very well, I can picture what you are doing.

We were in what is considered the danger zone for two and a half days but the passengers took very little notice of it. An occasional porpoise made some of them jumpy but the trip has been just like the others. Wouldn't I like to start straight back to my darling Mum, submarines or not!

I am keen on my work which, if successful, should go far to help to end the war. Harold knows what my duties are. I am to be well guarded night and day, and shall be most careful. The harder I work the more quickly shall I return to my darling Mother. I am well, vigorous, and tremendously anxious to win.

My love to everyone I love, and most for my darling Mother who is in my thoughts a thousand times a day.

ALFRED.

The *St. Paul* docked at New York on June 12. Northcliffe was one of the first of her passengers to step ashore—'projecting himself down the gangplank with more speed than is usual with distinguished Englishmen', according to one spectator of his arrival. 'A man of fifty-two, he looks ten years younger, despite a neck stoop—head thrust forward as if hurrying on his body.' The same observer noted the familiar white-dotted red tie and 'eyes that are restless and eager, the glance suggesting the general curiosity and irritability at everyone's slowness'. Balfour had arrived in a frock coat, which led to his being referred to in a newspaper as 'an interesting survival'. Northcliffe wore the blue serge suit of his perennial taste, with a soft felt hat, and a soft white collar instead of the starched linen of English convention. His informality in dress was an ingratiating factor of more than personal value in American estimates of him.

The ship reporters of the New York newspapers had gone out in a tug to meet the *St. Paul* in quarantine. Their interest in Northcliffe amounted almost to excitement. To them he was a formidable personage, headlined in their papers as 'The Old Gang's Scourge', 'Mentor of Ministers' and

'Breaker of Cabinets'. They were equally well aware of the exceptiona
romance of his career, begun in their ranks of the profession. They were
disappointed when he told them: 'I am not here to talk. I am engaged
in a gigantic task of organization.'

The *Times* Washington correspondent, Arthur Willert, was among
those who had gone out to meet him. Northcliffe asked him questions
about the Ambassador: was he likely to be difficult? Willert told him that
Spring Rice was a sick man. Northcliffe said that it was necessary in the
national interest that they should work together and that he, for his part,
would do his best to co-operate. They had corresponded on a friendly
basis when Spring Rice was at the Legation in Stockholm some years
before. It might be helpful, he suggested, if he sent a friendly word to the
Ambassador on landing. It could be given to the Embassy representative
on the quay. Willert then had to say that there would be no Embassy
representative there to greet him. Willert said that Northcliffe showed
'quiet concentrated anger'. His immediate response was to send a protest
to Lloyd George via the *Times* editor in London. He was so 'entirely
dissatisfied' by the treatment he had received, his message ran, that unless
steps were immediately taken to remedy it he would return and make a
public statement of his reason for so doing. Dawson replied that he had
seen the Prime Minister, who was 'exceedingly sorry' and hoped that
Northcliffe would communicate direct with him in the event of any
further difficulty. A few days later Northcliffe cabled Dawson again, instructing him to take a message to Bonar Law: *Absolutely decline to submit
to further flagrant incidents stop like your advice whether I should return stop
otherwise everything going perfectly and chaos and expense being reduced.*

Meanwhile, House had informed the President of the situation, saying
that Northcliffe had been 'angry beyond words'. At the same time, House
wrote to Northcliffe expressing pleasure at his safe arrival and offering any
help in his power. According to House, the Anglophobe William Randolph Hearst had sent his personal representative to call on Northcliffe,
who declined to receive him, saying that if Hearst wanted to see him he
could come himself. 'In the event he comes,' House told the President,
'Northcliffe would tell him some truths that would be good for his soul.'
Transmitting his account of the episode to Wilson, House may have
hoped to correct the President's bias against Northcliffe. That effect may
have been retarded by a further spate of adulation from Page in London,
who wrote to the President:

He is the friendliest of Englishmen to us. His papers have been singularly fair
to us. He knows and likes the United States, and it is very well worth our while
to show our appreciation of his friendliness and helpfulness. Any attention that
you yourself may show him will bear good fruit. He is perhaps the most

powerful man now living in Great Britain, how much by reason of and how much in spite of his methods, it would be hard to say. For the twenty years that I have known him he has done our country steady and useful service in his vast influence on British opinion.

A letter reached Northcliffe at the Hotel Gotham on his third day in New York from the American novelist, Mary Roberts Rinehart: 'Welcome to America. . . . I cannot tell you how very general is the satisfaction over your coming. For a long time, we have felt over here that you understood us when the rest of the world did not . . . and the feeling is really of gratitude for your appointment.' The New York Tribune echoed the note of appreciation in a leading article on June 13. He had the further consolation of being cordially welcomed by André Tardieu, the French High Commissioner in Washington. On June 14, Spring Rice cabled to Balfour: 'State Department appear to be quite reconciled to Northcliffe's arrival.' Balfour had a cable from Northcliffe that day: *Allow me to take this opportunity of saying your work here makes my humbler effort comparatively easy*. Accepting the fact of his presence in America, and impressed by the immense responsibility put on him by the War Cabinet, both House and Wiseman set about clearing the air in his favour. Thanks largely to them, the Embassy arranged for him to meet the President and other chief men of the administration without undue delay. Page, also, had used his influence. On June 16, Northcliffe cabled him: *Deeply grateful for warm reception obtained for me here*. Northcliffe still had to break down the obduracy of the Ambassador, Spring Rice, who was no doubt uncomfortably aware of his concurrence in the Prime Minister's view that in times of crisis 'diplomacy as usual' could not be allowed to prevail. Making no secret of it or, for that matter, of the Prime Minister's previous offer to him of the ambassadorship with extra powers, Northcliffe conducted himself with restraint if not with the utmost tact in his approaches to the Embassy at Washington.

His good will did not overcome the ambassadorial scruples. Emotionally and physically overwrought by the wartime stresses of his post, Spring Rice, a devoted public servant, could not accommodate himself to a situation in which a civilian might in certain circumstances supersede him. Personalities apart, ambassadors were not usually amenable to the sending of missions or commissions into their domain of influence. Spring Rice's explanation of the apparent lack of official civility was that 'strict orders had been given to keep Northcliffe's movements secret'. He said that Northcliffe took it as 'an intentional insult and that he felt inclined to go home again'.

While Northcliffe waited in Washington to be received by the Ambassador, he wrote to his mother:

(*Opened by the Censor.*)

Shoreham Hotel,
Washington.
Friday, 14th June, 1917.

Most sweet and adored,—I have now been here four days and so much goes on around me that it seems like four weeks. It is barely more than a fortnight since I resolved that it was my duty to make this great sacrifice and I have had to adjust and readjust my view of the tremendous task I have in hand, of which I will give you details when I have had more time at it.

I begin my work as at home, at about six o'clock. It is very hot at that hour and I miss my cool room at Poynters which I can see vividly as I write and I miss my darling, darling Mother. Six o'clock is of course twelve o'clock with you. I keep a clock and English time before me always. I cable every day, dear, and hope they arrive the same day. I get them off before 8 a.m. (two in the afternoon) so they *ought* to arrive the same day.

I am looking for a house in the country, about as far out as Poynters. I have seen one near golf and the sea, but the prices are appalling.

I have been very well, though the heat is very trying. The American Govt. is very nice to me. *They are a mighty people, these Americans, and will end the war.* They are beginning slowly, but surely. It is their final pressure, added to our glorious work and that of France, that will rid the world of these monsters.

The wife will give other news of me and I shall send you papers and clippings.

YOUR FIRSTBORN.

Northcliffe to G. A. Sutton: New York, 15 June, 1917.—*Send out dozen those little black pencils dear Sutton.*—Chief. Northcliffe to his Mother: New York, 19 June, 1917.—*Things going smoothly darling Mother.*—Northcliffe. New York, 20 June, 1917.—*Still busy and thinking of my darling Mother.*—Northcliffe.

On June 20, he sent a long letter to Sutton with the covering note: 'Will you please see Davies [Lloyd George's secretary] and see that this is read to the Prime Minister, and see that he listens?' Lloyd George reprinted the letter with significant omissions, in his war memoirs. Northcliffe wrote:

I know that the Prime Minister does not see letters or hear about them. It is essential, however, that he should hear about what is going on in this country, *where, as I told him in* 1914, the war will be decided.

After paying tribute to the War Mission staff, Northcliffe described his experiences as a newcomer to Washington. 'My reception from the President downwards could hardly have been better. My reception at the hands of the British Ambassador could not have been worse.' He referred to Sir Cecil Spring Rice as 'an odd person' and went on to tell the Prime Minister:

Here is an account of the amazing scene which took place in his room at the Embassy, which I dictated immediately after my return.

Let me preface the statement of this interview by saying that, outwardly, he treated me quite well, though he did not meet me at the station. I went to Washington, however, prepared to swallow a great amount of snubbing in view of the urgency of our national cause. I got it!

Northcliffe further told how, after a day of being introduced by the Ambassador to members of the American Government, Spring Rice had invited him to dine at the Embassy. He asked Northcliffe to arrive a little ahead of the stated time, as he wished to have a private talk. Northcliffe complied with that request.

He was sitting at a table before his red boxes, and, suddenly looking up, produced a cutting from the pro-German *Evening Post* which had appeared before my arrival and which said, as far as I can remember, that it was odd that a man who had criticized the Ambassador in scareheads and articles (a concoction) should be coming to this appointment.

He then suddenly rose, looked at me in a very queer way, and, pointing his finger at me, said: 'You are my enemy. Apart from these criticisms, you inserted four years ago an anonymous attack in *The Times* which nearly killed me; *and Lady Spring Rice declines to receive you on that account.*' (There are, fortunately, other charming ladies in Washington!)

Northcliffe answered that he had never criticized him, to which Spring Rice replied that he had been marked down in *The Times* for his prolonged absence from the Embassy and for travelling in German ships. He pointed out that his absence had been due to bad health and to diplomatic circumstances which were necessarily private. At that point, Northcliffe made a gesture of leaving the house.

I walked towards the door with the intention of doing so, when he rushed after me, put out his hand, and said: 'We have got to work together, whatever we may feel about each other.'

I accepted his hand and the incident was fortunately closed at that moment by the announcement of the French Ambassador.

The British Ambassador's subsequent account of the interview confirmed Northcliffe's version, except that it more emphatically charged him with being personally responsible for the criticisms in *The Times*. Northcliffe's opinion, conveyed in the same letter to Lloyd George, was that 'Sir Cecil Spring Rice is either overwrought by the strain of war, or is not quite right in his head'.

The President, on the other hand, was 'cordiality itself'. Colonel House, who was increasingly taken with Northcliffe—'I like him the more I see him'—may have toned down the President's suspicious attitude. House told the President what had passed between Northcliffe and Spring Rice who 'invited him to dinner. Strangely enough, he chose the occasion to insult him.'

Willert, of *The Times*, reported from Washington to his editor in London, on July 17: '. . . Northcliffe behaved with the greatest possible common sense and dignity. It was, however, a difficult situation largely owing to the attitude of the Embassy.' Willert told Dawson: 'Outwardly, since the first outburst, there has been civility. There is no co-operation whatsoever, unless the spasmodic passing on of half-digested or muddled problems can be called co-operation.' Northcliffe, Willert wrote a few days later, had started well and had made a good impression. 'The President, who had expected a political ogre reeking with the blood of those British radicals with whom he is fundamentally in sympathy, has expressed himself as agreeably surprised.'

In order to avoid a further clash with the Ambassador, Northcliffe had not taken a house at Washington, as the Prime Minister had suggested. He wrote to tell Lloyd George: 'I have taken a modest flat instead which will be an office for the Mission, and I am buying a cheap motor-car in order to be as unobtrusive when in Washington as possible.' The flat was on Massachusetts Avenue and it had a defect which its new tenant discovered too late—creaking floors; to him, always, one of life's abominations. His letter to the Prime Minister continued:

No effort at conciliation on my part will be lacking, even if my personal dignity suffers, in view of the fact that the war can only be won from here—when this mighty republic is awakened. And it is slowly awakening. When it wakes there will be thrown into the scales a weight that will settle the great struggle.

You need have no fear that I will have friction with the Ambassador, if it can be helped. If there be a change in the Embassy, I strongly urge, old as he is, Lord Bryce. He probably does not approve of me but I approve of him.

Yours sincerely,
NORTHCLIFFE

P.S. Life is not the bed of roses here that it is in Downing Street and Walton Heath.

House wrote to the President on June 19: '. . . you charmed Northcliffe in your few minutes' talk with him the other day. I have heard from many directions of his enthusiastic praise of you. You seem to have been a revelation to him. I am glad you treated him so kindly, for he has shown desire to work in harmony with every one.' Lord Eustace Percy (later Lord Percy of Newcastle), who had gone out with the Balfour Mission and was staying on in Washington, was communicating at the same time with Sir Eric Drummond at the Foreign Office: 'One of His Excellency's incalculable actions,' he wrote in reference to Spring Rice's behaviour to Northcliffe, 'a nervous attack.' Spring Rice felt intensely the strain of wartime service. The British poet, Alfred Noyes, who visited him in Washington, wrote that 'many traps were laid for him and there was one attempt at assassination'.* Reporting direct to Balfour, Lord Eustace Percy suggested that it was desirable to ignore the almost inevitable friction 'between those who will always be fools and those who will never be gentlemen'. He pointed out that in effect there was no British Ambassador at Washington, Spring Rice lacking the power to organize, control, direct or stimulate his staff. 'We cannot go on like this. There will be a mess. Northcliffe will become ambassador.'

*   *   *

In London, on June 21, Northcliffe's leadership of the British War Mission was attacked in the House of Lords by Lord Buckmaster (Lord Chancellor, 1915–16), who made what Geoffrey Dawson described as 'an elaborately malignant speech', arguing that Northcliffe was not qualified for such a post. Lord Curzon, replying, maintained that Northcliffe was 'supremely well qualified', but Dawson let Northcliffe know that Curzon's speech was 'characteristically lame'. *The Times*, on June 21, asked what patriotic purpose was served by the attack, which had come, the leading article said, from 'a little knot of ex-Ministers who had not themselves been conspicuously successful as organizers of victory'. Maxse's *National Review* (July 1917) was more sardonic: 'What future is there for the self-seeking lawyer and the inefficient nobleman who has for many years monopolized power in our unhappy country if men of capacity are brought into the sacred circle?'

In the House of Commons, Bonar Law defined the scope of Northcliffe's task in America and told the House that 'he is undertaking this highly important duty at the urgent request of the Government and at inconvenience to himself'. Northcliffe himself had demanded that the last-named point should be made, although 'sacrifice' was the word he had suggested, not 'inconvenience'. In the *National Review*, L. J. Maxse declared that Northcliffe was '*the* man for this Mission', and added provokingly: 'Though it may be exceedingly astute of the Prime Minister to expatriate at this critical moment a potentially formidable critic, and in a sense to "nobble" the Northcliffe press . . . we regret it, because Lord

* *Two Worlds for Memory*, Sheed & Ward, 1953.

Northcliffe's influence is indispensable at home. He has rendered en
during service throughout the war—necessarily making some mistakes—
and over and over again he has literally saved the situation.' Anothe
prominent editor, Austin Harrison, of the *English Review*, had writter
privately to Northcliffe: 'I implore you not to quit the objectivity of you
room by becoming an official of the Government.' The Asquithiai
Liberal newspapers, led by the *Daily News*, had no good word to say
'The Government have only to send Mr Horatio Bottomley as an envoy
extraordinary to Paris or Rome to satisfy the public that things are really
moving.' The same newspaper claimed to have received 'a great many
letters of protest against the appointment at a time when good relation:
with America are above all things necessary'. The American press, on the
whole, was friendly. 'He fits the opportunity', was the general view.
Ex-President Theodore Roosevelt greeted Northcliffe in a message as
'a splendid friend of America'. Northcliffe cabled Geoffrey Dawson that
the American press 'thoroughly understood the motives for the debate
in the House of Lords and were merely amused'.

Reporting more fully to Northcliffe, Dawson wrote: 'I saw the Prime
Minister. I have no doubt that he was genuinely annoyed to hear that no
sort of preparation had been made for your arrival. He sent for all the
papers while I was with him and undertook to go into the matter personally.' Dawson then disclosed, by implication, that Lloyd George himself was the source of the bother. 'The most astounding thing is that,
having once settled your letter of instructions [as Head of the British War
Mission], the Prime Minister seems to have thought that he had done all
that was necessary and to have taken no steps whatever to see that the
various authorities in America were informed. That sort of thing would
be inconceivable in any private concern, and confirms what we have
always known, viz. that the Prime Minister, with all his great qualities,
is a hopeless organizer, and does not know how to use the very considerable staff which he has collected about him.' Dawson concluded: 'I only
hope that things will go better after this unfortunate beginning, for I am
sure that on the Prime Minister's part there is not the slightest desire to
minimize your Mission or to go back on anything which he may have
said to you.'

This communication was followed by another in which Dawson informed Northcliffe: 'I saw both Lloyd George and Balfour. The former
was already in process of sending you a message, and the latter asked me
to assure you of his good will and support and of his hope that you would
carry the Mission through.'

The Prime Minister's message was 'most cordial'. Northcliffe took the
chance of expanding his cabled thanks into a report on some of the difficulties besetting the Mission. He prefaced it with a comment on the

House of Lords attack on himself: 'I am not at all disturbed by Old Gang carpings, except for the effect they may have on some of our officials at Washington, of whom not a few are under the belief that the Old Gang will return.'

The American public situation, he told Lloyd George, was unlike anything that he had known in his twenty-five years' American experience. 'Despite the Rt. Hon. A. J. Balfour's great personal triumph . . . a strong current is dragging one down, the perpetual workings of German propagandists and financiers. Wherever one turns, there is some mysterious force making for endless discussion and delay. The whole atmosphere of Washington is permeated by this mysterious influence.' The warning passed to him in 1909 by Medill McCormick, the Chicago newspaper proprietor, proved to have been well founded: anti-British views radiated strongly from the American universities, with their German affinities.* Northcliffe's impression was that the administration tried to do its best, 'but does not know how to'. Every decision was in the hands of the President. The smallest matters were referred to him.

In the cordial conversation he had with me he was obviously under no misapprehension as to the nature of our great task, but he lacks help, for beyond question the people around him, with one or two exceptions, are not at all of the calibre of those around you.

Six different buying agencies or smaller missions were at work in the United States, Northcliffe informed the Prime Minister. 'There is friction, jealousy, overlapping, over-expansion, but much ability.' Orders and counter-orders from England were causing many difficulties.

I do not wish to make further reference to the small attitude of the Ambassador. I am keeping out of his way as much as possible. I have taken a house near New York, so as to be away from Washington.

One of the most valuable people here is Sir William Wiseman, Head of our Military Intelligence. He is young, alert, and knows these people well. Another is Sir Richard Crawford, of the Embassy. Eustace Percy does good work. Royden and Salter, the shipping men, are essential to this Mission and should not be recalled. E. R. Stettinius, of Morgans, is a tower of strength.

May I express the hope that you and your colleagues are not being overworked? They may rely on me to do the utmost in my power. I know that the war is to be won here and, as far as is compatible with discretion, I will leave no stone unturned to help achieve victory.

Among the more obvious influences that hindered his labours was the Irish element. 'The Irish hurt us in all sorts of ways. I am seeing some of their leaders. One is up against the Irish influence in a variety of un-

* See page 384.

expected places—in coming to agreements, making contracts and so on.' Regard may or may not have been paid to his partly Irish family background in the deliberations leading up to his appointment as head of the British War Mission. It presumably counted for something as he went about his country's business on the American continent. 'I flatter myself that the British War Mission stands very well with the Irish here,' he wrote to his wife after he had been in America two months. 'I am on good terms with the Irish leaders in Senate and Congress.'

He wrote to Sutton on June 24: 'But for my implicit belief that the war will be won by the United States, I would not stop here for twenty-four hours.' To his mother on the same date, he wrote: 'I am getting a little more used to my unwilling exile, because I more and more realize that the war will be won from here. My department spends two million pounds a day. I have to hurry people up, stop friction, save money. I have no private life at all. Much past hospitality at Elmwood, Sutton Place and St. James's Place which we showed to Americans now comes back. I think of my darling Mother and all at home always. I want to push on the war and get back.' He wrote a little later that 'it was a most fortunate thing' that he had entertained Colonel and Mrs House in London, 'and that House had been more than once to the *Times* office, and that Mrs House had spent a day at Sutton Place'.

Sir Arthur Willert has since written that Northcliffe's avoidance of Washington hampered the Mission's co-ordinating work. It left the way open for the French and Italian missions to consolidate their contacts at the expense of the British. The French representative, Tardieu, was particularly active with his propaganda service, which belittled British sacrifices. Apparently Northcliffe thought it in the interests of the Mission that he and Spring Rice should have as little to do with each other as possible. 'I did not want to place him in a difficult position', Northcliffe told Tracy of the British Bureau of Information. Spring Rice had written favourably of him in a letter to London on July 5: 'Lord Northcliffe is making an excellent impression. He is on very good terms with M. Tardieu who is an old friend, this is a very important matter at the present moment.' Spring Rice had only just heard, from Northcliffe himself, that Northcliffe had been offered the ambassadorship 'some two or three months ago'. Cabling at once to London, Spring Rice asked if Balfour had any knowledge of it. A reply came the same day from Sir Eric Drummond saying that Balfour had no knowledge of it 'and doubts the fact'. Probably it was another instance of Lloyd George's habit of taking decisions without first referring them to his colleagues in office.

Telegraphing to Wiseman about persisting confusions, Willert said that 'the chief trouble is Northcliffe's refusal to settle in Washington', which was rapidly becoming a war capital. But New York was the centre of finance and commerce, a headquarters of world news and also of the nation's railway system. What Northcliffe had not immediately realized was that there were fears in Washington that Wall Street might find him too easily accessible in New York. Some of the Washington officials distrusted Sir Hardman Lever because of his contacts with Morgans, who were anathema to American liberals. 'I had to be careful not to mix in Morgans' circle, as Lever did to his detriment,' Northcliffe told Tracy. 'That is why I decided to have my headquarters up town and a very happy party we were, I truly believe. I certainly was so.'

Northcliffe informed Bonar Law that he had been able 'to effect much more good' through Colonel House 'than I have achieved at Washington'. Soon Willert was forced to admit that 'Northcliffe was a better judge of the situation than we were'. He wrote in his book that 'the dictator of Fleet Street was engaged in a task for which he did not find himself as competent as he thought he would be at first'. Northcliffe's letters make it clear that he had no such illusion. Now and again, it seemed to some of those who worked with him that he found the task too great. Lord Eustace Percy, reporting to Balfour, also thought it a possibility and suggested that Northcliffe might 'prepare an exit'. For example, Northcliffe had no grasp of the intricacies of high finance and within a few days of his arrival in America he was engaged in momentous transactions with the U.S. Treasury. A matter of pre-eminent concern was a British Government overdraft for 400,000,000 dollars arranged through Morgans. Northcliffe had his own nickname for the loan—'the sea serpent', because it had a way of rearing its head unpredictably in the midst of his negotiations. 'Northcliffe received a message from Lloyd George to come here and advise with me,' House wrote to the President (June 29, 1917). 'The British understood that we would take care of certain Russian obligations they have been carrying. What they need is 35,000,000 dollars on Monday, 100,000,000 dollars on Thursday and 185,000,000 dollars a month for two months beginning ten days from next Thursday. This is a staggering amount and indicates the load which Great Britain has been carrying for her Allies.' On House's recommendation, Northcliffe went to the Secretary of the Treasury, William C. McAdoo, in Washington, in regard to England's desperate need for money. There was a grave risk of financial collapse 'which would be worse than defeat in the field', Balfour cabled to House. In his reminiscences* McAdoo wrote:

I have met few men who had such a quick comprehension as Northcliffe. It was never necessary to explain anything to him twice. He was dynamic, his phrases were vital, his ideas crisp and clear, and he had a way of getting down at once to the vital thought in any question under discussion.

* *Crowded Years*, 1931.

But Northcliffe was not a financier, nor did he pretend to be one. His strong point was in determining how to do things—the shortest and surest road to accomplishment.

Northcliffe had a vivid cable phrase for the transactions in which he was secretly engaged at that time: 'If loans stop, war stops.' He reiterated it in his communications to Downing Street and its satellite departments. Frank about his want of qualifications to discuss national finance at the highest possible levels, he strongly supported the American Government's request that an ex-Cabinet minister or someone of similar status be sent out to take his place at the conference table. His feeling of inadequacy in that direction impelled him to make more intense efforts in others. Out of weakness came forth strength.

Chapter Twenty

Spending £2,000,000 a day

As head of the British War Mission, Northcliffe could not avoid the social life which was never to his liking even in leisurely times. For entertaining purposes, New York was more congenial to him than Washington, where protocol ruled the scene. 'The accusation against the embassy', he wrote, 'is that those there are a set of hermits who hold themselves aloof from other embassies and from members of the Congress and Senate. The British War Mission is determined to "mix" here as much as possible, but the price paid for the decision is a severe one. It means entertaining at the Gotham Hotel every day and being entertained at Washington at huge luncheon and dinner parties.' Moreover, at Washington there was always the Ambassador with his overriding powers. 'It is a curious experience,' Northcliffe confided to his family, 'to have only partial authority when one has been accustomed to absolute authority.'

Despite his often expressed distaste for social activities—'the severest part of my exile'—he appeared to enjoy presiding at interesting tables. On one such occasion, he was seated between Paderewski and William Randolph Hearst. Paderewski had no liking for Hearst, whose newspapers were pro-German, and he sat in sullen silence until Northcliffe turned on Hearst with the accusation: 'You are fooling your readers!' Hearst, he declared for all to hear, was 'backing the wrong horse'. The Allies were going to win the war—'and you ought to know it'. Hearst sat back in his chair like a suddenly winded man. Regaining his composure, he may have conveniently remembered Pulitzer's offer to Northcliffe in the first year of the century. 'Very well, Lord Northcliffe,' he said in his unattractive *falsetto*, 'I'll give you the freedom of the *New York American* editorial page for one day. You can write what you like in it.' Bringing his fist down on the table with a bang, Northcliffe accepted the offer. Hearst could match him in wealth and newspaper power, but Northcliffe had a place in the world which Hearst could not claim.

His flair for publicity was one of the causes of continuing disagreement between himself and British officialdom in Washington. As a journalist and newspaper owner, he had a far better appreciation than the diplomats of what could be done by publicity, above all in America. To them publicity was disreputable; an article written by Northcliffe was not so much a contribution to the common cause as a display of vulgar self-advertisement. Both Wiseman and Willert tried to persuade Northcliffe that propaganda was not one of his tasks as head of the Mission and that it was likely to embroil him in more difficulties with Washington, particularly as he had not hesitated to criticize the administration in some of his writings. Wiseman wrote: 'He is convinced that he is doing it in the best interests of the country and undoubtedly spares no effort to further our cause in the way which seems best to him.' The official view appears to have been voiced by Lord Hardinge of Penshurst, at that time Permanent Head of the Foreign Office. He wrote in *The Old Diplomacy*** that Northcliffe's purpose in America was to seek 'his own glorification'. In that bitter travesty of the truth can be heard the accents of outraged custom and propriety. Sir Arthur Willert suitably retorted in *The Road to Safety*:

If Northcliffe's unbridled publicity shocked Washington, it did much to make the country understand the meaning and demands of belligerency and without annoying it, for to the American public Northcliffe was not a high official behaving improperly, but a great and friendly English newspaper proprietor talking sense.

Propaganda for the British cause in the United States was constantly in his mind. 'The French, as is only natural, have convinced America that they are doing the lion's share of the war. Tardieu has this morning issued a statement greatly exaggerating France's position in the war. It will be on the front page of two thousand Sunday newspapers.' He wrote to Ambassador Page: 'The French have a very easy task here. Their historic friendship is a solid rock for them. It is said that nations have no gratitude, but Americans are certainly grateful for Lafayette and Rochambeau.'

The propaganda need had seemed to him so great that before leaving England he had released Pomeroy Burton, general manager of Associated Newspapers, to take charge of a Foreign Office inquiry which led to the establishment of a British bureau of information in New York under Geoffrey Butler, a young Cambridge don who had accompanied Mr Balfour's mission as its press officer. Burton had gone out in March and in a few days was cabling to Northcliffe: 'Already am convinced a

* Murray, 1948.

hundred times over of the urgent necessity for vigorous work in this field.' Northcliffe passed Burton's messages and recommendations to the Prime Minister, who had replied on April 4: 'We are sending over immediately a very strong mission to deal with all the subjects referred to in Mr Pomeroy Burton's cable. . . . I agree with Mr Pomeroy Burton that there is no time to lose.' The Balfour Mission was consequently well primed with Burton's findings. On April 26, John Buchan (later Lord Tweedsmuir), director of the Press Bureau at the Foreign Office, told Northcliffe that Burton's report had been invaluable. 'It will enable us to start our new bureau in New York on the best lines.'

Emboldened perhaps by the knowledge that his information was reaching the highest quarters, Burton began sending back proposals for reforming other branches of British war activity in the United States. Before his zeal had trespassed far, he received a cable from Northcliffe ordering him abruptly to stick to his brief. Northcliffe's own self-extended role regarding propaganda might have warranted rebuke too. Propaganda was not in the terms of reference handed to him by the Prime Minister on his appointment to the British War Mission. But there was no silencing him on that subject. 'For the sake of our position at the Peace Conference and our position in American history, it is essential that we should be better known here.'

The American press, he protested in another letter, never referred to British forces in action. 'I have not seen one English regiment mentioned since I got here, until this week, when in response to cables I sent home, we are now hearing of British regiments. I was telling a very friendly and well-read American of the glories of our Guards regiments. He was under the impression that they had been guarding Buckingham Palace and doing work of that kind.' To Page, again, he wrote: 'Our people do not understand your people, and I despair of ever teaching them. Here are generous, affectionate and easily moved people, thousands of miles away from the war, who are expected to understand the war through heavily censored war news.' From as far back as 1906 he had tried to dispel what he had then called the 'conspiracy of misunderstanding' between the two countries.

So urgently beset was he by the war propaganda question that several months before leaving for America he had expressed his readiness to serve under Buchan, 'and bring a small useful staff with me', when it was proposed to start a propaganda department in London. Saying that he hoped that the Government would not sanction the taking over of yet another hotel for the new department when 'four decent-sized rooms at the Royal Automobile Club would be enough', he told the Prime Minister: 'A wicked member of the Reform Club said yesterday that the large bath at the R.A.C. could be used for washing the Government's dirty linen.'

Then there was the censorship, its necessary principles applied with un-imaginative stringency and a source of irritation to Northcliffe not merely because it touched his professional sensibilities. 'It really is most unfair,' he complained, writing home. 'I cannot tell you how weary I am of the headline: "Another Loan To The British".' He went on to explain:

The Americans do not know that we lent over *six billion dollars* to our Allies before America came into the war and that we have since lent infinitely more to the Allies than has America. Our damnable policy of secrecy is coming home to roost with a vengeance. Some of the most highly placed members of the Government here are politely sceptical when I tell them of what we have done in the war. It causes me many anxious hours, begging interviews, wearisome train journeys to Washington. I cudgel my brains how to get round the difficulty, *how to make these people realise the immensity of our sacrifice.* The President knows, Col. House knows, Lane, the Minister of the Interior, knows, Houston, the Secretary for Agriculture, knows, here and there a friendly Senator or Congressman knows, but Washington in general does not know, and the Germans have poisoned the fountain of truth by saying that we are in the war for money, that we are accumulating large fortunes in shipping and war materials, that we retain a large army at home to defend ourselves, while the Canadian, Australian, French and Belgians are fighting for us. If it were not for the knowledge and friendship of Col. House, I should despair of the situation.

'My country has been stupid,' he told Josephus Daniels, United States Secretary of the Navy, in a talk about the operation of the censorship in America. 'Every day we are told, "Don't print this, don't print that",' and he insisted to Daniels that the people 'were entitled to the news, good and bad, and that knowledge would stimulate both patriotism and sacrifice'. Daniels saw Northcliffe as 'the new type of Englishman' and wrote that 'he had none of the hesitation that, for instance, marked Balfour, but spoke with a sort of American directness and emphasis'. The Navy Secretary considered that Northcliffe was 'the most dynamic of all the distinguished British visitors to Washington in 1917'. Studying the confidential documents relating to the British War Mission, it becomes plain that, after Balfour, Northcliffe was the one British representative in the United States with whom the leaders in Washington cared to do business.

* * *

If Lloyd George fancied that the ocean had insulated him from North-cliffe's stubborn attention, he was mistaken. 'His constant excursions to the Continent are irritating people here', Northcliffe wrote to Dawson of *The Times.* Lloyd George relied on Milner to keep Dawson on the right path. But Dawson was keeping Northcliffe regularly informed of the Prime Minister's conduct of affairs: 'he sends me a little political sketch every mail'. Writing on June 28, Dawson told Northcliffe:

Lloyd George's worst failing is that he gets an idea and pushes it to a very advanced point, involves all kinds of people, wastes weeks of their time, and then draws back in the face of some probably negligible opposition. There is no doubt that he actually offered Winston the Air Board and then yielded to protests. Since the only way out of the mess was to induce Cowdray to remain, the net result may not have been bad from the national point of view; but it was hard luck on Winston and this kind of thing adds to the growing opposition.

He has certainly done the same thing with Drink Control and State Purchase. To my knowledge, he wasted at least a fortnight of Lord Milner's very valuable time, to say nothing of using up that of innumerable less important people, and finally abandoned the whole business because of the combined agitation of brewers and prohibitionists. The Ministry of Health is another case in point— hung up, I imagine, because of the hostility of the insurance societies. So is Education, in which Herbert Fisher, after a brilliant beginning, finds it almost impossible to make headway. This last is a vital question and I am going to deal with it today or tomorrow.

No doubt Lloyd George has proved himself a great diplomatist and stands high in France and Italy. It is in domestic questions that he is likely to come to grief, and I put this down very largely to Bonar Law's incurable nervousness of the House of Commons.

Northcliffe had another well-informed correspondent in Printing House Square, Wickham Steed, the *Times* foreign editor. Steed wrote to him a few days later: 'Ll.G. seems to have been under all sorts of influences lately and to be more shifty than usual. By dint of scaring him we are trying to make him run straight.' Northcliffe stated in a letter to his private circle: 'Lloyd George is regarded here as soft and lacking in "punch" and "pep".'

Northcliffe could not have too much news of his family and friends, his businesses and staffs, or of Whitehall politics. He expected regular information about the state of his papers. He was closely in touch with Sutton who, inspired by his massive power of attorney, sent him the loyal if ungrammatical assurance: 'Everything of your own personal things are alright.' He conducted a correspondence from afar about salaries in the *Times* office, 'of some of which I am quite ashamed'. His letters show how much home was in his mind. 'On the whole, I am cheerful, though sometimes violently homesick. But there is so much to do that one has not time for vagrom thoughts.' He wrote again: 'The American robin's little note makes me very homesick, reminding me of my beautiful Sutton Place.'

He was writing from a century-old house called Bolton Priory, which he had taken furnished for its English atmosphere and the golf facilities that went with it. His tenancy agreement was for five months and twenty-three days, bringing it up to December 31. He had an option to continue it to July of the following year. 'It is about the most English thing in the United States. My English butler has the gentle tread and obsequious manner that seem so strange here. Mrs Fox, my English cook, who came here nine years ago with Sir somebody, cooks perfectly in the English way.'

Bolton Priory, at Pelham, Westchester County, on the shores of Long Island Sound, fifteen miles from New York, was described by Northcliffe as 'a grey stone, creeper-smothered, large rambling house in which generations have been born and lived. It is filled with pictures and books—mostly English books. Beside me, as I dictate, is a fine set of *State Trials*.' The house had an air of antiquity warranted less by age than by the manorial gravity of its style. He did not hide his pleasure in being able to return there at the end of the day's work in New York. It was as homelike and as comfortable as Elmwood. 'Inside the house I am in England', he wrote to his wife. His first thought, on going there to live, was where to hang the de Laszlo portrait of his mother which he had asked to be sent out from Sutton Place. He told her: 'I want it always before me.'

Hamilton Fyfe, who was at Bolton Priory with him, 'as a sort of *major domo*', a description that Fyfe would probably have resented, believed that Northcliffe enjoyed there 'a kind of happiness that he had not known before'. He delighted in the call of the mocking bird, the brilliance of the red cardinal. He was thrilled when he came on 'an amazing quantity of tiger lilies, growing wild'. He threw back his head and drew in the scent of 'a great clump of fragrant honeysuckle'. He showed the excitement of a boy when he found a tortoise on the fairway at golf. 'One gets all sorts of funny little surprises here.' He wrote one evening: 'If you ask me if I am happy, darling Mother, I can say that I really am. But I miss you every moment of the day and whenever I wake at night. My great consolation is that I believe I am helping to win the war. I know that I am popular with these people. They do many things that I ask.'

He appeared to be much less harassed by the great affairs in which he was engaged than he had been by the countless small worries of running his papers at home. For the first time, he was experiencing the exhilarations of the corporate life in which self-interest is eclipsed by a larger aim. It was agreed by those around him that he looked remarkably well and that, considering the weight of his work and responsibilities, he was youthfully flexible in body and mind. 'Perhaps it is because I am so preoccupied with this difficult and delicate task—this mountain of tasks—that I live in a mental world of my own, oblivious of surroundings', he wrote. He who was helping the Americans to discover their unrealized productive potential (which was to astonish them again in the Second World War) was finding in himself new resources of strength that enabled him to work as he had never worked before.

He wrote home: 'I think I must be a veritable salamander. The hotter it gets the more energetic I become, as the unhappy Price, to whom I dictate this, will attest. Up to now, I have begun the day's work every morning at about six o'clock, keeping at it continuously until late at night. Whenever possible, I get to bed at nine-thirty. The Almighty has granted me wonderful sleep.' The daytime temperatures were phenomenal. In New York, the death roll from heat was 995, 'mostly children', Northcliffe noted. He was moved by the spectacle of long lines of cars being driven out into the country each evening, every car filled with children being taken out of the humid city for 'a breath of cool, fresh air'. He still kept his weight book, its page for 1917 headed: 'A Fat Man's Gallant Fight Against Fate'. It showed that the furnace heat of that New York summer had almost no effect on his metabolism. Harder to bear than the heat were the long train journeys: 'very trying to my strength and patience'.

His evenings at Bolton Priory were usually given to gramophone playing, for him an unending source of entertainment. As of old at Elmwood, if he liked a record he played it with insatiable, and to others insufferable, adolescent delight. A visitor to the Priory remembered: 'I had to listen to one record through the whole of my evening there—a song from *The Maid of the Mountains* with the refrain: At seventeen, he falls in love quite madly, With eyes of tender blue. . . .'

Northcliffe to his wife:

Washington.
July 1st, 1917.

. . . In thinking about me you should always remember that time here is six hours later than with you. Thus, when I am having breakfast at eight, you are finishing lunch at two; when I am finishing golf at seven, it is one o'clock in the morning with you, and I hope you are fast asleep.

Remember also that I am never alone. I began life here with five secret officers about me. Remember, further, that we have to exercise the utmost care, for we are undoubtedly minutely watched by the Germans. For this reason I am using none but English assistants, straight from England.

The President has received me twice with very great kindness. He is a man who does not resemble his photographs at all. A determined-looking gentleman with whom one would not care to be in antagonism, he is about as tall as I am, more slightly built, very quiet in his manner, compresses more meaning into a few words than any other American I have met, uses more American in his speech than I had expected, is, I believe, with his family quite a hermit, is always surrounded with a bodyguard of detectives, does not entertain privately, bears his worries remarkably well, is quite humorous and amusing and, incidentally, the most powerful individual in the world. I should say that his fault is lack of power of delegation. He called himself to me 'the clearing house of the Government'. Everything has to be 'put up' to him. I like him thoroughly and believe that I shall get on with him.

I was suddenly ordered here the day before yesterday to see the President on an urgent begging mission of colossal scale. I slept for nine hours without waking before the interview, as I did last night after the interview.

He reported the ritual accompaniments of a visit to the President. 'At the door are the two huge black servants whom I remember from Roosevelt's time. They usher you to the ante-room. At the exact moment of the time appointed, the door of a large reception room is opened. In the middle of the room stands the President.' Northcliffe contrasted his own morning dress with the President's white trousers and blue serge jacket. The sole presidential insignia, he noted, was an American flag in rubies and diamonds, worn in the lapel. The President was 'an excellent listener and expects you to be a quick talker', a requirement which Northcliffe had no difficulty in meeting. The President told him: 'I had the choice of two courses; going early into the war with a reluctant people, or going when I did with a willing people.' He continued:

My chief duty is to make obeisance and genuflexion and *ask*.

As for the kindness received, considering that the English here are all beggars, it is overwhelming. I believe it to be largely due to the sacrifice that has been made on the battlefield. To me it is a constant source of marvel that the Americans are in the war at all. Those of them that are nearest to the war are 3,000 miles from it. Millions of them are 6,000 miles away.

I have received nice cables from the Prime Minister and Mr Balfour about my work and I have begun to realize that I am doing something useful. Robin [Geoffrey Dawson] may have told you of the great crises through which we are passing, and I realize that I, by my knowledge of the American character, and persistent energy, helped to achieve what looked like an impossibility. I do not think that people in England would have slept soundly in their beds if they knew of some of these crises.

I am much more cheerful about affairs than I was. I did not know that I would be able to effect anything. But every morning when I am awakened by the new sounds of birds to the fact that I am far from England, and my beautiful homes and happy circle, I think of those who are engaged at the Front and at sea, and that, after all, my bit is a very moderate one in proportion.

For his first meeting with the President he had armed himself with facts and figures about German imports from the United States *via* neutral countries. They helped the President in his decision to impose the vital embargo proclaimed on July 8. Northcliffe was also consulted officially about the United States air programme, for which the House of Representatives voted 600,000,000 dollars on July 14. Balfour cabled his 'best congratulations' on the success of the interview with the President. Sir Eric Drummond sent a note to J. T. Davies, the Prime Minister's secretary: 'Lord Northcliffe's visit to the President seems to have been a great success, but just one word of warning in your private ear. Don't let the P.M. think that the President likes N.' The hint of personal antipathy may have been misleading. President Wilson was said not to like contact with too powerful personalities because he found them devitalizing.

A member of the staff of *The New Republic*, the American radical weekly review, saw Northcliffe standing unobtrusively in the throng at one of the President's press conferences, apparently savouring the pleasure of being among men of his craft and kind. Seeing the *New Republic* man, William Hard, whom he had previously met, Northcliffe took his arm for the long descent of the Capitol steps. He showed signs of nervousness. 'I don't like heights', he said, his grip tightening on Hard's arm, as he 'walked down very slowly and carefully'. He dined with the *New Republic* editorial staff and left with them a memory of a genial guest who believed that Labour would come to power in England after the war. 'Watch the younger men in our Labour movement', and he named G. D. H. Cole as a possible Prime Minister. His belief in the ability of Labour to rule England was second only to his confidence in the ability of England to survive the experience. His *New Republic* hosts were impressed by the depth of his faith in the English future.

★　　　★　　　★

His mission leadership meant making speeches, a form of self-expression that he had never found congenial. 'There is a daily speech all the time, but I take care that very few are reported. I do not want to become cheap. I am supposed, in addition to my other duties, to be a sort of Encyclopædia Britannica about the war. The American Government consults me about a hundred topics. Yesterday, I had to address their Ministry of Munitions. One day this week I have to address their naval surgeons.' A subject that he found gripped every type of American audience was daylight saving, 'the invention', he was careful to point out, 'of an Englishman, Mr Willett'.

He wrote to the Prime Minister on July 17:

I have always in my mind the possibilities of friction between the American and British Governments. That is not in my department, but in that of the Ambassador's. I can do much, however, to keep this Government in good humour, but when the Government asks me, for example, for the personnel and power of the Air Board at home, in order to assist them in their discussions here, and no reply is sent to my pressing cable, my position then confirms what they already believed—that they only see us when we come to ask for something. I rushed that cable, so that a reply might reach me for a meeting of the Air Committee at Congress. There was ample time for the answer and I promised it. They telephoned continuously for it on the day it should have arrived. It arrived 7 days too late! This sort of thing simply will not do.

You know full well that I had no desire to come here and that I came only because my intimate knowledge of these people, extending over a quarter of a century, convinced me that I could help to win the war. I remain here only because I know that I am helping to win the war. It is that consolation which keeps me slaving in Washington and New York City in a shade temperature usually ranging from 80 to 92. I am doing all that I possibly can and 90% of the Englishmen whom I found engaged in our war work are men of energy, all doing their best. On their behalf I ask for better support and quick action at home.

Making his public appeals for good will and practical aid, he found the American people in the grip of what sometimes seemed to be a fearful apathy. The first Liberty Loan had been mainly taken up by the bankers; the public response was poor. In Iowa, where there were 475,000 men of military age, only 1,750 had volunteered. In Michigan, there was 'an almost total absence of interest in the war'. In Wisconsin, the general feeling 'was pro-German and pacifist'. In a number of places, Northcliffe heard the objecting cry: 'This is Wilson's war!' Eastward, in New York City, there was a more heartening mood.

On the hot evening of July 21, 1917, he braced himself to confront 'the largest audience I have ever addressed—14,000—in Madison Square Garden. They cheered for five minutes.' It was 'British Recruiting Week' in the United States and Northcliffe's speech signalized a change of sentiment that made it a part of the texture of history. He referred to the occasion 'as one of those milestones that mark the progress of humanity'.

Here tonight for the first time an appeal is being made to men of American and British birth to enlist in the armies which are to fight side by side for the common aim of their two countries. Here tonight we have what we have never had before—American and British speakers on the same platform with the same object in view, and that object the raising of forces to uphold the ideals which underlie our common civilization. . . .

In fact, many of those in the farther parts of the hall did not hear what he had to tell them. His voice had no declamatory ring. He was well received, even though he was not heard, because of his reputation in the world. The chairman, as at most of his meetings, had introduced him in conquering-hero terms. He told his mother in a letter that his meetings were invariably opened 'with very uncomplimentary references to the

Old Gang at home. I am announced as the man who gave Asquith "the once over", the "knock out", or as the man who "put it over" him, to use the slang.'

In Chicago we went out to what we had been told was a dinner of two or three men, but which turned out to be a gathering of seventy. It was, however, a really delightful evening, though I felt very sorry that one of the speakers, ignorant of the fact that there was present young Capt. Asquith, the very nice son of the ex-Prime Minister, aroused the table to enthusiasm by references to my attacks on Asquith, the 'wait and see' policy, and the 'Old Gang'. I am glad to say that I had made generous reference to Asquith's attitude towards the present Government and to his eloquence, but I saw that the young man looked pensive as the vigorous American speaker tackled his father's short-comings, waving his arms spectacularly in the American fashion.

As a speaker, Northcliffe was more successful at private assemblies. He did not pretend to oratory. He avoided rhetoric. His speaking style was that of a chairman of directors addressing a meeting of shareholders. He completely captured the hearts of two hundred Middle West newspaper editors in Kansas City. Fyfe, who was there, said that 'they went away chanting his praises'. All over the country, similar small influential groups came under his spell: bankers at Atlantic City, shipping men at Phila-delphia, manufacturers at Detroit. He told them the truth about the war as he saw it, and had seen it at first-hand, dissembling nothing. 'Like you, when we went into the war we were all purse and no fist. Pull yourselves together for a long struggle.' He showed no false modesty in putting before them the facts of Britain's desperate needs and of her sacrifices in the field. 'If we had spent as much on preparedness as we are spending now in a week, there would have been no war.' The impression that he made was so strong that more than one American leader was heard to say that he ought to be head not of a mission but of a government. That his warnings were acceptable to American public sentiment was shown by the fact that the Hearst newspaper policy was trimmed to reflect it. Hearst's *New York American* gave a half-page in bold type to his demand for a greater effort from the shipyards. There was an approach from the publishing house of Harper to bring out his speeches in book form.

He told in his letters home of the several departments of the Mission: 'the best staff I ever had, which is saying a good deal'. He emphasized 'the valuable services' of Charles Gordon, the Canadian financial expert, who was vice-chairman of the Mission, though one good judge thought him 'the wrong man in the wrong place'; the Hon. R. H. Brand of Lazard Brothers, 'a fellow of All Souls and a first-rate man', who, Northcliffe said, was 'curiously unable to make the right impression'; Sir Hardman Lever, Financial Secretary to the Treasury, 'who has given the most able assistance possible'; Sir Thomas Royden, deputy chairman of the Cunard Steamship Company, 'a tower of strength'; Ashley Sparkes, also of Cunard; and of 'a score of other Englishmen who have made the sacrifice to come here to win the war in the only place in which it can be won— the United States'. Caird, from Carmelite House, was proving a most adroit buyer of oil and other war materials, and had made 'some fine Scotch bargains already'.

Gordon, I am glad to say, is now 'Sir Charles'. It took several telegrams from me to drive into the heads of the people at home that a knighthood helps enormously here. Brand, unfortunately, is not a Sir or a Lord! Any Englishman who goes into a Government office as plain Mr might as well stay outside. If he is a Mr in England, he cannot be much! My experience of being the head of large affairs enables me to smooth over difficulties and make right combinations of men. Harold would smack his lips at some of the cutting down that has to be done. . . .

In another letter he spoke highly of the services of 'a delightful young Canadian, Colonel Campbell Stuart, who lunched at St. James's Place. He is the young man who raised the Irish-Canadian mixed Protestant-Catholic regiment', a feat of persuasion as well as of organization which Northcliffe admired. Stuart had joined the British War Mission as its military secretary, seconded from the British Embassy at Washington. It was a role that kept him constantly at Northcliffe's side, evoking sardonic comments from Spring Rice in his communications with London. Fyfe wrote that Northcliffe 'leaned on him as he had never leaned on any subordinate before', and it was Stuart who, above all, ensured the smooth running of the tours by which the Americans came to know Northcliffe and to see him as the embodiment of the British war spirit, a representative of the British people rather than of their Government. Becoming his right-hand man, Stuart quickly attained an intimacy with him that was unique in that its harmony was never disturbed. His knighthood, bestowed early in the following year, was a mark of the recognition given to Canada's indispensable hyphenating role in the great new transatlantic partnership. But for Campbell Stuart the British War Mission might have been a less efficient instrument of Anglo-American co-operation. That was its *raison d'être*, the condition of its survival, and the inspiration of its success.

In his offices, which covered a whole floor at 681 Fifth Avenue, North-cliffe was at the centre of an extraordinary web of specialized activity. His writ ranged far and wide over finance, shipping and the commodity markets. His Treasury experts, under Sir Hardman Lever, were at 23 Wall Street. His shipping men, under Sir Thomas Royden, were at 165 Broadway. His purchasing department, under J. W. Woods, a Canadian banker, was at 120 Broadway. (That department alone registered its 50,000th cable later in the year and made it an occasion for celebration.) His department of war supplies, under Sir Charles Gordon, and department of aeronautical supplies, under Brigadier-General J. D. Cormack, were at Munsey Building, a great office block in Washington. He had a group of inland waterway and dock experts, under Lieutenant-Colonel W. H. Owen, R.E., at Drummond Building, Montreal; sugar supply experts, under Sir Guy Granet, at 68 William Street, New York; and a wheat buying organization, under Herbert T. Robson, at 27 Beaver Street, New York. Oil and timber supplies were also under his control. He was responsible for two military missions and a Royal Flying Corps mission. The number of separate groups working under his leadership was twenty-eight. He told Sutton: 'This is like running a bunch of Standard Oil, United States Steel and International Harvester companies.' His secretary, Price, wrote to Mackenzie, his private accountant in London: 'We have real offices, where the general staff work, but the Chief does a lot of *his* work in his hotel bedroom—you know his taste.'

One of his main anxieties was that the Mission's heavy dealings in foodstuffs put up prices for the American housewife. A bulk purchase of condensed milk brought an outcry from the nation's mothers. He retorted, when pro-German newspapers drove the point home to their readers: 'At least it indicates an appreciation of American products, which are excellent.' To a friend in England, he wrote: 'John Bull wears heavy boots. He treads hard on people's corns over here.' He was much amused to see himself proclaimed in headlines as 'The Greatest Spendthrift in History'. Sending the clippings home to his wife, he wrote: 'I have to deal with ships, iron, steel, brass, copper, bacon, sugar, cotton, grain, shells, horses, railway trains, oil and money, money, money.' Having stopped the various British official agencies from outbidding each other, he was now faced with the increasingly difficult problem of competition from buyers for the American war departments.

'I have never worked so hard in my life.' He was writing to Walter Hines Page, at the American Embassy in London. 'I am shot backward and forward between Washington and New York like a shuttle in a loom.' He was continuously impressed by the fact of his Mission spending two million pounds a day, 'and sometimes more'. He mentioned it often in his letters home. 'I never dreamed I should have such a responsibility placed on me. I have a staff of ten thousand people, scattered all over America and Canada.' Memorizing the faces and names of hundreds of these people, he said, was 'not the least difficult part of my job. Also I have a correspondence impossible to cope with.'

At 681 Fifth Avenue there was an unending stream of callers: 'they, and correspondence, and telephone calls absorb the time which ought to be devoted to the great purposes of my Mission—that, added to the heat and cutting off from people to whom I am attached, does not improve my temper'. The callers were 'bankers, politicians, people with grievances, people who want to go to the war, inventors, Red Cross officials, salesmen who have nothing in stock but nerve; many others'. Mostly, they hardened him in his criticism of American 'unpunctuality and verbosity'.

He wrote home: 'I have not opened one of my newspapers while I have been here—for two reasons. First, I think I should concentrate entirely on the gigantic question of steel supplies and, second, on personally investigating and urging anti-submarine inventions, pressing forward shipbuilding, investigating and urging aeroplane construction, "keeping close", as one says here, to the Senate, Congress, and the Cabinet, securing the thirty-seven million pounds monthly with which partly to pay for what we are buying here, and pushing the recruiting of British subjects.'

Northcliffe to Sutton:

New York.
July 20, 1917.

My dear Sutton,—Many thanks for the admirable people you sent out. . . . It would be untrue to say that I like being here and that I do not miss my friends, my homes, my newspapers and my English life. I am glad that I came because I believe I am doing some good. The work, however, exceeds anything I have ever done in my life. It requires labour, tact, versatility and the digestion of an ostrich. The banqueting is absolutely essential. Business is conducted here entirely at golf clubs, restaurants and houses. Everything here is personal. Everything depends on personal relations with those you meet.

Naturally, I think about the businesses and cannot help worrying a good deal, though I know in what safe hands they are. People tell me the *Mail* is very flat, but they may be saying that to flatter me.

In a few minutes Edison arrives to pay me a ceremonial visit. He is as deaf as a post. I shall have to shout into his ear-trumpet. Still, it is a great compliment to me, as he never goes to see anybody.

I don't like the high ceremony here, I can assure you. Much as I delight in these people—and they are a splendid people—they are the greatest nation of time-wasters on God's earth. Life here, as you know, is a combination of ridiculous rush and waste of time.

Goodbye, my dear Sut,
Your devoted
CHIEF

'I am willing to remain here', he wrote to his family on July 26, 'for twice the three months agreed upon, if the Government want me to do so.' It was his first reference to any period of engagement. 'If they can find a man they think more suitable, I hope they will send him out, and I shall help him into the saddle and return.'

Northcliffe to Sutton (by cable): New York, July 26.—*Tell parents girl typists being carefully looked after stop shall endeavour take small house seaside for them during hot weather stop affectionate greetings dear Sut—Chief.*

As a postscript to a letter to Sutton on July 29, he wrote: 'The figures of the business are really wonderful. I congratulate you. I know that you have an immense burden to bear, and I am most grateful for the load you have taken from my shoulders.' He wrote to his mother the same day, heading his letter, 'Hot and thundery. 7 o'clock here, 1 a.m. with you', and telling her: 'Never was your firstborn so busy in his life. I have everything I want except my Mother, Wife and beloved newspaper work and happy brotherhood. Tell Dot, Harold, Cecil, Vi, Leicester, Hilder, Pop [Christabel], Vyvyan, Dick [Charles], Bonch [St. John] most of all, they are in my thoughts every day, and all the sweet nieces and nephews.' Spring Rice, in his correspondence with Drummond at the Foreign Office, had recently reported his impression that 'Northcliffe seems rather tired of business and regrets [his absence from] his London work'.

*　　　　*　　　　*

He wrote to Page, in London, that he 'had never been through such grave anxieties'. He was referring most particularly to the oil shortage which had brought him a midnight telegram from Balfour. A crisis situation had arisen in the Royal Navy. There was not enough oil in reserve to enable its larger units to fight a battle or even to play a full part in some lesser emergency. 'The telegram which set me to work was the most anxious one I have ever received, and it gave me the most anxious time I have ever had', Northcliffe wrote home. He told Page what had happened in another letter:

I had only been here a few days, but long enough to know that such fuel is already scarce here. I knew that that cable, if disclosed, would cause such a jump in the oil market as had never been known. I was up bright and early, I can assure you. A little cautious pussyfooting as to the oil situation brought no comfort: great demand, small supply—nothing doing. I read and re-read that telegram and finally called up the Standard Oil head man. We met, and I gave him that cable to read, despite its *Most Urgent Most Secret* inscription. He read it slowly twice, gave it back to me, saying: 'If it can be done, it will be done.' I said nothing whatever about price. Those people started in right there, and oil is pouring across the Atlantic with giant strides, and at a less price than we have averaged over here. They could have squeezed millions out of our trouble, had they chosen. When I thanked them they merely remarked: 'It's our war as well as yours.' I can imagine the panic at No. 10 if they had known I had disclosed that cable to the oil controllers.

Writing about the same episode, Northcliffe told his family circle that he had met the president of the Standard Oil Company, A. C. Bedford, two days before receiving Balfour's telegram. 'I had "sized him up" as a very large person and very pro-English. I felt sure that he would not take advantage of me as to price or in any other way. I knew he was the only man in the whole country who could do that which was wanted. He and, through his influence, a number of others, achieved the desired result.' Northcliffe subsequently wrote that the momentous telegram was 'in the nature of a personal appeal from Mr B. to me'. It has since been suggested that as British ships were carrying American troops to Europe, it was necessary only 'to ask the President or the Procurement Agency for oil'.* To that comment a feasible rejoinder is that Northcliffe's method appears to have served the situation with more dispatch. He had cabled to the Prime Minister and the Foreign Secretary: *You place on me tremendous responsibility of supplying oil for British Navy which I am willing to accept on condition that I have quicker co-operation London.*

Hardly less disturbing and far more persistent were his anxieties about the financial position. He wrote to the American Ambassador in London: 'Complaint is expressed in Government circles here that the British Government is not frank enough with your Government, and there is much justice in the charge that we expect them to hand out one hundred and eighty-five million dollars monthly as a matter of course.' His anxieties were deepened by the British Government's neglect of a Washington request for the services of Lord Reading in that connection, he having made a favourable impression on Washington during an official visit two years previously. The suggestion had been passed on to Northcliffe by House. Northcliffe regarded it as an inspiration. 'The United States Government being a Radical Government, they would like some distinguished Radical to come here to discuss financial matters with them.' He cabled the suggestion to London (July 15) and more than once thereafter. 'But the usual delay, which causes so much suspicion here, took place.' Conflict between the Chancellor of the Exchequer, Bonar Law, and the Governor of the Bank of England, Lord Cunliffe, had distant reverberations and Northcliffe's strong backing of Reading went unanswered. Meanwhile, he saw the taxpayers being plundered by the profiteers and wrote his disgust in letters home. He had already supplied the head of the United States war metals committee, Bernard Baruch, with figures showing 'criminal war profits' being made out of steel. He told of a day when Great Britain stood on the brink of financial collapse. He had signed the documents averting that calamity within minutes of the fatal hour, and Hamilton Fyfe said that 'he enjoyed the thrill'.

He complained to the Prime Minister that he was receiving Foreign

* Lord Beaverbrook, *Men and Power.*

Office instructions 'inevitably making for conflict with the embassy'. Giving details, he had written: 'You ask me to try to avert something that may happen by Monday and I am going to do my utmost both as regards money and oil. But the geographical difficulties are very great. House is seven hours north and the Ambassador three nights' journey away. Look at maps.' He wrote again to the Prime Minister: 'As you have landed me in the most difficult job I have ever had in my life, I want you to help me in every way in your power.' He pointed out that 'the Americans are not accustomed to our huge financial operations. . . . When I repeat the Chancellor's statement that the war is costing fifty million dollars a day, they are aghast.' He thought it necessary to tell the Prime Minister:

Members of the Cabinet should understand that our attitude towards the United States Government is that of beggars. The majority of people with whom one comes in contact (though not the President or Colonel House) have no notion of the immense sacrifices we have made or are making. I do not know who was responsible for the concealment of this information in the early days of the war, but whoever he was he has rendered our position here, as beggars on behalf of the British nation, most difficult.

Somewhat oddly, Lloyd George assumed this to be an appeal for the publication of casualty lists. Annotating it as such in his *War Memoirs*, he rejoined that every belligerent had withheld that information, thus discounting his testimony to Northcliffe's 'fundamental common sense' in the same place. Northcliffe's references to sacrifices were in the wider context.

* * *

A meeting with Henry Ford called for a suppression of personal feelings which might have aggravated the emergency it was designed to remove. Ford had offered to supply six thousand of his tractors at cost price to the British Government. The tractors were needed 'to keep starvation out', as Northcliffe put it. But there was a great demand for them in the United States and Ford was not disposed to tolerate prevarication from the British authorities. Northcliffe tried to make contact with him, 'but he has twice put me off. It may be necessary for me to go to Detroit and eat humble pie and if so I will gladly do so.' With the help of his friend Edison, Northcliffe was able to pin Ford down to an appointment. On the day he left for Detroit, he wrote home:

According to some American newspapers, Ford was vilely treated in England, so my task is not a rosy one, especially as my newspapers were particularly

565

hostile to him at the time of his ridiculous peace ship expedition to Europe. My Mother drives about, I understand, in one of his 'tin Lizzies'. I wonder what manner of man he is? Among other little pleasantries, I remember that we refused to print his advertisements in *The Times* and *Daily Mail*.

It was said that Ford thought that Northcliffe was a Jew and had not been forthcoming for that reason. At least thrice handicapped, Northcliffe went to Detroit—'though I have no further desire for long journeys'— and succeeded in getting on the right side of Ford, personally and nationally. The tractors were supplied. 'A less generous man would have kicked me out of the factory.' When Ford was explaining the multiple uses of his tractor, Northcliffe intervened with the remark: 'I hope you mean to stop at that, Mr Ford. If you go any further, your tractors will be printing newspapers and I shall be out of business.' He cabled to Churchill, with whom he was in close touch at that time, that it was 'a mistake to treat Ford as a commercial man', that he was an idealist who 'looks like the Bishop of London. He is no more interested in money than I am and knows as much as I do about it.' In the course of their talk, Ford had spoken of Cobbett's *Rural Rides*. Northcliffe arranged for an expensively bound copy of that work to be sent to him as a gift from London by embassy bag.

His understanding with Ford might have come to grief as a result of the fierce outcry from a section of the British motor industry when news of the tractor deal became known. That it held firm was a tribute to Northcliffe's personal success with Ford who, Geoffrey Dawson told Northcliffe in a letter of August 23, had 'behaved infinitely better than his British rivals', whose tactics had delayed the food production programme. That was no fault of Ford. 'He has submitted to all kinds of contradictory orders and broken pledges. He has virtually handed over all his patents, organization and skilled men to the British Government. In fact, he has done everything possible to serve the cause of the allies, while his rivals . . . have subsided into a mere campaign of detraction.'

Sending home a cutting from the *Detroit Free Press*, whose reporter with a German-sounding name had referred to him as 'the rotund English nobleman', Northcliffe wrote: 'In that single word "rotund" he got back on me for all that I have been saying about Germany for years', forgetting that in German eyes corpulence is a masculine virtue. A writer in *Collier's Weekly* suggested that 'in Lord Northcliffe's case a paunch is more accurately described as large engine capacity', and contended that it was 'an important element in many kinds of success'.

The cartoonists helped to make him better known than the reporters did. They drew him as John Bull, a characterization which neither fitted nor pleased him with its suggestion of implacable insularity. He was more amused when a pro-German newspaper depicted him as Satan on its front page.

*   *   *

The publishers of his book, *At the War*, Hodder & Stoughton, had made 'large payments' of his royalties to the Red Cross. 'It constitutes a record,' they informed him later that year, and 'we wonder whether it would not be an excellent idea to publish a volume from your pen entitled "America at the War".' Probably with that in view, he supplemented his correspondence by a series of long letters intended, as he wrote, 'for my family and a few chosen friends', naming Sutton, Dawson and Steed, and leaving it to Sutton to decide whether Max Pemberton was 'discreet enough' to be allowed to see them. He suggested that they would also be 'a much-needed tonic' for H. W. Wilson, the *Daily Mail* leader writer. At the top of the letters he scribbled different injunctions to secrecy: 'Most Private', 'Very Confidential', 'For Very Careful Distribution', and so on, indulging the childish love of mystification which was a characteristic of some of the Harmsworths. Reading the letters now, the extreme caution seems extravagant, but certainly there was a risk of his correspondence falling into the wrong hands. Talking to Americans, he liked to hint darkly at the attention he was receiving from enemy spies.

Threatening letters were sent to him at the Hotel Gotham; one was left for him in his bedroom there. A motor-car, intended to be mistaken for his dark green Rolls-Royce, drove up to the post office at Pelham with an occupant who said that he had been sent to collect Lord Northcliffe's mail. Allied mission offices in New York had been burgled for documents. A man was caught studying a blotter on his desk through a magnifying glass. In Chicago, he was advised by the authorities not to show himself in the streets, 'as there are more Germans than in Dusseldorf'. He wrote to Sutton: 'Germans are everywhere, in the Post Office, in the telephone service. Think what London would be like if it had nearly eight hundred thousand of them.' He was constantly escorted by a strong-arm guard, sometimes of six men. 'When they surround me, I can see nothing. I have not told you of McCahill—the nicest of the many detectives I have had. Amusing, loyal, very strongly built, armed to the teeth, carrying, as I always tell him, everything except a searchlight, resourceful and active, he never lets me out of his sight, though I sometimes pass the whole day without seeing him. He was one of the President's bodyguard of thirty-five.'

Northcliffe's privately communicated reports of that crucial summer are a profuse, discursive, vivid commentary on the awakening of the American people from their long indifference to the German peril and to what came foremost in his reckoning, the fate of England. Wickham Steed found them 'extremely illuminating and helpful', and wished that they could be circulated to all the members of the Government. Northcliffe's impressions were heightened by a sense of events being inexorably shaped into history:

When I arrived in New York, I hardly ever saw a uniform. Now the Park is crowded every morning with young men, in and out of uniform, drilling. Only the gigantic and obtuse blundering of Germany could have got these people into the war.

Travelling on duties which took him to many parts of the country, 'I continually ask myself why have these people come into the war? I agree with Lowell, the president of Harvard University, who said to me last week that it is instinct, the instinct of self-preservation.' He seeks out the leading American business men and finds it possible to be 'most touched' by their impatience to put their organizing genius into the nation's war effort. 'They will do so with tremendous effectiveness when they "get going".'

At this point, Price remarks that I am losing my ability to express myself in correct English. I hate to think that may be so, but it comes from continual talking with and telephoning to Americans. The President himself, who speaks the most perfect English, and, indeed, classic English, spoke to me of Mr Balfour having 'put something up to him'.★
I object strongly to many of these Americanisms. Why should they say 'check up' for 'check', and 'try out' instead of try, 'win out' instead of win? They seem to have a natural desire to use the longest words possible: why 'typewriter operator' instead of typist? Why should every little shop be a 'market', the long word 'elevator' be used instead of lift?

On a journey to Cleveland, 'the spectacle of the farms and factories of Ohio cheered me. If it were not that these people are practically allies, their prosperity would be irritating. Was there ever a land so overflowing with milk and honey?' He was 'very gratified' by the cordiality to England of many American Jews. 'After meetings, they often come up to me and shake hands, saying: "We are for the country of the square deal. We have always had that in England and we do not forget." ' At Washington he finds American red tape as hampering as the British kind, with an all-powerful President 'who does not seem able to cut the red tape'. The President, 'like our Prime Minister, has too much on his shoulders. He is a more orderly man than Lloyd George. He does not waste so much time, but has not Lloyd George's energy.'

★ In another letter Northcliffe expressed surprise at Balfour requesting him to 'speed up' certain action.

A cynical Englishman said to me, 'Look round Washington and you will find an exact replica of our government in 1914.' There is this difference, however: on top of all is a man with absolute power, patient, resourceful, but very determined when it comes to an issue. My own impression is that he could not have got his polyglot people into the war before he did.

Complacency at home about American affairs constantly disturbed Northcliffe, who sent cable after cable to London protesting against what he summarized as 'the pathetic ignorance' in Whitehall of the American system of government. 'The Government at home does not seem to understand that the United States is preparing a gigantic army of its own in France, and that the motto of those preparing the army is not unnaturally "America first". Congress, which rigidly examines the expenditure of every dollar lent to the Allies, or spent on American preparations, does not rush votes of credit as we do in the House of Commons. The Secretary of the Treasury is held to "strict accountability".' He found 'intense annoyance being caused here' by speeches of British politicians about 'the illimitable resources' of the United States. A serious feature was the growing fear of American bankers that a financial crisis would be caused by the successive loans to Britain and her allies.

I sometimes wonder if our Prime Minister has very much imagination. I remember that on January 1st, 1914, he wrote an article in the *Daily Chronicle* showing that he had no idea that a war with Germany was ever coming. He must be more and more aware of the fact that if the Americans withheld their payments to us for as much as twenty-four hours, there would be a financial crash that would mean a German victory. Since I have been here I have had but one short telegram from him. I quite understand his preoccupations, but I think that they are preoccupations of the wrong kind.

Northcliffe's impatience was often of 'the wrong kind'. As Lloyd George was to make clear later, 'in politics and diplomacy long intricate persuasion is an essential prelude to action. Lord Northcliffe had not even the experience of a provincial Mayor to guide him in the activities which depend more on co-operation than dictation. For a man of his dictatorial temperament and experience he did well.'

Northcliffe to T. E. Mackenzie (his accountant):

New York.
July 29, 1917.

My dear Mackenzie,—Though you do not hear from me you are very much in my thoughts, and you know that I am very grateful for the burden you take from my somewhat overburdened shoulders.

It would be quite impossible for me to endure the anxieties of this most responsible position if I had home worries. Roughly speaking, my work consists of the administration and expenditure of two million pounds daily, and the superintendence of some ten thousand people who are engaged in ordering and inspecting every sort of edible, every kind of gun, shell, all kinds of railway material—everything, indeed, that this vast continent produces. The task is rendered none the easier because of the unbusinesslike state of affairs at home. They hardly ever reply to my cables in reasonable time and sometimes never reply at all.

Let me know how you are and how my affairs are doing.

Yours always,
CHIEF

He wrote to his mother under the date line, 'Last Sunday in July, 1917', reminding her that it was within a few days of two months since he had come to America, 'and I am most grateful for the health and energy that have been given me through all this terrific heat. I think it is the mental concentration of beating the Germans that keeps me going. *This is the place where they are going to be beaten and no other.*' His letter concluded:

I am not so lonely now that I am getting home letters, but it is a great sacrifice to be away from all I love and to be unable to visit the war from time to time.

Get ready for your autumn change, darling Mother. Don't stay at Poynters too late, as last year.

Your devoted Firstborn

'Mother is still at Poynters,' his brother Rothermere wrote to him during the wettest August for forty years. 'She is extremely well and in excellent spirits. If there should be any recurrence of the cough she had last winter, I will see she is moved at once.'

Northcliffe had asked his brother to promote at home the idea of Lord Reading being sent to the United States to take over the increasingly delicate loan negotiations. Harold reported to him in the same letter, dated August 9: 'I put about what you said in regard to the L.C.J. [Lord Chief Justice]. [Lloyd] George is quite afraid to utilize his services. He fears a revival of the Marconi allegations. I shall be surprised if you see Reading in America.' Harold closed his letter with a fraternal suggestion: 'If you get thoroughly tired of your job and want to return, tell Lloyd George I will take it on. I have no palpitating desire to go to the States just now, but I am quite ready.' He signed himself 'Yours affectionately', an avowal on his side of the old regard which he had not often put into words. Northcliffe wrote to his mother that he thought it 'fine of Harold' to make the offer. The Minister of Munitions, Winston Churchill, was recommending to the Prime Minister the setting up of an all-embracing organization which he proposed should be called The American Board. It would absorb the many British official activities in the United States and Churchill intimated his readiness to support Northcliffe as its operating head. Geoffrey Dawson wrote to Northcliffe: 'I think that everyone here is beginning to appreciate the magnitude of your undertaking, the almost superhuman obstacles and the way in which you are tackling it' (August 7).

From his invalid's chair, St. John Harmsworth was sending his eldest brother messages of admiration and affection. 'We hear little of what is going on in America, little of your great task, but we realize its varied immensity and its decisive influence on the war. . . .' 'I have copies of your private letters, my dear brother. They are a tense synopsis of your tremendous work and anxieties. . . . How I wish you were nearer. . . .'

Sutton wrote to tell him that the *Daily Mail* 'is missing your personality'. Northcliffe replied: 'Please give my affectionate regards to the whole staff, editorial, business, mechanical. They are in my thoughts many times every day.' The tireless American interviewer, Isaac Marcosson, who had arrived in England to collect material for *Saturday Evening Post* articles, wrote to Northcliffe from the Savoy Hotel: 'With you out of England, there is something vital and definite and dynamic lacking in the whole structure of the nation.' H. W. Wilson, who was ostentatiously marking his gossipy letters 'V. Secret', told him: 'We in Carmelite House feel rather like a watch without a mainspring.' He mentioned that a Forces member of the staff visiting Carmelite House on leave from France had remarked that 'we have all aged very much'. Wilson said that he had replied that 'one cannot live through these times without feeling some sense of strain', and he went on to tell Northcliffe: 'All last week we heard the Flanders guns going incessantly. The noise at night is like the throbbing of some diabolical machine. And you have the twitter of robins', rhetorical tactlessness atoned for by the postscript:

I asked Swinton [Major-General Sir Ernest Swinton, K.B.E., D.S.O., afterwards Chichele Professor of Military History at Oxford], the man mainly responsible for the tanks, what his present attitude to you was. He told me that he was convinced we should have been beaten and made peace a year ago but for you; and he admitted that Kitchener was a failure, though he was much attached to him.

On August 7, Dawson, at Printing House Square, sent a letter marked 'Private and Confidential (Very)', which can hardly have failed to renew Northcliffe's doubts of Lloyd George. It disclosed that Arthur Henderson, the secretary of the Labour Party and a member of the Cabinet, who was described by Dawson as 'a man of mediocre capacity and very easily impressed', had undertaken to go to France with Russian emissaries as a preliminary to an International Socialist Congress at Stockholm, where British delegates would meet their opposite numbers from enemy countries. Henderson had acted without reference to his Cabinet colleagues and there was a sequel of complications from which neither he nor the Prime Minister, according to Dawson, 'came out with credit'. Dawson wrote that he was 'absolutely convinced, though I cannot prove it', that Lloyd George had 'personally encouraged Henderson's action'. His letter continued:

Of course, it does not mean for a moment that Lloyd George is despondent about the war and looking for a way out. Far from it. I am absolutely convinced that he was never more determined to win than he is just now. But he has such an unfortunate weakness for running hares and flying kites that he is a perpetual object of suspicion. Someone compared him the other day to one of those toys which they sell in the Strand—a little man who is always jumping out to the full extent of his elastic tether and then coming back to the same place. I have been present within the last week at some very plain talking to him by personal friends on the danger of these methods as affecting public confidence not only in this country but abroad. Nevertheless, I still think him by far the best man available just at the moment for his place, and he has a sufficient nucleus of steady colleagues to keep him approximately straight.

*　　*　　*

As the weeks went by, and the financial dealings between London and Washington became more urgent and much more difficult, Northcliffe chafed at the indecision of the War Cabinet about sending Reading, for whose 'skilled advice' McAdoo, Secretary of the Treasury, had specially asked. Probably for the reasons stated in Rothermere's letter of August 9, Reading himself had not been told of the plan. 'I cabled on July 13 and repeatedly, at the expressed wish of the U.S. Government, who know that he had worked at the Treasury with [Lloyd] George and McKenna,' Northcliffe wrote privately, 'but he was not informed of my cables till August 23. The delay has cost us many millions of pounds.' House had noted on August 25: 'Financial problems are continually arising and Northcliffe has not the technical training to deal with them.'

Sir William Wiseman had gone to London at the request of his highly placed Washington friends to try to expedite Reading's arrival. Dawson of *The Times* wrote to Northcliffe on August 23: 'If you think he [Wiseman] is moving slowly, it is because of the endless difficulties of his task. No one has really obstructed. You must clear out of your mind the notion that any responsible person here has anything but goodwill towards your

Mission. But the Cabinet, as always, has been terribly overworked.' He explained that Wiseman was 'paying innumerable visits' to members of the Cabinet and 'produces a favourable atmosphere', but without securing definite results. 'He is more tolerant of this than I am and thinks that Lloyd George is pondering matters deeply between-whiles, which I doubt.' About Lloyd George, Dawson wrote: 'As we all know, he is the worst organizer in the world and does not know how to get full value out of the first-rate men who are at his disposal. Also, he is all over the place and very difficult to catch.' Dawson added that 'Bonar Law coquettes with the idea of going out himself', but doubted whether it would be so satisfactory as the choice of Reading. 'Bonar Law would not make a good personal impression', although Northcliffe had told the War Cabinet on August 15: 'I learned from House that a very warm welcome would be given to Bonar Law if he can pay a long enough visit to discuss the financial future of the war.' Wiseman told Northcliffe what he was fully prepared to believe: 'The Treasury does not understand the American situation.' Sir Arthur Willert remembers Northcliffe's comment at the time: 'They don't want to understand it because to understand it would be to admit that London is now second fiddle to Washington.' He may not have known that on July 21 House had received a letter from the President, who mentioned the differing views on peacemaking by England and France on the one hand and the United States on the other. 'When the war is over we can force them to our way of thinking, because by that time they will, among other things, be financially in our hands.'

Writing in that same week to Wickham Steed, Northcliffe referred again to 'the ignorance at home of American personalities and American ways', and said that it caused him and his associates 'great anxiety'. His cables to England about financial and other pressing affairs had been met, he declared, 'with long silences and perpetual misunderstandings'. He had not grasped the fact that his unconventional way of handling official matters was likely to disturb the routine hidebound civil servants who were in a position to be obstructive. He had no one at this side who understood their stereotyped procedures. He could make allowances for diplomatic nuances involving delay. He was altogether intolerant of political blundering. He told Steed: 'Lloyd George's optimistic speech about the submarines did infinite harm here. It has paralysed our efforts to hasten ship construction.' He cabled an urgent message to Churchill pointing out the dangers of minimizing the U-boat threat. 'It paralyses the efforts of those Americans favouring shipbuilding policy. Opposed to such Americans are the builders of skyscrapers, bridges, automobiles, etc., who protest that their demand for steel and labour should not be interfered with.'

Lloyd George's pronouncement at that darkest period of the war may have stiffened the American Government's decision to confiscate ships being built for Great Britain in American yards. It was a potentially serious set-back, both politically and economically. The American attitude was considered to be based on jealousy of the British mercantile marine and to reinforce an ambition to rival it in the post-war years. It could have shaken the foundations of the new understanding between the two countries. At a War Cabinet meeting the shipping controller had stressed the dangerous position that might arise for the Allies from the requisitioning of the ships at such a critical time. Northcliffe drove himself hard to bring about a settlement. He wrote to the Prime Minister on August 21:

If H.M. Government were to send a strong and earnest protest to the United States I cannot believe that America would perpetrate a deed which would always be regarded as an example of unfriendly commercialism.

A splendid fight at Washington has been put up by Royden who assures me that if the President were emphatically told that confiscating Allies' ships purely to gain commercial advantage is an action not in conformity with the best traditions of civilized States, Wilson might alter his opinion.

The emphasis he lays on moral issues is well known to those about him. The issue is entirely in his hands. Without a doubt, he is much under the influence of McAdoo, his son-in-law, who is trying hard to secure political prestige as he may possibly in 1920 stand for the Presidency.

If we act at all we must act quickly. Anti-British prejudice in America has to be met and the Germans are directing powerful propaganda against our ships. There is great ignorance at Washington of the enormous sacrifices which the British mercantile marine has made during the War. If affairs were in my hands I would lodge an urgent protest with the President without delay.

I hope you will pardon me for exceeding my proper functions as this matter is urgent and our Ambassador is twelve hours distant from Washington.

Turning to House for aid, Northcliffe followed his representations with a letter, pointing out that 'our people are evidently very agitated about this most delicate and difficult question. My instructions are to point out that my Government will keenly feel the blow, which will be a very serious one to England.' He referred to the heavy losses already sustained by England at sea and underlined the fact that to be deprived of the ships on order 'must embarrass our military and naval activities'. He ended his appeal with the intimation: 'My Government places itself entirely in the hands of the President.'

He had thought it necessary to assure Balfour: 'You may rely on me never to use minatory language. I have been dealing with these people for thirty years. Nothing can be gained here by threats, much by flattery and self-abnegation.' His conduct in the ship requisitioning crisis conformed with some strictness to that precept. No War Mission negotiations had been more demanding of tact, patience and level-headed advocacy. The Americans had not solved their tonnage problem, in spite of much ballyhoo. Seizing the British ships, on which £17,000,000 had been spent, was a sign of weakness. The *Times* correspondent in Washington wrote to his editor in London: 'There seems to be an absence of any outstanding organizing ability. Desks are thumped and jaws are clenched but nothing happens.' A paragraph from Lloyd George's *War Memoirs* ends the story: 'Unhappily, despite our appeals and the strenuous efforts of Northcliffe and Royden in America, the influences antagonistic to British shipping interests won the day with the President, and 150 ships were confiscated by the American Government and added to its Government Fleet.' Sir Robert Borden, Prime Minister of Canada, recorded a conversation of October 5, when Northcliffe spoke of the American Government as 'very grasping and selfish'.

Such prodigious opportunism was disheartening to men of good will. The American Government had ample pleadings in extenuation. There was a fear, easy to whip up into alarm, that much of the money handed out so lavishly in the name of the American people was put to uses designed to buttress post-war commerce among the allied nations. There was loud talk of extravagance and graft at the expense of the American taxpayer. The loans were not being properly accounted for. In particular, it was believed that Great Britain was maintaining her world-wide trade in spite of the war. Lloyd George wrote: 'America was altogether doubtful of Europe.' Such was the scene in which Northcliffe played the most difficult role in his career.

* * *

Confirming in a letter to Northcliffe on August 27, that 'the Reading business is settled', Dawson asked: 'Have you considered Asquith for future use as a touring demonstration of British Liberalism?' The *Times* editor added some comments about the staff of that newspaper: 'our small but strong and rather wild team'. There was 'Steed, with his violent prejudice in foreign affairs, Repington, always with some game on hand, Fraser, who wants incessant watching and nursing. They're all as good and as loyal as can be, but there must be someone with no particular bias and in touch with Ministers and others who know what is really going on. We are very well found in the technical business of editing . . . but very weak in acquaintance with public men. Steed, Repington and Fraser practically include it all. Just at the moment, we are rather short of "balanced worldliness".'

Rothermere to Northcliffe:

23–9, Bouverie Street,
London, E.C.4.

My dear Alfred,—Mother keeps extraordinarily well. Although we have had an absolutely beastly summer in point of weather, she looks very fit. I am keeping an eye on her. I have told her she must go away for the winter. She is kicking very hard but if I see the least sign of a return of the cold she had last winter I will see she moves from Poynters at once. She does not seem in the least bit nervous in regard to the possibility of any raids near London. In the big raid, the German machines were quite close to Totteridge. She is quite imperturbable.

. . . I hear now that it is most likely Reading will go to America. I happened to meet Bonar Law at Margate last weekend, and he told me that the American Government as well as yourself were urging that he should be sent. Although Bonar Law did not say so, I conclude that there is going to be a change in the Embassy at Washington. Why do you not suggest Reading for the job? He is dying to get away from the Bench.

I hope you will take great care of yourself. Mother expects you back some time in November. At least, this is what I glean from what she says. I should think you could manage to come over, if not finally, at least for some weeks about that time.

Your loving brother,
HAROLD

Reading's arrival in New York early in September 1917, accompanied by Colonel E. D. Swinton and J. M. Keynes, was welcomed by none more sincerely than by Northcliffe, who was only too well aware of the financial tension. Even the Americans were staggered by the size of some of the bills which the Allies were running up, not to say by the still greater loans that were contemplated. The matter was more than one of high-powered accountancy. There were vital political implications and those, too, were beyond Northcliffe's scope. He had cabled to Reading on August 26, urging him to accept the War Cabinet's request. Reading had replied to him: 'Much impressed by your telegram', and announced his intention of sailing within a week. In urgently recommending Reading for the post of chief financial negotiator on behalf of Great Britain, Northcliffe rendered further conspicuous service. Ultimately, it led to the appointment of Reading as British Ambassador with plenipotentiary powers. Meanwhile, in order not to hurt Spring Rice's feelings, the purpose of Reading's visit was kept in the background. Sir William Wiseman, writing to Sir Eric Drummond, mentioned that Northcliffe's feelings were considered too. The impression was allowed to develop in Washington that Reading's main affair was the Morgans overdraft. In consequence, Reading was regarded simply as a Treasury representative.

It made his position difficult and another result was that he, in turn, tended to underestimate the power of the American administration.

House and Northcliffe had discussed the future of Spring Rice. House, who spoke of the Ambassador as 'an excitable invalid', insisted that it would be a mistake to dismiss him. 'They would say that Northcliffe had done it.' House thought that the solution was to give the Ambassador long leave of absence. 'Stick another title on him and give him something to wear on his coat at night.' In a communication to Lloyd George, House had said that 'Lord Northcliffe is helping to make Reading's visit a success'. Wiseman wrote to Drummond: 'Northcliffe accepted Reading's coming very well; in fact, all through, Northcliffe has shown a singleness of purpose which is very commendable. He does not seem to mind about his own position.' Wiseman added that 'the only two difficulties with him are, firstly, that he is not really fitted to organize enormous business undertakings, such as the British War Mission, and, secondly, that he cannot keep his hands off propaganda'.

On September 1, Dawson wrote to assure Northcliffe: 'Every Minister that I have lately seen has spoken most highly of all that you have been able to do with your Mission. The P.M. and Milner have both applauded it to me within the last few days. Even Bob Cecil (as the P.M. told me) is convinced that your path should be smoothed by prompt changes at the Embassy. For the moment your backing here is perfectly solid.'

Northcliffe wrote to his mother that day, saying: 'The work is terrific and little to show for it, *but I know the influence I am exerting here directly and indirectly is helping to win the war*. Give my fond love to every brother, sister, nephew, niece, Aunties and every one. All are in my thoughts always. Tonight I go to Canada.' His letter was written on 22 St. James's Place notepaper. Against that address he had scribbled: *I wish it were so*. Writing to his mother again a few days later, he told her: 'It is curious that I dream about home affairs almost nightly, and never about America.'

The opportunity to be in Canada gave him pleasure. He had always liked that country and was warm in his feelings for its people. *En route* to Toronto, he went to Rochester, N.Y., reputed to be the most pro-British of American cities. The university had invited his acceptance of an honorary degree. He had been charmed by his first sight of the university buildings—'much like ivy-covered, red-brick Harvard'. The ceremony closed with the spontaneous singing of *God Save The King*. He went on to speak to a thousand business men at the chamber of commerce. He told them that the submarine danger called for 'a superhuman effort', which would not bring peace by Christmas.

In Ottawa, where he was the guest of the Governor-General, the Duke of Devonshire, he gave his attention to the maladroit propaganda from London which encouraged the Canadians to believe that they were doing all the fighting. 'It floods Canada with news of Canadian troops and never mentions an English regiment, which helps the anti-conscription party in Canada to say: "We have done our share. Let John Bull have a turn at the war." ' Taking up the matter with leading political figures, he noted: 'I like the Canadian tone very much. The war has softened it.' There survives a memory of him enjoying himself in the company of Texan mule suppliers and French-Canadian staff officers at the British Army reservist centre in Montreal. 'He was far from being the brooding and petulant man we had expected. He was on entirely free-and-easy terms with everyone.' He foresaw Ottawa as the empire capital—'in fifty years', he told Willert of *The Times*.

At Government House, 'driving up to the portico in an English car with a couple of English chauffeurs, passing British sentries, with the round, smooth English butler and a crowd of long slim footmen in buff liveries, I was back in England'. It was agreeable, he wrote, 'to be away from all this new Americanism of jazz music, the cabaret and the roof garden, those abominations of New York', and he revels in his few peaceful days among the lakes, with their flights of wild duck and their mountain ash trees with scarlet berries.

I was fishing this morning for black bass in the midst of a beautiful lake when a small boat approached in which, bringing my mail and dispatches, was the unfortunate Price. To reach me he has a fifteen-mile trip in a Ford and then has to come through a chain of lakes in one of my host's motor-boats. His arrival had been heralded half an hour before by the rising of five wild duck into the sky.

Finding the money for Canadian munitions and food was the most difficult of the negotiations awaiting Northcliffe on his visits to Montreal, Toronto and Ottawa.

How to pay for all these vast supplies, when we have not a gold sovereign to send across the Atlantic, is an intensely difficult problem. It resolves itself into the old situation—that I am to go to Washington, this time with Sir Thomas White, Canadian Minister of Finance, and ask the United States to lend the money to Canada to pay for British munitions and food; in other words, the poor relation business again—the pawning of the British Empire to the United States, a position I foresaw plainly during my voyage across the Atlantic.

His case was not helped by the bungling of the authorities at home: as an example, an English buyer had been sent out to procure eight million pounds worth of cheese from eastern Canada. Nothing was known of the transaction by the British War Mission until the Treasury representative in New York received a demand for payment from the Canadian Government. Northcliffe wrote: 'We notified the Treasury at home and they replied that they had no eight millions to send.' It then became his task to persuade the Canadian Government to make funds available. 'And they did it. I have stopped all chance of a recurrence of that sort of costly muddle.'

The possibility that England might not be able to finance further war purchases in Canada led him to consider, gloomily, an economic and therefore political change of some magnitude that might ensue. In place of England, the United States would step in and buy all that Canada had to sell. 'The channel of trade, north and south, once thus established, will continue for all time, and the great work for which many of us have laboured for years, the creation and maintenance of inter-Empire trade, will be destroyed.'

While he was in Ottawa, he received an offer of £30,000 for the remainder of his lease of Sutton Place. It came from the Duke of Sutherland. Lady Northcliffe had not wanted to leave the beautiful home to which she had given not only her social graces but her heart. Northcliffe himself had grown tired of large houses. He had spent £70,000 in maintaining and improving Sutton Place. 'I'm quite happy in a bedroom on the fifth floor of the best hotel in Paris', he had told Millicent, Duchess of Sutherland. His first thought, on cabling his acceptance of the Duke's offer, was to make his wife a consoling gift of £5,000, to which he later added £30,000, the amount received for the furniture and other contents. His second thought was for his books at Sutton Place: 'Tell Butes to take care of them.' He reminded his wife in a letter that both Sir Robert Borden, the Prime Minister of Canada, and Sir Wilfrid Laurier, a former Prime Minister, had been their guests at Sutton Place 'and elsewhere', and that he had met Borden earlier that year at Brighton, 'when I honoured him by presenting him to Mother'. He had met other prominent Canadians, he said, who cherished their recollections of Sutton Place. 'I am truly glad it is disposed of,' he wrote to his mother. 'It served its purpose in our lives. I was never well there, but I do not regret a farthing of the fortune spent on it, for I helped to perpetuate a beautiful thing.'

In Ottawa, he dictated from his bed at Government House early one morning a brief résumé of what he called his 'kaleidoscopic life since the war began'.

First, those intense four days in 1914 of flogging those political jelly-fish into action, then the row about Kitchener and the shells and the bannings and burnings of my newspapers, then Ypres, Verdun, Gorizio and the Corso, among the Germans in Switzerland, then off to Spain, a few days' salmon fishing on the Tay (six fish in one day), the Battle of the Somme, more visits to France, more stirrings up of the Government, thirty-six hours in which to abandon the work of my life for the killing job of trying to push everything available in the United States across the Atlantic to Haig, and all the meat and wheat I can get for the people at home; then Washington, New York, Boston, Ottawa—most of them merely words to those who read these lines—but all of them self-centred worlds of their own and all gradually getting into the great vortex of the war.

★   ★   ★

Lloyd George had forecast that Northcliffe's work in the United States would be finished by September. Early that month, Northcliffe cabled him: 'Your prognostication cannot possibly be realized. The task is immense and ever growing. I have never worked so hard before.' He proposed returning home in November 'for a short visit'. Having that in view, he suggested, 'with respect', that his brother Rothermere should take his place *pro tem*. 'He knows the United States and would come here for two or three weeks before I leave.' There is no record in the Northcliffe archives of an answer from Lloyd George. As has been noted, the suggestion came in the first place from Rothermere himself. By the turn of events, he was shortly afterwards given a more important post. Wiseman to Sir Eric Drummond: 'I learn that Northcliffe proposes to return at the end of November for two months and is arranging for Lord Rothermere to take his place while absent.' Informed of this, Balfour inquired: 'Whom is Lord Northcliffe arranging this with?'

Northcliffe to his mother:

Home Island,
River St. Lawrence,
Canada.
7th September, 1917.

. . . The days of exile pass slowly without you, sweet Mother, despite innumerable daily tasks and great kindness from all kinds of Americans.

When this reaches you I shall know whether I can get leave in November for at least a month. I started out at such short notice, and I am glad I did, for I got to work the quicker for it, though I did not get about me a sufficient staff. I can demand leave, of course, or go home altogether, but I shall obey orders. *I know that I am helping to win.*

Your letters come regularly, sometimes two in two days, and I love them, my sweet.

Many people now write to me from England, including many strangers who think I ought to return to ginger up our very limp government.

I hope that if Poynters does not agree with you, you will *at once* go to any place you choose. I shan't easily forget how run down you got last autumn.

My fondest love to you, my darling Mother, and to all our circle, and to Mrs Jealous.

I have not seen an English paper since I left, *even my own*. I am deep in this task and spend my life at it.

I shall think of you on the 21st September, darling [her wedding anniversary]. I never forget *any* of our days.

Your devoted firstborn.

He made much of having no time to see his newspapers, which continued to arrive intermittently in bundles by the uncertain Atlantic mails. Despite his disclaimer, there is a memory of him reading the small feature in the *Daily Mail* called 'A Countryman's Diary', extracted for him by his secretary. He was keenly alert to the wartime fortunes of his Amalgamated Press, concerning which Sutton kept him dutifully informed. He was more than three thousand miles away, travelling by the Canadian Pacific Railway across Canada, when he wrote to Sutton: 'We are not active enough in the Midlands and the North', and expressed the opinion that 'the flaming balance sheets of Newnes, etc.' would stir up the enterprise of 'shrewd people like Hulton and others, and I have the power of seeing very far ahead, as you know'. Ten days later, he was telling Sutton that his mission work gave him no time for personal affairs, though he had 'looked at *Answers*'.

I have been so absorbed in the task of organizing this whacking great job that I have totally neglected all home private and business things. Picture an American arriving in England to take charge of Embassy, Times, Amalgamated Press, Mail, Evening News, Gravesend, Manchester, raw material, and expenditure of sometimes 2 millions daily, all his heads of depts. being either distraught volunteers, unpaid (such as Sir Thomas Royden, vice-chairman, Cunard), Civil Servants, or more or less useless enthusiasts. He has to deal with a hostile Press and Government (save for some real friends), he has many enemies in his own camp here and at home. His work is injured at the start by ambassadorial insults, backed up by minimizing debates in Parliament. The thing sounds an impossible job, especially as some of the branches of the Mission are in Canada, others in South America. In addition is certain ceremonial dining and speaking. Add to that a heat wave. . . .

Hope to be home on leave end of November for some weeks.

Life with detectives about you is a good deal of an annoyance, exile from Mother, home, friends, dear Elmwood, and my dear businesses a great trial. But as I awake to strange surroundings, or in moments of trial and discouragement, I feel that my sacrifices are nothing compared with those of other people. . . .

Caird has been A1 for oil purchases, a vital part of our work. What risks our fleet has run of fuel shortage!

U.S. Government insisted on Reading, and have *reduced financial supplies* pending his arrival. Poor Lever [Sir Hardman Lever, British Treasury representative in the U.S.] is in despair. Our weekly bills (10 to 12 millions) have to be met. If they're not, there would be the biggest financial crash in the world's history. Every secret German influence is trying to bring about that event.

He repeated to Sutton the opinion that he had given in several other letters: 'When the Americans are properly in the war, it will be very hard to get them out of it.' Taking tea in Washington with his American novelist friend, Mary Roberts Rinehart, he told her: 'The Pacific will be the strategic ocean of the future.'

The ex-Chancellor of the Exchequer (1915–16), Reginald McKenna, had a brother Ernest, who had written to Northcliffe because 'Sutton insisted that I must. I do it with fear and trembling'. He put the question: 'Do you realize that your Press does not stand where it did? That is the effect of your absence and the situation is slipping out of its hands. The Govt. is weakening so fast that one really does not know what a day may bring forth. There is no doubt that you are doing splendid work in America, but is America the real centre at this moment—whatever it may become in the future?' Northcliffe replied that he had not seen any of his newspapers since he left England, 'being deeply absorbed in the task of preventing a rupture between our country and the United States— always a grave danger'.

'The man is as full of energy as a caged lion, stalking up and down.' A reporter for the *Montreal Star* was describing Northcliffe dictating to Price, his principal secretary. 'Up and down, up and down across the room, he walked, talking the while. There was a large rug on the floor. On this, his feet made no sound, but when his heavy walking shoes struck the border of hardwood they gave out a crunching sound that added to the nervous tenseness of things. After a while, you felt like jumping out of the window to get away.' When Northcliffe left the room, the reporter said to Price: 'Yours must be a killing job.' Price replied: 'I had a rest for a year. I was at the Front.'

Hamilton Fyfe thought that Northcliffe's health was impaired by his prodigal war mission exertions. He was still more sure that Northcliffe's sense of proportion had suffered, that 'the constant flow of compliment and flattery, of eulogy and panegyric', had not been for the good of his soul. 'Speakers proclaim him everywhere as the most powerful man in Britain', and Fyfe, writing after he had become detached from the Northcliffe circle, said that Northcliffe himself 'began to believe it'. True, there was the repetitious emphasis on the immensity of the task, and Northcliffe may have dramatized his role in certain paramount emergencies. For those who knew him best, there was reassurance in the delighted surprise which ran through all his unofficial communications from America. It told them that he had not lost a memorable characteristic, what H. G. Wells in writing of him called 'the gleam of the ineradicable schoolboy'.

*　　　*　　　*

House had told Northcliffe that 'the President was absolutely aware of the great part we have played in the war'. Northcliffe was still far from satisfied with what was being done to make the facts known to the American people: for instance, 'nothing is heard of our fleet'. He agreed with the Foreign Office press representative, Geoffrey Butler, who was doing his best to improve the small existing British information bureau, that 'we need the visit of some very prominent war character. The highest authorities here cannot understand why we do not make our case better known.' Northcliffe sent a cablegram to Smuts, who replied: 'Your remarks are deeply appreciated. I would gladly come to U.S.A. and suitable opportunity might occur later in winter. I am deeply impressed with necessity for propaganda campaign in U.S.A.' Northcliffe became increasingly concerned about it. He sought stronger Foreign Office backing for the work that Geoffrey Butler was doing. 'His job is a very difficult one. Numbers of Americans believe that we tricked them into the war. Others object to joining "a bankrupt concern", as they describe England.' He summarized his misgivings:

. . . the United States Government has no notion of what we are doing in the war. Newspapers give the impression that the war is being fought by France and Canada. At a popular theatre here one of the scenes depicted nightly is of Canadian troops returning from the battlefield to their meals which are being cooked for them by British soldiers. This ignorance indirectly affects all our financial efforts at Washington.

Although it has since been held that Northcliffe had an exaggerated view of the war news situation in so far as it dealt with the exploits of the French and the Canadians, there is no denying that he genuinely believed otherwise and that he gave himself well and truly to the always congenial job of stirring up the appropriate authorities. In making his protests he had the important backing of Colonel House, America's most influential private citizen, whom he had completely won over as ally, counsellor and friend. After they had worked together with increasing intimacy, and when the time of Northcliffe's departure was not far away, House wrote of him: 'He does what he promises and he rings true.' Northcliffe informed his circle at home that 'one of the reasons for House's power is that he wants nothing for himself. He could have any office he chose', and he recorded again his satisfaction at having 'entertained him and Mrs House in London'. There was 'additional good fortune' in the fact that he had met Hugh Wallace, 'House's most intimate friend and agent, in London, and that Mrs Wallace had been with Mrs House to Sutton Place'.

House, soft-footed and soft-voiced, was the confidant to whom Northcliffe turned many times in his War Mission difficulties. An increasing personal regard for Northcliffe is reflected in House's papers. House had cabled to London on August 11: 'Northcliffe is doing good work and is getting on well with everyone.' Their most effective co-operation was on propaganda, a war weapon which Wilson, the President, mistrusted. Ignoring his Presbyterian scruples, Northcliffe and House reached their fullest measure of understanding on propaganda as an indispensable weapon in modern war. Dr Charles Seymour, of Yale University, who edited *The Intimate Papers of Colonel House*, stated that Northcliffe 'had already conceived the ideas which were carried into effect by the following spring'. Out of his deliberations with House there was to come an abundant harvest in the months ahead.

Northcliffe had cabled to the Prime Minister on August 15, informing him that House referred to the subject of propaganda 'again and again in the course of our interview', and that 'he said the war was being fought without imagination; that where the Germans have spent millions on propaganda we have only spent thousands'. German propaganda had helped to defeat the Italians at Caporetto. It was doing much damage to the Allied cause in Russia and Greece. He passed on the opinion that 'if a small portion of the money which has been expended in war material had been put into effective propaganda . . . the war would have nearly reached its conclusion'. Others were thinking along similar lines. Northcliffe's powerful convictions, strengthened by his experience of German war propaganda in Spain and the United States, gave wings to an argument which was carried to the highest quarters.

Northcliffe to W. J. Evans, editor of the *Evening News*:

New York.
26th September, 1917.

My dear Evans,—I ought to have written to you before, but this job leaves me no time for any kind of letters. It never ends and is infinitely the most difficult thing that I have ever attempted.

. . . I don't think I travel an unnecessary mile or make an unnecessary speech, but our propaganda is so wretchedly deficient here that we have no speakers and every one of the Mission has to turn to. I have a splendid and distinguished body under me, a capable staff—some 10,000 altogether. . . . Now that the United States is beginning to compete in the purchase of war materials and in tonnage, the task is going to become very difficult.

I may be home on leave in November, when I shall have the opportunity of telling the home government a few home truths about their slackness with regard to the United States.

Your attached
CHIEF

Northcliffe had implied in a letter to the Prime Minister (September 21) that he would be in New York through the winter. Now he was showing signs of restlessness. The indecision, frustrations, delays, attending so many of the transactions of officialdom bore heavily upon him. Lloyd George said that 'he was now in a world where the autocrat had to submit to being an all-round subordinate'. Northcliffe had written: 'The Prime Minister may get complaints about my ruthless methods, but I do nothing without the collaboration of Sir Hardman Lever, who may be relied on to check my brutality.' He told H. G. Wells that the power of instant dismissal given him by the War Cabinet had enabled him to 'cure at once' the squandering of millions of money, as well as 'friction, obstruction, and some swindling'.

'When you get this', he wrote to his mother on October 11, 'I ought to be less than a month from you. I shall be a great deal at Poynters to avoid travelling. I feel that I never want to see another train as long as I live, and I am almost as tired of motors.' At the same time, he wrote to Sutton: 'I shall choose the fastest and best armed ship I can get', adding: 'Our Govt. *cannot* apparently understand situation here.' Wilson, of the *Daily Mail*, had written to him shortly before: 'We do miss you. Lloyd George is very irresolute. He has not put through the Admiralty changes as he would have done if you were here.' Wickham Steed wrote (October 14): 'I was glad to hear that there is a chance of your coming back at least for a time, because I am sure your influence here is needed.' He referred to an attack on Lloyd George in *The Globe*. There was a belief that it had been prompted by Robertson, Chief of the General Staff. It posed the desirability of Asquith's return to power. German official propaganda was busy in Europe on the basis of the Reichstag resolution of July 1917 that Germany was ready for 'peace without annexations or indemnities'. Steed had no doubt that Lloyd George's 'fear of press criticism' was lessened during Northcliffe's absence. 'He imagines that as you are not here to bite him, public opinion as revealed in the press is a more negligible quantity.' There were others besides Steed who thought it timely for Northcliffe to return.

He wrote to his private circle on October 21: 'I am about to cross the Atlantic at a very stormy time of year, and a particularly periscopic period, in the hope that I may be able to get together a Government Department which will answer my cables and instil some understanding of these people into the "shirt fronts" and "rubber stamps" of whom two are members of our Cabinet. Now, I put it to you—who of the Cabinet is a notorious "shirt front" and who is an obvious "rubber stamp"?' On the previous day, Colonel Swinton had written from America to the secretary of the War Cabinet in London, Sir Maurice Hankey: 'Northcliffe is full of zeal and working very hard and has helped Reading a lot. He is as keen as mustard to try to do all he can for his own country. I firmly believe in his patriotism, but I think he is, with the best of intentions, talking a bit too much for American liking.'

In a letter to Dawson of October 26, Willert, in Washington, urged that no effort be spared in persuading Northcliffe to return to the United States in due course. 'Impress upon him that he must come back. If he fails, America will say that he was ousted by Reading who came out and found he was making a mess of things. S.R. [Spring Rice] is doing his best to spread that impression.' Willert explained: 'Northcliffe has done extraordinarily well with his propaganda work. . . . We need his great prestige.'

Northcliffe had been asked to speak in several cities in support of the second Liberty Loan, and on October 21 he went to Cleveland, Ohio, where almost nothing was known of Britain's part in the war. He wrote home during his train journey of 700 miles: 'The war news from home is bad; the temperature dropped twenty degrees in the night, as it does here; and I am miserable.' He found that only one British speaker had been in Cleveland before him. 'These entirely alien populations must have the war explained to them very simply and by people who have been in it.' He struck the vein of idealism in his far-off audiences of the American Middle West, the warm-hearted sentiment which, serving to restrain men's more violent ambitions, has had a profound effect on the American social system. He spoke of the soldiers' homecoming, of their changed attitudes to the past and what was good and bad in their national inheritance, and of the certainty of their will to demand 'conditions of existence which will show that they have not fought vainly to improve life all round'. He would say with firm conviction: 'And I consider that they will be well within their rights to do so.' His sincerity never failed to stir the people into loud approving applause.

In Chicago, a dinner was organized in compliment to him by Samuel Insull, the financier. Northcliffe was surprised, and appeared to be delighted, when he saw that the menu was a reproduction in miniature of an edition of *Answers*, with the correct shade of orange for its cover. Of his crowded day and a night in that city he spared two hours for talk at the Blackstone Hotel with an old Stamford School boy, Monckton Denes, who never forgot Northcliffe's consideration for him on that occasion. 'He confessed to retaining a rather hazy recollection of me as I was in our boyhood days; nevertheless, he was most kind and cordial at a time when men of national importance were waiting their turn to see him in the ante-room.' He was at a chamber of commerce function at St. Louis, Missouri, on October 26, and from there went on to Dayton, Ohio, to see Orville Wright and to inspect the field in which the Wright brothers' first flight was made. There was a formal side to the visit. At his instigation, the Royal Society of Arts had awarded its Albert Medal to Orville Wright and Northcliffe was asked by the British Ambassador to make the presentation. Katharine Wright, Orville's sister, had written to him on October 2: 'Almost every magazine I pick up refers to Langley as the inventor of the aeroplane', and feared that 'if this goes on much longer, it will be hard to change public opinion'. She asked Northcliffe to help her 'to get something done', as many people believed that the credit should go to Langley. 'Until the fraud of that particular trial of the Langley machine is made public in some striking way, nothing will change that opinion.' She added: 'Sometimes I think that I care more about it than Orville does, though I am sure I couldn't appreciate your friendship more than he does.'

Nearing the day of his departure from New York, Northcliffe wrote to Rothermere and Sutton (November 1): 'If anything should happen to me on my forthcoming voyage, or indeed in any other way, I want you to see that my secretary and friend, Mr H. G. Price, is well looked after. He knows who are my friends and that my wishes are that any of them, such as Max Pemberton, for example, should be taken care of, if what I have left them in my will is not sufficient.' The same day, he received a message from Downing Street signed 'Prime Minister'. He found it awaiting him at the hotel in New York. 'A pleasant surprise,' he wrote, 'quite unex-pected.' The message was as follows:

Before you return on leave I wish, on behalf of the War Cabinet, to thank you for the invaluable work you have done in the United States as head of the British War Mission. It was an appointment requiring exceptional tact and vigour and the War Cabinet desire to express to you their complete satisfaction with the manner in which you have fulfilled your mission. They would also like to congratulate you on the great energy and effect with which you have striven to explain what Great Britain has been doing and the needs of the Allies to the American public, and the success of your efforts to combat enemy attempts to sow dissension between the people of the U.S. and Great Britain.

At once, he had the substance of the message transmitted to his mother, who was staying at Warne's Hotel, Worthing. He followed it with a copy of a message sent him by the Prime Minister of Canada, Sir Robert Borden:

Your work in the United States has been crowned with great success and I was specially interested in your wonderful tour of the Middle West which cannot fail to be attended with immense advantage to the great cause we all have at heart.

The intelligence service arranged a melodramatic exit for him on November 3. His baggage was labelled for Canada. He was required to spend the night at 'the station for Canada'. Next morning, he showed up again at the Hotel Gotham, 'to be seen by spies'. He was then driven to the station in his Rolls-Royce. There he was smuggled into a police car which drove him at top speed to the dock where the *St. Paul* was lying. Lord Reading was going home in her, too, after achieving what North-cliffe wrote was his 'great personal success' at Washington. 'The secret service people think that if the Germans knew that he and I are on the *St. Paul* efforts will be made to catch us by submarine, or put infernal machines in the coal.' He was discouraged from saying goodbye to members of the War Mission staff, 'in order not to arouse suspicions as to my departure'. On November 2, one of the War Mission headquarters typists, Amy Cottell, wrote home: 'We are all dreading tomorrow when the Chief goes.' Saying farewell to him in the privacy of his flat at 105 West Fifty-fourth Street, where one wall was almost covered with framed photographs of Northcliffe, Louis Tracy remarked that 'there is little use in denying, even to oneself, the dangers of the trip'. At home, Cecil Harmsworth was writing in his diary (November 2): 'Northcliffe is leaving America by the *St. Paul* tomorrow and I am anxious to hear what steps are being taken to protect his ship. Ll.G. is concerned about this and urgent messages go to the Admiralty enjoining on them the necessity for fully adequate measures. If the Germans can drown him or take him prisoner in a submarine it will be no end of a score for them.'

Two days out from New York, Northcliffe was impelled to write: 'My last peep at the U.S. was radiantly beautiful.' He was taking with him a memory of 'the crimson leaves of the masses of oak trees, and the almost translucent gold and amber of the maples and poplars with the background of turquoise cloudless sky and dazzling sunlight'. It could not be pictured, he wrote, unless seen.

The titanic skyline of giant buildings, each a town of ten to fifteen thousand people and mostly of white building material, gleamed and dazzled in the brilliance as the old *St. Paul* slid out of the wonderful harbour. In the distance, they looked like the pipes of a vast organ.

The *St. Paul*, camouflaged in pale grey, green and yellow, was sailing with only a few passengers, among whom he found several known to him, apart from Lord Reading: Sir Thomas (later Lord) Catto, Governor of the Bank of England; Thomas Lamont, the American banker; and Colonel Swinton. Northcliffe impressed himself on Swinton as 'that amazing man, then at the height of his powers'. Continuing his notes, Northcliffe recorded that 'every one about to face the submarines affected an exaggerated gaiety, the accentuated grins and attitudes of "movie" stars.' He was given 'a grim-looking black rubber suit', like a diver's without the helmet. 'In front is a pouch. My valet, Paul, has already inserted a bottle of Horlick's tablets and a flask of brandy in mine.'

He went on to ruminate in writing on the inter-Allied council of which he had been a sponsor when it was first proposed some time before. The council was to scrutinize and co-ordinate Allied war needs before requests were passed on to the United States for loans and other help. From America Northcliffe had written to his wife: 'My great fear is that the Allies will muddle their relations with the United States and squander the products of this vast and bounteous continent. I am trying to arrange that there should be an Allied Committee in Paris, who should agree as to what this and that Power needs to win the war.' He wrote from the ship:

I ought to have been in Europe weeks ago. The Inter-Allied Council should have assembled on August 15, but the delays inseparable from Allied warfare have postponed and re-postponed this urgent gathering. Had the meeting taken place on the date indicated, I do not believe the Italian tragedy [the disaster at Caporetto] would have happened. However, America is to blame. She declined until October to participate. The conference arose out of a conversation between Mr McAdoo, Secretary of the Treasury, and the French High Commissioner and myself, as far back as June.

He referred in the same memoranda to Reading's negotiations at Washington, summing them up as 'a victory of a magnitude, financial and political, that will one day be realized. I cannot yet reveal it.' He rounded off his notes with the reflection:

A voyage gives me restful retrospect. . . . My general impression of five months in God's Own Country is of sunshine, lessening waste, increasing war spirit, parades and processions, too much train and motor for me, terrific work, wonderful sleep, universal kindness, splendid loyalty of a staff to me, not enough exercise.

Of the value of the American Giant to the Great Cause, it depends entirely on how he is used by those who direct, misdirect or intermittently direct the war. Wealthy beyond dreams in man power, machine power, money power, food power, steel power, copper power, oil power, cotton power, inventive power and enthusiasm, he is being confused by the conflicting demands of the Allies. Generous, but ignorant of the war, he has been giving with both hands. So far, little harm has been done. But the Giant must insist on co-operation, system and foresight on all our parts unless he, like Russia, the other Giant, be wasted. The Inter-Allied Conference is the first sign that he is getting impatient.

On the homeward voyage, Northcliffe talked more than once with Reading about the enhanced importance of the Washington embassy as a result of America's entry into world politics. There was need to bring all the British activities in the United States, political, diplomatic, financial, under one directing head. Reading knew that he was likely to be asked to take over that supreme responsibility. He was hesitant about accepting it. Northcliffe strongly urged him to do so. Reading's success at Washington could not be questioned; but he was undoubtedly aware of strong prejudices against him, and also against his German-Jewish wife, which did not exist in England, and he may have discovered that while McAdoo had welcomed his coming, the President had not shown the same interest.

They reached London on November 12. Northcliffe showed no obvious sign of tiredness or strain, but he had caught a chill in Liverpool and its effects were more real than apparent. Some of his friends thought he had aged. His head seemed more massive and to be set deeper in his shoulders. He resumed his communiques to the *Times* staff the next day in good humour: 'A very excellent *Times*. The leading articles are much the best of any paper', and the day following: 'It is a great treat to come back and open *The Times*. I did not see the paper between June 2nd and November 11th. It is immensely quoted in the United States.'

Of his having well and truly discharged the task put upon him by the War Cabinet five months before there could be no reasonable doubt. The Prime Minister had expressed the appreciation of the Government. Dealing with the Mission in his memoirs, Lloyd George wrote that Northcliffe had 'proved a striking success', and cited his achievement in gaining the confidence and good will of President Wilson, 'a man with a temper as autocratic as his own, but with a mind, training, character and outlook essentially different from his own'. Against that tribute from the highest authority it may be superfluous to set the statement of Lord Hardinge in *The Old Diplomacy* that Northcliffe 'was a complete failure', or the diary note of Geoffrey Dawson's friend, F. S. Oliver, the London drapery house director who wrote *Ordeal by Battle* (1915), that Northcliffe 'made a complete mess of everything he was charged with in America'. Northcliffe was deficient in the 'good business capacity' which had been part of the War Cabinet's commendation of him to the British Ambassador, Spring Rice, on May 30. Only the voice of prejudice could assert that he had failed in the larger purposes of his mission. He had succeeded where Balfour did not because he could not, for all his charm, experience and political wisdom. To most Americans, Balfour personified the 'effete civilization' which they were reluctant to defend. He was hardly the man to convince them that the people of the United Kingdom were as resourceful, or as virile, as themselves. He tended to confirm the notion that lords of the manor still held sway, that every nobleman was a great landed proprietor, every British soldier a 'redcoat'. It required a man of Northcliffe's calibre to remove those and more important misconceptions from the American mind. Triumphantly he did it.

There were impressive endorsements from the American administration. Robert Lansing, the United States Secretary of State, wrote to tell Northcliffe that he 'counted it a most fortunate thing for our two countries that one so competent to judge the temper of this people should have acquired a knowledge of the mental atmosphere of America and the countercurrents of public thought arising from our mixed population, which make our problems so complex'.

It will not be improper to insert here part of the testimony which Lord Reading telegraphed to Northcliffe after he had gone out to America for the third time to represent the Government, early in 1918. 'I should like you to know that the result of my survey and examination of the activities and organization of the British War Mission is eminently satisfactory. This should be gratifying to you who, as first Chairman of the Mission, were responsible for it before my appointment as High Commissioner.' A later message from Edward Hurley, chairman of the United States Shipping Board, may be brought forward: 'I want you to know that I sincerely believe that your being in America during the most trying period of the war, making speeches throughout the country, had more to do with arousing the interest of our people than any other one thing I know of. I don't believe you appreciate what a hold you have on the American people. We did not realize the seriousness of the situation until you presented it to us.' At Washington, they had expected to receive the self-centred demagogue of biased report. He had proved to be a statesman. His talks with the Americans were more decisive than the guns that thundered along the battle fronts at the Chemin des Dames, at Passchendaele, at Caporetto, at Cambrai. He created a closer link between the public opinion of Great Britain and the United States than any other Englishman and, in so doing, he rendered conspicuous and lasting service to the future of the free world.

Chapter Twenty-one

At the Summit

WELCOMED back to London by his wife and Geoffrey Dawson, Northcliffe hurried out to Totteridge for the reunion that meant so much more to him than any other. Next day he cancelled his afternoon appointments to visit his aunt Sarah Miller, the former 'belle of Kensington', described by Cecil as 'a woman of infinite jest and laughter, now greatly broken'. To Northcliffe she had a lifelong devotion. During his absence in America, he had arranged for flowers and fruit in season to be sent to her from Elmwood and Sutton Place, varied by hampers of good things from Fortnum & Mason's. Sitting with her that afternoon, he noted a trace of 'the old spirit' in the coquettish way she wore her lace cap.

Within a week he was at the centre of a public controversy that blew up like a squall, lashing the political scene into a flurry of bad tempers. The Prime Minister had talked to him on November 15 about the possibility of his taking over the newly created office of Air Minister. The chairman of the existing Air Board, Lord Cowdray, had been led by Lloyd George to believe that he would be the first holder of the new post. The following day, Northcliffe published a letter declining what he had evidently regarded as a definite offer. In Whitehall and Fleet Street, his letter was considered to be a sensational document. He had returned to London, he said, to find the Government continuing 'to dally with urgent questions', and he went on to declare: 'I feel that in the present circumstances I can do better work if I maintain my independence and am not gagged by a loyalty that I do not feel towards the whole of your Administration.' He had given 'anxious consideration' to the Prime Minister's 'repeated invitation' to take charge of the new ministry. He regarded it as 'a great honour and responsibility', and in declining it he had 'none but the most friendly feelings' towards Lloyd George.

I take this opportunity of thanking you and the War Cabinet for the handsome message of praise sent to me as representing the five hundred officials of the British War Mission in the United States, many of them volunteer exiles. Their achievements and those of their ten thousand assistants deserve to be better known by their countrymen. The fact that their work is not known is due to the absurd secrecy about the war which is still prevalent. Everything that these officials are doing is known to our American friends and, of course, to the Germans.

He could look the Prime Minister in the eye. He had faced danger and felt the better for it. He was braced also by his dealings with men who had at their command resources of power beyond any known to the rulers at home.

May I also take the opportunity of giving a warning about our relations with that great people from whom I have come? We have had the tragedy of Russia, due partly to lack of Allied propaganda to counteract that of the Germans. We have had the tragedy of Italy, largely due to the same enemy propaganda. There is one tragedy which I am sure we shall not have and that is the tragedy of the United States. But, from countless conversations with leading Americans, I know that unless there is swift improvement in our methods here, the United States will rightly take into its own hands the entire management of a great part of the war. It will not sacrifice its blood and treasure to incompetent handling of affairs in Europe.

It was a manifesto rather than a letter and no doubt its purpose was to make clear to the country the views of one who had seen the inner workings of personality and policy in relation to events which involved the future of the world. Lloyd George was adept at political intrigue, Northcliffe not even a struggling amateur. He had been driven to speak out in defiance of formal usage by an overriding sense of the public interest.

His publication of the letter without consulting the Prime Minister can now be seen as a mutation of political expediency which there is small profit in pursuing. For his immediate victim, Cowdray, with whom he had always been on friendly terms and with whom he had corresponded in that same week, Northcliffe had a sympathy which he was careful to make known. Cowdray put the blame on Lloyd George, who had talked with Northcliffe but not with him. Lloyd George ascribed to Cowdray's lasting resentment the 'widening of that schism in the Liberal Party that has led to its crumbling and collapse'. F. E. Guest, M.P., sent a note to Lloyd George on November 17, telling him that 'Cowdray's grievance is that you did not speak to him first of all. He quite understands N's rascality.' Carson and Austen Chamberlain condemned Northcliffe's violation of the code. Their voices echoed back from the walls of Westminster, making little stir beyond. At the Constitutional Club, Carson asked Northcliffe why he did not speak in the House of Lords, 'where he could be answered'. The railwaymen's leader, J. H. Thomas, publicly urged the Labour Party 'to stand four-square' against a press dictatorship. American journalism made much of the affair, summarizing it as an indictment of a weak Government. It became a nine-day's wonder, from November 15, when the Prime Minister first sounded Northcliffe, to November 24, when Northcliffe was made a viscount. 'Lloyd George must be tired of the Harmsworth family,' Cecil noted (November 15). 'Alfred has declined the Air Ministry, Harold the First Commissionership and the Ministry of Food, and I the post of Chief Whip of the Coalition.'

★   ★   ★

Certain people in high places were talking of peace. Northcliffe suspected Lloyd George of listening to their counsels, despite his parliamentary reassurances to the contrary. Before the month was out Lloyd George was telling C. P. Scott, of the *Manchester Guardian*, that 'there is a good deal of feeling in the War Cabinet towards peace'. Northcliffe was adamant in his view that the war must first be won decisively. His swift surprise stroke in dealing with the Prime Minister was a symptom of his impatience with the half measures and the temporizing. 'War is a very slow business to one who has been accustomed to the lightning round of a daily newspaper,' he told Caird. 'It seems to consist of one chaos after another.' There were men in the Government who, in his judgment, were not war winners: to House he named Balfour and Bonar Law. He spoke also to House about Lloyd George's 'incurable timidity at certain times, due to his humble origin and his fear of criticizing the aristocracy'. To his brother, Rothermere, he wrote: 'A lot of our troubles are due to Bonar Law, who is either overworked or understaffed.' He sent a memorandum to the office of *The Times*:

The words 'pacifist' and 'pacifism' occur too much in *The Times* and should be kept out. . . . I have been in England about a month. My work in connection with the British War Mission has brought me in touch with all sections of the population, and I have never yet met a pacifist. Advertising pacifism by continually printing the word is the way to promote it. . . . The publicity given to pacifism in the British Press produces deplorable results in Canada and the United States. I hope that the Staff will take these remarks very earnestly to heart.

The *Daily Mail* was addressed in similar terms. 'The word "pacifism" occurs too often in the paper. Let it be dropped.' Perhaps to demonstrate the damnable power of reiteration, he wrote in a communique to the *Times* office: 'Conan Doyle is an amusing example of the semipacifist who learns that he has been duped. Well do I remember seeing him hobnobbing with Henry of Prussia, when that arch-spy was throwing dust in the eyes of the London and provincial public by inaugurating what he called "Prince Henry's automobile tour of Great Britain".'

Pacifism was the inspiration of a notorious letter written by Lord Lansdowne, a former British Foreign Secretary, which the editor of *The Times* had declined to publish, deeming it 'a thoroughly mischievous document'. On November 28, the editor and Northcliffe were in sharp conflict, Northcliffe taking the view that the letter should have been printed and answered in a leading article. As a result, Dawson found himself awkwardly obliged to publish letters following up one which his readers had not been allowed to see. Policy apart, that to Northcliffe was bad journalism. Once again he found himself being denounced for a decision which he had not taken and did not approve: 'a shrieking chorus', Dawson wrote, accused Northcliffe of 'refusing publication'. H. W. Massingham, in *The Nation* of December 8, made it another excuse for decrying 'Northcliffe journalism'. Sir Norman Angell, in his autobiography, *After All*,* blamed Northcliffe for having 'decided that the British people—or as many of them as his papers reached—should not be allowed to know that responsible people were making such a suggestion', namely, 'an earlier and negotiated peace'. Northcliffe suffered often from that form of imputation. In a message to the *Daily Mail* office, December 24, 1917, he referred to criticisms of Lloyd George by Lovat Fraser, of the *Times* staff, being cabled to the United States under the catchline: 'Northcliffe Attacks Lloyd George.' On January 15, 1918, he wrote to H. G. Wells, who had complained about the presentation of one of his articles in the *Daily Mail*: 'My own particular reason for emphasizing personal expressions of opinion is in order to avoid the American-Canadian-Australian habit of cabling snippets with headlines to the effect that Northcliffe attacks Lloyd George, or Wells, or the Trinity, as the case may be.'

Interviewed by *The Globe*, he was asked whether he would change his mind about the offer of a ministerial post. He answered: 'My direct and indirect connection with the Government convinces me that it needs wholesale revision; some of its members are tired and some are unsuitable. The burdens borne by the Prime Minister, Lord Milner, General Smuts and others are beyond human endurance. I can best assist them by independent support in my Press and by returning to my duties in the United States.'

* Hamish Hamilton, 1951.

Thus, towards the end of 1917, he was aware of a new personal ascendancy in his dealings with the politicians. House, too, was aware of it and wrote after dining with the Prime Minister and Lord Reading: 'We talked of Northcliffe. He [Lloyd George] is evidently afraid of him and, unfortunately, Northcliffe knows it.' Earlier that day, Northcliffe had told House that he paid no attention to the censorship, which he considered 'stupid and useless', and that the British Government 'dare not interfere'. Here House added in an aside: 'He certainly is an unruly member.' Northcliffe, he recorded, insisted on attending the inter-allied conference in Paris. 'He handles himself just as if he were Dictator of England, and, in a way, he is, for the Government are afraid of him.' There was a possibly unexpected tribute from his brother Hildebrand. 'You are indeed a Triton among minnow, and we are all more than proud of you. As a family, we are not given to overpraise of one another, but the feeling is there all the same.'

In the public eye Northcliffe had become a figure of the summit, radiating a splendid faith in victory and a patriotism that could not be denied. That he had reached a height of popular regard at which he imagined the people would summon him to the foremost place was anyone's guess, ignoramus and jealous politician alike. The people realized that they had in him an inalienable champion. His near contemporary, Lord Beaverbrook, said that between 1916 and 1918 Northcliffe could have had Cabinet rank at any time he desired it. Northcliffe told a Canadian correspondent early in 1918: 'I am able to do things quicker now because I have a large body of public opinion at my back—so great, indeed, that I am unable fully to reach it through the medium of my newspapers.'

In his small personal circle the easy assumption that he craved the ultimate in political power was given no credence. To his closest friends and colleagues it seemed, indeed, incredible. They could not imagine him sacrificing his great solo position of newspaper statesman, or, for that matter, making himself even more vulnerable to the Fleet Street opposition. Marlowe told Price Bell, the American journalist: 'I do not believe that he wanted to be Prime Minister. He much preferred to be the donkey's driver.' As for being severed from his journalism, he more than once told Dawson that he 'had rejected high office in order that *The Times* may be independent'. At Carmelite House, his conduct over the letter to Lloyd George was received as a new demonstration of the audacity which had brought Kitchener down. H. W. Wilson had no doubt that 'the purpose of the letter was to strengthen Mr Lloyd George's hands against the stubbornness of those of his Ministers who hampered efficiency'. He claimed that one of its immediate effects was to bring about Admiralty changes and to expedite food rationing. Cecil Harmsworth, a popular

House of Commons personality, regarded it as an eruption of his brother's abiding scorn for professional politics, concerning which Hamilton Fyfe could testify: 'The politicians' fear of public opinion, fear of weakening their hold on office or their chance of it, fear of offending powerful interests, moved Northcliffe to derision.'

In *The Globe* interview, Northcliffe had spoken of returning to his War Mission work in America. House, who was strongly in favour of his going back, wrote to the President on November 16, the day of the publication of the letter to Lloyd George:

With this combination of Wiseman, Reading, and Northcliffe, things are being accomplished with more rapidity than I ever expected here. Northcliffe has been splendid. The Prime Minister has repeatedly offered him a seat in the Cabinet, which he has refused. He did not propose to relinquish the right to criticize when he thought it necessary.

Northcliffe lowered his tone in writing to Balfour on November 24: 'I am not sanguine about future matters with the U.S. Treasury. I pretend to no knowledge of finance. I will do my very best to bear the responsibility placed upon me.' He had not yet decided to return to New York. He notified Balfour that he proposed 'doing nothing about America' until he had seen Lord Eustace Percy, who was expected home and 'who has certain views worth attention'.* He protested that he had no further desire for exile, 'but I am quite willing to do anything that the Government ask me'.

On December 6, House wrote appreciatively to Northcliffe of the help 'given to me personally and to the United States Mission since we have been in England and France'. The same day House made a diary note that Northcliffe had spoken to him of 'someone being near Lloyd George'. The fact that House wrote down Northcliffe's utterance suggests that its possible significance did not escape him and that Northcliffe may have been visualizing himself in the intimate advisory kind of relationship with the Prime Minister that House had with the President. Political eminence with freedom of comment and action, power without responsibility: the prospect would no doubt have been pleasing to him. Whether a conjunction of Northcliffe and Lloyd George could have been successfully maintained is a question for the student of personality rather than of politics.

---

* Lord Eustace Percy (later Lord Percy of Newcastle) advised Northcliffe by letter that he had better not return because of Irish and pro-German influences which were being worked up against him in America. Writing in 1957, Lord Percy thought that he may have overestimated the strength of the anti-Northcliffe feeling at that time.

Travelling to and from the allied war conference in Paris and visiting Field-Marshal Haig and General Pershing, commander-in-chief of the American Expeditionary Force in France, Northcliffe was gravely attentive to the clamour of opinion about the battle of Cambrai, which had ended in an ignominious reverse for the British Army. It had opened with a brilliant tank assault on November 20. The Hindenburg Line was pierced. Church bells rang out in London. A week later, a German counter-attack won back the lost ground and penetrated to the original British defence line, behind which there had been inadequate reserves. In his memorandum to the *Times* staff on December 12, Northcliffe referred to it as 'one of the most ghastly stories in English history'. His feelings towards Haig appeared to change from that stage of the war.

Northcliffe to Sir Philip Sassoon:

Elmwood,
St. Peters, Kent.
13th December, 1917.

My dear Sir Philip,—. . . My knowledge of the temper of the people (quite apart from the temper of the Government, which will fall if there are many more Cambrais) shows me that they are at the end of their patience. There is the memory of a dead man, or the knowledge of a missing or wounded man, in every house. Outside the War Office, I doubt whether the Higher Command has any supporters whatever. Sir Douglas is regarded with affection by the Army, but everywhere people remark that he is surrounded with incompetents. . . . I should be no friend of the Commander-in-Chief, nor of anyone, did I not warn you of the intense resentment here about Cambrai.

War is war, and you may show this letter to anyone or make any other use you like of it. The only loyalty I feel is towards the Empire.

Yours very sincerely,
NORTHCLIFFE.

He was writing in the harshly generalizing mood which too often particularized his personal feelings. One of his nephews, Vyvyan Harmsworth, eldest son of Rothermere, had been a casualty at Cambrai, wounded for the third time. After his previous wounds, Vyvyan had insisted on being sent back to his men, though a staff job had been found for him. There was now little hope of his recovery. 'I am grieved for Harold,' Northcliffe told Caird. 'His youngest son—and last—is just going off to the war.' Harold had become the first Air Minister in a British Government.

Northcliffe went down to Elmwood immediately after returning from France. Passing through London, he cabled to his friend, Cyrus Curtis, proprietor of the *Philadelphia Public Ledger* and *Saturday Evening Post*: *I had the great pleasure of seeing New England troops guarding fair France stop need*

I say how great an encouragement this is to old England. Especially in his dealings with the Americans, his private good will was often a public service. Not so eager as he formerly was to be caught up in his manifold affairs, he had apparently committed his official future to the flux of events. In his businesses, he was leaving others to take action which formerly only he could make decisive. His main link with his newspaper staffs was the daily communique, usually dictated in bed each morning after he had read the morning editions brought to him about seven o'clock. 'It is quite natural that all my circle of sycophants should tell me how dreadful the paper was during my absence' (message to the *Daily Mail* staff, December 13, 1917). 'I believe nothing of the kind. The paper has been produced under very great difficulties, owing to the shortage of brainworkers.'

Humphrey-Davy, conducting himself as if he were gentleman-usher to a supreme being, was providing him with light entertainment by submitting long lists of territorial titles from which his master might make a choice appropriate to his viscountcy: 'Bolton ("because of The Priory") Pelham ("likewise"), Broadstairs, Elmwood, Chapelizod, Grand Falls, Newfoundland, Poynters, Thanet, Totteridge', etc., twenty-two names in all. Humphrey-Davy to Northcliffe: 'My Lord,—I have ventured, with some diffidence, to draw up a Memorandum on the subject of the Viscountcy. I fear it may seem rather a liberty, as the matter is essentially a personal and family one affecting your Lordship. Still, you have always been so kind to me that I feel you will not object to my humble intervention.'

Humphrey-Davy also compiled a list of peers who might sponsor Northcliffe's reintroduction to the House of Lords in his new style, in respect of which Northcliffe had received from the Secretary of State for Home Affairs a bill for £430, plus '2s. docquet fee'. Entrusted with the preliminary arrangements on behalf of 'the noble Viscount' (his reiterated phrase), Humphrey-Davy obviously revelled in his negotiations with Garter King of Arms, Richmond Herald, the Lord High Chancellor, and other officers of State. Having persuaded 'two noble Viscounts' to attend specially on the day of Northcliffe's presentation, Humphrey-Davy was put out by discovering that Northcliffe had arranged with Knutsford and Milner to present him, leaving his discomfited servitor to find consolation in supervising the alteration of 'the noble Viscount's' robes by Ede & Ravenscroft, of Chancery Lane, and by seeking precedents for a special remainder. Northcliffe wished his brother St. John to succeed him in the title. The matter was one for the Prime Minister in the first place and Humphrey-Davy made out an elaborate case for the Prime Minister's guidance. On January 15, two days later, Humphrey-Davy informed Garter King of Arms that 'Lord Northcliffe has decided not to take any further steps'. Northcliffe wrote shortly afterwards to the *Times* office: 'Humphrey-Davy is shocked at a paragraph under the Court Circular in which, while two Countesses get their full titles, I am reduced to a mere Baron. He is very much upset and thinks that *The Times* shows inconsistency, lack of deference, and want of decency!'

On the day of the House of Lords ceremony, Northcliffe received a letter from Claude Johnson, of Rolls-Royce, just back from the United States: 'I am furious at the insult to Royce, making him an O.B.E. Poor little man! He knows nothing about Honours and had no one to advise him, and he accepted it.' Northcliffe replied: 'I will get the matter put right.' In a further letter he referred to it as 'a scandalous thing that this modest genius should be so treated', and undertook to speak to the Prime Minister.

Down at Elmwood where the telephone bell rang all through the day, the servants hurrying into the garden with messages often found Northcliffe standing in his 'pulpit' in the flint wall, gazing across the meadows of Joss Farm to the sea. In London there were editorial and business executives daily expecting to be summoned. They received no sign. Pomeroy Burton, general manager of Associated Newspapers, was waiting tensely at the head of the queue. He had been 'sent to Coventry' several months before by Northcliffe for a speechmaking indiscretion in New York. 'I have taken my medicine fairly well—though it galled me to be humiliated among the high officials I have been working with, and to be shelved entirely by you. I want you to reconsider my position.' S. J. Pryor, Northcliffe's old colleague of the *Daily Mail* early days who was now somewhat obscurely on the staff of *The Times*, begged for a decision about his future: 'it only wants a word from you'. Pryor apologized for troubling him with a letter, 'but I cannot, nor ever could, speak with you directly without being sadly flustered'. The manager of *The Times* Book Club, Alfred Butes, hoped for an opportunity of laying before him personally 'a memorandum of progress', which would show a profit 'for the six months now ending of about £3,000. You have been so very patient with the White Elephant that I am very happy to make this statement. *The Times* Book Club is now the best book business in the country.' Dawson wrote to Willert: 'I have really seen extraordinarily little of Northcliffe myself.' When Horatio Bottomley desired to interview him at Broadstairs, Northcliffe sent him the cryptic answer: 'I am not doing any journalism just now.' A letter to the wife of the *Daily Mail* drama critic, James Waters, a popular office personality, was proof that 'the Chief's' warmer sympathies were not in abeyance. Waters had been gravely ill. 'Everybody at Carmelite House is devoted to dear Jimmy and the idea that he should be worrying about present or future finance is very distressing to us. If he lives to be a hundred he will receive his salary, and in any case you will receive one-third of his salary as a pension. And the boy will be looked after.' To which there came the reply: 'I am so grateful I cannot write. Jimmy is already better—it is your doing.'

Only Sutton and Stuart had direct access. Sutton brought news of a good year for the Amalgamated Press: net profit £324,000.

Northcliffe to Sutton:

> Elmwood,
> St. Peters.
> 13th [December]

My dear Sut,—The A.P. balance sheet is a monument to your loyalty, affection and industry. I have been thinking a great deal about the early days of the business and am particularly reminded of them by the Bungalow here.

I know how many anxious hours you must have had during the past twelve months and I realize the amount of tact required to deal with difficult people— all the little personal difficulties, the shortages, both human and otherwise. For all you have done so successfully, I am most grateful.

If my work has been a contribution to the war, it is because I was able to work in the United States with a mind free from A.P. worries.

I am more anxious today about our relations with the Americans than any other single factor in the war. The year 1918 will be the turning point in the history of the British Empire, and, unless the Americans are better handled than they have been, there will be trouble. Whether I shall be responsible for the British War Mission in London or in New York I do not yet know for certain, but in any case I shall retain the leadership of it, and I must work with a free mind, which I could not have if I had A.P. anxieties to contend with.

> Your devoted
> CHIEF.

Sutton to Northcliffe:

> The Fleetway House,
> Farringdon Street, E.C.
> December 17, 1917.

My dear Chief,—Many thanks for your kind letter of appreciation. My work is as much a pleasure now as it was in the Bungalow days so long ago, and I am just as keen as ever to show you that I realize the responsibility you gave me, and to prove also that I value the great help and many kind things you have done for

> Your affectionate
> SUT.

Deputations from the two professional bodies, the Institute of Journalists and the National Union of Journalists, met representatives of the Newspaper Proprietors' Association on December 14, to discuss salaries. Northcliffe asked for a report to be sent to him the next day. W. J. Evans, editor of the *Evening News*, wrote to him: 'Sir Edmund Robbins, for the Institute, made a long and flowery speech, winding up with a proposal that all proprietors should pay a bonus of 25 per cent on all salaries. The point was put to him whether he meant *all* salaries, whether a man getting £2,000 a year should be presented with a 25 per cent war bonus. He giggled and said "yes". After that deputation was got rid of, we received the deputation of the N.U.J., headed by a man named Mansfield, who, I believe, is on *The Times*. They put forward a reasonable set of proposals. The deputation seemed very fair-minded. By the by, an old letter of yours to the N.U.J. of October 2, 1912, was produced and read. They seemed to regard it as a charter of their union. It was framed.'

Northcliffe to W. J. Evans, a director of Associated Newspapers Ltd.:

Elmwood,
St. Peters,
December 15, 1917.

My dear Evans,—I am very glad to see that the journalists have at last had the courage to tackle the proprietors. We are rolling in money at Carmelite House and it is time we began to disgorge to the staff. I have been a constant advocate of increased remuneration since I was a reporter. I do not know of any occupation which is more ill-paid.

When Mr Pulitzer, of the *New York World*, died, evidence given at the inquest showed that his services to that paper were worth £50,000 a year. I feel that way about myself and should like a bonus!

Yours sincerely,
CHIEF.

Northcliffe to F. J. Mansfield, vice-president of the National Union of Journalists:

Elmwood,
St. Peters,
December 15, 1917.

My dear Mansfield,—I have not been able to devote more than four or five hours to newspaperdom since I returned.

It seems to me a pity that there should be two separate deputations to the N.P.A. [Newspaper Proprietors' Association]. You know that the Union will have my support in any negotiations with the newspaper proprietors.

I am one of the few newspaper owners who have been through the mill of reporting, sub-editing, and editing, and I have very vivid and resentful recollections of underpaid work for overpaid millionaires.

Yours sincerely,
NORTHCLIFFE.

His resentment was transferred in latter years to the 'amateur proprietors' (his term), who acquired newspapers as they acquired oil wells, factories or chain stores, and who had no experience of or special regard for newspaper working conditions. He had the professional jealousy of the man who has served his time and with him it was the more inflexible because his own apprenticeship had not been as complete as he claimed, for instance, in the letter just quoted. For some of his fellow members of the Newspaper Proprietors' Association he had little professional respect and he seemed determined to make as many difficulties for them as could be devised. When they rejected wage increases, he retorted by raising wages. He met their moves for conciliation with arbitrary action. There were some who believed that the bitter attacks on him by the 'Cocoa Press' were not the outcome of political animosity alone. That Christmas he ordered that an all-round bonus should be paid to the staffs at Carmelite House and if any fellow newspaper controller had objected to its possibly unsettling effect on the labour market of Fleet Street, Northcliffe might have flourished a letter written to him on December 23 by the scholarly and respected night editor of the *Daily Mail*, Charles I. Beattie. 'I am writing to thank you on behalf of myself and the night staff for your generosity and that of the firm, which is possible only because the firm is you. I need not tell you that you and Mr Marlowe have the entire loyalty of every one of us without such a pleasant surprise as that which we have had this Christmas eve, but I must add that the air of delight radiated throughout the office this evening would have rejoiced your heart had you seen it.' Northcliffe replied: 'Any share you or they get is none too large, as I have told my co-proprietors.' High profits interested him not less as a sign of success than as a source of benefactions for which, not unnaturally, he was pleased to receive the credit. In 1918, troubled about the need to hide the large profits of his newspapers, he gave thought to plans which resulted in the building of Northcliffe House.

To *The Times*, he wrote on December 29: 'The attention paid by *The Times* to Labour matters is bringing me remonstrances from some of our "Junkers" who think that we are encouraging Labour by mentioning it prominently. They seem to imagine that if we put it on a back page, Labour would disappear. I disagree. If I may be allowed to say so, I think the Editor shows great wisdom in dealing fully with Labour.' The *Daily Mail* had at that time a special writer on Labour affairs, Alexander M. Thompson, who had been with Blatchford on *The Clarion*. In some articles about a shipbuilding breakdown, he made light of certain Labour leaders' speeches. Northcliffe rebuked him in a message to the *Daily Mail* office: 'I have never liked his system of caricaturing speeches by Labour men, instead of reporting them. It will be remembered that I have mentioned this objection before.' Returning to the topic in a message to *The Times*, he wrote: 'The custom of blaming the shipyard workers is not more fair than the politician's trick of blaming the reporters.' Northcliffe's mental feelers were out, sensing the future. Many readers of *The Times*, in particular, thought that it was full of menace. An ominous new noun was occurring in the popular vocabulary: Bolshevik.

*   *   *

His private accountant, Mackenzie, had prepared some figures about current finance. His income was down to £120,000 for the year 1917. His outgoings were £106,000. He had paid £26,000 tax. Annuities to dependants amounted to £17,000. He had given £6,000 to a variety of obscure and needy charities: Woking Cabmen's Social; Windsor Congregational Church (for a new organ); the Advertising War Memorial Fund; Medical Scholarships for Serbian Girls' Fund; St. Mary's Home for Working Girls, Bow Road, London, E.; Printers' Medical Aid Fund; Redemptoristine Convent, Clapham Park (£30 for coal); St. Peters and District War Distress Association; and the Sandwichmen's Christmas Fund, were on the list. He was called on to wipe out the bank overdraft for the *Manchester Courier*, £34,711 8s. 3d.

Mackenzie was told to check the number of individuals receiving aid from Northcliffe's private purse. 'Madam,—Greater care will have to be taken in the expenditure on your son's school clothing. I am instructed not to pay further bills that I consider extravagant.' Northcliffe to the Rector of Chapelizod, his birthplace near Dublin: 'I am reducing all my donations on the principle that I think people should be taught to understand the war. With the money thus saved, I am paying the expenses of officers and men at the war, maintaining a private hospital and making special grants to young officers. When the war is over, I shall of course restore my little gift to the original amount. If there is any emergency case in the meanwhile, you can rely on me.' Lady Northcliffe's Hospital for Officers at 14 Grosvenor Crescent, London, accounted for £5,600; the maintenance of his several houses, £14,800. He had paid £214 for personal medical advice. He had given presents to the value of £4,569. Hamilton Fyfe to Northcliffe: 'My dear Chief,—How can I thank you for your great kindness? The cheque this morning filled me with grateful astonishment. It is munificent—just like you.' Two weeks later, Fyfe to Northcliffe again: 'I have just received the bag and dressing-case, and I really am overwhelmed with gratitude. I have never had such beautiful things in my life and never expected to have.' Louis Tracy to Northcliffe: 'My most grateful thanks for such a handsome gift', six Palm Beach suits. Northcliffe could invent novel forms of giving.

*   *   *

Withdrawn from a scene over which he had cast a pro-consular shadow, he may not have found it easy to readjust his perspectives. He had been given a marvellous insight into the human estate, a broad unfolding view of the economic systems linking the nations and of the infinite complexity of the connective tissue through which the world's energy coursed from pole to pole. *The Times*, the Anglo-Newfoundland Development Company, Associated Newspapers, and the Amalgamated Press, comprised an imposing edifice of capital, enterprise and social influence. Put beside the immense responsibility vested in him as head of the War Mission, they stood against a diminished horizon. He could not but feel that he had existed more commandingly in America, whose majesty, power and coming dominion were obsessively in his thoughts. Northcliffe to the *Daily Mail* staff (December 13, 1917):

I am worried by post and by people of all kinds about America. People want to know about the United States. The English know less of the United States than they do of Spain, and do not realize that the mass of Americans are as different from the mass of Englishmen as are the Spaniards. We are living on views of the United States of a quarter of a century ago.

'I am afraid I am not worrying about the war', he wrote to his nephew Esmond Harmsworth (Rothermere's youngest son), just after Christmas. He was saddened by the death of young Noel Ross, a correspondent of *The Times*, in whose career the King had shown an interest and who Northcliffe said was 'near to genius'. A member of Ross's family wrote to him: 'He was not only your admirer but your champion, and among the writings he left behind is a one-act play in which the good Samaritan is, evidently, yourself. Your name was on his lips almost to the last.' There was a letter from John Buchan enclosing one from Geoffrey Butler, who told how surprised he and his colleagues of the British Information Service in New York had been to find that Northcliffe 'was not the slap-dash and hurry-away individual' they had expected. They had been very much struck by Northcliffe's having 'gone full-tilt' at the task of pacifying Henry Ford, 'who was disgracefully treated by our Ministry of Munitions'. Butler's letter concluded: 'I have always come away from his office, after seeing him, feeling 150 per cent more vigorous and encouraged. I have a really genuine and deep admiration for Northcliffe and I shall be very glad when he is back.'* A letter, dated December 29, 1917, from Lloyd George's confidant, Sir George (afterwards Lord) Riddell, may have given him still more satisfaction. It contained the phrase: 'You will go down to history as one of the great figures of the war.'

* A member of the distinguished academic family, Geoffrey Butler (1887-1929) had been a major scholar of Trinity, president of the Union, and editor of the *Cambridge Review*. He was a Fellow of Corpus Christi and president of that college.

On Christmas Day, Admiral Sir John Jellicoe, the First Sea Lord, had resigned. The *War Memoirs* of Lloyd George tell us that the 'overriding vitality' of his successor, Sir Eric Geddes, was soon felt 'in every branch of activity'. Under Admiral Keyes, the German submarine base at Zeebrugge was stormed on St. George's Day, 1918. 'There was a quickening of action all round,' Lloyd George wrote. 'The convoy system at last had a fair chance. The attack on the submarine developed.' Behind the scenes, Northcliffe had been a critic of the Jellicoe regime. Writing to Northcliffe a few months afterwards, Wilson, the *Daily Mail* naval authority, recorded that 'there are other things which hardly occur in the *Mail* and which I know you to have done, e.g. *the Admiralty changes*. Hall [assumed to be Admiral Sir Reginald Hall, director of naval intelligence at the Admiralty] said at the conference last Friday that those changes saved the Allies. We could never have risked bringing the Americans over by the hundred thousand if the submarines had been able—as they were under Jellicoe—to get through the Straits of Dover. Posterity will regard this as being almost as important as the shell business.'

Northcliffe had written to a French woman journalist, Andrée de Tizac, that he expected to sail for New York in the first week in January, but that he had been asked to remain in England 'for certain work which the Government thinks essential'. At last, the propaganda question was being given full consideration by the War Cabinet. 'I gather that Northcliffe is prepared to return to America,' Dawson wrote to Willert, 'but that he increasingly reluctant to do so.'

Northcliffe to the directors of Associated Newspapers Limited:

Carmelite House,
E.C.
1st January, 1918.

Gentlemen,—I feel that the time has come when the Chairmanship of the Associated Newspapers Company, in addition to the many hours of work which I spend each day on the Company's newspapers, is more than I can bear, and I therefore propose to resign the Chairmanship as from today, the 1st January.

I suggest that, if he is willing, the Vice-Chairman, Mr Thomas Marlowe, should be appointed Chairman and that Sir Andrew Caird should become Vice-Chairman.

I am pleased to hear that it is proposed by the Directors to offer me some remuneration for the work which I am gladly contributing to the newspapers of the Company each day.

Yours sincerely,
NORTHCLIFFE.

The London headquarters of the War Mission was a small Georgian terrace house facing the House of Lords. For Northcliffe, the contrast in office amenities, after 681 Fifth Avenue, may have been amusing; it was certainly uncomfortable. Soon, he was complaining of the creaking floors and he welcomed the move to Crewe House, Curzon Street, the London home of the Marquess of Crewe; it still lends charm to surroundings that have been subject to constant change. Northcliffe had his desk and his big green-leather armchair installed there early in January. He considered Crewe House 'eminently suited' to his task of 'looking after the thousands of Americans who are passing through London'.

Northcliffe to Caird in America:

> Crewe House,
> Curzon Street, Mayfair, W.1.
> January 3rd, 1918.

My dear Sir Andrew,—The situation here has been undecided, owing to the slow action of the Government in regard to Lord Reading, but by the time this reaches you he should be on his way to Washington. The present arrangement is that I should stay here for two or three months organizing the British end of our Mission. We were first put into 29, Abingdon Street, an ancient house in which I really could not work.

There is a great deal of Mission work, difficult to describe, having to do with the Air Board, War Office, Ministry of Munitions and 10, Downing Street. . . . The indecision of the position here during the last six weeks has been very trying. It was only last night that I learned finally that Reading would take over the particular position in the United States of High Commissioner and that it would be better for me to remain here and organize what will become a very important department. I am glad to remain for other reasons. This Government is always on thin ice, half of it is just as wobbly as it has always been, and you can guess which half. The night before last the wobbly half sent out a pacifist communique to the Press in the name of the Government. The Editor of *The Times* happened to be dining with Ll.G., heard of this thing from the office, and the Press Bureau at once stopped its circulation. I watch these people vigilantly day and night.

Give my affectionate greetings to all my friends.

> Yours sincerely,
> CHIEF.

'My dear Sir Andrew' was Northcliffe's salute to Caird as one of the New Year knights. Caird had sent him 'very grateful thanks', asking him to believe that the recommendation, coming from 'the Chief', was as gratifying as the title. Judging by the fervent appreciation of his successful nominees, Northcliffe himself was regarded as the fount of honour. The King had lately instituted the new Order of the British Empire. Northcliffe was lavish in his commendation to the Prime Minister of War Mission colleagues of all ranks, down to the typists' pool. Paraphrasing Shakespeare's *King Henry V*, Basil Blackett, of the Treasury, who became one of the War Mission knights, wrote to Northcliffe: 'If it be a sin to covet honours (for others), you must be the most offending soul alive.'

He had procured a C.B.E. for Geoffrey Butler in New York. In an acknowledging letter, Butler wrote: 'I still pass the Gotham with a pang.' He had put forward the name of Arthur Willert for a knighthood and wrote that Willert's refusal 'upset my list completely', his recommendation holding good when Willert changed his mind. 'The currents and cross-currents in these matters are amazing', he wrote to Caird, and asserted that compiling a list of recommendations for honours 'is work requiring much experience, of which I have had little. Quite a number of people objected to Guthrie', a reference to Sir Connop Guthrie, the British shipping controller's representative in the United States. In a letter of the same week, he told Caird: 'The scramble for honours in which the worthy almost invariably get little is an abominable business.' For Sutton, whose 'Feed-The-Guns-With-War-Bonds' campaign for the Treasury Bonar Law said was 'simply invaluable', he demanded something superior to a K.B.E., and later obtained for him a baronetcy, although Sutton had no posterity to sustain it. He wrote again to Caird, with whom he was more friendly at a distance than at close quarters: 'I hope you will keep a careful eye for those who should have honours and those who want them. . . . I had a rare fight over some of my nominations.'

Caird had been particularly anxious that a higher degree of knighthood should be conferred upon Sir Charles Gordon, who was the vice-chairman of the British War Mission and who conducted his responsible duties with outstanding ability. He was an eminent Canadian, who ultimately became President of the Bank of Montreal. He was thought to be a Liberal in Canadian politics. Honours to Canadians now require the consent of the Canadian Government, and a good deal of correspondence passed between Northcliffe and Sir Robert Borden's Conservative Government before the honour was finally agreed to.

Northcliffe wrote to Gordon, whose knighthood he had originally helped to procure:

There is a lot of balderdash being written and talked in Canada about honours. It is quite impossible to fight a war without recognition of merit—both military and civilian. Canadians are very fond—if you will allow me to say so—of the word 'democracy'. There happens to be one real democracy in Europe—that of France, and nowhere are people more punctilious about honours than in France. Honours are chiefly objected to by inefficients who are not entitled to them. I am not speaking of hereditary honours—an entirely different matter. The Germans attach similar importance to honours. The Chinese, who know about most things, are very particular about titles; so, too, are the Japanese. The Americans love them and grab sham ones, such as those of General, Colonel and Professor. I am proud of the fact that I have got an extra step as a result of my American work, just as proud as a captain who becomes a major for services rendered.

Northcliffe at Elmwood

German 'Medal of Hate', 1917, showing Northcliffe sharpening a
quill pen, and an ink-pot containing 'propaganda ink'

Concerning peerages, he told Lord Newborough: 'The trend of the times is obviously to abolish hereditary peerages, though I am strongly in favour of those already in existence being continued. I am so, although not blessed in the possession of an heir myself.' He was receiving hints from American would-be recipients of the favours of the fifth King George. The *Saturday Evening Post* writer, Isaac Marcossan, of the ox-yoke shoulders and the loud-striped shirts, disclosed his interest in 'getting a decoration from the British Government'. Cecil Harmsworth wrote that Pomeroy Burton was 'pressing his claims', while Northcliffe was doing likewise for Edward Stettinius, of Morgans, who expressed his anticipatory pleasure with 'very affectionate regards'. From the New York office of the British Bureau of Information, Louis Tracy was solemnly commending to Northcliffe the idea of 'a special Order' to be created by the Sovereign for Americans who helped the British cause. A letter from Colonel House's son-in-law, Gordon Auchinloss, of the office of 'The Counselor for the Department of State', Washington, imparted a touch of hilarity to proceedings which might have become ponderous. Its long official envelope was addressed to 'Lord Rufus I. Northcliffe, Crewe House, London'.

★   ★   ★

'I assure you I often feel homesick for New York,' Northcliffe wrote to Caird later in January. 'I shall look for another house if Bolton Priory is not put in order.' His plans for the future, he said, depended on the term of Reading's stay in America. 'I daresay you think me very vague. I am doing practically no newspaper work', but his frequent messages to the *Times* and *Daily Mail* staffs frustrated any hope that he was losing his journalistic zest.

Northcliffe to Alfred Turner, editor of the *Evening News*:

Elmwood,
St. Peters,
January 5, 1918.

My dear Turner,—In the intervals of my heavy work for the British War Mission I write little reports for the *Daily Mail* which you ought to see. I have not written any for the *Evening News*—not from lack of interest in that paper, of which I am very proud, but because at the end of the day I am so tired (as I begin work long before daylight) that I do not think my observations would be worth reading or my judgment good.

I can assure you that I regard the paper not only with affection, as my first daily newspaper, but with personal pride at having selected so capable an editor.

Yours sincerely,
CHIEF.

He wrote to tell Caird that 'the English end of the Mission is growing like a prairie fire'. Its main purpose was to give effect to Reading's recommendations from America, as he explained more fully to a French official in London, M. Comert. 'Our chief function is to hurry the war. We utilize the knowledge of American affairs gained in the United States. If we are advised from New York or Washington that there is a delay in any Government Department here, we go to the Department concerned. We do a thousand and one things that a Government department cannot do.'

By the end of January, he was letting his friends in Washington know that he would be remaining in London as chairman of the War Mission. If he gave them the impression that the decision was his alone, they were not less cordial in their expressions of regret and esteem. The secretaries of state, war, commerce, agriculture, the interior, the navy and the treasury, all wrote appreciatively of his services and the compliments of some of them went well beyond the formal courtesies. He may not have been less touched by hearing from the wife of the *Times* correspondent in Washington that his 'black beauties', the two negresses who had looked after him in the Massachusetts Avenue flat, had wept when they were told that he was not going back.

When Austin Harrison, editor of *The English Review*, reproached him for his faith in salvation through America, Northcliffe answered: 'I do not know how you can possibly see a way to avoid indebtedness to the United States. If you can solve that problem, you deserve to go down in history.' In London, he showed himself to be even more sensitive to American good opinion than when he was working among the Americans. He took to heart the unfortunate impression said to have been made by some of the utterances of F. E. Smith, M.P., the Attorney-General, then visiting America. Northcliffe himself had proposed the visit in a letter to the Prime Minister on December 11, 1917. 'It is largely due to his lack of tact and, above all, to his complete ignorance of American character and conditions', Northcliffe was told by one of his well-placed informants on January 11.* Northcliffe's countering move was to tell American callers at Crewe House what President Wilson had said on reading the Attorney-General's speech to an assembly of New York lawyers, where he had begun his address with the words, 'Speaking as a lawyer to lawyers. . . .' The President had said: 'He may as well know that I and the whole country are fed-up with lawyers.'

In a confidential memorandum, which contained some exceedingly interesting information about President Wilson's private life, Northcliffe's

---

* In *Frederick Edwin, Earl of Birkenhead*, 1935, a biography by his son, the second earl, it is stated that Lord Reading, as British Ambassador, made it his business to inquire 'into hostile rumours about F. E. Smith's mission . . . they were wholly unfounded'.

informant of January 11 wrote: 'I had a rather pathetic letter last night, of farewell, from Spring Rice, written on the eve of his departure from Washington. He is quite broken by his recall, and deeply humiliated.' The retiring Ambassador had sent his last report to Balfour, the Foreign Secretary, on January 4. On January 12, he had composed, 'as a sort of spontaneous outpouring', his moving and subsequently widely known verses, *I Vow To Thee, My Country*. A month later he died.

Chapter Twenty-two

Word Power, the New Weapon

Russia's tremendous default was enabling more German divisions to be sent to the west. Obviously, they would seek a decision there before American power could be advantageously deployed. England and France faced 1918 with diminished reserves of strength. One of the greatest resources left to them was word power. Concentrated on a declining enemy morale, it was an invaluable and doubtless indispensable reinforcement of the Allied armies. Northcliffe's personal prestige and his unshakeable belief in the power of the word to influence the minds of men, helped to forge the propaganda weapon into a finally effective aid to victory.

John Buchan to Northcliffe:

> Department of Information,
> Foreign Office.
> January 23, 1918.

My dear Northcliffe,—I am concerned about the fate of my Department, for I must have a head who can help to get things done.

There are two ways of attaining this. One is to make the Department a Ministry and include under it both foreign and home propaganda . . . the other way would be to have a new member of the War Cabinet who would have a real interest in our work. There would be nobody half as good as yourself, and if I had you as my Chief we would get things done.

I wonder if it would be possible for you to speak seriously to the Prime Minister on the subject? He is so burdened with heavy matters that unless you take it up, I fear the thing will drift.

> Yours ever,
> JOHN BUCHAN.

A month later in one of his daily communiques (February 19, 1918), Northcliffe corrected a *Times* misstatement about himself: '*The Times* reports that I have been appointed MINISTER of Propaganda in Enemy Countries. Such an appointment would place *The Times* in a very difficult position. I am DIRECTOR, not Minister. I shall accept no position under the Government that would harass *The Times*, and I have lately again refused Cabinet office.' He wrote to the *Daily Mail* editor the same day: 'As a Minister I should be a member of the Government, which, with this present wobbly ministry in power, would mean the virtual extinction of the *Daily Mail* as an independent newspaper, for you would be obliged to support me in this Government.' Writing to the *Daily Mail* correspondent in New York, W. F. Bullock, he said: 'I have been offered a Cabinet job, but refused it. For one thing, the position is very difficult in regard to my own undertakings. They are not private concerns, which I could abandon, but public companies whose stock has a sale value of about fifty million dollars, and on which we have consistently paid a high rate of interest for years.' Wickham Steed stated, in *Through Thirty Years*, that the Cabinet post in question was that of Secretary of State for War. Rothermere and Beaverbrook together called on Campbell Stuart at Crewe House to ask whether he thought Northcliffe would accept that office. Apart from the references in his message to *The Times* and in the letter to Bullock, Northcliffe left no note of the matter in his private papers. Wickham Steed said that he warned Northcliffe not to accept a ministerial position. 'His health was not good and I was convinced that, should he attempt to work with permanent officials in a Department of State, he would soon be irritated into resignation.' Campbell Stuart made representations to the same effect. Derby had again threatened to resign as War Secretary and had gone to Haig for advice. Haig wrote in his diary: 'If he left, Lord Northcliffe would probably succeed him. This would be fatal to the Army and the Empire.'

Lloyd George informed the King on February 9: 'I have sought in vain for months for a man to put our propaganda right.' Possibly overstressing his zeal, for he was aware of the need to counter German propaganda in neutral countries, he could hardly have ignored Northcliffe. Northcliffe, not being a candidate, the Ministry of Information went to Beaverbrook, who rebounded with the suggestion that Northcliffe should be asked to take charge of propaganda against enemy countries. 'Ask him, then', was in effect Lloyd George's instruction, and an announcement of Northcliffe's acceptance was made on February 7. The framing of the announcement did not suit Northcliffe and Beaverbrook received a friendly rebuke. 'What is happening in regard to the Propaganda Department is that which happened in the matter of the British War Mission to the United States. When I was appointed, no proper official announcement was made here or in the States. As a natural result, a hostile debate took place in Parliament and to that debate the Prime Minister made no reply. I started in the United States without *locus standi*.' In short, declared North-cliffe, 'never again'. The point of difference was resolved by an agreement that his enemy propaganda department should be 'a separate entity, under the direct control of the Prime Minister'. He refused to work under Beaverbrook, while expressing his willingness to co-operate with his Ministry.

The organizing side of Northcliffe's department was left to Campbell Stuart, his deputy director. Northcliffe supervised its earliest operations from Elmwood, where persistent trouble with his throat kept him in semi-invalidism through most of that year. Although his attendances at Crewe House conferences were fewer than those of any other member of the effective committee, more than anyone else he inspired the labours of those who worked harder at the task than he did. His name was probably of greater value than his services. To the Germans, certainly, it meant relentless purpose. Down at Elmwood he was not beset by office routine and there was time to spare for other matters. The Irish settlement was one of them. Home Rule seemed to be no nearer practical realization than it had been in 1914 when it was placed on the statute book. He asked the *Daily Mail* not to make any statement of opinion about Ireland. 'I have strong political reasons.' Despite the injunction, the paper published a leading article, which, he complained, would 'injure some negotiations I am making'.

Sir Edward Carson to Northcliffe:

5, Eaton Place, S.W.
January 23, 1918.

Private.

Dear Lord Northcliffe,—I suppose the argument I am expected to use is something like this: 'You Ulster people are loyal and devoted to England. You have helped with men, money and ships. But the best way you can help us now is to agree to submit to a Govt. that you loathe and hate. This is your reward.' It is not easy.

Yours sincerely,
EDWARD CARSON.

Northcliffe's 'negotiations' are not a subject in his correspondence files for 1918, save for a letter written to the Prime Minister on February 14, in which he insisted on the importance of 'a large measure of fiscal autonomy, with certain safeguards', as one of the settlement essentials. 'Without a bold stroke, you will not get a settlement, either north or south. I know them.' To Lord Decies, he wrote on February 27: 'Ireland is being stirred up by German money.' Decies, as that exceptional being, an Irishman 'with no political axe to grind', had sent him a long memorandum. Cecil Harmsworth continued to be active in Irish affairs and was often in touch with his brother about them from 1916 onward. Northcliffe had another fount of information and advice in Lord Justice O'Connor, concerning whom a more closely trusted correspondent in Dublin, who had been assistant secretary of the Irish Convention, wrote to him: 'I believe that, in this matter, he is acting as the agent of the Roman Catholic Church. . . . I suggest that he be thanked and told that his letters are always of interest.' Northcliffe's vision of the Irish future was of a united British dominion. He seemed to regard Home Rule merely as a prelude to that fulfilment. Cecil Harmsworth, in his diary for April 15, 1918: 'With Ll.G. in his car to House of Commons. The little man shows unmistakable signs of wear and tear. I mention to him Northcliffe's desire for a firm assurance that, if he supports Home Rule with all vigour in his newspapers, he can rely on Ll.G. going through with it to a finish. Ll.G. most positive on the point, saying that he will resign if he cannot have his way in this matter.' From 1918 onward, Northcliffe increasingly exerted such influence as he had, or hoped to have, on Irish affairs, through *The Times*. His brother Leicester said that Northcliffe could not forget the Irish sacrifices at Gallipoli. Ireland was a recurring topic of his private office messages; for example (April 24, 1918), 'I am very glad to see the short, decided article on the Irish priests. I have lived among them and know that the object of the priests is to oppose Home Rule, which would bring about the end of their tyranny, the majority of the Irish members being secretly anti-clerical.' It was a dogmatic statement which could have been challenged on the domiciliary claim, if no other. The daily newspaperman, it is true, is required to know something about everything. In his dealings with *The Times*, Northcliffe often seemed to be under a compulsion not merely to know something about everything but to assert himself as an authority on everything.

Northcliffe to J. L. Garvin:

> Elmwood,
> St Peters.
> January 25, 1918.

My dear Garve,—I am on the eve of going away for a complete change with an easy companion. My mind will be at rest and in communion with yours, which will also, I hope, be at rest.

I had a talk with a very famous doctor the other day. He said that the vanity of middle-aged men hurries their end. They forget the silent passage of time and imagine that they can 'go it' to the giddy strains of the music of youth. It is only when staring at oneself in that great delineator, the shaving glass, that the truth reveals itself.

I hope you will rest, dear Garve. Walk on the heights of Lynton and spout as you go. That is what you need. I know the place well and should like to be with you, but this mission of mine calls for continuity, so I am going to the little wooden shed to which you and Christina [Mrs Garvin] escorted me one starry night.

With affection,
Yours,
N.

J. L. Garvin to Northcliffe:

Royal Castle Hotel,
Lynton, N. Devon.
January 28, 1918.

My dear Chief,—I came in from a long tramp by hill and coombe to find your letter and was infinitely touched that you had made time to think of me. All hail and good health to you in your eyrie [the bungalow at Clandon]. Well do I remember it under the stars. It reminded me of a thing I love—sleeping on deck when on long voyages.

Wise is your letter and reinforces my own mood. There is only one goal for us all. We pass. My desire is to be cheerful, keen and kindly to the end, and whatever else happens, to die with a smile—if I can remember to do so—as Geddy [his only son Gerald] . . . did when he had twenty wounds in his body from two German machine guns. There was stuff; and I think, quand même, there is plenty of stuff in me yet. Not that I would now willingly try to force life in any way; but it's not worth while unless we have courage, freshness and resource for emergency.

The next few years are going to be full of emergencies more testing for our profession than the war itself. We have an exacting but most interesting job—you in your vast way, I in my smaller—a job giving scope to everything in a man, to the steady flame of his maturity as well as to his youthful flare.

Necessarily, your biggest years are to come. That biggest will be demanded from you by the things I see clearly ahead. Heartily glad am I that after the heavy, the historic, burdens you have carried you are taking some rest now. It will be clear gain even if the American duty makes it only partial. I wish we were nearer each other.

I won't be tempted into a very long letter, though full of lots of things. 'Anno Domini', no doubt, is the universal enemy; but he is neither to be over estimated nor under estimated. To keep our vital spirits is the thing. That's why I am here. 'Anno Domini' is not what has been the matter with me. The boy's death (and my mother's) made it difficult for me to live. I went on staunchly but carried lead within. But after eighteen months the time has come to take this break (as they would wish) and recover my spirits. I mean to do it.

It's a land of golden afternoons, this—the walks beautiful and many—the air this January day as mild and blue as spring. . . . If I no longer spout on the hills (that old mood being gone for ever), I can laugh great human laughter, the more human now because of knowing so very much more of the sad.

God bless you and with heart's returns for every warm thought you have of me, count me always,

Your affectionate
GARVE.

Northcliffe's protracted absence from Fleet Street, his resignation as chairman of Associated Newspapers Limited, and his more strongly marked attachment to the quiet of Elmwood, were interpreted by some as indications of waning power. Writing thirty years after, Sir Campbell Stuart could say that he had noticed 'signs of decline' in Northcliffe during the first months of 1918. He was as acutely sharp as ever in spotting the news story that had been 'missed' by one or other of his papers. His discursive general knowledge was still displayed with the efficiency of a craftsman working with a row of tacks in his mouth. 'The writer of the article, "Dogs of War", is evidently unaware that before the war every military wagon belonging to the French carried a dog.' 'I should like to know the name of the careless sub-editor who wrote that paragraph about Lady Honywood's hotel in which he stated that she is the wife of the holder of the oldest baronetcy in England. That position is held by Sir Hickman Bacon, who is a reader of the *Daily Mail* and whose title is 49 years older than that of Lady Honywood's husband.' 'Follow up growing sunflowers. Years ago they were grown largely for chicken food but seem to have disappeared from the landscape.' His tendency to exaggerated professional reminiscence appeared again, without seriously distorting the truth. 'The article about London traffic was good but hysterical. How did we manage to get about 25 years ago? As a matter of fact, we walked then much more than we do now. I used to walk from Hampstead to Fleet Street and back every day. When I was on night work, I arrived home at six o'clock in the morning and none the worse for it.' Sometimes there was a compassionate note: 'A good *Daily Mail* this morning, but too much Litvinoff and too little of the sad story of the penniless officer who forged a cheque.'

A reduction in the size of the *Daily Mail* had brought him a letter from an anxious member of the staff. He replied in the morning bulletin: 'I shall do my best to keep every one. . . . Mrs Howarth has been with us from the first number of the paper. She must be provided with other work or be suitably pensioned.' He had been looking through the list of *Times* salaries. 'There appear to be great anomalies. I find a boy only recently arrived receiving £1 5s. a week, while the head messenger, who has been 34 years in the service, receives only £2 10s.' Style in writing was always subject to his scrutiny. 'I have often objected to the word "bus". It is just as vulgar as "stunt", "boom", "slump", or "pub".' He complained that '*The Times* is getting quite American. Yesterday in a headline, we had the term "speeded-up". Today on page 5, we have it stated that Charlie Chaplin is "drafted", an Americanism for "conscripted".' His eye roamed with untiring curiosity over the wartime London scene. 'I saw again this morning queues outside the Maypole Dairy shops. Is there any reason why this company should have queues? Is it a crude form of advertising?' He suggested that the *Daily Mail* art department should record what was then a phenomenon of the streets.

The bound volumes of his office messages copiously index Northcliffe's moods, which in 1918 were not those of significant temperamental change. He was still liable to indulge in the advantages of his position: 'I am coming to one of the office conferences, but no one will know when I am coming.' Announcing the promotion of young men to posts of responsibility, he was apt to cloud their satisfaction by the added surmise: 'I hope I am not making a mistake—some of my friends think I am.' He had not lost his knack of writing slogans: 'The power of the press is very great, but not so great as the power of suppress.' He could be heartening as of old: 'An excellent paper today, in all respects.' He still enjoyed impressing the groundlings: 'The statement in the leading article that we can soon look forward to the long-distance bombing of German towns would be true if we had any long-distance bombers.' He continued to enjoy the spectacle of senior staff men in the pillory, especially when he could contrive that they should pelt themselves with his rotten eggs: 'This is the last occasion on which I can tolerate Macleod's gross neglect and carelessness. He will read this message out to the editorial conference on Monday.' Lewis Rose Macleod, literary editor of the *Daily Mail*, was, just then, one of his two favourite victims, the other, Arthur Baker, art editor of the newspaper. 'Baker is as fond of that old photograph of a British soldier giving chocolate to French children as he is of ugly old women. Destroy the negative.' Macleod, who became editor of the *Rand Daily Mail*, was constantly assailed. 'He is not a man of resource and needs watching and driving.' Having endured that rebuke, Macleod had his faltering self-assurance revived by a private invitation: 'Will you and your lady please me by coming to lunch on Saturday?—N.' His vein of mordant humour was not yet worked out. 'Last night I was told by a well-known man that a member of the staff of the *Morning Post* told him that I was selling my controlling interest in *The Times*. I need scarcely say that there is no truth whatever in this assertion. The shares will not be available until a small paragraph has appeared about me on Page One—10s. 6d. for three lines or less, and 2s. 6d. for every additional line.' 'The *Daily Mail* heading for the front page can now be reduced in size. Please have made for me one three-quarters of the size of the present one. The Royal Arms may need sharpening up; the lion's face is beginning to look like that of the Prime Minister.' Reading these messages from 'the Chief', we discover no sign, either, that his sense of proportion was as yet seriously impaired. 'I don't suppose that one person in five thousand knows the name of the editor [of the *Daily Mail*]. We live in a little backwater of our own in Carmelite House and yet we imagine that we are a sort of Niagara and that all the world knows about us.' On January 12 he had given a written instruction that no mention of his name was to be made in the paper without his permission.

He was remaining obstinately inaccessible to a number of people on his staff who wanted to see him, their frustrations deepened by his perversity in summoning their juniors to his presence. There was an exceptional day when the *Weekly Dispatch* editorial staff was required to wait on him at Elmwood for a conference. They were given a lunch at which Northcliffe was embarrassingly silent. An elderly sub-editor, becoming unnerved, took too much wine and began to babble about his experiences at sea. 'I've been shipwrecked three times,' he began, when from the end of the table Northcliffe spoke, in his softest tone, 'Four times.' 'Three times, my lord,' was the confident reply. 'Four times,' insisted Northcliffe. 'Three times, sir,' the sub-editor protested, everyone else listening in fascinated dismay as the victim struggled to make his point. 'Four times,' Northcliffe said, with three months' notice in his voice. The sub-editor received it in writing at the end of the week.

As for the idea that Northcliffe's vitality was beginning to ebb in 1918, we find apprehensions rather than symptoms of it in his dealings with the doctors, in his preoccupation with the weight problem and with replenishing the medicine chest at Elmwood. He had dictated an order to a Broadstairs chemist for Glauber's salt, Eno's fruit salt, Carter's 'little liver pills', Friar's balsam, sal volatile, quinine tablets and tinctures, zinc ointment, milk of magnesia, iodine, and a large assortment of throat pastilles, jujubes, and lozenges. The doctors were diagnozing 'protracted bronchial and laryngeal catarrh'. He was watching his weight as if with a fear of something more profound. It was fairly steady at 13 st. 11 lb., but a new examination had made him unduly aware of the thyroid gland and the pathology of its derangement. One of the specialists thought there was a possibility of Graves's disease. Another told him: 'There is no sign of Graves's disease.'

He sent a memorandum to a number of his medical advisers, headed:

The Predicaments of a Patient

I have received the following note from a member of the platoon of quacks: 'I am very anxious to see you, as I am all against your taking thyroid.' Another of my medical friends writes: 'Thyroid should be taken at night and never in the morning, and always in liquid form.'

'Because I do not write often,' he wrote to Caird in New York on February 6, 'please do not think you are not in my mind. I am as attached to the Mission as though it were one of my own businesses. I know it has done a great deal of good, and I know that it will do much more good. I am well satisfied with the way the war is going up to now. The Austrians are very shaky.' The broad outlook confirmed his faith in the final result, but his satisfaction owed little, it appears, to the generals.

Northcliffe to Lord Rosebery:

> Crewe House,
> Curzon Street, W.
> February 17, 1918.

My dear Neighbour,—. . . Our losses from sheer ignorance on the part of those who issue orders are appalling. Vyvyan*, my brother Rothermere's son who died last week, said to me when lying wounded in hospital in France: 'I do not mind having been wounded three times, but I hate to think that I have been muddled three times.' He was a very able young man, and he told me that on all occasions when he sustained wounds, he had been in the thick of chaos and disorder, caused by ignorance of actual fighting conditions displayed by commanders.

Our losses last year make up a shocking tale. I should not like to say how many men were thrown away at Passchendaele and Cambrai. Unless you see the blunders, as I have done, it is incredible that they should have been committed. Is it believable that sane men would send masses of metal weighing thirty tons [tanks] into the mud at Ypres? The tank experts warned the commanders of what would happen to these invaluable weapons if they persisted.

He expressed to Rosebery a cause for anxiety to which he was more susceptible than the military men, namely, that 'many American officers are reporting adversely to Washington'. It might jeopardize the confidence which had granted the monthly subsidy of dollars for war purposes. Admiring Haig, he told Rosebery that he thought 'the riddance of Robertson a good thing', but that he wished Haig was more closely in touch with the fighting men of his armies. He considered that Haig led too circumscribed a life. 'Hindenburg and Ludendorff seem to be able to move around continually.' He wished also that the King was better informed about the blunders that were being made. 'He could have great influence on the army. Yet I am told on good authority that His Majesty protested against the removal of Robertson.' Northcliffe continued:

I blame the Prime Minister for these matters and tell him so. He is one of the most remarkable men who ever occupied the room which you adorned at Downing Street, but he is afraid of the House of Commons and of the newspapers. Were it not for the backing of Milner, who is overworked, I should be despondent about him. He has no power of organization or of delegation. He is a wonderful conciliator and convener of men. His cheeriness, his ability to recuperate, and his courage of a certain kind are almost without precedent.

* Captain the Hon. H. A. V. St. G. Harmsworth, M.C. He joined the Irish Guards a few days after the outbreak of war and went to the front in December 1914. He died on February 12, 1918, of wounds received in action.

He is a vitalizer, not an organizer. Had he the management of a great estate, or a great enterprise, rather than the upbringing of a provincial attorney, he would have realized that he cannot do everything himself. He would then realize that he should be chairman of his War Cabinet and that every member of that Cabinet should have distinct responsibilities.

I see today that Derby is described as 'spineless'. Added to that physical condition is a certain element of craft said not to be unknown at Newmarket.

You say you will not cross the channel again. That is no reason why you should not venture across the Tweed and watch the future of the Crown from the Lords. I am very anxious about the Crown. . . .

Yours very sincerely,
NORTHCLIFFE.

Garvin had written feelingly to him that day: 'The tragic, utterly unexpected news cast a gloom over us when we heard of Rothermere's second loss; and it made us sad to see how sad you looked in the *Daily Mirror* picture.' Although Vyvyan Harmsworth's death from wounds was not unexpected, it shocked Northcliffe into protesting from his desk as the news was brought to him: 'They are murdering my nephews!' Yet no one had been more insistent than he that every fit young man should play his part.

Lord Rosebery to Northcliffe:

5, Randolph Crescent,
Edinburgh.
February 21, 1918.

Confidential.

My dear Neighbour,—Let me say at once how grieved I was to see your brother's second bereavement. The lad, according to his pictures, seems to have had a singularly winning face and you say that he was able as well. Speaking metaphorically, the fountain of tears is nearly dry. One loss follows another till one is dazed. Please tell Harold how deeply I feel for him. I will not trouble him with a letter.

Your letter was very interesting but not less depressing. 'Lighten our darkness' is the prayer always in my mind, for it is difficult to see much light. Russia, on whom we depended so much, collapsed in treachery and anarchy, Greece a phantom, Rumania overwhelmed, the cursed havoc of the submarines and the damnable imbroglio of our party politics. Nevertheless, though all crumble round us, we shall be staunch. *Impavidum ferient ruinae.* Moreover, I cannot but think that our artisans earning high wages will scarcely submit to being rationed men when they have been living in luxury.

I can believe in a revolution against wealth, but not against the Crown, which would mean the immediate dissolution of the Empire. But perhaps we have Bolsheviks who would not mind that.

Sincerely,
R.

Northcliffe to Caird (February 21): 'You may have noticed several attempts to unseat Lloyd George. They have been very feeble, chiefly consisting of abuse of a Certain Wicked Viscount who does not very much worry about it!' Austen Chamberlain spoke in the House of Commons about the Government's relations with the newspaper proprietors, urging Lloyd George to break the connection. Northcliffe was chairman of one Government body and director of another. Rothermere was in charge at the Air Ministry, Beaverbrook, of the *Daily Express*, at the Ministry of Information. Riddell, of the *News of the World*, was intimately advising the Prime Minister, who was also on a close footing with another proprietor, Dalziel, of *Reynolds News*. 'You will have trouble', Bonar Law warned Lloyd George. Right-wing Conservative wrath erupted with some violence. It had been fanned by a *Daily News* leading article which declared that 'the newspaper proprietor is advancing from the sway of opinion to the throne of actual power. We are in some danger of having a newspaper Administration in this country.' There was an extra thrust of the dagger for Northcliffe as chairman of the War Mission: 'He knows little or nothing about America.'

Northcliffe's friend, George Dewar, sometime editor of *The Saturday Review*, wrote to him on February 26 about 'the humbugs—"Tory" and other—who are crying out against journalists and "newspaper people" daring to help in government. I know a good bit about these pompous but ineffectual asses. Lord Salisbury seems to be the leader of the journalists-must-not-apply tradition just now. I was at Oxford with him—a dull man with a loud voice and tumultuous prejudices. But, of course, being by a fluke born with a Cecil spoon in his mouth, he was a leader and constant spouter there.' A letter from Rawle Johnstone & Co., solicitors, of 1 Bedford Row, London, informing Northcliffe that the Marchioness of Ripon had left him a personal souvenir in her will, may have softened the impact of Dewar's anti-patrician outburst. An enfilading attack came from a fellow journalist, St. Loe Strachey of *The Spectator*, writing about the risks of 'a Northcliffe Ministry'. Geoffrey Dawson, amused by 'poor dear Strachey's solemn approach to the subject', retorted that 'if he had an ounce of common sense, he would realize that Northcliffe had neither the desire nor the power to form a ministry', but Strachey went on publishing letters gravely discussing the likelihood of such an event. He had known Northcliffe for a long time, and was a neighbour of his in Surrey, but, as Dawson pointed out, close acquaintance had not helped him to understand that 'there was never a less far-sighted schemer than Northcliffe in the history of the world. His strongest characteristic, and the secret of his success, is that he is so extraordinarily sensitive to the mood of the moment. No one was ever less like a Machiavelli.' Thus Dawson in February 1918. In February 1919 he believed that certain of Northcliffe's personal activities were directed towards 'establishing a political position for himself', and suspected, too, that an attack on Milner in the *Daily Mail* was the result of 'a deliberate policy of overpowering the Prime Minister by discrediting his most disinterested colleagues'.

The revolt against the press lords smouldered and sizzled for several days in the House of Commons. Austen Chamberlain had returned to the subject there and Northcliffe commented: 'He is absolutely like a bear with a sore head since his brother Neville was ejected and he has lost office.' Austen Chamberlain was sent for by the Prime Minister to take Derby's place as War Minister, but Derby withdrew his resignation. Northcliffe was writing to Reading, in America, on March 8:

The fact is, I think (Geoffrey Dawson, the editor of *The Times*, agrees with me) that quite a number of public men are getting rattled about the war. Carson certainly is. The Prime Minister is not. Bonar Law is better than he was. I cannot say that I am happy about the war, but I am not in the least depressed about it.

He told Reading that there were 'the customary intrigues against the Prime Minister of which the country took no notice'. He had been warned that a general election was planned for October, 'a long time to look forward to, and in war time as much may happen in a week as occupied half a century in peace time, as witness the recent alterations on the map'. He believed that when an election did come, Lloyd George would 'sweep the country'. His long letter to Reading continued:

The Prime Minister does not take enough care of his health. I do not see him often—about once a month. He is whiter and older looking than even when you left. He has wonderful recuperative powers and the faculty of auto-stimulation by conversation to a degree I have never seen in anybody else. The evening when he had returned from his recent spell of ill-health, I took Felix Frankfurter to see him. I merely wanted him to shake hands, and stayed in the room to take Frankfurter away, but Frankfurter had knowledge that the Prime Minister wanted to get, and in less than a minute he was full of life and energy.

I had to appear before the War Cabinet one day this week, when he was again full of life, but tired-looking. You know him a thousand times better than I do. You will know whether it is true that contact with men and conversation are the source of his vivacity. I cannot help thinking that the nation is drawing too much upon his strength, when he himself does not economize. Walton Heath is nominally golf on Saturday, but really dispatch boxes, telephones and visitors. Downing Street is a public breakfast, with thirty minutes' walk with someone who is probably trying to get something out of him. The War Cabinet right up to lunch time; Americans and other foreigners at lunch; deputations and interviews in the afternoon, and perhaps another War Cabinet; boresome and intense people like me at about six; very often people at dinner. Added to all this are speeches. Such instances happened this week, when he had to meet some hundred Unionists, stirred up by Lady Bathurst of the *Morning Post*, and Lords Salisbury and Selborne to discuss his alleged domination by the press. He wiped the floor with the Unionists, who passed a unanimous vote of thanks to him. Personally, I wish that he would see other people, like the leading ship owners. The 'national' ships have proved an absolute failure.

The previous night Northcliffe had been in an air raid at Totteridge while staying with his mother. 'The house shook exactly as in an earthquake, the old-fashioned bells all rang, and above was the noise of one of the new super-Gothas. One bomb made a hole as big as your large room in the Embassy.' A sensitive ear might have caught a jarring undertone in his voice as he dictated the last paragraph of his letter to Reading:

You are doing an immense service to the nation; you have a most interesting circle, great position, and are not liable to receive unexpected aerial messages to blow you to Kingdom Come. Nor do you have to worry as to whether you have lost your meat ration ticket, and you are probably eating excellent white bread with plenty of butter, which is a very scarce commodity here.

Northcliffe was beside himself with anxiety for his mother as the bombs fell on Totteridge. He begged her to go with him to the bungalow at West Clandon. She refused to leave Poynters Hall until other members of the family joined in the entreaties, when she took a small property called Southdown Lodge, near Hassocks in Sussex. She stayed there for long periods during the war with her invalid son, Dick, and retained the house as a summer residence until her death in 1925.

The work of the enemy propaganda department was accelerating. Northcliffe had to overcome his disinclination to be in London. 'My day is divided as follows,' he told Caird. '6.30 to 9.30 a.m. my newspapers [editions were delivered earlier in London than at Broadstairs]. Breakfast and small talk', the latter often contributed by colleagues from the office, who had found him more readily accessible. 'Get to Crewe House about 10.30. The rest of the day I see Americans and people connected with propaganda in enemy countries. London is becoming an American colony.'

He had initiated the work there by presenting what Balfour, the Foreign Secretary, acknowledged as 'a very lucid memorandum'—lucidity supplied by Wickham Steed—on the desirability of concentrating persuasive methods against the Habsburg empire. 'As you point out with unanswerable force,' Balfour replied, 'everything which encourages the anti-German elements in the Habsburg dominions . . . diminishes the efficiency of Austria-Hungary as a member of the Middle Europe combination.' There was the weakest spot. Northcliffe and his colleagues at Crewe House set about probing it.

His callers at Crewe House rarely saw him at his desk, with its silver-mounted blotting pad and massive crystal glass inkwells: 'I can never use a fountain pen.' He worked mostly in his green-leather armchair, files of documents on his knees, loose sheets around him on the floor. Golf had given his cheeks a healthy glow. His hair, lacking the bright lustre that had made him look youthful beyond his time, was smoothed down close to his head, and the Napoleonic forelock was now more like a butcher's curl. His clothes were of the finest stuff, as always, but now they draped rather than embellished his figure. A conspicuous object in the room was a thermometer. He constantly referred to it. Since his return from America, he had become sensitive to room temperatures. A fall below sixty degrees was likely to send him home.

Many of the callers were Americans, in and out of uniform, and some of the more discerning among them noticed that he talked to them as if he was not only the chief proprietor of *The Times* but also its principal leader writer. When he wrote to prominent Americans he now more usually did so on *Times* notepaper, although he had been to Printing House Square only once since his return from America.

A letter from T. W. Callender (M.A., Oxon), professor of Greek at Queen's University, Ontario, had asked help in collecting material for an effective rejoinder to an attack on Northcliffe's war record in the university magazine. The article had been written by a professor of philosophy (M.A., Oxon), who had worked on the *Morning Leader* before it was absorbed by the Liberal *Daily News*. Northcliffe wrote to Professor Callender on March 10:

This man is asking what I have done in the war. The only claims that I make are, after many visits to Germany and Austria, I persistently warned the public here that the war was coming. I did so also on your side of the Atlantic when I spoke at Winnipeg in 1909 and in the same year at Chicago and San Francisco. I do not suppose that I had more than two or three thousand supporters at that time, but among them was Lord Roberts, who was as violently abused in Canada and the United States as he was here. When I endeavoured to introduce the aeroplane to officials here, again the only support I got was from Lord Roberts. I had to encourage it by huge prizes for flights. Our Government ignored the aeroplane, but the German Government replied to my prizes by a steady stream of premiums awarded to Germans who broke the records of other nations.

Having told the professor that he 'had no intention of answering anyone connected with the notorious *Morning Leader*', Northcliffe went on to amplify his personal explanation:

When the war broke out I was silent about things that had gone wrong until, when at the front, I saw the lamentable spectacle of our men fighting the

Germans not with shells but with their bare breasts. The public had been lulled into a sense of preposterous optimism by the lies of politicians who thought that the war would be over before the lack of provision was discovered. You will remember that I exposed what I called the tragedy of the shells. The public, thinking that the war was actually won, were greatly incensed and my newspapers were burned all over the country and banned from every club. Their sales fell by 100,000. I received some five thousand abusive letters a day and had to take measures for my personal safety. At that time Mr Asquith had the audacity to go to Newcastle and say that there was nothing wrong with our equipment. The tide speedily turned in my favour because wounded men from the front began to spread the facts throughout the land. As a result of my exposure of the shells tragedy, the Ministry of Munitions came into being. However, I do not care to speak of myself and I never mind criticism. It is good for everyone.

The professor of philosophy had come down heavily on Northcliffe in his role of destroyer of reputations, notably Kitchener's, describing a *post mortem* criticism of Kitchener in the Northcliffe press as having been 'written for the gutter from the gutter'. This produced from Northcliffe the comment:

I knew that Lord Kitchener was successful in conducting small enterprises like the Sudan campaign in which he achieved efficiency, but this great war was totally beyond him. It is said that he prophesied that it would last three years, but I have never been able to find out when he said it. Anyone who paid any attention to the German preparations would have known that the war would be more likely to last six years than three. If you have a file of *The Times* or of Hansard, I suggest that you read Lord Kitchener's speeches in the House of Lords during the war. It is a thankless task to criticize the dead.

He ended his letter to the professor of Greek with the declaration: 'I shall go on exposing failure after failure. I am not a politician, nor am I interested in such people.' He disclosed his impatience in another letter: 'Ll.G. dislikes Haig. Robertson dislikes Ll.G. Bonar Law dislikes Churchill.'

The agitation against the newspaper proprietors flickered into oblivion. 'I do not know if the great Northcliffe debate in the Commons was published in the United States,' he wrote to Caird. 'It was a wicked waste of time and, personally, I have not read it.' He was scathingly critical of the possibility of Austen Chamberlain being taken into the Cabinet. 'At this moment the Germans are advancing on the Channel ports and the strongest men in the Empire are wanted for the War Cabinet. If this appointment is confirmed, political jobbery is a crime,' he stated in a message to the *Times* office. 'If he is appointed I shall not, after the passing of Home Rule, be able to go on giving the great support of my newspapers to the Government which I do now often with a twinge of conscience. I have so notified the Prime Minister.' His message continued:

The War Cabinet is feeble enough at present. It needs no more politicians, but one or two men of inflexible determination and untiring energy. Having to deal with the War Cabinet, I know very well that there are only two people in it who do anything—The Prime Minister and Lord Milner. We attacked the late Government because it was inefficient; the addition of Mr Chamberlain would bring the Government down to the level of Mr Asquith's.

When the resignation of the Minister of Food, Lord Rhondda, was a subject of rumour, Northcliffe was prompted to further harsh comment on party politics in one of his messages to *The Times*. Rhondda's reasons for leaving the Government, he asserted, were actuated by motives similar to his own. 'The Prime Minister is playing a small party trick, despite the German advance to the Channel.' He reported that Rhondda had written to him: 'I was in the House of Commons for twenty-three years, and saw something of political trickery. It certainly looks as though party considerations have influenced the selection of Austen Chamberlain, and it is to be very much deplored.'

Northcliffe to G. Murray Brumwell, night editor of *The Times*:

16th March, 1918.

My dear Brumwell,—Will you please see that in future Austen Chamberlain is reported in the third person? The speeches of political time wasters should be reduced to their proper length.

Members of Parliament have pointed out to me that our system of reporting these people so fully encourages them. We have neither the paper nor the space to devote much to them.

Yours sincerely,
NORTHCLIFFE

The House of Commons attacks had apparently sharpened Northcliffe's appetite for independence. He talked about putting a term to his service as director of enemy propaganda. He had not been invited into the inner circle of the Government and he was becoming more critical of the Prime Minister. It can be seen now as the beginning of a final stage of deterioration in the relations between the two men.

Northcliffe wrote to the editor of *The Times Weekly Edition*, W. A. Ackland: 'I now have no time to supervise my affairs. My official work occupies so many hours a day.' He was making a disclaimer and refuting it in practice, every day dictating his memoranda to his newspapers and keeping up with a correspondence which had grown in volume and variety since his return from America. *The Times* advertising was 'running amok', as he called it. 'I hope that the editorial staff will throw out as much of the advertising manager's raucous typography as possible.' A certain latitude was to be given to drapery establishments, 'which are news for readers living in the country'. Delane's biographer, Arthur Irwin Dasent, wanted to sell him the Delane papers. Northcliffe did not want them and offered to speak to 'one of the Walters'. Dasent replied quickly: 'I think I ought to tell you that Delane was not particularly enamoured of the Walter family.' 'The letters,' he said, 'contained many uncomplimentary references, particularly to John Walter whom you, I think, would not remember, but also to Arthur Walter, whom you do.' General Sir Arthur Sloggett, director of medical services, writing from British general headquarters in France, told Northcliffe: 'D.H. [Douglas Haig] is splendid—calm and not flustered. He shows up wonderfully at a time like this.' A prominent American soldier, General Leonard Wood, later Governor of the Philippines, sought Northcliffe's support for a plan of military operations in the Far East in conjunction with the Japanese, 'to prevent the Germans organizing Russia for their own ends'. Condemning some pictures in the *Daily Mail* of March 23 headed 'Street Snapshots At Maidenhead' as 'an absolute waste of space on the second day of the greatest battle of the world', Northcliffe further commented in his message to the office: 'Those photographs are almost as bad as Mr Asquith's talking—at the beginning of this great battle—about Free Trade, as he did yesterday. We cannot criticize him when we commit such follies ourselves.' Mr Justice Brandeis, of the Supreme Court of the United States, to Northcliffe (March 24, 1918): 'You have been much in my thoughts today, and I am glad that you are there, where a stout heart and resolute mind may give most in support. The supreme test of which you spoke seems to have come.' Northcliffe to W. F. Bullock, *Daily Mail* correspondent in New York (March 24, 1918): 'I have no doubt that I shall be back in America before the end of the war. I would very much like to return. One hates criticizing one's successors, but, judging from the cables which pass through my hands, I do not think that the practical part of the work of the British War Mission is being done as well as it used to be. As for affairs here, we are at the beginning of the great battle which may decide the future of the world for some centuries. I do wish our American friends were quicker.'

General Pershing, the American commander-in-chief, was in London. Northcliffe and he talked of the German push. Pershing afterwards said that Northcliffe was so moved as to be 'almost unable to speak'. He had looked into the heart of chaos. He had felt profoundly the death of his nephew, Vyvyan. He had spoken of 'rattled' politicians. He was unfaltering in his belief that Germany would go down in defeat. Four days after the unprecedented blow had fallen on the western front on March 21,

1918, he wrote in a message to *The Times* and the *Daily Mail*: 'It is difficult to think about newspapers or anything except the crisis of our fate. But I am confident.' That day, March 25, he wrote to R. B. Marston, editor of the *Fishing Gazette*:

It has long been my ambition to go to New Zealand for a fishing expedition, but I fear that my desire will never be fulfilled. However, I cannot grumble. I have killed salmon in British Columbia, Canada, Newfoundland, Scotland, Ireland and Spain. While in Canada last September, I caught a number of the most beautiful perch and pike. I say 'beautiful' because they were obviously our English perch and pike, but their colouring was much brighter. I often wonder if they were the offspring of fish that may have been taken out by the early settlers.

I have had good sport with trout in France, Germany and almost everywhere else. I have enjoyed many good days' roach fishing in the Thames, not to mention tarpon in the Gulf of Mexico and gudgeon in waters nearer home.

There had been a 'wonderful week of salmon fishing in the second year of the war', but he told Marston that recalling it made him feel 'very melancholy, for all those with whom I fished those waters have died'. Marston had asked him if he had read the articles and letters about the 'Northcliffe Administration' which Strachey had been publishing in the *Spectator*. Northcliffe replied:

I have no time for reading that kind of journal in these days of actualities. I have no desire to be Prime Minister. I have twice refused Cabinet rank because I believe that I can be more useful in my present position as an independent critic. A good many of our radical friends want to get me into the Government in order to shut me up.

In a message to the *Times* office on April 9, he wrote: 'One has not the heart to criticize a newspaper today. This morning's *Times* gives some indication of the tremendous losses of late, most of them unnecessary, and totalling 150,000, killed and wounded.' The same Periclean mood was on him, as of 'spring gone out of the year', when he wrote: '. . . our young airmen are now being killed at the rate of two or three a day at home training stations. There have been two such deaths close to my house in the last fortnight. Both fatalities could have been avoided.' Addressing himself to the staff at Printing House Square on April 13, he wrote: 'These are the most momentous issues of *The Times* since June, 1815, and our danger is infinitely greater than then. Personally, I am not anxious.'

There was a warning from the doctors, after a thorough overhaul. 'They say that I cannot go on at this pace.' He had cut his Saturday golf to twelve holes but was too tired to complete the round. A comb-out of men up to fifty added to his burdens. 'I do not know how I shall manage my concerns in the future.' To Bullock, in New York, he had written on April 6: 'I do not know how long Reading will remain. He is doing fine work. I have a fear that, if he comes back at all soon, the Government will ask me to go to Washington. I shall decline. He is a much better man than I am and he ought to be kept there if he possibly can be. I have not been really well since I came home.' He more than once referred to the chill that he had got in Liverpool, returning from the United States, as if it was a precursor of his health misfortunes of that year: 'I did not take care of myself', but he was more ready to blame the north-east wind which spoilt the spring of 1918. Bronchitis gave way to influenza, a sharp attack.

He retired to Elmwood again, 'feeling very low', but not so low as to be despondent about events and taking with him the little green deed-box full of letters awaiting answers. Northcliffe to Mme de Tizac, in Paris: 'As I have told you many times, whilst I am always anxious from day to day, I never worry about the war. The losses are terrible, but the thing had to be, and THE RESULT IS CERTAIN.' His faith was almost sublime. In London, his brother Cecil was noting: 'Not a cheerful face to be seen anywhere. In the House of Commons there is the utmost gloom. Men's heads are bowed and the lines on every face seem to have deepened. There is not merely anxiety; there is stupefaction and bewilderment at the hurried and confused retreat of our glorious army—just as if they were so many Italians or Rumanians.' He had seen Lloyd George, 'white-faced with apprehension'. Writing again to Mme de Tizac, Northcliffe, at Elmwood, told her: 'I am nearer the northern battlefield than you are. The windows rattle all day long from the terrific cannonade. I am glad to read of school children being sent away from Paris. If I had my way, I would never allow children to be brought up in cities at all. This may be the beginning of a great change.'

Sir Arthur Lee (later Lord Lee of Fareham), Director-General of Food Production, sent him a message (April 12): 'You will be glad to hear that, thanks to your shaking up, the Ford tractors are now arriving in a steady stream, which is threatening to develop into a most embarrassing spate.' L. J. Maxse, editor of the *National Review*, wrote: 'I do most earnestly hope that you, as one who has rendered such conspicuous service during the war, will reconsider your present disposition to back up Lloyd George and Co., as from all accounts they are at least as capable as Squiff [Asquith] and Co., if not more so, of going off round the corner, thoroughly rattled as the P.M. frequently is, and making a suicidal peace with the Boche.' Northcliffe to L. J. Maxse: 'My dear Leo,—I often hear remarks like those in your letter, but I never hear the names of any persons with whom to replace the present Government.' People grumbled to him, he told the *Times* staff on April 12, about the paper's pessimistic tone. 'I am glad that the paper does its best to get as much of the truth as possible, which is very difficult in view of the misleading, slovenly and late bulletins issued from G.H.Q. I have been present at the preparation of these things and know what poor brains produce them.'

Northcliffe to Beaverbrook (April 19): 'In regard to the London Headquarters of the British War Mission to the United States, whose work is increasing every week and whose scope will naturally widen as the United States and Great Britain become intertwined, I suggest, with respect, that Lieut-Col. Sir Campbell Stuart be appointed to the position held by me. . . . I will carry on the work for fourteen days more, so that there may be no possibility of confusion by a hasty change. Sir Campbell Stuart has done all the work since I have been ill.' To the same, on the same day: 'With regard to the Department of Propaganda in Enemy Countries, of the control of which I desire to be relieved, certain matters are pending which render it unwise for any sudden change to take place, and I am willing, therefore, to continue for four weeks longer. . . .'

Northcliffe to H. K. Hudson, secretary of the Enemy Propaganda Committee (April 19): 'Sir Campbell has no doubt told you that I have sent in my resignation to the Prime Minister, but I have had no reply—which is like him. I am particularly annoyed because he was negotiating with me about Home Rule all last week, and asking for my support. This I gave, little knowing what he was up to in connection with his vote-catching bargain with Mr Chamberlain. The net result of his proceeding has been to weaken himself greatly. He has practically got rid of Lord Milner from Downing Street. He did not like Lord Milner's firmness.'

Northcliffe to C. J. Phillips*: 'It is a very deep disappointment to me that I must sever myself from any association with this Government; but, after the happenings of this week, I am so filled with mistrust that I think it my duty to retire to a position from which I can watch them and pounce upon them when necessary. Men who carry out an intrigue like this can carry out an intrigue with the Germans or the Austrians. I do not know who is guilty—not Lord Milner, who has been away for a week. My brother Cecil, who is very close to the Prime Minister, was completely ignorant of it. I have today written to the Prime Minister, asking to be relieved of my tasks. I am sending you, dear Phillips, a little souvenir of our association, and I should like to say how much I appreciate your worth, diligence, precision and loyalty.'

Northcliffe to Sir George Lewis, Bt., of Lewis & Lewis, solicitors (April 21): 'The Duke of Sutherland is anxious to buy a newspaper. I have tried to dissuade him. . . . If he comes to you, I would strongly urge that

---

* C. J. Phillips, a civil servant, had been seconded to the Foreign Office from the Board of Education. He had been a member of Balfour's Mission to the United States, and subsequently he did much to facilitate Northcliffe's communications with Downing Street and the Foreign Office.

he be advised to go very slow about newspapers. He has, I believe, an immense sum of money lying at his bankers which he does not know what to do with. If he is not careful, he will find vampires. From my knowledge of Fleet Street vampires, they would make short work of any firm of family solicitors acting on behalf of a headstrong young nobleman like the Duke. Alas, I am not likely to be back in London just yet, as I am still in the hands of the medical vampires. I narrowly escaped pneumonia. Kind regards to the firm.' To J. L. Garvin he wrote: 'The Duke of Sutherland writes to me to ask if Lord Astor wants to sell *The Observer*. I wish you would let me have a letter saying "No" so that I can deal with the matter. He is itching to get into some newspaper trouble. I have done my best to warn him.' He sent a request to Geoffrey Dawson 'to support decimal coinage in the columns of *The Times*. It will save millions of hours of labour every year and this is the time to do it, when all values are changing' (April 30).

There were knowing smiles in the *Daily Mail* office when his communique for April 23 was put up on the notice board in the newsroom. 'The budget was extremely well done. Noting the nationality of our night sub-editors, I was amused at the tremendous prominence given to whisky prices. There must have been weeping at The Clachan last night. Price, to whom I am dictating this, says: "What's that?" When I was a reporter, there was a place called The Clachan, near Salisbury Square, and I understood the dose was known as "a half mutchkin".' The Clachan public house of which Northcliffe was thinking in 1918 is situated between Fleet Street and Mitre Court, Temple. It was long regarded as a haven for Scottish newspapermen in exile.

The new call-up was more worrying than those that had gone before. It threatened to deprive the professions, business and industry of their best brains. Technically, the problem for Northcliffe was a little eased by shrinking paper supplies, resulting from losses at sea, including one of his own paper boats. The *Daily Mail*, for example, was publishing a four-page paper twice a week (and its founder was regretting the necessity for dropping 'Teddy Tail', a feature for the very young). The situation required judgment and firm handling in steering his enterprises through circumstances that were becoming more difficult if not less profitable. The managerial side in particular would feel the effects of the withdrawal of key men. Editorially, he was chiefly concerned about *The Times*.

Northcliffe to Lord Milner:

Elmwood,
St Peters.
April 22, 1918.

My dear Lord Milner,—There are three matters to which I should like to draw your attention:

(1) *Geoffrey Dawson's position*: This is a subject on which I cannot be a good and impartial adviser. Dawson has for a long time been restless and anxious for soldiering. He came to see me on the subject last Saturday. It seems to me that the editorship of *The Times* is war work of prime importance. Dawson feels that he cannot advise men of his own age to enter the Army while abstaining himself. Both he and I attach the utmost importance to your judgment, and I should be very much obliged if you would advise him if he consults you, which I believe he will do.

(2) *Possibility of Secret Peace Negotiations*: I feel anxious at your disappearance from the War Cabinet. Recent events have made me distrust the Prime Minister. He was asking for my support of the Home Rule Bill through my brother Cecil, who is one of his Secretaries, but did not mention the Cabinet change. I greatly fear that such a secret habit may some day find us face to face with a secret peace negotiation.

(3) *Sir William Robertson*: There is a purely artificial agitation to bring back Robertson. It has no public support. Nor has it any backing from the Army in France. I was telling Geoffrey Dawson the other day that my barometer of public feeling is the thousands of letters addressed to the *Daily Mail* every week. A million copies of that newspaper are published every morning and it is undoubtedly read by five million people daily. We have had exactly two letters and one telegram about Sir William Robertson. As for the letters, they are both anonymous and come from the same person. I enclose one of them. The telegram was unsigned.

I notice that the letters which appear in the *Morning Post* and the *Star* which are trying to excite the public in the matter, are unsigned. I am writing this to you because I have personally found that the Prime Minister and his Secretaries are prone to be affected by spurious Press manifestations of this kind.

Yours sincerely,
NORTHCLIFFE.

Lord Milner to Northcliffe:

17, Great College Street,
S.W.

April 22, 1918.

Dear Lord Northcliffe,—Many thanks for your letter of today. I cannot do better than give a perfectly direct answer to your questions.

(1) Dawson. I have not a shadow of doubt that his duty lies in sticking to his present post, in which he has done admirable public service. I have told him so.

(2) I do not altogether like the *methods* of the Prime Minister. But I do not think any influence I have with him will be lessened by not being in the Cabinet. I have no fear of his engaging in secret peace negotiations. And despite great defects, which we all realize, I believe he is the best man we have to see us through the present intensely critical time.

(3) I entirely agree with you about Sir W. Robertson. He is a very good man, and has done excellent work in certain respects and whom I hope to see

employed again in the service of his country. But I believe the agitation to get him back as a sort of military dictator is quite artificial. Wilson is, in my opinion, a far abler man and much better fitted to be Chief of the Staff. He is doing extremely well and I think the prejudice against him, which was very strong at first and which that unprincipled scoundrel, Repington, has done his best to foster, is steadily disappearing.

> With kind regards,
> Yours very sincerely,
> MILNER.

Beaverbrook had reported to Northcliffe (April 22) that the Prime Minister 'had expressed himself in the strongest way' against Northcliffe abandoning his duties as chief propagandist against the enemy countries. 'He is sending you a copy of the report on Austria, obtained presumably from our secret agents there, and felt certain that when you read it you would go on with the work. As to the British War Mission in London, the Prime Minister is very anxious to have a personal talk with you. When you are well enough to come to town, will you go and see him?'

Northcliffe to Beaverbrook, in reply (April 23): 'I have not the slightest intention of continuing with the Departments mentioned for longer than the period I named. I am afraid that I did not make myself sufficiently clear in my letter. I want to get away from any connection whatever with this alleged War Cabinet, in order that I may say what I think of it.' He asked Beaverbrook to let the Prime Minister know his decision at once, 'as I propose making a public statement on the matter, but do not wish to embarrass him unnecessarily'. His doctor would not hear of his returning to London, he added, until the bronchitis had gone. 'The present weather has been much against me.'

Northcliffe wrote again to Beaverbrook on April 30, marking his letter 'Strictly Public' in reply to one from Beaverbrook (of April 29) marked 'Secret'. Northcliffe's was querulous. 'The indecision and lack of business training of the Prime Minister makes it very difficult for me to continue my work, but I will do so for a time, as I told you.' He gave examples of the indecision in regard to the enemy propaganda department. 'My slight experience of the Prime Minister', he observed with cryptic modesty, 'is that he is so heavily engaged in seeing the wrong people . . . that he never hears of these things. If he thought less of the House of Commons and politics and more of what thinking people are saying about him on these grounds, he would last much longer.'

Northcliffe's poor health prevented his regular attendance at meetings of the enemy propaganda advisory committee, but he had been successful in setting up a useful and doubtless indispensable inter-allied group to accelerate its work. He had written to Balfour in February 1918: 'It goes without saying that declarations on behalf of the British, French and Italian Governments, and, if possible, on the part of President Wilson . . . would, if promptly made, greatly facilitate my efforts.' His chief contribution, in the first months of 1918, was to impart a sense of urgency to plans designed to weaken Austrian morale. With his backing, Wickham Steed and R. W. Seton Watson had gone to Italy to start that process. Northcliffe had no difficulty in believing it to be a first essential towards the final liquidation of the Central Powers. There is no sign that he knew then that there were those, including Haig, who, perturbed by the Russian collapse and the slowness of American preparations, regarded it as a prerequisite of the compromise peace which they were willing to negotiate.

Political dissensions in Italy at first blunted the force of the new-style offensive. It consisted of novel ingenuities of assault and battery: rockets and mortars to shoot leaflets into the Austrian lines, aeroplanes and balloons to drop them in civilian zones, and gramophone records, played out in no-man's-land, to stir up feeling among the foreign elements in the lopsided Austrian armies. Northern Slavs (Czecho-Slovaks) in Bohemia and Moravia were particularly susceptible to appeals to their national aspirations. In Eastern Austria, there were Poles who were hostile to the cause for which they were required to fight. Rumanians in south-east Austria desired union with their parent country. The Southern Slavs (Yugoslavs) of Bosnia, Croatia and Dalmatia, yearned for a free Serbia. Before long, Austrian army orders began to reflect a growing uneasiness. More to the point for the directing committee at Crewe House was the news that fear of mass desertions among the Piave battle front had forced the Austrian high command to order machine-gun sections to undertake 'special duties' with divisions containing troops of the Habsburg subject races. Northcliffe's belief in the value of the propaganda weapon was beginning to be justified.

He had procured the printing of 15,000,000 leaflets in three days. His campaign against the Austrians and their satellite peoples took only five weeks to show important results, some of which may have been due to the reorganization of the Austrian forces which put them on the defensive for many months. When, at the end of April 1918 the Prime Minister passed on to him testimony from Italy to the effectiveness of his campaign, Northcliffe was sufficiently assured of success to demand somewhat peremptorily that he should be informed of any Cabinet change of policy in regard to Austria. 'You ask me,' he wrote to Lloyd George, 'to continue this very difficult task, and I reply that I will do so until you can find someone else. But I wish it to be clearly understood that an important condition must be observed.' Under his responsible direction, he asserted, 'a very precise impression has been conveyed that this country, at least, favours the liberation of the Habsburg subject races. I therefore regard myself as being entitled to be informed before any steps are taken, direct or indirect, public or secret, that might constitute a departure from this line of policy.' He added: 'It is not only a question of consistency of method. It is a question of keeping faith.'

Rothermere, who had held office as Secretary of State for Air for less than six months, resigned that post. Throughout he had been at logger-heads with his chief of staff, Trenchard, who from the first had been opposed to the Cabinet's decision to make a separate arm of the Royal Air Force. Overworked and bowed down by grief, Rothermere was under great strain. When Beaverbrook went to see him at that time, he found him 'worrying acutely . . . seeking forgetfulness in labour—and not suc-ceeding in finding it'. Northcliffe told Evelyn Wrench: 'Only my Mother and I know how ill Harold has been. We feared a complete breakdown.' Accepting his resignation, the Prime Minister had written: 'Your sacrifices to the national cause have been so heavy, and the strain imposed on you so cruel, that it would be impossible to deny you the right to some repose.' Rotheremere wrote to Northcliffe in reply to a birthday greeting on April 26:

My dear Alfred,—. . . I am getting better. The strain of the last four months was too much for me. If I had stayed on, I should have broken down. Of this I had much warning.

You are, I hope, taking great care of yourself. At fifty—I am that now—there is no longer any real resilience. When you are nearer London, I will come and see you.

George's Government is confronted by a strange intrigue. There is a great push among 'dud' politicians and 'dud' generals. The idea is to make Grey Prime Minister, and Robertson Secretary of State for War, with Jellicoe at the Admiralty. The Cecils are in it. Asquith, of course, will join and Carson, so it is said, will support on terms.

It is time the public were told again in plain Anglo-Saxon how entirely inadequate Robertson and Jellicoe are. These two warriors are being sedulously boomed. The public does not know Robertson was responsible for the ridicu-lously unsuccessful campaign at Ypres commencing on the 29th July last, and that Jellicoe failed at Jutland.

From what I hear this intrigue might, if George is in difficulties during the next month, pull off a Grey Premiership.

Always yours affectionately,
HAROLD.

P.S. Fancy Grey after the Blockade failure!

Writing appreciatively to the Prime Minister, 'for your kindness to me last week when I resigned', Rothermere told him: 'At this juncture, a continuance of the Trenchard regime would have meant paralysis and death in the Air within twelve months.' He expressed a further opinion. 'A continuance in office of myself would have been more and more difficult for your Government as the General Election approached. Beyond instructing my newspapers [*Daily Mirror, Sunday Pictorial, Glasgow Record*] not to criticize the appointment of Mr Austen Chamberlain, I have given them no directions since my appointment. This would have been an impossible position with a General Election looming and in progress.' He valued his freedom, he declared, because he could conduct his newspapers 'entirely from the point of view of upholding your Administration and beating the enemy'. There was a postscript to his letter: 'A counter-Press offensive is nearly due and I am prepared to take a hand in it.' Rothermere was thus acting in opposition to his brother's role of independent critic of the Government, though far from defying it. He and Lloyd George had established a friendship which, while not intimate, was firmly based. When Lloyd George fell from office in 1922, Rothermere wrote to him: 'You will find me a good foul weather friend.'

Early in May 1918 Northcliffe left Elmwood and went off to Canford Cliffs, near Bournemouth, to recuperate. The influenza attack had been severe. It appeared to reproduce some of the effects of the malarial crisis through which he had passed years ago. He complained of pain. He had put himself in the hands of a local doctor, who urged him to do deep breathing exercises. He suffered the usual bouts of despondency, which did not preclude him from studying his newspapers each morning and keeping up with the outflow of criticism, comment and compliment to the *Times* and *Daily Mail* offices. Possibly inspired by the nearness of Egdon Heath, he re-read some of the Hardy novels.

Northcliffe to Geoffrey Dawson:

Canford Cliffs.
May 4th, 1918.

My dear Robin,—I have been carefully reflecting upon the attitude of *The Times* to the Prime Minister, and I must say that the Paper, in my opinion, lacks independence.

The most urgent matter which I have in hand, so far as enemy propaganda is concerned, cannot be decided except by the Prime Minister. Would you believe it—that I am now waiting for weeks for a decision as to whether I am to distribute propaganda over the German lines by aeroplane or not? As it is, he is being bluffed by the Germans. The Prime Minister could settle the matter in five minutes. We are not helping him by letting him think that he has *The Times* in his pocket.

The Times has been very non-critical for months, and I do not wonder that it is regarded as a Government organ. It is certainly not that, for I have kept out of the Government partly in order that it should not become such. I do expect, in return for my attitude, that the Paper should be independent.

Yours ever,

N.

To Louis Tracy, in New York, he wrote: 'I, as you know, do not worry about the war. Our losses have been considerable . . . but the spirit of the people is magnificent. It is now nearly a year since I left England for America. On the whole, it was a very happy time.' He had been flattered by a request from General Pershing to be allowed to see copies of the private letters which he had circulated among his relatives and friends while in the United States. Message to *The Times*, May 17: 'On the whole, I think we gave enough to the Duke of Northumberland. I am not sure that the value of Dukes is very high during these important times.' There was another scolding for Lewis Rose Macleod, the long-suffering literary editor of the *Daily Mail*: 'This is the third time I am writing to tell you that you are not to put names on articles that we have cut to pieces. Imagine the anger of the writers.' There was a different tone on May 18: 'Anxious as I am to find fault with the paper every day, I can find nothing wrong with it this morning.'

Rothermere to Northcliffe:

Salehurst, Sussex.

Whit Monday, 1918

My dear Alfred,—I am glad mother is in such vigorous health. She is an amazing woman. Why can't we get her made a member of the War Cabinet? She would kill more trifling and nonsense than the rest together.

For nearly two years I have been feeling 50 and more. I never expected my health would allow me to stay long at the Hotel Cecil Air Ministry head-quarters, but I determined to stay long enough to knock out that dud Trenchard. He was establishing a Kitchener regime in the Air Force, and gave out quite openly to his intimates that he intended to be the autocrat of the new service. I simply waited for him and tripped him up.

Instead of being Chief of the Air Staff, he is now second string to Salmond in France. As Chief of the Air Staff, he was simply a Gargantuan joke. If he is the kind of man Haig surrounds himself with, I am not surprised we have done so badly in France. Milner is doing extraordinarily well. He is the best executive member of the War Cabinet.

I am never going to hustle again and I hope you won't do so. We have not Mother's health. At fifty she was twice as strong as you and I. We must be leisurely. If things go wrong, put them right without unnecessary nervous wear and tear. Seek sunshine and green fields. Avoid London with its bricks and mortar and depleted air. Collect something.

I overworked at the Royal Army Clothing Department. I did so with my eyes open. From the day I went there, scandal ceased, although there used to be about two scandals a week before I accepted the appointment.

If you could be sent on a special ambassadorial mission to Spain or Italy, it might amuse you for two or three months. Think it over. I am sure it could be easily managed.

Always your devoted
HAROLD.

*   *   *

Macleod, the literary editor, was under orders to send him, two or three times weekly, a batch of galley proofs of the short articles for the new *Daily Mail* leader page which Northcliffe had devised in response to the severe need for compression in a four-page paper. What had always been known as Page Four in a larger *Daily Mail* was now page two, but its contents continued to be referred to as 'fourth-page articles'. Northcliffe had gone back to his *Answers* formula. He proposed to fill the page with short articles, four days a week. They were to consist of two articles on food, two on women, one personality sketch and four on the war. Professional and amateur journalists were invited to submit contributions of not more than 500 words each which, if accepted, would be paid for 'at the highest rate in daily journalism', namely, three guineas. Telling Marlowe to publicize the offer, Northcliffe commented: 'We are creating something new in journalism.' Macleod was ordered to write 'a very nice letter to every manuscript sender', in place of the usual acknowledgment. Having established that practice, Macleod received a rebuke: 'I do not like the notepaper which you use for letters to contributors. There is nothing of the Literary Department about them. They look like memoranda forms which one expects to receive from Harrods.'

The page-four innovation was a success and not less so with Northcliffe than with the writers and the readers of the *Daily Mail*. It proved that his judgment was still sound, that he had not lost touch with the public taste. 'Our invitation to contribute is bringing in between 600 and 700 articles a week. We have abundant evidence from all over the country of the popularity of this new feature', he wrote to the editor of his *Evening News*, Alfred Turner. 'It takes me two hours a day to go through those that are sent to me by Macleod, who has a preliminary taste of them.' If the new *Daily Mail* 'literary page' represented literature at the Pickwickian level, there was no denying that it was well suited to a war-weary reading public. Northcliffe told Marlowe: 'We have to train our writers to write short articles. They do not seem to understand it. Max Pemberton, for example, though I told him the exact number of words to write and stood over him with a blue pencil, weighed in with between half and two-thirds of a column which I had to cut down.'

Northcliffe was extremely interested in his widely advertised 'new departure in daily journalism', which produced occasional gems of good writing and a steady level of competence. He developed an eccentric concern for contributors' names. William Pollock, a *Daily Mail* cricket reporter, opened the paper one morning to find that his name over a Page Four article had been changed to Pollock Pollock. Seeing the article in proof, Northcliffe had struck out 'William' with the remark, 'A good name for a butler', and written in 'Pollock'. The *Daily Mail* night news editor's name was C. Robert Mackenzie. 'In future when he writes an article for us, he will be known as "Crobert Mackenzie". It will not only distinguish him from our other office Mackenzies. It will look fine at the top of an article.' He told J. M. N. Jeffries, *Daily Mail* special correspondent: 'You and H. W. Wilson will never get the public to remember you with those initials.' He devised a number of the pen-names which became familiar to Page Four readers. One of the best known was 'January Mortimer', the pseudonym given by Northcliffe to Walter M. Gallichan, a one-time collaborator of Havelock Ellis and a prolific freelance contributor. Another successful writer for the page was a *Daily Mail* staff man, Sidney Howard, who had returned wounded from the war and had invented a character called 'Butterfly Bill', popular with *Daily Mail* readers. Northcliffe objected that Sidney was not a name to remember and inquired: 'What day were you born on?' Howard said that he would have to look it up. 'Never mind,' Northcliffe said. 'We will make it Thursday Howard—it's much better than Sidney.' Howard looked so distressed that the subject was dropped. 'The Chief' was specially well disposed to the contributions of Twells Brex, a name which everyone thought was a fake. It was the family name of a former solicitor's clerk who had been invited to join the *Daily Mail* staff earlier in the war. Northcliffe liked to see that name on Page Four. It suggested originality and would have caught his fancy even if the articles under it had been less well written.

The new page made life still more difficult for the literary editor. There were many nights when he was called back to the office at a late hour because Northcliffe had pulled the page to pieces. He would write an article himself just before edition time, causing expensive delay. 'I understand that the O.G. [Old Guard] weep copiously.' That year, 1918, he wrote a number of articles for the page but his enthusiasm as a contributor waned when he found that it was not he, but 'January Mortimer' on love and 'Butterfly Bill's' front line experiences that drew appreciative letters from readers.

H. G. Wells to Northcliffe:

52, St James's Court,
Buckingham Gate, S.W.
[Undated]

Private.

Dear Lord Northcliffe,—I wish I could have a long talk with you some time.

640

Curzon and Northcliffe

Rothermere and Northcliffe, with Courtenay Pollock, the sculptor, at Elmwood

Things move very fast, conditions change very rapidly, and the mind of the country does not move quickly enough to keep pace with its necessities. . . . It is a time when, given vigorous publicity, men of creative imagination might swing the whole world into a new phase. Our Government is mentally stale. The German is equally stale. Hardly anyone seems to have a clear purpose except Wilson and he is aloof and professorial. You seem to me—I'm not flattering you at all—in a position not only unique now but unique in history—for giving the lead into a new state of world politics. Napoleon failed in a like crisis because he was egotistical and vulgar and could see nothing more in his world situation than a chance to ape the Roman emperors. History never repeats itself and the future is for the men who have the courage to be new. Your department can be either a little bureau for scattering handbills among the enemy troops or it can over-stride the Foreign Office exactly as the Ministry of Munitions stepped over the Ordnance Department. With your press instrument also available, you can put on a hoarding before the whole world the outline of a settlement that would smash German Imperialism and unite the Atlantic and Mediterranean powers into one great dominant unity and secure the peace of the world.

Yours ever,
H. G. Wells.

Northcliffe's aunt, Sarah Miller, died on May 23. She had been a great figure in the family. 'Latterly she suffered from extreme ill-health and was almost blind, but she braved it out almost to the end with her elaborate coiffure and many rings and gewgaws', Cecil wrote in his diary. Northcliffe was with her in her last hours.

Northcliffe to G. S. Freeman, night editor of *The Times*:

Carmelite House,
E.C.4.
May 24, 1918.

Dear Freeman,—Lloyd George has been much with Haldane lately and also with Sidney Webb. If there is any sign of wobbling or peace talk, please deal with the Prime Minister drastically.

CHIEF.

Chapter Twenty-three

Germany's Confidence Shattered

NORTHCLIFFE's mother had a letter from Humphrey-Davy, written from The New Inn, Lechlade, Gloucestershire, on June 3, 1918: 'Lord Northcliffe is decidedly better. The perfect summer weather here, with a gentle west wind, has done him good and he enjoys his trout fishing.' The letter enclosed, 'at His Lordship's request', a cutting from the *Daily Express* about the baronetcy that had been conferred on Leicester Harmsworth. 'There are now three baronetcies in the famous Harmsworth family, a remarkable achievement.' Congratulating Leicester, Geraldine (the eldest Harmsworth daughter) wrote: 'In view of the paper shortage, I think the family ought to issue printed forms, viz.: *Many congratulations on your being made . . . .*' (with a blank space to be filled in according to the dignity bestowed). Leicester's baronetcy was to be followed by that conferred on Hildebrand four years after. Later, there came Cecil's peerage, making four baronetcies, three baronies, two viscountcies and one Privy Councillorship among the five eldest brothers. Northcliffe remained strict in his observance of the niceties of titular distinction. Dictating letters to his brothers, he always made sure that their style was set out in full.

He was getting up earlier than usual for his trout fishing in the upper reaches of the Thames, but first he went through his newspapers and dictated comments for 'Humpty-Dumpty' to pass on to the appropriate offices. Telegrams would be sent to the *Daily Mail* editor: 'Paper spoiled by bad make-up. Main page first edition better than second. Wasteful map without arrows. Much small news missed.' The unpleasant Pemberton Billing–Maud Allan libel case was sending up newspaper circulations; 'a horrible business', in his opinion, expressed to Marlowe. 'In a small Gloucestershire town the thing is arousing deplorable excitement,' he wrote to *The Times*. 'Evening newspapers are being fetched by cyclists who come many miles to get a copy.' Among the letters which Price had

642

put in the green deed-box was one dated June 2 from Lieut.-General Sir Hubert Gough, relieved of his command of the Fifth Army after the breaking of the British line in the March battles. 'I am impelled to write to you because I feel that the military situation is desperately critical and I know you to be a patriot before all else and a patriot who has the power to help us through this crisis; in fact, almost the only man in England who can do it.' The gist of the general's letter was that 'the immediate cause of the present situation in France is the shortage of men'. Northcliffe replied thanking him 'for a kind and interesting letter, with much of which I agree'. He told the general that he was in favour of reconstructing the War Cabinet by the addition of the strongest naval and military representatives. 'So strongly do I feel the necessity for reconstruction that I have declined to join the Government because it is not constituted for war.'

Informed on June 7 that *The Times* had made a record profit of £4,308 the previous week, he wrote to the office next day: 'I am glad to find that the Managerial Department is waking up to the needs of the army of women clerks at Printing House Square, and that they are to share the bonuses and be better looked after. It is about time.' He ordered Corbett, the manager, to improve the women's accommodation in the office. 'See that they have a good rest room.' The editor of the *Daily Mail* was told to take up the question of exemptions for farmers' sons. 'Last market day, in the little Gloucestershire village where I am staying, I counted sixty or seventy lusty young men in sporting costume.' He had been 'begged by the Gloucestershire chief police inspector to do something', he told *The Times* office. 'Farmers send their labourers into the army and retain their sons in safety.' Later it was disclosed to him that Dawson, of the Yorkshire acres, had resented those comments. Northcliffe proposed, also, to fight the battle of the men who would presently come home from the war. 'I do not think the *Daily Mail* quite understands the soldiers' land question. There are two projects which I have been told privately are backed by the great landlords who fear the break-up of their estates. One is to shunt as many soldiers out of the country as possible, the other to pen them up in what are called farm colonies. I happen to know that soldiers detest both these ideas. They want an individual home and an individual piece of land. I have talked with many of them. They have no desire to go to Australia or Canada. They want to come home. I should like a leader about it' (June 5, 1918). He cautioned the *Daily Mail* staff to 'watch very carefully the basis for the exchange of prisoners'; the Government had been 'shamefully cheated' by the Germans, 'owing to flabby negotiators'. There had been 'let loose Germans of great value', such as a certain prince and his wife, 'for whom we got only one decrepit colonel'. He was concerned about the German bank branches in London; 'every

Englishman knows there is some immense power obstructing the winding-up of these banks'. A house at Camberley was advertised so often in *The Times* personal column that he 'thought sometimes that the persistency of the advertisement indicated a code'. On what now seems to have been flimsy evidence, he reported the names of alien suspects to Basil (later Sir Basil) Thomson, of Scotland Yard. 'F——, who is interned, has a daughter who is employed at the Empire Theatre and who makes a point of paying special attention to young officers.' 'German is spoken at the house of H—— in New Road, Chatham. A man there is employed at the powder works and is fond of photography.' He was ready to listen to anyone who professed to have news of enemy activity in London or elsewhere on the home front. A Baker Street business man who wrote claiming to know that an Admiralty official was receiving £400 a year 'from an unnaturalized German' to disclose ship routes was asked at once to Carmelite House so that Northcliffe could question him.

Geoffrey Dawson was fishing with him at Lechlade—'a glorious summer's day in which we loafed by the river and through wonderful Gloucestershire villages. N. still bad, I thought, with his throat, though he professed himself full of energy and interest.' The day's amiability was a patch of blue in a stormy sky. Their clashes of policy and temperament were to make it a year of increasing difficulty for both. In *Geoffrey Dawson and Our Times*★ Sir Evelyn Wrench stated that Dawson's diary for 1918 contained more references to Northcliffe than any previous year. Dawson showed signs of being more impatient of the 'intimate association' of *The Times* with the Northcliffe press than of his personal relations with Northcliffe, increasingly difficult though they were. Northcliffe was tiring of Dawson's social affinities. They drew him too often to Cliveden for Northcliffe's liking.

★   ★   ★

Leaving Lechlade, Northcliffe went to stay with his mother at Totteridge. 'You should have a house near London *without a telephone*,' his brother Rothermere wrote to him. 'Cut off the one at Poynters.' While he was there he received an urgent letter from Wickham Steed with an enclosure which hardened his heart towards the Government. Steed's enclosure was a copy of a confidential letter from Clifford Sharp, editor of the *New Statesman*, who had been seconded from military duty to intelligence work in Stockholm, where he was given the nominal post of *The Times* correspondent. He had come to London on leave. Steed regarded his

★ Hutchinson, 1955.

letter as being 'so startling that action had to be taken at once'. He had
sent copies also to Balfour, and Hughes, the Prime Minister of Australia.
The letter disclosed a plan to make peace with the Germans at the expense
of Russia. After setting forth details of the plan, of which Milner was
named as the chief architect, Sharp had written:

The fact seems to be that the Cabinet or at any rate most of its leading
members have got cold feet. I've met none of them during my visit but I have
had their state of mind described to me by two or three most reliable people
who are in a position to know what they are talking about. It seems that they
are just 'afraid'. Their fear does not attach itself to anything definite, to any
specific prospect of danger, but is simply loss of nerve. . . . They seem rotten,
to have lost all their pluck, if they ever had any. Milner is perhaps an exception,
as far as keeping his head is concerned, but then in his heart he is more of a
believer in German culture than Haldane even.

It seems that we have no Englishman to lead us and express the mind of
Englishmen. If there *is* a Pitt he is mute and inglorious. . . . However, there is
still *The Times*! I have never been a Northcliffe enthusiast but I am certainly
leaving England with the feeling that amongst those in high places here he
more than any deserves the confidence of those of us who mean to see the
thing through. Of course we *shall* see it through, but heaven knows *how*, with
such a crew in Whitehall.

Steed reported that Balfour said that the letter 'appalled him'. Hughes
'telephoned to say that he was fully aware of the situation and had been
fighting against it, but was almost powerless'. Northcliffe had telephoned
from the country to hear Steed's suggestions. 'An article in *The Times*
might cause too much alarm.' Steed proposed instead 'a sensational article'
in the *Daily Mail*. Headed 'Watch Lansdowne and Others' it appeared
on June 21.

. . . Our ministers may be weak and foolish, but we have no right to think
them traitors; and traitors they would be were they to listen, even for an
instant, to any idea of giving Germany 'a free hand in the East'. They would
deserve to be, as they probably would be, hanged by their indignant fellow
countrymen and countrywomen, who would not suffer the war to end in so
shameful a betrayal.

Steed, and no doubt Northcliffe, had expected 'a furious outburst' in
reply. There was silence. Northcliffe telephoned to Steed: 'We've hit the
bull's eye!' No more was heard of what Steed recorded in his autobiography, *Through Thirty Years*, as 'the pacifist intrigue'. The episode
changed Northcliffe's attitude to Milner, who was referred to in communiques to *The Times* shortly afterwards (July 11). 'Some people are

trying to get me to modify my action on enemy aliens. . . . I find that the public think that the Government will not move because of Lord Milner. A statement as to Lord Milner's ancestry might be worth while.' (He was born in Germany, of English descent.) 'There is a widespread feeling that the leniency with which Germans are treated in this country was due to Lord Milner, and that the reason why Germans were not interned is that Lord Milner will have to be interned as well' (July 26).

By mid-June, Northcliffe was back at Elmwood, working and taking his meals under the trees, with H. G. Price bent sedulously over his short-hand notebook at all hours. H. G. Wells had sent him a propaganda suggestion. Northcliffe, in reply: 'May I say, with respect, that you are young at this game?' He desired the French President, M. Georges Clemenceau, to receive a Canadian friend of his, the Hon. Arthur Meighen, a member of the Canadian Cabinet. Making the request, Northcliffe dictated a peroration: 'Let me tell you with what intense interest, admiration and affection the English people are watching the glorious stand of France.' He sent an invitation to the Canadian Prime Minister, Sir Robert Borden, to stay with him, 'if you want to escape to some peaceful place'. Borden answered that his War Cabinet work would detain him in London. 'My forebears in the County of Kent took their departure for America in 1638. For nearly three hundred years before that they lived in the quiet village of Headcorn, in the Kentish Weald.' When the secretary of the Broadstairs & St. Peters Allotment Holders' Association solicited Northcliffe's patronage, he wrote in reply: 'I have lately found that every time I come to Broadstairs I am bombed, not only by the Germans, but by the inhabitants! I enclose cheque.'

He insinuated his technical authority into a message to *The Times* (June 13). 'Only those who like myself have sat many nights with the blue pencil in hand can realize the care and amount of detail work behind what is presented to the reader every morning. There is, as far as I know, nothing like the *Times* sub-editing in the world.' He thought it important to protect *The Times* from the charges of bias to which his *Daily Mail* was frequently exposed. 'The Clapham election should be reported with fairness to both sides' (June 18). 'I should have liked to have seen [*sic*] more of the Leverton Harris case', that of a parliamentary secretary to the Blockade Department who was accused of favouring a German firm. 'I hope it was not cut down because they are friends of my own household. This case explains the flabby blockade' (June 19).

The outpouring of criticism and comment went on intimidatingly, although on June 15 he had told the *Daily Mail* staff: 'Owing to the work I am doing in stirring up trouble in Austria I am unable to devote sufficient time to ensure such close comparison of the papers as I used to do.' It was not only as a publisher of books (Amalgamated Press) and chief proprietor of a bookshop (*The Times* Book Club) that he wrote a few days later: 'I do hope *The Times* will combat the suggestion of the Luxury Tax Committee that books are luxuries. The amount to be gathered by the taxation of books will be very small, and the distress of our men at the Front very great.' Receiving word that Sir Ian Hamilton was likely to be made Commander-in-Chief Home Forces, he wrote at once to the Prime Minister's secretary, J. T. Davies: 'Can this be true? Will you ask the Prime Minister if it is possible that yet another failure is to be promoted?' Asked by Max Pemberton to give his opinion of the Pelman system of mind training, Northcliffe thought it relevant to urge the Pelman Institute to 'teach people to sign their names properly. It would be a national achievement. My squad of secretaries performed a dance, accompanied by yells, at the glad news that postage had been increased to threehalfpence, but, alas, it has not had the desired effect. At least five per cent of our correspondents sign their names illegibly.'

There was disquieting news from George Curnock, one of the *Daily Mail* representatives in Paris. The German armies were within forty miles of the capital. A renewed and greater long-range gun bombardment was expected. The *Continental Daily Mail* staff stood ready to evacuate the paper to Nantes. Curnock sent long daily reports to Northcliffe, who seemed to be worried about the fate of his newspaper while remaining completely optimistic about the war in general. Rothermere wrote in his pessimistic vein: 'Perhaps we are played out. The Harmsworths may not be intended for very old bones. Certainly the only thing to do is not to take on any work or responsibility which we have not the health to carry out. There is an impression about that you are not at all well. I hope you are taking things very quietly.'

Physically, Northcliffe was complying with that precept. At Elmwood he was going to bed regularly at nine and getting up late. He was playing very little golf, taking no other exercise. Often his short evenings were given up to his old passion for the gramophone, his favourite record of the moment being one from America: *How 'ya gonna keep 'em down on the farm, now that they've seen Paree?* When there were no visitors to share his pleasure in it, he would sit and listen alone. In America, he had met Irving Berlin and rarely thereafter heard his name spoken without being impelled to say: 'Isn't it extraordinary that he doesn't know a note of music?' For some time he was under the spell of *Alexander's Ragtime Band*, the first of the jazz age classics.

Mentally, he was unceasingly active, in and out of bed. At Crewe House, Campbell Stuart had taken full charge of the departmental work, relieving him of routine committee duties and of all but policy responsibilities. Northcliffe was the better able to concentrate on securing the best results from a form of attack which caused the Germans to name him, in an

Army order, 'Minister for the Destruction of German Confidence'. That distinctive epithet was not earned for him simply by the impact of his name and reputation. The propaganda going out from Crewe House was the work of the ingenious minds which he had enrolled in its service. H. G. Wells to Northcliffe: 'Crewe House, Curzon Street, W.1., 27th June, 1918: Apart from amiable intentions towards yourself, I wish you were better in order to take hold, as you alone can do, of the whole of this Propaganda situation. There is still very great disorganization, waste and internecine conflict.' Wells, who had been given charge of the German section at Crewe House, complained, underlined, of 'an absence of a definite general scheme of action'. Englishmen, he said, 'do not seem to understand this necessary condition of intellectual team work. Propaganda is that and nothing else.' He demanded 'the clearest and most emphatic statement of the *leading ideas of our propaganda*, known to all the organization and accepted and loyally adhered to by everyone'. He insisted that these leading ideas should shape the policy also of Lord Beaverbrook and his Ministry of Information, if there was to be finally effective co-operation. 'I have been to him to ask him about his policy and so far as any general idea goes, he hasn't one.' Wells continued:

It must also be the policy of *The Times* in particular, because from a foreign point of view *The Times* still speaks for England. But while Crewe House is working its way towards certain definite ends, *The Times* is evidently running on Imperialist lines that are at least four years out of date, across and even counter to our activities. Next to the public utterances of leading statesmen, *The Times* is our chief medium for propaganda in enemy countries and unless *The Times* can be brought up to date, briefed upon our lines, and our memorandum used as its general instruction, our work will remain but half effective. . . . Unless we have better team work . . . this war is going to end in a worse muddle than the muddle that begot it.

Wells was agitated by the policy of a group known as the War Aims Committee, which was cutting across the work of Crewe House: 'antagonizing our people against anything and everything German'. Northcliffe's *Evening News*, he pointed out, was assisting that campaign, which was 'an infernal nuisance'. Such activities, he declared, helped to make Crewe House 'ineffective and a little absurd'. Another of Wells's subjects just then was Russia. 'I can find no shadow of a plan or a policy, or a scheme, or an outlook anywhere in regard to Russia.' According to him, the Ministry of Information was 'all over the shop' on that question. He exhorted Northcliffe to 'suppress, slay, stop, any official obstruction, General Headquarters arrangements, or freak journalism', which tended to thwart the plan which he and his like-thinkers had drawn up.

Northcliffe to H. G. Wells:

Elmwood,
St. Peters,
29th June, 1918.

Dear Mr Wells,—We think alike in some things but not in all.

As to the control of propaganda, my commission is direct from the Prime Minister and not from Lord Beaverbrook. I am not in Lord Beaverbrook's department, and I am not sure that he has any knowledge of organization. His training has not been that of an organizer but of a financier, which is a very different thing. I will see him as soon as the doctor allows me to use my voice continuously, and I will show him your letter.

I totally disagree with you on the question of the internment of Germans in England. I would intern every one of them who had been naturalized within five years of the outbreak of war. . . . The freedom of a good many of the Germans in England is due in a great degree to snobbery and worse in *very high places*.

About Russia, Northcliffe asked Wells: 'Is Russia an enemy country? If not, Crewe House cannot interfere with it.' The War Aims Committee he described as 'a scandalous series of jobs'.

The whole of these difficulties could be settled if the Prime Minister were a man of business, which he is not. If he would summon into a room these miscellaneous propagandists whom he has allowed to multiply and would define their territories and functions, we should get a move on. That is not the way of our gifted orator. Flashing about Europe like a dragonfly, from Edinburgh to Taranto and from Versailles to Downing Street, with one eye on the war and, as Colonel House said to me, the other on Mr Asquith, he has no time, even if he had the executive ability, to achieve practical results.

On the question of propaganda, Northcliffe had been angrily frustrated by the yielding of the Army Council to German threats of reprisal against Air Force officers captured with leaflet-dropping aeroplanes over the Western Front. He had protested against the handicapping of the work of Crewe House in that way, his information being that the Germans themselves were using the same method over the British lines. Moreover, there had been no ban on the use of aeroplanes for propaganda purposes on the Italian front. He wrote in his letter to Wells:

My own conceptions of propaganda are perhaps unusual. Having got permission to use the aeroplane (which the Prime Minister could give me by a stroke of the pen), I would deluge the German people with all sorts of American and English views, whether I agree with them or not. I lately asked *The Times* to publish the great Socialist Manifesto. I do not agree with much of it, but I had hoped to send it into Germany.

To Wells's wish for his better health, Northcliffe replied: 'I am making a great effort to be restored by the end of a fortnight.' He said that his illness was 'obstinate', and concluded his letter with a declamatory flourish that may have fallen short of impressing his correspondent: 'I have had to conduct all my many businesses singlehanded, owing to depletions of my staffs, to deal with Crewe House matters daily, and to carry on a public and private warfare with those in high places who have been bought and paid for by Germany', evidence for which seemingly reckless statement he could perhaps have supplied, though he was often the prey of rampant suspicion.

During his London sojourns that year, he made a habit of being driven up to Hampstead two or three mornings a week to take a walk over the Heath with his brother Leicester, who was living at the Old Court House. Northcliffe was intolerant of being kept waiting and someone was always posted behind the front door with ears strained to catch the sound of his Rolls-Royce. That duty was done one morning by the youngest son of the house, Geoffrey, home from his preparatory school for the summer holidays. When his face appeared at the open door, Northcliffe called out from the car: 'Where's your father, my boy? Still asleep, I suppose, like most of the Liberal party.'

There had been twenty-three Harmsworth nephews and to each of them, as to his fourteen Harmsworth nieces, he personified the best that an uncle could be. He enjoyed the relationship. He entered genially and affectionately into its obligations and sentiments. Schoolboy Harmsworths would be excited by his visits to Eton, Harrow and Winchester. He always replied promptly to their requests for famous autographs, foreign stamps and photographs of aeroplanes. There were school holidays at Elmwood where he would introduce nephews to the great and famous and give them the thrill of hearing him talk on the telephone to the Prime Minister. Four of the boys were lost in the war, acquainting him with a deeper grief than any he had known before. From it sprang much of his hatred of 'the muddles' of which he was a relentless critic. He wrote to Esmond Harmsworth, Rothermere's youngest and sole surviving son:

6th August, 1918.

My dearest Nephew,—We shall be delighted to see you at luncheon and all the meals you care for.

I never worry about the war. The Americans are not only sending troops, but are commencing to build ships and manufacture aeroplanes on a scale of which the world is not aware. The war will be long—very long, and will end with the total dispersal of the German tribes.

Your devoted
Uncle N.

★   ★   ★

His persistence secured the resumption of the use of leaflet-dropping aeroplanes over the German lines and beyond. He had refused to let the matter rest on the Army Council's decision. He brought it to the attention of Lord Milner and the War Cabinet. Many valuable weeks had been wasted. For that, he largely blamed Milner, who, he said, had been bluffed by the German threats of reprisal. There were close observers of the military scene who believed that if Northcliffe and his colleagues at Crewe House had been given a free hand, the war would have ended sooner. It was an ironic footnote to history. Northcliffe, sponsor of the aeroplane, was forced to be a balloon man. Instead of the intensive campaign that he had planned, he had to be content with sending over 100,000 leaflets at a time, their distribution at the mercy of every wind that blew. Despite the vagaries of men and of weather, 1,689,000 leaflets were showered over the German lines in June 1918. For July, the total was 2,172,000. Skilfully written and produced, the leaflets were of two types, 'stock' and 'priority'. They told the truth in simple language, illustrating it with map drawings. Because it was the truth, the Germans soon had to stop denying it. Reports from the front showed that many soldiers were being won over to the view that Northcliffe's paper war would prove to be more decisive than that of shot and shell. The grand campaign of propaganda against the Germans was largely based on a carefully composed statement of aims and methods drawn up by Wells. Northcliffe used it as the substance of a letter which he sent to Balfour, requesting the War Cabinet's approval. The letter became, in effect, the charter of the department over which Northcliffe presided. It asserted the will of the Allies to continue the war at all cost and their desire to avoid the necessity of a ruinous peace. That fate, it declared, would be Germany's if she persisted in her policy of conquest and subjugation. Balfour replied that Northcliffe's 'important letter' must be brought before the Cabinet. 'Thus we were able to go ahead', wrote Wickham Steed, who drafted the communications submitted to the Cabinet in Northcliffe's name.

Truth and hope were the watchwords of the propaganda against Germany. 'Propaganda that merely threatens achieves nothing unless it holds out hope also.' Wells stated it in the form of a proposition: 'Conquest or the League.' He invented suggestions for causing the enemy 'new and disturbing inconveniences to his national life', by way of promoting discouragement and fear. For example: 'We might start a newspaper controversy for and against the use of an absolutely non-existent poison bomb.' But, he urged, 'we can do better by being honest than by being cunning'. Wells recalled in his *Experiment in Autobiography**that he had undertaken the work of director of the German section at Crewe House after talking with Northcliffe in what had been the drawing-room there.

* Cresset Press & Gollancz, 1934.

Northcliffe had said to him: 'You want a social revolution. Isn't our sitting here social revolution enough for you?' Wells hoped for an opportunity of projecting into the realm of practical politics his ideas about a supra-national authority in the form of a league of free nations, with emphasis on 'free'. In his memorandum he had written:

The Allies now offer the world quite definitely the scheme of an organized League of Nations, a rule of law and justice about the earth. To fight for that and for no one conceivable end, the United States of America, with the full sympathy and co-operation of every state in the western hemisphere, has entered the war. The British Empire, in the midst of the stress of the great war, has set up in Dublin a Convention of Irishmen of all kinds of opinion, with the fullest powers of deciding the future of the country. If Ireland were not divided against herself, she could be free and equal with England tomorrow. It is the open and declared intention of Great Britain to develop representative govern-ment, where it has not hitherto existed, in India and in Egypt and to go on steadfastly increasing the share of the natives of these countries in the govern-ment of their own affairs, until they, too, become free and equal members in the world league.

He believed that Northcliffe had grasped what he had in mind. 'Or, to be more accurate, I think that at times—in exceptional gleams of lucidity—he sympathized with it and wanted to forward it. But his undoubtedly big and undoubtedly unco-ordinated brain was like a weather chart in stormy times . . . his skull held together, in a delusive unity, a score of flying fragments of purpose.' Wells's official propaganda had not departed from the principles which he had enunciated since the war began. He soon had to complain that Northcliffe, in that matter, was leading a double life. For the moment, Northcliffe was trying to settle a difficulty which had arisen between the Ministry of Information and the Foreign Office over policy matters.

Northcliffe to C. J. Phillips, Foreign Office:

Elmwood,
St. Peters,
7th July, 1918.

My dear Phillips,—You know my views as to providing Beaverbrook or anybody else not absolutely responsible with information that might affect the safety of this realm, but the specific charge he makes in his letter to the Prime Minister of refusal to allow propaganda in Japan is a matter that cannot be burked. I am hoping that the letter I have written to Mr Balfour will bring about some adjustment.

Beaverbrook's Ministry [of Information] is doing very well, especially in regard to the Canadian and American part. Things are improving in France, in Switzerland and in Spain. He has drive, but is apt to regard all permanent officials as fools. His influence behind the scenes in this Government is what you and I know it to be, and it does not seem to be beyond the wit of man to devise a solution by which the Foreign Office can work with him.

Yours very sincerely,
NORTHCLIFFE.

Writing to the same Foreign Office official five days later, Northcliffe said: 'As a people, we do not understand propaganda ways. . . . Propaganda is advertising and diplomacy is no more likely to understand advertising than advertising is likely to understand diplomacy. . . . If my throat was well enough to talk, I am sure I could settle the Beaverbrook Foreign Office matter.' He took up the subject with the Prime Minister the same day. 'The dispute between Beaverbrook and the Foreign Office is undoubtedly delaying propaganda and lengthening the war. . . .' The dispute, he told the Prime Minister, was 'more unfortunate than appears on the surface', particularly as, in his opinion, Beaverbrook's work had been a great success. He wrote privately to Balfour at the Foreign Office (July 7): 'Beaverbrook is not a particularly tactful man, but he is full of energy and his Ministry is doing excellent work.' He had no doubt that he could settle the dispute, 'if my doctor would allow me to use my voice'. Unknown to him or to the doctors then, a serious condition was developing in his throat.

Using his voice on July 8, he dictated: 'An admirable *Times* this morning, with a leading article that recompenses me for twice declining to take office in order that my newspapers might be independent.' The next day: 'I wish the paper would pay more attention to the underpayment of London women teachers.' Fidgety about the social proprieties and about Anglo-American relations, he cabled to Lord Reading on July 12 complaining that 'an important American lady states that she was received by the British passport office in New York by an official in shirt-sleeves and braces'. Urging the *Daily Mail* to persevere with its 'alien propaganda without being strident', he reported having been told 'on excellent authority' that certain Home Office officials were 'determined to protect their friends'. He called on July 13 for 'a leading article in which would be tabulated the names of all public bodies that have issued remonstrances against alien enemies. I have read of at least 100. This will be a reply to the Home Office contention that the agitation is a product of my wicked newspapers. We must watch this thing day by day.'

He spent his birthday, July 15, at Totteridge with his mother. There he dictated the day's message to Printing House Square: '*The Times* this morning gave me a nice birthday present in the shape of a fine complete paper.' Carmelite House also received an acknowledgment: 'The *Daily Mail* made me a very fine 53rd birthday present in the shape of an excellent paper this morning.' The *Daily Mail* office, in turn, passed to him a message which, read these forty years after, echoes history. 'Mr Marlowe says Handley Page desires privately to say that if Lord Northcliffe wishes the first Transatlantic flight to be of real influence in the aeronautic world, the flights ought to be open and competitive, that Lord Northcliffe should insist that the Air Board should give every manufacturer a fair field and no favour, and that the Air Board shall not insist, as Handley Page thinks it will, on the trial flights being Government affairs.' He sent a memorandum to Marlowe: 'Point out to Weir [Air Minister] that the Atlantic Prize will be the means of the construction of great Handley Pages and Capronis, and other machines sufficiently strong to fly the Atlantic regularly. I am personally quite sure that we are approaching this state of affairs in aviation.'

From Caird at Carmelite House came news that the National Society of Operative Printers & Assistants had given formal notice to the Newspaper Proprietors' Association to terminate its agreements 'covering labour conditions' then in force. It was an opportunity for Northcliffe to throw one of his pebbles into the pond of labour relations. He told Caird (July 20): 'The printers are realizing that the invention of the rotary press and wood pulp paper have enormously increased the power and profit of newspaper owners. As soon as the newspaper owners were hit by the war they doubled and in some cases trebled the price of their product. I have not yet heard that they have doubled or trebled the wages of their workers, whose cost of living has, in many cases, doubled and trebled.'

The following day he left for the bungalow at West Clandon, which he now called his 'famous sleeping place'.

★   ★   ★

H. G. Wells to Northcliffe:

Crewe House
[undated]

Dear Lord Northcliffe,—I can imagine nothing more utterly mischievous than this campaign to make every human being of German origin hate us as bitterly as possible and I can see no possibility of conducting a propaganda against the German government while it goes on.

Cannot we get to some better understanding in this matter with your newspapers? And not only in this matter but generally upon propaganda. Lord Northcliffe of Crewe House has sent Mr Balfour a very remarkable document indeed, embodying his conception of the Allied war aims. Will he not now induce Lord Northcliffe of Printing House Square and Carmelite Street to insist upon that document becoming the guiding memorandum upon foreign affairs of *The Times*, the *Daily Mail* and the *Evening News*? Cannot we educate our own people and people abroad to the conception of one clear steadfast purpose in our policy, instead of dissipating their energies in these waves of misdirected emotion? Under the influence of the War Aims Committee, which does nothing but rant at the Germans and holds out no sort of hope of a happy world after victory, and your penny papers, the country is getting nervy, hopeless, irritable and altogether rotten. We are not developing a victory psychology. We are developing an incoherent pogrom spirit. No man has anything like the power that you have to pull up this worried crowd of stragglers into line again.

Yours very sincerely,

H. G. WELLS.

Bye the bye, the enclosed photograph may interest you. There was an assistant master at Henley House school called Johnstone in your time. He is the manager of a bank in Natal and my brother took the snapshot a month or so ago. He looks rather like setting someone 'ten sums'.

Northcliffe to H. G. Wells:

16th July, 1918.

Dear Mr Wells,—Let me say at once that I entirely agree with the policy adopted by my newspapers, which I do not propose to discuss with anyone. I have not wandered about Prussia for two years without learning something, and if you will wait you will find that I will unearth much sinister and active Prussianism in England.

I was flattered to receive letters from two geniuses on the same subject. Both you and Kipling have written to me, but in very different terms.

Many thanks for the photograph. I do not remember Johnstone.

Yours very sincerely,

NORTHCLIFFE.

Wells replied by return post: 'I am sorry that you insist upon being two people when God has only made you one. I cannot, for my own part, separate the *Evening News* from Crewe House while you remain one person.' Angered by the enforced resignation from the Crewe House staff of a young man of German origin whom he described as 'my most useful assistant, a St. Paul's School boy of great literary ability', Wells himself resigned. Northcliffe wrote to him: 'I cannot say how sorry I am that you have deprived Crewe House of your valuable services, and I want to thank you for laying the foundations of the great work which will be carried on, now that we have at last received permission to use the aeroplane.' Northcliffe hoped that Wells would not leave the enemy propaganda committee, even though he would no longer direct a department. 'All committees need stimulus and criticism. I regard myself really as a trustee in this matter.' He and Wells retained a good opinion of one another, though they reached none of the closer stages of friendship.

Colonel House to Northcliffe:

> Magnolia,
> Massachusetts,
> 18th July, 1918.

Dear Lord Northcliffe,—Thank you for thinking to cable me on the anniversary of your first visit to Magnolia.

You do not know how much pleasure those visits gave us, nor how much I miss being in touch with you. I was reading today in our cable despatches from neutral countries nearby Germany, how much they were disturbed by 'the propaganda which Lord Northcliffe is directing against us. The English are doing more to defeat us in this way than the armies in the field.' This is the greatest tribute one could have.

With all good wishes, dear Lord Northcliffe,

> I am,
> Your sincere friend,
> E. M. HOUSE.

The news that aeroplanes were to be made available to him for propaganda duties over Germany had an exhilarating effect. 'My dear Beaverbrook,—I am delighted to hear that the War Cabinet have, at length, rendered it possible for us to carry out efficient propaganda in Germany. I am sure that we shall now be able to get on with our work, but the incident makes one despair of the brains of G.H.Q.' (July 19). It was not the end of the story of frustration and delay. The Air Board continued to be intimidated by the German attitude to pilots engaged in propaganda work. The leaflet-dropping was being done by French and Italian pilots.

Wells's place in the department had been taken by Hamilton Fyfe. Other colleagues to whom Northcliffe owed a large part of this particular success with which he was credited were the scholarly Dr (later Sir) J. W. Headlam-Morley; S. A. Guest, a civil servant who was seconded to propaganda activities earlier in the war and who, from one room and with only secretarial help, had organized a remarkable network of smuggling routes into Germany; Peter (later Sir Peter) Chalmers Mitchell, man of science; C. J. Phillips, valuable on the diplomatic side; the Earl of Kerry, liaison officer between Crewe House and the War Office; Commander (later Sir) Guy Standing, R.N.V.R., the naval representative; and Brigadier-General Sir George Cockerill, Director of Special Intelligence. Sir George Cockerill's department at the War Office had been carrying on the 'paper war' over Germany for two years. He subsequently complained in a book that the work had been smothered by the publicity given to Northcliffe and Crewe House, unaware no doubt that his own efforts may have originally been sanctioned and encouraged as a result of a letter written by Northcliffe to General Charteris, of Haig's staff, in August 1916, when Northcliffe urged that attempts should be made 'to produce by propaganda a state of mind in the German army favourable to surrender'. In the letter Northcliffe set out measures which, 'in my humble and uninformed opinion', might lead to that climax. They included the scattering of leaflets by aeroplane over the enemy lines, a reminder of his original proposal to General French as early as September 1914. He had closed his letter to General Charteris with the statement: 'I believe this bombardment of the German mind is almost as important as the bombardment effected by guns.'

At Crewe House, on the administrative side, there was Sir Campbell Stuart, who later published the volume called *The Secrets of Crewe House* (which Wickham Steed thought a needlessly melodramatic title) and who was known as the 'Senior Wangler'; C. S. Kent, the financial controller who had been brought over from Associated Newspapers, and H. K. Hudson, Sir Robert Hudson's brother, who was secretary of the main propaganda committee and of the various sub-committees. Of Northcliffe's personal services, Chalmers Mitchell wrote in the *Encyclopædia Britannica*, twelfth edition: 'The Director of Propaganda in Enemy Countries was patient in listening to the facts and arguments put before him, decisive in coming to a judgment on them, swift and powerful when action began.' The entry concluded: 'Steed's knowledge, Stuart's organizing tact, and Lord Northcliffe's driving force and far-reaching influence made Crewe House different in quality and energy from any pre-existing agency.'

Asking his support for an exhibition of British scientific products, the editor of *Nature*, Professor (later Sir Richard) Gregory, received a letter from Northcliffe undertaking to throw himself 'enthusiastically into the work of making the exhibition well known'. Wells, he wrote, had sent him a report 'which is one of the most fascinating things I have ever read on what has been done in the last four years to establish scientific industries formerly exclusively in German hands'. He enclosed a cheque towards the cost of the exhibition. 'I wish I could send more. I am shovelling money out all day long' (July 24). Northcliffe to F. W. Wile (July 24): 'Buy a sixpenny toothbrush and clean your typewriter; take your winkle pin and clear out the d's, a's, o's and other letters.'

He still did not believe that there would be an early end to the war. He told Fyfe: 'None of us here will see the end. No people of our age will be alive at the end', an example, Fyfe said, of the over-emphasis in which Northcliffe indulged since his return from America. He believed that his propaganda could offset the enemy's military superiority. Inspiring the policy of his organization, he combined his news instinct with psychological judgment. 'The Americans are pouring into France,' he told his

Crewe House staff. 'We must make the most of it. We must harp on it all the time.' When some of his colleagues showed eagerness to batter the enemy with that information, he advised caution. 'Let the Germans find out first how little they have gained by their latest attacks,' he said. 'Wait till they are feeling *down.*'

The last German onslaught in the west had opened on July 15. Ludendorff, who was in command of it, afterwards reported 'a perceptible deterioration in the spirit of the Army', and that 'our infantry did not everywhere offer a firm front' to the counter-attack launched by Foch three days later. German commanders had similar unpleasant experiences when a British surprise attack was launched on August 8, called by Ludendorff 'the black day of the German army in the history of this war'. Six or seven German divisions which had previously been regarded as efficient were completely shattered. Ludendorff recorded: 'The officers at many points lost control and allowed themselves to be swept away. . . . All that I had feared, all the perils against which I had given such endless warnings, had here become accomplished facts. Our fighting machine was no longer of high quality.' Blockade by sea, bombs from the air, the collapse of allies: Germany was encompassed by disaster, the facts of which were being driven home by an intensified British propaganda assault. In August, Crewe House caused 4,000,000 leaflets to be showered over Germany.

The leaflets told of greater air attacks to come on the German homeland, of the rapidly mounting numbers of American troops arriving in Europe, of the failure of the U-boat campaign. Those were not exaggerations. Northcliffe and his colleagues had fully concurred in Wells's dictum that 'lies are the least effective form of propaganda. The effect of a lie diminishes. The effect of a frank statement increases with the square of time that has ensued after it has been told.'

Northcliffe presided over the four-days' Inter-Allied Propaganda Conference which opened at Crewe House on August 14. It was the most important gathering held there. For the first time, high-ranking Service representatives as well as delegates from the Allied Governments sat round the conference table to discuss a general propaganda policy. Addressing them, Northcliffe made as his chief point the need for conceiving propaganda as something more than a war-winning instrument. It had an equally momentous part to play in peacemaking.

While the conference was going on, Prince Rupprecht of Bavaria was writing to Prince Max of Baden: 'Masses of propaganda leaflets have been thrown over to our troops by the enemy and are having a damaging effect on the morale of our exhausted soldiers.' Hamilton Fyfe wrote: 'We told the truth', which Lloyd George subsequently agreed was the 'deadly quality' of the Crewe House propaganda. Fyfe told how 'we addressed the Germans in the accents of comradeship; there was not one of the staff at Crewe House on whose lips those accents were false. What was emphasized and insisted on was that guilt lay upon the Imperial Government and that if this Government were overturned the German People would not be held responsible for its misdeeds.' The sincerity of three and a half months was to curdle into the cynicism of a generation.

*   *   *

Health problems continued to obtrude on Northcliffe's correspondence He had written to his mother's doctor on July 24, 1918: 'In Harley Street, I went into one of those shops with four brass plates on its door, and my chauffeur, who is a very old friend of mine, said: "Did they all have a go at you?" Had I followed your advice and stayed in bed at Poynters I should have been well long ago.' Dr Moon of Broadstairs, to Northcliffe (July 25): 'I was sorry to find how much you had gone back since you left here. I feel that at all costs you must procure fresh butcher's meat for your *daily* food', to which Humphrey-Davy replied on July 28: 'We have all noticed a considerable improvement in the Chief's appearance during the last three days since his change of diet.' It had been reported to him that there was a new exodus from the Thanet coast towns for fear of air-raids. He had ordered some articles to be written in his newspapers about the virtues of Thanet as a health resort. Moon wrote to him: 'There are now more people coming into Broadstairs than going out and we are all very grateful to you.' Soon there would be further cause for local indebtedness to him. He had started negotiations for the purchase of land which would give the district one of England's finest golf links, the North Foreland. Instructing William Graham to proceed with the legal part of the scheme, he wrote: 'I have made this great expenditure of capital in the hope of benefiting the whole Isle of Thanet and of reaping a moderate amount of interest for myself.' It cost him over £40,000.

His health liabilities of 1918 did not, seemingly, reflect a lessening of his mental resilience. Throughout the year, he was an exceptionally lively correspondent. To Hannen Swaffer, editing his *Weekly Dispatch*, he wrote: 'My dear Poet,—It is not true that all journalists want money. I am a journalist, have been since I was fifteen and a half years old, and have always detested money and the annoying people it brings around one.' Learning that the Lord Chancellor, Lord Finlay, had declared his disbelief in 'the Hidden Hand', he dictated 'a leading article for tonight' (July 28), drawing attention to 'Huns and semi-Huns who are allowed freedom of residence and occupations dangerous to the State'. It tallied with a public mood. Read today, it is like a leaf out of a war psychosis casebook. The *Daily Mail* literary editor, Macleod, came under fire again: 'What is the authority of the writer of "Naval Business Men"? How do you know it is true?' Northcliffe to the Prime Minister (August 2): 'Hoover [American food controller, later President of the United States], a friend of mine of many years, spoke to me very strongly of obstruction and intrigue at the Food Ministry. I said I would speak to you, but he did not wish it. Knowing Hoover, I have come to the conclusion that, to avoid a grave danger to the State, I ought to do so. Hoover, who loathes incompetence and politics, will, I am convinced, act drastically, and I, personally, don't want to starve.' Northcliffe to the *Daily Mail* (August 5): 'I wish we would pay more attention to British troops and to British affairs generally. This morning we gave plenty about French and American troops but very little about English troops who have played a great part in the battle. The only British people who are noticed are the Scots—and everybody at Carmelite House knows why.' Northcliffe to Beaverbrook (August 6): 'Any influence my newspapers and I possess has been derived from the fact that they are fearless as regards war winning. You have done a great deal to improve your Ministry—more than your critics know, but the war winning is hampered by your retention of numbers of men who are just as inefficient as the people in the Foreign Office, whom I am continually prodding.' One of the earliest *Answers* contributors was a sufferer from locomotor-ataxy. An appeal had been made to Northcliffe. 'See that he gets treatment. I will pay expenses.' He wrote asking Marlowe to convey his compliments to 'Miss Lawler, of our "Soldiers' Friend" department. She has answered 26,197 letters in the last six months. I suggest that her salary be raised.' He was proud of that department. 'I invented it and it is of immense public service. I shall continue it even though it demands the services of a hundred clerks.' He had heard of a group of United States Congressmen who had been officially invited to England and were 'wandering round without any attention being paid to them'. At twenty-four hours' notice, he entertained the party at his mother's house at Totteridge.

He had gone there to spend a few days before leaving for Scotland, where he hoped to breathe drier air. While he was with his mother, sleeping, as always in the bedroom next to hers, he was much occupied in going through piles of postcard entries in a competition which he had devised after a *Daily Mail* offer of a £10,000 prize to record-breaking shipyard workers had been turned down by the trade unions—'all the worse for them and their men', was his comment in a message to the office. He proposed re-offering the £10,000 to the best non-charitable war cause suggested by *Daily Mail* readers. There was to be a prize of £100 for the best suggestion. He ordered that an announcement, '£10,000 Going A-Begging', should be displayed prominently on the front page of the *Daily Mail* for August 2. His £100 prize offer drew 33,000 postcards. He wished to choose the winning postcard himself. The fourth-page sub-editor, Sidney Howard, invalided home with wounds, took the postcards to him at Totteridge. Northcliffe had put a screen across a corner of a ground-floor room as a temporary office. He and Howard worked at a card table. Northcliffe chose four winning postcards, dividing the £100 prize. One of the winning senders achieved fame later as a professional humorist and amateur politician, A. P. Herbert.

On August 16, Northcliffe was host to 150 representatives of the Dominions and foreign press, with the Prime Ministers of Canada, Australia and New Zealand, the sheriffs of the city of London, and other personages. He received the guests in what was described as 'a most beautiful pavilion', in fact a large marquee, put up in Printing House Square. 'He was in good form and treated his guests royally', wrote the same observer. Cecil Harmsworth said that 'Alfred made a fine strong speech'. He challenged the censorship again and spoke out against fatuous official reticence. 'We are rapidly being deprived of freedom of speech in this country. But I think we are still allowed to estimate. I estimate that in the past year our casualties numbered 900,000.' Also on August 16, he wrote to the Prime Minister suggesting that the enemy propaganda department should be fused into the London branch of the British War Mission, of which he was still chairman. He declared his willingness to continue in that role. It was perhaps a matter of more than greater efficiency. Ten days before, *The Times* had printed a letter written by him from Crewe House in which he credited Beaverbrook with the success of the Ministry of Information, while reaffirming that for his own department he was answerable not to that ministry but direct to the Prime Minister and the War Cabinet. The new formation would be more convincing proof of his independence. Beaverbrook was a younger man and becoming a force in journalism with his *Daily Express*, although his extraordinary energy was for the time being enrolled in the service of the Government. Northcliffe no longer ranked him among the Fleet Street trespassers. On his side, Beaverbrook let Northcliffe know in writing that he looked on him as 'the foremost figure in journalism in the whole world history of the profession'.

Some time during that month Lloyd George told his friend Riddell that he had reason to believe that Northcliffe was anxious to enter the Cabinet. Lloyd George thought that 'he would be difficult to work with if he could not have his own way'. Presumably, Lloyd George had the intimation from Beaverbrook, who has written (in *Men and Power*) that Northcliffe sought office in the middle of that year, 1918. 'He would become Lord President of the Council in a Lloyd George–Northcliffe administration.' The same source is authority for the information that on a journey to Scotland with Northcliffe 'Sir Campbell Stuart telephoned frequently on Northcliffe's instructions to ask for the Prime Minister's answer'. Lord Beaverbrook states that 'in making this overture for place and authority, Lord Northcliffe employed two intermediaries, Lord Reading and myself'. Finally, at Glasgow, says Beaverbrook, there came the Prime Minister's answer. It was 'a downright refusal'. The Northcliffe papers contain no reference to the subject, while Sir Campbell Stuart has since been unable to confirm from memory or documents the happenings described in Lord Beaverbrook's book.*

On the point of leaving for Scotland in the autumn of 1918, Northcliffe wrote to tell Sutton that he expected to be away for ten days, 'or for as long as I can get, for I am fairly done'. A letter-diary to his mother:

Wednesday.—Arriving at Stamford, found it completely changed. Alive with flying men, mostly Americans. Went to see my old school and hated it. Grantham also packed with English, Australians and Americans. *Thursday.*— Went to see Lincoln and loved it. Have been passing through a glorious harvest. Very meagre lunch and one of my coupons gone. Went on to York where Max [Pemberton] joined me. Hot as blazes. *Friday.*—We went across country through Carlisle, all full of life and money owing to the great Gretna Green munitions works, 10 miles long. A very lovely drive. Passed Gretna Bridge where Squeers kept school. *Saturday.*—Went to Moffat. Thence to St. Mary's Loch, lonely and lovely. Slept at Tibby Shiel, a little inn where Walter Scott, Hogg and other poets used to stay and drink. Walked five miles. *Sunday.*— Wet, very wet. Capital roast beef at Stirling, then on to Perth. Very dour this wet Sabbath; bells going and all off to kirk except Your Loving Firstborn.

He had proposed to F. W. Wile that, as an American, he should apply himself to producing a pamphlet for the enlightenment of American soldiers coming to England, called 'Explaining the British'. Wile wrote the pamphlet and sent a proof copy for Northcliffe's opinion, which he gave:

I hope you will not mind my saying that I am very disappointed with your 'Explaining the British'. The whole gist of the situation is that we held the fort until the Americans came, but were as unprepared for the war as they were; that we financed the Allies till the United States entered the war; that with our bare breasts we bore the onslaught of the Germans who were preparing for this particular war for nearly 50 years. I have not the time to write on all that you have omitted. . . . All that cricket reference is nonsense. The national game of Great Britain is Association Football. Cricket was nearly dead before the war. It died of the disease of elaboration, whereby a simple two hours' game was extended to a three-days' game.

* Lord Beaverbrook was under the impression that he had been told by Sir Campbell Stuart that he accompanied Northcliffe and carried on the telephone conversations. Lord Beaverbrook has since confirmed that Stuart could not have telephoned as he did not accompany Northcliffe on the journey to Scotland in 1918.

He was corresponding with the Countess of Strafford about the propriety of public references to the American troops as Yankees. 'When I was in the United States last year,' he wrote, 'they called themselves "Sammies". Objection was raised to that, and they then called themselves "Yanks", the term used in their official newspaper, *The Stars and Stripes*. They now officially ask to be called "Doughboys". We find objection to the use of the word "American" both from South Americans and Canadians. Canadians remind me that the United States is the smaller half of the North American Continent. South Americans point out that the South American States and Brazil are almost as large as the United States and Canada put together and are part of America.' When the countess asked him to dine, he replied that his throat condition prevented him from going out at night. 'If you honour me by looking in at Crewe House at any time, I shall be delighted to discuss with you the question of good relations with the United States—the chief interest of my life.'

He had gone to Scotland to protect himself 'from too much talking'. He also desired to consult Dr Walker Downie, 'one of the two leading throat doctors in Scotland'. Another item in his itinerary was a visit to the Newfoundland Forestry Corps headquarters at Kenmore. His voice was rasping but he went on dictating letters to the typist he had taken with him. To his department heads: 'I am hearing of cases (not in our business) of wounded soldiers coming back to their old jobs and being taken on at lower wages because of the pensions they are getting. I am sure you will see to it that none of your subordinates re-engage old employees on those terms.' To Moon, the Broadstairs doctor: 'I am inclined to believe that my throat is a sort of human barometer. It is certainly much affected by dampness and rain. My physical state was never better. I have seaweed baths (iodine); sleep like the giant sloth at the zoo; eat like a cormorant; drink little; smoke hardly at all, and read novels instead of dispatches; but, and it is a big BUT, my throat is still throwing down the gauntlet to Harley and Wimpole Streets.' Northcliffe to Stanley Washburn, who had been the *Times* correspondent in Russia: 'Do try to get really well. In my opinion, you have not got over your Russian experiences. . . . I, also, am a sufferer. I cannot get rid of my throat weakness. I am under the doctors' strictest orders about work. I have each day a great deal more to do than I should have.' Northcliffe to Lord Reading, on leave in London from Washington (September 5): 'Lest you fold up your tent and depart before I reach London, I write this to thank you for continually smoothing things in that complicated coming world centre on the banks of the Potomac. I am sorry that the Prime Minister has a high temperature and sore throat. I started that way in February last and, neglecting to take to my bed, as I should, have still the throat part of the trouble left.' The *Times* medical correspondent, Dr R. McNair

663

Wilson, had written to him: 'The arrival of women on the political scene seems to me to have made domestic health and child health and the care of the disabled men very burning questions', to which Northcliffe replied on October 4: 'I am paying great attention to women's votes just now', and passed on to the more compelling topic: 'Could you come to see me on Tuesday, at 3.30 p.m. at Crewe House, Curzon Street? Please bring with you a reflector for examining my throat.'

Coming home from Nairn, he had spent a day on the Clyde and wrote a note of it. 'I found that no attempt was made to interest the men in their work, and a director of one of the yards seemed quite surprised when I suggested that films should be shown of the ships the men make and what they do when they get to sea. Music would help to make the men contented', but music-while-you-work had to wait some years before becoming a feature of industrial life. He wrote to Thomas Hardy to tell him that his novels were not on sale in Perth. Mrs Hardy replied (October 16): 'If you had the opportunity of mentioning this to the Macmillans [Hardy's publishers] it would certainly be of great benefit. The sales of his books are not large, and if the booksellers will not stock them, that is hardly surprising. May I thank you for your kindness in writing to my husband and remembering him? So many of the friends who knew him years ago seem to have quite forgotten him . . . and his life is, in some respects, a very lonely one. He was delighted with your letter and immensely gratified at hearing from you. He has so often spoken with admiration of your great work for the nation, which no one appreciates more than he does.' Northcliffe pencilled in a top corner of the letter: 'Keep'. A letter to Mackenzie, his steward, concerned domestic discipline. 'Paul [his valet] is persistently late in the morning. I warned him that I would reduce his wages by £1 a month. This morning, when I was very busy, he was again late. Please, therefore, reduce him by that amount' (October 16). The next day, writing to the *Daily Mail* office, he touched another chord: 'I hope due attention will be given to the starving horses about which there is a meeting today. My attention was called to them—as people say when they write to the newspapers—at Brighton some time ago when I saw wealthy Orientals riding behind four-legged skeletons. Complaining to one of the drivers as to the state of the horses, I was told that horses had never had less food or so much work.'

Answering Mrs Thomas Hardy's letter: 'It is very surprising to me to hear that the sale of Mr Hardy's books is not great. So far as this household, and the households of most of my friends are concerned, Mr Hardy's books are part of our lives. Fortunately or unfortunately, like other true geniuses, your husband has no sense of self-propaganda.' Northcliffe enclosed a copy of the letter he had written to Sir Frederick Macmillan, Hardy's publisher (October 18):

Believing myself firmly that Hardy is the greatest writer we have produced in a hundred years, I should be very glad to use my Press to open up to as many minds as possible the enjoyment of his genius, but it is difficult to do so without an occasion. If you think of anything, I wish you would make a suggestion. The method in which much rubbish is poured out and puffed is not new, but the volume of trash is so great today, despite the paper restrictions, that great works of imagination like Hardy's are forgotten by the booksellers in their desire to meet the demand for topical novels that will be as dead as the German Empire in about the same time.

Thomas Hardy to Northcliffe:

> Max Gate,
> Dorchester.
> October 21, 1918.

Dear Lord Northcliffe,—I must send a line to thank you for your kindly interest in my books—now, alas, getting rather old, though I may say that your interest in them shows that you do not age much mentally.

I saw to my surprise in a paper on Saturday that the heroine of *A Pair of Blue Eyes* was one of my best. Tennyson also told me the same thing as being his opinion. If you ever meet with the novel, I should like to know what you think.

Believe me, with renewed thanks,

> Sincerely yours,
> THOMAS HARDY.

Northcliffe to Thomas Hardy:

> Carmelite House,
> London, E.C.4.
> October 24, 1918.

Dear Mr Hardy,—I could tell you the story of *A Pair of Blue Eyes* backwards. I am so dreadfully in love with Tess that I really cannot yield in that matter, though Charles Whibley is of the opinion of Tennyson.

> Sincerely yours,
> NORTHCLIFFE.

He dictated an excessively long letter to Sir Philip Sassoon at British general headquarters in France about the 'hopelessly insufficient' newspaper arrangements which had led 'to the gradual disappearance of the British army from the world's press'. The subject was evidently much on his mind just then.

I am now nearly well enough to return to London and hope to be there next week. I could not write before because I have had the most positive orders from a leading specialist to do absolutely nothing. . . .

I recently travelled by road from London to Scotland and passed through something like an avenue of wounded men—many blind, legless or one-legged; others armless or one-armed; yet others crippled in other ways or facially malformed. It is deplorable to think that, while we have had these terrible losses, the families of these men should know so little of what they have done in the war. The pointed lack of reference to our Army by public men in their speeches I attribute entirely to their belief that our casualties have been out of all proportion to our gains in the field. This may or may not be true. What is undoubtedly true is that the British public have had to face heavy casualties—so numerous that the newspapers are ashamed to print them; and, at the same time, the Press have had no continuous flow of descriptive writing, photographs and drawings from other correspondents and artists. . . .

Pershing is better known in this country already than Sir Douglas Haig; likewise, Mangin and Gouraud are far better known here than any British generals under him. . . .

If you will come and see me when next you are in London, I will give you my views very fully. . . .

He composed some paragraphs for his Sunday newspaper, the *Weekly Dispatch*. There was an accompanying letter to Hannen Swaffer who was in charge: 'My dear Swaffer,—Knowing that you are in trouble at the office and much criticized, I thought it would be kind to help you with the "Secret History" '—a column of political gossip.

Those who saw the Prime Minister on his return to town were rejoiced to find him in such good fettle. It is now an open secret that his place of rest was an interesting Tudor mansion [Danny Park] in the neighbourhood of Hurstpierpoint in Sussex, whither the wirepullers directed their motors from all points during Mr Lloyd George's period of seclusion.

Can it be true that that dashing *militaire*, Major Sir John Simon, is reported to be returning from the advanced trenches in France to his chambers in the Temple? This time he is not likely to escape criticism, as on previous occasions.

The reference to the Prime Minister came from personal observation. Northcliffe spent a day at Danny Park with Lloyd George. He had written to Riddell, Lloyd George's friend and press adviser, on October 3, telling him that he would be glad to help Lloyd George, but that he declined to work for the return of the 'Old Gang'.

My exact position may be summed up in the following words: I do not propose to use my newspapers and personal influence to support a new Government, elected at the most critical period in the history of the British nations, unless I know definitely and in writing, and can conscientiously approve, the personal constitution of the Government.

Lloyd George's answer, given through Riddell, was that he 'would not dream of such a thing'. Rothermere wrote to Northcliffe: 'I am glad you have made your views known to Lloyd George. Of course, at the present he may be elated at the outlook and have a fit of independence. But I think he knows the war is not nearly over. If we get through by 31st December, 1920, we shall be lucky. If he thinks this way he will now have to make arrangements in order to retain office until peace comes. With his Celtic temperament he may possibly agree with those who see the end next year, in which case you will find it difficult to bend him to your terms.' Northcliffe had heard from his brother Cecil, working in 'The Garden Suburb', as the secretariat huts adjoining 11 Downing Street were known, that Lloyd George could not be persuaded to give his mind to shipbuilding. Cecil wrote: 'Our efforts to goad him to activity have been only partly successful. It is odd that he should be so slack in this respect.'

The Prime Minister had just acquired a new suit of armour and he could now ride into the lists against his stoutest Fleet Street opponent with a more comfortable assurance. His business friends, headed by Sir Henry (soon Lord) Dalziel, Liberal member for Kirkcaldy and proprietor of *Reynolds News*, had bought the *Daily Chronicle*. That Liberal organ had been criticizing him in recent days. He had complained about its treatment of him. Now it gave him a power of attack where, before, it had not always provided defence. 'The Prime Minister has a positive craze for the Press,' *The National Review* had told its readers, 'being convinced that, given sufficient journalistic backing, nothing else matters.'

In that same week of October 1918, Northcliffe wrote to the United States Secretary of State, Franklin K. Lane: 'I had a day with the Prime Minister, inducing him to enable me greatly to increase the propaganda business. I could shorten the war if I had more support. If an opportunity should ever offer to speak to the President on the subject, I should be very grateful.'

Clement Shorter, editor of *The Sphere*, had written him a note of warning about the question of conscription in Ireland, 'which you say you are determined to promote'. It could only have the effect, Shorter believed, of bringing about wholesale bloodshed. 'We shall win the war whether Ireland be conscripted or not; but if you conscript Ireland you lose all the moral advantages of victory.' Northcliffe in reply (October 10): 'I have always heard that you have very little sense of humour, and I think that your letter shows it. Go on getting out your excellent *Sphere* and do not be so stupid.' Shorter rejoined with a blend of firmness and tact: 'I have always thought it was your own limitation that you had no sense of humour. . . . I am glad, in any case, that you admire *The Sphere* and never forget that it would not have come into existence had it not been for your kindness.'

An article in the *New York Herald* by T. P. O'Connor contained the careless statement that Lloyd George had 'added Northcliffe to his ministry'. 'T.P.' was called to order by Northcliffe, who wrote to him (October 18), after he had offered to print a correction:

I have no intention of exchanging my independence for a position in which I would have to say 'ditto' to Lord Milner, for example. What I said at the time was that I would not join the Prime Minister because I do not like his associates. If ever I take office, it will be on the distinct understanding that I join those who unswervingly desire to win the war. The Prime Minister does, but many of his satellites have frigid feet.

He informed the *Times* office on October 17: 'I have personally begged the Prime Minister to formulate a peace policy and let Washington know that we shall insist upon it, lest Wilson, sharing in the general American ignorance of our sacrifices (ignorance due to our censorship and to German propaganda), shall turn our victory into defeat for the British Empire— a possibility to be borne in mind.' The possibility was firmly in Northcliffe's mind. A message had been conveyed to him from a leading American journalist in Paris, through the British Embassy. It referred to President Wilson's proposed visit to Europe. 'If Wilson is coming it is very important that he should start soon. There are many influences in America against the war and these influences would be brought to bear in case of peace negotiations being set on foot—to obtain easy terms for the Germans. It is important that Wilson should be *away* from such influence.' Sir William Wiseman to Northcliffe (October 18): 'The Colonel [Colonel House] says he has put you on the list of those who will have to work overtime at the Peace Conference to keep things straight!' On October 25, Sir Douglas Haig wrote in his diary that Lord Derby had been to see him in Paris. 'Both he and Lord Milner agreed that the demands of the English Press (led by Northcliffe) for a humiliating peace with Germany were against the best interests of the British Empire.'

Northcliffe had been visited at Crewe House by the Air Minister, Sir William (later Lord) Weir, who at last brought his department's consent to the use of British aeroplanes and pilots for leaflet-dropping duties over Germany. Northcliffe's reception of the long-delayed permission and facilities might have been interesting to report. He had expressed some of his feelings in a message to *The Times* on October 9: 'It is not generally known that heads of the British Air Force have been frightened to allow their aviators to distribute my propaganda, despite the fact that a middle-aged man like D'Annunzio flew the whole journey to Vienna for that purpose.' He arraigned Milner in another office message as one of those responsible for 'backing down before the Germans when they impudently threaten reprisals against our leaflet-dropping airmen'. He gave it as his opinion that 'Milner is losing his grip' (October 21). The following day he wrote to the *Daily Mail*: 'It was in my mind the other day to revive the *Lusitania* picture. I am glad to see it. It is a sufficient answer to Lord Milner, Lord Lansdowne and company, and their "be kind to Germany".'

His immediate impulse, after the Air Minister's call, had been to give a print order for 3,000,000 leaflets which were scattered from the skies within the next few days. Crewe House had been unremittingly at work all through the summer with its paper-carrying balloons. It also used less spectacular and often secret methods. Much moral damage was done by a German trench newspaper edited and produced by Crewe House. Northcliffe was particularly pleased with it. He can hardly have overlooked the possibly nullifying effect on his labours of a German military success at that time. The *Times* correspondent with the American forces in France, Noble Hall, an American political journalist, who, Northcliffe made it known, had the confidence of President Wilson, wrote to him from American Press headquarters at Nancy on November 1: 'Dear Chief,— Germany is a long way from being beaten and her armies are not destroyed. It is not her military situation that is so desperate; it is the internal upheaval caused by your propaganda in enemy countries. It has shortened the war by three years.'

Ludendorff's testimony to the success of the British propaganda offensive has long been on record: 'The enemy propaganda assailed us ... with such cleverness and on such a scale that many people were no longer able to distinguish their own impressions from what the enemy propaganda had told them. . . . The shattering of public confidence at home affected our soldiers' readiness to fight. The moral attack on our home front and on the spirit of the army was now the chief weapon with which the Entente intended to conquer us, after it had lost all hope of a military victory.' The ex-Kaiser contributed his own verdict: 'Just as the English were more than our match with that terrible weapon of theirs, the tank— against which we could bring nothing of equal efficiency—so also were they superior to us with their very effective weapon of propaganda.' Lady Norah Bentinck, visiting the fallen emperor at Amerongen immediately after the war, said that she often heard Northcliffe's name spoken by him and his entourage. 'Ach, diese propaganda von Northcliffe! Es war Ko-loss-al!' While she was there a copy of *The Secrets of Crewe House* was sent for. The ex-Kaiser, Lady Norah wrote, 'regards Lord Northcliffe with intense bitterness'. It was expedient for the Kaiser, as for his commanders, to say that they had been defeated by propaganda rather than by force of arms.

* * *

On November 12, Northcliffe resigned his post as director of enemy propaganda. The Prime Minister wrote to him at once, agreeing that the armistice, announced the day before, had made the post unnecessary. 'In accepting your resignation, I wish to assure you how grateful I am for the great services you have rendered to the Allied cause while holding this important post. I have had many direct evidences of the success of your invaluable work and of the extent to which it has contributed to the dramatic collapse of the enemy strength in Austria and Germany.'

A little later there came the tribute of Colonel House: '. . . it may fairly be reported here that Northcliffe has never received the credit due to him in the winning of the war. He was tireless in his endeavours to stimulate the courage and energy of the Allies, and he succeeded in bringing them to a realization of the mighty task they had on their hands. He was among the first to grasp the significance of President Wilson's philippic against the German military autocracy, and the distinction he made between the Junkers and the German people. He caused these utterances of the American President to be sent into Germany by countless thousands, and did more than any single man, other than Wilson himself, to break down the enemy's morale behind the lines.'

Balfour, writing from the Foreign Office, regretted that his co-operation with Northcliffe had come to an end, 'though I rejoice in the cause'. There were messages from his newspaper staffs. The Compositors' and Readers' Chapel of the *Daily Mail* forwarded him a copy of a resolution, 'carried unanimously', in which he was thanked 'for the considerate manner in which we have been treated during the last four years', and complimented him on his contribution to the victory. 'We express our pride in the knowledge that we have been helping in our humble capacity.' Members of the National Society of Operative Printers and Assistants at Manchester telegraphed congratulations on his 'good work in endeavouring to bring the war to a satisfactory settlement'. The sentiments of his friends were epitomized in the letter written to him by Claude Johnson, managing director of Rolls-Royce: 'The amazing events of this month have not stunned me to such an extent as to leave me unmindful of the great and unforgettable part you have played in bringing about victory.'

On November 7, in Paris, Northcliffe had been present at a luncheon given for the staff of the *Continental Daily Mail*. Speaking of his propaganda labours, he was content to say: 'We have to some extent hastened the end.' He was well aware that the pressure of the Allied armies under Foch had been exerted toward the grand climax. Nor did he at any time claim the credit that accrued to him with the fixity of a legend as the central figure of the Crewe House organization. Lord Beaverbrook believed that he would have renounced it. The greatest satisfaction for him personally was in the knowledge that he had fought a bloodless battle, that

The Fiend: 'Welcome, Great Master! From you we shall at last learn the Science of Lying!' (From *Simplicissimus*, Munich)

his assaults against the enemy had not swollen the lists of British dead. He had not forgotten, and could never forget, what he had seen at Cambrai.

There was a letter from Wells: 'I am really sorry you are dropping the propaganda direction. But I hope it won't be the end of co-operation between us. You have the rare and precious gift of getting co-ordinated work out of discrete and narrow men.' Wells was writing on November 15, after attending a complimentary luncheon to Robert Donald, who had resigned the editorship of the *Daily Chronicle* in protest against its sale to Lloyd George's backers. Wells told Northcliffe that at the luncheon there had been 'strong denunciation' of the purchase of newspapers by 'special interests'. Donald, he reported, had been 'very good in his definition of your group of papers as being essentially journalistic in origin and spirit as distinguished from *bought* papers'.

Like others at Crewe House, where through that summer the staff had worked day and night, seven days a week, Northcliffe had taken no salary or other remuneration. One effect of their willing service was that when the bill for propaganda was made out it proved to be astonishingly small for what was accomplished: £31,460 4s. 9d. By several times that amount a grateful nation presently rewarded its generals.

Chapter Twenty-four

Changes at 'The Times'

AT 'the Chief's' prompting, the boards of his companies had marked the end of the war by giving two weeks' extra pay to all grades of the staff. An anonymous letter, in a hand later identified as that of a member of the foundry staff at Carmelite House, expressed thanks for the gesture and begged Northcliffe's acceptance of a small gift. 'I don't suppose you have had a lot given you. People think, of course, you don't need it.' The writer declared his pleasure in working on the Northcliffe newspapers, 'for it is my honest opinion that had it not been for you, and them, the war would not have been over by a long way yet', and signed himself 'Just One of Your Workmen'. Northcliffe was delighted. He had the letter reproduced on fine art paper and distributed to every department. 'The gift accompanying the letter', he revealed in an introductory note, 'was a box of very expensive Havana cigars.'

For the rank and file of his people he continued to be a good-natured presence watching from above. 'R—— [a sub-editor] must on no account be prejudiced for approaching me direct,' he wrote to the editor of the *Evening News*. 'On that aspect of affairs I am adamant.' The *bonhomie* of his office messages contained much similar reassurance. There were seniors who read them with a less warmly subjective interest. Evans and Caird, both directors, had been informed in a letter addressed to them jointly that 'the Chief' wanted 'no more arguments'; that in effect his word was thenceforward to be the unquestioned law. Pomeroy Burton had also received a letter thanking him for 'work well done' for the Paris *Daily Mail* and promising support for his claim to a knighthood 'for public services'. Taking it as a mark of favour restored, Burton had resumed sending comments and ideas to the fountainhead of decision. It may have been a shock for him to receive, towards the end of that month of rejoicing, a message telephoned from Broadstairs: 'His Lordship receives more letters from you than from all the rest of his staffs put together. If he gets any more letters he will sack you.' Peremptoriness had become intolerance. The head telephonists at Carmelite House, Printing House Square, and The Fleetway House were told: 'The Chief wishes you to warn your staff, and please convey the message to the night operators, that in the event of any private conversations taking place on any of the telephone lines, they are to be recorded.' Wareham Smith, the *Daily Mail* advertising manager, was blamed because Northcliffe had received ' a begging letter' from the King's Fund for the Disabled. 'If I get any more, I shall give the thing a sharp rap in the *Daily Mail.*' Another advertising man, Charles (later Sir Charles) F. Higham, 'had never had anything in the whole course of my career that hurt me quite as much as your message this morning. I feel sure you do not wish to hurt a fellow-being without some justification for it.' Higham, an up-and-coming advertising agent, had been successful in securing a contract for election publicity. Northcliffe thought the Prime Minister wrong in sanctioning it. 'My father died when I was eleven,' Higham wrote beseechingly out of the bitterness of his feeling as an ambitious man, 'and left me to fight life in the best way I knew how, without money and without influence. I need your help and goodwill.' Ignoring Higham's business-bringing potential, Northcliffe refused an interview: he had been prejudiced by reports of a minor lawsuit in which Higham was involved. Another correspondent was summarily rebuked through the post for having addressed a letter to him as Lord Northcliffe, not Viscount Northcliffe: 'It is a sign of ignorance.' Sir Eric Geddes, in charge of demobilization plans, was sent a letter from one of his officials who had addressed Northcliffe as 'Dear Sir'.

At the Amalgamated Press, where Sutton now virtually reigned supreme over sixty-nine periodicals, the activities of its prolific editorial staffs had never been a subject of regular comments from 'the Chief' of the kind that could make or mar the day for more vulnerable colleagues at Carmelite House or Printing House Square. While giving generous praise as well as power to Sutton, he was more extravagantly asserting his proprietorship when any new 'A.P.' production succeeded with the public. Thus it was 'my *War Illustrated*', 'my *Universal Encyclopædia*', and he had no personal part in the success of either. He was never heard to speak of 'my *Answers*', though he never failed to acknowledge it as the source of his fortunes and his Thursday visits to The Fleetway House were still dedicated to reading proofs of its articles and stories.

In Printing House Square, the self-glorification of 'my *Times*' was a continual irritant to Geoffrey Dawson, who was feeling the strain of a year in which his relationship with the chief proprietor had never been more sorely tried: 'probably the severest strain he ever had to endure', said his biographer, Sir Evelyn Wrench. The hardened directors at Carmelite House had long been immunized against Northcliffe's worst moods by the exhilarating impact of his best. Dawson was not susceptible to mercurial impulses and did not aspire to any subtlety in dealing with them. Like Marcus Aurelius, he saw no virtue in being temperamentally 'whirled about', to him a sign of instability which ill-accorded with the control of the world's greatest newspaper. He wrote to his friend Michael Furse, Bishop of St. Albans, that he had passed through 'much the worst time I've ever known . . . and I've been very near the breaking-point once or twice, both physically and professionally!' It was sufficient comment on the harassing nature of his work at *The Times*.

Northcliffe's own health state was worsening. A lump was now externally visible in his throat. Medical opinion was undecided about its character. Sir William Osler thought an operation was necessary. 'Sinister possibilities cannot be overlooked', Willert wrote to Dawson in a reference to Northcliffe's condition. When Steed saw Northcliffe in Paris the day after the armistice he was in bed 'almost gasping for breath and unable to speak above a whisper'. His inherent hypochondria no doubt aroused fears which were projected harshly on those around him. Wythe Williams, an American newspaperman who worked for the *Daily Mail*, was asked down to Broadstairs to see Northcliffe, who was telephoning to the *Times* office when he arrived. 'What have you done with the moon?' Northcliffe was shouting. 'I said the moon—the *moon*! Someone has moved the moon!' There was the clicking of a voice at the other end. Northcliffe broke in angrily: 'Well, if it's moved again, whoever does it is fired!' Williams recalled: 'He banged down the receiver and then peevishly explained that "some wretch at Printing House Square has put the weather report on a different page".' On December 2, at Elmwood, Dawson found him difficult to talk to, emphasizing his intention 'to have his own way' with *The Times* and hinting at the possibility of a parting, at which Dawson had spoken up firmly to say that he had no desire to stay if he was not wanted; and so on. The next day, Dawson saw him at the little furnished house in Buckingham Street. 'Butter wouldn't melt in his mouth.'

Yet at that period of increasing stress between them, Northcliffe was still capable of lacing his comments on *The Times*, if not those on its editor, with good humour. 'As I was walking across St. James's Park this morning, one of my toadies said "How good *The Times* has been lately". In this he was telling the truth' (November 15). 'An excellent *Times* this morning in every respect, except that the copy delivered at my house was printed on very yellow paper—not, I trust, a sign of any future tendencies in the direction or the tone of the journal' (November 16). For the final paragraph of the same communique, he dictated: 'I would like to call the attention of the staff to a very fine specimen of deferential journalism in this morning's *Morning Post*, dealing with the silver wedding of the Proprietor and Proprietrix [Lord and Lady Glenesk]. No such genuflexions took place in Printing House Square on the occasion of my silver wedding.' Reinforcing the no-fear-or-favour policy by which he had always run his newspapers, he complained to Freeman, deputy editor of *The Times*, that he was being 'plagued by people who wish their divorce cases kept out of *The Times*. Great pressure is being exercised on behalf of some well-known people who are about to appear in these cases. In one instance, an emissary was sent to me in the South of France. I trust the law department will do its full duty to all concerned in this and other legal matters' (November 17). On November 19: 'I have to thank many members of the staff for letters on the Armistice bonus. When I was a working journalist I always felt that the proprietor had too much of the swag. I am still of that opinion.'

He had commended *The Times* for giving 'full attention to labour matters, which is much to my liking' (November 14). In the *Daily Mail* he had ordered a column to be made available every day during the general election to Labour Party matters. His bulletin to that office on December 3 had the comments: 'I perceive that Bowerman, the printers' M.P., one of the most able and patriotic Labour men, who has prevented many trade disputes, is being opposed by the Coalition. Every newspaper should support him against this trickery. I am glad to see in this morning's *Daily Mail* that Mr Ernest Barker, of New College, holds my views with regard to the Coalition's un-English ways', a sniping shot at the Welsh leadership.

On November 30, Cecil Harmsworth had written in his diary: 'A message from Downing Street saying that the P.M. wants to see me urgently. Ll.G. discusses with me the reasons for Northcliffe's unfriendly attitude to him and his Govt. I tell him that I have not seen N. for many weeks and can only surmise that the reasons are (1) the fact of Ll.G's not having asked him to go to the Peace Conference and (2) the lack of any statement from Ll.G. about personnel of his Govt. in the new Parliament.' Cecil Harmsworth had found Lloyd George 'low-spirited about the Election', and had the impression that he wished 'he had not embarked on it. He paces up and down the Cabinet room more agitated in his manner than I have seen him during the war, save on one or two very critical occasions.' The diary entry continues:

After dinner I ring up N. who is at 'Elmwood', giving him hints on the situation and asking if there is any use in my coming down to Broadstairs to talk things over with him. 'Not the slightest', he says. He tells me to remind Ll.G. of a conversation between them in Paris, when N. urged him to cut adrift from his embarrassing high Tory alliances and go to the country as

'Ll.G.'. As it is, N. says, Ll.G. will be tied hand and foot to the Junkers of the Tory 'old gang' party.

After the jubilation of the streets, the bonfires and the fireworks, that had marked the end of one world war came the controversies and the bitterness that were to lead to another. The conflict that ended in 1918 had brought down the German warrior state and raised up in place of that menace a host of problems that finally wrecked the peace. Those problems were of a magnitude to exercise men's minds and try their souls far more desperately than had the equally grave but less complicated issues of 1914. They dwarfed the human intellect. They made men seem to be, after all, puppets of fate rather than creatures of destiny.

Northcliffe fumbled as blindly through the maze of post-war politics as any of the figures on the world stage at that time. New situations were forming on every side, a constantly frustrated crystallizing process in the foreign and domestic spheres, in politics, in economics, in industry. The fame of only one or two of the negotiators was soaringly enhanced. Many reputations were eclipsed and, in its public aspects, Northcliffe's was one of them. The new problems called for a more searching insight than the intuition which had served him in lesser affairs. They sharpened his awareness of his political deficiency, which handicapped him not less as an independent critic than it would have done had he been the pundit of a party. For want of it he was a periphery man, a situation that became more exasperating for him as the drama of Versailles moved to its portentous close.

* * *

On the strength of the pledge that 'those who started the war must pay to the uttermost farthing', the Coalition Government, in December 1918, was given the overwhelming support of the electorate. The pledge had been wrung from Lloyd George under pressure, largely Northcliffe's. 'He Has Not Said It' was 'banner-lined' and 'boxed' in Northcliffe's newspapers several days running. Lloyd George had originally gone to the people with the vague declaration: 'Germany shall pay up to the limit of her capacity.' A *Daily Mail* leading article on December 9 reflected Northcliffe's mistrust and impatience: 'That may mean anything or nothing.' A few days later, Lloyd George tiptoed a little farther along the Northcliffe *autobahn* to peace with justice: 'A trial for the Kaiser', and 'fullest indemnities'. Still suspicious of Liberal intentions, Northcliffe sketched a programme which he submitted to the electors for constituency use. It included 'full indemnity from Germany and ton for ton', the latter as restitution for British shipping losses. At Bristol, the Prime

Minister abandoned his qualifying clauses and came out for 'searching the pockets' of Germany for 'the whole cost of the war'.

Northcliffe's attitude to reparations was not mainly punitive, in spite of the clamour of his newspapers. He had acknowledged the sense if not the justice of a peace policy framed by his Crewe House colleagues before the armistice, a wholly reasonable document to which Hamilton Fyfe said 'he listened with attention, nodding approval now and then'. When the reading ended, Northcliffe turned to Price, his chief private secretary, and said: 'I want this to appear in all the principal newspapers of the world on the same day. Make the necessary arrangements, please.'

Political considerations apart, his American experience of the previous year had opened his eyes to certain facts of economic geography which he felt could not be ignored by the British side at the peace talks. He feared that they would be ignored if the talks were bedevilled by what he scorned as Liberal sentimentality. In spite of her certain and probable losses, Germany's economic assets were greater than those of the United Kingdom. The Ruhr coal deposits exceeded those of England, Wales and Scotland. Her iron ore resources were superior. Moreover, the Germans in retreat, with their own mines and industrial plants intact, had gone to work with high explosives and oxy-acetylene flame on the French and Belgian mines and factories with the object of eliminating future competition. Earnestly coached by H. W. Wilson in private letters and drafts for *Daily Mail* leading articles, Northcliffe believed that Germany might also eliminate British competition, notably in coal exports, by dodging reparations in cash and forcing British taxpayers to make yet more sacrifice in order to reconstruct their industries as well as to repay money borrowed from America to finance their allies. He did not suppose that in 1919 Germany could pay large sums in restitution. Neither did he doubt that, given a government of honest purpose, she had the productive power which could put her in a position to do so within a reasonable time.

He was unwilling to accept the Milner view, for example, that the Germans should be 'let off' in order that they might be free to deal with the Bolshevist threat. A letter from Stanley Washburn, the ex-correspondent of *The Times* in Russia, had warned him: 'That we are going to feel the effects of the Bolshevist movement all over the world for the next few years seems to me to be a certainty', and he had gone on to propose ways of 'forestalling this menace'. For the moment, Northcliffe was more impressed by information, which had come to him by secret sources *via* Crewe House, that the Bolshevik threat to Germany was being deliberately exaggerated by German agents who hoped to influence the peace talks. *Do not let paper exaggerate Bolshevism in news and headlines,* he had telegraphed to Marlowe of the *Daily Mail*. Marlowe had written privately to him, sounding a warning that chimed with his suspicions. 'Lloyd George is acting on the belief that Englishmen like to shake hands after a fight. So they do—but not this time.' Marlowe referred to 'the impertinence of British sportsmanship' being exploited by Lloyd George's 'international financier friends. I hope you will ram this "stunt" down his throat.' Northcliffe feared that the British people might be 'cheated'. That possibility supplied the motive for his newspaper campaigns which harassed the Coalition Government throughout the Versailles peace conference and the several conferences that followed. Underlying it was his deep mistrust of the politicians and a heightened sense of his own qualifications to speak for England in the Salle de l'Horloge. He had divined a missing element of fervour in Lloyd George's patriotism—love of England. That such a circumstance could be explained, understood, even approved by the emotionally mature, had no weight with Northcliffe, whose politics were of the heart and largely ineffectual because of it. Lloyd George had never intimidated him but he had intimidated Lloyd George and was capable for that reason of treating him with personal disrespect. During the general election preparations that December, for instance, he had taken Alexander M. Thompson, the *Daily Mail* writer on Labour, to see the Prime Minister at Downing Street. Thompson had just come back from a reporting tour of the industrial north and Northcliffe had thought that the Prime Minister should know what he had seen and heard. Lloyd George, who had not met Thompson before, clapped him genially on the back and began to talk of Russia. Northcliffe intervened almost at once. 'I didn't bring Thompson here to talk about Russia!' Thompson said that Northcliffe's voice was 'like the crack of a whip'.

A letter from Northcliffe to Dawson on November 30 was tactful but firm. It reiterated Northcliffe's mistrust of the Prime Minister, whom he accused of 'evading main issues', notably that of making Germany pay for the war. 'I do not believe that Lloyd George is a free agent in this matter and I am determined to bring pressure to bear.' He reaffirmed his sense of responsibility in the ownership of *The Times*. '. . . I must say, with much affection and respect, that I do not propose to speak any more with two voices.' *The Times* was not displaying the independence 'that it should.' It is difficult to quarrel with the proprietorial standpoint at this distance; as there defined, it was reasonable. To Dawson it was not even clear. He telephoned the next day to tell Northcliffe that he failed to understand his attitude. Northcliffe replied:

You certainly understood it in July . . . and you agreed with it. Last July you evidently saw the necessity for the formation of the strongest possible Cabinet.

Unless we speak now on the question as to who are the people the Prime Minister is going to put into his new Government, we may find that the pressure of Sir George Younger, who is a most able political boss, but who makes no pretence of dealing with any other task than that of running a party of wealth, may impose upon the Prime Minister reactionary Ministers who will not allow Lloyd George to carry out such reforms as will prevent revolution.

Northcliffe insisted that unless *The Times* spoke out strongly about the new Cabinet, 'the deadweight of the preponderance of reactionary Coalitionists will impose on the Prime Minister Old Gangers who have shown themselves in the last few years to be without prevision'. He doubted Lloyd George's power of judgment 'in selecting men who will be able to grapple with the difficulties at home and abroad which will confront this country in 1919—particularly difficulties in regard to the United States'.

I personally put this question to the Prime Minister in writing two months ago. I was promised a reply, but never got it. I put it to him again in Paris. Turning very red in the face, he 'side-slipped', saying that he was in a great hurry to catch his train, which he certainly was.

Northcliffe thought it necessary to remind the editor that there had been moments in history when *The Times* had rendered great service to the nation. He proposed that, as editor, Dawson could follow in that tradition by requiring the Prime Minister to tell the country who were the men it was being asked to vote for. 'If I have not made myself plain, then I am afraid that I am incapable of coherence', and a distracted editor might have acquiesced in the suggestion. Dawson felt that unreason prevailed in Northcliffe's mind. He could hardly have cited Northcliffe's argument on that occasion as evidence of it. The truth was that under Dawson *The Times* had become Northcliffe's greatest worry: elsewhere his tensions were less marked not only because at Carmelite House, for example, he ruled by the Napoleonic precept: 'The emperor has commanded. . . .' To the domination of the *Times* policy by that of the *Dail Mail* Dawson was implacably opposed: even if the precedence were reversed he would still have been resentful of the alliance. There was the heart of the matter. Dawson was borne along his course as anonymous public mentor by the conviction that he and his friends were 'in the right', a company of apostolic spirits who alone had the secrets of shaping policy and guiding government. Dawson did not consider that Northcliffe was qualified to assist those processes. His self-satisfaction, and that of some others in his circle, was immense. He was not vain in the cheap sense, but he was invincibly sure of himself. He relished the 'feel' of power, while desiring none of its trappings.

Cecil Harmsworth was sent for again by Lloyd George at that time to discuss Northcliffe. Cecil wrote that 'Ll.G. was gravely perturbed by N's opposition'. For his part, Northcliffe was 'genuinely perturbed at the electoral prospects', his brother told the Prime Minister. 'He evidently thinks that the old reactionaries—Walter Long, Austen Chamberlain, etc., are all more firmly fixed in the saddle than ever; that you will not be strong enough to master them and that an unprogressive Coalition may result in a dangerous feeling in the country.' That Northcliffe's price for the support of his newspapers was unreasonable remains a debating point. Winston Churchill had deemed it not improper to make a similar inquiry about the men with whom he might have to serve before deciding on his own course in that election. He, too, received a dusty answer. On November 27, Northcliffe had written to *The Times*:

The Staff should know that the Prime Minister originally told me that he would form a new Government of experts and go to the country immediately the new register became legal. When I was in Paris a few weeks ago, he pursued me vigorously, and when I saw him I asked for the names of the members of the new Government. I did not then know that Sir George Younger, the Conservative wire-puller and much the ablest person in English party politics, had frightened the Prime Minister, as he did in December, 1916. At this Paris interview, to my surprise the Prime Minister told me that he was unable to give me the names of the members of the new Government, to which I replied that I would not support a Government with whose personnel I was unacquainted, or as a well-known former supporter of Mr Lloyd George who holds my views, bluntly remarked, would not take shares in a company which declined to make public the names of its directors. When this proposed company is formed, it will be found that the directors are not, with two exceptions, experts in anything except politics.

There was influential, if not powerful, backing for him within the political inner circle. He told the *Times* office later that month: 'I happen to know that Lord Beaverbrook did his utmost to urge Mr Lloyd George to follow last summer's advice of *The Times* as to getting rid of "deadheads", but in vain.'

The rejection of Northcliffe's demand for information about the new Government marked the last phase in the estrangement between him and Lloyd George, who had thought it time to tell him to 'go to hell'. Northcliffe's manner after taking A. M. Thompson to Lloyd George for a second meeting suggested that there had been a clash on that occasion. Thompson left the Cabinet room before Northcliffe and waited for him in the hall of No. 10. 'In a few moments he came out or rather burst out like a volcanic eruption and, sweeping past me without a word, entered his car and drove away, evidently quite oblivious of my existence.' Another round in the duel came a few days before the people went to the poll that December. Northcliffe telegraphed to Lloyd George at Leeds urging him to be finally explicit on the subject of reparations and hinting that the alternative would be serious trouble in the country. Lloyd George's telegraphed reply ended with the admonition: *Don't be always making mischief*, a scolding which, coming from that quarter, seemed to stir echoes from the weird Druidic past.

Cecil Harmsworth's belief that 'the real cause of Northcliffe's resentment against Lloyd George was the refusal to associate him with the work of the Peace Conference', was also Lloyd George's. In *The Truth About the Peace Treaties* (1938), Lloyd George wrote: 'He was visibly astonished and upset by my declining to accede to his request.' Wickham Steed, in *Through Thirty Years*, did not accept the theory. 'He never gave me any hint that he cherished such an ambition', and Steed recorded that Northcliffe 'was far too unwell to undertake work so exacting'. Northcliffe himself told J. A. Spender that he 'greatly resented' the rumours which assigned that cause to his breach with Lloyd George. The originators of it, Northcliffe said, knew perfectly well that he was threatened with a serious operation at that time and that his doctors had told him he must do nothing else but prepare for it. Riddell, the newspaper proprietor, wrote in his diary that Lloyd George told him that 'N. wanted to be one of the British delegates at the Peace Conference', and that Lloyd George had said that he could not agree 'and would rather cease to be P.M.' Riddell concluded his diary note: 'Where Ll.G. got his information from he could not say.'

He may have had it from the editor of *The Times*. Dawson wrote in some notes on his last weeks in the editorial chair that Northcliffe had told him on two occasions 'that he hoped to make such a position for himself as to be a British Plenipotentiary at the Peace Conference'. That aspiration, Dawson mentioned, had been expressed 'much earlier'. Though often genial in manner and given to occasional flippancies, Dawson was a serious-minded man, capable of missing an inflexion. The *Times* history quotes Steed as having written to Dawson on August 15, 1938: '... I have asked Ll.G. about it and he never mentioned N's alleged ambition to be an official delegate to the Peace Conference. He said that "N. wanted to dictate", and that he (Ll.G.) would not be dictated to. The proposal N. meant to make to Ll.G. was something quite different; and when I explained it to Ll.G. some years ago, Ll.G. said he had never understood it.'

The 'quite different' proposal was a scheme for promoting peace propaganda in Germany following the armistice. Northcliffe hoped to secure French support for it, but first needed Lloyd George's approval. Sir Auckland (later Lord) Geddes saw both men on the day of the final break between them. He later wrote: 'Each described the other as impossible and intolerable. They were both very tired men and had been getting on one another's nerves for some time.' Geddes did not believe that Northcliffe had asked for a seat at the peace conference. 'If he had made such a request, Lloyd George would have blurted it out all over the place and there would have been a cloud of witnesses. When Ll.G. was thoroughly angry with anybody his utterances were not marked by what is ordinarily called discretion' (Letter to Geoffrey Harmsworth, December 9, 1953).

What emerged from the feverish political cross-talk was the fact that Lloyd George had led Northcliffe to think that his presence in Paris at the time of the peace conference might be desirable. He had suggested that Northcliffe should take a house there, to be available, with his Crewe House staff, for consultations about peace propaganda. Leaving Wickham Steed to make the arrangements, Northcliffe went to London on November 5. Steed told in his autobiography, *Through Thirty Years*, what happened, that when Northcliffe returned to Paris on November 12 he found the situation altered. 'Mr Lloyd George had changed his mind and had decided to put his friend, Sir George (afterwards Lord) Riddell, in charge of British publicity arrangements.'

Northcliffe had procured world-wide publication of his views on the peace-making which could have given offence by its unfortunate timing and the self-emphasis which sober-minded men deemed extravagant. Dawson had little doubt that the purpose was 'to advertise himself as the real author of British peace terms'. Sir Robert Donald, of the *Daily Chronicle*, who had a place on the Crewe House committee, wrote that Northcliffe 'wanted quick action' and to 'force the pace' in deciding a post-war reconstruction policy. Intentionally or not, the style of his declaration suggested that he wanted not simply to influence the proceedings at Versailles but to take command of them. As for his being one of the chosen five at the conference table, he can hardly have been so blinded by self-interest as to be unable to see the difficulty for the Prime Minister of dropping a Cabinet colleague in his favour or of making an appointment which would outrage other sections of the Press. The *History of The Times* may be quoted as giving an acceptable verdict: 'No written evidence that Northcliffe demanded the place of a full delegate at the Peace Conference has survived. That Northcliffe was conscious of making such a demand is improbable.'

*　　　*　　　*

Northcliffe to the *Daily Mail* office, December 9, 1918: 'Anglo-American relations are in a very delicate condition, and I suggest that the utmost care is used in what we print both from and about the United States.' Northcliffe to *The Times*, same date: 'Anglo-American relations are in a very delicate position.' He returned to the subject in his memorandum to *The Times* of December 11: 'Whoever wrote this morning's first leader understands something of the deep anxiety felt by those behind the scenes

in connection with British and American relations at the present moment.'
On December 12 he told the *Times* staff that he had received letters from
American friends who were anxious about the situation. One of them was
Thomas Lamont, the Wall Street banker, who had written forcibly to
him on December 5: 'The permanent peace of the world is at stake.' He
foresaw attempts at the Paris conference to 'twist the lion's tail'. Democrat
extremists behind President Wilson would insist on his firmness in the
matter of the freedom of the seas, which one of the President's Fourteen
Points for peace proposed to restrict. In his parting address to Congress,
the President had given the American navy the chief credit for trans-
porting the American armies to Europe, though the safety of the operation
was largely a British responsibility. 'The bulk of the American people
know nothing about our war efforts', Northcliffe told *The Times*: 'Very
few people realize that something like a struggle for world supremacy
between Great Britain and the United States will begin to be waged next
week from Paris.'

On December 13, he went to Paris 'to find out what is going on'.
H. W. Wilson referred to the visit as 'a mission of the utmost importance
and delicacy', which, allowing for Wilson's devotion, it may have been,
seeing that it resulted in an exclusive interview with the American
President. Once again, House had been the good friend. The interview
was given the prominence of five columns in *The Times* on December 21.
Northcliffe ordered it to be made available to other newspapers at home
and abroad. Its most significant paragraphs were those in which the President took note of 'the special international questions which arise from
the fact of Britain's peculiar position as an Island Empire'. By recognizing
the island situation of Great Britain, the American President dispelled
doubts and suspicions that had sprung from Number 2 of his Fourteen
Points: 'Absolute freedom of navigation upon the seas outside territorial
waters, alike in peace and war, except as the seas may be closed in whole
or part by international action.' It meant that the fleets would be deprived of all except the power of passive defence. It would tip the balance
in favour of the continental countries with larger armies.

Northcliffe outlined the British case to the President, believing from
his personal dealings with him that he could be made to see the sense
of it. There had been fears that Point Two would split the conference at
Paris. The Associated Press of America news agency representative in
Paris, Charles H. Thomson, wrote that by impressing the President with
the British view Northcliffe rendered 'one of those quiet but inestimable
services to his country'.

While he was in Paris, Northcliffe wrote to his brother Cecil saying
that he had spent some of his time 'in the midst of the returning soldiers
at the British Leave Club, a wonderful organization inaugurated by my

Daily Mail'. Thousands of men passed through the club every week and, he reported, most of them were filled with discontent.

It is my knowledge of this state of affairs and of the public mind in England that made me adopt the line I did in the Election. I believe that the Government of Tory reactionaries that we are going to have will be a direct incentive to dangerous discontent.

If you have watched my recent course of action, you will understand how anxious I am that these returning soldiers should get justice. They have been through horrors unspeakable, unwritable, unbelievable, and they must not be fobbed off with more promises and speeches. I will see to it that they are not so treated.

I hope you will get in with a good majority and that you will not lick the Party's boots. Take the line of sane and intellectual Labour, as befits the times.

Lord Reading wrote to Northcliffe: 'I hope you received my message congratulating you very heartily on *The Times* interview with the President—above all, I liked its tone. Altogether it was very valuable and opportune.' Dawson did not share Reading's approval. His opinion of the 'famous interview' was that it was 'appalling' in its presentation, 'another instance of Northcliffe's desire for self-aggrandisement'. His dislike of it would have been stiffened by a sight of the letter from Northcliffe to House, which twice referred to 'my *Times*', and he would certainly have thought his view justified had he seen the message passed to Marlowe by Humphrey-Davy on December 26: 'The Chief wants his writers to model their style on the descriptive writing in his book, *At the War*.' To Dawson, practically any display of egotism could be a morbid symptom. By that time, he was citing megalomania as the only possible explanation of Northcliffe's behaviour. Membership of a university *corps d'élite* was no guarantee of sensitiveness to latent tragedy.

* * *

Christmas 1918 was near. Northcliffe gave up a morning to going through his domestic accounts with Mackenzie, his steward. 'Estimated income for year ending March 31, 1919: £97,000, after payment of £44,624 tax.' He complained that 'Super-Tax and Excess Profits Tax have reduced what was a very large income to a bare sufficiency to cover my personal expenditure and the handsome allowances I make to a large family. I have no intention of ending my days in consuming my capital' (letter to John Walter, March 31, 1919). He had given cash presents amounting to £4,807, plus charity subscriptions of £3,510, with the Salvation Army still heading the list. He had paid another year's expenses of Lady Northcliffe's Hospital for Officers. He went through the annual list of recipients of his Christmas bounty in the form of cheques and banknotes. There were sixty-three names in it, not including relatives and his oldest friends, such as Mrs Jealous and Max Pemberton. The last-named had written to say that he was 'in a very tight place and at a loss to know how to carry on'. There were £25 cheques for young serving officers in the Army, among them Alfred Pemberton, Andrew Hands, son of Charles Hands, the *Daily Mail* reporter, and Harold Snoad, of the secretarial staff. He had given an extra donation 'to the poor of all denominations' at St. Peters. There were Christmas boxes for domestic staffs, gardeners, chauffeurs, golf caddies, the clerks at Coutts', servants of the Beefsteak Club, station masters, messengers at Carmelite House, Printing House Square and The Fleetway House. He ticked for renewal his subscriptions to the English Speaking Union, the Hakluyt Society, the Irish Literary Society, the Royal Geographical Society, the Colonial Institute and other bodies.

'Pardon me for taking the liberty of writing to you, but I feel it is my duty to thank you for your goodness to my sister, Olive C——.' It was a postscript (December 6) to another tale of Northcliffe's generosity to persons having no claim upon it save that of human feeling. A young woman who left the staff to marry a Canadian soldier had been deserted. Distracted, she appealed to 'the Chief'. He considered that she had been 'outrageously treated', and tried to get redress for her through the Canadian authorities. Through most of the year he contributed to her support; a wholly disinterested act of kindness. There was a considerable correspondence to be dealt with before he went away to a more soothing climate. He had just bought a lease of 1 Carlton Gardens, Pall Mall: 'unexpired term, 35 years, ground rent, £510 per annum', for £32,000. It was a Nash house with a notable past. Prince Louis Napoleon had rented it in 1839 from 'Prosperity' Robinson, M.P., who became the first Lord Ripon. Gladstone had occupied it. In these latter days it is the official residence of the British Foreign Secretary. Among the contents of the small green deed-box was a letter, dated December 24, from John Walter, sending Christmas greetings from Madrid. 'Especially must I thank you for having brought the Paper safely through all the difficulties of the war to a pitch of prosperity of which nobody would have dreamed a few years ago.' There was a letter from a lady-in-waiting to Her Majesty the Queen. 'Please forgive my troubling you, but from several quarters I hear people wishing that thanks could be given in all the papers for all that the Government has done during the war, so I thought I would like to ask you if it would be possible to do this in your papers?' Northcliffe appears to have composed his reply with some deliberation, as if he assumed that it might be seen by more exalted eyes at Court.

The Times,
Printing House Square, E.C.
29th December, 1918.

Dear Lady Bertha Dawkins,—I would have replied to your kind letter before, had I not been somewhat indisposed.

I think, on the whole, that the late Government did well, but may I say that it required an immense amount of urging to get it to move?

We now have a Government in process of formation which may be a replica of the old one, in which case I look for an accentuation of the grave unrest that prevails in England today. That unrest is in no way Bolshevik or anti-Monarchial [sic]. It is, in my view, caused by the inability of Governments to understand the legitimate aspirations of the people, together with the fact that the pound sterling is only worth about seven shillings to those who buy, as do the poor, in small quantities. . . .

Moreover, I feel equally certain that, unless the new Government has within it a sufficiency of Labour representatives, men who really know what the miner, the agricultural worker and the shipyard and cotton operative wants, there will be trouble in England of a nature that we have not had for a hundred years.

If the Prime Minister has the courage to ignore what are called Party 'claims' to office and appoints such men as I have indicated, my newspapers will ungrudgingly praise his Ministry. On the other hand, if he does not, we shall do our best to throw light on the situation in the hope that publicity will direct attention to wrongs that must be righted.

Yours sincerely,
NORTHCLIFFE.

The gallant defender of Kut, in Mesopotamia, General Townshend, had to be courteously rebuffed in his desire that Northcliffe should air his grievances against the War Office. Having referred to an 'indiscreet utterance attributed to you in a French evening paper of repute', Northcliffe pointed out to him: 'There is a very proper and necessary rule in the King's Regulations—binding upon all in the Services from privates upward—as to non-communication with the Press.' Northcliffe to Austin Harrison, editor of The English Review: 'Many thanks for your kind letter, which, however, gives me too much credit. Everyone has helped to win the war.' Harrison had insisted: 'Knowing much that is not known generally, I consider that you more than any other man in this country have really helped conspicuously and decisively towards the great Allied victory.' Northcliffe to the Daily Mail office (December 27): 'Someone described Mrs Woodrow Wilson as a pleasant looking little woman. She is a distinctly handsome lady of ample proportions.' The same, December 30: 'I liked Mr Clynes' Labour article. . . . The King was very pleased with Saturday's leader about Princess Patricia.' To The Times, December 30: 'I have my doubts as to the Prime Minister's courage to form a Cabinet independent of Party claims. From what I know of the desire and drastic methods of Sir George Younger he will stand no democratic trifling. His well-known Edinburgh ale is a very strong brew.' Northcliffe to Marlowe, ill from overwork: 'I want you to know how grieved everyone is at your trouble and how hopeful we all are of your return to health.' Northcliffe himself was moving towards an ominous state of exhaustion. Yet, out of the weariness of his own mind and body, Geoffrey Dawson could only see him then 'as a man whom at heart I regard as a fraud!' (letter to Dr Furse, December 23, 1918).

Northcliffe to Rothermere:

The Times,
Printing House Square,
E.C.
December 31, 1918.

My dear Harold,—I am greatly looking forward to being at your beautiful villa for a week of two. I will start as soon as the doctors have tested a new vaccine on me which they think may improve the condition of my throat which has now been out of order for more than ten months. During this time I must have coughed at least two hundred times daily, the grand total of which your arithmetical mind can easily assess. It is not the daily part that I mind so much, but the nocturnal noise which spoils my sleep. Everybody has something and I must not grumble.

The Prime Minister has an immense opportunity, but I doubt whether he will take it. The country would support him in a clean sweep of the Old Gang people. The nation would welcome it.

Your affectionate
ALFRED.

He wrote to Marlowe on January 1: 'I shall not come back until my throat is normal. I have now been afflicted—and it is a real affliction—since February, 1918.' In the letter, he invited Marlowe to be 'Chairman of our Associated Newspapers. It does not mean any extra work but it will mean some titular distinction which I should like you to have from this or the next Government.'* The doctors, he said, were sending him to the south of France. 'I may be away three months.' He rebuked Burton and Caird for their 'constant restlessness about money matters' (January 2).

The Secretary of the Labour Party to Lord Northcliffe:

33, Eccleston Square,
London, S.W.1.
3rd January, 1919.

Dear Lord Northcliffe,—At a meeting of the Executive Committee of the Labour Party held to-day to review the situation arising out of the recent general election, I was instructed to tender you the thanks of the Committee

* Marlowe did not receive a title.

688

on your generous offer of the free and uncontrolled use of the daily column in the *Daily Mail* during the period of the election. The Committee recognize the value of the opportunity afforded the Labour Party to place its policy before the large section of the public represented by the readers of your paper, and they appreciate the spirit of fair play which prompted you to place the space at the disposal of a party which is at present so seriously handicapped by the non-existence of an official Labour daily newspaper.

Yours sincerely,
ARTHUR HENDERSON.

A few days before, a Bedford Row solicitor and parliamentary agent had sent Northcliffe 'a sonnet, as an honest expression of what a good many of us feel'. The sender, W. J. Wenham, wrote as a member of the Labour Party.

LABOUR TO LORD NORTHCLIFFE

Not ours, my Lord, to yield you servile praise
In that you lately lent, of your own choice,
Your giant megaphone to Labour's voice.
This Jericho falls not in fifteen days
Even to such a trumpet. We must sap and raze.
Yet no mean blast was this in this mean fight,
And, as its challenge rang along the night
Through which the sun of freedom bright shall blaze,
Methinks you, prescient, knew it pealed the knell
Of cruel wrongs; and, gazing through the gloom,
Saw shapes of captains, calm, indomitable,
Riding to where our foes' alarm-guns boom,
While, on your ear, a mighty rhythm fell—
The tramp of Labour's army, vast as doom.

Northcliffe's response to the compliment is not on record; the degree of his appreciation was indicated by a pencilled note: 'Keep This'. No Labour supporter was ungenerous enough, it seems, to question Northcliffe's motives. Allowing for his sympathy with the workers' claims and hopes, and his editorial flair, the strength of his willingness, if not his wish, to embarrass Lloyd George might have been worth assessing.

His practical attitude to Labour was tested a day or two before he left London. An *Evening News* van driver was fined for drunkenness at the West London Police Court. The Carmelite House management dismissed the man. His union protested. When trouble looked like developing, Northcliffe was appealed to. His verdict was that he would be no party to the employment of a man who could fairly be regarded as a public danger and announced that rather than retain the man he would stop publishing newspapers. The affair was settled by his taking a more judicial view. He agreed to the man's reinstatement on condition that 'he takes the pledge for twelve months and is willing to do work not connected with machines'. To a letter from the man's representatives thanking him 'for the just and impartial decision', he replied: 'Please do not think that I was at all annoyed by the bringing forward of the recent little dispute. It was the first that we have ever had in our business since we started it. I realize that the matter was merely one of paying a little too much attention to comradeship and not enough to public interest.' The men's representative (Father of the Chapel) in the *Evening News* publishing and distributing department trusted that 'your lordship will not construe this incident as a sign of discontent in any shape or form'. The printing trade would be the focus of historic tensions between capital and labour in the years not far ahead. But now the men were coming back from the war to jobs that gave them fuller pay packets than the Services could provide and they were not yet ready to assert themselves as claimants of a more ample inheritance. Northcliffe's outlook was that of an impregnable employer whose benevolence did not encompass the hardships implicit in the exercise of his power. For the moment, he was in full command of the situation. He had stopped a strike.

Northcliffe to his mother:

8th January, 1919.

My dearest Mum,—Oh my, what an uncomfortable journey this is! A fairly rapid dash in an overcrowded train to Folkestone. A long, long wait while an amazing number of people pour into the ship. Goodness only knows where they are stowed away. After an hour and a half delay before starting a couple of hours of rough and tumble in the Channel. The scenes and sounds in the ladies' room, I understand, are not particularly savoury. At Boulogne more wait, wait, wait. Finally, after a long train journey and a slapdash dinner with sweet champagne in an overheated dining car, we groan on our way to Paris. Time— 12 hours and 10 minutes, rather longer than Charles Dickens used to take more than eighty years ago.

Your Firstborn.

Hurrying out to Fontainebleau, 'to avoid talking in Paris', while the blue Rolls-Royce was being made ready for the long journey south, he was handed an hotel bill which made him laugh. '£120 for three days: myself, Paul, and Humpty-Dumpty. Service excellent; waiters with manners like bishops' chaplains. Still, £40 a day ample.'

He lashed the Carmelite House editors for the inadequacy of their arrangements for reporting the coming peace conference—'the most complicated world drama that has ever been acted'. Doubting whether any of them had grasped the significance of it, he set about pulling their 'wretched little plans' to pieces and reconstituting them 'in the way we would have tackled this thing when we were twenty years younger'. He warned them, as he prepared to leave for the Riviera (January 8): 'You will get some hot wires from the south of France.'

* * *

White houses dazzling amid orange groves under a blue sky; beyond, a shimmering blue sea: Rothermere's villa, La Dragonnière, Cap Martin, was an incomparable setting for a rest cure, but his brother Northcliffe could not rest. The more he relaxed physically, the more active he was mentally. Two days after arriving in a landscape which he was delighted to hear an American soldier on leave there say made California 'look like thirty cents', he summoned 'Humpty-Dumpty' to take down his dictation of notes which, continued day by day, were in due course bound up and presented to his mother under the title of 'Lord Northcliffe's Throat Diary'. It reported the hardly beguiling symptoms and sensations of a man with a chronic cough which went with him by day and night like a vengeful pursuer.

Wednesday, 22nd January.—Put my face in very hot water to relieve congestion of the sinuses. *Thursday, 23rd January.*—Usual spraying at doctor's, with injection of arsenic and something else. I had a violent fit of coughing. *Saturday, 25th January.*—Had London vaccine and did not feel very well all the afternoon. *Monday, 27th January.*—I can see no change in my condition, except that the doctor, supported by my other symptoms, says that I am looking better. *Wednesday, 29th January.*—I am 20% anaemic and have an immense excess of uric acid. Very bad coughing. *Monday, 17th February.*—Adrenalin injection today. Unfortunately I could not tell the result owing to the fact that I had taken too much. My voice disappeared.

The self-emphasis was no more intense than that of most diarists. Many of his letters of those months referred directly or parenthetically to the state of his health and while his correspondents may have been sympathetic, he perhaps took their solicitude too seriously. But Northcliffe was becoming increasingly vulnerable to the lay students of psychology. They shook their heads knowingly on seeing his telegram to the *Times* Paris correspondent, George Adam, on January 21: *You may be chosen to represent me at conference stop hope you will realize honour and great responsibility stop Chief.* His doctors, on the other hand, were entertained in their varying degrees by a letter he wrote to them that same week. Sir Milsom Rees, the ear, nose and throat specialist, headed a list of eight consultants who received the letter:

I daresay you have heard of the proposal of the profession to erect a statue to me, and I hope I shall see your name on the influential committee that is to be formed.

It is suggested, I understand, that the figure should be one of the size known as 'heroic' and that the monument is to be placed in Cavendish Square. I hear that I am to be represented as standing erect with the right arm extended and pointing in the direction of Harley and Wimpole Streets and the left hanging by the side nonchalantly clasping an empty cheque book.

On one side of the plinth, which is to be of rich gilt, the following inscription, I am told, is to appear:

'*In the multitude of counsellors there is wisdom*',

while on the remaining three sides are to be engraved the names of the forty distinguished quacktitioners who have participated.

The doctors took the joke well enough, though of the quality of their appreciation we cannot be sure. Sir Milsom Rees was 'highly amused'. Dr McNair Wilson, the *Times* medical correspondent, thought 'quacktitioners' a 'lovely word'. Northcliffe wrote to him:

They say that 'whosoever hath himself for a patient hath a fool for his doctor', but is he any worse off than the victim of the guinea-grabbers of Harpole and Wimpley Streets?

As for operations, had I succumbed to suggestions of this sort, there would have been nothing left of me to operate upon. Arbuthnot Lane's suggestion ('removing the large bowel *in toto*') is not more radical than some of the others. You may tell me that many people think I have a 'kink', but I do not think it is in that part of the anatomy in which he specializes.

Please do not mind my chaff, but, really, Harpole and Wimpley Streets make me laugh. I daresay your friend Mackenzie [Sir James Mackenzie] himself laughs too, sometimes. I am really relying very much more on Dr Sol, a well-known practitioner in these parts.

In another department of his affairs where the atmosphere was unfavourable to humour of the sort in which he was indulging at the doctors' expense, badinage would have withered as if in a chilly blast. He was sending Dawson, at *The Times*, a series of telegrams which were entirely centred in the construction of the new Government as a result of Lloyd George's victory at the polls. He had written to Rothermere on January 13 expressing disappointment at Lloyd George's treatment of their brother Cecil, who had been given an under-secretaryship at the Foreign Office, 'despite his past heavy work and your special message about him to the Prime Minister. I am pretty sure', Northcliffe wrote, 'that if A.J.B. [Balfour] were asked, he would make him Assistant Secretary. Cecil will not put himself forward.' There was a passing reference to a prominent member of Lloyd George's entourage. 'I had a talk with Eric Geddes the day before I left England. Unless I am much mistaken, he is a greatly overrated man.' Northcliffe to Caird:

> La Dragonnière,
> Cap Martin.
> 12th January, 1919.

My dear Caird,—. . . Since August last I conducted a campaign regarding the General Election. The original plan was that the Prime Minister should go to the country on his own, forming a Government of 'All The Talents' and Parties beforehand. I was asked to join it, but declined. Then Sir George Younger stampeded the Prime Minister, and in *The Times* and the *Daily Mail* I did my utmost to point out what would happen if the Prime Minister was again frightened by Younger & Co., as he formerly had been when he formed his Ministry in December 1916.

Eventually even worse than what I foretold has happened. A Government that is a scandal has been formed, and yet the *Daily Mail* complacently licks its boots. It will be many a long year before I forget this. . . . That is why I wired yesterday that in my absence and in that of Marlowe the paper has ceased to be the *Daily Mail*.

I hope all will understand that I shall be watching the *Daily Mail* with double extra compound magnifying glasses. I shall have nothing else to do.

> Yours sincerely,
> CHIEF.

Dawson's position *vis-à-vis The Times* had become irksome to Northcliffe and the *History of The Times* suggests that the prelude to the breaking-point was the outpouring of criticism by telegram and letter from Northcliffe in those first weeks of 1919. Many of Dawson's diary entries for the period were replicas of the notes that he had made on Northcliffe's moods and conduct in 1913–14. 'N. rampaging on the telephone.' 'N. very troublesome.' 'I thought N. rather unbalanced.' 'Another day of great strain.' 'N. obviously ill and nervy.' Northcliffe had been particularly irritated by Dawson's attitude to the new Government and still more by the advance of Lloyd George in public esteem as shown by the general election result. He saw in the job given to Cecil Harmsworth one more 'cunning Welsh' attempt to placate him. 'The giving of office either to brothers or friends will not move me to the extent of a single colon or comma [Northcliffe to Dawson, January 19, 1919]. I now earnestly commend you to a study of Welsh character and history.' The patient who made fun of his doctors seemed to have no affinity with the proprietor who made such heavy going with the editor of *The Times*.

Matters came rapidly to a head over the editorship. The official history of *The Times* takes the line that Northcliffe planned and contrived the break with Dawson. Proprietorial nagging was wearing Dawson down. At the back of it was Northcliffe's dwindling faith in Dawson's loyalty to him, a state of doubt encouraged by Rothermere, who did not like Dawson. Northcliffe had always liked him. There is no evidence in what passed between them in the crucial days of January and February 1919 that Dawson had finally forfeited his personal regard. *I do not propose to terminate long pleasant relationship by acrimonious discussion*, was the gist of a telegram to Dawson on February 7.

Dawson was a member of what in these later days is identified as the Establishment, that incorporate thinking organism dedicated to the survival of England through any and every crisis of history and abrogating to itself, as some outsiders have thought, an influence capable of transcending the executive power. As one of the outsiders, but a no less passionate promoter of what he considered to be the best interests of England, Northcliffe was at the same time a natural rebel against any such concept of secret authority.

Dawson's undoing as editor of *The Times* was his resort to circles, social and political, in which there were men who were inimical to Northcliffe and whose views Northcliffe mistrusted. Milner was one of them, Waldorf Astor, of *The Observer*, another; and there was Dawson's position *vis-à-vis* Lloyd George, which had lately incurred Northcliffe's displeasure. A *Times* leading article of December 12, 1918, was full of praise of the Prime Minister. Above all, word was coming back to Northcliffe, sometimes through Rothermere, of indiscreet talk by Dawson within that circle of his friends, not every one of whom was as respectful of his confidence as he thought. Northcliffe considered that an editor's place was at his desk and not at the dinner tables of Mayfair. 'I am not a believer in the dining-out theory of the editorship of *The Times*,' he told G. S. Freeman of that newspaper. 'A very shrewd old woman, Lady Dorothy Nevill, told me that for many years Delane sank into the position of "an old Irish snob", to use her own words—pulled hither and thither by the exalted ones with whom he consorted.' He thought Dawson 'a child in the hands of skilled intriguers', a rash opinion which he communicated to Wickham Steed.

Whatever the faults on both sides, such a divergence between proprietor and editor could not continue; and the good of the paper had never ceased to be as important to Dawson as to Northcliffe. Dawson was one of the great servants of *The Times*. His standing in the editorial succession has since been debated. Some who saw his work at close quarters have held that he was a good editor not in spite of Northcliffe but because of him. Such a view ignores the truth that Dawson was one of the ablest men in England—Northcliffe himself used those words in speaking of him—and that the *Times* editorship fitted him like a glove. He was the right man in the right place—and he could have had any one of several places, in all of which he would have been right. He appeared to some to be vain in his complete self-assurance, which, incidentally, made him attractive to women. He had no touch of genius, none of Northcliffe's mercurial flair or intuition. He had no vices. He was a rock of integrity. While being attracted by Northcliffe's charm, he found it galling to have to accept him as the arbiter of his journalistic career. They were divergent men whose temperaments were bound to clash.

What the *History of The Times* refers to as 'the turning point in their relations'* came in the last days of January 1919. Northcliffe found cause for complaint in Dawson's not having acted on his suggestion that *The Times* should publish a dispatch about the overstaffing of British Government departments established in Paris for the peace conference. He wrote on January 25:

> My dear Robin,—. . . I have no intention of reverting to the unpleasantness of December last, but I assure you that I cannot acquiesce in any more of this kind of *non possumus*.
> If you do not like my attitude, I beg you to do either one of two things— endeavour to see eye to eye with me, or to relinquish your position. . . .
> My ownership and control of *The Times* are a great responsibility, and as long as I have the health I will act up to that responsibility to the full. In the last three months I have, against my will and owing largely to the inertia of ill-health, fallen far short of my conception of my duty.
>
> N.

The *Times* official history notes that at that stage Northcliffe had abandoned his familiar habit of subscribing himself to Dawson, 'Your attached Chief', and that his peremptory 'N.' at the foot of his letter of January 25 was an intimation of impending crisis. Those nuances seem trivial now; the historian omits the fact that Northcliffe had addressed Dawson in the letter as 'My dear Robin', as of old. Shortly afterwards, he reverted to the style, 'My dear Dawson', for the reason, probably, that the letters were part of a formal transaction.

Touching on Rothermere's part in the breakdown between Northcliffe and Dawson, the *History of the Times* also records that Rothermere did not believe in 'strong editors' and that he 'relished the opportunity' of irrtating his brother by passing on stories of Dawson's dinner-party frankness. Rothermere was never a journalist, though he was conveniently described as such in some of the early company articles of association. His attitude to editors remained that of a commercial manager for whom circulation and advertising were the pre-eminent departments of a newspaper. As has been seen, it had led to a clear definition of his responsibilities in both Harmsworth Brothers and Associated Newspapers. It is desirable also to

* It was also Dawson's phrase used in his notes of those events.

repeat that divergence on the business plane had never finally impaired the personal relationship of Northcliffe and Rothermere which at the period in question was marked by renewed regard on Rothermere's side. Northcliffe wrote to him on January 26 that he had 'derived much benefit' from being at the villa. 'My bronchial tubes have so far improved that I can now sleep on my left side which I have not been able to do for months—a disability of great inconvenience.' He had greatly enjoyed being at 'beautiful Dragonnière', and feared that his brother would 'find the bills high. For the rest and luxury I have had', he concluded, 'I am greatly obliged.'

Rothermere to Northcliffe:

> 71, Savoy Court,
> Strand, W.C.2.
> 29th January, 1919.

My dear Alfred,—I am very glad to hear that you are better. I do hope you will use the Villa in every way possible. My only wish is that you should get well and that quickly.

Mother has a small cold, but is in good spirits. I am going out to see her tomorrow.

I failed to sell my provincial papers—worse luck. I got a very handsome sum as deposit money, which I have annexed.

You seem to have heard the rumour that I am to be made a Viscount. I believe there is something in it, but I have heard nothing definite. On the principle of refusing nothing I shall accept it, although this kind of decoration has very little value in these times.

Cecil, if he had asserted himself, could easily have been Assistant Secretary. I was told that he was to be Assistant Secretary. Cecil, although wonderfully conscientious, and with considerable capacity, will never cut much ice in the political world. His failure to make himself felt at critical moments handicaps him beyond redemption.

Mind you stay at the Villa as long as you like and return there again if you wish to.

> Yours always affectionately,
> HAROLD.

The storm clouds that were gathering over Printing House Square only intermittently cast their shadow as far southward as La Dragonnière. There, Northcliffe kept up a bright and brisk correspondence from which no one could deduce mental stress, far less the grimmer possibilities envisaged by Dawson and his friends, one of whom, F. S. Oliver, had surmised in a letter to Dawson (November 7, 1918): 'Isn't Northcliffe just now a little bit—what shall we say?—affected in the cerebellum. . . . He is a poor turnip.' Northcliffe to John R. Rathom, of the *Providence Journal*, Rhode Island: 'With forty thousand officers dead and a total number of empty chairs amounting to close upon a million, you will readily believe that any scheme to make war very difficult in future—especially when that plan has the backing of the majority of people in this country and of a considerable number of persons in the United States—is warmly welcomed.' There was the inevitable reference to his throat. King George V's maxim that a man should bear his sufferings mutely like an animal had apparently not been commended to Northcliffe's notice. 'It is a bitter disappointment to me that my state of health prevents my being in Paris during this Conference. I could have helped, I think. I know that I could have stopped some of the blunders' (January 28). Northcliffe to Sutton (January 28): 'The Anglo-Newfoundland company, like all of our companies, wants new blood. We are all of us ageing, and we shall have to fight the coming generation. For that reason, we should arm ourselves by engaging members of that coming generation. As to my illness, the bronchial part of it is distinctly better, thanks to most careful medical treatment.' It was hardly with the hand of an invalid that he wrote to Mme de Tizac on January 29:

What do you mean by saying 'In the old days, I had the illusion that, outside business and your great kindness to me, you perhaps had some slight friendship for me. The illusion vanished and left me a little sad.' 'Gott in Himmel!' as the German royalties who inhabited Cap Martin up to 1914 would have said. I am *verstummt* at such a remark. You know that I am much attached to you. Perhaps I possess the heavy and tactless hand of John Bull. If so, please forgive me. 'On a souvent besoin d'une plus petite que moi', and I am well aware of that fact. I hope you will always remain on the Paris staff of the *Daily Mail*.

You appear to be anxious about the 'spoiling' of your dear French peasant folk. I find no sign of it anywhere. The tiny places where I usually lunch are just as cheap as before. Old Madame Dumaine, of Fontainebleau, has robbed me since I was a boy, yet I am going back to be robbed there again as soon as I am strong enough to stand it.

On February 13th, I celebrate the first anniversary of my cough and of its musical accompaniment known among our somewhat brutal country folk by the suggestive title of 'churchyard cough'. I do not mean to be beaten by it. That is why I will stay here and not come to the Peace Conference, to my very great disappointment.

That day, House had written to him: 'I do hope that your health is much improved and that it will be possible before long to have you with us in Paris.' Northcliffe to House: 'Please, my dear Colonel House, remember that health comes first.' Northcliffe to T. E. Mackenzie (January 29): 'It is obvious from the doctor's reports here that I shall be very little in London in future. I am making *some* progress, but it is very slow.' He expected, he told Mackenzie, to 'make much more use of the bungalow [at Clandon] than in the past', and gave Mackenzie instructions to make it more comfortable. 'I never liked the idea of having the bathroom next to the kitchen. If the old bathroom is repainted, please see that the record of my weight is not obliterated.' There was a long letter from the new Secretary of State for War, Winston Churchill, accompanying a file of papers 'for your secret and personal information', pertaining to 'demobilization problems and to the military policy which I consider necessary'. Churchill reported having 'found things in a very bad state'. Northcliffe, who shared his brother Rothermere's fear of revolution coming after the return of the troops to 'a land fit for heroes', replied by return: 'All my newspapers will do exactly what you wish', and followed that promise with the possibly disconcerting proposal that 'Army pay should be increased to the rate of pay of Americans or Australians.' The Secretary of State may have been relieved to be able to telegraph (February 3): *Our men are not much in contact with Americans and the Australians are going home as fast as ships can take them.* Northcliffe objected to a leading article in *The Times* on labour unrest in England. He telegraphed to Dawson (February 3): *Your writer is mistaken in supposing that strikes are against state stop strikes are against years of ill treatment by bad employers especially during war period.* To his brother St. John (February 6): *Dearest Bonch—I am very distressed about Mother and am unhappy here in consequence.* To his mother (February 10): 'Darling Mother,—I am glad that you are going to have a change at Savoy Court [Rothermere's town flat]. I only wish I could come and lunch with you there every day, as I used to when you were at the Ritz. There is no question that I am gradually getting better. I am much stronger and in excellent spirits. Your devoted Firstborn.'

Bold assumption, if not wild surmise, is written into the *Times* official record of Dawson's resignation, which occurred towards the end of February. 'What Northcliffe had counted on was being able to reduce the Editor to submission, to make him loyal to his own person, and his personal policy.' And again: 'He [Northcliffe] had decided to evict Lloyd George from the premiership.' Northcliffe had worked closely with Dawson for eight years. He had long known that he could not bend Dawson to his will. As for evicting Lloyd George, the 'khaki election' had just shown that the enormous suggestive force of the Northcliffe newspapers had no final influence on the voters. Northcliffe had told the *Times* staff on January 7: 'The daily message conveyed to the household in the form of the newspaper is an essential part of democratic government and it was the wish of the newspapers to help the government', a restatement of the answer he had given the previous day to Sir Eric Geddes, who complained to him of press criticism.

*   *   *

So Dawson left *The Times* and Wickham Steed reigned in his place. The final act of change was accomplished with credit all round. Northcliffe to Steed: 'I am glad that all went smoothly. Parting with dear Robin is a personal grief to me. But after pondering the sad business I felt that my duty to the paper was clear', and he took care to tell Steed: 'My family, though very fond of Robin, are in entire agreement with me.' Rothermere had telegraphed to Northcliffe on February 13: *So very glad to hear your decision regarding certain resignation hope nothing on earth will induce you to depart from it he is not your man.* Steed to Dawson (February 14): 'At Lord Northcliffe's suggestion I met him for a few hours last Thursday at Avignon. He showed me his correspondence with you up to that date. Into the merits of the questions at issue it is not for me to enter, but I know you are right in saying that you only remained at your post during a most trying period from a sheer sense of duty.'

Northcliffe to Geoffrey Dawson:

Mentone.
February 15th, 1919.

My dear Dawson,—Though, by Agreement, I have complete control of The Times Publishing Company and the appointments connected therewith, I am anxious that such control should revert to the Walter family at my death.

The state of my health since February, 1918, has been such as not to suggest that I shall outlive arrangements now made. I have therefore asked John Walter to carry out the details of the change resulting from your resignation.

. . . I should have liked to have been in England to express more earnestly than I can do on paper my great regret that our association in journalism—to me a very happy one—should not have continued. I believe that I am credited with greater knowledge of the history of *The Times* than most of those who serve at Printing House Square, and, as I have said to Walter, it is my opinion that the Paper has never stood in higher esteem both at home and abroad than under your leadership.

Yours sincerely,
NORTHCLIFFE.

Dawson wrote to Evelyn Wrench on February 26: 'Very likely I managed things badly, but there came a point at which no other course seemed decently possible.' At the same time, Marlowe wrote to Northcliffe: 'May I offer my hearty congratulations on the change at *The Times*? It is what I have for many months wished to see.'

Steed was continuing to do his peace conference work in Paris, Dawson having offered to stay on in Printing House Square until his successor was ready to take charge. Northcliffe to Steed: 'Dawson is a most conscientious and honourable man, but, inasmuch as one cannot serve two masters, nobody can at once be a servant of *The Times* and a seeker of fresh occupation in life', and Steed was urged to go to London. Northcliffe's letter closed with the policy guidance: 'There should be criticism of the government . . . but not nagging.' Steed to Northcliffe: 'Dawson behaved very well, and we parted on the best of terms. As no one in the office knew what was coming, I had no means of gauging how the change will be accepted by the staff, but I do not think it will be unpopular. . . . The Paper certainly lacks leadership, and will want a certain amount of pulling together. But I believe that the whole staff will respond readily to a good leader, and will be grateful for an opportunity to co-operate intelligently in carrying out the policy which you adumbrated to me at Avignon', subscribed 'Yours affectionately'. Campbell Stuart, whom Northcliffe had just made a director of the *Continental Daily Mail* (£1,000 a year), a director of the Anglo-Newfoundland Development Company (salary to be fixed), and managing director of *The Times* (£3,500 a year after tax), and who had been his emissary in the negotiations with Steed, reported that Steed 'would regard himself as your trustee as far as the policy of *The Times* is concerned, and will do everything in his power to safeguard and develop your property and especially to guard and increase your reputation'. The quotations, Stuart assured 'the Chief', contained 'Steed's exact message'.

That handsome assurance doubtless accounted for the seemingly irrational effect which Steed's volatile temperament had on Northcliffe. It calmed him. With the *Times* crisis point so happily passed, he recovered some of his old zest and charm. Dawson was a Yorkshire squire with a donnish mind. Steed looked and carried himself like an ambassador at the court of St. James's. When they walked abroad together, Northcliffe was glad to take Steed's arm; the old boy of Henley House School who had written an article in the school magazine on the greatest newspaper in the world with whose editor he was now on intimate terms. . . .

At Mentone, he was keeping to a prescribed regime of 'no telephone and not much talking'. He was still waking early to read the newspapers. He had a half-hour's inhaling before breakfast. He then did correspondence, much of it by telegram. By nine o'clock, sharp, he was at the villa of Stanley Rendall, M.D., who had practised many years on the Riviera. His exercise was golf, his indoor recreation re-reading Boswell's *Life of Johnson* and W. H. Hudson's *Far Away and Long Ago*. He was regularly abed by 9.30. Sometimes 'Humpty-Dumpty' was commanded to read him to sleep. Too often 'Humpty-Dumpty' himself would fall asleep, when Northcliffe would challenge him with having 'been at the port again' and threaten him with dismissal. The last entry in his 'Throat Diary' was: 'Gramophone came—thank God.' He liked to have it playing outside his bedroom door, sending him to sleep with dreamy waltz tunes. 'With regard to my health,' he wrote to the wife of his principal secretary, 'physically I feel as well as ever I did in my life and I am able to walk up and down these hills vigorously.' He went on to tell her that the judgment of his *Daily Mail* staff in Paris for the peace conference compared unfavourably with that of *The Times* men, who, he said, did not make foolish mistakes. 'Why not? Because they *know*.' He told a young member of the Paris staff who was suffering from overwork to 'draw a hundred pounds from the office and go off for a good holiday'. Inquiring about him a month later, Northcliffe learnt that he had been to Morocco with his wife, and was well again. 'But he couldn't have done it on a hundred pounds,' Northcliffe told Peter Goudie, managing editor of the Paris *Daily Mail*. 'See that he gets five hundred.'

Steed wrote to him on February 28: 'This morning I went for a walk in the Bois, muttering HEALTH FIRST! I will go every day. I know how big the task will be and I don't want to let you down.' John Walter to Northcliffe: 'The momentous change will take place more smoothly than might have been the case. Everyone, I think, regrets Dawson's departure keenly; but all find some consolation in the fact that Steed is to be his successor. Dawson himself has made everything as easy as possible.' Northcliffe to John Walter (March 9): 'Please let me thank you for your tact and discretion in a very delicate matter rendered easier by the good-will of all concerned. I have had many nice letters. It was a little unjust to me that Dawson should have published his letter (*vide* the Press Association) without giving me a chance of explaining, but I feel no grievance.' Later in the month John Walter reminded Northcliffe that the control of all appointments to the *Times* staff was vested in the directors. He wrote: 'I do not wish to labour this point in connection with the recent change of editor, which was a *fait accompli* before I heard of it.' Northcliffe replied on March 31: 'I am sorry I exceeded my authority. I have no desire at all to interfere with your directorate position. Prompt decisions I must make; indeed, the success of the last few years is entirely due to the fact that we, by very great quickness, have headed the procession. . . . Prestige goes to the first and not to the last.' He included in his letter a long extract from a passage written about *The Times* in a book published in 1873, in which the writer stressed the point that John Walter the Second, who had made the paper's reputation, was imbued with 'an ever present desire to be first whenever possible'. Northcliffe told John Walter the Fifth: 'I am sure you will agree that my policy throughout has been that of your ancestor. It is always my endeavour to be first whenever possible, and I will cringe to no Government.' Pointing out that 'with the help of a very willing staff' he had been able to raise the profits of *The Times* 'now to the rate of £200,000 a year', he wrote:

I have to remember that I am in my fifty-fourth year, and that I have had a grave warning in the shaking off of laryngitis, almost disappeared, that a healthy man would have got rid of in three weeks, whereas I have had it for fourteen months. It is my ambition to get around *The Times* every able young man who can be found, so that when I go the way of all flesh *The Times* will not be burdened by a number of old men. Unfortunately, young men are hard to get.

Chapter Twenty-five

A National Invalid

THE general election had confirmed that Northcliffe presided over a vast prismatic organization which reflected—some said distorted—events but did not influence them. During the war, there were occasions when he might have claimed the dual role. It is doubtful whether at any time he cherished the illusion of infinite power. He showed many signs of enjoying the sensation of flexing the power that he had, in this or that cause, but now it was 1919 and a tide was rising in the affairs of the nation which he may intuitively have decided would either engulf him or leave him washed-up. He had written to Howard Corbett at *The Times* on February 10: 'I am fifty-three and a half years of age and I am training Sir Campbell Stuart and others to relieve me of some of my responsibilities, in order that I may be able to see a little more of the world and not be a mere slave of the printing press.' To Sir Arthur Willert of *The Times* he wrote three days later: 'I have not broken fresh ground in travel since my acquisition of the control of *The Times* in 1908. I want to go to South America, the West Indies and the Far East.' It was something to look forward to, an escape which he may have been seeking longer than he knew.

Life was still attractive in the south of France, despite restrictions and prices, petrol at £1 a gallon, a cup of coffee 3s. 2d. He was enjoying his days there and was communicating the pleasures of them to his family in a series of circular letters to which he gave the heading, 'Leaves from a Peasant's Diary', the peasant conceit derived from the valley of Gorbio and the small farmhouse which he had taken at £40 a month. Dictating the diary, he ordered Humphrey-Davy to type a footnote: 'I am personally unacquainted with the lives of Italian peasants, but I am glad to know that they are in possession of a 1917 Rolls-Royce car, an extremely up-to-date secretary, with a valet and other entourage.—(Signed) M. Humphrey-

Davy.' The diary contains not a hint of the egotism that affronted the dons. It is picturesquely informative, entirely good-humoured, sometimes gay. Seeing ox-carts on the road: 'I compare the oxen to matrimony and the goad to public opinion which keeps a couple moving along in their uncomfortable state. Ladies of the family, Mother and Madame la Vicomtesse, please skip!' He is charmed by the young French mother who comes to sit at his table in the restaurant at Brignolles, 'to feed her baby as mothers always should, without being in the least ashamed'. Passing an empty chateau, on which much money had been squandered, he insists upon 'the futility of wealth'. When a Frenchman angrily complains about the American troops, 'they are a veritable epidemic', he reminds him that 'it was your Joffre who was sent to bring over the epidemic'. Driving to Marseilles: 'A huge passenger aeroplane passed over us, going at a hundred miles an hour. As I watched it disappear in space, I felt myself to be an old-fashioned man, belonging as I do to an age that is passing.' Farther up the valley there lived in a house with a turquoise roof, 'a very handsome lady, the wife of a well-known Member of Parliament whom I had met during my excursion to Nairn in Scotland, where I had taken my cough at the end of August last'. He pondered the etiquette of the situation. 'On the one hand, a fine handsome middle-aged man; on the other, an equally good-looking and much younger lady with a husband engaged in his Parliamentary duties at Westminster. Who should call, she being the resident, he the sojourner?'

If there were glimmerings of the idyllic, he was soon brought back to a prosaic level of existence by a visit from 'Sir Andrew McBlank [meaning Caird], of Carmelite House, who came down to talk of the expensiveness of things everywhere', or by letters of solemn import. There was one from the railwaymen's leader, J. H. Thomas, followed by the diary note: 'I am sedulously reading everything I can lay hold of about Labour.' Thomas had written: 'The outlook is very black indeed . . . a terrible crash is imminent. I am feeling very much worried. Labour is determined to have a place in the Social Order.' That pessimistic forecast was unlikely to have prompted Northcliffe to set about re-making his will, 'a dreary task', he told H. G. Price by letter (February 20), to which he gave more time than he had to drafting earlier versions. In it he made dispositions of an estate eventually proved at more than £3,000,000. He remembered his family, his oldest friends and his workers, a generously conceived document which, by the irony of circumstance, became the subject of almost bitter and certainly costly litigation, besides causing unforeseen dissatisfaction among members of the staffs who regretted its lack of discrimination between years of service. He wrote to H. G. Price: 'If I am taken, you will find that I have not forgotten those who do not forget me.' Making provision for his women relatives and friends, he said to Price: 'It is wiser

One of the last studio portraits of Northcliffe

Northcliffe and Paderewski

to leave them annuities. Lump sums would make them the prey of fortune hunters.' Many of the bequests which he wrote into his will that day in February 1919 provided handsome incomes for the recipients.

J. L. Garvin to Northcliffe:

9, Greville Place,
N.W.
26th February, 1919.

My dear old Chief,—I never long for anything much more than to join you as at Valescure just nine years ago, but fate has conspired against it. I have known now the meaning of de profundis down to the very bottom of the blackness of the pit; never had a human night's sleep for nearly three months. . . .

Except on the one point of super-indemnities from Germany—to which I am dead opposed as certain to mean a new deluge of blood sometime, as well as a clogging of all business and finance and the spread of Bolshevism at home and abroad—you and I just now are wonderfully at one in our feelings about public things. Success has made Ll.G. lose much of his insight for the time in the way that often happens. I saw him the other day and we had a tremendous tussle. I stood up to him without compromise and told him more truth about the public situation than he has heard from anyone for many a long day. For fifteen months I have been studying, in view of peace, the whole Labour question consecutively and thoroughly, and have been in close touch with all those who count in framing the mind of Labour.

Winston is going to play a big part, after all. No doubt of it.

Don't forget that I am the same old plain-spoken Garve. I am the same affectionate one; never changing in personal friendship and greatly attached to you. At the end, our lives will seem like smoke, as Turgenev says in that wonderful little novel, and waste of friendship after fifty is worse than waste of money. The old happy hours we can always renew.

Ever yours,
GARVE

Pursuing his own Labour studies, between rounds of golf, drives in the Rolls-Royce, and chef-prepared meals, Northcliffe read *My Days and Dreams*, by Edward Carpenter, the sandalled Socialist visionary. A passage about 'self-seeking blusterers and designing mis-leaders' who fed the people on 'fancied wrongs', but who could not prevail against 'the patient common-sense of the mass', moved him to insist: 'It ought to be pasted in the hat of every Member of Parliament and on the shallow pate of every pressman or other person who prattles about the tremendous subject of Labour without knowing anything about it.' Satisfied, undoubtedly, that he knew more about 'the tremendous subject' than most people, he wrote to G. S. Freeman, deputy editor of *The Times*, on March 10:

I felt very strongly that *The Times* was not giving the miners' side of the case. I know from personal contact with colliers both in the North and Scotland that the three chief causes of unrest are: 1. Just suspicion of excessive profits. 2. Old-fashioned methods of coal production, and 3. Loathsome domestic surroundings.

Our Labour correspondent—whoever he may be—is not apparently a man who knows much about Labour.* Now, I happen to employ almost every kind of labour—miners, sailors, engineers, railway workers, paper workers, printers, and other kinds of worker in various places on the other side of the Atlantic, in England (North and South) and in France, and I have never had any trouble with them. The reasons for this are: 1. I pay them properly. 2. I am interested in the way they live, and 3. They can communicate with me, or see me, with the greatest of ease.

He suggested to Freeman that 'the best advisers you can find on Labour questions are not masters or agitators, but clergymen—especially the clergy of the Church of England'. 'Such men,' he said, 'gently born and members of one of the senior universities, are broad enough to see both sides. Many of these clergy become what are loosely called Socialists.' The relations between masters and men in many industrial districts were 'simply damnable'. He thought, too, that the police had been 'systematically ill-treated for years'. In Buckle's day *The Times* had some 'very fine articles' on the police. The subject should be brought up to date. 'Lay hold of a copy of the mammoth book which every policeman has to study and see all that is expected of him for a very small wage.' Behind the sentiment for social justice there was a fear of disturbing change, of industrial unrest, of possible violence. Unlike his brother Rothermere, Northcliffe was not worried about his personal fortune. He did not feel any longer equal to new stresses. It was even a relief to him that his daily newspaper *post mortem* had been interrupted. His chief concern was the new *Times* editorship: he was anxious to see it successfully inaugurated. The *Daily Mail* was hammering away at indemnities from Germany. To some in political authority it was an embarrassment and Northcliffe was naturally blamed for it, as he was for much that was written and spoken in his name. 'I suppose we are all a little too inclined to ascribe everything to N.', Lovat Fraser had observed in a letter to Geoffrey Dawson not long before, when Northcliffe had been wrongly denounced for the publication of an attack on a member of the Government.†

Resuming his role of dilettante correspondent, he took up 'the hard case' of a *Daily Mail* correspondent's wife who had been deserted by her

* According to the *History of The Times*, an unwarranted suggestion.

† As a further example, on March 28, the Paris *Daily Mail* printed a leading article, 'Peace With Honour', which frustrated Lloyd George's intention to accord recognition to the Bolsheviks in Russia. Northcliffe was thought to have inspired it. Wickham Steed, writer of the article, stated categorically that 'Lord Northcliffe had nothing whatever to do with it'.

husband for a Frenchwoman; welcomed Seymour Price back to medical practice after four years' war service; sympathized with Marlowe, who was another bronchitis victim; instructed the architect, Basil Oxenden, to inspect 'the dreadful Board Room at *The Times* and suggest what can be done. I am ashamed of it'; issued orders to his editorial staffs to 'mention the motor of any aeroplane to which you refer—Rolls-Royce, Napier, and so on, the engine being nine-tenths of the aeroplane'; and warmed the heart of W. Lints Smith, the manager of *The Times*, by telling him (March 10): 'You have a very heavy burden and I do not spare you. That is my way, but none the less I am full of sympathy. As you know, I do not even spare myself.' To Wickham Steed he wrote: 'I am feeling considerably better, though my Lady, who is here, says she does not much like the look of me.' Garvin wrote: 'Homage to the lady who is rare among women. I always like you two being together and am invincibly old-fashioned about you both because you are inseparables in my memory and affections.' An ear, nose and throat specialist, Hunter Tod, arrived to examine him. A few days afterwards, on March 7, twenty-eight persons, including members of his family, received a telegraphed bulletin: *Report of London specialist on Lord Northcliffe's throat was most satisfactory and eventual cure only a question of time and care.*

Wickham Steed to Northcliffe:

> 55, Avenue Marceau,
> Paris.
> 15th March, 1919.

Personal.

My dear Chief,—I was talking this morning with Auchinloss [son-in-law of Colonel House] and Frazier [Arthur Hugh Frazier, First Secretary at the American Embassy in Paris] on sundry matters. Auchinloss raised the question of the Washington Embassy. He said 'Far and away the best man would be Lord Northcliffe'. Frazier backed this up and asked me to consider the suggestion very seriously. I said you had not been well, that you might not be fit to do much public speaking for some time, that you were very anxious about the situation at home and that you wished to use your papers to improve it. I was not at all sure that you would not feel your first duty to be to your own country. I left it at that. The suggestion may of course be Auchinloss's own or it may be a result of his trip from Brest with House and the President. In any case I think you ought to know of it.

Steed interpolated his own views in so far as the suggestion affected *The Times* and himself. 'If you were out of England and tied up in an official job during the next few years, I should pretty well despair of our pulling the country round. . . . Ll.G. and Co. would doubtless be delighted to get you out of the way, but, notwithstanding the great importance of the Washington embassy, I think your first duty is to the country and your papers. Besides,' Steed concluded, 'if ever you take office it ought to be at the top and goodness knows there are few enough men in England who are fit to be there.'

Steed was responding generously to Northcliffe's expressed wish 'that not even the most minute friction should arise between us'. Northcliffe's reply to his letter took the form of notes 'on the delicate posture of affairs between the British Nations and the United States', with special reference to the personality of the representative at Washington, a matter which he considered to be, not only in the light of his experience, 'vastly important'. He wrote as if he expected that his views might be transmitted to the President. 'I happen to know that it is only lately that the Prime Minister has got to understand the United States and what the new United States may be.' Considering the claims of various likely candidates for the embassy, he wrote: 'Robert Cecil has some of the qualifications. He is as well liked by the Americans as he is by the French, and is likely to become well known owing to his wise weekly interview with the American Press. But his wife is stone deaf and, with the increasing force of the women's movement in America, I think the personality of the Ambassadress is almost as important as that of the Ambassador.' He told Steed that he put forward the name of Herbert Fisher, later Warden of New College, Oxford, some time before. He still regarded him as the best possible choice.

Aga Khan to Northcliffe:

> Hotel Ritz,
> Place Vendôme,
> Paris.
> 31st March, 1919.

My dear Lord Northcliffe,—It is with reluctance that I approach you for I know that in yr. state of health you need rest. And I've been ill enough to know how welcome rest is.

But, on the other hand, you are to my mind and my convictions one of the great cosmic and world forces for good. It is to *you* and *yr.* faith that we owe *victory* over forces that were evil and without you a patched peace would have come about long ago with another war against Kaiserism.

Whatever other dangers face mankind today, Kaiserism, thanks to you, is dead and done with forever. But now the problem of *Imperial* reconstruction is no less difficult than that of home economic and social reconstruction and India, with 3/4ths of the population of the Empire, cannot be left aside. I am anxious that for the good of the Empire you and I both so passionately love and believe in, that you should agree to meeting at lunch any day you like to choose H.H. Maharajah of Bikanir and Lord Sinha, India's 2 delegates to the peace conference.

. . . Choose yr. own day and time. We will all be leaving by Saturday.

Shall I ask W. Steed? It might help if he heard the views that these 2 people will place before you.

Yrs. always

AGA KHAN

The scent of narcissi had given him a homesickness for Elmwood, which was always much in his thoughts at that time of year. 'I want my little house to be perfect,' he told Mackenzie, the steward. 'Mrs Gordon [housekeeper] is to have all the help needed. We shall then have the original establishment at Elmwood, as it was thirty years ago.' Happy *Answers* days! Mackenzie was to see to it that the door from the servants' hall was fitted 'with one of those American automatic shutters'. There must be a guaranteed hot water supply, 'an essential part of my cure'. How about the fire extinguishers: did anyone understand them? Had Gordon, the head gardener, a plan? 'Gardeners, I notice, are always inclined to grow what they eat themselves.' There must be melons and Gordon must be reminded again that 'I am very fond of violets and lilies-of-the-valley'. His interest in these small concerns was abruptly switched off by the discovery that *The Times* still used 'obsolete quadrupeds to race to the stations at night. I really groaned at my own inefficiency,' he wrote to Price at Printing House Square. 'I can hardly believe it. Get after John Bland' (head printer). He returned to Elmwood matters, ordering pigs to be kept, 'as an example to the district in economy', the local people being 'very wasteful', only to be affronted by a rumour that 'a man named Mackay Edgar' was claiming to be one of his associates in business. 'Who is he?' he angrily demanded of W. J. Evans, the channel of his information and displeasure. 'To the best of my knowledge I have never seen him and have only a vague notion that there was some financier of that name.' Evans to Northcliffe: 'I thought you were quite possessed of the facts. Mackay Edgar [a Canadian financier] holds a considerable number of Associated Newspapers deferred shares; roughly, about 100,000.'

Northcliffe to W. J. Evans:

Hotel de France et d'Angleterre,
Fontainebleau.

April 10, 1919.

My dear Evans,—It is admitted by those who work with me that I am an 'arbitrary gent'. It is equally admitted that my methods bring prosperity to all concerned. Those methods are based upon the fact that I do not regard newspapers as financial undertakings and have never done so.

The last people that I wish to have anything to do with are financiers. I have always said that financiers and newspapers should keep apart. That financiers should go about claiming to be my support is about the limit.

Yours sincerely,

CHIEF

The Riviera had become hot and dusty, not the atmosphere for throat recuperation. Northcliffe had begun his return to northern latitudes. He was staying again at his favourite hotel at Fontainebleau, opposite the chateau where in 1814 Napoleon had said farewell to his troops. Here he was once more within the peace conference penumbra, taking an energetic interest in the proceedings at Versailles. The vital issue now was the attitude of the United States to the future. That country had suffered no great war losses and the reparations question had little more than an academic interest for those who shaped its policies. Given assurance of American support for the League of Nations in the first place, the Allies might have modified their claims against Germany. There was at that stage no such guarantee and Great Britain and France felt that their only protection against a resurgence of the German power was to be secured through indemnities, by which Germany, having lost the war, would be prevented from winning the peace. Northcliffe therefore increased the tempo of criticism evoked by the more lenient policy towards which Lloyd George, despite his election pledges, now seemed to be veering. *They Will Cheat You Yet, Those Junkers!*—the slogan was printed regularly in the *Daily Mail* between April 7 and June 30, 1919, on Northcliffe's instructions.

Northcliffe had been confirmed in his resolve to force the Prime Minister's hand by an interview with 'a high authority' published in the *Westminster Gazette* on March 28 and based on a talk between Lloyd George himself and a Paris correspondent, Sisley Huddleston. No reader of it could doubt that it was a challenge to the make-Germany-pay school of thought and it lent considerable colour to the view of those who already believed that the British Prime Minister was 'going soft' on reparations. Wickham Steed said that the interview made Northcliffe 'anxious'. Another of its effects was to prompt Kennedy Jones, independent Member of Parliament for Hornsey, London, to ask Northcliffe's advice on what should be done. Northcliffe's anxiety had been deepened by private reports which Wickham Steed was sending him about the situation. Northcliffe made it clear to 'K.J.' that the strongest possible protest should be made to Lloyd George in the names of the constituencies. Failing some such demonstration, decisions might be made in Paris which would leave Great Britain impossibly in debt and facing, in consequence, incalculable social problems, unemployment among them. He telegraphed to Marlowe (April 5): *Unless you write very vigorously on Ramsay MacDonald and Company who are busy in Paris they will deprive our working men and business men of the reparation due to us,* and to Kennedy Jones: *You evidently do not know how serious situation is.* His nephew, Esmond Harmsworth, was on the Prime Minister's staff at the peace conference, and Northcliffe wrote to him: 'I have letters from all over England expressing the fear that your Chief is giving away the show. He always seems to be led by the nose by those who were at the bottom of the poll at the last election.' Still worrying, he telegraphed Marlowe again: *Anxious about reparations stop unless strongest pressure be placed upon George burden of war expenses will be transferred from German to backs of British workers and business men stop unless George is resolute forthcoming budget will form staggering weight upon British people period insist that he carries out his promises.* On April 8, 370 Members of Parliament signed a telegram to Lloyd George in Paris asking for reassurances. By then, the arguments at Versailles had become a noisy discord, with a firm-lipped American President threatening to go home. The following day the Prime Minister answered the telegram. He would abide by his general election promises. The constituencies, or their representatives, were satisfied. Northcliffe was not. He was well aware of what Woodrow Wilson's biographer, Ray Stannard Baker, later put on record, that Lloyd George was capable of expressing 'an unalterable determination on one day, and be unalterably determined some other way on the day following', and that Bonar Law had been sent to Paris to steady him on his course. Angered by criticism, as he invariably was, the Prime Minister resolved to defend himself before a press conference at the Hotel Majestic. But the M.P.s' telegram had upset him still more, particularly as he believed Northcliffe to have prompted it. Also, his Government had a by-election defeat at Hull. He reserved for the House of Commons the speech he had intended to make at the press conference.

Northcliffe knew, moreover, that during the President's absence in March the American delegates had been able to secure the Prime Minister's acquiescence in the 'fundamental principle' urged by the American Government that Germany's reparation payments were to be limited to 'actual damage' and would not include 'the cost of the war'. It was an open secret in Paris that Clemenceau had been astonished by what he called 'this surrender'. It bore out what Northcliffe had written about Lloyd George a few weeks before in one of his Fleetway House papers, the *New Illustrated* (formerly *War Illustrated*), that he had not 'that high moral courage which enables a man to stand alone. The most perilous defect in his character is that he is not sure of himself.'

Northcliffe to Rothermere (April 10): 'Unless the strongest pressure is put on the Government, there is no doubt that we are going to be left in the matter of indemnities. . . . The Germans are bluffing.' He had simplified the burning issue down to the proposition that there must be ample recompense for the sacrifices and sufferings borne by England and France during the last four years. 'I am very unhappy about the peace conference,' he told Claude Johnson, of Rolls-Royce. 'If they had sent a fighting man like Winston, we would have done much better.' A great amount of information was being passed to him at Fontainebleau from

Paris. He was constantly visited by Wickham Steed, who saw the conference becoming a parody of the Congress of Vienna and whose sweeping historical perspectives made him regard Wilson and Lloyd George as amateurs when compared with Castlereagh, Talleyrand and Metternich. Of his relations with Northcliffe at that time, Steed wrote in his *Through Thirty Years* that Northcliffe 'did not inspire, or seek to inspire, a single line that I wrote during the Peace Conference. Still less did he give me "instructions".' Northcliffe depended on Steed for more than information. His guidance in the politics of the confused European scene was invaluable. Lloyd George's pallid, dry-witted, right-hand man of the press, Sir George (later Lord) Riddell, was another of Northcliffe's confidants and disposed to be the more so as there was a decreasing sympathy between himself and the Prime Minister. Northcliffe felt entitled to tell his friend Claude Johnson: 'Of course I am on the inside of the conference.'

Northcliffe to Rothermere:

> Hotel de France et d'Angleterre,
> Fontainebleau.
> 10th April, 1919.

My dear Harold,—Esmond tells me that you are to see the Prime Minister. You will be doing a great service to the country and to the Prime Minister himself if you tell him the truth, that this uncertainty as to who is to pay for the war, Germany or those she attacked, and Bonar Law's halting statements as to financial reparation, are exasperating people to a degree which I suppose it is difficult for a man like the Prime Minister, engaged in daily conference, to understand. According to Esmond, he sees far too many people and has no time for reflection, talking at breakfast, lunch and dinner. According to the newspapers, he sees the wrong kind of people.

I, personally, have no intention of spending the rest of my life swotting to pay excess profits tax and supertax for the benefit of Germany, if I can help it. I do not believe the tales of German hard-up-ness. I know that if we let her, she will dodge and cheat.

> Yours affectionately,
> ALFRED

He followed that letter the next day by a long, carefully prepared statement of his views, which he desired his brother to study. 'The situation is so grave that I have asked the Ritz people to see that you have this immediately you arrive.' Clearly, he hoped that Rothermere would take the opportunity of his meeting with the Prime Minister to present the views contained in the statement. Corrected by Northcliffe in a barely legible hand, it reiterated his complaint about the Prime Minister seeing too many people and talking too much. 'No man can keep a sense of perspective or gather resolution who leads a life like that.' It jeered at his allegiance to the *Manchester Guardian*. 'I know its circulation figures, which are comic', an irrational comment from the chief proprietor of *The Times*, which likewise exerted an influence much in excess of its sales. 'I should like to support the Prime Minister, or, failing him, Winston, who is coming on, but I do not intend to support any policy that keeps me swotting for the rest of my life in order to get tax money that should be paid by Germany or helping to build up another Prussia.' Riddell had complained to him of the 'pressure of the Jews on the Sacred Four', at Versailles. Northcliffe told Rothermere: 'They had the nerve to send me a four-thousand-word telegram from Berlin through Holland, prepared by Rathenau [later German Foreign Secretary], head of the Electricity Trust with its two hundred million pounds capital. I sent them a reply that I did not deal with Huns, and Hun-like they responded with quite a civil answer.'

Northcliffe's memorandum to his brother reads now like the product of a tired nervous system. Rothermere may have been too busy with affairs to note more than casually that typed boldly across the top of page one was the somewhat incongruous reminder: THIRTY-SECOND ANNIVERSARY OF MY WEDDING DAY. Rothermere was the Prime Minister and afterwards went out to Fontainebleau to spend a day with Northcliffe. There was reason to suppose that he had arrived with overtures from the Prime Minister. At the end of a long discussion, much of it on the golf links, Rothermere left with his mission unfulfilled. Speaking about Lloyd George to Corbett, the *Times* manager, who was summoned to Fontainebleau, Northcliffe remarked: 'It's his big head on a little body that I don't like.' Not long after Rothermere's abortive attempt to make peace between them, Lloyd George attacked Northcliffe in what some people regarded as one of his most memorable parliamentary performances.

Situation as to finance changing for worse, Northcliffe wired to 'K.J.' on April 13. *Am asking Wickham Steed to go to London at once stop he will see you and others who may desire to learn the facts*. Fearing that the censorship would delay the message, he wrote to Kennedy Jones the same day:

The situation here is this. The German financial agents are at Senlis about twenty miles from Paris . . . bringing immense pressure to bear on the Conference, to this intent, that the Germans cannot pay much, and that if pressed to pay, will decline to sign the Peace Treaty, go Bolshevik, or allow the Allied armies to enter Germany. We hear a different story every day.

There are, of course, the usual sinister rumours about Lloyd George, none of which I believe. That he is being bluffed is obvious. His entourage say that the reason why the peace terms cannot be published is that the British Government would fall at once, as the people would realize that they had been had. We have been the weak element in the Conference—not Mr Wilson, who has been altruistic in some things but very practical. He is getting impatient at our vacillations.

According to Northcliffe's letter, Clemenceau was kept quiet by being told that if the peace terms were published the British Government would fall and the conference would begin all over again. Northcliffe thought it not too late to rectify matters.

An active participant with Lloyd George is Montagu [Secretary of State for India]. The French are very much surprised to find a Jew engaged in this business. I am not anti-Semite, as you know, but it is a deplorable thing that after all our sufferings and the sacrifice of all the gallant boys who have gone that in the end we should be beaten by financiers. You can easily put my statements to the test by having the Prime Minister interrogated. There can be no motive for hiding the peace terms other than what I have given, namely, that he is afraid to show them to the public. The French Press is unanimous in demanding publicity.

The President is worn out with these delays, but he has done his best for Great Britain, and his snubbing of the Irish delegations, who have been pestering him all the time, is the real test of his sincerity. You know how many votes these snubs are going to cost him.

He gave his glancing attention to a topic which he could have been excused for overlooking in the hectic circumstances of those days. The Actors' Association was in conflict with C. B. Cochran, the well-known producer. Agreeing that Cochran 'appears to pay better salaries than many other managers', he sent a memorandum to the deputy editor of *The Times* on April 15: 'There seems no doubt that the majority of small-part and chorus people are underpaid. They suffer from non-payment for re-hearsals and from suspension of salaries during even temporary illness.' He suggested that *The Times* should support the actors' case.

*　　*　　*

On April 16, in the House of Commons, Lloyd George, at the apex of his career, a victor in war, an architect of peace, struck back at Northcliffe. After referring to the peace talks and to his Government's attitude to the Bolsheviks of Russia—'we have received no approaches of any sort or kind from them'*—he visibly braced himself for a peroration by which he obviously hoped to make his greatest impression of the day and, not less specifically, to divert attention from the damaging *Westminster Gazette*

---

* 'The most egregious case of misleading the public, perhaps the boldest, that I have ever known', was the testimony of William C. Bullitt before the United States committee on foreign affairs in September 1919. Bullitt, who later became U.S. Ambassador to Russia, had breakfasted at Downing Street with the Prime Minister on March 28 and had then handed him official proposals from the Bolsheviks.

interview. Not mentioning Northcliffe by name, he spoke of 'ridiculous expectations', of 'diseased vanity', at that point, touching his forehead insinuatingly, of 'the crime of sowing dissension between great lands', of *The Times* being 'a threepenny edition of the *Daily Mail*'. It was a speech in his best form and his triumph was great. Tories of the Austen Chamberlain kind beamed their delight. Wickham Steed, who was there, wrote that the House 'showed no critical faculty whatever. In view of the gravity of the position in Paris, the spectacle was hardly a comforting one.' A few members looked pained and puzzled. After all, Northcliffe had been invited into the Cabinet by the Prime Minister. His war service had been outstanding. Amid a storm of buzzing approval and of waving order papers, the Prime Minister sat down, eyes afire, face flushed, hair falling over his ears. A watcher in the Press Gallery could scarcely forbear to laugh aloud at the recollection of Northcliffe's having said that in moments of agitation Lloyd George looked like 'a dishevelled conjuror'.

That Northcliffe had brought the attack down on himself was widely agreed. He and his newspapers had 'sniped at Lloyd George from behind every rock', as a member of his Paris staff, Valentine Williams, afterwards wrote. But in choosing attack as the best method of defence, the Prime Minister descended to the demagogic level, showing none of the broad magnanimity of the statesman. As he left the chamber to go to his private ministerial room, he met Cecil Harmsworth. Seeing the latter's stricken look, he said: 'I went too far.' Cecil Harmsworth wrote at once to Northcliffe offering to resign his post in the Government, 'in protest against an insult to a man who was my affectionate brother and best friend'. Northcliffe replied to him:

> Do not worry about the Prime Minister. He has succeeded in making about four hundred journalistic enemies among the staffs of *The Times* and my other newspapers. As far as I am concerned, the incident has simply brought me a great deal of amusement and public congratulation and has substantially increased the sale of both *The Times* and the *Daily Mail*. It has also, as you may have noticed, increased the volume of letters from public men in *The Times*.
> The attack was a little ungrateful in view of the abject letter of thanks the P.M. wrote to me for my assistance during the Marconi case.

Privately, and through his newspapers, Northcliffe received many expressions of contempt at the Prime Minister's attack. French reaction was particularly strong. For him it was merely another bruising scuffle in the political game; others thought it a knock-out. He told his chief editorial men on April 22 that he deprecated their tendency to hit back 'when the Prime Minister makes foolish remarks about me', and suggested to them that 'silence is a more effective and dignified weapon'. The *History of The Times* states that his attitude on that occasion 'amounted to a model of restraint'. A leading article in *The Times* brought the following comments from Northcliffe to Steed:

Many years of experience of newspapers have taught me that readers do not understand irony, and I notice that the reference to the Prime Minister's 'dignity, tact and truthfulness' is practically universally understood to be praise of him. An ironical reference by Max Beerbohm to the wickedness of the London Fire Brigade in putting out beautiful fires brought us thousands of letters from the public.

That was the only blemish on a very fine leader. Directly I saw it I said: 'The great public will not see what is meant.'

The intended compliment may have gone awry. *The Times* did not undertake to serve 'the great public', and Northcliffe may or may not have been justified in his estimate of the intellectual limitations of its readers.

'I hope the Prime Minister's speech satisfied his supporters,' he told Claude Johnson. 'I shall continue to expose his be-kind-to-Germany tricks, beloved of him and his financial friends. He has been trying to pull my leg and that of the new Editor [of *The Times*] for weeks, but we declined to have any communication with him. He finally wired for my brother Rothermere. We may expect more fireworks soon.' Dr McNair Wilson, the *Times* medical correspondent, who had studied economics as well as medicine, said that Northcliffe had 'a real fear that Lloyd George would give in to American or international money interests'. Northcliffe had no knowledge of economics as a science, but, quoting Dr Wilson, 'he seemed to have sensed the dangers of that possible situation'. To another of his medical advisers, Stanley Rendall, M.D., of Mentone, he wrote that 'the Prime Minister is quite angry at my exposure of his tricks and those of his pro-German financial friends. I shall continue to prod him.'

When he wrote to tell Rendall that he had spells of 'feeling weak' and that he 'tired easily', the doctor replied (April 14, 1919): 'Your letter sounds a little depressed', and surmised that a tonic 'would only make you worse'. At Fontainebleau, he was playing more golf with 'Sandy' Thomson and enjoying 'the beautiful course'. But he would not let go: the stream of dictation went on and on. To W. Lints Smith: 'I see that advertisements are now to be addressed to the Classified Advertisements Manager. I hate these modern innovations. They used to be addressed to the Chief Clerk. Let us revert to that good old Printing House Square style.' To Marlowe: 'I specially asked for no booming of the Asquith wedding as a political dodge [Violet Asquith's marriage to Maurice Bonham Carter]. When it takes place, give it modest publicity.' To C. I. Beattie, *Daily Mail* night editor: 'Do not use many of Tom Webster's

Northcliffe orders the removal of the statue of Lloyd George
from Printing House Square

cartoons and always put them at the bottom of the page', a decree which troubled Marlowe, the editor, who liked Webster's work and forecast for him the great success which he duly attained in the *Daily Mail* sporting pages. To Marlowe: 'Can you stop our political correspondent writing this rubbish, "one of the first tasks to which the Prime Minister will devote himself on his return from Paris . . ." That is a well-known 10 Downing Street trick to tell the public that nothing can be done without the Prime Minister.' He announced to his Carmelite House staff an offer of £500 in prizes 'to be distributed among those sending good suggestions and criticisms of the various offices and publications of Associated Newspapers Limited'. He ordered his management to extend the five-day working week throughout his offices, telling H. W. Wilson, of the *Daily Mail*, that there were a few things which he was proud to have done, 'and instituting the five-day week is one of them'. At first the printers and machine men were sceptical, fearing that the shorter week might at any time mean a wages cut. Northcliffe's advice to them was: 'Let us try it for three months and see how it works', saying at the same time to his directors: 'They'll become interested in gardening or some other hobby and then we shall hear no more objections to the five-day week.' Crediting him with that important step, The National Union of Journalists' official organ, *The Journalist*, recorded that he was 'a warm supporter of the principles on which the Union was founded and of many of the policies it is pursuing'. He backed the journalists' demand for the eight-guinea minimum which was secured that year. 'In my opinion,' he wrote to H. G. Price on April 4, 'a worker who does not join a union is a fool. The only wish I express is that no one will be forced to join who does not want to join.'

Northcliffe to Mme Andrée de Tizac:

Hotel de France et d'Angleterre,
Fontainebleau.

13th April, 1919.

My dear Andrée,—There are lovely and odd things here—'La Roche qui pleure', and 'Moret' whose church was consecrated by one of our Archbishops of Canterbury, Becket. I think one gets every kind of memory emotion in Fontainebleau. The rise and fall of Napoleon are well indicated in the various rooms he occupied at the Chateau when he was First Consul and by the sight of the gorgeous salons he made for himself as Emperor.

To play golf on a carpet of violets is new to me and can only be done at Fontainebleau. None the less, I shall be glad to get back to my Elmwood—now all daffodils and primroses, I hear.

You may rely at all times on my doing my best for France. The French have not been very wise in their handling of the Americans. Many people from the Crillon [the hotel headquarters of the American delegation] come to see me.

They all say the same thing—that the French are so different from what they expected. 'They keep us up to two o'clock in the morning, arguing about centimes. We did not like the English before, but we now find that they never argue about centimes.'

Yours affectionately,
CHIEF

On April 19 he announced through his senior secretary, Price, the part in his businesses to be played in future by Campbell Stuart, who would thenceforward be his main channel of decision. 'It will save me writing and telephoning.' The arrangement was a first step in his gradual withdrawal from supreme activity as a publisher and newspaper proprietor. His health future was becoming a more positive worry. The lump in his throat seemed to be larger. He had sensations of choking. But his weight remained fairly constant at 13 st. 10 lb. There was comfort in that.

He was diverted from self-centredness by developments in the wider scene, where there were many signs of combustible possibilities. The strike weapon was being brandished by the workers with far more confidence than they had ever mustered before. The miners, the railwaymen, and, surprisingly, the police, were all making demands with a new imperative ring in them. It was not simply that Disraeli's 'two nations' looked like being joined in mortal combat. The men who made the munitions and built the ships, the factory workers who had been getting 'good money' during the war, resented the flooding of the market by demobilization, a dangerously ugly manifestation of the Labour spirit.

Northcliffe perceived that the empirical approach would not meet the new problems of war debts, complicated taxation, and unprecedented budgets, that an age of specialization was about to break on Western society and he, like others of his time, felt his deficiencies the more. Economics, with J. M. Keynes as its prophet, was the master word of post-war reconstruction, the inspiration of a new political *élite*. 'It is unfortunate that there are so few people connected with the Press who understand anything about economics,' Northcliffe wrote to Rothermere from Fontainebleau on April 21. 'You are probably the only one in England. I wish you would help me. . . . You are debarred from being Chancellor of the Exchequer but by helping the *Times* Financial Department you could wield just as much power for good.' Looking up at the gathering Labour storm clouds, his essential optimism seemed to wilt. He spoke of 'the gravest anxiety' felt by those 'who have anything to lose', and declared to Rothermere his desire to do his best 'to avert the worst of the many ills that are threatening those who happen to have worked and accumulated'. He besought his brother: 'I want you to help me. Without advice, I go back rather helpless.'

That was an uncharacteristic mood of Northcliffe's and it may have had more meaning than was construed from it at the time. The specialist, Hunter Tod, had been summoned again. After examining Northcliffe's throat, he urged his patient to return to London by the end of April. 'Then we can decide what had better be done.' Diagnosis of thyroid morbidities was not so precise then as it has since become and Northcliffe cannot have been other than a worried man. He hardly showed it. 'Che sara sara . . .'

Northcliffe to Marlowe (April 24): 'Steed tells me that he heard I have given an order that there should be no reference to Bolshevism in the paper. To whom did I give such an order? The only order that I gave was that we should not play into the Germans' hands by exaggerating the spread of Bolshevism. The Germans use the threat of Bolshevism to inspire fear in our upper and middle classes.' Northcliffe to Jan Paderewski, Prime Minister of Poland: 'I am giving some gramophones and records to schools. I have been impressed by the opinions of Elgar and others as to the educational value of this method of reproducing music. I would be greatly obliged if you would kindly give me your views on the choice of the machines and music.' Paderewski to Northcliffe (April 25): 'I very much agree with you. Education by good music is essential to the mind-development of children in every country. We should all be careful of German propaganda by music, so active before the war and not yet dead.' Humphrey-Davy to Marlowe (by telegram, April 25): *Chief says no petty nagging of Lloyd George.* Northcliffe to Mme Andrée de Tizac (April 25): 'My ambition in life is to help forward an unbreakable chain between America, the five British nations, and France.' Northcliffe to H. G. Price (April 25): 'My dear Prigcliffe,—I do not want to find a huge "haunch" (as Sutton says) of letters awaiting me when I arrive at Elmwood. I want to have the morning alone in my little house. I am said to be looking well by my circle of sycophants. Still the throat will not stand the least cold wind and I think the growth is larger. I shall see Sir William Osler about it as speedily as possible.' Northcliffe to Wickham Steed: 'We have far too little matter of feminine interest in *The Times*. I well remember the remark of a leading *modiste* who, when asked to advertise in *The Times*, said: "No, thank you. I see the kind of women who read *The Times* going to *The Times* Book Club."'

Northcliffe to C. I. Beattie, director, Associated Newspapers Limited:

Hotel de France et d'Angleterre,
Fontainebleau.
April 29, 1919.

My dear Beattie,—In Monday's paper you make me say that 'it is not true that M. Clemenceau and Lloyd George approve President Wilson's manifesto on Fiume'. I did not say that because I know it is not true, and it is unfair that I should be saddled with statements like this.

It is very difficult for me, at this distance, to say how the Daily Mail is. Sycophants arriving from England tell me that it is very flat, but they always say that when I am away. To me here it seems good, but I am not comparing it with other papers, as I shall be on and after Thursday, when I return to full work after an absence of two years; first, with Civil Aviation, secondly, with American Mission, thirdly, with Propaganda in Enemy Countries, and, fourthly, with ill-health.

I was very glad to hear you were all right. I shall be better pleased still when I hear that you are having a five-day week.

Your attached
CHIEF

He was back at Elmwood by the last day of the month. He had warned Price: 'The big stick is ready. I am having some lead put at the end of it.' He could still command a gentler sentiment. When Price mentioned that his mother was staying in Ramsgate, Northcliffe at once stopped work, saying: 'Why didn't you tell me before? You must be with her', and sent for Pine, the chauffeur, telling him: 'Mr Price is having the afternoon off. I want you to take him and his mother for a nice drive in the country.'

Awaiting Harley Street appointments, he resolved to 'clear out the files'. Keeping up with the stream of dictation, Price and Humphrey-Davy, and Amy Cottell, the stenographer, were like runners in a relay race from Northcliffe's huge wickerwork *chaise-longue* on the lawn to the room in the house that was used as a temporary office. The bungalow had become little more than a museum. Everything there was as it had always been: the blackboard with faint chalk inscriptions, the old ink-stained desk from Paternoster Square, the polar bear rugs, the framed photographs which he had taken of Niagara years ago, the two young alligators from Florida which used to startle visitors with their snapping jaws, now stuffed as electric light holders and jarring taste rather than nerves. Every fine day (and that first post-war spring was very beautiful), Northcliffe would lie at full length with his soft white felt hat on his knees, so that it could be used as an eyeshade if necessary. After reading a letter, and answering it, he would drop it on the grass for others to pick up. His voice developed a grating hoarseness; occasionally it faded to a whisper. The surgeons had decided that a thyroid operation must be done.

Once again, the bulletin boards at Printing House Square and Carmelite House were the object of lively curiosity. 'Coming back to England, I notice that yet more newspapers have copied my small articles, so strongly objected to at the time of their introduction' (message to the Daily Mail, May 3, 1919). 'The editorial page is good and Rebecca West appears to be a consistently good writer' (message to the Weekly Dispatch, May 4).

'The 23rd Birthday Number of the *Daily Mail* did its best to approach the early numbers of the paper when the staff were working hard to provide the present staff with their enormous salaries' (message to the *Daily Mail*, May 5). A message to the *Times* staff of May 3 was an historical résumé that may have seemed patronizingly superfluous to some of the veterans:

I was comparing the fat *Times* of this morning with the meagre production for which I was suddenly pressed by some of the proprietors of *The Times* to deposit an immense sum of money some years ago. At that time . . . nearly all the advertisements had disappeared. The paper (the raw material itself) had been reduced in quality some 40 per cent. from its previous standard and the net sale was under 40 thousand a day.

With three exceptions, the editorial and commercial salaries were on a wretched scale. There are this day, Saturday, eight pages of small advertisements, almost as many as there were in 1865; the sale is nearly four times greater than when I joined forces; the editorial and other salaries have, in their totality, considerably more than doubled apart from bonuses; advertisers who left the paper years ago have returned; and the printing equipment is certainly the best in London. The 130 proprietors of *The Times* received a dividend at the outset and have had one ever since, though, as their uneasy visits to Printing House Square and litigation showed, they had long been without any.

I am such a severe critic of the paper that it is only right to acknowledge the services of the editorial, commercial, mechanical, and publishing staffs in reviving *The Times*.

His attack on the files showed that his mind was as nimble as ever in its play over the public and professional scene. Bernard Falk, editor of the *Weekly Dispatch*, to Northcliffe (May 1): 'Regarding your doubt as to my being a *bona-fide* member of the Ancient Race, are you not overlooking the variety of the natal products of the aforesaid race? There is Trotsky and there is Lord Reading. We have a race that is supposed to have invented capitalism deliberately seeking to destroy it—such is our variety. No, my dear Chief, I am true to type, but it is a different type.' Marlowe to Northcliffe (May 2): 'I am very grieved and disappointed to hear that you are not making a good recovery, as we had all hoped. I pray that the new symptoms may prove to be less serious than is suggested.' A rumour that he had cancer of the throat had caused uneasiness among some of the senior men at Carmelite House, who might have expected to be told the truth, but Northcliffe had still not outgrown his pleasure in being thought a sphinx or a mystery. W. J. Evans, a director whom he liked and respected, wrote to him on May 2, pointing out that his resignation from the chairmanship of the Northcliffe newspaper group had 'given rise to a feeling of anxiety for the future'. Evans recalled 'the Chief's' remark just before leaving for the south of France, that they 'might walk in some morning and find a new proprietor in Carmelite House'. Evans appealed to him: 'So, just as we have always placed our full confidence in you in the past, we ask you to give us your full confidence now', and, in the names of Pomeroy Burton and himself he offered to buy Northcliffe's controlling interest in Associated Newspapers Limited at £5 a share, 'or approximately one and a quarter millions sterling'. He assured Northcliffe that 'we have ample financial backing of the highest character'. It was believed to have been provided by Mackay Edgar. Northcliffe dismissed the offer by saying: 'Let Campbell Stuart deal with it', and proceeded with his correspondence.

To Marlowe: 'I was sorry to receive a letter in your own handwriting. It must have taken at least thirty-five minutes to write.' To Pomeroy Burton: 'I understand that you are one of those who think we ought to start an illustrated evening paper. We cannot produce even an unillustrated paper. Just look at the enclosed. *Vanitas vanitatum.*' To Mackenzie, his steward: 'A line to thank you for the great trouble you have taken about my dear little house. Things have been admirably done.' To Valentine Williams, of the *Daily Mail* peace conference staff, who sought leave to break the rule barring wives from being with their husbands in Paris: 'As the Conference looks like going on interminably, I suggest that you not only have your wife to live with you but start building a house there.' Humphrey-Davy to Alfred Pemberton, manager, small advertisement department, *The Times*: 'The Chief says there is something wrong about Page 2 today. See "Articles for Sale", where the following advertisement appears: "STOUT Gentleman WANTS good SECOND-HAND CLOTHING, also underwear." Why put this among "Articles for Sale"? The Chief says: "I have no personal feelings in the matter as I am not the gentleman mentioned." ' Northcliffe to Major-General Seely (later Lord Mottistone): 'My experiences of semi-official work have proved to me that newspapers and Governments cannot go hand in hand. Although I specifically did not see or communicate with my newspapers during the whole time I was in the United States, continual misrepresentations were made by public men that my newspapers derived benefit by reason of my being in possession of official secrets. I have made no communication to *The Times* or the *Daily Mail* about anything that has come before me officially.'

Procuring news was a problem which exercised Northcliffe's editors on more than grounds of professional rivalry. Quite apart from his own aloofness, his attitude to public men, and his attacks on them, could stop valuable sources of information and opinion, a kind of frustration which all his editors endured from time to time. For the editor of *The Times* it was a particularly vexatious position to be in, as Dawson had known only too well. The *Daily Mail* news editor, Walter Fish, told Northcliffe on May 5 that 'the paper's chief weakness at present is that most of the

Ministers and ex-Ministers are not sufficiently friendly with us to go out of their way to give us news'. There is no sign that Northcliffe fully considered the difficulty or appreciated the ingenuity and effort by which it was surmounted.

⋆   ⋆   ⋆

His visits to Harley Street showed that the growth in his throat, which was increasing in size, was an adenoma of the thyroid gland, a non-malignant but inflammatory condition and likely to become more so. The major operative risk, he was warned, was in after-bleeding. Ordered to 'feed up' in preparation, he was relieved to find that, far from losing weight, he quickly put it on: four pounds in four weeks. Evelyn Wrench wrote commiseratingly about the operation. Northcliffe replied: 'I rather rejoice, for I feel that I have not suffered during the war.' He wrote to Sir Milsom Rees, of Wimpole Street, that the decision had been reached 'after all the lavish expenditure of effort on the part of you and your friends and of cash on my part'. He had paid £430 in medical fees in the previous twelve months. He whiled away some of his waiting time by writing a parody of a *Lancet* news item which he ordered to be set up in the *Daily Mail* composing room and sent to twenty-one consultants, specialists and general practitioners who had attended him, among them such eminent members of the profession as Sir James Mackenzie, Sir Bertrand Dawson (later Lord Dawson of Penn), Sir Anderson Critchett, Dr (later Sir James) Dundas Grant and Sir William Osler.

A PROFITABLE COUGH
(An Extract from *The Chanceit*)

Considerable interest continues to be manifested in the well-known and profitable cough of Lord Northcliffe. Discovered in February, 1918, by a general practitioner, it has from time to time been a source of much augmentation of income, not only to local medical men, but also to the consultants of Harley and Wimpole Streets.

The emoluments so profusely scattered have hitherto fallen into the hands of physicians, but we are glad to state that there is now a prospect of the surgical branch of the profession coming into its due share. Nursing Home and massage circles are also looking forward to a proportion of the profits.

Northcliffe could afford to be frank with the doctors, far more so than most patients. When their prescriptions failed him, he let them know it, saying that this medicine was 'no good', that treatment 'useless'. A glass of good Burgundy, he would tell them, was better than all their tonics and pills and 'quackcines', and would add: 'The patient knows best.' He reserved his greatest respect for Sir James Mackenzie, of 133 Harley Street, to whom he was taken by McNair Wilson of *The Times*, who had been Mackenzie's assistant. Wilson said that the interview was 'the most nerve-racking' of his life. Northcliffe had complained of heart pain and feared *angina pectoris*. 'I want a frank opinion', he said to Mackenzie. There was a snap in his tone which the physician did not like. 'This is a place of science, not a newspaper office', the great consultant replied with quiet firmness. From that time when Northcliffe spoke of him, Mackenzie was 'that grand old Scotsman'.

Northcliffe to Wickham Steed:

Elmwood,
14th May, 1919.

My dear Steed,—I am very glad at length to see the word 'holiday' in one of your letters, and I mean to hold you to your bargain.

It is a lovely part of the world to which you are going. There is a rather decent golf course at Arachon, and near by, as you know, is the Chapon Fin. The proprietors of the *Petite Gironde* are friends of mine. You will find buried in the 'Bordelais' *patois* a good many English words reminiscent of our possessions in that part of the world 500 years ago. This time of year there is an excellent migratory pigeon to be eaten called palomba.

Overlooking Steed's need of a holiday, he wrote at greater length three days later stating that he was not interfering with the editorial opinions of *The Times*. Nonetheless, he objected to a leading article in which Lloyd George was credited with having summoned the Imperial War Cabinet. 'It was *The Times* and my other newspapers which agitated for that. Far from the Prime Minister being in advance of public opinion, he was behind it.' He expressed himself strongly against the 'puffing of the Prime Minister in the present state of affairs. The Welsh do not understand fair play. They regard that kind of attitude as cringing.' Then there was 'the ridiculous beslavering' of the Austrian delegates to the peace conference. Expressing his feelings about it, he spoke out in a tone of remonstrance that echoes down the years. 'There is a fat-headed geniality in the modern Englishman which is not a sign of virility in the nation, I fear.'

Steed had to be told about 'the growth', that it had 'doubled in size', that it was inflammatory but non-malignant, etc. 'It has been so pronounced by all the experts and I have seen many.' When Steed was back, and they could talk things over, the operation would take place. And so on. As for *The Times*: 'The prosperity and influence of the paper are wonderful. Without any reflection on Robin, his retirement has taken a great weight off the minds of the staff. I notice that Freeman [deputy editor] is not only getting stronger, but looking stronger in the face.' A casual reader of that comment might have thought it more than a 're-flection' on Dawson, that a vampirish power had been removed from

725

Printing House Square. 'Money is flowing in. It is also going out too fast', Northcliffe told Steed in his next letter. He looked to Steed 'to steady the whole of my Press on many matters'. For example, 'puffing the Prime Minister in the present state of affairs is a serious error'. Just then, he was pleasurably repeating a story sent to him by the *Daily Mail* correspondent in New York, W. F. Bullock. When Bullock showed Frank Cobb, a leading American newspaperman, a Paris message stating that the peace conference situation had resolved itself into a struggle between Wilson and Northcliffe for the soul of Lloyd George, Cobb retorted: 'That is what I call a damned small stake.' A message from a venerable French-woman, Madame Adam, of the Abbaye de Gif at Seimet, may have given him a slightly worthier satisfaction. She desired Madame de Tizac to let him know that she had met Gladstone at the house of Emile de Girardin, the great French journalist, just before the war of 1870 and that Gladstone had then said to her: 'We will stand at your side.' That abortive promise had renewed her old hatred for England, 'the England of Joan of Arc, of the Congress of Vienna, of Heligoland, where she gave up the sea into the hands of the Kaiser. But now I bless her because of Lord North-cliffe—in him is personified the British soul.'

★   ★   ★

On May 13, the news gathering side of the *Daily Mail* was alerted by a message which said that two British airmen, H. G. Hawker and Mackenzie Grieve, had taken off from Newfoundland in a Sopwith aeroplane in an attempt to win the *Daily Mail* prize of £10,000 for the first Atlantic flight. They had cheerfully faced the risk of unfavourable weather on hearing that an American seaplane, the Curtis N.C.4, was already in the air. Splendidly daring, Hawker and Grieve passed beyond the gaze of watchers at St. John's and thereafter all was silence for several days, an interval of anxious expectation during which the whole of the Western world was keyed-up with excitement. On May 25, a Danish ship arrived off the coast of Scotland with the two men on board. They had been rescued in mid-ocean. Northcliffe had gone to see Mrs Hawker to sym-pathize with her in her anxiety. Impressed by her faith and courage, he ordered the *Daily Mail* to announce that £10,000 would be divided between the airmen's next of kin if they did not return. Mrs Hawker wrote to him: 'While appreciating this as a very noble offer, I cannot and will not, as you know, believe that my husband is not alive. I am sure that he will soon return to hear of the generosity of the *Daily Mail*, and your personal kindness to me at this time.' Once again the staff, looking at the bulletin board, had cause to bow their heads in deference to 'the Chief's' superior information. Constantly he gave them facts which did not appear in the paper. 'Mrs Hawker is one of the most remarkable people I have ever talked to. When I went to see her on Wednesday to advance the question of a prize for her husband, I could not get near the topic. Her attitude was one of perplexity at the ignorance of the public of the airman's personality. "They don't understand what a man of resource my husband is", she said. Mrs Hawker had no doubt whatever as to his safety' (May 26, 1919). Hawker's return to London filled the streets with excited, cheering crowds. His car was unable to move and he completed his triumphant progress on the back of a cab horse. By Northcliffe's order, Hawker received a cheque for £5,000 'in recognition of the gallant and patriotic character of his attempt'.

The £10,000 prize remained to be won. Soon, it would be dramatically back in the headlines. Northcliffe, having 'cleared out' the files, was proposing *Daily Mail* improvements, not all of them of board room ponderosity. Northcliffe to Pomeroy Burton:

> Elmwood,
> St. Peters.
> 20th May, 1919.

Dear Burton,—Who is responsible for the state of the office typewriters? Are they ever cleaned? Some of the worst typewriting in London comes out of Carmelite House, and that is saying much. Please arm every man and woman with a winkle pin and brush.

> Yours sincerely,
> CHIEF

Politically, he was much less active than he had been for months. Field-Marshal Lord French had written to him from the Vice-Regal Lodge, Dublin, wishing that he 'would find time to come over and stay'. Northcliffe replied: 'I feel very strongly that your efforts at revealing the truth and thus guarding the reputation of hundreds of men who have been maligned as a result of public ignorance, need every possible support.' Invoking his 'impending throat operation' he regretted that he could not accept the invitation. 'I was born there and understand something of a very difficult problem.' Northcliffe to George Moore, the Irish novelist (May 22): 'I was abroad when you wrote to *The Times*, but I read the letter. In fact, I have read, I think, all that you have ever written. I remember you, but perhaps you do not remember me, when we were both members of the Yorick Club. If I were well, I would try to settle the Irish question, but, alas, I have an operation pending.'

Concentrating on the *Daily Mail*: 'I am glad to see our younger men coming forward,' he wrote; 'we are sadly lacking in youth.' His office communiques were tending to become longer, possibly because he was practising with the dictaphone, an office technique which appealed to him

727

rather more for its novelty than for its advantages. The daily bulletins were the pith and epitome of his journalism. His most ruthless critic could not find anywhere among them an incitement to the sensationalism with which he was frequently charged. Particularly at that time, they reflected his mind more faithfully than his newspapers did, displaying its essential discursiveness and the restless obsession with information. He mentioned someone, unnamed, who had told him that the 'young men in the office find them helpful as an aid to developing personality'. Inspired, maybe, certainly pleased, he expanded some of his comments to a length calling for a degree of devoted attention which it may not always have been politic to exhibit among the cynics of the newsroom.

I took up the *Daily Mail* rather wearily this morning, somewhat depressed by our recent efforts to produce a newspaper, and a little more anxious to hear the nightingale and tree pipit (which have come on my garden for the first time for twenty years) than to engage in the lugubrious task of finding the weak and timorous spots in our organization. It is delightful here by the sea and an excellent golf course at my door is an additional temptation not to read the paper. But to my surprise and great pleasure, I find an excellent *Daily Mail* this morning. (To the *Daily Mail*, May 13, 1919.)

That was a delightful and true article on the tree pipit's song in *The Times* last week which I have read and re-read and for which I would like to send my thanks to the author. (To *The Times*, May 13.)

There is nothing wrong about this morning's paper except that more should have been given about the death of Lady [Arthur] Paget. She was an American who held considerable sway in Royal circles. I do not suppose our society bird knew anything about it. I have often said that the whole paper is completely out of touch with the great world. An old and cynical member of the staff remarked to me, 'They are too closely in touch with Brixton.' (To the *Daily Mail*, May 21.)

I am not sure that we have given enough attention to the oil borings in Derbyshire and I want a 4th page article on the subject tonight by some expert, entitled 'If England Strikes Oil'. A hint on the subject will be found in *The Times* this morning. On no account must the writer paint rosy pictures and delude the public and there must be a strong emphasis on the 'if' throughout. (To the *Daily Mail*, May 23.)

The present prohibition movement in the U.S. began in the South, where the whites rightly determined that the blacks should not have alcohol. The movement, organized with American thoroughness, spread from city to city and was worked on that semi-blackmailing system by which so many American campaigns—the Red Cross, the Liberty Loan—are accompanied. The same movement will be attempted here and I propose to fight it without any connection with brewers, distillers, wine merchants, or the rest. We shall have to face accusations that we are concerned with these people and we shall have to be prepared to face lying statistics as to alcohol and efficiency. So far as I am concerned, it is not a question of prohibition but one of the individuality and individualism of our nation. (To the *Daily Mail*, May 26.)

What I think is a fine exclusive—for I did not see it in any other paper—is the sale of Berkeley Square. What a sensation that would have made before the war! Yesterday, at luncheon, I heard people discussing the extraordinary transfer of land without any particular emotion. Some of them expressed the opinion that it was good to have new blood among the landlords of England. 'Exclusives' such as these used to be the lifeblood of *The Times*.

The Editor of *Figaro* used to try to get one in every day, and his dictum was that an editor should throw a stone into the pool every day, so that its ripples might reach its utmost subscriber. Bogart, the American editor, said that the element of surprise is the most important factor in the news. A dog biting a man is not news; a man biting a dog is distinctly news. (To *The Times*, May 27.)

The first leading article was somewhat of a groan. I personally do not hold with these pessimistic views, and am absolutely confident of the future of our country. (To the *Daily Mail*, June 5.)

The £500 offer to the Carmelite House staff for 'suggestions and criticisms' had brought in a flood of new correspondence, 'invaluable in showing what is wrong with the paper', Northcliffe told Marlowe. 'As the time before my operation, which takes place on June 18, is very short, I have not been able to go into every matter as thoroughly as I should.' He read about two hundred of the letters. He devised a house organ which he called *The Carmelite* and filled its first issue with a selection from the suggestions received and his comments on them. He showed some eccentricity in awarding payments to the senders. Many received £4 and £6; none £5.

When the news editor of *The Times*, George Beer, proposed that Sir Ian Hamilton, of Dardanelles fame, should be invited to write military articles for the paper, Northcliffe replied (May 27): 'Surely you do not suggest that *The Times* should employ a man who murdered as many people as the general whom you mention. He is, in my opinion, an arch-humbug.' He took the opportunity of chiding Beer for writing his letter in his own hand.

Men with a thousand a year should not do what can be done by a three-pounds-a-week typist. It is reminiscent of the time when the then Mr Astor appointed an advertisement manager at a salary of two thousand a year. The manager hired a vehicle of those days—a horse brougham—for which he paid five guineas a week. Mr Astor was furious at this extravagance and told him that he ought to ride on omnibuses. To this the manager replied: 'Do you pay me two thousand a year to ride on omnibuses?' and left him to better himself, as servants always say when they want to leave.

Sometimes, he would abruptly stop dictating, start up from his favourite prone position, and go off to ruminate in the 'pulpit' in the wall. It was not always the seaward view that enticed him there. He came back from one of his soliloquies to dictate a letter to his friend Dewar at Cheyne Court, Chelsea: 'I would like you to do an article called "Birds in a Thanet Garden", touching particularly the nightingale, lesser white-throat, garden warbler, goldfinch and chaffinch.'

An electrocardiograph of his heart had 'not entirely satisfied' the experts of Harley Street. There were further consultations with the surgeon engaged to remove the growth in his throat, James Berry, of the Royal Free Hospital, a leading authority on thyroid pathology. Wickham Steed, who came over from Paris to see Northcliffe, referred to him as being 'very ill'. His correspondence, which he continued right up to the day of the operation, gives no hint of it. Steed wrote that Northcliffe 'faced the operation pluckily. He knew that it might be fatal or that, should he recover from it, it might seriously impair his powers. He said repeatedly that anything would be better than the suffering he had undergone during the past year.' He had asked the doctors about possible after-effects: might there be some reduction of mental capacity? There is no record of what answer he was given. He had great confidence in the surgeon. Steed returned to Paris before taking up his editorial post in London. He wrote to Northcliffe from there: 'When your operation is safely over . . . a big load will be taken off my mind. You may rely on me to do everything possible to lighten your burden but even you hardly understand how much I rely on you and your intuition.' Beaverbrook wrote: 'You may not know that the public is much concerned about your real condition and your doctors ought to issue a statement at an early moment.'

'Those heart specialists have begun to wobble a bit,' he said, coming away from another series of cardiac tests. He was not being a helpful patient. The doctors had asked him to rest completely before the opera-tion. His wife had taken a furnished house, 7 Carlton Gardens, Pall Mall, for that purpose, while their new town house, No. 1, was being got ready. He had no difficulty in staying away from Fleet Street, but his corre-spondence went on without interruption. Northcliffe to Wareham Smith (May 24): 'I am very glad to hear that Imber [advertisement manager of Associated Newspapers Ltd] may earn £6,000 this year. He is a delicate man, and his widow will probably want it.' To Sir George Lloyd, Governor of Bombay (May 24): 'I have spent much of my life in our out-of-the-way parts of the world and know that the man on the spot, unless he has been there too long, is nearly always right.' To Thomas Marlowe (May 31): 'As I personally remember when I was an employee, people will not tell the truth to the heads of a business for fear of getting the backs up of their immediate superiors. There is a great deal of that at Carmelite House.' To the same (June 1): 'My long absence, your absence, war fatigue and the fact that we are all much older—this speaks frankly of *anno domini* at Carmelite House. The sub-editors are overworked and dragooned. The reporters are made to write exactly like each other. The women are not treated properly in the office.' To E. H. Curtis, managing editor of the Manchester edition of the *Daily Mail* (June 1): 'A commission of enquiry is coming to Manchester and I write this as a friend to set your house in order and keep more in touch with your men.' To C. I. Beattie, night editor of the *Daily Mail* (June 1): 'I believe your night staff is on the edge of revolt. It looks as though I shall be obliged to spend a night in the office myself.' To Wickham Steed: 'The puffing of the Prime Minister continues in *The Times*. We are fighting a very astute organization—the Press Bureau of Downing Street.'

He begged his brother Cecil at the Foreign Office to do anything in his power to minimize the effects of the British blockade of Germany on Anglo-American understanding. He urged his news staffs to look into the 'scandal' of war stores at Richborough and Slough. He was pleased to learn that Thomas W. Lamont, the American banker who owned the New York *Evening Post* and who was serving on the American peace delegation in Paris, had told his newspaper staff (June 3): 'I should be grateful if you will bear in mind the fact that I know Northcliffe well, I esteem him highly, I have a great regard for him as a friend and that though we have political differences, whenever I see comments reflecting upon the sincerity of his motives, I am pained, because from my own knowledge of him, I do not believe they are just.' Colonel House to North-cliffe (June 4): 'I am distressed to know that you must undergo an operation, for you were never needed more than now.' Northcliffe to the manager of the *Evening News* (June 4): 'I understand that you have held over advertisements of clerks and others seeking situations in order to make room for advertisements of motor-cycles for sale. Please see that this does not occur again.' After another visit to Harley Street, he spent an afternoon standing at street corners in Oxford Street and Piccadilly, comparing the demand for his *Evening News* with that for *The Star*, *The Globe* and the *Evening Standard*. 'I watched with mixed feelings', having noted that the red paint of the *Evening News* delivery vans was not of 'the same good quality' as the yellow paint of *The Star* vans. H. G. Wells met him in Victoria Street, Westminster, 'looking in the shop windows', recommended as mental relaxation by one of Northcliffe's doctors.

Northcliffe to Mrs Herbert Ward:

> 7, Carlton Gardens,
> S.W.
> June 6, 1919.

My dear Sarita,—I was with my Mother last night and she showed me your letter about Herbert. I am distressed. We are about the same age, and it is curious that we should have both suffered from influenza with consequent heart trouble. Mine was in January last year and I am not over it yet. Herbert has a magnificent constitution. I remember what Stanley [Sir H. M. Stanley, the explorer] said, 'Ward, with his wonderful physique', and I put my money on his getting through.

My own case is that I undergo an operation on Wednesday week for the removal of a thing called adenoma of the thyroid gland. I cannot say that I am looking forward to it, but I am not afraid. What is to be will be.

> Yours always sincerely,
> NORTHCLIFFE

He told Steed, 'in the event of my not returning, I consider you are entitled to an agreement for five years and that if at the end of that time you desire to relinquish your position, you shall be entitled to a pension for life equal to two-thirds of your salary at your retirement'. The official historian of *The Times* chose to read into Northcliffe's proposal to Steed a subtlety not necessarily implicit in a wish to do him a good turn. The implication, according to the historian's rendering, was that Northcliffe desired 'to elevate his own personal dignity by making himself the Proprietor-Editor of *The Times*', and that he wished to use Steed as an instrument for achieving that purpose. During that month Northcliffe had written to Steed (June 5): 'It is always realized that quite apart from the immense labour involved in your position is the responsibility. In your absence in France I have borne this responsibility for six weeks and I can assure you that I am heartily relieved to think that you are back again to take it from my shoulders.' *The Times* official historian failed to note an intimation possibly more authoritative than his involved conjecture. Writing to Steed, Northcliffe said: 'I hope you have gone to golf today. I dreamed last night that I saw you looking very tired.'

Steed replied to Northcliffe that his letter was 'characteristic of your forethought for those who are privileged to work with you' (June 6). The wife of a Carmelite House foundry hand named Davies wrote to thank him for another kind of forethought, 'for making up my husband's wages while he was with H.M. Forces. Perhaps to you it may not seem much, but to me it was goodness itself.' Northcliffe to Mrs Davies (June 11): 'I have been very prosperous, and I like to feel that those who have helped to make the prosperity should share it. Believe me, dear Mrs Davies, I am very grateful for your letter.'

On June 13 he sent for Evelyn Wrench, of the Overseas League, 'to discuss Anglo-American relations'. Wrench found him 'full of energy' and 'much concerned' about the subject in hand. 'He is an extraordinary contrast,' Wrench wrote to his parents in Ulster. 'After discussing really big things, he switched on to arranging details with a member of his staff as regards the "Golden Slipper" he is offering in the *Daily Mail* for the actress with the smallest foot!' Wrench confessed himself baffled by 'this lack of discrimination in Northcliffe's make-up'. The Golden Slipper scheme was discussed and analysed in all its details. 'He threw just as much energy into the golden slipper stunt as he did into the problem of British representation at Washington!' Northcliffe to the directors of The Times Publishing Company (June 13): 'As a Director of *The Times*, I have undertaken, in the event of anything happening to me, that the services of Mr H. G. Price, Mr Humphrey-Davy and Miss A. Cottell, will be retained for a minimum period of five years.'

As the day of the operation drew near, there was conjecture about his fitness to stand it and about its outcome. To the lay mind, an operation on the thyroid gland sounded ominous, even grim. Nor were the specialists, then, given to being briskly optimistic about it. 'Severe but not dangerous', they felt entitled to tell the patient and Northcliffe passed on their opinion in a *Daily Mail* bulletin in which he thanked the many members of the staff who had written letters to him, wishing him well. While there were those who had no doubt that he enjoyed being a national invalid, about whose health public statements were issued, there were many others whose fear that he might vanish from the scene impelled them to expressions of deep feeling. Walter J. Evans to Northcliffe (June 14): 'I have always been cursed with an incurable shyness . . . and I am sure I could not really make you understand how deeply grateful I am for all your many kindnesses and how thoroughly I realize that one's success is for the most part due to being associated with you and profiting by your inspiration. I am always conscious of the fact that most of us must be rather disappointing to you, and that sometimes you must think you bear more than your share of the burden. It is so and I have always felt that we might say of you: "It is he who hath made us, and not we ourselves." ' Northcliffe replied that he was 'greatly touched by the kindness of the letter'. Marlowe to Northcliffe (June 15): 'Just one word of sympathy and affection to assure you that all our thoughts and hopes will be with you on Wednesday.'

★　　★　　★

On the night of June 14–15, two British airmen, John Alcock and Arthur Whitten-Brown, in a Vickers Vimy Rolls-Royce twin-engined biplane, made the first Atlantic flight. The news uplifted the nation, a considerable part of which had only a dim idea that Northcliffe had anything to do with the achievement. Even in his *Daily Mail* he had lately insisted that the reporters should not write as if his £10,000 prize offer 'was the important thing. The important thing is the flight itself', and he took the chance of stressing again that 'the most important part of an aeroplane is the engine. We should always give the name of the engine.' He wrote to Alcock on June 15: 'A very hearty welcome to the pioneer of direct Atlantic flight. Your journey with your brave companion, Whitten-Brown, is a typical exhibition of British courage and organizing efficiency.' He had no doubt, he said, when he first offered the prize in 1913, 'that it would soon be won', and he looked forward 'with certainty to the time when London morning newspapers will be selling in New York in the evening . . . and *vice versa*'. That first flight had been made 'more quickly than the average press message of 1919. We shall no longer suffer from the danger of garbled quotations due to telegraphic compression.' The effect would be to aid Anglo-American understanding; and having uttered that well-disposed cliché, he concluded with a reference to the airmen having arrived at the 'future happy and prosperous dominion of Ireland', which might have caused some of the political critics of 1919 to believe that he was as ill as rumour suggested. He wrote next day, June 16, to Whitten-Brown: 'I was not aware that behind the great number of British decorations you have earned was the hidden personality of an American born in Scotland. There is nothing I rejoice in so much as co-operation between the American and British peoples—the only thing that, in my opinion, can maintain the peace of the world.' *The Star*, the Cadbury's London evening newspaper which had jeered at the £10,000 prize when it was originally offered, made amends in a complimentary leading article written by its editor, James Douglas. 'Newspaper men, without a tinge of petty jealousy, will congratulate Lord Northcliffe and the *Daily Mail* on the fruition of their foresight and enterprise. We are glad that the feat has been accomplished in time to provide a tonic for Lord Northcliffe to help him through his operation on Wednesday.'

Northcliffe wrote to Steed on June 16: 'Is it true that the Clerical Editor of *The Times* is a man whose real name is Kirshbaum? I am really surprised to find that we have a man of German name, and probably a Jew, as Clerical Editor of *The Times*.' Steed replied in praise of Kirshbaum, 'who changed his name to Knight in the war because his wife was insulted in the streets', and Steed considered that there would be 'grave difficulty in replacing him by anyone so well up in Church affairs' (June 16). Northcliffe was content to reply: 'I don't like people who change their names.' Telling Marlowe: 'I had no notion what a topic of public conversation among all classes films have become', he ordered a weekly column of film criticism. 'New films should be reviewed in the *Daily Mail* exactly like new plays', and soon a new race of critics was born. Soon, too, he was telling the *Times* staff: 'I was delighted to see the word "boom" in quote marks on page 7. We must guard the portals of our language more vigorously than ever, now that the moving-picture screen is dumping horrid words upon us.' He forecast keen post-war competition from American periodical publishers and commanded J. H. Newton, the Amalgamated Press head printer, to improve the production of its chief publications. 'The specimen copies which are sent to me are carefully selected ones. I take no notice of them.'

He wrote to his mother's medical adviser, Dr H. J. W. Martin, of Mill Hill (June 16): 'The removal of the adenoma is likely to result in my being fuller of vigour and venom than ever before.' A younger member of the Printing House Square dynasty, Stephen Walter, wrote to him (June 16): 'I want to thank you for all the kindness that you have shown me.' Sympathetic and flattering resolutions were passed at company meetings . . . 'never was a time when his vigilance and energy were more needed by the nation', and so on. Northcliffe to Mrs Moberly Bell: 'Just one parting word—please do not sell your [*Times*] shares cheaply. The directors are, I believe, about to declare a 12½ per cent dividend.' He glanced back in his letter to Mrs Bell at recent events in the history of *The Times* (June 16): 'I had no personal quarrel with Geoffrey Dawson, from whom I have a very sweet telegram at this very minute. He and I did not agree about the vacillations of our present Government in the face of the enemy—that is what it amounted to.'

He told Mrs W. K. Clifford, the novelist: 'I go into the nursing home with only one anxiety—Anglo-American relations. They are very bad—infinitely worse than our Government or the public know—and if we are not very close to war with the United States before the end of the next Presidential election, I shall be a very happy man.' He had heard from Sir Arthur Willert, in Washington, on June 13 that the 'present situation is sinister'. Ireland, the British censorship and the British blockade against Germany were exacerbating factors. Northcliffe wrote: 'The Irish are creating great difficulties for us over there.' He sent a message to Marlowe on June 17: 'I hope there is no prospect of any speech at the Alcock luncheon likely to arouse the Americans.' More letters of good will and good wishes reached him on the morning of the operation, June 18: 'My dear Northcliffe,—This is only a line to wish you good luck in your operation and for a speedy restoration to good health. My wife joins me in this wish. —Winston S. Churchill.' There was an instruction for Sutton: 'I want Arthur Pearson's book, *Victory Over Blindness*, to be properly dealt with in my periodicals as well as my newspapers. We must not overlook the tragic fate of young men blinded in the war and the quiet heroism with which they learn at St. Dunstan's to overcome so serious a handicap in life.'

At 7.45 in the morning of June 18 he pencilled a note to his mother: 'Am feeling fine and joyous at thought of getting rid of my annoyance. Deep and tender love, most darling Mum.—The Firstborn. P.S. I slept perfectly, but am very hungry.' He then read the newspapers and telephoned his comments. To *The Times*: 'A good *Times* this morning. I like the Irish leader and judgment in giving the full text of the Irish accusations and our belated reply. But will anything but a garbled condensation appear in the American press? We have no one in the United States to see to these things.' To the *Daily Mail*: 'An excellent *Daily Mail* this morning. The *Evening News* was better last night than usual. Congratulate our boxing man. . . . There were too many dress pictures in the picture page, showing a lack of sense of proportion again.' Ten minutes later he was wheeled into the operating theatre.

The doctors made a public announcement. '*Wednesday, June 18th.*— Viscount Northcliffe was operated upon this morning. A deep-seated adenoma of the thyroid, which was causing considerable pressure, was removed. The patient's condition is satisfactory.' It was signed by James Berry, P. Seymour Price and E. G. Moon. The last-named was the Broadstairs general practitioner. Northcliffe had specially asked that he should be present and that his name should appear on the bulletin.

J. L. Garvin to Northcliffe:

9, Greville Place,
N.W.
18th June, 1919.

My dear old Chief,—I don't know when you will be allowed to read this, but hope they will let you see it soon to tell you that it carries with it the true unchanged affection of this friend. Tonight's bulletin relieves my mind about you; for amidst the rumours, some mild, some wild, I knew nothing with certainty. An operation of that kind must be a severe ordeal, in any case; but let me hope that it may restore you to perfect health. You are young in my eyes and capable of so many great things. When the Atlantic flight was accomplished I thought of you as a pioneer in one of the biggest wonders of human history and only today Lady Colvin was talking to me of the gentleness and courtesy you showed her, recently, as you often did in the old days to me and mine. In spite of the rubs inseparable from the public jostle, it is not easy for anybody who has ever been very fond of you to cease to be so. The human things and the human memories count with me more and more. So bless you; and when you are seeing people let me come to bring you a few minutes of good cheer.

Ever yours,
GARVE

Northcliffe and Winston Churchill

Sir Henry Royce (of Rolls-Royce) with Northcliffe at Kingsdown, Kent

Northcliffe to his mother: '11 & 12, *Beaumont Street, Portland Place, W*.1. 19th June, 1919. Sweet Mother,—The surgeons now say that I may tell you that all danger is past, but that I must go slowly for three months, one month, I hope, with my dearest Mother, in Scotland or Ireland. Your devoted Firstborn.' He pencilled a note to Steed: 'There are three reasons why I must go slow. Heart trouble caused by the adenoma. Elimination of the poison caused by the beastly thing. Disturbance of the thyroid caused by the operation. I mean to get really well for once and keep well. *Paper is A.1.*' Northcliffe to Campbell Stuart (June 23): 'The heart specialists are coming tomorrow to do and make their bit.'

Chapter Twenty-six

Storm Clouds over the Atlantic

NORTHCLIFFE could enjoy solitude only as an angler. He could not endure boredom: 'it was agony' to him, said Dr Macnair Wilson. After three days in the nursing home he grew restless and was temporarily solaced by the music of Chopin, played by his request on a piano brought into the corridor outside his door. Soon, he threw off the doctors' restraints, sent for H. G. Price and the green deed-box, and insisted on receiving more than the prescribed two visitors a day.

He had suffered thirty-six hours of severe neuralgia. Sumptuously pillowed, he looked like a bandaged Cæsar. Less harassed by his affairs than usual, he was free to display to perfection that consideration for others which he was capable of showing without its not infrequent reward of slavish gratitude. Immediately after the operation, he suggested that his personal physician, Seymour Price, should send in his bill. Seymour Price to Northcliffe: 'Thank you very much for your cheque, but I would like to thank you still more for the kindly thought that made you ask me for my account. Your unselfish thought for others has made everyone of us— doctors and nurses—deeply attached to you.'

The operation wound was 'healing nicely'. One of the doctors thought fit to confide in him: 'I can't tell you how relieved I am, now that the growth is extracted, to find that it was not malignant. *We never know.*' Northcliffe underlined the words in a letter to a friend. It was deeply pleasing to him to receive letters and telegrams from unknown well-wishers among the public; several hundred. He was moved especially by a message signed by sixty-seven women members of the staff at Carmelite House. 'We hope you will very quickly recover and be able to resume your active work among us all.' His devotion to the sex being what it was, no doctor could have prevented him from returning 'most grateful thanks' immediately.

He was only a little less gratified by messages from trade union groups, among them the members of the combined house chapels of the mechanical departments of his newspapers and periodicals, and from individual workers. He responded as if he had received a benediction when word was brought to him that the pupils of Christ Church School, Brighton, had prayed in class for his recovery. A letter was dictated at once to the head teacher, desiring 'the dear children' to be told that he was 'most humbly and deeply grateful'. Contrasting with those decent compulsions were others that belied the gentle smile and soft voice.

Northcliffe to Sir Basil Thomson, Director of Intelligence, Scotland Yard: 'I am confined to bed and do not suppose that my doctors would be pleased if they knew I was dictating even a short note. I happen to know a great deal about de Laszlo, who has painted three portraits for me', de Laszlo being a fashionable portrait painter of Hungarian-Jewish origin. 'I do not think a man of this type should be allowed to claim British nationality', and he contributed disparaging details which he hoped Sir Basil would 'show to the Attorney-General'. It was the Northcliffe of the story, raising the glass partition between the pike and the goldfish in the aquarium. Time hanging heavily in the nursing home, he seized the telephone at any impulse of the moment to speak to people in his various offices. Several were told: 'I may have something important to say to you later in the day', and were kept waiting in vain through hours of anxious anticipation. Annoyed by Corbett, the *Times* manager, he ordered Price to ring Corbett's home telephone number every half-hour through one evening as a reprisal.

There was a letter from Lovat Fraser, of the *Times* leader writing staff, giving him information about the 'Slough war depot scandal', which the *Daily Mail* had been exposing. Fraser insisted that much of the blame for concealing the truth about the affair lay with Dawson, the *Times* ex-editor. 'The night after the Armistice I returned from France and begged him to allow me to smash the scheme, which I knew to be a Glasgow "ramp". He put me off week after week, and I did not in the least realize that the true reason was that Lord Milner was involved. . . . Dawson and I were always good friends, and remain so now; but I cannot help feeling that in this matter, as in others, he put private before national interests' (July 8).

By the end of the first week in July, Northcliffe felt sufficiently well to begin sending comments on the paper in long letters to Marlowe, though he had not yet resumed his regular bulletins. More, he could again face a world with Lloyd George in it. Northcliffe to Marlowe (July 8): 'Downing Street is desperately anxious for our support. They approach me in every kind of way. You know well enough that my attitude is not a personal one. When the Prime Minister does what I think right I say so; when he does what I think wrong I equally say so. See to it that none of our people go near his Press Bureau.' A few days later he was complaining again to Marlowe: 'I am being pestered by politicians and I hear that the Lord Chancellor [Lord Birkenhead] wants to see me. Perhaps I should see him, though my doctors will only allow me to see absolutely essential people connected with our family or affairs. I greatly dislike these politicians trying to see me over the heads of my editors.'

The politicians were hoping to find him favourable to their plans for the Irish future, concerning which the English half of him seemed to be in the ascendant over the Irish half. It pleased him on occasions to say that he had lived in Ireland, though he had not done so since the age of two, and that he knew the Irish people, though he had rarely gone among them. His Irish sentiment was opportunist rather than profound. Primarily he regarded the problem of Ireland in the light of Anglo-American relations, which it was doing so much to bedevil. Willert, in Washington, had written to him (July 10): 'The whole future of Anglo-American relations depends on a solution', and had recorded his surprise at finding 'how many of the better Irish-Americans want an Irish settlement not so much on account of Ireland as because they feel that, after all, the decency of the world has its taproots in British institutions'. Such a view was entirely acceptable to Northcliffe, who was never an Irish partisan and for whom a settlement was important as a contribution to the larger aim.

'I now see numberless paragraphs that I am disappointed at not being appointed Lord Lieutenant of Ireland', he told Steed in a letter of August 9. 'Also that I have lately bought the old family mansion in Dublin, where I was born. As a matter of fact, I was *not* born in Dublin but in Chapelizod, which house I have long owned. It was my brother Cecil who bought the family mansion in Dublin. All these paragraphs come from Downing Street', where a Welshman (Lloyd George) and a Scot (Sir William Sutherland, his parliamentary secretary) persisted in regarding Northcliffe as an Irishman: 'the most eminent Irishman living', according to Lloyd George at that time.

Northcliffe warned Steed that 'the Prime Minister's next step will be to drop the Irish question', because Steed had published in *The Times* some special articles on peace in Ireland. As Steed told Walter Long, the First Lord of the Admiralty, 'we know enough of the Cabinet and of the Prime Minister to be sure that, if a scheme for an Irish settlement were inspired by God Almighty and were published first in *The Times*, it would be rejected by the Government because it had been published in *The Times*'. Alternatively, Northcliffe suggested, Lloyd George 'will say that we stole the scheme from him (he has made that suggestion more than once about our projects)'. He urged Steed: 'Push it. Keep at the subject.'

The secretary of the Irish Club in London had informed him of the views of many members of the club, that 'by birth, experience, and world-wide influence, you could be the saviour of Ireland'. His brother Cecil had written to tell him that 'eager Irish nationalists are running round the Lobbies tipping you for the place of Lord Lieutenant'. Northcliffe replied to him: 'Does any human being imagine that I would compromise my power and independence by a footman's job like that—or any other job? I am all for the abolition of the Lord Lieutenant and such flunkeys.' Joseph Devlin, the Nationalist leader, wrote to him from the National Club, Belfast, disagreeing with Northcliffe's policy for Ireland as set out in *The Times*, while recognizing it as 'a bold and statesmanlike attempt to solve the problem'. Devlin expressed the hope that Northcliffe would live 'to be the chief instrument in solving the Irish question upon lines which will bring satisfaction to Ireland and good will and enduring friendship between the Irish and the British people' (August 5, 1919).

*   *   *

'I feel awfully tired—an absolute jellyfish.' He was at 7 Carlton Gardens, writing to Stanley Rendall, M.D., at Mentone. 'Parting from my little friend [the adenoma] has left me very limp.' He was allegedly 'resting in the garden', but the letter flow, in and out, was beyond the province of the doctors. 'I know your impatient spirit chafes, but for the sake of England and the Empire, rest and let Nature do her healing in her own way', was the advice to him of one of the Empire's homegoing Prime Ministers, W. M. Hughes, of Australia. 'It is troubling me, my very dear brother,' the crippled St. John wrote to him, 'to see you labouring under such great weakness. You must take care, and very great care. You must throttle down your brain. Getting well is a zigzag business, so you must not be impatient with the initial progress which will be slow and variable. You must give yourself a long rest. Nothing else matters.'

Lord Birkenhead, who wrote personally, expressed himself 'glad that you got through your trouble so easily', and asked for the opportunity of 'a long talk about public affairs'. The *Daily Mail* leader writer, Wilson, likewise presuming a little too soon on Northcliffe's recuperative powers, proposed that 'the office should have no truck with Lloyd George until he has the decency to apologise to you for sneering at your illness, a caddish act on his part'. To that doggedly loyal suggestion, Northcliffe replied: 'My dear Wilson,—What is the matter with your liver?' When Marlowe touched on the same topic, he was told in an injured schoolboy tone: 'The Prime Minister, having taken occasion to attack a man whom he knew to be ill and not having had the courage to apologise, will find that the difficulty will never be overcome so far as my Mother, my Wife, and the Family are concerned.' At Printing House Square dignified shoulders were shrugged when he ordered W. Lints Smith (July 15):

741

'Please have a big flag put up on the flagpost here, with the words "The Times" in very large letters upon it. Get the biggest flag the pole will stand.' Eight days later there was another flourish of power from the sick-bed: 'I have asked Sir Campbell Stuart to have made a very large sign covering the whole of the building with gilt letters from four to six feet high, including the Royal Arms in colours. *The letters should dominate the building*—not the building the letters. Do not delay. They can very easily dominate the street if brains and imagination are used. Chief.' Laid aside, he may have had a sense of diminished personal force for which the sudden compulsive obsession with size was an over-compensation. The order for the huge gilt sign implicated the entire management of *The Times* in the *folie de grandeur* charge often made against Northcliffe, who told Price: 'Now the taxi-drivers will know the place when they see it.'

There had been a message of greeting to him after his operation signed by every member of the *Times* staff. He took an unconscionable time over composing a suitable acknowledgment. It proved to be an elaborate protestation of the part that he had been called on to play in the affairs of the paper. Not all the grave and reverent seniors of Printing House Square were likely to have read it. Those who did probably thought it redundantly proprietorial.

My connection with Printing House Square has not been of long duration compared with that of many of the signatories, yet my memory goes back to a very different paper; to a time when, just about a decade ago, against the advice of nearly every friend, and when, as at present, I was in ill-health, and at a time, too, when many people thought that *The Times* was dying, I suddenly found myself with the burden of the paper on my shoulders.

It did not seem probable then that old readers would return and that new ones would be found to a degree never contemplated in 1860, when *The Times* had reached the highest journalistic pinnacle ever attained before here or in any other English-speaking country.

The disastrous legal quarrels among some of the old proprietors, following upon the Parnell Commission, had almost felled the giant, and it was then that I first surveyed its decaying printing establishment and deserted advertising hall.

In the few years that have elapsed, much labour and the gay and vibrant enthusiasm of the workers at Printing House Square have resulted in placing *The Times* once more in the position of being not only the leading newspaper of the world, but the most prosperous journal in the world.

It is true that most of our prosperity leaves us in the form of Excess Profits Tax, but that matters little so long as politicians do not waste the fruit of our labour, for *The Times* is not an instrument of gain but of good government.

Our great fortune is the result of the work of many minds at home and abroad.

We have been much helped by the cordial sympathy of the Walter family. Many of the changes that we newcomers caused to be made at Printing House

Square may have seemed revolutionary to those who had the honour of being associated with *The Times* for so many decades, but in whatever we have done, we have had from the outset the unswerving support of John Walter.

Our achievement and the beautiful presentation from Printing House Square are a great solace to me at a time when good health seems to be a long way off, and they are a complete recompense for the thousands of hours that I have spent in the service of the Paper.

He was becoming garrulous and repetitive, symptoms of exhaustion. He sent Marlowe three identical letters of complaint about the politicians, who, he said, were trying 'to get at' him in the nursing home. It was necessary to fend them off with a statement of policy proclaiming his independence. Steed drew up a formula which he instantly adopted. A copy of it, neatly centred in the page, was sent to the chief editorial men on his newspapers.

Support no Government merely because it is a Government.
Attack no Government merely because it is a Government.
Judge all Governments, and all members of Governments, from the standpoint of the national welfare, never accepting their assurance at face value but giving support when their deeds bear out their words; and withholding support or attacking them when their words or their deeds seem to be dictated by party or personal interests.

Having thus delivered the tablets of his political commandments, he went to stay at the bungalow at Clandon, in Surrey. By his order, two members of the business staff of the Amalgamated Press telephoned him there on the eve of leaving for a first trip to America. He gave them a short homily. 'Criticize no one or anything. Express delight at everything. You will be told that America won the war. To that you must not demur. Don't wear spats. Goodbye and good luck.' While he was at the bungalow he was stricken by what he declared was 'the most excruciating agony of my life', apparently a bad attack of neuritis. Injections of morphine had no effect, 'nor did three heavy doses of opium'. Relief came through hyoscine—'what Dr Crippen gave a nagging wife'. There had been an accompaniment of swelling down the left side. He wrote to H. G. Price from the bungalow on *Times* notepaper:

Over a hundred business items have arrived during my few days' stay here. Mr Marlowe wants to see me. Is it really urgent? Sutton wants to see me on a much more urgent matter, but he does not propose to see me. Also Lord Rothermere wants to see me on much more important matters than any concerning Mr Marlowe. You should be sharper with these people.

The doctor says that the quicker I get away, the sooner I shall be free from these relapses. The last one was a severe warning, for the whole of my left side was out of order from the top of my head to my toes.

It is not fair to send me a serial story to read. I return it unread. The other day Hamilton Fyfe was on most of the day till we pulled out the telephone. None of these people realize, except Sir George Sutton who does realize it, that each is only one of hundreds. He also knows that this relapse has been very much more serious than the operation. Even deferential Humpty says that I look a wreck. *You* never bother me, but you have passed things on to me during the last few days when I ought to be far from doing work.

Your very wonky
CHIEF

'I could write a very good article on the effects of drugs', he told Marlowe, and wondered whether, because he could not share the amusement which others found in an article by Sir James Barrie in the *Daily Mail*, 'my illness has robbed me of my sense of humour. Some people could not see any fun in *The Young Visiters*. I have hardly ever laughed so much.' There was another letter to Marlowe the same day (July 24): 'I was warned that thyroid operations produced all sorts of queer results. I am just able to lie here and read my papers.' Yet he was quite unable to resist pointing out their defects. 'It is rather hard that, though I was practically the inventor of printed photographs, we should have so much trouble with them in the *Daily Mail*.' A famous opera singer, addressing him as 'Dear Big Man', had made an appeal to his heart for help for an old German servant of the Royal Opera House. She received an answer of a kind likely to affront an artist. 'My dear Melba,—There are so many English people who need help that I leave the support of any Germans in England to their own fellow-countrymen who have made fortunes here during the war.' Northcliffe to Steed: 'Au revoir! I feel like a deserter leaving you at this time of great troubles. . . . You are the centre of the policies of my newspapers and an hour's work from you a day in good health is all that I really want. You must not do so much.'

So saying, he left for Scotland, taking Max Pemberton with him. He had told Sir Courtauld Thomson that he was suffering from 'a heart complication'. To Sutton he had written: 'As to the state of my heart, the doctors are anxious to push me off.' In the light of later events, his heart condition in the summer of 1919 was probably more significant than was realized. He closed his letter to Sutton: 'We are all getting on in years and never know what may happen.'

Northcliffe to H. G. Price:

King's Arms Hotel,
Lockerbie.

1st August, 1919.

My dear Price,—Humpty has been plainly told that any more nocturnal goings on and carryings-on will incapacitate him from work later or even sooner. I have therefore given him eight weeks' rest, with free board and bed,

744

and have written him firmly and kindly that I cannot have about me a semi-invalid *noctambule*, fond as I am of him.

Now I have a 'hunch', as they say in N.Y., that after about three weeks of marine and rural serenity [at Elmwood] he will find excuse to get up to town and hike him off to the Canning Town Hippodrome or Peckham Palace; his damsels, owing to weak legs, never get nearer to town.

That must be stopped. I know that he 'doesn't like the country', and doesn't see why he 'shouldn't enjoy himself like others'. But apart from the urgent question of his health, my life and work *must* be considered, and I *cannot continue with him* in his recent state of mind blankness and red-nosed forgetfulness. Two doctors have said it is curable, if taken in hand *now*.

Am still wonky,

CHIEF.

'I am paying the price of so much work,' he told his mother, having arrived at the Royal Marine Hotel at Nairn. 'I am doing all the doctors say', and quite a lot that they did not say, seeing that they had explicitly told him: 'Keep away from business for three to six months.' A message awaited him from Sir James Mackenzie, of St. Andrews. 'Allow me to congratulate you on your recovery from the operation. As one who has appreciated your work during the war and who is grateful for what you have done, I read with concern the reference to your illness in the newspapers, while I was interested in you personally as one who had consulted me.' He was angry because his five-day week edict was not being fully observed at Carmelite House. 'The difficulty of getting things done there, my dear Price, is due to the fact that the heads are all middle-aged. Take care that Fish—a hard piece of human mechanism—knows my displeasure.' He notified George Curnock, organizer of many *Daily Mail* campaigns, 'I have ordered a five-day week and I mean to have it', his tone deriving some of its firmness from a letter written to him direct by a member of the reporting staff who described the 'intolerable working conditions' at Carmelite House; also there was trade union pressure. A further cause of irritable comment at that time was the misuse of their prerogative by his editors. He unburdened himself to Steed on that matter: 'Campbell [Stuart] is the only person I have yet found who understands the harmonizing of my newspapers, that is to say, chiefly stopping their pin-pricking habits. Just as nothing is so easy as spending other people's money, so to certain people nothing is more pleasant than wasting someone else's power and influence. . . . Though it is essential that *The Times* be kept absolutely separate from the other newspapers with which I am concerned, it is impossible that the head evening news-paper in the whole world [the *Evening News*] can, in the mind of the Government, be dissociated from the policy of Printing House Square.' There was an afterthought for Lints Smith: 'Please see that all the women

745

workers of Printing House Square have half a day, a morning or an afternoon, once a fortnight (in addition to Saturday afternoon) in order that they may see something of the world and of the shops.'

Thereafter, the death of Herbert Ward filled his thoughts. 'For days together we would talk of nothing else,' Max Pemberton said. 'Often, as we settled down in the car for a long day's journey, he would say: "Let us talk about Herbert." ' Northcliffe to his brother St. John: 'Herbert was one of my earliest recollections. I knew him long before you were born and can see him very vividly in my mind's eye now in his sailor suit, when we lived at Alexandra Road and I must have been less than 5. We left there in 1870. He was a real war victim, for he owed his death entirely to his sufferings from war service. I do not suppose that he and I exchanged half a dozen letters in our lives, yet we thought a great deal about each other.' Northcliffe to Sutton: 'Herbert Ward's passing tells me to go slow: when he was 54, he was a stronger man than I have ever been. I knew him 20 years before I saw my dear Sut. Allowed one hour's golf daily but still wonky. Hulton seems to waste a lot of money in these small towns.' Northcliffe to his mother: 'Herbert's passing was not a shock, but a surprise. Except Arthur Hendry, he was my earliest memory outside the family, Mrs Jealous perhaps excepted, also. I well remember him in a sailor hat, with a small boat and his fine fat silkworms. He was as strong as an ox, and the most varied man possible. Three years ago when he was my age, he was apparently in perfect health and tremendous spirits. A lesson to me, my sweet.—Your Firstborn.' He wrote to his mother again: 'Herbert Ward's passing has made me think a great deal of all sorts of things. Three years ago he was in far better health than I am now. It is a warning to me to be very careful.' His brother St. John wrote from 90 Wigmore Street: 'When I saw Herbert the last time he was a dead man and I think he knew it, as when I was leaving him he asked me to kiss him. He was a ghost. I know you will deeply feel the loss of Herbert. I do. He was a mystic creature, full of great affection for you, of whom he always talked when I ever saw him. He was what I always imagined General Gordon to be like.'

* * *

'Humpty-Dumpty', at Elmwood, was still keeping late hours, 'quite incompatible with the kind of work his position with me demands' (Northcliffe to H. G. Price). 'Frankly, I am very weary of him.' Price interceded on Davy's behalf and Northcliffe promised to give him a further trial until Christmas. But Davy was to accept conditions. '1. That you do not arrive at my work in the morning in a state of exhaustion due to nocturnal excursions. 2. That you pay more attention to your appearance and stop making old-man noises. 3. That you do not answer the telephone. 4. That you do not write letters about my affairs without first showing them to me. 5. That you do not interview anybody.' To which Davy replied: 'It makes me feel very sad to realize that, despite my affection for you and my efforts to please you, I have so ill succeeded in earning your approval of my work. Judging from your constant kindness to me, I was under the impression that I was giving satisfaction', and, carefully copying out his master's conditions, he promised 'to abide by them devotedly, My Lord.' By then, Northcliffe was in his father-of-my-people mood. 'Let us see how you go on', he told 'Humpty-Dumpty'. To W. A. Ackland, editor of *The Times Weekly Edition*: 'Do not take my criticism too much to heart. I always say what I think, but am not so outrageously unreasonable as some people think.' To the *Times* news editor, George Beer: 'Your deficiencies are those of a purely Fleet Street education, which I had the good fortune to escape, but I am your keen supporter in the office', and subscribed himself, 'Yours affectionately and sincerely'. To H. W. Wilson: 'What about your holiday? See that you get a good one.' Wilson was 'greatly cheered' by his 'kind and generous letter', and thus fortified wrote to point out the dangers of Marxism in factories. Northcliffe retorted by post: 'I do wish you would get this damned nonsense of Bolshevism out of your brain. You have never understood the British workman.' He approved again Price's management of his correspondence. 'You never send me anything that I should not have, which is a great comfort.' Northcliffe to Rothermere: 'I believe that I am very much better, but for some reason or other I am abominably tired after very little exertion.' Northcliffe to Sutton: 'Am slowly progressing but easily exhausted. Hope you go slowly in view of winter campaign. *Health first*. I notice that the women at the hotel are reading needlework papers.' He took pleasure in telling a number of his correspondents, among them Madame de Tizac in Paris, that when his stenographer, Amy Cottell, bought a new pencil in a Nairn shop, 'they put a penny on the bill for sharpening it'. The start of a commercial air service between Paris and London on August 25 was noted with no trace of self-congratulation. 'Few people realize how dense is the general mind. I have to write to Paris every day and yet have never heard any of my secretaries suggest that letters should go by air.' Northcliffe to Pomeroy Burton: 'I hope to see an improvement in the appearance of the front hall at Carmelite House when I return. It is no credit to you. Go to The Fleetway House and compare it. The lift girls' costumes and hair arrangements do not give one a favourable impression. When I was last there one of the girls received me and a distinguished American visitor, eating.'

Seeking a haven from the changing winds of literary circumstance,

Max Pemberton had revived a suggestion Northcliffe had made some time before, that there should be an authoritatively endowed school of journalism in London. Pemberton had secured the backing of the principal of the Pelman Institute, W. J. Ennever, who wrote confirming his interest to Northcliffe at Nairn. Northcliffe agreed with Pemberton that an institution of the kind might help to produce journalists for the new times that were coming. More particularly he wanted to help Pemberton. He allowed Pemberton to use his name, and out of the discussions there came the London School of Journalism, which has continued to function from that time.

Northcliffe to Marlowe:

The Royal Marine Hotel,
Nairn.

26th August, 1919.

My dear Marlowe,—It seems but yesterday that I said goodbye to you at Carlton Gardens, and here am I starting on another two months' holiday, while you are back at the treadmill.

What has been particularly noticed about the Associated Newspapers is that it is not developing people. When I look at The Fleetway House and Printing House Square and see how young men are being pushed on there to positions of great responsibility—take Freeman, Anderson and Linforth, for example, or Corbett and Campbell Stuart—I realize that what one of our enemies said of Carmelite House is true: 'You are all people of middle age and all advancing at the same rate into old age.' It is certainly true of me who am now in my 55th year and well aware of it. We have at Carmelite House two most admirable men, who I think are stumbling blocks to the discovery of new talent, Beattie and Fish. I have never known either of them find or develop anybody.

Many years ago Mr Pulitzer said to me: 'Holiday time is the time to find who's who in a newspaper office. Give your head men long holidays. It will do them good and develop the young ones.' I do not want to inject new blood arbitrarily from the outside, but I will have to do so if our young men do not get their chances.

As to my health, my heart is examined twice weekly and so far each time the doctor says it has increasing 'kick' in it (did I hear you remark that you thought so?). I am not taking any drug for it.

Did you notice that the Manchester edition, page 3, Monday, spoke of Newfoundland as being in Nova Scotia?

Your attached
N.

Under the same date, he wrote also to Freeman, deputy editor of *The Times*, deferring to Steed's editorial authority. 'As to my own suggestions, please remember that if ever I send any which happen to be in contradiction to those sent by Steed mine must give way.' During his long illness, he said, he had many hours in which to think of 'world affairs and newspapers'. His ponderings had yielded many ideas, 'some good, some, I daresay, bad'. It appeared that he was anxious to avoid the provocation which had injured his relations with Dawson. '*The Times* is of course not one-twentieth of the responsibility I have and it does not absorb a fiftieth of my time, owing to its good organization. It is only proper, therefore, that I should in all matters save those of basic principles, such as our relation to the United States, the Irish question, the size of the Navy and Labour questions, give way to those like you and Steed who devote their lives to one object.'

Colonel House, who was no longer a vitally active force in American policy-making, was staying with Lady Northcliffe at her little house at Crowborough. Northcliffe wrote to him from Nairn:

Here I am in an entirely different land, among the wild Highlands, 650 miles due North from you, close to the tiny battlefield of Culloden, where, in 1746, the Scots and the last of the Stuarts were defeated by the Anglo-Hun forces, aided by the treacherous Campbells, with the double result that our present Royal Family was firmly enthroned and the American Colonies and Canada received an immense influx of MacDonalds, Stuarts, Gordons, Frasers, MacIntoshes, and so on, who emigrated in thousands. Your dear little granddaughter who gave me the rose at Magnolia is very like the children here.

His overriding concern for the Anglo-American future prompted him to write to Lord Grey of Falloden on August 29, 'as one of many who are grateful for the sacrifice you are about to make'. Grey had been appointed to succeed Reading *pro tem* at Washington.

For more than five-and-twenty years, since my first visit to the United States, I have realized that our relations with its people are a paramount question. Labour troubles, economic questions, and the rest of our national worries may solve themselves, but on the other side of the Atlantic is a latent series of hostile elements that nullify the strong friendship and admiration felt for the British Empire in many and, I am glad to say, influential circles.

He told Grey that he was anxious about the period of the coming presidential election, 'one of extra danger', and said that it was a great solace to know that Grey would be in Washington. 'I hope that my fears may be proved wrong.' He passed to a theme not less congenial to them both:

You will be awakened every morning, as I was, by the voices of birds that were all of them new to me. You will find a growing movement there for nature study, as you no doubt heard from Theodore Roosevelt, who gave me a vivid account of his day with you.

There was word from Paris that the price of paper for the *Continental Daily Mail* was likely to go up by twenty per cent before the year was out. He allowed that matter to disturb his rest at Nairn where, he told Sutton, his recuperation was 'so much slower than it was ten years ago—a warning to you to get as much holiday as you can before the summer is over'. He was going on, he said, to see Sir James Mackenzie, 'the great heart man who, though retired, has taken much interest in my case'. He repeated his injunction to Sutton to watch his health. 'If I had taken more rest I should not be perpetually exiled, as I am, from friends and work.' He compared his golfing stamina of before the war with that of the Nairn holiday. 'I could and often did play two rounds a day. Here I can just do fifteen holes in a foursome.' He added the postscript: 'NOW GET MORE HOLIDAY.' Max Pemberton said that he was 'quite amazed' when in one of their talks during that Scottish holiday Northcliffe insisted that he had been at Stamford School after leaving Henley House, whereas the reverse was true. It was an aberration of memory which Pemberton cited as an indication of 'a certain failing' of Northcliffe's powers.

Northcliffe wrote to Sutton again, three days later. He had seen Mackenzie, 'a fine old leonine Scot, who used vigorous and profane language about the quacks of Harley Street and district', and who mentioned that he had been in America and had heard what Northcliffe had done there and of the distances he had travelled, of the audiences he had addressed, and so on. Northcliffe said that Mackenzie had thus addressed him:

'You are 54 years of age. You have overworked all your life. You have had a severe operation. If you were a manufacturer with two or three businesses, I would tell you to sell all but one. It is obvious that you cannot do that, therefore it would be well if you began work slowly and gradually and go on up to about *three days a week.*'

He announced himself to Sutton as 'heartily sick of semi-invalidism and golf. I want to get back to work', and, it appeared, to the politics he despised. While he was not actively influencing his newspapers just then, he said, he proposed to continue his attacks against 'Government waste establishments' which he called 'my road-to-ruin campaign'. He also intended to go on resisting the Prime Minister's overtures. 'I am taking none of them, nor shall I mix up in any of Beaverbrook's rather clumsy wire-pulling.' Steed had reported to Northcliffe that Lloyd George was referring to the 'unfriendliness' of *The Times* towards him and that some people thought he was 'offering an olive branch'. Cecil Harmsworth had written in his diary on August 19: 'Ll.G. in a reckless mood today. He talks of "going for" Northcliffe again, N. having been going for him vigorously in his Press of late.' Northcliffe was critical of Government expenditure.

He wrote to St. John: 'Even during the last few weeks the Government have, to my knowledge, been creating a number of fat jobs. There is no more mystery about cutting down national expense than there is in cutting down the expenses of a business. I learned that in America and at Crewe House, where I kept motor-cars and all expenses down to nothing, and took good care to pay for my own car, tyres and petrol as an example. The Prime Minister has an enormous and totally unnecessary entourage.' But when, on a visit to Manchester, Lloyd George was taken ill with a throat infection, Northcliffe instructed the manager of the Manchester office of the *Daily Mail*, H. J. Peddar, to 'convey a message of sympathy'. Peddar said that 'the Prime Minister appeared to be delighted. He asked for Lord Northcliffe's address at Nairn, saying that he would write to him.'

He had correspondence with Caird about expenses at Carmelite House. Caird gave him news of rising costs on every hand. 'The five-day week will cost us £90,000 a year.' Paper prices were not falling. Railways were almost certain to increase their rates; moreover, Caird wrote pessimistically, 'men are not working as they used to do. An extra page in the foundry brings a deputation downstairs for an interview. In one department last week a card was displayed bearing the words: *Don't hurry, don't worry*.' None of those things seemed to bother Northcliffe. 'What a gloomy devil you are,' he replied to Caird. 'Why should you expect the "workers" to hurry and worry when the capitalists such as myself and you are lying back in the heather listening to the humming of the bees, or waiting at each tee on an overcrowded links for a game that takes four hours to play? I have no fear whatever of our workers.' Speculating in his reply on 'how many *good* things you are keeping from me', he told Caird: 'If you will send me an outline of possible savings I will authorize them if I think fit, as I am in a most reasonable state of mind just now. Supposing I begin at the top!' (September 2).

Lord Grey of Falloden, replying to Northcliffe's letter of August 29:

> Falloden,
> Lesbury,
> Northumberland.
> 4th September, 1919.

Dear Lord Northcliffe,—I know you have always cared for good relations between us and the United States and felt them to be of the greatest importance. To me almost everything seems to depend on this, and I know that there are elements in the United States which make for co-operation with us, so that there are great possibilities; but there are other influences there, especially the Irish, which threaten to spoil everything. I am so glad that you have taken the line that you have about this, for I am sure it will need all our efforts to overcome this difficulty in the United States.

The Government here cannot do it without the Press, and the influence of *The Times* in putting Irish policy in a favourable light in America is invaluable. The Government, of course, must do their part in putting forward a good policy.

The failure of my sight, which severely limits my reading and prevents me from seeing faces, makes public work very laborious and difficult, so I have stipulated that I must be free to come away, and a permanent Ambassador must be appointed early next year.

I regret the loss of Roosevelt very much. He had a wonderfully trained ear and eye for birds and great knowledge of them. It was remarkable that he should have found time to acquire this in such a strenuous public life.

I am afraid that your illness must have been tedious and I hope that your recovery will not now be long.

Yours sincerely,
GREY of F.

Having seen Grey off to Washington from Southampton, Steed told Northcliffe that they had discussed the attitude of *The Times* to the Government regarding Ireland. 'I answered that *The Times* and you were determined that this Irish business should go through, not for the sake of journalistic or personal prestige but for the thing itself.' He considered it unlikely that Grey would have more than a *succès-d'estime* at Washington. 'Perhaps he was tired, but I got from him no impression of magnetic bigness—in fact, I have never got it from him.'

★　　　★　　　★

Northcliffe was trying to bring comfort to the victim of a terrible fate, Twells Brex, the popular young *Daily Mail* writer. Despite increasing and, for some time, undiagnosed pain, he had insisted on being at his place in the office, where he more than once collapsed. Northcliffe wrote to him on September 4: 'The only safeguard is several opinions. If you will read Sir James Mackenzie's book, which I send herewith, you will find that he, the greatest of his kind, practically knows nothing.' It was not then known that Brex was suffering from inoperable cancer. 'I shall be anxious to hear about you,' Northcliffe wrote. 'Please keep me informed. I have had about as much illness as most people, as you know, and begin to understand a little about it.'

Sir James Mackenzie had warned him again to be sensible and rest. 'He stripped me to the skin and examined me very vigorously indeed', and prescribed 'only three days' work a week in future'. Not all the skill of the Royal College of Surgeons could have severed Northcliffe from the monstrous connective tissue of his affairs, quivering with the new competitive impulses of the post-war world. He startled some of his older editorial men by asking them whether they had kept up their shorthand and told those who had not: 'Please practise it.' He had decided that it was essential to office competence, especially when he telephoned. 'It will relieve my voice of strain, if every one will set himself to take down my messages quickly.' There was the problem of Marlowe's deafness. He had given Marlowe gentle hints about it. 'You will understand that I am not allowed to raise my voice in future.' He sent a private message to Douglas Crawford of the *Daily Mail* foreign staff. 'If someone could induce Mr Marlowe to get the same kind of sound box that Lord Knutsford uses, it would be a boon', and not long afterwards he was complaining to Campbell Stuart of 'Marlowe's increasing slowness of mind'. Driving out with Max Pemberton, he was 'surprised to find the wonderful hold the *Daily Mail* has here in Scotland'. But its contents bills were bad and he demanded to be given every day the names of those who wrote them. 'There is no need to issue two different bills,' he notified Carmelite House, 'unless of course two events of equal importance take place, such as George Robey being made a peer and Winston assassinating Lloyd George.' There was a message from a President-to-be of the United States, writing from the Ritz Hotel, London: 'This is just a word of goodbye, thanks, and hopes that you will continue your great work in reduction of friction between our two countries, for in these times everybody's nerves are on edge and it requires patient far-seeing people to keep things going.—Herbert Hoover.' Northcliffe thought it necessary to write a long letter to Edward Price Bell, of the *Chicago Daily News*, about the ignorance and indifference' to American affairs prevailing 'in the highest quarters here'. He insisted: 'In my opinion, there should at once be established an American Department in the Foreign Office' (September 13, 1919).

★ ★ ★

He left Scotland in the last week of September, motoring homeward with his wife through York and Lincoln, 'in order to ransack the antique shops'. He wrote to his brother St. John: 'On Saturday, I hope to sleep for the first time in my new house, No. 1, Carlton Gardens, the seventh town house since my marriage. My typist says this ought to be a lucky number.' There was a memorandum from his principal secretary to Mackenzie, his steward: 'Sir James Mackenzie has started an institution for investigation into the early stages of disease and the conditions that favour its origin. The Chief has promised to help him with £500 a year for five years. The Chief has sent the £500 for this year direct to Sir James Mackenzie', and Sir James had written to the Chief: 'I thank you very sincerely for yr. cheque, which I have received. Your generosity has been of the greatest encouragement and help to me in tackling a very difficult problem.' Mackenzie's clinic at St. Andrews was to become world known, a centre of medical pilgrimage. Northcliffe's useful contribution owed much to Mackenzie's sterling character and something to McNair Wilson's advocacy of his aims. Mackenzie summarized his work in another letter. 'Some 35 years ago I started to study the early stages of heart disease, with the result that a revolution has taken place in regard to the manner in which hearts should be examined.'

Warned of 'the Chief's' impending return to Broadstairs, Humphrey Davy was reading every word in every issue of *The Times* and the *Daily Mail*, preparing himself for a current affairs cross-examination. He had received a message: 'I do not want to waste time explaining to you that we have lately fought a war, that a man called President Wilson is urging an association called the League of Nations, or that gardens have pergolas.' There was the further injunction: 'Do not let me arrive to find that you have forgotten the stationery required, or that the typewriter ribbon is worn out, or that the machine has not been cleaned for three months.' Humphrey-Davy may have been silently exasperated, for he was privately engaged with an idea of his which had been dormant since the war began but which might be suitably revived with some profit in esteem, if not glory, for himself, the 'All-British Shopping Movement', object: 'Industrial Patriotism, chairman the Rt. Hon. the Viscount Hill, vice-chairman and founder, F. H. Mountjoy Nelson Humphrey-Davy, Esq., O.B.E.' His vice-presidents and executive council were in themselves a glittering reward for his devotion to the cause. It cannot have been easy for him to reconcile stationery ordering and typewriter cleaning with dreams of recognition beyond the power even of 'the Chief' to bestow. Frustration was his lot. Northcliffe to F. H. M. N. Humphrey-Davy: 'I would much prefer you to concentrate on your duties.'

Twells Brex wrote to tell him that he had postponed the operation which the surgeons had advised and begged to be allowed to write again for the *Daily Mail*. 'I feel I cannot continue to draw my salary for no work. In any case, my brain does not share my body's affliction. Fighting calamity sharpens one's mind. Again thanks, dear Chief, for your solicitude and advice. My little wife has been deeply touched by your tender kindness to us.' Replying, Northcliffe was obliged to resort to the fiction writer's art (October 11):

The question of operation or no operation is one of profound difficulty. . . . Personally, I am of that disposition that I am not greatly interested in being alive or dead. I have absolutely no fear of death and no particular desire for life except as it affects those to whom I am dear. I am not saying these things with a view to comforting you, for probably your view of life is like mine. I say them because every person who is advised to have an operation must use his own judgment—more or less.

As to work, unless your advisers are against it, why not? I worked till 7.45 on the morning of my operation which took place at 8 o'clock, and I worked again in the afternoon, to the consternation of the doctors. Everybody is different, but I should think that you are rather like me.

Please do not worry about salary. I have not put in eighteen hours a day since I was fifteen in order that those who help me should be deprived in the hour of need.

*   *   *

In September, a strike of British railwaymen, who were bitter about unfulfilled Government promises, was sharply criticized in the *Daily Mail*. Northcliffe received a letter of objection. 'We, the machine managers, wish to enter a strong protest against the treatment that is being meted out to the National Union of Railwaymen in the columns of your press. Signed on behalf of the chapel, J. H. Isaacs.'

Northcliffe to J. H. Isaacs, Father of the Chapel:

Carmelite House,
E.C.4.
October 1st, 1919.

Dear Mr Isaacs,—Allow me to express my surprise at the ingratitude displayed in your letter today, in which you complain of the attitude of my newspapers in the present dispute.

You must be aware that my Press has always given great space to Labour matters. It will be within your memory that during the recent General Election I took the unprecedented step of placing valuable and prominent columns in these newspapers at the disposal of the Labour Party. I notice that, despite the shrunken sheets we are now issuing, Mr J. H. Thomas's long statement of yesterday was given in full, and that Mr Alexander M. Thompson, a known and respected Labour writer, voices the views of Labour practically every day.

I hope you will understand that I have no intention of allowing my newspapers to be influenced in this or any other matter by anyone.

For a long period my Press was assailed by the Asquith Government, its suppression was continually threatened, it was persecuted in the Law Courts, and proscribed in Parliament again and again.

During the war it was attacked by ignorant members of the public, burned in the street, boycotted by advertisers, and banished from most of the principal clubs and reading rooms.

Lately, it has been bitterly and vulgarly assailed by Mr Lloyd George because of its independent attitude at the Peace Conference.

I am entirely satisfied with the attitude of my journals towards this national calamity, and rather than be dictated to by anyone or any body of men I will stop the publication of these newspapers, and, in view of your letter, I have so informed the Newspaper Proprietors' Association.

I am forwarding a copy of this correspondence to Mr J. H. Thomas, M.P.

[General Secretary of the National Union of Railwaymen] and shall also publish it.

Yours faithfully,
NORTHCLIFFE

When the *Daily Mail* was going to press that night there was a demonstration in the machine-room in Northcliffe's favour. The men read his letter in type. 'Good old Chief!' one of them shouted and there was a loud response of cheers. 'Northcliffe is splendid!' wrote Wilson Pope, news editor of the Radical evening paper, *The Star*, to Marlowe. 'That's the stuff to give 'em! Congratulations that the father of the chapel is not to succeed you as editor.' That trade union functionary wrote on behalf of his supporters: 'We tender our thanks to Lord Northcliffe for his sportsmanlike attitude in printing the letters,—J. H. Isaacs.' Northcliffe to Sir George Riddell, of the *News of the World*: 'I told J. H. Thomas of my intention of stopping my newspapers in a certain eventuality, and received from him the cheerful assurance that I should not have the opportunity because I should not be here in a week's time: that, in fact, I should be the first to go. If it is a case of going in order of circulations, you will be pretty high on the list. In such a case I should loudly disclaim any priority and push you forward to the guillotine.' The head of the general federation of trade unions, W. A. Appleton, made it privately known that he appreciated Northcliffe's action 'in certain crises'. There were numerous approving letters from professional colleagues, headed by the veteran journalist, Sir Henry Lucy ('Toby, M.P.' of *Punch*), and from readers of Northcliffe's newspapers. Northcliffe was in a magnanimous mood. 'I know my workers and they know me. Mr Isaacs is a young man and it was his first day as father of the chapel.'

*   *   *

It had been part of Northcliffe's health history that he always recovered quickly after the deep exhaustions that intermittently beset him. That recuperative power was weakening. His tiredness in the autumn of 1919 was unduly prolonged. Wickham Steed, calling on him at Carlton Gardens, found him so completely exhausted as to feel 'unable to go on'. William Graham, the solicitor, passing on word of land for sale at North Foreland, received the answer: 'I do not want any land. I do not want anything.' A printers' strike had brought the *Continental Daily Mail* to a standstill in common with other Paris newspapers. He was loftily disinclined to negotiate, not simply because he may have believed that the great days of the paper had passed with the peace conference, when it was diligently read by the plenipotentiaries and their trailing hordes of delegates. He telegraphed to Peter Goudie, in charge of the Paris office: *Am not in the least anxious to start paper again until men are tired of strike*, nor did he show signs of relief when the strike collapsed after two weeks. There was a diminution of zest in him. Yet the mental activity continued at a scarcely altered tempo; there was no marked decline in his response to the ceaseless stimuli of proprietorial journalism. He was writing most days to *The Times* and the *Daily Mail*. No letter that reached him went unanswered, except those from more persistent members of the staff. 'The people I like best in the office,' he told Humphrey-Davy, 'are those who never write to me at all.'

He was having discussions with Sir Robert Baden-Powell on developments of far-reaching importance to the Boy Scout movement, by that time a million strong. Baden-Powell was seeking his assistance in promoting the international Boy Scouts Jamboree which he hoped to launch in the interests of world understanding. 'Your advice would be immensely helpful,' Baden-Powell wrote to him on October 21, 1919, 'and might be productive of big results.' Northcliffe invited him to the *Times* office and Baden-Powell afterwards expressed himself in grateful terms. To Steed, Northcliffe wrote that 'Lady Leslie, sister of Winston's mother, came to see me nominally to discuss Ireland. About two minutes after, I found that she had called on behalf of Lady Cunard . . . to try to get puffs for Beecham's Opera and there is no reason why we should give these people free advertising. If we do, I shall be burdened with other appeals. The greater part of my work today is dealing with various people who are asking for support for this, that, and the other' (November 24). He told Wareham Smith, the Carmelite House advertisement director: 'I can't afford to mix with people—they always want something from me.'

He was guiding the *Daily Mail* campaign against reckless Government spending. He was discreetly supporting his nephew Esmond Harmsworth, Rothermere's surviving son, in a Thanet by-election. He was taking up the case of British prisoners in Russia, worrying about the likelihood of burglary at 1 Carlton Gardens and the more immediate menace of creaking floors at Elmwood, and studying the *Times* library clippings on General Mannerheim, the Finnish leader, who was asking to see him. A silly little paragraph in the frivolous 'Letters of Eve' in *The Tatler*, which he considered an insult to Lady Northcliffe, tipped him almost alarmingly off balance. 'There are some things flesh and blood cannot stand and the thing that I cannot stand is an attack upon my wife', and William Graham was ordered to issue a writ. Northcliffe was prepared, it seemed, to enlarge the incident into a *cause célèbre*. He was finally appeased only by letters from Sir John Ellerman, chief shareholder in the *Tatler* group, and from the editor, Clement Shorter.

The *Daily Mail* had published an attack on a prominent personality. Letters of protest addressed to Northcliffe himself provided an occasion for reminding the staff of the commonly distorted view of newspaper proprietorship (November 5): 'I was once leaving a public meeting when I heard a working man say, "That's the man who writes the *Daily Mail*." Everybody thinks that I inspire every line in *The Times, Daily Mail, Evening News, Weekly Dispatch, Overseas Daily Mail, The Times Weekly Edition, The Times Literary Supplement, Answers* and *The Times Engineering Supplement*. A considerable part of the correspondence of my secretaries consists in dealing with the alleged expressions of my views in those papers.'

That winter he bought *Notes & Queries*. 'I do not want any further papers, but I do not like to see an historical and very useful journal passing out of existence' (Letter to H. K. Hudson, December 29, 1919). Soon, the circulation figures showed an upward rise, the first in twenty-five years. There may have been relief for Northcliffe in turning his attention to that relatively microscopic matter, for the strain of his large-scale affairs was undoubtedly telling on him. The finances of the Carmelite House group were becoming a cause of worry. There were healthy cash reserves, but heavily rising costs in all directions were creating current difficulties. Advertising rates had already been raised and a further rise was not yet practicable. There were anxious board meetings in those last weeks of the year. Northcliffe could not ignore the situation.

*   *   *

By the end of 1919, he seriously believed that there was a danger of war between Great Britain and the United States of America. He wrote again to Edward Price Bell in Chicago: 'Excuse a long letter. The subject is always on my mind, as was the war with Germany for twenty years before it came. *That* war could not be averted, though foresight could have provided preparations that would have shortened its duration. *This* one can be averted.' The basis of his fears was 'the very large and active propaganda having for its object the humiliation of this country'. A source of the infection was the *Chicago Tribune*, the Anglophobe proprietor of which newspaper was in London. Northcliffe undertook to see him. 'I will talk to him as plainly as one newspaper owner can to another' (November 10). He wrote in his *Daily Mail* comments on November 17: 'I wonder if anyone in the office ever reads the American newspapers and realizes the animosity against Britain manifested therein. The comfortable after-dinner "hands across the sea" nonsense talked at the Pilgrims' Club exists only in one or two small circles in New York and other eastern cities. Boston, which used to be the English centre, is now entirely Irish. Its leading newspapers are strongly anti-British.' The chief aggravating factors were Ireland, war debts and the League of Nations. He told Bell: 'There is no active anti-Americanism in this country yet, though I cannot tell you how much American news I suppress to prevent its growth— news of ship-grabbing and the like.' Bell did his best to allay Northcliffe's fears: '*I do not believe that hell itself could drive America into any policy designed to humiliate England*' (his italics).

Northcliffe to Lord Weardale, a trustee of the National Gallery: 'Anglo-American relations are my principal political preoccupation. There is no day on which I do not confer about them.' Northcliffe to Lord Reading: 'I am anxious about Anglo-American affairs. Carson often advises me about my newspapers. I feel inclined to advise him to go to the United States and make counter-propaganda. If he did so, they would then understand the justice of Dominion Home Rule for Ireland.' He told his secretary, Price: 'If it were not for my great responsibilities, I should get out of journalism and go into the Anglo-American propaganda business.' Willert was sending him full information from Washington and often valuable guidance with it. He wrote nothing to justify Northcliffe's possibly extreme view of the Anglo-American situation. A few weeks later Colonel George Harvey, who became American Ambassador in London in 1921, was writing to Northcliffe: 'The chief point I had in mind in my talk with Grey was to put a stop to the sinister growth of antagonism between England and America.' As an aid to restoring a better understanding between the two nations, Northcliffe proposed publishing a new journal to be called *The American Monthly*. Its style and format were to be those of *The Times Literary Supplement* and it was to contain articles by authoritative writers on both sides of the Atlantic. He asked J. W. Robertson Scott, formerly of the *Pall Mall Gazette*, to prepare a 'dummy', which was done. But Northcliffe's other interests and activities were too numerous and the project did not mature.

'It is a trying time for us all,' Reading had told him early in December 1919, 'and will be for the next year, I fear.' He acknowledged again Northcliffe's 'good feeling for America', and said that he was 'profoundly thankful' for the 'restraint in criticism' of America which was Northcliffe's policy, especially in *The Times*. Lord Grey was returning from Washington early in the new year and Willert wrote to Northcliffe: 'He is anxious to talk things over with you as soon as possible.'

Northcliffe wrote to Moberly Bell's widow (November 30): '*The Times* has been a back-breaking task, and much of my ill-health has been due to the thousands of hours I have devoted to it. You will probably get more applications from persons desiring to buy your *Times* shares. Pray resist them. That dividend is only a faint indication of the prosperity of

Printing House Square, which could not have been but for the fact that Moberly Bell held the fort in the most difficult period of the history of *The Times*.' A letter from Paris conveyed the personal regard of President Poincaré, who in a private talk with Northcliffe's correspondent, 'dwelt at great length on the services rendered to the common cause by *The Times*, the *Daily Mail* and the *Continental Daily Mail*', while Sir William Tyrrell (later Lord Tyrrell of Avon), who had accompanied Grey to Washington, besought Northcliffe's help in forming a more favourable American opinion. 'They are potentially the most powerful nation in the world. What they lack is the experience, balance and wisdom to make the best use of their position. I should like to see a relationship created in which they will seek our advice without our having to obtrude it on them' (November 27).

Wickham Steed sent him information about 'the intrigue' against Colonel House, who had been boycotted in Washington since President Wilson's breakdown. Steed's highly-placed informant had told him 'who was behind it', and Steed suggested that 'it would be discourteous to the Colonel' to publish news of the attack on him 'without turning it down contemptuously'. Steed had no doubt of the origin of the revised attitude to House. 'It is a piece of Jew revenge upon House for having done his best to prevent the international financiers from running the Peace Conference.'

Mrs Asquith wrote to Northcliffe from 20 Cavendish Square: 'I thought it *very* kind of you to say you wd help to boom my book when it comes out in April or May' (*The Autobiography of Margot Asquith*). She regretted the necessity for 'selling this beautiful old house', and explained: 'We are, as you can imagine, very hard up'.

Shortly before Christmas, he learnt that Coutts' Bank was being taken over by the National Provincial Bank. He and other members of his family had banked at Coutts' from the early days of their prosperity. Some of the Harmsworth companies had accounts there. Northcliffe took it as an affront that 'people so deeply concerned as we are' had not been told 'of the terms of the arrangement'. Writing on December 23, he may have disturbed the Christmas of the aged senior partner of Coutts', W. R. Malcolm. The letter was marked 'Not Private'.

I cannot say that I like the transaction, nor have I met anyone who does. We shall very carefully consider what to do about our accounts. The public are getting very anxious about these so-called fusions. There is an American touch about them; and the American Government has, as you know, set its face against these gigantic trusts.

One thing I do hope and that is that Messrs Coutts' directors will do something to cause these big banks to pay their servants properly. Considering the gigantic profits that are made, the rate of wages is scandalous, and if the wages are not improved my newspapers will take the matter in hand as they did that of the Army & Navy Stores.

Steed, who had been urged (December 18) by Northcliffe to 'deal firmly with the advertising people' who were 'plastering *The Times* with advertisements, to the disgust of many readers', wrote to him on the last day of the year: 'You understand most things but I don't know whether even you recognize all that your health and energy mean to the country and to *The Times*. You must do your utmost to conserve your driving power and your vision; and we at Printing House Square will do our utmost to back you up.' Steed wanted his advice on reviewing a controversial new book that was about to appear, J. M. Keynes's *Economic Consequences of the Peace*. He described it to Northcliffe as 'a bit of snake-in-the-grass work', done 'from the highest motives, by a cleverish, pro-German, pacifist, conscientious objector sort of Cambridge don'. Northcliffe agreed that Keynes was a man of great ability. 'But I wouldn't put him in charge of a business.'

Chapter Twenty-seven

Prelude to a Journey

FOR Northcliffe the year 1920 had a sombre beginning. The death in January of the young *Daily Mail* writer with the curious name, Twells Brex, affected him deeply. Brex had written him a heartrending letter telling of terrible suffering: 'Even the doctors don't come near me now.' Rallying from unconsciousness, the patient was enheartened by his sight of 'the Chief' sitting silently in a corner of the bedroom. Brex's wife told Hamilton Fyfe: 'He comes and sits with him so often. Yesterday he was here twice. The other day I happened to mention that we found it hard to get butter. He went half over London in his car trying to buy butter for us.' She wrote to Northcliffe: 'Out of all the terror and darkness there shines the wonder of your kindly care and constant thought.' In his last few days of life, Brex wrote down his reflections as a dying man and sent them to the *Daily Mail*. Published under the heading 'Towards Sunset', the article touched innumerable hearts. After the funeral, Northcliffe sent an instruction to Carmelite House: 'Will you send Mrs Brex a cheque for £1,000 and please also see that her late husband's salary is paid to her till the end of the year?' He arranged for her and her small son to stay at Elmwood for six weeks, and a telegram of greeting from him awaited their arrival. It was followed by a letter, 'the utter kindness of which broke down all my self-control tonight', the young widow wrote. 'During these first weeks of my widowhood, you have never let me feel the loneliness, distracting my thoughts by every kindness. Oh, *please*, dear Chief, will you understand why I stumble over this letter?' Wilson, the leader writer, wrote to him on January 2: 'Who could help being devoted to you? Who cannot but be proud to serve under you?'

His brother Leicester was impelled to send him a note of warning (January 31): 'You are back in the thick of it far too soon, in my opinion, after your operation. As one who observes you pretty closely, I say without hesitation that you are not looking well. You are in for very strenuous times with your papers, I think, and it would be wise of you, if I may say so, to get a little sunshine into your blood before the summer comes, and Home Rule, Bolshevism, falling exchanges, and a tottering Government absorb your energies.' Northcliffe to Lovat Fraser (February 5): 'The enemy is always crediting me with everything that goes into the paper, which is very annoying, but has to be borne. I hope you will keep on at Anti-Waste [the campaign against Government spending]. I distrust their promises. A man like the Prime Minister who has always a millionaire in his company—the Astors, the Sassoons, the Riddells, and the Inverforths— cannot keep a balanced mind about expenses. I have lived in that world and know it. It is especially difficult for a man who has no money of his own and never has had any. He does not know the responsibility of wealth.'

At Carmelite House that morning the staff had read in his office message: 'I cannot accept Mr Churchill's view that Labour is incapable of governing. It could not govern worse than he does.' Naming members of the Government: 'There is hardly one of them that I would support as a Director of Associated Newspapers.' In the same communique he wrote that 'it is about time we dropped the word "jazz" as an adjective. It is out of date and stupid.'

Northcliffe had warned Steed that Lloyd George was 'making advances to *The Times* through Churchill, and to my other newspapers via the Lord Chancellor' (Birkenhead). Steed sent under seal of secrecy some notes of a talk at Printing House Square with Lord Robert Cecil, who had gone there to put forward the name of Sir Edward Grey as a possible Prime Minister. He believed that Grey would accept, if circumstances proved favourable, though he was 'very cautious in expressing his feelings'. Steed put it to Northcliffe that 'what was in Cecil's mind' was the possibility that 'the succession might ultimately devolve on him'. Steed asked Northcliffe to 'think it over', with the reminder that 'it would be dangerous to write it to anybody or even to mention it to anybody who is not absolutely watertight' (February 1920). At that same period both Curzon and Grey were in touch with Northcliffe, sending him information and soliciting his views. Curzon 'very much regretted' the estrangement between Northcliffe and Lloyd George. Grey was 'constrained to admit that Lloyd George's frequent *gaffes* were a very heavy drawback to the whole of our foreign relations'.

* * *

A new threat of bronchitis sent Northcliffe to Mentone. *En route*, he wrote to Sutton (February 9): 'I do not want to hear anything about business. I am thoroughly tired of it.' He returned to take up residence for a few weeks at The Hive, Parkstone-on-Sea, rented furnished. He then left for a six weeks' tour of France, Spain and Morocco. From Angoulême on March 5 he wrote to his mother:

I do hope my darling Mother is preparing to go to Totteridge unless it be very cold. Yesterday, between here and Tours, there were little clusters of white and blue violets by the roadside. I picked one of each for you, dear.

I shall not be back till I and my throat are really well. I've had enough of illness lately to make me *detest* ill health.

I think of you many times each day.

Your devoted Firstborn.

He wrote to Sutton from Seville on March 20 about rumours of new company taxation. 'It seems that as regards The Amalgamated Press the person financially hit will be me.' He proposed to tell the shareholders that if they valued his service to the company they should pay for it. 'I hate to think of the years of hard work we have put in and all the profits of our toil being taken by that squandering Welshman. *There is waste in Spain, British Govt. waste*, I mean. Not possible, you say, but there is and something like corruption too. Now put me back on the Board and see that I am properly paid. I am very well indeed and quite willing to put my nose to the grindstone, whatever that may mean. Throat nearly right. Energy terrific.' Sutton took the chance, in replying on March 26, to point out the defects of his own position. '*You* will, I know, admit the value of my own personal efforts. Not having anything in the way of a partnership, or big shareholding, I never can have any permanent benefit.'

The British Agent in Tangier, Archibald Kerr,* wrote to Northcliffe saying that 'you will be interested to hear (and perhaps touched, too) that the Moors of Tangier were preparing a petition to you asking that Tangier should be given neither to the French nor the Spaniards'. Northcliffe replied: 'When asked whether I thought the British would support the Spanish authorities in their efforts to get Tangier, the only reply I could make was that my newspapers would oppose the passing of Tangier to either France or Spain. I have said that to everyone I met, adding, of course, that my newspapers are in no sense Government organs.' He told Kerr that 'at a long *audencia* with King Alfonso, he cooed and threatened, saying that England would want a friend in Europe one day. When he said that the Spaniards were a grateful people, I replied that the statue to celebrate the battle of Vittoria, in what we call the Peninsula War and what they call the War of Independence, practically ignores the fact of our participation in the expulsion of the French.'

Those various excursions did little more than confirm that for him the

* Sir Archibald Clark Kerr, later British Ambassador in Iraq, China, the U.S.S.R., and [Lord Inverchapel] the U.S.A.

circumference of his existence was more attractive than its centre, where there was no peace. He had spoken to his brother Harold about going to Grand Falls: 'It is seven years since I was there.' What he would have understood as an appetite for more experience might with greater truth have been interpreted as a longing for less.

In London, he would be constantly thinking of things to be done at Elmwood. At Elmwood, his thoughts turned restlessly to London. Staying recuperatively near Bournemouth, which he called 'Mournemouth' because of 'the numbers of sick people to be seen here', he saw a flight of swans on their way to Poole Harbour. 'Something that I had not seen before, a most curious sight, their wings making a noise like mouth-organs from within the dark recesses of miners' cottages in the north.' He was enjoying, he said, the tranquillity of his surroundings, but the same day he wrote to W. J. Evans asking about 'rumours that Mrs Edward Hulton is loud in public about the plans and intentions of the Hulton Press', and that 'Beaverbrook's new paper, the *Sunday Express*, is a failure'.

During a rare postal void, he was impelled to send a message of general benevolence: 'I am most anxious that all of our people should be happy.' He had been in brisk correspondence about a strike of Pearl Assurance agents for higher pay. 'You must get justice for these people,' he told Falk, of the *Weekly Dispatch*. 'Give the capital of the Company, names and addresses and private telephone numbers of directors, the profits, the company's case and the agents' case. I do not like to hear of such injustice.' He had heard that the *Times* messengers were being paid three pounds a week. Northcliffe to Howard Corbett, assistant manager of *The Times*: 'I do not wonder they are joining a Union. I understand that 77s. a week is the smallest sum on which a married man can live in the humblest circumstances in London. How would you or I like to do it? Personally, I should organize a strike.' Lints Smith, sending information about the wages paid to the women on the *Times* business side, received the reminder: 'Evil is wrought by want of thought, as well as by want of heart.'

A letter from the wife of an R.A.F. man at Farnborough described the hardships of trying to live on 33s. 6d. a week. She was expecting a child. 'I do not suppose my letter will reach you. Should it do so, it is my hope that you will be able to do something to improve pay and conditions in the R.A.F.' Northcliffe listened while Humphrey-Davy read the letter, in which the writer said: 'For years I have admired Mary Pickford's beauty and talent. Last week, I felt I hated her as she drifts over America and Europe trailing money-bags in search of pleasure, so easily earned.' Private inquiries producing a favourable report, he sent the airman's wife his cheque for £25 with the message: 'If this is not sufficient, I will send more when the baby comes.'

Seymour Price, his personal physician, had not found it easy to rebuild his general practice after four years' war service. Northcliffe lent him £2,400 without interest, 'in the hope that it may be of some use'. His solicitor pointed out that he had already lent the doctor £1,400. Northcliffe answered: 'I want to help him. He sacrificed everything for the country. It is the duty of rich people to help in such cases.' Sending thanks 'for all your goodness to me', Price remarked: 'If only we could divorce you from your 1,000 h.p. brain for a few weeks, how fit you would get!' Message to T. E. Mackenzie, the steward: 'The Chief wishes the old man who helps in the garden at Elmwood to receive more money. Presumably he has an old age pension. The Chief wants you to arrange that the increase does not invalidate the pension.' He had lately added to his private pension list a veteran named Kidman, his father's old clerk, who, fifty years before, had often escorted him as a child to Miss Budd's school in St. John's Wood.

He drove out from Broadstairs one day with Wickham Steed to see Canterbury Cathedral, because, he explained, he was interested in an official guide named McClemens, 'a man who ought to have gone farther in life'. He had asked the guide about his earnings. They were £5 a week, out of which he was paying £120 a year for the education of his daughter at Bedford College, London. 'You have bitten off more than you can chew,' Northcliffe wrote to him on *Times* notepaper. 'It is true that you have a delightful occupation, but I am bound to say that it is an extremely badly paid one. I will provide your daughter's college fees.'

Sir Campbell Stuart wrote to him that year: 'I seem to be always thanking you—and quite properly. You have been so good to me.' It would be easy for the cynics to say that Northcliffe's constant giving gratified his power sense. It was singularly free from patronage. He would remark that he felt humble to be so placed in life that he could help others.

A return of the throat swelling took him to Wimpole Street again. Examined by Hunter Tod, he was advised not to go to Canada. 'You would probably have another breakdown. I am very strongly of the opinion that you should not undertake the journey.' He went, instead, to Birmingham, where there was a doctor named Mackay who had a reputedly successful vaccine treatment. He took a course of injections and was cheerfully optimistic about the results. 'I am an entirely different man', he told Arthur Brisbane, the Hearst newspaper writer, and he was pleased to report to Wickham Steed after staying with Lady Northcliffe at Crowborough: 'I went round the links here without fatigue. It is one of the most tiring courses in England.'

His health graph, unsteady through the year, may have been a record of stresses from outside and particularly from Printing House Square, where there was a circulation slump and a bank overdraft. *The Times* did not interest women, 'which means that it will not get advertisements and will eventually die'. There were difficulties also about the position of Sir Campbell Stuart who, as the new managing director of *The Times*, had been arbitrarily put in authority over men who were more experienced, who were temperamentally averse from change, who resented new faces and who traditionally objected to members of the staff having titles. Moreover, Steed was less comfortable in the editorship than he had been during the first months of his accession. His steering of the paper was complicated by differences between the reigning member of the Walter family and Northcliffe about its Irish policy.

That policy had been framed in a long leading article (four columns) published on July 24, 1919, proposing the creation of two State legislatures in place of the Home Rule Act. The paper's treatment of Irish events in the autumn of 1920 involved its chief proprietors, the editor and his staff, in the possibility of reprisals by violent means. Threatening letters were received. A photograph of himself with a bullet hole marked on the forehead was delivered by hand to Northcliffe at *The Times*. Police guards were provided at Printing House Square and at his other establishments. 'I have no doubt that our present Irish policy is losing us readers,' he wrote to Freeman of *The Times*. 'The circulations of my papers have often suffered by the advocacy of unpopular measures, such as Conscription, for example, which caused the loss of many readers and also of advertisements. I have never allowed these considerations to have any weight.'

He was avoiding speech fatigue and public gatherings, but in May he was present at a luncheon at Printing House Square to celebrate the first attempted flight from Cairo to the Cape, made the previous February. The flight had been sponsored by *The Times* and it was an opportunity for him to tell his hearers that the development of commercial aviation was an Imperial necessity. He also warned them that Germany was already foreseeing a future war in terms of air supremacy.

When, some years ago, my newspapers introduced the aeroplane to the notice of the War Office, we were told by the civilian head of that Department that it was an interesting scientific discovery, but nothing was done. The only person who took much notice of our remarks about aeroplanes was the late Lord Roberts, who said that if men could ascend 500 feet to 600 feet in the air, the whole future of warfare in general, and of gunnery in particular, would be changed. . . . More money should be devoted to the air, principally to civilian aviation. If we develop civilian air work it will be quite easy, in the event of another war, to transfer the men to military occupations. We did it with great success in the case of the officers of our mercantile marine. Aviation should be continually put to the hard test of commercial success. That test will eliminate faults in design and of construction as speedily as did the war.

The force of the principle which he outlined that day was demonstrated by the rise of the Luftwaffe. Had his words been heeded by British ears, we might today be living in a different world. Apparently his warning had been heard in Downing Street, for not long afterwards Steed reported to Northcliffe that Lord Derby had been to see him with the suggestion that 'Lloyd George should make amends to you by asking you to do something for the Government; for instance, to inquire into the dangerous development of civil aviation in Germany'.

'The gigantic achievements you have made during the War must have been a great strain upon you—and still you endeavour to keep the cobwebs from all our eyes.' Royce, of Rolls-Royce, was writing to Northcliffe. 'I hear you are well, but need a rest from your strenuous life.' At Carmelite House six of the chief editorial men were away ill, including the editor, the news editor, the financial editor—'I have had a headache continuously for seven weeks'—and the picture editor. Northcliffe declared that for him it meant five hours a day on the telephone. He told John Walter of *The Times*: 'Steed is ageing greatly. Campbell Stuart, the ablest young man in my *entourage*, is better. Corbett is much better. Lints Smith is a little tired.' He asked Walter: 'If you get an opportunity of telling our young men to go a bit slow in view of their health, I shall be obliged.' He ordered Sutton away for a rest, saying 'if anything happens to you, I should have to go right back into The Amalgamated Press business'. It was not long before Northcliffe's face was throbbing with neuralgia again, an indicator registering an overload. Northcliffe to Sir James Mackenzie, at St. Andrews (June 10): 'I shall arrive on Saturday morning at 10.24 by train.' In the train he walked along the corridor looking for readers of the *Daily Mail*. 'Gracious, what a preponderance we have over the others! I never realized it before, as I travel little by train. The responsibility makes one think and think and think, and I always do think about this responsibility.' To Sir Campbell Stuart (June 13): 'Sir James Mackenzie says that if I go slow and rest in the afternoons, I shall last a long time.'

Northcliffe's way of justifying afternoon rest was to work twice as hard in the morning; 'besides, I feel so vigorous', he wrote home. 'Sir James says the thyroid flow has increased.' As proof of it, so had the telegram flow. Northcliffe to Macleod, *Daily Mail* literary editor: *Passed over one hundred charabancs in a single day stop they have not made appearance in south yet but we shall have them in due course stop get some articles stop.* To Caird, repeated to Stuart: *Our excellent Edinburgh correspondent receives same retainer and rate as in nineteen fourteen though prices here more than double stop presume same starvation wages apply to all other provincial correspondents stop no wonder they lack enthusiasm displayed by highly paid directors departmental heads linotype operators at Carmelite House stop let me know by telegram before I leave Edinburgh that matter has been put right all round Chief.*

Northcliffe to his mother:

Braids Hills Hotel,
Morningside,
Edinburgh.
14th June, 1920.

Darling Mum,—As I telegraphed you today, we start back tomorrow morning by the west route through Carlisle.

I want to see something of the great wall which the Romans built across the north of England. It was their way of keeping the Scotch out of England, and we have not been able to do so since then.

I saw Sir James Mackenzie whom I always regard as my head physician. He is, admittedly, the greatest authority in the world on fatigue and exhaustion. He was satisfied with my condition but insisted on my having as much rest as possible and I am trying to do what he said.

I think of you many times every day.

Your devoted Firstborn.

In 1920, the circulation of Northcliffe's *Daily Mail* was 1,350,000, the world's largest. Its advertising space, and notably its expensive front page, was booked for months ahead. Kennedy Jones deemed it timely to publish his testamentary work, *Fleet Street and Downing Street*, designed to remove any doubt about his role as a principal architect of the paper's fortunes. The book made it clear that in his view the rise of the *Daily Mail* had rested on a genius which had been justly and happily apportioned between Alfred Harmsworth and himself. Except for the dedication, 'to my colleagues of eighteen years', the book little more than casually acknowledged Northcliffe's part in founding the paper. Those who had never known Kennedy Jones wondered if there had been, after all, some disparity of public acclaim. Northcliffe was content to remark in a letter to Sutton: 'I have now received a third copy of K.J's heavy explanation of his failure in life. It does not seem to have made much stir in the ant hill.'

Steed of *The Times*, like Northcliffe's other editors, was counselled to be on the alert to the activities of the new-style functionaries who were springing up in Whitehall, the press or public relations officers. Northcliffe found his own name for them—'official excuse-makers'. He frowned on them and their jobs, telling his editors that it had been a mistake to abolish the Ministry of Information—'not a very patriotic procedure, as no contradictions of the lies published about us abroad are ever issued by our Government'. He told Steed (June 5): 'Those lies will bring us close to war with the United States.'

Returning to Elmwood he dictated a message to Mackenzie, the steward: 'I cannot tell you how delighted I am with the perfection of detail in all that you have done to my house here. The minute care that has been taken touches me deeply.' Another message asked Mackenzie to have the bed at the bungalow 'exactly copied, as it is the most comfortable bed I have ever slept in. It has a hole or dip in the middle', and he wanted one like it at Carlton Gardens. At Elmwood he ordered the staff to place his bed in the middle of the room with the head backed to the light from the window. He banned the use of white tablecloths, apparently because of increased optical sensitiveness. He was becoming tyrannical in the use of house bells. A footman with squeaky shoes was ordered to change them immediately. Ringing up one of the Carmelite House advertising managers at twelve-forty on a Saturday morning, he was angry that no one was in the department to answer his call. A telegram went forthwith from Broadstairs to the private address of the advertising director, Wareham Smith. It ordered him to arrange that he and two other senior advertising men would 'take it in turn in future to be there the whole of Saturday'.

His more considerate side was shown that same month when a party of incurably sick children was brought over at his invitation to Elmwood from Lawn House, Margate. 'What do they enjoy most?' he asked Father Keniry, who was in charge of the children. 'Music', was the answer. Northcliffe bought them a piano-player costing £150. It was delivered with twenty music rolls chosen by himself. A message from Brussels told him of the failing powers of an old editor, Arthur Pask, for whom he had written articles in his freelancing days with Pemberton. He wrote to the British chaplain: 'I am grateful for your news of my dear old friend whom I have known since I was a boy. It grieves me to think that he is suffering. If he wants anything, I will get it for him. I will gladly pay any medical fees, but please do not tell the doctors where the money is coming from.'

Who is the vulgarian who persistently describes Lord Robert Cecil as Lord Cecil? he demanded in a telegram to Goudie, managing editor of the Paris *Daily Mail. Let me know his name.* In the same telegram: *Who swallowed Bolshevik wireless about the lack of work in England? See page three. It is about time I paid a visit to stir things up.* Another telegram was for Caird at Carmelite House, in response to a proposal that Northcliffe should take a stand with Manchester newspaper owners against impending wage demands. *I will have nothing to do with northern masters who consistently underpay their people* (June 14).

He had drafted a *Times* Personal column advertisement for an assistant private secretary. 'The appointee will be one of a secretariat of three, and his credentials, demeanour and other qualifications will be minutely examined by the other two.' The successful applicant for the post, at £600 a year, was a young ex-officer of the King's Own Scottish Borderers, Charles Scott-Moncrieff, M.C., who has his place in literary history as the translator of Proust. He was transferred afterwards to the staff of *The Times*, marking the change in his career by thanking Northcliffe 'for all your kindness to me'. They were laughing in the *Times* office at the story told by Price, the senior secretary. He had sent out for a taxi for 'the Chief'. The messenger came back to say that he could only get a hansom cab. Northcliffe got into it. 'Where to, my lord?' the cabby asked through the roof flap. He was told in an exceedingly bored voice: 'To the nearest taxi.'

On June 19, the anniversary of his throat operation, he sent telegrams of greeting and thanks to the surgeons and physicians who had attended him and to the matron and staff of the nursing home in Beaumont Street. He announced his personal gift of £5,000 to the Westminster Abbey restoration fund, sponsored by *The Times*; in some sense a thank-offering, though his veneration for the Abbey had always been great. Dean Ryle wrote to him on June 24: 'From my heart I thank you for this generous act and for the enormous service which you are rendering us through *The Times*. You have conferred a great boon upon this glorious place; and if we can drag it out of the humiliating disability of its present position, you, my Lord, will have done a deed which all future lovers of the Abbey will wish to thank you for.' The dean's appreciation was echoed by Sir Robert Hudson: 'It is thanks to you and *The Times* that the Abbey today is far wealthier (with hard cash in the Bank of England) than it has been for two centuries. After all, that's a great thing to have done.'

His office communique of June 21 urged 'vigorous war against interested trade persons who are supporting the dangerous left-hand drive', for motor-cars. He mentioned that his recent journey back from Scotland had shown him that 'Prioleau [*Daily Mail* motoring correspondent] should pay a little more attention to road life itself and less to motor-cars'. He had a suggestion to make: 'Every mechanically propelled vehicle should be provided with a safety mirror for seeing what is behind it', an idea long since given the sanction of the law.

A tightening general economy made it probable that bank loans would be called in. Northcliffe was concerned about his Perrier guarantee of £40,000. He wrote to St. John: 'It is very obvious that the present state of affairs cannot continue. It must be a source of great anxiety to you.' St. John replied that he would 'rather Perrier at the bottom of the sea than it should be the cause of monetary arguments between us. Money questions corrode friendship and nothing could replace in my life even a weakening of your regard and affection, dearest Alfred.'

Northcliffe to William Blackwood, editor of *Answers:*

10th August, 1920.
My dear Blackwood,—I would like to say a word about the excellence of *Answers*. It has been topping lately. You know how fond I am of that paper,

than which no journal in the world has had a more romantic career and results. No other paper ever before produced two Peerages, five members of Parliament and, I suppose, about a hundred fortunes. I read every word of *Answers* every week.

Yours sincerely,
CHIEF.

One morning in that same month of holiday, he telephoned Carmelite House to ask whether particular notice had been taken of a photograph in the *Daily Mail* of a child with a sandcastle, alongside which 'Daily Mail' had been scratched in the sand. He said: 'Does no one realize that here is an idea for some of the best free advertising the paper could ever have?' He alone had spotted the possibilities of a competition which inscribed 'Daily Mail' on the sands of every leading seaside resort for many summers thereafter. Wareham Smith, the advertising director, wrote: 'It was one of the most successful stunts the paper ever ran. And it didn't annoy anybody.' Northcliffe made a tour of southern resorts to see for himself how the competition was catching on. The circulation director who went with him said that he was obviously as delighted by the pleasure it gave to the children on holiday as by its success in 'booming' the *Daily Mail.*

Rothermere was in one of his depressive states: 'I do not at all like the financial outlook. It looks as if a very bad time is coming.' He wrote again: 'It will be necessary to raise the morning papers to 1½d. before long.' Northcliffe was untroubled. 'I am not so anxious about the future as you are.' He had been plainly told by the trade union leaders, he said, that a fifteen per cent demand in wage increases was coming. 'I am not afraid of a fight', he wrote; but he was capable of being almost completely disorganized by another kind of fear.

In September, his mother was taken ill at Broadstairs. There were disquieting internal symptoms. Northcliffe's imagination enlarged them into disaster. He was almost beside himself with anxiety. *I am afraid of some medical muddle*, he telegraphed to Rothermere. He telegraphed to Leicester: *Mother's handwriting is feebler than I have ever known it.* He telegraphed to Cecil, on holiday, in the Isle of Wight, urging him to go to Broadstairs. Wickham Steed went down to Elmwood. His first question: 'What is the news of Mrs Harmsworth?' touched a nerve that set Northcliffe quivering. Steed said that Northcliffe called out to him in an agonized tone: 'I can't bear to see her suffer!' He begged Steed to telephone three Harley Street specialists with the question: Had they known of a case of a woman of eighty suddenly developing cancer? When all three gave reassuring answers Northcliffe 'threw up his hands with relief'. He had looked into the void and found it terrifying.

So consuming was his anxiety that at the funeral of his young nephew Robert, Leicester's third son, who had died from infective endocarditis, he added to the distress of some members of the family by ignoring them all except Leicester, whose arm he took, saying: 'You know, mother is still desperately ill.' There was nothing in the medical reports to warrant such an extravagance of feeling. A pathetic memento of the episode remains: Northcliffe's notes of the doctors' final diagnosis. It had evidently given him comfort to be able to write down in his own hand details which, after all, were not alarming.

Geraldine Harmsworth's illness, from which she made a good recovery, brought the older brothers together and gave them an opportunity to discuss the affairs of St. John and his Perrier Water business, which had suffered from the war, heavy overdrafts and his declining health. There was a letter from St. John's nurse, Sally McCalmont, with the private disclosure: 'Funds are low.' Pending a formal investigation of the Perrier position, the brothers undertook to provide St. John with £5,000 a year. As his most devoted brother, Northcliffe did not forget to remind the others of 'possible injury to Bonch's health by any firm action. We must think over carefully what we ought to do.' When he had proposed to St. John that the business should be sold, he was met 'by reproaches and tears'. Pathetically, the crippled brother had assured him (October 4): 'My heart is still courageous and my mental activity good, but my body drags slowly and painfully behind.'

Cecil noted it as 'a little disconcerting' to hear 'Charlie' Hands, *doyen* of Carmelite House reporters, speak of Northcliffe as 'the old man'. Committing his surprise to his diary, Cecil commented (September 28): 'Until now perennial youth has been an attribute of the great Chief of the Northcliffe Press.' Rothermere had a new worry, the war wealth levy which the Cabinet was said to be considering. 'I was rather in favour of it at first,' he told Northcliffe, 'but now I am full of forebodings.' Northcliffe said to Price, his secretary: 'My brother Harold is always worrying about money.' Leicester had just bought, 'eventually for my boys', *The Western Morning News*, the leading provincial newspaper serving south-western England. When Leicester informed him of the purchase, Northcliffe replied by picture-postcard from Spain: '*The Western Morning News* stands well in the public eye.' Leicester had made a surprise gift to their mother, the freehold of Hill Lodge, Campden Hill, an attractive Regency house which he, a connoisseur and collector himself, had adorned for her with many of his choicest treasures in furniture and pictures as a winter residence. Cecil, still at the Foreign Office, lived in one of the former ducal mansions of Bayswater, facing Hyde Park. Hildebrand, like Vyvyan before him, had heard the ancestral call of the countryside and was farming in Sussex. Charles was living the life of a recluse, smiling with secret contentment behind the high hedges of his mother's retreat in the South Downs.

'I do beg of you to realize that I am a much-occupied man', Northcliffe wrote to Olga Nethersole, the actress. She had founded The People's League of Health and in June he had subscribed £100 and given permission for the use of his name as one of the vice-presidents. 'Please do realize that the controller of one hundred and ten publications must have occasional leisure. I do not desire to be brusque, but my staff are getting restless under your correspondence and calls.' A few weeks earlier, Miss Nethersole had been strolling through the Vale of Health at Hampstead. She saw 'a thickset rather tired-looking man' looking over the gate of one of the smallest cottages. 'He appeared to be engrossed in thought.' It was not until he had walked away that she realized that he was Northcliffe, revisiting the scenes of his childhood.

Northcliffe to his cousin Everard Hamilton:

The Times,
E.C.4.
September 11th, 1920.

My dear Everard,—I have received the results of your many months of labour and shall study it carefully [*The Hamilton Memoirs*].

You know how much importance I attach to race, and how I almost invariably choose the officers of my organizations according to race, applying a Scot where caution is required, a County Down man where caution and judgment, generosity and fairness are needed, Canadians of British origin where new ideas are needed; and so on and so forth.

So it is with families. If they could only be induced to pick their fathers and mothers carefully and to avoid marrying cousins!

Helen [Hamilton] and I understand each other thoroughly and I am glad she is happy. She is the only relative I have among all the thousands of my co-workers. I make it a rule, in justice to all who follow my flag, that there should be no favouritism.

Yours very affectionately,
ALFRED

He complained about the contents of his Sunday newspaper, the *Weekly Dispatch*, which announced 'The Diary of a Policeman outside 10 Downing Street'. He asked in a message to the office: 'Have we come down to that? You might follow up with "Memoirs of a Rag and Bone Man" and "Bottle Washer", then with the "Diary of a Greengrocer's Assistant", and, as a sequel to these, "25 Years with Sam Isaacs—the Recollections of a Fish Frier".'

He told the staff in the same message: 'I motored yesterday along the coast to Gravesend, and, after a peep at the paper mills, crossed the river by ferry, landing at Tilbury. I passed through the desolate Essex flats and then into beautiful country to Dunmow, where I spent a delightful afternoon with Mr and Mrs H. G. Wells' (October 27, 1920).

774

There were some who chose to see in 'the *Daily Mail* hat' campaign of the winter of 1920–1 sufficient confirmation of new rumours about Northcliffe's 'queer behaviour'. He had suggested the idea as a means of 'lightening the paper'. The *Daily Mail* had published a picture of Clemenceau wearing a hat of novel shape. Northcliffe wrote in his bulletin: 'Why not get a specimen? Wire for it. It is about time men had a new hat. Offer £100 for a new design.' One of the first wearers of the *Daily Mail* hat was Winston Churchill, whose *penchant* for novel hat styles made him popular with the cartoonists. Despite his example, the idea failed and the implication of eccentricity in Northcliffe was changed to one of declining powers. The story was told that a dismissed member of the *Continental Daily Mail* staff was seen walking up and down outside Northcliffe's hotel in Paris, wearing the new hat in the hope of being reinstated.

Trade unionists in the machine-room of the *Continental Daily Mail* had no reason to concur in the belief that 'the Chief' had lost his touch. Two of their representatives sat stiffly in his room in the Paris office that November. They were told: 'If you have come to discuss increased wages, there is nothing doing. You are living partly by your work, but more largely by the enterprise and faith of those who have supported this paper all these long years. I have neither the nerve nor the desire to go back to London and tell our shareholders that men who receive the highest rate of pay in France now want even more money.' Exchange problems and rising costs made existence as difficult for the *Continental Daily Mail* as it did for individuals working on it. 'I have had more trouble here in Paris than anywhere. I am sorry to be brief and brusque but mine is a sixteen-hour-day. Good morning, gentlemen.'

He wrote to his secretary, Price, at the *Times* office: 'Have had a very pleasant time here. Not so restful as *you* would like, but plenty of critical and instructive work such as *I* like.' A focus of his keenest displeasure at that moment was Wareham Smith, the advertisement director, who was summoned to see him in Paris. Arriving at the hotel, Smith was warned by the acting secretary, Douglas Crawford, later foreign editor of the *Daily Mail*: 'I'm afraid you're for it!' Smith was called in to Northcliffe's private sitting-room, where a sculptor was working on a plaster model of his head. Northcliffe sprang at Wareham Smith, 'like a tiger—I thought he was going to knock me down. He raved at me for twenty minutes without a stop.' Humiliated before a third person, Wareham Smith could not find the nerve to walk out. He confessed: 'Northcliffe was the only man I was never able to stand up to. He always had me beaten.' When the outburst subsided, he apologized for recent sins of omission. 'Northcliffe's face brightened, his eyes shone with benevolence. He extended his hand and said: "My dear Wareham, I'm glad to see you looking so well! Sit down and tell me how business is."'

Arriving back in London, he was confronted with the prospect of a new clash with trade unionism. He addressed the men's leaders at Carmelite House on November 25: 'If any trade union action takes place, the directors, immediately, and with the deepest regret, well aware of the suffering that it will entail upon you and your families, will issue legal notice to terminate all contracts throughout the building and will stop the publication of our four newspapers. This is not a threat. I never threaten. It is a fact.' In making his Olympian pronouncements to Labour he was both fortified and burdened by his fair record as an employer and by his generous if often tactical encouragement of the aspirations of those whom he employed. As employer and as a publisher, he had nourished the thews of Demos. That sombre giant was now preparing to flaunt a more imponderable power.

In December, the National Union of Journalists put forward new wage demands and with them a programme of staff grading which Northcliffe promptly denounced as 'degrading', declaring that it would 'bring journalism down to jam factory level'. He wrote a *Daily Mail* leading article which envisaged a reluctant but complete shut-down. Two days later, the paper published a report of a N.U.J. meeting, heading it prominently by Northcliffe's command: 'Jam Factory Journalism.' One of its results was to produce from the National Union of Journalists an expression of gratitude for Northcliffe's past encouragement and of hope that it would not be dissipated by those later events. To many people, some of them members of the Union, it seemed that Northcliffe had gained the victory. He may have so regarded it, for he could sense movements but not necessarily divine their meaning. The settlement reached three months later was in fact an armistice. His *Daily Mail* was presently to be the focal point of the greatest eruption in British trades union history, though he would not live to see it.

He spoke out strongly against promoters who came into Fleet Street, not as journalists, but as seekers of money and power. Visiting the Advertising Exhibition, he was 'twice thanked for the stand we are taking against the poisoning of the Press by financiers'. It had seemingly not occurred to him that his own tremendous success had made the invasion easier and probably inevitable. His message to *The Times* of November 30 contained the reflection:

It is not pleasant to think that, owing to the gigantic wages paid in newspaper offices and the high price of paper, newspapers are now for the first time in their history, *entirely* subordinate to advertisers. I see no way out of this *impasse*, other than by maintaining a great daily net sale and thus keeping the whip hand of the advertiser. The situation is such as should make everyone in a newspaper office think.

Wickham Steed had remarked after a meeting with Northcliffe in the late autumn that he 'did not like the look of him'. Hamilton Fyfe had the impression that 'some insidious poisoning' was at work in his system, basing that judgment on Northcliffe's displays of temper which, though less frequent, were more explosive. There was a marked droop at the corners of his mouth. At times he looked angrily apprehensive, as if he was fighting a secret battle.

There was a deteriorating position at *The Times*. Steed was bothered by what he referred to as 'the J.W. problem', meaning the attitude of John Walter to the paper, Northcliffe and himself. The dynastic co-proprietor was alleged by Steed in a letter to Northcliffe (December 5, 1920) to be 'working steadily against you, the Paper, and me', and Steed affirmed, in the same letter, his loyalty to Northcliffe 'in deed, in thought, and in word. No one shall succeed in making bad blood between us, as many people would like to do.' Walter was more concerned about 'tone' than personalities. He feared that *The Times* was losing its authority, in regard to Irish affairs in particular. He desired a sharper definition of policy 'and greater conviction'. Northcliffe to John Walter (October 15): 'You always write me nice letters. I am not sure I deserve them.' John Walter to Northcliffe (October 16): 'You are right. You did not deserve the nice letter I wrote you on Tuesday', Walter having found after writing it that without consulting him as co-proprietor, Northcliffe was negotiating Campbell Stuart's future with the paper on a long-term basis. At the same time, a dwindling circulation and rising costs required that yet more money had to be found for *The Times*. 'Mr Walter and I, and the other proprietors, have been obliged to put our hands very deeply into our pockets', Northcliffe told the staff on December 11. For all that, he would make no concession on policy. 'I know that our policy is right. I also know that it is losing us week after week hundreds of readers.' His remedy was: More counter-attractions, 'strong attractive features'. His communique to Printing House Square for December 13 was a long one, covering his weekend activities, which had been much concerned with *The Times*. He had called 'three leading advertising experts' down to Broadstairs to discuss the paper's revenue weaknesses. 'I find they take a very serious view of the matter.' Later that day a messenger arrived with a letter from John Walter, inquiring if Northcliffe objected to his selling a large block of his shares in The Times Publishing Company to Sir John Ellerman. 'Nine-thirty to bed. Thoroughly weary of *The Times*.' The communique concluded:

Monday morning. Eight o'clock. Telephone from Printing House Square. Paper down again. Lowest figure for some years. Not the four thousand square miles of Newfoundland, with my ships and railways, social problems of the increasing population; nor the Paper Mills at Gravesend; nor the Amalgamated Press with seventy publications; nor the *Daily Mail*, whose circulation has increased even in the month of December, cause me even one featherweight of annoyance. Some day there will come a limit to my capacity to stand *The Times* annoyance.

He let Steed know that 'it would be wise and kind to issue a general warning to the staff that it may be necessary to reduce their numbers', telling Campbell Stuart at the same time: 'My long experience with the staff is that the only thing that ever moves them to efficiency is fear.' The daily sale of *The Times* had dropped to an average of 114,000 copies. He told William Graham, the solicitor: 'There never has been such an anxious time in the publishing world. Wages have increased one hundred and fifty per cent and the cost of paper five hundred per cent. New claims are being made against us every day.'

He had instructed Mackenzie, his steward, to suggest possible cuts in his Christmas box list. Among others, it contained the names of fifteen gardeners, four chauffeurs, and eight indoor male servants. His net income for the year, after paying £133,000 tax, was £153,000. He had spent £132,000. His personal assets stood at just under £2,000,000. A begging letter written from a London workhouse infirmary by a former editor named Hughes, to whom he and Pemberton had tried to sell articles in their freelance days, prompted the reminiscence: 'I well remember that ancient scoundrel whose office we frequented in the vain pursuit of non-existent guineas.' Mackenzie reported difficulty in suggesting Christmas box economies, 'except in regard to one or two odd job men'. Mrs Harriet Jealous to Northcliffe (December 23): 'If I could write as I feel, I would tell you how your constant kindly thought of me, year after year, touches me. You carry a world's weight on your shoulders and yet you think of the old lady who loved you, so long ago, when you were so young. So, dear, accept my thanks for all your kind remembrance of your old friend.' A new name was added to his regular allowances list, Esther Wood, sister of his father's old friend Fred Wood, £156 a year.

His generous impulses were still easily kindled; obversely, vindictiveness was sometimes potent within him. A day or two before Christmas, his news editors received the injunction: 'Until further notice, I wish no member of the staff to see or in any way communicate with Lord Lee [of Fareham, who gave the Buckinghamshire mansion of Chequers to the nation for the use of its prime ministers].' Northcliffe conceived Lee to be responsible for criticisms that had appeared in *The Outlook*. Lee's disclaimers went unheeded. Northcliffe's self-esteem had been hurt and the discomfort of it had to be deflected to some other victim. In that temper he was still using his communiques to spread despondency if not alarm.

'The editorial page is good. Mr McLeod has bucked up a good deal since he knew that someone was waiting for his job.' He wrote to Lord Stamfordham, private secretary to the King, on December 30, after a private tour of Windsor Castle: 'I have been much overworked lately. The mental change and the subjects for new thoughts that I received yesterday have done me as much good as a holiday.'

Northcliffe to Wickham Steed:

New Year's Eve, 1920.

My dear Steed,—I am going away to get up my health and strength in one final endeavour to get *The Times* situation right.

During 1920, the Paper has caused me more annoyance than any big operation that I have ever had. I told you yesterday that, unless the position improves, I shall most reluctantly transfer my obligation to other shoulders—the best that I can find in the interests of the paper. I am looking round.

Sir James Mackenzie has for the last six years continually urged me to relax. He again spoke strongly in June, and has written since. He considers it necessary that I should be examined every week, and on the whole with not unsatisfactory results.

The Times must cut its coat according to its cloth and set out to get features that will overcome its partially necessary unpopularity. It must be a lesser anxiety to me than it is.

The first essential is health on the part of all concerned. I shall not be acting as a friend if I did not tell you that people are always saying to me that you look tired.

Your attached,
N.

He was disturbed again by the Anglo-American situation which was still inflamed. Steed had written to tell him that 'the head of one of the biggest news organizations in the United States, a man whom I know well and who has always been Anglophil, writes it as his firm opinion that "this country [the United States] is consciously or unconsciously preparing for war with Great Britain, whether it comes in twelve months or in twelve years".' Northcliffe referred in a communique to *The Times* to 'a potential enemy with a semi-hostile population of a hundred and ten millions of people who have absorbed an immense share of the world's gold' (December 9). A *Times* leading article of December 30 dealt with the *idée fixe* of the Americans that Great Britain was secretly in agreement with Japan to join her against them. Northcliffe wrote to the *Times* office:

It is a mistake to suppose that the idea is confined to readers of the Hearst newspapers. The discovery of the existence of the Pact of London by President Wilson was a great shock to the whole American people. The whole atmosphere of Washington and that of the American newspapers is one of suspicion about

779

Great Britain. A letter from a friend in New York this week says 'my position as an Englishman here is almost unbearable. I am distrusted even by friends of ten years' standing.'

Secretly communicated information strengthened Northcliffe's suspicion that there was an American move to outbuild the Royal Navy. He passed it on to Lloyd George's friend Riddell. 'A peculiar and disagreeable fact is that Captain N——, the chief of the U.S. Intelligence Division, has been brought over here as American naval attaché. He is all smiles and pleasantness. I know him. He will find out anything that we have to keep secret. He is the man who wrote that British "navalisimus" is as dangerous to the world as German "militarismus".' The new *Times* correspondent in Washington, Willmott Lewis, intimated that Sir Auckland Geddes, the British Ambassador, was coming to London and desired 'a heart-to-heart talk with the Chief, for whom he has a great admiration'. A private communication from a member of Lloyd George's *entourage* caused Northcliffe to ponder the question: 'Where will France stand if we have to fight the United States?' He was given good reason to suspect that Lloyd George was preparing to abandon Great Britain's fundamental alliance. It hardened his attitude to the 'little Welshman'.

The Duke of Sutherland had told Northcliffe that the Prince of Wales 'much wanted' to see him. A meeting was arranged at Sutton Place. Northcliffe told Sir Robert Hudson (December 20, 1920): 'I had a long talk with the young man. He talks just as wisely and sensibly as he does in his speeches.'

★   ★   ★

Northcliffe to his mother, January 1, 1921 (by telegram): *Began New Year by thinking of you dearest.* His message to *The Times* mentioned that he had been rung up from the office overnight for information about Ford, the Kilburn printer of the Henley House School Magazine, who had just died and 'who claimed—he being the sixth or seventh person to do so—to have given me my first reportorial engagement. The first person who gave me journalistic work was the late Mr Jealous, a well-known member of the Savage Club and owner of the Hampstead paper.' Sentimental reminiscence was seemly in a message to Carmelite House; in the more sober context of *The Times*, a false quantity. As if from a resentful apprehension of the difference, he was sending in 1921 longer messages to *The Times*. Read now, they give an impression of largely wasted mental effort. It was only when he touched on the fortunes of the paper that he could expect the lively interest of a difficult staff. In his message of January 1, 1921, he posed a question:

To what is due the unpopularity into which the Paper has fallen in 1920?
We are not supporting lost causes. But we are supporting causes temporarily distasteful to the unthinking public.

We are for friendship with the United States, and nine people out of ten say 'Damn the Americans! Let them mind their own business.'

Then, again, we are supposed to be in sympathy with Sinn Fein.

We support the League of Nations, which most people are bored by and do not believe in.

Our sometimes tactless pinpricking of the Prime Minister in leading articles has created the impression—especially in clubs—that we have a personal vendetta against him.

Yet I believe that we must maintain all our policies. They are right.

The Times enters upon 1921 in a more anxious state than at any time in its history. A superhuman effort will be required to recover its position. If the Paper is to continue under its present Proprietary, the existing scale of expenses is impossible. We will dip our hands into our pockets no more.

The next day he left for Paris and the south. Arriving at the little story-book town of Roquebrune, he received a message from Lord Derby telling him that 'the authorities' were still hoping to designate him Lord Lieuten-ant of Ireland. He wrote to Stuart: 'Winston is here, but I am not seeing him, or Beaverbrook either.' The last-named was out of favour for the time being. When Campbell Stuart remarked to Northcliffe shortly after-wards that the Canadians were a misunderstood people, Northcliffe re-torted (May 16): 'Beaverbrook's ways make me think so.'

His stay at Roquebrune was cut short by a letter from Totteridge: his mother was grieving at the death of a granddaughter, the second family bereavement in a few months, and from the same cause, infective endo-carditis. He hurried back to be with her, driving out from town each evening to stay the night. By day, the *Times* advertising position in-volved him in many conferences and discussions. A report on it had been drawn up by J. C. Akerman, one of Fleet Street's penetrating business brains. It called for a bolder approach to the problem of bringing in the big London department store advertisers who year by year supported the *Daily Mail* with lavish contracts. Northcliffe was determined to 'do something' about *The Times*, with its many subsidiary publications, but inspiration did not come as easily as of old. He was as serious-minded as any of the Printing House Square veterans in desiring to preserve the paper's integrity and prestige, but the post-war world with its new economic developments and its changing social values was increasing his burden at a time of life when it needed easing. 'If it is true that I worry about *The Times*, it is because I am perhaps the only person who under-stands the real situation. The worst part of the position is that the ad-vertisers do not get a response to their announcements' (letter to Mme

Clemence Rose, January 17, 1921). He complained to Price: 'Trying to improve *The Times* is like biting a rusty file.'

From The Fleetway House, Carmelite House, Printing House Square, Grand Falls, the Imperial Paper Mills at Gravesend, the Empire Printing Ink Company, and the Educational Book Company, there came a ceaseless stream of matters requiring his personal decision. The pages of his engagement book were full of names: Dudley Field Malone, American attorney; Max Beerbohm; W. S. Crawford, advertising agent; Rosita Forbes, professional traveller; Senator Millen, of Australia; Sydney Walton, publicity expert; Evelyn Wrench; Walter Hard, of the *New Republic*; Newman Flower, of Cassell's; Sylvia Pankhurst; the Hon. J. McEwan Hunter, agent-general for Queensland; John Lawrie, managing director of Whiteley's; Burton J. Hendrick, American journalist and biographer; Sir John Lavery; Lord Robert Cecil; Sir Albert Stephenson, Lancashire newspaper proprietor; Keith Murdoch, the Australian editor: their appointments with him made a typical day at Printing House Square early in 1921. Price remembered him remarking wearily as the last of a long list of callers departed: 'There's no time to obey the calls of nature.'

H. W. Wilson ('your most devoted') had written to him: 'The more I read your war record the more I ask myself: Shall all this influence and executive capacity not find a higher use than it has at present, great though its power is?' In other words, would not 'the Chief' take a hand in governing the country?

Northcliffe to H. W. Wilson:

> The Times,
> Printing House Square,
> E.C.4.
>> 27th January, 1921.
>
> My dear Wilson,—Have you any knowledge of the financial state of affairs at Printing House Square and Carmelite House, and of our difficulties in facing this newspaper situation?
>
> Do you realize the fact that, if I enter political life, I have to abandon all connection with the Press, which is my sole source of power?
>
> Mine is a new kind of position in the world. I have been more or less forced into it, but I prefer it to any other as a means of getting things done.
>
> It is kind and affectionate of you to make the suggestion.
>> Your attached
>> CHIEF.

Unable to forget that he had a throat, he had resumed the vaccine treatment given by the doctor in Birmingham. On one of his journeys there he travelled with a woman contributor to the *Daily Mail* who was writing a book in which he was interested. He had promised to read the typescript in the train. Another woman passenger started to talk. Glaring at her over his glasses, Northcliffe demanded: 'How can I concentrate on my work when you chatter?' The incident troubled his companion for more than social reasons. It displayed an abruptness which was new in her experience of 'the Chief', whose consideration for her sex was legendary. She could only conclude that he was ill; when she met him at Euston station he had seemed 'tired, bored and lonely'. A few days afterwards he was telling Seymour Price that he felt 'a bit rocky'. He had attacks of nose bleeding. He wondered whether the Birmingham doctor's 'quackcines' were causing it. He returned to the Riviera with his wife and Mrs Belloc Lowndes. The eminent surgeon, Sir Frederick Treves, was also a guest. Treves prescribed Northcliffe 'a bromide course'. Northcliffe sent Pine, the chauffeur, on a round of the chemists' shops of Mentone, buying up their stocks of the sedative. He spoke to Mrs Lowndes of his plan to make certain changes at *The Times*. When she referred to the subject a few days later, he turned furiously on her, declaring it 'a monstrous thing' that a guest of his should speak of matters known to be secret. To Mrs Lowndes he was 'always an exhausting man'. She remained one of his greatest admirers.

A strike threat in Newfoundland was followed by another strike threat from Paris. Rothermere, who had been offered, and had refused, the post of First Lord of the Admiralty,* was writing gloomily about the likely effect of the first on the price of paper, while Northcliffe was taking more positive action about the second. He sent a telegram to Goudie, of the *Continental Daily Mail*: *If our men attempt to enforce this greedy demand shut down the paper.* It was a pleasurable relief to him to survey the relatively untroubled Amalgamated Press scene.

Northcliffe to A. E. Linforth, vice-chairman:

Villa Roquebrune,
Cabbé-Roquebrune,
Alpes Maritime.
29th January, 1921.

My dear Linforth,—When I look back to June, 1888, and that tiny room in Paternoster Square, not as big as the waiting room at Fleetway House, I feel very proud of the great harvest which we are gathering from the little seed then planted—especially proud that our publications do so much good to the rising generation.

The result has been achieved by the foresight of Sir George [Sutton], assisted by the zeal, initiative, energy, industry and loyalty of those who work with me at Fleetway House. Please let them know that I am very grateful.

Yours sincerely,
CHIEF.

* Cecil Harmsworth's diary, January 28, 1921.

He wrote to Price: 'I am afraid that I was very irascible in London, what with the persistent importunities of relations and of people who really have no claim upon me, the demands of a certain mineral water, and the infernal taxes which render it impossible for me to do what I should have liked for those who really form my inner circle—these things "get my goat", to use an expression employed in America. I know that I should not be so cross, but the fact is that I am.' Secretly, he had heard that Lloyd George was conniving in a political libel suit which might implicate *The Times*. Warning Campbell Stuart, he told him: 'Asquith did the same thing against *The Times*, and when he lost the case he disclaimed having had anything to do with it.' He now thought it 'particularly ungrateful' of Lloyd George because 'as you know, my hints on the stopping of pinpricks by my newspapers have been carried out by the Editors'. Northcliffe added: 'When my turn comes I do not propose to be as gentle with him as in the past. You might let his *entourage* know my views on this subject. His ordeal is yet to come.' When Caird sent him the name of the member of the night news staff who was responsible for the libel, he replied (February 28): 'He has been with us twenty years and should not be criticized, as he has great responsibilities at night.' He told Sutton that 'the position of a newspaper proprietor will be perfectly impossible if he is responsible for the mistakes which occur in the office at midnight. The whole fabric of editorial responsibility falls to pieces if the proprietors are held personally responsible for the servants of the company', a possibly significant utterance in view of the changing roles of proprietor and editor in the conduct of newspapers. Recovering his poise, he wrote a personal note of appreciation to old Sam Stimson, who had been 'on the door' at Carmelite House from the first day of its opening. 'My dear Stimson,— During all your years of service I have never received anything but warm praise of you from staff and callers. Allow me to trust that your retirement will be as happy as your working days. I cannot say more, for I know that you were as pleased to be with us as we were to have you.' He sent a picture postcard to T. E. Mackenzie with an 'x' marking the villa: 'Nice to have four homes and a villa, isn't it? Yes, but not so nice when you are kept on the move all the time by the exigencies of work. Signed: One Of The Idle Rich.' A glimpse while passing through Paris of the Rolls-Royce showroom with its blinds drawn prompted a letter of four close-typed pages to Claude Johnson on the importance of publicity. 'You ought to have your latest model standing at the kerb outside the showroom so that the ladies could look at it. I believe that women have as much to do with the buying of a car as men, and that *carrosserie* is of vital importance.' Always, from the beginning of the motoring era, he had been interested in Rolls-Royce affairs: 'the directors', Johnson wrote in reply to his latest suggestion, 'are deeply grateful to you'.

Northcliffe to the Directors of Associated Newspapers Limited:

Mentone.

March 2nd, 1921.

My dear Directors,—'God moves in a mysterious way, His wonders to perform.' When I review the various criticisms of my queer way of running a newspaper, I look at the net sale figures and the weekly balance sheet, and wonder what would have happened had I adopted those criticisms, which, none the less, will continue, I hope.

I have another suggestion to make now—that we establish an Advertisement Department. We have not got one. We have an Advertisement Collection Department, which is quite a different thing.

Your attached

CHIEF.

The cancer shadow fell across his days at Mentone that spring. His friend, General Sir John Cowans, the British Army quartermaster-general in the war, was dying. A message came from the hushed household: 'He always looks forward to your visits. They are a bright spot in his suffering.' He wrote to Campbell Stuart: 'I have been so busy about poor Jackie Cowans that I have not been able to do much else.' He had not shirked the saddest vigil, despite his lifelong dreads. There was the unfailing anodyne, work. It began at his bedside with the *café-au-lait* at six-thirty every morning; 'frightful arrears of correspondence that Humpty-Dumpty brought up here in a huge trunk, the *Mystery of the Daily Mail* booklet, and quite a lot of prompting and correcting of the Paris *Daily Mail*, keep me just as hard at it here as I am anywhere else', he wrote to Price. There was a postscript: 'Is there any reason why the ribbon of Davy's Corona [typewriter] should always be going wrong? It is a damned nuisance. The only relief that I get here is—no telephone.'

In a long letter to Caird of April 16, he announced the promotion to the board of E. H. Curtis, editor of the Manchester edition of the *Daily Mail*. 'He was with me two years before the *Daily Mail* started.' He ordered that Curtis's new appointment should be announced 'on the main page of the London and Paris editions', a compliment to Curtis's worth as a colleague. It was also an opportunity to inform Caird: 'I propose appointing short term directors henceforth, in view of the increasing age of the staff. I can see that *anno domini* is coming upon us very severely in some quarters. It is a horrible disease and very catching.' His letter to Caird continued: 'I find myself wondering whether I should consult some younger medical man than Dr Mackay, of Birmingham, who is about thirty-two, remembering that long before I was twenty-five I had organized many successful publications and travelled widely. Newspapers, more than any other under-

785

takings, demand a constant influx of youth. This is not aimed at you in particular—YET.' He urged Caird to read Bacon's essay, *Youth and Old Age*. 'You will see our case exactly put.' The writer of the *Daily Mail* pamphlet which he was editing, F. A. Mackenzie, had told him of the 'enthusiasm and loyalty' to be found in all departments of the paper. 'That is tremendously pleasing to me,' Northcliffe let Caird know, 'for, very often, when my throat is depressing my energy, I wonder why I should go on with this perpetual grind'.

The *Daily Mail* pamphlet, 'which, by the way, gives almost as much about the office tea room as it does about Newfoundland', he told Caird, was a source of considerable irritation to him. He wrote to the Picture Editor, Arthur Baker, on April 17: 'I hope you are mentally all right, though when I saw that horrible collection of Guy Fawkes photographs which you are alleged to have perpetrated for the forthcoming booklet, I had serious doubts.' He was astonished, he wrote, 'to notice that all the pushful people in the office have got in, while many of the chief workers there are not to be seen.' It seemed to him that 'the men with the worst clothes and the biggest feet are put in the foreground. H. W. Wilson looks as though he has not had a bath for a month.'

Young Harold Snoad, of his secretarial staff, asking for leave to go to a Territorial camp at Easter, received a picture postcard addressed: *Colonel Snoad, c/o The Viscount Price, The Private House, The Times, E.C.* 'Of course you must go to your training, dear Harold. If there are no trains you will find walking to Salisbury Plain very good for feet, figure and appetite.' At the same time, Price was instructed to send out a letter, dictated by Northcliffe, for posting up in all departments, asking for more consideration for 'the Chief's burdens'.

Rothermere, who was at Cap Martin, noted that Northcliffe 'looked so much better in health than for several years', and in expressing his pleasure by letter on April 25 signed himself 'Your devoted brother'. Northcliffe was having 'a new vaccine, which upset me very much, but I have complete faith in it'. Making another appointment with the Birmingham doctor, Mackay, he wrote: 'I am very grateful to you.'

The impression of renewed well-being was not obvious to all who saw him at the *Daily Mail* twenty-fifth anniversary celebration held at Olympia, London, on May 1, when seven thousand people greeted him with an unmistakable warmth of regard as he rose from his place at the top table and, without speaking, held up a little flag consisting of the Union Jack interwoven with the Stars and Stripes. The whole gathering rose in a spontaneous gesture of respect for 'the Chief', a myriad little flags of the same design fanning a roar of cheers to the roof. The scene before him symbolized all the striving, the strain, the achievement of his years. He gazed upon it with no sign of heartfelt pleasure, and certainly none of the exuberance with which he would have noted as *Answers* editor that 40,000 plates were required for the feast and with them, 75,000 knives, forks and spoons, or that 945 waitresses served the guests. Feelings were hurt by his turning aside from shaking the hands of editorial and advertising men and demanding the presence of George Isaacs, organizer and leader of one of the printing trade unions. When that future Minister of Labour and National Service (1945-51) was brought forward, he said: 'Now let me meet some of your people. *They*'—indicating the lined-up editors and advertising managers—'can wait.' Greeting women of the staff, it was noticed that he leaned forward to speak to some of them as if to share a confidence. Afterwards, it was found that he had whispered the same thing to each: 'My dear, what a charming hat!' Many of them who had served him longest were moved by the sight of him slowly escorting his mother round the gallery of the great hall so that she might have a panoramic view of the great spectacle below. He had long since laid his success at her feet. Some of those watching him thought that he looked seriously fatigued.

Grace was offered by the vicar of St. Jude-on-the-Hill, Hampstead Garden Suburb, the Rev. Basil Bourchier, who called for a blessing on 'Thy servant Alfred'. Cecil Harmsworth noted: 'It was heard with mixed emotions by some present and excited ribald merriment in Fleet Street.' He believed that 'Mr Bourchier, an earnest and devoted padre of exceptional ability and unconventional methods, was unconscious of anything extravagant in the terms of his prayer'. Marlowe to Northcliffe: 'I cannot let this wonderful day pass without offering you my hearty congratulations on the splendid demonstration, worthy of your long and crowded years of vigorous leadership, which we have witnessed this afternoon.' The *Morning Post* commented: 'On Sunday last Lord Northcliffe entertained 7,000 of his employees at Olympia. We understand that he has engaged Salisbury Plain in order to give a summer picnic to those who *have been* in his employ.' The venue had not been of his choosing. Referring to the anniversary plans in a letter to Price, he wrote: 'I am rather afraid of Olympia as the scene', but the tongues of enmity seized on the occasion as one more excuse for assailing him with the charge of unbridled self-importance.

★   ★   ★

He went down to Broadstairs the day following the 'great jamboree', travelling again after many years by the 5.10 train from Holborn Viaduct station and noting that the *Evening Standard* was being read mostly in the first-class coaches while his *Evening News* preponderated in the third-

787

class, a humiliating differential for which the circulation manager, George White, was sharply called to account the next morning. Accompanying his master, Humphrey-Davy took with him 'between two and three thousand unanswered letters', many of them, presumably, of a congratulatory kind. Northcliffe's hoarseness had returned. 'Today I can hardly dictate' (May 6), repeating the voice failure of his father, from whom he thought he derived his throat weakness. With the aid of his friend, Alfred Clark, managing-director of the Gramophone Company, he had some records made of his voice and submitted them to the judgment of the specialists. The recording session was 'a great strain; $4\frac{1}{2}$ minutes was more than I could stand'.

At Elmwood, breakfasting in bed on bacon-and-egg, fruit and Perrier water at eight-thirty sharp after having gone through the morning newspapers, he sent several times for Gordon, the head gardener, urging him to produce better crops, 'because food is going to be a world problem'. Relating the Elmwood kitchen garden to international economics may have seemed unrealistic to the dour Scots gardener, but Northcliffe liked to impress others, and particularly those of limited imagination, with his grand-scale perspectives, and Gordon was made to understand that asparagus and spinach were two crops indispensable to his own survival if not that of a wider comity. Mention of spinach was like a death-knell in Gordon's ear. He had so far grown thirty different varieties of it without finding one to finally gratify his lordship's taste, which relished spinach *purée*. He was also a connoisseur of asparagus for breakfast. 'I know nothing about gardens,' he told Mackenzie, 'but I know my garden is all wrong. The lettuces are disgraceful.' He had been studying the *Daily Mail* children's feature, 'Teddy Tail', and reported in his communique of May 4: 'A tiny mite of $2\frac{1}{2}$ years, the granddaughter of a very distinguished person, was brought to me yesterday so that I might tell her all the private life of Teddy Tail, in whose existence she implicitly believes.'

No doubt there was therapeutic value in those petty distractions. In April, he had been sufficiently free of *Times* annoyances to tell Campbell Stuart: 'I suppose it is because I am getting old, fat and complacent that I do not worry about Printing House Square, but I take the long view.' Inside three weeks the 'long view' had been foreshortened into a pseudo-dramatic crisis bringing urgently forward the possibility outlined in his letter to Steed of New Year's Eve, 1920.* 'All my other affairs are growing at a pace with which it is very difficult to compete and *The Times* is just that last straw which makes the load unbearable' (Northcliffe to Steed, April 24, 1921). *The Times*, he declared, was the only responsibility from which he could escape. He announced his intention of providing the paper with 'a proper and entirely British substitute for myself', someone well

* Page 779.

A Fat Mans gallant Fight against
~~Obesity~~
1920

Jan 10 (Horrible) 14 . 0 . 8

May 20 (Good Boy) 13 - 12 . 10

June 27 (Feels Fed up 13 . 13
            again)

July 10 (Holding my own) Same

Aug 20 13 . 13 . 3   worse

Sep 3   13 - 12 . 6   Ha! Ha!

Horror→ Nov 1   14 . 1

        29   13 . 13

    Dec   20   13 . 11 —

              1921   13 . 13 . 12

Jan 24

March 13   13 . 11 . 6

May 30   13 - 10 8

A page from Northcliffe's 'weight diary'

qualified to take his place and to play a fully active part in its affairs. His doctors, he stated, yet again, had told him that it was essential for him to reduce the load of his responsibilities.

You will know, my dear Steed, that I have no personal feeling in this matter. We have worked together in various relations for many years without, as far as I can remember, a single cross word or *arrière pensée*.

Steed had remained admirably unprovoked by Northcliffe's growing arbitrariness of temper, which he may have perceived to be pathological in origin. He prided himself, certainly in after years, on having noted significant change in Northcliffe's health before it became apparent to others. Through most of the spring of 1921 he had reason to believe that he was losing Northcliffe's support as editor if not his allegiance as a friend. Northcliffe realized that while Steed had eminent qualities, loyalty among them, he had proved to be a good editor of part of *The Times* but not of the whole paper. In European affairs his judgment was often superb. In other departments it was less acute. Coming to that conclusion, Northcliffe also arrived at one of his crises of near-hysteria, throwing off hints by letter, telegram and telephone of mysterious negotiations. *The Times* was 'getting him down'. The citadel which he had fortified against fate was still defying him to shape its destiny.

His private papers do not supply proof of the genuineness or extent of the negotiations in question. Reports were published in London and Paris of an impending transaction; then silence. In the Harmsworth family it was believed that his mother had been the chief prompter of his change of mind. Lady Northcliffe had certainly intervened.

★   ★   ★

The Times, Ireland and Anglo-American relations had weighed him down. Travel was the only possible palliative and there was always his doctors' advice to justify it. At what point he decided to set out on his longest journey is not clear. His correspondence does not indicate any relish of anticipation or elaborate planning. In the middle of May 1921 he went on a tour of the Midland, Northern and Scottish coalfields to see what he could of conditions that had caused a miners' strike. He seized the opportunity of his stay in Manchester to make a warmly respectful public reference to C. P. Scott, of the *Manchester Guardian*, who was having eye trouble. Scott wrote, in thanking him: 'Three English oculists whom I had consulted all wanted to take my eye out. The German oculist saved it, for which I confess I have been eternally grateful, and I owe the reprieve in some degree to you. Thank you for your kind thought for me then and now.' Northcliffe admired Scott and visited him at his home in Manchester. The city had another attraction for him; he said that he never had a headache there. He liked the people and particularly enjoyed going to lunch at Sam's Chophouse, where he could talk to the cotton men on Exchange days.

Receiving copies of his London *Evening News*, he was roused to protest yet once again about the type and display of advertisements: 'They are dreadful.' Never through his years of publishing had he come finally to terms with the advertising side, which he was now referring to as the 'You-Be-Damned' department because its managers, he said, no longer found it hard to sell space and were behaving like the man who broke the bank at Monte Carlo. The sight of one of his advertising managers, Horace Imber of the *Evening News*, going about his lawful occasions in the West End of London had prompted a sardonic mention in a *Daily Mail* communique of May 12:

We have promoted Imber to the peerage. He is to be known as Lord Imber of Golders Green in future. Getting out of his Rolls-Royce in Bond Street with eyeglass, stock and white spats, he looks more like a peer than most of my friends in the Lords and is, by the way, much better off than half of them.

He was also having 'the little articles' for Page Four of the *Daily Mail* sent to him in Manchester by train and he told Price, his secretary in London, that he gave a full hour each morning to choosing and editing them. 'I read most of them three times.' He complained of 'the infernal nuisance' of being well known. 'It robs me of privacy and time for reflection, which is the Almighty's antidote against hasty judgment.' Hearing of the death of a former *Answers* staff writer, Mrs D. M. Henry, to whom he had paid a retaining fee through several years of illness, he wrote to her son: 'It was about thirty years ago that your dear Mother joined our very small army. She was not only an excellent writer but had wonderful judgment of the writings of others. She was very kind to everyone and I was glad to do what we could at a time when she was unable to continue her work.'

A letter bearing the Coventry postmark stirred memories of his lodgings there thirty-five years before with the former governess, Miss Mercer, and of her tolerance of his piano vamping. A neighbour had written, without her knowledge, telling him of Miss Mercer's reduced circumstances and of the hardships she had suffered. Northcliffe responded at once by settling £100 a year on her for life, saying: 'She was always kind and good to me and foolishly generous.' Miss Mercer was overcome. In a heartfelt letter, she wrote to him: 'Can you imagine the affluence of £2 a week after trying for so long to live on 7s. a week?'

Northcliffe to Rothermere:

Midland Hotel,
Manchester.
20th May, 1921.

My dear Harold,—I am distressed to hear that you have started rheumatism. Time is making its mark on all of us. I went to Aix-les-Bains in 1882 with Mr Powys, who is a great believer in the place. I sometimes think I have a tendency to rheumatism, and at least once a week I take a very hot salt bath or mustard bath. I hope you will not be downcast about it.

I have just been on a tour of the coalfields—Yorkshire, Lancashire, and Lanarkshire. People said that if I went in a Rolls-Royce (a rather showy one at that), I should be attacked. Far from being attacked, the car was universally admired by the miners, especially when told that it was a hundred per cent British.

I immensely admire the fortitude of these strikers. Their only desire seems to be that their children shall get enough to eat.

The cut in wages was too sudden. That was the opinion of everyone I met, including some mine owners. The whole question is damnably complex.

Except in Glasgow, there is nothing Communistic or Bolshevik about the miners. Glasgow is not pleasant. There is practically no gas there and the electric light is very dim in the hotel.

Mother is, according to the latest news, in tremendous form.

Yours affectionately,
ALFRED.

He told Sir Robert Horne, President of the Board of Trade, that he intended sending a skilled miner to the United States to report on mechanical improvements in the industry there. He also proposed to buy 'two specimens of the dreadful dens in which some of the Scottish miners live', to be put on view at the *Daily Mail* Ideal Home Exhibition. 'I trust you will not regard this as an intrusion. My excuse is that I cannot remain idle having seen three hundred miles of people out of work.' Concerning the miners' homes, he wrote to John Robertson, Labour Member of Parliament for the Bothwell division of Lanarkshire and chairman of the Scottish Miners' Union: 'I have been shocked by the hovels in which the future generation are reared. The Japanese say, "Change of clothes, change of mind", and I am very sure that what applies to clothes applies to houses and environment. The marvel to me is that such beautiful children can come out of these single-room dens.' To a *Daily Graphic* man who wanted to work for him, he referred to 'the present difficult times', which precluded him from making new appointments, and added: 'I have just motored through the Midlands and the North. A thousand miles of people out of work is a sad sight.' He telegraphed a message to his editors regarding unrest in the mines: *Hope moderate tone will continue in all papers stop print both sides fully.* To a contributor who submitted an article about the possibility of a revolution among the Welsh miners, he wrote: 'England is ruled not by the Welsh but by the sturdy folk of Yorkshire, Lancashire and the North generally.'

When the editor of *The Communist*—'A Weekly Organ of the Third (Communist) International: Official Organ of the Communist Party'— Francis Meynell, wrote to him from 16 King Street, Covent Garden, asking him to provide printing facilities for that journal in the name of 'the rights of a free press', Northcliffe replied, not with full relevance, that the request reminded him of an Italian proverb which said that 'a man who is twice good to those who do not deserve it is a fool'. Against the advice of his associates, he declared, he had once helped the *Daily Herald* with a supply of paper at a critical moment. He had done so not because he shared in any respect its point of view, 'but because I am a journalist and believe in freedom of speech'. In return for that helping hand, he said, 'I received something more than my share of unfair abuse and denunciation from the *Daily Herald*, which apparently cares little for freedom of speech or fairness towards those with whom it does not agree' (May 31).

He attended the Manchester office celebrations of the *Daily Mail* twenty-fifth anniversary and was as attentive a listener as the rest of the company to the 'repeat' of his short speech which had been recorded for the great occasion in London three weeks before. It disclosed an unmistakable tiredness in his voice. Two days' international golf at Hoylake was spoilt for him by some mishandling of the arrangements for the American players. He claimed that he had himself settled 'a stupid difficulty'. He had written to Price a few days previously: 'Anglo–American relations and Americans occupy me much. Those who like us are getting really anxious about the state of affairs.' In another letter to Price he referred to 'a headache of three or four days produced by trying to understand the intricate mining problems explained in the various dialects of Scotland, Lancashire and Yorkshire'.

One of his opponents on the links at Southport was a Lancashire newspaper proprietor, Sir Albert Stephenson, who remarked on the firmness of Northcliffe's iron shots. Northcliffe held up his hands. 'These are some of the strongest wrists in England', he declared; a legacy, he might have added, from his 'boneshaker' days. A young journalistic aspirant named Vernon Bartlett, later a Member of Parliament and a master of the new medium of radio broadcasting, had called at Printing House Square to see Northcliffe a short time before. He noticed the same exceptional wrist development. 'I thought to myself, I should not like to be hit by a hand with *that* wrist behind it.'

For 'sleeping purposes', as he put it, he went down to the Surrey bungalow, for once taking no correspondence with him. It was merely a token severance from his world. He read the newspapers in bed, as always, and telephoned his comments on them to his offices. 'I must see dear Bennie before he leaves us', he remarked to Price one morning during dictation (June 1). 'There is a letter from him in the basket,' Price said, picking it out and handing it to 'the Chief'. It was an affectionate farewell from Charles Benham, the *Daily Mail* legal adviser for many years whom Northcliffe had spoken of as 'the noblest Jew I know'.

Not long before, Benham had irritated Northcliffe by overlooking a dubious legal point in a *Daily Mail* proof. His rebuke was harsh; it included an uncalled-for reference to Benham's ancestry. Repenting, Northcliffe sent a secretary out to buy a fresh salmon, which he himself laid on Benham's desk with a note of apology. Seeing Hannen Swaffer, the wit of Carmelite House, he asked him if he thought Benham would appreciate the salmon. 'P-p-probably, Chief,' Swaffer answered, 'he'd p-p-prefer a Gluckstein', and Northcliffe was much amused.

A message to the *Daily Mail* office of that date recalled to the staff one of the oldest subjects of 'the Chief's' public sympathies:

I would like more attention paid to the performing animals question. There is an abominable lot of cruelty about these totally unnecessary performances.

Personally, I hate to see performing animals, and I remember when I was a reporter finding out a good deal of the cruelty involved—especially in the matter of performing birds. We must keep an eye on the plumage matter until it is really through.

He had heard from the president of Standard Oil, A. C. Bedford, on the subject of Anglo–American friendship, which, Northcliffe assured him, his newspapers would do nothing to endanger, 'so far as I can ensure it'. Northcliffe wrote on the same subject to his fellow newspaper proprietor, Riddell. 'As to the United States. The fine publicity which was very properly achieved by Lord Beaverbrook for the Canadian Army completely eclipsed our wonderful effort. I was in the United States between seven and eight months and went through agonies in the knowledge that we (after France) were making the greatest sacrifice in the war, but the vast number of United States people did not know, and never will know, what we did.' Riddell had mentioned that visiting American Rotarians were being taken to Hampton Court. Northcliffe commented (June 9): 'What a capital idea! Why not keep them there?'

He returned to London to greet the new American Ambassador, his friend, George Harvey, the publisher, of whom he wrote to Garvin: 'I feel about Harvey that we had better be kind to him, *for we are certain to be asking him for something very soon*. I am anxious about Anglo–American relations.' He commended Harvey to his brother Cecil, at the Foreign Office, as a man to be cultivated for his personal qualities, apart from his official standing. He was the more annoyed to hear from Harvey that a document sent by his Embassy to the Foreign Office had brought no acknowledgment. Northcliffe to Cecil Harmsworth: 'That is rude.' As an aid perhaps to obliterating an unfortunate impression, he and Lady Northcliffe gave 'a big party' for the new Ambassador at 1 Carlton Gardens on June 7.

A letter, of that date, asked for an interview, 'with the object of ascertaining if a good understanding could be re-established between you and the Prime Minister', and suggested that it might be done without loss of independence on either side. The writer, Gerald Maxwell, who had worked on the *Daily Mail* some years previously, intimated the Prime Minister's personal interest in the proposal: 'I have, of course, already ascertained that this is his desire.' A peer, Lord Colwyn, had been active in the same cause. Northcliffe to Gerald Maxwell:

> The Times,
> Printing House Square,
> E.C.4.
> June 8th, 1921.

My dear Mr Maxwell,—. . . Politicians and newspapers and financiers and newspapers are best apart. Some politicians seem to think that newspapers act from personal motives. Mine certainly do not.

I have often expressed my great admiration for the part the Prime Minister played in keeping up the public spirit during the war. I saw him surrounded by his gloomy Cabinet at that time.

When he does what my newspapers conscientiously believe to be right, they will say so. I do not think he has been right about Ireland, a country I know as well as some people, and I do not think he is right about national expenses, and I shall say so.

I am much obliged for the trouble you have taken.

> Sincerely yours,
> NORTHCLIFFE.

His brother Cecil wondered whether 'anything could be done' about dissociating the family name from that of a firm of moneylenders trading under the name of Harmsworth. Northcliffe replied: 'I daresay lots of people believe we are in the moneylending business. What does it matter?' Receiving a letter from two elderly sisters named Harmsworth claiming a distant relationship with him and stating, more precisely, that they were 'in reduced circumstances', he sent Price to investigate. Price was not convinced; he could find no link with Northcliffe's family, but Northcliffe, 'preferring to be on the right side', made them a small regular allowance.

He reacted differently on learning from the *Times* Berlin correspondent that 'the German anti-Jewish movement' had named him as a member of the German-Jewish banking family of Stern, whose head was Lord

795

Michelham. Marking his letter 'very urgent', he wrote thanking the correspondent and asked him to make it publicly clear in Germany that he was born of an English father, 'a well-known barrister', and an Irish mother. As an insurance against further doubt in that quarter he sent his birth certificate.

Tragedy touched him when on June 11 he received a letter from his old colleague McManus. 'I am withdrawn from the stage. I cannot eat, drink, smoke or speak. Cancer has me by the throat, and but for sucking a little liquid food daily I am practically dead. Goodbye. I am glad to have worked for you and I believe that in doing my small bit to start the *Mail* in 1896 I did my bit to win the war and save the, Empire.' Northcliffe wrote: 'I should greatly like to clasp you by the hand, my dear McManus', feeling that it was the only comfort he had to offer. There was a letter from the son of old James Henderson, the publisher of Red Lion Square, asking him to see a young man who wanted a start in daily journalism. Northcliffe wrote (June 12): 'Your father was so kind to me when I was an aspirant that I would be delighted to see anybody you asked me to see.' Walking one afternoon at that time from Printing House Square to The Fleetway House with Corbett of *The Times*, he swung abruptly to the left at Ludgate Circus and crossed the street to take a roundabout route *via* Shoe Lane. 'We'll do best to keep to the byways,' he explained to Corbett. 'We might meet some of the men I've sacked—they sometimes lie in wait for me here.'

He was less often seen at Carmelite House, but his voice on the telephone still communicated his formidable personality. One of the younger reporters there recalled Northcliffe's 8 a.m. telephone calls to the office when he was at Elmwood in those days. 'The effect was electrifying. The voice of a switchboard operator trembled when he rang down to the newsroom to say that the Chief was on the line.' Northcliffe's questions would come 'like machine-gun fire'. He not only expected to be told what was the best news story in his newspapers that morning, *The Times* included, but what was the best in other papers. It was a difficult test and those reporters, old or young, who did not survive were likely to fall by the wayside. Those who did not fall, 'walked on clouds', in the reporter's words. 'Often there would be a £5 bonus, but one's pleasure could be turned sour next morning by one of the Chief's rockets of wrath.'

Northcliffe to Reginald Poole, of Lewis & Lewis, solicitors:

The Times,
E.C.4.
June 17th, 1921.

My dear Mr Poole,—Next month I enter my fifty-seventh year. My health is fairly good, but Sir James Mackenzie, who sees me twice a year, is insistent that I must go slower, and, rightly or wrongly, the people at my offices think that it would be better for the undertakings to have me for a long time in an advisory capacity than to bring about an early and final retirement owing to overwork.

The older James Gordon Bennett said, 'No man can control a newspaper unless he sleeps on the premises'. Far from sleeping on the premises, my ambition is to see a little of the world, for one reason that I have not travelled enough, and another reason is that sea voyages have proved to be the best form of rest for me.

I wish my position to be akin to that I have in regard to my Amalgamated Press, where I am remunerated for my advice. I hope I am not vain in thinking that my advice is valuable to any newspaper undertaking.

He proposed to resign from Associated Newspapers Limited, and to give up his directorship of The Times, both to take effect from July 15, 1921, his fifty-sixth birthday, reminding the solicitor that when he resigned from the board of The Amalgamated Press neither the price of the shares nor the progress of the company was affected. Ostensibly he wished to be free 'to visit the Pacific and learn about the tangled question of Anglo–Japanese–American relations', the reason he gave to Poole. An earlier draft of the letter showed that there were other reasons: the difficulties of his position as a newspaper proprietor who was held responsible for the mistakes of his editors. He wished to know whether there was any legal method of reducing that responsibility and the liabilities attaching to it. For example:

I find that I am held responsible for a libel action concerning Walter Long, whom I know and like, who behaved extremely decently in regard to a previous libel. I am also held responsible for another case which you have in hand, that of a member of Parliament of whom I know nothing. In this latter suit I am made liable for something that I actively objected to when I saw it. A day or two after my expressed dissent, I was warned by, I believe, an ex-Lord Chancellor, that some of the matter printed in the Daily Mail was very dangerous.

In the last five years I have been completely out of touch with the business, often for months at a time. Yet, despite the fact that the companies have appointed highly efficient and highly paid editors and directors—Steed of The Times and Marlowe of the Daily Mail receive, I believe, about six thousand a year each—I find myself in the ridiculous position of being defendant in a libel action in a matter in which I had already informed those rightly responsible was libellous.

I do not in the least object to responsibility, but I vigorously object to being responsible for that which I disapprove.

It may be that there is no solution, in which case do not trouble to reply.

Congratulations on the recent Daily Mail anniversary celebration arrived from India. Sir George (later Lord) Lloyd, Governor of Bombay, to Northcliffe (June 16): 'None of us who care for the Empire can ever forget the great service you rendered to us all in the war and what you went through in the face of public hostility and criticism in order to win the war.' The future pro-consul of Egypt appended a comment on India: 'We have failed miserably in developing this country and in training Indians to develop it, and we are reaping the results of our past negligence.'

On June 19, the matron of the Beaumont Street nursing home, Miss Carlin, opened a telegram which read: *Many thanks for your kindness to me two years ago.—Northcliffe.* There was an accompanying gift of flowers. It was the second anniversary of his thyroid operation. Similar telegrams were received in Harley Street and Wimpole Street—typical of Northcliffe's thoughtfulness. Between acknowledging a message from the King, who had privately expressed appreciation of the support of *The Times* and the *Daily Mail*, which had 'rendered possible the success of his visit to Belfast'; urging Campbell Stuart: 'I do beg of you to be more firm with *The Times*'; and writing to his brother St. John: 'There are those who say that a second Great World War is unthinkable and impossible, but Japan is undoubtedly preparing for war', his attention was caught by an item of news passed to him by Tom Clarke, the keen young *Daily Mail* news editor. It announced that American robins (*Turdus migratorius*) had been seen in East Anglia, Cumberland and Westmorland. The office was at once ordered to ring up the curator of birds at the London Zoo to check the reliability of the ornithologist who had sent in the report.

* * *

Abruptly, he began to behave like a man summoned to great affairs again. He was saying more often and more peremptorily to his chief secretary, 'Now, Price, immediate things only', leaving Price to cope alone with a heavier load of correspondence than usually fell to his lot. There was a message on July 6 from the British Embassy in Washington: 'The Ambassador [Sir Auckland Geddes] is endeavouring to arrange for an interview between Lord Northcliffe and the President.' Northcliffe to Rothermere (July 10): 'I am off on Saturday to try to find out what the Japanese are up to. They are very busy in all sorts of war ways.' Renouncing his political direction of Associated Newspapers, and resigning his seat on the board of The Times Publishing Company, did not mean a lessening of his vigilance. 'It is appalling to find that the *Evening News* is still being distributed in some districts by horse-drawn vehicles. Why not bullock wagons?' (July 13).

A member of the *Times* staff, Alan Pitt Robbins, had to take a typed copy of a speech to Northcliffe at 1 Carlton Gardens. The speech contained many figures. 'It was not one of his best days,' Pitt Robbins said. 'He had already kept his doctor waiting in an ante-room for an hour or so.'

Reading through the speech, he was irritated by the figures. He ordered Pitt Robbins to take down a memorandum for Steed, the editor. 'In future, no figures will appear in *The Times*. They will all be printed out in words.' Pitt Robbins took the message back to Steed. 'He looked at it and then said with a smile: "I see—and what about the Stock Exchange prices?" ' Nothing more was heard on the subject from Northcliffe.

One of his visitors at Printing House Square just before he left on his world journey was Mrs C. S. Peel, of the *Daily Mail* staff, who wrote afterwards that 'he seemed low, worried and irritable'. He had arranged for a new film projector to be demonstrated in the *Times* board room. He invited Mrs Peel to see it with him. 'The performance was remarkably bad and Northcliffe lost his temper. He seemed so ill and upset that I persuaded him to come upstairs to his own room again. At the door he paused and looked towards the abashed and disappointed operators. "I am sorry, very sorry. I should not have spoken like that", he said', and Mrs Peel saw that tears were streaming down his face.

His behaviour as a luncheon guest of Gordon Selfridge, of the Oxford Street department store, indicated that he had reached a danger-point of strain. Selfridge was then living at Lansdowne House, Berkeley Square. Northcliffe, welcomed by the host, glanced swiftly at the other guests and immediately showed agitation. He had noticed that the company numbered thirteen. Selfridge tried to laugh it off. 'I wouldn't be the thirteenth at any table in the land!' Northcliffe exclaimed vehemently and the situation was saved only by the courtesy of a more accommodating guest who retired from the scene.

Northcliffe to Mrs Belloc Lowndes:

> The Times,
> Printing House Square, E.C.4.
> July 15th, 1921.

My dear Mrs Lowndes,—. . . I should be unjust to *The Times* if I did not tell you the truth—that it is produced largely by people who do not go into what is called Society (on which *The Times* depends for its living), that such of their wives as I have seen are dowdily dressed, and that several of the editorial staff would have been much better as schoolmasters than as journalists. I am not blind to their many qualities, but I do feel that the Black Friars are much more cut off from the world than they were in monastic times. They never seem to know what is being talked about.

> Yours very sincerely,
> NORTHCLIFFE.

He was at Carmelite House that day holding a farewell conference of editorial staffs in Room One. As he took his place at the big desk, he snapped at a sub-editor in a corner of the room: 'What was the best story in this morning's *Daily Mail?*' The sub-editor promptly quoted the announcement: 'Viscount Northcliffe is leaving tomorrow on a world tour and will be away from England for several months.' There followed what one of the young men present, A. S. Frere, of the *Evening News*, described as 'a shocked silence'. Northcliffe looked stern. Then, turning to his secretary, he said: 'See that that man gets a hundred-pound bonus.' There was a murmur of surprise, rising to laughing appreciation. Northcliffe's stern expression remained. Later in the day he was at The Fleetway House, taking papers by the handful from the safe in his room and tearing them into small pieces which Price was ordered to throw down the lavatory. Price said that the clearing-up task occupied 'most of the afternoon'. One of 'the Chief's' parting letters was to Joseph Brunnbauer, his old valet, who had returned to live in his native Linz, Austria. 'Dearest Joseph,— I have your kind message. You never forget me and I never forget you' (July 15). Madame Rose, who acted as hostess for Wickham Steed when he entertained important foreign visitors at his flat in Holland Park, begged him to 'come back rested, brimming over with energy and full' of that urchin fun you have had so little leisure to delight others with' (July 14).

Sutton was once again given full power of action in his name. By Northcliffe's command, copies were made of Dr Johnson's dictum on the virtue of seeing the Great Wall of China and sent to members of his family and to his friends. In his baggage there was a box of volumes of history and travel, including accounts of the voyages and researches of Captain Cook and Sir Joseph Banks. There was also a set of Dickens's works. His mother had given him as a keepsake a little book of devotional thought called *Daily Light on the Daily Path*. He had drawn up for her a detailed itinerary of his journey so that she might follow his course precisely and read the little book at the same hour as he did every morning. Mackenzie made a last minute note: 'Insure Chief's false teeth.' Max Pemberton was apprehensive. 'I told him very frankly that by undertaking such a journey he might be signing his death warrant.' Pemberton was well acquainted with Northcliffe's health history and knew that Seymour Price had discovered a heart defect.

He sailed from England on July 16, the day after his fifty-sixth birthday, the night of which he spent at Totteridge. Before leaving early in the morning he dictated over the telephone a last memorandum for Caird: 'As Miss Rudge [Telephone Department] is one of those who went across the Atlantic in my service at the time of the submarine menace, I wish her position not to be interfered with during my absence abroad.' His mother received a radiogram from him on July 20: *Reading little book dearest.* He wrote to her from the *Aquitania* the same day: 'Most Sweet and Perfect. . . . I count the days till we are together again.' *The Times* and *Daily Mail*

Northcliffe at Elmwood with (*left*) his secretary, Humphrey-Davy, and Gonnoské Komai, the Japanese poet

Northcliffe with his mother at Poynters Hall, Totteridge, on his fifty-sixth birthday, before leaving on his world tour, July 1921

announcements of his departure had a proclamation ring, inciting *Punch*
to print an undergraduate skit on 'Lord Thanet's world pilgrimage', in
the course of which 'he will visit the North and South Poles, ascend
Mount Everest and descend to the centre of the earth'. The *Morning Post*
stopped just short of satire:

> Alas! Alack! What shall we do?
> Lord Northcliffe's gone on tour.
> Without him even two and two
> How dare we say make four?
>
> Why *now* the master-hand withdraw
> From *Times* and *Daily Mail*,
> That gave the Tables of the Law
> A more than million-sale?
>
> Too late to plead. His sail's unfurled.
> What comfort's to be found?
> For while 'the Chief' goes round the world,
> How will the world go round?

Chapter Twenty-eight

'I Dream only of England'

Lovat Fraser had written to tell Northcliffe that Horatio Bottomley, who was sixty, was planning a new Sunday newspaper. Northcliffe replied, June 30, 1921: 'I do not think that I shall be able even to conduct newspapers at sixty, let alone start them, and I imagine my vitality is as good as most.' Seen with his arm linked in Wickham Steed's on the deck of the *Aquitania* just before sailing, he looked not only tired of his crowded years, but exhausted by them. His face was florid and puffed and his eyes had lost their attentive brightness. He told Spedding, the purser, that he was 'suffering from brain fag'. His soft white collar, worn with the familiar red and white tie, was a size too large and showed the mark of his throat operation. His clerical-grey flannel suit hung loosely on him, its jacket buttoned primly down the front.

Appearance was deceptive; after two days at sea he was dictating a sparkling article called 'The Wonder Ship' for the *Daily Mail*; 'a country house at sea with just the right number of people in it and plenty of room for them all'. Spedding said that 'it was such a pleasure showing him things—he was so appreciative'. Every day he asked to see some new part of the ship. The purser, who had known him on other voyages, said that he had lost 'none of the old inquisitiveness'.

The New York reporters liked his voice; they described it as 'low and quiet'. Nor did he mentally belie their impression of a forceful personality. There were so many interviewers that he held an all-day reception for them in his room at the Gotham Hotel. His protests that he was on holiday and keener to read novels than newspapers evoked the sort of laughter that might have been heard in an interview with Machiavelli.

Out of his easy-going dealings with the newspapermen of New York there came a serious *contretemps*. An alleged interview with Steed referred to the King's part in the Irish negotiations. The so-called interview was cabled to London in Northcliffe's name and published in the Irish edition of the *Daily Mail*, before it was suppressed. Not much notice was taken of it in the United States. *The History of The Times* records that 'in England it exploded with the force of a bomb'. The detonation disturbed Northcliffe far less than it did some other people, including the Prime Minister, who cited the 'interview' as an example of 'criminal malignity', an indictment which, said the *National Review*, evoked the 'raucous cheers of Coalition K.B.E.s in *esse* and in *posse*'. It was the Premier's chance of revenge for the very sharp attack made on him in *The Times* of July 13, when he was described as 'probably the most distrusted statesman in Europe'. Northcliffe telegraphed to Buckingham Palace: *I gave no such interview*. Not stopping to check the facts, Lloyd George had advised the Sovereign to issue a formal repudiation of words attributed to him. Northcliffe to his mother: 'I daresay you saw a ridiculous fuss in the papers about something I was supposed to say about the King. A complete fabrication. I am afraid I didn't fuss at all but went on with my golf and novel reading as usual. I read a novel every day now.' At home, the reverberations rumbled back and forth between Fleet Street and Westminster. There was a meeting of directors at Carmelite House. Sir Robert Hudson appealed to Northcliffe to 'go slow'. Lady Northcliffe cabled: *Greatly distressed and ill with worry situation here intolerable quite understand you personally not responsible but you are regarded as responsible for your staff so fear personal position not much improved by denial do now refrain from politics and take complete holiday.* Rothermere urged him to 'get rid of Steed'. Northcliffe continued to stand firmly by him. 'Here, if you don't give an interview, they invent one', he told John Walter by letter.

It was Steed's first visit to the United States. Speaking to reporters 'off the record', he had assumed that none of his remarks would be printed. That expectation was ignored by one of the reporters, a Welshman working on a New York newspaper. He wrote a so-called interview with Steed which was inadvertently cabled to London by an inexperienced young assistant in the New York office of the *Daily Mail*. 'His folly follows me round the world', Northcliffe told Bullock, the *Daily Mail* correspondent in New York. *Hope newspapers published my denial of interview with King stop now wrench of parting over thoroughly enjoying myself.* That message to Price at Printing House Square on August 1 was followed by another the same day. *Wire Mother's health and circulation figures.* He wrote to his mother also that day: 'Most Sweet and Perfect,—Am more than sixteen days nearer to you than I was when I left. That thought is before me every morning and every evening when I read the little book. I think of you always and wonder whether you have yet gone to Southdown. [Her little house in Sussex where she went to stay with Charles, her invalid son.] When you are there give my love to Dick'—the family name for Charles. 'I will send him some picture postcards.' Sutton, it seemed, had not so easily got over 'the wrench of parting'. He cabled a business message to Northcliffe on August 3 which ended: *Fond love*. By that time news had reached Northcliffe of the Prime Minister's fierce comment in Parliament on the alleged interview referring to the King. He immediately cabled his protest against 'a totally and outrageously unjustified attack', and at the same time wrote to Lord Stamfordham: 'The editor of the *Philadelphia Public Ledger* commented on this outrageous fabrication on the morning of its appearance and considerably before the Parliamentary discussion.' The New York *Daily News* invented a postscript which made Northcliffe laugh. The newspaper reported that when the Prince of Wales read the alleged interview, he remarked: 'Lord Northcliffe has no daughter—if he had one, I've no doubt he would make me marry her.'

'I hope the office has recovered from its cold feet about the fabricated interview with me,' Northcliffe wrote to Caird at Carmelite House. 'Tell them not to believe it if they see that I have attacked the Queen, exposed the Prince of Wales, or made some slighting remarks about Queen Alexandra.' He found New York in 1921 'very like what it was in 1917. I had exactly the same rooms at the Gotham and most of the same servants were still there. Melville Stone [American newspaperman] is very old.' He had found time to go out to the Pelham manor house where he had lived in 1917. 'The door was opened by a sleek English butler as before.'

The *Times* criticism of July 13 had been focused also on Curzon, the Foreign Secretary. At his suggestion, British officials in Washington decided to boycott Northcliffe's visit. An Embassy reception was cancelled. When Northcliffe and Steed went to the White House to meet President Harding, the British Ambassador was not there to present them. In affecting to believe that Northcliffe did not count in the post-war world, the Foreign Office signally failed to impress the President and his advisers. President Harding kept Northcliffe and Steed talking with him for eighty minutes, the longest private audience then on record at the White House. Northcliffe reported to Stuart: 'I liked Harding immensely. He has grown bigger since I met him in 1917.' He described Harding as 'physically the most attractive' of the five American presidents he had met, 'a man of good-humoured patience and broad common sense'. Wickham Steed wrote to Northcliffe: 'Harding's popularity throughout the country has been greatly increased by the way he received you and me after Curzon's attempt to exclude you.'

Reinvigorated, as always, by the North American scene, Northcliffe soon found that he had 'altogether underestimated the secretarial side of the job. I could easily have managed with two more shorthand typists.' By

August 4 he was in the mood to write home to Price: 'I shall never come to the United States or Canada again. I had no idea that I was so well known. 1917 was a joke to 1921.' Deputations, with or without flowers, and surrounded by large crowds, waited on him at every train stop; many of the people who came to greet him waved copies of *Answers*. Telegrams showered in on him from places far distant along his 'world whirl' route. There were requests that he should stop at points not included in his itinerary. One such appeal from the mayor of Suva, Fiji, suggested that the liner *Makura* in which he was to cross the Pacific should be 'slowed down' so that he could be given a ceremonial greeting from the shore. 'I am just longing for a bed that doesn't hit you in the back all night. But the C.P.R. have done us proudly. Better organization I cannot conceive.' At some stations large parcels of autograph books awaited his attention. 'To turn this trip into a holiday tour is going to require the firmness of a Bismarck,' he wrote home. 'It is a triumph of Nemesis that I should be pursued round the world by a monster partly of my own creating—the Press. If one goes quietly about one's affairs, one is called haughty, as I have been.' He told Caird in a letter that 'cables of invitation are pouring in. It is going to be a tremendous fight to make this trip a holiday.'

As a companion-aide, he had taken with him John Prioleau, the *Daily Mail* motoring correspondent, who was helped by Harold Snoad as travelling secretary. The rest of the party consisted of Frederick Foulger, his valet, and Pine, his chauffeur, chosen because his was 'an old familiar face' and also because he was capable of forceful action as a bodyguard, if need be. Wickham Steed, who had travelled with Northcliffe to Vancouver, now turned back in order to be present at the Washington disarmament conference, making notes on the situation *vis-à-vis* America and Japan *en route*. With the troublesome New York incident in mind, Steed wrote pointedly to Northcliffe that he had subsequently given '160 interviews, in not one of which was I ever "let down" by an *American* reporter'. Northcliffe had conceived it to be in the public interest that he too should study 'the Pacific problem', the future impact on the world, and especially on the British part of it, of 'the teeming populations of Japan and China, increasing at the rate of 5,000,000 a year and within a fortnight's sail of the vast, unpopulated but immensely rich areas of Australia and New Zealand'. In British Columbia, Northcliffe insisted that his newspapers were not giving the facts. 'We have been supine and ignorant and duped', he told Steed.

His speech at the crowded Canadian Club in Vancouver called for 'mental disarmament'. Failure at the Washington conference, he said, 'would be a catastrophe', and in a reference to the unguarded frontier between the United States and Canada he wished that the condition of 'friends having no need of fleets and armies' prevailed over wider areas of the world. His tone was characteristically hopeful but it was also practical. There was still a great danger spot in Europe. 'Germany is unrepentant, vengeful and watchful.'

In Vancouver, also, he experienced again what he called 'the rising of the ghosts', the unexpected reappearance of friends and acquaintances of his earlier years. One of them was the *Bicycling News* sub-editor, Stephen Golder, another a son of a vicar of St. Peters, Thanet, who had played in the Elmwood garden as a child, another a Henley House School boy whom he did not recognize. There were pioneers of the original Grand Falls project and former patients of Lady Northcliffe's war hospital at Sutton Place. He was moved by 'the intense British loyalty' of the people he met in Canada. 'If we get into another warm corner, they will, I am sure, swarm over as they did before. At present they are disturbed about Japan.'

The buoyancy of the American part of his journey subsided as he crossed the Pacific, but he was no longer *distrait*. He was sending home long reports and comments on his travels to be circularized, as before, among his relatives, friends and colleagues. Every day he cabled to his mother. No week passed in which he did not write at least two letters to her. As he travelled farther away from her, his affection became more extravagant. He had not used the endearment of 'darling' so profusely before in writing to her or signed himself 'Yours adoringly'. He assured her: 'Little book is read every day. Hadn't time to get a case for it, so I have made a little nest for it in a cigarette box, which rests in front of your picture in my shrine of home photographs. You are always in my thoughts, darling Mother. I think of you wherever you may be—of your rooms and of your movements.' Sir Robert Hudson, sending him news about the Westminster Abbey appeal fund, wrote: 'It is due to you that the Abbey's finances are sound and secure for our time, and, as I believe, for *all* time.' Sir Robert also told him: 'Your lady is looking splendidly well.' Northcliffe let him know in reply: 'I have been thinking a great deal about her on this voyage. I have three of her portraits in my cabin.'

There were many days on which he showed the liveliest mental energy in dictating letters of several pages to various members of his staffs, in addition to the regular circular letter for his family and friends. To H. G. Price: 'I wonder if you have gone for your holiday or not. I never think about the newspapers or business at all. It is no good doing so. It is better for me and the business that my brain should lie fallow in that manner, but you know how much I think about all my friends there. Every day at waking they are in my mind; I try to imagine what they are doing. When I wake now it is just the time when they are leaving their offices. . . .' To Price again (August 17): 'I wonder what old Humpty-Dumpty is up to. Tell him I often think of him and despite his damnable Humptiness, tell him I am very fond of him.' To Sir Campbell Stuart (August 20): 'I often wish I had you with me on this trip. The correspondence has been tremendous and the difficulties innumerable. If I were an official person it would be quite easy. I am occupying a nebulous position, yet asked by everybody. I am always placed in a position where tact is essential. If you go to Government House, you get a very inferior lunch and see nothing; if you are entertained by the leading citizen you lunch in an exquisite tropical bungalow and have delightful excursions.' To his mother: 'Very hot. I sleep in the costume you gave me on the 15th July, 1865' (the date of his birth), and, two days later: 'How queer it is to be 12 hours in front of you. I read the dear little book, which I kiss every day at 7 in the morning, 7 o'clock at night with you.' Gloom awaited his arrival at Hamilton, New Zealand. His R.A.F. friend and airship pioneer, Air-Commodore Maitland, had been killed in the R.38 disaster at Hull. Maitland, 'so daring, so able, so handsome', had lunched with him at Carlton Gardens the day before he sailed.

He thought the Southern Cross 'a very poor constellation' compared with Charles's Wain, and the fauna of New Zealand disappointed him by the lack of birds, delighted as he was to hear 'English thrushes and blackbirds' on a golf course; 'very strange to hear them singing their nesting songs in August'. The boiling springs of Rotarua inflamed his imagination. He had seen a wonder of the world and it excited him to write pages of ardent description which read now like an *Answers* article of the early days. The sight of mountains, lakes and forests began to weary him; 'but I am not tired of volcanoes, boiling waterfalls, and geysers with their queer moods. The whole place is inconceivably interesting. I call it topsy-turvy-dom—parlourmaids in the summer earn seven pounds a week, tops of mountains are blown away sixty miles, your money turns black with the sulphur in the air, there are wingless birds, forty pound trout, caterpillars with trees growing out of their heads, and ferns as tall as Printing House Square.' Cooling down, he wrote to Campbell Stuart: 'Canadians who are travelling in New Zealand do not want to go home. They realize that they went to the wrong place.' At Wellington, there was another of the 'ghosts from the past', the President of the Wellington Club, who had been a neighbour of the Harmsworths at St. John's Wood in the 1880s. Yet another early acquaintance turned up with a copy of the first issue of the *Daily Mail*. Wherever Northcliffe went, there were ex-soldiers who pressed forward to shake his hand. 'They had been without shells in France', and they greeted him 'with terrific applause', reminding him that, 'just after the shells agitation', he had spent two days with the New Zealand forces at Armentières. But there was always the likelihood, he wrote in another of his letters home, that they came to see him for a less flattering reason—'they rarely do see anyone new in these out-of-the-way places'. He was sorry to leave New Zealand. 'It has been a great and pleasing surprise to me.'

Northcliffe to his mother:

> At sea 'twixt New Zealand
> and Australia.
> Monday, 5th September, 1921.
> (Many days nearer you)

Most Sweet and Precious,—I've said goodbye and I expect for ever, my dearest, to beautiful and prosperous New Zealand. Quite impossible to describe, and in forty-eight hours I land in mighty Australia.

Everywhere the 'rising of the ghosts'—the appearance of people one hasn't seen for years. At Sydney, there will meet me the wife's only brother, Henry, who left England when I was twenty-one.

On every ship in the world is a chronometer at Greenwich time, and every day I look at it so that I may know what my darling Mother is doing. Reading her little book, scolding Ridley (her butler), in her chair, playing her games, her Sunday night gatherings.

Give my love to everyone. I think of all when I read the little book each day. I am marking each page with the name of the ship or place I read it in.

With a thousand embraces, my dearest dear,

> Your Firstborn.

Both New Zealand and Australia formally welcomed him through their acting prime ministers. The unofficial greeting of Australia was expressed in the cheers of the 'diggers', the men who had returned from the campaigns in Europe and the Middle East and who knew that his good will and influence had supported them through more than one crisis of the war. He wrote in his private circular letter from Sydney: 'I have been overwhelmed by the reception here. Great crowds we meet everywhere I am announced to go, and always with cheers, headed by the returned Australian soldiers. No speech is made here without reference to the shell campaign and my criticism of the Gallipoli expedition (in which so many Australian fathers and mothers lost their sons), and especially our criticisms of the delegates to the disarmament conference at Washington, in which the whole of this continent may be involved.' He found himself 'in another world', teeming with amusements and cheap food. 'I cannot bear to contrast our vast slums with the sunshine and plenty here.' The glowing Australian sunlight was too strong for his eyes: 'it troubles me more than anything else'. In Sydney, 'some very nice people came to me bearing Auntie Miller's signed portrait and remembering our family in 1870!' The hour of his arrival in Melbourne coincided with that of a famed prelate, Archbishop Mannix. 'I was a little surprised to find that the crowd took absolutely no notice of him and came to cheer me.' More faces appeared from the past: 'Mr Bernard Parker, who transacted the sale of the *Evening News* (in 1894); Emma F——, daughter of the Wheatsheaf Inn landlord at St. Peters, where I stayed when I was twenty'; J. A. Newton, 'who was on the staff of *Bicycling News* with me', men 'who as boys had been at our camp at Broadstairs'. One night in Melbourne, 'I dreamt that I was down at Elmwood. Somehow or other, I entered it by the red brick gates of the gardens of the big red house opposite, and found my dear Elmwood filled with Bulgarians.'

Tasmania, 'as large as Ireland with the population of Peckham', reminded him of home, 'of the British Isles at their best'. He saw it becoming 'a great industrial country, without the squalor and filth of British industrial districts', a land which might flow with milk and honey if only it could find the settlers. A young man pushed his way through the crowd at Hobart to speak to him: 'he had been a picture-framer at Broadstairs and framed pictures for me twenty years ago'. Another of his 'ghosts' in Tasmania was 'assistant editor of the *Review of Reviews* with Stead'. What he had not seen in Tasmania, or in Australia and New Zealand, supplied the theme of a speech he made to trade unionists in Melbourne on his return there. 'The emptiness of your immense island is one of the great dangers to world peace.' Taking note of local labour conditions, he observed that the makers of strife, 'or Reds, are usually of Irish provenance'. Asked for a summary of his impressions, he issued a fresh warning: 'I leave lovely Australia haunted and subdued by the thought of your weakness. I am amazed at your indifference to events in the outside world and especially in Asia.' His words did not fall like music on every Australian ear. Official Labour was not amenable to any easing of the restrictions on the supply of workers. There were realists who congratulated him on his frankness. Bullock wrote to him from New York: 'Your parting speech from Australia created a sensation. I was lunching the day it was published with Mark Sheldon, the Australian Commissioner, and some other Australians, who all confessed that the speech had thrilled them.' Nor did he flinch from confronting them with certain facts about the war as a corrective to local notions about the decisive part played in it by Australian and New Zealand men. 'Unfortunately, the Australians and New Zealanders, who came into the war long after our best men had been slain, were put alongside weak British divisions as an encouragement to those divisions. They judge us by the men they met at that time.' He left Australia with a greatly enhanced esteem for the Australians and a profound sense of the emptiness of their country. He had been hugely impressed by the gaunt majesty of the natural scene. Not less striking for him had been the physical size of many of the men. 'I feel that I have been staying among giants. That feeling has been with me all the time.' Equally memorable, he wrote, was their quality of individualism which made them impatient of leadership and resentful of class divisions and especially of the State Governors' 'little courts'.

He cabled his mother on her wedding day, September 21: *Thinking of you, most darling stop lilac and chestnut blossom time here.* To Lord Montagu of Beaulieu he wrote on September 24: 'I can truly say the last month has been the most interesting in my whole life.' On September 29 he wrote to Price:

I am learning more about what I don't know than ever before in my life. These people are absolutely blind to the Japanese danger. They are too well fed, enjoy too much sunshine, have too many holidays, and too much beautiful scenery. They are thoroughly nice people. I like them all.

I should not care to live here with the Japanese Islands two and a half days off by steamer.

We talk about you all every day. You at your telephone. Helen [the cousin who worked at Printing House Square] demure at her desk. Dear old Humpty (I love him despite his mental freaks), muddling away at your side. Thorpe [an old Walter family retainer], the only respectable looking man of the lot, obsequious below.

By the time this reaches you our faces will be turned towards Printing House Square. Exactly the way of our return it is impossible to forecast; the boat situation is most difficult, especially as I don't wish to travel in Japanese ships.

Your devoted
CHIEF

While Northcliffe was voyaging through the Antipodean scene, at home in England the first Earl of Oxford and Asquith was noting in his diary that 'Northcliffe, who is somewhere in the Pacific', was said to have telegraphed to the King to announce that he was becoming a Roman Catholic. 'The King's alleged reply was, I thought, excellent: "Well, well—I can't help it." ' The librarian at Windsor Castle has no such telegram in his keeping and the story was contemptuously dismissed by Hamilton Fyfe in his reminiscent study, *Northcliffe* (1930), as 'malicious gossip'.

He left Australia for Japan on October 1, sailing in the *St. Albans*, 'a little steamer which really might be my own'. His friend Lord Inchcape, of the P. & O. Line, had arranged that the ship should 'stop wherever and whenever I wish it', a rare concession which he delighted thereafter to dwell on in recounting his experiences of the tour. No voyage ever pleased him more: it brought out the last vestiges of the boy in him, thrilling him with the possibility of calling at desert islands, 'of seeing a picture of boyhood's dreams come true', as, for example, at Cape York. 'The ship lay anchored about a mile away, hull and tall masts reflected in the polished sapphire of the bay. On the curving white coral beach the three ship's boats lay hauled up. A hundred yards inland, in the shade of stunted, wind-racked trees, the landing party (every mother's son of whom was, in imagination, armed to the teeth) were busy laying out a camp and building a fire of wreck wood.' They returned to the ship 'over a sea of gold and purple, with a blazing scarlet sun setting the whole sky on fire over our heads. For ten minutes the world was a riot of incredible colours, and then it was as if a giant hand had suddenly poured night out of a can over the whole thing, and it was dark.'

He wrote to his mother on October 7: 'I have heard nothing of my business and I have not seen any of my papers, though I often see people reading them. I want to give my mind a complete rest from them. I never even think of them. Curiously enough, I dream of Poynters or Elmwood or the bungalow every night. Never about business. I have had more public fuss than I like. Thank goodness, that is over at last. Give my love to everyone, all my brothers and sisters. Your most adoring Firstborn.' He mentioned his dreaming to Sir Robert Hudson in a letter of the next day: 'A curious personal feature of this trip is the fact that I have dreamt every night since I have been travelling. In no dream have I dreamt about the journey, or about my businesses, which I have completely dismissed from my mind. Most of my dreams are about my homes and always about England. Last night, for example, I was at a theatre in Birmingham trying to reach the front row of the stalls by walking along a narrow plank in the dress circle.' He wrote to Sutton that same day (October 8): 'If anything should happen to me while I am away, will you take notice that I desire one share of the shares in which my will is arranged to be given to my brother-in-law, Henry G. Milner, of Brisbane; failing him, his wife; failing his wife, to be divided among the children, to whom I desire to leave five hundred pounds each. They are the only people associated with me who have not shared my great prosperity. They are extremely nice people and Milner was my earliest boyhood friend.' Milner had a family of nine and Northcliffe 'enjoyed tracing their likenesses to their kinsmen at home'. They looked on his coming as 'a miracle', Harry Milner, a refrigeration engineer who had lost his business connections through the war, being at the end of his financial tether. He had not disclosed the state of his affairs to Northcliffe or to Lady Northcliffe, his sister, or indeed to any of his relatives or friends. Settling Milner's affairs and putting the family in his will (by means of a codicil later legally upset because it had not been correctly witnessed), Northcliffe wrote to Milner's mother: 'I have had the greatest pleasure in bringing him with me on this journey to Japan and China. He has picked up wonderfully.'

From Thursday Island, the route was northward to Borneo, the Philippines, Japan and China. Northcliffe to Mrs H. G. Price (October 9):

'I cannot tell you how many springs, summers and autumns we shall have had by the time we get home. A few weeks ago it was the snowdrop and daffodil (at Hobart, Tasmania), last week it was the tropical flowers (in Brisbane), shortly it will be the autumn leaves of China; then, one day, it will be the mimosa at Cap-d'Ail, and then daffodils again in England.' He reiterated in his letters that he 'never thought of newspapers'; but the pretence fell to pieces when he discovered that the New York correspondent of the *Daily Mail* was responsible for getting news out of the Philippines. 'Would you believe it?—Bullock, in New York, covers Manila!' The discovery shocked him: 'It is almost incredible. How the devil can Bullock cover Manila? It looks as if our correspondents are arranged by people who have never been anywhere.' The transmitter in the *St. Albans* was kept busy with his exclamatory messages on that topic. 'Gott in Himmel! Think of Bullock being responsible for Manila!'

Northcliffe to his mother:

At sea between China and Japan.
27th October, 1921.

On Tuesday next my face turns towards you, dearest, and I shall be travelling fast towards Totteridge.

I have written as often as I have had anything to say, except that I always want to say that I am devoted to my most sweet Mother.

You get the diary I send home, I trust. It is badly done and very jerky. Written at great speed.

I read and sleep a great deal and have never had such a rest in my life.

Every morning on waking up I think of you, my very dear one.

I am having a wonderful education, and should have done this long ago.

I expect to reach Marseilles on the 18th February (D.V.). Shall spend some days with wife on Riviera. I shall have to be careful after so much heat.

Your devoted Firstborn.

'My great regret is that I didn't make this tour when I was much younger,' he wrote to Rothermere on November 1. 'I could have been much more useful to the public if I had known what I know now.' Striving to avoid the official side of things, he applied himself even more strenuously to his exceptional fact-gathering opportunities. 'I had no desire to see lepers,' at Berhala, Borneo, 'but I thought it my duty to know something about these unfortunate people.'

At Manila he was given a welcome which, according to *The Philippines Herald*, 'surpassed all previous receptions given to any individual visitor'. His speech to members and guests of the Manila Rotary Club on October 21 both advocated and forecast a complete partnership of views and action in a world crisis arising from events in the Far East—'events which, possibly, we do not like to name', he said. The Washington Conference, he told his hearers, was 'dealing with the mysterious and puzzling circumstances of the future', and he 'dreaded to think' of what would happen if the conference failed. 'The mad race for armaments would continue until there came a war in all probability much more terrible than the worst phases of the conflagration that is even yet not quite extinct in Europe, a war in which so-called scientific weapons will be developed still further.'

Going through the schools of Manila, he doubted whether the children in them 'will ever become young Americans'. He wrote down the opinion of 'an eminent Filipino' who told him: 'It is better to have our own disorderly government than to be interfered with by Americans', an attitude which he was to find repeated at later stages of his journey among the subject peoples of the world. He was still interested in prison life, emotionally rather than sociologically, but the 'great gaol' of Manila, he wrote, 'did not please me very much'.

In Hong Kong, he was welcomed by an old member of the Sylvan Debating Club, Dr Pearce, of the Health Department, and mentioning the matter in a letter home he wrote: 'I hear that one of Cecil's boys is a member of the Sylvans, which pleases me much. I wish there was more desire for tradition in the family.' In Canton, he was greeted as 'big number one topside man', and noted with satisfaction that the Union Jack was prominently displayed in Canton and on the river. 'While the Japanese alliance has degraded our prestige in the eyes of the East, we are still a very considerable people.' For the alliance, he had two adjectives, 'hateful' and 'infernal'. He heard from the ship's radio operator 'of curious wireless quarrels between American and Japanese operators. They annoy each other and make contemptuous signs to one another.'

First sighting Japan, he thought it 'a noble coast—great cliffs and, beyond them, mountains'. Opposed to the alliance, he seemed the more staunchly resolved to be fair to the Japanese people, in whose name he had been publicly thanked for services rendered to Japan by his newspapers in 1914. He believed that their rulers were bent on world dominion, but he saw no reason for withholding his appreciation of a people who were too polite to stare at him in public places and many of whose traditions were rooted in lofty ideals and expressed with infinite charm. He told the *Osaka Asahi* newspaper: 'In a brief visit, I do not want to look at things with ugly meanings, like battleships.' He liked their tea drinking ritual, their houses and gardens. His visit to the Imperial Gardens at Kyoto was 'enchanting, bewildering, fascinating'. Politics spoilt a delightful memory.

We are sad to-day [November 6]. We were mixed up with the assassination of Hara, the Prime Minister here. I did not see Hara on purpose. I did not wish to get involved in any discussion with regard to the Anglo-Japanese agreement, which is detested by every European and American I have met. Hara was a forceful sort of man, and was determined to see me. He took advantage of a meeting of his supporters at Kyoto so that he might be able to meet me. Just before the train started from Tokyo he was assassinated.

There were fears for Northcliffe. He had declared his opposition to the Anglo–Japanese treaty in advance of his arrival in Japan. That had been a tactical move, designed to forestall official hospitality, which he considered a waste of time. For the Foreign Office in London it was an embarrassment, while his declaration had also unnerved the Tokyo correspondent of *The Times*, who 'didn't sleep for nights'. Northcliffe distrusted the military *clique* in Japan. 'They are as like Prussians as they can be—inquisitive, spying, flattering, even goose-stepping.' He told Price: 'All telephones tapped, everybody watched. The biggest spy and police force per square mile in the world.' He had seen and heard enough to convince him of the reality of Japan in the modern world, a brutal power which aimed first at mastering China and marching on to still mightier conquests. His assessment of the propaganda by which Japan was completing the first stages in her career of subjugation opened many eyes in Europe and the United States to future perils.

★   ★   ★

'On, on, on we go.' The phrase recurred in his letters home, giving a sense of continuous movement over vast distances. In Seoul, he asked whether the country had not really gained by exchanging the tyranny and corruption of the old Korean regime for the hygiene, education and greater efficiency of Japanese control. 'It was a question that the Koreans were unable to answer satisfactorily.' Asked in turn whether he thought that the Koreans could rule themselves, he answered: 'No, I don't. They strike me as being similar to the Egyptians and Filipinos—very polite, very suave, fond of writing letters and of oratory, but unpractical.' He praised their habit of tree-planting, felt 'a certain reverence for their villages, because it was through here that the converts of Persia passed through to Japan', and was delighted by a sight of 'our old friend the magpie again. I have not seen the real magpie since I was in France last.' He had looked out for the bird life at every stage of his route and had decided that the finest of all birds was the albatross.

Northcliffe to his mother:

Pekin.

12th November, 1921.

(In bed, 7 a.m.)

Very Sweet Mum,—I reached this wonderful town last night, and have seen nothing except a dinner party and the hotel—better than any we have.

My last little ride from Tokio–Pekin was 2,800 miles, yet I am quite fresh and could start round the world again.

I hear that you are well and rejoice thereat. I hear that my dainty little lady is in good spirits, too, and it rejoices me.

Yesterday at 7 p.m. (eleven in London) I celebrated Armistice Day in the train, alone in my little room.

Little book is always with me. Much is obscure, especially Old Testament, but I have learnt much from it, most sweet.

Health and sleep A.1., but FAT. Exercise difficult to get. Kiss all for me.

Your most loving Firstborn.

For him, Pekin was the most charming city in the world, 'the first place abroad where I have met British and American people who don't want to go home'. It was the Riviera, 'with a dozen added attractions'. He immensely enjoyed his visit, despite a State luncheon in his honour and various formal interviews. He liked the Chinese, 'who are not unlike us', and from whom, he later wrote, he was sorry to take his leave. Some of them called him 'Mr Northcliffe'. In Pekin he walked more than at any other time in the tour. He resented being drawn in a rickshaw, a form of vassalage which made him feel uncomfortable. He was also thinking about his weight.

If he looked at Pekin with the eyes of a tourist, he listened with the ears of a journalist who desired to be well-informed about matters more important than the prices of celadon. What he heard confirmed his belief that Japanese influence was extending in China and that it would ultimately be detrimental to Western interests. He sent a cable to Steed urging that *The Times* should advocate the immediate termination of the Anglo–Japanese treaty and work for 'the establishment of Anglo–American unity' (November 16). With his guiding approval, Steed made influential contributions of judgment and opinion in dispatches from Washington and in leading articles in *The Times* based on them. Soon, the abrogation of the alliance was being formally drafted.

Northcliffe to Rothermere:

Grand Hotel de Pekin,
November 13th, 1921.

My dear Harold,—This is to wish you and yours everything good in 1922, and to wish you one day a complete holiday such as I am having.

I touch wood when I say that I have never been so well before. Sir James Mackenzie told me that, between fifty and sixty, a man should have a holiday of at least six months away from his affairs with different people, different food, and different climate.

The whole thing here is vastly interesting. I am afraid that I shall find things at home very tame after it.

I have not seen a wave since I left Southampton and hardly a dark day.

I don't know what is happening to my business and I don't care. I feel so fit that if there is anything wrong I can put it right in a few months. Also, I shall come back with more knowledge than any of my competitors.

I do wish you were with me; I have wished it many times.

My only homesickness is to get near Mother again. I rejoice to hear she is so well.

I hope everything will go well with you, especially with your health. I know now that I was not well before I left home, and was talking and thinking too much about health. My energy has returned to the condition it was in thirty years ago.

> Yours affectionately,
> ALFRED.

Some of his weekly letters home were given a wider audience as articles in both British and American newspapers. When he wrote too hurriedly the articles were polished by correspondents who knew the territories he was writing about. The result was genial, glancing journalism mingling information with entertainment so successfully that a number of publishers asked for the book rights.* He wrote to tell Sir James Mackenzie at St. Andrews, that 'the intense interest I feel in all about me' helped to make him feel younger. 'The real holiday I am getting has made me feel twenty-five, though I am fifty-six and a half' (November 13). 'I have had a very remarkable world whirl, so far,' he wrote to Marlowe (November 22). ' "Some men see more riding on a Hampstead stage than others in a great tour of Europe", said Dr Johnson. I think I am of the seeing kind.' Mentioning that he had met old Carmelite House men 'all over the world', he remarked in the same casual strain: 'I heard in China that Kennedy Jones was dead. I have no means of knowing whether that be true.' Presumably, he could have asked for cabled information but he showed no interest in doing so. 'I touch wood many times when I say that I believe my health is better now than it has been for years. We are all getting on and must take it easy. I am already planning a trip to South America.' The *Daily Mail* had announced that he had stayed with the 'Governor of Victoria' instead of with the Governor-General of Australia. He remarked in the letter to Marlowe: 'My dear daily has the unfortunate habit of hurting itself by sheer ignorance.'

Kennedy Jones had died on October 19. He was the same age as Northcliffe. Northcliffe's letter to 'K.J.'s' widow, sent from Government House, Singapore, was hardly more than a polite expression of regret. 'His political work and my frequent absences abroad had rendered our meetings rarer of late, but I always preserved and shall always preserve my regard for a colleague of ability, worth and character.'

* *My Journey Round the World* by Lord Northcliffe (edited by St. John and Cecil Harmsworth was published by The Bodley Head in 1923.

While staying at Government House, Singapore, Northcliffe was unwell for two or three days and took to his bed. Two years later, the head of Reuters, Sir Roderick Jones, occupied the same room and bed as a guest of Sir Laurence Guillemard, the Governor. Sir Roderick, who had not known of Northcliffe's stay in the house, had a weird experience. Northcliffe appeared to him in a dream—'the most living dream I ever had in my life: it had a high and awful quality of reality', Sir Roderick relates in *A Life in Reuters*.* The Governor urged him to send a report to the Society for Psychical Research. 'I said I should. But I never did.'

Having told Marlowe that he proposed taking things more lightly on his return, Northcliffe informed Campbell Stuart (November 26): 'I shall devote nearly all my time to *The Times*. I am full of energy and ideas.' Northcliffe to his mother (November 28): 'I touch wood when I say that I've not felt so well for years. I needed a long change. I'm no longer tired in the evenings and can work more hours a day than I used, though at 56½ I shall go slower in future.' He wrote to Rothermere (November 29): 'Japan is aiming at the mastery of the Far East. Despite the perfection of her minor organizations, I believe that she is heading for a gigantic bump, such as Germany got. It will probably not come in our time', and he added the personal information: 'I am not tired now even after an eighteen-hour day.' To his mother he wrote (December 1): 'Getting nearer! Well, fat, keen. Reading little book regularly. Longing to be with my Mum.' Leaving Singapore, he addressed Price as 'my dear friend Wang Pri', and asked him: 'How would you like to be a Governor? Fine uniform, three palaces, red carpet, God-save-the-King and heaps of style, very little rhino, all things to all men, nasty paragraphs in local press, State yacht, State train, questions in Parliament about your table expenses, wet through all day in 95° in shade, private band, condensed milk and tinned butter, State banquet three times weekly, grievance mongers (Chinese, Malays, Tamils, Dyaks) with bombs, row with Colonial Secretary after seven years' perspiration, and Wimbledon on £1,000 per annum pension. Would Davy take it?'

He illustrated his journey for his family and friends by picture-postcards sent from many places on his route. 'Those who don't get cards from me will know that they have been stolen in the post, for I have missed *nobody*.' Housemaids and footmen at Elmwood, servants of his mother at Poynters Hall, printers, old friends, shared the largesse of his remembrance with Sutton at The Fleetway House, Campbell Stuart at *The Times*, and the directors at Carmelite House. It was a form of thoughtfulness which he never delegated to a secretary. Every card bore a personal message written by himself. Picture postcard sending gave him a chance to indulge the humour that came most readily to him. Price, his secretary, was

* Hodder & Stoughton, 1951.

variously addressed: 'The Gourmet of Soho, Printing House Square, E.C.4', 'The Very Rev. the Dean of Soho, D.D., c/o The Times, E.C.4', 'The Travel Hater, Printing House Square, E.C.4', 'The Hander-out of Doles, O.B.E., Printing House Square, London', 'The Clockwork Secretary, c/o The Times, London', and 'The Precise One, Printing House Square, London'. A less skittish warmth of feeling was induced in him by the sight of children travelling the high seas. He watched a very young baby. 'I notice that as we get farther and farther into the tropics the little mite gets paler and paler.' Fractious youngsters who annoyed the older passengers drew his sympathy. 'The poor little things do not get proper sleep in the day as they should.'

He wrote to Price (December 12): 'Touching wood, I feel that I have never been so well within my memory and *that* despite practically no exercise. It would be so like what happens in life if all the good of the holiday were done away with by injudicious rushing to cold England.' Meantime, he wished Price to see that 'the Red-Nosed One', meaning Humphrey-Davy, compiled a list of persons known to him who had recently died. 'I know very little, especially about personal things.' Seeing a film of his arrival at Singapore, he commented in a letter: 'I shall never be able to look a weighing machine in the face again.' He was becoming self-conscious about his increasing girth. 'My awful obesity', was his phrase for it in a letter to Price.

$\star \qquad \star \qquad \star$

In November, when he was in Japan, he had cabled urgently to the *Times* office: *Absolutely no further concessions Irish*, a hardening of policy towards a settlement that upset his mother, who considered that *The Times* was being unfair to Ulster, land of her forebears. Her cabled protest reached him in Java: '*Alfred—I will not have Ulster coerced.*' It was followed by a letter which Northcliffe described in his diary as 'a stiff one'. He cabled at once to her in reply, stating that information coming to him had shown civil war to be imminent (December 5). He wrote to her three days afterwards: 'I was very disturbed by your Ulster message, most darling one. I *hate* to think that while I'm whirling round the world you should be for a moment unhappy about a matter I am too far off to help. I pray God I shall soon be near you.' In another cablegram he announced his willingness to go home earlier, 'if it would reassure you'. He was not to know until his return of the urgency of her feeling on that occasion or of the steps she had taken to make it known in Printing House Square. Cecil Harmsworth wrote in his family notes:

The attitude of Ulster had been so unyielding and intransigeant throughout the settlement negotiations as to evoke sharp criticism in *The Times*. My mother, though she was not an Orangewoman herself, took strong exception to this. She sent for representatives of *The Times* to Totteridge and gave them a piece of her mind. On their return to town they called on me at the Foreign Office, seeking my advice as to what they should do.

I reminded them that from the moment of his coming into possession of the great newspaper, Northcliffe had laid it down that Printing House Square was his own peculiar province and that he would brook no interference in its control from any quarter. But, I said, the Old Lady of Totteridge was in a category apart, the only human being to whom Northcliffe yielded his opinion. My advice to them was to do what she wanted—to adopt, in short, a friendlier attitude to Ulster. This was accordingly done, and I do not know that Northcliffe made any sort of complaint about his mother's intervention when he returned home. . . .

His mother sent him another cable. *Alfred—I cannot make up my mind which of your two principal papers is the more vulgar this morning.* John Prioleau, who had known Northcliffe for ten years, said that he never saw him more troubled. Prioleau helped him to draft a reply indicating full compliance with her wishes. 'It took an hour to find a form of words that satisfied him.'

The editorial attitude at Printing House Square to the Irish negotiations is traced in detail in the official history of *The Times*. J. A. Spender, writing autobiographically, considered that the paper's influence on the drafting of the settlement proposals 'was one of the most powerful efforts in the journalism of my time'. The Lord Chancellor, Birkenhead, had told Marlowe, who had been to see him at Northcliffe's request, that the Government intended to carry out the policy which Northcliffe and his newspapers 'have so long advocated', and in making the acknowledgment he associated the name of the Colonial Secretary, Winston Churchill, with his own. Spender said of Northcliffe that during the negotiations 'the Irishman in him came to the top'. But at no time did Northcliffe show as much eagerness about the future of Ireland as he did about the Anglo-American future, which would benefit lastingly from the settlement. An American newspaperman, Samuel McCoy of the Philadelphia *Public Ledger*, cabled a request to Northcliffe for a personal expression of opinion on the coming of peace to Ireland. In reply Northcliffe told McCoy to 'write a statement and put my name to it', an act of faith which, McCoy wrote, 'pleased, astonished and saddened me'. Receiving news of the signing by Great Britain and the new Free State, Northcliffe cabled Campbell Stuart on December 11: *Hope we fullest credit Ireland stop fullest history of our work should be given.* The Times could at last forget the humiliations of the Parnell days.

Arriving at Saigon, he was given a message: Sir Arthur Pearson, his old publishing rival, had died. At once he dictated a postscript to his latest letter home (December 12): 'I have known him since 1884—a strange, erratic but noble character. He is much in my mind today.'

A French newsreel film, taken of his meeting with the Governor-General at Saigon, M. Long, did not show him as a happy traveller. He looked over-indulged, overweight and bad-tempered. He walked as if on uneven ground, his small feet pointing markedly outward. In Bangkok, he was a guest of the king. He asked for a newspaper which had been sent from home. Snoad could not find it. Northcliffe rushed at him with a bullying shove which sent him headlong through the swinging half-doors and down the palace stairs. He was picked up by four impassive purple-garbed servants of the king. Snoad wrote in his diary: 'My birthday—the worst day of the tour so far. The Chief has been most offensive to me in the very worst degree.' The next day they were to leave Siam. Northcliffe sent for Snoad. He gave no sign of remembering what had happened between them. 'Let us get away from these people, Harold,' he said in his gentlest tone. 'I want you to come for a drive with me. We will go in a car by ourselves and talk about our mothers.' He had allowed himself to be emotionally overcome by a small lapse in efficiency; physically, he was suffering badly from the heat. When it was reported to him that three gold watches had been stolen from his baggage, he showed no concern.

His notes for December 24 were headed 'Christmas Eve—Mother's Birthday'. Christmas messages, 'a huge sheaf of them', awaited him at Penang. 'I do not think that anybody at home has forgotten me, and I don't know any happier feeling than *that*, when one has been moving for months among strangers.' The cables he most liked receiving, he wrote, were 'from those I love'. But he was 'rather proud' of a Christmas message from President Harding—'for he is a very busy man'. On New Year's day: 'I woke at exactly seven minutes to six this morning, which was seven minutes to twelve last night in London. I thought of every one I am fond of, all the great armies of people who work for me on the St. Lawrence in Canada, in Newfoundland, Paris, Manchester, London, Gravesend and everywhere else. Not one single department forgot me this Christmas and New Year.' Thanking his mother for her New Year greetings, he told her (January 3, 1922): 'I am *learning so much*. I shall be a more useful member of society and I know more of the world.'

'Lord, Lord, Lord! How one has to travel to realize that one part of the world takes little interest in another,' he wrote to Sutton on January 5. 'There is not a word about my Mother's health. The report of the death of Robert Hudson's mother, who was younger than my Mother, makes me apprehensive. My peace of mind on this tour has depended entirely on her health. I was very worried by her cable about Ulster, not so much by the cable itself, but the fact that an old lady of 83 should be disturbed and anxious, which she cannot afford to be at that time of life.' Mentioning that her handwriting had deteriorated, he wrote: 'If only I could transport her to this beautiful climate of Nuwara Eliya, I could prolong her life for years. As it is, I never open a cable without a little perturbation.'

He wrote to Campbell Stuart the same day: 'Don't think I am coming home to grumble, but I dislike Mrs Asquith', meaning her reminiscences which *The Times* was serializing. 'She is bad from every point of view. It is old and dull stuff. Nobody takes any interest in elections of 1892. I don't even remember them.'

'The *Daily Mail* campaign for the reduction of prices is the proper use of newspaper power,' he wrote to Stuart on January 8. 'Our little trip is ending. I thought I knew something of the British Empire before I started, but I didn't. John Bull is very much top dog in the vast world of the Far East. How such a tiny island as ours does it I don't know, but it does.'

His pride in the British—for him primarily English—achievement gleams through his notes of the journey and his letters home. Looking back on their travels together, Prioleau wrote that Northcliffe's first ruling passion was not his newspapers but England, 'by a very, very long way the first—England right or wrong, but especially when the world considered her in the wrong'. Pine, his chauffeur, whom he counted also as a friend, asked what characteristic of 'the Chief's' he remembered best, replied at once: 'His innermost loyalty—there was nothing he wouldn't do for England.' It delighted him to meet 'an English inspector and an English driver' on the Federated States Railway in what has since become Malaya. He never failed to note the services rendered by Englishmen as leaders of local communities or advisers, 'like my host at Kuala Lumpur, Mr Stonor, an Etonian of the Camoys family'. He was greatly stirred by the sight of English flowers in an exile's garden. 'How heavenly it was—a little peep of English life', he wrote after visiting a planter's home. The strongest thread linking the many letters he wrote during the journey were love of kinsfolk and of country.

After a week in Ceylon, at the end of which time he felt entitled to claim that he had 'mastered the simpler Sinhalese affairs pretty well', he went on to India, to stay with the Readings at Viceregal Lodge, Delhi. Lady Reading wrote to Lady Northcliffe: 'I must tell you how well he looks, quite rejuvenated, so different from when I last saw him in London and he was in excellent spirits. I abjured dinner parties!' (January 18). Northcliffe was happy at Viceregal Lodge: 'A most hospitable and kindly house', he wrote. But he did not like India, 'a wearisome country', and he wondered: 'What do we want India for? Prestige? Perhaps. Cash? We certainly don't get any from it. The thousands of able men from home could do far better almost anywhere else.' He was made aware of an all-pervading anxiety about the future—'almost as anxious as in 1857'. The eighth Delhi, he was assured, would see the end of British rule in India, 'and this vast new Delhi, a wonderful pre-war conception which is unpopular with every one we meet . . . is the eighth Delhi'. He had seen Asia awakening. He predicted that soon in Asia 'centuries will be crammed into decades'. He summarized his impressions of the Asiatic world in a paragraph:

I do not presume to cast the horoscope of the East, but we Britons must look outward and study the great world movements at work in these distant lands and seas. The time must come when we shall find the East, from whence we first learned the trading instinct, knocking at the doors of the world markets.

He was invited to partake of the sumptuous hospitality of some of the princes, but he made his excuses. He enjoyed privilege as much as most men but he could surrender it more lightly than many. There was no private car for him on the long and dusty railway journey from Delhi to Bombay. 'I think it does people good to come down a peg', he wrote to his mother from the train. He thought there was virtue, too, in being made to mix 'at close range' with people in a ship. 'In your circle at home you pick your own associates, avoiding people you don't like. Here you are up against folks, whether you like it or not. I hope the experience is making me more tolerant of others.' Reflecting comparatively on the many sights that he had seen thus far, he made the summary comment: 'Give me Elmwood every time.' He wrote to Mrs H. G. Price: 'Be it ever so humble, there's no place like home or, failing that, a ship.'

In Ceylon, he had embarked on his 'thinning regime', as he called it. 'By not drinking an hour before meals and an hour after meals and depriving myself of everything that is pleasant to eat, I have removed about one stone of my charms.' He had weighed himself before leaving London: 'thirteen stone thirteen pounds'. His aim was twelve stones six pounds, 'and twelve stones six pounds it shall be at Marseilles'. He dieted rigorously on the voyage from Bombay to Suez in the P. & O. liner *Naldera*. He visibly lost weight. His complexion became tropically sallow.

From the start of the tour, Snoad had read Dickens to him in bed at night, often for two hours at a time. Nearing Aden, Northcliffe abandoned Dickens and took to dictating long verbose descriptions of his day's activity. Snoad typed them out every morning. Northcliffe rarely troubled to glance at the typescripts. Usually he tore them up. Snoad, in his early twenties, was lost in admiration at the flow of words which 'the Chief' poured out night after night. It might be eccentric behaviour but did not genius and eccentricity go together? At first, the sessions were not too long and enabled Snoad to improve his shorthand. When they were carried over into the early hours of the next day, he wondered whether eccentricity was the word for it.

There was a night when Northcliffe went to bed at nine o'clock. Shortly afterwards, he sent for Snoad and began dictating. By one in the morning Snoad's wrist ached. He asked for respite. From his pillows Northcliffe nodded assent. In a quarter of an hour he resumed, continuing until 3 a.m. Snoad took down just on six hours' dictation. The result was a fat wad of typescript. Northcliffe never asked to see it. From that time onward Snoad had his doubts about Northcliffe's mental state. There was no one to whom he could confide them. He had found Prioleau, the monocled old Harrovian, socially restrained. Pine, the chauffeur, was unlikely to be amenable to the suggestion that, after twenty years, there was any mood of Northcliffe's with which he was not familiar. Frederick Foulger, the valet, had no time for doubt about anything except when they would see the white cliffs of Dover again, for him a subject of ever-present anxiety.

A letter from his brother Leicester reassured Northcliffe on the subject of the Perrier business. 'You would be pleased if you saw the show of Perrier in the Far East,' he replied to Leicester. 'I have always believed in it, but I simply can't take any part in it. When a man is over fifty-five, every extra job is a nuisance to him.' Referring to Perrier reorganization, he told that brother: 'The only capacity I have as a man of business is to find men of business and leave them alone, which I do', and he ended his letter with the injunction: 'Give mother a double hug next time you see her. She and I read identical little books together each day. It keeps us very close together —Your devoted A.' Nearing the Middle East, he wrote to one of his secretaries at Carmelite House: 'I suppose by the time you get this I shall be in Palestine. I am told that it is very cold there in January. We must wear sheepskins—not the first time my affectionate critics will say that this wolf has gone forth so clad.' But for 'a certain old lady at Totteridge', he added, 'I would not hurry back. My throat seems cured and my energy is terrific.' He informed H. G. Price: 'I have already marked out my forthcoming routes. No. 1—West Indies, Panama Canal, and South American Republics (8 months). No. 2—all round Africa and up the middle (9 months). You will be dragged with me *whether you like it or not.* I will be quite willing to start off a week after arrival. I shall have to do these strenuous parts of the world before I get too ancient.' Humphrey-Davy was to be told to brush up his typing. 'That habit of his of using the "Corona" as combined spittoon and ashtray, and of occasionally oiling it with that deadly hair-restorer of his, is no good.'

He had possibly significant lapses of memory. Louis Tracy wrote mentioning Sir Philip Gibbs, the war correspondent, as a former member of the *Daily Mail* staff. Northcliffe replied that he had no recollection of

Gibbs on the paper. 'I met him in France, I think, once, but cannot recall having ever seen him before.' In his book, *Adventures in Journalism*,* Gibbs describes his *Daily Mail* job of editing the articles for Page Four and his contacts with Northcliffe. 'For a little while I was one of his favourites. He used to chat with me in his room and say amusing, indiscreet things, about other members of the staff, or his numerous brothers.' When Tracy wrote again, Northcliffe repeated: 'I have a good memory, but I have no recollection of Philip Gibbs's association with the *Daily Mail*.' His memory defaulted again when one morning in the liner *Naldera* he woke up with an urge to send an affectionate message to his Aunt Miller. He began writing out a cable to her and then remembered that she had been dead a year. Climate changes had not left him unscathed. At Aden, he was struck by a sudden pain in the left side, 'nothing paralytic', he explained to Price in a letter. His left leg was numbed for several days, causing him to 'hobble dolorously'.

Private affairs obliged Prioleau to leave the party at Suez. Snoad was being sent to London in advance to take business documents to Sutton. 'He is making a bee-line for the abode of love or the home of the giant sloth, or whatever you call your nook in Printing House Square', Northcliffe wrote to tell Price. Northcliffe went off alone in a French Government yacht to see the Canal. At Ismailia, 'I was a bit cold and cross: there were no home letters or papers for me'. To his mother, also from Ismailia: 'I am so close to my Most Perfect now that I could be with you in six days, which seems like nothing.' He wrote to Price again: 'The end of the world trip has almost come. When I get back I shall want to be in my homes. I hope Elmwood will be ready. Naturally, I am not coming back to exactly the same routine. I am getting too old for some of the detail. These thoughts have been much in my mind.' He did not forget to add his thanks for Price's watchful concern for his affairs. 'During these long voyages, when I am so out of touch with the world, I am very grateful for all that you have done. I need not tell you that.'

Northcliffe to Keith Murdoch of the *Melbourne Herald*:

S.S. Naldera,
January 24th, 1922.
My dear Keith,—As to my trip—the *Australian coast*, superb. *Philippines*: America's toy, Filipinos pampered. *Hong Kong*: made the Australian [his brother-in-law] throw out his chest when he saw this magnificent place, the Union Jacks, and heard the bugles blowing. Sydney people were very silent when they saw the harbour. In fact, we heard no more about harbours after Hong Kong. *Japan*: much more medieval than we expected. Busy, active, imitative, second-rate people, thoroughly German. *Korea*: very few Japanese have gone there. *Manchuria*: few Japanese but under Japanese control. *China*:

* Heinemann, 1923.

marvellous, Pekin the most interesting city we have seen. *Singapore, Malay States*: rolling in money. *French Indo-China*: wonderful, humbled us a bit. *Siam*: dear little country, tiny people, efficiently imitative, on the whole pro-British. *Ceylon*: beautiful gardens, full of native talkers (how cross the natives were with me for saying so). *India*: same old India, a place I have always disliked. I didn't want to go again, but Reading and Co. pressed me to. India wants watching closely. I said to an educated native lady, 'Why do Indians educated in England come back so bitter?' 'Because they discover that though they can pass examinations as well as the British, they lack backbone and character', was the reply.

Would you believe it, as soon as he got out of Australian waters, in touch with a.d.c.s and such like, Prioleau reverted to his eyeglass. One of his chief adventures of the trip was the breakage of that eyeglass, the cutting of his fingers with the bits and the search for another. Frederick [the valet] who was in the room while I was dictating this, said: 'You might remind Mr Murdoch that I, Frederick, had to go out hunting for monocles on several occasions.' At a certain Government House he was one of six wearing monocles. Incredible as it may seem, he has infected that Australian brother-in-law of mine!

My first visit to Australasia has given me a very great affection for that part of our English-speaking world. I am rather pleased with old man Bull's position on this globe.

Yours sincerely,
N.

It evidently gratified him to tell Sir Robert Hudson that through all his journeys 'there has always been somebody who knew all about me'. Many of those whom he met, he said, referred to his 'alleged relations' with Lloyd George. He reminded Hudson (Red Sea, January 27): 'I have never had any to speak of, as you know. I don't remember his having been to our house. I don't remember ever having been to his.' Writing to thank Lord Inchcape, chairman of the P. & O. Steamship Company, who had organized the smooth running of his itinerary by sea, he said (January 29): 'This voyage has given me ample time for reflection as to the position of the British Empire. On the whole, without being jubilant, I am not discontented. I do feel that we must have new British centres at the other end of the world. I intend to do all that within me lies to send people to Australia and New Zealand—a task well within the function of my newspapers.'

On January 30, in the Suez Canal, he noted that 'the little book full of wisdom which Mother gave to me to guide me', contained the Biblical quotation: 'It is good for a man that he bear the yoke in his youth.' He wrote in his diary for that day: 'I do often ask that my early "success" may not have spoiled me; but I did bear some yoke, a good deal more, in fact, than I like to talk about.' When the *Egyptian Gazette* headlined him as 'Northcliffe the King Maker', he wrote that 'it was perhaps a teeny-

825

weeny bit overdone'. After 'many tiresome interviews' at the Residency in Cairo he found 'real enjoyment' in being taken by his host, Lord Allenby, to a lake of wild duck and egrets. 'The water is alive with them, the trees are bowed down by them. Birds know sanctuary when they see it.' Shown a tame rhinoceros, he posed the question in his diary: 'Who wants to shoot these poor beasts?'

On February 6, he wrote: 'I don't suppose anyone except a stone image can enter the country of Christ without deep emotion. I, for one of millions, cannot.' He had entrained for Gaza, Ludd and Jerusalem. Along the route he received telegrams addressed to the 'King of the Press' beseeching him to receive delegations with local grievances. One delegation was followed by a crowd with sticks and stones and had to be stopped. He received Arabs, Christians, Zionists and Orthodox Jews: 'All tried hard to get me to express an opinion on their cause. All lie profusely; the Moslems outrageously, the Zionists artistically. I have seen and questioned over two hundred of the various disputants.'

Northcliffe to his mother:

> Government House,
> Jerusalem.
>
> 8.2.22.
>
> Our little book was placed on the stone on which Christ's body lay for the annointing, today, dearest.
>
> I have been greatly moved these three days at being in the places in which our Saviour moved and had his being, seeing the very hills and valleys he saw. I have picked and am bringing you flowers from the holy places.
>
> Today I drove through Bethany, down the mountain road many miles to the Dead Sea, oh, so salt, then through Jericho and the Jordan, where I got you a bottle of water of the holy river.
>
> Am tired after my long day and my visit to one of our friendly native chiefs, Amir Abdulla.*
>
> Your devoted Firstborn.

He concluded his diary notes of his visit of less than a week with the declaration: 'There will be trouble in Palestine.' He had seen for himself that the British troops 'hate their work of repression', and he believed that unless more regard was shown for Moslem and Christian rights the country would become 'a second Ireland'. He told the High Commissioner, Sir Herbert Samuel, in a letter (February 11): 'As a supporter of sane Zionism, I am frankly unhappy at many things that it is impossible to ignore. Time may obliterate many, but tact on the part of the overseas zealots and newcomers would do more. If Zionism be not ruined by its fanatics it can, in my very humble opinion, be eventually achieved peacefully and to the good of the world.' But he thought the 'National Home'

* Later King Abdulla of Jordan.

ideal a British mistake because it ignored Moslem sentiment and interests. He told Lovat Fraser: 'We mustn't suppose that because a man wears a turban or a tarboosh that he is a fool or slow or unable to combine.' One of the lessons of his journey, he said, was the discovery that 'these people are not so much unlike ourselves as we thought they were'.

At Port Said, he walked and talked with Arthur Moore, a special correspondent of *The Times* who was going out at his bidding to India, 'in view of the seriousness of the situation there', and at the request of the Viceroy. Moore recalled at a later date in *The Times* that Northcliffe had spoken then of the editorship of Geoffrey Dawson and their subsequent breach. He quoted Northcliffe's words: 'I liked Dawson very much. I had nothing against him except that he is just naturally pro-German. He can't help it.' Moore saw no sign of faltering mental powers in Northcliffe. 'His talk was perfectly sensible and always interesting.'

'What is one to say about the last day of a world tour?' Northcliffe asked in writing on February 17, during 'a lovely day off Corsica'. To him, it was an anti-climax. He wrote as one of his last diary notes of the tour: 'Every ship has its odd characters. Among those of the *Egypt* is a former fat man, now in skeleton class, who beginning life as a reporter at sixteen, is now said to have more papers than he can count and more money than brains. Is finishing whirl round world and ready for another tomorrow. Hasn't seen one rough or windy day', which was so remarkable a fact of his journey that the captain of the *Egypt* sailed in the shelter of the French coast, 'lest my wonderful world's record for weather should be broken'.

Heading his letter 'Off Corsica, where some of the Soho rascals come from', he wrote telling Price that he had made a list of twenty friends who had died during his absence. Among those he named were Sir Ernest Shackleton, Lord Halsbury, 'K.J.', Sir Arthur Pearson, 'old man Baker', who had worked in the garden at Elmwood, Lindsay Bashford, one of the numerous editors of Page Four of the *Daily Mail*, and 'Bill, the dog at the bungalow'. As if to strike a compensatory note he mentioned that 'more than that number *appeared* en route, who had *disappeared* for years'. He had received by letter and cable '14 invitations to speak on my tour'. Price was instructed to decline them all, 'except the Sylvan Club'. Earlier, Northcliffe had cabled to Lady Northcliffe for the names and length of service of members of the domestic staffs at his various houses. Receiving the information, he gave up some of the last hours of the journey to listing the presents he was bringing home for them. Pine had followed Snoad in going home ahead of Northcliffe, taking with him two monkeys and several parrots and canaries as souvenirs of the tour. 'Just a little appreciation of all your kindness to me, my dear Price,' he wrote as his ship drew near Marseilles. 'Your postal task has been a very difficult one.' The letter was followed by a picture postcard for Price, addressed to him c/o Printing House Square: 'To The Man Whose Good Times Are Nearly Over.' To his mother, he wrote: 'I've not been so close to my dearest for seven months and two days, and can now get to her within 30 hours at any time. I suppose it is crocus time at Totteridge. I shall be with you *directly* I get used to the cold', and he signed himself 'Your devoted, and very grateful for God's blessings, Firstborn'. As the ship entered harbour, he sent her a telegram: *Grateful God's protection during forty four thousand miles read thanksgiving at end of little book dearest Mother.*

The French gave him a formal but also fervent welcome at Marseilles. The long official proceedings were made more bearable for him by his satisfaction in having noticed that the large crowd which cheered him as he went ashore consisted 'of the ordinary working folk'. The *Daily Mail* reported that he 'appeared to be in the best of health'. His weight was what he had resolved it should be when he reached Marseilles, twelve stones six pounds. He replied to the official greeting with a speech in French written for him by Wickham Steed, who told him in a covering letter:

You probably hardly realize the personal and political importance you have acquired during the last few months. Both as regards the situation at home and the situation in Europe—to say nothing of America—you are now in the position of a statesman wielding far greater power than you have ever possessed and enjoying the peculiar advantage of immunity from overthrow by parliament or by electors.

Steed had a courtier's style but he was not given to pointless flattery. While he was skilled at framing a compliment, he was happier to state an opinion, preferring forthrightness to subtlety. He knew Northcliffe well, better than those who were subservient to him. He could make allowances for Northcliffe's self-esteem and be perfectly sincere in his feelings towards him. Often they amounted to admiration. His tactful letter may have had a palliative design. Steed had clashed with Rothermere over a matter affecting the *Times* policy. Rothermere was likely to refer it to Northcliffe.

Northcliffe asked Steed for a general political appraisal. Steed replied that the Government was 'very shaky'. It was not 'playing straight' with France. It was 'quite ready to play the fool with America'. It was disposed to be amiable to the Germans. It was hankering after the good will of the Bolsheviks, 'if only in order to show the Labour electorate how willing it would be to associate Lenin and Trotsky with the work of European reconstruction'. Steed's letter contained personal annotations of historical interest—that Lloyd George had become 'almost pathologically jealous' of Balfour, that Curzon had 'wept physically' over Allenby's policy for Egypt, that the Prince of Wales, writing home from India on matters of high administration there, had been 'wigged for butting in'.

Thus primed, Northcliffe left for a course of acclimatization at Cap d'Ail. 'Energy doubled', he wrote to Rothermere from the Eden Hotel as soon as he had arrived. His wife had gone there to join him. The war had separated their paths as it had those of innumerable married couples. Gossip hinted at a rift, but Lady Northcliffe continued to discharge and adorn her role with the distinction and efficiency which she had always brought to it. She never lost her admiration for Northcliffe and there was no moment in which he was not ready to demonstrate his respect for her. It pleased him, still, to think of new ways of expressing it in his letters. Apropos of the visit to Cap d'Ail, he wrote to his mother: 'Her Daintiness will be with me.' The statement in the *Times* official history that he was 'a failure in his private life' was written by a colder hand than his.

'Round the world without a headache', it pleased him to tell his friends. Back in Europe, he began at once to fuss about his health again. His catarrh returned, he caught a chill, his throat 'felt unsettled', his eyes were inflamed, 'my temper too'. There was disconcerting business news from Printing House Square. Not improbably, his hypochondriacal display was connected with it. He discharged his feelings in a telegram to Campbell Stuart, Wickham Steed, Lints Smith and Freeman, all of the *Times* staff: *In view appalling gross figures just received am returning immediately fullstop figures are worse than I predicted two years ago fullstop all those explanations and statistics with which it was attempted to dope me make very pathetic reading today fullstop.*

Steed was singled out for his displeasure in a telegram to Sutton in which Northcliffe objected to Steed's handling of news from the Far East. His 'constant censoring' of messages from the *Times* foreign correspondents could no longer be tolerated. *I am not cross with him but he must stop that sort of thing or shall give Stuart instructions to overrule him* (February 20).

Others beyond the Printing House Square pale had to share the burden of his displeasure. Northcliffe to the literary editor of the *Daily Mail*, L. R. Macleod: *Your article didn't say where Solomon Islands are fullstop you are getting vague fullstop map was wanted fullstop.* The first of his resumed *Daily Mail* communiques complained of the 'priggish nonsense' of using the word 'ectoplasm' in a leading article. 'Kindly have the name of the writer sent to me that I can deal with him direct.' The writer was Marlowe, who, Sutton reported on February 21, had been 'somewhat disgruntled', and was willing to retire, but his price for doing so was too high for Sutton to settle. 'I told him that it would be a matter for you', and Sutton also indicated that W. J. Evans was ready to go.

A telegram from Northcliffe to FitzHugh, acting editor of the *Evening News*: *Don't like vulgar tone of paper stop ten pound smile in Commercial Road disgusting stop please cease this sort of thing at once* (February 21), was followed by a written reprimand. 'Although we spend most of our advertising money on electric signs in the West End, you seem to think that your readers live in the New Cut, Bermondsey, Seven Dials, Houndsditch and the Mile End Road, the remainder occupying Rowton Houses.' In another message to the *Daily Mail* he ordered the editorial staff to 'leave out all top-heavy advertisements which ruin the paper, such as the bottle in Johnson's Prepared Wax and the large heading of Quaker Oats. If you do not leave them out, I shall ask the printers to do so.' He did not forget to thank his Carmelite House colleagues 'most heartily' for their work during his absence, commending their co-operation as 'splendid'. Printing House Square received no such compliment.

I have not returned to a bed of roses so far as P.H.S. is concerned. In spite of the warnings that I and others gave, readers have been deserting the Paper for years and recent editorial *gaffes* are, I am sure, losing us more.
    The unpopular policies I do not mind. I am responsible for them, as for the entire policy. The blunders I do mind, because they hurt the Paper and still further alienate its reading circle, now down to 108,000.
    I am not going to be quite as gentle in the future as in the past, and if pressure is put upon me by the other Proprietors, as seems likely to be the case, I shall institute a root and branch enquiry into the administration of *The Times*, the expenses thereof and the personnel.

He was pleased to praise individual issues of *The Times* but the paper had put an end to his boasted immunity from headaches. It was galling to him to know that his rejuvenated powers were to be employed in a task that was no longer congenial to him. He had 'saved' *The Times* before. To do so again would cost him more than transferred securities.

* * *

Trouble was blowing up for him in the *Continental Daily Mail* office. *En route* for England, he resolved to stay in Paris to deal with the situation in person. The printers' leaders were demanding more money. Their approach was harshly uncompromising. Northcliffe said: 'This is not trade unionism. It is a form of blackmail with which we are unacquainted in Great Britain. It is the kind of blackmail attempted by Continental lawyers of the baser kind and by *maîtres chanteurs*, as they are called.' He telephoned from his hotel: 'Have the men's leader at the office at eleven o'clock.' The man, A——, was in bed at his lodgings when the summons came. Scenting surrender, he rose, shaved and put on his best Sunday suit. Punctually at eleven he was shown into Northcliffe's room. 'How long have you been taking my money?' Northcliffe snapped at him and without waiting for a reply, added: 'You're a damned ungrateful swine!' The man stepped forward truculently. 'I won't have that word "swine",' he said. Northcliffe leaped from behind his desk, seized the man by the jacket collar and, exerting the full force of his powerful wrists, bundled him out of the room, giving him a parting kick as he went.

Arriving in England with his wife, Northcliffe drove to her house at Crowborough, enjoying the springtime scene with an exile's relish and writing notes about it for an article which does not appear to have been printed. The song birds of England were 'not equalled anywhere'. There was 'an unsurpassed mixture of undergrowth' to delight a homecoming eye. He was touched by the sight of 'Sussex children carrying primroses, violets, anemones', and by 'the stitchwort and wild arum green at the foot of those wonderfully neat hedges'. To one like himself, 'returning from the untidy new countries of South and West, and from the untidy old countries of the East, England seems very prim, precise, quiet and, after the glare of the Antipodean lands, *dark*'.

In the far-away places that Britain has peopled the dwellers will proudly tell you that they are ninety-eight per cent from the Old Country. They will show you their Romney Marsh sheep, their Clydesdales, their imported and acclimatized flora; but none of those places is exactly like the wonderful little piece of earth whence springs the conquering race that has no close parallel in history.

After looking at the faces of many peoples, I believe that we are the most individual, the most *un-like*, the least imitative people in the world.

Some of those who were at Victoria station to meet him on his brief return to London were troubled by his appearance. To them he 'looked haggard' and had 'no colour in his face'. One or two of the nephews found his handclasp disappointingly perfunctory. For others who had gathered on the platform he was too obviously anxious not to be detained. In fact, his first thought was to get to Totteridge as quickly as he could. One of his nieces was there with his mother. He seemed to be 'well and cheerful' but his niece noticed and remarked on his 'shrunken appearance'.

At Carlton Gardens the next morning Northcliffe telephoned personally to George Isaacs, the trade union leader who had freer access to him than any other. He asked Isaacs to call: 'Come at once, if you can.' Seeing Isaacs in the hall, Price, the secretary, who had not known of the telephone call, exclaimed: 'Good heavens—he's not wasting any time, is he?' Northcliffe asked Isaacs: 'What's happening?' He did not hide his displeasure when Isaacs told him that there was a move to cut wages.

Isaacs also told him that he had asked the Newspaper Proprietors' Association for 'dividend particulars' before he could agree to any discussion of the cuts. Northcliffe's comment was: 'Quite right.'

The newspaper proprietors were finding him an awkward member of their union, the association known as the NPA. On his side, he could not overcome his objection to lining up with the new men of business who had joined the proprietorial ranks. Of some of them, Beaverbrook of the *Daily Express* and the Berry Brothers of the *Sunday Times*, for example, he was probably a little jealous as they forged ahead in 'the Street' in which he had for so long been the dominant figure. He had begun drafting a pamphlet in which he proposed to set forth his opinions on the subject of newspaper proprietorship. 'We journalists have no objection whatever to capitalists owning newspapers and thus creating employment. But I object to being a member of a combination in which capitalists ignorant of Fleet Street dictate terms to those who have spent their lives trying to understand the complex questions of a newspaper.' George Isaacs went back to his headquarters with Northcliffe's assurance that there would be no wage cut. In fact, he had decided to leave the NPA.

The *Times* history places within the few days of that London visit of Northcliffe's a statement made to Wickham Steed by the eminent solicitor, Sir Charles Russell. 'When he lately lunched with Northcliffe, he found him so abnormal that he considered him incapable of business, and judging by his appearance, unlikely to live long.' Newman Flower, of Cassell's, was another who saw Northcliffe at that time. He received a telephone message asking him to go across to Printing House Square. What followed is told in Flower's autobiography, *Just as it Happened*.* 'In ten minutes I was in his private room. He greeted me. Then he said: "Flower, I've been to my thirty-second specialist today. I'm going to die." ' Flower told how Northcliffe walked up and down the room, 'talking all the time; his eyes on the carpet. About his illness. And that phrase occurred continuously: "I am going to die." ' He recalled his early work for one of the Cassell publications. 'I used to write for it at seven-and-six a column when I was young.' He asked Flower: 'Are my papers reviewing your books properly?' and told him: 'If you want anything done, and I can help you—ring me. Don't hesitate. But you'll have to do it soon. It won't be very long. . . .' Flower said that 'his face was somewhat drawn', but that there was no other noticeable change in him. There is the contrasting testimony of E. O. Hoppé, the photographer, who saw 'no sign of physical or mental fatigue' when Northcliffe called at his studio in Cromwell Place, South Kensington, in those early weeks of 1922; 'and I have a trained eye for that sort of thing'. Hoppé said that Northcliffe 'automatically assumed the profile pose', and that he talked animatedly

* Cassell, 1950.

Wickham Steed with Northcliffe, leaving the White House after seeing President Harding, July 1921

1 Carlton Gardens, Northcliffe's last London home, where he died, 1922

during the sitting about the possibility of bringing an art exhibition to London from Vienna, and admired a Jacob Epstein bust of one of the daughters of Tree, the actor. Shortly afterwards, Hoppé went to see Northcliffe at Carlton Gardens. 'He came bouncing down the spiral staircase with the spring of a young man.'

On March 3, the editorial conference at the *Times* office was held in the board room instead of in the editor's room. Word had gone forth that Northcliffe was sending a special message to the conference, which was accordingly enlarged by the unaccustomed presence of sub-editors. The message was read to the assembled company by Price, the secretary. He was ill at ease; his voice shook. The message referred to 'the unfortunate proprietors of *The Times*', and to the latest sacrifice required of them 'to save the positions and salaries of the staff'. He accepted full responsibility for 'the unpopular policies', but not for 'the blunders which hurt the paper, now down to a circulation of 108,000'. Unfortunately, outside the office he was also held responsible for 'the *gaffes*'. He declared: 'I am not going to be quite as gentle in the future as in the past', and announced a change in the price of the paper, from 3*d.* to 1½*d.* When Price stopped reading, the editor, Steed, inquired of him: 'Is that all?' Price answered 'That is all', and withdrew.

★ ★ ★

A memorandum, marked 'Strictly Private', which Northcliffe sent on March 5 to F. E. Bussy, the Carmelite House director responsible for the *Daily Mail* Ideal Home Exhibition and other extra-mural enterprises, seemed grotesquely out of key. 'Be very wary of B.P. [Baden-Powell]. He is not the inventor of the idea of Boy Scouts. . . . He well knows my view of him.' Max Pemberton, going to 1 Carlton Gardens to greet him as his oldest friend, was startled by the change in him. 'The robust figure, the upright bearing, the buoyant manner, were gone. I saw a stooping, wizened, shrunken old man and the first glance at him told me that he was doomed.'

New York messages reported that the world tour had 'severely strained' his health. Seymour Price, his private medical adviser, had no doubt that he had dieted too severely. Price had no reason, then, to think that the cardiac murmur which he had discovered several years before had assumed a menacing relevance. Lady Northcliffe, with him at Cap d'Ail and during the short visit to England, saw nothing exceptional in his manner and did not share the apprehensions that others, his brother Leicester, for instance, felt and expressed. H. W. Wilson, who saw him at Carmelite House, wrote that he noticeably tired more easily 'and worried more'.

Joseph Conrad to Northcliffe:

> Oswalds,
> Bishopsbourne, Kent.
> [Undated]

My dear Lord,—I had a scruple in adding even a small scrap of paper to occupy your time directly after your return. I venture it just now to tell you that you have been welcomed back in spirit in this house. . . . The greatest joy was the report of your Marseilles speech, because that one gave us positive assurance of your improved health, conveyed as it were in your own voice.

I must add that I have read all you have given us to read, finding in every line that directness of feeling and that simplicity of utterance which are a delight to a troubled spirit. For you have a 'style parlé' of marvellous perfection and altogether your own. A triumph of personality. I fancied I could hear your voice.

> Believe me, my dear Lord,
> Always affectionately yours,
> JOSEPH CONRAD

The Times was the focal point of the uncharacteristic worrying symptom which Wilson had noted. He was no longer chiefly animated by the desire for success or a fear of failure. 'I am a most unwilling controller and proprietor of *The Times* and would be most glad to be relieved of the burden. I do not propose to be made ridiculous by the paper, as I have been on so many occasions', another reference to the *gaffes* which, he complained, were constantly being made in the paper for which he said, exaggerating, that he too often had to take the blame. His resolve to reduce the price of *The Times* to 1½d. had caused consternation in Printing House Square, where some people feared again that it presaged a closer alignment with the *Daily Mail*. He had it well in mind that 'for some psychological reason the equivalent of the British three-halfpence, the American three cents, the French three sous, is the price of successful newspapers in many parts of the world'. His decision brought him a telegram from Rothermere: *Best wishes dearest Alfred for new Times development*, which put up the paper's circulation and also its rate of loss (to £1,000 a week). When Rothermere raised the question of costs, reminding him that 'there is such a thing as bankruptcy', Northcliffe repeated testily to Price: 'There's my brother, moaning about money again.' Admitting the truth of the statement 'by the hereditary Proprietor that the staff is enormous and expensive', he could not resist the sardonic reflection: '*The Times* is getting on. It is advancing by leaps and bounds. "22 Bishops Murdered" is equal to any attempt at a headline made by our American friends.' He was still willing, if no longer deeply concerned, to protect the paper's future, but the men who got it out day after day seemed to be ever more diligently devoted to its past, labouring under the delusion, he said, that 'news like wine, improves with keeping'. He was glad to return to the south of France.

On March 8, he sent a message to Carmelite House for the editorial staff of the *Evening News*. Agreeing that the paper had 'some excellent qualities', he pointed out that it was 'never quoted at home or abroad and is not taken very seriously'. The begrudging tone of the message, which he had ordered to be displayed in the office, irritated a hard-working acting editor, Fitzhugh, and his colleagues. It produced unexpected opposition. The notice was torn down and a meeting of the editorial chapel was called to discuss further action. Reporting the occurrence to Northcliffe in a letter, W. J. Evans, the editor-in-chief, told him: 'Had the meeting taken place, I am quite sure events would have taken a turn prejudicial to the business and very disconcerting to yourself. In the interests of the business and of discipline it was with some difficulty stopped.' Evans's letter was unusually frank. Drawing on his thirty years' association with Northcliffe he wrote:

That message you sent to be posted up was a profound mistake. Its effect on the staff is disastrous. Good men who are keen on their work *know* whether they are successful or not, they know every occasion on which they have been beaten and they know every time they have beaten the other man. They don't mind criticism and are ready to profit by it, but they resent unnecessary complaint and they won't stand abuse.

Evans told Northcliffe that he had reduced everyone around him 'to a state of simply watching your moods and saying whatever they think likely to please you without regard to any other consideration'. He was well aware, he said of Northcliffe's 'system of keeping young men up to the mark by alternately praising and blaming them'. It worked only with second-rate men: 'It doesn't pay with good men.' Evans then stated his personal attitude:

If you *want* a change and want to get rid of what I suppose you look on as 'the old gang', say so straightforwardly. I am prepared to talk it over with you. But I want you to understand quite clearly when I say that I can't be bullied or rattled and nagging has no effect upon me. I suppose I am one of the very few persons round you who cares as much for the business and for yourself as representing the business, as he does for his own position in it, and I don't like some aspects of recent happenings because they put you in a bad light with those who don't know you and don't make allowances for one who has so many cares, worries and responsibilities.

Evans gave it as his opinion that Northcliffe's resignation from the Newspaper Proprietors' Association had been ill-advised. He also wrote that the purely personal basis of negotiation which had been set up between Northcliffe and 'the man Isaacs' had 'dulled our reputation'. He concluded his letter to Northcliffe:

Please let me know what you are aiming at, and how I can meet you in the matter. Don't telegraph back and say, 'Talk it over with Caird', because I won't talk it over with Caird. If, as I fear, you are not so well as you seem, and don't want to be worried, let Sutton know what your aims and plans are and I will have a talk with him.

Northcliffe replied from Paris, on his way south. He may have noted that it was the first time in their thirty years as colleagues that Evans had not addressed him as 'My dear Chief'. He wrote in a far from tyrannical mood (March 14):

My dear Evans,—You know that I like frank criticism. People in my position are very apt to be at the mercy of flatterers and sycophants. I hope I am *not* so swell-headed as to be oblivious to that situation. Only this week I found that one of my directors had been warned that he should not insert in his report that a certain competitor was growing rapidly. It might offend me!

But, let me be frank too. W.J.E. is very touchy and inclined to take for himself reproofs in no way intended for him. Were I so touchy I might be vexed that after 8 months' absence the only important associate from whom I received no word of greeting was W.J.E. I was not hurt. I ascribed the silence to work and preoccupation with the difficult problems we all face at C.H.

Yr. affectionate
CHIEF

He told John Prioleau, writing to him on March 15, that he felt 'very strong and full of pep, punch and kick'. He assumed that Prioleau had noticed, as he had, that his colleagues were 'older, balder, fatter, as we on our part no doubt are'. He mentioned that he had concluded his diary of the world trip with a note saying: 'Prioleau and I went round the world without a single *contretemps*, which says much for Prioleau.'

Chapter Twenty-nine

A False Aurora

HE appeared to find relief from the troubles of *The Times* in turning to the *Daily Mail*, the most consistently efficient journalistic expression of his personality and purpose. It brought him more satisfaction than *The Times* and far less worry of the obdurate nerve-wearing kind. Its circulation stood at 1,735,000—'a stupendous figure', he told Keith Murdoch of the *Melbourne Herald*. It pleased him to be planning serial stories again. 'Ours are the best serials and they must be kept the best', he informed Mrs Violet Price, wife of his principal secretary, whom he had asked for 'the woman's view' of them. 'What happiness they must bring to lonely farmers in the north and elsewhere', perhaps not a wholly realistic understanding of the habits of farmers anywhere. Turning also to the smooth-running affairs of the Amalgamated Press, he told one of the directors: 'My heart is always with my first-born—*Answers* in particular. Nothing gave me greater pleasure when going round the world than to find *Answers* everywhere. It is the universal paper.'

On his way through Paris he had called on 'the great eye specialist', Landolt, of the rue de Berri, who told him that, for his age, his sight was excellent. He then went to see Lord Derby, the British Ambassador, for whom he had a private nickname, 'the Brewer's Drayman'. 'I came to the conclusion that he cannot make up his mind,' Northcliffe wrote to his mother on March 15. 'He evidently wants to be Prime Minister, but he is frightened of the criticism of Lloyd George's newspapers, and of Birkenhead and Winston.' Northcliffe's opinion influenced a character study of Lord Derby which appeared in the *Daily Mail*. The 'Old Lady of Totteridge' was piqued into inquiring about its source. Northcliffe answered her at once:

Yes, dearest, I am a little at the bottom of it. I consider that if Lord Derby joined the present government, it will temporarily strengthen this wretched gang of people who are making us pay six shillings in the pound Income Tax, causing us trouble in India, Egypt, Palestine, and making the French hate us, and all the rest of it. I told him, firmly but kindly, that my newspapers would be hostile to his joining.

I sometimes think England wants a little quiet. We should let the country alone for a bit and not worry business men with constant interference. I remember during the coal strike last year, feeling, as I went among the miners and mine owners in the north of England, that if they were left to themselves they would soon come to terms, and you will remember that they did.

I am physically extremely well and feeling the benefit of my whizz round the world. I know your movements to the minute, and think of you in all of them.

Relays of heads of departments from Carmelite House, Printing House Square and Fleetway House were summoned to join him at Pau. 'Many of them, I fear, have rough Channel crossings, but I get to know them by this means and they get to know me.' After morning discussions on office topics he would send them off to enjoy themselves at his expense on the golf links or in the casino, while he stayed behind to savour the view of the snow-capped Pyrenees which, he said, 'quietens the nerves'. His thoughts must often have taken him back over the years to 1909, when from that same hotel he had gone forth as an eager observer of man's earliest attempts to conquer the air.

'I am fighting the good fight, and retain my figure and eat very little, and only drink at one meal daily', and his mother was further informed: 'Seven of my workers are here, so that the time passes quickly enough. They come in succession and have very useful talks. Oh, the snow, the beautiful snow! But I want it to leave Pau and Poynters, so that we may both get out' (March 23).

Northcliffe to C. I. Beattie, director, Associated Newspapers Limited:

Pau.
25th March, 1922.

My dear Beattie,—You realize that the crouching tiger of Pau will shortly be within springing distance and the present complacency that reigns at the end of the long passage on the third floor at Carmelite House will be very rudely disturbed.

I do not know whether you are transmitting my wishes to the staff, but I hope you are. The secretive and cautious habit of the Scot often prevents the transmission of some of my voltage. Please do not short circuit me.

Your attached
CHIEF

A telegram that day from Rothermere reported 'considerable anxiety throughout the newspaper trade' on account of wage demands from the printing trade unions. It was followed by another, more urgent. North-cliffe to H. G. Price: 'Sir George Sutton, who has been with me for days, talked over every subject and never referred to it', namely, the situation which disturbed Rothermere. 'Any person in my office who accentuates my brother's tendency to panic will earn my most permanent hostility.' He believed that Rothermere was getting moral support from Caird and Fish at Carmelite House. 'It is with much difficulty that, in view of my Mother's advanced age, I have succeeded in averting family friction.' It was unusual for him, even in his most intimate office circles, to disclose a critical attitude towards a member of the family. He had marked his letter to Price 'Secret'. Touching on the printers' demands, he said that if they tried to dictate *how* he should run his business, he would fight them. 'But,' he added, 'I am not likely to join combinations of rich men for grinding down poor men', another dig at the new millionaires of Fleet Street who were not journalists, like himself, and who regarded newspapers as an extension of the commodity markets. 'Monsters of the Fleet Street deep', was one of his phrases for those men.

His attitude to labour relations had become that of an autocrat whose benevolence of intention was too often expressed in impulsive action. He had always been a protagonist of the printing and allied trade unions. He had long urged his men to support them and over the years he paid many individual workers' dues. Challenged by the power he thus en-couraged, he was apt to exhibit the independent and sometimes oppressive spirit which had brought the unions into being. Insisting that every printer should be able to own a car, he upset the balance of wage negotia-tions. An insurance company which had been tardy in settling printers' accident claims had its Harmsworth business cancelled and given to a rival company. As a generous subscriber to the Printers' Pensions Corporation, he demanded that its benefits should be made available to unapprenticed men of the National Association of Operative Printers & Assistants.

He held that Fleet Street competition was entirely domestic, involving no outside rivalries. Therefore, he maintained, high wages for printers did not affect the nation's external trading position. He was still more emphatic about the loss, through low wages, of good printing craftsmen to America, overlooking the fact, as they did, that higher wages in America went with a higher cost of living. He showed scant consideration for the aims and efforts of the joint industrial council which had been working for months to find a policy acceptable to both sides. Negotiations within the complex printing trades had always been difficult. For Northcliffe, who rationalized his refusal to argue by saying that argument was a waste of time, there was only the method of arbitrary decision. In his use of it, he was both perverse and generous.

Always, he was staunch in upholding the right to strike and it is possible to imagine him, a natural rebel, born under another star as a Labour leader of the expansive and intimidatingly powerful American kind. When T. E. Naylor, M.P., of the London Society of Compositors, wrote offering his mediatory services in the disputes of March 1922, Northcliffe replied to him: 'We in Great Britain invented trade unionism. Its name stands high before the world. I have often said in public that I could not produce these great numbers of newspapers without trade unionism. Throughout the whole of my career my relations with compositors, which began at the age of fifteen and a half, have been most pleasant.' He wrote with feeling about the likely effect of the wage reductions which were being urged by some of his rivals. 'Many of our workpeople, as a result of their recent prosperity, are able to send their children to better schools. I do not want them to have to take them away.' His critics might say that it was largely a relationship of expediency, but there were many craftsmen who remembered him kindly in their years of retirement. 'He was a jolly good employer, one of the best.' 'He had a kind thought for us all.' 'The best friend we printers ever had'—extracts from a bulging file of reminiscent tributes. On March 22, 1922, he received a message expressed in terms rarely heard since in trade union negotiations. The compositors at Carmelite House united in sending him 'heartfelt gratitude' for his refusal to join in the wage cut discussions. 'They wish to add the hope that when you return to your employees at home it will be in that perfect health which they desire should be yours.'

Northcliffe to Sir Andrew Caird:

> Pau.
> 30th March, 1922.
>
> My dear Caird,—I suppose things are doing very badly and that we are losing barrels of money every week. As you know, that is my particular *penchant*. I hope we shall continue to do so.
>
> You have heard, no doubt, that 'the Chief' is gradually approaching England and that the happy and peaceful days of somnolence, customary during his absence, are nearly over. He hopes once more to make the building vibrate with energy, and to pursue with vigorous communiques the numberless Die-Hards—'We'd Better-Nots', 'We've Never Done It Before', and 'It Can't Be Doners'.
>
> Seriously, I am very grateful for all the good work you do.
>
> > Your attached
> > CHIEF.

He wrote in the same week to another of his Scottish directors, Charles I. Beattie, complaining about a heading in the *Evening News* written by a Scottish sub-editor. 'I am all for the Scots, being maternally of a family which lived on the same farm for 710 years, but they have to be caught

840

young, and when you civilize them, apply them to the proper places. They are excellent fellows, these pawky folk, but humour, apart from the Dean Ramsay type, is not their strong point. Please do not lock this in your desk, but pass it round to every member of the staff.'

At Pau, his golf 'pro', Thomson, was troubled because 'the Chief gets tired now at the twelfth hole'. Thomson told Tom Clarke, the *Daily Mail* news editor: 'There's something on his mind. He starts all right, and then goes off, and you can tell his thoughts are off the game. . . . He's worrying.' Tom Clarke was making his own observations and notes. 'He looked quite twenty years older. He seemed a little undecided in his movements as he rose and bade us his usual "Good night, boys", and he lingered about for a moment like an old man, and mumbled a word or two I did not catch. . . .' 'Humpty-Dumpty' was reading him to sleep with nightly instalments of the first post-war best-selling novel, *If Winter Comes*, by A. S. M. Hutchinson. Asked his opinion of the novel, he answered: 'I cannot understand why it is so popular. I read it because it is important to me to know why five hundred thousand copies of it have been sold. It is like sawing through damp wood.'

St. John Harmsworth to Northcliffe:

> 90, Wigmore Street,
> W.1.
> April 1, 1922.

You seem to be having the same blue-nose weather as we are in London, dear Alfred. I hope your throat has not been affected.

The sweet Mother is well, tho' she feels the cold very much. She came into town with me this morning with two pigeons of uncertain morals in a basket, bent on doing some kind of swap with a bird merchant in some mean street in Kensington. She's a wonder!

> Devotedly
> ST. JOHN

Sir Roderick Jones, the chairman of Reuters, was staying at the hotel at Pau with his wife, Enid Bagnold, novelist and playwright. Sir Roderick had long talks with Northcliffe about the future of Reuters. Northcliffe twice visited him and Lady Jones in their suite: 'on each occasion, the same manner, collected, reasonable, charming', Lady Jones recalls. He wore his usual navy-blue suit with the white-dotted red tie, 'hair carefully brushed'. After one of his visits, Lady Jones went out on to the balcony. A full moon was rising over the valley. She saw Northcliffe standing on the balcony of his rooms with another man. 'He was pointing. Then he shook his head and went in.' Shortly afterwards, in London, Lady Jones met Northcliffe's companion of that evening. He asked her what she remembered about Northcliffe on that occasion: 'How was he—how did he seem?' He then explained: 'I had just arrived from London when Northcliffe came back after his talk with you. He went out with me on to the balcony and pointed to the moon. "How many moons do you see?" he asked me. "One." "I thought so," he said, "but I see two." '

Strangely, until Wickham Steed arrived at Pau, with Sir William Beach Thomas of the *Daily Mail*, none of those around Northcliffe regarded him as the doomed invalid of Sir Charles Russell's and Max Pemberton's imagination. The *Times* official history, which is diligent in its pursuit of evidence to support a verdict of 'unsound mind' against the man whose personality supplied the material for its most readable chapters, states that Steed 'was struck by the incoherence of his talk and the sensitivity of his nerves. The slightest noise startled him as though it had been a pistol shot.' The intolerance of noise, shared by other members of the Harmsworth family, had been noted far back in his boyhood by young Alfred's old Hampstead neighbour, Mrs Jealous, and in his middle years by J. L. Garvin, who cited instances of his exceptionally acute hearing powers. Beach Thomas heard rumours about Northcliffe's health from Steed, as they travelled to Pau. 'We were delighted to find him altogether himself, merry and full of enjoyment.' Northcliffe wrote to his mother from Pau: 'I have this consolation—that spring will be deferred by this weather so that when I walk by your side at Poynters we can look at the shoots of the spring bulbs together. I do feel so greatly the consolation that I am within a day of you and living at exactly the same *time*.' And to his wife: 'On the whole, this is a quiet nook. Many people call it deadly dull and complain that the gambling is very mild. Personally, I do not go to those places. I do not think it is because I am older. I never did like them.'

The Times had perpetrated another *gaffe*, his word for the missed news story among other sins of omission and commission with which he charged the staff. The marriage of a well-known lady of title had been ignored. 'It is not necessary for us to be libellous, but it is necessary for us to be alive', he wrote in vexation to Campbell Stuart.

There is an amount of babyism about that queer conglomerate of men forming the *Times* editorial staff which would be amusing if they were not content to draw the proprietorial pap so complacently. I am going to inject a little pep—not pap. *The Times* must be made more *interesting*.

He dictated a letter to Seymour Price: 'You may remember a former housekeeper at Elmwood, who married and who is now Mrs Jackson, of Barton, near Preston, Lancashire. She is slowly dying of cancer. Having, as you know, sat by some cancer death beds in the last two or three years, I cannot bear to think of anyone I know enduring this horrible tragedy. If anything can be done, I should like it to be done.' He tele-graphed £100 to Mrs Jackson and followed it with a letter offering more money and arranging for her to have in addition 'the best medical advice and treatment', if necessary, in London. 'What I send is out of the abund-ance with which the Almighty has blessed me.' He further assured her: 'Should misfortune overtake you and Mr Jackson, I shall see that your little girl is properly brought up, schooled and started in the world.' When Seymour Price reported that 'the patient had been brought to London for X-ray treatment, but that there is no hope of a cure', Northcliffe wrote to her again: 'I propose sending you £90 a month. If that is not enough, let me know', and told her to write direct to him at *The Times*. To H. G. Price, he dictated the reflection: 'In the little book my Mother gave me, I found the following words: "Unto whomsoever much is given, of him shall much be required, and to whom men have committed much, of him will they ask more." How true that is.'

Impatient with his travelling secretaries, Humphrey-Davy and John Duncan, whom he nicknamed 'Dilly and Dally', after two popular cartoon figures in the *Evening News*, he was dictating shorter letters and longer telegrams. Northcliffe to C. I. Beattie (March 27): *Inform Fitzhugh* [acting editor, subsequently editor, *Evening News*] *in audible voice in presence of whole staff that in view of improvement in paper am continuing his trial for thirty days longer when decision as to his position may be made but request him to be considerate and gentle in handling people especially women stop.* Northcliffe to Campbell Stuart: *Beg you to go away for two or three days stop health comes first stop Elmwood or my bungalow at your disposal stop we shall all have to be in bestest form next week stop do be reasonable.*

The plea for reasonableness may have sounded ironical in Stuart's ear. Northcliffe was assailing him almost hourly with exhortations to greater activity at Printing House Square and Carmelite House. Stuart's health reserves, never ample, were running low: he was feeling the strain of working for 'the Chief', who wrote to Price: 'I feel that I am driving everyone very hard', and underlined his conviction that '*at my age, it is now or never with the Old Lady of Printing House Square*'. He advised Price: 'Read Bacon's essay on "Youth and Age". By sixty, I shall probably become as strong a "Die-Hard" as any at Carmelite House and, no doubt, President of the It-Can't-Be-Done Club, also Chairman of the We'd-Better-Not Association.' The prophets of his doom would have been confounded by the good humour of his letters at that time, but he con-fessed: 'I dread the coming summer with its inquisitive overseas Premiers and enthusiastic young Chinese students, who will have to be received and entertained. I simply cannot do it.'

He decided to reorganize his secretariat and his working day—'a change forced on us from without, not from within', he told Price. 'I think that it is because I am better known in the world. I was rather struck by a remark which a woman in the Far East made when I was introduced. She said: "I thought Lord Northcliffe was someone who had been dead some time and that he founded some Press to which his name had been given."' He had noticed, he said, 'that at this Pau hotel people wait about the hall to see me go out, and wait about the golf course to see me drive (or foozle)'. At which point he added: 'However, my dear Price, I shall begin to become one of your correspondence bores if I don't stop.'

Staying at the sumptuous Hotel de France et d'Angleterre at Fontainebleau on his way home again, he was welcomed by the *grande dame* who owned it. She said to him: 'I hear that you have sold *The Times*. Is it possible?' To which he replied: 'I may have to do so to pay your bill.' Hildebrand and St. John were among his guests there. A freelance foreign correspondent, Sisley Huddleston, who was about to join *The Times*, was touched by Northcliffe's 'solicitude for his crippled brother'.

Some days he sent twenty telegrams to London. *The Times* published Winston Churchill's photograph twice in a week: *Fashion picture would have been better*. The *Evening News* cartoonist, Poy, depicted France being kicked out of the international conference at Genoa: *I think if this cartoon is reproduced in France it will hurt I have telegraphed to stop it*. The *Daily Mail* was not paying enough attention to its youngest readers: *I am receiving many complaints about Teddy Tail*.

Telling Campbell Stuart of his plans for finally reforming *The Times*, he added the all too prophetic assertion: 'It is now or never.' His journey across the world, he said, had given him a new outlook on many things. It had also given him a new view of some of his associates. 'In talking to Steed, who is in many ways well informed, I feel now that I am talking to a pinhead. He knows a great deal about that small but comparatively unimportant part of the world, Central Europe, but his *gaffes* in regard to the Far East have been as bad as his encounter with the *New York Times*', a reference to the bogus interview of the previous year which had stirred up so much trouble for Northcliffe. Steed, he ordered, was not to have 'anything to do with' a projected leading article on the Prince of Wales's visit to Japan (April 3). The *Times* history suggests that relations between the two men were seriously strained and that Northcliffe was plotting Steed's downfall as editor. Their correspondence of the period continued to be amiable enough. Each was signing himself 'Yours affectionately'. Dealing with Northcliffe's attitude to *The Times* and its editor at that point, 'the Paper's' official historian supplements his history with thought-reading, presuming to report categorically what was in Northcliffe's mind; for example, that 'he decided to be absolute master in Printing House Square before he died', and that he aspired to be 'in his own person, the greatest single [*sic*] journalist the world had ever known'. But, the historian admits, 'about this he had, so far, said nothing to anybody, at least in Printing House Square'.

Returning to London in the second week of April, Northcliffe attended what he referred to in an office message as 'a very moving gathering—two hundred of our Fathers of Chapels and other comrades of the great companionship of Carmelite House, Printing House Square and Fleetway House'. It was an opportunity for him to state again his opinion of the new type of proprietor in Fleet Street. 'Some of the multi-millionaires who have plunged into Fleet Street in the last five years are trying to drive the men's wages down. One of them confessed to me that he did not know the difference between a rotary machine and a rotarian. They know nothing of the lives, habits and ambitions of those who are the very aristocracy of British labour. *The Times*, the *Daily Mail*, and our other publications are asked to join in this combination of rich men and I suggest that we have nothing to do with them. On the other hand, I suggest that the Bolsheviks who nearly prevented the issue of *The Times* the other night should be hammered good and hard every time they show their heads, as we lately hammered them in the Paris *Daily Mail* office.'

His speech drew a note of fervent appreciation from the undemonstrative news director, Walter Fish. 'As a reporter, I have listened to thousands of speeches and never before have I known an audience held absolutely spellbound for eighty minutes. I estimate that you spoke at an average rate of 100 words a minute. Therefore you must have spoken four columns of *The Times*.' The subject of the Fleet Street interlopers, as he called them, lay heavily on his mind. He protested to his fellow proprietors, Burnham and Riddell. 'Capitalists have come into Fleet Street who have made fortunes in other industries with no experience of newspapers at all. It is unreasonable that they should take part in dictating the wages of printers who have been associated with newspapers all their lives.'

★　　　★　　　★

As a result of his fleeting visit to Palestine he was importuned for interviews and support by London Zionists. They did not find him entirely responsive. He had written to Albert M. Hyamson, of the Department of Labour in the Government of Palestine (April 13): 'I went out of my way to revisit Palestine, knowing nothing of the state of affairs that I found there. What impressed me most was the unhappiness of British officials, the over-pushfulness of the Zionists, and the fact that England, which cannot afford it, is committed to a high annual expenditure to keep the peace in that country.' His mind reverted to 'our Palestine commitments', he said, when he saw 'the mournful processions of unemployed in London'. As for charges that he was anti-Semitic, 'I believe that the

Jews have greatly contributed to the attainment of the high position held in the world by the British Empire'.

Meeting the Jews in their promised land had not been an altogether happy experience. He found them rebounding from the bondage of the ghetto with violent social assertiveness. Sir Herbert Samuel, the High Commissioner, had written to him on March 26 saying that 'our political difficulties are considerable', and concurring in Northcliffe's opinion that the excessive demands put forward by some of the Zionist leaders had greatly contributed to the difficulties of the existing situation which was 'far from satisfactory'. Northcliffe had been provoked into admonishing the general secretary of The Zionist Organization, Israel Cohen. 'You are overdoing it with this telephoning and general pushfulness, just as you are overdoing it in Palestine.' Cohen wished Northcliffe to know that 'Dr Chaim Weizmann is exceedingly anxious to see you'.

The *Daily Mail* was taking the line that the British taxpayer could not afford to support Zionist ambitions towards which the paper was otherwise sympathetic. Weizmann, whom destiny had marked out to be the first president of the Jewish national homeland, wanted to put before Northcliffe personally the proposition that the British troops in Palestine would have to be garrisoned in Egypt or elsewhere at probably greater cost. He was asked to lunch at Carlton Gardens. Northcliffe also asked the ardent defender of English interests everywhere, L. J. Maxse. According to Dr Weizmann's published account of what happened (in his autobiography, *Trial and Error**), Northcliffe sat himself between them after lunch and announced that he would umpire their discussion, but that it was Northcliffe who did the talking. Quoting Weizmann, 'this conception of the functions of an umpire was new to me, and suggested that I was probably wasting my time, so I shortly made my excuses and withdrew'. H. G. Price was present. He supplemented Weizmann's account from his own recollection. 'When the two men were seated, the Chief took out his watch and said: "Now, gentlemen, you each have five minutes in which to state your case." ' He handed the watch to Price, who was told to call out 'Stop!' at the end of each speaker's five minutes. He ordered Price to 'take a careful note' of what was said. When the speeches were over and the two men had gone, Price asked Northcliffe if he wanted the notes typed out. 'Good Lord, no!' Northcliffe said. 'Forget it.'

On the morning of April 28, Price was called up to Northcliffe's bedroom to take a message for the *Daily Mail* staff. Northcliffe was angry at the sight of the paper that day, 'plastered all over by advertisements that would have been refused by the *News of the World*', a comparison intended to hurt 'Lord Imber', the advertising director.

* Hamish Hamilton, 1949.

Some years ago an American friend of mine was told by his printer and machine-room staff that they could not print pictures. 'Very well,' he said, 'I will print pictures.' He brought the captain of his yacht into the office and in a fortnight the yachtsman produced excellent pictures.

I propose asking Mr Glover, the handsome hall porter at Carmelite House, to come to me for a week for training. If the present state of affairs be ever repeated on any one day, I will put him in charge of the Advertisement Department.

He harped on the advertisement theme in a succession of bulletins. 'For twenty-five years I have been emphasizing: "Do not let the advertisements rule the paper."' Now, he proclaimed, his patience was at an end. 'I can make the only appeal left, and that is to force. Mr Glover, who has been appointed head critic of the advertisements, strips in the ring at 18 stone and has a reach longer than Dempsey's.' Referring to a rumour that 'the Old Man is a bit off his head', he commented: 'The Old Man, the Mr Alfred of earlier days, may be off his head, but he has stopped the big bludgeoning advertisements getting into the paper.'

The Glover episode has been made much of in Fleet Street memoirs, in which it is cited as proof of Northcliffe's mental instability. Robert Glover was a fine upstanding ex-Guardsman who commanded the entrance to the *Daily Mail* office for thirty years. He spoke French and for that reason he was a conspicuous figure also at the annual *Daily Mail* Ideal Home Exhibition, which drew many foreign visitors. Physically, he was formidable enough to fend off a threat by a notorious American negro boxer who, accompanied by his black retinue, appeared at Carmelite House with a demand to see the editor of the *Daily Mail*, which had printed something that the boxer did not like. Neither he nor his supporters got past Glover.

Northcliffe asked Glover to lunch with him at Carlton Gardens to talk about offensive advertising. Afterwards, advertising men from Carmelite House assembled there to be addressed by the commissionaire in his new role of advertisement critic. Uneasily fingering one of 'the Chief's' largest cigars, he made a speech which Northcliffe commended in his bulletin the next day. No more was heard of Glover as censor of advertisements. Northcliffe had given him an extra £100 a year. Wareham Smith, the advertisement director, saw 'nothing inconsistent in it with Northcliffe's innate impishness'. H. G. Price saw Northcliffe immediately after the meeting. He was sitting with his head in his hands, his shoulders heaving with laughter, 'like a schoolboy who has played a successful trick'.

On Easter Sunday, he was at church at Totteridge with his mother, accompanied by Duncan, of his secretarial staff. During the sermon Northcliffe sent Duncan out to telephone to friends with whom he was to lunch at Iver, Bucks. 'Tell them the sermon is longer than I expected. I shall be late.' He sent two more messages before the service ended. As soon as he reached the house he spoke on the telephone to *The Times*. During the conversation, he lost his temper and for the first time his hostess, who knew him in most of his moods, heard him use an expletive. He appeared to be unusually irascible.

On Easter Monday he was at Carmelite House and 'in great form', according to Tom Clarke's diary. 'How he shook everything up!' He was at his desk in Room One, looking as if he had never left it through all the busy years. 'Blue-pencil in hand, he peered at us through his horn-rimmed spectacles, the old eagerness in his manner, the old impatience of talk. "I want to get this paper of ours up to two millions."' There were to be new features, a new free insurance scheme, a new net sales campaign. The women's page was to be improved. He himself would write a special article, 'Watch Japan', which would be cabled round the world. Price heard him say on the telephone: 'Yes, journalism is a great game—and the stakes are human liberty.' He wrote to Murdoch in Australia (April 18): 'I feel very much that Great Britain is a wonderful country.' His recent world voyaging had given him the idea that there should be a shipboard newspaper for transatlantic travellers. The *Atlantic Daily Mail* was launched in the following year, 1923. Optimism glowed forth from him, as if his lucky star was shining more brilliantly than ever. Tom Clarke wrote: 'I have never seen him so enthusiastically at work before.' It was a false aurora, a manifestation of the 'spes endocarditis' of Horder's definition, the 'bright mentality' symptom of the disease which was soon to lay him low. Those phases alternated with others in which he appeared to be spent. H. W. Wilson, who saw him at that time at Carlton Gardens, said that 'after an hour's work or discussion, he would throw himself back in his chair with the words, "I'm done."'

He looked 'pale and nervous, but not ill' (Wilson's description) when, on May 4, a *Daily Mail* anniversary day, he presided at a farewell luncheon to Evans, the retiring editor-in-chief of the *Evening News*, whose twenty-eight years' service was rewarded with a cheque for £10,000 and a pension of £2,500 for ten years, with £1,000 a year thereafter. 'The Chief' made two speeches. In the first, he spoke easily and humorously. In the second he showed emotion. He had been called to his feet by overwhelming acclamation. His voice sank almost to a whisper.

This morning, in order to discuss this gathering, Sir Andrew Caird and I went for a walk at Hampstead and saw the house where my mother brought up seven children. Four houses away was the house of a gentleman who was at that time secretary of the Savage Club and also the proprietor of the *Hampstead & Highgate Express*.

When I was five years old he gave me a present of a small case of type, and I knew how to set type before I was seven. I wrote for his paper while I was at school.

★   ★   ★

Carmelite House would not see him again. At the Evans luncheon, many of his colleagues looked on him for the last time, though his office bulletins told them that he was still observant of their work. They learnt that he had been up and out at five o'clock on several mornings, watching the distribution of his papers to the newsagents' shops, the railway bookstalls and the street sellers, recapturing the thrill of earlier days when he watched the newsboys racing through the streets with his newspapers. Taking with him the *Daily Mail* sub-editor who wrote the contents bills, or a junior member of some other department, he drove in the Rolls-Royce to Hyde Park Corner, Oxford Circus or to some equally busy point in the City, and made a spotting game of it. 'Here comes the *Morning Petticoat*,' his name for Lady Bathurst's *Morning Post*, he would exclaim, peering into the approaching traffic. 'Two lengths ahead of the *Telegraph*—and *The Times* nowhere!' Later in the day he would sally forth again, observing the distribution of the evening newspapers. 'I followed a shabby yellow motor delivery van that goes along Seymour Street in the very busy Kentish Town district. It was a melancholy spectacle to me, the arrival of the excellent *Evening News* too late for its public.' He was in the machine-room at Carmelite House one morning at half-past four. Seeing 'several tired-looking men', he vowed to stop the technical process known as 'plate changing' which kept them working late. To him, it meant editorial mind-changing, which formerly he would have applauded as enterprise. Now, he demanded: 'Stop this nonsense.'

Rumours about his mental health were more insistent. Corroboration mainly came from Printing House Square, where Steed was considered the oracle. Campbell Stuart thought that Steed was dramatizing the facts; he saw nothing abnormal in 'the Chief's' behaviour. At Carmelite House no one seemed to have authentic information, while Sutton, at The Fleetway House, remained coldly immune to the suspicion that after thirty years he was not acquainted with all 'the Chief's' tempers and distempers. Pine, who had a closer bond with 'Lordy', as he always called Northcliffe, than most chauffeurs with their employers, saw nothing unfamiliar in his manner or behaviour and was strict in refuting what to him were slanderous opinions. Neither did Price, the principal secretary, take kindly to the implication that he was shorter sighted than people who saw far less of Northcliffe than he did. To him, 'the Chief' was as autocratic, as restless, as impulsively generous, as incalculable, as he had always been. He was still briskly attentive to his correspondence and his daily comments on his newspapers were not less lively than of old.

Northcliffe to Olga Nethersole: 'I thought I told you before that I was unable personally to attend to such matters as The People's League of Health. Some charming ladies have no sense of proportion.' Northcliffe to Valentine Williams, foreign editor of the *Daily Mail*, whose new 'Club-foot' novel was about to be published: 'No man can serve two masters.' George Moore, the Irish novelist, to Northcliffe: 'I believe your influence won us the war.' Northcliffe to Sir James Barrie: 'I wish you would write a few lines about *If Winter Comes* for *The Times*. The book has a great many enemies and I feel it so important that we should, in the interest of national propaganda, have successful books to combat the epidemic of American books. I am doing my utmost to help it.' Sutton to Northcliffe, concerning Markwick, who was associated with *Answers* at the beginning: 'He may write to you. I have had to stop his legal work for *Answers* owing to the wrong replies he is sending and getting us into hot water. He is out of date and getting old.' Northcliffe to T. E. Mackenzie by telegram: *Ask Mother if she will permit telephone extension to morning room Totteridge stop it would enable me to work Totteridge and be with her more.* Valentine Williams to Northcliffe: 'Price has told me of the magnificent present you are making to me as a personal gift on my leaving your service and I want to tell you how touched and grateful I feel at your very kind thought of me.' Northcliffe had told Price: 'If Williams writes a nice letter, he is to go to the Goldsmiths' and Silversmiths' Company and choose anything he likes up to two hundred pounds.' The Viceroy of India, Lord Reading, to Northcliffe: 'I want to thank you very warmly for your help in England and for all the support you give me. It is a great encouragement. You know and understand the difficulties of the task here.'

Edgar Wallace to Northcliffe:

> 71, Clarence Gate Gardens,
> N.W.1
> 5th May, 1922.

My dear Lord Northcliffe,—I have just finished reading your tribute to Evans and my mind went back to my own association with you, and all that I owed you. I don't know whether you realize that when you gave me my chance I was a semi-illiterate—a man entirely without education or any of the advantages which men had, even if they had only graduated in Fleet Street.

It was a most wonderful experience to find such an inspiration near at hand, visible tangible genius. Something in a red-spotted tie that was human in form. Why, it was like meeting Courage in a top-hat or Faith wearing gloves! In a sense it was disastrous, for it seemed to one who lacked in some degree, balance and ballast, so easy a thing to be great; so easy to acquire a beautiful rosewood office. So easy, in fact, to ape greatness. I don't want from you any more than I have had. I don't even want to contribute to any of your newspapers or magazines, though I shall in the ordinary course of business. I have vague dreams of magnificent windfalls when I shall stalk into Sutton's office and say, 'How much do I owe Lord Northcliffe?' but even that may not materialize. I shall be a spendthrift all my days. But I will pay you, in my heart, and by my spoken and written word the homage and love which I feel for you.

Yours sincerely,
EDGAR WALLACE

On May 8, Northcliffe described some of his world tour experiences at a full meeting of the Sylvan Debating Club. Cecil, his brother, said that 'Alfred was in good form'. Three days later, he was the guest of honour at a luncheon marking his return by the Empire Press Union, with Lord Burnham of the *Daily Telegraph* in the chair. He was annoyed because the reporters had not been adequately provided for, an excuse for him to remind the *Daily Mail* staff in an ensuing bulletin: 'When I was a reporter . . .', but that dubious claim to early professional status had worn thin. He had a topical point to make: 'Since the advent of the N.U.J. [National Union of Journalists] reporters have become more humble.' His brother Leicester, who was one of the guests, said that he was 'very fidgety and jumpy—and undoubtedly ill'. Yet his speech was successful. It brought him repeated bursts of cheering and, at its close, prolonged applause.

He was giving luncheon parties at Carlton Gardens and to his guests he was the well-pleased host who took little part in the conversation and yet kept it alive. On May 10, Sir Edward Elgar was there with Lord Cowdray and Gordon Selfridge. A few days before, he had asked Tom Webster, the *Daily Mail* sports cartoonist, to bring Jack Dempsey, the heavyweight boxing champion of the world, and also present were Brigadier-General Groves, the self-sacrificing organizer of the Air League of the British Empire, and Major-General Swinton, the soldier whose imaginative exertions had helped to make the tank the greatest tactical surprise weapon of the late war. Dempsey brought Northcliffe's old boyish smile into play by announcing, when he was asked to speak: 'I can't make a speech, but I'll fight anybody in the room!' The champion refused the menu, choosing to eat an apple and dry toast, a frugal preference which the *Times* historian mistakenly ascribed to Northcliffe as a sign of his ebbing vitality. He always liked to see 'plenty of fruit' on the dining table. His favourite luncheon beverage was now Pouilly diluted with Perrier water.

Laurence Binyon, the poet and scholar, was told by a friend of his who was a guest at one of Northcliffe's luncheons that there was mention in conversation of 'the oldest more-or-less intact human body in existence' being on display at the British Museum. Northcliffe appeared to be abnormally interested. He ordered cars to be ready immediately after the luncheon to take him and his guests to the British Museum, where they gazed on the object of their visit, the corpse of a Stone Age man shown in a crouching position in the mummy room.

At that period, Sisley Huddleston, the newly appointed *Times* correspondent, was called to Carlton Gardens on several occasions. He was there when Northcliffe decided to reinvigorate the photographic department at *The Times*, that innovation of his which was to become a valuable adjunct of the company. Huddleston wrote of his meetings with Northcliffe: 'In my experience, he was not in the least tyrannical, though he could not suffer fools gladly and resented inefficiency and time-wasting. On the contrary, I saw numerous acts of extreme generosity and I listened to kind words to subordinates that came from an affectionate heart. He could be easily irritated but he could still more easily be touched. "My bark is worse than my bite", he said.'*

Northcliffe to *The Times* (May 13): 'I think that the Prime Minister has outlived his usefulness. He does not like Steed and Steed does not like him. He does not like me because, after urging, begging and cajoling me to join him, I wrote that letter which *The Times* and every other newspaper published at that time', November 15, 1917. Protesting that it was impracticable to combine the responsibilities of an editor with the duties of a foreign correspondent, Steed had gone to Genoa in April to attend the international economic conference which was to recognize Bolshevik Russia and to examine, among other things, the possibilities of trade with that country. Northcliffe called it 'shaking hands with murder', blowing into flame Lloyd George's smouldering wrath against him. Sending Sir Edward Grigg on his behalf to meet the journalists, Lloyd George sought to appeal through them to the public at home 'not to believe any statements about the Genoa Conference that are made in *The Times* or the *Daily Mail*', saying that he would deal with them in Parliament. Grigg had been a member of the *Times* staff (he had a warm place in his heart for Northcliffe) and the newspapermen received the message with every sign of being amused by it.

A misunderstanding that was never finally explained to the satisfaction of all the parties gave Lloyd George a resounding opportunity to pronounce judgment against *The Times* as a reliable newspaper. He had hoped to find salvation for his shaky Coalition Government by bringing back from Genoa a solution to Great Britain's major post-war problem, unemployment. Steed had never believed that the conference would succeed. He foresaw it making 'European confusion worse confounded'. In a dispatch to *The Times* he disclosed that Lloyd George had made representa-

---

* *In My Time*, Jonathan Cape, 1938.

tions to the French which suggested 'a parting of the ways' between France and England. Quoting from Wickham Steed's account of the episode, given in *Through Thirty Years*: 'Mr Lloyd George declared it to be totally unfounded, and M. Barthou [leader of the French delegation], under British insistence, ended by denying its verbal precision. But, as the chief delegates at Genoa knew, and as documentary evidence in my possession shows, its substantial accuracy could not be challenged.'

The episode is examined at some length in the *History of The Times*, where it is shown that in a supplementary dispatch Steed had mistakenly imputed to M. Barthou similar statements made by Lloyd George to the foreign editor of *Le Petit Parisien*. The full dispatch as it appeared in *The Times* gave readers the impression that the Prime Minister had threatened to repudiate the *entente*. 'There is not a word of truth in it. The French delegation is outraged by it', Lloyd George telegraphed to Austen Chamberlain in London, at the same time telling the press representatives at Genoa that the statements made in *The Times* were 'just the ravings of a person who is insane with desire to wreck the Conference'. The House of Commons was told by Chamberlain that 'the account in *The Times* is a wicked and malicious invention' (cheers). The *Times* official history shows that Steed's dispatch from Genoa came very much nearer to the truth than Lloyd George wished to admit, but, the historian states, 'the combination of denials by the Prime Minister, Chamberlain and Barthou placed Printing House Square in a situation that was as uncomfortable as it was unfamiliar'.

Northcliffe had entered the fray on May 9 with a telegram to Steed: *Hearty congratulations you have saved the entente he daren't go back on it now*, Steed having disclosed to Northcliffe on the previous day the sources of the information on which he had based his dispatches. Then Barthou, under pressure, made his denial, and Steed received a message from Stuart: *Chief's telegram written in ignorance Barthou's denial he thinks you have been duped again none the less he believes good will result*. Flicking off the perhaps unnecessary allusion to the notorious New York interview, Steed telegraphed to Northcliffe further evidence of the veracity of his dispatches to *The Times*. He received an answering telegram which, not unreasonably, he may have considered proof of his belief that Northcliffe's mental powers were at the mercy of an insidious disease: *Amazed disgusted your reply fullstop*.

Sutton to Northcliffe:

The Fleetway House,
Farringdon Street,
E.C.4.
12th May, 1922.

My dear Chief,—Just before I went to the South of France, Hamwick [code name for Wickham Steed] told me that if at any time you were anxious to part with him, it would simply be a matter of terms.

In view of recent events, I would like you to consider carefully whether that time has not now arrived.

Stuart and I have had several discussions on the subject, and are convinced that it is a wise step to take now, otherwise you and the old paper [*The Times*] will be continually involved in some trouble. His daily messages since the Barthou incident seem to indicate that he has completely lost his balance.

I would like you to think this over very carefully, and I would suggest that you ask Robert's [Sir Robert Hudson's] views on the matter. I know that you have great faith in his judgment.

Affectionately,
SUT.

The Genoa episode bore heavily on Northcliffe: '. . . my friends say that the reputation of *The Times* has suffered. When I point out that we believe that Mr Steed told the truth, they say: "Why did M. Barthou deny it? Therefore, what are we to accept, a man who was tricked in America, or a very distinguished French statesman?" I give it up. I hope that this wretched stage of *The Times* history is finished', but he returned to it in his communique six days later, on May 19: 'The paper has been terribly hurt.' His impatience with Steed took the form of taking Steed's name off the list of those who received the communiques.

Lloyd George was contemplating the possibility of a libel action arising out of Steed's dispatches. Garvin, Northcliffe's old admiring friend, spoke out strongly in support of the Prime Minister. There was no end to the worries of controlling the world's most responsible newspaper. Pomeroy Burton, seeing Northcliffe at the Hotel Cecil on May 16, thought that he 'looked tired' and told him so. 'I was thoroughly tired', Northcliffe agreed, writing to Burton on May 19. Burton had suggested a holiday. 'I am always obliged for your advice, whether I take it or not. It has been very wrong sometimes, as you know. I am going away for perhaps five or six weeks.' He had referred to that intention the previous day in a speech to the Australian and New Zealand Club in London, hinting that he would be visiting Germany. Drawing on his recent experiences in the countries of his hosts, his speech was frank, informative and colourful. He sat down amid a storm of cheers. Just before he rose to leave, he told the company: 'This is the last invitation I shall accept this season.' It was in fact his last public function.

German newspapers reacted at once to the proposed visit. Their readers were reminded that 'Northcliffe is the one man in the whole world who hates Germany most. We trust that employers, officials and workmen who are in contact with him will not forget it.'

*　　*　　*

Suddenly, he flared up about 'office nepotism', complaining in bulletins and in memoranda to heads of departments about 'employees' relatives who have been smuggled into the office'. He told Sutton: 'The office is a honeycomb of relationships. I find that two men who have been in the office for years are brothers masquerading under different names. I do not care whether they are trade unionists or not. I am not going to allow this corruption to go on.' H. W. Wilson had been notified 'that his brother cannot remain at Carmelite House'. Imber, the advertising director, was ordered to dismiss his nephew. Sir Andrew Caird was informed that his brother William, employed on the *Weekly Dispatch*, must go. The *Times* staff was likewise called to heel. A departmental head was denounced in a bulletin for introducing one of his relatives into the office and had the discomfiture of reading that 'his engagement is now subject to a fortnight's notice'. The bulletin further proclaimed that 'six persons have been dismissed today as a beginning. Any person employed in the office, however humbly, can help the proprietors by stopping this scandal.' Behind the shattering arbitrariness there was at least cause for righteous indignation. He had found, in the first place, that one of his general managers was employing a brother under an assumed name. Thundering forth his edicts, casting out the sinners, he might have been obeying an instinct of the blood drawn from some elder of the kirk on his mother's Scottish side.

His pamphlet, *Newspapers and their Millionaires*, was published that month. It made a considerable stir in Fleet Street, if nowhere else. It was highly contentious in its attitude to the members of what Northcliffe called 'the sacred caste' of the Newspaper Proprietors' Association, from which he had resigned on May 3. One of them, Sir William Berry (later Lord Camrose) publicly stated that it was 'not quite fair'. Its tone, intended to catch the ear of a wider audience, seemed to some readers to be mischievous. Qualified approval came from an unexpected quarter, the *New Statesman*. Its editor, Clifford Sharp, wrote that 'Lord Northcliffe is perfectly justified in poking fun at his "millionaire" colleagues'. Discussing, in a reasoned review of the pamphlet, the effect of certain kinds of proprietorship on the journalist's work and security, Sharp wrote that conditions had arisen in which 'journalists of all political colours are almost driven to pray for more Northcliffes'.

Northcliffe to Clifford Sharp:

Elmwood,
St. Peters.
25th May, 1922.

Dear Mr Sharp,—I notice your kind comments on my work. You ask why my newspapers are technically excellent. The explanation is very simple. There is not the bullying and sacking in my offices that take place elsewhere. Indeed, I am afraid there are many old passengers on our boat.

We pay three times the salaries paid elsewhere. We have bonus systems. We give pensions. No man works more than five days a week.

You know how muddly people are. Many think that I am a Jew, a Roman Catholic, that I am extremely eccentric, that I drink, and the rest of it.

My boast is that I have never lost a good man yet.

Yours sincerely,
NORTHCLIFFE

One morning at Elmwood, Price found him standing in his room surrounded by copies of his numerous periodical publications scattered over the floor. 'I can't think they do any harm in the world', he said quietly, as if talking to himself. On a table were copies of the newspapers he controlled, all except *The Times*. 'The publications with which I am connected have a total net sale greatly exceeding twenty million copies weekly.' He was dictating a letter 'to advertisers and advertising agents', setting forth the advantages of the 'net sales' certificate as 'a much-needed reform' designed to check the practice of issuing false circulation claims on behalf of newspapers and other publications for which the 'returns' (unsold copies) were heavier than their proprietors cared to disclose. As men's motives are rarely simple, and Northcliffe's were often complex, it may be assumed that he had aims other than the purification of circulation departments. He hoped, in fact, that his campaign would produce more advertisements for his newspapers. He had not foreseen that 'net sales' would inevitably strengthen the authority of the advertising department, a development which he had resisted all through his working years. He conceded in his letter to the advertising men that there were kinds of circulation which, though small, were more valuable to the advertiser than some involving larger figures. He did not believe 'that any hardship would be inflicted upon owners of class and technical journals of limited sale if they also disclosed their net sales'.

His insistence on the quantitative aspect of circulations made difficulties for numbers of specialist publications, including journals of cultural value. The larger the circulation the greater the price paid for space, a form of budgeting which forced down the value of space in newspapers and periodicals with modest sales. Consequently, some were hard put to it to continue. In the course of his campaign, Northcliffe received much private information about circulation cheating: for example, a well-known 'society' weekly which told its advertisers that its circulation was sixty thousand printed an average of eleven thousand copies a week; and so on. His case was stronger than most critics cared to admit, but it produced evils greater than those it was supposed to cure. Circulations were artificially inflated by 'free insurance' and 'gift schemes' promoted by hordes of canvassers who knocked at every street door with bribes for new readers. It was the final justification of Kennedy Jones's only known epigram: 'We found journalism a profession and left it a branch of commerce.'

★   ★   ★

The New York *Evening Post* stated that William Randolph Hearst was likely to be received by King George V, with Viscount Northcliffe as his sponsor. When Bullock, the *Daily Mail* man in New York, referred the report to London, he was told to issue an immediate denial on Northcliffe's behalf. Bullock also reported that laudatory articles on the British Royal Family were appearing in the Hearst press and that a cartoon, highly flattering to Northcliffe, had been published in the same newspapers. 'People here are talking about the possibility of Hearst being presented to the King.' The suggestion was put privately to Northcliffe that Hearst should be encouraged to make a formal application for presentation through the American Ambassador, so that there might be 'an emphatic refusal'. Northcliffe did not appear to be interested. Hearst was about to sail for Europe in the *Aquitania*. Some people thought it explained Northcliffe's decision to leave England.

His message to *The Times* and *Daily Mail* of May 25 was a *pronunciamento* in which his old love of mystery was reasserted. 'Before this reaches you all I shall be out of England on a very interesting mission of which you will hear nothing and of which you know nothing whatever now, though you may think you do.' Sir George Sutton, 'a very much overworked man', had again been given power of attorney. 'I have asked him to let me know the names of those who trouble him during my absence ... he does not want to be asked about the humdrum side of newspaper making. In case of any real injustice he may be appealed to. He knows my views on that sort of thing.' He told Filson Young: 'I'm tired. I'm going to get out of newspapers.'

At Elmwood, where he had been preparing for his visit to Germany, the domestic staff never remembered him being more irritable or harder to please. To John Walter, who saw him on May 24, Northcliffe appeared to be normal. To the staff at Elmwood he seemed to be permanently angry. Gordon, the head gardener, wrote to Mackenzie, the steward, saying that he and his wife, the housekeeper, could not put up 'with his lordship's tempers. They felt that they must leave', after their eleven years' service. Northcliffe had complained that there were no new peas in May, 'and no broadbeans the size of threepenny bits'. Gordon, he said, must go to France 'to learn how to grow salads'. He was extremely restless. Instead of reclining under the trees on the lawn as he had always liked to do, he strode hurriedly back and forth among the daffodils like an angry commander unsure of the course of a battle. Spring at Elmwood, which he had enjoyed for thirty years, had lost its balm. The view from the 'pulpit' attracted him no longer. The gramophone was silent. He disappointed the Amalgamated Press circulation director who reported 'a great success' with a new periodical, *Popular Wireless*, by showing no interest. Two years before, he had been eager to promote the 'wireless concerts' of the Marconi company experimenting at Chelmsford.

A member of the household staff at Elmwood said to Pine, the chauffeur: 'No one seems to realize how ill he is.' Price, the secretary, called down from London, became worried when he saw that 'the Chief', pencilling some drafts for *Daily Mail* contents bills, had written 'Maily Dail—Million Sale'. The chef, Peyronelle, used all his arts to tempt his master's palate, with no effect. One day he produced a luscious sucking pig for lunch. Northcliffe would not look at it. 'Cold beef,' he snapped. He lost his temper when meals were not on the table for serving at the hour he had ordered. 'When I say lunch at one, I mean it to be here at one'—banging the dining-room table—'not ready in the kitchen at one.' Hot coffee had to be available all through the day. Receiving a formal invitation to attend a local military function in his capacity of honorary colonel of the Thanet battalion of the Kent Volunteer regiment, he protested anxiously that he was 'not the man for the job', and discovered an urgent reason for being in London.

Early one morning William, the footman, ran into the garden with a message for Gordon: 'His lordship wants to see you urgently.' Northcliffe was in his upstairs workroom: he no longer used the bungalow of happy memories. Gordon found him overwrought, 'thoroughly keyed up'. He spoke breathlessly, ordering Gordon to arrange at once for fire alarms to be put into Elmwood, saying that 'some people may be coming down from London to set fire to the house'.

Chapter Thirty

Into the Shadows

IN 1902, motoring in France, he had gazed eastward from the Vosges to see Germany for the first time. It had been an emotional experience. 'I shall never forget my first sight of Germany', he had written in the diary. Now, twenty years after, he was going to Germany as if at the bidding of a Wagnerian fate.

There was no compulsive professional reason why he should go. Germany had not been included in the extensive future travel programme which he had drawn up during the last stages of his recent world journey. Before his office staffs knew that he had left London, he had arrived at the Hotel Christol at Boulogne which had been the scene of his no less mysterious movements in 1908, when he was awaiting the climax of his negotiations for *The Times*. He signed the hotel register as 'Leonard Brown'. The senior stewards of the cross-Channel steamers knew him well. One of them, S. Mason-Springay, who saw him during that crossing, recalled: 'It was plain to us when he came on board that he was on the verge of a breakdown. He was in a very angry mood.' The stewards agreed among themselves that nothing should be done to upset him; but the cabin steward was too attentive and greatly annoyed Northcliffe who made a strong protest before leaving the ship. The chief steward waited until Northcliffe's tirade had ended and then said quietly: 'Ah, well, my lord, that's the worst of being so popular.' There was a breathless silence. Then Northcliffe smiled. 'All right, Connor,' he said to the chief steward, 'let's forget it.' He shook hands with all the stewards, including the offending one, and left the ship.

With him were Sandy Thomson, the golf 'pro', Pine, the chauffeur, and William, a temporary valet. He showed Pine a revolver, saying that it might be needed for his protection in Germany. Receiving a message from Printing House Square, he wired to Price: *Have forgotten business want no figures fullstop reading French fullstop every time you wire causes me trouble fullstop very cold here.* That demand for respite was followed by a letter asking Price's attention to a number of minor office matters, in the course of which Northcliffe mentioned that he was 'sleeping ten hours and putting on a little weight'. He also said that he had received a threatening letter at the hotel, written in German, although every precaution had been taken to keep both his identity and his whereabouts secret. He announced to Price his intention of working more in future at 1 Carlton Gardens and of giving up his room at the *Times* office. 'I do not work when there, I find.'

At Boulogne, he received through the *Times* office an invitation to stay with the Commander-in-Chief of the British Army on the Rhine, General Sir Alexander Godley, whose headquarters were at Cologne. Northcliffe to Godley: 'I was on my way to meet my lady in Switzerland when I received your most unexpected telegram. I had no intention of going to Germany till July and should have, *of course*, asked your permission to come. My "Blue Butterfly" Rolls-Royce is far too well known a car for the Rhineland. I propose motoring to the Belgian frontier *douane* and should be grateful if some one could pick up me and my valet there. If *nobody talks or wires or whispers* I'm not in the least afraid.'

Acknowledging the Commander-in-Chief's invitation in Northcliffe's absence, Price, at Printing House Square, had told Sir Alexander Godley: 'We are receiving many threatening letters here.' Godley to Northcliffe: 'Of course there is always the possibility of an attempt to boycott you if you do come. There is no doubt that at this moment you are probably the Englishman who is most hated in Germany. Therefore, I think you should understand that you are running certain risks, though, frankly, I am of the opinion that they are slight.' There were more German protests against his coming. 'The man we can thank for our misery. . . . In him, we are not dealing with an honourable and sincere enemy. If he came to us, we would shut the door in his face.' The *Neueste Nachrichten* said that 'nobody had been so hated in Germany since Napoleon'. Copies of the 'Hate' medallion of him which the Germans had struck during the war were being put on sale again in the shops of the Rhineland. 'I am sorry to say that I am very cheap in Germany,' he wrote '—only six marks.'* There was attempted Foreign Office obstruction in the form of 'an extraordinarily fierce telegram' from the Permanent Secretary, Sir Eyre Crowe, who had complained that Northcliffe was 'carrying on an outrageous campaign against the Government and the Prime Minister and for this purpose he does not hesitate to promote misunderstanding and dissension between the French

---

* Occupying Paris in the Second World War, the Germans searched the offices of the *Continenta Daily Mail* in the rue du Sentier and removed only one object, a large framed photograph of Northcliffe, their old enemy.

and ourselves. I have no doubt that his visit to Occupied Territory is intended to serve the same object'. The Permanent Secretary saw no reason 'for His Majesty's Representative showing him any special civilities or indeed taking any notice of him'.

Northcliffe left for Brussels in the blue Rolls-Royce on May 29. 'Roads worn out by war,' he wrote on a picture postcard to his mother. 'Immense parks of captured German cannon about. I hope you continue to buck up, darling. Am in good form.' He visited Ypres, Vimy Ridge and 'the terrible region round Lens'. In wooded parts of the journey, he stopped the car and practised revolver shooting, with trees as targets. By the time he reached Brussels that evening, he was extremely fatigued. Before going to his rooms he gave Pine a telegram to be sent to Sutton and to each of his newspaper editors. It read: *Lloyd George must not be attacked personally.* The Prime Minister's standing in the country was high again; Birkenhead said 'incomparably so'. The criticisms of *The Times* had rebounded in his favour, another reason for Northcliffe revising his judgment of Steed's suitability as editor.

Referring again to possible risks, Northcliffe wrote that 'a dozen interesting old German friends' whom he was seeing in Brussels thought that there was 'little danger and that I am so thin that nobody will recognize me'. He wrote to Godley: 'I don't want to meet local Germans or anybody', though he had introductions to local government officials at Cologne, among them the deputy mayor, Conrad Adenauer. 'I just want your views for two days and must then proceed with my journey to Switzerland.' Godley shared his amusement with his staff on receiving a telegram from Northcliffe in Brussels saying that he was sending him a letter by train. 'It will be brought to you by a lame man. I shall be glad if you will have him met.' The 'lame man' was Pine—'quite a lame Sherlock Holmes!' Godley wrote home.

Northcliffe motored from Brussels to Cologne on May 31. The Commander-in-Chief had sent a staff car to meet him at the Belgian frontier. During the drive Northcliffe became unwell, developing what were thought to be symptoms of food poisoning. He arrived at Cologne in 'a state of collapse and went straight to bed', according to Godley, who wrote afterwards to his cousin, Lord Kilbracken, that his guest had spent the whole of the next day in the garden, until in the evening he was persuaded to go for a short drive into the country. He drank large quantities of barley water and seemed to his host to be 'obviously a very sick man'. Godley found him 'extremely egotistical', and said that he 'talked incessantly' and showed no inclination to listen to anyone.

Apart from members of the Commander-in-Chief's staff, he saw only an American general, the *Times* correspondent and the editor of the British Army newspaper, the *Cologne Post*, so Godley wrote ten days after the visit. Years later, Godley recorded in his *Life of an Irish Soldier*★ that Northcliffe, sitting in the garden, received visitors 'of every nationality', a contradiction of his earlier statement which makes biography more difficult than autobiography. At the time, Godley thought it strange that in view of announcements that he would be writing about Germany, Northcliffe did not choose to meet any Germans. Expressing his surprise in a letter to his cousin, Lord Kilbracken, Godley received the reply: 'The Northcliffe episode was delightful. I happened to be writing to Austen Chamberlain; he has, as you may remember, a special feud of his own with Northcliffe. I could not help imparting to him the contents of your letter. He wrote back, delighted.' The soldiers had not realized that Northcliffe's purpose in seeing the *Times* correspondent and the editor of the *Cologne Post* was to secure from them the information he wanted for his proposed articles. There were jocular references to the possibility of suspicion regarding Northcliffe's illness falling on a German maid who helped in the kitchen of the Godley household. Northcliffe himself was inclined to blame his imprudence in eating ice cream in Brussels; he was also prepared to believe that he had been overcome by the heat. 'I was absolutely spent. I cannot say why.' A few days later he was letting it be known at Carmelite House: 'I have had a curious illness. Some people think I was poisoned. Personally, I cannot believe that but I know I have been very bad.' There could be no doubt that, apart from his physical state at the time, he was subject to exceptional strain from the fact of his being on German soil. Godley said that he was 'in a great state of jumpiness and living entirely on his nerves'.

That impression of him was reinforced by his reaction when it was made known to him that an officer of the British Army on the Rhine, aged thirty-five, had captured the affections of a niece of Lady Northcliffe's, aged eighteen. Northcliffe became extremely agitated and much of the 'incessant talking' which Sir Alexander Godley described was on that topic. Northcliffe could not dismiss it from his mind; it obsessed him. The suitor he thought to be a fortune hunter—'and she has *no* fortune', he reiterated again and again. There were protests from another guest in the house, Mrs Brinton, the former Mrs Willie James, a noted Edwardian hostess. Northcliffe thought she was trying to 'get at him', on the officer's behalf. General Godley wrote that there was 'a desperate set to' between Northcliffe and Mrs Brinton. Northcliffe sent home a series of furious telegrams about the affair. By doing so he increased the area of tension, causing distress in Lady Northcliffe's family circle.

Although he had tried to check the flow of business reaching him from London, he may have had cause to be grateful for the distractions it provided. There were letters from Sutton reporting John Walter's wish to

★ Murray, 1939.

part with his interest in *The Times* because he found it no longer possible to co-operate with Northcliffe. To Sutton's inquiry: 'What is your idea of the value of Walter's shares?' Northcliffe replied: 'Please, please, please, please, please don't consult me about the Old One. Will do exactly what you choose', the *cri de coeur* of an exhausted man. He sent a reassuring telegram to Totteridge before leaving for Boulogne on June 2: *Am very well and always thinking of my darling Mother—Alfred.* He travelled by the night train to Ostend to join Sandy Thomson, whom he had left at Boulogne. Northcliffe to Godley: 'I want to thank you and her Ladyship most cordially for the extreme kindness which I received at your quiet house. I had not expected a certain grievous annoyance which, however, you and her Ladyship did your best to relieve', a reference to his clash with Mrs Brinton. 'For the rest, every moment with you was happiness. My kind regards to all those who were nice to me.'

In the breakfast car of the night train he had been recognized, he said, by two Germans, 'one of whom I had known slightly before the war'. They had talked 'rather offensively', using his name. He had said to them: 'Will you kindly cease shouting my name in that tone or I will request the guard to put you off the train at the next stop.' They bowed, clicked heels and apologized. After breakfast, Northcliffe wrote, 'we had a very reasonable chat'. The next day he wrote again to Godley asking him to deny, 'in the most emphatic manner', rumours of the engagement of his niece. He threatened, 'if we hear any more of the matter', to publish 'a prominent contradiction'.

Telegrams and letters about the rumoured engagement awaited him on his return to Boulogne on June 3. Sandy Thomson, with whom he had arranged to play golf at Wimereux before leaving for Paris and Evian-les-Bains, was found 'horribly drunk'. It was the last straw on Northcliffe's load of exasperation. Thomson was dismissed. More telegrams flashed to and from London. To H. G. Price (June 4): *Do you realise that I have over hundred letters and telegrams here from London Paris containing some biggest problems in business stop wire immediately result office golf stop urgent rates.* He communicated none of his worries to his mother, wiring to her that day: *Am resting quietly darling*, and to his wife at Evian-les-Bains: *Hope you are enjoying the flowers dear stop had very interesting and adventurous time among the Bosche*, followed by another complaining that he had had 'only one night's real sleep'. Also on June 4, he sent a letter of six pages to Sir Robert Hudson at Evian. It might be considered a casebook document.

You have with you the most distinguished medical man in the world [Sir Frederick Treves]. Will you kindly ask his opinion as to my sanity? I have begun to have doubts whether it is too little work and too much money, or whether it is simply decay of my faculties; I do not know, but I think I am going mad. Please wire me at once to relieve my suspicions.

I dreamt the other night that I had run off with Princess Mary and had started a boarding house at Blackpool, and she said to me: 'Thank you, we are doing very well.' That was a dream.

He knew it for a dream, he said, but was uncertain about the affair of Sandy Thomson: was it dream or reality? 'I gave him a very important letter for the committee of the Wimereux Golf Club. We left him apparently all right, if I am any judge of anyone being all right, which I doubt', and then Thomson vanished. 'I wonder if I am right or if it is an hallucination.' Thomson, he said, was carrying a cheque for £1,000 as a gift to the golf club, 'which is hard up'. The rest of a long letter overflowed with anguish about his niece, 'darling S., the daughter I prayed for who never came to me. I am more stirred up about it than I have been for years about anything. I cannot eat, I cannot sleep.' Going to bed that night, he complained of a smell of escaping gas in his room. Various people were brought into the room; none could smell gas. He could not be appeased until Pine moved into the adjoining bedroom, to be at hand in an emergency.

Another niece, on the Harmsworth side, was less affectionately regarded in a letter of his written the following day to his sister Christabel, Mrs Burton. The burden of the letter, however, was a complaint that he never saw his mother except in the presence of his eldest sister, Dot (Lady King). 'She will never leave me alone with Mother.' Because of it, he had reduced the yearly allowance he had been making to Lady King. He was now willing to restore it to the original amount, £1,400.

The sweet Mother's days are shortening. Every hour I spend with her is golden to me and, I believe, to her. I go out to Totteridge often after sixteen hours' work, when I would much prefer to sleep in London, and I want to see Mother and Mother only.

Northcliffe to the directors of Associated Newspapers Limited, Carmelite House (June 5): *Telegraph me this morning whether my overpaid directors are carrying out my instructions in regard to relations stop if not, I shall come home for forty-eight hours and do it myself stop Caird's case scandalous.* That matter, too, had assumed an obsessive disproportion in his mind. A telegram to Price later in the day threatened again his return in forty-eight hours to *dismiss every relation fullstop you know that I have gone through great worry with my family and even with my dear mother because I will not take relations.* The number of his telegrams on that subject on June 5 was seven. In one of them he mentioned that he was 'very tired after anxious German visit'. But when Price passed on office replies to his messages he in turn replied: *I just want telegrams from those I love and nothing else.* He wrote to Sutton (June 5): 'As to Wickham Steed, I am not anxious that he should leave *The Times*. As a special correspondent in Europe, he is unexcelled. I am extremely fond of him and regard him as a naughty boy. He loses his head when in a difficulty.' He telegraphed to Lord Reading at Viceregal Lodge, Delhi (June 6): *My newspapers are always at your disposal dear Reading stop greatly admire wisdom you have shown and your absence of jumpiness stop wish I knew someone in London to whom I could confide in about you stop am in touch with no member of present government.*

A young telephonist of the *Times* staff who was also a shorthand writer had been sent to Boulogne as a temporary secretary to Northcliffe. His name was Douglas Reed and when, in after years, he embarked on a career of authorship, he described in one of his books, *Insanity Fair,*★ his experience of that time. He had been warned by his mentors at Printing House Square that he would have to 'strain his wits' in the effort to please. To Reed, it appeared in retrospect that 'the shadows were already closing in' on Northcliffe, who seemed to him to be an extremely sick man.

He felt himself surrounded by treachery. He put his hand under the pillow and brought out a little black silk bag. 'Look at this,' he said, 'it was left here for me, for Mr Leonard Brown, by a man who wouldn't give the porter his name. How do they know that I am here? You see the colour? It is the colour of death!'

He reprimanded Price by telegram for sending him a letter 'with a little black circle on back', a morbid reference to the *Times* monogram. The stream of telegrams from Boulogne became a torrent. To Sir Robert Hudson, who had gone on to Evian to await his arrival: *Am quite ill not with dangers my German visit but with anxiety about niece stop what with that matter and Thomson its been worst week of my life stop fond love to my lady.* To Lady Northcliffe: *Am growing daily more anxious about S. [the niece] stop please read my letters very carefully dearest stop I slept only four hours last night and find it difficult to work in this anxiety.* To Sir Frederick Treves: *Am growing daily more anxious about S.* To the news editor of *The Times*: *Your Cologne correspondent completely misrepresented me stop will you get rid of him stop about time you exposed dangers Channel flying stop I have kept quiet about it in hopes of encouraging British aviation but whole thing is in rotten hands except perhaps Instone.* To H. G. Price: *Considering I risked life for old one [The Times] they are giving my articles a very small advertisement.* To W. L. Warden, editor of the *Continental Daily Mail*: *Your advertisement my articles very feeble stop make it much bolder stop after all I risked my life for Paris Daily Mail.* To Oscar Pulvermacher, night editor of the *Daily Mail*, Carmelite House: *Considering I risked my life for Daily Mail think display of advertisement my forthcoming articles very meagre.* To his

★ Cape, 1938.

mother: *Of course not going back to Germany my dear stop I went through very great danger and had quite enough of it stop but it was most interesting and I hope you will like my articles.*

To Price he sent a letter of five pages, undated, saying that on account of his niece he 'had been through such anxiety that I have not slept'. He was anxious about Carmelite House: 'It seems to be out of control.' He was anxious about Sandy Thomson: 'that business has been an absolute nightmare'. He had found it difficult to write his articles on Germany, 'and that is a fact'. The letter continued: 'I like Mr Reed extremely. He has been with me during one of the worst weeks of my life, and has not been gushing but quietly sympathetic. I thank you for choosing him. I am hoping tremendously that this will be a permanent engagement.' Reed, whose shorthand could hardly keep pace with Northcliffe's fevered loquacity, drew no assurance of security from that ingratiating wish.

'I am sending one article,' Northcliffe told Price, 'which is very bad.' Two of his articles, *Incognito into Germany*, were printed in *The Times* and the *Daily Mail*. They were superficial and discursive. A third and a fourth article showed mental confusion and were referred to Sutton, who agreed with the editors that they should be withheld. 'I beg that I receive nothing,' Northcliffe told Price. 'I want nothing to read', but in the same letter he also wrote: 'I want the circulation figures every day and I want *The Times*, *Weekly Times*, *Daily Mail* and *Evening News*.' He continued:

I do not like the tone of John Walter's letter. He refers to constant differences with Lord Northcliffe. What are they? Criticisms of Sisley Huddleston's articles, criticisms of the pictures and little things like that.

I am getting very weary of our overpaid directors, their idleness and blunders.

Tell Marlowe that I am very pleased with the editorials. Tell Tom Clarke and Pemberton that I like the news. Tell Pulvermacher and Fisher that I like the make-up. Tell Baker that the pictures are better. Tell Bussy I am delighted with the writing in the sky [by aeroplane].

As to *The Times*, I think it will require an entire shake-up, and if I get control of those shares I will do it.

Lady Northcliffe telegraphed to him from Evian-les-Bains on June 7: *Come as soon as possible dear our rooms at the Royal will be delightful*. In Northcliffe's life there was to be no more delight.

* * *

He had telegraphed to Steed on June 8, inviting him to Paris for a meeting at the Hotel Plaza-Athénée on June 10. On June 9, the telegraphic spate reached its fullest flood: twenty-four separate messages at urgent rates.

Several of them belittled Price's capabilities and services. One of fifteen hundred words contained implications that for him were too painful to be borne. Nerve-worn and deeply distressed, he left his room in Printing House Square to seek relief from an intolerable strain. He was the subject of an humiliating repudiation in Northcliffe's last communique to the *Daily Mail*, sent that same day: 'I wish this communique to be prominently posted in a hundred different rooms. There is an idea that Mr Price knows my views. He does not know my views and many mistakes occur through asking him. Any person who in future asks Mr Price any question whatever will incur my severe displeasure. As for my whereabouts, Mr Price rarely knows. When I am abroad it is known only to my family.' The long telegram, rambling through successive states of disorder and lucidity, accused Price of disloyalty and conspiracy: *You know nothing at all about what is going on fullstop you do not even know that I have bought the entire Walter interest fullstop sincerely hope you will not wear that grey suit fullstop blue serge is best fullstop we are all getting older except you and me fullstop dear Price it is about time you did something to help me fullstop I hate London and I loathe beastly dirty Times offices* . . . and, receiving it, Price was impelled to write in the margin: 'Poor Chief.'

One of the telegrams on June 9 was to Steed: *Have purchased entire Walter interest thus sacking two of your chief enemies Lints Smith and Walter fullstop am very pleased you are coming.* To Rothermere: *Do wish you would give my pamphlet a little lift dear Harold fullstop do give me a lift.* That plaintive appeal to his brother was for publicity on behalf of his *Newspapers and their Millionaires* pamphlet in Rothermere's newspapers, the *Daily Mirror* and *Sunday Pictorial*. Fleet Street read it eagerly; outside London, there was still no strong response. Northcliffe ordered that each reprint of a thousand copies should be boldly marked 2nd edition, 3rd edition and so on; he was as anxious as ever not to be identified with a failure.

On legal as well as on personal grounds, Sutton would have been shown the long incoherent message which had upset Price. Within twenty-four hours Sutton telegraphed to Northcliffe in a cautionary tone that did not hide his concern. *Sorry you have been ill fullstop afraid you are overworked fullstop suggest you drop all detail work and telegrams in view of heavy work on your return fullstop Price broken up with your messages and gone away fullstop your health only concern fullstop please do not worry fullstop big business going well fullstop liked your article this morning fullstop much affection always.—Sut.* Northcliffe replied at once that he was not overworked ('dearest Sutkin'). He had suffered 'a sort of blood poisoning', which some people thought had been deliberately activated in Germany, 'but I don't believe it'. He complained of Price's neglect to send him 'news telegrams', but was careful to say: 'Be very kind to Price for I love him.' Sutton was also asked to convey a message to Marlowe of the *Daily Mail*: 'Tell him I am devoted to him but my weak throat and his deafness makes our friendship impossible.'

Sutton's phrase, 'big business going well', referred to the purchase on Northcliffe's behalf of John Walter's 215,000 ordinary shares in The Times Publishing Company. Particulars of the transaction are given in the *History of The Times*, where it is stated that, as a prelude to it, Northcliffe had devised 'every means to irritate, fatigue and affront Walter'. By acquiring Walter's shares, we are told in the same place, Northcliffe was able to achieve 'a supreme coup; to obtain now what he had so long wanted: undisputed and absolute mastery, proprietorial and editorial, of this proud, mysterious, unique newspaper'. There is the further statement that 'by skilful arrangement and planned extravagance', Northcliffe had depressed the value of the ordinary shares which he had for so long wished to procure. Extravagance had been charged against him from the beginning of his career; but it may be disputed that he had ever wilfully planned its indulgence or that he had the patience to exercise the subtlety which such an operation would have required, in the circumstances, over many years. The *Times* historian states that Northcliffe intended taking over the editorship himself. Acquiring John Walter's shares, he had gained the whiphand over the 'old gang'.

John Walter had terminated the historic association of his family with the *Times* newspaper. Northcliffe seemed genuinely to regret it. He told Sutton to offer Walter the life chairmanship of the company, which could be continued through his son. After demurring, Walter agreed on conditions. While the negotiations were going on, Northcliffe prepared to leave for Paris. Repeatedly, he had told his family, his friends and colleagues, that he had 'been quite ill' but was better again. His nervous tensions remained. The hotel manager at Boulogne, having felt the lash of his tongue, was avoiding him. His young temporary secretary, Reed, whose salary had been impulsively raised to £10 a week, was given £150 in cash and sent to London to buy himself a possession which Northcliffe thought it shameful that any secretary of his should be without, a silver-fitted crocodile leather suitcase. He telegraphed his surprise to 'my dearest Sutkin' at hearing that his private room at The Fleetway House was 'being used by others'; another of his ill-founded suspicions. Mackenzie, the conscientious steward, was accused of 'communicating with Price', for which the penalty was dismissal or 'employment in some minor capacity'. A telegram was directed to the female staff at Carmelite House: *Now girls be good fullstop I shall be back in few weeks to find out whether you have been very good.* Another went to Gordon Robbins, the day editor at Printing House Square: *Reporter here from London says you swagger up and down Fleet Street in a tall hat stop I hope that horrible statement is not true stop tall hats are now for undertakers only not for members of my newspapers except on certain occasions.* Telegram number ten that day commanded Price to send *Who's Who* and a thousand pounds. Telegram number nineteen bade him *For Gods sake give your dirty grey suit away.* A telegram to Northcliffe's mother on the same day (June 10) told her that he was 'very well' and enjoying 'lovely weather'. A further telegram to Sutton begged him to complete the purchase of John Walter's shares. *We are going to make a fortune although I am not keen on making money as you know.* He was annoyed by the terms of John Walter's response, telegraphed that morning, to the offer of the *Times* chairmanship. Walter wished to make it conditional on his having the option to purchase Northcliffe's controlling interest. Northcliffe dictated, but did not send, a letter to Brumwell, assistant editor of *The Times*, on June 11. It was a statement of his views of impending change at Printing House Square.

For the first time I shall have freedom. There is going to be a strong Board to look after the commercial end, which, as you know, I don't understand. They will have no power to interfere with you in any way whatever, but they will cut down some of the preposterous expenses. . . .

It is not at all sure that we shall appoint an Editor at all. You are Associate Editor and Director. The whole of our little company of badly used proprietors has entire confidence in you and your staff. If I retain Steed it will be purely as Travelling Correspondent, and on condition that he goes exactly where we tell him, and describes exactly what we want.

His grip on *The Times*, as on all his responsibilities, as on life itself, was fast failing. As this work proceeds to record the forlorn happenings of Northcliffe's last phase, it is fitting to insert here the final verdict on his services to *The Times* pronounced by the official historian of that newspaper.

To him, *The Times* owes its transformation from a bankrupt nineteenth-century relic into a flourishing twentieth-century property. To him the paper owes its being as a national daily newspaper and register, the epitome of the world designed for the whole range of executive, professional and political men and women who, by their calling, intelligence and education, rank as the most influential constituency in Great Britain. *The Times* would have foundered without him. Northcliffe alone had the genius. It was he, his work, his inventions and his changes that alone re-established the property.

*　　*　　*

He left for Paris. Reed was dismissed. Saying goodbye to him, Northcliffe turned away with the words: 'You'll never see me again in this world.' It had not occurred to Reed then, or after, that Northcliffe's mental balance was in question: 'no such thought entered my head'. He had been told to expect 'a most imperious man', whose orders must be instantly and strictly obeyed. 'I found that an understatement, but when I think back it seems to me that he was essentially the kind of man I had been led to expect, possibly with his usual characteristics made more prominent by ill-health.'

Reaching Paris, he was so exhausted that he had to be supported on the platform. Colonel House and his wife were in the vestibule of the Hotel Plaza-Athénée when Northcliffe entered. He greeted Mrs House with a crude embrace that shocked House, who told Steed, two hours after the incident: 'Northcliffe is gone! He won't live long now.' When Steed went to Northcliffe's room at the appointed hour, Northcliffe clutched his hand and was effusive in his expressions of regard, saying that he 'felt terribly' their separation. 'How long is it since we left England?' he called to the valet. 'Is it seventeen years or seventeen days?' He put out his tongue. It was black. Steed noted that his eyes were wild and, particularly, that 'his left eye had a strange squint in an upward diagonal direction'. Steed had seen 'a squint' in the eye of a friend of his who had died of general paralysis of the insane. He believed that Northcliffe was a victim of that catastrophe. The medical findings completely dismissed the theory. Some distortion of the eye has been noted as a factor in bacterial endocarditis, the disease which had Northcliffe in its grip.

He kept on talking. He told Steed that he intended to edit *The Times* personally in future. He said that he had made a mistake in accepting a peerage. When he was better he would take steps to become 'plain Mr Harmsworth' again. Steed sat at his bedside from eight o'clock one evening until a quarter-past one in the morning, listening. Two or three times Northcliffe produced his Colt revolver from under the pillow. Once he threatened to use it, mistaking his dressing-gown hanging on the door for an intruder. During one of his visits to the bathroom, Steed unloaded the revolver; it had a bullet in every chamber. Steed returned to the hotel at five o'clock that morning. Peter Goudie, manager designate of *The Times*, who was there, said that Northcliffe was manifestly ill but Goudie saw and heard of no violent behaviour. Steed wrote in some notes dictated a few days after he returned to London:

Lord Northcliffe asked me to go through the manuscript of his second article on Germany. I did so, and found some passages in it so insane that I told him they must be suppressed. They referred to his revolver and to his ability to shoot seven Germans at sight through his pocket. He flew into a rage when I suggested the suppression of these passages, but immediately consented when I told him that people would think he was afraid of the Germans.

He sent his last communique to *The Times* on June 11. It was largely an attack on the professional competence and integrity of Sir Maurice Craig, the mental specialist whose name was prominent in the trial of Ronald True, a young man of mysterious social antecedents who had murdered a girl. Northcliffe believed, perhaps not exclusively, that there were law-perverting influences behind the trial, which greatly agitated him.

He, Wickham Steed, Peter Goudie, Sisley Huddleston, Miss Rudge (a *Daily Mail* telephonist), and his valet, William, left Paris for Evian-les-Bains on June 12. Pine had gone on in advance with the Rolls-Royce. As soon as the train had started, Northcliffe sent for Huddleston and told him that he was no gentleman because he had a red silk handkerchief hanging loosely out of his pocket; moreover, his teeth were bad, his breath foul. Huddleston, upset, left the train at Dijon. The president of the P-L-M had placed his private dining-car at Northcliffe's disposal, a rare courtesy. A chef was in charge of it with orders to cook for no one else. Northcliffe refused to use the car or to eat the chef's food. There was dismay. Steed had no doubt that the French railway authorities would be deeply affronted. He wrote:

During the rest of the journey, Northcliffe wished me to sit with him in his compartment, where he talked incessantly. The compartment was darkened. I must have spent more than nine hours of the ten and a half hours of the train journey, listening and replying to his ceaseless stream of indistinct and mostly disjointed talk. In it were intervals of uncanny lucidity. At one point, he called Mr Goudie to him, gave him instructions to return from Switzerland to London and to dismiss at once 120 people from *The Times* staff. He accused us of being deaf because we could not always catch his indistinct remarks, and ended by telling some improper stories to Miss Rudge. After luncheon he said to me: 'Did I go a little too far with that girl? Don't you think I am mad? Am I mad?'

Quoting Steed again, as the train drew near Bellegarde, 'he had, or simulated, a choking fit, accompanied by dry retching. He screamed, shook his fist in my face, and seemed entirely beside himself.' During the journey, he had insulted various members of the train staff. Seeing Pine at the railway station, he gasped: 'Oh, my dear Pine, I've had a hell of a time since you left me!' He made Pine drive at breakneck speed over the narrow, winding road to Evian, and then shrieked that they would all be killed.

They arrived at Evian at eight-thirty in the evening. When the manager of the hotel came forward to welcome him, Northcliffe drove him away with an insult. Otto Kahn, an old friend, was waiting to greet him. Northcliffe made a grimace and pushed past him without a word. He scattered the waiting pageboys. He threatened the hall-porter. Lady Northcliffe saw him immediately after he had been put to bed by his valet. He insulted her with a shamelessness that sent her trembling from the room. North-cliffe by telegram to his mother, the next day (June 13): *I am in a delightful place where intend spend some time with my dear wife among wild flowers stop am therefore announcing my indisposition in newspapers though in reality am perfectly well.* Posted to him that day was a grateful acknowledgment of what was to be the last of his many givings to charity. It was from St. Joseph's Hospice for the Dying, Mare Street, Hackney, London, E.

A discussion between Treves, Steed and Hudson resulted in a decision to call in a Lausanne neurologist. He arrived with a trained nurse and a male attendant. Northcliffe was induced to see the specialist, only on being assured that he was an authority on 'German poisons'. The *Times* history states: 'He certified Northcliffe as insane.' Wickham Steed's notes contain the phrase: 'The specialist from Lausanne, who is a brilliant French professor and holds many British medical degrees, wrote a certificate that Lord Northcliffe was out of his mind.' Steed afterwards said that he did not see the certificate but 'certainly heard of it'. In fact, he was not at Evian at the time that it was supposed to have been written. The Lausanne specialist is dead.

Seymour Price, who went to Evian to take over the case from the local medical men, had assured Leicester Harmsworth that there had been no certificate of insanity. Sir Thomas Horder wrote to Leicester Harmsworth on October 21, 1926: 'I am writing to confirm the fact which Dr Price has already stated, viz. that Lord Northcliffe was never certified as insane. I am able to substantiate Dr Seymour Price's denial very emphatically.' On October 26, 1926, Seymour Price confirmed his opinion in writing to Leicester Harmsworth: 'Lord Northcliffe was never at any time certified insane. I was his private medical adviser for eleven years. He could not have been certified without my knowledge or consent. There is a world of difference between insanity and the delirium caused by such an illness as his.' There is also the important testimony of Lady Northcliffe herself, the only surviving witness, who was at Evian with Northcliffe. She heard nothing of the alleged certifying. Later, Horder made a signed statement confirming that Northcliffe was not insane within the accepted meaning of the term and that no certificate of insanity was issued. Discussing the *Times* history in 1953, Horder dismissed the insanity statement as 'completely false'.

In 1954 Steed wrote privately: 'I did not invent the story [of Northcliffe having been certified insane]. It was discussed with me by Sir Robert Hudson and Sir George Sutton.' Northcliffe's behaviour to the hotel manager and staff had increased the likelihood, Steed wrote, that he might be reported 'as a dangerous lunatic' to the Prefecture of Haute-Savoie. 'This is why I got my friend, Senator Victor Berrard [Chairman of the Foreign Relations Committee of the French Senate, 1922] to ask Poincaré to instruct the Prefecture not to take action pending the removal of Northcliffe to London. Poincaré promised to do this.'

Steed's observations showed that Northcliffe's mental state at Evian swung constantly between confusion and clarity. He had always been a man of extravagant moods. They were now amplified by a demonic force which transformed ill-humour into paroxysms of rage and simple kindness into a grovelling desire to please. There were long periods when apparently his every thought had to be given utterance; the flow went on and on, unchecked, before exhaustion brought uneasy rest. From the notes that Steed made after his return to London there emerges a clinical record of the breakdown of lifelong inhibitions, of the patient's uncanny awareness of attempts to deceive him, of friends being distorted into enemies, of love turning to hate, of personality degraded by the processes of an incalculable disease.

Yet nothing of that dark shadow lies across the recollection of Stephen Dowling, the shorthand writer from the Paris *Daily Mail* who saw Northcliffe every day of the stay at Evian. Regularly each morning at 5.30 he was called to 'the Chief's' bedside. Dowling thought that his 'dreamy and inconsequential talk' was due to his not having slept well. 'He seemed to be still only half awake and to be talking aloud to himself about the various ideas which had passed through his mind the previous night. Then he gradually awoke, asked me about the weather, and told me to be sure that he received the newspapers as soon as they arrived at the hotel. He never failed to tell me to have a good breakfast and to be sure to ask for anything I wanted.' Receiving *The Times* of the previous day, he scribbed his notes down its margins with a 6B lead pencil, as of old. He inquired about Dowling's wife, whether she was happy at being left behind in Paris. 'Ask her if she would like a trip to London. I will pay the expenses. She shall have a new dress to go in', and he gave Dowling a cheque for £50.

He had himself sent for Seymour Price, telegraphing: *If I am not depriving any patient of your great services wish you get in train at once come Royal Hotel Evian was poisoned by Germans fullstop anxious to get home as my lady is worn out nursing me.* Seymour Price, Sutton and Leicester Harmsworth travelled together to Evian. It had been agreed by the brothers at home that Leicester was best fitted temperamentally to deal with Northcliffe in his illness. With their arrival there came a change of routine. Dowling was told that it was his duty to circumvent Northcliffe's attempts to communicate with the outside world. The young stenographer played his part in the deception with no conviction of the need for it. To him, 'the Chief' was an exceptional being, larger than life, his behaviour extravagant but not abnormal. Sir Frederick Treves was often called into Northcliffe's bedroom to hear Dowling read the leading article for *The Times* which Northcliffe dictated. One of the themes was the German future. 'He was certain that in the long run Germany would plot and plan her revenge against us.' Dowling saw none of the scenes described by Steed, the ravings, the struggles, the revolver brandishing. He heard nothing about a certificate of insanity. He remembered a conversation with Seymour Price. 'He said that he did not believe that there was any question of insanity. He regarded Lord Northcliffe as a victim of extreme fatigue.' Seymour Price telegraphed to London his opinion that Northcliffe would recover, although for the time being 'sense of proportion nil'. That was demonstrated by the many telegrams which Steed said that he privately suppressed. Northcliffe was also writing by hand long indecipherable letters that gave every sign, in form and content, of flickering mental powers.

He dictated a telegram to his mother on June 14: *Always thinking of you darling* and begging her to discount rumours about his illness. *George Sutton will tell you they are untrue stop I have been unwell but am now well again.* Sutton and Steed returned to London on June 13. Rothermere telegraphed an appeal to his brother that day to 'cease immediately all work'. He told Northcliffe: *Your health worries me dear Alfred you are putting severe strain on your heart and might easily lead to further valvular trouble,* an echo of the diagnosis of 1910. Steed had borne the brunt of Northcliffe's worst attack. He could stand no more. The *Times* history asserts that Northcliffe had tried 'to break Steed's nerve with every kind of indecent insult', a charge which places responsibility where at such phases of Northcliffe's illness it could not logically be assumed. Northcliffe's brothers thought that Steed himself was a disturbing influence. Cecil had asked Leicester to try 'to persuade Wickham S. to leave Alfred. If not, it may be possible to induce him to "go slow" and not excite A. to fresh mental activities.'

On June 14, writs against Northcliffe were issued and later withdrawn by Sir Andrew Caird, general manager of Associated Newspapers Limited, and Walter G. Fish, assistant editor of the *Daily Mail*. They alleged that he had libelled them concerning their attitude to his wages policy for printers. Also on June 14, a cable from Milwaukee announced that when Northcliffe was mentioned in a speech at the convention there of the advertising clubs of America, the large company spontaneously rose and cheered his name.

He telegraphed to his mother again: *Believe nothing you hear about my health stop Sutton coming to see you stop cannot stop these rumours.* Except for a telegram to his sister Christabel on that same day, June 15, in which he told her that he had been 'very near to death', few of his messages reached London. Every kind of subterfuge had to be used to outwit him. He counted the number of words in each message and was not satisfied until an official receipt had been shown to him. Some messages were diverted to private addresses. Sir Robert Hudson wrote to Sutton: 'Let me repeat my warning that I may at any moment fail to intercept these messages. He may give them to a waiter and they may be on the wires before I know.' The following day, June 16, Hudson wrote again to Sutton: 'This business is the devil! He is driving everyone round him into a condition which will *soon resemble his own*! Everyone is to be dismissed as soon as he gets back to London, *so pack your kit*!' A message to his mother that day read: *Very well and merry stop shall be with you in a few days.* No doubt Sutton faithfully carried out the instruction to convey reassurance to Totteridge. His task was not an easy one. He had seen and heard for himself that 'the Chief' was a woefully changed man. By then other members of the family were forced to realize the seriousness of the illness. *My tenderest devotion*, St. John wired to Northcliffe on June 16. Fleet Street, more knowing than Harley Street, had already filled in with rumour what it could not establish as fact. 'Northcliffe has gone mad!' That day, the first announcement about his health appeared in the *Daily Mail*: 'On account of indisposition, Lord Northcliffe has been ordered by his physicians to abstain from work for the present. The publication of his articles on Germany will therefore be temporarily suspended.'

He left Evian for London on June 17, overcoming his reluctance to travel only on being assured that his mother longed to see him. Recalling that it was the third anniversary of his thyroid operation, he sent telegrams of 'thanks and grateful remembrance' to the doctors who had attended him at that time. Other telegrams Hudson felt obliged to intercept. One denounced Sutton for his 'astounding lack of imagination'. Another to Sutton, about instructions that had not been carried out, complained: *I cannot make head or tail of you all.* A message to his mother was allowed to go through: *Starting this evening merry party stop very well dearest stop fondest love.*

He was driven in the Rolls-Royce to Bellegarde to entrain for Paris. With him were his brother Leicester, Seymour Price and Sir Robert Hudson. On the way, he was so overcome by fatigue that he ordered Pine to stop the car, begging Seymour Price: 'Let me lie by the roadside and die.' The French President, M. Poincaré, had sent his private railway coach to Bellegarde for the homeward journey across France. Northcliffe was seen standing alone in the corridor of the coach, gazing angrily out of the window. His fingertips were pressed white against the glass. Leicester Harmsworth said that on the way to Calais, Northcliffe insisted that he must go to Fontainebleau, 'to make a will'. He talked, ramblingly, of the future of his newspapers, 'after I am dead'. He told Leicester that he wanted him to 'have *The Times*'. During the journey he became 'restless and difficult'. He had the furtive look of one who fears an unseen assassin.

At Calais, the stewards of the waiting cross-Channel steamer did not immediately recognize him: 'he looked so much older'. Greeted by the purser, he said: 'Well, Crush, they've got me at last—they've killed me!' At Dover, seeing the familiar face of Donald White, Cook's representative, whom he had known for many years and whose boy he had offered to educate, he waved and called 'Hullo, Donald!' His hand was limp, his voice faint, and White said that he moved along the quay 'like a paralysed man'. Another spectator of his distress that day at Dover was Sir William Orpen, the portrait painter, who was startled by Northcliffe's appearance. In the train to London he drank thirteen bottles of Perrier water. Sutton was at Victoria Station to meet him. In response to his greeting Northcliffe turned on him with loud abuse. The doctors still believed that he might get better. On June 19, Steed had to accept that possibility, which denied his own prognosis, when Caird telephoned to say that Rothermere had given him reassuring news. The doctors at Evian had told both Sutton and Hudson that 'with prolonged rest and quiet there was a good hope of recovery'. Fearing that Northcliffe might carry out his threat to go down to Printing House Square and 'fire the lot', Lints Smith, the manager of *The Times*, had a guard put on the door.

From *The Times* of June 20, 1922: 'Viscount Northcliffe has returned from the Continent. He has been advised to undergo a course of treatment on account of heart weakness, accentuated by an attack of ptomaine poisoning.' He had been seen the previous day by Horder. When Seymour Price introduced Horder, Northcliffe exclaimed: 'One of George's bloody knights!' and took a revolver from under his pillow. 'He did not—as has been reported—fire at me,' Horder wrote afterwards. 'The revolver was not loaded.' It had been deliberately left in his possession because it appeared to give him a sense of security. That outburst was followed by a calm in which he dictated a message to be sent by hand to his mother at Totteridge: 'I shall try to fetch Pretty [his cocker spaniel] tomorrow, darling. I will give up using the telephone for six months from today, dearest.' His brother Leicester thought him 'decidedly better', but had no doubt that his 'tornado days of business activity have got to be ended'. St. John Harmsworth, thinking that the crisis period had passed, went back to his home by the sea. He wrote to Leicester: 'We are all under a deep debt of gratitude to you for the masterly way you have handled the sad and difficult situation.'

Seymour Price had discovered a 'tender, round, movable lump' in the right lower part of the patient's abdomen. Considered in conjunction with the fever and other symptoms, acute appendicitis was suggested. Further examination disclosed an enlargement of the spleen. There was also a heart murmur of organic significance. 'These signs', Horder wrote, 'raised the question of septic endocarditis of a sub-acute type.' It was a disease on which he was one of the few authorities. Downstairs, in the small study at 1 Carlton Gardens, Leicester and Cecil Harmsworth waited.

When Horder explained to them the possible implications of his new diagnosis, they asked him to take charge of the case. From that day, 1 Carlton Gardens became a one-patient hospital. Lady Northcliffe moved to the Ritz Hotel. No one was allowed in the house without Seymour Price's permission. Northcliffe did not wish to see Horder again. Horder therefore remained in supervisory control. On June 25 he called in the senior consulting surgeon of Guy's Hospital, F. J. Steward, for consultation. Leicester Harmsworth let Lady Northcliffe know the following day that it was the consultants' 'strong opinion' that the source of Northcliffe's illness was 'a disordered appendix'.

The diagnosis gave relief to all, not least the patient. 'Alfred is fully aware that it is appendix trouble,' Leicester wrote. 'Dr Price thinks that Alfred has been worried greatly as to the cause and nature of this illness. I believe this phase of the matter is going to help us greatly. I have felt very strongly all along that a great deal of Alfred's hostility to doctors was based upon a dread that there was something radically wrong with him, that his delirium, for example, indicated brain disturbance. Alfred has apparently made a pretty considerable study of medical matters, especially as affecting himself. He knows all about appendicitis. It does not frighten him, whereas, on the other hand, if he be satisfied that it is appendicitis, his other fears disappear. I really think things are going on in the right way with him.'

Three days later he upset the hopeful view by attacking one of the male nurses with a poker. That such an instrument was at hand showed that the medical advisers were satisfied that his illness was not primarily a mental one. Throughout its course he was subject to the mildest restraints; chiefly, not being allowed to go beyond the confines of bedroom and bathroom. Convinced that the patient was in an increasing state of septicæmia, Horder called in a pathologist who discovered that the bloodstream had been invaded by a streptococcus of the kind known to be characteristic of the disease which Horder had suspected. Horder wrote in his report: 'There was no other abnormal finding and the W.R. [Wassermann reaction] test for venereal disease was negative.' Horder wrote to Leicester Harmsworth on July 11: 'My fears are confirmed. I cannot avoid the conclusion that the heart has become infected.' In 1954, he looked up the notes he had kept of the case and wrote:

Those were the pre-penicillin days and we had at that time no specific treatment for a septicæmia which owed its existence to the colonization of the germ in the valves of the heart. Very rarely we saw the disease 'die out', but, in the main, it justified the sinister name given to it at that time, malignant endocarditis. The form of the disease from which Lord Northcliffe suffered had only recently been described and its characters were just then being recognized by the profession, through the work of Osler, Libman and myself. It is probably the most insidious type of blood poisoning known to us. It may be present for several months before it declares itself by one or other of its complications. As is frequently the case, it is not possible to say how long it had been present in the case of Lord Northcliffe, almost certainly for months rather than weeks. It explained the gradual loss of strength, the increasing pallor (the *café-au-lait* complexion is a feature of the disease) and, in so dynamic a personality as his, the active nature of the delusional state which supervened.

The *British Medical Journal*, reviewing the course of Northcliffe's illness (August 19, 1922), suggested that he had suffered from the streptococcal infection 'for at least a year'. The journal stated that 'very often the history of this extremely fatal form of endocarditis suggests that the infection, having reached the blood, attacks one of the valves of the heart which may have been damaged, perhaps by rheumatism, many years before'. Remittent fever, with all its well-known accompaniments, including delirium, is one of the usual manifestations of the disease. In Northcliffe's case, the fever and its delirium recurred through another six weeks, with intermissions of lucidity and calm that were convincing enough to give hope of his subsequent recovery.

Optimism faded when Seymour Price admitted, after more talks with Horder, that he was 'very worried'. Price wrote to Leicester Harmsworth: 'We shall fight every inch of the way with redoubled energy, but the issue must be in higher hands.' Receiving the news, St. John wrote: 'It would seem, dear Leicester, that Alfred has passed into the hands of God. It may be that his mission on earth is fulfilled. He has been a great captain and has always done his duty, above all, to the family.'

Leicester Harmsworth consulted Horder about the advisability of offering a large cash sum for a cure. 'I put it to him whether it was not likely that there were doctors in this or other countries striving for a cure of this complaint, with perhaps ideas that are in front of general medical knowledge of the subject. Horder said it was quite possible.' Rothermere had said at once: 'Put me down for £10,000.' He and Leicester fixed the offer at £25,000. A letter from Cecil gave them second thoughts. 'The more I think of it, the more alarmed I am at its probable effect on Mother. Such an announcement must necessarily imply that the best medical advice we know of is helpless in the matter.' It was considered to be wise caution. Geraldine Harmsworth had not been told of the mental effects of Northcliffe's illness, but she had been warned early in July that its nature might prove to be more serious than had at first been supposed. Instead of offering a spectacular reward, the brothers agreed not to 'spare any expense in consulting any specialist in America or in any other part of the globe, unless probably Germany' (Leicester Harmsworth to Horder, July 19, 1922).

On the strength of that decision, Horder consulted Sir James Mackenzie, the most eminent British cardiologist, and the American specialist, Dr Emanuel Libman, who had been attending Madame Sarah Bernhardt in France. Libman told Horder: 'I believe in fighting the case as long as possible. I have had seven recoveries.' Mackenzie's visit provoked delusions of poverty in the patient. 'My shoes are all I have left in the world. I can't afford to get them soled and heeled.' The two consultants had little to advise that was new. Libman believed that treatment should be the same as in cases of advanced tuberculosis, namely, building-up. In Northcliffe's case, the intermittent high fever, during which the temperature was often at 103, showed no sign of abating. By the third week in July, hope for him had run low. He was given a blood transfusion. His brother Vyvyan was the willing donor. He had been asking for his mother, who had designedly been kept away from his bedside. She was allowed to see him on July 22, her first and last visit to him during his illness. As she entered the room, her thoughts must have gone back to the time when she had held her first-born in her lap to nurse through one crisis after another. With the exclusive private insight of a mother, she asked the doctor in attendance: 'Is it his head?'

In one of his later diminishing periods of consciousness he exclaimed: 'Tell mother she is the only one!' The male nurses had occasion to restrain him from further violence on one or two occasions, but the attacks were of lessened force. Sometimes the darkened room oppressed him and he would tumble out of bed in a sudden fleeting access of energy and switch on all the lights. There were days when he fasted, saying that it was a religious exercise. He prayed aloud, often he wept, sitting on the side of his bed, head in hands.

On August 3 he called Seymour Price into his room and told him: 'I made a big mistake about Price.' Seymour Price asked if he meant his secretary, H. G. Price. Northcliffe said: 'Yes. I made a big mistake about him and I want him to know that I now know I was quite wrong.' Seymour Price ensured that the message was at once sent to his namesake, who wrote a letter to Northcliffe that same day:

My dear Chief,—I am so delighted to get your kind message through Dr Price. It cheered me very much.

My affection for you is as it has ever been, and, beyond everything else, I hope that you will continue to improve and soon be restored to complete health.

My love and best wishes to you, dear Chief. I think of you all day and every day.

Yours always,
H. G. PRICE

He wished also to rid himself of the feeling that he had behaved unfairly to his brother-in-law, Percy Burton, the advertising agent, with whom he had never been temperamentally at ease. He asked to see his sister Christabel, Mrs Burton, and told her: 'My dear, I was very unjust to Percy.' He desired to make amends by increasing her share in his will.

There were heavy hearts in Carmelite House, where his writ had run most powerfully and for so long. Tom Clarke, the *Daily Mail* news editor, wrote: 'There was a feeling of anxious expectancy everywhere in the office. Reporters went about with glum faces. Even sub-editors, a much more phlegmatic species, looked up wonderingly at people who entered or left the room. Upstairs the compositors tapped away diligently at their linotypes; downstairs the machine hands got ready the giant presses . . . but they tugged at the coat of any editorial man who passed their way and whispered, "What's up with the Chief?" ' It was understood that he was too ill to speak on the telephone. Oscar Pulvermacher, the night editor of the *Daily Mail*, was therefore startled to be told one evening that 'the Chief wants you'. Pulvermacher said: 'His voice was hardly audible. He wished to give me instructions designed to remove him from captivity, poor man.' Sutton, however, said that it was impossible for Northcliffe to have spoken as all the lines from Carlton Gardens had been cut off to prevent him from 'worrying the office'. But Northcliffe had remembered that there was a telephone in his wife's boudoir. It was from there that he whispered his last telephone call.

At Printing House Square, the prevailing emotion was less personal: What will happen to *The Times*? The completion of the sale of John Walter's shares to Northcliffe had necessarily been delayed. Now it was a question whether Northcliffe himself was a competent party to negotiations of any kind. Sutton and Stuart (who had returned hurriedly from Canada on August 7) still had power of attorney and invoking it was among the matters which were being privately and actively discussed. Northcliffe's exhaustion had become dire; and while his life was ebbing to a close, he was the central figure in a drama of which he knew nothing. A cast of *Times* proprietors and executives, solicitors, doctors and relatives, with Lloyd George and some of his business friends waiting to be called on to the stage if required, moved busily through several acts which reached only anti-climax. It was believed that Lloyd George might be interested not only in having a say in directing the paper's policy but in actually occupying the editorial chair. That possibility is examined at some length in the official history of *The Times*, in which it is shown that the discussions, if they never reached a negotiating stage, were at times devious, if not mysterious. Lloyd George was working closely in the matter with Birkenhead; another of the schemers was Sir Warden Chilcott, M.P.

Meanwhile Northcliffe had drafted in his own handwriting and signed two new wills. The first, dated July 7, was signed 'Northcliffe'. The second, revoking that of July 7, was signed 'Alfred Charles William Harmsworth' and was dated July 22.* The phraseology and language employed in both documents revealed the clouded state of Northcliffe's mind. He spoke of his 'suffering from one dangerous disease, Indian Jungle fever' and 'poisoning by ice-cream supplied on the Belgian frontier'. There were attacks on members of his family. 'I invented the *Daily Mirror*. It was a failure at first and Rothermere ran for his life.' He bequeathed, subject to an annuity of £10,000 a year to 'my Darling Mother', everything he possessed to his wife and 'I particularly wish that my darling wife shall remarry if she thinks fit'. Horder, who refused to add his signature as a witness to the wills, has left on record his own verdict: 'I never saw Lord Northcliffe in a state of mind capable of understanding the nature of a legal document from the day of his arrival in England up to his death.'

Northcliffe's friends and office colleagues were receiving a daily message about him from Seymour Price. The public was given news of him in a weekly bulletin, which in August became a daily one, when his condition worsened. The bulletins were carefully phrased and approved by Leicester Harmsworth out of consideration for his mother. There were so many personal inquiries at Carlton Gardens that a policeman was put on duty to keep inquisitive sightseers away from the portals. A cable from New Delhi expressed the Viceroy's 'alarm'. The American Ambassador, George Harvey, called with a warm-hearted tribute which Northcliffe never received. The *Daily Mail* received many letters from readers who had followed the paper's fortunes from its first day. Ex-Servicemen of the late war showed concern for one who had done so much for them. People called at Carmelite House with offers of 'certain cures'.

On August 9, Horder decided that the patient must have 'all round the clock' fresh air, and the roof of 1 Carlton Gardens was inspected to see whether a revolving shelter could be put there. When it was found unsuitable, the Duke of Devonshire, who owned the adjoining house, gave permission for his roof to be used. Spaces had to be cut through ceilings to allow the hoisting of a stretcher. Northcliffe showed pleasure at seeing the twin towers of Westminster Abbey across St. James's Park. Seymour Price noted down his last whispered utterance:

I wish to be laid as near Mother as possible at North Finchley and I do not wish anything erect from the ground or any words except my name, the year I was born, and this year, upon the stone.

In *The Times* I should like a page reviewing my life-work by someone who really knows and a leading article by the best man available on the night.

* It was not admitted for probate as a result of subsequent legal proceedings. The will of March 1919 was allowed to stand.

He passed into a twilight of consciousness in which he was disturbed only by the sound of rain falling on the shelter roof. At his mother's request, prayers were being said for him daily in the parish church of St. Andrew at Totteridge. On August 12 the Bishop of London asked for prayers throughout his diocese. They were offered in St. Paul's Cathedral and in churches outside London.

He died at twelve minutes past ten on the morning of Saturday, August 14, 1922. The bulletin stated that 'the end was perfectly peaceful'. He was fifty-seven. The cause of death was ulcerative endocarditis. His brothers Cecil and Vyvyan were with him at the last. They clung to a belief that he had faintly recognized them before they heard the sigh of death. On the wall, facing his bed, was an illuminated portrait of his wife. Seymour Price had put the little book, *Daily Light on the Daily Path*, which he had read each day on the world journey, into his clasped hands, telling Leicester Harmsworth in a letter: 'I think his Mother would wish it to stay with him.' His nephews took turns at keeping an all-night vigil in the room next to the one in which he lay. Those of the family who saw him before he was finally borne beyond the sight of men were startled by a change in his appearance. Death had given him back his youth.

*   *   *

Within a few hours messages were flooding in from kings, presidents, prime ministers, political and industrial leaders, ambassadors, representatives of many races, personages of many countries. Their tributes crowded the communications systems for two days. Newspapers at home and overseas were black-bordered. At *The Times* and the *Daily Mail* offices there were special deliveries of bags containing letters of condolence. The obituary notices from the press of Great Britain and the United States alone filled two immense albums of the page size of *The Times*.

At a quarter-past eleven on the morning of Tuesday, August 17, the doors of Westminster Abbey were thrown open to admit the greatest mourning congregation known there for many years. Wave after wave of people poured into the nave and spread out on either side until every place was filled. The chapter clerk's plans for seating them were severely tried. Even the organ loft was packed. An old member of the Abbey staff who said that he had been present at 'all the great war ceremonials' could not recall a bigger funeral service. Sorrowfully surveying the scene, Cecil Harmsworth noted 'some conspicuous absences' which he said he 'could never forget'. The enmities of politics were reduced to pettiness by the public's sense of loss. Northcliffe was being honoured by a breadth of esteem that even his most devoted admirers could hardly have expected.

Followed by his brothers, and by young nephews, among whom there

I wish to be laid as near Mother as possible at North Finchley and I do not wish anything erect from the ground or any words except my name, the year I was born and this year upon the stone.

In THE TIMES I should like a page reviewing my life-work by someone who really knows and a leading article by the best man available on the night.

Northcliffe's last wishes, dictated to his doctor

were facial resemblances almost unbearably poignant to some who had known him over the years, he was carried to the foot of the sanctuary steps. His coffin was covered by the splendid Abbey pall of white brocade embroidered with the Cross, the crowned Tudor rose and the crowned portcullis of Westminster. At head and feet and at either side were great golden candlesticks bearing spears of flame. Beyond was the purple-fronted altar with its gleaming gold cross; all around, the newly cleaned stone and the marble of monuments and tombs whose mellow beauty had been made visible once more by the mason's faithful hand in concord with the journalist's generous heart.

After the choirboys' serene and passionless treble, singing his mother's favourite hymn, *Hark, hark my soul!* came the daringly confident strains of the Funeral March of Chopin, swelling upward and outward until the whole great fabric seemed to tremble. Then began the long walking-pace progress to the grave at St. Marylebone Cemetery, a cavalcade of ninety cars passing through seven miles of streets between Westminster and North Finchley, not a single yard without its sign of public respect. In Parliament Square, at Victoria, at Hyde Park Corner, at Marble Arch, the crowds stretched far back until they seemed like the multitude that gathers to watch the passing of a king. 'All were made common acquaintances by the rights of a common grief.' Bus drivers stopped their engines and doffed their caps; passengers rose in respect from their seats. In many of the streets the shop blinds were lowered. The last part of the journey was through the scenes of his boyhood: Maida Vale, Swiss Cottage, St. John's Wood. Of the day's solemnities, none was more full-hearted or more moving than London's wayside tribute. As the farewell words were spoken in the cemetery, an aeroplane, high overhead, dipped in salute.

Throughout the following weekend new crowds gathered by the grave where he had been laid beside his father and grandfather. Among them were many men of the generation that had fought and suffered at Mons, Gallipoli, Passchendaele and the Somme. They made common cause with the compositors and machine-men and other trade unionists who, not content to join in corporate expressions of sympathy, had added their private and personal tokens to the greatest mass of flowers ever seen in that place.

*　　*　　*

So ended the reverberating life of Alfred Charles William Harmsworth, Viscount Northcliffe. His singular destiny had helped to make an epoch, and many who had known him in the years of his ascendancy felt that his death marked its close. More certainly, they were assured of never seeing his like again.

Bibliography

This bibliography has been prepared for the student of Northcliffe and his immediate contemporaries and times. Those books which have been referred to in the present work have also been acknowledged in the text.

★   ★   ★

I. THE HARMSWORTH DESCENT

THE GENEALOGY OF THE FAMILY OF HARMSWORTH
Compiled by Mrs V. Heddon and registered at the College of Arms, 1954.

A SHORT HISTORY OF THE FAMILY OF MOFFAT OF THAT ILK
Compiled by Robert Maxwell Moffat: The Beresford Library, Jersey, 1908.

HAMILTON MEMOIRS
Compiled by Everard Hamilton, B.A.: Dundalgon Press, Dundalk, 1920.

★   ★   ★

II. BY NORTHCLIFFE

HENLEY HOUSE SCHOOL MAGAZINE
Founded and Edited by Alfred C. Harmsworth. No. 1, Vol. I, March 1881: Printed by Ford & Son, Kilburn Gate, London N.W. Last issue edited by Alfred Harmsworth is dated December 1881. In the May 1890 issue (No. 35) see: 'A Short History of a Henley House Boy', by J. V. Milne.

PHOTOGRAPHY FOR AMATEURS
Alfred C. W. Harmsworth: *Youth*, November–December 1882.

WILFRID GRANT'S DOUBLE
Alfred C. W. Harmsworth: *Youth*, February–March 1883.

BLACKTHORPE'S, A SCHOOL STORY
A. C. W. Harmsworth: *Youth*, March 28, 1883.

THE QUEEN'S MESSENGER
A Story by A. C. W. Harmsworth: *Youth*, September 26, 1883.

A THOUSAND WAYS TO EARN A LIVING
Tit-Bits Office, Burleigh Street, Strand: Carr & Co., 26 Paternoster Square, 1888.

ALL ABOUT OUR RAILWAYS
Tit-Bits Office, Burleigh Street, Strand: Carr & Co., 26 Paternoster Square, *c.* 1888.

SEA FISHING: TARPON
A. C. Harmsworth: *The Badminton Library of Sports and Pastimes,* Longmans, Green, 1895.

HARD TRUTHS FROM INDIA
Alfred C. Harmsworth: *Daily Mail* Office, 1897.

MOTORS AND MOTOR DRIVING
Alfred C. Harmsworth: *The Badminton Library of Sports and Pastimes,* Longmans, Green, 1902.

JOURNALISM AS A PROFESSION
Arthur Lawrence, with a Chapter entitled 'The Making of a Newspaper' by Alfred C. Harmsworth: Hodder & Stoughton, 1903.

AT THE WAR
Lord Northcliffe: Hodder & Stoughton, 1916. George H. Doran, New York, 1916. (A LA GUERRE) Librairie Payot & Cie., Paris, 1917.

LORD NORTHCLIFFE'S WAR BOOK: WITH CHAPTERS ON AMERICA AT WAR
A. L. Burt, New York, 1917.

THE RE-MAKING OF IRELAND
Lord Northcliffe: privately printed by Clement Shorter, London, 1917.

BEOWULF
Translated by C. K. Scott-Moncrieff with an Introduction by Viscount Northcliffe: Chapman & Hall, 1921.

NEWSPAPERS AND THEIR MILLIONAIRES
Viscount Northcliffe: Associated Newspapers, 1922.

MY JOURNEY ROUND THE WORLD
Alfred, Viscount Northcliffe, edited by Cecil and St. John Harmsworth: John Lane, The Bodley Head, 1923.

★　　★　　★

III. BIOGRAPHIES AND MEMOIRS OF NORTHCLIFFE

NORTHCLIFFE: BRITAIN'S MAN OF POWER
William E. Carson: Dodge, New York, 1918.

LORD NORTHCLIFFE
Andrée Viollis: Librairie Bernard Grasset, Paris, 1919.

LORD NORTHCLIFFE: A MEMOIR
Max Pemberton: Hodder & Stoughton, 1922.

THE REAL LORD NORTHCLIFFE: SOME PERSONAL RECOLLECTIONS OF A PRIVATE SECRETARY, 1902–1922
Louise Owen: Cassell, 1922.
NORTHCLIFFE'S RETURN
Hannen Swaffer: Foreword by Lord Beaverbrook: Hutchinson, 1925.
THE COMING AGAIN OF NORTHCLIFFE
The Rev. J. W. Potter: The Society of Communion, 1926.
LORD NORTHCLIFFE: A STUDY
R. Macnair Wilson: Ernest Benn, 1927.
NORTHCLIFFE: AN INTIMATE BIOGRAPHY
Hamilton Fyfe: Macmillan, New York, and Allen & Unwin, 1930.
NORTHCLIFFE: THE FACTS
Louise Owen: Privately Printed and Published, 1931.
MY NORTHCLIFFE DIARY
Tom Clarke: Victor Gollancz, 1931.
WITH NORTHCLIFFE IN FLEET STREET: A PERSONAL RECORD
J. A. Hammerton: Hutchinson, 1932.
NORTHCLIFFE IN HISTORY: AN INTIMATE STUDY OF PRESS POWER
Tom Clarke: Hutchinson, 1950.
LORD NORTHCLIFFE
A. P. Ryan: Collins, 1953.
NORTHCLIFFE: THE NAPOLEON OF FLEET STREET
Harry J. Greenwall: Allan Wingate, 1957.

★

DICTIONARY OF NATIONAL BIOGRAPHY (1922–1930)
Harmsworth, Alfred Charles William, Viscount Northcliffe: Biography contributed by Geoffrey Dawson.
ENCYCLOPÆDIA BRITANNICA
Northcliffe, Alfred Charles William Harmsworth. Biography contributed by H. W. Wilson.

★　★　★

IV. THE NORTHCLIFFE PRESS

THE RISE AND PROGRESS OF THE HARMSWORTH PUBLICATIONS
F. A. McKenzie: Published by B. W. Young, 24 Tudor Street, 1897.
THE ROMANCE OF THE AMALGAMATED PRESS
Compiled by George Dilnot: Amalgamated Press, 1925.

★

THE ROMANCE OF THE 'DAILY MAIL'
Alfred C. Harmsworth, 1903.

THE RISE OF THE 'DAILY MAIL'
Lord Northcliffe, 1916.

'SCARE-MONGERINGS' FROM THE 'DAILY MAIL' 1896–1914
Compiled by Twells Brex, *c.* 1915.

THE 'DAILY MAIL' AND THE LIBERAL PRESS. A REPLY TO 'SCAREMONGERINGS' AND AN OPEN LETTER TO LORD NORTHCLIFFE
Reprinted from *The Star, c.* 1915.

THE MYSTERY OF THE 'DAILY MAIL' 1896–1921
F. A. McKenzie: Associated Newspapers, 1921.

NEWS IN OUR TIME: GOLDEN JUBILEE BOOK OF THE 'DAILY MAIL' 1896–1946
Associated Newspapers, 1946.

FIFTY YEARS OF THE 'DAILY MAIL' 1896–1946
G. Ward Price [MS, unpublished].

★

THE ROMANCE OF THE 'DAILY MIRROR' 1903–1924
With a Foreword by Lord Rothermere. The Daily Mirror Newspapers, Ltd.

PUBLISH AND BE DAMNED!
Hugh Cudlipp: Andrew Dakers Ltd., 1953.

★

THE HISTORY OF 'THE TIMES'—The 150th Anniversary and Beyond, 1912–1948.
Part I, Chapters I–XII, 1912–1920.
Part II, Chapters XIII–XXIV, 1921–1948.
Written and published at The Office of *The Times*, Printing House Square, London, 1952.

★

The files of *Answers* from 1888 to 1922, the *Daily Mail* from 1896 to 1922 and of *The Times* from 1908 to 1922, should also be studied. The files of the *Newspaper Owner* (later the *Newspaper World*) also contain much valuable information covering the period of Northcliffe's active life in Fleet Street.

★ ★ ★

V. JOURNALISM

STRANGE STREET
Beverley Baxter: Hutchinson, 1935.

A REBEL IN FLEET STREET
Comyns Beaumont: Hutchinson, 1944.

POLITICIANS AND THE PRESS
Lord Beaverbrook: Hutchinson, 1925.

THE LIFE AND LETTERS OF C. F. MOBERLY BELL
By his daughter, E. H. C. Moberly Bell; Introduction by Sir
Valentine Chirol: The Richards Press, 1917.

R. D. B.'S DIARY 1887–1914
R. D. Blumenfeld: Heinemann, 1930.

R. D. B.'S PROCESSION
Ralph D. Blumenfeld: Ivor Nicholson & Watson, 1935.

THE STORY OF 'THE TIMES'
William Dodgson Bowman: Routledge, 1931.

BRITISH NEWSPAPERS AND THEIR CONTROLLERS
Viscount Camrose: Cassell, 1947.

THE PRESS AND A CHANGING CIVILIZATION
A. J. Cummings: John Lane, 1936.

THE ADVENTURES OF A NEWSPAPER MAN
Frank Dilnot: Smith, Elder, 1913.

BEAVERBROOK
Tom Driberg: Weidenfeld & Nicolson, 1956.

MASTERS OF ENGLISH JOURNALISM
T. H. S. Escott: T. Fisher Unwin, 1911.

HE LAUGHED IN FLEET STREET
Bernard Falk: Hutchinson, 1933.

FIVE YEARS DEAD
Bernard Falk: Hutchinson, 1937.

SIXTY YEARS OF FLEET STREET
Hamilton Fyfe: W. H. Allen, 1949.

J. L. GARVIN: A MEMOIR
Katharine Garvin: Heinemann, 1948.

ADVENTURES IN JOURNALISM
Philip Gibbs: Heinemann, 1923.

NEWSPAPER LORDS IN BRITISH POLITICS
C. J. Hambro: Macdonald, 1958.

CHILD OF WONDER—AN INTIMATE BIOGRAPHY OF ARTHUR MEE
Sir John Hammerton: Hodder & Stoughton, 1946.

C. P. SCOTT
J. L. Hammond: G. Bell & Sons, 1934.

IN AND OUT OF FLEET STREET
B. M. Hansard (Dedicated to Lord Northcliffe): No publisher
given, 1935.

THE MAKING OF MODERN JOURNALISM
Harold Herd: George Allen & Unwin, 1927.

THE MARCH OF JOURNALISM
Harold Herd: George Allen & Unwin, 1952.

BRITISH JOURNALISTS AND NEWSPAPERS
Derek Hudson: Collins, 1945.

FLEET STREET AND DOWNING STREET
Kennedy Jones: Hutchinson, 1919.

FRONT EVERYWHERE
J. M. N. Jeffries (Correspondent of the *Daily Mail*, 1914–1933):
Hutchinson, 1935.

A LIFE IN REUTERS
Sir Roderick Jones: Hodder & Stoughton, 1951.

MOBERLY BELL AND HIS TIMES
F. Harcourt Kitchin ('Bennet Copplestone'): Philip Allan, 1925.

MY LIFE STORY
Arthur Lynch: John Long, 1924.

BEAVERBROOK
F. A. Mackenzie: Jarrolds, 1931.

ADVENTURES IN INTERVIEWING
Isaac F. Marcosson: John Lane, The Bodley Head, 1920.

BEAVERBROOK
Edgar Middleton: Stanley Paul, 1934.

THE TRUTH ABOUT A JOURNALIST
Sydney A. Moseley: Sir Isaac Pitman & Sons, 1935.

NEWSPAPERS TODAY
Alan Pitt Robbins: Oxford University Press, 1956.

'WE' AND ME
J. W. Robertson Scott: W. H. Allen, 1956.

SPILT INK
Wareham Smith: Ernest Benn, 1932.

LIFE, JOURNALISM AND POLITICS (2 vols.)
J. A. Spender: Cassell, 1927.

WITH THE DICTATORS OF FLEET STREET
Russell Stannard: Hutchinson, 1934.

THROUGH THIRTY YEARS 1892–1922 (2 vols.)
Henry Wickham Steed: Heinemann, 1924.

ST. LOE STRACHEY—HIS LIFE AND HIS PAPER
Amy Strachey: Gollancz, 1930.

A TRAVELLER IN NEWS
Sir William Beach Thomas: Chapman & Hall, 1925.

GEOFFREY DAWSON AND OUR TIMES
John Evelyn Wrench: Hutchinson, 1955.

* * *

VI. THE FIRST WORLD WAR

POLITICIANS AND THE WAR 1914–1916
Lord Beaverbrook:
Vol. I, Thornton Butterworth, 1928.
Vol. II, The Lane Publications, 1932.

MEN AND POWER 1917–1918
Lord Beaverbrook: Hutchinson, 1956.

THE MEMOIRS OF PRINCE MAX OF BADEN (2 vols.)
Authorized Translation by W. M. Calder and C. W. H. Sutton:
Constable, 1928.

FIELD-MARSHAL SIR HENRY WILSON—HIS LIFE AND DIARIES
Major-General Sir C. E. Callwell: Cassell, 1927.

AT G.H.Q.
Brigadier-General John Charteris: Cassell, 1931.

THE WORLD CRISIS 1911–1918 (6 vols.)
Winston Churchill: Thornton Butterworth, 1923–1931.

WHO'S WHO IN THE BRITISH WAR MISSION TO THE UNITED STATES OF
AMERICA, 1917—CHAIRMAN VISCOUNT NORTHCLIFFE
Published by Edward J. Clode, New York, 1917.

HAIG
Duff Cooper: Faber & Faber, 1935.

BRITISH SECRET SERVICE DURING THE GREAT WAR
(Dedicated to and a Foreword by Lord Northcliffe): Nicholas
Everitt: Hutchinson, 1920.

THE DIARY OF LORD BERTIE OF THAME 1914–1918 (2 vols.)
Edited by Lady Algernon Gordon Lennox: Hodder & Stoughton,
1924.

THE FIFTH ARMY
General Sir Hubert Gough: Hodder & Stoughton, 1931.

THE LETTERS AND FRIENDSHIPS OF SIR CECIL SPRING RICE (2 vols.)
Edited by Stephen Gwynn: Houghton Mifflin Co., Boston and
New York, and The Riverside Press, Cambridge, 1929.

WAR MEMOIRS OF DAVID LLOYD GEORGE (6 vols.)
Ivor Nicholson & Watson, 1933–1936.

MY WAR MEMORIES 1914–1918 (2 vols.)
General Ludendorff: Hutchinson, 1919.

FALL OF THE GERMAN EMPIRE 1914–1918 (2 vols.)
Hoover War Library Publications, No. 1. Selected and Edited by
Ralph Haswell Lutz: Stanford University Press, California, and
Oxford University Press, 1932.

BRITISH WAR MISSIONS TO THE UNITED STATES 1914–1918
Colonel W. G. Lyddon: Oxford University Press, 1938.

PERSONALITY AND DIPLOMACY IN ANGLO–AMERICAN RELATIONS 1917
Stanley Morison—Reprinted from Essays presented to Sir Lewis Namier.

THE FIRST WORLD WAR 1914–1918 (2 vols.)
Lieut.-Colonel C. à Court Repington: Constable, 1920

LORD RIDDELL'S WAR DIARY 1914–1918
Ivor Nicholson & Watson, 1933.

LORD RIDDELL'S INTIMATE DIARY OF THE PEACE CONFERENCE AND AFTER 1918–1923
Victor Gollancz, 1933.

THE INTIMATE PAPERS OF COLONEL HOUSE (4 vols.)
Charles Seymour: Ernest Benn, 1926–1928.

AMERICAN DIPLOMACY DURING THE WORLD WAR
Charles Seymour: The Johns Hopkins Press, Baltimore, 1934.

LIFE OF HERBERT HENRY ASQUITH, LORD OXFORD AND ASQUITH (Vol. II)
J. A. Spender and Cyril Asquith: Hutchinson, 1932.

BRITISH PROPAGANDA AT HOME AND IN THE UNITED STATES FROM 1914 TO 1917
James Duane Squires: Harvard University Press, 1935.

SECRETS OF CREWE HOUSE
Sir Campbell Stuart: Hodder & Stoughton, 1920.

THE TIMES HISTORY AND ENCYCLOPÆDIA OF THE WAR
Part 263, September 23, 1919—British Missions in America.
Part 270, December 30, 1919—British Propaganda in Enemy Countries.

⋆   ⋆   ⋆

VII. GENERAL

MY POLITICAL LIFE (Vol. II)
L. S. Amery: Hutchinson, 1953.

AFTER ALL
Sir Norman Angell: Hamish Hamilton, 1951.

MEMORIES AND REFLECTIONS 1852–1927 (2 vols.)
The Earl of Oxford and Asquith: Cassell, 1928.

THE HOUSE IS SITTING
Arthur Bader: Blandford Press, 1958.

THE TRUMPET SHALL SOUND
(Foreword by Hannen Swaffer): Maurice Barbanell: Rider & Co. 1933.

FREDERICK EDWIN, EARL OF BIRKENHEAD—THE LAST PHASE
By his son The Earl of Birkenhead: Thornton Butterworth, 1935.

THE HISTORY OF THE SYLVAN DEBATING CLUB
T. Livingstone Baily: The Field Press, 1931.

BIBLIOGRAPHY

THE UNKNOWN PRIME MINISTER—THE LIFE AND TIMES OF ANDREW BONAR LAW 1858–1923
Robert Blake: Eyre & Spottiswoode, 1935.

PILGRIMS AND PIONEERS
Sir Harry Brittain: Hutchinson, 1946.

5,000 MILES IN A BALLOON
(With a contribution 'Aerial Navigation as a Practical Possibility' by Lord Northcliffe): Frank Hedges Butler: Horace Cox, 1907.

AT THE SIGN OF THE WORLD'S END
G. K. Chesterton: The Harvest Press, 1930.

LIFE OF LORD CARSON
Ian Colvin: Gollancz, 1936.

AS I KNEW THEM
Ella Hepworth Dixon: Hutchinson, 1930.

AN ENGLISH WIFE IN BERLIN
Anon: Dutton, New York, 1920.

SOUTH AFRICAN MEMORIES
Sir J. Percy Fitzpatrick. Prepared for the Press from the Manuscript of the Author by G. H. Wilson: Cassell, 1932.

MEMOIRS (2 vols.)
Sir Almeric Fitzroy: Hutchinson, 1925.

JUST AS IT HAPPENED
Sir Newman Flower: Cassell, 1950.

HEARTS AND POMEGRANATES
Dame Katharine Furse: Peter Davies, 1940.

ETON: AS SHE IS NOT
J. Goodwin: Eton, R. Ingalton Drake, n.d.

AN AUTOBIOGRAPHY
Richard Burdon Haldane: Hodder & Stoughton, 1929.

A SONG OF SPEED
W. E. Henley: David Nutt, 1903.

IN MY TIME
Sisley Huddleston: Jonathan Cape, 1938.

LETTERS OF ARTHUR, LORD KILBRACKEN, G.C.B., AND GENERAL SIR ALEXANDER GODLEY, G.C.B., K.C.M.G., 1898–1932
Cheltenham Press, n.d.

POWERS AND PILLARS: INTIMATE PORTRAITS OF BRITISH PERSONALITIES
Rudolf Kircher (trans. Constance Vesey): Collin

THINGS I KNOW ABOUT KINGS, CELEBRITIES AND CROOKS
William Le Queux: Eveleigh Nash & Grayson, n.d.

TEMPESTUOUS PETTICOAT
Clare Leighton: Gollancz, 1948.

MODERN MEN OF MARK
    Mrs Stuart Menzies: Herbert Jenkins, 1921.
THE MIRRORS OF DOWNING STREET
    A Gentleman with a Duster: Mills & Boon, 1920.
MASTER AND BROTHER
    Lieut.-Colonel the Hon Arthur C. Murray: John Murray, 1945.
LORD LANSDOWNE
    Lord Newton: Macmillan, 1929.
TWO WORLDS FOR MEMORY
    Alfred Noyes: Sheed & Ward, 1953.
TEMPESTUOUS JOURNEY—LLOYD GEORGE: HIS LIFE AND TIMES
    Frank Owen: Hutchinson, 1954.
THE POMP OF POWER
    Anonymous: Hutchinson, 1922.
UNCENSORED CELEBRITIES
    E. T. Raymond: Fisher Unwin, 1919.
INSANITY FAIR
    Douglas Reed: Jonathan Cape, 1938.
MORE PAGES FROM MY DIARY 1908–1914
    Lord Riddell: Country Life, 1934.
MEN AND MEMORIES: RECOLLECTIONS 1872–1900
    Sir William Rothenstein: Faber & Faber, 1931.
THE REAL LE QUEUX: THE OFFICIAL BIOGRAPHY OF WILLIAM LE QUEUX
    N. St. Barbe Sladen: Nicholson & Watson, 1938.
WEETMAN PEARSON, FIRST VISCOUNT COWDRAY 1856–1927
    J. A. Spender: Cassell, 1930.
SIR ROBERT HUDSON—A MEMOIR
    J. A. Spender: Cassell, 1930.
OPPORTUNITY KNOCKS ONCE
    Sir Campbell Stuart: Collins, 1952.
THE WAY OF A COUNTRYMAN
    Sir William Beach Thomas: Michael Joseph, 1944.
JOHN, LORD MONTAGU OF BEAULIEU
    Lady Troubridge and Archibald Marshall: Macmillan, 1930.
EDGAR WALLACE: BY HIMSELF
    Hodder & Stoughton, 1932.
TRIAL AND ERROR
    Dr Weizmann: Hamish Hamilton, 1949.
THE WORLD OF WILLIAM CLISSOLD
    H. G. Wells: Ernest Benn, 1926.
EXPERIMENT IN AUTOBIOGRAPHY
    H. G. Wells: Victor Gollancz and The Cresset Press, 1934.

THE ROAD TO SAFETY
   Sir Arthur Willert: Derek Verschoyle, 1952.
FROM QUEBEC TO PICCADILLY AND OTHER PLACES
   Beckles Willson: Jonathan Cape, 1929.
THE HISTORY OF UNILEVER (Vol. I)
   Charles Wilson: Cassell, 1954.
DOCTOR'S PROGRESS
   R. McNair Wilson: Eyre & Spottiswoode, 1938.
UPHILL
   John Evelyn Wrench: Ivor Nicholson & Watson, 1934.

★   ★   ★

VIII. NOVELS

A NAPOLEON OF THE PRESS
   Marie Connor Leighton: Hodder & Stoughton, 1900.
LORD LONDON—A ROMANCE OF TODAY
   Keble Howard: Chapman & Hall, 1913.
CALIBAN
   W. L. George: Methuen, 1920.

★   ★   ★

IX. PLAYS

THE WORLD
   J. B. Fagan.
WHAT THE PUBLIC WANTS
   Arnold Bennett.
HIGH TREASON
   Noel Pemberton Billing.

★   ★   ★

X. PORTRAITS

SEYMOUR LUCAS, R.A.
   A portrait in oils of Alfred Harmsworth, aged twenty-nine, exhibited at the Royal Academy, 1894. In the collection of Mr Alfred Harmsworth. (See frontispiece.)
THE MARCHIONESS OF GRANBY (THE LATE VIOLET, DUCHESS OF RUTLAND)
   A pencil drawing of Alfred Harmsworth, in his early thirties, inscribed 'Napoleon'. In the collection of Viscount Rothermere.
SIR WILLIAM ROTHENSTEIN, A.R.C.A.
   An unfinished portrait of Northcliffe (c. 1906) was lost during the artist's move from Church Row, Hampstead, to Oakhill Park (see Men and Memories, Faber & Faber, Vol. 2, p. 91, 1932).

PHILIP DE LASZLO

A portrait in oils of Northcliffe, 1911. The original painting is at New Carmelite House. There are copies at Printing House Square, Northcliffe House and in the Parliament Buildings, Ottawa.

SIR JOHN LAVERY, R.A.

A portrait in oils of Northcliffe, in profile, 1921. Geraldine House. A smaller version is in the collection of Mrs Ivy Clark.

A full face portrait in oils by Sir John Lavery is in the Municipal Art Gallery, Dublin.

* * *

XI. BUSTS

A bronze plaque of Alfred Harmsworth, in profile, by Edith Bell, 1900, was regarded by the late Lord Harmsworth as the best likeness at that time. There is a copy in the National Portrait Gallery.

A portrait bust of Northcliffe by Courtenay Pollock, 1919. Northcliffe House.

A portrait bust of Northcliffe by Lady Hilton Young, resting on a plinth designed by Sir Edwin Lutyens, R.A., 1930. In the forecourt of St. Dunstan's-in-the-West, Fleet Street.

A portrait bust of Northcliffe by Arthur G. Walker, A.R.A. Exhibited at the Royal Academy, 1930.

* * *

XII. RECORDING

A recording of Northcliffe's voice was made by H.M.V. on April 28, 1921. It is entitled: 'Short Address by Viscount Northcliffe. For the luncheon at Olympia, on May 1, 1921, commemorating the Twenty-Fifth Anniversary of the founding of the *Daily Mail*.' For private distribution only.

Index

Index

FITZHUGH (*Evening News*), 830, 835
FLOWER, Newman (Cassell), 832
FOCH, General—views on N., 506
FORD (Kilburn printer), 36, 780
FORD, Henry—N's meeting with, 565, 566, 605
Forget-Me-Not—Harmsworth paper for women, 128*ff*, 166
FOREIGN quotations—N's dislike of, 346
FOULGER, F. (valet), 823
Fox, Frank (Australian journalist), 513
FRANKFURTER, Felix, 623
FRASER, Lovat—writes for *Answers*, 83; on *The Times*, 471, 473, 479, 595, 739, 763
FRAZIER, A. H. (American Embassy in Paris), 707
FREEMAN, G. S. (*T.T.*), 641, 676, 694, 705, 725
FRENCH, Viscount (Earl of Ypres)—and the shell-shortage, 474*ff*; invites N. to Ireland, 727
FRERE, A. S. (*Evening News*), 800
FURSE, Mrs K., 382
FYFE, Hamilton—edits *Daily Mirror* (1903), 278, 282; with N. in America, 554, 559, 582; at Crewe House, 656, 658, 678; views on N's health, 777

GALSWORTHY, John—correspondence with N. on Anglo-German relations, 361, 362; visits German prison with N., 367; writes to N. on possible aerial warfare, 416; N. asks him to crusade for humane slaughtering, 440
GARDINER, A. G. (editor, *Daily News*)—denounces *T.T.* war policy in 1914, 463; 'open letter' to N., 470
GARVIN, James Louis (editor, *The Observer*), 291, 519, 615, 616; views on N., 350; friendship for, 358; views on characterization of N. in play, 363; writes to N. about *The Observer*, 364; advises N. to rest, 366; N. concerned about his health, 371; writes to N. about 1909 Budget, 377, 378; accompanies N. to St. Raphael, 392; writes on N's health, 393, 394; parts political and journalistic company with N., 414*ff*; writes to N. on peace terms, 705; sends good wishes after N's operation, 736; supports Lloyd George in Genoa episode, 854
GATEHOUSE, G. (Iliffe), 66
GEDDES, Sir Auckland, 682, 693, 798
GENOA conference (1922), 852*ff*
GEORGE V, King—message from on visit to Ireland, 798
GEORGE, Tom (head printer, Carmelite House), 320, 342

GERALDINE Press, 150, 216
GERMANY—N's concern about ambitions, 152, 232; *D.M.* warnings, 232; N. in 1900 forsees war, 252; his first visit to, 272; *D.M.* Berlin correspondent reports on British ambassador's attitude to *D.M.*, 301; *T.T.* correspondent described as 'a first-class swine', 327; Admiral von Tirpitz's talk with *D.M.* correspondent, 332; N. orders compilation of memorandum on war preparations, 331; Prof. Delbruck's statement, 337; N. and Galsworthy write on dangers, 361; N. gives interview to German news agency, 366; arranges for *D.M.* articles by 'A German in England', 368; gives impressions of visit to Imperial Press Conference delegates, 369; N. interviewed in America, 383; commissions Blatchford to visit Germany; articles published, 384, 388, 389; German Emperor lectures British military attaché in Berlin, 403; interview, 425; Prof. Delbruck states German case in *D.M.*, 425; N. plans to print newspaper in Berlin, 426, 427, 443, 445; N. suppresses American interview with German Emperor, 434; *D.M.* Berlin correspondent continues warning messages, 443, 454; nephew asks N. to support Anglo-German friendship club at Oxford, 455; the ex-Kaiser regards N. with intense bitterness, 669; N's article *Incognito into Germany*, 866
GIBBS, Sir Philip (*Daily Chronicle*), 426; (*D.M.*), 823, 824
Girls' Reader (Harmsworth publication), 419
GLADSTONE, William Ewart—comment on *Answers*, 138; message to N. on *D.M.*, 202
Glasgow Daily News (Henderson), 45
Glasgow Echo (Harmsworth publication), 188
Glasgow Evening Mercury (Henderson), 45
Globe, The, 293, 585, 595
GLOVER, Robert (Carmelite House), 847
GLYN, Elinor, 486
GODLEY, Gen. Sir A.—entertains N. in Cologne, 860*ff*
Golden Soil—N. idea of paper, 359
Golden Stories, 159
GOLDER, S. (*Bicycling News*), 806
GOLF—N's interest in, 233, 400*ff*, 435, 440, 629, 659, 716, 793, 841
Golf—published by Leicester Harmsworth, 264